POLITICAL PARTIES OF THE WORLD

Other current affairs reference titles from John Harper Publishing include:

Border and Territorial Disputes
The Council of the European Union
Directory of European Union Political Parties
Directory of Pressure Groups in the EU
The European Commission
The European Courts
The European Parliament
Political Parties of Eastern Europe, Russia and the Successor States
Revolutionary and Dissident Movements
Trade Unions of the World
Treaties and Alliances of the World

POLITICAL PARTIES OF THE WORLD

5th edition

edited by Alan J. Day

JOHN HARPER PUBLISHING

Political Parties of the World, 5th edition

Published by John Harper Publishing
Editorial enquiries: 27 Palace Gates Road, London N22 7BW, UK. E-mail: jhpublish@aol.com
Sales enquiries: Turpin Distribution Services Ltd, Blackhorse Road, Letchworth, SG6 1HN, UK. E-mail:
books@turpinltd.com

Distributed exclusively in the United States and Canada, and non-exclusively outside North America, by Gale
Group Inc., 27500 Drake Rd., Farmington Hills, Michigan 48331, USA

1st edition (1980), Longman Group UK Ltd
2nd edition (1984), Longman Group UK Ltd
3rd edition (1988), Longman Group UK Ltd
4th edition (1996), Cartermill International Ltd

This edition first published 2002
© John Harper Publishing 2002
ISBN 0-9536278-7-X

Page makeup by Fakenham Photosetting Ltd
Printed in Great Britain by Bookcraft (Bath) Ltd

Table of Contents

Introduction

Political Parties of the World was first published (at that time under the Longman imprint) in 1980, since when immense changes have occurred to the world political landscape. In 1980 the Soviet Union and the eight communist countries of Eastern Europe were single-party states; that region has since fragmented into 27 countries, mostly with vigorous party systems and between them accounting for more than 530 of the parties profiled in this new edition. In 1980 much of Africa was likewise ruled by single-party regimes, often installed in the aftermath of independence; since that time Africa has experienced a wave of democratization, peaking in the early 1990s, followed by a partial retreat to renewed dominance by ruling parties. Many former authoritarian regimes in Latin America have made a transition to freer and more pluralist politics. In the developed democracies the socialist parties of 1980 have almost universally come to accept the central role of the market in driving economic progress, Marxist parties have collapsed, retreated to the fringes or adopted democratic socialism, and conservative parties have faced internal conflict, and in some cases fracture, as they have struggled to define their position between the conflicting claims of moderate traditionalism and right-wing radicalism. Despite a pattern of declining electoral participation in most developed democracies, in the world as a whole there has been a great expansion in the number and diversity of political parties.

Reflecting these changes, the number of political parties profiled in this 5th edition has increased to over 2,550, notwithstanding the deletion of numerous lapsed, trifling or inactive parties and editorial criteria excluding numbers of new self-described "political parties" that have established a presence on the Internet but nowhere else. The new edition includes coverage of well over 400 parties that have been created since the last edition in 1996, with many examples of such parties now playing a major role in political life. Features of the worldwide party scene that emerge from this new edition include (i) the growing importance of racial and/or religious identity as a determinant of party political affiliation and the often related rise of regional political movements demanding greater autonomy and in some cases outright separation; (ii) the parallel trend towards formal international co-operation between national parties within supra-national bodies such as the European Parliament; and (iii) the emergence of a strong anti-globalization current in many countries, notably in the Green parties which have become an established feature of the party scene in developed countries but also in parts in the developing world.

As with previous editions, illegal, guerrilla and terrorist movements have not usually been included: these are dealt with in the Publishers' companion volume *Revolutionary and Dissident Movements*, a new edition of which will appear during the course of 2002. Some exceptions have been made, however, in respect of certain countries where the exercise of political power is particularly fluid, where such banned organizations exercise de facto political power in part of the territory, or where exclusion would otherwise render understanding of the overall political situation impossible. Defunct parties are not described except in the context of the historical antecedents of existing parties.

The most important information source for the present volume was the parties themselves, many officials of which took the trouble to reply to requests for current data. More than 750 parties maintain Internet websites and even more may be contacted by email. Both sorts of address are given in party entries where available, together with traditional contact data. Also utilized were the websites of the five main international party organizations (the memberships of which are given in Appendix A of the present volume) and those of the party groups in the European Parliament (see Appendix B). Of other sources used, particular mention should be made of Wilfried Derksen's estimable "Elections around the world" website (www.electionworld.org), which provides data on the most recent national elections as well as links to many party websites. Also useful for party and other political links was the "Political Resources on the Net" website (www.politicalresources.net). For authoritative information on electoral systems (though not always on election results), the *Parline* database of the Inter-Parliamentary Union (www.ipu.org/parline) has been valuable, while the monitoring reports of the OSCE's Office for Democratic Institutions and Human Rights (ODIHR) have been an important source on recent elections in Eastern Europe (www.osce.org/odihr).

Alan J. Day
London, November 2001

Layout of entries

Within country sections, parties are described in alphabetical order according to an English-language version of their name. However, where in wholly or partly English-speaking countries a party specifically employs a non-English language name (such as the *Parti Québécois* in Canada), this non-English version is used. Similarly, some non-English party names are so generally used in English sources, such as *Likud* in Israel, that to list them under a translated version would be redundant and anomalous. For most countries the parties are sub-divided with more significant parties profiled first, with details of minor parties following in a separate alphabetical order sequence. Various variations exist country-by-country: for example, the regional parties of Spain, France and Italy are covered in separate sections. Dependencies are covered as sub-sections in alpha order under the name of the colonial authority: for example, Gibraltar under the United Kingdom and Greenland under Denmark.

Within party entries, cross-references to other parties with entries under the same country are denoted (at first reference) by a → symbol; cross-references to parties in other countries are denoted by the →→ symbol.

Contributors

The Editor compiled the entries for European and various Pacific and other countries, as well as international party organizations. Contributions of material for the rest of the world were made by the following:

Shirin Akiner (Kazakhstan, Kyrgyzstan, Tajikistan, Turkmenistan, Uzbekistan)
Chris Baker (Thailand)
Peter Calvert (Bolivia, Guatemala, Panama, Paraguay)
William Case (Malaysia)
Keane Clyde (Guyana)
Marc Cole-Bailey (Argentina, Belize)
Peter Ferdinand (China, Indonesia, Japan, Koreas, Taiwan)
Robert Funk (Chile)
Richard German (various African and Middle East)
F.J. Harper (USA, Canada, various Caribbean)
Lawrence Joffe (Bahrain, Chad, Egypt, Israel, Jordan, Kuwait, Lebanon, Palestinian Entity)
Roger Kershaw (Brunei)
R.J.May (Myanmar, Papua New Guinea, Philippines)
Raymond Miller (New Zealand)
Alfred Oehlers (Singapore)
Francisco Panizza (Brazil, Uruguay)
Lloyd Pettiford (Costa Rica, Honduras)
George Philip (Mexico)
Pasuk Phongpaichit (Thailand)
Steven Ratuva (Fiji)
David Roberts (Cambodia)
Emily Rudland (Myanmar)
D.J. Sagar (various South and Central American, African and Middle East)
Alan Sanders (Mongolia)
Martin Stuart-Fox (Laos)
Elizabeth Taylor (various African)
Carlyle A. Thayer (Vietnam)
David Washbrook (Bangladesh, Bhutan, India, Nepal, Pakistan, Sri Lanka)

Afghanistan

Capital: Kabul

Population: 21,500,000 (2000E)

The Islamic State of Afghanistan was proclaimed in April 1992 as successor to the Soviet-backed regime of President Mohammed Najibullah, which had been overthrown by opposition *mujaheddin* ("holy warriors") following the end of the 1979–89 Soviet military intervention. Following further conflict, the Taleban militia took power in Kabul in September 1996, and in October 1997 proclaimed the Islamic Emirate of Afghanistan. Forces of the deposed government of President Burhanuddin Rabbani had meanwhile established the United National Islamic Front for the Salvation of Afghanistan (UNIFSA). The Islamic State of Afghanistan (with UNIFSA "Northern Alliance" forces holding some northern areas) retained the recognition of the UN and much of the international community, while the Taleban consolidated de facto control of most of the country, including the capital. Continuing sporadic conflict was given impetus by the ethnic hostility of minority northern Uzbeks and Tajiks to the (majority) Pushtun-dominated Taleban.

Following terrorist attacks on New York and Washington on Sept. 11, 2001, the USA charged the Taleban regime with providing shelter to Osama bin Laden, regarded as the instigator of the attacks. After a period of unsuccessful pressure on the Taleban to surrender Bin Laden, the USA commenced overt military operations in support of the Northern Alliance on Oct. 7. Parallel efforts (involving the UN and also Pakistan, previously the Taleban's principal sponsor) were also underway to prepare for the creation of a government of national unity, representative of the various ethnic groups. The fall of Kabul to the Northern Alliance was reported on Nov. 13.

No general elections have been held in Afghanistan since April 1988 and political parties do not function. Allegiances within the country are primarily on an ethnic or clan basis.

Islamic Emirate of Afghanistan
Taleban Islamic Movement of Afghanistan (TIMA)
Leadership. Mullah Mohammad Omar (Spiritual Leader)
The Taleban ("Seekers") Movement emerged in September 1994 as a militant armed force then composed mainly of Islamic fundamentalist Sunni Pushtun "students" who sought the overthrow of the government in Kabul and the installation of "genuine" Islamic rule. They captured Kabul in September 1996, ousting the government of President Burhanuddin Rabbani and executing former President Najibullah, who had been sheltering in a UN compound since being overthrown in 1992. Mullah Mohammad Omar, the Taleban's Spiritual Leader, became de facto leader of the new regime. As of mid-November 2001, the Taleban regime retained diplomatic recognition only from Pakistan, its original sponsor (which had nonetheless also said it favoured the creation of a new broad-based government), and had lost control of Kabul.

Islamic State of Afghanistan
United National Islamic Front for the Salvation of Afghanistan (UNIFSA)
Email. info@hezb-e-islami.org
Website. www.jamiat.com
Leadership. Burhanuddin Rabbani (chairman)
The UNIFSA was created in June 1997 by the principal *mujaheddin* groupings that had held power until the →Taleban takeover in September 1996. Its political leader, President Burhanuddin Rabbani, retained the recognition of much of the international community. Its military leader, former Defence Minister Gen. Ahmed Shah Masud, was assassinated immediately prior to the Sept. 11, 2001 attacks in the USA. The various factions opposed to the Taleban were reported to be fragmented, recognizing different warlords as leaders, and with Rabbani's leadership being nominal.

Albania

Capital: Tirana

Population: 3,490,000 (2000E)

After the then communist government had in December 1990 bowed to popular pressure by authorizing the formation of parties to compete with the ruling Party of Labour of Albania (PLA), the Republic of Albania was proclaimed under an interim constitution adopted on April 29, 1991 (replacing the Socialist People's Republic of Albania in existence since 1946). In June 1991 the PLA was renamed the Socialist Party of Albania (PSSh). Under a new democratic constitution approved by referendum on Nov. 22, 1998, by 93.5% of those voting, supreme political authority is vested in the unicameral People's Assembly (*Kuvënd Popullore*), whose 140 members are elected for a four-year term by universal suffrage of those aged at least 18 years. Of the total, 100 deputies are elected in single-member constituencies in two rounds of voting; the other 40 seats are filled from national party lists according to the proportional first-round share of parties with at least 2% of the total vote. Electoral legislation enacted in February 1991 banned "extremist" parties and those based exclusively in ethnic minorities. The Albanian President is elected by the Assembly for a five-year term once renewable (and may not hold party office); the Assembly also approves the Prime Minister and Council of Ministers designated by the President. Having been proclaimed an atheist state in 1967, Albania opted for freedom of religion in April 1991. Some 70% of the population espouse the Islamic faith.

General elections in March 1992 were won outright by the new Democratic Party of Albania (PDSh), which also obtained a large majority in the next contest in May–June 1996. However, most international observers endorsed claims by the PSSh and other opposition parties that the 1996 poll had not been fairly conducted. New Assembly elections were held in June–July 1997 in which the PSSh won a decisive majority. Retaining its advantage in further parliamentary elections on June 24 and July 8, 2001 (with re-runs being held later in 10 constituencies), the PSSh won 73 seats (with 42.0% of the proportional vote), while a five-party Union for Victory alliance headed by the PDSh took 46 seats (37.1%), five small parties 19 seats between them and independents 2.

Albanian Agrarian Party
Partia Agrar e Shqipërisë (PASh)
Address. Rr. Budi 6, Tirana
Telephone/Fax. (+355–42) 27481
Leadership. Lufter Xhuveli (chairman)
Supports the agrarian interest and won three seats in the mid-2001 Assembly elections.

Albanian Republican Party
Partia Republikane Shqiptar (PRSh)
Address. Bul. Deshmoret e Kombit, Tirana
Telephone. (+355–42) 32511
Fax. (+355–42) 28361
Leadership. Fatmir Mediu (vice-chairman); Çerçiz Mingomataj (secretary-general)
Founded in January 1991 with support from the →→Italian Republican Party, the PRSh has its main power base in southern Albania. In the mid-2001 Assembly elections the PRSh was part of the losing Union for Victory alliance headed by the PDSh.

Democratic Alliance
Aleanca Demokratike (AD)
Address. c/o Kuvënd Popullore, Tirana
Leadership. Neritan Çeka (chairman); Edmond Dragoti (secretary-general)
The centre-right AD was founded in October 1992 by dissident elements of the ruling →Democratic Party of Albania opposed to the "autocratic rule" of President Berisha, who accused it of having pro-Serbian tendencies.

The AD presented its own list in the 1997 Assembly elections, winning two seats and subsequently joining a centre-left coalition government headed by the →Socialist Party of Albania. It improved to three seats with 2.4% of the vote in 2001.

Democratic Party of Albania
Partia Demokratika ë Shqipërisë (PDSh)
Address. Rruga Konferenca e Perez 120, Tirana
Telephone. (+355–42) 23525
Fax. (+355–42) 28463
Email. pd@albannet.al
Website. www.albania.co.uk/dp
Leadership. Sali Berisha (chairman); Jemin Gjana (chairman of parliamentary group); Ridvan Bode (secretary-general)
The PDSh was launched in December 1990 as Albania's first authorized opposition party since World War II, on a platform of human rights' observance, a free enterprise economy, better relations with neighbouring states and eventual membership of the European Union. It was derived from a movement of dissident intellectuals led by the writer Ismail Kadare. Teachers and students at Tirana University founded the PDSh immediately after the ruling PLA central committee had endorsed the legalization of opposition parties. The PDSh won 75 of 250 Assembly seats in the first post-communist elections in March–April 1991, after which it opted in June to join a "non-partisan" coalition government with the →Socialist Party of Albania (PSSh, formerly the PLA), until withdrawing in December 1991 in protest against the slow pace of reform.

The PDSh won a landslide victory in the March 1992 Assembly elections. PDSh chairman Sali Berisha was the following month elected President of Albania by the Assembly, following which the PDSh became the dominant formation in a coalition with the →Social Democratic Party (PSD) and the →Albanian Republican Party (PRSh), under the premiership of Aleksander Meksi. The party chairmanship passed to Eduard Selami. Serious post-election tensions in the PDSh were highlighted by the departure of six moderate leftists in July 1992 to form the →Democratic Alliance. The PDSh-led government was accused of increasing authoritarianism in 1993–94, although the party took steps to expel several declared right-wing extremists. Concerned with the status of ethnic Albanians in the Yugoslav province of Kosovo, the PDSh maintained close ties with →→Democratic League of Kosovo.

The rejection of a new government-proposed constitution in a referendum on Nov. 6, 1994, represented a major setback for the party, which was accused of seeking to increase presidential powers at the expense of the People's Assembly. President Berisha responded by carrying out a major government reshuffle in December, retaining Meksi as Prime Minister but losing the PRSh and the PSD as formal coalition partners. At a special PDSh conference in March 1995, Selami was dismissed as party chairman, having opposed the President's plan to hold another referendum on the new draft constitution. He was replaced in March 1996 by Tritan Shehu, as the PDSh launched its election campaign on a platform of lower taxes and more privatization. The following month Selami and seven others were ousted from the PDSh national council.

Amid opposition charges of electoral fraud and intimidation, the PDSh was officially stated to have won 122 of the 140 seats in the May–June 1996 parliamentary elections; but the descent into near-anarchy and north-south conflict early in 1997 forced the PDSh to surrender the premiership to the PSSh in March. For the new Assembly elections in June-July 1997 the PDSh headed the Union for Democracy seeking to rally the centre-right; but the party slumped to 28 seats out of 155 (and 25.7% of the vote), whereupon Berisha vacated the state presidency and the party went into opposition to a government led by Fatos Nano of the PSSh.

The shooting of a PDSh deputy by a PSSh member in September 1997 provoked a PDSh boycott of the Assembly which was to last, with short intervals of participation, for nearly two years. The murder of prominent PDSh deputy Acem Hajdari in September 1998 produced a new crisis in which Berisha and the PDSh were accused of attempting a coup in Tirana. The resignation of Nano at the end of September was welcomed by Berisha, who gave qualified support to the new government of Pandeli Majko (PSSh). New strains developed over the PDSh boycott of a constitutional referendum in November 1998 and its rejection of the result on the grounds of low turnout. However, from March 1999 the PDSh gave general backing to the government's line on the NATO–Yugoslavia hostilities over Kosovo and in July called off its latest boycott of the Assembly.

In September 1999 then PDSh parliamentary leader Genc Pollo called on the centre-right opposition parties to unite under PDSh leadership. However, at a party congress the following month Pollo failed to unseat Berisha, who was re-elected PDSh chairman unopposed following a purge of moderate members of the party executive. The moderates subsequently regrouped within the party as the Democratic Alternative, which attracted the support of eight PDSh parliamentary deputies.

The PDSh suffered major reverses in local elections in October 2000, winning only about a third of the vote and losing control of Tirana to the PSSh. The party contested the mid-2001 parliamentary elections at the head of an Alliance for Change and advanced to 42 seats, but remained in opposition to a further PSSh-led government.

Human Rights Union Party
Partia për Mbrojtjen e te Drejtava te Njeriut (PMDN)
Address. c/o Kuvënd Popullore, Tirana
Telephone. (+355–42) 27170
Fax. (+355–42) 28361
Leadership. Vasil Melo (president); Thoma Mico (secretary-general)

The PMDN was launched in February 1992 principally to represent Albania's ethnic Greek population (perhaps 3% of the total, concentrated in southern Albania in what used to be called Northern Epirus), following the enactment of legislation banning parties based on "ethnic principles". The new law was directed in particular at the Democratic Union of the Greek Minority (Omonia) which had won five seats in the 1991 Assembly elections. In the early 1990s Omonia agitation contributed to the flight of many ethnic Greeks from Albania to Greece, amidst increasingly serious border incidents and alleged ethnic Greek subversion within Albania.

In further Assembly elections of March 1992 the new PMDN (including Omonia representatives) won two of the 140 seats with 2.9% of the first-round vote. In May 1994 six activists of the outlawed Omonia, including chairman Theodhori Bezhani, were among many ethnic Greeks arrested in a government crackdown, five of them being convicted in September 1994 on treason and other charges. By early 1995, however, all five had been released, as the Albanian government sought to accommodate ethnic Greek grievances.

In the 1996 elections the PMDN won three seats, and in 1997 four, when it was allocated one portfolio in a coalition headed by the →Socialist Party of Albania. In the mid-2001 Assembly elections the party slipped to three seats with 2.4% of the vote.

Movement of Legality Party
Partia Lëvizja e Legalitetit (PLL)
Address. Rr. P. Shkurti pall. 5/1, Tirana
Leadership. Ekrem Spahia (chairman)

The PLL was relaunched in February 1991 as the political wing of the Albanian monarchist movement, having originally been founded in 1943 to support the unsuccessful attempt of King Zog (deposed in 1939) to regain the throne. The PLL backs the restoration of the exiled royal family now headed by Zog's son, Leka Zogu.

Leka Zogu returned in April 1997 "to share the suffering" of the Albanian people at a time of social crisis, successfully calling for a referendum on whether the monarchy should be restored. The non-binding consultation was held simultaneously with the first round of Assembly elections on June 29, 1997, the PLL leading the "yes" campaign and later dismissing as fraudulent official results showing a "no" vote of 66.7%. The party won only two seats in the Assembly elections, in which it was a component of the Union for Democracy headed by the →Democratic Party of Albania (PDSh). During the campaigning Leka Zogu held a rally of armed supporters at which one person was shot dead; he was later convicted *in absentia* of trying to organize a coup attempt.

In the mid-2001 Assembly elections the PLL was part of the losing Union for Victory headed by the PDSh.

National Front
Bashkimi Kombëtare (BK)
Address. c/o Kuvënd Popullore, Tirana
Leadership. Abaz Ermenji (chairman)

Claiming descent from the anti-communist wing of the World War II resistance, the right-wing BK was revived following the collapse of communist rule in 1990–91. BK leader Abaz Ermenji returned to Albania in October 1995 after 49 years in exile. In the mid-2001 Assembly elections the PLL was part of the losing Union for Victory headed by the PDSh.

Social Democratic Party
Partia Social Demokratike (PSD)
Address. Rr. Asim Vokshi 26, Tirana
Telephone. (+355–42) 26540
Fax. (+355–42) 27485
Leadership. Skënder Gjinushi (chairman); Gaqo Apostoli (general secretary)

Tracing its descent from pre-communist workers' parties, the PSDS was founded in March 1991 on a democratic socialist platform and won seven Assembly seats in the March 1992 elections, subsequently joining the coalition government headed by the →Democratic Party of Albania but withdrawing in 1994. For the 1996 legislative elections the PSD formed the "Pole of the Centre" alliance with the →Democratic Alliance, both formations joining in the opposition boycott of the June run-off voting. In the mid-1997 Assembly elections the PSD won eight seats in alliance with the →Socialist Party of Albania (PSSh) but in the mid-2001 Assembly elections it declined to four seats, taking 3.6% of the vote.

Claiming a membership of 20,000, the PSD is a full member of the Socialist International.

Socialist Party of Albania
Partia Socialiste e Shqipërisë (PSSh)
Address. Bul. Deshmorete e Kombit, Tirana
Telephone. (+355–42) 23409
Fax. (+355–42) 27417
Leadership. Fatos Nano (chairman); Gramos Ruçi (general secretary)

The PSSh is descended from the former ruling Party of Labour of Albania (PLA), which held power in a one-party state from the 1940s. Under its leader Enver Hoxha, the PLA presided over a regime that adopted rigid Stalinist methods in a backward rural society, Albania remaining one of the most closed societies in the world, hostile to both the West and to Soviet bloc Eastern European countries.

Hoxha died in April 1985 and was succeeded as party leader by President Ramiz Alia, who moved to end Albania's isolation but who initially took a hardline stance against the post-1989 political changes in Eastern Europe. In November 1990, however, a PLA congress conceded limited pluralism. Popular demonstrations in December 1990 yielded the legalization of several opposition parties, but the PLA's strong rural base enabled it to win a two-thirds majority in multi-party elections in March–April 1991.

In May 1991 President Alia surrendered the PLA leadership, while the following month a party congress, featuring unprecedented criticism of past actions, adopted the new PSSh name to signify an abandonment of Marxist precepts and elected a new leadership, former Prime Minister Fatos Nano becoming party chairman. Concurrent popular demonstrations forced Alia to appoint a "non-partisan" government under Ylli Bufi of the PSSh and including representatives of former opposition parties. But continuing unrest obliged the PSSh to surrender the premiership in December 1991. In further Assembly elections in March 1992 the PSSh was heavily defeated by the →Democratic Party of Albania (PDSh) and went into opposition, while Alia resigned as President in April.

In 1993 the PSSh was weakened by the prosecution of Alia, Nano and other leaders for alleged corruption and abuse of power under the previous regime. Nano was convicted on various charges in April 1994 and sentenced to 12 years' imprisonment (later reduced), while in July Alia was also found guilty, although his nine-year sentence was later reduced prior to his release in July 1995, when he vowed to resume active politics. Despite his conviction, Nano remained PSSh chairman, with deputy chairman Servet Pellumbi becoming acting chairman. Pressure on the PSSh was maintained with the conviction in June 1995 of Ilir Hoxha (son of Enver) for "inciting national hatred" by denouncing the PDSh government and praising the former communist regime. In September 1995 the Supreme Court rejected Nano's appeal against his conviction.

In November 1995 the PSSh deputies were among those who unsuccessfully opposed legislation requiring senior public officials to be screened for their activities in the communist era. Under this so-called Genocide Act, a number of proposed PSSh candidates were barred from contesting the 1996 legislative elections, the actual conduct of the first round of which in May was widely regarded as riddled with fraud and intimidation. The PSSh accordingly led an opposition boycott of the second round and was credited with only 10 seats when the official results were published.

The PSSh led popular opposition to the subsequent PDSh-led government, assisted by general outrage from early 1997 at the collapse of fraudulent "pyramid" savings schemes and the resultant descent into general anarchy. In March 1997 the PSSh joined a "government of reconciliation" headed by Bashkim Fino and was boosted by the release of Nano on a presidential pardon. In further Assembly elections in June–July 1997 the PSSh returned to power with 101 of the 155 seats and 52.8% of the vote. In July 1997 Rexhep Majdani of the PSSh replaced Sali Berisha (PDSh) as President, whereupon Nano was appointed to head a five-party coalition government.

Further instability resulted in Nano being replaced as Prime Minister in September 1998, his successor being PSSh general secretary and leading reformist Pandeli Majko. Internal party strains caused Nano to announce in January 1999 that he intended to resign as PSSh chairman in order to launch "an emancipating movement" to restore hope among the people. At a PSSh congress in October 1999, however, Nano was re-elected chairman by a narrow majority over challenger Majko, who therefore resigned as Prime Minister. Majko was replaced by Deputy Premier Ilir Meta, who was seen as on the PSSh reformist or "Euro-socialist" wing but was more dependent on Nano and his conservative PSSh faction.

In October 2000 the PSSh registered substantial local election advances, winning over 50% of the popular vote and 252 out of 398 local authorities, including Tirana, hitherto a PDSh stronghold. The party lost some ground in the mid-2001 parliamentary elections but remained dominant by winning 73 of the 140 seats, so that Meta was able to form a new government.

The PSSh is a consultative member of the Socialist International.

Other Parties

Albanian Communist Party (*Partia Komuniste Shqiptare, PKSh*), formed in June 1991 by a faction of the Party of Labour of Albania opposed to its conversion into the →Socialist Party of Albania. The PKS was legalized in November 1991, banned in mid-1992 as an extremist organization but re-legalized in April 1998.
Leadership. Hysni Milloshi (chairman)

Christian Democratic Party of Albania (*Partia Demokristiane e Shqipërisë, PDK*), based in the Catholic areas of northern Albania, member of Christian Democrat International.
Address. Rr. Dëshmorët e Shkurtit 4, Tirana
Telephone. (+355–42) 30042
Fax. (+355–42) 33024
Leadership. Zef Bushati (chairman)

Party of National Restoration (*Partia per Rimekembjen Kombëtare, PRK*), extreme nationalist formation founded in early 1996 that advocates the unification of all Albanian-populated lands in the Balkans, by force if necessary.
Leadership. Abdi Baleta (chairman)

Algeria

Capital: Algiers

Population: 30,000,000 (2000E)

The Democratic and Popular Republic of Algeria, under an amendment to its 1976 constitution adopted in 1989, moved from the status of one-party state in which the National Liberation Front (FLN) was the "vanguard, leadership and organization of the people with the aim of building socialism" to being a qualified multi-party democracy. The constitution provides for an executive President, who is directly elected by universal suffrage of those aged at least 18 for a renewable five-year term and who appoints and presides over a Council of Ministers.

After a hiatus following the cancellation of the second round of parliamentary elections in January 1992 because of the imminent victory of the Islamic Salvation Front (FIS), a new parliamentary structure approved in a constitutional referendum in November 1996 provides for a bicameral Parliament (*Barlaman*) consisting of (i) an upper Council of the Nation (*Majlis al-Oumma*) of 144 members, of whom one-third are appointed by the President and two-thirds indirectly elected for six-year terms by a college of local government representatives; and (ii) a lower National People's Assembly (*Majlis Ech Chaabi al-Watani*) of 380 members (eight representing Algerians abroad), directly elected for five-year term by proportional representation from party lists. The 1996 constitutional referendum also approved the proscription of political parties based on religion, language, gender or region.

Assembly elections on June 5, 1997, resulted as follows: National Democratic Rally (RND) 156 seats (36.3% of the vote); Movement of Society for Peace (MSP) 69 (16.0%); National Liberation Front (FLN) 62 (15.3%); Renaissance Movement (*Nahda*) 34 (9.4%); Socialist Forces Front 20 (4.8%); Rally for Culture and Democracy 19 (4.6%); Workers' Party 4 (2.0%); Progressive Republican Party 3 (0.7%); Union for Democracy and Liberties 1 (0.5%); Social Liberal Party 1 (0.4%); independents 11 (4.9%).

In controversial presidential elections on April 15, 1999, Abdelaziz Bouteflika of the FLN, who was supported by the military and also by the RND, the MSP and *Nahda*, was declared the winner with 73.8% of the vote. However, the withdrawal of the six other candidates shortly before polling (though their names appeared on ballot papers) tainted the result, amidst opposition claims that the vote had been rigged and that the turnout had been drastically lower than the official figure of 60.9%.

Islamic Salvation Front
Front Islamique du Salut (FIS)
Website. www.fisalgeria.org
Leadership. Abassi Madani (president); Ali Belhadj (vice-president); Anouar Haddam (spokesman in exile)

Formed from student and other Islamist groups dating from the early 1970s, the FIS obtained official recognition in February 1989 amid a rising tide of opposition to the government of the →National Liberation Front (FLN). In municipal elections in June 1990 FIS candidates took 55% of the popular vote, winning control of 853 municipalities and 32 out of 48 provinces. Serious clashes between FIS supporters and the security forces resulted, in June 1991, in the postponement of Assembly elections and the arrest of hundreds of FIS activists, including Abassi Madani and Ali Belhadj. Divisions between moderates and extremists in the remaining leadership resulted in the former prevailing in their view that the FIS should contest the elections, set for December 1991, and call off street demonstrations. Led in the elections by Abdelkader Hachani and presenting candidates for all 430 seats, the FIS took a commanding lead in the first-round voting, winning 188 seats outright (and 47.5% of the vote). With the FIS poised to secure a substantial overall majority in the second round, Hachani made it clear that an FIS government would seek an early presidential election and, "should that be the people's demand", embark upon constitutional reform; he gave no specific commitment to the multi-party system, but stressed that Islamicization would be pursued by legal means.

Hachani and Rabeh Kebir were among several FIS leaders arrested in January 1992 following the cancellation of the second electoral round and the military's effective assumption of power. Upon petition by the High State Council, the FIS was banned by a court ruling in March 1992 (upheld by the Supreme Court in April) on the grounds that it had violated the 1989 law prohibiting a religious basis for parties. In a major clamp-down on FIS activists, many thousands were arrested and detained in desert concentration camps. FIS moderates, committed to non-violence, sought political accommodation with the regime (and the FIS leadership denied any involvement in the assassination of head of state Mohammed Boudiaf in June 1992); but the initiative passed increasingly to radical splinter-groups favouring armed struggle, notably to the Armed Islamic Group (GIA). In July 1992 both Madani and Belhadj were sentenced to 12 years' imprisonment after being convicted on insurgency charges. The following month Kebir escaped from detention and was later granted political asylum in Germany, together with Ossama Madani, son of Abbasi. In September 1993 the German authorities refused an Algerian extradition request for these two, who had both been sentenced to death *in absentia* for their alleged part in a bomb attack at Algiers airport in August 1992.

In 1993–94 attacks on security personnel and foreign nationals mounted, as did arrests and executions of FIS militants, bringing the country to a state of virtual civil war. In February 1994 the new Zéroual government released two senior FIS figures in an effort to promote political talks; but a subsequent unofficial dialogue involving FIS representatives produced no agreement. In September Madani and Belhadj were transferred from prison to house arrest in a regime move to promote further dialogue; when this did not occur, both were reimprisoned in November. The release of the two FIS leaders was the main demand of the hijackers of a French airliner at Algiers in December; presumed to be members of the GIA, all four hijackers were killed by French security forces at Marseilles. The episode generated press speculation on whether the GIA and the official armed wing of the FIS, called the Islamic Salvation Army (AIS), had merged. French sources put the death toll in Algeria's internal conflict in 1994 at some 40,000, the majority of them civilians.

In January 1995 the FIS was represented at a conference of Algerian opposition parties held in Rome, but a draft peace plan drawn up on that occasion found little favour with the Algerian government. The following month several prominent FIS members were among many killed when the Algerian security forces put down a revolt by Islamist prisoners at the Serkadji prison in Algiers. Talks between FIS leaders and the government were initiated in April 1995, initially in secret, but broke down in July, with the government claiming that the FIS had entered new conditions at a late stage and had refused to give a commitment to pluralist democracy. Having again been released to house arrest during the talks, Madani and Belhadj were again returned to prison when the talks failed. The FIS boycotted the November 1995 presidential elections, claiming after the result was declared that the turnout had been only about 30% rather than the 75% cited by the Algerian authorities. Growing divisions in the Islamist opposition were highlighted in December 1995 by the execution by a GIA firing squad of two aides of the FIS leader who had criticized the GIA's campaign of violence.

In April 1997 the FIS participated in a Madrid meeting of opposition parties which called for the opening of a peace dialogue. The FIS urged a boycott of the June 1997 parliamentary elections, following which Madani and Hachami were conditionally released from prison in July in a gesture of conciliation by the new government headed by the →National Democratic Rally (RND). Although secret negotiations made little immediate progress, and Madani was returned to house arrest in October, the AIS declared a unilateral truce from Oct. 1, 1997. In March 1998 FIS spokesman Anouar Haddam was sentenced to death *in absentia* for his alleged involvement in various killings.

In April 1999 newly-elected President Abdelaziz Bouteflika declared that the FIS would not be re-legalized, although former FIS members would be allowed to join legal parties. In June the AIS announced the permanent ending of its armed struggle, reportedly being joined by some 1,000 GIA defectors (although GIA violence continued), while the approval of Bouteflika's new "civil concord" in a referendum in October 1999 generated new hopes for peace. Despite the assassination of Hachami in Algiers in November, in January 2000 the AIS announced that it would disband, reports suggesting that former AIS activists would join government forces in fighting the GIA and other militant groups. After some initial confusion, the President granted a blanket pardon to all former AIS members. With the FIS remaining banned, many Front members joined the new →Wafa party, although in May 2000 the Interior Minister expressed reluctance to authorize legal recognition for the new formation.

Movement of Society for Peace
Harakat Moudjtamaa as-Silm
Mouvement de la Société pour la Paix (MSP)
Address. 63 rue Ali Haddad, El Mouradia, Algiers
Telephone. (+213–2) 272572
Fax. (+213–2) 675024
Email. info@hms-algeria.net
Website. www.hms-algeria.net
Leadership. Sheikh Mahfoud Nahnah (president); Magharia Mohamed (vice-president for political relations); Farid Hebbaz (vice-president for co-ordination)

This moderate Islamist party was formed in 1990 as the Movement for an Islamic Society (*Hamas*), being unrelated to the Palestinian movement with the same acronym. Declaring its opposition to the radicalism of the →Islamic Salvation Front (FIS), it advocates the gradual creation of an Islamic state and respect for individual liberties and the democratic process. The party failed to win a seat in the first round of the December 1991 Assembly elections and was subsequently supportive of the regime's anti-fundamentalist campaign, being the only significant party to participate in the "national consensus conference" convened by the government in January 1994. Sheikh Mahfoud Nahnah was a candidate in the November 1995 presidential elections, coming in second place with 25.4% of the vote. After the result was declared, Sheikh Nahnah asserted that 4 million names added to the electoral register since 1991 could not be justified by population growth; he also claimed that his supporters and monitors had been intimidated by the authorities. Nevertheless, in January 1996 Hamas accepted two portfolios in a government reshuffle announced by President Zéroual.

The party renamed itself the MSP in light of the November 1996 referendum decision proscribing religious identification for parties. In the June 1997 parliamentary elections it took second place, with 69 of the 380 seats and 16% of the vote, although Sheikh Nahnah claimed that the polling had been rigged and that the MSP had won 100 fewer seats than its real entitlement. The party nevertheless entered a new coalition government headed by the →National Democratic Rally (RND), seeking to rally moderate Islamist opinion against the extremists. In the December 1997 indirect elections to the Council of the Nation the MSP took only two of the 96 elective seats.

After Sheikh Nahnah had been barred from standing in the April 1999 presidential elections (because he had not proved that he had participated in Algeria's war of independence), the MSP backed the successful candidacy of the Abdelaziz Bouteflika of the →National Liberation Front (FLN) and was again included in the subsequent government. The party supported Bouteflika's "civil concord" peace plan approved by referendum in November 1999.

National Democratic Rally
Rassemblement National Démocratique (RND)
Address. c/o Barlaman, Algiers
Leadership. Ahmed Ouyahia (secretary-general)
The creation of the RND was announced in March 1997 by supporters of then President Liamine Zéroual with the aim of providing a vehicle for the ruling establishment in the June 1997 parliamentary elections. The new party declared itself to be in favour of political democracy, social justice and modernization of the economy by privatization and to be determined to crush the "extremism" of the →Islamic Salvation Front (FIS) and other Islamist groups. In the June elections the RND became substantially the largest Assembly party, winning 156 of the 380 seats with 36.3% of the vote, although its success was tainted by charges of vote rigging and electoral fraud. The party thereupon formed a coalition government headed by Ahmed Ouyahia which included the →National Liberation Front (FLN) and the →Movement of Society for Peace (MSP).

At the first RND congress in April 1998 Tahar Benbaibeche was confirmed as secretary-general heading a 15-member national bureau. However, Benbaibeche's resistance to RND endorsement of the army-backed presidential candidacy of Abdelaziz Bouteflika (FLN) precipitated his dismissal in January 1999 and replacement by Ouyahia (who had vacated the premiership the previous month). Following Bouteflika's controversial victory in the April 1999 presidential elections, the RND continued to be the leading component in the government coalition, which was extended to the →Renaissance Movement (*Nahda*), although a non-party Prime Minister was appointed. The

RND gave strong backing the Bouteflika's "civil concord" peace plan approved by referendum in September 1999.

National Liberation Front
Jabha al-Tahrir al-Watani
Front de Libération Nationale (FLN)
Address. 7 rue du Stade, Hydra, Algiers
Telephone. (+213–2) 592149
Fax. (+213–2) 591732
Leadership. Boualem Benhamouda (secretary-general)
The FLN was founded at Cairo in November 1954 under the leadership of Ahmed Ben Bella and other nationalists as an anti-colonialist, socialist, non-aligned, pan-Arabist and pro-Islam movement dedicated to ending French rule. After achieving independence and coming to power in 1962, it experienced internal strife in which Ben Bella was initially victorious but which eventually resulted in his replacement in July 1965 by Col. Houari Boumedienne, who held the government and party leadership until his death in December 1978. The FLN was then reorganized and given a new statute at its fourth congress in January 1979, at which Bendjedid Chadli was elected party leader and designated as sole candidate for the presidency in elections the following month. Re-elected unopposed in January 1984, Bendjedid embarked upon a programme of economic reform, emphasizing "pragmatic" socialism and the virtues of the private enterprise, to the chagrin of the FLN's socialist old guard. He also, following anti-FLN riots in late 1978, sought to democratize political structures, to which end the posts of head of state and party leader were made incompatible by decision of an FLN congress in November. Bendjedid was succeeded as FLN secretary-general by his brother-in-law, Abdelhamid Mehri, and himself took the new post of party president.

The move to multi-party democracy in 1989 revealed the extent of popular discontent with the FLN, which suffered a serious rebuff in local elections in June 1990 marking the emergence of the fundamentalist →Islamic Salvation Front (FIS) as a major force. Subsequent anti-government demonstrations resulted in the formation in June 1991 of the first post-independence government not dominated by the FLN, Bendjedid resigning as party president the same month. In Assembly elections in December 1991 the FLN trailed a poor third in the first-round voting despite putting up 429 candidates, after which the military intervened to prevent a likely FIS victory in the second round and Bendjedid resigned as President.

Although the new regime included many figures associated with the years of FLN rule, the party itself effectively went into opposition, joining other parties in calling for a transitional government of national unity and condemning the use of military courts to enforce emergency regulations banning fundamentalist political activity. It also declined to join a regime-sponsored National Patriotic Rally, announced in June 1992 as a new "foundation" for political co-operation; for its pains the FLN was dispossessed of its state-owned properties, including its party headquarters in Algiers. In March 1994 the FLN joined other parties in opening a dialogue with the new Zéroual government, while in January 1995 Mehri attended the Rome conference of Algerian opposition parties at which a peace plan was drawn up, although without substantive effect. A member of the FLN central committee, Ahmed Kasmi, was found beheaded in February 1995, apparently the victim of Islamic militants. The FLN joined the opposition parties' boycott of the November 1995 presidential elections, after which Mehri made a conciliatory statement calling on the government to enter into real dialogue with the FIS.

The FLN participated in the June 1997 parliamentary elections, coming in third place with 62 of the 380 seats and 15.3% of the popular vote, while in the December indirect elections to the Council of the Nation it took 10 of the 96 elective seats. Its participation in the new coalition government headed by the →National Democratic Rally (RND) precipitated divisions between FLN "reformists" led by former Prime Minister Mouloud Hamrouche who favoured accommodation with the FIS and the more hard-line leadership of Boualem Benhamouda, who asserted his authority at an FLN congress in March 1998. With military backing, the FLN nominated former Foreign Minister Abdelaziz Bouteflika as its candidate for the April 1999 presidential elections, while Hamrouche entered the contest as the nominee of a new alliance of six parties called the Group of National Forces (GFN). Bouteflika was also backed by the RND, the →Movement of Society for Peace (MSP) and the →Renaissance Movement (*Nahda*) and was controversially elected with 73.8% of the vote, after the other candidates had withdrawn shortly before polling.

The FLN continued to participate in the government, backing Bouteflika's "civil concord" peace plan approved by referendum in September 1999. In February 2001 a new party called the →Rally for National Concord (RCN) was launched to provide a broader political base for the President.

Progressive Republican Party
Parti Républicain Progressif (PRP)
Address. 10 rue Ouahrani Abou-Mediêne, Cité Seddikia, Oran
Telephone. (+213–5) 357936
Leadership. Slimane Cherif (secretary-general)
The moderate PRP was established as a legal party in 1990 under the then leadership of Khadir Driss. In the June 1997 parliamentary elections it won three of the 380 seats with 0.7% of the national vote.

Rally for Culture and Democracy
Rassemblement pour la Culture et la Démocratie (RCD)
Address. 87 rue Didouche Mourad, Algiers
Telephone. (+213–2) 738487
Fax. (+213–2) 738472
Email. rcd@rcd-dz.org
Website. www.rcd-dz.org
Leadership. Saïd Sadi (president)
Based in the Berber community, the secular RCD was formed in February 1989 on a platform of "economic centralism" and official recognition of the Berber language. It took third place in the June 1990 local elections (which were boycotted by the rival Berber-based →Socialist Forces Front), winning 5.7% of the vote and majorities in 87 municipalities and the province of Tizi Ouzou. In the December 1991 Assembly elections, however, none of its 300 candidates were elected in the first round. The RCD joined other mainstream parties in opposing the military-led regime installed in January 1992, launching the broad-based Movement for the Republic (MPR) in November 1993 to rally support, until Liamine Zéroual's accession to the presidency in January 1994 heralded a more conciliatory government stance, enabling political dialogue to commence in March. Saïd Sadi (then RCD secretary-general) was a candidate in the November 1995 presidential elections, winning 9.3% of the vote.

In the June 1997 parliamentary elections the RCD won 19 of the 380 seats (and 4.6% of the national vote), including 15 of the 24 Algiers seats, but claimed that it had been particularly damaged by electoral fraud. The party therefore boycotted the December 1997 elections to the new Council of the Nation and organized large protest demonstrations in Algiers. After the second RCD congress in February 1998 had elected Sadi as party president, the RCD announced in February 1999 that it would boycott the forthcoming presidential elections.

Rally for National Concord
Rassemblement pour la Concorde Nationale (RCN)
Address. c/o Barlaman, Algiers
Leadership. Sid Ahmed Abachi (chairman)

The RCN was launched in February 2001 with the stated aim of providing "a popular base" for President Bouteflika, who had been a member of the →National Liberation Front (FLN) when he was elected in 1999. Claiming to represent over 7,000 national and local associations, the RCN undertook to give support to the President against those trying to obstruct his national reconciliation programme and against the forces of sedition.

Renaissance Movement
Harakat al-Nahda (Nahda)
Mouvement de la Renaissance (MR)
Address. 4 ave des Ecoles, Place des Martyrs, Algiers
Telephone. (+213–2) 667666
Fax. (+213–2) 667666
Leadership. Lahib Adami (secretary-general)
This moderate Islamist party sprang from a Constantine University movement of the 1970s and was called the Islamic Renaissance Movement until early 1997, when it dropped the "Islamic" descriptor to conform with the new constitutional ban on parties of religious orientation. It was unsuccessful in the December 1991 Assembly elections and subsequently declared itself in favour of dialogue to bring about a national consensus, being boosted by the government as an alternative to the extremist →Islamic Salvation Front (FIS). Its leader participated in a conference of Algerian opposition parties held in Rome in January 1995 and endorsed a resultant draft peace agreement, but this text did not impress the regime in Algiers.

Nahda joined other opposition parties in boycotting the November 1995 presidential elections, but participated in the June 1997 parliamentary elections, winning 34 of the 380 seats and 9.4% of the vote. It opted not to participate in the subsequent coalition government headed by the →National Democratic Rally (RND), following which internal divisions developed between long-time *Nahda* leader Sheikh Abdallah Djaballah and secretary-general Lahib Adami over whether the party should back government candidate Abdelaziz Bouteflika of the →National Liberation Front (FLN) in the April 1999 presidential elections. The outcome was the dismissal of Djaballah as leader in January 1999 (and his formation of the breakaway →Movement of National Reform), whereupon the rump *Nahda* supported Bouteflika in his successful but highly controversial candidacy and was subsequently included in a new coalition headed by the RND.

Socialist Forces Front
Front des Forces Socialistes (FFS)
Address. 56 ave Souidani Boudjemaa, 16000 Algiers
Telephone. (+213–2) 593313
Fax. (+213–2) 591145
Email. ffs.idf@wanadoo.fr
Website. www.f-f-s.com
Leadership. Hocine Aït Ahmed (president); Mustapha Bouhadef (first secretary)
Originally founded in September 1963 and revived and legalized in November 1989 after 14 years of clandestine existence, the FFS espoused democratic socialist principles as contrasted with the state centralism of the then ruling →National Liberation Front (FLN). Its founder and leader, Hocine Aït Ahmed, is one of the surviving *neuf historiques* who launched the Algerian war of independence against France in November 1954. Following independence in 1962, he instigated an unsuccessful Berber revolt against the Ben Bella government in 1963. Arrested in October 1964, Ahmed was sentenced to death in April 1964 (the sentence being commuted to life imprisonment) but escaped abroad in May 1966.

After Ahmed had returned to Algeria from Switzerland in December 1989, the FFS held its first post-legalization congress in March 1991. After an abortive attempt to create a broad coalition to oppose the →Islamic Salvation Front (FIS), the FFS emerged as the leading non-Islamist party in the first round of Assembly elections in December 1991. It put up 317 candidates and won 25 seats outright with 15% of the vote, on a platform advocating a mixed economy, regional autonomy and recognition of the Berber language. Having ruled out a second-round alliance with either the FLN or the FIS, Ahmed strongly criticized the subsequent military intervention and returned to exile in Switzerland.

Calling for a government of national unity and an end to anti-FIS repression, the FFS rejected affiliation with the National Patriotic Rally launched by the government in June 1992 and also boycotted the "national consensus conference" convened in January 1994. Nevertheless, having urged moderate army elements to join with the democratic opposition, the FFS responded to the conciliatory overtures of the new Zéroual government in March 1994, while insisting that political dialogue must result in a resumption of multi-party democracy. In January 1995 Ahmed attended the Rome conference of Algerian opposition parties at which a putative peace plan was formulated. Following its rejection by the government, the FFS was one of several opposition parties that boycotted the November 1995 presidential elections. Ahmed returned to Algeria in March 1996 to attend the second FFS congress, at which he was elected party president (having hitherto been secretary-general) and which appealed for national dialogue to achieve civil peace.

In January 1997 Ahmed criticized government policy of promoting the creation of local anti-Islamist militias, contending that they were involved in smuggling, organized crime and vendettas between families and clans. In the June 1997 parliamentary elections the FFS took fifth place (just ahead of the rival Berber-based →Rally for Culture and Democracy), winning 20 of the 380 seats and 4.8% of the vote. It thereafter remained in opposition to the new government headed by the →National Democratic Rally (RND), urging it to move towards legalization of the FIS. In the December 1997 indirect elections to the Council of the Nation it took four of the 96 elective seats.

A special FFS congress in February 1999 nominated Ahmed as the party's candidate for the presidential elections in April; however, together with other opposition candidates he withdrew shortly before polling in protest against intervention by the military to rig the ballot in favour of Abdelaziz Bouteflika of the →National Liberation Front (FLN). The third FFS congress in May 2000 reaffirmed the party's opposition to Bouteflika's "civil concord" peace plan approved by referendum in September 1999, calling instead the election of a constituent assembly to bring about genuine "democratic alternance".

The FFS claims a membership of 30,000 and is a member party of the Socialist International.

Workers' Party
Parti des Travailleurs (PT)
Address. 2 rue Belkheir Belkacemi, Hassan Badi, El Harrach, Algiers
Telephone. (+213–2) 753637
Fax. (+213–2) 753698
Website. www.multimania.com/tribune
Leadership. Louisa Hanoune (president)
The leftist PT was represented by Louisa Hanoune at the Rome conference of opposition parties in January 1995. The party won a creditable four seats in the June 1997 parliamentary election with 2% of the national vote. In January 1999 the PT central committee nominated Hanoune as the party's candidate for the April 1999 presidential elections, but she was barred from standing because she was deemed to have provided less than the required 75,000 signatures of support.

Other Parties

The large number of legal minor parties in Algeria was reduced by an announcement by the authorities in May 1998 that 30 parties had been banned for failing to meet new rules pertaining to such organizations, including a provision that a party must have at least 2,500 individual members.

Democratic Social Movement (*Mouvement Démocratique et Social, MDS*), launched in October 1999 as successor to the Challenge (Ettahaddi) movement, itself created in January 1993 as successor to the Socialist Vanguard Party (*Parti de l'Avant-Garde Socialiste*, PAGS), itself descended from the Algerian Communist Party (CPA) founded in the 1930s. *Ettahaddi* boycotted the the 1997 parliamentary and 1999 presidential elections, its conversion into the MDS signifying a renewed commitment to the democratic process and the mixed economy, as well as opposition to any compromise with Islamic extremism.
Address. 67 blvd Krim Belkacem, Algiers
Telephone. (+213–2) 420336
Fax. (+213–2) 429723
Email. mds@mds.pol.dz
Website. www.mds.pol.dz
Leadership. Al-Hashemi Cherif (secretary-general)

Wafa Party, founded in early 2000 mainly by former members of the banned →Islamic Salvation Front (FIS) following the Bouteflika presidency's new accommodation with the FIS accepting that FIS activists could join other legal parties.

Andorra

Capital: Andorra la Vella   **Population**: 71,000 (2000E)

Andorra effectively gained independence on May 4, 1993, with the entry into force of its first written constitution, adopted by referendum on March 14. The sovereignty hitherto vested in the President of the French Republic and the Bishop of Urgel (in Spain) as Co-Princes was transferred to the "parliamentary co-principality" of Andorra. The Co-Princes were retained with the status of a single constitutional monarch, with much reduced powers, and were still represented by their respective Permanent Delegates, and locally by the *Veguer de França* and the *Veguer Episcopal*. The unicameral legislature, the 28–member General Council of the Valleys (*Consell General de las Valls d'Andorra*), is elected for a four-year term by universal franchise of Andorran citizens aged 18 and over, 14 members being elected on a national list system and two each from the seven constituent parishes. Most residents are ineligible to vote, being French or Spanish nationals. The General Council, under the new dispensation, selects the Head of Government (*Cap del Govern*) who presides over an Executive Council or Cabinet (*Govern d'Andorra*); neither the Head of Government nor the ministers may be members of the General Council.

Political parties were legalized by the 1993 constitution, which also formalized trade union and civil rights and the separation of the judiciary from the executive and legislative branches. Various ad hoc groupings had contested earlier elections, and the General Council balloting on Dec. 12, 1993, marked the development of these groups into political parties. In elections to the General Council on March 4, 2001, the Liberal Party of Andorra won 15 seats (with 46.1% of the vote), the Social Democratic Party 6 (30.0%), the Democratic Party 5 (23.8%) and the Lauredian Union 2.

Democratic Party
Partit Demòcrata (PD)

Address. c/o Consell General, Casa de la Vall, Andorra la Vella

Leadership. Lluís Viu Torres (chairman); Josep Garrallà Rossell (chairman of parliamentary group)

The PD was formed prior to the 2001 General Council elections as the successor principally to the centre-right National Democratic Grouping (*Agrupament Nacional Democratica*, AND) and was also joined by the Union of the People of Ordino (*Unió del Poble d'Ordino*, UPd'O).

The AND had been founded in 1979 by Oscar Ribas Reig, who presided over the Executive Council in 1982–84 and 1990–94, latterly for a ten-month period as the first Head of Government under the 1993 constitution. Modernizing reforms introduced under Ribas Reig included the abolition of capital punishment, implementation of the new constitution, a customs union with the European Union and admission to the United Nations in July 1993. More controversially, he proposed to widen indirect taxation beyond sales to cover banking, insurance and other sectors to finance infrastructural development, and it was on this issue that his government fell in November 1994. However, two AND members who helped to vote in the successor government headed by the →Liberal Party of Andorra (PLA) did so only on condition that it agreed to implement a broadly similar budget. In the February 1997 General Council elections, the AND slipped from eight to six seats and remained in opposition to a further administration headed by the PLA.

The UPd'O had been based in the constituency parish of Ordino, from which it had elected two representatives in the February 1997 elections, both of whom joined the PLA parliamentary group.

In the March 2001 General Council elections the new PD won a disappointing five seats (and remained in opposition), with a national vote share of 23.8%.

Lauredian Union
Unió Laurediana (UL)

Address. c/o Consell General, Casa de la Vall, Andorra la Vella

Leadership. Marc Pintat Forné (leader)

Based in the parish of Sant Julià de Lòria, the UL was part of the victorious list of the Liberal Party of Andorra (PLA) in the 1997 General Council elections. Standing in its own right in the March 2001 contest, it won the two parish seats for Sant Julià de Lòria, its two elected members joining the PLA parliamentary group.

Liberal Party of Andorra
Partit Liberal d'Andorra (PLA)

Address. Edif. Elan 1°/4a, Avda. del Fener 11, Andorra la Vella

Telephone. (+376) 869708

Fax. (+376) 869728

Email. pla@andorra.ad

Website. www.partitliberal.ad

Leadership. Marc Forné Molné (president); Antoni Martí Petit (chairman of parliamentary group); Estanislau Sangrà Cardona (secretary-general)

Granted legal status in July 1992, the PLA is a centre-right formation advocating deregulation of the economy and greater openness to foreign investment.

In the December 1993 elections the PLA secured five seats on the General Council in its own right, with 22 per cent of the national vote, while four allied independents were elected from two parish constituencies. The Liberal group voted against the nomination of Oscar Ribas Reig of the National Democratic Grouping (AND) as Head of Government in January 1994. When Ribas Reig's coalition partners in New Democracy withdrew their backing for budget proposals in November 1994, PLA leader Marc Forné Molné garnered sufficient votes from other parties (including two from AND) to form a new administration with six other Liberal members and three non-party ministers.

In the February 1997 elections the PLA formed the core of the Liberal Union (*Unió Liberal*) alliance, which included *Unitat i Renovació* in the parish of Canillo, an independent Liberal grouping in La Massana and the →Lauredian Union in Sant Julià de Lòria. The alliance won a total of 16 seats (with 42.3% of the national vote) and the Liberal group in the General Council was also joined by the two representatives of the Union of the People of Ordino. Forné Molné was accordingly confirmed as Head of Government with a substantially improved majority. He continued in office after the March 2001 General Council elections, in which the PLA won 15 seats in its own right with a 46.1% national vote share, its parliamentary group being increased to 17 by the adhesion of the two elected Lauredian Union (UL) councillors.

The PLA has been a member of the Liberal International since 1994 and became a full member of the European Liberal, Democratic and Reformist (ELDR) organization in June 2001.

Social Democratic Party
Partit Socialdemòcrata (PS)

Address. c/Verge del Pilar 5, 3r/1a, Andorra la Vella

Telephone. (+376) 820320

Fax. (+376) 867979

Email. ps@andorra.ad

Leadership. Albert Salvadó Miras) (president); Jaume Bartumeu Cassany (chairman of parliamentary group & secretary-general)

The centre-left PS was founded in 2000, partly on the basis of the New Democracy (*Nova Democracia*, ND) grouping, which had won five seats in the 1993 General Council elections and two in 1997. The PS also attracted most of the National Democratic Initiative *Iniciatíva Democratica Nacional*, IDN), which had also won two seats in the 1997 elections. The new party performed creditably in its first General Council elections in March 2001, winning six seats with a 30% share of the national vote, but remained in opposition to the →Liberal Party of Andorra.

The PS is a consultative member of the Socialist International.

Angola

Capital: Luanda

Population: 12,00,000 (2000E)

Angola achieved independence from Portugal in November 1975 as the People's Republic of Angola, with the Popular Movement for the Liberation of Angola (MPLA) becoming the sole ruling party in Luanda. By early 1976 the MPLA government, assisted by Cuban military forces, had established control over most of Angola, although the competing Union for the Total Independence of Angola (UNITA), backed by South Africa and the USA, remained active in the south. Following the signature in December 1988 of the Brazzaville Agreement, providing for the withdrawal of Cuban and South African troops, the MPLA in December 1990 abandoned Marxism–Leninism and embraced "democratic socialism". The Lisbon Accord of May 1991 provided for an end to the civil war with UNITA and for reform of the political structure, including the introduction of a multi-party system. Under constitutional amendments adopted in August 1992, the country was renamed the Republic of Angola and provision made for a "semi-presidential" system headed by an executive President, directly elected for a five-year term in two rounds of voting, who appoints a Prime Minister. Legislative authority is vested in a National Assembly (*Assembléia Nacional*) elected for a four-year term by universal adult suffrage and proportional representation, with 130 members being returned nationally, 90 from provincial constituencies and possibly three by Angolans living abroad.

A law enacted in May 1991 specifies that political parties "must be national in character and scope". Specifically prohibited are parties that "are local and regional in character; foster tribalism, racism, regionalism or other forms of discrimination against citizens or affect national unity and territorial integrity; use or propose the use of violence to pursue their aims…; adopt a uniform for their members or possess clandestine parallel structures; use military, para-military or militarized organization; [or] are subordinate to the policy of foreign governments, bodies or parties". The 1991 law also makes provision for registered parties to receive state financial assistance on the basis of their support in the most recent general election and the number of candidates presented.

Multi-party elections to the new National Assembly on Sept. 29-30, 1992, produced the following results: MPLA 129 seats (53.7% of the national vote), UNITA 70 (34.1%), Social Renewal Party 6 (2.3%), National Front for the Liberation on Angola 5 (2.4%), Liberal Democratic Party 3 (2.4%), Democratic Renewal Party 1 (0.9%), Social Democratic Party 1 (0.8%), Party of the Alliance of Angolan Youth, Workers and Peasants 1 (0.4%), Angola Democratic Forum 1 (0.3%), Democratic Party for Progress–Angolan National Alliance 1 (0.3%), Angolan National Democratic Party 1 (0.3%). By agreement of the parties, the three seats reserved for Angolans abroad were not filled. In concurrent presidential elections, incumbent José Eduardo dos Santos (MPLA) won 49.6% of the first-round vote, just short of the 50% needed to make a second round unnecessary, although this was not held. A newly-appointed transitional government headed by the MPLA included representatives of four smaller parties, while posts were also allocated to UNITA. The latter nevertheless disputed the official election results and resumed military activities. Direct negotiations between the two sides opened in Lusaka in November 1993 after UNITA had declared its acceptance of the September 1992 election outcome. This process yielded the signature of a ceasefire and power-sharing agreement in the Zambian capital on Nov. 20, 1994.

Shortly before the expiry of its four-year term, the Assembly on Nov. 13, 1996, adopted a constitutional amendment extending its mandate for up to four years. In April 1997 UNITA representatives at last took up their Assembly seats and their posts in a "government of national unity and reconciliation". However, as warfare in the country intensified, the government in January 1999 formally repudiated the Lusaka agreement. Although President dos Santos promised in March 2000 that presidential and Assembly elections would be held in 2001, continuing hostilities forced the abandonment of this plan, the mandate of the Assembly being extended indefinitely on Oct. 17, 2000.

National Front for the Liberation of Angola
Frente Nacional de Libertação de Angola (FNLA)

Address. c/o Assembléia Nacional, Luanda

Email. fnla@ifrance.com

Website. www.fnla.org

Leadership. Holden Roberto (president); Ngola Kabangu (secretary-general)

The FNLA was founded in March 1962 as a merger of the *União das Populações de Angola* (UPA) led by Holden Roberto and the *Partido Democrático Angolano* (PDA), two northern nationalist movements which had launched an anti-Portuguese peasants' revolt the previous year. Based in what was then Zaïre and backed by President Mobutu (Roberto's brother-in-law), the FNLA the following month formed the "revolutionary Angolan government-in-exile" (GRAE), with Roberto as prime minister. Although vigorously anti-communist, the FNLA secured the backing of China, which switched its support from the pro-Soviet →Popular Movement for the Liberation of Angola (MPLA) in December 1962; it was also at various times aided by South Africa and the USA. In 1966 it was weakened by the formation of the breakaway →National Union for the Total Independence of Angola (UNITA), but it subsequently allied itself with UNITA in a pre-independence struggle for supremacy with the MPLA, interspersed with the signature of abortive "unity" pacts with the latter.

Following the left-wing military coup in Lisbon in April 1974, Portugal signed ceasefire agreements with the FNLA and UNITA, but a powerful pro-Soviet faction of the new Portuguese regime favoured the MPLA. In January 1975 all three Angolan movements received OAU recognition and formed a transitional government, but hostilities between them resumed almost immediately, with the FNLA–UNITA alliance receiving active military support from South Africa. On the MPLA's declaration of an independent People's Republic of Angola in November 1975, the FNLA and UNITA declared a rival Democratic Republic. However, following the withdrawal of South African forces in early 1976, Cuban-backed MPLA troops established control of most of Angola, driving FNLA forces into Zaïre and winning a decisive victory over them at Kifangondo in November 1977. The FNLA then ceased to be a significant force and President Mobutu transferred Zaïrean support to UNITA, which continued to resist the MPLA in the south. Expelled from Zaïre in 1979 (and subsequently from Senegal and Gabon), Roberto was eventually granted asylum in France.

Following the signature of the May 1991 Lisbon Accord between the MPLA government and UNITA, Roberto returned to Angola at the end of August and announced his candidacy for the presidency in the planned multi-party elections. After some dispute over whether it had a military wing (possession of which was supposed to disqualify parties), the FNLA was registered as a political party and in October 1991 joined the pro-democracy National Opposition Council. In the September 1992 elections Roberto came fourth in the first-round presidential balloting, with 2.1% of the vote, while the FNLA won five of the 220 seats in the new National Assembly.

Although the FNLA was named as a member of the "unity" government announced in December 1992, it subsequently played no part in the governance of the country and did not figure in the further "national reconciliation" government announced in April 1997. It thereafter maintained outspoken opposition to the MPLA regime from its overseas headquarters in Paris, although internal divisions became apparent in Angola between the Roberto leadership and a group led by Lucas Ngonda favouring accommodation with the government. A congress convened by Ngonda's faction in February 1999 at which he was elected FNLA president was followed by another in May at which Roberto's leadership was reaffirmed.

National Union for the Total Independence of Angola
União Nacional para a Independência Total de Angola (UNITA)

Address. c/o Assembléia Nacional, Luanda
Leadership. Jonas Malheiro Savimbi (president); Gen. Paulo Lukamba Gato (secretary-general)

UNITA was founded in March 1966 by a breakaway faction of the →National Front for the Liberation of Angola (FNLA) consisting mainly of elements of the former *União das Populações de Angola* (UPA) led by Savimbi, who had resigned as foreign minister in the FNLA-sponsored "revolutionary Angolan government-in-exile" (GRAE) in July 1964. Based in the Ovimbundu and Chokwe tribes of central and southern Angola, UNITA had Maoist ideological roots but had moved to an anti-leftist stance as it adopted a policy of co-operation with the Portuguese authorities against the dominant Soviet-backed →Movement for the Liberation of Angola (MPLA). After the left-wing military coup in Lisbon in April 1974, UNITA signed a separate ceasefire agreement with Portugal in June. In 1975, following the collapse of an OAU-sponsored transitional government of all three liberation movements, UNITA forces, allied with the FNLA, came increasingly into conflict with the MPLA, receiving substantial military support from South Africa. According to later South African accounts, the 2,000 South African troops sent into Angola could have taken the whole country by late 1975 had not Savimbi insisted that he wanted control only of areas of UNITA support in the interests of reaching a settlement with the MPLA.

Following the declaration of the independent People's Republic of Angola by the MPLA in November 1975, Cuban-supported government troops launched an offensive against the FNLA and UNITA, whose capacity to resist was seriously weakened by the withdrawal of South African forces across the Namibian border early in 1976. By late February UNITA had been forced to vacate all its positions and to resort to guerrilla warfare in the bush. A UNITA congress at Cuanza (central Angola) in May 1976 called for intensified armed struggle "against the regime imposed by the Cubans and Russians" and approved a reorganization of UNITA structures, including the creation of an armed people's militia. Subsequent clashes between UNITA and forces of the MPLA led to widespread losses and chaotic conditions, especially in the south. From 1982 onwards UNITA attacks were increasingly directed at economic targets, including the Benguela railway from the coast to what was then Zaïre; abduction of foreign specialists and their families also become a regular UNITA practice. In September 1985 the South African government admitted that it had provided military and humanitarian aid to UNITA for a number of years with the aim of halting "Marxist infiltration and expansionism". In mid-1985 the US Congress voted to repeal the 1976 Clarke Amendment which had prohibited US financial or military aid for UNITA. Savimbi paid an official visit to Washington in January 1976, reportedly securing a pledge of covert US aid from President Reagan.

After military setbacks for UNITA and South African forces in early 1988, UNITA came under further pressure later that year when it was agreed that South African and Cuban forces would be withdrawn from Angola as part of the Namibian peace settlement. The MPLA–PT government showed its willingness to negotiate by releasing 700 UNITA detainees in June 1988 and by conceding UNITA's demand for multi-partyism (as endorsed by an MPLA–PT congress in December 1990). Talks in Lisbon resulted in the signature in May 1991 of the Estoril Accord providing for a ceasefire, demobilization of forces and democratic elections. Savimbi returned to Luanda in September 1991 and in December UNITA published an election manifesto identifying the economic upliftment of the people as a central aim. In early 1992 UNITA was damaged by the defection of two senior members, amid charge and counter-charge cataloguing nefarious activities on both sides. Tending to sour UNITA–US relations, the episode deprived UNITA of support in Cabinda (where the defectors came from) and narrowed its ethnic base to the Ovimbundu in the south.

In the September 1992 Assembly elections UNITA came a poor second to the MPLA, winning only 70 of the 220 seats; but Savimbi did better in the simultaneous presidential poll, taking 40.1% of the first-round vote and helping to deny President dos Santos of the MPLA an outright majority, although no second round was held. Despite the verdict of international observers that the polling had been fair in the main, UNITA alleged widespread fraud in both contests and ordered its troops, most of whom had evaded demobilization, to resume armed struggle. The naming of a "unity" government in December 1992 with one cabinet and five other posts reserved for UNITA did not resolve the crisis. Conflict of unprecedented ferocity ensued, with UNITA making major advances not only in the south but also in central and northern Angola. It continued unabated after the opening of peace talks in Lusaka in November 1993 on the basis that UNITA would accept the 1992 election results. Factors impelling UNITA to negotiate included the USA's decision to recognize the MPLA government in May 1993 (implying the end of US backing for UNITA) and the imposition of a mandatory UN oil and arms embargo against UNITA in September. Factors impelling it to continue fighting included the temporary weakness of Angolan government forces, many of which had been demobilized under the 1991 accord.

Despite continued fighting between UNITA and government forces, the Lusaka talks on power-sharing made headway in mid-1994, as UNITA suffered serious military reverses. A ceasefire and power-sharing agreement was at last signed in Lusaka on Nov. 20, 1994, but Savimbi

11

signalled his displeasure with continued advances by government forces by leaving the signature to the then UNITA secretary-general, Gen. Eugénio Manuvakola. Amidst efforts by UN mediators to consolidate the Lusaka agreement, a UNITA congress at Bailundo (in Huambo province) in February 1995 was marked by serious divisions between those favouring the accord and hardliners. On Savimbi's proposal, delegates voted to accept the agreement; but a senior UNITA defector, Col. Isaac Zabarra, claimed subsequently that Savimbi in reality opposed the Lusaka accord and had instructed his military leaders to use the ceasefire to reorganize UNITA forces. According to Col. Zabarra, several UNITA leaders identified with the peace process were under detention, including Gen. Manuvakola. At the Bailundo congress, the latter was replaced as UNITA secretary-general by Gen. Gato.

Savimbi had talks with President dos Santos in Lusaka in June 1995 and again in Gabon in August, reportedly agreeing in principal to accept a vice-presidency in the government and to implement the other power-sharing clauses of the November 1994 accord. However, the MPLA regime's insistence on the prior disarming of UNITA guerrillas and their confinement to barracks pending the creation of a national army remained a major obstacle to implementation of the accord.

In April 1997 four UNITA ministers and seven deputy ministers at last took up their designated posts in a government of national unity and reconciliation, while UNITA National Assembly representatives took their seats in the National Assembly. However, Savimbi not only refused to become a Vice-President but even to attend the new government's inauguration, as UNITA and Angolan government forces fought a proxy war in Zaïre, the former backing President Mobutu in his efforts to retain power and the latter the rebels led by Laurent Kabila. Kabila's victory in what became the Democratic Republic of the Congo was a setback for UNITA, although its capability as a fighting force in Angola appeared to be little affected, despite the imposition of UN sanctions on UNITA from October 1997.

In Luanda a split developed in late 1997 between pro-Savimbi and anti-Savimbi UNITA factions, the latter headed by former secretary-general Gen. Manuvakola and backed by the MPLA. After most pro-Savimbi UNITA officials had fled the capital in July 1998, the following month UNITA members were suspended from the Assembly, as the MPLA-led regime sought to promote the pro-peace UNITA–Renewal faction (see next entry). Savimbi dismissed as "irrelevant" the activities of the breakaway faction, which held what it described as the ninth UNITA congress in Luanda in January 1999. Most UNITA Assembly members refused to join UNITA–Renewal, notably parliamentary leader Abel Chivukuvuku.

UNITA's apparent responsibility for the downing of two UN planes in December 1998 and January 1999, with the loss of 23 lives, sharpened UN condemnation of the movement's perceived unwillingness to end the civil war, although the MPLA-led government was also blamed. In July 1999 the UN launched an investigation into UNITA involvement in the illegal diamond trade, as UNITA forces were accused of massacring 50 women and children in the southern village of Sachitembo. Military reverses for UNITA in late 1999 continued in early 2000, but a UNITA counter-offensive in eastern Angola in April 2000 was attributed to the movement's receipt of new weaponry despite the UN sanctions. In 2001 the two sides remained locked in conflict.

National Union for the Total Independence of Angola–Renewal
União Nacional para a Indepêndencia Total de Angola–Renovar (UNITA–R)
Address. Rua Comandante Bula 71-73, S. Paulo, Luanda
Email. info@unita.org
Website. www.unita.org

Leadership. Eugénio Ngolo Manuvakola (president)
UNITA–R was launched in September 1998 by Luanda-based elements of the →National Union for the Total Independence of Angola (UNITA) opposed to the perceived intransigence of the Savimbi leadership towards a negotiated peace settlement. Backed by the government headed by the →Popular Movement for the Liberation of Angola (MPLA), UNITA–R included government minister Jorge Alicerces Valentim, although almost all UNITA Assembly members declined to join the breakaway group. In mid-January 1999 UNITA–R held what it described as the ninth UNITA congress in Luanda, electing as its president Eugénio Ngolo Manuvakola, who as UNITA secretary-general had signed the 1994 Lusaka peace agreement. The government then formally repudiated the 1994 agreement and declared that in future it would recognize UNITA–R as the legitimate representatives of the movement.

Popular Movement for the Liberation of Angola
Movimento Popular de Libertação de Angola (MPLA)
Address. c/o Assembléia Nacional, Luanda
Leadership. José Eduardo dos Santos (president); João Lorenço (secretary-general)
The MPLA was founded in 1956 as a merger of two nationalist movements, the *Partido da Luta Unida dos Africanos de Angola* and the (Communist) *Movimento para a Independencia de Angola*, initially under the leadership of Mário de Andrade and, from 1962, that of Agostinho Neto. Backed by the USSR, it played a leading part in the struggle against Portuguese rule, sometimes in collaboration but usually in conflict with the two other nationalist movements, the →National Front for the Liberation of Angola (FNLA) and the →National Union for the Total Independence of Angola (UNITA). On Portugal's transference of sovereignty to "the Angolan people" in November 1975, the MPLA proclaimed the People's Republic of Angola in Luanda, with Neto as President and do Nascimento as Prime Minister, and secured recognition from many states (although not the USA). By February 1976 the MPLA government, assisted by Cuban forces, was in control of the greater part of the country, although UNITA continued to conduct military operations in the south.

Pre-independence dissension within the MPLA resurfaced in 1976, when Andrade and other leaders of his *Revolte Activa* faction were arrested; the following year another dissident faction attempted a coup in Luanda. At its first congress in December 1977 the MPLA restructured itself as a Marxist–Leninist "vanguard of the proletariat" and added the suffix Party of Labour (*Partido de Trabalho*, PT) to its title to signify its claim to unite the working and intellectual classes. Further internal divisions in 1978 resulted in the abolition of the post of Prime Minister in December 1978 and the dismissal of do Nascimento and other ministers. Neto died in Moscow in September 1979 and was succeeded as President and party leader by José Eduardo dos Santos, whose preference for a negotiated settlement with UNITA and rapprochement with the West was resisted by the hardline pro-Soviet faction. At the second party congress in December 1985 the MPLA–PT central committee was enlarged to give the President's supporters a majority, three veteran hardliners being dropped from the resultant political bureau.

The third congress in December 1990 ratified a central committee recommendation that Angola should "evolve towards a multi-party system", dos Santos acknowledging that the collapse of communism in Eastern Europe indicated a need for democratic reform and that collectivist policies had failed. The congress approved the jettisoning of Marxist-Leninist ideology, which was to be replaced by a commitment to "democratic socialism", including a free enterprise economy and protection of private property and foreign investment. Under the May 1991 Lisbon Accord with the UNITA, the MPLA–PT government made provision for the legalization of competing parties and for multi-party elections. These changes were approved by a special MPLA–PT congress in May 1992, when reformers secured the enlargement of the central committee from 180 to 193 members and the election to it of representatives of the business community, intellectuals and some former dissidents.

Elections in September 1992 resulted in the MPLA–PT winning a decisive majority in the new National Assembly, while dos Santos took a commanding 49.6% in the first round of simultaneous presidential balloting. UNITA's rejection of the results and resumption of armed struggle meant that the second presidential round could not be held. A new "unity" government appointed in December 1992 was dominated by the MPLA–PT but included nominees of four small parties as well as, notionally, UNITA representatives. In 1993 MPLA–PT hardliners regained some influence with criticism of the dos Santos leadership for precipitate army demobilization under the Lisbon Accord, to the advantage of UNITA in the renewed civil war. By then the MPLA had officially dropped the Party of Labour suffix to demonstrate its inclusive aspirations and commitment to democratic socialism.

In May 1993 the USA at last recognized the MPLA-led government, signalling an end to its support for UNITA, which in November indicated its acceptance of the September 1992 election results. Peace talks then resumed in Lusaka between the government and UNITA on an agenda which included power-sharing at national and provincial level. After intensified conflict from mid-1994, a ceasefire and power-sharing agreement was signed in the Zambian capital on Nov. 20, 1994, as government forces made important advances against UNITA. A year later, however, the agreement remained unimplemented, despite two face-to-face meetings between dos Santos and UNITA leader Jonas Savimbi in June and August 1995, principally because of the difficulty of arranging for the disarming of guerrilla forces.

Although UNITA representatives at last took up posts in a government of national unity in Luanda in April 1997, the MPLA continued to be in open conflict with UNITA in the country. After the government had effectively severed relations with the Savimbi UNITA leadership in August 1998, opponents of the peace process gained the ascendancy at the fourth MPLA congress held in December 1998, when João Lorenço was elected secretary-general in place of Lopo do Nascimento, hitherto regarded as likely successor to the ailing dos Santos. In January 1999 the MPLA-led government formally repudiated the Lusaka peace agreement and accorded exclusive recognition to the anti-Savimbi →National Union for the Total Independence of Angola–Renewal. Having already voted a four-year extension of the parliamentary mandate in November 1996, the MPLA-dominated Assembly in October 2000 approved an indefinite extension, as plans for presidential and Assembly elections in 2001 were abandoned amid undiminished hostilities between government and UNITA forces.

The MPLA is an observer member of the Socialist International.

Other Parties

Liberal Democratic Party of Angola (*Partido Liberal Democrático de Angola, PLDA*), centrist pro-democracy formation which won three Assembly seats in the 1992 elections with 2.4% of the vote, although the PLDA leader came tenth in the presidential contest with only 0.3%. The PLDA is a member of the Liberal International.

Address. Rua Che Guevara 181, Luanda
Email. pld@ebonet.net
Leadership. Analia de Victoria Pereira Simea (president)

National Democratic Union of Angola (*União Democrática National de Angola, UDNA*), founded by exiles in London in the 1980s, registered in Angola in 1999. Espousing the political principles of Montesquieu, the party is associated with the International Democrat Union through the Democrat Union of Africa.
Leadership. Francisco J. Pedro Kizadilamba (president)

Republican Party of Angola (*Partido Republicano de Angola, PreA*), founded in 1997 in opposition to the dos Santos government headed by the →Popular Movement for the Liberation of Angola, accusing it of war crimes, institutional corruption, nepotism and denial of free speech.
Address. C.P. 3626, Luanda
Telephone. (+244–2) 347739
Email. preasecretariadogeral_org@yahoo.com
Leadership. Carlos Contreiras (president)

Cabinda Movements

Various movements and factions seeking separate independence for Cabinda—an oil-rich coastal enclave which is not contiguous with Angola proper, being bordered by Congo and the Democratic Republic of the Congo (formerly Zaïre)—are descended from the **Front for the Liberation of the Enclave of Cabinda** (Frente para a Libertação do Enclave de Cabinda, FLEC), which was founded in 1963. Encouraged by the Portuguese colonial authorities as an ally of sorts against the →Popular Movement for the Liberation of Angola (MPLA), FLEC refused to co-operate with other nationalist movements and rejected the claim of the MPLA government installed in Luanda at independence in November 1975 that Cabinda was part of Angola. Forced on the defensive by Cuban-supported government troops, FLEC was also weakened in the late 1970s by internal divisions which resulted in the creation of several factions. Two of these declared "independent" governments in Cabinda and one claimed in 1979 to control 30% of Cabindan territory. But guerrilla action by the FLEC factions was sporadic in the 1980s, being usually directed at state oil installations and similar targets.

The withdrawal of Cuban troops in 1990–91 prompted a revival of FLEC, which condemned the May 1991 Lisbon Accord between the government and the →National Union for the Total Independence of Angola (UNITA) for its failure to contemplate Cabindan independence. In 1992 the various FLEC factions came together to mount actions designed to disrupt the September Assembly elections, subsequently claiming that the participation rate of under 20% in Cabinda demonstrated a desire for independence. In May 1993 FLEC declared that the US recognition of the government in Luanda did not extend to Cabinda and warned foreign nationals to leave the territory if their companies supported "the extermination of the Cabindan people". The Angolan government claimed that FLEC was being armed by "Congolese politicians" and was reported to be seeking an alliance with a FLEC splinter group to offset the perceived possibility of a FLEC–UNITA joint front.

By the late 1990s the most active FLEC faction appeared to be FLEC-Renewal (*Renovada*), or FLEC-R, which in January 1997 elected a more militant leadership in the persons of António Bento Bember (president) and Arture Tchibassa (secretary-general).

Antigua and Barbuda

Capital: St John's

Population: 68,000 (2000E)

Antigua and Barbuda became internally self-governing in 1967 and independent from the United Kingdom in 1981. The head of state is the British sovereign, represented by a Governor-General who is appointed on the advice of the Antiguan Prime Minister. Legislative power is vested in a bicameral parliament, the lower 17-member chamber (House of Representatives) of which is directly elected for up to five years. The Prime Minister and Cabinet are responsible to parliament and are appointed to office by the Governor-General acting upon its advice. Barbuda, the smaller of the country's two inhabited constituent islands, maintains a considerable degree of control over its local affairs.

Elections to the House of Representatives elections on March 9, 1999, resulted in the Antigua Labour Party winning 12 seats (with 52.9% of the vote), the United Progressive Party 4 (44.4%) and the Barbuda People's Movement 1 (1.4%).

Antigua Labour Party (ALP)

Address. St Mary's Street, St John's
Telephone. (+1–809) 462–1059
Leadership. Lester Bird (leader); Vere Bird Jr (chairman)

Long affiliated with the Antigua Trades and Labour Union (of which Vere Bird, Prime Minister and ALP leader until 1994, was a founder member), the domestically-conservative ALP was continuously in power in the colony from 1946 to 1971. Returned to office in 1976, the ALP has since remained the ruling party, most recently securing a sixth successive term with 12 of the 17 seats in the House of Representatives in the March 1999 general election. Since 1994 the party has been led by Vere Bird's son, Lester Bird.

Barbuda People's Movement (BPM)

Address. c/o House of Representatives, St John's
Leadership. Thomas Hilbourne Frank (leader); Fabian Jones (chairman)

The BPM campaigns for separate status for Barbuda. It controls the local Barbuda Council, and has won the single Barbudan seat in the House of Representatives in recent general elections. Strains between the BPM and the central government of the →Antigua Labour Party (ALP) intensi-

fied early in 2001 over whether the BPM or the ALP should chair a new joint consultative council to be set up on the recommendation of the Commonwealth to oversee relations between the two islands and to promote economic development in Barbuda.

United Progressive Party (UPP)

Address. c/o House of Representatives, St John's
Leadership. Baldwin Spencer (leader); Vincent Derrick (chairman); Burton Barnes (general secretary)

The UPP was formed in early 1992 by the merger of the Antigua Caribbean Liberation Movement (founded in 1977 as a "new left" organization), the Progressive Labour Movement (established in 1970, and the ruling party from 1971 to 1976), and the United National Democratic Party (a formation identified with business and professional interests, which arose from the merger of the small United People's Movement and National Democratic Party in 1986).

In the 1994 general election the UPP was runner-up with five of the 17 lower house seats, winning nearly 44 per cent of the vote. It slipped to four seats in the 1999 election, despite increasing its share of the vote to 44.4%.

Argentina

Capital: Buenos Aires

Population: 36,570,000 (2000E)

Upon returning to civilian rule in 1983 following seven years of military rule by successive juntas, most of the constitutional structure of 1853 was restored. The Republic is composed of an autonomous Federal District, 23 provinces and the National Territory of Tierra del Fuego. Each province has its own elected governor and legislature, concerned with all matters not delegated to the federal government. A new constitution entered into effect on Aug. 24, 1994, under which the President, hitherto appointed by an electoral college, is directly elected for a four-year term (reduced from the six years allowed under the 1853 constitution) with re-election allowed for only one consecutive term. Run-off elections for the presidential and vice-presidential posts take place unless a candidate obtains 45% of the vote (or 40% with a 10% advantage over the second-placed candidate). The new constitution also allows for an autonomous government for the capital, Buenos Aires, with a directly-elected mayor. As previously, in the absence of the President, the president of the Senate assumes the presidency. The cabinet is appointed by the President, who exercises executive power and is head of state.

The federal legislature consists of a Chamber of Deputies of 257 members elected for four-year terms with half of the seats renewable every two years, and a 72-member Senate. Until 2001, two senators were nominated by the legislature of each of the 23 provinces for nine-year terms (one third of the seats being renewable every three years), and a third senator was directly elected from each province. Under new arrangements introduced in 2001, all senators became directly elected.

The late 1990s were a period of retreat for the Peronist Justicialist Party (PJ), which had retained control of the presidency and the Chamber of Deputies in the presidential and legislative elections of May 14 1995. In the congressional elections of Oct. 26 1997, in which 127 of the 257 seats in the Chamber of Deputies were at stake, the opposition Alliance (*Alianza*), a coalition of the centre-left Radical Civic Union (UCR) and the Front for a Country in Solidarity (FREPASO) secured 45.6% of the popular vote compared with the 36.1 percent secured by the PJ. Although the PJ secured 118 seats as against the *Alianza*'s 110, the balance of power shifted to the *Alianza* and smaller provincial parties (which collectively held 29 seats).

In the presidential election of Oct. 24, 1999, Fernando de la Rúa, the *Alianza* candidate, defeated Eduardo Duhalde of the PJ, thus ending a decade of Peronist domination of the presidency. De la Rúa and his FREPASO running-mate, Carlos "Chacho" Alvarez, secured 48.5% of the popular vote against 38.1% for Duhalde. Domingo Cavallo of the Action for the Republic (AR) won 10.1% of the popular vote. In simultaneous legislative elections, in which 130 of the 257 seats in the Chamber of Deputies were contested, the *Alianza* won 63 seats, increasing its representation in the Chamber to 127 seats—two seats short of an overall majority. The PJ secured 50 seats, increasing its strength to 101 seats and the Action for the Republic won 9 seats, increasing its representation to 12 seats. Following the 1999 elections 17 seats were held by minor, mainly provincial, parties.

Action for the Republic
Acción por la República (AR)

Address. Congreso de la Nación, 1835–1849 Buenos Aires 1089

Telephone. (+54–11) 4502–6800

Email. fervaloni@cavallo.org.ar

Website. www.ar-partido.com.ar

Leadership. Domingo Cavallo (1999 presidential candidate); Alfredo José Castañón (congressional president); Armando Caro Figueroa (executive committee chairman); José Luis Fernández Valoni (secretary-general)

The centre-right AR was established in April 1997 by Domingo Cavallo, a former Economy Minister (1991-96), as a vehicle to support his bid for a congressional seat in the October 1997 legislative elections and for a possible candidacy in the 1999 presidential elections. In the 1997 elections the party secured three seats. In the presidential election of 1999 Cavallo secured 10.1% of the popular vote, while in the simultaneous legislative elections the AR increased its representation from nine seats to 12. Cavallo joined the *Alianza* government as Economy Minister in March 2001. The addition of an AR politician to the cabinet coincided with the fact that, for the first time since the *Alianza*'s 1999 election victory, there were no ministers of the →Front for a Country in Solidarity (FREPASO) serving in the cabinet, although FREPASO deputies officially remained within the *Alianza* bloc in the Chamber of Deputies.

Broad Front
Frente Grande} (FG)

Address. Congreso de la Nación, 1835–1849 Buenos Aires 1089

Leadership. Carlos "Chacho" Alvarez (1999 vice-presidential candidate)

A left-wing grouping, the FG was launched in October 1993. In the elections for the Constituent Assembly in April 1994, the party won 12.5% of the popular vote and secured 31 seats. The FG fought the 1997 legislative and 1999 presidential and legislative elections as part of the →Front for a Country in Solidarity (FREPASO), a coalition of left-of-centre parties, which was in turn a component of the *Alianza*.

Christian Democratic Party of Argentina
Partido Demócrata Christiano de Argentina (PDCA)

Address. Combate de los Pozos 1055, Buenos Aires C1222AAK

Telephone. (+54–11) 4304–2915

Fax. (+54–11) 4306–8242

Email. juntanacional@dc.org.ar

Website. www.dc.org.ar

Leadership. Eduardo Cúneo (president); Gerardo Marturet (secretary-general)

Dating from 1954, the PDCA was one of the five small parties in the *Multipartidaria* democratic movement whose PDCA presidential candidate won 0.3% of the national vote in the October 1983 elections and obtained one seat in the Chamber of Deputies. A rapprochement with the Peronist →Justicialist Party (PJ) in 1984 led to a conflict in the party which caused a majority of the centre-left Humanism and Liberation faction to split away and join the →Intransigent Party (PI). In the congressional elections of September 1987, the party received only 0.2% of the national vote despite greater unity within the party. To improve their electoral chances the PDCA joined the FREJUPO electoral alliance supporting the Peronists' presidential candidate Carlos Saúl Menem, who won the election on May 14, 1989. The Christian Democrats' support was rewarded with the appointment as Social Security Minister of António Erman Gonzalez, who in December 1989 was transferred to the important Economy Ministry. The PDCA withdrew from the FREJUPO alliance in October 1990 in protest against Gonzalez' economic measures.

The PDCA fought the 1997 legislative and 1999 legislative and presidential elections as part of →Front for a Country in Solidarity (FREPASO), the coalition of centre-left parties of which it had been a founder member of in 1994. The party secured just one seat in the 1999 elections. At a party convention in November 2000, the PDCA decided to withdraw from the *Alianza* of FREPASO and the →Radical Civic Union (UCR) in protest at the economic policy of the *Alianza* government.

The PDC is affiliated to the Christian Democrat International and the Christian Democrat Organization of America.

Democratic Socialist Party
Partido Socialista Democratico (PSD)

Address. Rivadavia 2307,1034 Buenos Aires

Website. www.geocities.com/CapitolHill/Senate/1137/

Leadership. Alfredo Bravo (congressional president}

The leftist PSD currently has four seats in the Chamber of Deputies, two of whom were elected in 1997 and two of whom were elected in 1999. The party fought the 1997 and 1999 legislative elections as part of the →Front for a Country in Solidarity (FREPASO) coalition.

Front for a Country in Solidarity
Frente Pais Solidario (FREPASO)

Address. Congreso de la Nación, 1835-1849 Buenos Aires 1089

Email: frepaso@sion.com

Website. www.frepaso.org.ar

Leadership. Carlos "Chacho" Alvarez (1999 *Alianza* vice presidential candidate; Dario Pedro Alessandro (congressional president)

One of the newest and one of the most important parties in Argentina, FREPASO was launched in late 1994 as a moderate left coalition designed to incorporate the →Broad Front (FG), the →Christian Democractic Party (PDC),

15

→Open Politics for Social Integrity (PAIS) and Socialist Unity (US). It includes a number of independent communists and socialists. The Front's presidential candidate, Jose Octavio Bordon, secured second place behind Carlos Menem on May 14, 1995, polling 29.2% of the vote. FREPASO as a whole secured 26 seats in the simultaneous legislative elections leaving the Front third overall. On May 17, 1995, FREPASO came into being as a permanent structure.

A coalition arrangement (*Alianza*) between FREPASO and the →Radical Civic Union (UCR) brought electoral success to both parties in the legislative elections of 1997 and the presidential and legislative elections of 1999. In the 1997 legislative elections the UCR-FREPASO *Alianza* secured 110 seats based upon 45.6% of the popular vote. In the 1999 presidential elections Carlos "Chacho" Alvarez the FREPASO running mate of Fernando de la Rúa was elected vice president and, in simultaneous legislative elections in which 130 of the 257 seats in the Chamber of Deputies were at stake, FREPASO secured 36 seats.

The UCR-FREPASO *Alianza*, however, came under the twin stresses of a corruption scandal, which prompted Alvarez's resignation from government in October 2000 in protest at de la Rúa's retention of two ministers implicated in the scandal and FREPASO displeasure at austerity measures announced by the government in late 2000 and the first few months of 2001. Although FREPASO had not officially withdrawn its support from the *Alianza* as many as 14 deputies had expressed their intention to withdraw their support from the government by the end of April 2001 and the FREPASO Minister of Welfare Marcos Makon and the FREPASO Chief of Staff to the President, Ricardo Mitre, had resigned from the government in March 2001 in protest at proposed cuts in public spending. Following a reshuffle in March 2001, the cabinet contained no FREPASO ministers for the first time since the election of the *Alianza* government in 1999.

Intransigent Party
Partido Intransigente (PI)

Address. Riobamba 482, 1025 Buenos Aires
Website. www.pi.org.ar
Leadership. Gustavo Cardesa (president); Jorge Drkos (secretary)

The PI originated in a left-of-centre split from the →Radical Civic Union (UCR) in 1956 and the formation of the UCR *Intransigente* (UCRI), which changed its name to Intransigent Party in 1972 after the rival People's UCR had won the exclusive right to the UCR title. For the presidential elections of 1973 the party joined forces with the →Communist Party of Argentina (PCA) and two other small parties and fielded Oscar Alende as their candidate, who, however, polled only 7.4% of the vote. Following the coup of 1976 the PI was banned and many activists were imprisoned and tortured.

In the first presidential election following Argentina's return to democracy, in October 1983 Alende, with Lisandro Viale as his running-mate, came third but won only 2.3% of the valid vote. With its support waning, the PI joined the FREJUPO alliance backing the Peronist Justicialist Party (PJ) candidate, Carlos Saul Menem, for the May 1989 elections. Menem won the presidency with a majority in the electoral college (48.5% of the national vote). The PI left FREJUPO in October 1990 in protest at the government's economic policies. It won one chamber seat in 1993 and none in 1995. In the congressional elections held in October 1997 the party secured just one seat, which it retained in the 1999 parliamentary elections.

Justicialist Party
Partido Justicialista (PJ-Peronist)

Address: Matheu 128, 1082 Buenos Aires
Telephone. (+54–11) 4952–4555
Fax. (+54–11) 4954–2421

Email. bpj@hcdn.gov.ar
Website. www.pj.org.ar
Leadership. Carlos Saul Menem (president); Rubén Marin (first vice-president); Carlos Reutemann (second vice-president); Eduardo Duhalde (1999 presidential candidate); Humberto Jesús Roggero (congressional president); Eduardo Bauza (secretary-general)

Founded in 1945, the PJ is populist in outlook, encompassing groups from the far right to the far left. Formerly the Justicialist Nationalist Movement (*Movimiento Nacionalista Justicialista,* MNJ) the PJ grew out of the nationalist *Peronista* movement led by Lt.-Gen. Juan Domingo Peron Sosa during his 1946-55 presidency. Peron returned to power in 1973 after he was deposed by a military coup in 1955 but his government was overthrown by a second coup in March 1976.

In the October 1983 elections which followed the Falklands/Malvinas war and the collapse of the military regime, the Peronists lost to the →Radical Civic Union (UCR) in both the presidential and congressional elections but beat the UCR in the provincial governorship elections. The party, with Isabelita Peron (the third wife of Gen. Peron) as its figurehead, obtained 40.5% of the vote, which translated into 111 seats in Congress, while its presidential candidate—Italo Luder—came second (with 40.2% of the vote) to Raul Alfonsin of the UCR. This defeat resulted in a long period of internal turmoil which split the Peronist movement into two main rival factions with parallel leaderships: the right-wing *oficialistas* (official wing) and the *renovadores* (renovator wing). A party congress in July 1985, intended to reunite the party, resulted in an *oficialista* takeover of the party machinery. All *oficialista* candidates were confirmed for the forthcoming congressional elections because of a boycott by the left wing, which subsequently put forward alternative candidates under the name of the *Frente Renovador* (Renovation Front), led by Antonio Cafiero. Neither the official PJ, which fought the election as the leading party in the FREJULI alliance, nor the Renovation Front did well, overall PJ representation in the congress being reduced by 10 seats.

Despite further splits within the two factions in 1986, which produced four distinct PJ blocs in Congress, the Peronists began to gain in popularity. Benefiting from widespread discontent with the UCR government's austerity measures and its lenient treatment of the army, the PJ won the highest number of votes (41.5%) in the September 1987 congressional elections and narrowed the gap between the PJ and UCR representation in Congress. As well as increasing their congressional seats to 105, the PJ won 16 provincial governorships, including that of the crucial province of Buenos Aires. With the general election of 1989 in view, the PJ regrouped. Isabelita Peron was finally replaced as the party's president and a leadership comprising *oficialistas, renovadores* and the Federalism and Liberation faction, linked to Carlos Saul Menem, was elected. Small left-wing and right-wing factions were ignored and Herminio Iglesias' right-wing group, which had contested the elections separately as the October 17 Party, was expelled in December 1987.

The modern PJ defined from 1989 when Menem gained the leadership of the party and the nation. The dominant *menemista* faction, promoting a free-market economy and privatization, moved the party sharply to the right. Menem took office in July 1989 and struggled with a fundamentally destabilized economy with policies as diverse as rationing, an expansion of the state privatization programme, and large reductions in the workforce of the state iron and steel plants. Although Menem largely continued his UCR predecessor's policy of leniency towards the military, measures such as an amnesty for crimes perpetrated during the so-called "dirty war" of 1976-83 could not prevent increasingly vocal discontent over army low pay and lack of status.

The PJ's electoral performance between 1989 and 1997 was a strong one, and Menem himself overcame a long period of unpopularity in his party for his perceived abandonment of Peronism. In congressional and gubernatorial elections held in August, September, October and December 1991, the PJ increased its seats in the Chamber of Deputies from 112 to 119, and won the governorships of 14 provinces. The Peronists won the Chamber elections (for 127 seats) in October 1993, increasing their total number of seats to 125; this total was further raised, to 137 seats, in the elections (for 130 seats) in May 1995, when they also took nine of the 14 provincial governorships at stake. The Peronists had won 136 seats in the elections held in April 1994 to the new 305-member Constituent Assembly, which was responsible for drawing up a new constitution.

Menem was re-elected President in May 1995 with 49.8% of the vote and was sworn into office on July 8 along with the majority of the previous cabinet. In a Senate election for the federal district of Buenos Aires in October 1995 the PJ won only 22.6% of the vote, against 45.7% for the centre-left →Front for a Country in Solidarity (FREPASO) coalition and 24.3% for the UCR. Nevertheless, the Peronists held power in 14 of the 23 provinces following provincial elections staged between July and October 1995.

The party's electoral success came to an end in the October 1997 congressional elections, in which 127 of the 257 seats in the Chamber of Deputies were contested. The PJ secured 36.1% of the popular vote compared with the 45.6% won by the *Alianza*. The PJ's representation in the Chamber was reduced to 118 compared with the *Alianza*'s 110, leaving the balance of power in the hands of the *Alianza* and smaller parties which collectively held 29 seats. The defeat was ascribed to public concern at rising unemployment and the imposition of orthodox economic policies.

In the presidential election on Oct. 24 1999, a decade of Peronist rule was ended when Eduardo Duhalde, the PJ candidate, was defeated by Fernando de la Rúa of the opposition *Alianza*. De la Rúa and his FREPASO running-mate, Carlos "Chacho" Alvarez, secured 48.5% of the popular vote compared with Duhalde's 38.1%. In simultaneous legislative elections, in which 127 of the 257 seats in the Chamber of Deputies were at stake, the PJ won 50 (with 33.7% of the vote), so that its representation fell to 101 seats.

In opposition, the PJ experienced familiar internal dissension in 2000. The party's difficulties increased in May 2001 when Menem was subpoenaed by a federal judge to testify in an investigation of illegal arms supplies to Croatia and Ecuador during his presidency.

The PJ is a member of the International Democrat Union, the Christian Democrat International and the Christian Democrat Organization of America.

Open Politics for Social Integrity
Politica Abierto para la Integridad Social (PAIS)
Address. Congreso de la Nación, 1835–1849 Buenos Aires 1089
Email. bpais@hcdn.gov.ar
Leadership. Jose Octavio Bordon
PAIS was launched in September 1994 by an anti-Menem →Justicialist Party (PJ) senator, Jose Octavio Bordon. The party contested the 1995 legislative and 1999 presidential and legislative elections as part of the left-wing →Front for a Country in Solidarity (FREPASO).

Popular Socialist Party
Partido Socialist Popular (PSP)
Address. Entre Rios 1018 1080 Buenos Aires
Telephone. (+54–11)4304–0644
Website. www.psp.org.ar
Email. pspcn@abaconet.com.ar
Leadership. Ruben Giustiniani; Guillermo Estévez Boero; Edgardo Rossi
Affiliated to the Socialist International, the party currently has four deputies in the Chamber of Deputies and contested the 1999 legislative elections as part of the →Front for a Country in Solidarity (FREPASO) coalition.

Progressive Democratic Party
Partido Democrata Progresista (PDP)
Address. Chile 1934, 1227 Buenos Aires
Email. bdprogresista@hcdn.gov.ar
Leadership. Alberto Adolfo Natale (congressional president)
The PDP participated in the 1980 talks with the military regime negotiating the normalization of political activities and in August of the same year it joined the →Union of the Democratic Centre (UCeDe). In the presidential elections of 1983, however, the party's then leader, Rafael Martinez, stood as candidate of the Democratic Socialist Alliance against the UCeDe's Alvaro Alsogaray and obtained 0.3% of the vote. The PDP contested the partial congressional elections of 1985 as a separate party and gained 0ne seat in the Chamber of Deputies. In the elections of September 1987 the party's share of the national vote was 1.3%and it increased its representation in the Chamber to two seats.

The PDP thereafter joined forces again with the UCeDe and in the May 1989 presidential elections, in which Alberto Natale was running-mate to the UCeDe's Alsogaray, who came third with 6.4% of the vote. The party won three lower house seats in 1995, two on a joint ticket with the →Corrientes Liberal Party (PLC). One PDP candidate secured election to the Chamber of Deputies in the legislative elections of 1997, to be joined by two others in the elections of 1999.

Radical Civic Union
Union Civica Radical (UCR)
Address. Alsina 1786, 1088 Buenos Aires
Telephone. (+54–11) 449–0036
Email. info@ucr.org.ar
Website. www.ucr.org.ar
Leadership. Fernando de la Rúa (president); Horacio Francisco Pernasetti (congressional president)
As Argentina's largest centrist/moderate left party, the UCR has been the dominant mainstream opposition to the Peronist →Justicialist Party (PJ). The party dates from the late 19th century, when the radical faction split away from the mainstream Civic Union and led an unsuccessful revolt against the Conservative government. One of the party's main demands was the enfranchisement of all adult male Argentinians, and it did not participate in any elections until 1912, when that demand was met. In 1916 the UCR formed its first government and remained in power until 1930, when President Hipólito Yrigoyen was ousted by a military coup. After losing both the 1945 and the 1951 elections to the Peronists, the UCR suffered internal problems which culminated in a dramatic split in 1956, caused by the nomination as the UCR's presidential candidate of Arturo Frondizi of the Intransigent faction, who was favourable to some co-operation with the Peronists. Frondizi became the candidate of the newly-formed UCR *Intransigente* (UCRI, later the →Intransigent Party) and, with assistance from the Peronists, won the presidency in 1958.

The conservative wing of the party, led by the former UCR presidential candidate Ricardo Balbin, formed the People's UCR (UCR *del Pueblo,* UCRP) in 1956, which was to become the official UCR in 1972, when a court ruling awarded it the sole right to the name. The UCRP supported the military coup against Frondizi in 1962 and in the subsequent elections of 1963 the UCRP's candidate, Arturo Umberto Illía, was elected President. He was himself overthrown in 1966 in another military coup which was supported by the UCRI. Balbin stood again in the 1973 presidential elections for the now renamed UCR and was heavily defeated by Peronists in both the April and September polls.

In 1981 the UCR helped to form a five-party democratic alliance opposed to the latest military junta (in power since 1976), which called for the restoration of democracy. Following the deposition of the military regime in 1982, UCR candidate Raul Alfonsin Foulkes won a major victory in presidential elections in October 1983. He took 317 of the 600 seats in the electoral college, which gave him 51.8% of the electoral college vote. The UCR also won a majority of Chamber of Deputies seats (129 out of 256) but only 16 of the 48 Senate seats and seven of the 24 provincial governorships, including Buenos Aires.

Inaugurated in December 1983, Alfonsin proceeded to make good his election promises of reorganizing the armed forces and putting an end to the cycle of political instability and military intervention. Over half the military high command was forced into retirement and members of the military juntas since 1976 were prosecuted for murder, torture and abduction, some being sent to prison. However, after uprisings in a number of army garrisons in April 1987 and persistent rumours of an impending coup, Alfonsin introduced the law of "Due Obedience", dropping all prosecutions against lower-ranking army and police officers indicted for human rights violations. Further military uprisings by officers demanding greater army spending and an extension of the military amnesty to higher-ranking officers nevertheless followed in January and December 1988, followed in January 1989 by an incident, thought to have been provoked by the armed forces, in which a left-wing group attacked La Tablada barracks in order to suppress a rumoured military coup.

Spiralling inflation and a highly unstable economy forced Alfonsin to relinquish power to Carlos Menem of the JP in July 1989, five months before the expiry of his presidential mandate. Two months earlier Menem had comfortably won presidential elections in which the defeated UCR candidate was Eduardo César Angeloz. The UCR became the main opposition party, and in February 1990 Angeloz refused an invitation from President Menem to join his cabinet. Instead, he called for all political parties to sign a pact under which a plan for effective government would be drawn up to preserve and consolidate democracy in an extreme social and economic crisis.

Such proposals, and the UCR's criticism of government policies did not improve the party's electoral performance. In the 1991 mid-term elections the UCR lost five Chamber seats, its strength thus falling to 85 seats, while in the gubernatorial elections the UCR retained only three governorships. One of the victims of this poor showing was Alfonsin himself, who, following strong criticism from within the UCR, resigned the party leadership in mid-November 1991. Upon his resignation, Alfonsín announced the formation of an internal faction within the UCR, the Movement for Social Democracy (*Movimiento por la Democracia Social,* MDS), which called for the defence of traditional UCR democratic principles. The eventual outcome was his re-election as party leader by an overwhelming majority in November 1993. In the 1995 presidential elections, the party's nominee, Horatio Massacesi, came a disappointing third with 17.1% of the vote. However, in legislative balloting the UCR retained the second highest Chamber representation with 69 seats.

The UCR contested the 1997 legislative elections in an alliance (*Alianza*) with the →Front for a Country in Solidarity (FREPASO) which won 45.6% of the popular vote against the 36.1% for the PJ. Although the PJ secured 118 seats compared with the *Alianza*'s 110, the balance of power shifted to the *Alianza* and smaller provincial parties which collectively held 29 seats. In the October 1999 presidential elections, Fernando de la Rúa, the *Alianza* candidate, defeated Eduardo Duhalde of the PJ, thus ending a decade of Peronist domination of the presidency. De la Rúa and his FREPASO running-mate, Carlos "Chacho" Alvarez, took 48.5% of the popular vote against 38.1% for Duhalde. In simultaneous legislative elections, in which 127 of the 257 Chamber seats were contested, the *Alianza* won 63 seats, increasing its representation in the Chamber to 127 seats, two seats short of an overall majority.

In 2000 the government of President de la Rúa, and the stability of the UCR-FREPASO *Alianza*, were shaken by a corruption scandal in which ministers were accused of having bribed legislators in order to secure the enactment of labour reform. Also damaging was a new collapse in confidence in the economy in late 2000 and early 2001.

Republican Force
Fuerza Republicana (FR)
Address. Pte. Peron 318, P.I Of.5, 1008 Buenos Aires
Email. bfrepublicana@hcdn.gov.ar
Leadership. Gen. (retd.) António Domingo Bussi (president)
A right-wing party, founded in 1989 and strongly based in the north-western Tucumcin district, the FR had loose links with the previous military regime and increased its seats in the Chamber of Deputies from two to four in the October 1991 mid-term elections. The party went on to win three lower house seats in October 1993, adding another in 1995. The party secured two seats in the legislative elections of 1997 and won a third seat in the legislative elections of 1999.

Union of the Democratic Centre
Union del Centro Democratico (UCeDe)
Address. Av. R. S. Peña628, P.I Of.2, 1008 Buenos Aires
Email: bucd@hcdn.gov.ar
Leadership. Alvaro Alsogaray (president)
More right-wing than centrist, the UCeDe is a conservative party standing for a free market economy and a reduced public sector. Originally a coalition of eight small centre-right parties, the UCeDe was formed in 1980 under the leadership of Alvaro Alsogaray, who had held an important position in the post-1976 military government. In the October 1983 elections the party won only two seats in the Chamber of Deputies, Alsogaray receiving only 0.3% of the presidential vote. In order to improve its chances in the Federal Capital of Buenos Aires in the November 1985 elections, the UCeDe formed the "Popular Centrist Alliance" coalition with the Capital Democratic Party (PDC) and Federalist Centre Party (PFC). The vote for the alliance increased to 3.5% of the national vote.

Although Alsogaray was elected as the UCeDe presidential candidate in June 1988, the party leadership at the same time decided to support the campaign of the Peronist →Justicialist Party (PJ), hoping thereby to raise the UCeDe's profile. This strategy led to the party polling 9.5% of the national vote, giving the UCeDe nine seats out of the 127 up for election in the May 1989 elections. Alsogaray came third with 6.4% of the presidential vote.

In May 1989 with Alsogaray as its candidate the party polled 6.4% *of* the presidential vote, placing them a disappointing third overall. The party's legislative vote was only 2.6%, increasing only slightly to 3.0% in 1995.

Other Parties

Civic and Social Movement (*Movimiento Civico y Social, MCS*), returned one deputy to the Chamber of Deputies in 1997 and another in 1999.
Leadership. Mario Héctor Bonacina (president)

Communist Party of Argentina (*Partido Comunista de la Argentina, PCA*), founded in 1918 and in long-term decline from its early importance. The party was unable to secure parliamentary representation in the legislative elections of 1997 and 1999. It is currently part of the United Left (*Izquierda Unida*) alliance.
Address. Av. Entre Rios 1033, 1080 Buenos Aires
Telephone. (+54–11) 4304-0066
Email. central@pca.org.ar
Website. www.pca.org.ar
Leadership. Patricio Echegaray (general secretary); Jorge Kreyness (director)

Corrientes Liberal Party (*Liberal de Corrientes, LdC*), returned one deputy to the Chamber in 1997.

Email. blcorrientes@hcdn.gov.ar
Leadership. Luis María Díaz Colodrero (president)

Corrientes Self-Government Party (*Autonomista de Corrientes, AdC*), based in the province of Corrientes, elected one candidate to the Chamber of Deputies in 1999.
Email. bacorrientes@hcdn.gov.ar
Leadership. Ismael Ramón Cortinas (president)

Development and Justice (*Desarollo y Justicia*), returned one candidate to the Chamber in 1997.
Email. bdyjusticia@hcdn.gov.ar
Leadership. Arturo Jorge Moreno Ramírez (president)

Entre Rios Social Movement (*Movimiento Social y Entrerriano, MSE*), returned one candidate to the Chamber in 1997.
Leadership. Juan Domingo Zacarías (president)

Mendoza Democratic Party (*Demórata de Mendoza*), based in the province of Mendoza, returned two deputies to the Chamber in 1997 and a third in 1999.
Email. bdmendoza@hcdn.gov.ar
Leadership. Carlos Mario Balter (president)

New Party Front (*Frente Partido Nuevo, FPN*), returned two deputies to the Chamber in 1997 and another in 1999.
Email. bfrepanu@hcdn.gov.ar
Leadership. Catalina Méndez de Medina Lareu (president)

Popular Fueguino Movement (*Movimiento Popular Fueguino, MPF*), returned one deputy to the Chamber in 1997.
Email. bmpfueguino@hcdn.gov.ar
Leadership. Ernesto Adrián Löffler (president)

Popular Neuquino Movement (*Movimiento Popular Neuquino, MPN*), returned one deputy to the Chamber in 1997 and another in 1999.
Leadership. Pedro Salvatori (president)

Renewal Crusade (*Cruzada Renovadora, CR*), returned one member to the Chamber in 1997.
Email. bcrenovadora@hcdn.gov.ar
Leadership. Luis Segundo Varese (president)

Salta Renewal (*Renovador de Salta*), returned one deputy to the Chamber in 1997 and a second in 1999.
Email. brsalta@hcdn.gov.ar
Leadership. Ricardo Gómez Diez (president)

San Juan Bloc (*Bloquista de San Juan, BSJ*), based in the province of San Juan, elected one deputy to the Chamber in 1999.
Email. bbsanjuan@hcdn.gov.ar
Leadership. Julio César Conca (president)

Social and Civic Front (*Frente Civico y Social, FCS*), returned one deputy to the Chamber of Deputies in 1997 and another in 1999.
Email. bfcsocial@hcdn.gov.ar
Leadership. Simón Fermín Guadalupe Hernández (president)

Unity Buenos Aires (*Unidad Bonaerense, UB*), based in Buenos Aires, returned one deputy to the Chamber in 1999.
Website. www.angelfire.com/ar2/pub/
Leadership. Miguel Antonio Jobe (president)

Armenia

Capital: Yerevan   **Population**: 3,750,000 (2000E)

The former Soviet republic of Armenia declared independence as the Republic of Armenia in August 1990 and became a sovereign member of the Commonwealth of Independent States (CIS) on the latter's creation in December 1991. Independent Armenia retained its Soviet-era constitution, with some adjustments to cater for multi-partyism, until the approval by referendum on July 5, 1995, of a new text establishing a democratic "presidential" system. Directly elected for a five-year term, the executive President appoints the Prime Minister and other ministers and may dissolve the National Assembly and call new elections. Legislative authority is vested in the unicameral National Assembly (*Azgayin Zhoghov*), whose 131 members are elected for a four-year term by universal adult suffrage, 75 by majority voting in single-member constituencies and 56 by proportional representation from national lists of parties obtaining at least 5% of the vote.

In presidential elections on March 16 and 30, 1998, non-party candidate Robert Kocharyan was elected with 59.5% of the second-round vote against 40.5% for Karen Demirchyan (later of the People's Party of Armenia). In legislative elections held on May 30, 1999, only six parties or blocs surmounted the 5% barrier in the proportional section (out of 21 which submitted lists), although some others won constituency seats. The results were as follows: Unity Bloc (of the People's Party of Armenia and the Republican Party of Armenia) 55 seats (41.7% of the proportional vote), Communist Party of Armenia 11 (12.1%), Armenian Revolutionary Federation (*Dashnak*) 9 (7.8%), Justice and Accord Bloc 7 (8.0%), Country of Law Party 6 (5.3%), National Democratic Union of Armenia 6 (5.2%), Pan-Armenian National Movement 1 (1.2%), Democratic Party of Armenia 1 (1.0%), Mission 1 (0.8%), independents 32, invalid contests 2. The successful formations usually took other names, and in some cases new compositions, in the new Assembly.

Armenian Revolutionary Federation
Hai Heghapokhakan Dashnaktsutiune (HHD/Dashnak)
Address. P.O. Box 123, Yerevan 375010
Telephone. (+374–2) 535623
Fax. (+374-2) 531362
Email. buro@arf.arm

Website. www.arf.am
Leadership. Hrand Margaryan (chairman of world bureau); Armen Rustamyan (leader of Armenian executive); Davit Lokyan (parliamentary group chairman); Giro Manoyan (executive director)
Dating from 1890, *Dashnak* was the ruling party in pre-

Soviet independent Armenia (1918-20) and retained a large following in the Armenian diaspora after it had been outlawed by the Bolsheviks in 1920. Re-established in 1990 as a nationalist opposition party of socialist orientation (and also calling itself the Armenian Socialist Party), *Dashnak* put up the actor Sos Sargsyan in the October 1991 presidential election but received only 4% of the vote. The party became a fierce critic of the conduct of the war in Nagorno-Karabakh by the government of the →Pan-Armenian National Movement (HHSh), which claimed in response that *Dashnak* leaders in exile had co-operated with the Soviet security authorities. *Dashnak* parliamentary leader Gagik Ovanessian was expelled from the party in June 1994 for publicly criticizing its "Bolshevik" methods.

In late December 1994 the *Dashnak* was "temporarily suspended" by presidential decree, on the grounds that it had engaged in terrorism, political assassination and drug-trafficking. It therefore did not participate as a party in the July 1995 legislative elections, although party members stood in many constituencies and one was elected. Some 30 *Dashnak* activists were put on trial in March 1996 charged with involvement in an alleged coup attempt during the elections, those receiving prison sentences including chairman Vahan Hovhanisyan and executive council member Hrant Margaryan. However, they were all released in February 1998 when the ban on the party was lifted, a week after the resignation of President Ter-Petrosyan (HHSh).

Dashnak backed the successful candidacy of Robert Kocharyan (non-party) in the March 1998 presidential elections, following which Hovhanisyan became a presidential adviser and the party obtained two ministerial portfolios in the new government. In the May 1999 Assembly elections *Dashnak* achieved third place with nine of the 131 seats and 7.8% of the proportional vote, subsequently obtaining one portfolio in the new government coalition.

Dashnak held its 28th world congress in Tsaghkadzor in February 2000 (its first in Armenia since 1919), electing Margaryan as chairman of the party's world executive bureau and establishing the party's head office in Yerevan. The Armenian executive subsequently appointed Armen Rustamyan as the principal *Dashnak* representative in Armenia. In June 2001 *Dashnak* again warned that it would oppose any government concessions on the →Nagorno-Karabakh issue that it considered to be a danger to national unity.

Dashnak is a consultative member of the Socialist International (having joined the pre-World War I Second International in 1907).

Communist Party of Armenia
Hayastani Komunistakan Kusaktsutyun (HKK)
Address. 22 Khorenatsi Street, Yerevan
Telephone. (+374–2) 567933
Fax. (+374–2) 523506
Leadership. Vladimir Darpinian (first secretary); Hrant Voskanian (chairman of parliamentary group)
Having been Armenia's sole ruling party in the Soviet era, the HKK could manage only second place in multi-party legislative elections in 1990 and was suspended in September 1991. Many of its members in the state bureaucracy joined the new ruling →Pan-Armenian National Movement; others opted for the →Democratic Party of Armenia. Re-legalized in 1994, the HKK took a poor third place in the 1995 Assembly elections, winning 12% of the proportional vote and only seven out of 190 seats.

In the September 1996 presidential elections then party leader Sergey Badalyan came third with 6.3% of the vote. He also stood in the March 1998 presidential contest, improving his support to 11% in the first round but coming fourth. The party's call for Armenia's accession to the new Russia-Belarus Union was an important plank in its platform for the May 1999 Assembly elections, in which it took second place with 12.1% of the proportional vote and 11 of the 131 seats.

Badalyan died of a heart attack in Moscow in November 1999 and was succeeded in January 2000 by Vladimir Darpinian, who had served as Armenian SSR Interior Minister in the 1970s. The following month the party joined the government led by →Republican Party of Armenia (HHK), thereby taking office for the first time since losing power in 1990.

Country of Law Party
Orinants Erkir (OE)
Address. 2 Arshakuniatis Street, Yerevan
Telephone. (+374–2) 563584
Leadership. Artur Baghdasaryan (chairman); Sergo Yeritsyan (parliamentary leader)
Launched in March 1998, the right-wing OE backed the successful presidential candidacy of Robert Kocharyan (non-party), subsequently becoming a core supporter of the new President. In the May 1999 Assembly elections the party took fifth place in the proportional section, with 5.3% of the vote, and obtained six of the 131 seats.

Democratic Party of Armenia
Hayastani Demokratakan Kusaktutyun (HDK)
Address. 14 Koryun Street, Yerevan
Telephone. (+374–2) 525273
Fax. (+374–2) 525273
Leadership. Aram Sarkisyan (chairman)
The HDK was established in late 1991 as the would-be successor to the former ruling →Communist Party of Armenia (HKK), which was suspended in September 1991 after having secured the second-largest number of seats in the 1990 legislative elections. Many senior Communists switched allegiance to the ruling →Pan-Armenian National Movement (HHSh) rather than to the HDK, which was also weakened by the revival of the HKK in 1994. In the 1995 legislative elections the HDK took only 1.8% of the vote and failed to win representation.

The resignation of President Ter-Petrosyan (HHSh) in February 1998 produced a partial revival for the HDK, whose chairman became a foreign policy adviser to the new non-party President, Robert Kocharyan. In the May 1999 Assembly elections the HDK won one seat and 1% of the proportional vote.

Justice and Accord Bloc
Iravunk yev Miabanutyun (IeM)
Address. 50A Eznik Koghbatsi Street, Yerevan
Telephone. (+374–2) 532725
Fax. (+374–2) 532676
Leadership. Artashes Geghamian (chairman)
The IeM was originally launched in March 1998 by seven left-inclined nationalist parties supportive of the successful presidential candidacy of Robert Kocharyan (non-party) but was subsequently reduced to, principally, National Accord (*Miabanutyun*) led by Artashes Geghamian and the Union of Constitutional Rights (*Sahmanadrakan Iravunqi Miutyun*, SIM) led by Hrant Khachatryan, who had obtained 0.3% of the first round vote in the 1998 presidential elections. In the May 1999 Assembly elections the bloc took third place in the proportional section with 7.97% of the vote and fourth place overall with seven seats out of 131.

Following the 1999 elections Geghamian became increasingly critical of successive governments headed by the centre-right →Republican Party of Armenia. At a *Miabanutyun* congress in May 2000 Geghamian argued that far greater state involvement was needed to overcome Armenia's economic crisis, subsequently conducting exploratory talks on a formal alliance with the →People's Party of Armenia. In September 2000 Geghamian launched a national campaign for the calling of new elections, although without obvious support from Khachatryan's SIM grouping.

Mission
Araqelutiun
Address. 15 Njdeh Street, Giumri
Telephone. (+374–69) 34350
Leadership. Artush Papoyan (chairman)
This formation was launched shortly before the May 1999 Assembly elections, in which it won only 0.8% of the proportional vote but secured one constituency seat.

National Democratic Union of Armenia
Azgayin Zhoghorvrdavarakan Miutyun (AZhM)
Address. 12 Abovian Street, Yerevan
Telephone. (+374–2) 523412
Fax. (+374–2) 563188
Leadership. Vazgen Manukian (chairman)
The centre-right AZhM was formed by Vazgen Manukian following his resignation as Prime Minister in September 1991, when he also left the then ruling →Pan-Armenian National Movement (HHSh). In mid-1994 the AZhM organized demonstrations against the HHSh government in Yerevan. The party won 7.5% of the vote and five Assembly seats in the 1995 Assembly elections, while in the September 1996 presidential contest Manukian was runner-up with 41.3% of the vote, subsequently claiming that the result had been rigged.

Manukian stood again in the March 1998 presidential elections, being eliminated in the first round with 12.2% of the vote. Having failed to find alliance partners for the May 1999 Assembly elections, the AZhM slipped to 5.2% of the vote but increased its representation to six seats. Although critical of the presidency of Robert Kocharyan, the party accepted a ministerial post in February 2000. In September 2000 Manukian ruled out entering an alliance with the main ruling →Republican Party of Armenia or any other formation, although at an AZhM congress in December he favoured qualified co-operation with the Kocharyan presidency, therefore coming under criticism from party members who advocated a return to outright opposition.

The AZhM was weakened in early 2001 by the breakaway of at least two dissident groups and the creation of the →National Democratic Bloc and the →National Democratic Party.

Pan-Armenian National Movement
Hayots Hamazgain Sharzhum (HHSh)
Address. 27 Khanjyan Street, Yerevan
Telephone. (+374–2) 557982
Fax. (+374–2) 570470
Leadership. Alexander Arzoumanian (chairman)
Established in November 1989, the HHSh originally grouped pro-independence elements of the then ruling →Communist Party of Armenia (HKK). Its early leaders included Levon Ter-Petrosyan, who in the Soviet era had been a prominent member of the unofficial Karabakh Committee advocating the transfer of the Armenian-populated enclave of Nagorno-Karabakh from Azerbaijan to Armenia. In his youth Ter-Petrosyan had been arrested in 1965 at a demonstration in Yerevan marking the 50th anniversary of the Turkish massacre of Armenians during World War I.

Calling for Armenia's negotiated withdrawal from the Soviet Union, the HHSh swept the May 1990 legislative elections and subsequently led Armenia to full independence. Following the dissolution of the HKK, Ter-Petrosyan secured a popular mandate in October 1991 when he was directly elected President with 83% support from those voting. HHSh dominance was not seriously affected by the formation of the breakaway →National Democratic Union of Armenia in 1991, nor by the revival of the HKK in 1994. In the 1995 legislative elections it headed the victorious Republic Bloc (*Hanrapetoutioun*), which also included the →Republican Party of Armenia, the →Armenian Christian Democratic Union, the →Democratic Liberal Party of Armenia and the →Social Democratic Hunchakian Party.

As the governing party, the HHSh sought to pursue the conflict with Azerbaijan to a successful conclusion, by which it meant the transfer of Nagorno-Karabakh to Armenian sovereignty with territorial adjustments to make it contiguous with Armenia proper.

The election of Yerevan mayor and former Interior Minister Vano Siradeghyan as HHSh chairman in July 1997 precipitated internal divisions culminating in the formation of the breakaway →Homeland movement in September 1997. The sudden resignation of Ter-Petrosyan as President in February 1998 increased the party's difficulties. Although it backed the successful candidacy of Robert Kocharyan in the March 1998 presidential elections and was included in the new government, by the end of 1998 it had become an opposition party, amidst strong criticism of the Ter-Petrosyan presidency by non-HHSh Kocharyan supporters, particularly of Siradeghyan's record as Interior Minister in 1992–96. Accused of instigating the murder of political opponents in that period, Siradeghyan went abroad in January 1999 two weeks before the Assembly voted to strip him of parliamentary immunity from prosecution.

In March 1999 Siradeghyan was nevertheless re-elected as HHSh chairman at the party's 11th congress, which launched a fierce attack on the "criminalization" of the government under Kocharyan and the creation of a "military-police system". Siradeghyan returned shortly before the May 1999 Assembly elections and was promptly arrested. The elections demonstrated the marginalization of the HHSh, which was reduced to a single seat (won by Siradeghyan in a constituency contest) and only 1.2% of the proportional vote.

Siradeghyan again fled abroad in April 2000 and was replaced as HHSh chairman by former Foreign Minister Alexander Arzoumanian, who was confirmed in the leadership by the party's 12th congress in December 2000. Arzoumanian called upon the HHSh to form a united front with other centre-left parties.

People's Party of Armenia
Hayastani Zhoghovrdakan Kusaktsutyun (HZhK)
Address. 24 Moskovian Street, Yerevan
Telephone. (+374–2) 581577
Leadership. Stepan Demirchyan (chairman)
The HZhK held its foundation congress in Yerevan in February 1999, proclaiming a commitment to "democratic and popular socialism" and to reversing post-Soviet "deindustrialization". The party had been launched in 1998 by Karen Demirchyan on the strength of his support in the March 1998 presidential elections, when he had been runner-up to Robert Kocharyan (non-party) with 30.7% in the first round and 40.5% in the second. Karen Demirchyan had been first secretary of the then ruling →Communist Party of Armenia from 1974 until his dismissal in 1988 for failing to clamp down on Armenian nationalism.

The HZhK contested the May 1999 Assembly elections in an alliance with the →Republican Party of Armenia (HHK) called the Unity Bloc (*Miasnutiun*), which dominated the contest by winning 55 of the 131 seats and 41.7% of the proportional vote. While the then HHK leader became Prime Minister, Karen Demirchyan was elected Speaker of the new Assembly. However, in October 1999 he was one of eight political leaders, including the Prime Minister, slain by intruding gunmen during an Assembly debate. He was succeeded as HZhK chairman in December by his younger son, Stepan Demirchyan, while Armen Khachatrian of the HZhK became Speaker.

Although Stepan Demirchyan initially pledged the HZhK's continued participation in the Unity Bloc, his criticism of government policies intensified following the appointment of HHK chairman Andranik Markarian as Prime Minister in May 2000. The divisions sharpened in September when HHK deputies led an attempt to oust Khachatrian from the Speakership, following which Demirchyan in October refused to commit the HZhK to supporting the Markarian government.

Republican Party of Armenia
Hayastani Hanrapetakan Kusaktsutyun (HHK)
Address. 23 Toumanian Street, Yerevan
Telephone. (+374–2) 580031
Fax. (+374–2) 581259
Leadership. Andranik Markarian (chairman)
The centre-right HHK was relaunched in mid-1998 as a merger of the Yerkrapah Union of Veterans (of the Nagorno–Karabakh war) and the original HHK, which had been founded in May 1991 by a moderate faction of the →National Self-Determination Union and had been part of the victorious Republic Bloc in the 1995 Assembly elections. Yerkrapah leader and then Defence Minister Vazgen Sarkisyan was elected chairman of the new HHK, which espoused free market economic policies.

The HHK stood in the May 1999 Assembly elections in an alliance with the left-leaning →People's Party of Armenia (HZhK) called the Unity Bloc (*Miasnutiun*), which dominated the contest by winning 55 of the 131 seats and 41.7% of the proportional vote. As leader of the stronger partner, Vazgen Sarkisyan became Prime Minister of a government in which smaller parties were also represented. However, in October 1999 he was one of eight political leaders assassinated by gunmen who invaded an Assembly debate. He was succeeded as Prime Minister by his younger brother, Aram Sarkisyan, and as HHK chairman by Andranik Markarian.

In May 2000 Aram Sarkisyan was dismissed as Prime Minister by President Kocharyan and replaced by Markarian, who was quickly faced with dissidence from the HHK's Yerkrapah wing, which formed a separate Assembly group (*Hayastan*) strongly critical of President Kocharyan. Also undermining the *Miasnutiun* alliance in late 2000 was the increasing disaffection of the HZhK. In February 2001 Aram Sarkisyan resigned from the HHK and announced his intention to form a new "conservative opposition" party, together with Albert Bazeyan, the former mayor of Yerevan, and the *Hayastan* faction. A statement from the two accused Markarian of becoming "the appendage of a vicious government" and showing "total neglect of the rule of law".

Other Parties and Blocs

The following selection from the large number of minor parties and constantly changing party blocs active in Armenia focuses on those which made some sort of showing in the May 1999 National Assembly elections.

Armenian Christian Democratic Union (ACDU), founded in 1990 and supportive of the post-communist government of the →Pan-Armenian National Movement. It formed part of the victorious Republic Bloc in the 1995 legislative elections. Advocating Christian democracy on the West European model but adapted to Armenian conditions, the ACDU is an affiliate of the Christian Democrat International.
Address. 8 Abovian Street, Yerevan
Telephone. (+274–2) 561067
Fax. (+274–2) 561963
Leadership. Azat Arshakian (chairman)

Free Armenia Mission (*Azat Hayq Arakelutyun, AHA*), right-wing formation dating from 1990, won 0.6% of proportional vote in the 1999 Assembly elections.
Address. 27/25 Nor Aresh Street, Yerevan
Telephone. (+274–2) 457308
Leadership. Rouben Mnatsakanian (chairman)

Homeland (*Hairenik*), launched in September 1997 by Edouard Yegorian and a dozen dissident moderate deputies of the →Pan-Armenian National Movement; the 1999 Assembly elections were contested by Yegorian's Democratic Homeland (*Zhoghovrdavarakan Hayrenik*), which took 1.2% of the proportional vote, and the more nationalist Powerful Homeland (*Hzor Hayrenik*), which won 2.3%.

Address. 12 Vagharshian Street, Yerevan
Telephone. (+374–2) 351530
Fax. (+374–2) 341055
Leadership. Edouard Yegorian (chairman)

Nation State (*Azgain Petutiun*), right-wing formation dating from 1993, won 0.5% of the proportional vote in the 1999 Assembly elections.
Address. 8/28 Zaqian Street, Yerevan
Telephone. (+374–2) 589066
Fax. (+374–2) 628011
Leadership. Samvel Shahinyan (chairman)

National Democratic Bloc, founded in April 2001 by a dissident faction of the →National Democratic Union of Armenia (AZhM) led by Arshak Sadoyan, who had opposed the parent party's support for the post-1999 government headed by the →Republican Party of Armenia. In June 2001 Sadoyan called for the state to retain a majority stake in the energy and other strategic industries.
Leadership. Arshak Sadoyan

National Democratic Party, founded in February 2001 by a dissident faction of the →National Democratic Union of Armenia (AZhM) opposed the parent party's support for the post-1999 government headed by the →Republican Party of Armenia.
Leadership. Shavarsh Kocharyan

Self-Determination Union (*Inqnoroshum Miavorum, IM*), Christian-oriented formation which contested the 1995 Assembly elections as an opposition party, winning 5.6% of the national vote and three seats; contested the 1999 elections in the AIM+ alliance with the Homeland-Diaspora Union (*Hayrenik-Spiurq Miutiun*, HSM) led by Hrach Ter-Esayan, which obtained only 2.3% of the proportional vote and no seats.
Address. 15 Grigor Lusavorich Street, Yerevan
Telephone. (+374–2) 563321
Fax. (+374–2) 562916
Email. pharikyan@aimusd.am
Website. www.aimusd.am
Leadership. Paruyr Hayrikian (chairman)

Shamiram Women's Party (SWP), women-only party which took as its title the Armenian version of the name of the legendary Queen Semiramis of Assyria reputed to have built the Hanging Gardens of Babylon; won an impressive 17% of the vote and eight seats in the 1995 Assembly elections, to become the largest single opposition party and the best-represented women's formation in Europe (and probably the world). But it slumped to 0.2% of the proportional vote and no seats in the 1999 elections.
Leadership. Gayane Saroukhyan (chairwoman)

Social Democratic Hunchakian Party (*Sotsial Demokratalkan Hunchakian Kusaktutiun, SDHK*), dating from 1887, registered in modern Armenia in 1991, formed part of the victorious Republic Bloc in the 1995 Assembly elections, but made no impact in 1999 elections, in which it contested three constituencies.
Address. 70 Pushkin Street, Yerevan
Telephone. (+374–2) 251781
Leadership. George Hakobyan (chairman)

Union of Communist and Socialist Parties (*Komunistakan yev Sotsialistakan Kusaktsutyunneri, KSK*), headed by the United Progressive Communist Party of Armenia (*Hayastani Arajadimakan Miatsial Komunistakan Kusaktsutiun, HAMKK*), which was founded in January 1998 as the self-proclaimed successor to the Soviet-era Communist Party and in opposition to the perceived revisionism of the →Communist Party of Armenia. The KSK received 2.5% of the proportional vote in the May 1999 Assembly elections, none of its 29 candidates being elected.

Address. 1/3 Pavtos Piuzand Street, Yerevan
Telephone. (+374–2) 584522
Leadership. Vazgen Safarian (chairman)

Union of Right-Wing Forces (URF), launched in May 2000 as a merger of the Democratic Liberal Party (*Ramkavar Azatakan*) led by Vigen Khachtrian (which won 0.7% of the proportional vote in the 1999 elections), Freedom (*Azatutiun*) led by Hrant Bagratyan) (which won 1%), the 21st Century Party led by David Shahnazarian and the *Armat* grouping led by Babken Ararktsyan. The constituent formations mostly derived from breakaway factions of the →Pan-Armenian National Movement. The new movement's founding congress in Yerevan accused President Robert Kocharyan of having "seized power" on the resignation of Levon Ter-Petrosyan in February 1998.

Union of Socialist and Intellectual Forces (USIF), incorporating the Union of Intellectuals (*Mtavorakanneri Miutsiun*, MM) led by Felix Safaryan and the Social Democratic Party of Armenia (*Hayastani Sotsial Demokratakan Kusaktsutiun*, HSDK) led by Arman Martirossyan, presented 47 candidates in the proportional section of the 1999 Assembly elections but won only 0.2% of the vote.
Leadership. Ashot Manchurian (chairman)

Worthy Future (*Arzhanapative Apaga, AA*), centrist grouping supporting a free market economy, social justice and human rights, led by a former Soviet deputy, won 3.3% of the proportional vote in the 1999 Assembly elections.

Address. 4/16 Amirian Street, Yerevan
Telephone. (+374–2) 520156
Leadership. Ludmilla Harutinian (chairperson)

Nagorno-Karabakh Parties

Legally an autonomous republic of Azerbaijan, the Armenian-populated enclave of Nagorno-Karabakh made a unilateral declaration of independence in 1996 and has since held presidential and legislative elections which have been declared illegal by the Azerbaijani authorities.

Armenakan Party, won one out of 33 seats in elections to the Nagorno-Karabakh legislature in June 2000.

Armenian Revolutionary Federation (*Hai Heghapokhakan Dashnaktsutiune, HHD/Dashnak*), Nagorno-Karabakh wing of the Armenian party (see above), won nine out of 33 seats in legislative elections in June 2000.

Democratic Artsakh Party, supportive of "President" Arkady Gukasyan, who was elected in November 1997 in succession to Robert Kocharyan after the latter had been appointed Prime Minister of Armenia. The party headed the poll in elections to the Nagorno-Karabakh legislature in June 2000, winning 13 of the 33 seats.

Australia

Capital: Canberra, ACT

Population: 19,200,000 (2000E)

The Commonwealth of Australia is a parliamentary democracy with the British monarch as non-executive head of state, represented by a locally nominated Governor-General. Australia comprises six states, each with its own directly-elected assembly with extensive powers, and two territories. There is a bicameral federal Parliament. The membership of the Senate is currently fixed at 76: 12 members from each state, directly elected for a six-year term (with half the seats renewed at three-year intervals), and two members each from the Northern Territory and the Australian Capital Territory (ACT), directly elected for three-year terms. The members of the House of Representatives–currently totalling 148 – serve a three-year term. Either the House or both chambers may be dissolved early by the Governor-General, whose powers are by convention exercised in accordance with the advice of the Australian government.

Elections to the House, and to most state lower chambers, use the alternative vote system in single-member constituencies; those to the Senate, and the Tasmanian lower house, use proportional representation in multi-seat constituencies. Federal and state elections are on the basis of universal and (with some exceptions) compulsory suffrage. The Governor-General appoints the Prime Minister, who is normally the majority leader in the federal House of Representatives, and who exercises executive power along with a cabinet drawn from and answerable to Parliament; broadly similar arrangements apply at state level, each state having its own constitution and a government led by a state premier.

The activities of political parties are regulated principally by the Commonwealth Electoral Act and the Australian Electoral Commission. On the recommendation of an all-party parliamentary committee in 1994, the Act was amended to increase public funding of parties, also imposing stricter requirements to disclose donations to party funds. Federal funds are allocated to those registered parties and independent candidates obtaining at least 4% of state or territory first-preference votes in elections for either the federal House of Representatives or the Senate. In the 1998 general elections the rate of funding was set at A$1.62 per first-preference vote and the total paid out to 13 parties and 16 independent candidates was A$33,920,787 (House A$17,002,468, Senate A$16,918,319), of which the Australian Labor Party (ALP) was the largest beneficiary with A$14,010,512. Under half-yearly indexing in line with the consumer price index, the rate per first-preference vote was set at A$1.69 for the second half of 2000.

After winning five general elections in a row, the ALP lost power on March 2, 1996, to the Liberal–National Party coalition. The coalition was given a further mandate in House of Representatives elections on Oct. 3, 1998, which resulted in the Australian Labor Party winning 67 seats (with 40.0% of first-preference votes, the Liberal Party of Australia 64 (34.1%), the National Party of Australia 16 (5.6%) and an independent 1. As a result of simultaneous elections for 40 of the 76 Senate seats, the composition of the upper house became Liberal Party of Australia 31, ALP 29, Australian Democrats 9, National Party of Australia 4, Australian Greens 1, One Nation 1, independents 1.

Five states have bicameral legislatures, whereas Queensland and the Northern Territory have single-chamber assemblies and the ACT's unicameral House of Assembly has a non-legislative role.

New South Wales. Australia's most populous state has a 93-member Legislative Assembly and an upper Legislative Council with 60 members. Assembly elections are held at maximum intervals of four years, a quarter of Council seats being also renewed at each election. In elections on March 27, 1999, the ALP retained power with 55 Assembly seats, to 33 for the Liberal-National coalition and five independents.

Queensland. The Legislative Assembly's 89 members represent single-seat constituencies and are elected for three-year terms. In elections on Feb. 27, 2001, a strong vote share for One Nation damaged the Liberal-National alliance and enabled the ALP administration to retain power, the ALP winning 66 seats, the National Party 12, the Liberal Party 3, One Nation 3 and independents 5.

South Australia. The House of Assembly has 47 members, serving a three-year term, and the Legislative Council has 22 seats. In elections on Oct. 11, 1997, the Liberals narrowly retained power by winning 23 Assembly seats, with the ALP winning 21, independent Liberals 2 and the National Party 1.

Tasmania. Australia's island state has five constituencies, each returning five members for a four-year term in the House of Assembly. The 19-member Legislative Council is directly elected, each member serving for six years; three seats are renewed each year and four every sixth year. In elections on Aug. 29, 1998, the ALP ousted the ruling Liberals by winning 14 Assembly seats, against Liberals 10 and Greens 1.

Victoria. The 88 members of the Legislative Assembly are elected every three years, along with half of the 44 Legislative Council members, who serve a six-year term. In elections on Sept. 18, 1999, the Liberal–National coalition lost its majority, winning 43 of the Assembly seats against 42 for the ALP and independents 3. The ALP formed the new government with support from the independents.

Western Australia. The Legislative Assembly, with 57 members, is subject to election every four years. Half of the Legislative Council's 34 members are also elected at four-year intervals, serving for six years. In Assembly elections on Feb. 10, 2001, a strong vote (although no seats) for One Nation resulted in the incumbent Liberal–National coalition losing power to the ALP, which won 32 seats, while the Liberals won 16, the National Party 5 and independents 4.

Australian Capital Territory. The directly-elected Legislative Assembly, with 17 members, advises the federal government on ACT affairs. In elections held on March 17, 1998, under a new system of proportional representation the Liberals retained power with seven seats, with the ALP winning 6, the Greens 1 and independents 3. In July 1998 one of the Liberals formed the United Canberra Party.

Northern Territory. The sparsely-populated NT's unicameral Legislative Assembly has 25 members directly elected under a two-party preferred vote system. In elections on Aug. 30, 1997, the Country Liberal Party increased its majority by winning 18 seats against the ALP's 7. In a referendum held simultaneously with the federal elections on Oct. 3, 1998, NT voters rejected a government offer of statehood.

Australian Democrats
Address. PO Box 4089, Kingston, ACT 2604
Telephone. (+61–2) 6273–1059
Fax. (+61–2) 6273–1251
Email. inquiries@democrats.org.au
Website. www.democrats.org.au
Leadership. Meg Lees (leader); Michael Macklin (national president); Samantha Hudson (national secretary)
Founded in May 1977 by former →Liberal Party cabinet minister Donald L. (Don) Chipp, by a merger of the Australia Party and the New Liberal Movement, the Democrats (as the party is informally known) pursue a centre-left agenda. The party emphasizes its independence from business and organized labour, and favours higher public investment in education, welfare and poverty reduction.

The Democrats have never won a seat in the House of Representatives, but under proportional representation have been represented in the Senate continuously since 1977. In October 1998 they won 5.1% of the vote in elections to the House, but no seats, while in elections to the Senate they won nine seats, with 8.5% of the vote. The party holds the balance of power in the Senate.

Australian Greens
Address. GPO Box 1108, Canberra, ACT 2601
Telephone. (+61–2) 6247–6305
Fax. (+61–2) 6247–6455
Email. frontdesk@greens.org.au
Website. www.greens.org.au
Leadership. Catherine Moore (national convenor); Stu Cook (national secretary)

Declining to describe themselves as a party or their officers as leaders, the Australian Greens were established in August 1992 as the federal co-ordinating body for numerous state, territorial and local ecologist parties. The movement drew many adherents from the →Nuclear Disarmament Party, which had been launched by →Australian Labor Party (ALP) dissidents in 1984.

The Greens have never won a seat in the House of Representatives (taking 2.1% of the vote in the October 1998 elections) but have one seat in the Senate and have influenced the programmes of other parties, notably the ALP.

Australian Labor Party (ALP)
Address. 2 Centenary House, 19 National Circuit, Barton, ACT 2600
Telephone. (+61–2) 6273–3133
Fax. (+61–2) 6273–2031
Email. natsec@alp.org.au
Website. www.alp.org.au
Leadership. Kim Beazley (leader); Simon Crean (deputy leader); Greg Sword (national president); Geoff Walsh (national secretary)
Founded in 1901 as the political arm of the trade union movement (with which it retains close links) the democratic socialist ALP is Australia's oldest national political party, and since 1922 the only one to have held power other than in coalition. It first formed a government in 1904.

The party was seriously affected by ideological divisions during the Cold War and was out of office from 1949 until 1972 when, under the leadership of of Gough Whitlam, it returned to government. The Whitlam administration abolished compulsory military service, pulled Australian forces out of the Vietnam War, established diplomatic ties with China and lowered the voting age to 18. But its failure to secure a Senate majority in May 1974 brought on a constitutional crisis, culminating in Governor-General John Kerr's controversial intervention to dismiss the Whitlam government in November 1975. The ALP lost the following month's general elections.

The ALP recovered some ground in the October 1980 elections under the leadership of William (Bill) Hayden, a former president of the Australian Council of Trade Unions (who later became Governor-General of Australia). His successor in the union post, Robert (Bob) Hawke, was chosen to lead the party into the March 1983 elections and Hawke then led the party to successive election victories in 1983, 1984, 1987 and 1990.

Under Hawke's leadership the ALP discarded many of its traditional commitments and pursued an anti-inflation economic policy. Disputes between the party's traditionalist socialist left, based especially in the trade union movement, and pragmatic parliamentary caucus came to a head. In April 1989 a left-wing faction broke away, leaving the pragmatists in control. During 1991 Hawke's leadership was twice challenged by the federal Treasurer, Paul Keating. Succeeding at the second attempt in December, Keating took over as Prime Minister at a time of considerable economic difficulties but in March 1993 elections the government won a fifth consecutive term, winning 80 seats for a lower house majority of 13.

In June 1995 Prime Minister Keating (of Irish Catholic descent) published plans for a referendum to complete the transition to republican status in 2001, envisaging that the place of the monarch would be taken by an elected President. However, such aims did not enthuse voters sufficiently for Labor to win a sixth term in the March 1996 elections, when it retained only 49 seats (on a 38.8% first-preference vote share) and went into opposition. Keating resigned as ALP leader immediately after the contest and was succeeded by Kim Beazley, the former Deputy Prime Minister.

The ALP recovered some ground in the October 1998 national elections, winning 67 seats and 40% of first-preference votes, but remained in opposition. In a constitutional referendum in November 1999 the ALP's advocacy of a republic was rejected. In mid-2001 the ALP at state level was in power in New South Wales, Queensland, Tasmania, Victoria and Western Australia. Its retention of power in Queensland and its victory in Western Australia in February 2001 partly resulted from a strong vote for the populist →One Nation party to the detriment of the →Liberal and →National parties.

The ALP is officially committed to having at least 35% women parliamentarians at federal and state levels by 2002. There is an autonomous Young Labor Association. The ALP is affiliated to the Socialist International and the Asia-Pacific Socialist Organization.

Country Liberal Party (CLP)
Address. PO Box 4194, Darwin, NT 0801
Telephone. (+61–8) 8981–8986
Fax. (+61–8) 8981–4226
Email. ntclp@bigpond.com
Website. www.clp.org.au
Leadership. Denis Burke (leader); Suzanne Cavanagh (president); Charlie Taylor (general secretary)
Conservative in outlook and closely aligned to the federal →Liberal Party of Australia, the CLP (formally registered as the Northern Territory Country Liberal Party) has governed the Northern Territory (NT) since the first territorial legislative election in 1974.

In its eighth consecutive victory, the CLP increased its majority in NT elections in August 1997, winning 18 of the 25 seats. However, its advocacy of statehood for the NT was rejected in a referendum held simultaneously with the

October 1998 federal elections, in which the CLP also lost its one federal seat.

Liberal Party of Australia
Address. PO Box E13, Kingston, ACT 2604
Telephone. (+61–2) 6273–2564
Fax. (+61–2) 6273–1534
Email. libadm@liberal.org.au
Website. www.liberal.org.au
Leadership. John W. Howard (leader); Tony Staley (federal president)
The Liberal Party (as it is invariably called) has been, since its foundation by Sir Robert Gordon Menzies in October 1944, the main anti-socialist party in Australia, representing views ranging from the centre to the conservative right. Its core values are support for free enterprise and individual initiative, for the family and for "a common set of Australian values" in a multi-cultural society. It opposes state ownership of other than essential public services and advocates conservative economic policies, including rewarding enterprise through low levels of personal taxation.

The party originated in succession to the United Australia Party, which merged with other forces opposed to the →Australian Labor Party (ALP). The Liberals went into coalition with the (then) Country Party to form a federal government in 1949 and the party then remained in office until 1972, when the ALP returned to power. Invited by the Governor-General to form a minority government in November 1975, Liberal leader Malcolm Fraser secured a majority for the alliance in elections in December, and retained office in 1977 and 1980. Returned to opposition by the March 1983 elections, the Liberals subsequently underwent an intricate series of leadership changes. Andrew Peacock, who took over as leader after the 1983 defeat, was replaced by John Howard in September 1985. The alliance with the →National Party (the former Country Party) temporarily collapsed in 1987. Following the July 1987 federal election, in which the Liberals lost two seats in the House to hold 45, Peacock was appointed Howard's deputy, eventually ousting him and being reappointed leader in May 1989. But when the 1990 election saw the opposition fail to overturn Labor's majority, Peacock again resigned, to be succeeded by Dr John R. Hewson. Unpopular budget measures proposed by Hewson, including a 15% goods and services tax (GST) and cutbacks in the welfare state, were seen as contributing to the opposition's failure to oust an embattled Labor government in 1993, and Howard made another, unsuccessful bid for the Liberal leadership. Hewson stepped down in May 1994, to be succeeded by Alexander Downer. However, after eight months in the post, during which he secured the abandonment of the GST plan but got into political difficulties on other issues, Downer gave up the Liberal leadership in January 1995. Howard was elected unopposed to the post, completing his comeback at a time of auspicious opinion poll ratings for the opposition.

The Liberals expressed reservations about the ALP's proposal to abolish the Australian monarchy, although the issue caused some friction with the firmly monarchist National Party. The outcome was a Liberal pledge to convene a 'people's convention' to consider the constitutional options before any decision was taken. Howard declared, on resuming the leadership, that the Liberals were opposed to tax increases and favoured reductions in public expenditure, this platform taking the party to a sweeping victory in the March 1996 general elections (with 76 seats on a 39.1% first-preference vote share), after which Howard formed a coalition government with the National Party.

The Liberal–National government came under challenge in 1997 from the new →One Nation party, which attracted considerable support from conservative voters for its anti-immigration and pro-protection policies, which Howard was accused of not attacking sufficiently vigorously. Nevertheless, the coalition retained power in the October

1998 federal elections, in which Liberal representation in the lower house fell to 64 seats on the strength of a 34.1% first-preference vote share. Howard therefore continued as Prime Minister and played an important role in the November 1999 referendum rejection of an Australia republic by opposing the abolition of the monarchical system.

The Liberal Party has an official membership of 80,000 and is structured in seven autonomous state and territory divisions (the exception being the Northern Territory, where it is associated with the ruling →Country Liberal Party). In mid-2001 Liberals were also in power in South Australia and the Australian Capital Territory (having lost power in Western Australia in February 2001 because many of its supporters opted for One Nation).

The Liberal Party is affiliated to the International Democrat Union and the Pacific Democrat Union.

National Party of Australia

Address. PO Box E265, Kingston, ACT 2600
Telephone. (+61–2) 6273–3822
Fax. (+61–2) 6273–1745
Email. npafed@ozemail.co.au
Website. www.nationalparty.org
Leadership. John Anderson (leader); Mark Vaile (deputy leader); Helen Dickie (federal president); John Sharp (federal secretary)

A conservative force traditionally identified with rural interests, what is now the National Party emerged from Western Australia's state parliament in 1914 and developed a federal platform within two years under its original title of the Country Party. Its electoral appeal has been based on defending free enterprise, family values, national security and national economic development while emphasizing the concerns of people outside the relatively populous south-eastern coastal areas.

The party has participated in many federal coalition governments with the →Liberal Party of Australia, although the two conservative parties have differences in emphasis, in geographical spread and on policy matters and electoral strategy. The Nationals have shown a strong ideological commitment to the preservation of the monarchy, on which the Liberals have been divided, and the parties have sometimes disagreed on whether they should refrain from contesting each other's safe seats. The Country Party entered a federal coalition pact with the Liberals in 1949 and, as the junior partner, shared power with it until 1972. After changing its name to the National Country Party in 1974, it returned to federal office, again in partnership with the Liberals, from 1975 to 1983. By the time it reverted to opposition it had assumed its present title.

The National Party's strongest base is in Queensland, where the state government was led for two decades by the controversial right-winger Sir Johannes Bjelke-Petersen; he resigned in December 1987 after failing in a bid to take over the party's federal leadership (and was later criticized by a commission inquiring into allegations of gerrymandering). At national level, the party lost two seats in the June 1987 election, leaving it with 19 members in the House, but picked up a sixth Senate seat. Leader Ian Sinclair was replaced by Charles Blunt, who lost his seat in the party's election disaster of 1990 and was succeeded by Tim Fischer. Left with only 14 seats in the House, the party was severely dented by the findings of an official inquiry into corruption in the Queensland state administration. Over 200 officials and businessmen, Bjelke-Petersen included, faced criminal charges.

The fifth successive federal election victory of the →Australian Labor Party (ALP) in 1993 heightened the National Party's differences with the Liberals, leading to demands for an increased share of shadow cabinet portfolios for the smaller party. These problems were overcome, however, and the Nationals participated in the defeat of the ALP in the March 1996 federal elections, again becoming the junior government partner with the Liberals. In 1997 the National Party came under challenge from the new Queensland-based →One Nation party, which attracted considerable support in rural areas for its anti-immigration and pro-protection policies. In the Queensland state election in June 1998 One Nation successes resulted in the National-Liberal government being replaced by an ALP administration.

Nevertheless, the federal Liberal-National coalition retained power in the October 1998 national elections, in which the Nationals lost only two of their 18 seats, on a first-preference vote share cut from 8.2% to 5.6%. In July 1999 Timothy Fischer resigned as party leader and Deputy Prime Minister, being succeeded in both posts by deputy leader John Anderson, who retained ministerial responsibility for transport and regional services. In November 1999 the National Party helped to secure a decisive referendum decision against abolishing the monarchical system and moving to a republic. In February 2001 the party failed to regain power in Queensland, again being defeated by the ALP because of a strong vote for One Nation.

With an official membership of 125,000, the National Party is affiliated to the Pacific Democrat Union within the International Democrat Union.

One Nation

Address. PO Box 428, Ipswich, Queensland 4305
Telephone. (+61–7) 3281–0077
Fax. (+61–7) 3281–0899
Email. plh@gil.com.au
Website. www.onenation.com.au
Leadership. Pauline Hanson (leader)

One Nation was launched in March 1997 by Pauline Hanson, a former fish-and-chip shop proprietor who had been elected to the federal House of Representatives as an independent from Queensland in March 1996 and had gained national prominence for her outspoken populist views. The party has called for curbs on immigration from Asia, cuts in what it regards as disproportionately large welfare provision for Aborigines and the reversal of recent court decisions establishing the land title rights of the Aboriginal people. It also advocates tariff barriers to protect Australian enterprises from "unfair" foreign competition.

Drawing particular support from relatively disadvantaged rural voters, One Nation stunned the established parties by winning 23% of first-preference votes in the Queensland state elections in June 1998, thereby taking 11 of the 89 seats. In the federal elections in October 1998, however, it failed to win a single lower house seat (Hanson narrowly losing hers), despite taking 8.4% of first preferences, and returned only a single member to the Senate.

In February 1999 10 of the 11 One Nation members of the Queensland legislature left the party and one resigned his seat in protest against the party's "autocratic and undemocratic structure". Hanson offered herself for re-election, which she achieved by a unanimous vote at a party conference in late February. In August 1999 the Queensland Supreme Court ruled that One Nation's registration as a political party had been "induced by fraud and misrepresentation". In January 2000 the police raided One Nation offices in Queensland and New South Wales and seized hundreds of documents relating to the party's membership and finances. Two state One Nation branches subsequently lost their registered status, and the party appeared to be on a downward spiral. However, in state elections in Queensland and Western Australia in February 2001 One Nation bounced back, winning around 9% of the vote (and three seats in Queensland), effectively ensuring ALP victories in each state by taking votes from the →Liberal and →National parties.

Other Parties

Advance Australia Party, "economic nationalist" formation, advocating tariff protection for Australian manufacturing industry and assimilation of immigrants instead of multiculturalism.
Address. 41 Market Street, Wollongong, NSW 2500
Telephone. (+61–2) 4228–9292
Fax. (+61–2) 4225–8221
Website. www.lisp.com.au/~aap
Leadership. Rex Connor

Australian Republican Movement (ARM), formed to advance the campaign for the removal of the British monarchy from the Australian constitution.
Address. PO Box A870, Sydney South, NSW 1235
Telephone. (+61–2) 9267–8022
Fax. (+61–2) 9267–8155
Email. republic@ozemail.com.au
Website. www.republic.org.au
Leadership. Greg Barns (chairman); James Terrie (national director)

Australian Women's Party (AWP), established in Queensland but with branches in all states and territories, the AWP advocates constitutional change so that men and women are guaranteed equal representation in the federal parliament.
Address. PO Box 95, Red Hill, Queensland 4059
Telephone. (+61–7) 3217–1989
Fax. (+61–7) 3217–5699
Email. awp@powerup.com.au
Website. www.isis.aust.com/awp

Christian Democratic Party (CDP), also known as the Fred Nile Group after its leader, promotes Christian values in parliament and evaluates all legislation on biblical principles. It won 0.6% of the national vote in the October 1998 federal lower house elections and returned two members to the New South Wales upper chamber in March 1999.
Address. PO Box 141, Sydney, NSW 2001
Website. www.christiandemocratic.org.au
Leadership. Rev. Fred Nile (chairman)

City Country Alliance (CCA), launched in December 1999 by five dissident →One Nation members of the Queensland state legislature elected in June 1998 who had become disaffected with the vigorous style of leader Pauline Hanson.
Address. PO Box 287, Burpengary, Queensland 4505
Telephone. (+61–7) 3293–0115
Fax. (+61–7) 3293–0066
Email. gwb@gwb.com.au
Website. www.gwb.com.au
Leadership. Bill Feldman (leader)

Nuclear Disarmament Party (NDP), formed in June 1984 by elements of the →Australian Labor Party to campaign for the prohibition of nuclear weapons, nuclear power and the mining of uranium. Also advocates aboriginal rights.
Address. 38 Sheehan Street, Pearce, ACT 2067
Telephone. (+61–2) 6286–4650
Fax. (+61–2) 6286–7626
Email. info@nucleardisarmament.org
Website. www.nucleardisarmament.org
Leadership. Michael Denborough (chairman)

Shooters' Party, seeking to represent the rights of law-abiding firearms owners, its leader sits in the New South Wales upper house.
Address. PO Box 376, Baulkham Hills, NSW 1755
Telephone. (+61–2) 9686–2396
Fax. (+61–2) 9686–2396
Email. secretary@shootersparty.org.au
Website. www.shootersparty.org.au
Leadership. John Tingle (president)

Unity Party, also known as "Say No To Hanson", founded in 1998 to oppose Pauline Hanson's populist →One Nation and to maintain and enhance "an Australia that is truly multicultural". Drawing particular support from the ethnic Chinese community, the party won 0.8% of the vote in the October 1998 federal elections.
Address. PO Box K1222, Haymarket, NSW 2000
Telephone. (+61–2) 9211–4411
Fax. (+61–2) 9211–6801
Email. info@unity.org.au
Website. www.unity.org.au
Leadership. Peter Wong (president)

Austria

Capital: Vienna   **Population**: 8,050,000 (2000E)

First founded in 1919 following the demise of the Austro-Hungarian Empire in World War I, the Republic of Austria was re-established after World War II and obtained international recognition as a "sovereign, independent and democratic state" under the Austrian State Treaty signed on May 15 1955 by Austria, France, the UK, the USA and the USSR. The Austrian constitution provides for a parliamentary system of government based on elections by secret ballot and by "free, equal and universal suffrage"; as amended in 1945, it proscribes any attempt to revive the pre-war Nazi Party. There is a bicameral parliament consisting of a 183-member lower house called the National Council (*Nationalrat*) and a 63-member upper house called the Federal Council (*Bundesrat*), both together forming the Federal Assembly (*Bundesversammlung*). The *Nationalrat* is elected for a four-year term under an exact proportional representation system (subject to a minimum requirement of 4% of the national vote) by all citizens over 19 years of age. Members of the *Bundesrat* are elected for from four to six years by the legislatures of the nine Austrian provinces (*Länder*), each of which has an elected assembly (*Landtag*). The President of the Republic (*Bundespräsident*) is elected for a six-year term (to a maximum of two terms) by universal suffrage, the functions of the post being mainly ceremonial but including the appointment of the Federal Chancellor (*Bundeskanzler*) as head of government, who recommends ministeral appointments for confirmation by the President. Each member of the government must enjoy the confidence of a majority of members of the *Nationalrat*. Austria joined what became the European Union on Jan. 1, 1995, and elects 21 members to the European Parliament.

Under the Parties Financing Act of 1975, parties represented in the *Nationalrat* are granted federal budget support (for publicity and campaigning) in the form of a basic sum and additional amounts in proportion to the

27

number of votes received in the previous election, subject to at least 1% of the valid votes being obtained. Parties also receive state contributions to their national and European Parliament election expenses. The total amount of such financial support paid in 1998 was 201,718,700 schillings (about $15 million), rising to 475,689,591 schillings (about $35.6 million) in 1999, in which both national and European elections were held. Of this funding, the total amount available to the Social Democratic Party of Austria (SPÖ) in 1999 was 261,501,373 schillings (about $19.6 million). Separate state assistance is available to research foundations linked to the parties, totalling 123,768,389 schillings (about $9.3 million) in 1999, of which, for example, the SPÖ-linked Karl Renner Institute received 38,715,936 schillings (about $2.9 million).

Elections to the *Nationalrat* on Oct. 3, 1999, resulted as follows: Social Democratic Party of Austria (SPÖ) 65 seats (with 33.2% of the vote), Freedom Party of Austria (FPÖ) 52 (26.9%), Austrian People's Party (ÖVP) 52 (26.9%), The Greens–Green Alternative 14 (7.4%). In presidential elections on April 19, 1998, Thomas Klestil, an independent backed by the ÖVP, was re-elected for a second six-year term with 63.4% of the vote.

Austrian People's Party
Österreichische Volkspartei (ÖVP)

Address. Lichtenfelsgasse 7, A–1010 Vienna
Telephone. (+43–1) 401–260
Fax. (+43–1) 4012–6000
Email. info@oevp.at
Website. www.oevp.or.at
Leadership. Wolfgang Schüssel (chairman); Andreas Khol (parliamentary group leader); Maria Rauch-Kallat (secretary-general)

Founded in 1945 from pre-war Christian democratic groups, the ÖVP was the leading government party in 1945–66, in coalition with what later became the →Social Democratic Party of Austria (SPÖ). In sole power from 1966, the ÖVP was narrowly defeated by the SPÖ in the 1970 election, after which it was in opposition for 16 years. Although it lost ground in the 1986 election, simultaneous SPÖ losses dictated the formation of a "grand coalition" of the two major parties, which survived through the 1990 election and beyond, with the ÖVP as junior partner. Meanwhile, the party had become enmeshed in public controversy over the wartime record of Kurt Waldheim, whose election as President in 1986 with ÖVP backing was accompanied by claims that as a Germany Army officer he had participated in Nazi atrocities in the Balkans during World War II.

Waldheim's successor as President, Thomas Klestil, was elected in 1992 as the ÖVP-backed nominee. But provincial elections in the early 1990s showed falling support for the ÖVP, mainly to the benefit of the right-wing →Freedom Party of Austria (FPÖ). This trend was confirmed in the October 1994 federal election, in which the ÖVP's representation fell from 60 to 52 seats and its share of the vote to a low of 27.7%. The party nevertheless continued its coalition with the SPÖ, this being the only viable option if the FPÖ was to be excluded from the government. But Vice-Chancellor Erhard Busek later paid the price of the ÖVP's election setback, being replaced as party chair in April 1995 by Wolfgang Schüssel, who therefore also became Vice-Chancellor.

The ÖVP/SPÖ coalition unexpectedly collapsed in October 1995 over budget policy differences, precipitating a new federal election on Dec. 17. To general surprise, the ÖVP emerged with slightly higher representation of 53 seats, on a vote share of 28.3%, and in March 1996 entered a further coalition headed by the SPÖ. In Austria's first direct elections to the European Parliament in October 1996 the ÖVP headed the poll with 29.6% and seven seats, following which Klestil was re-elected as President in April 1997 with ÖVP backing. Strains arose in the coalition in March 1998 when the SPÖ insisted on maintaining Austria's neutrality, whereas the ÖVP favoured a commitment to NATO membership. In the June 1999 Euro-elections the ÖVP slipped to second place behind the SPÖ in percentage terms, although it improved to 30.6% of the vote and again won seven seats.

The governmental dominance of the SPÖ, combined with the rise of the FPÖ at provincial level, culminated in the ÖVP being reduced, very narrowly in terms of the popular vote, to third-party status in the October 1999 national elections, in which its vote share was a post-war low of 26.9%, although it retained 52 seats. Party leader Schüssel initially announced that the party would go into opposition, but in February 2000 took the controversial step forming a coalition with the FPÖ. Although it was stressed that the new government's programme included none of the FPÖ's more radical policies, the presence of the FPÖ in the coalition caused the EU to impose diplomatic sanctions on Austria. Schüssel stood his ground, however, and the sanctions were eventually lifted in September 2000.

At provincial level, the ÖVP in mid-2001 held the governorships of Lower Austria, Upper Austria and Styria in coalition with the SPÖ and FPÖ, of Salzburg and Tyrol in coalition with the SPÖ and of Vorarlberg in coalition with the FPÖ, while also participating in the coalition governments of Burgenland, Carinthia and Vienna. Claiming a membership of c.300,000, the ÖVP is affiliated to the International Democrat Union and the Christian Democrat International. The party's seven representatives in the European Parliament sit in the European People's Party/European Democrats group.

Freedom Party of Austria
Freiheitliche Partei Österreichs (FPÖ)

Address. Esslinggasse 14–16/Mezzanin, A-1010 Vienna
Telephone. (+43–1) 512–3535
Fax. (+43–1) 512–3539
Email. bgst@fpoe.at
Website. www.fpoe.or.at
Leadership. Susanne Riess-Passer (chairperson); Herbert Scheibner (deputy chairman); Peter Westenthaler (parliamentary group leader); Gilbert Trattner (business manager)

Usually described by the international media as a far-right or even "neo-Nazi" formation because of its opposition to immigration and other populist policies, the FPÖ has rejected such descriptions, pointing out that it is fully democratic and that its aim is to preserve the country's cultural identity and the employment prospects of the Austrian people. In January 1995 the party adopted the name Die Freiheitlichen (DF) after deciding that public antipathy to traditional party politics was so great that the word "party" should be dropped from its official title. But it continues to use the FPÖ title for most public purposes.

The FPÖ had been formed in 1956 as a merger of three right-wing formations, notably the League of Independents, which had won 14 lower house seats in 1953 on a platform of opposition to the post-war party system (*Proporz*) under which all state jobs were shared out between the two main parties. FPÖ representation languished in the 1960s and 1970s, although some of its policies, including more precise proportional representation in elections, were enacted. In 1983 it won 12 seats and joined a coalition government with what later became the →Social Democratic Party of Austria (SPÖ). Subsequently, the moderate federal leadership of Norbert Steiger came into increasing ideological conflict with the right-wing provincial Carinthian FPÖ, which contested the 1984 provincial election on a platform of opposition to the provision of bilingual education for the Slovene minority. This argument culminated in Steiger being replaced by youthful populist Jörg Haider in September 1986.

The SPÖ responded to Haider's elevation by terminating the ruling coalition, but in the resultant federal elections in November 1986 the FPÖ almost doubled its vote share to 9.7%, on a populist platform which included opposition to foreign immigration. In 1989 Haider became governor of the southern province of Carinthia in a coalition between the FPÖ and the →Austrian People's Party (ÖVP), but was obliged to resign two years later after asserting in a *Landtag* debate that "an orderly employment policy was carried out in the Third Reich, which the government in Vienna cannot manage". Developing its populist policies in the 1990 federal election, the opposition FPÖ increased its vote to 16.6%, thereafter also making a series of major gains in provincial elections. The party failed in 1993 to bring about a national referendum on the immigration issue, and Haider's opposition to the government's aim of European Union membership failed to prevent the Austrian electorate voting decisively in favour in June 1994. Nevertheless, after registering a further advance in the Vorarlberg provincial election in September 1994, the FPÖ's share of the vote rose to 22.6% (and 42 seats) in the October federal elections, although the party remained in opposition.

Following the collapse of the federal coalition of the SPÖ and the ÖVP in October 1995, general elections in December resulted in an unexpected failure to progress by the FPÖ, which slipped to 40 seats and 21.9%. The party nevertheless quickly recovered forward momentum against a new SPÖ/ÖVP federal coalition, winning 27.5% of the vote and six seats in Austria's first direct elections to the European Parliament in October 1996. Its subsequent advances at provincial level featured a 42% vote share in Carinthia in March 1999, as a result of which Haider again became provincial governor (in coalition with the SPÖ and the ÖVP).

In the June 1999 Euro-elections the FPÖ fell back to 23.5% and five seats. But Haider achieved a major advance in the October 1999 federal election, his party's 26.9% vote share being slightly greater than the ÖVP's and giving it 52 *Nationalrat* seats, the same number as the ÖVP. The eventual outcome in February 2000 was the formation of a highly controversial ÖVP–FPÖ coalition government in which the FPÖ took half of the ministerial posts, although the coalition agreement made it clear that none of the FPÖ's more radical policies were part of the government programme. Haider himself not only did not figure in the new ministerial team but also bowed out as FPÖ chairman, being succeeded by the new Vice-Chancellor, Susanne Riess-Passer. He nevertheless remained effective leader of the party as governor of Carinthia, campaigning in particular against enlargement of the EU to Austria's ex-communist neighbours without safeguards against migration of workers thereafter.

The FPÖ federal ministers generally kept a low profile, so that EU diplomatic sanctions imposed on Austria because of the party's arrival in office were eventually lifted in September 2000. However, majority Austrian opinion against foreign interference in the domestic democratic process did not benefit the FPÖ in provincial elections in Burgenland, Styria and Vienna in late 2000 and early 2001, in each of which the party lost substantial ground. After the Vienna defeat in March 2001, Haider blamed the party's participation in a federal government which "needed to show more concern for the common people". Independent observers attributed the FPÖ's electoral decline in part to the surfacing of allegations that the party had regularly obtained security information on its political opponents from FPÖ supporters in the police force.

Apart from heading the Carinthia government, the FPÖ in mid-2001 also participated in the administrations of Lower Austria, Upper Austria, Burgenland and Styria in coalition with the ÖVP and the SPÖ and in that of Vorarlberg in coalition with the ÖVP. Claiming 50,000 members, the FPÖ was an affiliate of the Liberal International until being replaced in that organization by the breakaway →Liberal Forum. The movement's five representatives in the European Parliament are part of the "unattached" contingent.

The Greens–Green Alternative
Die Grünen–Die Grüne Alternativen (GA)
Address. Lindengasse 40, A–1070 Vienna
Telephone. (+43–1) 5212–5201
Fax. (+43–1) 526–9110
Email. bundesbuero@gruene.at
Website. www.gruene.at
Leadership. Alexander Van der Bellen (spokesperson); Madeleine Petrovic (parliamentary group leader); Michaela Sburny (secretary-general)

The GA was formed in 1987 as a union of three alternative groupings which had won a total of eight seats in the 1986 federal election, although the conservative →United Greens of Austria subsequently opted to retain their organizational independence. Its component groups had already become influential campaigning on environmentalist issues, their biggest success being the referendum decision in 1978 not to proceed with the commissioning of the country's first nuclear power station at Zwentendorf. As a parliamentary party, the GA has not only sought to bring environmental concerns to the forefront of economic and industrial decision-making but has also pressed for the dismantling of the *Proporz* system whereby the two main post-war parties have shared out the top posts in government bodies and nationalized industries.

The GA increased its representation to 10 seats in the 1990 federal election and thereafter unsuccessfully opposed the government's policy of joining the European Union. In the October 1994 federal elections the formation advanced to 7% of the national vote, giving it 13 seats, but it fell back to 4.8% and nine seats in the December 1995 elections. In Austria's first direct elections to the European Parliament in October 1996, the GA improved to 6.8%, which gave it one seat. It doubled this tally to two seats in the June 1999 Euro-elections (with 9.2% of the vote) and then advanced to 14 *Nationalrat* seats in the October 1999 federal elections (with 7.4% of the vote).

At provincial level the GA was in mid-2001 represented in the parliaments of eight of the nine Austria provinces (the exception being Carinthia), in opposition in each case. The party took particular pleasure in its advance to 12.5% of the vote in the Vienna elections in March 2001.

Claiming an individual membership of 3,000 as well as many affiliated groups, the GA is a member of the European Federation of Green Parties. Its two representatives in the European Parliament sit in the Greens/European Free Alliance group.

Liberal Forum
Liberales Forum (LIF)
Address. Reichsratstrasse 7/10, A–1010 Vienna
Telephone. (+43–1) 402–7881
Fax. (+43–1) 402–7889
Email. lif@lif.at
Website. www.lif.or.at
Leadership. Heide Schmidt (leader); Gerhard Kratky (secretary-general)

The LIF was launched in February 1993 by five lower house deputies of the →Freedom Party of Austria (FPÖ). The dissidents disagreed with the strident right-wing and anti-foreigner stance of the FPÖ's post-1986 leadership headed by Jörg Haider. The chief defector, Heide Schmidt, had been the FPÖ presidential candidate in 1992, winning 16.4% of the first-round vote. The Forum backed the successful government line in favour of EU membership in the June 1994 referendum. In the October 1994 federal elections it prevented an even bigger advance for its parent party by itself winning 11 seats on the strength of 5.7% of the popular vote. In the December 1995 contest, however, it fell back to 10 seats and 5.5%.

In Austria's first direct elections to the European Parliament in October 1996 the LIF won 4.3% of the vote and one seat. Heide Schmidt was again the party's candidate in the 1998 presidential election, winning 11.1% of the vote. But in the June 1999 Euro-elections the LIF failed to surmount the 4% barrier and so lost its single seat. It also failed in the October 1999 parliamentary elections, winning only 3.7% of the vote and so ceasing to be represented in the *Nationalrat*. At provincial level, the LIF was in mid-2001 represented in the provincial parliaments of Styria and Vienna, in opposition in each case.

In 1993 the LIF was designated to replace the FPÖ as the Austrian affiliate of the Liberal International. The party has a membership of 2,000.

Social Democratic Party of Austria
Sozialdemokratische Partei Österreichs (SPÖ)

Address. Löwelstrasse 18, A–1014 Vienna
Telephone. (+43–1) 53427
Fax. (+43–1) 535–9683
Email. international@spoe.or.at
Website. www.spoe.at
Leadership. Alfred Gusenbauer (chairman); Doris Bures & Andrea Kuntzl (general secretaries)

The SPÖ is descended from the Social Democratic Workers' Party dating from 1874, which advocated social revolution and the transformation of the Austro–Hungarian Empire into a federal state of coexisting nations. It had no direct political influence before World War I, although it became the largest parliamentary party on the strength of universal male franchise. On the establishment of the Austrian Republic in 1919 it was briefly in government under Karl Renner, but went into opposition in 1920, remaining committed to "Austro–Marxism" and prepared to resort to armed struggle if the bourgeoisie sought to resist social revolution. The party came under increasing pressure in the early 1930s, as the pro-fascist Dollfus government adopted authoritarian methods, dissolving the *Nationalrat* in March 1933 and introducing rule by decree. The party's paramilitary Republican Defence League, itself already banned, responded by mounting an uprising in Vienna in February 1934 but was quickly defeated. Following the proclamation of a quasi-fascist constitution three months later, the party went underground and participated with other democratic forces in anti-fascist resistance until German forces occupied Austria in 1938.

On the re-establishment of the Republic in 1945, the SPÖ adopted a pro-Western stance and participated in a broad-based coalition government including the →Communist Party of Austria. From November 1947, however, it became the junior partner in a two-party coalition with the →Austrian People's Party (ÖVP) that endured until 1966, when the SPÖ went into opposition. In 1970 it returned to power as the sole governing party under the leadership of Bruno Kreisky, forming a minority government until 1971, when it gained an absolute majority in the lower house which it retained in the 1975 and 1979 elections. A party congress in 1978 renounced public ownership as a necessary requirement of democratic socialism.

Losing its overall majority in the 1983 election, the SPÖ formed a coalition with the →Freedom Party of Austria (FPÖ) and Kreisky handed over the government and party leadership to Fred Sinowatz. The latter resigned in June 1986 as a result of the controversial election of Kurt Waldheim as President and was replaced as Chancellor by Franz Vranitzky. In September 1986, because of the FPÖ's move to the right, the SPÖ terminated the coalition but lost ground sharply in November elections. It therefore formed a "grand coalition" with the ÖVP in January 1987, under Vranitzky's chancellorship, thereby provoking the resignation of Kreisky as SPÖ honorary chairman. Later that year

an SPÖ congress gave qualified support to the government's privatization programme.

The SPÖ/ÖVP coalition was maintained after the October 1990 elections, in which the SPÖ remained substantially the largest party. In 1991 the party renamed itself "Social Democratic" rather than "Socialist", retaining the SPÖ abbreviation. The government's key external policy of EC/EU membership was endorsed by the electorate in June 1994 by a 2:1 majority. In the October 1994 federal elections, however, the SPÖ vote slipped to a new post-war low of 35.2% and the party opted to continue its coalition with the ÖVP. In October 1995, however, the coalition collapsed over budget policy differences, with the result that new lower house elections were held in December. Against most predictions, Vranitzky led the SPÖ to a significant electoral recovery, yielding 71 seats and 38.1% of the vote. In March 1996 he was appointed to a fifth term as Chancellor, heading a further coalition between the SPÖ and the ÖVP.

Austria's first direct elections to the European Parliament in October 1996 produced a slump in SPÖ support, to 29.2% and six seats. In January 1997 Vranitzky resigned as Chancellor, a week after the SPÖ had pushed through the controversial privatization of the Creditanstalt, the country's second-largest bank. The architect of the privatization, Finance Minister Viktor Klima, succeeded him as Chancellor and, in April 1997, as SPÖ chairman. Subsequent regional elections showed an erosion of SPÖ support, which recovered only to 31.7% in the June 1999 European Parliament elections, in which the party increased from six to seven seats.

The October 1999 parliamentary elections produced a setback for both federal coalition parties, the SPÖ falling to 33.2% and 65 seats. As leader of still the largest party, Klima was asked to form a new government, but this attempt failed and the SPÖ went into opposition to a controversial new coalition of the ÖVP and the FPÖ. Klima resigned as party chairman in February 2000 and was succeeded by Alfred Gusenbauer. At provincial level the SPÖ in mid-2001 held the governorships of Burgenland (in coalition with the ÖVP and FPÖ) and of Vienna (in coalition with the ÖVP); it also participated in the governments of the other seven provinces.

The SPÖ has an official membership of 700,000 and is a founder member of the Socialist International. Its seven representatives in the European Parliament are members of the Party of European Socialists group.

Other Parties

Citizens' Initiative against the Abandonment of Austria (*Bürgerinitiave gegen den Ausverkauf Österreichs*). It contested the 1994 parliamentary elections under the electoral designation "No" (*Nein*) in opposition to EU and NATO membership and in favour of Austrian neutrality, winning 0.9% of the vote; in the 1999 elections it took 0.4% of the popular vote.

Communist Party of Austria (*Kommunistische Partei Österreiches, KPÖ*), founded by pro-Soviet Social Democrats in 1919. It was in government in 1945–47 and represented in the lower house until 1959; reputedly one of the richest Austrian parties on the strength of industrial holdings acquired under the post-war Soviet occupation. It took only 0.3% of the vote in 1994 parliamentary elections, improving to 0.5% in 1999.
Address. Weyringergasse 33/5, A–1040 Vienna
Telephone. (+43–1) 503–6580
Fax. (+43–1) 503–411/499
Email. kpoe@magnet.at
Website. www.kpoenet.at
Leadership. Walter Baier (chairman)

The Independents (*Die Unabhängigen, DU*), opposed to

the post-war party system; Lugner won an impressive 9.9% of the vote in the 1998 presidential election, but the DU managed only 1% in the 1999 parliamentary elections.
Address. Gablenzgase 11, Vienna 15
Telephone. (+43–1) 98140
Fax. (+43–1) 98140
Email. service@ldu.at
Website. www.ldu.at
Leadership. Richard Lugner (chairman)

Azerbaijan

Capital: Baku

Population: 7,750,000 (2000E)

The Azerbaijan Republic declared independence from the USSR in August 1991, becoming a sovereign member of the Commonwealth of Independent States (CIS) created on the dissolution of the USSR in December 1991. Interim constitutional arrangements based on the 1978 Soviet-era text applied until the adoption of a new constitution in November 1995, providing for an executive President, who is directly elected by universal adult suffrage for a five-year term and who appoints the Prime Minister and other ministers. Legislative authority is vested in a 125-seat National Assembly (*Milli Majlis*), also elected for a five-year term, with 100 members being returned from single-member constituencies by simple majority and 25 proportionally from party lists which obtain at least 6% of the national vote.

Since independence Azerbaijan has moved to a limited multi-party system, qualified by the exigencies of hostilities with Armenia over Nagorno-Karabakh, internal political conflict and the continuing preponderance of former Communists in the state bureaucracy. Stringent registration requirements for Assembly elections held on Nov. 12 and 26, 1995, and Feb. 4, 1996, resulted in only eight parties being deemed eligible to stand (and about a dozen being deemed ineligible), with the consequence that a UN/OSCE monitoring mission subsequently concluded that the elections, producing an overwhelming majority for the ruling New Azerbaijan Party (YAP), had not been conducted fairly.

Similar criticism was directed at the conduct of presidential elections held on Oct. 11, 1998, in which Geidar Aliyev (YAP) was re-elected with an official tally of 76.1% of the vote against five other candidates. International pressure resulted in a last-minute relaxation of registration requirements for Assembly elections held on Nov. 5, 2000, in which 12 parties and one bloc were allowed to stand, although the process was again strongly criticized by both the domestic opposition and international observers. The results were annulled in 11 electoral districts, where further polling took place on Jan. 7, 2001. According to the official results, the YAP won 75 seats (with 62.5% of the proportional vote), the Azerbaijan Popular Front 6 (10.9%), the Civil Solidarity Party 3 (6.4%), the Azerbaijan Communist Party 2 (6.3%), the New Muslim Democratic Party (*Musavat*) 2 (4.9%), the Azerbaijan National Independence Party (AMIP–*Istiqlal*) 2 (3.9%), other parties 5 and independents 29 (one seat being unfilled). The two AMIP–*Istiqlal* deputies were subsequently expelled from the party.

Azerbaijan Communist Party
Azerbaycan Kommunist Partiyasi (AKP)
Address. 29 Hussein Javid Prospekti, Room 637te, Baku
Telephone. (+994–12) 380151
Leadership. Ramiz Ahmedov (chairman)
The AKP governed the republic during the Soviet era, latterly under the hardline rule of Ayaz Mutalibov. In elections to the 360-member Azerbaijan Supreme Soviet in September-October 1990, the AKP won 280 of the 340 seats contested (with 78% of the vote) and Mutalibov was re-elected President unopposed in post-independence direct elections in September 1991 which were boycotted by the opposition parties. Following military setbacks in Nagorno-Karabakh, Mutalibov was forced to resign in March 1992 and fled to Russia after a shortlived return to power in May (for which alleged coup attempt criminal charges were later preferred against him). The AKP was effectively suspended under the subsequent government of the →Azerbaijan Popular Front (AKC), which replaced the Supreme Soviet with an interim 50-member National Assembly dominated by AKC members. Nevertheless, party members remained preponderant in the state bureaucracy and former AKP deputies continued to regard the 1990 Supreme Soviet as the legitimate legislative body.

In November 1993 an attempt was made to relaunch the party as the Azerbaijan United Communist Party (AVKP), the aim being to rally the opposition to the government of Geidar Aliyev of the →New Azerbaijan Party (YAP). On Sept. 1, 1995, the Supreme Court banned the AVKP in light of Justice Ministry allegations that the party had engaged in

anti-state activities by advocating union with other ex-Soviet republics. On Sept. 19, however, the Court reversed its decision, which it described as "groundless and illegal", thus enabling the party to contest legislative elections in November 1995, although it failed to win representation.

Divisions in Communist ranks resulted in the effective relaunching of the AKP as a registered party for the October 1998 presidential elections, although candidate Firudin Hasanov received only 0.9% of the vote. Whereas the AVKP was renamed the →Azerbaijan Communist Workers' Party in August 2000, the rump AKP achieved registration for the November 2000 Assembly elections. It was allocated two seats, being officially credited with having just surmounted the 6% barrier to representation in the proportional section.

Azerbaijan National Independence Party
Azerbaycan Milli Istiqlal Partiyasi (AMIP–Istiqlal)
Address. 179 Azadliq Prospect, 370087 Baku
Telephone. (+994–12) 622917
Fax. (+994–12) 980098
Email. nipa@azeri.com
Web. www.amip.azeri.com
Leadership. Etibar Mamedov (chairman)
The right-wing AMIP was founded in July 1992 by Etibar Mamedov, who had been a prominent leader of the then ruling →Azerbaijan Popular Front (AKC) but had defected in light of resistance to his hardline nationalist approach to the Nagorno-Karabakh conflict with Armenia. Mamedov

had been an initial candidate for the June 1992 presidential election but had withdrawn claiming that the arrangements favoured the AKC candidate. He found no more acceptance of his line from Geidar Aliyev of the →New Azerbaijan Party (YAP) when the latter came to power in June 1993 and refused a post in the Aliyev government. Thereafter Mamedov and the AMIP vigorously opposed the government's willingness to accept the deployment of Russian troops in Azerbaijan to help guarantee a Nagorno-Karabakh settlement.

The AMIP was officially stated to have won three seats in the November 1995 Assembly elections on the basis of a national vote share of 9%. The party gravitated thereafter to an outright opposition stance, highlighted by Mamedov's candidacy in the controversial October 1998 presidential elections, in which he was runner-up to President Aliyev with 11.8% of the vote (and later failed in a legal challenge to the outcome). In April 1999 the AMIP parliamentary deputies joined a new opposition Democratic Bloc, as the party participated in broader opposition fronts such as the Movement for Democracy and the National Resistance Movement. Having boycotted the December 1999 local elections, in April 2000 the AMIP entered into a bilateral co-operation pact with the →Democratic Party of Azerbaijan.

Registered for the November 2000 legislative elections, the AMIP was stated to have polled well below the 6% threshold for seats in the proportional section. Two candidates elected on the AMIP ticket in constituency seats were quickly expelled from the party. Mamedov joined in opposition demands for the elections to be annulled because of widespread gerrymandering by the government.

Claiming a registered membership of over 20,000, the AMIP was admitted to the International Democrat Union in September 1999.

Azerbaijan Popular Front
Azerbaycan Khalq Cabhasi (AKC)

Address. 1 Injasanat Street, 370000 Baku
Telephone. (+994–12) 921483
Fax. (+994–12) 989004
Leadership. Ali Kerimov (leader of "reformist" faction); Mirmahmud Fattayev (leader of "conservative" faction)
The AKC was founded in 1989 under the leadership of Abulfaz Elchibey (then a teacher of oriental philosophy) as a broad-based opposition movement calling for reform of the then Communist-run political system. The movement took a broadly pan-Turkic line, supporting nationalist calls for the acquisition of Azeri-populated areas of northern Iran. In January 1990 AKC members were among 150 people killed by the security forces in Baku and elsewhere in disturbances arising from AKC-led anti-Armenian demonstrations. Allowed to contest the Supreme Soviet elections of September–October 1990, the AKC-led opposition won only 45 of the 360 seats (with a vote share of 12.5%). Together with other opposition parties, the AKC boycotted the direct presidential election held in September 1991 but subsequently brought about the resignation President Mutalibov in March 1992. In a further presidential election in June 1992, Elchibey was returned with 59.4% of the vote against four other candidates.

In government, the AKC blocked ratification of Azerbaijan's CIS membership but came under increasing pressure from opposition groups, notably the →New Azerbaijan Party led by Geidar Aliyev and the forces of Col. Surat Guseinov. Replaced as head of state by Aliyev in June 1993, Elchibey fled to Nakhichevan and disputed the official results of an August referendum (boycotted by the AKC) in which only 2% of voters were said to have expressed confidence in Elchibey. Aliyev secured popular endorsement as President in September 1993, in direct elections that were also boycotted by the AKC. The authorities subsequently launched a crackdown against the AKC, raiding its headquarters in Baku in February 1994 and arresting 100 AKC supporters for "resisting the police". AKC leaders claimed

that weapons said to have been found at the building had been planted by the police. Nevertheless, the AKC was able in 1994-95 to command substantial popular support for its opposition to the Aliyev government's policy of seeking a Nagorno-Karabakh settlement via close relations with Russia.

In May 1995 Elchibey repeated the AKC's call for the creation of a "greater Azerbaijan", to include the estimated 15 million ethnic Azeris inhabiting northern Iran (twice as many as the entire population of Azerbaijan proper). The Iranian authorities responded by cutting off electricity supplies to Elchibey's stronghold of Nakhichevan. In the same month Shahmerdan Jafarov, an AKC deputy, was stripped of his parliamentary immunity and accused of setting up illegal armed groups in Nakhichevan, where Elchibey's residence was reportedly surrounded by government troops. On June 17 Jafarov was shot in a clash in the enclave, subsequently dying of his injuries, while in October 1995 former Foreign Minister Tofik Gasymov of the AKC was arrested and charged with involvement in a coup attempt earlier in the year.

In the November 1995 Assembly elections the AKC was officially credited with winning three proportional seats on the basis of a national vote share of 10%, taking a fourth seat in balloting for unfilled seats in February 1996. Proceedings against AKC members early in 1996 included the sentencing to death *in absentia* of former Defence Minister Rakhim Gaziyev for treason, although his sentence was commuted to life imprisonment on his extradition from Moscow to Baku in April. Some AKC leaders were released under a presidential amnesty in July 1996 and in October 1997 Elchibey returned to Baku after four years in internal exile.

The AKC opted not to participate in the October 1998 presidential election, following which Elchibey was put on trial for insulting the head of state. That the proceedings were called off in February 1999 on the initiative of President Aliyev was widely attributed to international pressure. Thereafter the AKC continued to be the leading component in various opposition fronts and in local elections December 1999 won 754 seats out of about 10,000 at issue. However, the party became riven by internal divisions which led to an open split in August 2000, coinciding with the death of Elchibey in Turkey from cancer. A "reformist" faction led by former AKC deputy chairman Ali Kerimov favoured some accommodation with the regime, while the "conservative" wing led by Mirmahmud Fatayev maintained an uncompromising line.

The Fatayev AKC was barred from presenting candidates in the November 2000 Assembly elections, instead forming an alliance with the →New Muslim Democratic Party (*Musavat*). The Kerimov AKC was allowed to stand, being credited with 10.8% of the vote in the proportional section and six seats (including one won in re-runs for 11 seats in early January 2001). In the wake of the balloting both factions joined in opposition condemnations of its validity. In mid-January 2001 the Kerimov AKC announced jointly with the →Civil Solidarity Party that its deputies would participate in the work of the new Assembly, but in order to campaign for new elections.

Civil Solidarity Party
Ventendash Birliyi Partiyasi (VBP)

Address. c/o Milli Majlis, 2 Mehti Hussein, Baku
Leadership. Ayaz Mutalibov (chairman)
The VBP was established in April 2000 as the political vehicle of ex-President Ayaz Mutalibov, the former leader of the →Azerbaijan Communist Party who had lived in exile in Moscow since May 1992. The party was among the first to be registered for the November 2000 Assembly elections, which it contested as the leading component of the Democratic Azerbaijan bloc, also including the groupings Courage (*Geyryat*) led by Ashraf Mekhtiev, Education (*Maarifchilik*) led by Mahmed Hanifa Musayev and Honour (*Namus*) led by Togrul Ibragimli. It was officially stated to have just surmounted the 6% barrier to representation in the proportional section of the balloting and was allocated three seats.

Mutalibov was formally elected chairman at the party's

second congress in December 2000 and declared his intention to contest the presidential elections due in 2003. In mid-January 2001 the VBP announced jointly with the "reformist" wing of the →Azerbaijan Popular Front that its deputies would participate in the work of the new Assembly, but in order to campaign for new elections.

New Azerbaijan Party
Yeni Azerbaycan Partiyasi (YAP)
Address. 6 Landau Street, 370073 Baku
Telephone. (+994–12) 393875
Leadership. Geidar Aliyev (chairman); Ali Ahmedov (secretary-general)
The YAP was founded by Geidar Aliyev in September 1992 as an alternative to the then ruling →Azerbaijan Popular Front (AKC) following his exclusion from the June 1992 presidential election because he was over a newly-decreed age limit of 65. At the time he held the presidency of the Azerbaijani enclave of Nakhichevan and had previously been a politburo member of the Soviet Communist Party and first secretary of the party in Azerbaijan (from 1969); he had also served as a Soviet deputy premier until being dismissed by Mikhail Gorbachev in 1987 for alleged corruption. Returning to Nakhichevan, he had become chairman of its Supreme Soviet in September 1991 and had conducted an independent foreign policy for the enclave, signing a ceasefire with Armenia and developing relations with Russia, Turkey and Iran. The new party pledged itself to the defence of the rights of all individuals, regardless of nationality, and the creation of a law-based state.

Aliyev used the YAP to rally opposition to the AKC government of Abulfaz Elchibey, who was deposed in June 1993 with assistance from Col. Surat Guseinov, a former wool merchant who had recently been dismissed as commander of Azerbaijani forces in Nagorno-Karabakh. Elected interim head of state, Aliyev appointed Col. Guseinov as Prime Minister and received popular endorsement of sorts in a presidential election in October 1993 (for which the 65-year age limit was rescinded), being credited with 98.8% of the vote against two other candidates, neither of whom represented major opposition parties. Meanwhile, at Aliyev's urging in September, parliamentary approval had at last been given to Azerbaijan's membership of the CIS. The new government launched a crackdown against the AKC, while Aliyev moved to improve Azerbaijan's regional relations and sought a settlement of the conflict with Armenia involving the deployment of Turkish troops in Nagorno-Karabakh and the return of a limited Russian military presence in Azerbaijan proper.

In a further power struggle in October 1994, Col. Guseinov was dismissed as Prime Minister and replaced by Fuad Kuliyev. The YAP regime accused Col. Guseinov of treasonable activities, reportedly in connivance with opposition groups and the Russian authorities. The episode therefore marked a distinct cooling between the YAP government and Moscow. In the November 1995 legislative elections (completed in February 1996) the YAP formed a front with the →Azerbaijan Independent Democratic Party, the →Motherland Party and →United Azerbaijan, being credited with 62% of the national vote in its own right and winning an overwhelming majority of Assembly seats when pro-government independents were included in the tally.

Firmly entrenched in power, Aliyev secured a predictable victory in the October 1998 presidential elections as the YAP candidate, being credited with 76.1% of the vote against five other contenders. International bodies criticized widespread irregularities in the polling, the official result of which was rejected by the opposition parties. Aliyev nevertheless reappointed Artur Rasizade as Prime Minister of a YAP-dominated government and in December 1999 was re-elected YAP chairman at the party's first congress. Five deputy chairmen also elected included the President's son, Ilham Aliyev, whom the YAP newspaper had described as his natural successor because his "genetic code does not belong to an ordinary person".

Ilham Aliyev headed the YAP list for the proportional section of legislative elections held in November 2000 and January 2001. Amid opposition cries of widespread fraud, the ruling party won another commanding majority of 75 seats (with 62.5% of the proportional vote) and could also expect backing from most of the 29 "independents" also elected.

New Muslim Democratic Party
Yeni Musavat Partiyasi (YMP-Musavat)
Address. 37 Azerbaijan Prospekt, 370001 Baku
Telephone. (+994–12) 981870
Fax. (+994–12) 983166
Leadership. Isa Gambarov (chairman); Vergun Ayub (secretary-general)
The YMP (usually referred to as Musavat) was founded in June 1992, indirectly descended from the pre-Soviet Musavat nationalists, of moderate Islamic, pan-Turkic orientation. It was closely allied with the →Azerbaijan Popular Front (AKC) under the 1992–93 government, when Gambarov was president of the interim National Assembly. The party came into sharp conflict with succeeding government of Geidar Aliyev of the →New Azerbaijan Party and won only one seat in the legislative elections held in November 1995 and February 1996. In December 1997 *Musavat* was temporarily weakened by the formation of the breakaway →National Congress Party by dissidents who objected to Gambarov's leadership style.

Musavat boycotted the October 1998 presidential election but participated in local elections in December 1999, winning 618 of some 10,000 seats at issue. In February 2000 *Musavat's* Baku headquarters were ransacked by around 100 armed men from Nakhichevan who reportedly objected to recent coverage of the enclave in *Yeni Musavat* (the party's newspaper), although some observers saw the government's hand in the action. Initially refused registration for the November 2000 Assembly elections, *Musavat* was in the end allowed to present candidates and won two constituency seats (having taken only 4.9% of the vote in the proportional section). The party subsequently joined with other opposition formations in condemning the balloting as fraudulent and immediately expelled a newly-elected Musavat deputy who had disregarded the party's boycott of the new Assembly.

Other Parties

Note: Parties in the Armenian-populated enclave of Nagorno-Karabakh, which is legally an autonomous republic of Azerbaijan but which made a unilateral declaration of independence in 1996, are covered under Armenia.

Democratic Party of Azerbaijan (*Azerbaycan Democrat Partiyasi, ADP*), founded in 1994 as the vehicle of exiled former Assembly Speaker Rasul Guliyev; active in the opposition to the Aliyev government, the ADP achieved official registration in February 2000 but was initially excluded from the November Assembly elections, until international pressure persuaded the authorities to allow it to run, although won only 1.1% of the proportional vote and no seats.
Leadership. Rasul Guliyev & Ilyas Ismailov (co-chairmen); Sardar Jalaloglu (secretary-general)

Independent Azerbaijan Party (*Müstaqil Azerbaycan Partiyasi, MAP*), whose chairman unsuccessfully contested the June 1992 presidential election, being at that time head of the Democratic Union of Azerbaijan's Intelligentsia. The MAP is closely allied with the →New Azerbaijan Party headed by President Geidar Aliyev. Suleymanov was again unsuccessful in the October 1998 presidential election, although he came a creditable third with 8.2% of the vote.
Address. 11/28 Keçid, 370073 Baku
Telephone. (+994–12) 394602
Leadership. Nizami Suleymanov (chairman)

Social Democratic Party (*Sosial-Demoktarik Partiyasi,*

33

SDP), founded in 1989 by Araz Alizade, who withdrew as a candidate for the September 1991 presidential elections in protest against the government's conduct of the poll. Prior to the November 200 Assembly elections the party headed the Union of Azerbaijan Forces with other small centre-left formations. The SDP is an observer member of the Socialist International.

Address. 3/28 May Street, Apt. 11, 370014 Baku
Telephone. (+994–12) 933378
Fax. (+994–12) 987555
Leadership. Araz Alizade (chairman)

Bahamas

Capital: Nassau

Population: 295,000 (2000E)

The Bahamas gained independence from the United Kingdom in 1973 after two centuries of colonial rule. The head of state is the British sovereign, represented by a Governor-General and the head of government is the Prime Minister. Legislative power is vested in a bicameral parliament consisting of an appointed 16-member Senate and a popularly-elected House of Assembly. The size of the Assembly was reduced from 49 to 40 seats prior to the general elections of March 14, 1997, in which the Free National Movement retained power by winning 34 seats (with 57% of the vote), while the Progressive Liberal Party won 6 (with 42%)

Free National Movement (FNM)
Address. PO Box N–10713, Nassau
Telephone. (+1–242) 393–7863
Fax. (+1–242) 393–7914
Leadership. Hubert Ingraham (leader); Roston Miller (secretary-general)

The conservative FNM was founded in the early 1970s by Kendal Isaacs as a merger of the United Bahamian Party and an anti-independence dissident faction of the →Progressive Liberal Party (PLP). Reconstituted in 1979 as the Free National Democratic Movement, the organization absorbed defectors from the now-defunct Bahamian Democratic and the Social Democratic Party, and was recognized as the official opposition in 1981 (subsequently reverting to the name FNM).

In the 1992 elections the FNM ended the PLP's long reign by winning 33 seats out of 49 in the House of Assembly (later being awarded an additional seat) and formed a new government under the premiership of Hubert Ingraham. The FNM retained power in the March 1997 general elections, winning 34 seats in an Assembly reduced to 40 members. Ingraham stated on being reappointed Prime Minister that it would be his last term. In September 1997 the FNM gained an additional Assembly seat in a by-election. In January 2000 Ingraham reduced the number of cabinet ministers from 20 to 15.

Progressive Liberal Party (PLP)
Address. PO Box N–547, Nassau
Telephone. (+1–242) 325–2900
Leadership. Perry G. Christie (leader); Kelsey Johnson (secretary-general)

The populist PLP was founded in 1953 as a mainly Black-supported party. A leading proponent of Bahamian independence and aspiring to overturn White economic dominance of the islands, the party came to power in 1967 and took the Bahamas to independence in 1973 under the premiership of Sir Lynden Pindling. Having won five successive general elections on a platform of economic self-reliance and greater government involvement in a mixed economy, the PLP lost power dramatically in the 1992 elections when it secured only 16 of the 49 House of Assembly seats. In January 1993, moreover, the electoral court awarded one seat previously given to the PLP to the now ruling →Free National Movement (FNM).

The PLP suffered a further bad defeat in the March 1997 Assembly elections, winning only six seats out of 40, although its share of the vote in the constituency-based system was 42%. Pindling retired from politics in July 1997 and was succeeded as leader by Perry Christie. The PLP promptly lost Pindling's Assembly seat to the FNM in a by-election in September 1997.

Other Parties

Bahamas Democratic Movement (BDM), advocating economic modernization and the development of natural assets such as tourism.
Address. PO Box SS–5685, Nassau
Telephone. (+1–242) 341–3991
Email. stuart1@bahamas.net.bs
Leadership. Cassius V. Stuart

Bahaman Freedom Alliance (BFA), an unrepresented opposition grouping.
Address. PO Box CB12412, Nassau
Telephone. (+1–242) 324–2948
Leadership. Holston Moultry

Survivors' Party
Address. PO Box N1703, Nassau
Telephone. (+1–642) 326-6191
Leader. Kenneth Taylor

Bahrain

Capital: Manama

Population: 634,000 (2000E)

The State of Bahrain, fully independent since 1971 having previously been a British protected state, is an absolute monarchy whose Emir governs through an appointed Cabinet. The 1973 constitution provided for a National Assembly consisting of the Cabinet and 30 other members to be elected by popular vote. Elections were held in

1974. However, the last National Assembly was dissolved in August 1975 for being "dominated by ideas alien to the society and values of Bahrain". In January 1993 the Emir appointed a 40-member Consultative (*Shura*) Council with limited law-making authority of its own. Denied legal political parties, opponents of the Emir expressed themselves via clandestine groups, mainly based in the majority Shia Muslim community. Others joined groups in exile, such as the London-based, Islamically oriented Bahrain Freedom Movement (BFM). Bahraini authorities suppressed overt Shia unrest, which began with a mass petition in December 1994 and later included bomb attacks.

In March 1999 Sheikh Hamad ibn Issa Al Khalifa succeeded his father as Emir of Bahrain, and in October 2000 announced a National Charter that accepted the principle of free expression, constitutional monarchy and the establishment of an elected second chamber by 2004. The charter received 98% approval in a national referendum held in February 2001. Women voted for the first time, and even London-based oppositionists supported the reforms. Later in the year Bahrain ended its ban (imposed in 1984) on Sheikh Issa Qasim's Islamic Awareness Society. The state also pardoned nearly 900 opponents, and freed BFM leader, Sheikh Abdul Amir al-Jamri, after three years under house arrest. In July 2001 Islamists formed a loose umbrella group, the *Al-Wefaq* National Islamic Society.

Bangladesh

Capital: Dhaka   **Population:** 129,000,000 (2000E)

The People's Republic of Bangladesh achieved sovereignty in 1971, having previously formed the eastern part of Pakistan (which had become independent from Britain in 1947). After a brief period of parliamentary democracy until August 1975, the country was then ruled by a series of military dictatorships, albeit with increasing scope for party activity, until Lt.-Gen. (retd.) Hussain Mohammed Ershad was finally forced to resign in December 1990. Under amendments to the 1972 constitution approved by referendum in September 1991, full legislative authority was restored to the unicameral National Parliament (*Jatiya Sangsad*) of 330 members elected for a five-year term. Of these, 300 are returned from individual constituencies by universal suffrage of those aged 18 and over, and can be of either sex, and the other 30 are women elected by the directly elected members. The country's President is elected by the *Jatiya Sangsad*, also for a five-year term, and has largely ceremonial powers. Executive power is vested in the Prime Minister and Council of Ministers, formally appointed by the President but responsible to the *Jatiya Sangsad*.

In February 1991 general elections to the *Jatiya Sangsad* resulted in victory for the Bangladesh Nationalist Party (BNP) with the Awami League in second place. After a long political crisis, general elections on Feb. 15, 1996, were boycotted by the main opposition parties and resulted in the ruling BNP winning an overwhelming majority. Amid continuing deadlock, the new BNP government resigned at the end of March 1996, a neutral caretaker Prime Minister being appointed pending new elections later that year. These resulted in the Awami League taking 176 of the 330 seats, with the BNP taking second place with 116. The Awami League's leader, Sheikh Hasina Wazed, formed a new government, initially with the support of the National Party, which had come third with 33 seats. In 1998 the National Party split and its majority joined the BNP-led opposition in walking out of parliament and launching a civil disobedience campaign to force an early general election. However, the government served its full term and resigned in favour of another neutral caretaker Prime Minister on July 12, 2001. A general election on Oct. 1, 2001, resulted in victory for the BNP, which took 191 seats.

Awami League (AL)
Address. 23 Bangabandha Avenue, Dhaka
Leadership. Sheikh Hasina Wazed (leader)
The AL was founded in 1949 as the Awami (i.e. People's) Muslim League by left-wing Bengali nationalists opposed to the right-wing orientation of the Muslim League after the 1947 partition. It headed coalition governments in East Pakistan in 1956–58 and was concurrently represented in the central government, although it was weakened by secession of pro-Soviet elements in 1957. In elections held in 1970 the AL won 151 of the 153 East Pakistan seats in the central parliament on a pro-independence and secular platform. Led by Sheikh Mujibur Rahman, it then brought about the secession of what was renamed Bangladesh, assisted by the Indian Army, and became the ruling party on the establishment of the new state in 1971. In 1972 the AL underwent a split when young advocates of "scientific socialism" broke away to form the →National Socialist Party. In January 1975 Sheikh Mujib introduced a presidential form of government and moved to a one-party system by creating the Bangladesh Peasants' and Workers' Awami League, within which all existing parties were required to operate. However, Sheikh Mujib was overthrown and killed by the military in August 1975, the AL being temporarily banned.

Resuming activity under the leadership of Sheikh Hasina (Mujib's daughter), the AL headed the Democratic United Front coalition which backed the candidacy of Gen. Mohammed Ataul Ghani Osmani in the June 1978 presidential election, won by Gen. Ziaur (Zia) Rahman of what became the →Bangladesh Nationalist Party (BNP). In the 1979 parliamentary elections the AL won 40 of the 300 elective seats, while in the November 1981 presidential contest the AL candidate, Kamal Hossain, was officially credited with 25.4% of the vote in a disputed result. Following Lt.-Gen. Ershad's seizure of power in March 1982, the AL was prominent in demanding a return to democracy, forming a 15–party left-wing alliance, which in September 1983 joined the BNP and its allies in creating the Movement for the Restoration of Democracy (MRD). Leftist elements of the AL broke away in July 1983 to form the Peasants' and Workers' Awami League (which was reintegrated with the parent party in 1991).

MRD pressure produced a partial resumption of legal party activity from January 1986 and the calling of parliamentary elections for May 1986. But the MRD parties were divided on whether adequate concessions had been made, with the result that the BNP and its allies boycotted the poll whereas the AL and seven associated parties opted to participate, being credited with 76 of the 300 elective seats in disputed results. AL and other opposition members boycotted the opening of parliament in July in protest at the slow progress of democratization, setting up a "people's parliament", of which Sheikh Hasina was elected leader. Both the AL and the BNP boycotted the October 1986 presidential contest, after which efforts by the Ershad government to entice the AL to attend parliament were eventually rebuffed.

The AL was then a leading organizer of a series of mass demonstrations and strikes demanding Ershad's resignation, culminating in the "siege of Dhaka" of November 1987, when over two million opposition supporters sought to immobilize government activity in the capital, Sheikh Hasina being briefly held under house arrest as a result. Both main MRD parties declined to participate in the March 1988 parliamentary elections. Renewed opposition demonstrations from October 1990 yielded the departure of Ershad in December and the holding of parliamentary elections in February 1991, when the AL came a poor second to the BNP in terms of seats although with a similar percentage share of the popular vote.

In December 1994 the AL began a boycott of parliament intended to force the government's resignation. Although this action was declared unconstitutional by the High Court, in January 1995 Sheikh Hasina called the boycott "irrevocable" and the AL thereafter stepped up its campaign of strikes and other actions aimed at forcing new elections under a caretaker government. Elections eventually held in February 1996 were boycotted by the AL and the other main opposition parties, with the result that new elections were held in June. These resulted in the AL taking the largest number of seats, enabling Sheikh Hasina to form a coalition government that included the →National Party. However, in 1998 the BNP and other opposition parties (including a section of the National Party) walked out of parliament to orchestrate a campaign of civil disobedience, similar to that led by the Awami League in 1994 and aimed at forcing another early general election. This failed, but the AL lost the election of October 2001, declining to 62 seats.

Bangladesh Islamic Assembly
Jamaat-i-Islami Bangladesh (JIB)
Address. 505 Elephant Road, Bara Maghbazar, Dhaka 1217
Leadership. Maulana Matiur Rahman Nizami (leader)
The Islamist JIB was originally founded in 1941 under the British Raj and opposed the creation of a separate Muslim state as being contrary to the principles of Islam. It combined this line with pronounced anti-Hindu and anti-Indian attitudes. After the 1947 partition its main strength was in West Pakistan, but its leader Gholam Azam built up a considerable following in East Pakistan. Opposed to the secular socialism and Bengali nationalism of the →Awami League (AL), the JIB campaigned against the Bangladesh independence movement in 1970–71. On the creation of the new state, the party was banned and Azam was deprived of his citizenship for alleged collaboration with Pakistan.

Following the overthrow of the AL government by the military in 1975, the JIB regained legal status in 1977 within the Islamic Democratic League, but was weakened in 1978 when its dominant liberal wing joined the new →Bangladesh Nationalist Party. The party's fundamentalist wing responded by relaunching the JIB in May 1979 under the leadership of Abbas Ali Khan as proxy for Azam, who had returned from exile. After the March 1982 military coup, the JIB maintained its distance from the main opposition alliances, although it made similar demands that the Ershad regime should restore democracy. In the May 1986

parliamentary elections JIB candidates were returned in 10 of the 300 elective seats.

The resignation of Ershad in December 1990 served to sharpen the JIB's Islamist profile, which in the 1991 parliamentary elections yielded 18 elective seats and, by dint of post-election co-operation with the BNP, two of the 30 seats reserved for women. In December 1991 Azam was elected to resume the party leadership, even though his lack of Bangladeshi citizenship made this technically illegal. Popular pressure then mounted, led by the AL, for Azam to be brought to trial for crimes allegedly committed during the 1970–71 independence struggle. Such demands were resisted by the BNP government, which accepted a High Court ruling in April 1993 that Azam should be granted citizenship (this being upheld by the Supreme Court in June 1994).

In 1994 the JIB was prominent in the fundamentalist campaign against the Bangladeshi writer Taslima Nasreen. In 1995 the party participated in AL-led strikes and civil disobedience aimed at forcing the government's resignation. With other opposition parties it boycotted elections held in February 1996 but it won three seats in re-run elections later that year. However, and in spite of the resulting change of government, the JIB continued to line up with the parliamentary opposition: this time, from 1998, joining the BNP in a civil disobedience campaign against the AL's administration. From this time, too, it stepped up its fundamentalist activities, protesting against judicial secularism and against the influence of foreign (western) non-governmental organizations in the country. In late 2000 Gholam Azam was replaced as party leader by another cleric, Maulana Nizami, who was also accused by opponents of complicity in war crimes by Pakistan in 1971. Allied with the BNP, the JIB took 18 seats in the October 2001 election.

Bangladesh Nationalist Party (BNP)
Bangladesh Jatiyatabadi Dal
Address. Sattar House, 19/A Road No. 16, Dhanmondi R/A, Dhaka 9
Leadership. Begum Khaleda Zia Rahman (leader)
The centre-right BNP was launched in September 1978 by the then President, Gen. Ziaur (Zia) Rahman, on the basis of the Nationalist Front which had successfully campaigned for his election in June 1978. In the parliamentary elections of February 1979 the BNP obtained 49% of the vote and two-thirds of the seats on a platform of inscribing Islam into the constitution and pursuing social justice rather than socialism. Martial law and the state of emergency were lifted in the course of 1979, and the BNP attracted various defectors from other parties. President Zia was assassinated in May 1981 in an apparent coup attempt and was succeeded by Vice-President Abdus Sattar, senior BNP vice-chair, who secured a popular mandate in presidential elections in November 1981. On Lt.-Gen. Ershad's seizure of power in March 1982 the BNP went into opposition, joining with the →Awami League (AL) and other parties in creating the Movement for the Restoration of Democracy (MRD) in September 1983. In January 1984 Begum Khaleda, the late President's widow, succeeded Sattar as leader of the main BNP (the party having in 1983 suffered defections by elements opposed to confrontation with the Ershad regime).

MRD pressure produced a partial resumption of legal party activity from January 1986 and the calling of parliamentary elections for May 1986. But the MRD parties were divided on whether adequate concessions had been made, with the result that the BNP and its allies boycotted the poll whereas the AL and its major allies opted to participate. MRD co-operation resumed after the legislative elections and both the BNP and the AL boycotted the October 1986 presidential contest. The BNP was then involved in demonstrations and strikes demanding Ershad's resignation, Begum Khaleda being briefly held under house arrest as a result. Both main MRD parties declined to participate in the March 1988 parliamentary elections, after which the BNP was again distracted by internal factionalism.

Renewed opposition demonstrations from October 1990 yielded the departure of Ershad in December. In parliamentary elections in February 1991 the BNP ended up with a comfortable majority of seats (although it took only some 35% of the popular vote) and Begum Khaleda was sworn in as the country's first woman Prime Minister. In October 1991 the BNP nominee, Abdur Rahman Biswas, was elected President by the new *Jatiya Sangsad*). In government, the BNP dropped its previous aim of restoring presidential government but found itself in renewed conflict with the AL, now the main opposition party.

From May 1994 the BNP government faced an opposition boycott of parliament and other protest action aimed at forcing early general elections. Amid mounting pressure, Begum Khaleda in September 1995 offered to hold talks with the opposition parties, while rejecting their demand for a caretaker government. As civil disturbances continued, President Biswas in November 1995 announced the dissolution of parliament, preparatory to general elections that were eventually held in February 1996. With the main opposition parties boycotting the poll, the BNP won almost all the elective seats and formed a new government under Begum Khaleda. However, amid undiminished civil disobedience by the opposition, the BNP leader resigned at the end of March, giving way to a neutral caretaker Prime Minister until new elections in June, in which the BNP was decisively defeated. Restive in opposition, in 1998 Begum Khaleda walked out of parliament and launched her own civil disobedience campaign against the new AL government. In the October 2001 election the BNP regained power, taking 191 of the 330 seats.

National Party
Jatiya Dal

Address. 104 Road No. 3, Dhanmondi R/A, Dhaka 9
Leadership. Lt.-Gen. (retd.) Mohammad Ershad (leader)
The *Jatiya Dal* was launched in January 1986 as a political base for Lt.-Gen. Ershad, who had seized power in March 1982, and succeeded an earlier National Front of pro-Ershad formations headed by the People's Party (*Jana Dal*). The new formation, which was joined by all the then government ministers, advocated national unity on the basis of independence and sovereignty, faith in Islam, nationalism, democracy and social progress. In the May 1986 parliamentary elections the *Jatiya Dal* won 180 of the 300 elective seats. In September 1986 Ershad was elected as party chair (having resigned as Army Chief of Staff) and the following month was returned as President with 83.6% of the vote in a presidential election boycotted by the main opposition parties.

Having gained an even bigger majority (251 elective seats) in the March 1988 parliamentary elections, which were also boycotted by the opposition, the *Jatiya Dal* government was gradually paralyzed by renewed popular agitation. Shunned by opposition leaders and in the end deserted by the military establishment, Ershad resigned in December 1990 and was later arrested, put on trial and convicted, together with several close associates. The *Jatiya Dal* continued under new leadership, which in January 1991 "begged forgiveness" from the people for the Ershad years. In the February 1991 parliamentary elections, the party won 35 of the 300 elective seats, with some 10% of the popular vote, and became part of the opposition to the new →Bangladesh Nationalist Party (BNP) government. In September 1993 a pro-Ershad faction of the party formed the National Party (Nationalist), which quickly established overall control of the party.

In 1994-95 the *Jatiya Dal* participated in the opposition campaign to force the resignation of the Zia government and the calling of new elections. Having joined the opposition boycott of the February 1996 elections, the *Jatiya Dal* took 33 seats in the re-run elections later that year. It then joined a coalition government headed by the →Awami League, reportedly in return for a promise that Ershad would be released on parole, which he was soon afterwards. Ershad's decision to accept office generated some internal dissent and provoked the resignation from the party of its former parliamentary leader, Moudad Ahmed. However, in 1998, Ershad led his (majority) faction of the party away from the AL government benches, joining an opposition 'walk out' from parliament led by the BNP. He also co-operated with the BNP in its civil disobedience campaign against the new AL government. In May 2001, he abandoned his alliance with the BNP and his faction won 14 seats in the October 2001 elections.

National Socialist Party (Rab)
Jatiya Samajtantric Dal (Rab) (JSD-Rab)

Address. c/o Jatiya Sangsad, Dhaka
Leadership. A.S.M. Abdul Rab
The JSD-Rab is derived from one of the several factions of the original JSD, which had been founded in 1972 by left-wing →Awami League dissidents, including Abdul Rab and Shajahan Siraj. The JSD gained an urban following for its militant opposition to the AL government and was banned in 1975 after its armed wing, called the Revolutionary People's Army, had allegedly attempted to seize power. It welcomed the military coup of August 1975 and played a prominent role in elevating Gen. Ziaur (Zia) Rahman to power later that year. Nevertheless, Gen. Zia disowned the JSD, whose leaders were arrested and brought to trial in 1976 on sedition charges, one being executed. Reactivated from November 1978, the JSD won nine of the 300 elective seats in the February 1979 elections, but its presidential candidate in November 1981 forfeited his deposit.

JSD factional strife intensified following the Ershad military takeover of March 1982, with the result that in January 1984 Abdul Rab formed the breakaway JSD (Rab), the rump party becoming known as the JSD (Siraj). Both factions joined the Movement for the Restoration of Democracy and were among the eight AL-led opposition parties which contested the May 1986 elections, the JSD (Rab) obtaining four seats and the JSD (Siraj) three. Thereafter, both factions adhered to the general opposition boycott of the electoral process under the Ershad regime, although they ceased to be formally allied with the AL. Following the restoration of democracy, the JSD (Siraj) won one seat in the 1991 parliamentary elections but the JSD (Rab) failed to register. In August 1993 the JSD (Siraj) became part of the →People's Forum and another faction led by Hasanul Huq Inu joined the new →Left Democratic Front in April 1994. In contrast, the JSD (Rab) remained a separate formation, won one seat in the June 1996 elections and was included in the new coalition headed by the AL (Abdul Rab becoming Minister of Special Affairs). This relationship lasted until the completion of the AL's term of office in July 2001.

Other Parties

Communist Party of Bangladesh (CPB), founded in 1948 as the East Pakistan section of the Communist Party of Pakistan (CPP), itself an offshoot of the Communist Party of India. In East Pakistan the pro-Soviet wing in 1968 formed an independent party, which was renamed the CPB on the creation of Bangladesh in 1971. Following the exit of President Ershad in December 1990 and the restoration of parliamentary democracy, the CPB won five of the 300 elective seats in the 1991 parliamentary elections. Meanwhile, the collapse of communism in Europe had inspired new thinking in the party leadership, with leader Saifuddin Ahmed Manik advocating the abandonment of Marxism-Leninism but being opposed by a majority of the CPB central committee. Eventually, in June 1993, the Manik faction broke away, later joining the new →People's Forum, while in April 1994 the rump CPB became a component of the →Left Democratic Front. However, neither faction won any seats in the 1996 or 2001 general elections.

Democratic Unity Alliance (*Ganotantrik Oikya Jote, GOJ*). This assemblage of nine mainly centre-right parties was launched in October 1994, none of them having parliamentary representation. It was headed by the National People's Party (*Jatiya Janata Dal*, JJD), which had been founded in 1976 by the Bangladeshi military commander in the 1971 war of independence, Gen. (retd.) Mohammed Ataul Ghani Osmani.

Left Democratic Front (LDF) (*Bam Ganotantrik Front*). The LDF was launched in April 1994 as an alliance of eight left-orientated parties, including a faction of the →National Socialist Party (JSD) led by Hasanul Huq Inu, the →Communist Party of Bangladesh, and the →Workers' Party of Bangladesh (WPB). However, it failed to win any seats in the 1996 general elections.

National Democratic Alliance (NDA). The NDA was created in February 1993 as an alliance of 10 Islamic parties of conservative and moderate Islamist orientation, headed by the Democratic (*Ganotantrik*) League of Khandaker Moshtaque Ahmed and the Freedom Party of Lt.-Col. (retd.) Khandaker Abdur Rashid.

Moshtaque Ahmed was briefly President of Bangladesh following the overthrow of Sheikh Mujubur Rahman's →Awami League (AL) government in August 1975 and founded the Democratic League the following year. Abdur Rashid was one of the three principal leaders (the so-called "majors") of the 1975 coup, in which Sheikh Mujib and members of his family were killed.

People's Forum (PF) (*Gano Forum*). The PF was founded in August 1993 by a dissident faction of the →Awami League (AL) led by Kamal Hossain, who had been the first Law Minister of independent Bangladesh, the framer of its constitution and later Foreign Minister in the 1971–75 AL government. It advocated "violence-free politics, economic progress at the grass-roots and basic amenities for all". Influential PF recruits included Saifuddin Ahmed Manik, who had vacated the leadership of the →Communist Party of Bangladesh after failing to persuade it to renounce Marxism-Leninism. The PF also included the faction of the →National Socialist Party led by Shajahan Siraj. However, it failed to win any seats in the 1996 elections.

Barbados

Capital: Bridgetown **Population**: 275,000 (2000E)

Barbados gained its independence from the United Kingdom in 1966. The head of state is the British sovereign, represented by a Governor-General, with the head of government being the Prime Minister. There is a bicameral parliament (with colonial era origins dating back to 1639), consisting of a 28-member House of Assembly and a 21-member Senate. Elections to the House are on the Westminster model, with MPs elected for five-year terms by universal adult suffrage on the first past the post single-member constituency system. Senators are appointed to office for a five-year term by the Governor-General (12 on the advice of the Prime Minister, two on that of the Leader of the Opposition, and seven at the discretion of the Governor-General to represent social, religious and economic interests).

In the most recent general election, held on Jan. 20, 1999, the Barbados Labour Party (BLP) (in office since 1994) was re-elected, winning 26 of the House of Assembly seats with 65% of the popular vote, while the Democratic Labour Party (DLP) took two seats and 35% of the vote. Barbados has a tradition of political stability and the BLP and DLP have been the two main parties since independence, sharing considerable ideological common ground.

Barbados Labour Party (BLP)
Address. Grantley Adams House, 111 Roebuck Street, Bridgetown
Telephone. (+1–246) 429–1990
Email. hq@blp.org.bb
Website. www.blp.org.bb
Leadership. Owen Arthur (chairman and political leader); Mia Amor Mottley (general secretary)
Founded in 1938, the moderate, social democratic BLP held office in the pre-independence period from 1951 to 1961 under the leadership of Sir Grantley Adams. It then went into opposition until the 1976 elections when, led by J.M.G. (Tom) Adams (Sir Grantley's son), it was returned to power. The party was affected by factional splits after Tom Adams's death in 1985 and was defeated heavily in the polls the following year. It then remained in opposition until a general election in September 1994 when, under the leadership of Owen Arthur, it won 19 of the 28 House of Assembly seats with just over 48% of the votes cast.

In the January 1999 elections the government ran on its success with the economy, with a campaign slogan of "one good term deserves another". It won 26 of the 28 House

seats (the biggest ever victory in a Barbados election), taking 65% of the vote.

The BLP is a member party of the Socialist International.

Democratic Labour Party (DLP)
Address. George Street, Belleville, St Michael
Telephone. (+1–246) 429–3104
Fax. (+1–246) 429–3007
Email. dlp@dlpbarbados.bb
Website. www.dlpbarbados.org
Leadership. David Thompson (leader and party president); George Pilgrim (general secretary)
The DLP was formed in 1955 principally by dissident members (led by Errol Barrow) of the →Barbados Labour Party (BLP). It was seen as standing somewhat to the left of the BLP and has traditionally been strongest among the urban electorate. Between 1961 and 1976 it was the governing party (during which time it led Barbados to independence), but then spent the following ten years in opposition before returning to power in the 1986 elections. The party leader and Prime Minister, Errol Barrow, died in 1987 and was succeeded by Erskine Sandiford. The party won the 1991 elections, but suffered a resounding defeat in the September

1994 polls (called early by Sandiford in response to an internal DLP revolt). Leadership of the party, whose parliamentary strength fell to eight seats, was assumed by David Thompson.

In the January 1999 election campaign the DLP charged that under the BLP lower and middle income people had been excluded from increasing prosperity, and crime had increased, but it suffered a sweeping defeat, retaining only two seats (one of them Thompson's).

Other Parties

National Democratic Party (NDP), formed in February 1989 under the leadership of Richard (Richie) Haynes, a former Finance Minister, following his resignation and that of three other MPs from the then ruling →Democratic Labour Party. The party lost its four seats in the 1991 elections, but regained one (won by Haynes), taking nearly 13% of the vote, in the 1994 polls. In the 1999 election, however, the NDP did not put up candidates, Haynes calling on his supporters to vote for the BLP, saying that it had implemented NDP policies.
Leadership. Richard Haynes

Belarus

Capital: Minsk

Population: 10,370,000 (2000E)

The Soviet Socialist Republic of Byelorussia declared independence from the USSR in August 1991, adopted the name Republic of Belarus the following month and became a sovereign member of the Commonwealth of Independent States (CIS) on the demise of the USSR in December 1991. The ruling republican Communist Party was suspended at independence and, on its revival in 1993, appeared to have lost the allegiance of most of the Soviet-era personnel who remained in control of government and state structures. A new constitution approved in March 1994 and substantially amended in November 1996 provides for an executive President, who is directly elected by universal adult suffrage for a five-year term (once renewable) and appoints the Prime Minister and Council of Ministers. The President may be impeached and removed from office in certain circumstances, but has the right to dissolve the legislature "in the event of systematic or gross violation of the constitution".

The legislature is the bicameral National Assembly, consisting of an upper Council of the Republic (*Soviet Respubliki*) of 64 members (56 indirectly elected for a four-year term by regional councils and eight appointed by the President) and the 110-member House of Representatives members (*Palata Predstaviteley*) directly elected for a four-year term in two rounds of voting, with successful candidates requiring an overall majority in a turnout of more than 50% of eligible voters. The introduction of the new parliamentary structure in 1996 was strongly opposed by parties dominant in the previous unicameral Supreme Council, a rump of whose members elected in 1995 rejected the legitimacy of the new legislature. Also controversial was the signature in December 1999 of a long-delayed treaty of union under which Belarus and the Russian Federation supposedly became a confederal state.

In presidential elections in June-July 1994, an independent candidate, Alyaksandr Lukashenka, was elected in the second round with 80% of the vote. Under a controversial referendum decision in November 1996 his five-year term was extended by two years to 2001. Equally contentious elections to the House of Representatives on Oct. 15 and 29, 2000 (with re-runs being held in 13 constituencies on March 18 and April 1, 2001), were boycotted by most of the opposition parties and resulted in "presidential" parties obtaining all but three of the 110 seats. When new presidential elections were eventually held on Sept. 9, 2001, Lukashenka was declared the victor with 75.65 per cent of the vote, after an electoral process regarded as deeply flawed by the opposition and most international observers.

Agrarian Party of Belarus
Agrarnaya Partiya Belarusi (APB)
Address. 86/2 Kazintsa Street, Minsk 220050
Telephone. (+375–17) 220–3829
Fax. (+375–17) 249–5018
Leadership. Syamyon Sharetski (chairman)
Established in 1994, the APB provides a national political framework for agrarian interests associated with the communist-era agricultural system, being opposed in particular to the restoration of individual peasant ownership of the land. It emerged as the most powerful agrarian party in the 1995 legislative elections, winning 33 out of 260 seats. In January 1996 APB leader Sharetski was elected to the chairmanship of the then unicameral legislature. Broadly supportive of President Lukashenka, the APB won five out of 110 lower house seats in the October 2000 legislative elections.

Belarusan People's Patriotic Union
Belaruski Norodna Patryatchny Soyuz (BNPS)
Address. c/o Palata Predstaviteley, Minsk
Leadership. Viktor Chykin (executive secretary)
The BNPS was created in September 1998 as a political alliance of some 30 conservative parties supportive of President Alyaksandr Lukashenka. It included the →Communist Party of Belarus (KPB), whose leader, Viktor Chykin, was elected as its first executive secretary, as well as the right-wing ethno-nationalist →Liberal Democratic Party of Belarus and the →White Rus Slavonic Council.

The BNPS effectively succeeded the Popular Movement of Belarus (*Narodni Dirzhenie Belarusi*, NDB), formed in 1992 as an alliance of pro-government conservative groupings favouring a cautious approach to political and economic reform and aiming to counter the influence of the pro-democracy →Belarusan Popular Front—Renaissance (NFB-A). Such elements had formed the core of the NDB, which had naturally embraced

The NDB had embraced both the conservative left and

the pan-Slavic right on a joint platform advocating the maintenance of close relations with Russia and resistance to Western capitalist encroachment. Its leaders had mostly prospered under the Soviet-era rule of the republican Communist Party, the suspension of which in August 1991 had not affected the predominance of former Communists in the government and in the Supreme Soviet elected in 1990. The election of Mechyslau Hryb as head of state in early 1994 had strengthened the position of the NDB hardliners, as shown by the introduction of a new presidential constitution in March 1994, the signature the following month of a monetary union treaty with Russia and moves to participate in CIS collective security arrangements.

In the mid-1994 presidential elections, however, the hardliners had been unexpectedly outmanoeuvred by the NDB's more moderate wing. Standing as an independent, hardliner Vyacheslau Kebich had secured only 17.3% of the first-round vote, ahead of the NFB-A candidate but well behind Alyaksandr Lukashenka, then regarded as a moderate, who had headed the poll with 44.8% on the strength of his reputation as an anti-corruption minister. In the second round, Lukashenka had registered a massive 80.1% of the vote, while Kebich managed only 15.1%, despite being backed by most sitting deputies.

In power, Lukashenka proved to be as authoritarian, pro-Russian and anti-Western as any of his predecessors and as wedded to preserving the economic and social structures of the Soviet era. Supported by the BNPS and the forces of state power, he secured a predictable sweeping victory in the September 2001 presidential elections.

Belarusan Popular Front–Renaissance
Narodni Front Belarusi–Adradzhennie (NFB-A)

Address. 8 Varvasheni Street, Minsk 220005
Telephone. (+375-17) 231–4893
Fax. (+375–17) 239–5869
Email. bpf@bpf.minsk.by
Website. pages.prodigy.net/dr_fission/bpf
Leadership. Vintsuk Vyachorka (chairman)
The NFB-A was launched in June 1989 (as the NFB) at a conference held in Vilnius (Lithuania) of representatives of groups and organizations united by the belief that Belarus should be governed by its own independent authorities rather than by Moscow. The then Communist Party regime had refused to allow the conference to be held in the republic and had denounced its organizers as "extremists". Elected party leader at the Vilnius session was Zyanon Paznyak, an archaeologist who in 1988 had published evidence of mass graves found at Kurapaty, near Minsk, on the site of a detention/execution camp established on Stalin's orders in 1937.

As European communism began to crumble from late 1989, the new movement had some impact in Belarus, where Belarusan replaced Russian as the official language in January 1990 and where opposition candidates were allowed to run in the April 1990 Supreme Soviet elections. However, the entrenched position of the →Communist Party enabled it to win a large majority, the NFB-A being confined to 34 seats in the 360-member legislature. Thereafter, the NFB-A sought to accelerate the government's hesitant moves to assert sovereignty and was strongly critical of its initial support for the attempted coup by hardliners in Moscow in August 1991. It therefore welcomed the resultant downfall of the Minsk conservatives and the advent of the Shushkevich government, supporting the latter's declaration of independence in late August. But the simultaneous suspension of the Communist Party deprived the opposition of a valuable target: although effectively a continuation of the previous regime, the new government could depict itself as independent.

The NFB-A opposed the new presidential constitution introduced in March 1994, on the grounds that a democratic parliament had not yet been elected. It also opposed the treaty on monetary union with Russia signed by the government in April and Belarusan participation in the CIS security pact. In the direct presidential elections of June-July 1994, Paznyak stood as the NFB-A candidate but received only 13.5% of the first-round vote and was eliminated. In the second round, NFB-A support swung overwhelmingly behind Alyaksandr Lukashenka as apparently being the more reformist of the two candidates on offer.

Opposed to the government's policy of close integration with Russia, the NFB-A won no seats in the 1995 parliamentary elections, following which Paznyak went into exile in the USA. Following the signature of a treaty of union by Belarus and Russia in April 1996, NFB-A leaders came under pressure from the authorities for organizing protests against constitutional amendments tabled by the government to replace the unicameral Supreme Council with a bicameral legislature. The approval of the amendments in a referendum in November 1996 was rejected as invalid by the NFB-A.

The political impasse continued over the next four years, during which the NFB-A was at the core of regular opposition demonstrations. In May 1999 the NFB-A was a principal organizer of "alternative" presidential elections, which unofficially yielded a two-thirds majority for Paznyak (although the exercise was called off before the results were declared). Thereafter the government combined repression of NFB-A leaders and other opponents with periodic attempts, under pressure from Western governments, to initiate a dialogue with the opposition, although with no substantive outcome.

The sixth NFB-A congress held in Minsk in August 1999 featured deep divisions between critics of Paznyak's leadership in exile and his supporters. The following month the latter minority faction broke away to form the →Conservative Christian Party, of which Paznyak was declared leader, while Vintsuk Vyachorka was elected NFB-A chairman. The NFB-A boycotted the October 2000 legislative elections and formed part of the anti-Lukashenka →For a New Belarus front in the September 2001 presidential elections.

As a pluralist organization which includes a strong Christian democratic current, the NFB-A is affiliated to the Christian Democrat International.

Belarusan Social Democratic Party
Satsiyal–Demokratychnaya Partiya Belarusi
(SDPB/Hramada)

Address. 13/28 Vasnyatsova Street, Minsk 220017
Telephone. (+375–17) 246–4691
Fax. (+375–17) 245–7852
Leadership. Mykola Statkevich (chairman)
The SDPB was founded in 1991 as a latter-day renaissance of the Revolutionary *Hramada* (Assembly) Party (founded in 1903), which spearheaded the early movement for the creation of a Belarusan state but was outlawed following the declaration of the Soviet Socialist Republic in January 1919. The revived party, also known as the *Hramada*, participated in the opposition →Belarusan Popular Front-Renaissance, supporting the latter's unsuccessful candidate in the first round of the June-July 1994 presidential elections. In the 1995 legislative elections the SDPB won two seats and later formed a 15-strong parliamentary group which also included the →Social Democratic Party of Popular Accord.

The SDPB was prominent in the opposition to the Lukashenka presidency in the late 1990s, its chairman being on several occasions being brought to court. In September 2000 unidentified thugs carried out a raid on the party's headquarters in Minsk. Unlike most of the opposition, the SDPB participated in the October 2000 legislative elections, but failed to win any seats.

The SDPB/*Hramada* is an observer member of the Socialist International.

Communist Party of Belarus
Kommunisticheskaya Partiya Belarusi (KPB)

Address. 52 Varanyanskaga Street, Minsk 22007

Telephone. (+375–17) 226–6422

Fax. (+375–17) 232–3123

Leadership. Viktor Chykin (chairman)

The Soviet-era Communist Party had originated as a regional committee of the Russian Social Democratic Labour Party (formed in 1904) covering both Belarus and Lithuania. Established as the ruling Communist Party of the Soviet Socialist Republic of Byelorussia in 1920, the party suffered heavily during Stalin's terror of the 1930s, when almost all of its leaders were liquidated and party membership fell by more than half. Enlarged by Soviet territorial acquisitions from Poland in World War II, the Byelorussian SSR was given UN membership in 1945 but its ruling party and government remained wholly subservient to Moscow.

From mid-1989 the republican leadership came under official Soviet criticism for lacking "tolerance…and readiness to make compromises". It therefore allowed candidates of the opposition →Belarusan Popular Front—Renaissance (NFB-A) to contest the April 1990 Supreme Soviet elections, correctly calculating that its control of the levers of power would ensure a decisive Communist victory. But the conservative Minsk leadership miscalculated when it backed the abortive coup by hardliners in Moscow in August 1991. In the immediate aftermath, the hardline Chairman of the Supreme Soviet (head of state), Nikalai Dzementsei, was replaced by the reformist Stanislau Shushkevich; independence from the USSR was declared; the first secretary of the republican Communist Party, Anatol Malofeev, resigned from the Soviet politburo; and the party itself was suspended and its property nationalized.

The party remained under suspension for 18 months, although the government structure and the legislature continued to be under the control of people appointed or elected as Communists. At government level, Shushkevich came into increasingly bitter dispute with the hardline Prime Minister, Vyacheslau Kebich, who commanded majority support from the so-called Belarus Group of conservative deputies for his resistance to political and economic reform. The re-legalization of the Communist Party in February 1993 did little to clarify true allegiance, in part because government members preferred to retain the "independent" label. There were, moreover, competing versions of the party owing to a leadership dispute: in addition to the party led by Vasil Novikau as chairman and Malofeev as (again) first secretary, another faction emerged under the leadership of Viktor Chykin, who in October 1993 founded the Movement for Democracy, Social Progress and Justice as a merger of seven hardline communist groups. However, the various factions came under the umbrella of the loose alliance of conservative parties called the Popular Movement of Belarus (NDB), which backed the ousting of Shushkevich in January 1994 and his replacement by hardliner Mechyslau Hryb. According to Shushkevich, this change marked "the restoration of *nomenklatura* power".

Having embraced the concept of multi-partyism, the Novikau–Malofeev KPB contested the June–July 1994 presidential elections in its own right, with Novikau as candidate. Its problem was that voters had other "establishment" candidates to choose from, including Kebich and Shushkevich, both standing as independents. The result of the first round was last place out of six candidates for Novikau, who managed only 4.5% of the vote. But forecasts that "*nomenklatura* power" would ensure victory for Kebich proved wide of the mark: relegated to a poor second place in the first round, he was heavily defeated in the second by another independent, Alyaksandr Lukashenka, a moderate conservative who in his parliamentary role as anti-corruption supremo had played a key role in the ousting of Shushkevich. Lukashenka subsequently received the support of the new "presidential" →Belarusan Patriotic Movement, but the KPB's stronger organization enabled it to become the largest formal party in the 1995 legislative elections, in which it won 42 seats.

Having established leadership of the rump KPB, Chykin

in September 1998 became executive secretary of the pro-Lukashenka →Belarusan People's Patriotic Union, grouping some 30 conservative parties which backed the proposed Belarus–Russian union treaty. In contrast, both Hryb and Shushkevich joined the anti-Lukashenka opposition, later becoming leading members of the →For a New Belarus movement launched in May 2001. Meanwhile, the rump KPB had obtained six seats in the October 2000 legislative elections.

For a New Belarus

Leadership. Uladzimir Hancharyk (2001 presidential candidate); Vasil Lyavonau (chairman)

This movement was launched in May 2001 as a support organization for candidates planning to oppose incumbent Alyaksandr Lukashenka in the presidential elections scheduled for September 2001. Joined by Mechyslau Hryb and Stanislau Shushkevich, both former leaders of the →Communist Party of Belarus, the new movement backed a pledge by five declared presidential candidates (Mikhail Chyhir, Uladzimir Hancharyk, Syamyon Domash, Syarhey Kalyakin and Pavel Kazlouski) to reach an agreement on one of them becoming a single challenger to Lukashenka. The chairman of the movement, Vasil Lyavonau, was a former Agriculture Minister who had been imprisoned under the Lukashenka regime.

In July 2001 Uladzimir Hancharyk, head of the main Belarus trade union federation, was endorsed as the movement's agreed presidential candidate. In the elections in September he was officially credited with only 15.65% of the vote, subsequently claiming that the polling had been riddled with fraud and government manipulation.

Liberal Democratic Party of Belarus
Liberalna–Demokratychnaya Partiya Belarusi (LDPB)

Address. 22 Platonava Street, Minsk 220056

Telephone. (+375–17) 269-5909

Fax. (+375–17) 247-7257

Leadership. Syargey Gaydukevich (chairman)

The right-wing pan-Slavic LDPD is the Belarus fraternal party of the →Liberal Democratic Party of Russia and therefore advocates close links with Russia. In September 1998 the LDPB was a founder member of the pro-Lukashenka →Belarusan People's Patriotic Union, grouping some 30 conservative parties which backed the proposed Belarus-Russian union treaty, including the →Belarus Popular Party and →Communist Party of Belarus. The party won one seat in the October 2000 legislative elections.

Social Democratic Party of Popular Accord
Satsiyal–Demokratychnaya Partiya Narodnaya Zgody (SDPNZ)

Address. 10 Karl Marx Street, Minsk 220050

Telephone. (+375–17) 248–0221

Leadership. Leanid Sechka (chairman)

The SDPNZ dates as such from 1997, when the Party of Popular Accord (PNZ) adopted the Social Democratic rubric. The PNZ had been founded in 1992 as a technocratic party emphasizing the need for economic reform, independent of the competing pro-democracy and conservative alliances, although it backed the →Belarusan Popular Front—Renaissance candidate in the 1994 presidential elections after then PNZ leader Henadz Karpenka had failed to meet the nomination requirements. The party won eight of the declared seats in the 1995 legislative elections and joined a 15-strong parliamentary group which included the →Belarus Social Democratic Party. The SDPNZ won one seat in the October 2000 legislative elections.

Other Parties

Belarusan Ecological Green Party, founded in 1998 as a merger of the Ecological and Green parties, which had each won one seat in the 1995 legislative elections.

Leadership. Alyaksandr Mikulich, Mikalay Kartash,

Belarusan Party of Labour and Justice (*Respublikanskaya Partiya Pratsy i Spravyadlivasti, RPPS*), founded in 1993, won one seat in the 1995 legislative elections and two in 2000.
Address. 7 Amuratarskaya Street, Minsk 220004
Telephone. (+375–17) 223–9321
Fax. (+375–17) 223–8641
Leadership. Anatol Nitylkin (chairman)

Belarusan Peasants' Party (*Belaruskaya Syalanskaya Partiya, BSP*), founded in 1990 as a reincarnation of the pre-Soviet agrarian movement, pledged to securing the restoration of peasant land ownership. It associated itself with the opposition →Belarusan Popular Front—Renaissance in the pressure for political and economic reform. In the 1994 presidential elections, however, it presented its own candidate, Alyaksandr Dubko (chairman of the Agrarian Union of Belarus), who won 6% of the first-round vote. In the 1995 legislative elections, the BSP was heavily outpolled by the pro-collectivism →Agrarian Party of Belarus, winning only one seat.
Address. 38/1 Gaya Street, Minsk 220068
Telephone. (+375–17) 277–1905
Fax. (+375–17) 277–9651
Leadership. Yaugen Lugin (chairman)

Belarusan Women's Political Party–Hope (*Nadzeya*), founded in 1994, advocating priority for protection of the family.
Address. 21 Masherov Avenue, Suite 707, Minsk 220126
Telephone. (+375–17) 223–8957
Fax. (+375–17) 223–9040
Email. zmn@sfpb.belpak.minsk.by
Web. www.nadzeya.org
Leadership. Valentina Polevikova (president)

Christian Democratic Party of Belarus (*Khrystsyanska Demokratychnaya Partiya Belarusi, KDPB*), centrist pro-democracy formation which is an observer member of the Christian Democrat International.
Leadership. Gennady Grushevoy (chairman)

Conservative Christian Party (*Konservativnaya Khrystsiyanska Partiya, KKP*), launched in September 1999 by supporters of 1994 presidential election candidate Zyanon Paznyak, who had been effectively ousted the previous month as leader in exile of the →Belarusan Popular Front–Renaissance. Strongly opposed to the Belarus-Russia union treaty, the party joined the general opposition boycott of the October 2000 legislative elections.
Leadership. Zyanon Paznyak (chairman)

National Democratic Party of Belarus (*Natsyianalna-Demokratychnaya Partiya Belarusi, NDPB*), founded in 1990 as a pro-market, nationalist formation. It later became a constituent party of the →Belarusan Popular Front—Revival and opposed the Belarus-Russia union treaty.
Address. 97/140 Labanka Street, Minsk
Telephone. (+375–17) 271–9516
Fax. (+375–17) 236–9972
Leadership. Viktar Navumenka (chairman)

United Civic Party of Belarus (*Abyadnanaya Grazhdanskaya Partiya Belarusi, AGPB*), pro-market formation founded in 1995 as a merger of earlier parties; it won nine seats in the 1995 elections and later became part of the opposition →Belarusan Popular Front – Renaissance. It is a member of the European Democrat Union.
Leadership. Stanislau Bahdankevich (chairman)

Belgium

Capital: Brussels

Population: 10,250,000 (2000E)

The Kingdom of Belgium is a constitutional monarchy with a parliamentary democracy in which most political parties are based in the country's linguistic communities, principally the majority Flemish-speaking population in the north and the French-speaking Walloon community in the south. The constitutional monarch, as head of state, has limited powers, with central executive authority residing in the Prime Minister and the Council of Ministers being responsible to a federal bicameral legislature. The lower house is the Chamber of Representatives (*Chambre des Représentants* or *Kamer van Volksvertegenwoordigers*), reduced from 212 to 150 members from 1995 and elected for a maximum four-year term by universal compulsory suffrage of those aged 18 and over according to a complex system of proportional representation. The Chamber has virtually equal powers with the upper house, which is the 71-member Senate (*Sénat/Senaat*), 40 of whose members are elected directly and the remainder indirectly, also for a four-year term. Belgium was a founder member of what is now the European Union and elects 25 members to the European Parliament.

A lengthy process of constitutional reform, inaugurated in 1970 and involving the phased devolution of substantial powers to the linguistic regions, culminated with the final parliamentary approval on July 14, 1993, of legislation transforming Belgium into a federal state. Under the changes, the country is divided into three regions (Flanders, Wallonia and bilingual Brussels), each with a government and directly-elected legislature (of 118, 75 and 75 members respectively) endowed with broad economic and social powers, and into three communities (Flemish, French and German) for cultural purposes. The Flemish community council is identical with the Flanders regional council; the French community council is indirectly constituted by the 75 Wallonia regional council members and 19 from the Brussels council; and the 25-member German community council is directly elected.

Although there is no direct public funding of parties in Belgium, those already represented in the federal legislature benefit from certain facilities during election campaigns, amounting to indirect state subsidy sufficient to cover the maximum authorized expenditure of BF40 million (about $1.2 million) on such campaigns.

Elections to the federal Chamber of Representatives on June 13, 1999, resulted as follows: Flemish Liberals and Democrats–Citizens' Party 23 seats (14.3% of the national vote), Christian People's Party (Flemish) 22 (14.1%), Socialist Party (Walloon) 19 (10.1%), Liberal Reformist Party/Democratic Front of French-Speakers (Walloon) 18 (10.1%), Flemish Bloc 15 (9.9%), Socialist Party (Flemish) 14 (9.6%), Ecologist Party (Walloon) 11 (7.3%), Christian Social Party (Walloon) 10 (6.1%), Live Differently (Flemish) 9 (7.0%), People's Union (Flemish) 8 (5.6%), National Front (Walloon) 1 (1.5%).

Christian People's Party
Christelijke Volkspartij (CVP)
Address. Wetstraat 89, B-1040 Brussels
Telephone. (+32–2) 238–3814
Fax. (+32–2) 230–4360
Email. inform@cvp.be
Website. www.cvp.be
Leadership. Stefaan de Clercq (president); M. Van Peel (chairman in federal Chamber); Chris Taes (secretary-general)

Historically descended from the *Katholieke Vlaamse Volkspartij*, which was the Flemish wing of the pre-war Belgian Catholic Party, the CVP was created in 1945 as the Flemish counterpart of the French-speaking →Christian Social Party (PSC), initially within a single party structure. From 1947 the CVP/PSC participated in successive coalition governments, except for the period 1954–58. By the mid-1960s the CVP and the PSC had effectively become separate parties, the former considerably larger than the latter in terms of electoral support. Consistently the strongest single parliamentary party, the CVP provided the Prime Minister in coalitions, with the Socialists and the →Democratic Front of French-Speakers of Brussels in 1979–80; with the Socialists and Liberals briefly in 1980; with the Socialists in 1980–81; with the Liberals in 1981–88; with the Socialists and the →People's Union in 1988–91; and with the Socialists in 1992-99.

In the November 1991 Chamber elections the CVP's representation fell from 43 to 39 seats out of 212 and its share of the vote from 19.5% to 16.7%. After 13 years of almost continuous incumbency as CVP Prime Minister, Wilfried Martens gave way to Jean-Luc Dehaene in the government formed in March 1992. In the June 1994 European Parliament elections the party took 17% of the vote (compared with 21.1% in 1989) and four of the 25 Belgian seats. In further Chamber elections in May 1995 the CVP unexpectedly increased its vote share to 17.2%, winning 29 out of 150 seats, so that Dehaene remained head of a federal coalition with the Socialists. In simultaneous elections for the 118-member Flemish regional council the CVP won a plurality of 35 seats (with 26.8% of the vote), providing the minister-president of Flanders in the person of Luc van den Brande, who headed a coalition with the Flemish Socialists.

From 1996 the CVP shared in the Dehaene coalition's deep unpopularity over official mishandling of a gruesome paedophile case, amidst widespread protest against expenditure cuts introduced to enable Belgium to qualify for the single European currency. On the eve of the June 1999 general, regional and European elections, moreover, two major food safety scares proved to be the death-knell for the government. Support for the CVP fell to 14.1% in the Chamber elections, its resultant 22 seats relegating it to second place behind the →Flemish Liberals and Democrats (VLD), with the result that the party went into opposition for the first time since 1958. The CVP also lost ground in the Flemish regional council elections (taking 22.1% of the vote and 28 seats) and was obliged to surrender the post of minister-president to the VLD. In the Euro-elections the CVP declined to 13.5% of the vote and its representation from four to three seats.

The CVP is a member of the Christian Democrat International and the European Union of Christian Democrats. Its three representatives in the European Parliament sit in the European People's Party/European Democrats group.

Christian Social Party
Parti Social Chrétien (PSC)
Address. Rue des Deux Églises 41/45, B-1040 Brussels
Telephone. (+32–2) 238–0111
Fax. (+32–2) 238–0129
Email. info@psc.be
Website. www.psc.be
Leadership. Joëlle Milquet (president); J.-P. Poncelet (chairman in federal Chamber); Jean-François Brouillard (secretary-general)

The PSC has its historical origins in the Catholic Union, one of several such organizations set up in Belgium in the 19th century. It is directly descended from the Belgian Catholic Party (PCB) created in 1936 and more specifically from the *Parti Catholique Social* (PCS), the PCB's French-speaking section. As the country's strongest party, the PCB took part in coalition governments before and during World War II, the PCS providing Belgium's wartime Prime Minister. At Christmas 1945 the PCB was reconstituted, the PCS becoming the PSC and the Flemish wing becoming the →Christian People's Party (CVP), at that stage within one overall party structure. Having confirmed its dominant position in the 1946 elections, the joint party entered a coalition with the Socialists in 1947. Thereafter the PSC/CVP tandem participated continuously in the central government until 1999, except for the period 1954–58.

From the mid-1960s the PSC and CVP effectively became two separate parties, the former becoming substantially the smaller of the two. The PSC has therefore been a junior partner in recent coalitions headed by the CVP, with the Socialists and the →Democratic Front of French-Speakers of Brussels in 1979–80; with the Socialists and Liberals briefly in 1980; with the Socialists in 1980–81; with the Liberals in 1981–88; with the Socialists and the →People's Union in 1988–91; and with the Socialists since 1992. In the November 1991 Chamber elections PSC representation slipped from 19 to 18 seats out of 212 and its vote share from 8% to 7.8%. In the June 1994 European Parliament elections the PSC retained two of the 25 Belgian seats but its vote share fell to 6.9% from 8.1% in 1989. This setback coincided with disclosures of financial corruption in the Brussels section of the party. Nevertheless, in the May 1995 Chamber elections the PSC retained a 7.7% vote share, winning 12 of the 150 seats, and took third place in the simultaneous elections to the Walloon regional council, with 16 of the 75 seats and 21.6% of the vote. Thereafter, in addition to remaining in the federal coalition, the PSC also maintained its coalition with the Walloon Socialists in the regional government of Wallonia.

In simultaneous federal, regional and European elections held in June 1999, support for the PSC fell to 6.1% in the Chamber elections and its representation to 10 seats, with the result that the party went into federal opposition for the first time since 1958. In the Walloon regional elections the PSC fell to 17.1% of the vote and 14 seats and likewise vacated the regional government. In the Euro-elections the CVP declined to 4.9% of the vote and its representation from two seats to one. The PSC leadership subsequently passed from Philippe Maystadt to Joëlle Milquet and the party relaunched itself as the "New" PSC.

The PSC is a member of the Christian Democrat International and the European Union of Christian Democrats. Its single representative in the European Parliament sits in the European People's Party/European Democrats group.

Democratic Front of French-Speakers
Front Démocratique des Francophones (FDF)
Address. Chaussée de Charleroi 127, B–1060 Brussels
Telephone. (+32–2) 538–8320
Fax. (+32-2) 539–3650
Email. fdf@fdf.be
Website. www.fdf.be
Leadership. Olivier Maingain (president); Claude Desmedt (chairman in federal Chamber); Didier van Eyll (chairman in French community council); François Roelants du Vivier (chairman in Brussels council); Serge de Patoul (secretary-general)

Founded in May 1964 with the aim of preserving the French character of the Belgian capital, the FDF incorporated various militant francophone groupings of Brussels. Its three Chamber seats in the 1965 elections were increased to 10 by 1977, after which it joined a coalition government with the Christian Socials and Socialists and assisted with the enactment of the 1978 Egmont Pact on regional devolution. Under the plan, Brussels was to become a separate (bilingual) region, i.e. not included in surrounding Flanders as some Flemish nationalists had demanded. Having risen to 11 seats in 1978, the FDF went into opposition again from 1980 and slipped to six seats in 1981. Two of these deputies defected to the Walloon →Socialist Party in March 1985 and the FDF was reduced to three seats in the October 1985 elections, retaining them in 1987 and 1991.

The FDF retained representation in the May 1995 Chamber elections by virtue of an alliance with the →Liberal Reformist Party (PRL). In simultaneous elections, the PRL/FDF alliance became the largest bloc in the Brussels regional council, winning 28 of the 75 seats (with 35% of the vote), and the second largest in the Walloon regional council, with 19 of the 75 seats and a 23.7% vote share. The FDF was allocated one portfolio in the six-party Brussels regional government.

The PRL–FDF alliance was maintained in the June 1999 elections, retaining 18 federal Chamber seats on a slightly reduced vote of 10.1%, improving to 21 seats (24.7% of the vote) in the Walloon regional council and slipping to 27 seats (34.4%) in the Brussels regional council. In the simultaneous European Parliament elections the FDF was allied with both the PRL and the →Citizens' Movement for Change (MCC), the joint list winning three seats on a 10% vote share. The FDF received no portfolios in the new federal government which included the PRL, but was represented in the new regional administrations of Wallonia and Brussels.

Ecologist Party
Ecologistes Confédérés pour l'Organisation de Luttes Originales (ECOLO)
Address. Rue du Séminaire 8, B–5000 Namur
Telephone. (+32–81) 227–871
Fax. (+32–81) 230–603
Email. info@ecolo.be
Website. www.ecolo.be
Leadership. Jacky Morael & Jean-Luc Roland (federal secretaries)

Originally founded in 1978 by Walloon environmentalists, ECOLO was reorganized for the 1981 elections, in which it co-operated with the Flemish →Live Differently (AGALEV) grouping and won two Chamber seats. Having established a significant local government presence, ECOLO increased its Chamber tally to five seats in 1985 (standing independently), but slipped back to three seats in 1987. The November 1991 elections brought a major advance, to 10 seats out of 212, with 5.1% of the vote, double the party's 1987 share. In the June 1994 European Parliament elections ECOLO won 4.8% of the national vote and one seat, compared with 6.3% and two seats in 1989. Its share in the May 1995 Chamber elections fell back to 4.0%, giving it six of the 150 seats, while in simultaneous regional polling it won eight and seven seats respectively on the 75-member Walloon and Brussels regional councils (with 10.4% and 9.0% of the vote respectively).

ECOLO resumed its electoral advance in the June 1999 federal, regional and European elections. Its representation in the federal Chamber almost doubled to 11 seats (from a vote share of 7.3%); it won 14 seats in both the Walloon and Brussels councils (with 18.2% and 18.3% respectively); it again took three seats on the 25-member council of the German-speaking community (with 12.7% of the vote); and it increased its European Parliament representation to three seats (with 8.4% of the vote). It alsoIn July 1999 ECOLO joined a new federal coalition headed by the →Flemish Liberals and Democrats, Isabelle Durant being appointed Deputy Prime Minister and Minister for Mobility and Transport. The ECOLO and AGALEV members in the federal Chamber form a single group under the chairmanship of Jef Tavernier.

ECOLO is a member of the European Federation of Green Parties. Its three representatives in the European Parliament sit in the Greens/European Free Alliance group.

Flemish Bloc
Vlaams Blok (VB)
Address. Madouplein 8 bus 9, B–1210 Brussels
Telephone. (+32–2) 219–6009
Fax. (+32–2) 217–1958
Email. vlblok@vlaams-blok.be
Website. www.vlaams-blok.be
Leadership. Frank Vanhecke (pesident); Karel Dillen (founder and honorary president); Roeland Raes (deputy president); Gerolf Annemans (chairman in federal Chamber); Filip Dewinter (chairman in Flemish council)

The ultra-nationalist Flemish Bloc first came into being for the December 1978 elections as an alliance between the Flemish People's Party, established in 1977 by Lode Claes following a split in the →People's Union (VU), and the Flemish National Party, led by Karel Dillen and also founded in 1977. Having won one seat in that contest, the two parties formally merged under Dillen's leadership in May 1979 on a platform of opposition to the 1978 Egmont Pact on devolution on the grounds that it demanded too many concessions of Flemings. Having increased its Chamber tally to two seats in 1987, the Bloc experienced a surge of support in the 1990s on a platform which now emphasized opposition to immigration. In the November 1991 elections the Bloc's representation in the Chamber increased to 12 seats and its vote share to 6.6%, ahead of the VU, for long the main vehicle of Flemish nationalism. During the campaign brown-shirted VB militants were involved in numerous violent incidents involving foreigners.

In the June 1994 European Parliament elections the Bloc won two seats and increased its vote to 7.8% (from 4.1% in 1989) on a platform which combined anti-immigration policies with opposition to the Maastricht process of European union. It made further advances in local elections in October 1994, winning representation in 82 of the 308 municipal councils and a total of 202 seats nationally. The Bloc headed the poll in Antwerp, winning 29% of the vote and 18 of the 55 seats, but its leader in the city, Filip Dewinter, was excluded from the mayorship by a combination of the other parties represented. The VB again registered 7.8% of the national vote in the May 1995 Chamber elections, giving it 11 out of 150 seats, while in simultaneous polling for the 118-member Flemish regional council it won 15 seats with a 12.3% vote share.

The VB made a further advance in the June 1999 federal, regional and European elections, winning 15 seats in the federal Chamber (with 9.9% of the vote) and 20 seats on the Flemish regional council (with 15.5% of the vote), also also retaining two European Parliament seats (on an increased vote share of 9.4%). In local elections in October 2000 the VB registered major gains in several cities, winning 33% of the vote in Antwerp and consolidating its position as the largest party on the city council, although it remained in opposition because none of the main parties would form a coalition with it.

The VB's two representatives in the European Parliament are among the "unattached" contingent. The party claims a membership of about 25,000.

Flemish Liberals and Democrats–Citizens' Party
Vlaamse Liberalen en Demokraten (VLD)–Partij van de Burger
Address. Melsensstraat 34, B–1000 Brussels
Telephone. (+32–2) 549–0020
Fax. (+32–2) 512–6025
Email. vld@vld.be
Website. www.vld.be
Leadership. Karel de Gucht (president); H. Coveliers (chairman in federal Chamber); Clair Ysebaert (secretary-general)

The VLD is descended from the historic Belgian Liberal

Party, which was founded in 1846 as the country's earliest political formation. It was in power in 1857–70 and 1878–84 but was then overtaken on the left by the new Belgian Labour Party, becoming the country's third political force behind the Catholics and Socialists. Having participated in a succession of coalitions after World War II, notably the 1954–58 Socialist-Liberal government, the Liberal Party was reconstituted in 1961 as the Party of Liberty and Progress (PLP). In 1970 the Flemish wing (*Partij voor Vrijheid en Vooruitgang*, PVV) became an autonomous formation, leaving the PLP as a Walloon party. Having participated in various coalitions in the 1970s, both the PVV and its Walloon counterpart, by now called the →Liberal Reformist Party (PRL), were in government with the →Christian People's and →Christian Social parties in 1981–88, being regarded as the right-wing component of the coalition. In the November 1991 general elections the opposition PVV increased its Chamber representation from 25 to 26 seats out of 212 and its vote share from 11.5% to 11.9%.

In November 1992, in a move to broaden its support base, the PVV switched to its current VLD designation, also using the sub-title Party of Citizens (*Partij van de Burger*). In the June 1994 European Parliament elections the VLD took 11.4% of the vote and three of the 25 Belgian seats, against 10.6% and two seats for the PVV in 1989. In municipal and provincial elections in October 1994 the VLD replaced the Flemish Socialists as the second-largest party in Flanders. It made a further advance in the May 1995 Chamber elections, winning 21 of the 150 seats with 13.1% of the vote, but not enough to oust the incumbent coalition. In simultaneous regional polling the VLD consolidated its position as second party in Flanders, winning 26 of the 118 seats in the Flemish regional council. In light of the party's relatively disappointing performance, Guy Verhofstadt resigned as leader and was succeeded in September 1995 by Herman de Croo.

Verhofstadt resumed the VLD presidency in 1997 and led the party to a significant advance in the June 1999 federal, regional and European, assisted by the deep unpopularity of the incumbent government. The party's representation in the federal Chamber increased to 23 seats (from a vote share of 14.3%); its seat tally in the Flemish regional council improved to 27 (with 22% of the vote); and it again won three European Parliament seats (with an increased vote share of 13.6%). In July 1999 Verhofstadt became Prime Minister of a new federal coalition which also included the PRL, the two Socialist parties, the →Ecologist Party and →Live Differently.

Claiming a membership of 80,000, the VLD is a member party of the Liberal International. Its representatives in the European Parliament sit in the European Liberal, Democratic and Reformist group.

Liberal Reformist Party
Parti Réformateur Libéral (PRL)
Address. Rue de Naples 41, B–1050 Brussels
Telephone. (+32–2) 500–3511
Fax. (+32–2) 500–3500
Email. prl@prl.be
Website. www.prl.be
Leadership. Daniel Ducarme (president); D. Bacquelaine (chairman in federal Chamber); Jacques Simonet (secretary-general)
Descended from the historic Belgian Liberal Party and its successors (see previous entry), the French-speaking PRL came into being in June 1979 as a merger of the Party of Reforms and Liberty of Wallonia (PRLW) and the Brussels Liberal Party. Of these, the PRLW had been formed in November 1976 as successor to the Party of Liberty and Progress (Parti de la Liberté et du Progrès, PLP), which had continued as the main Walloon Liberal party after the Flemish wing had become a separate formation in 1970, later becoming the →Flemish Liberals and Democrats (VLD). The Brussels Liberals had adopted the party's historic name in June 1974 as successor to the distinct Liberal

Democrat and Pluralist Party (PLDP) founded in January 1973. The PLP and the successor PRL (with the Flemish Liberals, who were consistently the stronger) participated in various coalitions, most recently with the →Christian People's Party and the →Christian Social Party in 1981–88, being regarded as the coalition's right-wing component.

In the November 1991 general elections, the opposition PRL's representation in the Chamber fell from 23 to 20 seats out of 212 and its vote share from 9.4% to 8.2%. In the June 1994 European Parliament elections the PRL won 9.0% of the vote and three seats compared with 8.7% and two seats in 1989. For the May 1995 Chamber elections the PRL presented a joint list with the →Democratic Front of French-Speakers (FDF) of Brussels, winning 18 out of 150 seats on a 10.3% vote share. In simultaneous elections, the PRL/FDF alliance became the largest bloc in the Brussels regional council, winning 28 of the 75 seats (with 35% of the vote), and the second largest in the Walloon regional council, with 19 of the 75 seats and a 23.7% vote share. The PRL was allocated two portfolios in the six-party Brussels regional government.

The PRL–FDF alliance was maintained in the June 1999 elections, retaining 18 federal Chamber seats on a slightly reduced vote of 10.1%, improving to 21 seats (24.7% of the vote) in the Walloon regional council and slipping to 27 seats (34.4%) in the Brussels regional council. In the simultaneous European Parliament elections the PRL was allied with both the FDF and the →Citizens' Movement for Change (MCC), the joint list winning three seats on a 10% vote share. In July 1999 the PRL joined a new federal coalition headed by the VLD, while the party also provided the minister-presidents of the new Brussels regional and French-speaking community governments, respectively Jacques Simonet and Hervé Hasquin.

Claiming a membership of 40,000, the PRL is a member party of the Liberal International. The PRL members of the European Parliament sit in the European Liberal, Democratic and Reformist group.

Live Differently
Anders Gaan Leven (AGALEV)
Address. Brialmonstraat 23, B–1210 Brussels
Telephone. (+32–2) 219–1919
Fax. (+32–2) 223–1090
Email. postmaster@agalev.be
Website. www.agalev.be
Leadership. Jos Geysels (political secretary); Luc Lemiengre (secretary)
This Flemish environmentalist formation won two Chamber seats in the 1981 elections standing jointly with the Walloon →Ecologist Party (ECOLO). Established as an independent party in 1982, AGALEV increased its representation to four seats in 1985, six in 1987 and seven in November 1991, when its share of the poll was 4.9%. In the June 1994 European Parliament elections, it retained one seat with 6.7% of the vote (as against 7.6% in 1989), while in the May 1995 Chamber elections it slipped to 4.4% of the national vote, winning five out of 150 seats. In simultaneous regional balloting, AGALEV took 7.1% of the vote in Flanders, winning seven of the 118 regional council seats.

AGALEV resumed its electoral advance in the June 1999 federal, regional and European elections. Its representation in the federal Chamber almost doubled to nine seats (with a vote share of 7.0%); it won 12 seats in the Flemish regional council (with 11.6% of the vote); and a joint list of AGALEV and the Flemish →Socialist Party (SP) won two seats on the Brussels regional council (with 3.1% of the vote). In the simultaneous European Parliament elections AGALEV improved from one to two seats (with 7.5% of the vote). In July 1999 AGALEV joined a new federal coalition headed by the →Flemish Liberals and Democrats, Magda Aelvoet being appointed Minister of Consumer Protection, Public Health and Environment. The AGALEV and ECOLO members in the federal Chamber form a single group under the chairmanship of Jef Tavernier.

45

AGALEV is a member of the European Federation of Green Parties. Its two representatives in the European Parliament sit in the Greens/European Free Alliance group.

National Front
Front National (FN)

Address. Clos du Parnasse 12/8, B–1050 Brussels
Telephone/Fax. (+32–2) 511–7577
Email. fn@frontnational.be
Website. www.frontnational.be
Leadership. Daniel Féret (president); Guy Hance & Alain Sadaune (vice-presidents); Jacqueline Merveille (secretary-general)

The extreme right-wing FN, modelled on the ⇒National Front of France, was founded in 1983 on a platform of opposition to non-white immigration. Based mainly in the French-speaking community, it achieved a breakthrough in the November 1991 elections, winning one Chamber seat with 1.1% of the vote. A further advance came in the June 1994 European Parliament elections, when it took 2.9% of the vote and one of the 25 Belgian seats. In October 1994 the FN leadership announced the expulsion of a member who had been shown on television desecrating a Jewish grave. In local elections the same month the party doubled its share of the vote in Wallonia compared with the previous contest in 1988. In the May 1995 Chamber elections the NF advanced to 2.3% of the national vote, winning two seats, while in simultaneous regional balloting it won six seats on the 75-member Brussels regional council (with 7.5% of the vote) and two seats in Wallonia (with 5.2% of the vote).

The FN lost ground in the June 1999 elections, winning only one Chamber seat (with 1.5% of the vote), two on the Brussels regional council (with 2.6%) and one in Wallonia (with 4.0%). It also lost its single European Parliament seat, taking only 1.5% of the vote in that contest. The party claims a membership of 1,000.

People's Union
Volksunie (VU)

Address. Barrikadenplein 12, B–1000 Brussels
Telephone. (+32–2) 219–4930
Fax. (+32–2) 217–3510
Email. secretariaat@volksunie.be
Website. www.volksunie.be
Leadership. Fons Borginon (president); Geert Bourgeois (chairman in federal Chamber); Dirk De Cock (chairman in Flemish council); Laurens Appeltans (secretary-general)

The VU was founded in December 1954 as a nationalist party seeking autonomy for Flanders on a "socially progressive, tolerant, modern and forward-looking" platform. It made a breakthrough in the 1965 Chamber elections, winning 12 seats, which it increased to 20 in 1969 and to 22 in 1974. It fell back to 20 seats in 1977, in which year it entered government for the first time, in coalition with the Christian Socials, Socialists and →Democratic Front of French-Speakers (FDF) of Brussels, with the task of enacting regional devolution plans. Enshrined in the 1978 Egmont Pact, these were opposed by many VU militants as being inimical to Flemish interests, the result being the secession of a VU faction which later became part of the →Flemish Bloc (VB). The VU retained only 14 seats in the December 1978 elections and reverted to opposition status. Rebuilding its strength, it won 20 seats in 1981 but slipped again in 1985 to 16. Having again won 16 seats in the December 1987 elections, it accepted participation in a coalition with the Christian Socials and Socialists formed in March 1988 but withdrew in September 1991 over an arms export controversy.

In the November 1991 elections the VU retained only 10 seats (and 5.9% of the vote), being overtaken by the VB. In the June 1994 European Parliament elections it slipped to 4.4% of the vote, from 5.4% in 1989, while retaining one seat. The May 1995 Chamber elections yielded a further setback for the VU, which fell to 4.7% of the national vote and

five seats (out of 150). In simultaneous regional elections it won 9% of the vote in Flanders and nine of the 118 regional council seats, while in Brussels it won one seat and was allocated one portfolio in the six-party Brussels regional government.

The VU gained ground in the June 1999 national, regional and European elections, winning eight federal Chamber seats (with 5.6% of the vote) and 11 on the Flemish regional council in an alliance with the →Complete Democracy for the 21st Century (ID21) grouping (with 9.3%), although it lost its single seat on the Brussels regional council. In the simultaneous European elections the VU-ID21 advanced to two seats on the strength of a 7.6% vote share.

In 2000 the VU became divided over the leadership's support for federal government plans for further constitutional reform under which responsibility for trade policy and agriculture to the regions. In early 2001 Patrik Vankrunkelsven was succeeded as VU chairman by Fons Borginon, although the party continued to support the changes. In May 2001 the VU Interior Minister in the Flemish regional government, Johan Sauwens, was forced to resign over his attendance at a meeting of former Belgian members of Hitler's Waffen SS.

The two VU–ID21 members of the European Parliament sit in the Greens/European Free Alliance group.

Socialist Party
Parti Socialiste (PS)

Address. Blvd de l'Empereur 13, B–1000 Brussels
Telephone. (+32–2) 511–6966
Fax. (+32–2) 512–4632
Email. international@ps.be
Website. www.ps.be
Leadership. Elio Di Rupo (president); Maurice Bayenet & Philippe Moureaux (vice-presidents); Cl. Eerdekens (chairman in federal Chamber); Jean-Pol Baras (secretary-general)

Dating as a separate French-speaking party from October 1978, the PS is descended from the Belgian Labour Party (POB) founded in April 1885 with its base in industrial Wallonia and its support in organized labour. After obtaining universal male suffrage through a general strike, the POB was well-represented in the Chamber from 1894 and was admitted to the government-in-exile formed at Le Havre (France) in 1915 during World War I. In 1938 Paul-Henri Spaak became Belgium's first POB Prime Minister, but the German occupation of Belgium in 1940 forced the party underground under the leadership of Achille van Acker. Reconstituted in 1944 as the Belgian Socialist Party, with direct membership rather than group affiliation, it took part in post-war coalition governments until 1949 and again (with the Liberals) in 1954–58. Thereafter it was in coalition with the Christian Socials in 1961–66 and 1968–72; with the Christian Socials and Liberals in 1973–74; and with the Christian Socials, the →Democratic Front of French-Speakers (FDF) and the →People's Union (VU) in 1977–78. In October 1978 the Socialists emulated the other main Belgian political formations by formalizing the separation of their Flemish and French-speaking wings into autonomous parties, respectively the PS and the SP (see next entry).

Both the PS and the SP participated in coalitions with the Christian Socials and the FDF in 1979–80; with the Christian Socials and Liberals briefly in 1980; and with the Christian Socials in 1980–81. Both parties were then in opposition until, having become the largest lower house force in the December 1987 elections (for the first time since 1936), they joined a coalition with the Christian Socials and the VU in March 1988. Following the VU's withdrawal in September 1991, both Socialist parties lost ground in Chamber elections the following month (the PS falling from 40 to 35 seats out of 212 on a vote share of 15.6%) and joined a new coalition with the two Christian Social parties in March 1992. Concurrently, the PS also headed the regional governments of Wallonia and Brussels, championing the channelling of redevelopment resources to French-speaking areas and the maintenance of a large nationalized sector.

The murder in Liège in July 1991 of André Cools (a former PS Deputy Prime Minister) led eventually to the uncovering of the Agusta scandal, involving allegations of financial corruption in the party leadership in connection with a 1988 government contract for military helicopters awarded to an Italian firm. In January 1994 the disclosures resulted in the resignations of Guy Coëme (as federal Deputy Prime Minister), Guy Spitaels (as minister-president of Wallonia) and Guy Mathot (as interior minister of Wallonia), although all three denied any impropriety and the main focus of investigations was on the SP rather than the PS. In European Parliament elections in June 1994, the PS vote share slipped to 11.3% (from 14.5% in 1989 and 13.6% in the 1991 national balloting), so that it won only three of the 25 Belgian seats.

The May 1995 elections demonstrated the party's resilience, the PS winning 21 out of 150 seats on an 11.9% vote share and remaining a member of the federal centre-left coalition headed by the →Christian People's Party. In simultaneous regional elections the PS remained by far the strongest party in Wallonia, taking 30 of the 75 regional council seats with a 35.2% vote share, so that the party retained the leadership of the regional government. In the Brussels region the PS won 21.4% and 17 seats out of 75, enabling Charles Picqué of the PS to remain head of government in charge of a six-party administration.

Corruption allegations continued to dog the PS in the late 1990s, the party's headquarters being raided by the police in January 1997 after new evidence had emerged about financial contributions in return for government contracts. Having resigned as president of the Walloon regional assembly in February, Spitaels was indicted the following month on charges arising from the affair (which he denied). His trial and that of other PS and SP figures opened in September 1998 and resulted in December 1998 in all being found guilty and given suspended prison sentences.

The PS shared in the ruling coalition's general unpopularity in the June 1999 elections, being reduced to 19 seats in the federal Chamber (with 10.1% of the vote), to 25 seats in the Walloon regional council (with 29.5%) and to 13 seats on the Brussels regional council (with 16.0%). In simultaneous European Parliament elections the PS retained three seats but its vote share slipped to 9.6%. In July 1999 the PS entered a new federal coalition, this time headed by the →Flemish Liberals and Democrats and also including the two Green parties. The party also retained the leadership of the Walloon regional government, with Elio Di Rupo as minister-president.

The PS is a full member party of the Socialist International. Its three European Parliament representatives sit in the Party of European Socialists group.

Socialist Party
Socialistische Partij (SP)
Address. Keizerslaan 13, B–1000 Brussels
Telephone. (+32–2) 552–0293
Fax. (+32–2) 552–0255
Email. info@sp.be
Website. www.sp.be
Leadership. Patrick Janssens (chair); Dirk Van Der Maelen (chairman in federal Chamber); Hedwig Van Roost (national secretary)
As the Flemish section of the post-war Belgian Socialist Party, the SP had its origins in the *Belgische Werklieden Partij* founded in October 1885 as the Flemish wing of the Belgian Labour Party; it became an autonomous party on the formal separation of the two Socialist wings in October 1978. Before and subsequently it participated in all the central coalition governments of which the Walloon PS was a

member (see previous entry). Having formally renounced Marxism and class struggle in 1980, the SP became more "social democratic" in orientation than its Walloon counterpart, distancing itself in particular from the pro-nationalization line of the latter. For long the weaker of the two parties electorally, the SP maintained its Chamber representation at 32 seats out of 212 in December 1987 but fell back to 28 seats in November 1991. In the June 1994 European Parliament elections the SP retained three Belgian seats but its vote share slipped to 10.8%, from 12.4% in the 1989 Euro-elections and 12.0% in the 1991 national poll.

Following the appointment of Willy Claes (then SP Deputy Premier and Foreign Minister) to the post of NATO secretary-general in October 1994, Frank Vandenbroucke replaced him in the government and was succeeded as SP chair by Louis Tobback, hitherto Interior Minister. In March 1995 Vandenbroucke became the most senior casualty to date of the Agusta bribery scandal, resigning from the government after admitting that in 1991 he knew that the party held a large sum of undeclared money in a bank safe deposit. Also implicated was Claes, who as Economic Affairs Minister in 1988 had been closely involved in the helicopter contract at the centre of the bribery allegations. Despite these difficulties, the SP advanced to 12.6% in the May 1995 general elections (ahead of the Walloon Socialists), winning 20 of the 150 Chamber seats. In the simultaneous regional polling, it took 25 of the 118 Flemish council seats (with a 19.4% vote share) and continued to participate in the Flanders government, while winning two seats on the Brussels regional council (with 2.4%)

In October 1995 Claes was obliged to resign his NATO post when the Belgian parliament voted in favour of his being brought to trial. Court proceedings opened in September 1998 and resulted in December in Claes and 12 other defendants being found guilty of corruption and given suspended prison sentences. Claes said that he would appeal to the European Court of Human Rights.

The SP shared in the ruling coalition's general unpopularity in the June 1999 elections, being reduced to 14 seats in the federal Chamber (with 9.6% of the vote) and to 19 seats in the Flemish regional council (with 15.0%), while retaining two seats on the Brussels regional council on a joint list with →Live Differently (AGALEV) which took 3.1% of the vote. In simultaneous European Parliament elections the SP lost one of its three seats on a reduced vote share of 8.8%. In July 1999 the SP entered a new federal coalition, this time headed by the →Flemish Liberals and Democrats and also including the two Green parties. The party also provided the new minister-president of the German-speaking community (Karl-Heinz Lambertz), having won four of the 25 council seats with a 15.0% vote share.

Claiming a membership of 76,000, the PS is a full member party of the Socialist International. Its two European Parliament representatives sit in the Party of European Socialists group.

Other Parties

Many minor parties contested the June 1999 elections at federal, regional or European level, most of them failing to achieve 0.1% of the respective vote totals. The following list focuses on the better-supported groupings but is not exhaustive.

Alive (*Vivant*), French-speaking formation urging abolition of taxes and social charges on the workplace and a big increase in VAT to compensate; won 130,703 votes (2.1%) in 1999 federal Chamber elections (but no seats) and one seat on Brussels regional council (with 1.5%).
Address. Blvd du Midi 25–27, 4ème étage, B–1000 Brussels
Telephone. (+32–2) 513–0888

Fax. (+32–2) 502–0107
Email. cadministratie@vivant.be
Website. www.vivant.be
Leadership. Dirk Vangossum

Christian Social Party (*Christlisch Soziale Partei, CSP*), the Christian Social party of Belgium's small German-speaking minority, secured one seat in the 1994 and 1999 European Parliament elections (with only 0.2% of the overall vote), on the ticket of the (Flemish) →Christian People's Party; the CSP MEP sits in the European People's Party/European Democrats group.
Leadership. Mathieu Grosch (president)

Citizens' Movement for Change (*Mouvement des Citoyens pour le Changement, MCC*), founded in 1998 by Gérard Deprez on the strength of public outrage at official mishandling of the Dutroux paedophile controversy; allied with →Liberal Reformist Party and →Democratic Front of French-Speakers in the 1999 national, regional and European elections, it secured four representatives in the various assemblies, Deprez being elected to the European Parliament and chosing to join the European People's Party/European Democrats group.
Address. Ave Générale de Gaulle 40, B-1050 Brussels
Telephone. (+32–2) 640–4047
Fax. (+32–2) 640–0241
Email. info@lemcc.be
Website. www.lemcc.be/mcc
Leadership. Nathalie de T'serclaes (president)

Communist Party (*Parti Communiste, PC*), French-speaking formation (autonomous since 1992) descended from the historic Belgian Communist Party (PCB/KPB) founded in 1921, powerful after World War II on a pro-Soviet tack but in decline since the mid-1950s, unrepresented in the Chamber since 1985, has renounced Marxism-Leninism in favour of socialist democracy.
Address. Rue Rouppe 4, B–1000 Brussels
Telephone. (+32–2) 548–0290
Fax. (+32–2) 548–0295
Leadership. Pierre Beauvois (president)

Communist Party (*Parti Kommunistische, KP*), Flemish formation (autonomous since 1992) descended from the historic Belgian Communist Party (PCB/KPB) founded in 1921 (see previous entry).
Address. Galgenberg 29, B–9000 Ghent
Telephone. (+32–9) 225–4584
Fax. (+32–9) 233–5678
Email. kp@democratisch-links.be
Website. www.democratisch-links.be

Complete Democracy for the 21st Century (*Integrale Democratie voor de 21ste Eeuw, ID21*), right-wing Flemish grouping, contested June 1999 Flemish council and European elections on joint list with →People's Union (Volksunie).
Address. Noordstraat 80, B–1000 Brussels
Telephone. (+32–2) 223–3933
Fax. (+32–2) 223–3934
Email. info@id21.be
Website. www.id21.be

Democratic Right (*Droite Démocratique, DD*), radical right-wing formation.
Address. Ave des Bécassines 29, B–1160 Brussels
Telephone/Fax. (+32–2) 675–8274

Website. users.skynet.be/dd
Leadership. Christian Galloy

New Front of Belgium (*Front Nouveau de Belgique/Front Nieuw België, FNB*), a "democratic nationalist party", founded in 1997; won one seat on Brussels regional council in June 1999 with 1.3% of the vote, but only 0.4% in federal Chamber elections and 0.6% in Walloon regional council elections (and no seats).
Address. Rue de la Cambre 336, B–1200 Brussels
Telephone/Fax. (+32–2) 770–8866
Website. www.fnb.to
Leadership. Marguerite Bastien

Party of Belgian German-Speakers (*Partei der Deutschsprachigen Belgier, PDB*), founded in 1971 to campaign for equal rights for the German-speaking minority; won three seats in 1999 elections for German-speaking community council.
Address. Kaperberg 6, B–4700 Eupen
Telephone. (+32–87) 555–987
Fax. (+32–87) 555–984
Email. guido.breuer@skynet.be
Website. users.skynet.be/pdb
Leadership. Guido Breuer

Social-Liberal Democrats (*Sociaal-Liberale Democraten, SoLiDe*), Flemish-based centre-left party, won 0.1% of the vote in 1999 federal Chamber elections.
Address. Th. Donnéstraat 59, B–3540 Herk-de-Stad
Telephone. (+32–13) 441–483
Fax. (+32–13) 461–902
Email. solide@ping.be
Website. www.ping/be/solide
Leadership. Anouk Sinjan (president)

Walloon Party (*Parti Wallon, PW*), left-wing nationalist party advocating a socialist Wallonia, founded in 1985 as a merger of the Rassemblement Wallon (RW) and other radical Walloon groups under the leadership of Jean-Claude Piccin. Founded in 1968, the RW had participated in a coalition government with the Christian Socials and Liberals in 1974–77, helping to secure the passage of the Egmont Pact on devolution; but it had been weakened by defections of moderates to what became the →Liberal Reformist Party. Whereas the RW won two Chamber seats in the 1981 elections on a joint list with the →Democratic Front of French-Speakers, in 1985 the PW failed to gain representation and was no more successful in subsequent electoral contests, winning only 0.2% in the 1999 federal Chamber elections.
Address. Rue du Faubourg 14, B–1430 Quenast
Telephone. (+32–67) 670–019

Workers' Party of Belgium (*Partij van de Arbeid van België/Parti du Travail de Belgique, PvdA/PTB*), founded in 1979 in opposition to the reformism of the →Communist Party, part of the All Power to the Workers (*Alle Macht Aan de Arbeiders*, AMADA) movement in the 1979 Euro-elections, unsuccessful then and subsequently in securing representation; won 0.5% of the vote in the 1995 and 1999 federal Chamber elections.
Address. Lemonnierlaan 171/2, B–1000 Brussels
Telephone. (+32–2) 513–7760
Fax. (+32–2) 513–9831
Email. ptb@ptb.be
Website. www.wpb.be
Leadership. Nadine Rosa-Rosso

Belize

Capital: Belmopan

Population: 236,000 (2000E)

Belize became independent within the British Commonwealth on Sept. 21, 1981. A Legislative Assembly has been in existence since 1935 and was given responsibility for internal self-government under the former constitution of 1954. Under the 1981 constitution the head of state is the British monarch, represented by a Governor-General. The head of government is the Prime Minister. The Governor-General formally appoints the Prime Minister, who is the leader of the party able to command a parliamentary majority. The Governor-General is also advised by an appointed Belize Advisory Council. There is a bicameral National Assembly, comprising an appointed eight-member Senate and a House of Representatives with 29 elected members.

Belize uses the first-past-the-post electoral system, with successful candidates requiring a simple majority in one of the 29 single-member constituencies. Members of the Senate are officially appointed by the Governor-General: five on the advice of the Prime Minister, two on that of the Leader of the Opposition and one after consulting the Belize Advisory Council. The National Assembly sits for a five-year term subject to dissolution.

In elections held on Aug. 27, 1998, the People's United Party (PUP) returned to power after five years with 59.4% of the vote and 26 seats in the new House, while the formerly governing United Democratic Party (UDP) took 39.1% of the vote and three seats.

People's United Party (PUP)

Address. 3 Queen Street, Belize City
Telephone. (+501–2) 32428
Fax. (+501–2) 33476
Website. www.pupbelize.org
Leadership. Said Musa (leader)

Founded in 1950, the centrist PUP has traditionally drawn more of its support from Catholics, Indians and Spanish-speakers than from the black population. The party was founded as a reformist party motivated by co-operatist ideas and supported by the General Workers' Union and the Roman Catholic Church. It campaigned for independence from Britain, a position which helped it win a comprehensive victory in the 1954 general election, following which (under the leadership of George C. Price from 1956) it remained the leading party through to independence in 1981.

In the first post-independence election in 1984, however, the PUP won only seven seats in the enlarged 28-member House. The party returned to power in the 1989 general election, when it won 15 seats, narrowly defeating the UDP, which took 13. During Price's post-1989 term of office the country identified itself more closely with the region, being accepted as a member of the Organization of American States (OAS) in January 1991. In September 1991 diplomatic relations were established with neighbouring Guatemala, which had long claimed sovereignty over the country.

In an early general election called by Price in June 1993, the PUP was unexpectedly defeated, retaining only 13 seats against 16 for the UDP. Price resigned as leader in October 1996 and was succeeded by Said Musa, a lawyer and hitherto PUP chairman. In the August 1998 legislative elections, the PUP benefited from the relatively poor performance of the Belizean economy, the introduction of an unpopular business tax by the UDP government and the widespread perception that inquiries into corruption allegations against leading PUP figures were politically motivated. Following his decisive victory by 26 seats to only three for the UDP, Musa was sworn in as Prime Minister on Sept. 1. In local elections in March 2000, the PUP retained control of six of the seven municipalities, winning a total of 51 seats against only five for the UDP.

United Democratic Party (UDP)

Address. South End Bel-China Bridge, PO Box 1898, Belize City, Belize
Telephone. (+501–2) 72576
Fax. (+501–2) 76441
E-mail. info@udp.org.bz
Website. www.udp.org.bz
Leadership. Dean Barrow (leader); Douglas Singh (chairman); Philippa Griffith-Bailey (secretary-general)

Founded in September 1973, the conservative UDP has a predominantly black (Creole) ethnic base but also claims to have support from the Mayan and Mestizo communities.

The UDP was created by the fusion of the previous National Independence Party, Liberal Party and People's Development Movement as a right-wing opposition to the dominant →People's United Party (PUP). In the 1979 general election, it won 46.8% of the vote and five seats on the basis of a campaign charging that the PUP government was influenced by communism. The party opposed early independence from Britain in view of Guatemala's territorial claim on Belize.

Manuel Esquivel became leader of the UDP in 1982 and led the party to power in 1984. However, in September 1989 the UDP lost office to the PUP. In September 1991 Belize established diplomatic relations with Guatemala and the party leadership's support for this resulted in some dissidents breaking away in February 1992 to launch the →National Alliance for Belizean Rights (NABR). The UDP expectedly returned to power in the June 1993 general elections, winning 16 of the 29 seats.

In the August 1998 general elections the party slumped to only three seats, although taking 39.1% of the vote. Having lost his own seat, Esquivel resigned as party leader and was succeeded by Dean Barrow as interim party leader. At the party's national convention in October 1999, Barrow was unanimously elected as leader of the party.

The UDP is affiliated to the Caribbean Democrat Union.

Other party

National Alliance for Belizean Rights (NABR), founded in February 1992 by former →United Democratic Party (UDP) members disaffected by maritime concessions to Guatemala (resulting in the conclusion of a non-aggression pact between the two countries in April 1993). Although a splinter group of the UDP, the NABR campaigned with the parent party in the 1993 elections and was subsequently included in the UDP government. It is not currently represented in the House of Representatives but participates in the National Advisory Commission (NAC) set up by the government in March 2000 to coordinate a united national front in the face of Guatemala's revival of its territorial claims.

Benin

Capital: Porto Novo

Population: 6,400,000 (2000E)

Benin achieved independence from France in 1960 as Dahomey, was renamed the People's Republic of Benin in 1972 and became the Republic of Benin in 1990. The People's Republic was proclaimed following a military coup led by Mathieu Kérékou, who installed a Marxist–Leninist regime with the People's Revolutionary Party of Benin (PRPB) as the sole ruling party. The Republic of Benin was proclaimed under new constitutional arrangements approved by referendum on Dec. 2, 1990, and providing for multi-party democracy (the PRPB having dissolved itself in April). The executive President, who appoints the Council of Ministers, is directly elected for a five-year term. Legislative authority is vested in a unicameral National Assembly (Assemblée Nationale) of 83 members, which is elected for a four-year term according to a department-based system of proportional representation and which may not be dissolved by the President.

Presidential elections held in 1991 were won by Nicéphore Soglo (backed by a coalition of parties), who defeated Gen. Kérékou (standing without party attribution). The following year President Soglo became identified with the new Benin Renaissance Party (PRB). Elections to the National Assembly in March and May 1995 resulted in the PRB and its allies becoming the largest bloc with 28 seats, although the other 55 seats went to nine anti-Soglo parties. In subsequent presidential elections in March 1996, President Soglo was defeated in the second round by Kérékou.

In further legislative elections on March 30 1999, the PRB won 27 seats, the Party of Democratic Renewal (PRD) 11, the Action Front for Renewal and Development (FARD-Alafia) 10, the Social Democratic Party (PSD) 9 and the African Movement for Democracy and Progress (MADEP) 6. Eleven other parties won 20 seats between them. Presidential elections on March 4 and 22, 2001, were contested by 17 candidates. In the second round, boycotted by second-placed Soglo and third-placed Adrien Houngbedji (of the PRD) amid claims of election irregularities, Kérékou was re-elected with 84% of the vote.

Action Front for Renewal and Development
Front d'Action pour le Renouveau et le Développement (FARD-Alafia)
Address. BP 925 Cotonou
Leadership. Jérôme Sacca Kina
Proclaiming itself to be a party of national unity on its foundation in 1994 by five opposition deputies, the FARD-Alafia formed part of the anti-Soglo group of parties in the 1995 Assembly elections, in which it won 14 seats. In the legislative elections in March 1999, the party lost four of its seats but remained the third largest group in the Assembly.

Benin Renaissance Party
Parti de la Renaissance du Bénin (PRB)
Address. BP 2205 Cotonou
Leadership. Nicéphore Soglo (president); Rosine Soglo
The formation of the PRB was announced in March 1992 by President Soglo's wife, Rosine Soglo, and was intended as a new political base for the President, who had been elected in March 1991 with the backing of the Union for the Triumph of Democratic Renewal (*Union pour la Triomphe du Renouveau Démocratique*, UTRD). A former World Bank official, Soglo had been named Prime Minister in February 1990 by a National Conference charged with establishing a new political structure for Benin. After heading the first-round balloting in the subsequent presidential contest, Soglo had secured a decisive 68% advantage over President Kérékou in the second, thus becoming the first successful challenger to an incumbent head of state in black continental Africa.

The three component parties of the UTRD were the Democratic Union of Progressive Forces (UDFP) led by Timothée Adanlin, the Movement for Democracy and Social Progress (MDPS) led by Joseph Marcelin Degbe and the Union for Freedom and Development (ULD) led by Marius Francisco. In the February 1991 Assembly elections the UTRD had become the largest grouping with 12 of the then 64 seats, the UTRD contingent forming the nucleus of the broader Renewal (*Renouveau*) Group which by mid-1992 numbered 34 deputies and thus gave the government a working majority. In July 1993 President Soglo effectively assumed the leadership of the PRB, saying that he would "come down into the political arena" and promote the new party as a "catalyst" for the country's emerging democracy. His decision contributed to strains within the presidential coalition in the Assembly, where 15 members of the Renewal Group defected in October 1993, claiming that they had been "marginalized" by the President. Later the same month, however, 11 pro-Soglo parties and associations, including the UTRD rump (but not the PRB), formed the African Rally for Progress and Solidarity (RAPS), thus restoring the government's Assembly majority.

Further strains were apparent in September 1994, when President Soglo declared his intention to introduce the latest budget by decree, thus ignoring parliamentary opposition to the measure. In October 1994 the PRB absorbed the small Pan-African Union for Democracy and Solidarity (*Union Panafricaine pour la Démocratie et la Solidarité*, UPDS). But presidential efforts to elevate the PRB into the dominant party were confounded by voters in the 1995 Assembly elections, in which the PRB won only 21 of the 83 seats (and its allies a further seven), while anti-Soglo parties aggregated 55 seats. In July 1995 the PRB was formally joined by a majority of the RAPS leadership.

In that he also held French citizenship, Soglo's quest for a second term in the 1996 presidential elections appeared at first to be ruled out by the passage in September 1995 of a law barring anyone with dual nationality from standing. In the event, he entered the contest in March 1996 and was unexpectedly defeated in the second round by the resurrected Gen. Kérékou, who had retained powerful support in the state bureaucracy. Having at first complained of electoral fraud, Soglo accepted the voters' verdict on April 2.

In legislative elections in March 1999, the PRB increased its representation to 27 seats, so remaining the largest single party in the Assembly. Soglo stood again for the presidency in elections in March 2001, gaining 29% of the votes to Gen. Kérékou's 47% in the first round. However, he boycotted the second round (as did the third-placed →Party of Democratic Renewal candidate), claiming that there had been electoral irregularities, although his allegations were not upheld by the Constitutional Court.

Party of Democratic Renewal
Parti du Renouveau Démocratique (PRD)
Address. c/o Assemblée Nationale, BP 371, Porto Novo
Leadership. Adrien Houngbedji
Website: www.prd-bj.net
The PRD contested the February 1991 Assembly elections in an alliance with the National Party for Democracy and Development which came in second place, although together they won only nine of the 64 seats. Party leader Adrien Houngbedji was subsequently elected president of the National Assembly, despite not having the backing of the then President Soglo. In the 1995 Assembly elections the PRD headed the victorious group of anti-Soglo parties, winning 18 of the 83 seats in its own right. In that he also held French citizenship, Houngbedji's candidacy for the 1996 presidential election appeared to be blocked by the passage of a law in September 1995 banning anyone with dual nationality from standing for the presidency. However, he did stand, taking third place with 17% of the vote in the first round on March 3 and subsequently announcing his support for Gen. Kérékou in the second.

In the March 1999 legislative elections, the PRD emerged as the second largest party again, but with a lower tally of 11 seats. Houngbedji contested the first round of the March 2001 presidential poll, winning 12% of the vote. But he refused to enter the second round run-off against Gen. Kérékou following the withdrawal of Soglo, the second-placed candidate, on the grounds of electoral irregularities.

Social Democratic Party
Parti Social–Démocrate (PSD)
Address. BP 04–0772 Cotonou
Leadership. Bruno Amoussou
The PSD was formed on the introduction of multi-partyism in 1990 and presented candidates in the November 1990 local elections. It contested the February 1991 Assembly elections in alliance with the National Union for Solidarity and Progress, registering a joint tally of eight of the 64 seats. It retained eight seats in the 1995 elections (out of 83), forming part of the victorious group of anti-Soglo parties. In the 1999 legislative poll, the PSD increased its representation to nine seats. Despite having come only fourth in the first ballot of the March 2001 presidential elections (mirroring his performance in the 1996 poll), party leader Amoussou contested the second round run-off against Gen. Kérékou following the withdrawal of the second- and third-placed candidates amid allegations of electoral irregularities. However, he gained only 16% of the vote.

The PSD is affiliated to the Socialist International as a consultative member.

Other Parties

African Congress for Renewal (*Congrès Africain pour le Renouveau, CAR-DUNYA*), won three seats in the 1999 Assembly elections.
Leadership. Albert Sina Toko

African Movement for Democracy and Progress (*Mouvement Africain pour la Démocratie et le Progrès, MADEP*), registered in December 1997, won six seats in the 1999 Assembly elections.
Leadership. Séfou Fagbohoun

Alliance SURU, four-party coalition of *Union pour la Patrie et le Progrès* (UPP), *La Démocratie et la Moralité (FDDM), Forum National pour l'Éveil Civil et Civique (FONEC)* and *Union pour la Démocratie et la Reconstruction Nationale (UDRN)*; won one seat in the 1999 Assembly elections.
Leadership. Guiriguissou Gaso

Communist Party of Benin (*Parti Communiste de Benin, PCB*), granted legal registration in September 1993, being the successor to the Dahomey Communist Party (PCD) founded in 1977 in opposition to the brand of Marxism–Leninism propagated by Kérékou regime. The PCD had boycotted the 1990 negotiations on transition to multi-partyism, most of its leaders remaining in exile. By 1993, however, many had returned to Benin and, undeterred by the demise of communism elsewhere in the world, had reconstituted the party under the PCB rubric. The party won one seat in the 1995 Assembly elections, on a platform of opposition to President Soglo, but ceased to be represented in 1999.
Address. BP 2582 Cotonou
Leadership. Pascal Fantondji (first secretary)

Democratic Party of Benin (*Parti Démocratique du Bénin, PDB*), registered in October 1996, secured one seat in the 1999 Assembly elections.
Address. BP 407 Cotonou
Leadership. Soule Dankoro

Impulse for Progress and Democracy (*Impulsion pour le Progrès et la Démocratie, IPD*), won two Assembly seats in 1995 as part of the anti-Soglo opposition, increasing its representation (as Alliance IPD) to four seats in March 1999.

Movement for Citizens' Commitment and Awakening (*Mouvement pour l'Engagement et le Réveil des Citoyens, MERCI*), registered prior to the 1999 legislative elections, in which it won two seats.

National Together Party (*Parti National Ensemble*), gained one Assembly seat in the 1999 elections.

Party of Salvation (*Parti du Salut, PdS*), won one seat in the 1999 Assembly elections.
Leadership. Damien Alahassa

Rally for Democracy and Panafricanism (*Rassemblement pour la Démocratie et le Panafricanisme, RDP*), founded in mid-1994 by a faction of the Pan-African Union of Democracy and Solidarity that opposed the latter's merger with the →Benin Renaissance Party. It won one seat in the 1999 Assembly elections.
Address. BP 03–4073 Cotonou
Leadership. Dominique Houngninou

Rally for National Unity and Democracy (*Rassemblement pour l'Unité Nationale et la Démocratie, RUND*), registered in early 1995, gained one seat in the 1999 Assembly elections.
Leadership. Idrissou Ibrahima

Star Alliance (*Alliance Étoile*), won four seats in the 1999 Assembly elections.

Bhutan

Capital: Thimphu   **Population:** 2,000,000 (2000E)

The Kingdom of Bhutan is an hereditary monarchy in which power is shared between the King (assisted by a Royal Advisory Council), the Council of Ministers, the National Assembly and the monastic head of Bhutan's Buddhist priesthood. The Council of Ministers is appointed by the King and may be dismissed by him with the consent of the National Assembly, which was established in 1953 as the principal legislative body. The unicameral National Assembly has 154 members, of whom 105 are directly elected on a non-partisan basis, 12 represent religious bodies, and 37 are appointed by the King to represent various interests. There are no legal political parties, with opposition to the government primarily based in ethnic Nepali groups exiled in Nepal or India, including the Druk National Congress (DNC).

Bolivia

Capital: La Paz   **Population:** 8,328,000 (2000E)

Bolivia claimed independence from Spain in 1825 and its first constitution was written in November 1826. From World War II until the 1990s the leading political formation was the Nationalist Revolutionary Movement (MNR) under its veteran leader, Victor Paz Estenssoro, who first came to power in the popular revolution of 1952. Bolivia was subsequently under the rule of military juntas almost continuously between 1964 and 1982, when it was returned to civilian rule under President Hernán Siles Zuazo.

The present constitution dates from 1947 and was revived after a coup in 1964. Executive power is vested in the President, who appoints the Cabinet, the nine departmental prefects and the country's diplomatic representatives, and nominates archbishops and bishops. The bicameral Congress comprises a 27-seat Senate and a 130-seat Chamber of Deputies. The President is elected by direct suffrage for a four-year term and is not eligible to serve two consecutive terms. If no candidate emerges from the election with an absolute majority the newly-elected Congress appoints a President. Senators (three for each of the nine provinces) and deputies are elected by proportional representation, also for a four-year term. There has been universal suffrage in Bolivia since the 1952 popular uprising and voting is compulsory.

Bolivia has a highly fragmented party system characterized by frequent splits, personalism and populism. In the first round of the 1997 presidential elections, no candidate received a majority of the popular vote. Gen. (retd.) Hugo Bánzer Suárez of the Nationalist Democratic Action (ADN) won a congressional run-off vote on Aug. 5, 1997, after forming a "mega-coalition" with the Movement of the Revolutionary Left (MIR), Civic Solidarity Union (UCS), Conscience of the Fatherland (Condepa), New Republican Force (NFR) and the Christian Democratic Party (PDC). In concurrent congressional elections, the ADN-led coalition won an overwhelming majority in both the Chamber of Deputies and the Senate. President Bánzer resigned because of illness in August 2001 and was succeeded by Vice-President Jorge Fernando Quiroga Ramírez.

Bolivian Communist Party
Partido Comunista de Bolivia (PCB)
Address. c/o Camara de Diputados, La Paz
Leadership. Marcos Domic (secretary-general)
Founded in 1950 by dissident members of the Party of the Revolutionary Left (PIR) youth section, the PCB attained legal status after the 1952 revolution. Its line was orthodox communist before the collapse of the Soviet Union, since when internal disputes have plagued the party.

The party at first supported the government of the →Nationalist Revolutionary Movement (MNR) but soon became critical of its effective one-party rule and stood against it in the general elections of 1956, in alliance with the PIR, winning only 1.5% of the vote. In 1960, when the PCB contested an election by itself for the only time in its history, the party found support among only 1% of the voters. In 1965 the PCB split into pro-Soviet and pro-Chinese factions and both were banned in 1967 even though their involvement with the guerrillas of Che Guevara's National Liberation Army, then attempting to ignite a domestic revolution, was limited to some pro-Soviet PCB

youth section members who were subsequently expelled. Although the ban was later lifted, the PCB was again driven underground during the Bánzer military regime of 1971 to 1978.

Under new leadership, the PCB fought the 1985 general elections in the United People's Front alliance with the Revolutionary Party of the National Left (PRIN) and two dissident factions of the →Movement of the Revolutionary Left (MIR), which won four congressional seats. In September 1988 it became a founder member of the →United Left (IU), within which it has contested subsequent elections.

Christian Democratic Party
Partido Demócrata Cristiano (PDC)
Address. Casilla 4345, La Paz
Telephone. (+591–2) 32–1918
Fax. (+591–2) 32–8475
Leadership. Benjamín Miguel Harb (president); José Roberto Castro (secretary-general)
The PDC is a centre-left Roman Catholic grouping that was

founded by Remo di Natale in 1954 as the Social Christian Party, taking its present name at its 1964 congress.

In the 1962 partial elections PDC leader Benjamin Miguel obtained the party's first congressional seat. Although it boycotted the 1966 general elections called by the military junta, the following year the PDC accepted the labour portfolio, which it resigned when President René Barrientos sent in the army to quell protesting miners. The PDC opposed all subsequent military regimes, which eventually led to the exile of both Miguel and the party's organizing secretary, Felix Vargas, from 1974 until 1978. In the 1979 elections the PDC, in an alliance with the →Nationalist Revolutionary Movement (MNR) and three minor parties, won nine seats in the Chamber of Deputies and three in the Senate. It was given a cabinet post after democracy was restored in October 1982.

In the 1985 elections the PDC's presidential candidate, Luis Ossio Sanjines, won only 1.4% of the vote, while the party's representation in Congress dwindled to three seats. In the run-up to the May 1989 elections, the PDC tried to negotiate an alliance with the left-wing →Movement of the Revolutionary Left (MIR). When the talks broke down in January 1989, it agreed to join forces with the right-wing →Nationalist Democratic Action (ADN), Ossio Sanjines becoming Gen. Hugo Bánzer's running-mate in his successful candidacy in the May 1989 presidential elections. In August 1989 Ossio Sanjines accordingly became Vice-President of the new Patriotic Accord (AP) coalition government.

Having contested the 1993 elections within the AP, in 1997 the PDC campaigned as a member of the "mega-coalition" which supported Bánzer's successful presidential candidacy, but failed to win any congressional seats.

The PDC is an affiliate of the Christian Democrat International and of the Christian Democrat Organization of America (ODCA).

Civic Solidarity Union
Union Civica Solidaridad (UCS)
Address. Calle Mercado 1064, La Paz
Telephone. (+591–2) 36–0297
Fax. (+591–2) 37–2200
Leadership. Max (Johnny) Fernández Rojas
An offshoot of the National Civic Union (Union Civica Nacional, UCN), the UCS was founded in 1988 as a vehicle for the presidential campaign of Max Fernández Rojas. He won a surprising third place in the May 1989 election with 22.8% of the vote but his candidacy was subsequently nullified by the Electoral Court after he was found to have forged 40,000 of the 60,000 votes he received. He nevertheless announced his candidature for the 1993 presidential elections, in which he polled 13.1% of the votes cast.

Following the 1993 elections, in which Gonzalo Sánchez de Lozada of the →Nationalist Revolutionary Movement (MNR) won the presidency, the UCS, with 21 seats in the Chamber of Deputies, was invited to be one of three parties in a new government coalition with the MNR and the →Free Bolivia Movement (MBL). In the 1997 presidential election the party ran its own candidate, Ivo Kuljis, who obtained 16% of the votes cast. In the concurrent congressional elections the party again won 21 seats in the Chamber and increased its representation from one to two in the Senate. It thereafter formed part of a coalition government headed by →Nationalist Democratic Action (ADN).

Kuljis subsequently left the party to form the Unity and Progress Movement (MUP). The party unsuccessfully contested the mayoralty of La Paz in 1999 with Moisés Jarmusz as its candidate.

Conscience of the Fatherland
Conciencia de Patria (Condepa)
Address. c/o Camara de Diputados, La Paz
Leadership. Remedios Loza (president)
The centre-left Condepa was founded in 1988 by a well-

known singer and broadcaster, Carlos Palenque. In the May 1989 general elections, Condepa won nine seats in the Chamber of Deputies and two in the Senate. During the presidential run-off in the Congress in August, the party threw its support behind Jaime Paz Zamora, candidate of the →Movement of the Revolutionary Left (MIR), but the party remained in opposition to the subsequent Patriotic Accord (AP) government. In the municipal elections of December 1991, Condepa candidate Julio Mantilla Cuellar was elected mayor of La Paz with 26.4% of the vote, and the party also won the major neighbouring city of El Alto with 34% of the vote, the results representing the party's most significant achievement to date. Mantilla pledged to use his office to bring justice to the poorest sectors of the population.

Condepa was placed fourth in the 1993 legislative balloting, winning 14 seats overall. Palenque died in March 1997 and was succeeded as Condepa leader by Remedios Loza, who in June 1997 became the first female Indian to run for the presidency, winning 16% of the vote. As a member of the "mega-coalition" led by Gen. (retd.) Hugo Bánzer Suárez of the →Nationalist Democratic Action (ADN), Condepa increased its strength to 17 seats in the Chamber of Deputies and won three in the Senate. The party was included in the resultant ruling coalition headed by the ADN, but was dropped from the government in August 1998 because of its internal divisions. The Condepa candidate, Jorge Dockweiler, polled 5.4% of the votes for the mayoralty of La Paz in 1999.

Free Bolivia Movement
Movimiento Bolivia Libre (MBL)
Address. Edificio Camiri, Oficina 201, Calle Comercio 972 esq., Yamacocha Casilla 10382, La Paz
Telephone. (+591–2) 34–0257
Fax. (+591–2) 39–2242
Website. www.bolivian.com/mbl
Leadership. Antonio Aranibar Quiroga (president)
This nominally left-wing party was founded in 1985 by the then secretary-general of the main →Movement of the Revolutionary Left (MIR), Antonio Aranibar Quiroga, after he and a left-wing section of the MIR split away in protest against participation in the government of Hernán Siles Zuazo of the →Leftist Nationalist Revolutionary Movement (MNRI). Aranibar fought the 1985 election as the presidential candidate of the left-wing People's United Front alliance and won 2.2% of the vote, while the alliance obtained four seats in Congress.

The municipal elections of 1987 showed an increase in the MBL's support, the party winning in Bolivia's legal capital Sucre and coming second in Cochabamba. In 1988 its electoral success brought the MBL to the leadership of the newly-formed →United Left (IU), as whose candidate Aranibar contested the May 1989 presidential elections but won a negligible percentage of the vote. In February 1990 the MBL left the IU alliance and was subsequently prominent in protracted opposition dialogue with the Patriotic Accord (AP) government over such issues as the independence of the Supreme Court and the establishment of a new electoral system presided over by a impartial electoral court.

In the 1993 presidential election Aranibar polled 5.1% of the vote and his party won seven seats in the Chamber of Deputies. In the June 1997 elections, the MBL's representation fell to four seats. It currently has no Senate seats and its candidate, Hernán Zenteno, gained only just over 1% of the votes in municipal elections in La Paz in 1999.

Movement of the Revolutionary Left
Movimiento de la Izquierda Revolucionaria (MIR)
Address. Calle Ingavi 600, Casilla de Correo 7397, La Paz
Telephone. (+591–2) 31–0416
Fax. (+591–2) 40–6455
Email. mir@ceibo.entelnet.bo
Website. www.cibergallo.com
Leadership. Jaime Paz Zamora (president)

Founded in 1971, the MIR professes to be left-wing but in power has usually proved to be conservative. Having its main power base in the liberal urban middle class, the party was formed in opposition to the 1971 military coup as a merger of small left-wing groups and young Christian democrats. It drew considerable support from the radical student movement and was linked to the insurgent National Liberation Army (ELN) in the early years of the military dictatorship of Gen. Hugo Bánzer Suárez (1971–78).

The MIR gradually moved away from its Marxist roots but nevertheless remained in strong opposition to the military regime, which continued to persecute and imprison members of the party, among them Bánzer's future political ally, Jaime Paz Zamora. The party contested the elections of 1978, 1979 and 1980 as part of an alliance led by the Leftist Nationalist Revolutionary Movement (MNRI) with Paz Zamora as running-mate of the victorious but ill-fated MNRI leader, Hernán Siles Zuazo, in 1979 and 1980.

Paz Zamora came third with 8.8% of the vote in the July 1985 presidential contest and in the simultaneous congressional elections the depleted MIR won 16 seats. When Congress had to vote in the second round of the presidential elections, the MIR joined with other centre-left parties in electing the presidential runner-up, Victor Paz Estenssoro of the →Nationalist Revolutionary Movement (MNR) in preference to ex-dictator Bánzer.

Having failed to form an alliance with the →Christian Democratic Party, the MIR contested the May 1989 elections alone, winning 41 congressional seats. In the presidential race Paz Zamora was placed a close third with 19.6% of the vote. In the absence of a conclusive winner, the runner-up, Gen. Bánzer, withdrew and switched the 46 congressional votes of the →Nationalist Democratic Action (ADN) to Paz Zamora, who in August was duly elected President by Congress. The price exacted for this support was the necessity for the MIR to share power with the ADN in the Patriotic Accord (AP). In an August 1991 major cabinet reshuffle, three MIR ministerial posts were allocated to members of the MIR-New Majority (MIR–NM) faction, which, due to the domination of the ADN, had previously been circumspect in its support for the MIR's involvement in the AP coalition. In March 1992, however, the MIR–NM confirmed its support for Bánzer as AP candidate in the 1993 presidential elections.

After persistent criticism of his presidency, Paz Zamora entered into "permanent" retirement in March 1994, but returned less than eight months later following the arrest on drugs charges of the party's secretary-general, Oscar Eid Franco. In the June 1997 presidential elections Paz Zamora came third with 16.7% of the votes cast and his party won 25 seats in the Chamber and six in the Senate. The party was included in the resultant ruling coalition government headed by the ADN. The MIR candidate, Jorge Torres, obtained 15.9% of the votes in municipal elections in La Paz in 1999, by which time the party was officially calling itself the MIR–NM.

The party is a member of the Socialist International.

Nationalist Democratic Action
Accion Democrática Nacionalista (ADN)
Address. c/o Camara de Diputados, La Paz
Website. www.bolivian.com/adn
Leadership. Jorge Fernando Quiroga Ramírez (President of the Republic); Ronald Maclean (2002 presidential candidate)
The ADN was formed as a vehicle for former dictator Gen. (retd.) Hugo Bánzer Suárez (1971–78) for the July 1979 general elections, in which he came third with 14.9% of the vote. In the 1980 general election his share of the vote increased slightly to 16.9% and the ADN won 30 congressional seats, which were finally taken up when Congress was recalled in September 1982. The ADN initially supported the July 1980 coup led by Gen. Luis Garcia Meza, but in April 1981 this backing was withdrawn. A month later Bánzer was arrested on a charge of plotting a counter-coup.

The general elections of July 1985 resulted in Bánzer winning the largest share of the vote (28.6%) in the presidential contest, while the ADN obtained 51 seats in Congress. However, because no presidential candidate had obtained a clear majority, a centre-left alliance in Congress elected Victor Paz Estenssoro of the →Nationalist Revolutionary Movement (MNR) as President. For the May 1989 elections the ADN entered into an alliance with the →Christian Democratic Party (PDC). Bánzer, the alliance's joint candidate, won 22.7% of the vote in the presidential contest and was narrowly outpolled for second place by the MNR candidate, Gonzalo Sánchez de Lozada. Personal dislike between the two candidates precluded an ADN–MNR pact and ensured that neither was elected President by Congress, which opted for Jaime Paz Zamora of the →Movement of the Revolutionary Left (MIR). The resultant Patriotic Accord (AP) coalition government led by the ADN and the MIR assumed power in August 1989. In return for the presidency, Jaime Paz Zamora awarded the ADN 10 out of 18 ministerial posts, including the most important portfolios of finance, defence and foreign affairs. Bánzer personally took the chairmanship of the Political Council of Convergence and National Unity, a post which gave him effective control over government policy.

In March 1992 MIR leaders ratified Bánzer as the AP's 1993 presidential candidate. However, although the AP secured 43 seats in the Chamber of Deputies and eight in the Senate, Bánzer himself could only manage second place in the presidential elections, victory going to Sánchez de Lozada of the MNR. The AP was consequently dissolved in August 1993, with Bánzer resigning as ADN leader in November. In February 1995, however, Bánzer changed his mind, returning to leadership of the ADN.

In August 1997 Bánzer again became President, having headed the popular polling in June with 22.3% of the vote and securing election in a congressional vote with the support of an ADN-headed "mega-coalition" which included the MIR, →Conscience of the Fatherland (Condepa) and the →Civic Solidarity Union. In the June 1997 congressional elections the ADN headed the poll, winning 33 Chamber seats and 13 in the Senate. The party was therefore dominant in the resultant coalition government.

In August 2001, announcing that he was suffering from cancer, Bánzer resigned both the state presidency and the party leadership.

The ADN is an associate member of the International Democrat Union.

Nationalist Revolutionary Movement
Movimiento Nacionalista Revolucionario (MNR)
Address. Jenaro Sanjines 541, Pasaje Kuljis, La Paz
Telephone. (+591–2) 37–8295
Website. www.bolivian.com/mnr
Leadership. Gonzalo Sánchez de Lozada (former President of the Republic)
The right-wing MNR was founded in 1941 and over the decades has ha spawned various factions with suffixes in their title, reflecting internal party divisions. Most recently, the main party current was known as the Historic Nationalist Revolutionary Movement (MNHR). The MNR's founders included Victor Paz Estenssoro, the left-wing Hernán Siles Zuazo and the fascist sympathizer Carlos Montenegro. The party's original policies reflected Paz Estenssoro's World War II attempt to combine the nationalist developmentalist ideas of the →→American Popular Revolutionary Alliance Party (APRA) of Peru with those of European fascism, as enunciated by Italian dictator Benito Mussolini. The MNR first participated in government in 1943-33 under President Gualberto Villaroel.

When the military overthrew Villaroel in 1946, numerous MNR leaders were killed or exiled. Paz Estenssoro fought the 1951 elections from exile as the MNR's presidential candidate and won the highest vote, although not an outright majority. The incumbent President handed power to a military junta which, less than a year later, was toppled by an MNR-led popular uprising, known thereafter as the 1952 Revolution, assisted by the police and tin miners. Paz Estenssoro was allowed to return from Argentina and was appointed President in April 1952.

Paz Estenssoro's coalition government with the Labour Party introduced a number of progressive reforms, including the nationalization of the mines, agrarian reform and the enfranchisement of illiterates. The MNR remained in power for two more terms, with Siles Zuazo taking the presidency in 1956 and Paz Estenssoro being elected President again in 1960.

In November 1964, following widespread strikes and disorder, Paz Estenssoro was overthrown and forced into exile by his Vice-President, Air Force Gen. René Barrientos Ortuño, who took power with the assistance of the army. The MNR was thrown into disarray and only re-emerged onto the political scene in 1971 as supporters of the military coup of Gen. Hugo Bánzer Suárez (→Nationalist Democratic Action, ADN).

The MNR participated in Bánzer's government until 1974, when it was expelled for protesting that the promised process of democratization had not begun. By then, the left wing of the party, led by Siles Zuazo, had broken away and formed the →Leftist Nationalist Revolutionary Movement (MNRI), to which Paz Estenssoro's faction, the MNRH, came second in the 1979 and 1980 presidential elections. Paz Estenssoro was beaten by Siles in both elections, winning 35.9% and 20.1% of the vote respectively. The MNRH, however, won 44 seats in the Congress in 1979.

Following another period of military government (1980-82) and three years of opposition to an MNRI government, Paz Estenssoro once again made a bid for the presidency. In the June 1985 elections he obtained 26.4% of the vote, 2.2% less than Bánzer of the ADN. However, in a run-off congressional vote in August 1985, the centre-left parties added their votes to those of the 59 MNRH congressmen and brought Paz Estenssoro to power again. He quickly introduced a strict austerity programme to reduce rampant inflation, a policy persisted with despite the collapse of the international tin market in late 1985.

Faced with general labour unrest, Paz Estenssoro found greater common ground with the right-wing ADN than with his erstwhile supporters of the centre-left. A "pact for democracy" between the MNRH and the ADN was duly signed in October 1985. In the municipal elections of December 1987 the MNRH polled poorly, amid widespread discontent with the government. This was further fuelled by the US-assisted anti-drug programme, which threatened the livelihood of many peasant coca growers, whose numbers had been swollen by unemployed miners. Nevertheless, in the May 1989 general elections the MNRH presidential candidate, Gonzalo Sánchez de Lozada (former Minister of Planning), headed the popular poll with 23.1% of the vote. A run-off election in the newly-elected Congress, in which the MNRH had 49 seats, did not produce a renewal of the pact with the ADN. Personal animosity between Sánchez de Lozada and ADN leader Bánzer resulted in the ADN switching its support to Jaime Paz Zamora of the →Movement of the Revolutionary Left (MIR), who was elected President.

Three months after the election of Paz Zamora as President, the 84-year-old Paz Estenssoro announced his desire to resign the MNR leadership. At the next party congress in mid-1990 the decision was formalized and Sánchez de Lozada was elected as his successor, although in 1992 he briefly stood down following a death threat from an MNR congressional deputy. In the June 1993 elections Sánchez de Lozada again defeated Bánzer, winning 33.8% of the popular vote and this time obtained congressional endorsement as President, with Víctor Hugo Cárdenas Conde of the →Tupaj Katari Revolutionary Movement–Liberation

(MRTK-L) becoming Vice-President. In the simultaneous legislative balloting the MNR/MRTK-L alliance raised its representation to 69 out of 157 seats, thus confirming the MNR's status as the dominant ruling party.

In the June 1997 presidential elections, the MNR candidate, Juan Carlos Durán Saucedo, came a poor second, winning only 17.7% of the vote, while in the concurrent congressional elections the party's representation was cut to 26 seats in the Chamber of Deputies and three in the Senate. The MNR's Guido Capra came second with 16% of the votes cast for the mayoralty of La Paz in 1999, whereas Percy Fernandez of the MNR was an easy winner in Santa Cruz de la Sierra. Paz Estenssoro died in June 2001 at the age of 93.

Tupaj Katari Revolutionary Movement–Liberation
Movimiento Revolucionario Tupaj Katari–Liberación
(MRTK-L)

Address. 939 Avda. Baptista, Casilla 9133, La Paz
Telephone. (+591–2) 35–4784
Leadership. Victor Hugo Cárdenas Conde (president); Norberto Pérez Hidalgo (secretary general)

A splinter group of the mainly Amerindian Tupaj Katari Revolutionary Movement (MRTK), the MRTK-L outpolled its weak parent party in 1985, winning two congressional seats, both of which were subsequently lost in 1989. In the June 1993 presidential elections the MRTK-L leader, Victor Cárdenas, was the running-mate of Gonzalo Sánchez de Lozada of the →Nationalist Revolutionary Movement (MNR), which was seeking to broaden its popular appeal. They were successful and the party has since then run in alliance with the MNR.

United Left
Izquierda Unida (IU)

Address. c/o Camara de Diputados, La Paz
Leadership. Marcos Domic (→Bolivian Communist Party)

The IU alliance was formed for the 1989 elections following the demise of the previous leftist coalition, the United People's Front (*Frente del Pueblo Unido,* FPU). The IU fielded the →Free Bolivia Movement (MBL) leader, Antonio Aranibar Quiroga, as its presidential candidate with Walter Delgadillo of the Patriotic Alliance (AP) as his running mate. The IU won 12 congressional seats, a poor result compared with that achieved by its component parties in the 1985 elections, as Aranibar won a negligible percentage of the total vote. In the municipal elections of December 1989 the IU maintained the MBL's hold on power in the judicial capital, Sucre. Two months later, however, the MBL left the alliance, leaving it in a state of disarray.

The IU put forward Ramiro Velasco of the Socialist Party-One as its presidential candidate in the 1993 election, at which it polled less than 1% of the vote and lost all 10 of its legislative seats. In 1997 it supported the successful presidential candidature of Hugo Bánzer of the →Nationalist Democratic Action (ADN) and won four seats in the Chamber of Deputies.

Other Parties

April 9 Revolutionary Vanguard (*Vanguardia Revolucionaria 9 de Abril, VR-9*), obtained 17% of the vote in municipal elections in Sucre in 1999.
Address. Avda. 6 de Agosto 2170, Casilla 5810, La Paz
Telephone. (+591–2) 32–0311
Fax. (+591–2) 39–1439
Leadership. Dr Carlos Serrate Reich (president)

Assembly for the Peoples' Sovereignty (*Asamblea por la Soberania de los Pueblos, ASP*), leftist nationalist party which contested 1997 elections as part of the →United Left (IU).
Leadership. Evo Morales

Left Revolutionary Front (*Frente Revolucionario de Izquierda, FRI*), formed by a splinter group of the →Movement of the Revolutionary Left (MIR) prior to the 1985 elections, in which it was allied with the →Nationalist Revolutionary Movement (MNR), gaining the Senate presidency for then leader Oscar Zamora Medinacelli. He achieved similar success in 1989 by backing the MIR–ADN coalition which yielded him the job of labour minister in the government of his nephew, Jaime Paz Zamora. In August 1991, the FRI joined the Patriotic Accord government and he re-obtained the Labour portfolio in an August 1991 reshuffle. This post he resigned in 1992 to accept the vice-presidential position in the unsuccessful presidential campaign ticket of the ADN's Hugo Bánzer, the former military dictator. The party contested the 1997 elections as part of the →United Left (IU).
Leadership. Mónica Medina (president)

Leftist Nationalist Revolutionary Movement (*Movimiento Nacionalista Revolucionario de Izquierda, MNRI*), founded after the left wing of the →Nationalist Revolutionary Movement (MNR) split away in the early 1970s. Led by MNR founding member and former President (1956–60) Hernán Siles Zuazo, the MNRI was the leading force of the Popular Democratic Unity (UDP) alliance in the 1978 elections. Siles Zuazo won both the 1979 and the 1980 presidential elections with 36% and 38.7% of the vote, but each time was prevented from taking power by a military coup. In October 1982 he was finally allowed to return from his Peruvian exile and take office. His UDP government rapidly lost support from the left, the unions and the peasantry as it failed to implement social reforms. The 1985 elections resulted in the heavy defeat of the MNRI presidential candidate, Roberto Jordan Pando, who received a mere 4.8% of the vote, with the party obtaining only eight seats in the Congress. The MNRI proceeded to split into a number of factions, including the centre-right *Movimiento Nacionalista Revolucionario–Vanguardia Revolucionaria 9 de Abril* (MNR-V) and the Leftist Nationalist Revolutionist Movement–One (MNRI-l), each of which subsequently campaigned separately with little electoral success.

National Leftist Revolutionary Party (*Partido Revolucionario de Izquierda Nacionalista, PRIN*), founded in 1964 as a splinter from the →Nationalist Revolutionary Movement (MNR), representing the Miners' Federation (FSTMB) and the Bolivian Workers' Federation (COB). It currently has no seats in Congress.
Address. Calle Colón 693, La Paz
Leadership. Juan Lechín Oquendo (president)

Nationalist Katarista Movement (*Movimiento Katarista Nacionalista, MKN*), emerged among the Aymara Indians in the early 1970s. Indigenist and pluri-national, it was named in memory of Tupaj Katari, an Aymara leader who led an anti-colonial uprising in 1781. The MKN is the present name of the rump of the Tupaj Katari Revolutionary Movement (*Movimiento Revolucionario Tupaj Katari,*

MRTK*)*, following the secession of the →Tupaj Katari Revolutionary Movement–Liberation (MRTK-L) in 1985. It polled 12,627 votes in the 1993 legislative elections but won no seats. Other factions include the Front of Katarista Unity (FULKA) led by Genaro Flores and Katarismo National Unity (KND) led by Felipe Kittelson.
Leadership. Fernando Untoja

New Bolivia Nationalist Front (*Frente Nacionalista Nueva Bolivia, FNNB*), founded in May 2001 by prominent businessman Nicolas Valdivia Almanza to support his intended candidacy in the 2002 presidential elections.
Leadership. Nicolas Valdivia Almanza (president)

New Republican Force (*Nueva Fuerza Republicana, NFR*), supported the successful candidacy of Gen. Hugo Bánzer of the →Nationalist Democratic Action (ADN) in the 1997 presidential elections; holds no seats in Congress and in the 1999 municipal elections its candidate for mayor of La Paz, Gregorio Lanza, obtained only 1.4% of the vote. The party was expelled from the government coalition in February 2000 when leader Reyes Villa opposed an increase in water rates in Cochabamba, where he was mayor.
Leadership. Manfred Reyes Villa (president)

Popular Patriotic Movement (*Movimiento Popular Patriótico, MPP*), led by a former member of →Conscience of the Fatherland (Condepa), who secured less than 1% of the vote in the 1999 municipal elections.
Leadership. Julio Mantilla Cuellar (president)

Revival Axis (*Eje Pachakuti, EJE*), indigenous socialist party standing for independence and multiculturalism. It polled 18,176 votes and elected one deputy in the 1993 legislative elections.
Leadership. Ramiro Barrenechea Zambrana (president)

Revival Movement (*Movimiento Pachakuti, MP*), founded in November 2000 as one of several formations aiming to represent Amerindians, led by the president of the CSUTCB peasant organization.
Leadership. Felipe ("Mallku") Quispe (president)

Revolutionary Workers' Party–Masses (*Partido Obrero Revolucionario–Masas, POR–Masas*), Trotskyist party with limited support and three prominent internal factions, founded as the Revolutionary Workers' Party (POR) in 1934; affiliate of the Fourth International. It did not contest the 1997 elections.
Leadership. Guillermo Lora Escobar (president)

Socialist Party (*Partido Socialista, PS*), founded in 1989 as the Socialist Vanguard of Bolivia (VSB), which secured only 1.4% of the vote in the 1997 elections and subsequently changed its name.
Leadership. Jerjes Justiniano

Bosnia and Hercegovina

Capital: Sarajevo

Population: 3,800,000 (2000E)

The Republic of Bosnia & Hercegovina declared its independence from the Socialist Federal Republic of Yugoslavia (SFRY) in March 1992 and was admitted to the UN in May 1992. Its pre-independence ethnic composition by main group was 44% Muslim (or "Bosniak"), 31% Serb and 17% Croat, a mixture which precipitated a bloody conflict from 1992-95 (Bosniaks and Croats having supported independence in a 1991 referendum while the majority of Serbs opposed it). Bosnian Serbs, with support from Serbia and the Serb controlled Yugoslav National Army, during 1992 seized large swathes of territory, ethnically cleansed non-Serbs (leading to the largest refugee crisis in Europe since World War II) and proclaimed their intention to incorporate the land they controlled in a "Greater Serbia". In 1993 a separate war between Croats and Muslims broke out in parts of the remaining territories, which was resolved with US mediation in March 1994, when the Federation of Bosnia-Hercegovina was established on the Muslim and Croat controlled territories.

A shift in the military balance, assisted by US-led air attacks that forced Serb forces to abandon their three-year long siege of Sarajevo, paved the way to the ending of military conflict through the Dayton Agreement of November 1995. The Agreement specified that the Republic of Bosnia & Hercegovina would remain a single sovereignty but would consist of two "entities", namely the Federation of Bosnia & Hercegovina (comprising 51% of the country's territory) and the Republic Serbska (*Republika Srpska*, RS) of Bosnia & Hercegovina (comprising 49%). The Agreement made provision for the return of all refugees as a precondition for reconstruction and redevelopment, a process which is still underway.

The administration of Bosnia & Hercegovina has some aspects of an international protectorate. Implementation of the Dayton Agreement is underwritten by the "Contact Group" consisting of representatives of the US, Great Britain, Germany, France and Russia. A High Representative, based in Sarajevo, is elected by and reports directly to the Contact Group. The Office of the High Representative (OHR) oversees all aspects of the implementation of the Agreement and has wide ranging powers and responsibilities to intervene in domestic politics. The international community also maintains a military (NATO-led SFOR stabilization force) and police (IPTF –international police task force) presence in the country. Bosnian politics are additionally affected by the operations of the International Tribunal for War Crimes in former Yugoslavia, established by the UN in 1993 and based in The Hague, which has resulted in the indictment and in some cases arrest of prominent (primarily Serb) political leaders.

Under the remarkably complex Dayton structure, the central government is primarily responsible for foreign relations, trade and customs, monetary policy and communications. It is headed by (i) a three-person Presidency —one Muslim, one Croat and one Serb—elected from the three ethnic communities for four-year terms, and (ii) a Council of Ministers, headed by a Premier. The Council of Ministers is responsible to a bicameral Parliament (*Skupština*), consisting of (i) an upper 15-member House of Peoples (*Dom Naroda*) indirectly elected for a two-year term by the legislatures of the "entities" (10 from the Federation of Bosnia & Hercegovina and five from the Serbian Republic), and (ii) a 42-member House of Representatives (*Zastupnički Dom*) directly elected for a two-year term from each "entity" (28 from the Federation and 14 from the Serbian Republic).

The Federation of Bosnia & Hercegovina is headed by a President and Vice-President, each elected by the Federation's legislature for four-year terms and drawn alternately from the Muslim and Croat communities. The Federation's President, with the agreement of the Vice-President, nominates the Federation Prime Minister and Council of Ministers for endorsement by the bicameral legislature, consisting of an indirectly-elected upper House of Peoples of 74 members, of whom at least 30 must be Muslims and at least 30 Croats, and a directly-elected House of Representatives of 140 members. The Serbian Republic of Bosnia & Hercegovina is headed by a President, who is directly elected for a four-year term and who nominates the Prime Minister and Council of Ministers for approval by the directly-elected unicameral 83-member People's Assembly. Under the Dayton accord, all elections in Bosnia & Hercegovina are organized and verified by the Organization for Security and Co-operation in Europe (OSCE).

In elections for the pan-Bosnian collective Presidency on Sept. 12–13, 1998, the successful candidates were Alija Izetbegović (Party of Democratic Action, SDA), who won 86.8% of the Muslim vote; Zivko Radišić (Socialist Party of the Serbian Republic, SPRS), who took 51.2% of the Serb vote; and Ante Jelavić (Croatian Democratic Union, HDZ), who obtained 52.9% of the Croat vote. In the Serbian Republic, presidential elections on Nov. 11, 2000, resulted in victory for Mirko Sarović of the Serbian Democratic Party (SDS) with 50.1% of the vote.

Elections to the pan-Bosnian House of Representatives on Nov. 11, 2000, resulted as follows: Social Democratic Party of Bosnia & Hercegovina 9 seats (18.0% of the vote), Party of Democratic Action 8 (18.8%), Serbian Democratic Party 6 (17.8%), Croatian Democratic Union 5 (11.4%), Party for Bosnia & Hercegovina 5 (11.4%), Party of Democratic Progress 2 (6.4%), Party of Independent Social Democrats/Democratic Socialist Party 1 (5.1%), Socialist Party of the Serbian Republic 1 (2.6%), Serbian People's Union–Biljana Plavšić 1 (1.9%), New Croatian Initiative 1 (1.6%), Democratic People's Union 1 (1.2%), Bosnian-Hercegovinan Patriotic Party 1 (1.1%), Democratic Pensioners' Party 1 (1.1%).

Elections to the House of Representatives of the Federation of Bosnia & Hercegovina on Nov. 11, 2000, resulted as follows: Party of Democratic Action 38 seats (26.8% of the vote), Social Democratic Party of Bosnia & Hercegovina 37 (26.1%), Croatian Democratic Union 25 (17.5%), Party for Bosnia & Hercegovina 21 (14.9%), Democratic People's Union 3 (2.1%), Bosnian–Hercegovinan Patriotic Party 2 (1.7%), New Croatian Initiative 2 (1.6%), Pensioners' Party of the Federation 2 (1.3%), Bosnian Party 2 (1.1%), Croatian Party of Rights 1 (1.0%), Democratic Pensioners' Party 1 (0.9%), Liberal Democratic Party 1 (0.9%), Republican Party 1 (0.6%), Croatian Peasant Party 1 (0.5%), Croatian Christian Democratic Union 1 (0.4%), Civic Democratic Party 1 (0.4%), Party of Independent Social Democrats 1 (0.1%).

Elections to the People's Assembly of the Serbian Republic on Nov. 11, 2000, resulted as follows: Serbian Democratic Party 31 seats (36.1%) of the vote), Party of Independent Social Democrats 11 (13.0%), Party of Democratic Progress 11 (12.2%), Party of Democratic Action 6 (7.6%), Party for Bosnia & Hercegovina 4 (5.2%), Social Democratic Party of Bosnia & Hercegovina 4 (5.0%), Socialist Party of the Serbian Republic 4 (4.9%), Democratic Socialist Party 4 (4.2%), Democratic People's Alliance 3 (3.5%), Serbian People's Alliance–Biljana Plavšić 2 (2.3%), Pensioners' Party of the Serbian Republic 1 (1.3%), New Croatian Initiative 1 (0.7%), Democratic Party of the Serbian Republic 1 (0.6%).

Muslim Parties

Bosnian-Hercegovinian Patriotic Party
Bosanskohercegovačka Patriotska Stranka (BPS)
Address. Hakije Kulennovića 9, Sarajevo
Telephone. (+387–33) 216881
Fax. (+387–33) 216881
Leadership. Sefer Halilović (chairman)
Led by a war-time Chief of Staff of the B–H Army in 1992–1993, and supported mostly by Muslim immigrants from Sandjak (south Serbia/north Montenegro). In the November 2000 elections the BPS won one seat in the union lower house and two in the Federation lower house. Halilović was indicted at The Hague in September 2001.

Democratic People's Union
Demokratska Narodna Zajednica (DNZ)
Address. Pucara Starog 23, Velika Kladuša
Telephone. (+387–37) 770407
Fax. (+387–37) 770407
Email. dnzbih@bih.net.ba
Leadership. Fikret Abdić (chairman)
The DNZ, established in 1996, is the dominant party in the isolated north-west Bosnia Muslim-inhabited region of Velika Kladuša, but has no support outside that area. Its founder and leader, Fikret Abdić, was a local political strongman and entrepreneur in the Yugoslav period. He won the largest number of votes in elections to the collegial presidency in 1990 as a candidate of the →Party of Democratic Action (SDA) but was subsequently passed over by the SDA in favour of Alija Izetbegović in making its nomination for the president of the republic. During the Bosnian war, Abdić in 1993 established the "autonomous province of Western Bosnia", reaching an accommodation with Serb forces that brought him into bitter conflict with the Bosnian army.

Abdić won second place in the Muslim section in the September 1998 elections to the collective presidency, but with only 6.2% of the Muslim vote. In both 1998 and 2000 elections the DNZ took one seat in the union lower house and three in the Federation lower house.

Party of Democratic Action
Stranka Demokratske Akcije (SDA)
Address. Mehmeda Spahe 14, Sarajevo
Telephone. (+387–33) 667274
Fax. (+387–33) 650429
Email. sda@bih.net.ba
Leadership. Sulejman Tihić (chairman)
The SDA is a nationalist Muslim party founded in May 1990. It became the largest Assembly party in elections in November–December 1990, with party leader Alija Izetbegović also becoming president of the republic and then leading it to the declaration of independence from Yugoslavia in March 1992 and through the war period. In the first post-Dayton elections (September 1996) the SDA maintained its hold on the Muslim vote. Izetbegović was elected as the Muslim representative on the collective presidency, with over 80% of the Muslim vote, while the SDA won 19 of the 42 seats in the lower house of the union legislature and 78 of 140 seats in the Muslim-Croat Federation lower house. Edem Bičakčić of the SDA accordingly became Federation Prime Minister. In the September 1998 elections the SDA participated in a coalition including the →Party for Bosnia and Hercegovina (SBiH). Izetbegović, as the candidate for the Coalition for a Single and Democratic Bosnia & Hercegovina (KCD), was re-elected to the collective presidency with 86.8% of the Muslim vote (and about 32% nationally). Although the KCD won only 17 seats in the union lower house and 68 in the Federation lower house, Bičakčić continued as Federation Prime Minister (but was later disqualified from any public office by the High Representative).

In mid-1999 the SDA was threatened with sanctions by the OHR for its alleged failure to implement local power-sharing accords. The Federation President Ejup Ganić of the SDA was expelled from the party in May for refusing to resign over the SDA's poor showing in local elections the previous month. Standing on its own in the November 2000 legislative elections, the SDA won only eight of the union lower house seats and only 38 in the Federation lower house, being challenged in both legislatures by the multi-ethnic →Social Democratic Party of Bosnia & Hercegovina. Prior to the elections, Izetbegović retired as a member of the union collective presidency (being succeeded by Halid Genjać of the SDA), although he continued as SDA chairman until October 2001.

Pensioners' Party of the Federation
Stranka Penzionera Federacijie (SPF)
Address. Uzunovića Put 1/A, Zenica
Telephone. (+387–32) 287604
Fax. (+387–32) 285057
Leadership. Husein Vojniković (chairman)
A Muslim party promoting the interests of old-age pensioners, it won one seat in the November 2000 elections to the Federation lower house.

Croat Parties

Croatian Christian Democratic Union
Hrvatska Kršćanska Demokratska Unija (HKDU)
Address. Kulina Bana bb, Tomislavgrad
Telephone. (+387–34) 52051
Fax. (+387–34) 52051
Leadership. Ante Pašalić (chairman)
Affiliated to the Christian Democrat International, the HKDU in November 2000 won one seat in the House of Representatives of the Bosnian-Croat Federation.

Croatian Democratic Union
Hrvatska Demokratska Zajednica (HDZ)
Address. Kneza Domagoja bb, Mostar
Telephone. (+387–36) 319478
Fax. (+387–36) 315024
Leadership. Ante Jelavić (chairman)
Email. hdzbih@hdzbih.org
Web. www.hdzbih.org
The HDZ, a nationalist Croat party with close links to the Bosnian Catholic hierarchy, was launched in Bosnia-Hercegovina in August 1990, partly on the initiative of the then ruling →→Croatian Democratic Union of Croatia. In the pre-independence Assembly elections of November–December 1990 it took most of the ethnic Croat vote. The party withdrew from the central government at the height of the Bosnian war in 1993 and became the main proponent of the breakaway Croatian Republic of Herceg-Bosna in the western Hercegovina region. This precipitated a Croat-Muslim war, during which the HDZ and Croat Defense Council (HVO) lines of responsibility intermingled (later leading to the indictment at The Hague of the wartime HDZ President Dario Kordić for war crimes).

International pressure on Zagreb, however, resulted in HDZ participation in the March 1994 agreement to end the Croat–Muslim conflict and set up a (Muslim–Croat) Federation of Bosnia & Hercegovina in the territory not under Bosnian Serb control. The moderate Krešimir Zubak became Federation President in May 1994. After protracted resistance by hardline Croats, Zubak in August 1996 signed an agreement for the abolition of Herceg-Bosna and full Croat participation in the Federation. In the first post-Dayton elections (September 1996), Zubak was elected as the Croat member of the union collective presidency with overwhelming support from Croat voters, whilst the HDZ won seven of 42 seats in the all-Bosnia House of Representatives and 35 of 140 in the Federation lower house. In March 1997 Zubak was succeeded as Federation President by Vladimir Šoljić of the HDZ.

The election of Croat nationalist Ante Jelavić as HDZ chairman in May 1998 precipitated the exit of Zubak and his supporters, who formed the →New Croatian Initiative (NHI), while the OSCE banned some HDZ candidates from running in the September 1998 elections because of their close links with Croatia. Nevertheless, the HDZ remained dominant among Croat voters. In the November 2000 legislative elections, the HDZ took five seats in the union lower house and 25 in the Federation lower house.

Croatian Party of Rights
Hrvatska Stranka Prava (HSP)
Address. Fra Petra Bakule 2, Ljubuški
Telephone. (+387–36) 834917
Fax. (+387–36) 834917
Leadership. Zdravko Hrstić (chairman)
The ultra-nationalist HSP believes in the unification of Bosnia and Hercegovina with Croatia. In common with the World War II Independent State of Croatia it regards Bosnian Muslims as ethnic Croats of Muslim faith. Following the November 2000 elections it has one seat in the Federation House of Representatives.

Croatian Peasants' Party
Hrvatska Seljačka Stranka (HSS)
Address. Radićeva 4, Sarajevo
Telephone. (+387–33) 441987
Fax. (+387–33) 441897
Leadership. Ilija Šimić (chairman)
The moderate HSS is the counterpart in Bosnia & Hercegovina of the →→Croatian Peasants' Party in Croatia. It won one seat in the Federation lower house in the November 2000 elections.

Democratic Pensioners' Party
Demokratska Stranka Penzionera (DSP)
Address. Bosanske 6e 51, Tuzla
Telephone. (+387–66) 151390
Fax. (+387–75) 280555
Email. dsp.bih@bih.net.ba
Leadership. Alojz Knezović (chairman)
A Croat party promoting the interests of pensioners, taking one seat in the November 2000 elections to the all-Bosnia lower house and one in the Federation lower house.

New Croatian Initiative
Nova Hrvatska Inicijativa (NHI)
Address. Sime Milutinovića 2/II, Sarajevo
Telephone. (+387–33) 214602
Fax. (+387–33) 214603
Email. nhi@nhi.ba
Leadership. Krešimir Zubak (chairman)
The moderate NHI was launched in June 1998 by Krešimir Zubak, then the Croat member of the union collective presidency, who had broken with the dominant →Croatian Democratic Union (HDZ) after hardliner Ante Jelavić had replaced him as HDZ leader the previous month. It won one seat in the union lower house and two in the Federation lower house in the elections in November 2000. It is a member of the Christian Democrat International.

Serb Parties

Democratic Party of the Serbian Republic
Demokratska Stranka Republike Srpske (DSRS)
Address. Kneza Miloša 28, Bijeljina
Telephone. (+387–55) 401951
Fax. (+387–55) 401951
Email. dsrs@bn.rstel.net
Leadership. Dragomir Dumić (chairman); Gavrilo Antonić (general secretary)
Founded in 1995 the moderate DSRS won one seat in the 83-member People's Assembly of the RS in November 2000.

Democratic People's Alliance
Demokratski Narodni Savez (DNS)
Address. Jespejcka 1, Banja Luka
Telephone. (+381–51) 215542
Fax. (+381–51) 216951
Leadership. Dragan Kostić (chairman)
The DNS was launched in July 2000 as a breakaway from the →Serbian People's Alliance–Biljana Plavšić (SNS–BP) and won three seats in the November 2000 elections for the RS Assembly.

Democratic Socialist Party
Demokratska Socijalistička Partija (DSP)
Address. Kralja Alfonsa 9, Banja Luka
Telephone. (+381–51) 212614
Fax. (+381–51) 211026
Leadership. Nebojša Radmanović (chairman)
The DSP was created in March 2000 by a breakaway faction of the →Socialist Party of the Serbian Republic (SPRS). It opposed the SPRS's decision to leave the moderate coalition supporting the RS premiership of Milorad Dodik of the →Party of Independent Social Democrats (SNSD). In the November 2000 elections, the DSP was allied with the SNSD for the all-Bosnia lower house elections, their joint list winning one seat. Standing on its own in the RS Assembly elections, the DSP drew on former SPRS support to win four seats.

Party of Democratic Progress
Partija Demokratskog Progresa (PDP)
Address. Vojvode Momčila 66, Banja Luka
Telephone. (+381–51) 218078
Fax. (+381–51) 218115
Email. pdp@blic.net
Leadership. Mladen Ivanić (chairman)
The moderate PDP was launched in September 1999 by Mladen Ivanić. In November 2000 it took 11 of the 83 seats in the Serbian Assembly. Ivanić became Serbian Republic Prime Minister in January 2001 at the head of a loose coalition which included the →Socialist Party of the Serbian Republic, one Muslim and one member of the →Serbian Democratic Party (SDS).

Party of Independent Social Democrats
Stranka Nezavisnih Socijaldemokrata (SNSD)
Address. Petra Kočića 5, Banja Luka
Telephone. (+381–51) 218936
Fax. (+381–51) 218937
Email. snsd@inecco.net
Web. snsd.tripod.com
Leadership. Milorad Dodik (chairman); Branko Nesković (secretary-general)
The SNSD was founded in March 1996. It won two RS Assembly seats in November 1997, following which party leader Milorad Dodik became RS Prime Minister in January 1998, heading a non-partisan administration and moving the seat of government from the Pale stronghold of the hardline →Serbian Democratic Party (SDS) to Banja Luka. In early 1999 Dodik, with Western support, successfully resisted efforts by RS President Nikola Poplašen of the ultra-nationalist →Serbian Radical Party (SRS) to replace him as Prime Minister. In elections in November 2000 Dodik came a poor second in the contest for the RS presidency. Although the SNSD improved its representation in the RS Assembly to 11 seats (and also won one in the Federation lower house), Dodik was succeeded as RS Prime Minister by Mladen Ivanić of the →Party of Democratic Progress.

Pensioners' Party of the Serb Republic
Penzionerska Stranka Republike Srpske (PSRS)
Address. Grečka 19, Banja Luka
Telephone. (+381–51) 301212
Fax. (+381–51) 214789

Leadership. Stojan Bogosavac (chairman)
Promotes the interests of pensioners and won one seat in the November 2000 elections to the RS Assembly.

Serbian Democratic Party
Srpska Demokratska Stranka (SDS)
Address. Kralja Alfonsa 13/1, Banja Luka
Telephone. (+381–51) 212738
Fax. (+381–51) 217640
Leadership. Dragan Kalinić (chairman)
The SDS was launched in July 1990 as the political voice of Bosnian Serb nationalism and secured most of the ethnic Serb vote in the November–December 1990 elections. It joined a post-election coalition with the (Muslim) →Party of Democratic Action (SDA) and the →Croatian Democratic Union (HDZ), arguing that Bosnia & Hercegovina should remain within a federal Yugoslavia. When the government opted for independence, the SDS withdrew from the Assembly in Sarajevo and in March 1992 led the proclamation of the Serbian Republic of Bosnia & Hercegovina in Serb-controlled territory, with its own assembly at Pale. The SDS leadership was thereafter prominent in the prosecution of the war against the Bosnian republic.

Under the leadership of Radovan Karadžić, the SDS secured the Bosnian Serbs' rejection of successive international peace plans, on the grounds that they involved the surrender of too much Serb-controlled territory and did not guarantee sovereignty for a Bosnian Serb entity. The SDS leadership came under increasing Yugoslav and international pressure in 1995 to accept a settlement preserving the nominal sovereignty of Bosnia–Hercegovina and reducing the Bosnian Serbs' effective control to around half of the state's territory. In consequence, serious divisions became apparent in the SDS. In April 1995 Karadžić was named as a suspected war criminal by the UN War Crimes Tribunal at The Hague. Under the US-brokered peace agreement concluded at Dayton, Ohio, in November 1995, indicted war criminals were specifically excluded from standing for office in post-settlement political structures. Bowing to international pressure, Karadžić relinquished the RS presidency and the SDS leadership to the Biljana Plavšić in mid-1996, but remained very much in control behind the scenes.

The SDS maintained its hold on the Serb vote in the first post-Dayton elections in September 1996. Hardliner Momčilo Krajišnik was elected as the Serb member of the new collective presidency of Bosnia–Hercegovina, while Plavšić was elected as RS President. Plavšić quickly came into conflict with Karadžić and was expelled by the SDS in July 1997, subsequently forming what became the →Serbian People's Union–Biljana Plavšić (SNS–BP). In further RS elections in November 1997 the SDS was reduced to 24 seats, with the result that Gojko Klišković (SDS) was succeeded as RS Prime Minister by Western-backed moderate Milorad Dodik of the →Party of Independent Social Democrats (SNSD).

In June 1998 hardliner Dragan Kalinić became SDS chairman and in the September 1998 elections for the RS presidency the SDS backed Nikola Poplašen of the ultra-nationalist →Serbian Radical Party (SRS), ensuring his easy victory over Plavšić. The SDS lost ground in legislative elections, however, and Krajišnik failed to secure re-election as the Serb member of the union collective presidency. The SDS staged a recovery in the November 2000 elections, securing the election of SRS hardliner Mirko Sarović as RS President with 50.1% and taking 31 seats in the 83-member RS Assembly. From its restored dominance, the SDS agreed in January 2001 to support a new RS government headed by Mladen Ivanić of the →Party of Democratic Progress, who appointed one SDS minister to his "non-partisan" administration despite Western opposition to SDS participation.

Serbian People's Alliance–Biljana Plavšić
Srpski Narodni Savez–Biljana Plavšić (SNS–BP)
Address. Srpskih junaka 4, Banja Luka
Telephone. (+381–51) 218339
Fax. (+381–51) 218213
Email. sna@blic.net
Leadership. Biljana Plavšić (chairperson)
The SNS was launched in September 1997 by Biljana Plavšić, who had been elected as President of the Serbian Republic (RS) in September 1996 as the candidate of the →Serbian Democratic Party (SDS). Plavšić, a wartime hardliner who subsequently adopted a more moderate position, was expelled from the SDS when she acted to dissolve the SDS-dominated RS Assembly in July 1997. New RS Assembly elections were held in November 1997 and resulted in the SNS winning 15 of the 83 seats, mainly at the expense of the SDS. Plavšić was therefore able to appoint a "non-partisan" RS government headed by Milorad Dodik of the →Party of Independent Social Democrats (SNSD) and to move the seat of government from Pale to Banja Luka.

In the September 1998 elections Plavšić was defeated in the RS presidential contest by Nikola Poplašen of the ultra-nationalist Serbian Radical Party (SRS), who was backed by the SDS, and in the RS Assembly elections SNS representation was reduced to 12 seats. In June 2000 the party split, with Dragan Kostić forming the breakaway →Democratic People's Alliance. In the November 2000 elections the SNS-BP was reduced to two seats in the RS Assembly and won one seat in the union lower house. Plavšić surrendered to The Hague tribunal following her indictment in January 2001.

Serbian Radical Party
Srpska Radikalna Stranka (SRS)
Address. Svetozara Markovića, Banja Luka
Telephone. (+381–51) 308886
Fax. (+381–51) 308886
Leadership. Nikola Poplašen(chairman); Mirko Sarović (deputy chairman)
The ultra-nationalist SRS originated as the Bosnian Serb wing of the →→Serbian Radical Party of Yugoslavia. It opposed the 1995 Dayton Agreement ending the war. In the September 1998 elections, SRS leader Nikola Poplašen, to Western dismay, won the RS presidency, running with the backing of the →Serbian Democratic Party (SDS). Poplašen's subsequent effort to install a new RS Prime Minister, in place of Milorad Dodik of the moderate →Party of Independent Social Democrats (SNSD), led the UN High Representative to dismiss him as President in March 1999 for "abuse of power". Poplašen's unwillingness to depart produced a political impasse, with his Vice-President, Mirko Sarović, also considered unacceptable. However, Sarović took his revenge in the November 2000 elections by winning the RS presidency with 53% of the vote, benefiting from SDS backing to defeat Dodik. In return, the SRS supported SDS candidates in the RS Assembly elections, enabling the latter party to recover its numerical dominance. In January 2001 Sarović appointed Mladen Ivanić of the →Party of Democratic Progress as RS Prime Minister, heading a "non-partisan" government which included an SDS representative, to further Western dismay.

Socialist Party of the Serbian Republic
Socijalistička Partija Republike Srpske (SPRS)
Address. Kralja Petra 1og Karadjordjevića 1, Banja Luka
Telephone. (+381–51) 215336
Fax. (+381–51) 215336
Leadership. Živko Radišić (chairman)
The SPRS was founded in 1993 as effectively the Bosnian Serb wing of the then ruling →→Socialist Party of Serbia (Yugoslavia) of Slobodan Milošević. In the post-Dayton period it opposed the dominant →Serbian Democratic Party (SDS) then led by Radovan Karadžić, in line with

60

Belgrade's increasing disenchantment with the latter's hard-line opposition to the Dayton Agreement. In September 1998 party chairman Radišić, running as the candidate of the moderate Accord (*Sloga*) alliance, won election as the Serb member of the union collective presidency. The SPRS withdrew from the *Sloga* alliance ruling coalition in January 2000. However, the SPRS ministers remained in the government, and in March a dissident SPRS faction opposed to the withdrawal broke away to form the →Democratic Socialist Party (DSP).

In the November 2000 elections, the rump SPRS was damaged by the impact of the new DSP, its representation falling to four seats in the RS Assembly and to one in the all-Bosnia lower house.

Multi-ethnic Parties

Bosnian Party
Bosanska Stranka (BOSS)
Address. Stari Grad 9, Tuzla
Telephone. (+387–35) 251035
Fax. (+387–35) 251035
Email. boss.bh@delta.com.ba
Leadership. Mirnes Ajanović (chairman)
BOSS, which is mainly Muslim based, took two seats in the Federation lower house November 2000 elections.

Civic Democratic Party
Gradjanska Demokratska Stranka (GDS)
Address. Maršala Tita 9A/V, Sarajevo
Telephone. (+387–33) 666621
Fax. (+387–33) 213435
Leadership. Ibrahim Spahić (chairman)
The GDS, which has mainly Muslim support, won one seat in the Federation lower house in the November 2000 elections.

Liberal Democratic Party
Liberalno Demokratska Stranka (LDS)
Address. Maršala Tita 9A, Sarajevo 71000
Telephone. (+387–33) 442349
Fax. (+387–33) 664540
Email. liberali@bih.net.ba
Leadership. Rasim Kadić (president); Tarik Kupusović (secretary-general)
An affiliate of the Liberal International, LDS support comes mainly from non-sectarian Muslim voters and it won one seat in the Federation lower house in the November 2000 elections.

Party for Bosnia and Hercegovina
Stranka za Bosnu i Hercegovinu (SBiH)
Address. Maršala Tita 7A, Sarajevo
Telephone. (+387–33) 214417
Fax. (+387–33) 214417
Leadership. Haris Silajdžić (president)
The SBiH is a centrist party aiming to rally moderate non-sectarian opinion, but having mainly Muslim support. It was founded in April 1996 by Haris Silajdžić, who had resigned as Prime Minister of the Bosnian government in January over what he saw as Islamic fundamentalist tendencies in the dominant →Party of Democratic Action (SDA). In the first post-Dayton elections in September 1996, Silajdžić came second in the contest for the Muslim member of the collective presidency and he was then one of the two union Prime Ministers from December 1996 until the move to a single Prime Minister in June 2000. The SBiH contested the September 1998 elections within the SDA-led Coalition for a Single and Democratic Bosnia and Hercegovina (KCD). Standing alone in the November 2000 elections, the SBiH won five union lower house seats and 21 in the Federation lower house.

Republican Party of Bosnia & Hercegovina
Republikanska Stranka Bosne i Hercegovine (RSBiH)
Address. Maršala Tita 9A, Sarajevo
Telephone. (+387–71) 525038
Fax. (+387–71) 664987
Email. republ94@bih.net.ba
Leadership. Stjepan Kljuić (chairman); Nedim Sarija (secretary-general)
The centre-right multi-ethnic RSBiH was founded in June 1994 by Stjepan Kljuić, a former leader of the →Croatian Democratic Union (HDZ) who had split with the HDZ because of his opposition to the partition of Bosnia on an ethnic basis. It won one seat in the Federation lower house in the November 2000 elections.

Social Democratic Party of Bosnia & Hercegovina
Socijaldemokratska Partija Bosne i Hercegovine (SDPBiH)
Address. Alipašina 41, Sarajevo
Telephone. (+387–33) 664044
Fax. (+387–33) 664042
Leadership. Zlatko Lagumdžija (chairman); Karlo Filipović (general secretary)
The SDPBiH was created by merger in February 1999 of the Social Democrats of Bosnia & Hercegovina (SDBiH) and the Democratic Party of Socialists (DSS), formerly the Union of Bosnian Social Democrats (ZSDB) under the leadership of Selim Bešlagić, the Muslim mayor of Tuzla. Affiliated to the Socialist International (which had pressed for the merger), the SDPBiH aims to be a social democratic party on the West European model, favouring a regulated market economy and opposing ethnic nationalism.

Between them the SDBiH and DSS in September 1998 elections won six seats in the union lower house and 25 in the Federation lower house. In the November 2000 elections, however, the new SDPBiH did better than its predecessor parties had separately, winning nine of the 42 seats in the union lower house, and second place in the Federation lower house, with 37 of the 140 seats. The party also won four seats in the Serbian Republic Assembly. While deriving particular support from Muslims disaffected from the nationalist →Party of Democratic Action (SDA), as well as from Bosnians of mixed ethnic background, the party has emphasized its inter-ethnic character in the composition of its lists.

Botswana

Capital: Gaborone

Population: 1,576,500 (2000E)

The Republic of Botswana became independent from Britain in 1966. Under its 1966 constitution, executive power is vested in the President as head of state, elected for a renewable five-year term by an absolute majority of the elected members of the National Assembly, which has legislative authority. Under a constitutional amendment adopted in 1997 (but not retrospectively applicable to the then current incumbent), no person may serve more than two presidential terms. The President appoints a Vice-President from among the members of the Assembly as well the members of the Cabinet, over which he presides. The Vice-President succeeds to the presidency in the event of the resignation or death in office of the President. The National Assembly, also having a term of five years, consists of 40 members directly elected from single-member constituencies by universal suffrage of those aged 18 and over, as well as four members elected by the elected Assembly members (from a list of eight submitted by the President) and three ex-officio members (the Speaker, the non-voting Attorney-General and the President). There is also a 15–member House of Chiefs, composed of representatives of the principal ethnic groupings, which considers draft legislation on constitutional or chieftaincy matters (but has no veto) and may make representations to the President on tribal matters.

In elections for the elective seats in the National Assembly on Oct. 16, 1999, the Botswana Democratic Party won 33 (with 57.2% of the vote), the Botswana National Front 6 (26%) and the Botswana Congress Party one (11.9%). Festus Mogae, who had succeeded to the presidency in April 1998 on the resignation of Sir Ketumile Masire, began his first full term as President of Botswana on Oct. 20, 1999, when he was elected by the members of the new National Assembly.

Botswana Congress Party (BCP)
Address. POB 2918, Gaborone
Leadership. Michael Dingake
The BCP was formed in July 1998 following a split in the →Botswana National Front (BNF) at an acrimonious BNF party congress in April 1998. Its founder, Michael Dingake, had served as deputy leader of the BNF. The BCP (with 11 members in the National Assembly) superseded the BNF as the official opposition party for the remainder of the current term of the Assembly. In the 1999 Assembly elections, however, the BCP won only one seat (Dingake being among its defeated candidates).

Botswana Democratic Party (BDP)
Address. POB 28, Gaborone
Telephone. (+267) 352564
Fax. (+267) 313911
Leadership. Festus Gontebanye Mogae (president); Pontashego Kedikilwe (chairman); Daniel Kwelagobe (secretary-general)
The BDP was founded in 1962 as the Bechuanaland Democratic Party, adopting its present name in 1965, when it won a decisive majority in pre-independence elections. Favoured by the British colonial authorities and white residents for its relative moderation, the party led Botswana to independence in September 1966, its then leader, Sir Seretse Khama, becoming President. Pursuing conservative domestic policies and adopting a pragmatic line externally (notably in regard to South Africa), the BDP was returned to power with further large majorities in the 1969, 1974 and 1979 elections. On Khama's death in 1980, he was succeeded as President and party leader by Vice-President Quett (later Ketumile) Masire. The BDP won further landslide victories in the 1984 and 1989 elections but faced increasing popular unrest in the early 1990s as well as opposition charges of graft and corruption. In March 1992 the report of a commission of inquiry into land allocations resulted in the resignations of Peter S. Mmusi as Vice-President and of Daniel Kwelagobe as Agriculture Minister, both men also losing their senior party posts. However, at a BDP congress in June 1993 Mmusi and Kwelagobe were elected party chairman and secretary-general respectively, while some senior cabinet ministers failed to secure election to the BDP central committee. Thereafter, tensions increased between the Mmusi/Kwelagobe faction and the traditional leadership of southern cattle-raisers typified by Lt.-Gen. Mompati Merafhe. Also apparent was a struggle for the succession to the ailing Masire.

The BDP retained an overall majority in the October 1994 Assembly elections, but its support slipped sharply to 53.1% (from 64.8% in 1989) and several cabinet ministers lost their seats. Mmusi died during the election campaign. The new Assembly re-elected Masire as President, while the post-election government included Kwelagobe as Minister of Works, Transport and Communications. In July 1995 the Presidential Affairs and Public Administration Minister,

Pontashego Kedikilwe, was elected as BDP chairman. Festus Mogae, who had served as Vice-President since 1992, automatically succeeded Masire as President (for the remainder of the current term) when Masire retired from politics at the end of March 1998. Mogae also became BDP party president. The BDP won 33 seats (with 57.2% of the vote) in the October 1999 Assembly elections. The Assembly subsequently elected Mogae to the Presidency in his own right. President Mogae appointed Lt.-Gen. Seretse Ian Khama, former commander of the Botswana Defence Force and son of Botswana's first President, as his Vice-President.

The BDP is associated with the International Democrat Union through the Democrat Union of Africa.

Botswana National Front (BNF)
Address. POB 1720, Gaborone
Telephone. (+267) 351789
Leadership. Kenneth Koma (president); Badziyili Nfila (secretary-general)
The centre-left BNF was established shortly before independence in 1966 by opposition elements seeking to provide an alternative to the dominant →Botswana Democratic Party (BDP). It won three Assembly seats in 1969, two in 1974 and 1979 and four in 1984, this last tally increasing to seven by late 1985 as a result of a by-election victory and two BDP defections. In 1989 the BNF fell back to three elective seats, although its share of the vote increased from 20.4% in 1984 to 26.9%. Based in the urban working class, the BNF had a Marxist orientation in the 1980s (and was portrayed as subversive by the BDP government) but moved to a social democratic stance after the 1989 elections. In 1991 it joined other opposition groups in the Botswana People's Progressive Front (BPPF), which called for the creation of an all-party commission to supervise the next elections, claiming that the previous contest had been rigged.

Revelations of corruption in ruling circles in 1992 generated increasing support for the BPPF alliance, which staged a series of mass protest demonstrations calling on the government to resign. In 1993, however, dissension developed within the BPPF over whether the alliance should boycott the next elections if its demands for electoral reform were not met. In the event, the BNF contested the October 1994 elections in its own right, substantially increasing its vote share (to 37.7%) and winning 13 elective seats, including all four in Gaborone. In July 1998 its Assembly representation was reduced to two when 11 of its deputies formed the →Botswana Congress Party (BCP). In the 1999 elections the BNF won 26% of the vote (compared with the BCP's 11.9%) and, with six seats, regained its former status of official opposition party in the National Assembly.

The BNF is an observer member of the Socialist International.

Other Parties

Independence Freedom Party (IFP), formed through a merger between the Botswana Freedom Party and the Botswana Independence Party. The IFP contested the 1999 general election in alliance with the →United Action Party.
Leadership. Motsamai Mpho (president)

United Action Party (UAP), founded in 1998, allied with the →Independence Freedom Party in the 1999 general election, in which that alliance won 4.7% of the vote and no seats.
Leadership. Lepetu Setshwaelo

Brazil

Capital: Brasilia

Population: 169,590,693 (2000E)

The Federative Republic of Brazil became independent from Portugal in 1822 and a federal republic in 1889. It comprises 23 states, three territories and a federal district (Brasilia). National legislative authority rests with the bicameral National Congress, comprising a 513-member Chamber of Deputies which is directly elected every four years by a system of proportional representation, and an 81-member Federal Senate whose members are elected for eight-year terms at four-year intervals for, alternately, one-third and two-thirds of the members. Congressional elections are by universal and compulsory adult suffrage. Executive power is exercised by the President who appoints and leads the Cabinet. A new constitution which entered into effect on Oct. 6, 1988, confirmed a five-year presidential term, and removed many of the restrictions imposed under military rule between 1964 and 1985. On May 25, 1994, congressional deputies voted by 323 to 29 to amend the constitution reducing the presidential term from five to four years.

Each state has its own government, with a structure that mirrors the federal level, enjoying all the powers (defined in its own constitution) which are not specifically reserved for the federal government or assigned to the municipal councils. The head of the state executive is the Governor, elected by direct popular vote under the federal constitution. The one-chamber state legislature is a State Assembly. The state judiciary follows the federal pattern and has its jurisdiction defined so as to avoid any conflict or superimposition with the federal courts.

Presidential elections in October 1998 were won by the incumbent, Fernando Henrique Cardoso of the centre-left Brazilian Social Democratic Party (PSDB). Heading a six-party alliance, Cardoso was re-elected with a resounding 53.6% absolute majority. The three main parties of the governmental alliance, the PSDB, the Party of the Brazilian Democratic Movement (PMDB) and the Liberal Front Party (PFL), gained the larger number of seats in simultaneous legislative elections. Cardoso was sworn in as President, with Marco Maciel as Vice-President, on Jan. 1, 1999, when a new coalition government of 21 ministers took office, featuring a mixture of politicians and independent technocrats. The governmental alliance won a majority large enough to give the new President broad support in Congress. As of mid-2001 the parties supporting Cardoso were the PSDB, the PFL, the Progressive Brazilian Party (PPB), the PMDB, the Brazilian Labour Party (PTB) and the Social Democratic Party (PSD).

Brazilian Labour Party
Partido Trabalhista Brasileiro (PTB)
Address. SLCN 3030 BL, Sala 105 Brasilia–DF, 70735-530
Telephone. (+55-61) 226–0477
Fax. (+55–61) 225–4757
Email. ptb@org.br
Website. www.ptb.org.br
Leadership. José Carlos Martinez (president)
Founded in 1980, the centre-right PTB is a direct successor of the pre-1965 Brazilian Workers' Party founded in the 1940s by former President Getúlio Vargas. It elected 31 deputies in the 1998 elections and is part of the governmental alliance that has supported President Cardoso since his first election in 1994.

Brazilian Social Democratic Party
Partido da Social Democracia Brasileira (PSDB)
Address. CP 07–1045, 70359–970 Brasilia DF
Telephone. (+55–61) 328-0045
Fax. (+55–61) 328–2660
Email. tucano@psdb.org.br
Website. www.psdb.org.br
Leadership. Fernando Henrique Cardoso (honorary president); José Aníbal (president); Sérgio Machado (Senate leader); Jutahy Magalhães (Chamber leader); Márcio Fortes (secretary-general)
The centre-left PSDB was founded in June 1988 with a manifesto advocating social justice, economic development, land reform and environmental protection. It also called for the establishment of a true parliamentary system within four years. The party was broadly modelled on the European social democratic tradition, although it had no organized working-class support. The PSDB is strong in the state of São Paulo and other states of the south-east as well as in the north-eastern state of Ceará.

The PSDB was formed by members of the *historicos* faction of the Party of the →Brazilian Democratic Movement (PMDB) opposed to the perceived corruption and lack of political principles of the PMDB's leadership, President Sarney's retention of the presidential system and his determination not to shorten his term of office. The catalyst, however, was the unsuccessful challenge by Mario Covas, PMDB leader in the Constituent Assembly, for the PMDB leadership. The new party also attracted defectors from the →Liberal Front Party (PFL), the →Brazilian Socialist Party (PSB) and the →Brazilian Labour Party (PTB). Soon after its formation the PSDB became the third largest party in Congress, with eight senators and 60 deputies.

In 1994 the party joined the PFL, the PTB and the →Liberal Party (PL) in supporting the successful presidential campaign of its leader, Fernando Henrique Cardoso. During Cardoso's two terms in office the party has moved to the centre of the political spectrum, supporting the President's programme of economic modernization. Cardoso's electoral successes have benefited the PSDB,

63

which in the 1998 elections won 99 seats in the Chamber of Deputies and 16 seats in the Senate, making it the second largest party in Congress, behind the PFL.

The PSDB is an observer member of the Christian Democrat Organization of America (ODCA).

Brazilian Socialist Party
Partido Socialista Brasileiro (PSB)
Address. Cam. Dep. Anexo II Bl. Lideranças, Sl. 18 BSB, Brasilia, DF 70160–900
Telephone. (+55–61) 318–5198
Fax. (+55–61) 224–8493
Email. psb@bauru.net
Leadership. Miguel Arraes de Alencar (president)
Founded in 1986, the PSB is an independent leftist party whose lineage goes back to the PSB of the 1946–65 period. The party managed to send only one deputy and two senators to Congress in the elections of November 1986. However, in the 1990s the party established itself as part of the left-wing opposition and increased its representation in the Chamber of Deputies to 11 seats in 1990 and 15 in 1994.

In the 1994–98 and 1999–2001 periods the party has been in opposition to the government of President Cardoso. In 1998 the PSB supported the presidential candidacy of Luís Inácio (Lula) da Silva of the →Workers' Party, winning 19 seats in the Chamber of Deputies.

Communist Party of Brazil
Partido Comunista do Brasil (PCdoB)
Address. Rua Major Diogo, 834 Bela Vista, São Paulo, SP CEP: 01.324–001
Telephone. (+55–11) 232–1622
Fax. (+55–11) 232–4245
Email. pcdobc@org.br
Website. www.pcdob.org.br
Leadership. João Amazonas (chairman)
The PCdoB originated in a Maoist faction within the Brazilian Communist Party (PCB, now the →Popular Socialist Party, PSP). It split away from the PCB and set up as a separate party under the PCB's original name after the Communist Party had abandoned internationalism. Banned as soon as it was founded, the PCdoB worked within what became the →Party of the Brazilian Democratic Movement, the official opposition party. After the death of Mao and the arrest of the "Gang of Four" in 1976, the PCdoB turned away from China and became pro-Albanian.

An official amnesty in 1979 allowed the party to operate more openly, although it remained officially illegal until June 1985.

Following the defeat of the →Workers' Party (PT) candidate, Lula da Silva, in the 1989 presidential elections, the PCdoB again campaigned by itself in the 1990 congressional elections and won five seats in the Chamber. It gave further backing to Lula in the 1994 and 1998 presidential elections.

As part of a left-wing opposition bloc, the PcdoB has strongly opposed the policies of President Cardoso of the →Brazilian Social Democratic Party since his election in 1994. The party won 10 Chamber seats in 1994, and seven in 1998.

Democratic Labour Party
Partido Democrático Trabalhista (PDT)
Address: Av. Marechal Câmara 160, 4° AND Ed. Orly, Sl. 417/420/RJ, 20020-080
Telephone. (+55–21) 262–8834
Fax. (+55–21) 262–8834
Email. redepdt@uol.com.br
Website. www.pdt.org.br
Leadership. Leonel de Moura Brizola; Sebastião Rocha (Senate leader); Miro Teixeira (Chamber leader); Manoel Dias (secretary-general)
Founded by Leonel Brizola, Doutel de Andrade (party vice-president until his death in January 1991) and other exiled

members of the old →Brazilian Labour Party (PTB) after their return to Brazil under the 1979 amnesty, the party had to adopt its current name after a dissident group won a court case over the old party name in 1980. The PDT had the support of 10 deputies from the start and in the general election of 1982 it increased its representation to 24 deputies and one senator thus forming the largest labour bloc in Congress.

Although the party had thrown its weight behind Tancredo Neves, the victorious Democratic Alliance candidate in the 1985 presidential elections, it was one of the few parties to take an early stand against the economic policies of his running-mate and replacement, President Sarney. This unpopular stand, however, was vindicated in 1988, when, following social and industrial tensions, the PDT made major gains in the November municipal elections at the expense of the ruling →Party of the Brazilian Democratic Movement (PMDB). In the 1989 first-run presidential election Brizola came very close to the two frontrunners, Lula da Silva of the →Workers' Party and Fernando Collor de Mello of the National Reconstruction Party, of whom the latter went on to win the second-run election.

The PDT recovered in the October 1990 congressional and gubernatorial elections, increasing its representation in the Chamber of Deputies from 24 to 46 seats and thus becoming the third largest party. However, Brizola's personalist style of leadership alienated voters and led to prominent politicians leaving the party. Brizola went on to stand as the PDT presidential candidate in 1994, coming in fifth place with a poor 2.6% of the vote and 34 seats in the Chamber.

In 1998 the PDT supported the further presidential candidacy of Lula da Silva, but its share of congressional votes continued to decline and the party won only 25 seats in the Chamber and two seats in the Senate. It thereafter maintained strong opposition to the presidency of Fernando Henrique Cardoso of the →Brazilian Social Democratic Party, claiming that he had deceived the people in his 1998 re-election campaign.

The party is a full member of the Socialist International.

Liberal Front Party
Partido da Frente Liberal (PFL)
Address. Senado Federal, Anexo I 26° andar, Brasilia, DF 70165–900
Telephone. (+55–61) 311–4305
Fax. (+55–61) 224–1912
Email. pfl25@pfl.org.br
Leadership. Jorge Konder Bornhausen (president); José Carlos Aleluia (secretary-general)
The centre-right PFL has its traditional stronghold in the underdeveloped north-east of the country and has been accused of appealing to traditional political practices such as patronage to gather electoral support. The party was founded in 1984 and was formed by the liberal faction of the right-wing Social Democratic Party (PDS) following disagreements over the appointment of Paulo Salim Maluf as the party's candidate for the 1985 presidential ejections. The PFL, with José Sarney (president of the military's official party ARENA, 1970-79, and president of the PDS, 1979-84) and the Brazilian Vice-President Antonio Aureliano Chaves de Mendonca among its leaders, and 72 deputies and 12 senators having sworn allegiance to the party, became Brazil's third largest party in parliament almost overnight. Although the PFL was not officially a legal political party until June 1985, it nevertheless formed a democratic alliance with the Party of the Brazilian Democratic Movement (PMDB) in order to contest the indirect presidential elections of January 1985, which José Sarney won.

In September 1987 the PFL officially withdrew from the Democratic Alliance, claiming that it was too dominated by the PMDB, although some PFL members retained their cabinet and other government posts. Sarney finally acquiesced to the popular demand for early elections, called in

November 1989. The PFL's candidate for the presidency was Sarney's Minas and Energy Minister, Antonio Aureliano Chaves de Mendonca, who obtained only a small percentage of the valid votes. In the elections of the following year, however, his party won the highest number of state governors' posts and again proved to be the second most popular party, winning 92 seats in the Chamber of Deputies.

The PFL supported the successful presidential candidacy of Fernando Henrique Cardoso of the →Brazilian Social Democratic Party in 1994 and 1998 and has been a key member of his coalition government. In 1998 the PFL became the largest party in Congress, electing 106 deputies and 20 senators.

The party is a member of the Christian Democrat Organization of America (ODCA).

Liberal Party
Partido Liberal (PL)
Address. Câmara dos Deputados anexo I, Gab. 2608, Brasilia, DF 70160–900
Telephone. (+55–61) 318–5899
Fax. (+55–61) 223–9444
Email. plnacional@persocom.com.br
Website. www.pl.org.br
Leadership. Valdemar Costa Neto (president)
Founded in 1985, the centre-right PL secured seven seats in the Chamber of Deputies and one Senate seat in the 1989 elections, bringing this number up to 15 in the 1990 elections. As a small party the PL stands for the country's tradesmen and supports free enterprise and fair wages for all. In 1994 the party supported the successful presidential candidacy of Fernando Henrique Cardoso of the →Brazilian Social Democratic Party. In 1998 it moved to the opposition, supporting the left-of-centre presidential candidacy of Ciro Gomes. In that year's parliamentary election the PL won 12 seats in the Chamber of Deputies.

Party of the Brazilian Democratic Movement
Partido do Movimento Democrático Brasiliero (PMDB)
Address. Câmara dos Deputados, Ed. Principal, Brasilia, DF 70160–900
Telephone. (+55–61) 318–5120
Fax. (+55–61) 223–5408
Email. dnacional@pmdb.org.br
Website. www.pmdb.org.br
Leadership. Michel Temer (president); Renan Calheiros (Senate leader); Geddel Vieira Lima (Chamber leader); Saraiva Felipe (secretary-general)
The centrist PMDB is the successor to the Brazilian Democratic Movement (MDB) created in 1966 as a legal outlet of opposition to the military regime of the time. Renamed the PMDB in 1979, the party played an important role in the process of transition to democracy in the late 1970s and early 1980s. Its campaign for democratization attracted support from a wide section of society, ranging from left-wing forces, such as the illegal Communist Party (now the →Popular Socialist Party) and trade unions, to moderate conservatives.

In November 1986 the PMDB became the most powerful party in Brazil, with 22 governorships, 260 out of 487 seats in the Chamber of Deputies and 46 out of 72 seats in the Senate, and thus also dominated the Constituent Assembly which President Sarney established in February 1987 to draft the 1988 constitution. However, by September 1987, with the economy in turmoil, an agrarian reform plan held in disrepute and a raging controversy regarding the length of his presidential mandate, the PMDB-led Democratic Alliance was dissolved. Sarney agreed to hand over power in March 1990 and in September 1988 endorsed Ulysses Guimarães' bid to become his successor.

In the 1990s the PMDB became an electoral machine with very little internal discipline or ideological coherence. The party also became tainted by allegations of corruption against several of its leaders. In March 1991 the 20-year party leadership of Guimarães finally ended, when he was defeated in a party election by the former governor of São Paulo, Orestes Quercia. In October the following year Guimarães was killed in a helicopter crash. In 1994 Quercia himself was forced to resign amid allegations of corruption.

As the largest component of the coalition supporting the presidential candidacy of Fernando Henrique Cardoso of the →Brazilian Social Democratic Party (PSDB) in 1994, the PMDB won 107 seats in the Chamber of Deputies, 22 seats in the Senate and nine of the 26 governorships. In the 1998 congressional elections, however, the PMDB came third behind the →Liberal Front Party and the PSDB, securing 82 seats in the Chamber and 27 in the Senate.

Popular Socialist Party
Partido Popular Socialista (PPS)
Address. Praça dos Tres Poderes, Anexo II, Camara dos Deputados, 70.169–970 Brasilia–DF
Telephone. (+55–61) 311–2164
Fax. (+55–61) 323–6389
Email. webmaster@pps.com.br
Website. www.pps.org.br
Leadership. Roberto Freire (president); Paulo Hartung (Senate leader); Rubens Bueno (Chamber leader); Francisco Inácio de Almeida (secretary-general)
Originally founded in 1922 as the Communist Party of Brazil, the party was renamed as the PPS in January 1992 under the leadership of Roberto Freire. It supported the liberation of the former Soviet Union, describing Marxism-Leninism as "corruption by Stalin of the thoughts of Marx, Engels and Lenin". In 1992 the party opted for the pursuit of socialism through democratic means, effectively becoming a moderate left-of-centre organisation. The PSP mainly campaigns for job creation, the abolition of "unproductive landholdings" and the autonomy of Amazonia.

In 1998 the PSB, in alliance with the small →Liberal Party, supported the presidential candidacy of Ciro Gomes, a dissident of the →Brazilian Social Democratic Party and governor of Ceara. Gomes did well in the presidential election, polling almost 11% of the votes, but his popularity did not help the PPS, which won only three seats in the Chamber of Deputies.

Progressive Brazilian Party
Partido Progressista Brasileiro (PPB)
Address. Anexo I do Senado Federal, 17 Andar –Brasilia/DF, 70165–900
Telephone. (+55–61) 311–3041
Fax. (+55–61) 226–8192
Email. webmaster@ppb.org.br
Website. www.ppb.org.br
Leadership. Paulo Salim Maluf (president)
A centre-right party based in Brazil's south and south-east, the PPR was formed in 1993 as a merger of the Social Democratic Party (PDS) and the Christian Democratic Party (PDC). Since its origins, what is now the PPB has changed its name several times and has undergone multiple splits as well as mergers with other parties. Although not an original member of the coalition supporting the successful presidential candidacy of Fernando Henrique Cardoso of the →Brazilian Social Democratic Party in 1994, the PPB later joined the government alliance. The party depends heavily on the political popularity of its leader, the former governor of São Paulo, Paulo Salim Maluf. In the 1998 elections the PPB won 60 seats in the Chamber of Deputies and five in the Senate, making it the fourth larger party in Congress.

Workers' Party
Partido dos Trabalhadores (PT)
Address. Rua Silveira Martins, 132, Centro SP
Telephone. (+55–11) 233–1313
Fax. (+55–11) 226–9762
Email. ptbrasil@ax.apc.org
Website. www.pt.uol.com.br

Leadership. Luíz Inácio (Lula) da Silva (presidential candidate); José Dirceu (president)

The PT was founded by the leader of the powerful United Confederation of Workers (CUT), Luis Inácio da Silva (known universally as Lula), Jaco Bitar and Airton Soares and emerged from the growing São Paulo *autentico* independent trade union movement in the late 1970s. The party also received strong support from the progressive branch of the Catholic Church and members of small left-wing groups as well as from former supporters of the former →Brazilian Labour Party (PTB), which had backed Presidents Vargas and Kubitschek in the 1950s. The party has since remained closely associated with the main trade union umbrella organisation, the CUT. Although chiefly supported by urban industrial workers, the party is also active in rural areas.

In its first congressional elections in 1982, the PT received only six seats in the Chamber of Deputies. The more open elections of 1986 gave the party 19 seats in the Chamber. However, opposition to President Sarney's austerity measures and support for the strikes and demonstrations called by the CUT greatly broadened the PT's electoral appeal. This became evident in the municipal elections of 1988 when the PT won control of 36 important towns and Luiza Erundina da Souza became mayor of São Paulo, the first woman mayor in Brazil. In the presidential election of November 1989, the PT formed a Popular Front with the →Brazilian Socialist Party (PSB), the →Communist Party of Brazil (PCdoB) and other left-wing parties. Standing in the subsequent presidential election, Lula da Silva came a close second to Fernando Collor de Mello in 1989.

In the 1990s the party underwent a progressive change of identity, abandoning its radical socialist proposals in favour of a more moderate programme aimed to appeal to wider sections of the electorate. In both the 1994 and the 1998 presidential elections Lula da Silva came second to Fernando Henrique Cardoso of the →Brazilian Social Democratic Party (PSDB), with 27% and 31.7% of the popular vote respectively. In the 1998 congressional elections the PT won 58 seats in the Chamber of Deputies and seven in the Senate. It has since acted as the main opposition party to the Cardoso administration.

Other Parties

Christian Social Party (*Partido Social Cristão, PSC*), centrist formation which won two seats in the Chamber of Deputies in the 1998 elections.
Address. R. Pouso Alegre 1390, Floresta, BH–MG, 30140–080
Telephone. (+55–31) 467–1390
Fax. (+55-31) 467–6522
Email. gms.mkt@uol.br
Leadership. Jorge Abdala Nossels (president)

Democratic Socialist Party (*Partido Socialista Democrático, PSD*), won three seats in the Chamber in 1998.

Address. Rua Moaci 329, Bairro da Moema, São Paulo, 04083–000
Telephone. (+55–11) 539–2683
Fax. (+55–11) 886–6585

Green Party (*Partido Verde*), small ecologist party which won one seat in the Chamber in 1998.
Address. Rua dos Pinheiros 812–Pinheiros, São Paulo, Brazil 05422–001
Telephone. (+55–11) 883–1722
Fax. (+55–11) 524–6875
Email. pv@pv.org.br

Humanist Solidarity Party (*Partido Humanista da Solidaridade, PHS*), won one Chamber seat in 1998.

National Labour Party (*Partido Trabalhista Nacional, PTN*), won one Chamber seats in 1998.
Address. Rua Antônio de Barros 2391, Conj. 33, 3 andar, Tatuape/SP 03401-001
Telephone. (+55–11) 522–6274

National Mobilization Party (*Partido da Mobilização Nacional, PMN*), won two Chamber seats 1998.
Address. Rua Bernardo Gimarães 1298 Apt.402, BH–MG, 30140–080
Telephone. (+55–11) 964–3634
Email. pmn@bitsnet.com.br

National Order Reconstruction Party (*Partido da Reedificaço da Ordem Nacional, PRONA*), far-right party at the service of its populist leader; won two Chamber seats in 1998.
Address. Rua Visconde de Piraja 414, Grupo 603, Ipanema, Rio de Janeiro, RJ, 22410–002
Telephone. (+55-21) 267–0432
Fax. (+55-21) 267–0432
Leadership. Enéas Carneiro

National Solidarity Party of Brazil (*Partido Solidarista Nacional de Brasil, PSNB*), centrist formation with observer membership of the Christian Democrat Organization of America (ODCA).
Leadership. Philippe Guedon (president)

Social Labour Party (*Partido Social Trabalhista, PST*), small right-wing party which won one Chamber seat in 1998.
Address. Av. Ipiranga 1071, 11 andar, Conj. 1101 a 1103, SP 01039000
Telephone. (+55–11) 228–7411

Social Liberal Party (*Partido Social Liberal, PSL*), won one Chamber seat in 1998.
Address. SBS.Q2 Bl S. Sl. 510/511–BSB–Ed. Empire Center, Brasilia, DF 70070-904
Telephone. (+55–61) 225–2680
Fax. (155-61) 325–7491

Brunei Darussalam

Capital: Bandar Seri Begawan

Population: 336,376 (including migrant workers)

The Sultanate of Brunei, having been a British protectorate since 1888, became internally self-governing in 1959 and fully independent in 1984. Under the 1959 constitution, supreme executive authority was vested in the Sultan. He is formally assisted by a Council of Cabinet Ministers, a Privy Council and a Religious Council. However, the Legislative Council (*Majlis Mesyuarat Negeri*) – non-elective since 1970 – was abolished shortly after full independence. Since then there has been little meaningful political party activity under an absolute monarchy which has codified its principles in a state ideology called "Malay Islamic Monarchy", with major emphasis on the tenets of conservative Islam.

The Sultans (Omar Ali Saifuddin III until 1967, followed by his son Hassanal Bolkiah) have ruled substantially by decree since December 1962. In that month, the left-wing nationalist Brunei People's Party (PRB), which had won all the elective seats in the first elections in August 1962 on a platform of opposition to merger with Malaysia, staged a revolt, believing that the Sultan and the British were preparing to impose merger. The revolt was put down by British forces, and the party was banned under a State of Emergency which has been in force continuously since then. After new elections in 1965, but still without responsible government, a People's Independence Front was formed as an amalgamation of all existing political formations, with a view to pressing the British for democracy and independence. But this move was partly diverted by Sultan Omar's abdication. By the time of independence in 1984, party politics had been moribund for 18 years, during which a neo-monarchical polity was consolidated, funded by astronomical oil wealth.

Brunei was proclaimed to be "democratic" under its 1984 independence declaration, following which some political association was allowed. Two new parties were granted registration: the Brunei National Democratic Party (PKDB) in 1985 and the Brunei National Solidarity Party (PPKB) in 1986. In March 1988, however, the government announced that it had dissolved the PKDB, while the PPKB became moribund until resurfacing in the 1990s.

Brunei National Solidarity Party
Partai Perpaduan Kebangsa'an Brunei (PPKB)
Leadership. Mohamad Hatta bin Zainal Abidin

The PPKB is Brunei's only registered political party. It was established in 1985 under the leadership of Jumat bin Idris and Mohamad Hatta bin Zainal Abidin, as a breakaway from the Brunei National Democratic Party (*Partai Kebangsa'an Demokratik Brunei*, PKDB), which had originally been led by Abdul Latif bin Abdul Hamid and Abdul Latif bin Chuchu.

The PKDB had proclaimed itself as a party of "Brunei Malays" connoting almost any indigenous Muslim. The PKDB leaders were arrested in January 1988, the party being banned shortly afterwards (and Latif bin Abdul Hamid dying in 1990). The grounds given for the ban were that the party had breached its terms of registration by opening connections with a foreign organization, the Pacific Democratic Union (of regional centre-right parties).

The PPKB invited membership from all indigenous Bruneians, regardless of religion but was restricted by the ban on government officials joining political parties. Its lack of success in recruiting members resulted in de-registration but it re-emerged in February 1995 when it was allowed to hold its first national assembly. Its president, former PKDB leader Abdul Latif bin Chuchu, soon resigned under government pressure. The party subsequently revived with Mohamed Hatta bin Zainal Abidin (who had been its first secretary-general in 1985) as its new president. The party now expressed support for the government's determination to investigate the Amedeo scandal, centring on the affairs of the over-stretched conglomerate of Prince Jefri, who was simultaneously director of the Brunei Investment Agency (BIA). This "revival" of the party, with leave to direct critical if oblique attention towards a member of the royal family, prompted speculation as to inter-factional intrigue within the Palace, as also at the time of the original breakaway from the PKDB.

Following Prince Jefri's dismissl from the BIA (in July 1998), Mohamed Hatta bin Zainal Abidin came under fierce criticism from government sources, prompting speculation that the brief period of "openness" had passed with the weathering of the crisis.

Brunei People's Party
Partai Ra'ayat Brunei (PRB)
Leadership. Ahmad Azahari bin Mahmud (president); Zaini bin Ahmad (secretary-general)

This left-wing nationalist party, long since banned, and existing, if at all, only in exile, had won all the elective seats in the first elections in August 1962 on a platform of opposition to merger with Malaysia. Believing that the Sultan and the British were prepared to impose merger, it staged an unsuccessful revolt in December 1962 and was banned. Since then Azahari has spent most of his life in Indonesia. Zaini escaped from detention in 1973 and fled to Malaysia, but returned in 1994 to make his peace with the Sultan.

Bulgaria

Capital: Sofia

Population: 7,800,000 (2000E)

The Republic of Bulgaria was proclaimed as a multi-party parliamentary democracy in November 1990, replacing the People's Republic which had existed since the Bulgarian Communist Party (BCP) came to power after World War II. Under a new constitution formally effective since July 1991 and declaring Bulgaria to be a "democratic, constitutional and welfare state", the President is directly elected (with a Vice-President) for a five-year term and nominates the Prime Minister and Council of Ministers for parliamentary endorsement. Legislative authority is vested in a unicameral National Assembly (*Narodno Sobraniye*), whose 240 members are elected for a four-year term by universal suffrage of those aged 18 and over. Elections are held under a system of proportional representation, the threshold for representation being 4% of the national vote. The 1991 constitution guarantees freedom of political activity with the exception of parties with separatist aims or likely to promote ethnic or religious divisions.

In presidential elections on Oct. 27 and Nov. 3, 1996, Petar Stefanov Stojanov of the Union of Democratic Forces (SDS) was the victor in the second round with 59.7% of the votes cast, defeating the candidate of the Bulgarian Socialist Party (BSP). Elections to the National Assembly on April 19, 1997, gave an overall majority of 127 seats to the SDS-led United Democratic Forces (ODS). In the next Assembly elections on June 17, 2001, however, the new Simeon II National Movement (NDSV), headed by the former Bulgarian monarch, came to power by winning 120 seats (with 42.7% of the vote). The ODS took 51 (18.8%), the Coalition for Bulgaria (headed by the BSP) 48 (17.2%) and the Movement for Rights and Freedoms 21 (7.5%).

Bulgarian Agrarian People's Union
Bulgarski Zemedelski Naroden Sayuz (BZNS

Address. Vrabtcha Street 1, Sofia 1000
Telephone. (+359–2) 874070
Leadership. Petko Iliev (chairman of main faction); Anastasia Dimitrova-Moser (chairperson of BZNS-NS faction)

The BZNS is descended from a peasant party founded in 1899. After World War I a BZNS government was in power from 1920 under Aleksandur Stamboliyski, until being overthrown by a right-wing coup in 1923 in which Stamboliyski was killed. During World War II left-wing BZNS elements participated in the Fatherland Front led by the Bulgarian Communist Party (BCP), which came to power in 1944 following the ejection of German forces by the Red Army. The anti-Communist wing of the party, led by Nikola Petkov, refused to participate in the obligatory Front list for the October 1946 elections, the Front's victory in which entrenched the BZNS pro-Communists. Petkov was hanged for alleged treason in September 1947. Under the subsequent People's Republic, the BZNS was always represented in the Assembly (with about a quarter of the seats) as well as in successive governments (usually holding the agriculture portfolio). The party had no record of ever contesting BCP decisions, and its vetted membership was limited to 120,000.

As East European communism began to crumble in late 1989, the BZNS asserted its independence of the BCP by replacing its long-time leader (and Deputy Premier), Petur Tanchev, and by refusing to participate in the government formed in February 1990. Meanwhile, the party's anti-communist faction led by Milan Drenchev had formed the separate Bulgarian Agrarian National Union-Nikola Petkov (BZNS–NP). Advocating full political democracy and a market economy based on private agriculture, the BZNS–NP became a component of the opposition →Union of Democratic Forces (SDS) and figured in the SDS list of candidates for the June 1990 Assembly elections, while the rump BZNS won 16 of the 400 seats and in December 1990 joined a national unity coalition with the →Bulgarian Socialist Party (the former BCP) and elements of the SDS. In early 1991 a faction of the BZNS–NP reunited with the parent party to form BZNS–United for the October 1991 elections, while the bulk of the remaining BZNS–NP opted to stand independently of the SDS. Neither list surmounted the 4% threshold for representation.

Thereafter various unity schemes proved abortive and other splits occurred. In February 1992 Drenchev was replaced as BZNS–NP leader by Anastasia Dimitrova-Moser, who advocated co-operation with the SDS minority government by then in office. The following month the BZNS–NP faction which had remained in the SDS opted to set up its own organization within the SDS, while most of the BZNS–United became the →Bulgarian Agrarian National Union-Aleksandur Stamboliyski (BZNS-AS), so that there were now at least three separate Agrarian parties deriving from the historic BZNS. Dimitrova-Moser's faction contested the December 1994 Assembly elections within the People's Union (*Narodni Sayuz*, NS) alliance with the →Democratic Party (DP), which won 18 of the 240 seats, while the remainder of the BZNS-NP participated in the defeated SDS electoral front and the BNZS-AS was part of the victorious BSP-led alliance.

Both BZNS–NP factions backed the successful SDS candidacy of Petar Stoyanov in the autumn 1996 presidential elections, in which Todor Kavaldzhiev became Vice-President identified simply by the BZNS label. Thereafter the NS returned to the SDS umbrella, with the result that the two anti-BSP Agrarian factions were part of the victorious

United Democratic Forces (ODS) alliance headed by the SDS in the April 1997 Assembly elections, taking about a dozen seats between them. Familiar strains quickly developed, however, with Vice-President Kavaldzhiev complaining in October 1999 that the BZNS was being sidelined by the senior coalition partners, while in January 2001 two BZNS deputies withdrew from the SDS Assembly group. In the June 2001 Assembly elections the BNZS shared in the heavy defeat of the ODS by the →Simeon II National Movement.

The BZNS is affiliated to the Christian Democrat International and is an associate of the European People's Party (EPP).

Bulgarian Agrarian National Union–Aleksandur Stamboliyski
Bulgarski Zemedelski Naroden Sayuz–Aleksandur Stamboliyski (BZNS–AS)

Address. c/o Narodno Sobraniye, Sofia 1000
Leadership. Dragomir Shopov, Svetoslav Shivarov

The BZNS-AS designation was adopted by factions of the →Bulgarian Agrarian National Union (BZNS) favouring alliance with the →Bulgarian Socialist Party (BSP) rather than the centre-right →Union of Democratic Forces. The BSP/BZNS-AS ticket (which included the →Ecoglasnost Political Club) won a decisive victory in the December 1994 Assembly elections, following which two BZNS–AS ministers were included in the BSP-led government formed in January 1995.

In the autumn 1996 presidential elections the BZNS–AS backed the defeated BSP candidate, while in the April 1997 Assembly elections it shared in the heavy defeat of the BSP. Opposition to the party's link with the BSP culminated in mid-2000 in the withdrawal from the alliance of a majority BZNS–AS faction which opposed the BSP's support for EU and NATO membership.

Bulgarian Social Democratic Party
Bulgarska Sotsialdemokraticheska Partiya (BSDP)

Address. 37 Ekzarch Yossif Street, 1504 Sofia
Telephone. (+359–2) 390112; 831962
Fax. (+359–2) 390086
Leadership. Petar Dertliev (chairman); Stefan Radoslavov (general secretary)

The BSDP traces its descent from the historic BSDP founded in 1891 and more especially from the non-revolutionary "broad" party resulting from the secession in 1903 of the "narrow" revolutionary wing that in 1919 became the Bulgarian Communist Party. The BSDP opposed right-wing regimes of the inter-war period. During World War II left-wing Social Democrats joined the Communist-dominated Fatherland Front, which came to power in 1944 on Bulgaria's liberation by the Red Army. The party's anti-Communist wing, calling themselves Independent Socialists, was powerless to resist the post-war consolidation of Communist power. Following the declaration of a People's Republic in December 1947, the BSDP was merged with the Communist Party in 1948 (although it was never formally banned). Over the next four decades exiles kept the party alive as the Socialist Party, which was re-established in Bulgaria in 1989 under the leadership of Dertliev, a veteran of the pre-1948 party and a former political prisoner.

In March 1990 the party reverted to the historic BSDP title in view of the imminent decision of the Communist Party to rename itself the →Bulgarian Socialist Party (BSP). As a component of the opposition →Union of Democratic Forces (SDS), the BSDP took 29 of the 144 seats won by the

SDS in the June 1990 Assembly elections. The following month Dertliev was the initial SDS candidate for the presidency but withdrew to allow SDS chair Zhelyu Zhelev to be elected unopposed in the sixth round of Assembly voting. The BSDP supported the decision of some SDS elements to enter a BSP-dominated coalition government in December 1990 but thereafter came into increasing conflict with the SDS pro-market wing. Whereas the latter advocated fullscale economic liberalization, the BSDP favoured a welfare market economy (including private, co-operative and state sectors) and argued that privatized industries should become co-operatives where possible. In the October 1991 Assembly elections it headed a separate SDS-Centre list, which failed to surmount the 4% representation threshold.

The BSDP backed Zhelev's successful candidacy in the January 1992 direct presidential elections and thereafter sided with the President in his developing conflict with the SDS minority government. Following the appointment of a non-party "government of experts" in December 1992, the BSDP warned that it marked a reassertion of Communist influence. In March 1993, seeking to establish a credible third force between the BSP and an SDS seen as moving to the right, the BSDP launched the Bulgarian Social Democratic Union, which the following month was enlarged into a Council of Co-operation of centre-left parties, two of them with Assembly representation. Further alliance building by the BSDP resulted in the formation of the Democratic Alternative for the Republic (which included the →Green Party) for the December 1994 Assembly elections, but its vote share of 3.8% was below the 4% minimum required for representation. An extraordinary BSDP congress in April 1995 endorsed the established line of seeking an alliance of all social democratic forces, rejecting a minority argument that the party should federate with the ruling BSP.

The BSDP supported the successful SDS candidate in the autumn 1996 presidential elections and contested the April 1997 Assembly elections as part of the victorious SDS-led United Democratic Forces (ODS). However, left-inclined BSDP elements opposed the party's centrist orientation, with the result that in late 1998 the party split into a pro-SDS faction and an anti-SDS majority faction led by Dertliev. In January 2001 Dertliev took the majority faction into a New Left alliance headed by the BSP, while the minority BSDP remained within the SDS fold. In the event, both factions were on the losing side in the June 2001 Assembly elections, which were won by the new →Simeon II National Movement.

The BSDP is a full member party of the Socialist International.

Bulgarian Socialist Party
Bulgarska Sotsialisticheska Partiya (BSP)

Address. 20 Positano Street, Sofia 1000
Telephone. (+359–2) 989–4010
Fax. (+359–2) 980–5219
Email. bsp@bsp.bg
Website. www.bsp.bg
Leadership. Georgi Parvanov (chairman)

The BSP dates from April 1990, when the then ruling Bulgarian Communist Party (BCP) changed its name, abandoned Marxism–Leninism (although not Marxist theory) and embraced democratic socialism. The BCP traced its descent from the Bulgarian Social Democratic Party (BSDP), founded in 1891, which in 1903 split into left-wing "narrow" and non-revolutionary "broad" parties. The BCP as such dated from 1919, when the pro-Bolshevik "narrow" party became a founder member of the Third International (Comintern), later organizing armed opposition to right-wing regimes of the inter-war period and renaming itself the Workers' Party in 1927. Finally banned in 1934, the party was for a decade based in Moscow, where many of its exiled leaders were executed in Stalin's purges.

During World War II (in which Bulgaria was allied with Nazi Germany until mid-1944) the party played a leading role in the anti-Nazi resistance, its activities being directed by Georgi Dimitrov, Bulgarian secretary-general of the Comintern. In September 1944 the Communist-dominated Fatherland Front (FF), including left-wing Agrarians and Social Democrats, took power in Sofia, assisted by the conquering Red Army. In the post-war period the Communists consolidated their position, Dimitrov becoming Prime Minister after the October 1946 elections and a People's Republic being declared in December 1947. In 1948 the rump of the BSDP was merged with the Workers' Party, the resultant formation readopting the BCP rubric. It thus effectively became the sole ruling party, although the →Bulgarian Agrarian National Union (BZNS) remained a component of the Front, the smaller members of which were dissolved in 1949.

On Dimitrov's death in 1949 the BCP leadership passed to Vulko Chervenkov, but he was replaced in 1954 by Todor Zhivkov after being accused of fostering a personality cult. Under Zhivkov's long rule Bulgaria remained closely aligned with the USSR and participated in the 1968 Soviet-led intervention in Czechoslovakia. At one stage he even proposed that Bulgaria should become a constituent republic of the USSR. In 1971 Zhivkov added the post of head of state to his BCP leadership and subsequently appeared to be grooming his daughter Lyudmila for the succession, until her sudden death in 1981. At the 13th BCP congress in April 1986 he announced a reform programme reflecting the Gorbachev *glasnost* and *perestroika* initiatives in the USSR; but reform proved difficult to accomplish because of party in-fighting. Amidst the rapid collapse of European communism in late 1989, Zhivkov was replaced as BCP leader and head of state by Petur Mladenov, whose palace coup was supported by those concerned at Zhivkov's repression of ethnic Turks and apparent grooming of his playboy son Vladimir for the succession. A purge of Zhivkov and his supporters followed, accompanied by denunciations of 35 years of "feudal, repressive, corrupt and incompetent" government.

The BCP's "leading role" in society and the state was terminated under constitutional amendments enacted in January 1990, following which an extraordinary party congress on Jan. 30-Feb.2 renounced "democratic centralism", replaced the BCP central committee with a supreme council and its politburo and secretariat with a presidium, and opted for a "socially-oriented market economy". In keeping with a pledge to separate state and party functions, the party leadership passed to Aleksandur Lilov (a prominent BCP reformer of the Zhivkov era), with Mladenov remaining head of state. Later in February 1990, paradoxically, the BCP was obliged to form the first openly all-Communist government in Bulgaria's history when the BZNS, now asserting its independence, opted to go into opposition and the new →Union of Democratic Forces (SDS) refused to join a national unity coalition. Dissatisfaction with the pace of change led in February to the emergence of a reformist BCP faction called the →Alternative Socialist Association; in the same period the Communist Youth League and the official trade union federation reconstituted themselves as bodies independent of the BCP, while the FF became the Fatherland Union. In April 1990, following a ballot of party members, the BCP officially renamed itself the BSP, which in multi-party elections in June resisted the East European trend by being returned to power with 211 of the 400 seats. Although the SDS did well in Sofia and other cities, the ruling party's organizational strength in rural areas made the difference.

In July 1990 Mladenov resigned as head of state, after disclosures about his role in the suppression of anti-government demonstrations in December 1989. He was succeeded by SDS leader Zhelyu Zhelev in August, in which month the BSP's headquarters building in Sofia was burnt down during an SDS-led demonstration. In December 1990 the BSP also vacated the premiership, although it remained the largest component in a coalition with the SDS and the BZNS. The adoption of a new democratic constitution in July 1991 was followed by political dissension over the BSP's attitude to the August coup attempt by hardliners in Moscow, seen by many as initially supportive. In further elections in October 1991 the BSP was allied with eight small parties and organizations on a platform of preserving the "Bulgarian spirit and culture", including the moderate →Bulgarian Liberal Party, the →Christian Republican Party and the nationalist →Fatherland Party of Labour, but was narrowly defeated by the SDS. It therefore went into opposition for first time since 1944 and in November 1991 the BSP Assembly group adopted the name Union for Social Democracy. At a party congress in December 1991, described as the 40th (i.e. since 1891), Lilov was replaced as leader by Zhan Videnov, who advocated a "modern left socialist party" and easily defeated the candidate of the reformist social democrats, Georgi Pirinski. The BSP also suffered a narrow defeat in the direct presidential election held in January 1992, its preferred candidate securing 46.5% of the second-round vote.

In September 1992 the decision of the (ethnic Turkish) →Movement for Rights and Freedoms (DPS) to withdraw support from the SDS minority government enabled the BSP to reassert its influence. A "government of experts" headed by Lyuben Berov (non-party), appointed in December, was backed by most BSP deputies (although a faction led by former leader Lilov voted against) in effective alliance with the DPS. Thereafter, as the government achieved a degree of stability by not hurrying privatization and deregulation of the economy, the BSP was content to avoid direct governmental responsibility during a period of transition, while relying on the Communist-era establishment network and the party's strength in the Assembly to influence government decision-making. By mid-1993 the BSP was again the largest Assembly party, due to the steady erosion of SDS affiliation. Dissent rumbled on in the party, however, as indicated by the launching in June 1993 of the centre-left Civic Alliance for the Republic, which included some BSP dissidents. In May 1994 a proposal by Berov to appoint a BSP member as Economy Minister was successfully opposed by the DPS on the grounds that it would signify BSP control of the government.

On the resignation of the Berov government in September 1994, the BSP declined the opportunity to try to form a new administration, preferring early elections. These were held in December, the BSP being allied principally with the →Bulgarian Agrarian National Union–Aleksandur Stamboliyski and →Ecoglasnost. The outcome was an overall Assembly majority for the BSP-led list and the formation of a coalition government in January 1995 under the premiership of Videnov which committed itself to a socially-oriented market economy and integration into European institutions. In local elections in October-November 1995 the BSP consolidated its position as the strongest party, winning 41% of the first-round vote in its own right.

In the autumn 1996 presidential elections the BSP sought to attract centrist support by nominating Pirinski (by now Foreign Minister), but he was ruled ineligible because he had been born in the USA. The BSP replacement was Culture Minister Ivan Marazov, who stood on the 'Together for Bulgaria' label but who was defeated by Petar Stoyanov (SDS) in the second voting round in early November on a 60%-40% split. Videnov accordingly resigned as both Prime Minister and BSP chairman, being replaced in the latter capacity by Georgi Parvanov in December 1996. Despite resistance by the BSP, President Stoyanov installed a caretaker administration and called early Assembly elections in April 1997. The BSP ran as leader of the Democratic Left alliance (again including BZNS and Ecoglasnost factions) but was heavily defeated by the SDS-led United Democratic Forces (ODS), the BSP-led alliance being reduced to 58 seats and 22% of the vote.

In opposition, the BSP in December 1998 formed the Social Democracy Union with other left-wing forces, while also establishing an alliance with the →Euro-Left Coalition with a view to broadening its popular base for the 2001 Assembly elections. In mid-2000 the pro-BSP faction of the BZNS broke into two groups, the main one withdrawing from the alliance in opposition to the BSP's support for NATO and EU membership. In January 2001 the BSP launched another alliance of left-wing parties, this one called the New Left, which was committed to "the values of modern social democracy and the European left".

Yet another title, Coalition for Democracy, was adopted by the BSP and its allies in the Assembly elections held in June 2001. However, the party's hopes of a return to power were dashed by the surprise victory of the new →Simeon II National Movement, in the face of which the BSP-led alliance could manage only 48 seats and 17.2% of the vote. After the elections, Parvanov accepted "full responsibility" for his party's defeat but received a vote of confidence from its executive council.

Democratic Party
Demokratiecka Partiya (DP)

Address. 8 blvd Dondoukov, 1000 Sofia
Telephone. (+359–2) 800187
Fax. (+359–2) 803411
Leadership. Aleksandur Pramatarski (chairman)

Descended from the conservative Christian party of the same name founded in 1896, the DP was revived in 1989 and joined the opposition →Union of Democratic Forces (SDS). Following the SDS victory in the October 1991 elections, DP leader Stefan Savov was elected president of the National Assembly. However, shortly before the fall of the minority SDS government, he resigned from the Assembly post in September 1992, after being named in a censure motion tabled by the opposition →Bulgarian Socialist Party and supported by some SDS dissidents. For the December 1994 Assembly elections the DP broke with the SDS, forming the People's Union with a faction of the →Bulgarian Agrarian National Union. The alliance took third place, with 18 of the 240 seats and a vote share of 6.5%.

The DP backed the winning SDS candidate, Petar Stoyanov, in the autumn 1996 presidential elections and subsequently rejoined the SDS-led alliance, called the United Democratic Forces (ODS). In April 1997 it shared in the landslide victory of the ODS in Assembly elections, taking seven of the 134 seats won by the alliance. Savov died in January 2000 and was succeeded as DP leader by Aleksandur Pramatarski. In the June 2001 Assembly elections the DP shared in the heavy defeat of the ODS by the new →Simeon II National Movement.

The DP is affiliated to both the International Democrat Union and the Christian Democrat International and is an associate member of the European People's Party (EPP).

Ecoglasnost Movement
Dvizhenie Ekoglasnost}

Address. 28 Marin Drinov Street, 1504 Sofia
Leadership. Edwin Sugarev (chairman)

The Ecoglasnost dissident movement was formed by anti-communist environmentalists in April 1989 under the leadership of the zoologist Petur Beron and the actor Petur Slabakov. Ecoglasnost was the principal organizer of the popular demonstrations which surrounded the downfall of Todor Zhivkov in November 1989 and became a leading component of the opposition →Union of Democratic Forces (SDS). On the election of Zhelyu Zhelev as President in July 1990, Beron succeeded him as SDS chair but was forced to resign in December by disclosures about his past role as a government informer. His successor, Filip Dimitrov, was also from Ecoglasnost and led the SDS to a narrow victory in the October 1991 Assembly elections, becoming Prime Minister of an SDS minority government. In those elections, a radical Ecoglasnost faction, taking the name →Green Party, presented a separate SDS-Liberal list with other left-of-centre groups but failed to secure representation.

Following the fall of the Dimitrov government in October 1992, the Ecoglasnost Movement became concerned at the rightward drift of the SDS. Some elements moved to centre-left alliances initiated by the →Bulgarian Social Democratic Party, while the main faction opted for alignment with the →Bulgarian Socialist Party (BSP) for the December 1994 elections. It was therefore on the winning side and was allocated the environment portfolio in the resultant BSP-led government. In the April Assembly 1997 elections, however, Ecoglasnost shared in the defeat of the BSP-led Democratic Left alliance, while in the June 2001 elections Ecoglasnost elements also participated in the equally unsuccessful BSP-led Coalition for Bulgaria.

Movement for Rights and Freedoms
Dvizhenie za Prava i Svobodi (DPS)
Address. 50/B/55 Petar Topalov Shmid, Ivan Vazov Street, 1408 Sofia
Telephone. (+359–2) 519822
Leadership. Ahmed Dogan (chairman); Osman Oktay (deputy chairman)
The DPS was founded in January 1990 based mainly in the Muslim ethnic Turkish community, forming some 10% of Bulgaria's population. The policies of compulsory assimilation practised in the 1980s by the Zhivkov regime, resulting in the flight of many ethnic Turks to Turkey and elsewhere, formed the background to the DPS's aims, which included full political, cultural and religious rights but excluded any fundamentalist or separatist objectives. In the June 1990 Assembly elections the DPS won 23 of the 400 seats at issue with 6% of the national vote. From December 1990 it participated in a national unity coalition under a non-party Prime Minister, together with the dominant →Bulgarian Socialist Party (BSP) and the →Union of Democratic Forces (SDS). In further elections in October 1991 it improved its positition, winning 24 of 240 seats with 7.6% of the vote.

From November 1991 the DPS gave crucial parliamentary backing to a minority SDS administration, being rewarded with the lifting of a ban on optional Turkish-language instruction in secondary schools. But the SDS government's subsequent pro-market policies were described as "blue fascism" by the DPS, which withdrew its support in September 1992, thereby precipitating the government's fall in October. After the BSP had failed to fill the political vacuum, the DPS successfully nominated a non-party Prime Minister (Lyuben Berov) to head a "government of experts" which included semi-official DPS representation. In the Assembly vote to endorse the new government in December 1992, the DPS was supported by most BSP deputies and by some SDS dissidents. In 1993 the DPS backed the Berov government but was weakened by internal dissension and by continuing emigration of ethnic Turks. In March 1994, after Berov had suffered a heart attack, the DPS Deputy Premier, Evgeni Matinchev (an ethnic Bulgarian), became acting Prime Minister. In May 1994 the DPS successfully opposed the ailing Berov's proposal to appoint a BSP member as Economy Minister.

Weakened by the launching of at least two breakaway parties in 1994, the DPS slipped to 5.4% of the vote and 15 seats out of 240 in the December 1994 elections, therefore reverting to opposition status. It won 8.2% of the vote in municipal elections in October 1995, following which the party mounted a protest campaign against the decision of the authorities to annul its victory in the south-eastern town of Kurdzhali on the grounds of voting irregularities. The DPS backed the successful candidacy of Petar Stoyanov of the SDS in the autumn 1996 presidential elections.

Prior to April 1997 Assembly elections, a majority decision by the DPS not to join the SDS-led United Democratic Forces (ODS) caused a pro-SDS faction to form the breakaway →National Movement for Rights and Freedoms. For the elections the rump DPS headed the Union for National Salvation (ONS), including the →Green Party

and the →New Choice Union, which won 19 seats on a 7.6% vote share. In opposition, the DPS in July 1998 participated in the launching of the four-party Liberal Democratic Alliance, while in January 2000 the Party of Democratic Change (PDP), one of the 1994 breakaway groups, rejoined the DPS.

The DPS contested the June 2001 Assembly elections at the head of an alliance which included the Liberal Union and the Euro-Roma formation. Notwithstanding predictions that the emigration of ethnic Turks to Turkey had reduced the level of natural DPS support, the alliance won 7.4% of the national vote and 21 seats. It subsequently agreed to join a coalition government headed by the new →Simeon II National Movement.

Simeon II National Movement
Natsionalno Dvizhenie Simeon Ytori (NDSV)
Address. 30 Shishman Street, 1000 Sofia
Email. simbul@mad.servicom.es
Website. www.seker.es/simeon
Leadership. Simeon Saxe-Coburg-Gotha (chairman); Plamen Panayotov (parliamentary leader)
The NDSV was launched in April 2001 to rally anti-government opinion around the person of Simeon Saxe-Coburg-Gotha, who as Tsar Simeon II had lost the Bulgarian throne in 1946 at the age of nine and had later become a successful businessman in exile in Spain. He stressed that his movement was not seeking the restoration of the monarchy, instead setting out an 800-day programme to eradicate government corruption, to improve living standards and to create a healthy market economy to enable Bulgaria to become a member of the European Union. The movement also favours Bulgarian membership of NATO.

The NDSV was based in part on the Kingdom of Bulgaria (*Tsarstvo Bulgariya*) alliance formed for the October 1991 elections (in which it won 1.8% of the vote) to advocate the restoration of Simeon II. It included the Committee for the Restoration of Parliamentary Monarchy, the Constitutional Union of Plovdiv, the Crown Movement of Gabrovo, the Kingdom of Bulgaria Union of Rousse, the Prosvetlenie Association of Sofia, the St John of Rila Club of Sofia, the Third Bulgarian Kingdom Committee of Sofia, the Nadezhda Union of Dobrich and the Union of Simeon the Great of Lovich. In the April 1997 Assembly election a Union for the Monarchy (*Obedenenie za Carja*) had obtained 1.1% of the vote.

Having been refused registration in its own right by the courts, the NDSV resorted to forming an alliance with two legal parties (the Movement for National Revival and the Bulgarian Women's Party) and using the NDSV title for the alliance in the June 2001 National Assembly elections. It swept to victory over the incumbent government headed by the →Union of Democratic Forces (SDS), winning 120 of the 240 seats with a vote share of 42.7%. Spokesmen complained that the movement would have won a clear overall majority if voters had not been confused by the presence on the ballot paper of two spoiling lists called the →Simeon II Coalition and the →National Union for Tsar Simeon II, which obtained 5% of the vote between them.

Simeon himself did not stand for election to the Assembly, but was not barred from becoming Prime Minister under the Bulgarian constitution. In post-election meetings with the NDSV leader, President Stoyanov stopped addressing him as "Your Majesty" and instead, out of "respect for the Bulgarian Republic", opted to address him as "Mr Saxe-Coburgotski", i.e. by the Bulgarian version of his original German family name. After some indecision, the former monarch agreed to become Prime Minister of a government which included representatives of the ethnic Turkish →Movement for Rights and Freedoms.

Union of Democratic Forces
Sayuz na Demokratichnite Sili (SDS)
Address. 134 Rakovski Street, Sofia 1000

Telephone. (+359–2) 981–2992
Fax. (+359–2) 981–0522
Email. udf-ir@bsbg.net
Website. www.sds.bg
Leadership. Ekaterina Mihailova (chairman); Nadezhda Mihailova (parliamentary leader); Plamen Ivanov (secretary-general)

The SDS was established in December 1989 by 10 fledgling pro-democracy movements, notably the Support (*Podkrepa*) independent trade union federation (formed in February 1989 by Konstantin Trenchev), the →Ecoglasnost environmentalist movement and →Citizens' Initiative (GI). The other founder members were the "Nikola Petkov" faction of the →Bulgarian Agrarian National Union (BZNS); the →Bulgarian Social Democratic Party (BSDP); the Independent Association for the Defence of Human Rights in Bulgaria, led by Ilya Minev; the Club of Persons Illegally Repressed After 1945, led by Dimitur Bakalov; the Committee for Religious Rights, Freedom of Conscience and Spiritual Values, led by Hristofor Subev (a priest); the Federation of Clubs for Democracy, led by Petko Simeonov (later founder of the →Liberal Party); and the Federation of Independent Student Societies. In the period up to the June 1990 elections the SDS was also joined by the →Radical Democratic Party (RDP); what became the →United Christian Democratic Centre (OHZ); the →Democratic Party (DP); the →Christian Democratic Union (HDS); and the →Alternative Social–Liberal Party (ASP). The →Bulgarian Democratic Forum (BDF) and the →Republican Party (RP) became observer members of the SDS.

Chaired by Zhelyu Zhelev (a dissident philosophy professor of the Zhivkov era), the SDS entered into talks with the ruling Bulgarian Communist Party (BCP) in January 1990, first on ethnic Turkish rights (which the SDS supported) and then on the country's political future. The SDS was permitted to launch its own newspaper (*Demokratsija*) and negotiated detailed arrangements for multi-party elections, but it refused to join a coalition government with the BCP at that stage. The SDS campaign for the Assembly elections held in June 1990 was seen as negative and flawed by over-gearing to international opinion, the result being a decisive victory for the →Bulgarian Socialist Party (BSP), the new name of the BCP. Nevertheless, following the resignation of the BSP incumbent, the new Assembly elected Zhelev as President of Bulgaria in August 1990. SDS deputies and their supporters in the country kept up vigorous opposition to the BSP government, which resigned in November 1990 and was replaced in December by a coalition, headed by a non-party Prime Minister, consisting of the BSP, elements of the SDS and the rump BZNS. Also in December 1990, SDS chairman Petur Beron (who had succeeded Zhelev on his elevation to the presidency) was obliged to resign following disclosures about his past activities as a government informer. He was succeeded by Filip Dimitrov, also of the SDS environmentalist wing.

Despite being in government, the SDS maintained an opposition mode and in August 1991 made much political capital out of the BSP's ambiguous response to the abortive coup by hardliners in Moscow. However, dissension between moderate and radical elements resulted in the presentation of three distinct SDS lists in the new Assembly elections of October 1991. The party components of the SDS proper, also designated the SDS-Movement and still embracing various civil movements, included the ASP, the BDF, two dissident factions of the BSDP, the GI, the main DP, part of the Ecoglasnost movement, the RDP, the RP and the UDC. An SDS-Centre alliance was headed by the main BSDP and included the →Alternative Socialist Association and factions of the DP and Ecoglasnost. An SDS-Liberal list included the →Green Party, the OHZ, a faction of the DP and the Federation of Clubs for Democracy. The outcome was a narrow plurality for the main SDS, which won 110 of the 240 seats and 34.4% of the vote, just ahead of the BSP.

Neither the SDS-Centre (3.2%) nor the SDS-Liberals (2.8%) secured representation. The main SDS proceeded to form Bulgaria's first wholly non-communist government since World War II, headed by Dimitrov, with the parliamentary support of the (ethnic Turkish) →Movement for Rights and Freedoms (DPS). In direct presidential elections in January 1992, Zhelev secured a popular mandate as the SDS candidate, winning 53% of the second-round vote (following an inconclusive 45% in the first).

The minority SDS government quickly fell out with the trade unions (including the *Podkrepa* federation), which opposed aspects of its pro-market economic programme. Serious strains also developed between President Zhelev and the Dimitrov government, while the SDS Assembly group, harbouring over 20 distinct party groupings, became riven with dissension. Having been told by Zhelev in August 1992 to end its "war against everyone", the Dimitrov government fell in October after the DPS had withdrawn its support and made common cause with the BSP in a no-confidence vote. The successor DPS-proposed "government of experts" under Lyuben Berov was approved by the Assembly in December 1992 with the support of most BSP and some 20 SDS deputies. The latter included the ASP deputies (who later joined the Bulgarian Social Democratic Union headed by the BSDP) and those of what became the →New Union for Democracy. Seen as increasingly conservative in orientation, the anti-Berov SDS in mid-1993 mounted demonstrations against President Zhelev for his alleged connivance with "re-communization". In June 1993 the Vice-President elected with Zhelev in January 1992, the poet Blaga Dimitrova, resigned and was not replaced.

By early 1994 SDS numbers in the Assembly had fallen to some 90 deputies, less than the BSP's committed parliamentary strength, while the Berov team was widely credited with having restored political stability. In April 1994 Zhelev sought to re-establish his SDS credentials by withdrawing political support from the government, charging it with having delayed privatization and with failure to attract foreign investment. The Berov government survived no-confidence votes in May but the validity of the results was disputed by the SDS, which in June launched a boycott of proceedings in the Assembly. Following the resignation of the Berov government in September 1994, the SDS declared a preference for new elections but was further weakened by the formation of the separate People's Union by former SDS formations.

Held in December 1994, the elections resulted in defeat for the SDS, which won only 24.2% of the vote and 69 of the 240 seats. Soon afterwards Dimitrov was replaced as SDS leader by Ivan Kostov (a former Finance Minister), who headed a party which, as the principal opposition formation, was now more cohesive by virtue of previous defections. Having failed to secure the passage of a motion of no confidence in the government in September 1995 (although it attracted 102 votes), the SDS won 24.7% of the first-round vote in municipal elections the following month.

Public dissatisfaction with the BSP-led government facilitated a comeback for the SDS in the autumn 1996 presidential elections, in which SDS candidate Petar Stoyanov, a relatively unknown lawyer, was elected with just under 60% of the vote in the second round. He eventually succeeded in calling early Assembly elections for April 1997, in which the SDS, heading an alliance called the United Democratic Forces (ODS), won 137 of the 240 seats. Kostov became the new Prime Minister, heading an SDS-led government.

The SDS-led government survived for the full four-year parliamentary term and was regarded as having overseen significant economic progress. In the June 2001 Assembly elections, however, it went down to a heavy defeat at the hands of the new →Simeon II National Movement, retaining only 51 seats with 18.2% of the national vote. Kostov accepted responsibility for the defeat and was succeeded as SDS leader by one of his close aides, Ekaterina Mihailova.

Other Parties

Bulgarian Democratic Forum (*Bulgarski Demokraticheski Forum, BDF*), of conservative orientation, successor to the pre-communist Union of Bulgarian National Legions, became observer member of →Union of Democratic Forces.
Address. 82 G.S. Rakovski Street, 1505 Sofia
Leadership. Vasil Zlatarov

Bulgarian National Radical Party (*Bulgarska Natsionalna Radikalna Partiya, BNRP*), won 1.1% of the vote in the 1991 elections, falling to 0.1% in June 2001 contest.
Address. 6 Alen Street, 1000 Sofia
Leadership. Ivan Georgiev (chairman)

Christian Democratic Union (*Hristiyan Demokraticheska Sayuz, HDS*), affiliate of the Christian Democrat International, participant in the →Union of Democratic Forces.
Address. 134 Rakowski Street, 1000 Sofia
Leadership. Julius Pavlov (chairman)

Democratic Party 1896 (*Demokratiecka Partiya 1896*), founded in 1994 by a faction of the →Democratic Party which opposed the creation of the People's Union and preferred to stay in the →Union of Democratic Forces.
Leadership. Stefan Raychevski (chairman)

Democratic Party of Justice in the Republic of Bulgaria (*Demokraticheska Partiya na Spravedlivostta v Republika Bulgariya, DPSRP*), founded in 1994 as a breakaway of the ethnic Turkish →Movement for Rights and Freedoms, led initially by Chief Mufti Nedim Gendzhev; won only 0.3% in June 2001 Assembly elections.
Leadership. Ali Ibrahimov (chairman)

Euro-Left Coalition (*Koalicija Evrolevica, KEL*), pro-EU formation launched in February 1997 by two left-leaning parties, including the Civic Union of the Republic led by Aleksandur Tomov and some dissident deputies of the →Bulgarian Socialist Party (BSP); won 14 seats with 5.6% of the vote in April 1997 Assembly elections. The grouping in December 1998 reached agreement with the BSP on the creation of a broad left-wing front for the June 2001 elections, but a faction called the Bulgarian Euro-Left stood independently and won 1% of the vote. The KEL is an observer member of the Socialist International.
Leadership: Aleksandur Tomov (chairman)

Georgi Ganchev Bloc (*Georgi Ganchev Blok, GGB*), created in March 2000 as successor to the Bulgarian Business Bloc (BBB), which had been founded in November 1990 by leading businessman Valentin Mollov as a right-wing, pro-market formation advocating the conversion of Bulgaria into a tariff- and tax-free zone so that it could act as a conduit for commerce between the former Soviet republics and the West. It won 1.3% of the vote (and no seats) in the 1991 elections but attracted growing support under the new leadership of the charismatic Georgi Ganchev, a former fencing champion whose accounts of a colourful past attracted much media publicity. In the December 1994 Assembly elections the BBB broke through to representation, winning 4.7% of the vote and 13 of the 240 Assembly seats. In the autumn 1996 presidential elections Ganchev attracted an impressive 21.9% in taking third place in the first voting round.

In the April 1997 Assembly elections the BBB improved slightly to 4.9% of the vote but its representation fell to 12 seats. By September 1997 two expulsions and a resignation from the BBB Assembly group had reduced its size to below the 10 deputies required to qualify for group status. Its relaunching as the GGB failed to arrest the decline, the party winning only 0.4% of the vote (and no seats) in the June 2001 Assembly elections.
Leadership. Georgi Ganchev (president)

Green Party (*Zelena Partiya, ZP*), derives from the →Ecoglasnost Movement of anti-communist environmentalists which played a key role in bringing an end to one-party Bulgarian communism in 1989-90 as part of the →Union of Democratic Forces (SDS).
Address. 3 Alabin Street, 1000 Sofia
Leadership. Aleksandur Karakachanov

Internal Macedonian Revolutionary Organization (*Vnatresno Makedonska Revolucionerna Organizacija, VMRO*), Bulgarian branch of the Macedonian nationalist movement of the same name, representing people in Bulgaria originating from original Macedonian territory; won two Assembly seats in 1997 Assembly elections within alliance headed by the →Union of Democratic Forces (SDS); contested June 2001 elections in alliance with George Day (*Gergyovden*) movement, winning 3.6% of the vote, thus failing to surmount the 4% threshold.
Address. 5 Pirotska Street, 1301 Sofia
Telephone. (+359–2) 876455
Email. vmro-mo@iname.com
Leadership. Krasimir Karakachanov (chairman)

National Movement for Tsar Simeon II list which won 1.7% in June 2001 Assembly elections, apparently attracting votes intended for the victorious →Simeon II National Movement.

New Social Democratic Party (*Nova Sotsialdemokraticheska Partiya, NSDP*), founded in 1994 by a faction of the →Bulgarian Social Democratic Party which opted to remain under the umbrella of the →Union of Democratic Forces.
Leadership. Vasil Mihailov (chairman)

Radical Democratic Party (*Radikalna Demokraticheska Partiya, RDP*), descended from a pre-war party, revived in 1989 and a participant in the →Union of Democratic Forces in recent elections, member of the Liberal International.
Address. 34 blvd Dondukova, 1000 Sofia
Leadership. Elka Konstantinova & Aleksandur Yordanov

Simeon II Coalition, list which won 3.4% in June 2001 Assembly elections, apparently attracting votes intended for the victorious →Simeon II National Movement.

United Christian Democratic Centre (*Obedinen Hristijandemokratitcheski Zentar, OHZ*), affiliated to the Christian Democrat International and the International Democrat Union, participant in the →Union of Democratic Forces (SDS), originally as the United Democratic Centre, part of the SDS-Liberal coalition for the 1991 elections.
Address. 134 Rakwski Street, 1000 Sofia
Leadership. Stefan Sofianski (chairman)

Burkina Faso

Capital: Ouagadougou

Population: 11,950,000 (2000E)

Burkina Faso achieved independence from France in August 1960 and was called Upper Volta until August 1984. After 20 years of alternating parliamentary and military rule, a military coup in 1980 led to the installation of a radical left-wing regime by Capt. Thomas Sankara, who was overthrown (and killed) in a further coup in 1987 led by Capt. Blaise Compaoré at the head of an army faction called the Popular Front. Following the African trend, the government brought military rule to an end in June 1991 on the approval by referendum (and immediate promulgation) of a new constitution providing for multi-party democracy. Under its terms, an executive President is directly elected for a seven-year term by universal adult suffrage in two rounds of voting if no candidate secures an absolute majority in the first. The President appoints the Prime Minister and Council of Ministers subject to parliamentary approval. Legislative authority resides in the Assembly of People's Deputies (*Assemblée des Députés Populaires*), which is popularly elected for a five-year term on a constituency basis. The Assembly has 111 members (increased from 107 by a constitutional amendment adopted in Jan. 1997).

Presidential elections on Dec. 1, 1991, were boycotted by the opposition parties, with the result that Compaoré was elected unopposed in a turnout of only 28%. Assembly elections on May 24, 1992, resulted in victory for Compaoré's Organization for Popular Democracy–Labour Movement (ODP–MT), which won 78 seats, and several smaller allied parties in the Popular Front. In 1996 the ODT–MT was superseded by the pro-Compaoré Congress for Democracy and Progress (CDP), which was returned to power in the next Assembly elections on May 11, 1997, with 97 seats initially, and another four following a further round of voting in June. The Party for Democracy and Progress took six seats, the African Democratic Rally two, and the Alliance for Democracy and Federation two.

The presidential elections on Nov. 15, 1998, returned Compaoré for another seven-year term with over 87% of the vote, although several opposition parties again boycotted the poll. Prime Minister Kadre Desiré Ouedraogo resigned in November 2000, to be replaced by Paramanga Ernest Yonli presiding over a government with representatives from 10 political parties, including some opposition groupings.

African Democratic Rally
Rassemblement Démocratique Africain (RDA)
Address. BP 347, Ouagadougou
Leadership. Gérard Kango Ouedraogo (secretary-general)
The RDA is descended from the nationalist movement of the same name founded in 1946 to promote independence in French West Africa, its local branch, the Voltaic Democratic Union (UDV), becoming the dominant party in the two decades after independence in 1960. Revived in 1991, the RDA selected Gérard Kango Ouedraogo (a former Prime Minister) as its presidential candidate, but in the event the party joined the general opposition boycott of the December 1991 election. It participated in the May 1992 Assembly elections, achieving third place with six seats, and subsequently secured one portfolio in the broad coalition government appointed in June. In the May 1997 legislative elections the RDA retained two seats, while in the 1998 presidential poll its candidate, Frédéric Guirma, took third place but with less than 6% of the vote.

African Party for Independence
Parti Africain pour l'Indépendance (PAI)
Address. 01 BP 1035, Ouagadougou 01
Leadership. Philippe Ouedraogo (secretary-general)
The PAI was active as a pro-Soviet Marxist party in the 1970s but was banned following the 1983 Sankara coup. Following the 1987 Compaoré coup, it became a component of the ruling umbrella Popular Front (FP). It backed Compaoré's candidacy in the December 1991 presidential poll and won two seats in the May 1992 Assembly elections. The party was unsuccessful in the 1997 polls, but obtained representation in the government appointed at the end of 2000.

Alliance for Democracy and Federation
Alliance pour la Démocratie et la Fédération (ADF)
Address. BP 1943, Ouagadougou

Leadership. Herman Yaméogo
The ADF was launched in December 1990, its leader (son of a President deposed in 1966) having in 1978 founded the opposition National Union for the Defence of Democracy (UNDD). He later became leader of the →Movement of Progressive Democrats (MDP) but broke away to form the ADF after the MDP had been expelled from the ruling umbrella Popular Front in June 1990 because of his alleged "irresponsible" behaviour. In February 1991 the ADF issued a joint statement with the →Alliance for Democracy and Social Development calling for a transitional government and the exclusion of the ruling Popular Front parties from elections. Yaméogo was appointed Agriculture Minister in June 1991 but he and two other ADF ministers resigned in August in protest against the slow pace of democratization. The ADF boycotted the December 1991 presidential election but Yaméogo again accepted a cabinet post in February 1992. The party won four seats in the May 1992 Assembly elections but lost two in the May 1997 polls, although it obtained representation in the government formed in late 2000.

Congress for Democracy and Progress
Congrès pour la Démocratie et le Progrès (CDP)
Address. c/o Assemblée des Députés, Ouagadougou
Leadership. Roch Marc Christian Kaboré (president)
Website: www.cdp.bf
The CDP was created early in 1996 as a merger of President Compaoré's Organization for Popular Democracy–Labour Movement (ODP–MT) and some 10 other pro-regime parties. The ODP–MT had been created in April 1989 by a merger of the Burkinabe Union of Communists (UCB) and a faction of the Union of Communist Struggles (ULC), from which the UCB had previously split. It was intended originally to provide a single-party base for the Compaoré regime by unifying "all political tendencies in the country" and became the leading component of the pro-Compaoré

Popular Front (*Front Populaire*, FP), first created in October 1987 and reorganized in 1991. Meanwhile, the first ODP-MT secretary-general, Clément Ouedraogo (former UCB leader), had been dismissed in April 1990 for "serious failures of principle and party policy". At a congress in March 1991, the ODP–MT formally renounced Marxism-Leninism and embraced a free enterprise, pro-Western philosophy, while remaining unenthusiastic about multi-party politics.

Asserting its autonomy and dominance within the FP, the ODP–MT backed Compaoré's (uncontested) presidential candidacy in December 1991 and in May 1992 unexpectedly won a large majority in Assembly elections (which were condemned as fraudulent by the opposition parties). The ODP–MT was the leading party in the post-election coalition government headed by Youssouf Ouedraogo, which included six other parties, several of them outside the FP. In March 1994 Ouedraogo was replaced by Roch Marc Christian Kaboré after failing to reach a wage agreement with the trade unions in the wake of the devaluation of the CFA franc. In January 1995 the leader of the ODP–MT youth wing, Moumouni Ouedraogo, was killed in disturbances preceding local elections the following month.

On the creation of the CDP in February 1996, Kaboré was replaced as Prime Minister by Kadre Desiré Ouedraogo, who remained in office until November 2000, when he was replaced by Paramanga Ernest Yonli. During Kaboré's premiership, the CDP won the May 1997 legislative elections with a massive majority, taking 101 of the 111 Assembly seats, and President Compaoré was returned to office in the November 1998 poll.

Movement for Progress and Tolerance
Mouvement pour le Progrès et la Tolérance (MPT)
Leadership. Noyabtigungu Congo Kabore
Founded as an "anti-imperialist and nationalist/progressive" party, the MPT has been more prepared for co-operation with the Compaoré regime than other opposition parties and obtained representation in the government formed in November 2000.

Panafrican Sankarist Convention
Convention du Partis Sankaristes (CPS)
Leadership. Ernest Nongma Ouedraogo
The CPS was established in 1999 to pursue the leftist policies of the 1983–87 Sankara regime. It obtained representation in the government formed in November 2000.

Party for Democracy and Progress
Parti pour la Démocratie et le Progrès (PDP)
Address. BP 606, Ouagadougou
Telephone. (+226) 362190
Fax. (+226) 362902
Leadership. Joseph Ki-Zerbo
The PDP came into being as a result of a power struggle in the National Convention of Progressive Patriots–Social Democratic Party (CNPP–PSD) in 1993. Prof. Ki-Zerbo had been placed fourth in presidential elections in 1978 as candidate of what became the socialist-oriented Voltaic Progressive Front (FVP), which was banned after the 1980 Sankara coup. On the restoration of multi-partyism in 1991, Ki-Zerbo returned to Burkina Faso and became associated with the CNPP–PSD, heading the allied Union of Independent Social Democrats (*Union des Sociaux-Démocrates Indépendants*, USDI) in the May 1992 Assembly elections, in which it won one seat.

Ki-Zerbo broke with the CNPP–PSD following the retirement of its leader in May 1993, complaining of the "suspicion, internal quarrels and absence of motivation" generated by the resultant succession struggle. His new PDP was formally constituted at a congress in April 1994, when it claimed to have the support of nine of the 13 CNPP-PSD/USDI deputies and thus to be the second strongest party in the Assembly. In the May 1997 legislative elections, the PDP won six seats to become the second largest party and the main opposition in the Assembly.

The PDP inherited the FVP's membership of the Socialist International.

Union of Greens for the Development of Burkina
Union des Verts pour le Développement du Burkina (UVDB)
Leadership. Ram Ouedraogo
The party was founded in 1991 and its leader was the first declared candidate for the December 1991 presidential election, although he later withdrew along with all other opposition nominees. In the 1998 presidential poll (again subject to opposition boycotts), Ouedraogo came second to the incumbent, Blaise Compaoré, but with only 6.6% of the vote. The party obtained representation in the government formed in November 2000.

Burundi

Capital: Bujumbura

Population: 6,054,000 (2000E)

Burundi was granted independence as a monarchy in 1962, having previously been administered by Belgium since the termination of German rule during World War I, first under a League of Nations mandate and from 1946 as a UN trusteeship. The overthrow of the monarchy in 1966 and the declaration of the Republic of Burundi was followed, from 1976, by a series of military regimes and one-party government. After a coup in 1987, Maj. Pierre Buyoya came to power. Following the African trend, Buyoya published a National Unity Charter in May 1990, under which Burundi moved to civilian rule and "controlled" multi-partyism; but the transition served to unleash conflict between the majority Hutu ethnic group and the minority Tutsis who had traditionally exercised dominance. A new constitution approved in March 1992 provided for an executive President, directly elected by universal adult suffrage for a five-year term (renewable once) who appointed the Prime Minister. Legislative authority was vested in a unicameral 81-member National Assembly (*Assemblée Nationale*), directly elected for a five-year term by proportional representation from party lists, subject to a minimum requirement for representation of 5% of the overall vote. Political parties were required, to obtain registration, to subscribe to the 1990 National Unity Charter, eschew racial, religious and royalist identification and have founder members from each of Burundi's 15 provinces. A "convention of government" concluded by the main parties in September 1994 (and incorporated into the constitution) provided for formalized power-sharing in government structures between representatives of the Hutu and Tutsi ethnic groups.

The first round of presidential elections on June 1, 1993, resulted in an outright victory for Melchior Ndadaye of the Burundi Front for Democracy (FRODEBU), who secured 64.8% of the vote, against 32.4% for incumbent Buyoya (candidate of the Union for National Progress, UPRONA) and 1.4% for a candidate of the People's Reconciliation Party (PRP). In Assembly elections on June 29, 1993, FRODEBU won 65 seats and UPRONA the other 16. Ndadaye was killed in an attempted coup in October 1993 and was succeeded in January 1994 by Cyprien Ntaryamira (FRODEBU), who under emergency constitutional revisions was elected by the National Assembly rather than by popular vote. Three months later, on April 6, 1994, Ntaryamira himself died in an air crash and was succeeded by Sylvestre Ntibantunganya (FRODEBU).

From early 1995 Hutu guerrilla groups launched a campaign against the army. Mounting insecurity culminated in a further military coup on July 25, 1996 that brought Buyoya back to power. Buyoya tried to form an ethnically mixed government and announced a three-year transition to civil rule, initiating a "national debate". This led by mid-1998 to a partnership agreement between the executive and the FRODEBU-dominated National Assembly, and the adoption of a new transitional constitution. This enlarged the National Assembly to 121 members and created two new vice-presidents (Frederic Bamvuginyumvira of FRODEBU and Mathias Sinamenye of UPRONA). Buyoya was officially sworn in as President(head of state and government) on June 11, 1998.

The transitional process has since been undermined by continuing ethnic violence, despite a peace agreement between the government and most of the rebel groups in August 2000, facilitated by former President of South Africa, Nelson Mandela. In April 2001 junior army officers staged an unsuccessful coup attempt.

Burundi Front for Democracy
Front pour la Démocratie au Burundi (FRODEBU)
Address. c/o Assemblée Nationale, Bujumbura
Leadership. Jean Minani (president)
FRODEBU began as an informal alliance of opposition groups which campaigned for a "no" vote in the March 1992 constitutional referendum on the grounds that the Buyoya regime had refused to convene a full national conference to agree the transition to multi-partyism. Following the promulgation of the new constitution, FRODEBU registered as a political party, containing both Hutus and Tutsis. The first round of presidential elections on June 1, 1993, resulted in an outright victory for Melchior Ndadaye, the FRODEBU leader, who secured 64.8% of the vote, against 32.4% for incumbent Buyoya, of the →Union for National Progress (UPRONA). In Assembly elections on June 29, 1993, FRODEBU won 65 of the 81 seats with 71.4% of the vote. The accession to power of Ndadaye, a member of the majority Hutu ethnic group, marked an interruption of centuries of rule by the Tutsi minority, although UPRONA members were allocated the premiership and six portfolios in the post-election coalition government. Ndadaye was killed in an attempted coup by militant Hutu dissidents in October 1993 and was succeeded in January 1994 by Cyprien Ntaryamira (FRODEBU), also a Hutu, who likewise appointed a Tutsi (and UPRONA member) as Prime Minister of a broad coalition government charged with promoting inter-ethnic peace. Nevertheless, some FRODEBU leaders were implicated in Hutu revenge attacks on Tutsis.

On April 6, 1994, Ntaryamira himself died in an unexplained air crash near Kigali (together with the President of Rwanda) and was succeeded by Sylvestre Ntibantunganya (FRODEBU), a Hutu, who was formally endorsed by the National Assembly on Sept. 30, 1994. Immediately prior to his endorsement, FRODEBU signed the "convention of government" providing for power-sharing with other parties. Following Ntibantunganya's inauguration on Oct. 1, a new government included representatives of FRODEBU (the dominant party), UPRONA (which continued to hold the premiership) and five other parties. Subsequent strains between the main coalition partners were partially resolved in January 1995 by the election of Léonce Ngendakumana of FRODEBU as Assembly speaker with UPRONA support, while the controversial original nominee for the post, Jean Minani, became FRODEBU president in place of President Ntibantunganya.

FRODEBU continued to participate in the new power-sharing government installed in March 1995, holding 10 portfolios. In May President Ntibantunganya rejected suggestions that the territories of Burundi and Rwanda should be reorganized into ethnically pure Hutu and Tutsi states. The following month he was rebuffed by his own FRODEBU Assembly deputies when he sought approval to rule by decree, amid a serious deterioration in the internal security situation. In September 1995 FRODEBU and other "presidential bloc" ministers, calling themselves the Force for Democratic Change (*Force pour le Changement Démocratique*, FCD), issued a statement criticizing the UPRONA Interior Minister for having rejected an assertion by the US ambassador to Burundi that the security situation caused him "deep concern". The same statement accused the Interior Minister of refusing to apply the law on political parties and of failing to take action to curb the continuing violence.

Upon the resumption of executive power by Maj. Buyoya in July 1996 and subsequent dialogue with the FRODEBU-dominated National Assembly, transitional constitutional measures were adopted, including the appointment in mid-1998 of a FRODEBU representative, Frederic Bamvuginyumvira, as one of two vice-presidents.

Guarantor of the Freedom of Speech in Burundi
Inkinzo y'Igambo Ry'abarundi
Address. c/o Ministry of Culture, Bujumbura
Leadership. Alphonse Rugumbarara (president)
Although not represented in the Assembly elected in June 1993, *Inkinzo* was included in the broad coalition government appointed in February 1994, its president becoming Minister of Culture, Youth and Sports. It signed the September 1994 "convention of government" and was also included in the successive multi-party cabinets installed in October and March 1995, holding one portfolio.

People's Reconciliation Party
Parti de la Réconciliation du Peuple (PRP)
Leadership. François Mbesherubusa (president)
The PRP was founded in September 1991 by elements favouring a restoration of the (Tutsi) monarchy and power-sharing between ethnic groups in a parliamentary system. It secured official registration in July 1992, notwithstanding a provision in the new parties law enacted in April debarring parties with royalist aspirations (among other categories). Its presidential candidate, Pierre-Claver Sendegeya, trailed a poor third in the June 1993 voting, winning 1.4% of the vote; later the same month the PRP failed to win a seat in Assembly elections. The party was nevertheless included in the broad coalition government appointed in February 1994 and signed the September 1994 "convention of government" on power-sharing between the main parties.

Rally for Democracy and Economic and Social Development
Rassemblement pour la Démocratie et le Développement Economique et Social (RADDES)
Leadership. Cyrille Sigejeje (chairman)
RADDES was founded on the move to multi-partyism in

1992 but failed to make any impact in the June 1993 Assembly elections. It was nevertheless included in the broad coalition government formed in February 1994, the then party president Joseph Nzeyimana becoming Minister of Trade and Industry after having protested vigorously about an initial allocation of portfolios. RADDES signed the September 1994 "convention of government" on power-sharing between the main parties and was also included in the coalition government appointed in October. It retained the Trade and Industry portfolio in the new government appointed in March 1995.

Rally of the People of Burundi
Rassemblement du Peuple du Burundi (RPB)

Leadership. Emmanuel Sindayigaya

Founded in 1992, the mainly Hutu RPB was third-placed party in the June 1993 Assembly elections, although without surmounting the 5% barrier to representation. It was nevertheless included in the coalition government appointed in October 1994, having backed the power-sharing "convention of government" concluded the previous month. In March 1995 the RPB leader, Ernest Kabushemeye, was killed in renewed inter-ethnic fighting and replaced as Minister of Energy and Mines by Emmanuel Sindayigaya.

Union for National Progress
Union pour le Progrès National (UPRONA)

Address. BP 1810, Bujumbura

Leadership. Luc Rukingama (president)

Founded in 1959 by Prince Louis Rwagasore, UPRONA has over the years undergone various adjustments in its French title, although all have retained the UPRONA acronym. It was in the forefront of the struggle against Belgian rule, winning an overwhelming majority in Assembly elections in 1961 (after which Prince Rwagasore was assassinated) and leading Burundi to full independence as a monarchy the following year. Having retained its majority in the 1965 Assembly elections (and lost two more Prime Ministers by assassination), UPRONA was proclaimed the sole ruling party on the overthrow of the (Tutsi) monarchy by the Tutsi-dominated army in 1966, whereupon Michel Micombero was installed as President. He was ousted in 1976 by Col. Jean-Baptiste Bagaza (a Tutsi), who declared the Second Republic and reorganized UPRONA as the ruling party. At its first congress in December 1979 UPRONA adopted a new charter and statutes, defining the party as a democratic centralist organization dedicated to the struggle against exploitation and imperialism and in favour of self-reliance, the preservation of national culture, and co-operation in community development.

A new constitution for Burundi, drafted by the UPRONA central committee and providing for a return to civilian rule, secured referendum approval in November 1981. In August 1984 Bagaza was re-elected President as the UPRONA (and only) candidate, but in September 1987 he was overthrown (while out of the country) by a military coup led by Maj. Pierre Buyoya, another Tutsi and a then little-known UPRONA central committee member. Although Buyoya dismissed the incumbent UPRONA central committee, he was backed by the party's national secretariat, which was instructed to establish a new structure for UPRONA. Full party activity was resumed in 1989 (after a spate of Tutsi-Hutu conflict), with Nicolas Mayugi (a Buyoya nominee and a Hutu) as UPRONA secretary-general. Under a National Unity Charter published by Buyoya in May 1990, the UPRONA central committee in December 1990 took over the functions of the Military Committee for National Salvation.

Having at that stage shown a preference for "democracy within the single party", Buyoya in May 1991 declared his support for a measure of pluralism, which was enshrined in the new constitution adopted in March 1992. At an extraordinary congress the same month UPRONA delegates elected a new 90-member central committee and also endorsed Mayugi as party president in succession to Buyoya (who stood down in accordance with the new constitution). That Mayugi and a majority of the new central committee were Hutus (despite UPRONA's membership being 90% Tutsi) reflected the regime's sensitivity to charges that it was dominated by the minority Tutsis.

The stratagem did not help Buyoya in the presidential elections of June 1993, when he was defeated outright in the first round by the Hutu candidate of the →Burundi Front for Democracy (FRODEBU). UPRONA was also decisively defeated in Assembly elections later the same month, winning only 16 of the 81 seats, after which the party complained of "ethnic manipulation" by FRODEBU. Nevertheless, UPRONA accepted representation in the post-election government, the premiership going to Sylvie Kinigi, a Tutsi and former UPRONA member, who became Burundi's first woman Prime Minister. Following the murder of President Ndadaya in October 1993, UPRONA again charged FRODEBU leaders of fomenting anti-Tutsi violence but accepted participation in a broad coalition government formed in February 1994 and headed by UPRONA member Anatole Kanyenkiko, a Tutsi.

The death of President Ntaryamira in April 1994 gave rise to fears of a tribal bloodbath on the Rwandan scale, to avert which UPRONA eventually co-operated in the elevation to the presidency of the FRODEBU Speaker of the National Assembly, a Hutu, and continued to participate in the coalition government. The intitial UPRONA candidate for the presidency had been Charles Mukasi, who replaced Mayugi as party president. UPRONA was a signatory of the September 1994 "convention of government" providing for power-sharing between the main parties. Following the parliamentary confirmation of the FRODEBU President in September 1994, UPRONA was the second-strongest party in the new broad coalition appointed in October, with Kanyenkiko continuing as Prime Minister. However, the latter was expelled from UPRONA in January 1995 (for having dismissed two UPRONA ministers at the President's behest) and was eventually replaced by Antoine Nduwayo after UPRONA had mounted anti-Kanyenkiko demonstrations.

In June 1995 most UPRONA Assembly deputies supported the President's unsuccessful request to be allowed to rule by decree. The following month UPRONA unsuccessfully demanded the dissolution of the Assembly and new elections, claiming that many FRODEBU deputies had fled the country. In September Nduwayo and the UPRONA Interior Minister, Gabriel Sinarinzi, came under attack from FRODEBU and other members of the government for downplaying the extent of violence in Burundi and for allegedly resisting multi-party democracy. He was dismissed from the government in October 1995.

Amid increasing insecurity and ethnic violence, the military again seized power in July 1996 under Maj. Buyoya, who subsequently negotiated a partnership agreement with the FRODEBU-dominated National Assembly. Buyoya was officially sworn in as President (head of state and government) in June 1998, and Mathias Sinamenye of UPRONA assumed one of two new vice-presidential posts.

Cambodia

Capital: Phnom Penh   **Population:** 11,400,000 (2000E)

The Kingdom of Cambodia achieved its independence in 1953 after 90 years of French rule, with King Norodom Sihanouk becoming head of state but vacating the throne in 1955 in order to preserve his political authority. Prince Sihanouk (as he then became) steered a neutral and non-aligned course until 1966, when visiting Chinese emissary Zhou Enlai persuaded him to permit the North Vietnamese to extend the Ho Chi Minh Trail through Cambodia. He was deposed in 1970, in what many believe to have been a US-backed coup d'état, and replaced by the pro-US Lon Nol. This further inflamed the continuing insurrection by the Chinese-backed communist Khmers Rouges (KR), who seized power in 1975, proclaimed Democratic Kampuchea (DK) in 1976 and engaged in a three-year reign of terror under Pol Pot.

In 1979 the DK regime was overthrown by Vietnamese-backed nationalists, who established the People's Republic of Kampuchea (PRK) in 1981 under the leadership of the pro-Soviet and strongly independent Khmer nationalist Kampuchean People's Revolutionary Party (KPRP). The Khmers Rouges and an unlikely coalition of Royalists and Buddhist Liberals formed the Coalition Government of Democratic Kampuchea (CGDK), headed by Prince Sihanouk but dominated by the KR. It lay concealed along the Thai border, enjoyed UN recognition and pursued a guerrilla war against the PRK government and the Vietnamese army in Cambodia. It was, however, a coalition in the weakest sense, regularly split by infighting, and acted as a conduit through which Western and Chinese aid could pass to the *Khmers Rouges*. Civil war raged for more than a decade, with women and children the main victims of the millions of land mines indiscriminately laid by all sides.

The PRK was renamed the State of Cambodia (SoC) in 1989, as Vietnamese forces finalized their withdrawal, facilitating the signature of a UN-brokered peace agreement in Paris in October 1991. This instrument provided for the country to be administered by a United Nations Transitional Authority in Cambodia (UNTAC) pending democratic elections and the formation of a new government. A Supreme National Council (SNC), originally formed in September 1990 under the chairmanship of Prince Sihanouk, supposedly embraced the main contending factions. However, amid continuing hostilities, the KR (now calling themselves the Party of Democratic Kampuchea, PDK)) boycotted UN-supervised elections in May 1993, allowing the Sihanoukist United National Front for an Independent, Neutral, Peaceful and Co-operative Cambodia (FUNCINPEC) to win a narrow majority over the ex-KPRP, now called the Cambodian People's Party (CPP). A coalition government of FUNCINPEC, the CPP and two smaller parties was formed and on Sept. 21, 1993, a new constitution was promulgated re-establishing the monarchy in the context of a pluralistic, liberal and democratic political system. Three days later a seven-member Throne Council elected Sihanouk to resume the throne he had vacated 38 years earlier.

Elections to a 120-member Constituent (later National) Assembly, held between May 23 and 28, 1993, and producing a remarkable 89.6% voter turn-out, resulted in FUNCINPEC winning 58 seats (with 45.5% of the vote), the CPP 51 (38.2%) and other parties 11. An uneasy power-sharing coalition was installed, with Prince Norodom Ranariddh (FUNCINPEC) as First Prime Minister and Hun Sen (CPP) as Second Prime Minister, which eventually degenerated into open conflict in July 1997, when Hun Chen ousted Ranariddh and effectively seized power. In elections to a 122-member National Assembly on July 26, 1998, the CPP reversed the 1993 result by winning 64 seats (with 41.4% of the vote), against 43 (31.7%) for FUNCINPEC and 15 (14.3%) for the new Sam Rainsy Party (SRP).

The losers' challenge to the legitimacy of the Assembly elections was eventually resolved by an agreement in November 1998. This provided for the formation of a CPP–FUNCINPEC coalition government headed by Hun Sen and the creation of an unelected upper house, the Senate, to provide more legislative posts for the parties to allocate to adherents. Under the agreement, Chea Sim of the CPP became chairman of the Senate and his previous position as chairman of the National Assembly was taken by Ranariddh of FUNCINPEC. Legislation approved by the National Assembly in March 1999 created a Senate of 61 members, of whom 57 are appointed on a proportional basis by the parties in the Assembly, two are elected by the lower house and two are chosen by the reigning monarch.

Cambodian People's Party (CPP)
Kanakpak Pracheachon Kampuchea
Address. Chamcarmon, Norodom Blvd., Phnom Penh
Telephone. (+855–23) 723405
Fax. (+855–23) 722906
Email. cpp@camnet.com.kh
Website. www.cppusa.net
Leadership. Chea Sim (chairman); Hun Sen (vice-chairman); Heng Samrin (honorary chairman); Say Chhum (general secretary and chairman of permanent committee)
The CPP was launched in October 1991 as a non-communist successor to the communist Kampuchean People's

Revolutionary Party (KPRP), then the ruling party in Phnom Penh. The KPRP was itself descended from the Indo-Chinese Communist Party (ICP) founded by Ho Chi Minh in 1930, which had divided into separate sections for Cambodia, Laos and Vietnam in 1951. Following the end of French rule in 1953, the KPRP in Cambodia for some years conducted peaceful opposition to the Sihanouk government, operating within the Masses Party and also seeking to infiltrate the ruling Popular Socialist Community Party. In 1960 the party was radicalized at a secret congress which opted for armed struggle and elected younger, Paris-trained intellectuals to the leadership, including Tou Samouth as general secretary and Pol Pot (then called Saloth Sar), Ieng Sary and Son Sen to other leading posts.

Pro-Chinese and Maoist in orientation, the Pol Pot faction became known as the *Khmers Rouges* (KR) and launched a peasant revolt in north-western Cambodia in 1967. The advent of the pro-US Lon Nol regime in 1970 produced an uneasy reconciliation between the KR and the CPK's pro-Vietnamese (and pro-Soviet) wing, the party as a whole joining the Beijing-backed government-in-exile headed by Prince Sihanouk. From 1973, however, Pol Pot began purging pro-Vietnamese elements from the CPK, with the result that, following the fall of the Lon Nol regime in 1975, the KR-dominated faction of the CPK was able to take power in Phnom Penh in 1976. In September 1977 it was officially confirmed that the ruling party in Democratic Kampuchea was the CPK led by Pol Pot.

The response of the pro-Vietnamese faction was an armed revolt and the formation in "liberated" areas of the Kampuchean National United Front for National Salvation (KNUFNS). This body was composed of less ideological, but nevertheless anti-Pol Pot individuals. With assistance from Vietnamese forces, the KNUFNS overthrew the Pol Pot regime in January 1979, in which month a "reorganization" congress in Phnom Penh decided that the CPK should revert to the KPRP rubric and elected a new leadership with Pen Sovan as general secretary. Under the 1981 constitution, the KPRP was confirmed as the sole legal party and the leading force of the Kampuchean United Front for National Construction and Defence (KUFNCD) as successor to the KNUFNS. Following an apparent internal power struggle, Pen Sovan was replaced as KPRP general secretary by Heng Samrin in December 1981. Although Pen Sovan was rumoured to be dead at this time, he reappeared in the 1998 elections.

The signing of the Paris Peace Agreement in October 1991 impelled the KPRP to change its name to the Cambodian People's Party, which renounced Marxism–Leninism and formally embraced multi-party democracy (a mixed economy having been the practice since 1985). Other decisions included the removal of the hammer and sickle from the party's emblem and the merging of the former politburo and secretariat into a single standing committee of the central committee. In leadership changes, the relatively hardline president of the National Assembly, Chea Sim, became party leader and the moderate faction leader, Prime Minister Hun Sen, became deputy leader, while Heng Samrin was allocated the cosmetic post of honorary chairman. In the UN-supervised Assembly elections of May 1993, the CPP benefited from a boycott followed by the KR, then called the Cambodian National Unity Party (CNUP), to win 51 of the 120 seats, in close second place behind the Sihanoukist →United National Front for an Independent, Neutral, Peaceful and Co-operative Cambodia (FUNCINPEC).

The CPP were left with an excess of candidates for a reduced number of positions in the new National Assembly – an inevitable consequence, in Cambodia's case, of moving from a single to a multi-party polity. Older party ideologues were sacrificed for younger technocrats, and 32 CPP nominees resigned their positions. This was unrelated to a short-lived "secession" led by Gen. Sin Song and Prince Norodom Chakrapong. Rather than an objection to developments in Cambodian politics broadly, the effort was aimed at securing personal aggrandisement, and had no bearing on the resignations, or upon the manner in which the CPP proceeded to force FUNCINPEC into an electorally unrepresentative, but otherwise realistic, 50–50 power-sharing coalition.

A feature of the new government was the appointment of the CPP's powerful organization chief, Sar Kheng, to the influential post of Deputy Prime Minister and Interior Minister, in which he was seen as a rival to Hun Sen, the CPP Second Prime Minister. This move was, however, balanced by the appointment of Chhun Lom, a pro-Hun Sen member and SoC ideologue. Reflecting a key characteristic of the CPP's recent history, his appointment was an attempt to create an internal balance of power that would ensure Hun Sen's continued primacy, but which would prevent internal party disintegration. Accordingly, after the 1993 elections CheaSim was again elected as chairman of the National Assembly, thus satisfying the needs of two of Hun Sen's rivals within the party.

Political cohesion within the CPP was maintained by continuing to prevent opposition parties, most notably FUNCINPEC, from wresting grass-roots power from the CPP. However, escalating tension resulted in a violent confrontation between the police, militia and military of Hun Sen and those of the FUNCINPEC leader, Prince Norodom Ranariddh, in the capital city in July 1997. Hun Sen's forces prevailed in two days of intense fighting and Ranariddh fled the country, whereupon relative calm returned with Hun Sen now in effective power. Although the government coalition with FUNCINPEC was maintained, the submissiveness of the new FUNCINPEC First Prime Minister ensured continued stability within CPP ranks.

The July 1998 Assembly elections further consolidated the power of the CPP, which outpolled FUNCINPEC by nearly half a million votes and won 64 of the 122 seats. Both FUNCINPEC and the new →Sam Rainsy Party (SRP) challenged the results, the solution arrived being the creation of an upper house (Senate) to accommodate the institutional and personal interests of FUNCINPEC and the SRP. This necessitated a reallocation of positions within the CPP, with Chea Sim becoming chairman of the Senate so that the returned Ranariddh could take the chairmanship of the Assembly. The outcome for CPP was that internal balances of power were maintained without compromising the party's authority over both the opposition and the Cambodian people.

Sam Rainsy Party (SRP)
Kanakpak Sam Rainsy
Address: 71 Sotheros Road, Phnom Penh
Telephone. (+855–23) 211336
Fax. (+855–23) 217452
Email. samrainsy@bigpond.com.kh
Website. www.samrainsyparty.org
Leadership. Sam Rainsy (president); Chhai Eang (secretary-general)

The SRP was launched in March 1998 and derives from another party established by Rainsy, the Khmer Nation Party (KNP). The KNP had been formed in exile in November 1995 after Rainsy had been ejected from both the →United National Front for an Independent, Neutral, Peaceful and Co-operative Cambodia (FUNCINPEC) and the National Assembly following his dismissal in October 1994 as Finance Minister, in which post had had become popular for his anti-corruption stance. However, Rainsy's deputy in the KNP, Kong Mony, declared himself president in open defiance of Rainsy. A court battle over the rights to the party's name ensued, but the legal system did not provide a solution in time for the 1998 elections, so that Sam Rainsy renamed his party eponymously.

In its election campaign the SRP resorted to racial slurs to garner support. Rainsy was repeatedly cautioned for his pejorative use of the term *yuon* ("savage") referring to Vietnamese people in Cambodia, whose relations with Khmers had been unstable for several decades. Rainsy drew on this mistrust to generate support for an otherwise weak political platform. After coming a respectable third, with 14.3% of the vote and 15 seats, Rainsy was vituperative regarding the outcome and challenged the dominant →Cambodian People's Party (CPP) to recounts. Rainsy then joined Prince Ranariddh of FUNCINPEC in refusing to enter into talks on a new government and led anti-CPP protests, some of which erupted into serious violence. Rainsy eventually conceded electoral defeat in November 1998, when agreement was reached with the CPP on the creation of a new upper house (Senate) as the solution to the impasse. The SRP accordingly took its seats in the new Assembly and accepted seven seats in the new Senate, becoming the parliamentary opposition to a new CPP–FUNCINPEC coalition government.

United National Front for an Independent, Neutral, Peaceful and Co-operative Cambodia
Front Uni National pour un Cambodge Indépendant, Neutre, Pacifique et Coopérative (FUNCINPEC)

Address. 11 Motha Vithei Preah Monivong, Sankat Srah Chak, Khan Daun Penh, Phnom Penh
Telephone. (+855–23) 217768
Fax. (+855–23) 426471
Email. info@funcinpec.org
Website. www.funcinpec.org
Leadership. Prince Norodom Ranariddh (president); Princess Norodom Monique & Nhiek Tioulong (vice-presidents)

FUNCINPEC was launched in March 1982 by King (as he later again became) Sihanouk as the political wing of the Sihanoukist National Army (ANS), then in conflict with the Kampuchean People's Revolutionary Party (KPRP) in power in Phnom Penh. FUNCINPEC was seen as the successor of Sihanouk's Confederation of Khmer Nationalists and included several earlier pro-Sihanouk movements which had opposed the 1970–75 Lon Nol government and 1975–79 regime of the *Khmers Rouges* (KR) headed by Pol Pot. Despite this recent history, in June 1982 FUNCINPEC renewed its earlier alliance with the KR by forming the Coalition Government of Democratic Kampuchea (CGDK), which also included the Khmer People's National Liberation Front (KPNLF), later renamed the →Buddhist Liberal Democratic Party (BLDP).

Under the titular leadership of Prince Sihanouk, the CGDK was dominated by the KR, as armed struggle against the Phnom Penh regime was interspersed with bouts of conflict between the CGDK components. Despite much international condemnation of the excesses of the Pol Pot regime, combined Chinese and US influence ensured that the CGDK retained UN recognition. US and other Western aid was overtly channeled to FUNCINPEC and the KPNLF, with covert Western and Chinese aid reaching the *Khmers Rouges*. However, the non-communist components of the CGDK forces remained ill-disciplined and poorly motivated compared with the KR.

Following the announcement of the completion of Vietnam's military withdrawal in 1989, UN-brokered negotiations produced agreement in September 1990 on the creation of a Supreme National Council (SNC) representing both the CGDK and the government of what was by now called the State of Cambodia (SoC). Having become chairman of the SNC, Prince Sihanouk resigned as FUNCINPEC and ANS leader and was succeeded by his son, Prince Norodom Ranariddh. However, notwithstanding assertions of his political neutrality by Prince Sihanouk, FUNCINPEC remained loyal to its founder.

On the strength of the Paris Peace Agreement of October 1991, FUNCINPEC and the other CGDK parties were authorized to return to Phnom Penh.This facilitated the development of a tactical alliance between FUNCINPEC and the →Cambodian People's Party (CPP) against the KR and the latter's new political wing, the Cambodian National Unity Party (CNUP). The CNUP's decision to boycott the May 1993 Assembly elections left the way open for FUNCINPEC to become the largest party, with 58 of the 120 seats, followed by the CPP with 51. Prince Ranariddh became First Prime Minister in the subsequent coalition government of FUNCINPEC, the CPP, the BLDP and the National Liberation Movement of Kampuchea (MOULINAKA), while Prince Sihanouk himself was restored to the Cambodian throne in September 1993.

Assisted by KR/CNUP intransigence, FUNCINPEC's alliance with the CPP mainstream held during 1994. Within FUNCINPEC, however, there remained considerable suspicion of the CPP's real intentions, given the latter's powerful organizational base. Accordingly, some FUNCINPEC elements advocated the formation of an anti-CPP alliance with the KR, pointing out that such a rapprochement would be likely to have the backing of China. Other strains within the party were evident in October 1994 in the dismissal of the popular anti-corruption Finance Minister, Sam Rainsy, in the interests of what Prince Ranariddh termed the need for "unity and cohesion", and the resignation of Prince Sereivuddh as Foreign Minister out of solidarity with Sam Rainsy, who later announced the creation of the Khmer Nation Party, which in turn became the →Sam Rainsy Party (SRP).

By 1996 relations had all but disintegrated between FUNCINPEC and the CPP. Many in the former were concerned about poor leadership on Ranariddh's part and his failure to secure a share of grass-roots power from the entrenched CPP. Local posts had been promised to the party faithful for their election work and political loyalty; when they were not forthcoming, disgruntlement set in and party splits appeared which were exploited by the CPP. In an attempt to force the CPP to accept grass-roots power-sharing, Ranariddh threatened to walk out of government after the 1996 FUNCINPEC congress (the first since the 1993 elections). When CPP leader Hun Sen dared him to leave, Ranariddh tried to recreate the old alliance with the remnants of the *Khmers Rouges*, still outlawed but holed up in the north-west of Cambodia. After this failed and the CPP secured a mass desertion from the KR under Ieng Sary, tensions rose yet further. Ranariddh was apprehended smuggling in weapons disguised as machinery, while KR documents recovered later revealed that the Prince was plotting with the KR to remove the CPP from power. In early July 1997 matters came to head when open hostilities erupted in Phnom Penh between the respective armed forces of the CPP and FUNCINPEC. The CPP quickly reasserted its authority and Ranariddh fled into exile.

FUNCINPEC retained its position of leadership in the Assembly and continued to function in Ranariddh's absence. An internal party election resulted in the FUNCINPEC presidency being taken by Foreign Minister Ung Huot, whose policy stood in stark contrast to his predecessor's. According to the new incumbent, accommodating Hun Sen and the CPP permitted a "win-win" situation to develop. Indeed, levels of hostility between the heads of the two parties declined markedly, while FUNCINPEC experienced further splintering and the formation of as many as eight breakaway parties, some of which were pro-CPP. These included the National Unity Party led by Toan Chhay (governor-general of Siem Reap), the New Society Party led by Loy Sim Chheang, the Khmer Citizen Party led by Nguon Souer and the Khmer Unity Party led by Khieu Rada.

Ranariddh was eventually allowed back into the country after receiving an amnesty from the King on charges of smuggling and co-operating with an illegal organization (the KR). Reassuming the leadership of FUNCINPEC (Ung Huot having departed to lead his own party), Ranariddh then led his party to second place in the July 1998 Assembly elections. However, the Prince was unhappy with the outcome and joined with the →Sam Rainsy Party (SRP) in challenging the CPP on irregularities and demanding recounting. After initially refusing to form a new government (in breach of the constitution), Ranariddh's FUNCINPEC relented when the CPP proposed that a new upper house (Senate) would be created. The FUNCINPEC leader demanded and received the chairmanship of the Assembly, succeeding the CPP's Chea Sim, who took the chairmanship of the new Senate.

FUNCINPEC continued thereafter to co-operate with the CPP, accepting the latter's pre-eminence but retaining its own agenda in terms of development.

Other Parties

The 1998 elections were contested by a total of 39 parties. Other than the three described above, only one has serious significance in contemporary Cambodian politics.

Buddhist Liberal Democratic Party (BLDP)
Kanakpak Preacheathippatai Serei Preah Puthasasna
Address. 197 Mao Tse Tung Blvd., Phnom Penh
Telephone. (+855–23) 26175
Leadership. Ieng Mouli, Son Soubert (presidents of competing factions)
The BLDP was founded in 1992 as the successor to the Khmer People's National Liberation Front (KPNLF), itself the political heir of the 1970–75 pro-US regime of Lon Nol. The KPNLF was launched in 1979 by Son Sann (a Prime Minister under the pre-1970 Sihanouk regime), first in France and then on the Thai-Cambodian border, as a democratic, non-communist movement opposed to the pro-Vietnam regime installed in Phnom Penh that year. Initially also opposed to the *Khmers Rouges* (KR), the KPNLF was the political wing of the Free Khmers (*Khmers Serei*) guerrilla army, which raised a considerable anti-communist following on the strength of US and ASEAN aid. In June 1982, however, the KPNLF joined the Coalition Government of Democratic Kampuchea (CGDK) in alliance with Sihanoukist forces and the KR, Son Sann becoming the CGDK Prime Minister.

Military reverses for the KPNLF in the 1980s were compounded by internal divisions, so that the Front had little influence in shaping the Paris peace agreement of October 1991. However, it did take two seats on the 12-member Supreme National Council (SNC) established by the contending factions the previous year for the purpose of sharing and distributing political authority for the period of transition during which the UN would establish electoral and other mechanisms whereby political authority would be determined by the Cambodian electorate, rather than unelected elites.

Authorized to establish a presence in Phnom Penh, the KPNLF transformed itself into a political party in May 1992, the chosen BLDP rubric being intended to demonstrate its non-communist, traditionalist but pro-market/democratic orientation. In the Assembly elections of May 1993, the BLDP won only 10 of the 120 seats but was subsequently included in the new coalition government headed by the Sihanoukist →United National Front for an Independent, Neutral, Peaceful and Co-operative Cambodia (FUNCINPEC) and the pro-Vietnamese →Cambodian People's Party (CPP). In July 1995 Son Sann was replaced as BLDP leader by Ieng Mouli, who had the public backing of FUNCINPEC and the CPP. In response, Son Sann formed the eponymous Grandfather Son Sann Party (*Kanakpak Ta Son Sann*), seeking to benefit from traditional respect for age and venerability in Khmer society. Further further splits occurred prior to Son Sann's death in December 2000 at the age of 89. As a result, there were in 2001 two parties named the BLDP, with Son Sann's son, Son Soubert, the leader of one, whilst Ieng Mouli retained the leadership of the other. Both were formally registered as political parties with the Ministry of the Interior.

Cameroon

Capital: Yaoundé

Population: 15,422,000 (2000E)

French-administered (East) Cameroon achieved independence in 1960 and the following year was united with the southern part of British-administered (West) Cameroon, both areas having been under German colonial rule until World War I. A one-party state established in 1966 under the National Cameroon Union, renamed the Cameroon People's Democratic Movement (CPDM) in 1985, gave way to a multi-party system in 1990. Under its 1972 constitution as amended, the Republic of Cameroon has an executive President who is elected for a seven-year term (once renewable) by universal suffrage of those aged 20 and over, requiring only a relative majority in a single voting round. The President is head of state and government, appointing the Prime Minister and other members of the government. There is a National Assembly (*Assemblée Nationale*) of 180 members directly elected by proportional representation for a five-year term. Legislation to establish a second parliamentary chamber, the Senate (*Sénat*), was enacted in 1996 without specifying any timetable for the implementation of bicameralism (which was still awaited in 2000). Under laws enacted in 1990–91, political parties may not be based on regional or tribal support and may not form coalitions for electoral purposes. Registered parties are eligible for financial support from state funds for their electoral campaigns.

Assembly elections held on May 17, 1997, resulted as follows: CPDM 109 seats, Social Democratic Front (SDF) 43, National Union for Democracy and Progress (UNDP) 13, Democratic Union of Cameroon (UDC) 5, Cameroon Youth Movement (MLJC) 1, Union of the Peoples of Cameroon (UPC) 1, Movement for the Defence of the Republic (MDR) 1. The seven remaining seats (in three constituencies whose May results were annulled) were won by the CPDM in further elections in August 1997, giving the CPDM a final total of 116 Assembly seats. A presidential election held on Oct. 12, 1997, was won by Paul Biya of the CPDM, this being his fourth consecutive victory, but the first since the introduction of a constitutional amendment limiting future Presidents to a maximum of two terms. The 1997 presidential election was also contested by candidates from six minor parties, who received in aggregate 7.4% of the votes cast (the election having been boycotted by the main opposition parties).

Cameroon People's Democratic Movement (CPDM)
Rassemblement Démocratique du Peuple Camerounais (RDPC)
Address. BP 867, Yaoundé
Telephone. (+237) 23–27–40

Leadership. Paul Biya (president); Joseph Charles Doumba (secretary-general)
The CPDM is the successor, created in March 1985, to the Cameroon National Union (UNC), which was established as the sole ruling party in 1966 as a merger of the francophone

Cameroon Union (UC) and five other parties, including three of anglophone identity. The UC had taken Cameroon to independence in 1960 under the leadership of Ahmadou Ahidjo (a Muslim), whose post-1966 one-party UNC government claimed credit for economic advances. When Ahidjo unexpectedly resigned in November 1982, he was succeeded as President and party leader by Paul Biya (a Christian), who had held the premiership since 1975. After surviving coups attempts in 1983 and 1984, Biya was confirmed in office in an April 1988 one-party presidential election (officially with 100% of the vote). Meanwhile, the UNC had renamed itself the CPDM, against strong internal opposition from the party's anglophone wing.

From mid-1990 the CPDM government accepted opposition demands for a transition to multi-party democracy, although Biya refused to convene a sovereign national conference on political change. In Assembly elections in March 1992 the CPDM maintained its dominance, although its 88-seat tally was short of an overall majority. The CPDM benefited from a boycott by some opposition parties and from its following in the francophone Christian south, but gained little support in the anglophone west or the Muslim north. In the October 1992 presidential election, Biya as CPDM candidate won a narrow victory over the nominee of the →Social Democratic Front, which made vigorous allegations of electoral fraud. In November 1992 the post-April coalition government of the CPDM and the small →Movement for the Defence of the Republic was expanded to include the other two parties represented in the Assembly. In 1993–94 the government came under persistent pressure from the political opposition and also faced growing secessionist tendencies in anglophone areas. It was reported in September 1994 that an assassination plot against President Biya had been foiled the previous May. In legislative elections held in May 1997 (and completed in August 1997) the CPDM won 116 seats. A presidential election held on Oct. 12, 1997 (and boycotted by the principal opposition parties) resulted in the re-election of Paul Biya with 92.6% of the recorded vote. The CPDM held virtually all the posts in the Cabinet appointed in December 1997 (the exceptions being three appointees from the →National Union for Democracy and Progress and one from the →Union of the Peoples of Cameroon).

Democratic Union of Cameroon
Union Démocratique du Cameroun (UDC)

Address. BP 1638, Yaoundé
Leadership. Adamou Ndam Njoya (president)
The UDC achieved legal status in April 1991, its president having been a senior minister under the pre-1982 Ahidjo regime. Together with the →Social Democratic Front (SDF), it headed the boycott of the March 1992 Assembly elections by some opposition parties on the grounds that the electoral arrangements gave an unfair advantage to the ruling →Cameroon People's Democratic Movement. It changed tack for the October 1992 presidential poll, in which Njoya came in fourth place with 3.6% of the votes cast. Thereafter strains developed betweem the UDC and the SDF: in January 1993 the UDC vice-president, Benjamin Menga, was fatally injured in an attack in which the SDF was implicated. The UDC won 5 seats in the May 1997 legislative elections. It boycotted the October 1997 presidential election in protest at the Government's failure to establish an independent electoral commission. In February 1998 the UPC announced its intention to form a "common opposition front" with the SDF.

Movement for the Defence of the Republic
Mouvement pour la Défense de la République (MDR)

Address. BP 895, Yaoundé
Leadership. Dakole Daissala (president)
The MDR was founded on the eve of the March 1992 Assembly elections, in a move to divide Muslim allegiance in northern Cameroon at the expense of the opposition

→National Union for Democracy and Progress (UNDP). Previously a prominent dissident, the MDR leader had spent seven years in detention in connexion with a coup attempt in 1984. Based particularly in the Kirdi ethnic group, the MDR won six of the 180 Assembly seats, enough to give it the immediate balance of power between the ruling →Cameroon People's Democratic Movement (CPDM) and the opposition parties. Daissala and four other MDR nominees were appointed to the CPDM-led government which was installed in April 1992 and expanded in November to include the other two parties represented in the Assembly. The MDR won only one seat in the May 1997 Assembly elections and was not represented in the next government.

National Union for Democracy and Progress
Union Nationale pour la Démocratie et le Progrès (UNDP)

Address. BP 656, Douala
Leadership. Maigari Bello Bouba (chairman)
The UNDP was founded in 1991 mainly by supporters of ex-President Ahidjo and was based in the Muslim community (forming 22% of the population). In early 1992 its first leader, Samuel Eboua, was displaced by Bello Bouba, who had been Prime Minister in 1982–83 following Ahidjo's resignation but had later been implicated in an alleged plot to restore Ahidjo. Having initially decided to boycott the March 1992 Assembly elections, the UNDP changed its mind and proceeded to win 68 of the 180 seats at issue, only 20 seats behind the ruling →Cameroon People's Democratic Movement (CPDM). In the October 1992 presidential election the UNDP leader came in third place with 19.2% of the vote and afterwards joined the leader of the →Social Democratic Front in challenging the validity of the official results. Nevertheless, in November 1992 the UNDP accepted participation in a coalition government of all four Assembly parties under the leadership of the CPDM.

The basic impasse persisted in subsequent years. In November 1994 UNDP deputies launched a boycott of the Assembly in protest against the arrest of some 30 party activists four months earlier. The party called off the boycott the following month (without securing the release of its members), but a presidential initiative to achieve reconciliation quickly collapsed when the UNDP and other parties refused to participate in a "constitutional consultative committee". The UNDP won 13 seats in the May 1997 Assembly elections, but boycotted the October 1997 presidential election in protest at the Government's failure to establish an independent electoral commission. Three UNDP members (including the party chairman) were appointed to Cabinet positions in December 1997.

Social Democratic Front (SDF)

Address. PO Box 490, Bamenda
Telephone. (+237) 36–39–49
Fax. (+237) 36–29–91
Website. www.sdfparty.org
Leadership. John Fru Ndi (chairman); Tazoacha Asonganyi (secretary-general)
Founded in early 1990, the SDF gained legal recognition in March 1991 after a year in which its anti-government rallies had frequently been subject to official repression. Based in the English-speaking north and west, the SDF opted to boycott the May 1992 Assembly elections but changed its line for the October 1992 presidential contest. Standing as the SDF candidate, John Fru Ndi attracted support from anglophone and francophone voters, winning 36% of the popular vote and thus coming a close second to incumbent Paul Biya of the →Cameroon People's Democratic Movement (CPDM). Supported by many foreign observers, the SDF claimed that the presidential poll had been fraudulent, but its petition was rejected by the Supreme Court. In November 1992 the SDF refused to join a new CPDM-led coalition government, calling instead for the convening of an all-party

national conference on the country's political future. It then initiated the formation of a 10-party opposition alliance called the Union for Change (*Union pour le Change*), with Fru Ndi as its leader, which launched a campaign of popular protests against the Biya government. The latter responded in March 1993 by banning demonstrations involving "a risk of violence" and by arresting over 100 opposition activists.

In June 1993 Fru Ndi refused to participate in a government-proposed "grand national debate" on constitutional reform, the idea of which generated some dissension within the SDF between moderates and radicals. An SDF congress in August 1993 endorsed the moderates' call for acceptance of the 1992 election results and participation in constitutional talks; but renewed harassment of Fru Ndi (who briefly took refuge in the Netherlands embassy in November 1993) reopened the government-opposition divide. In May 1994 Siga Asanga was suspended as SDF secretary-general for making unauthorized contact with the government on possible SDF participation in a national unity coalition. He subsequently left the party to form the →Social Democratic Movement. In July 1994 the SDF reacted to a major cabinet reshuffle by repeating its call for a sovereign national conference and for an interim government involving "all the nation's active political forces".

The SDF participated in the May 1997 Assembly elections, winning 43 seats, but boycotted the October 1997 presidential election in protest against the Government's failure to set up an independent electoral commission. In February 1998 (after the reported failure of talks with the CPDM on possible SDF participation in a coalition government) the SDF announced its intention to form a "common opposition front" with the →Democratic Union of Cameroon. A party congress in April 1999 re-elected Fru Ndi as party chairman (in a contested election) and voted not to enter into dialogue with the government until an independent electoral commission was established in Cameroon.

The SDF is a member of the Socialist International.

Union of the Peoples of Cameroon
Union des Populations du Cameroun (UPC)
Addresses. Ntumazah faction: BP 8647, Douala. Kodock faction: c/o Assemblée Nationale, Yaoundé.
Leadership. Ndeh Ntumazah & Augustin Frederic Kodock (leaders of rival factions)
The UPC was founded in the late 1940s as a Marxist–Leninist party opposed to French rule, under which it was banned in 1955. Relegalized at independence in 1960, it won 22 seats in the 1961 Assembly elections but became split into pro-Soviet and Maoist factions, both of which went underground in armed opposition to the one-party regime created in 1966. By 1970 the UPC insurgency had been largely suppressed, party leader Ernest Ouandié being executed in January 1971 after being convicted of "attempted revolution". Led by Ngouo Woungly-Massaga, the UPC survived in exile (based in Paris) and regained legal status in February 1991 as a social democratic formation. Meanwhile, Woungly-Massaga had left the UPC to form the →People's Solidarity Party, after failing to persuade his colleagues to join an anti-Biya united front and being accused by them of abuse of office. The leadership passed to Ndeh Ntumazah, a UPC founder, who led half the party into a boycott of the March 1992 Assembly elections, while the other half followed Augustin Frederic Kodock (UPC secretary-general) in putting up candidates, 18 of whom were elected. The split in the party deepened when Kodock alienated many of his colleagues by accepting a ministerial post in the coalition government formed in November 1992.

In 1996 Kodock was dismissed from party office. He subsequently formed a rival UPC faction with himself as leader, often referred to as the UPC(K) to distinguish it from the UPC(N) of Ntumazah (although both factions claimed to be entitled to unqualified use of the original party name). A member of the UPC(K) faction won one seat in the May 1997 legislative elections. A UPC candidate, Henri Hogbe Nlend, won 2.5% of the vote in the October 1997 presiden-

tial election and subsequently accepted a ministerial post in December 1997.

Other Parties

Dozens of other parties have been legalized in Cameroon since 1991. The listing below focuses on those for which there is evidence of recent political activity.

Action for Meritocracy and Equal Opportunity Party (AMEC), whose leader received less than 1% of the vote in the 1997 presidential election.
Leadership. Joachim Tabi Owono

Cameroon Anglophone Movement (CAM), originally a pro-federalist movement, has more recently supported separatist demands for the establishment of an independent republic in predominantly anglophone provinces of Cameroon.

Cameroon Youth Movement (*Mouvement pour la Jeunesse du Cameroun, MLJC*), won one seat in the May 1997 legislative elections.
Leadership. Marcel Yondo

Democratic Progressive Party of Cameroon (*Parti Démocratique et Progressif du Cameroun, PDPC*), an observer member of the Christian Democrat International.
Address. BP 6589, Yaoundé
Leadership. François Mama Etogo

Democratic Rally of People without Frontiers (*Rassemblement Démocratique du Peuple sans Frontières, RDPF*), founded in 1997. Its candidate received less than 1% of the vote in the 1997 presidential election.
Leadership. Antoine Demannu

Integral Democracy of Cameroon (*Démocratie Intégrale du Cameroun, DIC*), legalized in February 1991. Its leader received less than 1% of the vote in the 1997 presidential election.
Address. BP 8647, Douala
Leadership. Gustave Essaka

Liberal Democratic Alliance (LDA), anglophone grouping launched in 1993 to campaign for speedier constitutional reform.
Leadership. Henri Fossung

Movement for Democracy and Progress (*Mouvement pour la Démocratie et le Progrès, MDP*), founded in 1992 by a former leader of the →National Union for Democracy and Progress, who received 2.4% of the vote in the 1997 presidential election.
Leadership. Samuel Eboua

People's Solidarity Party (*Parti de la Solidarité du Peuple, PSP*), founded by Ngouo Woungly-Massaga in 1991 following his break with the →Union of the Peoples of Cameroon, presented 25 candidates in March 1992 elections, without success.

Popular Development Party (*Parti Populaire pour le Développement, PPD*), founded in 1997. Its candidate received 1.2% of the vote in the 1997 presidential election.
Leadership. Albert Dzongang

Progressive Movement (*Mouvement Progressif, MP*), legalized in August 1991, in January 1994 joined opposition front with →Social Democratic Party of Cameroon, →Social Movement for New Democracy and other groups.
Address. BP 2500, Douala
Leadership. Jean-Jacques Ekindi

Social Democratic Movement (SDM), founded in 1995 by a former secretary-general of the →Social Democratic Front following a split in that party.
Leadership. Siga Asanga

Social Democratic Party of Cameroon (*Parti Social-Démocrate du Cameroun, PSDC*), legalized in December 1991, in January 1994 joined opposition front with →Progressive Movement, →Social Movement for New Democracy and other groups.
Leadership. Jean-Michel Tekam

Social Movement for New Democracy (*Mouvement Social pour la Nouvelle Démocratie, MSND*), founded in 1991 by a former Bar Association president who was active in the early pro-democracy movement and served a prison term in 1990; in January 1994 joined opposition front with →Progressive Movement, →Social Democratic Party of Cameroon and other groups.
Address. BP 1641, Douala
Leadership. Yondo Mandengue Black

Social Programme for Liberty and Democracy (*Programme Sociale pour la Liberté et la Démocratie,*

PSLD), an opposition party whose leader was arrested in February 1995.
Leadership. Massok Mboua

Southern Cameroons National Council (SCNC), a separatist movement established in 1995 to campaign for the establishment of an independent republic in anglophone Cameroon. The SCNC proclaimed the establishment of a "Federal Republic of Southern Cameroon" in December 1999, and in April 2000 named a judge, Frederick Ebong Alobwede, as the president of the self-styled republic.
Leadership. Sam Ekontang Elad (chairman)

Union of Democratic Forces of Cameroon (*Union des Forces Démocratiques du Cameroun, UFDC*), legalized in March 1991, boycotted March 1992 Assembly elections in protest against electoral law banning party alliances; the party's leader was detained in November 1992 for alleged anti-government activities.
Address. BP 7190, Yaoundé
Leadership. Victorin Hameni Bialeu

Canada

Capital: Ottawa

Population: 31,300,000 (2000E)

The Dominion of Canada is a member of the Commonwealth with the British sovereign as head of state represented by a Governor-General. The Governor-General formally appoints the Prime Minister (the head of government) and, on the latter's recommendation, the members of the Cabinet. The federal legislature (Parliament) comprises a Senate of 105 members and a House of Commons of 301 members. The House of Commons is elected (on the Westminster model) for a period of up to five years by universal adult suffrage under the first past the post system in single-member constituencies (ridings). Appointment of Senators is controlled by the Prime Minister and follows party lines: thus of the 58 Senators appointed by Prime Minister Jean Chrétien since the Liberals returned to power in 1993, 56 have been Liberals and two independents. Canada comprises 10 provinces and (since the creation of the territory of Nunavut, with 25,000 mainly Inuit inhabitants, in April 1999) three territories. There is considerable decentralization of authority to the provincial governments, with the territories having lesser powers.

Political parties exist at both federal and provincial levels and one provincial party, the Quebec separatist Parti Québécois (PQ), has had particular significance in the development of Canadian politics. Elections Canada is the agency responsible for the registration of parties and conduct of elections at federal level. To achieve registration at federal level a party must endorse a candidate in at least 50 electoral districts in a general election: 11 registered parties competed in the most recent general election in November 2000. There is no limit on the amount that may be contributed to a candidate or political party, although donations from foreign sources are prohibited. However, the names of persons or organizations making contributions above $200 to a party or candidate must be disclosed. In addition, there are limits on spending by parties and candidates, varying by riding, and detailed restrictions on campaign activities. There are also relatively low ceilings on "third-party" advertising by individuals or organizations in support of candidates, in part to prevent circumvention of the limits on party spending. Candidates elected or receiving at least 15% of the vote in their riding, and parties receiving at least 2% of the votes cast nationally or 5% of the votes in the ridings where they present candidates, are entitled to reimbursement of (respectively) 50% and 22.5% of election expenses. Legislation and agencies regulating the registration of political parties and their finances also exist at provincial level.

In the most recent federal general election, held on Nov. 27, 2000, the centrist Liberal Party of Canada (LPC), in office since 1993, retained power, winning 172 of the 301 seats in the House of Commons and 40.8% of the popular vote. The neo-conservative Canadian Alliance won 66 seats with 25.5% of the vote, the separatist Bloc Québécois (BQ), with candidates only in Quebec, won 38 (10.7%), the democratic socialist New Democratic Party (NDP) 13 (8.5%) and the moderate conservative Progressive Conservative Party (PCP) 12 (12.2%). Six other registered parties each took a fraction of 1% of the vote and won no seats. The results underscored the deep divisions between the different regions of Canada, showing fault-lines between east and west and between Quebec and the rest of the country. The Canadian Alliance, campaigning on a programme of opposition to "big government" in Ottawa, won 60 of the 74 available seats in the three western provinces of Saskatchewan, Alberta and British Columbia. In contrast, it won only six seats elsewhere in Canada, while the Liberals won 100 of the 103 seats in the most populous province of Ontario. In mainly French-speaking Quebec (the second most populous province) the separatist BQ took fewer votes but won more seats (38) than did the Liberals (36). Although the Quebec electorate narrowly rejected independence in a referendum in October 1995 this remains a goal of the BQ and the governing party in the province, the Parti Québécois (PQ).

At provincial level the relative strength of the various parties does not overlap in a clear way with electoral performance at federal level. Thus although the Liberals came a poor second to the Canadian Alliance in the November 2000 federal election in British Columbia, winning only 27.7% of the vote, they won 77 of the 79 seats in the provincial legislature, with 58.5% of the vote, in May 2001. Similarly, although the right-wing Canadian Alliance won 10 of the 14 seats in Saskatchewan, and 47.7% of the vote, in the November 2000 federal elections (repeating the victory of its predecessor, the Reform Party, in 1997), the left-of-centre NDP is in office at provincial level.

Seats in the provincial legislatures were distributed as follows as a result of the most recent elections (the months of which are shown in parentheses): *Alberta* (March 2001) – PCP 74, LPC 7, NDP 2; *British Columbia* (May 2001) – LPC 77, NDP 2; *Manitoba* (September 1999) – NDP 32, PCP 24, LPC 1; *New Brunswick* (June 1999) – PCP 44, LPC 10, NDP 1; *Newfoundland and Labrador* (February 1999) – LPC 32, PCP 14, NDP 2; *Nova Scotia* (July 1999) – PCP 29, NDP 12, LPC 11; *Ontario* (June 1999) – PCP 60, LPC 34, NDP 19; *Prince Edward Island* (April 2000) – PCP 26, LPC 1; *Quebec* (November 1998) – PQ 76, LPC 48, Action démocratique de Québec (ADQ) 1; *Saskatchewan* (September 1999) – NDP 29, Saskatchewan Party (SP) 25, LPC 4.

Elections in the new territory of *Nunavut* and in the *Northwest Territories*, held in February 1999 and December 1999 respectively, resulted in all 19 seats in each legislature being won by independents. However, in the Northwest Territories six unsuccessful candidates ran under the NDP banner, introducing party politics for the first time. Elections to the *Yukon* legislature in April 2000 resulted in the LPC winning 10 seats, the NDP 6 and the Yukon Party one.

Canada evidences the decline in voter participation seen in other developed countries. Turnout was 61.2% in the 2000 general election, compared with 67.0% in 1997, 69.6% in 1993 and 75.3% in 1988.

Bloc Québécois (BQ)
Quebec Bloc

Address. 3750 Crémazie Blvd. East, Suite 307, Montreal, Quebec, H2A 1B6
Telephone. (+1–514) 526–3000
Fax. (+1–514) 526–2868
Email. info@bloc.org
Website. www.blocquequebecois.org
Leadership. Gilles Duceppe (leader)

The BQ was founded under the leadership of Lucien Bouchard in 1991 as the federal voice of Quebec separatism, committed to the achievement of sovereignty for the predominantly French-speaking province. It won 54 of the 295 seats in the House of Commons in the federal elections of October 1993, becoming the second largest party and the official opposition despite having seats in only one province. In support of the provincial →Parti Québécois (PQ), Bouchard campaigned intensively in the run-up to the October 1995 referendum on independence, which was lost only by the narrowest of margins. In the wake of the referendum, Bouchard became Premier of Quebec in January 1996, having been elected unopposed as leader of the PQ. In the June 1997 federal elections the BQ again came first in Quebec, winning 44 seats, although it lost its position as the official opposition in Ottawa to the Reform Party.

In the November 2000 federal election the BQ won fewer votes in Quebec than the Liberals, but emerged with 38 seats to the Liberals' 36, and came third nationally. During the campaign, BQ leader Gilles Duceppe emphasized the central importance of achieving sovereignty, although in September 2000 Bouchard had said "we sense a great fatigue on this issue". The BQ considers itself to be "Quebec's representative to Canada" and on the international stage and says that it will cease to exist when Quebec has achieved its independence.

Canadian Alliance

Address. #600, 833–4th Avenue SW, Calgary, Alberta, T2P 3T5
Telephone. (+1–403) 269–1990
Fax. (+1–403) 269–4077
Website. www.canadianalliance.ca
Leadership. Stockwell Day (leader); Clayton Manness (president)

Registered as the Canadian Reform Conservative Alliance, the Canadian Alliance was formed in March 2000 as the outcome of a two-year process aimed at unifying the right against the ruling →Liberal Party of Canada (LPC) at federal level. The Alliance failed to unseat the LPC in the November 2000 federal election, but consolidated its status as the main opposition party.

The roots of the Alliance lie in the mix of western populist neo-conservative politics and hostility to the federal government, seen as dominated by the eastern provinces of Ontario and Quebec, that had led to the formation in 1987 of the Reform Party (RP) under the leadership of Preston Manning. The RP had itself been in a populist tradition exemplified by Alberta's Social Credit Party, for which Preston Manning's father, Ernest Manning, had been premier of Alberta from 1943–68. The RP opposed bilingualism and multiculturalism, also advocating fiscal reform, a reduction in immigration and decreased powers for the federal government. In the 1993 federal general election it won 18% of the vote (predominantly in western Canada), giving it 52 seats in the House of Commons. It thus became the main voice of the right, eclipsing the party of traditional moderate conservatism, the →Progressive Conservative Party (PCP).

In the 1997 general election the RP retained its position as the principal opposition party, but won all of its 60 seats in just four western provinces (Manitoba, Saskatchewan, Alberta and British Columbia). In that contest the RP and the PCP in aggregate polled a similar proportion of the total vote to the Liberals, but under the first-past-the-post system won only half as many seats. This stimulated a drive, led by Manning, to create a unified conservative movement that could achieve success on a fully national basis, initially known as the "United Alternative". In March 2000 the RP voted to fold the party into what had become known as the Canadian Alliance, but in July 2000 Alberta Treasurer Stockwell Day defeated Manning in a membership ballot for leadership of the Alliance.

The Alliance ran in the November 2000 federal election on a platform that called for the downsizing of federal government, a single rate of taxation and mandatory balanced budgets. Other Alliance themes included the need for reform of the appointed, patronage-based Senate, extension of direct democracy through means such as initiative and recall and referenda, and an end to affirmative action and discriminatory quotas and other policies seen as unfairly assisting minorities. However, the PCP declined to ally itself with the Alliance, which won only six seats more than had the RP in 1997. While it won by a wide margin in Alberta,

Saskatchewan and British Columbia, it failed to make any breakthrough in the eastern provinces. It took only two seats (of 103) in Ontario (although with 23.6% of the vote) and none in the Atlantic provinces, where the Progressive Conservatives remained the principal opposition to the Liberals.

In May 2001 a number of Alliance members in the Commons, dissatisfied with Day's leadership, announced that they would caucus separately, while remaining in the party. Day criticized those in the party who, he said, wished it to be a "regional splinter". On July 17, 2001, he announced that in view of the "deep divisions" that had developed in the Alliance he had called on the party's national council to initiate a leadership election.

Liberal Party of Canada (LPC)

Address. 81 Metcalfe Street, Suite 400, Ottawa, Ontario, K1P 6M8

Telephone. (+1–613) 237–0740

Fax. (+1–613) 235–7208

Website. www.liberal.ca

Leadership. Jean Chrétien (leader); Stephen LeDrew (president); Terry Mercer (national director)

Founded in 1867, the Liberal Party was the ruling party in Canada for the greater part of the 20th century. It has had only seven leaders since 1887, reflecting the party's long-term stability. It is preeminently the party of national unity, resisting the forces of regional separatism threatening to tear Canada apart, which it counters with an emphasis on multiculturalism and respect for minorities. In respect of the problem of Quebec it has sought to steer a difficult course aimed at heading off separatist sentiment by accommodating many of the demands of the francophone majority in Quebec while attempting not to alienate the anglophone majority in the rest of Canada, many of whom believe Quebec enjoys preferential treatment.The Liberal Party favours free markets tempered by a social welfare system closer to Western European models than that of the USA.

In recent decades, the Liberals were returned to office under the leadership of Pierre Trudeau at federal general elections in 1968, 1972, 1974, and again in 1980, following a brief minority →Progressive Conservative Party (PCP) administration. However, in 1984, in the face of increasing unpopularity, Trudeau resigned and the party was decisively beaten at the polls by the PCP, which then retained power until 1993. In the October 1993 election the Liberals returned to office, winning 177 seats under Jean Chrétien (party leader since 1990), who went on to lead the successful campaign by pro-federalists against separatism in the October 1995 Quebec referendum.

The Chrétien government was re-elected in June 1997 (when it won 155 seats with 38.5% of the vote) and again in November 2000 (when it won 172 seats and 40.8% of the vote). However, although the Liberals (unlike any other party) won seats and took at least 20% of the vote in every province in the 2000 election, they were heavily defeated by the right-wing →Canadian Alliance in the western provinces of British Columbia, Alberta and Saskatchewan. Of the Liberals' successful candidates, 100 were elected in the single province of Ontario, where the Liberals won all but three of the seats. The Liberals had claimed during the campaign that the Canadian Alliance programme would lead to the disintegration of a unified country, survival of the fittest, tax cuts for the rich and the introduction of two-tier health care. The Liberals positioned themselves as champions of federalism and moderation, encouraging free markets while preserving Canada's traditional welfare state.

Despite the Liberals' victory at federal level in three successive elections, as of July 2001 they held power in only two provinces, British Columbia and Newfoundland and Labrador. Although the Liberals won nearly all the seats in Ontario in the federal elections of both 1997 and 2000, at provincial legislature level the Progressive Conservatives hold a comfortable majority following elections in 1999.

The party is affiliated to the Liberal International.

New Democratic Party (NDP)

Address. 85 Albert St., Suite 802, Ottawa, Ontario, K1P 6A4

Telephone. (+1–613) 236–3613

Fax. (+1–613) 230–9950

Email. ndpadmin@fed.ndp.ca

Website. www.ndp.ca

Leadership. Alexa McDonough (leader); Dave MacKinnon (president)

Established in 1961, the democratic socialist NDP was the third main party at federal level behind the →Liberal Party of Canada (LPC) and the →Progressive Conservative Party (PCP) until the 1993 general election, when it slipped to fifth in terms of vote share (6.6%) and retained only nine of the 43 seats in the House of Commons which it had won in the 1988 polling. In 1997 it won 21 seats with 11.0% of the vote, but in the November 2000 general election it subsided to 13 seats, taking 8.5% of the vote.

The NDP nationally has not succeeded in displacing the Liberals as the principal anti-conservative party. The NDP's vote is comparatively scattered geographically (other than for having virtually no presence in Quebec), a weakness given that Canadian politics have become highly polarized regionally and legislators are elected on the first past the post system. However, it has had more success at provincial than at federal level, including holding office in the most populous province, Ontario, in 1990–95. As of July 2001 the NDP formed the government in Manitoba and Saskatchewan (the latter being a traditional NDP stronghold), notwithstanding it not being the strongest party in either province in the November 2000 federal election. It lost power to the Liberals in a landslide in British Columbia in May 2001.

The NDP is supported by the Canadian Labour Congress, the national federation of trade unions. The NDP's campaign in the November 2000 elections focused on what it saw as the threat to replace Medicare with US-style two-tier health care. Following its poor performance at the polls it initiated a review of its policy positions.

The NDP is a member party of the Socialist International.

Parti Québécois (PQ)
Quebec Party

Address. 1200 av. Papineau, Suite 150, Montreal, Quebec, H2K 4R5

Telephone. (+1–514) 526–0020

Fax. (+1–514) 526–0272

Email. info@pq.org

Website. partiquebecois.org (French only)

Leadership. Bernard Landry (leader)

Founded in 1968 by René Lévesque, the separatist PQ was the governing party in the province of Quebec from 1976 to 1985 and its strength was reflected in a range of measures to consolidate and promote the French linguistic and cultural identity of the province. The vigorous enforcement of these measures precipitated the departure from the province of many from the anglophone community. However, the PQ failed in a referendum in 1980 to obtain a mandate to negotiate "sovereignty-association" with the federal government, and was subsequently weakened by divisions between moderate and hardline party factions over the separatist issue.

In December 1985 the PQ was ousted by the →Liberal Party of Canada, which retained office until the provincial elections in September 1994, in which the PQ, under the leadership of Jacques Parizeau, won a comfortable majority of seats (although only by a margin of 44.7% to 44.3% of the vote). A new referendum on independence for Quebec took place in October 1995, resulting in a very narrow victory for the opponents of separation. Factors in the result included the potential loss of subsidies from the rest of Canada. Parizeau subsequently resigned and was replaced in January 1996 as PQ leader and Quebec Premier by Lucien Bouchard, the leader of the →Bloc Québécois in Ottawa. Following the referendum defeat the PQ focused on issues such as Quebec's public finances, health and education, while proposing to hold a further referendum when circumstances were deemed favourable. Hardline separatists continued to press for early action to secure independence and further legislation to enforce the use of French. The PQ retained power in provincial elections in November 1998, winning 76 of the 125 seats. In January 2001 Bouchard announced he would stand down as party leader and Premier of Quebec, saying that "the results of my work are not very convincing" and that he wished to hand over to someone who could renew the fight for sovereignty. He was succeeded in March 2001 by Bernard Landry, formerly the Deputy Premier and Finance Minister.

Progressive Conservative Party (PCP)

Address. 141 Laurier Avenue West, Suite 806, Ottawa, Ontario, K1P 5J3
Telephone. (+1–613) 238–6111
Fax. (+1–613) 238–7429
Email. pcinfo@pcparty.ca
Website. www.pcparty.ca
Leadership. Joe Clark (leader); Bruck Easton (president); Susan Elliott (national director)
The PCP (referred to as the Conservatives or Tories), with a history dating back to 1854, has been historically (with the →Liberal Party of Canada) one of the two major Canadian national parties, although it has more commonly constituted the opposition rather than the government. It is essentially a moderate and traditionalist conservative party which has proved resistant to the populist, radical, anti-government and evangelical Christian streams of thought that have influenced most right-of-centre North American parties in recent times.

The period from 1963 to 1984 was spent almost entirely in opposition to Liberal administrations, although a minority PCP government was briefly in power under Joe Clark from May 1979 until its collapse nine months later. Under the leadership (from June 1983) of Brian Mulroney, the party won the 1984 federal election by a substantial majority. Having retained power in the 1988 elections, PCP popularity diminished to an unprecedented level in the face of economic recession and the rise of the neo-conservative western-based Reform Party, and the party was decimated in the October 1993 federal polls, retaining only two seats. Kim Campbell, who had replaced Mulroney in June 1993 to become Canada's first woman Prime Minister, subsequently resigned and was replaced by Jean Charest, a strong federalist.

In the 1997 election the PCP won 20 seats but its eclipse in the western region was confirmed, the party taking no seats at all in Saskatchewan, Alberta and British Columbia, where the Reform Party won a total of 57 seats. In April 1998 Charest stood down and former Prime Minister Joe Clark returned to public life to be elected leader in November 1998. However, the November 2000 election repeated the 1997 pattern with the →Canadian Alliance (the successor to the Reform Party) almost totally shutting the PCP out of the west, although Clark was elected as the sole PCP member from Alberta. The PCP remained the main challenger to the Liberals only in the Atlantic provinces of Newfoundland and Labrador, Prince Edward Island, Nova Scotia and New Brunswick, prompting comment that it had become an "Atlantic rump". Following the election Clark charged that the Canadian Alliance had "played to prejudice" and that the PCP, which had "founded the country" would be "here for centuries to come". In June 2001, however, he announced a series of round tables with other parties to try to build a coalition to oppose the dominance of the Liberals.

Despite its recent marginalization at federal level, the PCP as of July 2001 was in government in five provinces, these being Alberta (where it won 74 of the 83 seats in March 2001 provincial elections despite having taken only 13.5% of the vote and one seat in the November 2000 federal elections), New Brunswick, Nova Scotia, Prince Edward Island and Ontario.

The party is affiliated to the International Democrat Union.

Other Parties

Action démocratique de Québec (ADQ) (Democratic Action of Quebec), launched in 1993 by former members of the →Liberal Party of Canada; backed the unsuccessful separatist cause in the 1995 referendum; won one seat in the provincial general election of November 1998.
Address. 5115 rue de Gaspé, Bureau 420, Montreal, Quebec, H2T 3B7
Telephone. (+1–514) 270–4413
Fax. (+1–514) 270–4469
Email. adq@adq.qc.ca
Website. www.adq.qc.ca

Alberta Independence Party, founded in January 2001 ahead of provincial elections in which it won 7,400 votes; calls for provincial autonomy, the "preservation of Western culture", smaller government, and direct democracy.
Telephone. (+1–403) 254–1419
Website. www.albertaindependence.com
Leadership. Cory Morgan (interim leader)

Canadian Action Party, founded in 1997 by Paul T. Hellyer (a minister in the Trudeau government in the 1960s); argues that Canada must "reclaim its sovereignty" in the face of "corporate rule" and absorption by the US and calls for abrogation of the Canada–US Free Trade Agreement and NAFTA; took 0.2% of the vote in the November 2000 general election.
Address. 99 Atlantic Avenue, Suite 302, Toronto, Ontario, M6K 3J8
Telephone. (+1–416) 535–4144
Fax. (+1–416) 535–6325
Email. info@canadianactionparty.ca
Website. www.canadianactionparty.ca
Leadership. Paul Hellyer

Christian Heritage Party of Canada (CHP), bases its principles on "Biblical ethics"; has a mainly conservative agenda but says it is "falsely tagged" as part of the "religious right".
Address. Heritage Place, 155 Queen Street, Suite 200, Ottawa, Ontario, K1P 6L1
Telephone. (+1–819) 669–0673
Fax. (+1–819) 669–6498
Email. edchp@ottawa.com
Website. www.chp.ca
Leadership. Ron Gray (national leader)

Communist Party of Canada, founded 1921 and historically an orthodox pro-Soviet party. Coinciding with the disintegration of the Soviet Union a reform group briefly came to prominence but was denounced as petty bourgeois reformists and purged in 1992 by Marxist–Leninist traditionalists; took 0.1% of the vote in the November 2000 general election.
Address. 290A Danforth Avenue, Toronto, Ontario, M4K 1N6
Telephone. (+1–416) 469–2446
Fax. (+1–416) 469–4063
Email. pvoice@web.net
Website. www.communist-party.ca
Leadership. Miguel Figueroa

Communist Party of Canada (Marxist–Leninist), founded in 1970 in succession to "The Internationalists"; took 0.1% of the vote in the November 2000 general election.
Address. 396 Cooper Street, Suite 200, Ottawa, Ontario K2P 2H7

Telephone. (+1–613) 565–6446
Email. office@cpcml.ca
Website. www.cpcml.ca
Leadership. Sandra Smith (national leader)

Equality Party, Quebec-based party which believes that the English-speaking minority in Quebec is denied the protections given to the French-speaking minority elsewhere in Canada. It argues that if Quebec unilaterally breaks away from the rest of Canada it would have to be partitioned to protect those of its communities that wished to remain in Canada.
Address. PO Box 21, NDG Station, Montreal, Quebec, H3A 3P4
Telephone. (+1–514) 488–7586
Fax. (+1–514) 488–7306
*E-mail.*canadian@equality.qc.ca
Website. www.equality.qc.ca
Leadership. Keith Henderson (leader)

Green Party of Canada, federal organization of Green parties formed at provincial level from 1983, influenced by developments in Western Europe. The Greens have been unable to gain legislative representation at federal or provincial level under the first-past-the-post system and are campaigning for proportional representation. Nationally the Green Party took only 0.8% of the vote in the November 2000 general election. However, the Green movement scored its most substantial success to date when, although it took no seats, the Green Party of British Columbia won 12.4% of the vote in provincial elections on May 16, 2001.
Address. 244 Gerrard Street East, Toronto, Ontario, M5A 2G2
Telephone. (+1–416) 929–2397
Fax. (+1–416) 929–7709
Email. info@green.ca
Website. www.green.ca
Leadership. Chris Bradshaw (interim leader)

Libertarian Party of Canada, small group that opposes government restrictions on personal freedom; its leader was imprisoned in November 2000 as an outcome of his persistent refusal to wear a car seat belt.
Address. 1843 Ste. Marie, Embrun, Ontario, K0A 1W0
Phone. (+1–613) 443 5423
Website. www.libertarian.ca
Leadership. Jean-Serge Brisson

Marijuana Party, became a registered party in November 2000, immediately prior to the federal general election in which it took 0.5% of the vote. It campaigns on a single issue: the legalization of marijuana.

Address. PO 361, Station "C", Montreal, Quebec, H2L 4K3
Telephone. (+1–514) 528–1768
Email. info@marijuanaparty.org
Website. www.marijuanaparty.com
Leadership. Marc-Boris St-Maurice (leader)

Saskatchewan Party (SP), founded in August 1997 and led by former Reform Party agriculture spokesman Elwin Hermanson. In the September 1999 provincial general election it won more votes than the →New Democratic Party but fewer seats, with the NDP subsequently forming a coalition with the three Liberals elected. It opposes what it sees as the big government and high taxation policies of the NDP and calls for direct accountability of members of the legislature to the electors through recall.
Address. PO Box 546, Regina, Saskatchewan, S4P 3A2
Telephone. (+1–306) 359–1638
Fax. (+1–306) 359–9832
Email. skparty@sk.sympatico.ca
Website. www.saskparty.com
Leadership. Elwin Hermanson (leader)

Western Canada Concept, founded by Douglas Christie in 1980, advocating an independent nation of Western Canada. It calls for the introduction of referendum, initiative and recall to make politicians accountable, mandatory balanced budgets, and an end to immigration. It emphasizes individualism, Christian values and the English language as unifying forces.
Address. Box 143, 255 Menzies Street, Victoria, British Columbia, V8W 2G6
Telephone. (+1–250) 727–3438
Fax. (+1–250) 479–3294
Website. www.westcan.org
Leadership. Douglas Christie (leader)

Yukon Party (YP), believes in self-sufficiency and fiscal responsibility for the Yukon territory and advocates that north of latitude 60° should be a zone without gun controls. It won seven of the 17 seats in the Yukon legislature in elections in October 1992 and formed a minority administration that held office until 1996 when the →New Democratic Party came to power. The YP won only one seat in elections in April 2000 in which the Liberals came to power for the first time in Yukon.
Address. Box 31113, Whitehorse, Yukon, Y1A 5P7
Telephone. (+1–867) 668–6505
Fax. (+1–867) 667–7660
Email. yukonparty@mailcity.com
Leadership. John Ostashek (leader)

Cape Verde

Capital: Praia

Population: 400,000 (2001E)

The Republic of Cape Verde achieved independence from Portugal in 1975 and had a one-party system under what became the African Party for the Independence of Cape Verde (PAICV) until moving to multi-partyism under legislation enacted in September 1990. The 1980 constitution as amended in 1990 provides for an executive President who appoints the government and who is directly elected for a five-year term by universal suffrage of those aged 18 and over. Legislative authority is vested in a unicameral National People's Assembly (*Assembléia Nacional Popular*) of 72 members, who are directly elected for a five-year term from 21 multi-member constituencies.

National Assembly elections were held in early 1991, the decisive victory of the Movement for Democracy (MPD) marking the first ever constitutional transfer of power to an opposition party in West Africa. In the next Assembly elections held on Dec. 17, 1995, the MPD comfortably retained power winning 50 seats and 61.3% of the vote; the PAICV won 21 and 29.7%; and the Democratic Convergence Party 1 and 6.7%. In a presidential election on Feb. 18, 1996, the MPD candidate, António Mascarenhas Monteiro, was re-elected unopposed, having in 1991 defeated the then incumbent PAICV nominee by 73.5% to 26.5%.

In early 2001 the PAICV were returned to power after a ten-year absence. In the legislative elections on Jan. 14, the party gained 40 of the 72 seats, while the MPD took 30 and the Democratic Alliance for Change 2. In the presidential poll held over two rounds on Feb. 11 and 25, 2001, PAICV candidate Pedro Verona Rodrigues Pires very narrowly defeated Carlos Alberto Wahnon de Carvalho Veiga of the MPD.

African Party for the Independence of Cape Verde
Partido Africano da Independência de Cabo Verde (PAICV)

Address. CP 22, Praia, São Tiago
Telephone. (+238) 612136
Fax. (+238) 615239
Website. www.paicv.org
Leadership. José Maria Neves (president)

The PAICV originated as the islands' branch of the African Party for the Independence of Guinea and Cape Verde (PAIGC), which had been founded by Amilcar Cabral in 1956 to oppose Portuguese colonial rule. The PAIGC led both Guinea-Bissau and Cape Verde to independence in 1974–75, becoming the sole ruling party in each. Following the November 1980 coup in Guinea-Bissau, the Cape Verde party reconstituted itself as the PAICV in January 1981, under the leadership of President Arístides Maria Pereira. Under the 1980 constitution the PAICV was defined as the leading force in society and nominated all candidates in legislative elections. However, an extraordinary PAICV congress in February 1990 endorsed constitutional changes providing for the introduction of a multi-party system, to herald which Pereira resigned as party general secretary in July and was replaced the following month by Gen. Pedro Verona Rodrigues Pires, the Prime Minister since 1975. In multi-party elections in January 1991 the PAICV was heavily defeated by the opposition →Movement for Democracy (MPD), winning only a third of the popular vote and only 23 of the 79 seats. The following month Pereira, standing effectively as the PAICV candidate, went down to an even heavier defeat in presidential balloting, managing only just over a quarter of the vote.

In opposition for the first time, the PAICV underwent some internal strains and suffered a further rebuff in local elections in December 1991. In August 1993 a party congress elected Pires to the newly-created post of president, while Arístides Lima, the PAICV leader in the Assembly, took the vacated job of general secretary.

Having been defeated again in the December 1995 Assembly elections (taking only 21 of 72 seats), the PAICV returned to office in early 2001, securing an overall majority with 40 seats in the legislative polling, and a narrow victory in the presidential elections. PAICV candidate Pires (who had relinquished the party presidency to José Maria Neves) defeated his MPD rival in the second round of voting by just 17 votes. Neves was appointed as Prime Minister of the new PAICV government.

The PAICV is a full member of the Socialist International.

Democratic Alliance for Change
Aliança Democrática para a Mudança (ADM)

Address. c/o Assembléia Nacional Popular, Praia
Leadership. Eurico Correia Monteiro (president)

The ADM was founded in 2000 as an alliance of the →Democratic Convergence Party (PCD), the →Party of Labour and Solidarity (PTS) and the →Cape Verde Independence and Democratic Union (UCID). In the January 2001 Assembly elections, the ADM won only two seats with 6.1% of the vote.

Democratic Convergence Party
Partido da Convergência Democrática (PCD)

Address. c/o Assembléia Nacional Popular, Praia
Leadership. Eurico Correia Monteiro (chairman)

Founded in 1994 by dissidents of the →Movement for Democracy, the centrist PCD won only one seat in the December 1995 legislative elections, with 6.7% of the popular vote. It contested the January 2001 Assembly elections as part of the →Democratic Alliance for Change (ADM), whereas in the following month's presidential poll the party nominated Jorge Carlos de Almeida Fonseca, who won 3.9% of the vote.

Movement for Democracy
Movimento para Democracia (MPD)

Address. c/o Assembléia Nacional Popular, Praia
Leadership. Carlos Alberto Wahnon de Carvalho Veiga (chairman)

The MPD was founded by Lisbon-based exiles who in April 1990 issued a manifesto demanding the introduction of multi-party democracy and a free enterprise economy. The concurrent move of the ruling →African Party for the Independence of Cape Verde (PAICV) in that direction enabled the MPD leaders to return to Praia and to negotiate on a timetable for elections with the government. In mid-1990 the MPD signed a co-operation agreement with the →Cape Verde Independent and Democratic Union in an attempt to extend its influence throughout the islands.

In the Assembly contest in January 1991 the MPD registered a landslide victory, winning 56 of the 79 seats and nearly two-thirds of the popular vote. In presidential balloting the following month, moreover, the MPD candidate and then leader, António Mascarenhas Monteiro (a former PAICV member), overwhelmingly defeated the PAICV incumbent, winning nearly three-quarters of the vote. The resultant MPD government under the premiership of Carlos Veiga quickly experienced tensions between radical and more cautious reformers. The dismissal of Jorge Carlos Fonseca as Foreign Minister in March 1993 intensified internal divisions, which erupted in February 1994 when the reappointment of Veiga as MPD chairman provoked the resignations of several leading party members. Nevertheless, the MPD won a further convincing victory in legislative elections in December 1995, while President Monteiro was re-elected unopposed in February 1996.

In the legislative elections on Jan. 14, 2001, the MPD lost 20 of its seats and its share of the vote fell to about 40%, so relinquishing power back to the PAICV. Having resigned as Prime Minister in July 2000 in order to contest the presidential elections in February 2001, Veiga was marginally beaten by PAICV candidate Pires over two rounds of voting.

Other Parties

Cape Verde Independent and Democratic Union (*União Caboverdiana Independente e Democrática, UCID*), founded in 1974 by exiles opposed to the government of the →African Party for the Independence of Cape Verde (PAICV), registered in 1991; allied with the →Movement for Democracy in the 1990s, it was part of the →Democratic Alliance for Change (ADM) in the January 2001 elections.
Leadership. Celso Celestino (president)

Democratic Renovation Party (*Partido da Renovação Democrática, PRD*), contested the January 2001 Assembly elections, attracting just over 3% of the vote but gaining no seats.
Leadership. Jacinto Santos

Party of Labour and Solidarity (*Partido de Trabalho e Solidariedade, PTS*), founded in 1998, formed part of the →Democratic Alliance for Change (ADM) in the January 2001 Assembly elections.
Leadership. Onesimo Silveira (president)

Social Democratic Party (*Partido Socialista Democrático, PSD*), founded in 1992. It has failed to win any representation in Assembly elections, gaining less than 0.5% of the vote in January 2001.
Leadership. João Alem

Central African Republic

Capital: Bangui

Population: 3,510,000 (2000E)

The Central African Republic (CAR) became independent from France in 1960 and a one-party state from 1962. Military rule was imposed in 1966 by Col. Jean-Bedel Bokassa, who created the Central African Empire in 1977 but was deposed in 1979 by ex-President David Dacko, who revived the CAR. Military rule under Gen. André Kolingba from 1981 gave way in 1986 to a semi-civilian one-party regime under Kolingba's Central African Democratic Rally (RDC), which in turn gave way to multi-party democracy in 1991. Under a new constitution introduced in January 1995, the previous "semi-presidential" arrangements gave way to a fully presidential system in which the President, directly elected for a six-year term (renewable once), was to "embody and symbolize national unity" and was empowered to give policy direction to the Prime Minister. The latter is responsible to a National Assembly (*Assemblée Nationale*), with 109 members (increased from 85 for the 1998 polls) directly elected for a five-year term by universal adult suffrage in two rounds of voting. The 1995 constitution also provided for the establishment of directly-elected regional assemblies.

Assembly elections held on Aug. 22, Sept. 19 and Oct. 3, 1993, resulted as follows: Central African People's Liberation Party (MLPC) 34 seats; RDC 13; Patriotic Front for Progress (FPP) 7; Liberal Democratic Party (PLD) 7; Alliance for Democracy and Progress (ADP) 6; others 18. Presidential elections held on Aug. 22 and Sept. 19, 1993, resulted in the election of the MLPC candidate, Ange-Félix Patassé, with 52.5% of the second-round vote.

Since 1996 there have been frequent military mutinies against the government, necessitating intervention by French troops and latterly the deployment of a United Nations peacekeeping force which oversaw the legislative elections at the end of 1998 and the presidential poll in September 1999. In the Assembly elections held on Nov. 22 and Dec. 13, 1998, the MLPC won 47 seats; RDC 20; Movement for Democracy and Development 8; FPP 7; Social Democratic Party 6; ADP 5; Party for National Unity 3; Democratic Forum for Modernity 2; PLD 2; Civic Forum 1; People's Union for the Republic 1; independents 7. The presidential polling on Sept. 19, 1999, returned the incumbent Patassé to power with 51.6% of the vote, while Kolingba won 19.3% and Dacko 11.1%.

At the end of May 2001 there was a further unsuccessful coup attempt by disaffected soldiers in Bangui. Kolingba and the RDC were accused by the Patassé regime of complicity.

Alliance for Democracy and Progress
Alliance pour la Démocratie et le Progrès (ADP)
Address. c/o Assemblée Nationale, Bangui The ADP was launched in 1991 and became a founder member of the opposition Consultative Group of Democratic Forces (CFD) headed by the →Patriotic Front for Progress. The ADP suffered a setback in October 1992 when its first leader, Jean-Claude Conjugo, was killed by security forces during a trade union demonstration. In March 1993 the party expelled its first general secretary, Tehakpa Mbrede, when he accepted a ministerial post under the Kolingba regime. In the 1993 presidential elections the ADP supported the unsuccessful CFD candidate, while the simultaneous legislative elections gave the ADP six of the 85 seats. In October 1993 the ADP broke with the CFD by accepting representation in a coalition government headed by the →Central African People's Liberation Movement. In the 1998 elections, the ADP secured five seats in the enlarged 109-member Assembly.

Central African Democratic Rally
Rassemblement Démocratique Centrafricain (RDC)
Address. c/o Assemblée Nationale, Bangui
Leadership. André Dieudonné Kolingba (leader); Laurent Gomina-Pampali (general secretary)
Founded in May 1986 as the sole ruling party of the regime of Gen. Kolingba, who had come to power in a bloodless military coup in 1981, the RDC held its inaugural congress in February 1987. Launched as the country moved to semi-civilian rule, the RDC was intended to represent all political

and social tendencies except those seeking "to impose a totalitarian doctrine". The RDC provided the only authorized candidates in elections held in July 1987. The RDC at first resisted the post-1989 world trend against one-party regimes, but in April 1991 President Kolingba announced his conversion to multi-partyism and his party followed suit. At an extraordinary party congress in August 1991, he resigned as RDC leader with the aim of "putting himself above all political parties". Thereafter Kolingba and the RDC resisted opposition demands for a sovereign national conference and instead promoted the idea of a "grand national debate", which was boycotted by most other parties when it was held in mid-1992. The first attempt to hold democratic elections, in October 1992, was aborted by the authorities, reportedly with the opposition well ahead of the RDC.

In the first round of rescheduled presidential elections in August 1993, Kolingba trailed in a poor fourth place as the RDC candidate, winning only 12.1% of the vote and therefore being eliminated. Attempts by him to suppress the results were successfully resisted by the opposition, so that the RDC was obliged to hand over power to the →Central African People's Liberation Movement (MLPC) after the second round in September. In simultaneous Assembly elections the RDC also polled weakly, winning only 13 of the 85 seats, although this tally made it the second strongest party after the MLPC. Having resumed effective leadership of the RDC, Kolingba was stripped of his military rank in March 1994, under a 1985 law (which he had signed as President)

90

banning army officers from participating in elections or holding public office. This move, and the concurrent arrest of two senior RDC members on charges of "creating pockets of social tension", caused Kolingba to declare that democracy had been dangerously derailed.

In the 1998 legislative elections the RDC, although again emerging the second strongest party, won only 20 of 109 seats in the Assembly. Kolingba similarly failed in his bid to secure the presidency in September 1999, trailing the incumbent Patassé with only 19.4% of the vote. Following a coup attempt in late May 2001, the government suspended the activities of the RDC for alleged complicity.

Central African People's Liberation Movement
Mouvement pour la Libération du Peuple Centrafricain (MLPC)

Address. c/o Assemblée Nationale, Bangui
Leadership. Ange-Félix Patassé (president); Francis Albert Oukanga (secretary-general)

The MLPC was founded in Paris in mid-1979 by exiles led by Patassé, who as Bokassa's Prime Minister from September 1976 had overseen the creation of the Central African Empire in December 1976. Dismissed in July 1978 and forced to flee the country, he had then disclosed details of the barbarism and corruption of the Bokassa regime. The MLPC opposed the succeeding Dacko government established in September 1979 and Patassé, who returned to Bangui, spent a year in prison for "fomenting unrest", emerging to take second place in the March 1981 presidential election. Again forced into exile in April 1982 (this time in Togo), Patassé was ousted as MLPC leader in September 1983 by a majority which favoured a leftist orientation and alliance with what became the →Patriotic Front for Progress (FPP). The new leadership involved the MLPC in attempts to overthrow the Kolingba regime, but Patassé regained control by the time of the transition to multi-partyism, securing legalization for the MLPC in September 1991.

As MLPC presidential candidate, Patassé was well-placed in the first round of October 1992 elections, which were aborted by the authorities. In February 1993 Patassé accepted membership of a government-appointed transitional legislature but in April the MLPC refused to join a coalition administration. Concurrently, the MLPC leader dismissed as "slander" public allegations by the FPP leader that Patassé had links with international diamond merchants and right-wing mercenary groups. In resumed elections in August–September 1993, Patassé headed the field in the first ballot (with 37.3% of the vote) and won the run-off (with 52.5%) against the FPP leader. In simultaneous Assembly elections the MLPC became substantially the strongest party, although its 34 seats out of 85 left it without an overall majority. It therefore formed a coalition government, under the premiership of Jean-Luc Mandaba (MLPC vice-president), with the →Liberal Democratic Party, the →Alliance for Democracy and Progress and the six Assembly supporters of ex-President David Dacko (later organized as the →Movement for Democracy and Development).

President Patassé's powers were significantly enhanced under the new constitution introduced in January 1995 following approval in a referendum the previous month. In April 1995 Mandaba was forced to resign as Prime Minister after more than half the Assembly deputies had signed a no-confidence motion tabled by his own MLPC and citing government corruption, maladministration and lack of consultation. He was succeeded by Gabriel Koyambounou, a technocrat close to the President, at the head of a new government coalition of the "presidential majority" parties.

The MLPC retained power after the legislative elections of 1998 (winning 47 of the 109 Assembly seats) and the presidential contest in September 1999 (in which Patassé was re-elected with 51.6% of the vote).

Civic Forum
Forum Civique (FC)

Address. c/o Assemblée Nationale, Bangui
Leadership. Gen. (retd.) Timothée Malendoma (president)

The FC was one of many newly-founded parties which in late 1991 joined the opposition Consultative Group of Democratic Forces (CFD) headed by the →Patriotic Front for Progress. Its CFD membership was suspended in August 1992, however, when it opted to participate in the "grand national debate" convened by the then Kolingba government. Its relations with the CFD worsened in December 1992 when Malendoma was appointed Prime Minister, although they recovered somewhat in February 1993 when the FC leader was dismissed by Kolingba for "blocking the democratic process". Malendoma won only 2% of the vote in the presidential election first round in August 1993, while the FC secured only one of the 85 Assembly seats in concurrent legislative elections. In the Assembly elections in November–December 1998, the FC retained its one seat.

Democratic Forum for Modernity
Forum Démocratique pour la Modernité (FODEM)

Address. c/o Assemblée Nationale, Bangui
Leadership. Charles Massil

The FODEM secured two seats in the 1998 legislative elections, but party leader Massil gained only 1.3% of the vote in the presidential poll in September 1999.

Liberal Democratic Party
Parti Libéral-Démocrate (PLD)

Address. c/o Assemblée Nationale, Bangui
Leadership. Nestor Kombo-Naguemon (president)

The PLD was launched amid the transition to multi-partyism in 1991–92. Advocating a deregulated market economy, the party won seven of the 85 Assembly seats in the 1993 legislative elections and accepted representation in the coalition government formed in October 1993 under the leadership of the →Central African People's Liberation Movement. The PLD retained only two seats in the 1998 legislative elections. It was reportedly represented in April 2001 in the MLPC-led government under new Prime Minister Martin Ziguélé.

Movement for Democracy and Development
Mouvement pour la Démocratie et le Développement (MDD)

Address. c/o Assemblée Nationale, Bangui
Leadership. David Dacko (president)

The MDD was launched in January 1994 by ex-President Dacko, who had led the CAR to independence in 1960 and had established one-party rule in 1962 through the Movement for the Social Evolution of Black Africa (MESAN). He was overthrown in 1966 by his cousin, Col. Jean-Bedel Bokassa, who appropriated MESAN as his political vehicle and placed it under new management. In 1976 Dacko accepted appointment as a special adviser to Bokassa, shortly before the latter's controversial self-elevation to the status of Emperor, but in 1979, with the assistance of French paratroops, led the ousting of Bokassa and the re-establishment of the republic. Installed as President again, Dacko in March 1980 founded the Central African Democratic Union (UDC) as the sole ruling party, but later accepted multi-party competition under a new constitution promulgated in February 1981.

Declared the victor in disputed presidential elections in March 1981, Dacko was overthrown six months later by Gen. André Kolingba and thereafter was a key figure in the exiled anti-Kolingba opposition. Returning to the CAR on the introduction of multi-partyism, Dacko held aloof from party identification, standing as an independent in the August 1993 first round of presidential elections, in which he was placed third with 20.1% of the vote. In the concurrent Assembly elections, nominally independent candidates identified with Dacko won six of the 85 seats and in October

1993 became part of a coalition headed by the →Central African People's Liberation Movement. The subsequent creation of the MDD was intended to provide a party framework for the pro-Dacko element of the new government.

The MDD secured eight seats in the 1998 legislative elections, but Dacko came a distant third in the September 1999 presidential poll with 11.1% of the vote.

National Convention
Convention National (CN)
Address. c/o Assemblée Nationale, Bangui

The CD was founded in October 1991, immediately becoming a founder member of the opposition Consultative Group of Democratic Forces (CFD) headed by the →Patriotic Front for Progress (FPP). It backed the unsuccessful CFD/FPP candidate in the August–September 1993 presidential election, while winning three of the 85 seats in simultaneous Assembly elections. The party was reportedly represented in April 2001 in the MLPC-led government under new Prime Minister Martin Ziguélé, although it had failed to win any seats in the 1998 legislative elections.

Party of National Unity
Parti de l'Unité Nationale (PUN)
Address. c/o Assemblée Nationale, Bangui
Leadership. Jean-Paul Ngoupande

The PUN gained three seats in the Assembly elections in late 1998, and party leader Ngoupande (who had been Prime Minister from June 1996–January 1997) contested the September 1999 presidential poll, attracting 3.1% of the vote to take sixth place. The party was reportedly represented in April 2001 in the MLPC-led government under new premier Martin Ziguélé.

Patriotic Front for Progress
Front Patriotique pour le Progrès (FPP)
Address. BP 259, Bangui
Telephone. (+236–61) 5223
Leadership. Abel Goumba (president); Patrice Endjimoungou (secretary-general)

The FPP was launched in 1981 as the (Congo-based) Ubangi Patriotic Front–Labour Party after veteran anti-Bokassa campaigner Goumba had broken with the post-Bokassa Dacko government. During the late 1980s the party co-operated closely with the →Central African People's Liberation Movement (MLPC) when the latter was under left-wing leadership. It also forged links with the European democratic left, becoming an affiliate of the Socialist International. The party obtained legal recognition as the FPP in August 1991, but not before Goumba had spent six months in prison for participating in an unauthorized opposition attempt to initiate a national conference on political reform. In late 1991 the FPP took the lead in the formation of the Consultative Group of Democratic Forces (CFD), with 13 other parties and six trade unions, which refused to participate in a "grand national debate" proposed by President Kolingba.

Standing as the CFD candidate in the October 1992 presidential elections, Goumba was reported to be leading the first-round count when the elections were aborted. In February 1993 Goumba accepted membership of a government-appointed transitional legislature, but the CFD formations refused to join a coalition administration. When the electoral process was resumed in August 1993, Goumba took second place in the first round of presidential balloting, winning 21.7% of the vote. He therefore went forward to second round in September but was defeated by the MLPC candidate by 52.5% to 45.6%. In simultaneous legislative elections, the FPP won seven of the 85 seats in its own right. After the elections the CFD was weakened by the decision of the →Alliance for Democracy and Progress to join an MLPC-led coalition government. Nevertheless, the FPP became an active focus of opposition to the new Patassé administration, opposing the move to a presidential constitution in January 1995.

In the 1998 legislative polling, the FPP retained its seven-seat representation in the enlarged 109-member Assembly. Goumba stood again for the presidency in September 1999, achieving fourth place with 6% of the vote.

The party has observer status within the Socialist International.

Social Democratic Party
Parti Social-Démocrate (PSD)
Address. c/o Assemblée Nationale, Bangui
Leadership. Enoch Dérant Lakoué (president)

Founded in 1991, the PSD distanced itself from the main anti-Kolingba opposition, favouring instead an accommodation with the then ruling →Central African Democratic Rally (RDC). The PSD leader was a candidate in the aborted October 1992 presidential election and in February 1993 accepted President Kolingba's invitation to become Prime Minister. However, he failed in his quest to bring other major opposition parties into the government, his role in which precipitated wholesale defections from the PSD. Standing again for the presidency, Lakoué obtained only 2.4% of the vote in the August 1993 first round, while in Assembly elections the PSD took three of the 85 seats. Thereafter it formed part of the opposition to the new Patassé administration.

The PSD increased its representation in the Assembly to six seats in the 1998 legislative elections, but Lakoué managed to attract only 1.3% of the vote in the September 1999 presidential poll. The party was reportedly represented in April 2001 in the MLPC-led government under new Prime Minister Martin Ziguélé.

Chad

Capital: N'Djaména

Population: 8,420,000 (2000E)

The Republic of Chad achieved independence from France in 1960 and became a one-party state in 1962 under N'Garta Tombalbaye's Chadian Progressive Party. Tombalbaye's overthrow in 1975 ushered in a lengthy north-south civil war and a series of shortlived regimes, leading in late 1990 to the seizure of power by the Patriotic Salvation Movement (MPS) led by Col. Idriss Déby. In October 1991 the new regime agreed to legitimize political parties that renounced "intolerance, tribalism, regionalism, religious discrimination ... and violence". In April 1993 a sovereign national conference planned for a transition to multi-party democracy. Déby remained head of state, but the conference itself elected a transitional Prime Minister and a 57-member Higher Transitional Council (*Conseil Supérieur de Transition*) pending general elections. Initially, transition was to last a year; but 12-month extensions were decreed in April 1994 and May 1995.

In light of continuing rebel activity, the government in May 1994 established a National Reconciliation Committee to serve as a framework for the achievement of peace. In November 1995 a timetable was published scheduling presidential and legislative elections. Signed by the government and 13 opposition parties on March

9, 1996 the so-called Franceville Accord advocated a new constitution modeled on that of France. A national referendum approved the Accord in a 63.5% vote on March 31.

This paved the way for two-stage National Assembly elections in January and February 1997, which resulted in a small but absolute majority – 63 out of 125 seats – for the President's party, the Patriotic Salvation Movement (*Mouvement Patriotique du Salut*, or MPS). To foster national reconciliation, two opposition parties, the National Union for Democracy and Renewal (UNDR) and the Union for Democracy and the Republic (UDR), joined the MPS in government. Nonetheless, clashes in southern Chad continued between rebels and the army in late 1997, and re-erupted in 2000 after a peace agreement of May 1998 had appeared to restore calm. Increasingly, smaller opposition parties banded together in coalitions, like the 13 member Coordinated Armed Movements and Political Parties of the Opposition (CMAP) in late 1999, and the four-member *Comité Politique d'Action et de Liaison* (CPAL) in early 2000.

Presidential elections on May 20, 2001 saw Idriss Déby returned to office on a high turnout. He won 67.4% of the vote, compared with 13.9% for his nearest rival, Ngarlejy Yorongar. Allegations of fraud led to the detention of all six losing candidates, and heralded suppression of press and public protest.

Action Forces Front for the Republic
Front des Forces d'Action pour la République (FFAR)
Leadership. Ngarlejy Yorongar (also known as Lemohiban)
This is a strongly anti-Déby group. In 1996 party leader Yorongar, a Christian, federalist and ecologist, led a campaign against alleged kickbacks that the government was receiving from the Elf petroleum company. The party won a single seat in the 1997 assembly elections. In the 2001 presidential elections, however, Yorongar garnered 13.9% of the vote in a run-off with Déby, gaining national prominence through his criticism of governmental weapons acquisition, corruption and neglect of enduring famine. Yorongar accused the government of electoral fraud; his subsequent detention aroused international protest.

Action for Unity and Socialism
Action pour l'Unité et le Socialisme (ACTUS)
Leadership. Fidèle Moungar (president)
ACTUS originated as a faction of the Transitional Government of National Unity (GUNT), which had been created in 1979 to unite the forces of Hissène Habré and Goukhouni Oueddei but disintegrated in 1980. In 1990 ACTUS backed the successful offensive against the Habré regime by the →Patriotic Salvation Movement (MPS) led by Idriss Déby. After Déby assumed power in December 1990, ACTUS re-emerged as a distinct formation under Fidèle Moungar, a prominent surgeon. In May 1992 Moungar was appointed Education Minister in an MPS-dominated coalition government. In April 1993 he was elected Prime Minister by the sovereign national conference which planned the transition to multi-party elections. In October 1993, however, he was forced to resign after the transitional legislature had passed no-confidence motion, apparently inspired by Déby.

ACTUS took two seats in the 1997 elections. In December 1999 it joined 12 other parties in a coalition grouping called →Co-ordinated Armed Movements and Political Parties of the Opposition (CMAP).

Chad National Liberation Front
Front de Libération National Tchadien (FROLINAT)
Leadership. Goukhouni Oueddei (chairman)
FROLINAT was officially founded in 1966 by Libyan-backed Muslim northerners opposed to the southern-based Tombalbaye government (1960–75). It subsequently underwent repeated splits and fragmentation. After the overthrow of President Felix Malloum in 1979, FROLINAT factions were key elements of the governments of both Goukhouni Oueddei (1980–82) and Hissène Habré (1982–90). Libya continued backing rebel alliances led by the ousted Oueddei during the 1980s. In 1987 some FROLINAT forces, assisted by the USA and France, combined with the national army to expel Libya from most of the north. Based in Algeria, Oueddei was marginalized by a new rival, →the Patriotic Salvation Movement (MSP), which toppled Habré and assumed power in December 1990.

Oueddei made a highly publicized return to N'Djaména in May 1991 for talks with President Déby on a transition to multi-party democracy. Back in Algiers he led a faction of FROLINAT called the Provisional Council of the Revolution. Oueddei publicly eschewed armed struggle, and attended the reform conference convened by the Déby government in N'Djaména in early 1993. Some two thirds of delegates were former FROLINAT faction leaders. By then, however, the initiative had passed to the MSP and other parties. In August 1995 Oueddei was reported to be fighting alongside southern-based rebels. FROLINAT did not compete in the 1997 elections.

Co-ordinated Armed Movements and Political Parties of the Opposition
La Coordination des mouvements armés et partis politiques de l'opposition (CMAP)
Leadership. Antoine Bangui (president of council)
The CMAP was founded in December 1999 in Benin as an umbrella for 13 opposition groups from Chad. Antoine Bangui was a former minister, ambassador, and Chad representative to UNESCO. He also leads one of the constituent parties, the Front Extérieur pour la Rénovation (FER). The other 12 parties included →FROLINAT/CPR, →Action for Unity and Socialism (ACTUS), and the →National Front of Chad Renewed (FNTR).

Movement for Democracy and Development
Mouvement pour la Démocratie et le Développement (MDD)
Leadership. Gaileth Bourkou Mandah (secretary-general)
The MDD was founded Nigeria in 1991 by exiled supporters of ex-President Hissène Habré, who had been overthrown in December 1990 by the →Patriotic Salvation Movement (MSP) led by Idriss Déby. The MDD's military wing, the Western Armed Forces (*Forces Armées Occidentales*, FAO), invaded Chad in late 1991, but was repelled in January 1992. Soon afterwards MDD leaders were reportedly kidnapped from Nigeria, among them Goukhouni Guët. In early 1993 the MDD/FAO split, and Guët's faction participated in the reform conference held in N'Djaména in early 1993. A militant pro-Habré faction called the National Armed Forces of Chad (*Forces Armées Nationales du Tchad*, FANT) led by Brahim Malla continued the armed struggle. The MDD agreed in 1995 that selected MDD guerrillas would be integrated into the national army. Gaileth Bourkou Mandah, formerly head of the Democratic Revolutionary Council–Rejection Front (CDR-FR) subsequently replaced Guët as party leader. Malla led his MDD/FANT faction into the →Coordinated Armed Movements and Political Parties of the Opposition (CMAP) alliance in December 1999. Bourkou Manda was said to have formed the →Movement for Unity and the Republic in February 2000. In July 2000, MDD party president Moussa Medella signed an accord with the Chad government, while in Sudan, but was expelled from the party on

his return to N'Djaména that same month. Issa Faki was president of another MDD faction as of May 2001.

Movement for Democracy and Socialism in Chad
Mouvement pour la Démocratie et le Socialisme en Tchad (MDST)

Leadership. Salomon (Ngarbaye) Tombalbaye (president), Abderahman Hamdane (executive secretary)

The MDST was founded in Nigeria in 1988 by anti-Habré exiles, including Salomon (Ngarbaye) Tombalbaye, son of independent Chad's first President (who was assassinated in 1975). Allied with the →Patriotic Salvation Movement (MPS) in its successful offensive against the Habré regime in late 1990, the MDST elected Tombalbaye as its president in April 1992 and was legalized in June. Almost alone among the crop of new parties in Chad, the MDST advocated a socialist programme, while stressing the importance of full multi-party democracy. In May 1994 Tombalbaye rejected President Déby's offer become Chad's Health Minister.

National Action for Development
Action Nationale pour le Développement (AND)

The AND won two seats in the 1997 elections.

National Alliance for Democracy and Development
Alliance Nationale pour la Démocratie et le Développement (ANDD)

Leadership. Salibou Garba (president)

The ANDD was one of a number of parties formed in early 1992 on the fringes of the ruling →Patriotic Salvation Movement (MPS). The Prime Minister appointed in May 1992, Joseph Yodemane, was at first described as being "close" to the ANDD, while one of his ministers, Nabia Ndali, was an actual party member. However, Ndali resigned in July 1992 as a result of a dispute between ANDD leaders and Yodemane, who was formally disowned by the party and later formed the →National Alliance for Democracy and Renewal.

National Alliance for Democracy and Renewal
Alliance Nationale pour la Démocratie et le Renouveau (ANDR)

Leadership. Joseph Yodemane (president)

The ANDR was created by Yodemane after he had broken with the →National Alliance for Democracy and Development in July 1992. He served as Prime Minister of a coalition government from May 1992 to April 1993.

National Front of Chad Renewed
Front National du Tchad Rénové (FNTR)

Leadership. Ahmat Yacoub (secretary-general)

Based in central-eastern Chad, the rebel FNT under Alarit Bachar signed a peace agreement with the Déby government in October 1992 providing for its political and military integration into national structures. However, most FNT elements continued military activities, stepping them up in 1994. Bachar disowned a further ceasefire agreement signed with the government by a renogade faction in October 1994. The FNT reconstituted itself as the FNTR in April 1996, in Brussels. Under its new leader, Ahmat Yacoub, the FNTR was committed to a social democracy and opposed tribalism, regionalism and corruption. FNTR joined the → Co-ordinated Armed Movements and Political Parties of the Opposition (CMAP) opposition alliance in December 1999.

National Rally for Democracy and Progress
Rassemblement National pour la Démocratie et le Progrès (RNDP)

Leadership. Delwa Kassiré Koumakoyé (president)

The RNDP, also called *Viva*, was founded in early 1992. Its French-educated legalist leader became spokesman of the National Co-ordination of the Opposition (CNO) created in May 1992, but later gravitated towards the ruling →Patriotic

Salvation Front (MPS). He failed in a bid to become chairman of the sovereign national conference convened in January 1993. In June 1993 Koumakoyé accepted the post of Justice Minister in a transitional coalition government and in November was elevated to the premiership. His main stated aims were the further demobilization of armed forces, a social pact with the trade unions, the preparation of elections and reconciliation with unreconciled rebel movements. In April 1995, however, he was dismissed by decision of the legislative Higher National Council, apparently at the instigation of President Déby. Koumakoyé condemned what he termed the government's "drift towards totalitarianism and dictatorship". In 1996 he spent three months in jail on charges of illegal possession of arms. The RNDP nonetheless participated in the 1997 elections, and won three seats. Koumakoyé contested the 2001 presidential election, but received little support beyond his southern stronghold of Tandjilé.

National Salvation Council for Peace and Democracy
Conseil de Salut National pour la Paix et la Démocratie (CSNPD)

Leadership. Col. Moise Nodji Tchiete (president)

The southern-based CSNPD was founded in mid-1992 by deserters from the northern-dominated national army. After bloody clashes with the government in 1993, the two sides met peaceably in the Central African Republic, and negotiated a ceasefire agreement in August 1994. Government forces withdrew from the south and CSNPD fighters rejoined the national army, including party leader Tchiete, hitherto a lieutenant, who was now made a colonel. In April 1995 Tchiete was appointed Minister of Environment and Tourism in the new government headed by the →Patriotic Salvation Movement.

National Union for Democracy and Renewal
Union National pour la Démocratie et le Rénouvellement (UNDR)

Leadership. Saleh Kebzabo

The UNDR won 12 seats out of 125 in national assembly elections in 1997, making it the third strongest party in Chad after the MPS and URD. Its leader, Saleh Kebzabo, is a former news agency director and journalist whose stronghold lies in the south of Chad. In September 1995 he was arrested and charged with making illegal contacts with rebel groups. Formerly an opposition grouping, after 1997 the UNDR rallied to support President Déby. Kebzabo entered the cabinet as minister for mining. In May 1998 he returned to opposition with two other ministers from his party, and in 1999 led a campaign against restrictions on press freedom. Kebzabo returned to government as agriculture minister in 2000, but lost this post in an April 2001 reshuffle. He contested presidential elections in May 2001, coming a poor third behind the winner, Déby, and runner-up, Ngarlejy Yorongar.

Party for Freedom and Development
Parti pour la Liberté et le Développement, (PLD)

Founded in late 1993 by Ibn Oumar Mahamat Saleh and Paul Saradori, following the former's dismissal in May as Minister of Planning and Co-operation, advocating the "rehabilitation" of Chad. The party won three seats in the 1997 elections.

Patriotic Salvation Movement
Mouvement Patriotique du Salut (MPS)

Leadership. Idriss Déby (president), Maldom Bada Abbas (chairman)

The MPS was founded in March 1990 by Sudan-based and Libyan-backed opponents of the regime of Hissène Habré. The MPS leader, a northern Muslim from the Zaghwa tribe, was formerly a top adviser to the French-backed Habré, who had held power in Chad since 1982. He then led forces against pro-Libyan troops in the east. Déby participated in a coup attempt in April 1989, and was the only one of the three principals to escape when it failed. At first the MPS included Déby's April 1 Action (*Action du 1 April*) based in the Zaghwa and Hadjerai tribes of central Chad; the southern-based Movement for Chadian National Salvation (*Mouvement pour le Salut National du Tchad*, MOSANAT); and remnants of the Chadian Armed Forces (*Forces Armées Tchadiennes*, FAT).

The MPS adopted a pro-democracy stance and advocated "neither capitalism nor socialism". It then launched a major offensive against the Habré government which brought it to power in N'Djaména, and Déby to the presidency, in December 1990. The MPS emphasized political reconciliation, and attracted the allegiance of other groups, including the Chadian People's Revolution (*Révolution du Peuple Tchadienne*, RPT) led by Adoum Togoi and a faction of the →Chad National Liberation Front (FROLINAT). Internal strains were highlighted by the arrest in October 1991 of MPS vice-president Maldom Baba Abbas for an alleged coup attempt, but he was later rehabilitated.

From May 1992 President Déby expanded the political basis of the government to include several new parties, notably →Action for Unity and Socialism (ACTUS), the →National Alliance for Democracy and Development, the →National Rally for Democracy and Progress, the →Rally of the Chadian People, the →Union for Democracy and Progress, the →Union for Democracy and the Republic (UDR), the →Union for Renewal and Democracy and the →Union of Democratic Forces. In January 1993 the president hosted a sovereign national conference on the country's political future. He ensured that some 75% of the delegates (representing 66 parties and organizations) were MPS supporters. In April 1993 it adopted a transitional charter which left Déby as head of state and commander-in-chief. However, the conference elected the Prime Minister (initially, Fidèle Moungar of ACTUS) and an interim legislature, pending multi-party general elections. These were delayed by internal strife until January–February 1997, when the MPS achieved a bare absolute majority with a tally of 63 seats in the 125-seat national assembly. Idriss Déby was reelected president in May 2001.

Rally for Democracy and Progress
Rassemblement pour la Démocratie et le Progrès (RDP)
Leadership. Lol Mahamat Choua (president)
The RDP was launched in December 1991 under the leadership of Lol Mahamat Choua (mayor of N'Djaména). In 1979, as head of a FROLINAT offshoot group, he had briefly been President of an abortive national unity government. He later held ministerial office under the post-1982 Habré regime. Strong in the Kanem tribe around Lake Chad, the RDP came under heavy pressure from the security forces for its alleged involvement in the Kanem-backed coup attempt of January 1992. The party was nevertheless one of the first to be legalized in March 1992 and in May joined the National Co-ordination of the Opposition (CNO). It participated in the sovereign national conference of January-April 1993. Its leader was elected chairman of the interim legislature pending general elections. When the initial transitional period of 12 months was extended by a further year in April 1994, Choua complained that the Déby government had failed to make adequate preparations for democratic elections. Ousted from the CST chairmanship in October 1994, he claimed that the government had ordered the assassination of two RDP journalists and had arrested a dozen other RDP members. Choua came a distant fifth in the first round of the 1996 presidential elections. The RDP won three seats in the 1997 elections.

Rally of the Chadian People
Rassemblement du Peuple Tchadien (RPT)
Leadership. Dangbe Laobele Damaye (president)
The RPT obtained legalization in April 1992 and the following month a party member, Jeremie Beade Toiria, was appointed Minister of Trade and Industry in a new coalition government. He resigned at his party's request in October 1993 after the government had placed a temporary ban on trade union activities.

Union for Democracy and the Republic
Union pour la Démocratie et la République (UDR)
Leadership. Keibla Djimasta, Jean Alingué Bawoyeu
The UDR was still awaiting official recognition when, in March 1992, it elected Jean Alingué Bawoyeu as its president on his appointment as Prime Minister by President Déby of the →Patriotic Salvation Movement. The UDR leader ceased to be Prime Minister in May 1992, although the party remained in government. In April 1995 the UDR regained the premiership in the person of Keibla Djimasta. It won four seats in the 1997 elections, and initially backed the MPS government.

Union for Renewal and Democracy
Union pour le Renouveau et la Démocratie (URD)
Leadership. Wadal Abdelkader Kamougue (president)
Founded in March 1992 and legalized two months later, the URD consisted of supporters of Lt.-Gen. Kamougue. He was born in Gabon to parents from the Mbaye ethnic group, from the south of Chad. First appointed a minister in 1975, he had commanded anti-Habré forces in southern Chad in the 1980s and had been a vice-president of the Libyan-backed Transitional Government of National Unity (GUNT). Kamougue founded the Mouvement pour la Révolution Populaire (MRP) in the late 1980s, but abandoned his creation to form the URD. Following the sovereign national conference held in early 1993, he was in April 1993 appointed Minister of Civil Service and Labour but was dismissed in May 1994 in the wake of a strike by civil servants. Kamougue contested the 1996 presidential elections, and came second to the winner, Idriss Déby, with nearly 31% of the vote, thus making him the strongest southern politician. In the general elections of early 1997, the URD came second to the ruling MPS, with a tally of 29 seats. It initially joined in a national coalition government, but subsequently distanced itself from Idriss Déby. In May 2001 Kamougue came a poor fourth in presidential polls, with just over 5% of the votes cast.

Other Parties and Movements

Chadian Democratic Union (*Union Démocratique Tchadienne, UDT*), led by Abderhamane Koulamallah, a businessman.

Chadian Social Democratic Party (*Parti Social-Démocrate du Tchad, PSDT*), a southern-based movement led by Niabe Romain, a businessman.

Convention of Chadian Social Democrats (*Convention des Social-Démocrates Tchadiens, CSDT*), led by Younous Idedou, founded in April 1992 by (among others) several former ministers of the Habré regime, dedicated to creating a "new Chad" and ending decades of civil war. The CSDT won one seat in the 1997 elections.

Democratic Revolutionary Council (*Conseil Démocratique Révolutionnaire, CDR*), led by A-Cheikh Ibn Omar. Under previous leader, Aboubakar Adzalo Barraka, it had allied itself to the Oueddei faction of the →Chad National Liberation Front.

Democratic Union for Chadian Progress (*Union Démocratique pour le Progrès Tchadien, UDPT*), led by Elie Romba.

Movement for Democracy and Justice in Chad (MDJT), led by Youssouf Togoimi, a former Defence Minister under

President Déby. In 1998 the MDJC launched a major revolt against the Déby government. On 7 December 1999, the MDJT became the leading force in a four-party rebel grouping called le Commite Politique d'Action et de Liaison (CPAL). Other parties included the Movement for Unity and the Republic (MUR) and the Democratic Revolutionary Council of A-Cheikh Ibn Omar. Their union was reinforced in February 2000. Five months later the MDJT claimed to have captured a key northern town. Heavy fighting continued into 2001, despite the President's call for ceasefire.

Movement for Unity and Democracy in Chad (*Mouvement pour l'Unité et la Démocratie au Tchad, MUDT*), led by Julien Marabaye.

Movement for Unity and the Republic (*Mouvement pour l'Unité et la République, MUR*), created on Feb. 11, 2000, and led by Gaileth Bourkou Mandah, formerly head of the CDR-FR. MUR immediately allied itself with two other rebel groupings, →the Movement for Democracy and Justice in Chad (MDJT), and →the Democratic Revolutionary Council (CDR).

National Council for the Recovery of Chad (*Conseil National de Redressement du Tchad, CNRT*), a southern-based movement led by Idriss Agar Bichara, formed in mid-1992 by Col. Abbas Koty (an ex-member of the Déby government). Koty was killed by security forces in August 1993 shortly after negotiating a reconciliation and integration pact with the Déby government. It thereafter continued its armed struggle.

National Movement of Chadian Renovators (*Mouvement National des Rénovateurs Tchadiens, MNRT*), an opposition party led in exile by Ali Muhammad Diallo, allied with the Oueddei faction of the →Chad National Liberation Front.

National Union (*Union National, UN*), led by Abdoulaye Lamane (a former ambassador) and Mahamat Djerba (a former deputy leader of the Oueddei faction of the →Chad National Liberation Front), founded in March 1992.

Rally for Development and Progress (*Rassemblement pour le Développement et le Progrès, RDP*), led by Mamadou Bisso, founded in December 1991, the target of government reprisal attacks following the January 1992 attempted takeover by the →Movement for Democracy and Development. The party won three seats in the 1997 elections.

Revolutionary Council of the Chadian People (*Conseil Révolutionnaire du Peuple Tchadien, CRPT*), led by Hamed Jacob.

Chile

Capital: Santiago

Population: 15,153,797 (2000E)

The Republic of Chile won its independence in 1818. Prior to a right-wing military coup led by Gen. Augusto Pinochet Ugarte in September 1973, Chile had been a parliamentary democracy with an executive President and a National Congress elected by universal adult suffrage. After the coup, absolute power rested with the military junta, and increasingly with Pinochet, who in June 1974 was designated Supreme Chief of State, and in December, President of the Republic (although he did not formally assume that title until March 1981). The junta proclaimed various "constitutional acts" in 1976 purporting to establish an "authoritarian democracy", with executive and legislative authority vested in the President and the junta, assisted by a Cabinet.

In accordance with the March 1981 constitution, as amended and approved by referendum in July 1980, Chile is a democratic republic; executive power lies with the President, who is directly elected for a six-year term. Legislative power is held by a bicameral National Congress, comprising a 49-member Senate serving an eight-year term (of whom 38 members are elected and nine are designated, while two former Presidents of the Republic sit as lifetime senators) and a 120-member Chamber of Deputies elected for a four-year term. A binomial electoral system requires that parties present lists of two candidates per constituency. When a list attains over twice the number of votes of its nearest rival, it wins both seats. If it fails to do so, one of its candidates is elected together with one from the next most popular list.

This electoral system, together with the National Security Council, the Constitutional Tribunal, and the presence of designated senators and other measures comprise "authoritarian enclaves" which have prevented a full redemocratization of the political system.

In a plebiscite held on Oct. 5, 1988, a majority of nearly 55% voted against Pinochet remaining in office for a further eight years upon the expiry of his term in 1990. In the resulting presidential elections held on Dec. 14, 1989, Patricio Aylwin Azócar of the Christian Democratic Party (PDC), representing a 17-party Coalition of Parties for Democracy (CPD), was the clear winner. He took office on March 11, 1990. Since then the CPD has retained control of the presidency with the election in December 1993 of Eduardo Frei Ruíz-Tagle of the PDC and Ricardo Lagos Escobar, of the Socialist Party of Chile, on Jan. 16, 2000 (by a vote of 51.3% in a run-off election). In congressional elections on Dec. 11, 1997, the CPD parties won 60 of the 120 seats in the Chamber of Deputies.

Alliance for Chile
Alianza por Chile (ApC)
Leadership. Joaquín Lavín Infante (1999 presidential candidate); Sebastián Piñera
The ApC is the latest incarnation of the coalition of right-wing parties, previously known as the Union for Chile (*Unión por Chile, UpC*), whose constituent parties polled strongly in the December 1997 congressional elections. In the December 1999 presidential elections, the Alliance backed the candidacy of Joaquín Lavín Infante of the →Independent Democratic Union (UDI), whose narrow defeat in the run-of polling in January 2000 confirmed the ApC parties as the effective opposition in Chile.

The ApC constituent parties are the UDI, →National Renewal (RN) and the →Party of the South (*Partído del Sur*).

Christian Democratic Party
Partido Democrata Cristiana (PDC)

Address. Alameda B. O'Higgins 1460, Santiago
Telephone. (+56–2) 252–7408
Fax. (+56–2) 252–6257
Leadership. Patricio Aylwin Azócar (president)

The PDC was created in July 1957 as a merger of the National Falange (founded in 1934) and the majority faction of the Social Christian Conservative Party. The party's then leader, Eduardo Frei Montalva, came third in the presidential elections of 1958. The party built up its support in rural areas, especially through illegal rural unions. In 1961 the PDC became the largest party in Congress and remained so under the 1970–73 Allende government, to which it formed an effective and hostile opposition.

The 1973 military coup was welcomed by many within the PDC, including its president, Patricio Aylwin Azócar. However, its support for the junta diminished as evidence emerged of human rights abuses and as Gen. Pinochet developed his own political agenda. In 1977 the PDC was banned, along with all other parties.

In August 1983 the party founded the Democratic Alliance (AD), a centre-left grouping which superseded the *Multipartidaria* alliance formed only months earlier. In 1986 the party announced its acceptance of the military's 1980 constitution as an instrumental strategy for overthrowing the Pinochet regime. At the same time it became the main force in the AD's campaign for free elections and was a signatory to the National Accord, an opposition document outlining the agenda for a transition to democracy.

Aylwin became the spokesman for a 13-party opposition alliance that successfully campaigned against the extension of Pinochet's term as President, an issue submitted to a plebiscite in October 1988. The popular support, energy and enthusiasm generated by the "no" vote was harnessed to establish the →Coalition of Parties for Democracy (CPD), a 17-member electoral alliance led by the Christian Democrats. In July 1989 the CPD parties agreed to support Aylwin as the main opposition presidential candidate. His campaign programme included pledges to investigate human rights abuses, improve education and health care and increase the minimum wage within the context of a sound economic programme designed to boost exports and control inflation. In the December 1989 elections, Aylwin was elected President with 55.2% of the valid votes and the PDC became the largest party in Congress.

Having won a third of the available votes in the 1992 municipal election, the PDC provided the successful presidential candidate in the December 1993 elections, Eduardo Frei Ruíz-Tagle. However, in the primaries for the 1999 presidential elections the PDC candidate, Andrés Zaldívar, lost to the candidate of the →Socialist Party of Chile (a CPD member), Ricardo Lagos Escobar, who was elected in December 1999. The primaries represented a period of decline for the PDC, although it remained the party with the largest congressional representation. As a result of the 1997 parliamentary elections, there were 39 deputies and 14 senators belonging to the PDC.

The PDC suffered serious internal difficulties in the run-up to the December 2001 congressional elections. As a result, Aylwin was persuaded to return for his eighth stint in the party presidency.

The PDC is an affiliate of the Christian Democrat International and the Christian Democrat Organization of America (ODCA).

Coalition of Parties for Democracy
Concertación de los Partidos por la Democracia (CPD)

Leadership. Ricardo Lagos Escobar (President of the Republic)

The centre-left CPD alliance was founded in its present form in November 1988, arising out of the Democratic Alliance led by the →Christian Democratic Party (PDC) and the "Command for the No Vote" opposition alliance which successfully campaigned to prevent Gen. Pinochet from extending his presidential term of office beyond 1990, a view subsequently endorsed in a plebiscite held in October 1988. The other main members of the CPD are the →Socialist Party of Chile (PS), the →Party for Democracy (PPD) and the →Radical Social Democratic Party.

In order not to fragment the pro-democracy vote in the December 1989 presidential elections, the CPD's 17 member parties officially decided in July 1989 to back Patricio Aylwin Azócar, who was already the PDC candidate. After his inauguration in March 1990, President Aylwin formed a CPD coalition government with cabinet posts allocated to the main alliance parties proportionate to their representation in Congress. The new President had the difficult task of implementing the coalition's election promises while adopting a conciliatory approach towards the military and the two main right-wing parties. Thus Aylwin allowed Pinochet to remain commander-in-chief of the armed forces.

The CPD repeated its 1989 success in the December 1993 presidential elections, securing victory for Eduardo Frei Ruíz-Tagle (PDC), the son of an earlier Christian Democratic President. In 1999, however, the leadership of the CPD shifted to the Socialists and the PPD, with the election of Ricardo Lagos Escóbar (PPD) as the coalition's presidential candidate. Lagos effectively tied with his opponent in the first round of the December 1999 elections, but narrowly won the second round in January 2000 with 51.3% of the vote.

Communist Party of Chile
Partido Comunista de Chile (PCCh)

Address. San Pablo 2271, Santiago
Telephone. (+56–2) 671–9608
Email. pcchile@excite.com
Website. www.pcch.00politics.com
Leadership. Gladys Marín (president)

Formed by Luis Emilio Recabarren as the Socialist Workers' Party, the Communist Party adopted its present name in 1922, the year it joined the Third International (Comintern). The party contested the 1949 general election, obtaining six seats in the Chamber under the name National Democratic Front, which it retained until the PCCh was legalized in 1958. Joining forces with the →Socialist Party (PS) in 1952, it supported the unsuccessful presidential campaign of Salvador Allende and continued to do so in the elections of 1958, 1964 and 1970, when Allende was elected. The party's representation in the lower house rose throughout the 1960s. By the time it was invited into the Allende government in 1970, the PCCh was one of the largest Communist parties outside the Eastern bloc.

The PCCh was banned following the September 1973 military coup and many of its leaders and activists were imprisoned. Some leaders, including the party's longstanding secretary-general, Luís Corvalán Lepe, were sent into exile in 1976. Like other Marxist parties, the PCCh was not permitted to register in 1987 and for the December 1989 elections the party relied on the support of the Christian Democrat-led →Coalition for Democracy (CPD) and on PCCh-sponsored lists in exchange for the Communists' support elsewhere. Relations with other opposition parties, however, were strained because of the attempted assassination of General Pinochet in 1986, which the party supported. In January 1990, however, the PCCh finally renounced its policy of violent struggle by declaring that it had severed all links with the Manuel Rodríguez Patriotic Front *(Frente Patriotica Manuel Rodríguez,* FPMR), an active left-wing guerrilla group.

In the 1989 elections PCCh candidates won a total of 300,000 votes, but largely due to the binomial electoral system the party gained no seats in Congress. Despite regularly polling between 5% and 10% of the vote, the PCCh remains unrepresented in parliament. In the December 1999 presidential elections Gladys Marín garnered only 3.2 % of the vote.

Independent Democratic Union
Union Democrática Independiente (UDI)
Address. Suecia 286, Providencia, Santiago
Telephone. (+56–2) 244–2331
Fax. (+56–2) 233–6189
Email. udi@udi.cl
Website. www.udi.cl
Leadership. Pablo Longueira Montes (president)
The right-wing UDI was founded in the early 1980s under the leadership of Julio Dittborn Cordua and Jaime Guzmán. Its original platform included the creation of a nominal parliament in order to counteract growing popular demands for a transition to democracy, thereby ensuring the continuation of the military's political legacy. The UDI merged with two other groups to form the →National Renewal (PR) party in 1987, but was expelled in April 1988. It supported Gen. Pinochet's attempt to extend his presidency, voted down in the October 1988 plebiscite. The party then attempted to distance itself from the military regime by backing the presidential candidacy of Hernán Buechi, the Finance Minister and an independent right-wing technocrat, who came second in the December 1989 elections.

The UDI was dealt a serious blow in April 1991 when its president, Jaime Guzmán, was assassinated by left-wing terrorists. However, in recent years it has strengthened its claims to be the principal right-wing party. In 1997 it took 17 seats in the Chamber of Deputies, coming third behind the →Christian Democratic Party and National Renewal Party. In the first round of presidential elections in December 1999, its candidate, Joaquín Lavín Infante, the former mayor of a prosperous Santiago suburb, came close to defeating the candidate of the →Coalition of Parties for Democracy, winning 47.5% of the vote, thereby forcing a run-off election, which he narrowly lost (by a margin of 2.6%). Since then UDI has made major gains in municipal elections and in 2000 Lavín was elected mayor of Santiago.

National Renewal
Renovacion Nacional (RN)
Address. Antonio Varas 454, Providencia, Santiago
Telephone. (+56–2) 373–8740/244–3939
Email. prensa@rn.cl
Website. www.rn.cl
Leadership. Sebastián Piñera (president); Rodrigo Hinzpeter (secretary-general)
The right-wing RN was founded in 1987 as a merger of the National Union, the National Labour Front and the →Independent Democratic Union (UDI, which was expelled a year later). The RN campaigned in the 1989 elections as the party that would protect the 1980 constitution installed by the Pinochet military regime. It subsequently distanced itself from the regime. Following the October 1988 plebiscite rejection of an extension of Pinochet's presidency, the party tried to project a moderate image by declaring itself willing to negotiate with the pro-democracy movement. In early 1989 the RN put pressure on Pinochet to consider the constitutional reform proposals put forward by the →Coalition of Parties for Democracy (CPD).

In the 1997 parliamentary elections the RN won 23 seats, second only to the →Christian Democratic Party. However it has lost ground on the right to the UDI, reflecting its reduction in influence within the →Alliance for Chile, the result of personality conflicts, the electoral success of Joaquín Lavín of the UDI and the RN's continued distancing from the military.

The RN is affiliated to the Christian Democrat International.

Party for Democracy
Partido por la Democracia (PPD)
Address. Erasmo Escala 2154, Santiago
Tel. (+56–2) 671–2320
Email. ppd@ppd.cl
Website. www.ppd.cl

Leadership. Guido Girardi Lavín (president)
The PPD was founded in December 1987 by Ricardo Lagos Escobar as a political vehicle of the then illegal →Socialist Party of Chile (PS), in which all PPD members and leaders retained their membership. The party supported the "no" campaign leading up to the October 1988 plebiscite and was a member of the →Coalition of Parties for Democracy (CPD) from its inception in November 1988. After the CPD victory in the December 1989 general election, the PPD became a major player in Congress. In the 1997 elections it came fourth in number of seats won in the Chamber of Deputies (16). Its greatest political success to date has been the election of its founder, Ricardo Lagos, to the presidency in January 2000.

The PPD is a member of the Socialist International.

Radical Social Democratic Party
Partido Radical Social Democráta (PRSD)
Address. Miraflores 495, Santiago
Telephone/ (+56–2) 639–1053
Email. prsd_2000@yahoo.com
Leadership. Anselmo Sule Candia (president)
The PRSD was originally founded in 1863 as the Radical Party (*Partido Radical,* PR) and is the country's oldest extant party. It was Chile's main progressive party in the decades around the turn of the century and was in government from 1938 to 1952. The party lost power following bitter factional fights and subsequent division. It held some ministerial posts in the National Party government of Jorge Alessandri (1958–64). In 1969, after the defection of its right-wing faction to Alessandri's camp, it joined the broad Popular Unity (UP) alliance backing the presidential candidacy of Salvador Allende of the →Socialist Party of Chile, Radicals holding important portfolios in the 1970–73 Allende government.

Following the overthrow of Allende in September 1973, the party shared in the military's repression of the UP parties and other democratic elements. In the 1980s the Radical Party became an influential force in the →Coalition of Parties for Democracy (CPD). Having polled very poorly in the 1993 elections, the party adopted its present name. In the 1997 congressional elections it won four seats in the House of Deputies.

The PRSD is a member of the Socialist International.

Socialist Party of Chile
Partido Socialista de Chile (PS or PSCh)
Address. Concha y Toro 36, Santiago
Telephone. (+56–2) 696–1638
Fax. (+56–2) 695–2444
Email. pschile@terra.cl
Website. www.pschile.cl
Leadership. Camilio Escalona Medina (president); Pamela Pereira Fernández (general secretary)
The centre-left PS has the distinction of being one of Chile's oldest political parties. It was founded in 1933 by a merger of six parties which had supported the Socialist Republic proclaimed by Col. Marmaduke Grove, which lasted for 13 days. The PS won 19 seats in the Chamber of Deputies in the 1937 elections as part of a left-wing Popular Front alliance. After several conflicts with the →Communist Party of Chile (PCCh), the PS suffered a major split in 1948. A reunited party under the leadership of Saldavor Allende Gossens joined the Popular Unity (UP) alliance in 1969. With Allende as its candidate, the UP won the 1970 presidential elections, the PS receiving 22.8% of the overall UP vote.

Allende's reforms included the full nationalization of the copper industry, a price freeze and an increase in wages. Holding four ministerial posts, the Socialists were initially the most radical force in the Allende government, supporting land and factory seizures, but then increasingly called for moderation, as the government faced increasing opposition. Dogged by spiralling inflation, a US embargo, economic sabotage by the business sector and pressure from the army, the Allende government made increasing concessions to the right and in late 1972 included members of the military in the cabinet. This did not prevent a military coup in September 1973, in which Allende lost his life and many PS leaders were killed, imprisoned, tortured or exiled.

The party fragmented thereafter. For the December 1989 presidential elections the main PS faction joined the →Coalition of Parties for Democracy (CPD) supporting the victorious campaign of Patricio Aylwin Azócar of the →Christian Democratic Party (PDC). As a result the PS obtained cabinet representation under Aylwin's presidency and that of his PDC successor, Eduardo Frei Ruíz-Tagle.

The PS polled disappointingly in the December 1997 congressional elections, following which it held 11 seats in the Chamber and four in the Senate. Nevertheless, together with its allies in the →Party for Democracy (PPD), the PS effectively led the CPD alliance in the December 1999 presidential elections, in which the CPD candidate was Ricardo Lagos Escobar, a member of both the PDD and the PS. The narrow 51.3% to 48.7% victory of Lagos in the run-off voting in January 2000 re-established the PS as one of the dominant forces in Chilean politics.

The PS is a member of the Socialist International.

Other Parties

Humanist Party (*Partido Humanista, PH*), left-leaning "alternative" and pro-environment formation founded in 1984, a member of the Humanist International. Its presidential candidates won 1.2% in 1993 and 0.5% in 1999.
Address. Alameda 129, 4° piso, Santiago.

Tel. (+56–2) 632–6787
Email. juanepe@netup.cl
Website. www.partidohumanista.cl
Leadership. Tomás Hirsch Goldschmidt

Liberal Party (*Partido Liberal, PL*), founded in 1998 by centrist dissidents.
Address. Huelén 102, 2° piso, Providencia
Tel. (+56–2) 235–3752
Fax. (+56–2) 264–0792
Website. www.partidoliberal.cl
Leadership. Adolfo Ballas Azócar (president)

New Democratic Force (*Nueva Fuerza Democrática, NFD*), centre-right party affiliated to the International Democrat Union, through the Americas Democrat Union.

Party of the South (*Partido del Sur, PdS*), regional right-wing party which won one Chamber seat in 1997 as part of the Union for Chile (→Alliance for Chile).

Progressive Central-Central Union (*Union de Centro-Centro Progresista, UCCP*), populist party which won one Chamber seat in 1997 on the "Chile 2000" ticket, supplementing its single seat in the Senate. It was represented in the 1999 presidential elections by Arturo Frei Bolívar, who had left the ruling →Christian Democratic Party in protest over the arrest of Gen. Pinochet in London and who took only 0.4% of the vote.
Address. Dr Barros Borgoño 217
Telephone. (+56–2) 264–2615
Leadership. Carlos del Campo Correa

China

Capital: Beijing

Population: 1,272,050,000 (2000E)

The People's Republic of China (PRC) was proclaimed in 1949 on the victory of Mao Zedong's Communist Party of China (CPC) in a long civil war with Chiang Kai-shek's Nationalists. The first three PRC constitutions were promulgated in 1954, 1975 and 1978, the second and third specifically enshrining the leading role of the CPC. The 1982 constitution, the PRC's fourth and currently in force, describes China as "a socialist state under the people's democratic dictatorship led by the working class". It makes no reference to the role of the CPC in its main articles, although its preamble asserts that the Chinese people are "under the leadership of the CPC and the guidance of Marxism–Leninism and Mao Zedong Thought". The preamble also makes reference to "a broad patriotic united front" headed by the CPC and "composed of democratic parties and organizations", eight such parties being in nominal existence within this front, which is manifest in the China People's Political Consultative Conference (CPPCC).

Legislative authority is vested in the unicameral National People's Congress (*Quanguo Renmin Daibiao Dahui*), whose members are indirectly elected for a five-year term by the people's congresses of China's 22 provinces, five autonomous regions and four municipalities (themselves elected by all citizens aged 18 and over) and by the People's Liberation Army (PLA). All these candidates are approved by the CPC but are not necessarily party members. In addition delegates are selected from the newly created Special Administrative Regions of Hong Kong and Macao. The National People's Congress (NPC) meets annually, legislative authority being exercised in the interim by a 155-member Standing Committee elected by the NPC, which also elects the President and Vice-President of the PRC for a concurrent five-year term. All effective power, however, resides in the leadership bodies of the CPC. Elections to the ninth NPC were held in March 1998 and resulted in the return of 2,979 deputies approved by the CPC.

Communist Party of China (CPC)
Zhongguo Gongchan Dang
Address. CPC Central Committee, Beijing
Leadership. Jiang Zemin (general secretary), Li Peng, Zhu Rongji, Li Ruihuan, Hu Jintao, Wei Jianxing, Li Lanqing (other members of the politburo standing committee)
According to its authorized history, the CPC was founded in 1921 at a congress in Shanghai attended by a dozen dele-

gates (among them Mao Zedong) from Marxist groups with a total membership of 57. Independent accounts say that the inaugural congress took place a year earlier but was expunged from later official histories because one of the founders (Zhang Shenfu) was rapidly expelled from the party. The accounts agree that Chen Duxiu became general secretary of the new party. The CPC's first programme advocated "science and democracy", the nurturing of

Chinese culture and the abolition of feudalism. Party membership rose to 1,000 by 1925 and to 58,000 by 1927. Among its sources of support was the patriotic May 4 Movement, which had originated in Chinese outrage at the 1919 transfer of the leased port of Qingdao from Germany to Japan.

Inspired by the 1917 Bolshevik revolution in Russia, the CPC followed Soviet instructions to co-operate with the Nationalist government (headed by Chiang Kai-shek from 1925) and to infiltrate the ruling *Kuomintang* (KMT) party organization. Elected a politburo member in 1924, Mao took charge of the CPC peasant department in 1926 and advanced the then controversial thesis that the key revolutionary force in China was the poor peasantry (i.e. the "property-less class") not the (then small) industrial proletariat.

In 1927 Chiang broke with his increasingly numerous CPC allies in Shanghai. A period of confusion followed, in which Chen Duxiu was replaced as CPC general secretary by Qu Qiubai and then by Li Lisan. Mao was sent to Hunan to organize a peasant revolt, but the "autumn harvest uprising" was a failure and Mao lost his seat on the politburo. He and about 1,000 followers nevertheless set up headquarters in mountains on the Hunan-Jiangxi border, where he was joined in 1928 by Zhu De, who was to become the outstanding Communist military leader of the revolutionary period. From this base the Communists took control of most of Jiangxi and of large parts of Hunan and Fujian, where a Chinese Soviet Republic (CSR) was established in 1931 under the leadership of Mao and Zhu De. Meanwhile, Li Lisan had been removed from the CPC leadership in 1930 and Mao's belief in the revolutionary potential of the peasantry had begun to gain acceptance.

The CPC central committee, which had been operating underground in Shanghai, joined Mao in Jiangxi in 1931, after which the CSR declared war on Japan in light of its invasion of Manchuria. Policy differences resulted in Mao's removal from his military and political posts in 1932–4, as KMT forces mounted a series of offensives against the Communists. The fifth such onslaught, involving some 900,000 troops, compelled the Communists to evacuate Jiangxi in October 1934 and to start out on their Long March to the remote north-west. During the march a conference at Zunyi (Guizhou province) in January 1935 elected Mao as chairman of the CPC military affairs committee (and thus effective party leader) and Zhang Wentian as general secretary. After a 6,000-mile trek, only 4,000 of the 86,000 people who had set out on the Long March reached Shaanxi and established a headquarters at Yenan.

In 1937 a revolt among his own followers impelled Chiang Kai-shek to enter into an alliance with the Communists to resist Japanese aggression. This broke down in the early 1940s, when KMT troops began attacking CPC units. From then on Chiang combined passive resistance to the Japanese with military operations against the Communists, who by 1944 were holding down two-thirds of the Japanese occupation forces. By 1945 the Communists controlled a large area of rural northern China and had some 900,000 regulars and over 2 million militia under arms, facing 4 million KMT troops holding all the main towns.

The seventh CPC congress, held at Yenan in 1945, elected Mao as central committee chairman, adopted a new constitution embracing Mao Zedong Thought and noted that party membership had risen to 1,210,000. Under Moscow's instruction to come to terms with the KMT, Mao solicited US support for the formation of a post-war coalition government, but Chiang had Washington's ear. Renewed civil war broke out in 1946. Numerical superiority gave the KMT the advantage at first, but the tide turned in 1948 and Communist forces gained control of most of China in 1949. The People's Republic of China (PRC) in Beijing on Oct. 1, 1949, with Mao as Chairman (President) and Zhou Enlai as Prime Minister of a nominal coalition government including some small non-communist parties (see below).

The new regime was confronted by an economy ruined by years of war, its problems soon being exacerbated by China's involvement in the Korean War of 1950-53. Communist China was therefore dependent for some years on Soviet economic and military aid, its first five-year plan (1953–57) being concentrated on the development of heavy industry. From 1955, however, Mao set out to develop a distinctively Chinese form of socialism, pushing through the collectivisation of agriculture in 1955 and the transfer of private enterprises to joint state-private ownership in 1956. Following Khrushchev's denunciation of Stalin at the 20th Soviet party congress in 1956, the eighth CPC congress the same year approved the deletion of references to Mao Zedong Thought from the party constitution. It also revived the post of general secretary (vacant since 1937), to which Deng Xiaoping was elected, and created a new five-member standing committee of the CPC politburo (the first members being Mao, Deng, Zhu, Liu Shaoqi and Chen Yun). Party membership was reported to the congress as 10,734,385. Mao had by then enunciated the slogan "Let 100 flowers bloom, let 100 schools of thought contend", which he developed in 1957 by launching a "rectification campaign" in which the people were encouraged to criticize government and party officials. The response was so great that the campaign was changed into one against "rightists" (defined as critics of the regime). The non-communist ministers were dropped from the government.

In 1958 the CPC launched China on the Great Leap Forward, a grandiose attempt to develop Chinese socialism at high speed. Industrial and agricultural targets were repeatedly raised, agricultural co-operatives were grouped into large communes that also undertook small-scale manufacturing, and over 2 million "backyard furnaces" were set up for the local production of iron and steel. This policy quickly led to economic and political crisis. A CPC central committee meeting in December 1958 adopted a critical resolution and Mao was forced to yield the PRC chairmanship to Liu Shaoqi in April 1959.

A concurrent deterioration in relations with the USSR, mainly over ideological questions but also involving territorial issues, resulted in the termination of Soviet aid in 1960 and the onset of the Sino–Soviet dispute. This became official when the CPC broke off relations with the Soviet Communist Party in 1966, after which the only ruling Communist party to back China was that of Albania. Meanwhile, a series of disastrous harvests in the early 1960s had caused mass starvation and had impelled Deng and Liu not only to allow peasants to cultivate private plots but also to introduce bonuses and incentives in the industrial sector.

Regarding such policies as leading to a restoration of capitalism, or at least to Soviet-style revisionism, Mao in 1962 enunciated the slogan "Don't forget the class struggle". He was supported by Marshal Lin Biao, the Defence Minister, who promoted the study of Mao Zedong Thought in the army and in 1964 published a compendium of the leader's ideas in the famous *Little Red Book*. Opposition in the CPC leadership remained strong, however, and in October 1965 Mao moved from Beijing to Shanghai, which became his base for the campaign which became known as the Cultural Revolution. With army backing, he forced the CPC politburo, meeting in Shanghai on May 16, 1966, to issue a circular calling for a purge of "those who have sneaked into the party, the government, the army and various spheres of culture".

Demonstrations against such elements began at Beijing University later in May 1966, followed by the formation of Red Guard units of students and schoolchildren, who terrorized those suspected of bourgeois tendencies. Returning to Beijing, Mao presided over a CPC central committee meeting on Aug. 1–12, 1966, which issued instructions for the conduct of the Cultural Revolution. On Aug. 18 Mao and Marshal Lin (by now second in the party hierarchy) reviewed a parade of more than a million Red Guards in the capital. They received support from Zhou, who nevertheless endeavoured to moderate the excesses into which the Cultural Revolution quickly descended.

Having generated much public uneasiness, in 1967 the Red Guards were replaced as the main agents of the Cultural Revolution by the Revolutionary Rebels, consisting of adult workers. Pitched battles between rival factions followed in many parts of China, producing a state of virtual anarchy and obliging Mao to fall back on the support of the army. The party and government disintegrated, as almost all the leading members came under attack and were replaced. The most virulent campaign was directed against Liu Shaoqi (the "number one capitalist roader"), who was removed from the chairmanship of the PRC in 1968 (the post being left vacant), expelled from the party and put in prison, where he died in 1969. Also purged was Deng Xiaoping ("number two capitalist roader"), whose post of general secretary was abolished by the 9th CPC congress in 1969. At that congress Marshal Lin became Mao's designated successor, Mao Zedong Thought was reinstated in the party constitution and a new politburo was elected, dominated by Lin's military associates and recently-promoted politicians.

The new leadership was soon split over foreign policy, however. In the light of deepening Sino–Soviet rift, Mao and Zhou favoured détente with the USA, but this policy was opposed by Lin, whose supporters began to plan a coup. After the announcement in July 1971 that US President Nixon would visit China in 1972, Mao again withdrew to Shanghai to rally support. When he returned to Beijing, Lin fled the country in September 1971 and was killed when his plane crashed or was shot down in Mongolia, whereupon his supporters on the CPC politburo were arrested.

Mao's failing health in his last years obliged him to live in seclusion. He presided over the 10th CPC congress in 1973 but apparently took no part in its deliberations. These ushered in a new power struggle between the moderates, led by Zhou and the extremist "gang of four" politburo members headed by Mao's fourth wife, former actress Jiang Qing, who had the advantage of being able to claim that Mao supported them. Zhou secured the rehabilitation of many of those disgraced during the Cultural Revolution, including Deng, who became a Deputy Premier in 1973 and was readmitted to the CPC politburo in 1974. Zhou died in January 1976, however, and was succeeded as Prime Minister by Hua Guofeng, who took an anti-moderate line, assisted by serious disturbances in Beijing on April 5, 1976, that were labelled "counter-revolutionary". Later that month Deng was again removed from all his offices, accused of being an "unrepentant capitalist roader".

Following Mao's death in September 1976 (at the age of 82), Hua Guofeng took over as CPC chairman (and chairman of the central military commission) and turned against the radicals. The "gang of four" and their supporters were arrested in October 1976 on charges of plotting to seize power and in July 1977 Deng was again rehabilitated to his former party and government posts. A massive campaign was launched against the alleged misdeeds of the "gang of four", of whom Jiang Qing and one other were, in 1981, sentenced to death and the other two to long prison sentences, as were six former associates of Lin Biao. (The executions were not carried out, and Jiang committed suicide in 1991.)

Under Deng's influence, the theories and practices of the Great Leap Forward and the Cultural Revolution were gradually abandoned and earlier critiques of revisionism were admitted to be incorrect. The communes were dismantled and land was allocated to households on a contract basis. Central economic planning was relaxed and wages were related more closely to output. The formation of small private enterprises was encouraged and former capitalists' confiscated property was restored to them. Loans were accepted from external sources and foreign investment in joint enterprises was permitted. However, Deng defined the limits to change in his Four Principles of early 1979, requiring China to keep to the socialist road, uphold the people's democratic dictatorship, maintain the CPC's leading role

and stay true to Marxism–Leninism and Mao Zedong Thought. Thus Deng broke with the radical pro-democracy April 5 movement (named after the 1976 clashes in Beijing), the better to deal with opposition to his reforms from the politburo conservatives headed by Hua.

The power struggle between Hua and Deng culminated in the former's replacement as Prime Minister in September 1980 and as CPC chairman in June 1981, respectively by Zhao Ziyang and Hu Yaobang, both Deng associates who had been disgraced during the Cultural Revolution. Deng himself became chairman of the powerful CPC central military commission (as well as a member of the politburo's standing committee). In this phase some 100,000 people disgraced after 1957 were rehabilitated, many of them posthumously (including Liu Shaoqi), and a 1981 central committee resolution condemned most of Mao's post-1957 policies, while conceding that his contribution had outweighed his mistakes. The 12th CPC congress in September 1982 abolished the post of party chairman, Hu being elected to the strengthened post of general secretary (which had been revived in 1980), while Hua was excluded from the new politburo. A revised CPC constitution retained the reference to Mao Zedong Thought, but defined it as representing the distilled wisdom of the party rather than a programme of action. Under the new PRC constitution adopted in December 1982, Li Xiannian (a former close associate of Zhou) was elected to the restored post of President of China in June 1983.

There followed an extensive reorganization and relative rejuvenation of party and government bodies, with many of the "old guard" figures being replaced by supporters of Deng's pragmatic policies. The economy embarked on a phase of rapid expansion (growing at nearly 10% a year through the 1980s) and its integration into the world system gathered pace. This process was boosted by the signature in September 1984 of an agreement with Britain under which Hong Kong would revert to Chinese sovereignty in 1997 but retain its existing capitalist system for at least 50 years thereafter. Nevertheless, greater reliance on market forces led to increased corruption among party cadres, which in turn aroused popular discontent over the slow pace of political liberalization. Pro-democracy student demonstrations in several cities began in late 1986 and were stamped out only after some delay. Hu Yaobang was forced to resign as CPC general secretary in January 1987, being accused by Deng and others of excessive leniency to the demonstrators, and was replaced by Zhao Ziyang, who embarked on a campaign against "bourgeois liberalization".

Zhao was formally confirmed in office at the 13th CPC congress in October–November 1987, when Deng stood down from the politburo's standing committee while retaining the chairmanship of the central military commission. Endeavouring to attune his policies to Deng's thinking, Zhao pushed ahead with economic reform, proposing in mid-1988 that state price controls should be abolished within five years. Although this reform was quickly postponed (so that Zhao was left isolated), popular pressure for political reform, led by intellectuals and focusing on official corruption and rapidly rising prices, gathered impetus in late 1988 and early 1989.

The sudden death in April 1989 of Hu Yaobang, shortly after he had delivered an impassioned critique of government policy to the CPC politburo, gave renewed impetus to the pro-democracy movement. Demonstrations in Beijing's Tiananmen Square sparked similar protest rallies in other cities, gathering strength in mid-May during an historic visit to Beijing by Mikhail Gorbachev to mark the normalization of Sino-Soviet relations. For the demonstrators, mostly students but also including workers and intellectuals, Gorbachev's reformist policies in the USSR merited emulation. Zhao favoured a conciliatory approach but lost the argument to the hardliners led by Prime Minister Li Peng. On June 3–4 army units were sent in to clear the square, this being accomplished in bloody fighting which left up to

1,000 demonstrators dead and many thousands injured. Similar crackdowns followed in other parts of China, although on a less violent scale. In the inevitable conservative backlash, Zhao and his supporters were ejected from their politburo and other party posts, the position of CPC general secretary going to Jiang Zemin, hitherto party secretary in Shanghai. He joined a politburo standing committee enlarged to six members, whose dominant figure at that time was Li Peng. Also in the conservative camp was Yang Shangkun, a politburo member who had been elected President of the PRC in April 1988 in succession to Li Xiannian.

At a CPC central committee meeting in October-November 1989 Deng Xiaoping finally vacated the chairmanship of the central military commission, his only remaining post, and was replaced by Jiang Zemin. But Deng remained the effective leader of the regime as China's "elder statesman", issuing instructions that economic reform should be suspended and an austerity drive launched to curb inflation. In mid-1990 fears of an economic downturn led to a resumption of economic reform, while in 1991 some Zhao supporters were rehabilitated. Nevertheless, on the third anniversary of the Tiananmen Square massacre in June 1992, new regulations were published which placed even tighter restrictions on demonstrations. A 1992 codification of Deng's speeches asserted that the response to the "turmoil" of June 1989 had been correct. Differences persisted, however, as highlighted by the contrast in May–June 1992 between Li Peng's further warning against "bourgeois liberalization" and Jiang Zemin's criticism of "leftists" (i.e. conservatives) for using revolutionary slogans to "confuse the people".

The 14th CPC congress, held in October 1992, was told that party membership stood at around 52 million and elected a central committee (of 189 full and 130 alternate members) on which nearly half the members were new. Jiang was re-elected CPC general secretary (and chairman of the central military commission) and three of the other six members of the standing committee were also re-elected, although a majority of the other politburo members were also new, most of them Dengists. Features of the changes included the demotion of both President Yang and his half-brother, Yang Baibing, who had been prominent Dengists but were reportedly seen as an alternative power centre, and the inclusion of only one army representative (Gen. Liu Huaqing) on the new politburo.

At the eighth National People's Congress (NPC) in March 1993, the first session elected Jiang as President of the PRC in succession to Yang Shangkun. It also re-elected Li Peng as Prime Minister, although an unprecedented 330 votes were cast against him, indicating strong underlying disapproval of his role in the 1989 events. Jiang thus became the first Chinese leader since Hua Guofeng (in the immediate post-Mao period) to hold the three top posts of party leader, chairmanship of the central military commission and head of state or government. However, despite being designated "core leader", he remained in the shadow of Deng until the latter's death in February 1997. The broad Dengist line of economic liberalization combined with political conservatism continued to deliver success in terms of economic expansion: according to the IMF in March 1993, China had become the world's third-largest economy after the USA and Japan on the basis of purchasing power parity. Nevertheless, concern about inflation and other negative phenomena continued to generate strains within the leadership, highlighted by regular switches of economic policy priorities.

A CPC central committee session in November 1993 adopted a new blueprint for what was termed a "socialist market economic system" and appeared to mark a crucial victory for those favouring rapid economic change. In April 1994, however, there was a renewed crackdown on prominent dissidents in the run-up to the anniversary of the 1989 events. A session of the CPC central committee in September 1994 resolved that the "extensive and profound social change currently taking place in China" required the party "to do better in upholding and improving democratic centralism". In May 1995 Jiang launched a campaign against high-level corruption, requiring all state and party officials (and their children in some cases) to declare their incomes from all sources. At the same time, the *People's Daily* (organ of the CPC) began citing the teachings of Confucius – once denounced by the Communists as the creator of Chinese feudalism – on the need for social and political harmony.

At the 15th congress of the CPC, held in September 1997, Jiang Zemin was re-elected general secretary and, at the next session of the NPC in March 1998, head of state. Also at the NPC Zhu Rongji was elected Prime Minister in place of Li Peng (who became chairman of the NPC), whilst a representative of the next generation of party officials, Hu Jintao, was elected Vice-President of the country. In 1999 he also became deputy chairman of the central military commission. This made him Jiang's likely successor.

The 15th party congress was told that CPC membership had risen to 58 million, one-fifth being women and 22.4% aged under 35. A rise in the educational level of the membership was also apparent: 43.4% had at least graduated from senior high school and almost 18% were university graduates. At the same time, the central committee was becoming more "technocratic": 92% had university degrees (44% in engineering). The new generation of politicians coming to the fore were expected to compose a majority of the politburo after the next congress in 2002.

The run-up to the 2002 congress saw new thinking on the position of the CPC in society. In February 2000 Jiang Zemin launched the concept of the "three representations", i.e. the party should represent the advanced forces of production, the forward direction of advanced culture and the fundamental interests of the majority of the Chinese people. In mid-2001 he went a step further by changing party rules so that entrepreneurs could become CPC members, although old-style Maoists derided this. There were calls in some quarters for competitive elections for party posts.

In 2001 the NPC approved the tenth five-year plan for the economy covering the period 2001–05. This envisaged an average annual growth rate of 7% as compared with the 8.3% achieved between 1996 and 2000. Yet despite the optimism of these figures, society was becoming more turbulent. Tides of migrants flocked to and between cities, while peasants continued to mount sporadic demonstrations over difficult living conditions and "exploitation" by officials. Large numbers of workers in loss-making state-owned enterprises faced unemployment, and public opinion became increasingly exercised by growing social and geographical inequality and by increasing levels of crime and corruption. The party responded by stepping up campaigns against official corruption (a Vice-Chairman of the NPC being executed) and against crime in general (Amnesty International calculating that the PRC now carries out more judicial executions than the rest of the world combined), as well by launching a programme to "open up" the western part of the country. It also cracked down brutally on real or perceived opponents.

The CPC leadership in the late 1990s was also concerned by the rise of the Falun Gong Buddhist movement, which organized a demonstration of over 10,000 people outside the central leadership compound in Beijing in April 1999. This took the regime entirely by surprise. The subsequent investigation further unsettled the leadership by revealing that senior officials in the government and the army were members of the sect. Even though the Falun Gong were no contender for political power, their stubborn persistence in continuing to organize demonstrations despite persecution served as a reminder that alternative ideas were challenging the legitimacy of CPC leadership.

Other Parties

Eight other "democratic" parties are permitted to exist in China on the basis of participation in a "united front" with the CPC. Officially they are recognized as having co-operated with the CPC in the "war of resistance" against Japan (1937-45) and in the "war of liberation" against the *Kuomintang* (KMT), and as having played a role, as members of the China People's Political Consultative Conference (CPPCC), in the formulation of the first PRC constitution. Not allowed to operate during the Cultural Revolution, these essentially powerless parties re-emerged in the late 1970s. They are customarily allocated about 7% of the seats in the National People's Congress.

Pro-democracy activists failed in 1998 in several attempts to register the **Chinese Democracy Party**. Three leaders of the party – Wang Youcai, Xu Wenli and Qin Yongmin – received lengthy prison sentences and many activists were detained.

China Association for Promoting Democracy (*Zhongguo Minzhu Cujin Hui*), founded in 1945 to represent literary, cultural and educational personnel, emphasizes the importance of education in building a socialist society, running over 230 schools.
Address. 98 Xinanli Guloufangzhuangchang, 100009 Beijing
Leadership. Xu Jialu (chairman)

China Democratic League (*Zhongguo Minzhu Tongmeng*), founded in 1941 as the League of Democratic Parties and Organizations of China to unite intellectuals against the KMT, membership drawn from scientific, educational and cultural intellectuals.
Address. 1 Beixing Dongchang Hutong, 100006 Beijing
Leadership. Ding Shisun (chairman)

China National Democratic Construction Association (*Zhongguo Minzhu Jianguo Hui*), founded in 1945, membership drawn from industrialists and businessmen, promotes contact with overseas Chinese.

Address. 93 Beiheyan Dajie, 100006 Beijing
Leadership. Cheng Siwei (chairman)

China Party for Public Interests (*Zhongguo Zhi Gong Dang*), founded in San Francisco in 1925, descended from 19th-century secret society for overseas Chinese, advocates "reform and construction under the banner of socialism and patriotism".
Leadership. Luo Haocai (chairman)

Chinese Peasants' and Workers' Democratic Party (*Zhongguo Nonggong Minzhu Dang*), descended from pre-war movement of anti-Chiang Kai-shek Nationalists who abandoned the objective of a bourgeois republic in 1935 and joined forces with the Communist Party of China. Adopted present name in 1947, despite which it is based in the medical and scientific professions and gives priority to health and educational issues.
Leadership. Jiang Zhenghua (chairman)

Chinese Revolutionary Committee of the Kuomintang (*Zhongguo Guomindang Geming Weiyuanhui*). Founded in 1948 in Hong Kong by notional KMT members opposed to Chiang Kai-shek, "carrying forward Dr Sun Yat-sen's patriotic and revolutionary spirit" by seeking the "peaceful reunification of the motherland", membership drawn from health, finance, culture and education sectors.
Leadership. He Luli (chairman)

September 3 Society (*Jiu San Xuehui*), founded in 1946 in Sichuan as the Democracy and Science Forum, renamed to commemorate the date of the Japanese surrender in 1945, membership drawn from scientists and technologists.
Leadership. Wu Jieping (chairman)

Taiwan Democratic Self-Government League (*Taiwan Minzhu Zizhi Tongmeng*), founded in 1947 by pro-PRC Chinese from Taiwan, promotes contacts with Taiwan to further the goal of reunification.
Leadership. Zhang Kehui (chairman)

Hong Kong Special Administrative Region

Population: 6,796,700 (2000E)

The former British colony of Hong Kong returned to Chinese sovereignty on July 1, 1997, to become a special administrative region (SAR) of the People's Republic under the basic principle of "one country, two systems" guaranteed for 50 years. After the British and Chinese governments signed the 1984 Joint Declaration providing for the reversion, they had agreed to allow election instead of selection of some members to the Legislative Council (LegCo), but they had argued over the precise figures. Changes introduced by the last UK Governor were bitterly opposed in Beijing, which responded with a plan for an alternative Provisional Legislative Council (PLC). Immediately after the transfer of sovereignty, the new SAR Chief Executive, Tung Chee-hwa, dissolved LegCo and replaced it with the PLC. This laid down the detailed framework for implementing the Basic Law for the SAR that had previously been promulgated in Beijing and then it arranged for elections to a restored LegCo in May 1998 for a two-year term. New elections were held in September 2000. Voter turnout was 53% in 1998 but only 43% in 2000.

LegCo now has 60 members, of whom 30 are elected directly from geographical constituencies, 24 elected from functional constituencies and six chosen indirectly by the 800 directly-elected representatives on the Election Committee. The Basic Law states that all LegCo seats will be directly elected at an indeterminate date in the future. Since 1997 Hong Kong has sent 36 delegates to the National People's Congress in Beijing.

Citizens' Party (CP)
Address: Room 319, 88 Commercial Building, 28–34 Wing Lok Street, Sheung Wan

Telephone. (+852) 2893–0029
Fax. (+852) 2147–5796
Email. enquiry@citizensparty.org

Website. www.citizensparty.org
Leadership. Alex Chan (chairman)
Formed in 1997 by Christine Loh, the CP proclaims a belief in liberal democratic values and openness. Loh was the only CP candidate who won a seat in LegCo in 1998 (she had been an independent member in 1995). In the summer of 2000 she announced that she would not contest the next round of LegCo elections and would instead concentrate on political activity outside. In 2001 Alex Chan succeeded her as party chairman.

Democratic Alliance for the Betterment of Hong Kong (DABHK

Address. 12/F, 83 King's Road, North Point
Telephone. (+852) 2528–0136
Fax. (+852) 2528–4339
Email. info@dab.org.hk
Website. www.dab.org.hk
Leadership. Jasper Tsang Yok-sing (chairman)
Founded in 1991, its main orientation has been to co-operate with the mainland authorities in looking after the interests of the people of Hong Kong. In 1991 it failed to win any seats, but as the disputes between London and Beijing became embittered, it picked up support by encouraging moderation, whilst occasionally standing up to Beijing. In 1995 it won six LegCo seats and was rewarded with 42 seats on the PLC. Since 1997 it has made great efforts to collaborate with the government on day-to-day issues and now has over 2,000 members. In 1998 it gained 10 seats with around 25% of the vote and in 2000 11 seats with around 35%, though one seat was later lost in a by-election.

Democratic Party (DP)

Address. 4/F Hanley House, 776–8 Nathan Road, Kowloon
Telephone. (+852) 2397–7033
Fax. (+852) 2397–8998
Email. info@dphk.hk
Website. www.dphk.hk
Leadership. Martin Lee (chairman)
Founded originally in 1991 as the United Democrats of Hong Kong, this party has consistently won most electoral support. It gained 12 out of 18 geographical seats in the 1991 elections and 19 out of 20 in 1995. It has consistently pushed for full democracy in Hong Kong and the observance of human rights on the mainland. This has led it into regular clashes with Beijing. Its leaders mounted a symbolic demonstration against the dissolution of LegCo in July 1997 and it refused to co-operate with the PLC. In 1998 it won in nine out of 20 geographical constituencies and in four func-tional ones with 43% of the vote, making it the largest party in LegCo. In 2000 this slipped to just under 35% and 12 seats. In August 2001 it claimed 586 members.

The Frontier

Address. Flat B, 9/F, 557–9 Nathan Road, Yaumati, Kowloon
Telephone. (+852) 2524–9899
Fax. (+852) 2524–5310
Leadership. Emily Lau Wai-hing
Founded in 1996 by the current unofficial leader, Emily Lau Wai-hing, and two other members of LegCo, this formation was the most intransigent critic of London and Beijing over the handover of power. More loosely organized and rejecting the designation of a party as such, it has limited funds. It has sought to play a moral role in Hong Kong society by defending human rights, chiefly through operating in other environments than LegCo. Nevertheless, it won three geographical constituencies there in 1998 and two in 2000.

Hong Kong Progressive Alliance

Address. 11/F, 1 Lockhart Road, Central
Telephone. (+852) 2377–3030
Fax. (+852) 2377–2211
Website. www.hkpa.org.hk
Leadership. Ambrose Lau Hon-chuen (chairman)
Formed in 1994 by Ambrose Lau Hon-chuen, on encouragement from mainland officials who felt that the →Democratic Alliance for the Betterment of Hong Kong was too independent-minded, it has stayed closer to the line from Beijing. It gained three seats in 1995 and subsequently was rewarded with the largest proportion of seats (47) on the PLC. In 1998 it gained a total of five seats, though none were directly elected.

Liberal Party

Address. 7/F, Printing House, 6 Duddell Street, Central
Telephone. (+852) 2869–6833
Fax. (+852) 2533–4238
Leadership. James Tien Pei-chun (chairman)
Founded in July 1993, this party is most associated with the interests of business. In the 1991 LegCo it had 15 seats. Subsequently its status declined as it was squeezed on the one side by the rise of more overtly pro-mainland parties and on the other by the success of the →Democratic Party, which took up traditional "liberal" values such as human rights and the rule of law. In 1995 and 1998 it won 10 seats, falling to eight in 2000, but none of these were directly elected. The party strongly opposes proposals to abolish the functional constituencies.

Macau Special Administrative Region

Population: 437,312 (1999E)

Macau followed Hong Kong in returning to Chinese sovereignty in December 1999 as a special administrative region (SAR) of the People's Republic under the same basic principle of "one country, two systems" guaranteed for 50 years. Like Hong Kong, the Macau SAR has a Legislative Council (LegCo). In pre-reversion elections in September 1996, eight out of the 23 members were elected by popular vote by proportional representation, eight were elected indirectly and seven were appointed by the Chief Executive. In new elections on Sept. 23, 2001, 10 members were directly elected from among 15 groups and 10 were elected indirectly from functional constituencies representing 625 registered business, labour and community organizations, while a further seven continued to be appointed by the Chief Executive.

There are no political parties as such in Macau, but 12 civic groups put forward lists of candidates for direct election in 1996. Macau has yet to see ardent pro-democracy movements, as exist in Hong Kong. The main issues in elections tend to be economic development, healthcare, education and bureaucratic administration. However, the September 2001 elections resulted in 2 of the 10 directly elected seats being won by the "pro-democracy" New Democratic Macau Association, led by Ng Kuok-cheong, other seats being taken by various social and pro-Beijing groups.

Colombia

Capital: Santafé de Bogotá　　　　　　　　　　　　　　　　　　　　　　　**Population:** 39,700,000 (2000E)

The Republic of Colombia gained independence from Spain in 1819 after liberation by the forces of Simón Bolívar and, after several boundary changes, became a Republic in 1886. Colombian parliamentary politics have long been dominated by the Liberal Party (PLC) and the Conservative Party of Colombia (PCC), which were both founded in the 1840s. Colombia's only military government this century was overthrown in 1958, when the two rival parties joined forces and formed a National Front coalition government which lasted from 1958 until 1974. Under the terms of the 1991 constitution, executive authority is vested in the President, who is elected directly for a four-year term by direct universal suffrage and may not serve a second consecutive term. A Vice-President, Fiscal General, and Defender of the People assist the President in policy-making. The President is also assisted by a Cabinet, which he appoints.

Legislative power is vested in a bicameral Congress, consisting of a 102-seat Senate and a 161-seat House of Representatives. Members of Congress cannot hold any other public post. A system of proportional representation operates for the election of members of both houses, who are also elected for a four-year period. The Senate has 99 nationally elected members; indigenous people in specific regions have two appointed senators selected in special elections and one elected senator. Each of the 23 departments, four intendencies and five commissaries (32 states) elects two members of the House of Representatives and further seats are allotted to each state on the basis of population. Governors are elected directly in the 27 departments and intendencies. All Colombian citizens aged 18 or over are eligible to vote, except members of the armed forces on active service, the national police and people who have been deprived of their political rights. Women obtained the vote in 1957. The indigenous population enjoys judicial autonomy in minor internal disputes within certain recognized territories.

Legislative elections held on March 8, 1998, took place against the backdrop of a violent guerrilla offensive in the country, as left-wing rebels continued to oppose government security forces in the country's nearly 30-year-old civil war. Altogether more than 6,500 candidates, representing 64 political parties, contested the 263 seats at stake. Final results gave the PLC a renewed clear majority in both chambers. In the House of Representatives the PLC won 98 seats, the PCC 52 and other parties took 11 seats. In the Senate the PLC won 58 seats and the PCC 28 seats and other parties 16 seats. In presidential elections held on May 31 and June 21, 1998, the PCC candidate, Andrés Pastrana Arango, polled 50.6% of the vote, defeating the candidate of the ruling PLC, Horacio Serpa Uribe, who won 46.5% of the vote. Pastrana, whose victory ended 12 years of PLC rule, took office in August.

Conservative Party of Colombia
Partido Conservador Colombiano (PCC)
Address. Avenida 22 No.37–09, Bogotá de Santafé
Telephone. (+57–1) 369–0212
Fax. (+57–1) 369–0187
Email. secretaria@partidoconservador.com
Website. www.partidoconservador.com.co
Leadership. Enrique Gomez-Hurtado (president); Humberto Zuluaga Mondero (secretary-general)

The PCC was founded in 1849. The party stands for law and order and traditional religious values, its doctrine being based upon the encyclicals of the Roman Catholic Church. The PCC was founded by Mariano Ospina Rodriguez, a leading member of the conservative Popular Societies, and supporters of President Jose Ignacio Marquez (1837-42). The party drew its members and leaders chiefly from the landed classes and business. It originally stood for protectionism and a centralized state controlled by the traditional elite, their power being legitimized by the Roman Catholic Church which was given an important role in society.

Belisario Betancur of the PCC was inaugurated as President in August 1982 and his administration, hampered by a Congress dominated by the →Liberal Party of Colombia (PLC), still managed to pass a variety of social and economic reforms. In November 1982, in an attempt to bring about peace, Betancur announced an amnesty for the country's guerrilla groups and in mid-1984 secured agreement for a year-long ceasefire with the three main groups. However, this first step towards reconciliation was quickly overshadowed by an escalating war with the powerful drug cartels. After the murder of Justice Minister Rodrigo Lara Bonilla in May 1984, Betancur imposed a state of siege and in November of the following year, with the internal situation rapidly deteriorating, he declared a state of economic and social emergency. In the subsequent congressional elections of March 1986, and the presidential elections in the following May, the PCC was defeated by its old rival, the PLC, its seats in the Senate being reduced to 45 and in the House of Representatives to 82.

In late May 1988 the former PCC presidential candidate, Alvaro Gomez Hurtado, was abducted by the M19 guerrilla group for two months, which caused widespread protests against the government and demands for his release. Gomez broke with the PCC in 1990 to form the →National Salvation Movement (MSN), a move that greatly damaged the Conservatives. In the congressional elections of March 1990, the PCC again came second to the PLC, and in the presidential elections in May Rodrigo Lloreda Caicedo of the PCC finished only fourth with 12.2% of the vote. In 1994, moreover, the PCC's presidential candidate, Andres Pastrana Arango, lost to Ernesto Samper of the PLC, although by less than 1% of the vote in the second round. The party had again been defeated by the PLC in the earlier legislative elections (taking 56 seats in the House of Representatives and 21 in the Senate).

The PCC returned to power in the mid-1998 presidential poll, with Andres Pastrana defeating the PLC candidate in the run-off. A few months earlier, however, the PLC had managed to retain a narrow overall majority in both houses of Congress. The elections had been marred by guerrilla attacks aimed at disrupting polling, with some 250,000 troops and police being deployed to ensure the safety of voters. The PCC suffered a severe setback in departmental and municipal elections held in October 2000, winning control of just two departmental capitals and failing to win a single governorship. The elections were marked by a considerable degree of violence and intimidation, including the kidnapping of seven congressmen by the United Self Defence Forces of Colombia (AUC), a right-wing paramilitary organization, and the assassination of dozens of local candidates across the country by both leftist and right-wing groups. As of mid-2001 it remained to be seen whether President Pastrana's efforts to forge meaningful negotiations with the country's main guerrilla groups would bear fruit.

The PCC is a member of the Christian Democrat International, the Christian Democrat Organization of America (ODCA) and the International Democrat Union.

Democratic Alliance–April 19 Movement
Alianza Democratica-Movimiento 19 de Abril
(AD-M19)
Address. Transversal 28, No. 37–78, Santafé de Bogotá
Telephone. (+57–1) 348–9436
Leadership. Diego Montana Cuellar
This left-wing party and former guerrilla group dates from 1973. The M19 had been formed by →National Popular Alliance (ANAPO) supporters as the party's armed wing in reaction to the disputed April 19, 1970, election results. The group's ideology was originally an amalgam of Marxism-Leninism and the radical liberal ideas of Jorge Eliecer Graitan (assassinated 1948), which attracted dissident members of the Revolutionary Armed Forces of Colombia (FARC) guerrilla group to M19. As its first public act, M19 seized Simón Bolívar's sword and spurs in January 1974. ANAPO, which had shifted to the right, disassociated itself from M19 soon after.

Specializing in kidnappings and sabotage of multinational companies, M19 started its guerrilla activity in 1976 with the abduction and killing of a trade union leader whom M19 suspected of having links with the CIA. In early 1982 the guerrillas suffered heavy losses in counterinsurgency operations and clashes with the new right-wing paramilitary group Death to Kidnappers (MAS). In August 1984, M19, by now Colombia's most prominent guerrilla group, announced its intention to become a political party. In May 1988 M19, in an attempt to force the government to hold peace talks, kidnapped the presidential candidate of the →Conservative Party of Colombia (PCC), Alvaro Gomez Hurtado. Partly as a result of this action, the government put forward a new peace plan the following September. The M19 called a unilateral ceasefire, and negotiations began in January 1989. An agreement with the government on reintegration of the M19 into civilian life was signed two months later and in October the M19 was constituted as a political party – incorporating a number of other left-wing groups. In March 1990 the guerrillas signed a final peace treaty with the government and surrendered their arms. In exchange the government guaranteed the M19 a general amnesty, full political participation in elections and the holding of a referendum on the question of a new constitution.

In April 1990 the M19 leader and presidential candidate for the newly-formed Democratic Alliance M19 (AD-M19) Carlos Pizarro Leongomez was gunned down, at the instigation, it was thought, of the Medellín drugs cartel. He was replaced as candidate in the May presidential elections by Antonio Navarro Wolff, who came third with 12.6% of the vote. The M19 won the majority of the 19 seats secured by the AD-M19 in the Constitutional Assembly also elected, and as the largest opposition block made an important contribution to the drawing-up of the constitution which came into effect in July 1991. However, in the municipal elections of March 1992 the party suffered big losses, especially in the capital, Santafé de Bogotá.

In the March 1994 legislative elections the party saw its representation fall sharply, to only two seats in the House of Representatives and one in the Senate. In the first round of presidential balloting in May 1994, Navarro Wolff (who had served as Health Minister in the early 1990s) was again well beaten with a meagre 3.8% of the vote. Subsequently, a dissident faction, led by Carlos Alonso Lucio, a former guerrilla commando, split away from the main party. The party failed to make any impact in the 1998 legislative and presidential elections, although it retained a small presence in the House of Representatives.

The AD-M19 is an observer member of the Socialist International.

Liberal Party of Colombia
Partido Liberal Colombiano (PLC)
Address. Avenida Caracas No.36–01, Santafé de Bogotá
Telephone. (+57–1) 323–1000
Fax. (+57–1) 287–9740
Website. www.partidoliberal.org.co
Leadership. Luis Guillermo Velez Trujilo (president); Maria Teresa Uribe Bent (vice president); Eduardo Verano de la Rosa (secretary-general)
Founded in the 1840s, the progressive centrist PLC has been a mainstay of the country's political history, standing in recent times for free enterprise and privatization, improved living standards and combating drug-trafficking. The party emerged from the rise of the American-born Spanish middle-classes influenced by European republican and radical utopian ideas. Although its major founding forces were the political discussion clubs which opposed Simón Bolívar, the PLC's classic liberal reforms, such as the abolition of slavery, reduction of church power, decentralization of government, an end to state monopolies and the introduction of freedom of the press, were inspired by the earlier independence movement.

In the mid-1950s the PLC and the →Conservative Party of Colombia (PCC) agreed on a power-sharing arrangement whereby the presidency would be held by each party in rotation and cabinet posts divided equally between them. This National Front agreement was approved by a referendum in December 1957, and in the subsequent elections the Liberal candidate (and former President), Lleras Camargo, became the first National Front President. Even though the parity agreement officially expired in 1974, the Liberals, who won the elections of 1974 and 1978, continued to award half the cabinet portfolios to Conservatives.

Successive Liberal governments proved largely ineffective against the illegal drugs trade and the escalating violence, which in 1988 alone saw an estimated 18,000 political and drug-cartel-related killings. In the political turmoil of 1989 leading PLC members were among victims of the growing spate of assassinations of politicians. Nevertheless, in the March 1990 poll the PLC increased its representation in the Senate to 72 seats and in the House of Representatives to 120. The victory was crowned in the presidential election of May 1990, which PLC candidate César Gaviria Trujillo won with 47% of the vote.

President Gaviria's inauguration pledge to continue his predecessor's campaign against "narco-terrorism", but not his policy of extraditing drug traffickers, soon came to fruition. He issued a decree offering drug barons, who called themselves the *extraditables*, a guarantee that they would not be extradited to the USA if they surrendered to the authorities. Although this was generally seen as a concession to the Medellín cartel, the deal was followed by the surrender of several major drug traffickers and an end to all-out war between the government and the drug cartels. This in turn had the desired effect of stabilizing the country for economic growth. At the end of 1991 Gaviria announced major investment in infrastructure to assist this trend. The PLC government also continued the peace initiatives with the country's guerrilla groups, so that by the time of the opening of the Constitutional Assembly in February 1991 peace agreements with some groups had been signed.

The resignation of Alfonso Lopez Michelsen as PLC leader in April 1992 ushered in a period of internal strife within the party that forced four successive factional leadership changes in a four-month period. Coming from the party's left-wing faction, the PLC's 1994 presidential candidate, Ernesto Samper Pizano, narrowly defeated the PCC contender. The Liberals were also successful in legislative elections held in the same year, retaining congressional majorities with 89 seats in the Chamber of Representatives and 52 seats in the Senate. The PLC retained its control of Congress in the 1998 legislative elections, but the defeat of PLC candidate Horacio Serpa Uribe in the subsequent presidential elections ended 12 years of Liberal rule.

Following PLC criticism of his proposal for a referendum on rooting out corruption from the political system, President Pastrana reshuffled his government in July 2000, bringing in two members of the PLC (Juan Manuel Santos Calderón as Finance Minister and Consuelo Araújo Noguera as Culture Minister). However, then PLC leader Serpa Uribe insisted that the new Liberal ministers were acting in a "personal capacity" and denied that a coalition government had been formed. The Liberals performed well in departmental and municipal elections held in October 2000, securing 15 out of 30 governorships in contention and winning control of 13 out of 30 departmental capitals (including Medellín).

The PLC is a full member of the Socialist International.

National Popular Alliance
Alianza Nacional Popular (ANAPO)
Address. Carrera 18, No. 33–95, Santafé de Bogotá
Telephone. (+57–1) 287–7050
Fax. (+57–1) 245–3138
Leadership. Maria Eugenia Rojas de Moreno Díaz (president)
ANAPO was formally inaugurated in 1971 by Gen. Gustavo Rojas Pinilla, who had been President in 1953-57, and his daughter, Maria Eugenia Rojas de Moreno Diaz. From the outset ANAPO campaigned for a "Colombian socialism" on a Christian social basis. In 1975 Rojas de Moreno assumed the leadership of the party on the death of her father. Under her leadership ANAPO gradually lost influence, its various factions failing to achieve significant results in subsequent elections. In the 1998 legislative polling the party won only one seat in the Senate.

Other Parties

Bolivarian Movement (*Movimiento Bolivariano, MB*), won one Senate seat in 1998.

Citizens' Defence Movement (*Movimiento Defensa Ciudadana, MDC*), won one Senate seat in 1998.

Colombian People's Party (*Partido Popular Colombiano, PPC*), won one Senate seat in 1998.

Democratic Reconstruction Movement (*Movimiento Reconstruccion Democrática, MRD*), won one Senate seat in 1998.

Education, Work and Social Change (*Educacion, Trabajo y Cambio Social, ETCS*), won one Senate seat in 1998.

Independent Conservative Movement (*Movimiento Conservatismo Independiente, MCI*), won one Senate seat in 1998.

Independents Front of Hope (*Independientes Frente de Esperanza, FE*), won one Senate seat in 1998.

Indigenous Authorities of Colombia (*Autoridades Indigenas de Colombia, AIC*), won one Senate seat in 1998.

Let's Go Colombia (*Vamos Colombia, VC*), won one Senate seat in 1998.

Movement C4 (*Movimiento C4, MC4*), won one Senate seat in 1998.

Movement 98 (*Movimiento 98, M98*), won one Senate seat in 1998.

Movement Civic People's Convergence (*Movimiento Convergencia Popular Civica, MCPC*), won one Senate seat in 1998.

Movement Colombia My Country (*Movimiento Colombia mi Pais, MCP*), won one Senate seat in 1998.

Movement Social Indigenous Alliance (*Movimiento Alianza Social Indigena'as, MASI*), won two Senate seats in 1998.

National Conservative Movement (*Movimiento Nacional Conservador, MNC*), increased its number of seats in the Senate from one in 1991 to eight in 1998.
Address. Carrera 16, No. 33–24, Santafé de Bogotá
Telephone. (157–1) 245 4418
Fax. (157–1) 284 8529
Leadership. Juan Pablo Cepera Marquez

National Progressive Movement (*Movimiento Nacional Progresista, MNP*), won two Senate seats in the 1998 legislative elections.
Address. Carrera 10, No. 19-45, Bogota
Telephone. (157-1) 286 7517
Fax. (157-1) 341 9368
Leadership. Eduardo Aismak Leon Beltran

National Salvation Movement (*Movimiento de Salvacion Nacional, MSN*). Founded in 1990 by a splinter group of the →Conservative Party of Colombia (PCC) led by Alvaro Gomez Hurtado, who had been PCC presidential candidate in 1974 and 1986 and who came second in 1990 with some 24%, almost twice the PCC vote. The MSN played a significant legislative role in the early 1990s, but after the assassination of Gomez Hurtado in 1995 declined in importance, retaining only one seat in the Senate.

New Democratic Force (*Nueva Fuerza Democratica, NFD*), a conservative party that won one Senate seat in 1998.

Oxigen Liberal Movement (*Movimiento Oxigeno Liberal, MOL*), won one Senate seat in 1998.

Seculars for Colombia Political Movement (*Movimiento Politico Laicos por Colombia, MPLC*), won one Senate seat in 1998.

Comoros

Capital: Moroni

Population: 578,400 (2000E)

The Federal Islamic Republic of the Comoros (comprising Grand Comore, Anjouan and Mohéli, but not Mayotte) achieved independence from France in 1975. It later became a one-party state under the Comoran Union for Progress (UCP or UDZIMA) but moved to a multi-party system in 1989–92. Following an all-party national conference, a new constitution was approved by referendum in June 1992. It provided for an executive President, directly elected for a six-year term by universal suffrage of those aged 18 and over, with the power to appoint the Prime Minister and government. Legislative authority was vested in a bicameral parliament consisting of a 42-member Federal Assembly (*Assemblée Fédérale*) as the lower house, directly elected for a five-year term in two rounds of voting, and a 15-member Senate (*Sénat*) as the upper house, chosen by an electoral college for a six-year term. A new constitution was adopted in October 1996, enhancing the power of the President, abolishing the Senate and increasing the membership of the Federal Assembly (as the unicameral parliament) to 43.

A presidential election on in March 1990 resulted in Saïd Mohamed Djohar, as candidate of the UCP/UDZIMA, being re-elected in the second round with 55.1% of the vote. An attempted coup in September 1995 raised question-marks over the position of President Djohar, who took refuge on the French island of Réunion until, in January 1996, it was agreed that he would return to Moroni, assume a "symbolic" role as head of state and be effectively excluded from seeking a further presidential term by dint of an agreement that candidates should be aged between 40 and 70. In a presidential election on March 9 and 16, 1996, Mohamed Taki Abdoulkarim of the National Union for Democracy in the Comoros (UNDC) was elected with nearly two-thirds of the second-round vote. Legislative elections held on Dec. 1 and 8, 1996, resulted in an overwhelming victory, with 39 seats, for the National Rally for Development (RND), a newly-established broad alliance of parties and a political vehicle for President Taki. Three other seats were won by the National Front for Justice (FNJ) and one by an independent. Parties opposed to the President refused to take part in the electoral process.

Increasing political instability and violence arose from 1997 as the islands of Anjouan and Mohéli sought to secede from the Comoros, and then in November 1998 President Taki died in office. On April 30, 1999, the military seized power from interim President Tajiddine Ben Said Massounde in a coup led by army chief of staff Col. Azali Assoumani, who became head of state. The Federal Assembly was dissolved and the constitution suspended.

Forum for National Recovery
Forum pour le Redressement National (FRN)

Leadership. Abbas Djoussouf, Saïd Hassan Saïd Hachim

The FRN was created as an opposition alliance in January 1994, a month after Assembly elections in which the presidential →Rally for Democracy and Renewal (RDR) had won a substantial majority. Five of the FRN parties had hitherto comprised the National Union for Democracy and Progress (*Union Nationale pour la Démocratie et le Progrès*, UNDP), namely: the oppositon rump of the Comoran Union for Progress (*Union Comorienne pour le Progrès*, UCP/UDZIMA) led by Omar Tamou; the Movement for Renovation and Democratic Action (*Mouvement pour la Rénovation et l'Action Démocratique*, MOURAD) led by Abdou Issa; the National Union for Democracy in the Comoros (UNDC) led by Mohamed Taki Abdoulkarim (who later broke away from the FRN); the Rally for Change and Democracy (*Rassemblement pour le Changement et la Démocratie*, RACHADE) led by Saïd Ali Youssouf; and the Socialist Party of the Comoros (*Parti Socialiste des Comores*, PASOCO) led by Ali Idarousse.

The UCP/UDZIMA had been founded as the sole government party in 1982 under President Ahmed Abdullah Abderrahman and had been inherited in 1989 by his successor, Saïd Mohamed Djohar. Having backed the latter's successful re-election campaign in 1990, the party became increasingly estranged from Djohar and went into opposition in 1991 in protest against the formation of a coalition government as a prelude to the move to multi-partyism. The UCP/UDZIMA participated in the national conference of early 1992 but opposed the resultant constitution and did not contest the October 1992 Assembly elections, in part

because its leaders had been implicated in a coup attempt the previous month.

Of the other FRN participants, RACHADE was founded in December 1990 by UDC/UDZIMA dissidents, joined the coalition government formed in 1992 and approved the new constitution, although it later called for President Djohar's resignation. The PCDP also derived from the UDC/UDZIMA, Ali Mroudjae having held high government office under both Abdullah and Djohar; standing for his new party in the March 1990 presidential elections, Mroudjae came fourth and in 1991 took the PCDP into the opposition camp. The FPC leader had also contested the 1990 presidential elections, subsequently joining the transitional government of 1992 and backing the new constitution, as did the FDC, whose leader had previously been imprisoned for alleged involvement in a 1985 coup attempt and had also stood for the presidency in 1990. The MDP also backed the 1992 constitution and joined the interim government, its leader having been another unsuccessful presidential contender in 1990; it polled strongly in the November 1992 Assembly elections and was the largest single party at the dissolution in June 1993. The Islamist PSN won one seat in the 1992 elections and became alienated from Djohar by the growing influence of the President's son-in-law, Mohamed Saïd Abdullah M'Changama.

The UNDC-led alliance won 18 of the 42 Assembly seats in the December 1993 Assembly elections, the official outcome of which was described as a "masquerade" by the opposition. Contesting the results and the resultant appointment of an RDR Prime Minister, the opposition parties nevertheless acknowledged that their divisions had assisted what they described as Djohar's "political coup" and the "brutal interruption of the transition to democracy". They therefore agreed in January 1994 to form the FRN as a focus of joint opposition.

Following an abortive coup by rebel soldiers and mercenaries in September 1995, the FRN accepted representation in a new "unity" government announced in early November. However, in presidential elections in March 1996 Abbas Djoussouf, as FRN candidate, was easily defeated by Taki Abdoulkarim of the UNDC. The FRN opposed the new constitution approved in October 1996 following a referendum, and boycotted the legislative elections the following December.

After President Taki's death in office in November 1998, his interim replacement appointed a coalition government led by the FRN (with six cabinet seats and Djoussouf as Prime Minister), but this was deposed by the military coup in April 1999.

Islands' Fraternity and Unity Party
Chama cha Upvamodja na Mugnagna wa Massiwa (CHUMA)
Leadership. Prince Saïd Ali Kemal (president); Sy Mohamed Nacer-Eddine (secretary-general)

CHUMA was founded in the late 1980s as an anti-Abdullah "patriotic alliance" of exiled groups under the leadership of Kemal, grandson of the last Sultan of the Comoros. He took third place in the first round of the March 1990 presidential elections (with 13.7% of the vote) and backed Djohar in the second, being rewarded with a cabinet post. CHUMA was also a member of the interim government formed in 1992 and endorsed the new constitution.

CHUMA supported the successful presidential candidacy of UNDC leader Mohamed Taki Abdoulkarim in March 1996. However, it rejected Taki's proposal that those political groupings which had backed him should disband in order to form a single party with a parliamentary majority (established in October 1996 as the →National Rally for Development), and subsequently aligned itself with the opposition →Forum for National Recovery.

National Front for Justice
Front National pour la Justice (FNJ)
Leadership. Ahmed Abdallah Mohamed, Ahmed Aboubacar, Soidiki M'Bapandza

An Islamist formation, the FNJ won three seats in the Federal Assembly in the December 1996 elections, so qualifying as the opposition to the →National Rally for Development.

National Rally for Development
Rassemblement National pour le Développement (RND)
Leadership. Ali Bazi Selim (chairman)

The RND was formally established in October 1996. A pro-presidential grouping, it was formed by the merger of most of the parties which had supported Mohamed Taki Abdoulkarim in the second round of the presidential elections the previous March, including the National Union for Democracy in the Comoros (*Union Nationale pour la Démocratie aux Comores*, UNDC). In the legislative polling in December 1996, the RND won 39 of the 43 Assembly seats (many of which were unopposed due to an opposition boycott). President Taki died in office in November 1998. His interim replacement appointed a coalition government, including four RND Cabinet members, but this was deposed by the military in April 1999.

Rally for Democracy and Renewal
Rassemblement pour la Démocratie et le Renouveau (RDR)
Leadership. Mohamed Abdou Madi (secretary-general)

The RDR was created immediately prior to the December 1993 elections as a political vehicle for President Djohar. The latter had come to power in 1989 following the assassination of President Ahmed Abdullah Abderrahman and had inherited the latter's one-party regime of the Comoran Union for Progress (UCP/UDZIMA). He had nevertheless permitted opposition candidates to contest the March 1990 presidential elections, in which he was the comfortable second-round victor with the official backing of the UCP/UDZIMA. On the formal move to multi-partyism in 1991–92, the UCP/UDZIMA ceased to be the government party. In Assembly elections in November 1992 Djohar backed the Union for Democracy and Development but there was no clear overall majority.

After a period of political instability, the President dissolved the Assembly in June 1993 and new elections were eventually held in December. For these the RDR was created as a merger of the *Mwangaza* party (headed by the President's controversial son-in-law, Mohamed Saïd Abdullah M'Changama) and dissident groups of other parties. The outcome was an RDR victory, which was hotly contested by what became the opposition →Forum for National Recovery (FRN), and the appointment of the RDR secretary-general as Prime Minister in January 1994. In major government changes in October 1994, however, Mohamed Abdou Madi was replaced as Prime Minister by Halifa Houmadi, amid dissension within the RDR over privatization plans supported by the former but opposed by M'Changama. Houmadi was replaced in April 1995 by Caabi el-Yachroutou Mohamed, a former Finance Minister.

In late September 1995 the Comoros experienced its 17th coup attempt since independence, when a group of rebel soldiers backed by foreign mercenaries seized power in Moroni and held it until being overcome early in October by forces sent in by France. Restored to office, President Djohar proceeded to form a "unity" government headed by the RDR but including representatives of the FRN. This lasted until a presidential election in March 1996 was won by the candidate of the National Union for Democracy in the Comoros (→Forum for National Recovery).

Congo

Capital: Brazzaville

Population: 2,830,000 (2000E)

The Republic of Congo achieved independence from France in 1960, became a one-party state in 1963, was renamed the People's Republic of Congo in 1970 but reverted to its original name in 1991 on moving to a multi-party system. Drawn up by a national conference convened in February 1991, a new constitution approved by referendum in March 1992 provided for an executive President, directly elected for a five-year term (once renewable) by universal suffrage of those aged 18 and over, with the power to appoint the Prime Minister and other ministers. Legislative authority was vested in a bicameral parliament consisting of a 125-member National

Assembly (*Assemblée Nationale*) as the lower house, elected for a five-year term in two rounds of voting, and a 60-seat Senate (*Sénat*), with members indirectly elected for a six-year term.

Legislative elections held in May–June 1993 and re-runs in 11 constituencies in October 1993 resulted as follows: Presidential Tendency 65 seats, of which the Pan-African Union for Social Democracy (UPADS) won 47, the Rally for Democracy and Development 6, the Union of Democratic Forces 3, the Congolese Renewal Party 2, the Union for Congolese Democracy 1, the Union for Development and Social Progress 1, and others 5; Opposition Coalition 56, of which the Congolese Movement for Democracy and Integral Development (MCDDI) won 28, the Congolese Labour Party (PCT) 15, the Rally for Democracy and Social Progress (RDPS) 10, the Union for Democratic Renewal 2 and an independent 1; the Union for Democracy and the Republic 2; the Patriotic Union for National Reconstruction 1; and an independent 1. Presidential elections held on Aug. 2 and 16, 1992, had resulted in a second-round victory for Pascal Lissouba (UPADS) over the MCDDI candidate, Bernard Kolelas. The PCT candidate and former President, Denis Sassou-Nguesso, was eliminated in the first round.

Subsequent clashes between the army and the opposition, whose leaders maintained dedicated militias, degenerated into civil war from June 1997, despite earlier peace accords and the inclusion of MCDDI and RDPS members in government with the UPADS from January 1995. Sassou-Nguesso and his militia forces (assisted by Angolan government troops) succeeded in deposing President Lissouba and Kolelas (who had been appointed Prime Minister in August 1997), and the PCT leader assumed the presidency on Oct. 25, 1997. The 1992 constitution was suspended. The elected assembly was dissolved and replaced in early 1998 by a 75-member National Transitional Council (appointed by the President) pending the approval of a new constitution and the organization of fresh national elections which had, however, not taken place by November 2001.

Congolese Labour Party
Parti Congolais du Travail (PCT)

Leadership. Gen. Denis Sassou-Nguesso (president); Léon Zokoni (secretary-general)

The PCT was launched in 1969 as the sole ruling party of the military regime of Capt. Marien Ngouabi, replacing the National Movement of the Revolution. Forming Africa's first Marxist–Leninist government, the party was riven by factional struggle in the 1970s: among several purges, one in 1972 ousted Ambroise Noumazalaye as first secretary and resulted in him being condemned to death, although he was later amnestied. The PCT establishment took a back seat to the military regime of 1977–79, but was then instrumental in the replacement of Gen. Jacques-Joachim Yhombi-Opango by Col. (as he then was) Sassou-Nguesso, who was elected party chairman and thus head of state at an extraordinary congress in March 1979. Victims of a purge of "leftists" in 1984 included Jean-Pierre Thystère-Tchikaya, who was subsequently condemned for involvement in bomb attacks but amnestied in 1988. Yhombi-Opango was later to found the →Rally for Democracy and Development (RDD) and Thystère-Tchikaya the →Rally for Democracy and Social Progress (RDPS).

In mid-1990 the PCT opened the way for President Sassou-Nguesso's decision of October that year to accede to pressure for a transition to multi-partyism. In December 1990 a PCT congress opted to abandon Marxism-Leninism and to embrace democratic socialism; it also reinstated Noumazalaye, who was elected to the new post of secretary-general. In early 1991 the party participated in the national conference which drafted a new constitution, although a hardline PCT faction bitterly criticized the surrender of authority to the conference and the resultant transitional government. From mid-1991 the latter took steps to remove PCT cadres from their entrenched position in the state bureaucracy, some prominent members being convicted of corruption. Paradoxically, the PCT's surrender of power meant that popular discontent now focused as much on the transitional government as on President Sassou-Nguesso and the former ruling party. Nevertheless, in the mid-1992 elections the PCT came in third place, with 19 Assembly and three Senate seats, while Gen. Sassou-Nguesso also took third place in the first round of the August 1992 presidential elections (with 16.9% of the vote) and was therefore eliminated. Accepting his defeat "with serenity", Sassou-Nguesso endorsed the successful candidacy of Pascal Lissouba of the →Pan-African Union for Social Democracy (UPADS) in the second round and the PCT accepted membership of a post-election coalition government dominated by the UPADS.

Reports that a formal PCT/UPADS alliance had been agreed proved to be exaggerated, however. In late October 1992 the PCT deputies combined with those of the →Union for Democratic Renewal (URD) to defeat the government on a no-confidence motion, as a result of which President Lissouba dissolved the Assembly and called new elections. In December 1992 both the PCT and the URD were included in an interim national unity government, which kept the peace until the elections began in May 1993. But opposition charges of electoral fraud in the first round of voting, and a joint PCT/URD boycott of the second round in June, were accompanied by escalating violence. Rejecting the official results giving the UPADS and its allies a comfortable overall Assembly majority, the PCT/URD axis refused to recognize the new UPADS-dominated cabinet headed by Yhombi-Opango (RDD) and named a parallel government headed by Thystère-Tchikaya (RDPS). Growing civil unrest, featuring bloody clashes between government and opposition militias in Brazzaville and elsewhere, was stemmed by a Gabonese-brokered accord concluded in August 1993 under which the disputed elections were re-run in 11 constituencies in October. Seven of these contests were won by the opposition (so that the PCT's final tally was 15 seats and one pro-PCT independent), but the UPADS and its allies still had an overall Assembly majority.

Further fighting ensued, especially around the PCT/URD stronghold of Bacongo in south Brazzaville, until the signature of a precarious ceasefire at the end of January 1994. The following month an international panel ruled that a further nine 1993 election results were invalid, but the government took no immediate steps to hold re-run contests. Nor was there was much progress in disarming the contending party militias, among which Sassou-Nguesso's so-called "Cobras" (including many former presidential guards) achieved particular notoriety. Amid continuing violence, the PCT in September 1994 announced the formation of a new opposition alliance called the →United Democratic Forces.

Civil unrest involving clashes between government forces and the opposition militias, including the Cobras, simmered throughout 1995 and 1996, culminating in civil war from June 1997. Sassou-Nguesso emerged as the dominant political figure, deposing the Lissouba regime and assuming the presidency in October 1997, since when he has presided over a transitional administration pending a new constitution and national elections.

Congolese Movement for Democracy and Integral Development
Mouvement Congolais pour la Démocratie et le Développement Intégral (MCDDI)

Leadership. Bernard Kolelas; Michel Mampouya (secretary-general)

Founded in 1990, the centre-right MCDDI was a member of the broad Forces of Change coalition which spearheaded the transition to multi-partyism in 1991, Bernard Kolelas becoming an adviser to the Prime Minister of the resultant transitional government. In the mid-1992 legislative elections, the MCDDI became the second-strongest party, with 29 Assembly and 13 Senate seats. In the August 1992 presidential contest, Kolelas likewise took second place in the first voting round (with 22.9% of the vote), thus going on to the run-off, in which he was defeated by Pascal Lissouba of the →Pan-African Union for Social Democracy (UPADS) by 61.3% to 38.7%. The MCDDI had meanwhile formed the seven-party →Union for Democratic Renewal (URD), which opted to oppose the new UPADS-dominated government and procured an alliance with the former ruling →Congolese Labour Party (PCT) for this purpose. Having brought down the government in October 1992, both the MCDDI-led URD and the PCT joined an interim national unity government formed in December 1992 pending new Assembly elections. These began in May 1993, but Kolelas claimed that "monstrous irregularities" had been perpetrated by the government in the first voting round and led an opposition boycott of the second in June. After Kolelas had urged the army to intervene to restore law and order (without result), the MCDDI/URD boycotted the new Assembly and participated in the formation of an alternative government to oppose the new UPADS-dominated coalition. The immediate crisis was partially resolved by an electoral re-run in 11 constituencies in October 1993, as a result of which the final MCDDI tally in the 125-member Assembly was 28 seats (out of 56 held by the opposition parties).

Clashes between government forces and militiamen of the URD/PCT axis intensified in late 1993 and early 1994, until the signature of a ceasefire agreement in late January 1994 by UPADS and MCDDI representatives brought some respite. In July 1994 popular anti-government feeling in Brazzaville was demonstrated by the election of Kolelas as the capital's mayor. But the incipient accommodation between the MCDDI/URD and the UPADS-led government was consolidated in January 1995 when the URD accepted representation in a new coalition, thus apparently breaking with the PCT. The MCDDI's strong support in the capital was demonstrated in by-elections in May 1995; but the party was weakened the same month by a split that yielded the creation of the →Party for Unity, Work and Progress. The MCDDI continued to co-operate with the UPADS in the coalition formed in September 1996.

As the country subsided into civil war from mid-1997, Kolelas was appointed in August as prime minister by President Lissouba. However, his appointment was short-lived as the government was deposed by PCT leader Sassou-Nguesso and his forces in October 1997. Kolelas and Lissouba both fled the country into exile.

Congolese Renewal Party
Parti Congolaise du Renouvellement (PCR)

Leadership. Grégoire Lefouaba (president)

The PCR was founded in late 1992 by Grégoire Lefouaba, who had previously been a member of the →Congolese Labour Party. Forming part of the Presidential Tendency alliance in the mid-1993 Assembly elections, the party won two seats in its own right.

Pan-African Union for Social Democracy
Union Panafricaine pour la Démocratie Sociale (UPADS)

Leadership. Pascal Lissouba; Martin Mberi (secretary-general)

The left-of-centre UPADS emerged from the opposition National Alliance for Democracy, formed in July 1991, and contested the 1992 elections in its own right, having attracted defectors from other parties. Its leader, Pascal Lissouba, had served as Prime Minister in 1963–66 and had narrowly failed to be elected head of the transitional government formed in mid-1991 as a result of the national conference. The UPADS became the largest party in the legislative elections of June–July 1992, winning 39 Assembly and 23 Senate seats. Lissouba then won the presidential elections of August 1992, heading the first-round vote with 35.9% and taking 61.3% of the second-round vote, thanks in part to being endorsed by the outgoing President, Denis Sassou-Nguesso of the →Congolese Labour Party (PCT). The UPADS/PCT axis did not last long, as the PCT formed an opposition alliance with the →Union for Democratic Renewal (URD). The post-election UPADS-dominated coalition government lost a vote confidence at the end of October 1992, whereupon President Lissouba dissolved the Assembly the following month and called new elections.

A national unity government appointed in December 1992, including both the PCT and the URD, kept the peace until the elections began in May 1993. But opposition charges of electoral fraud in the first round of voting, and a joint PCT/URD boycott of the second round in June, were accompanied by escalating violence. On the strength of official results giving the UPADS and its allies a comfortable overall Assembly majority, Lissouba appointed a UPADS-dominated government headed by the leader of the →Rally for Democracy and Development (RDD). It faced a parallel government named by the PCT/URD and growing disorder, as government forces and opposition militias fought regular battles in Brazzaville and elsewhere. Under a Gabonese-brokered accord concluded in August 1993, re-run elections were held in 11 constituencies in October, seven being won by the opposition. This outcome still left the UPADS and its allies with an overall Assembly majority of 65 seats. Further bloody clashes ensued, until the signature of a precarious ceasefire at the end of January 1994.

The UPADS remained the dominant formation in a new coalition formed in January 1995 (again under the premiership of the RDD leader) and succeeded in persuading the URD to break with the PCT (by now heading the →United Democratic Forces) by accepting ministerial representation. Immediately after the new government formation, however, 12 UPADS Assembly deputies resigned from the party, complaining that they had been marginalized.

In September 1996 a new government was appointed, headed by Charles David Ganao (of the →Union of Democratic Forces) and including the →Congolese Movement for Democracy and Integral Development and the →Rally for Democracy and Social Progress as well as UPADS. However, continuing civil unrest intensified in mid-1997 culminating in the overthrow of the government by PCT leader Sassou-Nguesso and his militia in October 1997. Lissouba fled abroad into exile.

Party for Unity, Work and Progress
Parti pour l'Unité, le Travail et le Progrès (PUTP)

Leadership. Didier Sengha

The PUTP was launched in May 1995 by a dissident faction of the →Congolese Movement for Democracy and Integral Development (MCDDI), the breakaway party's leader, Didier Sengha, claiming that the MCDDI had ceased to care about "democracy, freedom, equity, legality and fraternity". The MCDDI leader, Bernard Kolelas, responded by accusing Sengha of financial misappropriation and embezzlement.

Patriotic Union for National Reconstruction
Union Patriotique pour la Réconstruction Nationale (UPRN)

Leadership. Mathias Dzon

The UPRN was formed prior to the 1993 Assembly elections as a party at that stage independent of both the government and the opposition alliances. It won one seat in that contest and in September 1994 joined the opposition →United Democratic Forces alliance headed by the →Congolese Labour Party.

Rally for Democracy and Development
Rassemblement pour la Démocratie et le Développement (RDD)
Leadership. Gen. Jacques-Joachim Yhombi-Opango; Saturnin Okabe (chairman)

The RDD was founded in 1990 as a political vehicle for Gen. Yhombi-Opango, who had become President of a military government in 1977 but had been ousted in 1979 and expelled from the then ruling →Congolese Labour Party. The RDD was at first an influential element in the broad Forces of Change alliance, which dominated the transitional government formed after the 1991 national conference. But by April 1992 the party was openly criticizing the Prime Minister for alleged misuse of public funds for electoral purposes. In the mid-1992 Assembly elections the RDD won five seats and thereafter aligned itself with the opposition to the newly-dominant →Pan-African Union for Social Democracy (UPADS). However, in further Assembly elections in mid-1993 the RDD formed part of the UPADS-led Presidential Tendency alliance, winning six seats in its own right, whereupon Gen. Yhombi-Opango accepted appointment as Prime Minister in a new coalition government. In January 1995 he was reappointed as head of a broader coalition, still dominated by the UPADS but also including the →Union for Democratic Renewal, but resigned the premiership in August 1996.

Rally for Democracy and Social Progress
Rassemblement pour la Démocratie et le Progrès Social (RDPS)
Leadership. Jean-Pierre Thystère-Tchicaya

The RDPS was founded in 1990 by Thystère-Tchicaya, once an ideologist of the former ruling →Congolese Labour Party (PCT), before being purged as a "leftist" in 1984. It won nine Assembly and five Senate seats in the mid-1992 elections, although Thystère-Tchicaya came a poor fifth in the first round of presidential elections in August, winning only 5.9% of the vote. The party was thereafter a member of the opposition →Union for Democratic Renewal (URD) led by the →Congolese Movement for Democracy and Integral Development, whose post-election axis with the PCT resulted in the fall in late October of the coalition government dominated by the →Pan-African Union for Social Democracy (UPADS). The RDPS participated in the opposition boycott of the second round of new Assembly elections in June 1993, when Thystère-Tchicaya was named as head of a parallel government set up by the URD and the PCT. Following electoral re-runs in 11 constituencies in October 1993, the RDPS tally in the Assembly was 10 seats. As a constituent party of the →Union for Democratic Renewal (URD), the RDPS lined up initially in opposition to the UPADS-dominated Lissouba administration. But in January 1995 the URD accepted representation in a new coalition government headed by the UPADS, and similarly participated with UPADS in subsequent administrations from September 1996 until Sassou-Nguesso's assumption of power in October 1997.

Union for Congolese Democracy
Union pour la Démocratie Congolaise (UDC)
Leadership. Félix Makosso (chairman)

The formation of the UDC was announced in November 1989 in neighbouring Côte d'Ivoire, where its founder, Sylvain Bemba, a former government official and associate of President Fulbert Youlou (1960–63), had been in exile for some 25 years. It was one of the first groups to challenge the one-party rule of the →Congolese Labour Party and joined the National Alliance for Democracy, becoming closely aligned with the →Pan-African Union for Social Democracy (UPADS). As part of the UPADS-led Presidential Tendency alliance in the mid-1993 Assembly elections, the UDC won one seat in its own right.

Union for Democracy and the Republic
Union pour la Démocratie et la République (UDR)
Leadership. André Milongo

The UDR was founded in 1992 by Milongo (a former World Bank official), who in June 1991 had been elected transitional Prime Minister by the national conference convened to determine the country's constitutional future. He had then represented the broad coalition of pro-democracy parties called the Forces of Change (FDC), which designation was used by him in the 1992 legislative and presidential elections, although by then many of its original components were in open opposition to his government. In the legislative elections of June-July 1991, the FDC failed to win a seat in the Assembly and won only one in the Senate. In the August 1992 presidential elections, Milongo came in fourth place in the first round, with 10.2% of the vote. Launched after his electoral failure, the UDR gave broad support to President Pascal Lissouba and the new government dominated by his →Pan-African Union for Social Democracy (UPADS), without becoming a member of the Presidential Tendency coalition. In the 1993 Assembly elections, the UDR was at first credited with six seats on the strength of the disputed balloting of May-June, but its tally fell to two seats as a result of the re-runs in 11 constituencies in October. By the latter date, however, Milongo had been elected president of the Assembly.

Union for Democratic Renewal
Union pour la Renouveau Démocratique (URD)
Leadership. Bernard Kolelas (MCDDI), Jean-Pierre Thystère-Tchicaya (RDPS)

The centre-right URD was created at the time of the mid-1992 elections as an alliance of seven parties, notably the →Congolese Movement for Democracy and Integral Development (MCDDI) and the →Rally for Democracy and Social Progress (RDPS), both with their main strength in central and southern Congo. Joining a post-election opposition axis with the former ruling →Congolese Labour Party (PCT), the URD helped to bring about the fall in late October 1992 of the coalition government dominated by the →Pan-African Union for Social Democracy (UPADS). It became a member of the interim national unity government formed in December 1992 but again came into conflict with the UPADS-dominated administration of President Pascal Lissouba when new elections were held. Claiming that the first round of voting in May 1993 had featured massive electoral fraud by the authorities, the URD and the PCT boycotted the second round in June and set up their own parallel government under the premiership of Thystère-Tchicaya, amid a descent into bloody civil conflict.

The impasse was partially resolved by repeat elections in 11 constituencies in October 1993, seven of them won by the opposition. As a result, however, the UPADS and its allies still had an overall majority in the 125-member Assembly and the opposition parties 56 seats, of which the URD parties held 40 (including two won by candidates standing under the URD rubric rather than for constituent parties). Further serious violence between government forces and the URD/PCT axis in late 1993 and early 1994 was temporarily stemmed by a ceasefire agreement of late January. The URD also welcomed the finding of an international panel in February 1994 that the 1993 election results were invalid in a further nine seats, although its demand for re-runs met with no immediate response from the UPADS-dominated government. However, little progress was subsequently made in disarming the opposing militias, that of the URD being concentrated in the south Brazzaville stronghold of Kolelas, who was elected mayor of the capital in July 1994.

The URD at first aligned itself with the opposition →United Democratic Forces (FDU) launched in September 1994 under the leadership of the PCT; but in January 1995 it broke with the FDU by accepting representation in a new coalition government headed by the UPADS. It similarly participated with UPADS in subsequent administrations from September 1996 until Sassou-Nguesso's assumption of power in October 1997.

Union for Development and Social Progress
Union pour le Développement et le Progrès Social (UDPS)

Leadership. Jean-Michel Boukamba-Yangouma (president)
The UDPS was formed prior to the mid-1993 Assembly elections by a dissident group, headed by trade union leader Boukamba-Yangouma, of the →Union for Social Progress and Democracy. As part of the Presidential Tendency alliance in those elections, it won one seat in its own right.

Union of Democratic Forces
Union des Forces Démocratiques (UFD)

Leadership. Sebastian Ebao (chairman)
Grouping a number of parties, the UFD formed part of the Presidential Tendency alliance in the mid-1993 Assembly elections, in which it won three seats in its own right. The UFD's David Charles Ganao was an unsuccessful contender for the Assembly presidency, despite receiving opposition backing because of his reputed political objectivity. He subsequently served as Prime Minister of a coalition government under President Lissouba from September 1996 to mid-1997.

United Democratic Forces
Forces Démocratiques Unies (FDU)

Leadership. Gen. Denis Sassou-Nguesso (PCT), Alfred Opimba (CAD), Nicéphore Fyla (PLR), Pierre N'Ze (UNDP), Mathias Dzon (UPRN), Gabriel Bokilo (URN)
The FDU was launched in September 1994 as an opposition alliance of six parties headed by the →Congolese Labour Party (PCT) and including the →Convention for the Democratic Alternative (CAD), the →Liberal Republican Party (PLR), the →National Union for Democracy and Progress (UNDP), the →Patriotic Union for National Reconstruction (UPRN) and the →Union for National Recovery (URN). The FDU's leaders came mainly from northern Congo, in contrast to the central and southern provenance of the →Union for Democratic Renewal (URD),

then the FDU's ally in opposition to the government headed by President Lissouba's →Pan-African Union for Social Democracy (UPADS). In January 1995 the FDU parties refused to participate in a new UPADS-led coalition, whereas the URD accepted representation.In October 1997 the PCT leader, Sassou-Nguesso, deposed the elected Lissouba regime and assumed the presidency. The FDU has reportedly changed its name to the Forces Démocratiques et Patriotiques (FDP).

Other Parties and Alliances

Citizens' Rally (*Rassemblement des Citoyens, RC*), founded in March 1998.
Leadership. Claude Alphonse Silou

Movement for Democracy and Solidarity (*Mouvement pour la Démocratie et la Solidarité, MDS*), a member party of the Christian Democrat International.
Leadership. Paul Kaya

National Union for Democracy and Progress (*Union Nationale pour la Démocratie et le Progrès, UNDP*), founded in 1990, was prominent in the early pro-democracy movement, but lost support to the →Pan-African Union for Social Democracy, joined the opposition →United Democratic Forces in 1994.
Leadership. Pierre N'Ze

Patriotic Movement of Ninja Forces (*Union Patriotique des Forces Ninjas*), formed in 1999 as the political wing of the militia supporting former presidential candidate and Prime Minister Bernard Kolelas.

Union for Social Progress and Democracy (*Union pour le Progrès Social et la Démocratie, UPSD*), founded in 1991 by former prominent members of the →Congolese Labour Party, joined the opposition National Alliance for Democracy, won two Assembly seats in the 1992 elections, thereafter gravitating to the anti-Lissouba opposition, weakened by the formation of the splinter →Union for Development and Social Progress, failed to win representation in the 1993 elections. Party leader Poungui was Prime Minister in 1985–89.
Leadership. Ange-Édouard Poungui

Democratic Republic of the Congo

Capital: Kinshasa

Population: 51,965,000 (2000E)

The Democratic Republic of the Congo (DRC, known as Zaïre from 1971–97) achieved independence from Belgium in 1960. Mobutu Sese Seko, who took power in a military coup in 1965, was President from 1970–97, ruling through the Popular Movement of the Revolution (*Mouvement Populaire de la Révolution*, MPR), which was the sole legal party until 1990, when the introduction of a multi-party system was announced. By February 1991 a large number of new parties had been established. In mid-1991 a National Conference on the political future of the country began, its claims to sovereignty leading to conflict with President Mobutu. The National Conference, which sat until December 1992, dissolved the National Legislative Council (which had been elected in 1987 from a list of MPR-approved candidates) and replaced it with a 453-member transitional legislature, the High Council of the Republic (HCR), but President Mobutu refused to sanction this action.

Political stalemate between the President and the opposition-dominated HCR, which had resulted by early 1993 in the appointment of two rival Cabinets, was broken in January 1994. The HCR and the National Legislative Council (which had been reconvened by Mobutu) were reconstituted as a single body to be known as the High Council of the Republic–Parliament of Transition (*Haut Conseil de la République-Parlement de Transition*, HCR-PT), which the following April endorsed legislation entrusting it with the task of overseeing the activities of a transitional government. The legislation strengthened the position of the Prime Minister and the Cabinet in relation to the President, and set the duration of the transition to democracy at 15 months, during which time a constitutional referendum, as well as presidential and legislative elections, would have to be organized. In June 1994 Léon Kengo Wa Dondo of the Union for the Republic and Democracy was appointed, controversially, to the post of Prime Minister, in which capacity he named a new transitional administration including pro-Mobutu and opposition members. In May 1995 the government confirmed that multi-party elections, scheduled for July 1995, would be postponed, whereupon the HCR-PT voted the following month to extend the transition period for a further two-years.

In the wake of the 1994 Rwanda genocide, long-standing ethnic tensions between Tutsi and Hutu inhabitants in the east of the country worsened. In October 1996 the Tutsi *Banyamulenge*, led by Laurent Kabila, and other rebel groups formed the Alliance of Democratic Forces for the Liberation of the Congo (AFDL) and began a revolt against the Mobutu regime. The AFDL made dramatic military gains against the Zaïrean army, entering the capital Kinshasa on May 17, 1997. Mobutu fled to Morocco (where he subsequently died) and Kabila declared himself President, head of both state and government.

Progress towards political reform and the holding of fresh elections, scheduled for April 1999, was derailed by renewed conflict and regional intervention from mid-1998. As Kabila's relations with his former Ugandan and Rwandan backers deteriorated, he ordered all foreign troops to leave. However, anti-Kabila Congolese rebels, now supported by Uganda and Rwanda, began to take control of large areas of the east and north of the country from August 1998. Meanwhile, Zimbabwe, Angola and Namibia intervened on the President's behalf. The Lusaka ceasefire agreement, setting out a framework for national dialogue and reconciliation, was signed in the autumn of 1999, but there was little subsequent progress towards a lasting settlement.

On Jan. 16, 2001, Laurent Kabila was assassinated, and was succeeded as President by his son, Joseph Kabila. The new head of state undertook to implement the Lusaka agreement, and in February 2001 all parties agreed a timetable for troop withdrawal and the demobilization of irregular forces operating in the country. In May 2001 President Kabila announced the lifting of the restrictions on party political activity maintained by his father, although it remained to be seen whether he was sincere in his stated intention to build a multi-party democracy.

Alliance of Democratic Forces for the Liberation of the Congo
Alliance des Forces Démocratiques pour la Libération do Congo (AFDL)

Address. c/o President's Office, Mont Ngaliema, Kinshasa
Leadership. Joseph Kabila

The AFDL was formed under the leadership of Laurent Kabila by anti-Mobutu rebels in October 1996. Kabila claimed the Presidency in May 1997 on Mobutu's flight abroad and formed a new administration. In early 1999 he announced that the ADFL was to be dissolved and local People's Power Committees created. The unstable internal security situation, however, undermined progress towards political reform, and then in January 2001 Kabila was assassinated. He was replaced as head of state and government by his son, Joseph.

Democratic and Social Christian Party
Parti Démocrate et Social Chrétien (PDSC)

Leadership. André Boboliko Lokanga (chairman)

The PDSC was founded in 1990, achieved legal status the following year, and joined the anti-Mobutu opposition grouping, the →Sacred Union of the Radical Opposition. The party is an affiliate of the Christian Democrat International.

Democratic Rally for the Republic
Rassemblement Congolais Démocratique (RCD)

Leadership. Ernest Wamba dia Wamba; Emile Ilunga

The RCD, an anti-Kabila rebel movement initially supported by both Uganda and Rwanda, was formed in 1998. However, in May 1999, the movement split into two factions, one led by Ilunga (backed by Rwanda) and the other by Wamba dia Wamba (with Ugandan support).

Political Forces of the Conclave
Forces Politiques du Conclave (FPC)

Established in 1993, the FPC was an alliance of pro-Mobutu groups, led by the →Popular Movement of the Revolution. In January 1994 the major constituent parties of the FPC and the opposition →Sacred Union of the Radical Opposition (with the exception of the →Union for Democracy and Social Progress) signed an agreement to form a government of national reconciliation. In June 1995 political consensus was reached between the FPC and the opposition resulting in the extension of the period of national transition by two years.

Popular Movement of the Revolution
Mouvement Populaire de la Révolution (MPR)

Leadership. Kithima bin Ramazani (secretary-general)

The MPR was launched in 1967 by late President Mobutu Sese Seko, advocating national unity and African socialism, and opposing tribalism. As the main vehicle of the Mobutu regime, it became the sole legal political party in 1969 and, until political liberalization in 1990, party membership was deemed to be acquired automatically by all Zaïreans at birth. President Mobutu was deposed in May 1997, fleeing to Morocco where he subsequently died.

Sacred Union of the Radical Opposition
Union Sacrée de l'Opposition Radicale (USOR)

The USOR developed in the course of 1991 as an umbrella group of organizations opposed to the Mobutu regime. Originally drawing on the ranks of the →Union for Democracy and Social Progress, the →Union of Federalists and Independent Republicans (which was subsequently expelled) and the →Democratic and Social Christian Party, the USOR linked some 130 anti-Mobutu movements and factions. The existence within the transitional legislature of an expanded radical opposition grouping, known as the Sacred Union of the Radical Opposition and its Allies (USORAL), was announced in late 1994.

Union for Democracy and Social Progress
Union pour la Démocratie et le Progrès Social (UDPS)

Leadership. Etienne Tshisekedi wa Malumba

The UDPS emerged in the early 1980s as an attempt to establish an opposition party within Zaïre to counter the "arbitrary rule" of the Mobutu regime. Various of its members suffered consequent arrest and imprisonment, and serious splits in its leadership were subsequently reported. The party was legalized in 1991. The UDPS leader, Etienne Tshisekedi, was elected Prime Minister in August 1992 by the national conference, but the legitimacy of his government was resisted by President Mobutu who, in early 1993, appointed a rival administration, so heightening the political impasse. The UDPS did not sign the agreement in January 1994 on the formation of a government of national reconciliation.

The UDPS is associated with the International Democrat Union through the Democrat Union of Africa.

Union of Federalists and Independent Republicans
Union des Fédéralistes et Républicains Indépendants (UFERI)
Leadership. Jean Nguza Karl-I-Bond (leader)

Founded in 1990 and seeking autonomy for Shaba/Katanga province, the UFERI was initially one of the most prominent groups in the →Sacred Union of the Radical Opposition. However, after party leader Nguza Karl-I-Bond had controversially accepted nomination by President Mobutu for the post of Prime Minister in November 1991, the UFERI was expelled from the Sacred Union coalition.

Other Parties

Congo Liberation Movement (*Mouvement pour la Libération du Congo, MLC*), a Ugandan-backed, anti-Kabila rebel organization formed in 1998.
Leadership. Jean-Pierre Bemba

Congolese National Movement-Lumumba (*Mouvement National du Congo-Lumumba, MNC-Lumumba*), formed in September 1994 as a coalition of parties supporting the nationalist aims of former Prime Minister Patrice Lumumba.
Leadership. Antoine Gizenga

Rally for a New Society (*Rassemblement pour une Nouvelle Societé, RNS*), founded in October 1996 and calling for the liberalization of political life in the DRC as a prerequisite to national reconciliation.
Leadership. Alafuele M. Kalal (president)

Renovated Sacred Union (*Union Sacrée Rénovée, USR*), formed in 1993.
Leadership. Kiro Kimate.

Union for the Republic (*Union pour la République, UPR*), formed in 1997 by former members of the →Popular Movement of the Revolution.
Leadership. Charles Ndaywel

Costa Rica

Capital: San José

Population: 3,711,000 (2000E)

Costa Rica gained independence from Spain in 1821 and was a member of the United Provinces of Central America until 1838. Following civil war in 1948 a new constitution was promulgated and the army was disbanded, boosting the country's claim to be the longest-lasting democracy in Latin America. A social democratic political tradition, represented by the National Liberation Party (PLN) dominated politics until 1990. A more conservative tradition, represented in a coalition by 1978, has shared power more recently in the form of the Social Christian Unity Party (PUSC).

Under the 1949 constitution, a unicameral Legislative Assembly is made up of 57 members. Executive power rests with the President, who appoints a Cabinet. A presidential candidate may not be a member of the clergy, related to an incumbent President or have served either as a cabinet minister or as a director of an autonomous state agency or as a member of the Electoral Tribunal or the Supreme Court in the period immediately preceding the electoral campaign. The President is elected directly by universal adult suffrage for a four-year non-renewable term. Members of the Legislative Assembly are elected by proportional representation for the same period to coincide with the presidential term. Voting is compulsory for all men and women between 18 and 70 years of age, although "abstentionism" has increased at recent elections.

Constitutional reforms in 1997 provided for the state funding of political parties as well as establishing the obligations of parties to provide information on their other sources of funding. The articles specify that a percentage of GNP should be allocated to parties receiving at least 4% of the vote at national or regional level.

Miguel Angel Rodríguez of the PUSC won the presidential election held on Feb. 1, 1998, with 46.9% of the vote, taking office on May 8. Simultaneous elections to the Legislative Assembly resulted as follows: PUSC 27 seats (with 47.0% of the vote), PLN 23 (44.6%), Democratic Force Party 2 (5.3%), Libertarian Movement Party 2 (1.8%), National Integration Party 1 (1.8%), Agricultural Labour Action Party 1 (1.2%), Costa Rican Renovation Party 1 (0.9%).

Agricultural Labour Action Party
Partido Acción Laborista Agricola (PALA)
Address. c/o Asamblea Legislativa, 1000 San José
Leadership. Carlos Alberto Solis Blanco (president)

Formed in the late 1980s, PALA might be described as an important provincial party, being based in Alajuela, or as a local party with national ambitions. Its programme seeks a recognition of the still predominantly agrarian nature of Costa Rican society and therefore of the importance of Costa Rica's *campesino* population. The party favours various reforms to social security provision to better suit the needs of rural workers and is against large government subsidies for agriculture, contending that they tend only to benefit a small number of large producers. The party won one seat and 1.2% of the vote in the 1998 legislative elections.

Costa Rican Renovation Party
Partido Renovación Costarricense (PRC)
Address. c/o Asamblea Legislativa, 1000 San José
Leadership. Carlos Avendano Calvo (president)

Formed in 1995, the PRC stresses the importance of values in society, claiming to be a party of 'God, the nation and the family'. Its programme defends the right to work and to enjoy the fruits of that labour, advocating that support should be given to small and medium-sized enterprises and that provision of social security must be balanced with productivity of the economy. The party won one seat and 0.9% in the 1998 legislative elections and its presidential candidate, Sherman Thomas Jackson, took 1.4% of the vote.

Democratic Force Party
Partido Fuerza Democrática (PFD)
Address. c/o Asamblea Legislativa, 1000 San José
*Leadership.*Isaac Felipe Azofeifa (president)
Having originated in the run-up to the 1994 elections as an alliance of mainly left-wing parties, the PFD is against the neo-liberal economic model and in favour of social solidarity. The party campaigns for social justice, workers' rights, a reduction in indirect taxes and regulation of the cost of basic public services such as electricity. It campaigns against tax evasion and other forms of corruption. The party won two Assembly seats in both 1994 and 1998 (and 5.3% of the vote on the latter occasion), its presidential candidate in 1998, Vladimir de la Cruz de Lemos, coming third with 3% of the vote.

Libertarian Movement Party
Partido Movimiento Libertario (PML)
Address. c/o Asamblea Legislativa, 1000 San José
Email. otto@libertario.org
Leadership. Otto Guevara Guth (president)
Founded in 1995 the PML advocates material and spiritual well-being and seeks a "moral revolution". Standing on a political programme combining anti-inflation measures, reducing the size of the state and more police on the beat with more popular participation in politics, the party won two seats in the 1998 elections.

National Integration Party
Partido de Integración Nacional (PIN)
Address. c/o Asamblea Legislativa, 1000 San José
Email. wmunoz@ongreso.aleg.go.cr
Website. www.pin.co.cr
Leadership. Walter Muñoz Céspedes (president)
The PIN calls for the promotion of small business, better provision for children and senior citizens, provincial autonomy, and resistance to privatization in order to allow longer-range planning. The PIN won one seat in the 1998 legislative elections (and 1.8% of the vote) and party leader Walter Muñoz Céspedes took 1.5% in the presidential contest.

National Liberation Party
Partido de Liberación Nacional (PLN)
Address. Sabana Oeste, San José
Telephone. (+506) 232–5133
Fax. (+506) 296–0916
Email. palina@sol.rcsa.co.cr
Website. www.pln.org
Leadership. Sonia Picado Sotela (president); Rolando Araya Monge (2002 presidential candidate)
Founded in October 1951, the PLN is nominally social democratic though has been relatively conservative in office. The successor to the Social Democratic Party (PSD) (founded in 1948), the PLN was formed around José "Pepe" Figueres Ferrer, who promised socio-economic reforms, restructuring of the government and better management of the state-run sector. The party lost the presidential elections in 1958 but regained the presidency in 1962 and held it from 1970–1978, 1982–1990 and 1994–1998. Until recently the PLN has had near continuous control of the Legislative Assembly (the exception being 1978–1982).

The nomination of Oscar Arias Sánchez as presidential candidate in 1986 marked a rupture with the old guard in the party who had a conservative pro-USA foreign policy and were hostile to the Sandinistas in Nicaragua. Arias gained international status for his Central American peace plan and received the Nobel Peace Prize in 1987. Domestically, however, the effects of foreign debt and pressure for economic restructuring, including the privatization of the state sector and banking reform, saw the PLN's moderate social democratic wing squeezed. Drug-related scandals involving prominent party figures, including Daniel Oduber Quirós, party president in 1974–79, damaged the PLN's image and

the shift in policy failed to restore it. The party's conservative candidate for the 1990 presidential elections, Carlos Manuel Castillo, was defeated and, symbolic of the end of PLN domination, long-time party leader José Figueres Ferrer died later that year.

In the February 1994 presidential elections Figueres' son, José María Figueres Olsen, defeated the candidate of the →Social Christian Unity Party (PUSC) by 49.6% to 47.5% of the vote, the PLN also winning a majority in the Assembly. In the February 1998 contest, however, PLN presidential candidate José Miguel Corrales Bolaño won only 44.4% and was defeated by the PUSC nominee, the PLN also losing its Assembly majority.

After some rather fractious internal politics in the 1990s, the PLN's situation was further clouded after 1998 as former President Oscar Arias Sánchez sought constitutional changes which would allow him to run for the presidency in 2002. As it turned out, the amendments which would have made this possible, as proposed by Otto Guevara Guth of the →Libertarian Movement Party, were rejected by the National Assembly by a substantial majority. As a result, defeated 1998 candidate Corrales emerged as joint front-runner for the PLN nomination, along with Rolando Araya Monge a 53-year-old chemical engineer and vice-president of the Socialist International. In the end, Araya's victory in a party election by 53% to 32% was graciously accepted by Corrales, and the PLN appeared to have re-established unity.

The PLN is a member party of the Socialist International.

Social Christian Unity Party
Partido Unidad Social Cristiana (PUSC)
Address. Apartada 725–1007, Centro Colón, San José
Telephone. (+506) 234–8395
Fax. (+506) 234–8683
Website. www.pusc.org
Leadership. Rina Contreras López (president); Abel Pacheco (2002 presidential candidate); Carlos Palma (secretary-general)
The right-wing Christian democratic PUSC was originally formed in 1978 as the four-party Unity (*Unidad*) alliance of the Christian Democratic Party (PDC, founded in 1962), the Calderonist Republican Party (PRC, founded in 1970), the Popular Union Party (PUP, founded in 1974) and the Democratic Renewal Party (PRD, founded in 1971). The coalition combined the right-wing republican tradition of ex-President Rafael Angel Calderón Guardia (1942–44) and the conservatism of the "coffee barons" with the guiding principles of Christian democracy. The *Unidad* presidential candidate, Rodrigo Carazo Odio, was successful in the 1978 elections and the alliance took 28 seats in the Assembly, one short of an absolute majority. Carazo's government clashed with the trade unions and cooled relations with Cuba and Sandinista Nicaragua. The *Unidad* candidate, Rafael Angel Calderón Fournier, lost the 1982 presidential elections and the party's strength in the Assembly was reduced to 18 seats. In the following year the PUSC title was adopted by the alliance.

In 1986 the PUSC's Calderón, standing on a platform that advocated opposition to agrarian reform, cuts in public spending and the privatization of state assets, came second in the presidential race to the candidate of the →National Liberation Party (PLN); but the party increased its number of seats in the Assembly. In opposition, the PUSC pressed for the breaking of diplomatic relations with Nicaragua, tax reforms and increased law and order. Calderón finally gained the presidency in February 1990, and the party a majority in the Assembly, promising more moderate economic measures and new social packages for the majority of the population. Instead, the government implemented drastic IMF-approved economic shock measures in June 1990, provoking widespread opposition, particularly from public sector trade unions. Government attempts to form a social pact with the trade unions and business sector failed, as did its attempt to gain public acceptance for a plan to deal with poverty.

As President Calderón's popularity plummeted, many PUSC officials and representatives in the Assembly publicly criticized the government's emphasis on economic readjustment as "excessive" and argued that more pressing social problems were being neglected. Nevertheless, the conditions for a third phase of the government's economic structural readjustment policies were finalized with the IMF in early 1992. The result was that in a close election contest in February 1994, Miguel Angel Rodríguez of the PUSC lost in the presidential race to the PLN candidate by 47.5% to 49.6% of the vote, while PUSC representation in the Assembly fell to 25 seats.

However, indicative of the genuinely two-party nature of Costa Rican democracy in the 1990s, the PUSC returned to power in February 1998, when Miguel Angel Rodriguez narrowly defeated his PLN opponent by 46.6 to 44.6% of the vote, winning the presidency with a smaller percentage than he had achieved in losing in 1994. The PUSC also again became the dominant party in the Assembly with 27 seats.

In stark contrast with the selection of a 2002 presidential candidate by the PLN, the contest within the PUSC was bitter and divisive. In February 2001 former President Calderón (1990-94) accused leading contender Abel Pacheco of emotional instability, triggering much insult-slinging and allegations of fraud. In the event, 67-year-old Pacheco beat off the challenge of the slightly younger Rodolfo Méndez Mata with a landslide victory. However, Méndez conceded defeat without mentioning his opponent's name, let alone endorsing his candidacy.

The PUSC is a member of the Christian Democrat International and of the Christian Democrat Organization of America.

Other Parties

Smaller parties appear and fold with great frequency. In addition many parties operate purely at the regional and local levels. Of the parties listed below, those that put up candidates in the 1998 presidential elections collectively received less than 2% of the votes.

Costa Rican Sun Movement Social Party (*Partido Social Costarricense Movimiento del Sol*), formed in late 1998 by a breakaway group of the →National Liberation Party, promising to fight the 2002 elections on the basis of a less selfish and instrumental brand of politics.
Leadership. Walter Coto

Democratic Party (*Partido Democráta, PD*), won 1.5% of the vote in the 1998 Assembly elections, with its presidential candidate, coming sixth and last with 1%. It calls for Costa Rican solutions to Costa Rican problems and autonomous development.
Leadership. Alvaro González Espinosa (1998 presidential candidate)

Independent Party (*Partido Independiente, PI*)**,** declaring itself to be neither of the right nor the left but in an "uncontaminated space", seeking to appeal to those who want change but who reject extremism.
Leadership. Eugenio Jiménez Sancho

National Christian Alliance (*Alianza Nacional Cristiana, ANC*), formed in 1981 with an explicitly Christian orientation; fought the 1998 election campaign on the basis of combating excessive state bureaucracy and greater stakeholder involvement in government decisions.
Leadership. Víctor Hugo González Montero

National Independent Party (*Partido Nacional Independiente, PNI*), promises a government free from outside influence and employing those with the qualities necessary to lead a "moral and spiritual" regeneration of Costa Rican society.
Leadership. Jorge González Marten

National Recovery (*Rescate Nacional, RN*), originally known as the Patriotic Front and registered with the election tribunal in 1997. It stands for a rejection of liberal economics.
Leadership. Marina Volio Brenes

New Democratic Party (*Nuevo Partido Democrático, NPD*) Seeks democratic, pluralist and popular changes as a genuine alternative to the two main parties.
Leadership. Rodrigo Gutiérrez Scwanhäuser

United People (*Pueblo Unido, PU*), left-wing alliance which won 1.1% in the 1998 Assembly elections, linked politically to the →Democratic Force Party.
Address. Calle 4, Avdas 7 y 9, San José
Telephone. (+506) 223–0032
Leadership. Alberto Salom Echeverría

Côte d'Ivoire

Capital: Abidjan

Population: 15,980,000 (2000E)

The Republic of Côte d'Ivoire achieved independence from France in 1960 and was a de facto one-party state until 1990, when a multi-party system was introduced. Executive power is vested in the President, who is directly elected for a renewable seven-year term (extended from five years under constitutional changes in 1998) by universal adult suffrage of those aged 21 and over and who appoints the Prime Minister and Council of Ministers. A controversial electoral code enacted in December 1994 (and reinforced in 2000) required all future presidential candidates to be Ivorian by birth and born of Ivorian parents, never to have renounced Ivorian citizenship and to have resided in the country for at least five years up to the election. Legislative authority is vested in a unicameral National Assembly (*Assemblée Nationale*) of 225 members (increased from 175 for the December 2000–January 2001 elections), who are elected on a constituency basis, also for a five-year term.

The official results of presidential elections held on Oct. 22, 1995 (but boycotted by most opposition parties), showed a turnout of less than 50% and a victory for incumbent Henri Konan-Bédié of the Democratic Party of Côte d'Ivoire (PDCI), who was credited with 95.3% of the vote. Assembly elections on Nov. 26, 1995, resulted in an overwhelming number of seats for the PDCI.

During the second half of 1999 the political atmosphere in Côte d'Ivoire deteriorated rapidly. Violent clashes between the security forces and opposition Rally of Republicans (RDR) supporters led to the arrest and detention of RDR leaders. On Dec. 24, 1999, 40 years of civilian rule came to an abrupt end as a military coup led by Gen. Robert Guei ousted the Konan-Bédié regime. A government of national unity was formed and Gen. Guei pledged an early return to democracy, a revised constitution being endorsed in a referendum in July 2000.

In early October 2000 the Constitutional Chamber of the Supreme Court ruled that only five of 19 originally nominated candidates for presidential elections later that month were eligible to stand. The main exclusions were RDR leader Alassane Ouattara (on nationality grounds) and PDCI candidate Claude Bombet, whose parties jointly represented some two-thirds of the electorate. The Oct. 22 polling was fought chiefly between Gen. Guei and the Ivorian Popular Front (FPI) leader, Laurent Gbagbo. Guei's attempt to claim victory led to a popular uprising by Gbagbo's supporters who successfully ousted Guei and his forces from power. The National Electoral Commission subsequently declared Gbagbo the winner with 60% of the vote. Further violence between FPI and RDR followers ensued in late October before Ouattara acknowledged Gbagbo's election victory and his new civilian administration.

Legislative elections were held on Dec. 10, 2000, and Jan. 14, 2001, again in controversial circumstances as Ouattara was once more disqualified from standing by the Supreme Court, resulting in a divisive RDR boycott of the polls. In the final results the FPI took 96 seats and the PDCI 94, with the remainder shared between minor parties and independent candidates.

Democratic Party of Côte d'Ivoire
Parti Démocratique de la Côte d'Ivoire (PDCI)

Address. c/o Assemblée Nationale, Abidjan

Leadership. Laurent Dona-Fologo (general secretary)

The PDCI was founded in 1946 as the local section of the pro-independence movement of French West Africa called the African Democratic Rally (*Rassemblement Démocratique Africain*, RDA), which designation is still a suffix of the PCDI's full official title. The party's Ivorian founder, Félix Houphouët-Boigny, sat in the French National Assembly from 1946 to 1959 (also holding ministerial office during this period), before returning home to lead Côte d'Ivoire to independence in 1960. For the next 30 years the PDCI was the only authorized party, although a one-party system was never formalized by law. Every five years a PDCI congress would draw up a list of Assembly candidates for endorsement by the electorate and would also renominate Houphouët-Boigny as the sole presidential candidate. By 1990 he had served six consecutive terms and was Africa's longest-serving head of state, running an administration committed to a free enterprise system, open access for Western capitalists and close relations with France (which remained Côte d'Ivoire's financial and military guarantor).

Bowing to a new wind of change in black Africa, Houphouët-Boigny in May 1990 publicly endorsed a transition to multi-partyism. The change was approved by a PDCI congress in October 1990, when changes in the party's structure were also agreed, including the revival of the post of general secretary (abolished in 1980) and the creation of an 80-member central committee with executive responsibilities. The congress also again endorsed Houphouët-Boigny as the PDCI candidate in the presidential election due later that month, resisting internal pressure from the party's "new guard" for the nomination of Henri Konan-Bédié, who as Assembly president was next in line to the President under a 1985 constitutional amendment. Houphouët-Boigny was duly re-elected with nearly 82% of the popular vote (according to official figures), defeating a candidate of the →Ivorian Popular Front (FPI), who claimed that the elections had been fraudulent. In multi-party Assembly elections in November 1990, the PDCI swept to a landslide victory, winning 163 of the 175 seats, although again the results were disputed by the FPI. The PDCI therefore remained in power, despite a sharp deterioration in economic and social conditions since the late 1980s.

The move to multi-partyism served to reveal long-suppressed tribal divisions within the PDCI, reflecting broader tensions between Côte d'Ivoire's predominantly Muslim north and the Christian south of Houphouët-Boigny. The election of Laurent Dona-Fologo as party general secretary in April 1991 was in line with the President's ruling that the post should be held by someone not from his own ethnic background. Nevertheless, tension increased between heir apparent Konan-Bédié (a southerner) and then Prime Minister Alassane Ouattara (a northern Muslim), being sharpened by the death of Houphouët-Boigny in December 1993. An attempt by Ouattara to assume supreme power (with army backing) was successfully resisted by Konan-Bédié (with French backing), who proceeded to appoint a new Prime Minister and was succeeded as Assembly president by Charles Donwahi of the PDCI. Thereafter, the PDCI government resisted calls from some opposition parties for a national conference to determine the country's future political structure.

In April 1994 President Konan-Bédié was unanimously elected PDCI chairman, thus ensuring his candidacy for the ruling party in the 1995 presidential elections. The following month Ouattara resigned from the PDCI and subsequently became identified with the breakaway →Rally of Republicans. Assisted by the enactment in December 1994 of new presidential qualifications that effectively barred Ouattara from being able to stand, Konan-Bédié won 95.3% of the vote in the presidential elections of October 1995, his only opponent being a candidate of the →Ivorian Workers' Party. The following month the PDCI retained its overwhelming majority in the Assembly.

In the wake of serious civil unrest, 40 years of PDCI rule was brought to an end in December 1999 as President Konan-Bédié was deposed by Gen. Robert Guei in a military coup. Under subsequent plans for a return to representative government, presidential elections were scheduled for the autumn of 2000. Claude Bombet was selected as the PDCI candidate, but he was declared ineligible by the Supreme Court, prompting a PDCI boycott of the Oct. 22 polling. Gen. Guei's attempt to rig the result led to a popular uprising in support of the FPI candidate, who was subsequently declared the winner. In the legislative elections in December 2000–January 2001, the PDCI won 94 of the 225 seats making it the second largest party in the Assembly.

The PDCI is associated with the International Democrat Union through the Democrat Union of Africa.

Ivorian Popular Front
Front Populaire Ivorien (FPI)

Address. c/o Assemblée Nationale, Abidjan

Website. www.fpi.ci

Leadership. Laurent Gbagbo (chairman); Abou Dramane Sangare (secretary-general)

The FPI was founded in France in 1982 by the then exiled Laurent Gbagbo (a history professor), who was granted an amnesty on his return in September 1988 but was harassed by the authorities in his moves to establish the party in Côte d'Ivoire. At its founding (illegal) congress in November 1989, the FPI committed itself to a mixed economy with a private sector emphasis, thus placing itself to the left of the ruling →Democratic Party of Côte d'Ivoire (PDCI). Legalized in May 1990, the FPI became the acknowledged leader of an opposition coalition which included the →Ivorian Workers' Party, the →Ivorian Socialist Party and the Union of Social Democrats. This coalition endorsed Gbagbo's candidature for the October 1990 presidential elections, as agreed the previous month by the first legal FPI congress. But sparse finance and organization compared with the resources of the PDCI contributed to Gbagbo's heavy defeat, the official results showing support of less than 18% for the FPI candidate. This outcome was hotly disputed by the FPI, which also denounced alleged government fraud in Assembly elections the following month, when the FPI was awarded only nine of the 175 seats. Its support in that contest came mainly from the north-east of the country and from the more affluent districts of Abidjan.

Amid growing popular unrest in 1991, the FPI declined to endorse a call by other opposition parties for a national conference to determine the future political structure; instead, it demanded the outright resignation of Houphouët-Boigny and announced a campaign of civil disobedience. Arrested in February 1992 amid anti-government demonstrations in Abidjan, Gbagbo and his chief lieutenant, Mollé Mollé, were sentenced the following month to two years' imprisonment, but were amnestied in July 1992 on the recommendation of the President. In October 1992 the FPI launched a new attack on the government for its failure to deal with the deteriorating economic and social situation; but it remained outside an opposition front of 15 other parties formed in December 1992. In the prelude to the death of Houphouët-Boigny in December 1993, the FPI publicly backed the Assembly president, Henri Konan-Bédié (PDCI), for the succession as provided for under constitutional law. However, when newly-installed President Konan-Bédié failed to offer Gbagbo the premiership, the FPI rejected his proposal that it should join a coalition with the PDCI and returned to opposition mode, although it did not join the →Group for Solidarity formed by 19 opposition parties in April 1994.

In December 1994 Gbagbo was endorsed as the FPI candidate in the 1995 presidential elections, but the party subsequently decided to boycott the contest. The FPI assailed the new presidential qualifications code as being "xenophobic and dangerous", joining with the →Rally of Republicans in mounting anti-government demonstrations. In June 1995 an FPI leader, Abou Dramane Sangare, was beaten by police while in the office of the Security Minister; the same month the pro-FPI weekly *La Patrie* was suspended for three months and two of its journalists were sent to prison after being convicted of conspiring to give offence to the President. Having not contested the October 1995 presidential contest, the FPI won 12 seats in the following month's Assembly elections.

A military coup brought an end to the PDCI government of President Konan-Bédié in December 1999 following serious civil unrest. Under subsequent plans for a return to representative government, presidential elections were scheduled for the autumn of 2000. Gbagbo was again selected as the FPI candidate, his eligibility to stand being approved (unlike other leading opposition figures) by the Supreme Court. After a successful popular uprising by FPI supporters against the attempt by the incumbent, Gen. Guei, to manipulate the results of the Oct. 22 polling, Gbagbo was declared the winner with about 60% of the vote by the National Electoral Commission. Despite further street violence, Gbagbo's victory was subsequently acknowledged by the other main parties and he nominated a new government. In the legislative elections in December 2000–January 2001, the FPI won 96 of the 225 seats making it the largest party in the Assembly.

Strongly based in the trade union movement, the FPI is a member of the Socialist International.

Ivorian Workers' Party
Parti Ivorien des Travailleurs (PIT)

Address. c/o Assemblée Nationale, Abidjan
Leadership. Francis Wodié (leader)

The left-of-centre PIT achieved legalization in May 1990 and joined a pro-democracy opposition alliance headed by the →Ivorian Popular Front (FPI), backing the latter's unsuccessful candidate in the October 1992 presidential elections. In Assembly elections the following month the PIT was the only opposition party apart from the FPI to gain representation, Wodié winning a seat in the affluent Cocody suburb of Abidjan. Three PIT leaders were among those sentenced to prison terms in March 1992 for their participation in anti-government demonstrations the previous month, although all the detainees were amnestied four months later. Thereafter the PIT and the FPI drifted apart, with the latter declining to endorse the former's demand for a fullscale national conference to decide the country's future political system.

In December 1992 the PIT joined with 14 other opposition parties (excluding the FPI) in an alliance called the Union of Democratic Forces. Shortly before President Houphouët-Boigny's death in December 1993, the PIT and five other parties called for the creation of a transitional all-party government. Wodié was the only opposition candidate in the October 1995 presidential election, being credited with 3.8% of the vote. He also contested the October 2000 presidential poll, attracting 5.7% of the vote. In the subsequent legislative elections in December 2000–January 2001, the PIT won four seats.

Rally of Republicans
Rassemblement des Républicains (RDR)

Leadership. Alassane Ouattara (president); Henriette Diabate (secretary-general)

The RDR was formally launched in October 1994 by a dissident faction of the ruling →Democratic Party of Côte d'Ivoire (PDCI) consisting mainly of "old guard" elements. Claiming to have the support of 31 Assembly deputies, the new party was joined by several former PDCI ministers. Its posters featured pictures of Alassane Ouattara, the former (northern Muslim) Prime Minister who had resigned from the PDCI in May 1994 six months after losing the power struggle for the succession to President Houphouët-Boigny. Ouattara had then taken up a post with the IMF in Washington and was thought likely to be the RDR candidate in the 1995 presidential elections. However, he was effectively barred from standing because his previous alleged citizenship of Burkina Faso and overseas residence ran foul of a new qualifications code enacted in December 1994 by the PDCI Assembly majority. In the run-up to the elections, the RDR took a prominent role in anti-government demonstrations calling in particular for the electoral code to be rescinded. Having not contested the October 1995 presidential elections, the RDR won 13 seats out of 175 in the following month's balloting for the Assembly.

From August 1999 violent clashes between the security forces and RDR supporters led to the arrest and detention of RDR leaders, including secretary-general Henriette Diabate. On Dec. 24, 1999, 40 years of civilian rule in Côte d'Ivoire came to an end as a military coup led by Gen. Robert Guei ousted the PDCI regime. Under subsequent plans for a return to representative government, presidential elections were scheduled for the autumn of 2000. In early October 2000 the Constitutional Chamber of the Supreme Court ruled Ouattara was ineligible to stand, again on nationality grounds. RDR supporters boycotted the Oct. 22 poll, and later clashed with Ivorian Popular Front (FPI) followers whose leader successfully claimed victory against the incumbent, Gen. Guei, after a popular uprising. Ouattara recognized the FPI's presidential victory, but was again disqualified from standing in the December 2000–January 2001 legislative polling by the Supreme Court, prompting a further RDR electoral boycott.

Other Parties

Group for Solidarity (*Groupement pour la Solidarité, GPS*), created in April 1994 as an alliance of 19 centre-left opposition parties under the leadership of the chairman of the Alliance for Social Democracy (ASD); it included the →Ivorian Workers' Party (PIT), which had one seat in the National Assembly. The GPS was a broader successor to the Union of Democratic Forces (*Union des Forces Démocratiques*, UFD), created in December 1992 as an alliance of 15 opposition parties headed by the PIT. The main opposition →Ivorian Popular Front did not join either alliance because it disagreed with the other opposition parties' demand for a sovereign national conference to draw up a new political structure for Côte d'Ivoire.
Leadership. Achi Kouman (ASD)

Ivorian Communist Party (*Parti Communiste Ivoirien, PCI*), registered in 1990.Ivorian Socialist Party (Parti Socialiste Ivoirien, PSI), led by a former vice-president of the National Assembly, registered in 1990.
Leadership. Mandaouadjoa Koukakou

National Union for Democracy (*Union National pour la Démocratie, UND*), founded in 1990.

Party for Social Progress (*Parti pour le Progrès Social, PPS*), registered in 1990, based in the Djoula ethnic group.
Leadership. Bamba Morifère

Rally for National Consensus, launched in May 2000 to support the candidature of Gen. Robert Guei in the presidential election later that year.
Leadership. Souleymane Coulibaly

Union for Democracy and Peace (UDP), founded in February 2001, seeking to liberalize the economy, attract foreign investment and promote regional co-operation.
Leadership. Paul Yao Akoto

Croatia

Capital: Zagreb

Population: 4,280,000 (2000E)

The Republic of Croatia declared independence from the Socialist Federal Republic of Yugoslavia in June 1991 and was admitted to UN membership in May 1992. Meanwhile, hostilities between Croatian forces and the Serb-dominated Yugoslav Federal Army had resulted in the declaration of what became the Republic of Serbian Krajina in Serb-populated areas of Croatia. The pre-independence ethnic composition of the republic was Croats 74.6% and Serbs 11.3%, with Muslims, Slovenes, Hungarians, Italians and Czechs forming small locally-significant other minorities. A census conducted in early 2001 showed that the ethnic Serb minority had fallen to only 5% of the population.

The 1990 constitution provided for a presidential form of government, with the President as head of the executive branch. However, under amendments approved in November 2000, Croatia moved to a system of parliamentary democracy under which the Prime Minister and Cabinet became fully accountable to the legislature, which could only be dissolved by the President on its recommendation. The President nevertheless retained substantial powers in the foreign and security policy spheres and continued to be directly elected for a five-year term. Legislative authority is vested in the Parliament (*Sabor*), which under the constitutional amendments promulgated in March 2001 became unicameral (having previously consisted of an upper Chamber of Districts and a lower Chamber of Representatives). The legislature has up to 151 members elected for a four-year term, 140 by proportional representation from multi-member constituencies, up to six to represent Croatians abroad and five to represent ethnic minorities whose share of the population is at least 8%.

Under legislation first enacted in 1993, state financial support is available to all parties represented in the *Sabor* in proportion to their number of members, the current arrangements specifying that the total sum available in a given year is equivalent to 0.056% of central state expenditure in the previous year. The total sum available to the parties in 2000 was 19.2 million kuna (about $2.4 million).

Elections to the House of Representatives on Jan. 2–3, 2000, resulted as follows: alliance of the Social Democratic Party of Croatia (SPH), the Croatian Social Liberal Party (HSLS), the Littoral and Highland Region Alliance (PGS) and the Slavonia and Baranja Croatian Party (SBHS) 71 seats (with 38.7% of the vote); Croatian Democratic Union (HDZ) 40 (26.7%); United List of the Croatian Peasant Party (HSS), the Istrian Democratic Assembly (IDS), the Croatian People's Party (HNS) and the Liberal Party (LS) 25 (14.7%); alliance of the Croatian Party of Rights (HSP) and the Croatian Christian Democratic Union (HKDU) 5 (5.2%); ethnic minority communities 5 and Croatians resident abroad 6.

In presidential elections on Jan. 24 and Feb. 7, 2000, the HNS candidate, Stjepan Mesić, headed the first round with 41.1%, against 27.7% for Dražen Budiša of the HSLS (and backed by the SPH) and 22.5% for Mate Granić of the HDZ, who was therefore eliminated. In the second round Mesić defeated Budiša by 56% to 44%.

Croatian Christian Democratic Union
Hrvatska Kršćanska Demokratska Unija (HKDU)
Address. Tkalčićeva 4/1, 10000 Zagreb
Telephone. (+385–1) 424111
Fax. (+385–1) 422494
Website. www.posluh.hr/hkdu

Leadership. Ivan Cesar (president)
The right-wing HKDU was formed in December 1992 as a merger of the Croatian Christian Democratic Party (HKDS) led by Ivan Cesar and a faction of the →Croatian Democratic Party (HDS) led by Marko Veselica. Founded in October 1989, the HKDS had won two seats in the 1990 pre-

independence elections and had participated in the subsequent coalition headed by the →Croatian Democratic Union (HDZ). It had failed to win a seat in the lower house elections of August 1992, when Cesar had come seventh out of eight candidates in the presidential balloting with 1.6% of the vote. The HDS had been founded in November 1989 by HDZ dissidents opposed to the parent party's reluctance to reject socialism. It had won nine seats in the 1990 elections but had failed to secure representation in 1992, when Veselica had come sixth in the presidential balloting with 1.7% of the vote.

Having failed to obtain representation in the February 1993 upper house elections, the merged party won one seat in the October 1995 lower house elections, in which it formed part of the centre-right Joint List bloc. The HKDU contested the January 2000 lower house elections in alliance with the nationalist →Croatian Rights Party (HSP), again winning one seat (out of five secured by the alliance).

The HKDU inherited the HKDS's affiliation to the Christian Democrat International.

Croatian Democratic Union
Hrvatska Demokratska Zajednica (HDZ)
Address. Trg Žrtava Fašizma 4, 11000 Zagreb
Telephone. (+385–1) 455–3000
Fax. (+385–1) 455–2600
Email. hdz@hdz.hr
Website. www.hdz.hr
Leadership. Ivo Sanader (president); Vladimir Šeks (parliamentary group chairman); Joso Škara (secretary-general)
Formally launched in June 1989 in opposition to the then communist regime, the HDZ spearheaded the drive both to multi-party democracy and to independence from the Yugoslav federation. A nationalist party, it was joined by many of the elite of the Yugoslav regime, although Franjo Tudjman himself, a history professor with a military background, had been a prominent dissident in the 1970s and 1980s. Contesting the 1990 multi-party elections on a pro-autonomy platform, the HDZ won a landslide parliamentary majority, by virtue of which Tudjman was elected President in May 1990 by vote of the deputies. The HDZ government secured a 94% pro-independence verdict in a referendum in May 1991 and declared Croatia's independence the following month. In further elections in August 1992, the HDZ retained an overall parliamentary majority and Tudjman was directly re-elected President with 56.7% of the popular vote. Thereafter, the HDZ government was riven by dissension about how to deal with the civil war in neighbouring Bosnia & Hercegovina; also controversial was its maintenance of much of the communist-era panoply of central economic control, despite the party's claim to be of the centre-right. Nevertheless, the HDZ in February 1993 won 37 of the 63 elective seats in the upper house, thereafter accepting the small →Croatian Peasant Party (HSS) into the government.

In October 1993 a special HDZ congress approved a new party programme espousing Christian democracy, describing the HDZ as the guarantor of Croatian independence and defining the liberation of Serb-held Croatian territory as the government's most important task. In addition to re-electing Tudjman as party president, the congress elected the hardline nationalist Defence Minister, Gojko Sušak, as vice-president but also, on Tudjman's urging, replaced some other hardliners with moderates on the HDZ presidium. But the impact of this move was diminished by Tudjman's proposal that Jasenovac in southern (Serb-held) Croatia, site of the camp where the wartime pro-Nazi *Ustaša* regime had exterminated Serbs, Jews and Gypsies, should also commemorate "all the victims of communism" (including *Ustaša* officials executed after the war) as well as the Croatian dead in the 1991 war with Serbia. In February 1994 President Tudjman publicly apologized for having, in an earlier book, doubted the veracity of received accounts of the Nazi extermination of Jews during World War II; the following month he also apologized for the role of the *Ustaša* regime in such extermination.

In April 1994 the HDZ was weakened by the formation of the breakaway →Croatian Independent Democrats by liberal elements which favoured alliance with the Muslims of Bosnia & Hercegovina against the Serbs and also objected to Tudjman's dictatorial tendencies. Further internal conflict was evident in the resignations of two prominent HDZ hardliners in September 1994, Vladimir Šeks (as Deputy Prime Minister) and Branimir Glavaš (as party chairman in Osijek), in what appeared to be the start of a purge of the party's radical right wing. Nevertheless, Šeks's popularity among HDZ deputies was demonstrated the following month when he was elected HDZ leader in the lower house. Buoyed by Croat military successes against the Serbs, the HDZ retained an overall majority in lower house elections in October 1995, although short of the two-thirds majority required for constitutional amendments and with a vote share of 45.2%. The party also retained its majority in the upper house in April 1997, following which Tudjman was re-elected President two months later with 61.4% of the vote.

In the late 1990s, as Tudjman's health deteriorated, the HDZ became increasingly divided between hardliners and moderates, amidst rising popular discontent with economic and social conditions. Following Tudjman's death in December 1999, the HDZ was heavily defeated in Assembly elections in early January 2000, retaining only 40 of the 151 seats (with 26.7% of the vote) and going into opposition to a centre-left government headed by the →Social Democratic Party of Croatia. In presidential elections in late January, moreover, outgoing Deputy Premier and Foreign Minister Mate Granić failed to overcome the HDZ's new unpopularity, despite resigning his party offices on the eve of polling, and was eliminated in the first round with only 22.5% of the vote.

In unaccustomed opposition, the HDZ was further weakened by an exodus of leading members, including Granić in March 2000, as evidence began to emerge of extensive corruption under the Tudjman regime. In April 2000 the party presidency was conferred on Ivo Sanader, reputedly a moderate nationalist, who set as his first objective the restoration of the HDZ's public image. In November 2000 HDZ deputies unsuccessfully opposed the conversion of Croatia into a parliamentary democracy.

Claiming a membership of over 400,000, the HDZ is affiliated to the Christian Democrat International and has observer status in the European People's Party and European Democrat Union.

Croatian Party of Rights
Hrvatska Stranka Prava (HSP)
Address. Primorska 5, 10000 Zagreb
Telephone. (+385–1) 377–8016
Fax. (+385–1) 377–8736
Email. hsp@zg.tel.hr
Website. www.hsp.hr
Leadership. Boris Kandare (president); Anto Djapić (parliamentary group chairman)
Descended indirectly from a pre-war nationalist party of the same name, the far-right HSP was founded in February 1990 by Dobroslav Paraga and had considerable support among Croats outside Croatia. It advocates "national-state sovereignty throughout the whole of [Croatia's] historical and ethnic space", which has been taken to imply a territorial claim not just to the Croat-populated areas of Bosnia-Hercegovina but to the whole of that state. To these ends, the party formed a military wing called the Croatian Defence Association (*Hrvatski Obrambeni Savez*, HOS), which became heavily involved on the Croat side in interethnic conflict in Bosnia (and was seen by many as the modern counterpart of the wartime pro-fascist *Ustaša* movement). The party won five lower house seats in the August 1992 elections and Paraga came fourth in the concurrent presidential contest, winning 5.4% of the national vote. It failed to win a seat in the February 1993 upper house

elections, after which Paraga and three other HSP leaders were charged with terrorism and inciting forcible changes to the constitutional order. The government also applied to the Constitutional Court for a ban on the HSP.

In July 1993 Zagreb police evicted the party from its headquarters in the capital, on the grounds that its occupation of the state-owned building since 1991 was illegal. Steps were also taken by the authorities to curtail the independence of the HOS by integrating its forces into units controlled by the Defence Ministry. Meanwhile, Paraga had come under criticism for his leadership, this resulting in his being replaced by Kandare at an extraordinary congress in September 1993, when a new main committee was elected as the party's governing body. Having been acquitted of the charges against him in November 1993, Paraga proceeded to form the new →Croatian Party of Rights 1861. In the October 1995 lower house elections the HSP just surmounted the 5% representation threshold winning five seats.

In the January 2000 parliamentary elections the HSP was allied with the →Croatian Christian Democratic Union (HKDU), their joint list winning 5.2% and five seats, four of which went to the HSP. In the presidential elections later the same month HSP-HKDU candidate Anto Djapić took only 1.8% of the first-round vote.

Croatian Peasant Party
Hrvatska Seljačka Stranka (HSS)
Address. Ulica Kralja Zvonimira 17, 10000 Zagreb
Telephone. (+385–1) 455–3624
Fax. (+385–1) 455–3631
Email. hss-sredisnjica@hss.hr
Website. www.hss.hr
Leadership. Zlatko Tomčić (president); Stjepan Radić & Ivan Stančer (deputy presidents); Luka Trconić (parliamentary group chairman); Stanko Grčić (general secretary)
The HSS is descended from a co-operative party founded by the Radić brothers in 1904, which became a standard-bearer of Croat nationalism in inter-war Yugoslavia but was suppressed by the wartime pro-Nazi *Ustaša* regime in Croatia. Revived in November 1989 and committed to pacifism, local democracy, privatization and rural co-operatives, the HSS won three seats in the August 1992 lower house elections and five in the February 1993 upper house balloting. It then effectively entered a coalition with the then ruling →Croatian Democratic Union (HDZ). On succeeding Drago Stipac as HSS president in December 1994, however, Zlatko Tomčić vacated his post as Minister of Urban Planning, Housing and Construction. In the October 1995 lower house elections the HSS won 10 seats as part of the opposition Joint List (ZL) bloc.

In the January 2000 lower house elections the HSS was again part of the ZL, which included the →Istrian Democratic Assembly, the →Liberal Party and the →Croatian People's Party (HNS). The HSS took 16 of the 25 seats won by the alliance and obtained two portfolios (including agriculture) in the new centre-left coalition government headed by the →Social Democratic Party of Croatia. In addition, Tomčić was elected president of the new chamber. In presidential elections in January-February 2000 the HSS backed the successful candidacy of Stjepan Mesić of the HNS.

Croatian People's Party
Hrvatska Narodna Stranka (HNS)
Address. Ilica 61, 10000 Zagreb
Telephone. (+385–1) 484–6106
Fax. (+385–1) 484–6109
Email. hns@hns.hr
Website. www.hns.hr
Leadership. Vesna Pusić (president); Radimir Čačić (president of board); Savka Dabčević-Kučar (honorary president); Srećko Ferenčal (general secretary)
The HNS was founded in October 1990, although its core leadership had formed a coherent dissident group since the

attempt in 1970–71 to liberalize the then ruling League of Communists of Croatia. It advocates "modernity" in political and economic structures, private enterprise, regionalism and the creation of a "civil society", drawing considerable support from ethnic Serbs. On its creation, it attracted the backing of five Assembly deputies elected under other labels in 1990 and in the August 1992 elections it won six lower house seats, while its president came third in the concurrent presidential contest with 6% of the national vote. In the February 1993 upper house elections the HNS won one of the elective seats. For the October 1995 lower house elections it was part of the centre-right Joint List (ZL) bloc, winning two seats.

The HNS retained its two lower house seats in the January 2000 parliamentary elections, again standing as part of the ZL, which included the →Croatian Peasant Party, the →Istrian Democratic Assembly and the →Liberal Party. One HNS minister was appointed to the resultant centre-left government headed by the →Social Democratic Party of Croatia. The HNS also secured the election of its vice-chairman, Stjepan Mesić, as President of Croatia in the subsequent presidential elections, in which he stood as the HNS/ZL candidate. Against most initial predictions, Mesić led in the first round with 41.1% of the vote and was elected in the second with 56%.

Croatian Social Liberal Party
Hrvatska Socijalno Liberalna Stranka (HSLS)
Address. Trg Nikole Šubića Zrinskog 17/1, 10000 Zagreb
Telephone. (+385–1) 481–0401
Fax. (+385–1) 481–0404
Email. hsls@hsls.hr
Website. www.hsls.hr
Leadership. Dražen Budiša (president); Djurdja Adlešić (parliamentary group chairman); Dorica Nikolić (secretary-general)
The HSLS was founded in May 1989 as a liberal party on the classic European model, emphasizing the "democratic and European tradition and orientation of Croatia". Having made little impact in the 1990 pre-independence elections, it became the second-strongest party in the lower house elections of August 1992, winning 14 seats, while its president took second place in the simultaneous presidential contest with 21.9% of the national vote. In the February 1993 upper house elections, the party won 16 of the 63 elective seats. Opposed to the government of the →Croatian Democratic Union (HDZ), the HSLS participated in an opposition boycott of parliament from May to September 1994 in protest against irregularities in the election of new presidents of the two houses in the wake of the formation of the →Croatian Independent Democrats. In the October 1995 lower house elections the party took 11.6% of the vote and 12 seats, confirming its status as the strongest single opposition party.

For the January 2000 Assembly elections, the HSLS was allied with the →Social Democratic Party of Croatia (SPH), together with two small regional formations, and won 24 seats in the anti-HDZ victory. The party was allocated six portfolios in the resultant six-party coalition government headed by the SPH. In the presidential elections three weeks later HSLS chairman Dražen Budiša, backed by the SPH, took second place in the first round with 27.7% of the vote and therefore contested the second round in early February, but was defeated by the candidate of the →Croatian People's Party (HNS) by 44% to 56%.

Claiming a membership of 15,000, the HSLS is a member of the Liberal International and an associate member of the European Liberal, Democratic and Reformist (ELDR) organization.

Istrian Democratic Assembly
Istarski Demokratski Sabor (IDS)
Sieta Democratica Istriana (SDI)
Address. Splitska 3, 52100 Pula
Telephone. (+385–52) 23316

Fax. (+385–52) 213702
Email. ids-ddi@pu.tel.hr
Leadership. Ivan Jakovčić (president); Damir Kajin (parliamentary group chairman)

The centre-right IDS confines its activities to the Istrian region, where it represents the aspirations of ethnic Italians and other minorities, advocating the creation of a "transborder" Istria encompassing Croatian, Slovenian and Italian areas. It has been especially exercised by Croatian-Slovenian border definition issues and by the Croatian-Italian dispute over compensation for Italians who left Yugoslavia in the wake of the Istrian territorial gains by the latter after World War II.

In the August 1992 lower house elections, the IDS was allied with →Dalmatian Action and the →Rijeka Democratic League in a regionalist front, winning four of the six seats taken by the alliance. In the February 1993 upper house elections the IDS won one elective seat and was allocated two more under the President's prerogative. In the same month it won 72% of the Istrian vote in local elections. In the October 1995 lower house elections it formed part of the centre-right Joint List bloc (ZL), winning four seats.

The IDS remained part of the ZL alliance in the January 2000 lower house elections, winning four of the ZL's 25 seats. The party subsequently joined the new government headed by the →Social Democratic Party of Croatia (SPH), its chairman becoming Minister for European Integration. In June 2001, however, the party withdrew from the ruling coalition, complaining that the government was almost as hostile to regional autonomy as the previous Tudjman regime had been.

Liberal Party
Liberalna Stranka (LS)

Address. Ilica 16/I, 10000 Zagreb
Telephone. (+385–1) 483–3896
Fax. (+385–1) 483–3799
Email. liberali@bbm.hr
Website. www.liberali.hr
Leadership. Zlatko Kramarić (leader); Vesna Pusić (parliamentary group chairperson); Helena Štimac Radin (secretary general)

The centrist LS was founded in February 1998 by unsuccessful 1997 presidential candidate Vlado Gotovac after he had been ousted from the leadership of the →Croatian Social Liberal Party (HSLS). In the January 2000 parliamentary elections the party was part of the Joint List (ZL) alliance headed by the →Croatian Peasant Party, obtaining two seats and one ministerial post in the resultant six-party coalition government headed by the →Social Democratic Party of Croatia (SPH). At the party's second congress in October 2000, Zlatko Kramarić was elected LS chairman in succession to Gotovac, who died two months later.

Claiming a membership of 4,500, the LS is a member of the Liberal International and an associate member of the European Liberal, Democratic and Reformist (ELDR) organization.

Littoral and Highland Region Alliance
Primorsko Goranski Savez (PGS)

Address. Ciottina 19, 51000 Rijeka
Telephone. (+385–51) 335359
Fax. (+385–51) 335418
Email. pgs@kvarner.net
Leadership. Nikola Ivanić (president and parliamentary group chairman); Franjo Butorac (secretary)

The PGS was established in September 1996 as the successor to the Rijeka Democratic League (*Riječki Demokratski Savez*, RDS), which had been founded in 1990 as a pro-market left-of-centre formation based in the ethnic Italian population of Rijeka to articulate issues of cultural expression, minority rights and education. The RDS had contested the August 1992 lower house elections in a regionalist alliance with →Dalmatian Action and the

→Istrian Democratic Assembly, winning one of the six seats accruing to that alliance. It retained representation in the October 1995 elections.

The change of name to the PGS reflected the party's aspiration to broaden its base beyond its ethnic Italian base in the city of Rijeka and surrounding area. In the January 2000 lower house elections the PGS was part of the victorious alliance headed by the →Social Democratic Party of Croatia (SPH), obtaining two seats. However, the resultant SPH-led government's declared commitment to regional autonomy and minority rights came under question within the PGS.

Serbian People's Party
Srpska Narodna Stranka (SNS)

Address. Trg Mažuranićev 3, 10000 Zagreb
Telephone. (+385–1) 485–5631
Fax. (+385–1) 485–5631
Leadership. Milan Dukić (president)

Founded in May 1991, the SNS represents ethnic Serbs who regard Croatia as their homeland and rejects separatist solutions. Although Croatia's Serb-populated areas were in 1991 largely outside the control of the Zagreb government, the SNS won three seats in the August 1992 lower house elections. In mid-1995 the party's support base was sharply reduced by the flight of most ethnic Serbs from the Krajina on its recapture by Croatian government forces, while the reduction of guaranteed Serb seats in the lower house narrowed its representative scope.

In October 1995 SNS leader Milan Dukić asserted that at least half of the Krajina's former ethnic Serb population of 250,000 wished to return and condemned the government's rejection of a mass return to the area. In lower house elections in the same month the SNS took two seats. In January 2000 the party won only one seat.

Slavonia and Baranja Croatian Party
Slavonsko-Baranjska Hrvatska Stranka (SBHS)

Address. Županijska 6, 31000 Osijek
Telephone. (+385–31) 200721
Fax. (+385–31) 212122
Email. sbhs@os.tel.hr
Leadership. Damir Jurić (president)

The SBHS mainly represents ethnic Croats in territories occupied by Serbian forces in 1991 but mostly recovered in 1995. The party contested the October 1995 lower house elections as part of the opposition Joint List bloc, winning one seat. In the January 2000 elections the SBHS was part of the victorious alliance headed by the →Social Democratic Party of Croatia (SPH), obtaining one seat.

Social Democratic Party of Croatia
Socijaldemokratska Partija Hrvatske (SPH)

Address. Trg Iblerov 9, 10000 Zagreb
Telephone. (+385–1) 455–2055
Fax. (+385–1) 455–2842
Email. sdp@sdp.tel.hr
Website. www.tel.hr/sdp
Leadership. Ivica Račan (president); Mato Arlović (deputy president and parliamentary group chairman); Željka Antonović (deputy president)

The SPH is descended from the Croatian Communist Party (created in 1937 when Yugoslavia's Communist movement was reorganized by Josip Broz Tito) and from the succeeding League of Communists of Yugoslavia (LCY), created as the ruling party in 1952. Croatian elements were prominent in periodic attempts to liberalize and reform the LCY regime from within; but in the post-1989 move to independence and multi-partyism the Croatian LCY was rapidly sidelined by the rise of the new →Croatian Democratic Union (HDZ). Seen as tainted with "Yugoslavism", the LCY lost much of its membership to the HDZ and other parties, failing to stem the outflow by changing its name to Party of Democratic Reform (SDP) and committing itself to democratic socialism and a market economy. In the 1990 pre-independence elections, the SDP trailed a poor second to the HDZ, winning 75 of the 349 legislative seats in its own right and a further 16 on joint lists with other parties. In further changes in 1991, the SPH title was adopted (the SDP rubric being temporarily retained as a suffix) and the party deferred to pro-independence sentiment by acknowledging Croatia as the "national state of the Croatian people", while stressing the need to accommodate non-Croat groups.

Advocating economic modernization combined with preservation of a welfare state, the SPH-SDP was reduced to 11 seats in the August 1992 lower house elections and failed to secure representation in its own right in the February 1993 upper house balloting, although it was allocated one seat by virtue of a pact with the →Croatian Social Liberal Party (HSLS). It performed better in the October 1995 lower house elections, winning nearly 9% of the vote and 10 seats, while in the June 1997 presidential elections SDP candidate Zdravko Tomac took second place with 21% of the vote.

Following the death of President Tudjman of the HDZ in December 1999, the SPH contested the January 2000 Assembly elections in tandem with the HSLS and two small regional formations. It became the dominant party by winning 44 of the 71 seats won by the alliance (on a 38.7% vote share) and formed a six-party centre-left coalition government headed by SPH chairman Ivica Račan. In immediately succeeding presidential elections, the SPH backed the HSLS candidate in both voting rounds, but applauded the eventual victory of Stjepan Mesić of the →Croatian People's Party, which was a member of the new ruling coalition.

The SPH is a member party of the Socialist International.

Other Parties

The listing below from the multiplicity of minor parties in Croatia focuses on those that contested the January 2000 elections to the Chamber of Representatives.

Croatian Christian Democratic Party (*Hrvatska Kršćanska Demokratska Stranka, HKDS*), founded in 1990, one of several competing Christian democratic formations, associate member of European People's Party.
Address. Ivana 8, 10000 Zagreb
Telephone/Fax. (+385–1) 218847
Email. endom@inet.hr

Croatian Citizens' Peasant Party (*Hrvatska Gradjansko Seljačka Stranka, HGSS*), founded in 1995, seeking to represent the urban and rural middle class.
Address. Poljička 13, 10000 Zagreb
Telephone. (+385–1) 611–0389
Fax. (+385–1) 611–9650

Croatian Dalmatian Home (*Hrvatski Dalmatinski Dom, HDD*), regional party founded in Split in May 1996, represented at district level.
Address. Bana Jelačića 4/II, 21000 Split
Telephone. (+385–21) 343402

Croatian Democratic Party (*Hrvatska Demokratska Stranka, HDS*), the rump formation remaining when then leader Marko Veselica led his supporters into the new →Croatian Christian Democratic Union in December 1992.
Address. Tkalčićeva 4, 10000 Zagreb
Telephone. (+385–1) 422062
Fax. (+385–1) 424111
Leadership. Anto Kovačevic (chairman)

Croatian Democratic Peasant Party (*Hrvatska Demokratska Seljačka Stranka, HDSS*), centre-right rural formation founded in 1994.
Address. Strossmayerova 9, 40000 Čakovec
Telephone/Fax. (+385–40) 364440

Croatian Democratic Republican Party (*Hrvatska Demokratska Republike Stranka, HDRS*), founded in October 2000 as a merger of the Croatian Spring (HP), the National Democratic Party (NDS) and the Croatian Peasants' National Party (HSNS).
Leadership. Josko Kovač (chairman)

Croatian Green Party (*Hrvatska Stranka Zelenih, HSZ*), one of several distinct environmental formations in Croatia.
Address. Aleja A. Augustinčića 18, 10000 Zagreb
Telephone. (+385–1) 233–5853
Fax. (+385–1) 383–0787

Croatian Independent Democrats (*Hrvatski Nezavisni Demokrati, HND*), founded in 1994 by a moderate group of the then ruling →Croation Democratic Union (HDZ) led by Stipe Mesić (then president of the lower house) who accused President Tudjman of authoritarian tendencies and bigotry; in the October 1995 lower house elections the HND returned one candidate in the constituency section, but it failed to secure representation in 2000.
Address. Frankopanska 2, 10000 Zagreb
Telephone. (+385–1) 484–8476
Fax. (+385–1) 484-9089
Leadership. Stipe Mesić (president)

Croatian Party of Pensioners (*Hrvatska Stranka Umirovljenika, HSU*), established in 1996 seeking to promote the interests of the retired.
Address. Trnsko 34a, 10000 Zagreb
Telephone. (+385–1) 652–5170

Croatian Party of Rights 1861 (*Hrvatska Stranka Prava 1861, HSP-1861*), launched in July 1995 by Dobroslav Paraga, former leader of the far-right →Croatian Party of Rights, who had won 5.4% in the 1992 presidential election and who had been acquitted of terrorism and other charges in 1993; taking its name from the foundation year of Croatia's original nationalist party, the HSP-1861 failed to win representation in the 1995 and 2000 elections.
Address. Šenoina 13, 10000 Zagreb
Telephone. (+385–1) 483–9938
Fax. (+385–1) 483–9939
Email. hsp1861@hsp1861.hr
Leadership. Dobroslav Paraga (chairman)

Croatian Peasant Labour Party (*Hrvatska Seljačka Radnička Stranka, HSRS*), left-wing rural party founded in February 1997.
Address. Novo Selo 9, 33404 Špišić Bukovica

Croatian Popular Party (*Hrvatska Pučka Stranka, HPS*), centrist formation founded in December 1997.
Address. Ozaljska 93/II, 10000 Zagreb
Telephone. (+385–1) 363–3606
Fax. (+385–1) 363–3749

Croatian Pure Party of Rights (*Hrvatska Čista Stranka Prava, HCSP*), right-wing formation established in December 1992.
Address. Frankopanska 2/II, 10000 Zagreb
Telephone/Fax. (+385–1) 484–8473

Croatian Republican Union (*Hrvatska Republikanska Zajednica, HRZ*), centre-right party founded in 1991 as successor to a movement founded by Croatian exiles in Argentina in 1951.
Address. Tkalčićeva 71c, 10000 Zagreb
Telephone/Fax. (+385–1) 466–8038
Email. hrz@zg.tel.hr

Dalmatian Action (*Dalmatinska Akcija, DA*), founded in December 1990 to represent the people of Dalmatia (many of them non-Croats), for which it seeks greater autonomy. In

the 1992 lower house elections it participated in a regional-ist alliance with the →Istrian Democratic Assembly and what later became the →Littoral and Highland Region Alliance (PGS), winning one seat. In October 1993 the Zagreb authorities launched a crackdown on DA activists, several of whom were arrested and charged with terrorist offences and illegal possession of arms. The party failed to win representation in the 1995 and 2000 national elections.
Address. Ulica Bana Jelačića 4/I, 21000 Split
Telephone/Fax. (+385–21) 344322
Leadership. Mira Ljubić-Lorger (president)

Green Movement of Croatia (*Zeleni Pokret Hrvatske, ZPH*), launched in March 2001, one of several environmen-talist parties in Croatia.
Address. Nehajeva 17, 23000 Zadar

Green Party (*Zelena Stranka, ZS*), founded in July 1996 as the Green Movement, changed name in 1999, one of several environmentalist parties in Croatia.
Address. Savska Ulica 183, 10000 Zagreb
Telephone/Fax. (+385–1) 302–4074
Email. info@zelena-stranka.hr

Homeland Civic Party (*Domovinska Gradjanska Stranka, DGS*), right-wing formation established in 1992
Address. Savski Gaj III, put br. 12, 10000 Zagreb
Telephone. (+385–1) 652-4988

Independent Democratic Serbian Party (*Samostalna Demokratska Srpska Stranka, SDSS*), founded in Zagreb in 1995, now based in Vukovar, seeking to represent the interests of ethnic Serbs.
Address. Borovo Naselje, Radnički Dom, 32000 Vukovar
Telephone. (+385–32) 65116
Fax. (+385–32) 66177

Istrian Independent Party (*Istarska Nezavisna Stranka, INS*), a regionalist formation established in 1990.
Address. Trg na Iokvi 3, 52210 Rovinj
Telephone/Fax. (+385–52) 816360
Leadership. Franko Šturman (chairman)

Istrian Party (*Istarska Stranka, IS*), a regionalist formation established in 1992.
Address. Flanatička 29, 52100 Pula

Movement for Human Rights – Party of Ecologically Conscious Citizens (*Pokret za Ljudska Prava–Stranka Ekološki Svjesnih Gradjana, POL*), launched in May 1999.
Address. Andrije Žaje 31, 10000 Zagreb
Telephone. (+385–1) 309–2201

Fax. (+385–1) 364–6115
Email. pravda@pol.hr

New Croatia (*Nova Hrvatska, NH*), established in November 1999.
Address. Ulica Grada Vukovara 23/II, 10000 Zagreb

Party of Croatia's Renaissance (*Stranka Hrvatskog Preporoda, SHP*), founded in Split in October 1999.
Address. Cesta Mira 27, 21000 Split
Telephone. (+385–21) 314992
Fax. (+385–21) 523951

Party of Democratic Action of Croatia (*Stranka Demokratske Akcije Hrvatske, SDAH*), Croatian section of the predominantly Muslim →→Party of Democratic Action in Bosnia & Hercegovina, supportive of the rights of Bosniaks in Croatia.
Address. Mandaličina 17, 10000 Zagreb
Telephone. (+385–1) 377–2212
Fax. (+385–1) 377–1288
Email. sdah@sdah.hr

Social Democratic Action of Croatia (*Akcija Socijal-Demokrata Hrvatske, ASH*), founded in June 1994 by vari-ous small left-wing groupings, aiming to mount an electoral challenge independent of the →Social Democratic Party of Croatia, but won only 3.2% in the October 1995 elections; contested January 2000 elections in alliance headed by →Croatian Peasant Party but failed to win a seat.
Address. Gundulićeva 21a/III, 10000 Zagreb
Telephone. (+385–1) 485–4262
Fax. (+385–1) 485–4258
Email. ash@hinet.hr
Leadership. Miko Tripalo (chairman)

Social Democratic Union of Croatia (*Socijalno-demokratska Unija Hrvatske, SDUH*), formed in 1992, won 3.2% in the 1995 lower house elections.
Address. Tratinska 27/1, 10000 Zagreb
Leadership. Branko Horvat (chairman)

Socialist Labour Party of Croatia (*Socijalistička Radnička Partija Hrvatske, SRP*), left-wing formation established in October 1997.
Address. Palmotićeva 70/II, 10000 Zagreb
Telephone. (+385–1) 483–9958
Fax. (+385–1) 483–9826
Email. srp@srp.hr
Leadership. Stipe Šuvar (chairman); Djuro Lazić (general secretary)

Cuba

Capital: Havana
Population: 11,140,000 (2000E)

The Republic of Cuba, ceded by Spain to the United States following the Spanish–American war of 1898, became independent in 1902. The United States, however, retains the right to have military bases on the island (currently the Guantinamo naval base). Under the 1976 constitution (as modified in 1992) executive authority resides with the President of the Council of State, Fidel Castro Ruz, who has held power since January 1959 (fol-lowing the revolutionary overthrow of the Batista regime). Nominal legislative authority is vested in the uni-cameral National Assembly of People's Power (*Asamblea Nacional del Poder Popular,* ANPP), which sits for a five-year term, holds twice-yearly ordinary sessions and elects a Council of State to represent it in the interim. Executive and administrative authority is held by a Council of Ministers, which is appointed by the ANPP upon the recommendation of the President. The majority of office-holders are members of the Communist Party of Cuba (PCC), the only authorized political party.

Direct elections to an enlarged ANPP were held in January 1998. Only candidates nominated by the PCC were permitted to contest the election. Figures released by the National Electoral Commission showed that all 601 PCC candidates for the 601 posts had obtained the necessary 50% of the votes to be elected. The turnout amongst the 8 million registered voters was officially put at 98.35%.

Communist Party of Cuba
Partido Comunista Cubano (PCC)
Address. c/o National Assembly of People's Power, Havana
Website. www3.cuba.cu/politica/webpcc
Leadership. Fidel Castro Ruz (first secretary); Raul Castro Ruz (second secretary)

The PCC was founded in 1961 as the Integrated Revolutionary Organizations (*Organizaciones Revolucionarias Integradas,* ORI), a coalition of the political and military groupings which had defeated the Batista dictatorship in the revolution of 1956–59. The components were Castro's rural guerrilla army, the July 26 Movement (*Movimiento* 26 *de Julio*); the communist Popular Socialist Party *(Partido Socialista Popular,* PSP); and the Revolutionary Directorate *(Directorio Revolucionario,* DR). No other political organizations were permitted to function after 1961. The ORI was transformed into the United Party of the Cuban Socialist Revolution in 1962, and adopted its present name in 1965.

The first PCC congress, held in 1975, approved a party constitution and programme, and the special status of the party as the leading force of society and the state was enshrined in the 1976 constitution. The second congress was held in 1980 and the third in 1986, at which time major changes in structure and personnel were approved. At its fourth congress in 1991, the PCC endorsed direct election to the ANPP, abolished the party secretariat, approved a substantially restructured politburo and removed the requirement that party members must be atheists.

The fifth congress, held in 1997, adopted a cautious programme up to 2002 which re-emphasised the need for political stability. The politburo was reduced from 26 to 24 members and reshuffled. This allowed the promotion of six younger members, but did not affect the body's ideological composition or balance.

Although regionally isolated, both diplomatically and economically (particularly by the United States), the PCC government supported numerous "anti-imperialist" revolutionary movements around the world in the 1960s and 1970s. It maintained close relations with the then Soviet Union and its allies until the demise of their communist regimes at the end of the 1980s. The PCC has since reiterated its continuing hardline commitment to Marxist–Leninist ideology and the revolution.

Illegal Opposition Groups

Christian Democratic Party *(Partido Demócrata Cristiano, PDC),* an affiliate of the Christian Democrat and People's Party International and the Christian Democratic Organization of America.
Address. PO Box 558987, Miami, FL 33155, USA
Email. pdc@pdc-cuba-org
Website. www.pdc-cuba-org
Leadership. Rafael A Sánchez, Siro Del Castillo, José Ignacio Rasco

Cuban Liberal Union (*Unión Liberal Cubana, ULC*), an affiliate of the Liberal International.
Address. Av. Mendendez Pelayo, No. 83 bajo dcha, 28007, Madrid, Spain
Website. www.cubaliberal.org
Leadership. Carlos Alberto Montaner (president)

Cuban Social Revolutionary Democratic Party (*Partido Social Revolucionario Democrático de Cuba*, PSRDC)
Address. PO Box 351081, Miami, FL 33135, USA
Email. soreb123@aol.com

Cuban Socialist Democratic Current (*Corriente Socialista Democrática Cubana, CSDC*)
Address. 5430 W. 7th Ave., Hialeah, FL 33012, USA
Email. micael@netzero.net
Website. www.corriente.org

Democratic Solidarity Party (*Partido Solidaridad Democrática, PSD*), an observer member of the Liberal International.
Address. PO Box 310063, Miami, FL 33131, USA
Email. gladyperez@aol.com
Website. www.ccsi.com~ams/psd/psd.htm
Leadership. Fernando Sánchez Lopez (president)

Liberal Democratic Party (*Partido Liberal Democrático, PLD*), the third Cuban affiliate of the Liberal International.
Leadership. Osvaldo Alfonso Valdes (president)

Cyprus

Capital: Nicosia

Population: 870,000 (2000E, including TRNC)

The Republic of Cyprus achieved independence from the UK in 1960 on the basis of a constitution that involved power sharing between the majority Greek Cypriots and the minority Turkish Cypriots. Guaranteed by the UK, Greece and Turkey, this arrangement broke down by 1964, amid an escalation of inter-communal conflict. In 1974 the territorial division between the two communities was solidified by the military intervention of Turkey, whose forces facilitated the effective partition of the island into a Greek Cypriot sector and what in 1983 became the Turkish Republic of Northern Cyprus (TRNC). The TRNC's self-proclaimed "independence" in about 40% of the island's area has been recognized only by Turkey. UN-sponsored talks, aimed at producing a federal settlement which preserved Cyprus as one sovereign state, had made no substantive progress by mid-2001. Under the 1960 constitution, which the Greek Cypriots continue to observe where possible, the Republic of Cyprus has an executive President, who is directly elected for a five-year term, by compulsory universal suffrage of those aged 18 and over, and who appoints the government. Legislative authority is vested in a unicameral House of Representatives (*Vouli Antiprosópon* in Greek, *Temsilciler Meclisi* in Turkish), which theoretically has 80 members elected for a five-year term by proportional representation, 56 by the Greek Cypriot community and 24 by the Turkish Cypriots. Since 1964, however, the Turkish Cypriot community has declined to participate in these arrangements and has set up its own political structures (see separate section below). Three representatives are elected by the Armenian, Maronite and Latin religious communities and have a consultative role in the House.

Political parties in the Republic of Cyprus are eligible for state financial support if they, alone or in coalition, receive at least 3% of the electoral vote. Of the total sum available, 40% (or CY£200,000 in 1994) is divided equally among qualifying parties or coalitions, while 60% (or CY£300,000 in 1994) is allocated to qualifying parties in proportion to the percentage vote received in the most recent parliamentary elections.

Elections on May 27, 2001, for the 56 Greek Cypriot seats in the House of Representatives resulted as follows: Progressive Party of the Working People (AKEL) 20 (with 34.7% of the vote), Democratic Rally (DISY) 19 (34.0%), Democratic Party (DIKO) 9 (14.8%), Movement of Social Democrats (KISOS) 4 (6.5%), New Horizons (NEO) 1 (3.0%), United Democrats (EDI) 1 (3.7%), Fighting Democratic Movement (ADIK) 1 (2.2%), Cyprus Green Party 1 (2.0%). In Greek Cypriot presidential elections held on Feb. 8 and 15, 1998, Glafkos Clerides (DISY) was re-elected for a second five-year term with 40.1% in the first voting round and 50.8% in the second.

Cyprus Green Party
Kinima Oikologon Perivalontiston
Address. 3 Nicos Kazantzakis, Acropolis, Strovolos, 2007 Nicosia
Telephone. (+357) 2251–8787
Fax. (+357) 2251–2710
Email. cyprusgreens@hotmail.com
Website. www.cycentral.com/greens
Leadership. George Perdikis (spokesman)Officially called the Ecologist and Environmentalist Movement, the Greens were launched as a national political movement shortly before the May 1996 parliamentary elections, in which they won a 1% vote share and therefore failed to gain representation. In the late 1990s the party achieved a higher profile as environmental issues came to the fore, notably over its campaign for the preservation of the unique Akamas peninsula as a haven for rare flora and fauna. In the May 2001 elections the Greens advanced to 2% of the vote and therefore obtained one seat in the new House.

The Cyprus Greens are part of the European Federation of Green Parties.

Democratic Party
Dimokratiko Komma (DIKO)
Address. 50 Grivas Dighenis Ave, PO Box 23979, 1687 Nicosia
Telephone. (+357) 2266–6002
Fax. (+357) 2266–6488
Email. diko@diko.org.cy
Website. www.diko.org.cy
Leadership. Tassos Papadopoulos (chairman); Nicos Cleanthous (vice-president & parliamentary spokesman); Andreas S. Aggelides (general secretary)
DIKO was founded in May 1976 as the Democratic Front, a centre-right alliance supporting President Makarios's policy of "long-term struggle" against the Turkish occupation of northern Cyprus. It became the largest party in the 1976 parliamentary elections, winning 21 of the 35 available seats in a pro-Makarios alliance which included the (communist) →Progressive Party of the Working People (AKEL) and the EDEK Socialist Party, which later became the →Movement of Social Democrats (KISOS). Having succeeded Makarios as President on the latter's death in August 1977, then DIKO leader Spyros Kyprianou was elected unopposed in his own right in January 1978 and re-elected in February 1983, when he received 56.5% of the first-round vote.

Meanwhile, DIKO had been weakened by defections and its parliamentary representation had slumped to eight seats in the 1981 elections (held by proportional representation), when its vote share was 19.5%. Kyprianou nevertheless retained the reins of power, supported by AKEL until the latter ended the alliance in late 1984 because it objected to the President's alleged intransigence in inter-communal talks. In early elections in December 1985 DIKO increased its vote share to 27.7% and its seat total to 16 in a House enlarged to 56 Greek Cypriot members. But Kyprianou

failed to obtain a third presidential term in February 1988, receiving only 27.3% in the first round of voting and being eliminated.

DIKO mounted strong opposition to the policies of the new AKEL-endorsed independent President, George Vassiliou, particularly his handling of the inter-communal talks. It was strengthened in 1989 when it absorbed the small Centre Union party led by Tassos Papadopoulos. Nevertheless, in parliamentary elections in May 1991 DIKO remained the third party, falling to 11 seats and 19.5% of the vote. Thereafter it formed a tactical alliance with the EDEK Socialists to oppose the 1992 UN plan for Cyprus, claiming that it formalized the island's partition. In the February 1993 presidential elections, DIKO and EDEK presented a joint candidate, Paschalis Paschalides, who obtained only 18.6% of the first-round vote and was eliminated. In the second round, official DIKO support was given to Glafcos Clerides of the →Democratic Rally (DISY), who won a narrow victory over Vassiliou. In return for this support, President Clerides included five DIKO ministers in the new 11-member government.

DIKO slipped further to 10 seats and 16.4% of the vote in the May 1996 elections, following which Kyprianou was elected president of the House of Representatives, the second highest post in the state hierarchy. The February 1998 presidential elections occasioned serious divisions within the party, which officially joined with AKEL to back the independent candidacy of George Iacovou, whereas a minority faction supported the candidacy of DIKO deputy chairman Alexis Galanos. Galanos obtained only 4% of the first-round vote, in which Iacovou headed the field with 40.6%; but Galanos' endorsement of Clerides in the second round was sufficient to give the incumbent a second term by a narrow margin. Rewarded with a presidential advisory post, Galanos subsequently formed the →Eurodemocratic Renewal Party, while other DIKO rebels were appointed to a new "national unity government".

The rump DIKO formed part of the opposition in the second Clerides presidency, articulating criticism in particular of the President's handling of the continuing impasse on the Cyprus problem. In October 2000 Kyprianou was succeeded as DIKO chairman by Papadopoulos, an outspoken critic of the government's conduct of UN talks on Cyprus. In the May 2001 parliamentary elections, however, DIKO continued its downward trend, falling to nine seats with 14.8% of the vote. The party then backed the successful candidacy of the AKEL leader to succeed Kyprianou as president of the House of Representatives.

Democratic Rally
Dimokratikos Synagermos (DISY)
Address. 25 Pindarou Street, PO Box 25305, 1308 Nicosia
Telephone. (+357) 2288–3000
Fax. (+357) 2275–2751
Email. epikinonia@disy.org.cy
Website. www.disy.org.cy

Leadership. Nicos Anastasiades (president); Panayiotis Demetriou (deputy president); Demetris Syllouris (parliamentary spokesman); George Liveras (director-general)

DISY was founded in 1976 by Glafkos Clerides as a conservative, pro-Western union of elements of the former Progressive Front and United and Democratic National parties. As president of the House of Representatives, Clerides had previously been acting President of Cyprus in the wake of the right-wing coup and the resultant Turkish invasion of mid-1974, until the return of Archbishop Makarios as head of state in December 1974. The new party won 27.5% of the vote in the 1976 parliamentary elections but failed to obtain a seat because of the constituency-based system then in force. In that contest DISY condemned the victorious alliance of the centre-right →Democratic Party (DIKO), the left-wing →Progressive Party of the Working People (AKEL) and the EDEK Socialists (later the →Movement of Social Democrats) as being communist-inspired.

Held under a proportional system, the 1981 parliamentary elections gave DISY 32% of the vote and 12 of the 35 available seats, while the 1983 presidential balloting resulted in Clerides winning 34% in the first round and being defeated by the DIKO incumbent, Spyros Kyprianou. During 1985 DISY attacked President Kyprianou for his alleged intransigence in the UN-sponsored negotiations on the status of Cyprus, combining with AKEL to force early parliamentary elections in December 1985. These resulted in DISY supplanting AKEL as the largest single party, its support increasing from 31.9% in 1981 to 33.6%, which gave it 19 seats in a House enlarged to 56 Greek Cypriot members.

In the presidential election of February 1988, Clerides was again defeated, winning 48.4% of the second-round vote against the victorious AKEL-supported independent candidate, George Vassiliou. In parliamentary elections in May 1991 DISY's share of the vote, on a joint list with the small →Liberal Party (KTP), rose to 35.8%, which yielded 20 seats (of which one went to the KTP). Thereafter, DISY gave broad support to President Vassiliou's conduct of the inter-communal talks, including his acceptance of a new UN plan tabled in 1992 demarcating Greek Cypriot and Turkish Cypriot areas of administration in a federal state, whereas DIKO and EDEK contended that the plan would entrench the island's partition. In the February 1993 presidential elections, however, Clerides astutely distanced himself from the UN plan and emerged as the unexpected victor against Vassiliou, his narrow 50.3% winning margin in the second round being in part due to the transfer to him of DIKO and EDEK voting support. Six DISY and five DIKO ministers were included in the new government appointed by President Clerides, who stood down as DISY leader in light of his election. In further talks, Clerides reverted to broad acceptance of the UN plan and sought to use his longstanding personal relationship with the Turkish Cypriot leader, Rauf Denktash, to expedite a settlement, although to no avail as at mid-2001.

DISY remained the strongest party in the May 1996 elections, winning 20 seats in its own right with 34.5% of the vote. In the February 1998 presidential elections Clerides came second in the first round (with 40.1%), behind an independent candidate backed by AKEL and most of DIKO, but narrowly secured re-election in the second round (with 50.8%) by dint of attracting dissident DIKO support. He then formed a "national unity government" which included DISY, EDEK, Liberal and rebel DIKO members as well as what became the →United Democrats (EDI). However, EDEK withdrew its two ministers in January 1999 in protest against Clerides' decision to abandon a controversial plan to deploy Russian-made surface-to-air missiles in Cyprus. In August 1999 allegations of improper ministerial participation in the 1999 stock market boom prompted the resignation of two DISY ministers.

In parliamentary elections in May 2001, DISY lost its position as the largest party, slipping to 19 seats and 34.0%

of the vote. When the new House convened in June, DISY leader Nicos Anastasiades was defeated by the AKEL leader in a contest for the vacant presidency of the legislature.

Having an official membership of 30,000, DISY is affiliated to the European People's Party as well as to the International Democrat Union and the European Democrat Union.

Eurodemocratic Renewal Party
Komma Evrodimokratikis Ananeosis (KEA)

Address. 3 Theokritou Street, Office 3, 1060 Nicosia
Telephone. (+357) 2243–1625
Fax. (+357) 2243–2627
Leadership. Antonis Paschalides (president)

The KEA was founded in October 1998 by former House of Representatives president Alexis Galanos, who had broken with the →Democratic Party (DIKO) before the February 1998 presidential elections because he disagreed with DIKO's decision to back the (ultimately unsuccessful) independent candidacy of George Iacovou. Galanos had himself obtained 4% in the first round of that contest, the switch of his dissident DIKO support contributing to the victory of incumbent Glafcos Clerides of the →Democratic Rally (DISY) in the second round.

The KEA contested the May 2001 parliamentary elections in alliance with the →Movement of Social Democrats (KISOS) but failed to secure representation.

Fighting Democratic Movement
Agonistiko Dimocratico Kinima (ADIK)

Address. c/o Vouli Antiprosópon, Nicosia
Leadership. Dinos Michaelides (president)

ADIK was launched by Dinos Michaelides following his resignation as Interior Minister in March 1999 amidst allegations of corruption (of which he was later substantially cleared). Michaelides had previously been a member of the →Democratic Party (DIKO), but had been among the DIKO dissidents who refused to follow the party's decision to back the (ultimately unsuccessful) independent candidacy of George Iacovou in the February 1998 presidential elections. In the May 2001 parliamentary elections ADIK obtained 2.2% of the vote and one seat, Michaelides being returned in the Limassol district.

Movement of Social Democrats
Kinima Socialdimokraton (KISOS)

Address. 40 Byron Ave., PO Box 21064, 1096 Nicosia
Telephone. (+357) 2267–8617
Fax. (+357) 2267–8894
Leadership. Yiannakis Omirou (president); Marinos Sizopoulos (first deputy president); Sofoklis Sofokleous (second deputy president); Vassos Lyssarides (life honorary president)

KISOS was launched in February 2000 as a merger of the Unified Democratic Union of Cyprus (EDEK Socialist Party) and smaller centre-left groups, its declared aim being to spearhead the process of Cyprus' integration into the European Union and to build a classic European social democratic party in Cyprus.

Founded in 1969 by Vassos Lyssarides, EDEK contested the 1970 parliamentary elections as the Democratic Centre Union, winning two seats. In the early 1970s it opposed both Greek interference in Cyprus and the Turkish invasion of the island of 1974, which some of its members actively resisted. It supported the return to power of President Makarios in late 1974 and in the 1976 elections participated in a pro-Makarios alliance with the centre-right →Democratic Party (DIKO) and the left-wing →Progressive Party of the Working People (AKEL), winning four seats. It fell back to three seats in 1981 campaigning independently, and in the 1983 presidential election Lyssarides, presented as the candidate of the broader National Salvation Front, took third place with 9.5% of the vote, despite having withdrawn from the contest at the last minute. EDEK increased its House representation to six seats in the 1985 elections, winning 11.1% of the vote, being at that time broadly supportive of President Kyprianou's tough line in the Cyprus inter-communal talks.

Lyssarides stood again in the February 1988 presidential elections but was eliminated in the first round, with only 9.2% of the vote. In the second round EDEK transferred its support to the AKEL-backed independent candidate, George Vassiliou, who was elected by a narrow margin. But EDEK quickly came to oppose President Vassiliou's more accommodating line in the inter-communal talks, making common cause on this issue with DIKO against AKEL and the conservative →Democratic Rally (DISY). In the May 1991 parliamentary elections EDEK won 10.9% of the vote and seven seats. Thereafter it mounted strong opposition, with DIKO, to Vassiliou's acceptance of the UN plan demarcating Greek Cypriot and Turkish Cypriot areas of administration in a federal Cyprus, claiming that the proposals amounted to partition of the island.

In the February 1993 presidential elections, EDEK and DIKO presented a joint candidate, Paschalis Paschalides, who obtained only 18.6% in the first round and was eliminated. In the second round, EDEK gave its support to Glafkos Clerides of DISY, who was narrowly victorious over Vassiliou. In the May 1996 legislative elections EDEK fell back to five seats with 8.1% of the vote. Lyssarides stood for the third time in the February 1998 presidential elections, being eliminated in the first round with 10.6% of the vote. Although EDEK did not formally back Clerides in the second round, his narrow victory was followed by the appointment of a "national unity government" in which EDEK took two portfolios.

Increasingly unhappy with Clerides' conduct of foreign policy, EDEK withdrew from the government in January 1999 in protest against the President's decision to abandon a controversial plan to deploy Russian-made surface-to-air missiles in Cyprus. It thereafter became an opposition party, maintaining this stance after the creation in February 2000 of KISOS, of which Lyssarides was elected president. Subsequent moves towards a merger between KISOS and the →United Democrats proved abortive.

In the May 2001 parliamentary elections, KISOS fell back to four seats and 6.5% of the vote, whereupon Lyssarides tendered his resignation as leader. He was succeeded in July by Yiannakis Omirou.

KISOS is a member party of the Socialist International.

New Horizons
Neoi Orizontes (NEO)
Address. Byzantiou Street 9, Strovolos, Nicosia
Telephone. (+357) 2276–1476
Fax. (+357) 2276–1144
Email. neo@neoiorizontes.org
Website. www.neoiorizontes.org
Leadership. Nicos Koutsou (president)
The right-wing NEO was founded in early 1996 by elements close to the Greek Orthodox Church. Its platform on the Cyprus question differed from those of other parties in that, while they all accepted the concept of a federal Cyprus, the NEO argued in favour of a unitary state and a single government. It failed to gain representation in the May 1996 elections, taking only 1.7% of the vote, but in May 2001 obtained one seat on the strength of a 3% vote share.

Progressive Party of the Working People
Anorthotiko Komma Ergazomenou Laou (AKEL)
Address. 4 Akamantos Street, PO Box 1827, Nicosia
Telephone. (+357) 2276–1121
Fax. (+357) 2276–1574
Email. k.e.akel@cytanet.com.cy
Website. www.akel.org.cy
Leadership. Demetris Christofias (general secretary); Andreas Christou (parliamentary spokesman)
AKEL is directly descended from the Communist Party of

Cyprus, which held its first congress in 1926 but was declared illegal by the British authorities amid the political and social unrest of 1931. Reconstituted as AKEL in 1941, the party emerged after the war as an orthodox pro-Soviet Marxist–Leninist formation and was again banned by the British in 1955. Legalized again in December 1959, it consolidated its dominant position in the trade union movement after independence in 1960. In the 1976 parliamentary elections it was part of a victorious alliance with the (centre-right) →Democratic Party (DIKO) and the EDEK Socialists (later the →Movement of Social Democrats.

Following the death of President Makarios in 1977, AKEL gave general backing to the new government of President Spyros Kyprianou (DIKO) and headed the poll in the 1981 parliamentary elections, winning 32.8% of the vote and 12 of the 35 seats then available. The alliance with DIKO was terminated by AKEL in December 1984 on the grounds that the President was showing insufficient flexibility in inter-communal talks with the Turkish Cypriots. In the December 1985 parliamentary elections AKEL slipped to third place, winning 27.4% and 15 seats in a House enlarged to 56 Greek Cypriot members.

For the February 1988 presidential elections AKEL opted to endorse an independent candidate, George Vassiliou, who was elected in the second round by a narrow 51.6% margin over Glafkos Clerides of the →Democratic Rally (DISY), receiving support from EDEK and many DIKO voters. In early 1990 AKEL appeared to be weakened by the formation of the breakaway Democratic Socialist Reform Movement (ADISOK), when the leadership declined to revise the party's Marxist–Leninist principles and mode of operation. However, the collapse of communism elsewhere in Europe and the demise of the Soviet Union in 1991, although regretted by AKEL hardliners, inevitably brought the party onto a democratic socialist path.

In the May 1991 parliamentary elections, AKEL increased its vote share to 30.6% and its representation to 18 seats (while ADISOK won none). AKEL again endorsed Vassiliou in the February 1993 presidential elections, but the opposition of DIKO and EDEK to his handling of the national question resulted in their supporters swinging behind Clerides (DISY) in the second round, in which Vassiliou was defeated by a 50.3% to 49.7% margin. Later in the year the ex-President launched the Movement of Free Democrats, but this centre-left formation, which later became the →United Democrats when it merged with ADISOK, was seen as more of a threat to DIKO and EDEK than to AKEL.

AKEL gained ground in the May 1996 parliamentary elections, winning 19 seats and 33% of the vote, but failed in its aim of overtaking DISY as the largest party. In the February 1998 presidential elections, AKEL joined with DIKO to back the independent candidacy of George Iacovou, who led the first-round vote with 40.6% but was narrowly defeated by incumbent Clerides in the second round. AKEL maintained its opposition stance and was rewarded in the May 2001 parliamentary elections by overtaking DISY as the largest single party with 20 of the 56 seats on a 34.7% vote share.

An immediate benefit was the election in June 2001 of AKEL leader Demetris Christofias as the new president of the House of Representatives (the second highest post in the state hierarchy), with support from DIKO deputies. This was seen as indicating the likely constellation of political forces in the presidential elections due in 2003.

United Democrats
Enomeni Dimokrates (EDI)
Address. 8 Iassonos Street, PO Box 23494, Nicosia
Telephone. (+357) 2266–3030
Fax. (+357) 2266–4747
Leadership. George Vassiliou (president)
The centre-left EDI was created in December 1996 as a merger of the Movement of Free Democrats (KED) and the

Democratic Socialist Reform Movement (ADISOK), which had been founded in 1990 by an anti-communist faction of the →Progressive Party of the Working People (AKEL).

The KED had been launched in April 1993 by ex-President Vassiliou following his unexpected failure to secure a second term in the February 1993 presidential elections. A wealthy businessman, he had been elected to the presidency in 1988 as an independent candidate with the backing of AKEL, which had again supported him in 1993. The KED was described as a centre-left formation which aimed to contribute to "the struggle of our people to solve the national problem" and to promote the admission of Cyprus to the European Union.

The KED won 5.1% of the vote and two seats in the May 1996 parliamentary elections, these going to Vassiliou and his wife Androulla. The formation then reached agreement to merge with ADISOK to create the EDI, of which Vassiliou was elected president at the founding conference in December 1996. However, the new movement made little subsequent progress in its declared aim of becoming the dominant centre-left party in Cyprus.

In the February 1998 presidential elections Vassiliou obtained only 3% of the first-round vote, following which the party joined a "national unity government" and Vassiliou was appointed as Cyprus' chief negotiator on European Union accession. In the May 2001 parliamentary elections EDI obtained only 2.2% of the vote and one seat (retained by Androulla Vassiliou).

Turkish Republic of Northern Cyprus (TRNC)

The "independent" TRNC was proclaimed in November 1983 as successor to the Turkish Federated State of Cyprus (TFSC), itself created in February 1975 as successor to the Turkish Cypriot Autonomous Administration dating from December 1968. Under its 1985 constitution, the TRNC has an executive President directly elected for a five-year term by universal adult suffrage and a 50-member Assembly of the Republic (*Cumhuriyet Meclisi*), also elected for a five-year term by proportional representation of parties winning at least 5% of the vote. Assembly elections on Dec. 6, 1998, resulted as follows: National Unity Party (UBP) 24 seats (with 40.3% of the vote), Democratic Party 13 (22.6%), Communal Liberation Party 7 (15.4%), Republican Turkish Party 6 (13.4%). In the first round of presidential elections on April 15, 2000, Rauf Denktash (standing as an independent) obtained 43.7% of the vote and was declared elected by default after the withdrawal from the second round of the UBP runner-up.

Only Turkey has recognized the TRNC. The Greek Cypriot government regards the TRNC government and Assembly as illegal, although it accepts the legitimacy of the political parties operating in the Turkish Cypriot sector. Under the TRNC's 2001 budget, a total of 758,000 million Turkish lira was allocated in financial support for the parties represented in the Assembly in proportion to their number of seats.

Communal Liberation Party
Toplumcu Kurtuluş Partisi (TKP)
Address. 13 Mahmut Pasa Street, Lefkosa/Nicosia
Telephone. (+90–392) 72555
Leadership. Mustafa Akinci (leader); Hüseyin Angolemli (general secretary)
The left-of-centre TKP (sometimes known as the Socialist Salvation Party) was founded in 1976 with the support of then Turkish Cypriot leader Fazil Küçük and espoused the principles of Mustapha Kemal Atatürk, founder of the modern Turkish state. It won six Assembly seats in 1976 and 13 in 1981. In the latter year the TKP presidential candidate, Ziya Rizki, came second with 30.4% of the vote. The party fell back to 10 seats in the June 1985 Assembly elections (winning 16% of the vote) and its presidential candi-

date, Alpay Durduran, came third with 9.2% of the vote. It then joined a coalition government with the →National Unity Party (UBP), but withdrew in August 1986 amid differences on economic policy.

In 1989 the TKP absorbed the Progressive People's Party (AHP), itself the product of a 1986 merger between the Democratic People's Party (DHP) and the Communal Endeavour Party (TAP). Of these ingredients, the DHP had been founded in 1979 by two former UBP Prime Ministers, Nejat Könük and Osman Örek, of whom the former had in 1983–85, by then an independent, again been Prime Minister of a coalition government. The centre-right TAP had been founded in 1984, and neither it nor the DHP had won representation in the 1985 Assembly elections.

In the 1990 elections the TKP's seat tally slipped to seven. In those of December 1993, which it contested as part of the Democratic Struggle alliance with →Republican Turkish Party and the →New Dawn Party, it declined further to five seats. In the first round of TRNC presidential elections in April 1995, TKP leader Mustafa Akinci came in fourth place with 14.2% of the vote. By then the party had become the most "moderate" of the main TRNC parties on the Cyprus issue, favouring a federal solution which preserves Cyprus as a single sovereignty and the island's entry into the European Union, even without Turkey's accession.

The TKP advanced to seven seats and 15.4% of the vote in the December 1998 legislative elections, becoming in January 1999 the junior partner in a coalition government headed by the UBP. The party strongly supported the UN-sponsored "proximity" talks with the Greek Cypriots that opened in December 1999. In the April 2000 presidential elections, however, Akinci won only 11.7% of the first-round vote. The Turkish Cypriot withdrawal from the UN talks in November 2000 exposed the TKP's differences with the UBP, which favoured separate sovereignty for the TRNC. In May 2001 the TKP was abruptly ejected from the government and replaced by the →Democratic Party.

Democratic Party
Demokrat Partisi (DP)
Address. 10 Mersin Street, Lefkosa/Nicosia
Telephone. (+90–392) 83795
Fax. (+90–392) 87130
Email. yenidem@kktc.net
Leadership. Salih Cosar (leader); Hursit Eminer (general secretary)
The DP was launched in mid-1992 by a dissident faction of the →National Unity Party (UBP) which advocated a more conciliatory line in the inter-communal talks than that favoured by the then UBP Prime Minister, Derviş Eroglu. Backed by President Denktash (formerly a UBP member), the new party had the support of 10 of the 45 UBP Assembly deputies elected in 1990–91. In October 1992 it was formally joined by Denktash, who was precluded by the constitution from leading a political party or submitting to party discipline.

In the December 1993 Assembly elections, the DP came close to supplanting the UBP as the leading party, winning 15 of the 50 seats against 17 for the UBP. The then DP leader, Hakki Atun, was appointed Prime Minister of a majority coalition government embracing the →Republican Turkish Party (CTP). The coalition policy agreement, while not following a pro-partition line, offered little accommodation on the Cyprus question, favouring joint sovereignty and a rotational presidency. The DP backed Denktash's successful re-election bid in April 1995, after which Atun was reappointed to the premiership of a further DP/CTP coalition.

In May 1996 Atun was replaced as DP leader by Serdar Denktash, son of the TRNC President, following which the coalition with the CTP was ended in July 1996 and replaced the following month by a UBP/DP government in which Serdar Denktash became Deputy Prime Minister. Despite absorbing part of the small →Free Democratic Party in

September 1998, in legislative elections in December the DP slipped to 13 seats (with 22.6% of the vote) and went into opposition to a coalition of the UBP and the →Communal Liberation Party (TKP). The DP backed Rauf Denktash's successful re-election bid in April 2000, following which internal divisions resulted in Serdar Denktash being succeeded as party leader by Salih Cosar in November 2000. In June 2001 the DP replaced the TKP as the UBP's coalition partner.

National Unity Party
Ulusal Birlik Partisi (UBP)

Address. 9 Atatürk Meydani, Lefkosa/Nicosia
Telephone. (+90–392) 73972
Leadership. Derviş Eroglu (leader); Vehbi Zeki Serter (general secretary)

The centre-right UBP was founded in 1976 by Rauf Denktash, leader of the Turkish Cypriot community, and had its origins in an earlier National Solidarity (UD) movement. Espousing the political principles of Mustapha Kemal Atatürk, founder of the modern Turkish state, the party won three-quarters of the seats in the 1976 Turkish Cypriot Assembly elections. Its then general secretary, Nejat Konuk, became the first Prime Minister of the TFSC, but resigned in March 1978, as did his successor, Osman Örek. Both participated in the formation of the breakaway Democratic People's Party, which later became part of the →Communal Liberation Party (TKP). Having been formally elected to the Turkish Cypriot presidency in 1976, Denktash was re-elected in 1981 as the UBP candidate with 51.8% of the vote. In the 1981 Assembly elections, the UBP was reduced to 18 deputies but remained the largest party and in August 1981 formed a new government, which fell on a no-confidence vote in December 1981, whereafter the UBP formed a coalition with two other parties.

Following the declaration of the TRNC in November 1983, the UBP continued as the main ruling party and increased its representation to 24 seats out of 50 in the June 1985 elections, with 37% of the vote. In the same month, Denktash was re-elected to the TRNC presidency as the UBP candidate, with 70.5% of the vote. A new coalition government between the UBP and the TKP broke down when the latter withdrew in August 1986, to be replaced by the →New Dawn Party. Standing this time as an independent, Denktash was in April 1990 re-elected TRNC President with 66.7% of the vote. In the May 1990 Assembly elections, the UBP won an absolute majority of 34 of the 50 seats, increasing this tally to 45 in by-elections in October 1991.

Strains then intensified between Denktash and the UBP Prime Minister, Derviş Eroglu, with the latter advocating the formal partition of Cyprus on the basis of the existing territorial division, whereas the President then favoured further exploration of a bicommunal solution in UN-sponsored talks. This divergence resulted in July 1992 in the formation of the breakaway pro-Denktash →Democratic Party (DP), which included 10 former UBP deputies. The rump UBP, following Eroglu's pro-partition line, remained the largest single party in the early Assembly elections of December 1993, but with only 17 seats (and 29.6% of the vote) it was unable to prevent the formation of a coalition of the DP and the →Republican Turkish Party (CTP).

Eroglu came in second place in the first round of TRNC presidential elections in April 1995 (winning 24.2% of the vote), but was easily defeated in the second by Denktash. In August 1996 Eroglu returned to the premiership, heading a coalition of the UBP and the DP. In the December 1998 legislative elections the UBP advanced to 24 seats (with 40.3% of the vote), so that Eroglu continued as Prime Minister, although the TKP replaced the DP as the UBP's junior coalition. In the April 2000 presidential elections Eroglu again came second with 30.1% of the first-round vote, helping to deny Denktash an outright majority, but he withdrew from the second round in protest against voting irregularities.

Having given qualified support to President Denktash's participation in UN-sponsored "proximity" talks from November 1999, the UBP strongly backed the decision to withdraw from the talks in November 2000. Increasing strains with the pro-settlement TKP impelled the UBP to terminate the coalition in May 2001 and the following month to form a new coalition with the DP, with Eroglu continuing as Prime Minister.

Republican Turkish Party
Cumhuriyetçi Türk Partisi (CTP)

Address. 99A Sehit Salahi Street, Lefkosa/Nicosia
Telephone. (+90–392) 73300
Fax. (+90–392) 81914
Leadership. Mehmet Ali Talat (chairman); Mustafa Ferdi Soyer (general secretary)

The CTP was founded in 1970 by Ahmed Mithat Berberoghlou as a Marxist–Leninist formation espousing anti-imperialiism, non- alignment and a settlement of the Cyprus question "on the basis of top-level agreements between the leaders of the two communities". In 1973 Berberoghlou stood unsuccessfully against Rauf Denktash, then of the →National Unity Party (UBP), for the vice-presidency of (then undivided) Cyprus. He also contested the 1976 presidential election in the TFSR, again losing to Denktash, while the CTP won only two out of 40 Assembly seats.

Under the new leadership of Özker Özgür, the party increased its representation to six seats in 1981, when the CTP leader came in third place in the presidential elections with 12.8% of the vote. In the June 1985 presidential contest, Özgür improved to second place with 18.4% of the vote, while in Assembly elections the same month the CTP won 12 out of 50 seats with 21% of the vote. In 1988 the CTP's financial viability came under serious threat when a TRNC court awarded President Denktash over £100,000 in damages for an alleged libel in the party newspaper. The CTP did not contest the April 1990 presidential election, while in the May 1990 Assembly balloting it won only seven seats, standing as part of the Democratic Struggle alliance with the →Communal Liberation Party and the →New Dawn Party.

Having eschewed Marxism–Leninism in favour of democratic socialism, the CTP recovered in the December 1993 Assembly elections, winning 13 seats standing in its own right. It subsequently entered a coalition government led by the recently-formed pro-Denktash →Democratic Party (DP). Özgür took third place in the April 1995 presidential elections (winning 18.9% of the vote), whereafter the CTP joined a new coalition government with the DP. This alliance collapsed in November 1995 when President Denktash vetoed two CTP-approved cabinet changes, but was re-established the following month. In January 1996 Özgür was ousted as CTP leader by Mehmet Ali Talat, who in July 1996 took the party into opposition.

The CTP fell back to six seats (and 13.4% of the vote) in the December 1998 legislative elections, remaining in opposition. In the April 2000 presidential elections Talat came fourth in the first round with 10% of the vote.

Other Parties

Freedom and Justice Party, right-wing formation launched in August 2000, apparently as successor to the Unity and Sovereignty Party (*Birlik ve Egemenlik Partisi, BEP*) founded in 1990.
Leadership. Arif Salih Kirdağ (chairman)

Liberal Party (*Liberal Partisi, LP*), launched in January 2001 as an alternative to "the dirty atmosphere, degenerated cadres and cliques" of the existing parties.
Leadership. Kemal Bolayir (chairman)

National Revival Party (*Ulusal Dirilis Partisi, UDP*), nationalist formation founded in 1997 by Enver Emin, a former general secretary of the →National Unity Party who in 1994 had launched the breakaway National Birth Party and who in 1996 had taken the latter into →the Democratic Party, from which he had broken within a year. The UDP won 4.6% in the December 1998 Assembly elections.
Address. 10 Mersin Street, Lefkosa/Nicosia
Leadership. Enver Emin (chairman)

Nationalist Justice Party (*Midiyetçi Adalet Partisi, MAP*), right-wing pro-Turkey party founded in 1991, formed part of the unsuccessful National Struggle Party (MMP) alliance in the 1993 Assembly elections. Following the 1998 elections it was joined by Kenan Akin, a Turkish settler who had been elected to the Assembly for the →Democratic Party.

New Dawn Party (*Yeni Doğus Partisi, YDP*), centre-right formation originally founded in 1984 and mainly representing Turkish settlers. It won four Assembly seats in 1985 and joined a coalition with the →National Unity Party in 1986; declined to one seat in 1990 (within the opposition Democratic Struggle alliance) and failed to secure representation in 1993, whereupon it merged with the →Democratic Party until being revived in 1997.

New Democracy Party, centre-right grouping founded in December 2000.
Leadership. Esref Düsenkalkar, Çetin Atalay

Our Party, Islamist grouping founded in 1998, won 1.2% in the December 1998 Assembly elections.
Leadership. Ökyay Sadikoglu, Seyh Nasim Kibrisi

Patriotic Unity Movement (*Yurtsever Birlik Hareketi, YBH*), left-wing formation established in 1998 as successor to the New Cyprus Party (YKP), which had been founded in 1989 by Alpay Durduran, the 1985 presidential candidate of the →Communal Liberation Party who won 1.8% of the first-round vote in the 1995 presidential contest. The YBH was also joined by Özker Özgür, former leader of the →Republican Turkish Party. Advocating a federal settlement for Cyprus and opposing separate sovereignty or union with Turkey, the YBH won only 2.5% in the December 1998 Assembly elections. In the April 2000 presidential contest, YBH candidate Arif Hasan Tahsin took 2.6% of the first-round vote.
Address. 10 Mersin Street, Lefkosa/Nicosia
Telephone. (+90–392) 74917
Fax. (+90–392) 88931
Email. ybh@north-cyprus.net
Leadership. Rasih Keskiner (spokesman); Izzet Izcan (general secretary)

Czech Republic

Capital: Prague

Population: 10,300,000 (2000E)

The Czech Republic became independent on Jan. 1, 1993, as a result of the dissolution of the Czech and Slovak Federative Republic, which had been under Communist rule (under various names) from 1948 to 1989 and had then become a multi-party democracy. Under the Czech constitution of December 1992, legislative power is vested in a bicameral Parliament of the Czech Republic (*Parlament České Republiký*), of which the lower house is the 200-member Chamber of Deputies (*Sněmovna Poslancu*), elected by proportional representation for a four-year term by universal suffrage of those aged 18 and over. The threshold for representation is 5% of the national vote for single parties, 10% for coalitions of two parties, 15% for coalitions of three parties and 20% for coalitions of four or more parties. Under constitutional implementing legislation enacted in September 1995, there is also an 81-member Senate (*Sénate*) as the upper house, whose members are directly elected from single-member constituencies for a six-year term, with one third being renewed every two years (although all 81 were elected in the inaugural poll in 1996). Executive power is vested primarily in the Council of Ministers responsible to parliament, although considerable authority resides in the President, who is elected for a five-year term by the members of the legislature.

Under the 1991 Law on Political Parties as subsequently amended, state financial support is available to each party which obtains at least 3% of the national vote, the current rates being a basic annual subsidy of CzK6 million plus CzK200,000 for each 0.1% of the party's vote. A further CzK900,000 is payable to parties for each seat obtained in either chamber of the national legislature, while CzK250,000 is payable for each seat won in regional assemblies.

To assure the transition to separate sovereignty, the National Council elected in the Czech Lands on June 5–6, 1992, under the federation became the Chamber of Deputies of the independent Czech Republic. The first post-separation elections were held on May 31–June 1, 1996, and the second on June 19–20, 1998, the latter resulting as follows: Czech Social Democratic Party (ČSSD) 74 seats (32.3% of the vote), Civic Democratic Party (ODS) 63 (27.7%), Communist Party of Bohemia and Moravia (KSČM) 22 (10.0%), Christian Democratic Union-Czechoslovak People's Party (KDU-ČSL) 20 (9.0%), Freedom Union (US) 19 (8.6%). Partial elections to the Senate in November 2000 resulted in its full composition becoming: ODS 22 seats, KDU–ČSL 21, US 18, ČSSD 15, KSČM 3, independents 2.

Christian Democratic Union–Czechoslovak People's Party
Křestánskodemokratická Unie-Československá Strana Lidová (KDU- ČSL)
Address. Karlovo nám. 5, 12801 Prague 2
Telephone. (+420–2) 2492–3871
Fax. (+420–2) 2491–7630
Email. gs@kdu.cz
Website. www.kdu.cz
Leadership. Cyril Svoboda (chairman); Jaroslav Kopriva (first deputy chairman); Jan Kasal (Chamber group chairman); Jiří Šenkýř (Senate group chairman); Petr Rybar (secretary-general)
The KDU-ČSL is descended from the Czechoslovak

People's Party founded in 1918 as the new state's main Catholic formation and represented in most inter-war governments until it was dissolved in late 1938 in the aftermath of the Munich crisis. Revived as a component of the Communist-dominated National Front in 1945, the People's Party was allowed to continue in existence as a Front party after the Communists took sole power in 1948. From late 1989 it sought to free itself from its recent history as a satellite of the outgoing Communist regime, undertaking personnel and policy changes designed to re-establish itself as an independent pro-democracy formation. Having joined the broad-based coalition government appointed in December 1989, the People's Party in June 1990 removed Josef Bartončik as party chairman amid allegations that he had been secret police informer. The party contested the elections of the same month in an alliance with other groups allied as the Christian and Democratic Union, which won nine of the 101 Czech seats in the federal lower house (with 8.7% of the vote), six of the 75 Czech seats in the federal upper house (with 8.8% of the vote) and 19 seats in the 200-member Czech National Council (with 8.4% of the vote).

Included in the post-1990 Czech coalition government, the Christian and Democratic Union was weakened in late 1991 by the departure of the Christian Democratic Party (KDS) to form an alliance with the new →Civic Democratic Party (ODS). In April 1992 the remaining constituents officially became the KDU-ČSL, which in the June 1992 elections won 15 seats in the Czech National Council (with 6.3% of the vote) as well as seven and six of the Czech seats in the federal lower and upper houses respectively. The party became a member of the ODS-led Czech coalition government which took the republic to independence in January 1993, after which it no longer advocated autonomy for Moravia, where it had its strongest popular support. A hankering after old borders is apparent in the party's retention of "Czechoslovak" in its sub-title.

Following the separation, the KDU-ČSL became an advocate of the free-market economy and Czech membership of Western economic and security structures. In late 1995 its parliamentary party was strengthened by the defection to it of five KDS deputies opposed to their party's decision to merge with the ODS. In the 1996 lower house elections the KDU-ČSL won 18 seats on a vote share of 8.1% and was included in another ODS-led government, now with minority status. However, political and economic difficulties in 1997 impelled the KDU-ČSL and the other junior coalition party to withdraw in November 1997, causing the government's resignation, following which the party was represented in a transitional administration pending new elections.

In the early lower house elections in June 1998, the KDU-ČSL advanced to 20 lower house seats and 9% of the vote, but went into opposition to a minority government headed by the →Czech Social Democratic Party. In June 1999 long-serving party chairman Josef Lux was succeeded by Jan Kasal, who took the KDU-ČSL into an opposition Coalition of Four with the →Freedom Union (US), the →Civic Democratic Alliance and the →Democratic Union, which planned to present joint candidates and prospective ministers in the 2002 elections. In the November 2000 partial Senate elections the KDU-ČSL advanced strongly within the opposition alliance, becoming the second largest party with 21 of the 81 seats.

In January 2001 KDU-ČSL deputy chairman Cyril Svoboda was unexpectedly elected leader of the Coalition of Four, ahead of the party's official candidate, Jaroslav Kopriva. Two months later Svoboda resigned from the post, in protest against the inclusion in the Coalition's shadow cabinet of a former KDU-ČSL minister with a dubious past, and was replaced by the then US leader. Resultant turmoil within the KDU-ČSL resulted in Svoboda ousting Kasal as party chairman in May 2001.

Having an official membership of 55,000, the KDU-ČSL is an affiliate of the Christian Democrat International and an associate member of the European People's Party.

Civic Democratic Alliance
Občanská Demokratická Aliance (ODA)

Address. Štefánikova 21, 15000 Prague 5
Telephone. (+420–2) 5732–7072
Fax. (+420–2) 5732–7072
Email. usek@oda.cz
Website. www.oda.cz
Leadership. Michael Žantovský (chairman); Daniel Kroupa (Senate group chairman)

The conservative ODA was launched in December 1989 and contested the June 1990 multi-party elections as part of the victorious Civic Forum (*Občanské Fórum*, OF), becoming a member of both the federal and the Czech republican governments. Set up as an independent party on the fracturing of the OF in early 1991, the ODA contested the June 1992 elections its own right, winning 14 of the 200 Czech National Council seats (with 5.9% of the vote) but none in either house of the Federal Assembly. As a member of the subsequent Czech coalition government headed by the →Civic Democratic Party (ODS), it supported the creation of a separate Czech Republic from January 1993. Its pro-market policy line was very similar to that of the ODS, the main differentiation lying in its greater emphasis on regional self-government and on the need for a reduction of the state's role.

Under the leadership of Jan Kalvoda, the ODA won 13 lower house seats in the mid-1996 elections, on a 6.4% vote share, and continued as a government coalition partner. But both the government and the ODA became increasingly beset by scandal, as the country experienced a major financial crisis. Kalvoda resigned as Deputy Prime Minister in December 1996 over a claim that he had pretended to have a doctorate and was succeeded as party chairman in March 1997 by Michael Žantovský, a former ambassador to the USA and spokesman for President Havel. Internal divisions intensified, however, with the result that Žantovský stood down in November 1997, as the withdrawal of the ODA from the government forced its resignation and the calling of early elections, pending which the ODA participated in a caretaker administration.

The next ODA chairman, Deputy Premier Jiři Skalický, lasted only until February 1998, when he was forced to resign from the government and the party leadership by allegations of illegal party funding, being replaced as ODA chairman by Daniel Kroupa. Meanwhile, the defection of a group of dissidents in January had further weakened the ODA, which opted not to contest the June 1998 lower house elections, instead urging its supporters to vote for other centre-right parties. The party nevertheless continued to be represented in the Senate, where Kroupa chaired a joint group of the ODA and the →Freedom Union (US).

In September 1999 the ODA joined an opposition Coalition of Four with the US, the →Christian Democratic Union-Czechoslovak People's Party (KDU-ČSL) and the →Democratic Union (DEU), which planned to present joint candidates and prospective ministers in the 2002 elections. In June 2001 Žantovský returned to the ODA chairmanship, being elected unopposed by a party conference after Kroupa and another contender had withdrawn their candidacies.

The ODA is a member of the International Democrat Union.

Civic Democratic Party
Občanská Demokratická Strana (ODS)

Address. Snìmovní 3, 11800 Prague 1
Telephone. (+420–2) 311–4800
Fax. (+420–2) 2451–0731
Leadership. Václav Klaus (chairman); Vlastimil Tlusty (Chamber group chairman); Mirek Topolánek (Senate group chairman)
Email. foreign@ods.cz

Website. www.ecn.cz/env/ods

The ODS came into being in early 1991 as a result of a split in the original pro-democracy Civic Forum (*Občanské Fórum*, OF), which had been launched in November 1989 by various anti-communist groups, notably the Charter 77 movement, under the acknowledged leadership of dissident playwright Václav Havel. Together with its Slovak counterpart, the OF had then brought about the "velvet revolution", quickly forcing the regime to give up sole state power. In December 1989 Havel had been elected President by a federal parliament still dominated by Communists, while the OF itself had triumphed in the Czech Lands in the June 1990 Czechoslovak elections, winning 68 of the 101 Czech seats in the 150-member federal lower house (with 53.2% of the Czech vote) and 127 of the 200 seats in the Czech National Council (with 49.5% of the vote). It had then entered a federal coalition government with other pro-democracy parties (in which Klaus became Finance Minister) and had headed the Czech government in the person of Petr Pithart. In October 1990 Klaus had been elected as first official chairman of the OF, announcing his intention to steer the movement to the right.

Once in power, the OF had experienced the inevitable internal strains between its disparate components. In February 1991 Klaus and his supporters formally launched the ODS, while elements preferring the maintenance of a broad-based movement converted the OF into the Civic Movement (*Občanské Hnuti*), which later became the Free Democrats, which in turn became the →Free Democrats–Liberal National Social Party (SD-LSNS). A third OF breakaway party was the →Civic Democratic Alliance (ODA). The ODS quickly built a strong organization and concluded an electoral alliance with the Christian Democratic Party (KDS). In the June 1992 elections the ODS/KDS combination became the leading formation both at federal level (with 48 of the 99 Czech seats in the lower house and 33.9% of the Czech vote) and in the Czech National Council (with 76 of the 200 seats and 29.7% of the vote). The resultant Czech-Slovak federal coalition was headed by Jan Stráský (ODS), while Klaus preferred to take the Czech premiership at the head of a coalition of the ODS, the KDS, the ODA and the →Christian Democratic Union-Czechoslovak People's Party (KDU-ČSL).

In dominant governmental authority, the ODS moved swiftly to implement its programme of economic reform, including wholesale privatization of the state sector, especially in the Czech Lands. But its main immediate concern was the constitutional question and in particular the gulf between the Slovak demand for sovereignty within a federation and the Czech government view that preservation of the federation only made sense if it had a real role. Opinion polls at that stage showed that a majority of both Czechs and Slovaks favoured a continued federal structure. But the failure of Václav Havel to secure re-election as President in July 1992, due to Slovak opposition in the federal legislature, served to harden attitudes. The upshot, probably desired more by the Czechs than by the Slovaks, was a formal separation as from the beginning of 1993, when the Czech coalition headed by the ODS became the government of the independent Czech Republic, with Klaus as Prime Minister.

In January 1993 Havel was elected President of the new Republic on the proposal of the ODS and its government allies, although foreign policy differences between the (non-party) head of state and the ODS emerged subsequently. Whereas the former promoted the Visegrad Group (with Hungary, Poland and Slovakia) as a Central European framework of economic reform and progress, the Klaus government saw speedy integration with Western economic and security structures as the priority. In 1994–95 the Klaus government remained the most stable in ex-communist Europe. In local elections in November 1994 the ODS headed the poll, with 28.7% of the vote.

In November 1995 the ODS voted in favour of a formal merger with the KDS (under the ODS party name), although the decision of half of the 10-strong KDS parliamentary party to join the KDU-ČSL rather than the ODS reduced the impact of the merger. The KDS had originated in the mid-1980s as an unofficial ecumenical Christian group calling for party pluralism and had been established as a distinct political party in December 1989. It espoused family values and strong local government, opposed abortion and easy divorce, and favoured a market economy and integration with Western Europe. At first a component of the broad pro-democracy Civic Forum (OF), the KDS had left the OF to contest the June 1990 elections within the broader Christian and Democratic Union. Included in the post-election Czech government headed by the OF, the KDS had opted in late 1991 to form an electoral alliance with the new ODS, while its erstwhile partners had later become the KDU-ČSL. Having won 10 seats in the 1992 Czech National Council elections, the KDS had been included in the consequential Czech coalition headed by the ODS.

Despite the merger with the KDS, the ODS lost ground in the 1996 lower house elections, winning only 68 seats on a 29.6% vote share. Klaus was nevertheless reappointed Prime Minister of a further coalition with the KDU-ČSL and the ODA, now with minority status and dependent on the qualified external support of the →Czech Social Democratic Party (ČSSD). Mounting difficulties in 1997, including a major financial crisis in May and allegations that the ODS had accepted illegal funding, led to the resignation of the Klaus government in November.

Although Havel secured parliamentary re-election as President in January 1998 on the proposal of the ODS, divisions in the party resulted in the creation of the breakaway →Freedom Union (US) and a sharp decline in ODS membership. In early lower house elections in June 1998 the ODS slipped to 63 seats and 27.7% of the vote, being overtaken by the ČSSD. It opted thereafter to enter into a so-called "opposition agreement" under which it undertook to give external support to the resultant ČSSD minority government, thus ending its previous centre-right alliance. In partial Senate elections in November 2000 the ODS won eight seats (its representation in the 81-member upper chamber falling to 22), while in simultaneous regional elections its vote share fell to 23.8%.

In March 2001 the ODS and the ČSSD government agreed to continue the "opposition agreement" until the parliamentary elections due in 2002. The following month, however, Klaus criticized newly-elected ČSSD chairman Vladimir Spidla as being "too left-wing" and warned that the ODS would terminate the agreement if the ČSSD replaced Miloš Zeman as Prime Minister.

The ODS is affiliated to the International Democrat Union and the European Democrat Union.

Communist Party of Bohemia and Moravia
Komunistická Strana Čech a Moravy (KSČM)

Address. Politických Vězňu 9, 11121 Prague 1
Telephone. (+420–2) 2289–7111
Fax. (+420–2) 2289–7207
Email. kscm@kscm.cz
Website. www.kscm.cz
Leadership. Miroslav Grebeníček (chairman)

Founded under its present name in March 1990, the KSČM is directly descended from the Communist Party of Czechoslovakia (KSČ), which was founded in 1921 by the pro-Bolshevik wing of the →Czech Social Democratic Party (ČSSD). The KSČ won nearly a million votes in the 1925 elections and was the only East European communist party to retain legal status in the 1930s, under the leadership of Klement Gottwald. It was eventually banned, as a gesture of appeasement to Nazi Germany, in the authoritarian aftermath of the 1938 Munich agreement, its leaders mostly taking refuge in Moscow. They returned at the end of World War II in the wake of the victorious Red Army as the dominant element of a National Front of democratic parties and in the 1946 elections became the largest party in the Czech Lands and the second strongest in Slovakia. Gottwald became Prime Minister and Communists thereafter used their control of the security apparatus to eliminate serious opposition to the party's designs. A government crisis of February 1948 enabled it to assume sole power, although most other Front parties were allowed to remain in existence in a subservient role throughout the subsequent 40 years of Communist rule (the exception being the Social Democrats, who were obliged to merge with the KSČ). Elections in May 1948 were held on the basis of a single National Front list controlled by the Communists, after which Gottwald took over the Czechoslovak presidency.

Purges of the KSČ leadership in 1951 in the wake of the Soviet–Yugoslav breach led to show trials and the execution of 11 prominent Communists in 1952, among them Rudolf Slánský, who had succeeded President Gottwald as party leader. They had been found guilty of being "Trotskyist-Titoist-Zionist-bourgeois-nationalist traitors". Following Gottwald's sudden death in 1953 (from pneumonia contracted at Stalin's funeral in Moscow), Antonín Novotný was elected to the revived post of party leader and later became President. Nikita Khrushchev's denunciation of Stalin in 1956 resulted in the rehabilitation of most of those executed in Czechoslovakia in 1952 (posthumously) and also of those imprisoned in that era, including Gustáv Husák. But no serious attempt was made to introduce political reform, pressure for which grew in the 1960s within and outside the party. Major economic reforms in 1967, largely inspired by Prof. Ota Šik, were aimed at decentralization and the creation of a "socialist market economy" but failed to stem the tide in favour of change. In January 1968 Novotný was replaced as KSČ leader by Alexander Dubček and as President by Gen. Ludvík Svoboda. Hitherto Slovak Communist leader, Dubček initiated what turned out to be the short-lived Prague Spring.

In April 1968 the KSČ central committee elected a new presidium dominated by reformers and also adopted an "action programme" promising democratization of the government system (although not party pluralism), freedom of assembly, the press, foreign travel and religion, curbs on the security police, rehabilitation of previous purge victims, and autonomy for Slovakia. Inevitably, this policy of "socialism with a human face" seriously alarmed the Soviet leadership and its Warsaw Pact satellites. Increasing pressure on the Prague reformers culminated in the military occupation of Czechoslovakia in August 1968 by forces of the USSR, East Germany, Poland, Hungary and Bulgaria (although not of Romania), on the stated grounds that they had been invited in by KSČ leaders, including Husák, who believed that the reform movement was out of control. Dubček and his immediate supporters were taken to Moscow as prisoners. They were quickly released on the insistence of President Svoboda, but the reform movement was effectively over. After anti-Soviet riots in early 1969, Gustáv Husák replaced Dubček as party leader and initiated a major purge of reformist elements which reduced KSČ membership from 1,600,000 to 1,100,000. Those expelled from the party included Dubček and other leaders of the Prague Spring.

Over the following two decades, Husák combined rigorous pro-Soviet orthodoxy and repression of political dissidents with a measure of economic liberalization. Having become President in 1975, Husák in December 1987 surrendered the party leadership to Miloš Jakeš, another political hardliner. But the post-1985 reform programme of Mikhail Gorbachev in the USSR had its inevitable impact in Czechoslovakia, with the complication that the party leadership could not easily subscribe to reforms which they had been brought into power to eradicate. The upshot was that the Communist regime crumbled with remarkable rapidity following the opening of the Berlin Wall in early November 1989, amid an upsurge of massive popular protest. At the end of November Jakeš was replaced as KSČ leader by Karel Urbánek and the following month Husák resigned as

President, having sworn in the first government with a non-Communist majority for over four decades, although it was led by a KSČ member. After Dubček had been elected chairman of the Federal Assembly (as a co-opted member), Husák was succeeded by the dissident playwright Václav Havel, who was elected head of state by a parliament still dominated by KSČ deputies. In late December 1989 an extraordinary KSČ congress elected Ladislav Adaméc to the new post of party chairman and issued a public apology for the party's past actions.

The Czech component of the KSČ responded to events by relaunching itself as the KSČM in March 1990, with Jiří Svoboda as leader and with a socialist rather than a Marxist-Leninist orientation. Hitherto, the KSČ had embraced the Communist Party of Slovakia but had had no Czech counterpart to that organization. In the June 1990 multi-party elections, the Czech Communists took second place in the Czech National Council, winning 32 of the 200 seats with 13.2% of the vote; they were also runners-up in the Czech balloting for the Federal Assembly, winning 15 of the 101 Czech lower house seats (with 13.5% of the vote) and 12 of the 75 Czech upper house seats (with 13.8%). The Communists then went into opposition for the first time since 1945, amid a continuing exodus of party members. In October 1990 the KSČM declared itself independent of the federal KSČ, shortly before the passage of a law requiring the KSČ to hand over to the government all of its assets at end-1989. In mid-1991 the KSČ was officially dissolved, but both the KSČM and its Slovak counterpart remained "Czechoslovak" in orientation.

In the June 1992 elections, the KSČM headed the Left Bloc Party, which included the Democratic Left Movement, the Left Alliance and the Movement for Social Justice. The Bloc won 35 of the 200 Czech National Council seats (with 14.1% of the vote) as well as 19 of the 99 Czech seats in the federal lower house and 15 of the 75 Czech seats in the upper house. Still in opposition, the KSČM mounted ultimately abortive resistance to the dissolution of the federation. Following the creation of the independent Czech Republic in January 1993, the party experienced much internal strife, including the resignation of Svoboda as leader over the rejection of his proposal to drop "Communist" from the party's title. He was replaced in June 1993 by the conservative Miroslav Grebeníček, whose election precipitated the formation of the breakaway →Democratic Left Party. A further split in December 1993 resulted in the creation of the →Left Bloc. These secessions meant that the KSČM had lost the majority of its deputies elected in 1992; it had also ceased to be supported by the former party newspaper *Rudé Právo*, which now favoured the Social Democrats (and later dropped "*Rudé*", meaning "Red", from it masthead).

The KSČM nevertheless retained substantial core membership and organizational strength, as well as a significant public following for its advocacy of a "socialist market economy" based on economic democracy and co-operatives and for its opposition to NATO membership and to absorption into the "German sphere of influence". In local elections in November 1994 it won 13.4% of the overall vote. In the 1996 parliamentary elections it took 10.3% of the national vote and 22 lower house seats, effectively becoming the main opposition to a further coalition headed by →Civic Democratic Party, given that the →Czech Social Democratic Party (ČSSD) agreed to give the new government qualified support. In the January 1998 parliamentary election for the presidency, KSČM candidate Stanislav Fischer, an astrophysicist, failed to progress to the second round against incumbent Václav Havel.

In April 1998 the KSČM joined the far-right →Association for the Republic–Czechoslovak Republican Party in voting against NATO membership in the decisive parliamentary division on the Czech Republic's accession. In the early June 1998 elections the KSČM advanced marginally to 24 lower house seats on an 11% vote share, remaining in opposition, now to a minority government of the ČSSD. In regional elections in November 2000 the KSČM advanced strongly to 21% of the vote.

Czech Social Democratic Party
Česká Strana Sociálně Demokratická (ČSSD)
Address. Hybernská 7, 11000 Prague 1
Telephone. (+42–2) 2421–9911
Fax. (+42–2) 2422–2190
Email. info@socdem.cz
Website. www.socdem.cz
Leadership. Miloš Zeman (leader); Vladimir Spidla (chairman); Bohuslav Sobotka (Chamber group chairman); Ladislav Svoboda (Senate group chairman)

Founded in 1878 as an autonomous section of the Austrian labour movement, the ČSSD became an independent party in 1911. Following the creation of Czechoslovakia after World War I, it won 25.7% of the vote in the 1920 elections (an inter-war record) but was weakened by the exodus of its pro-Bolshevik wing in 1921. Strongly supportive of the post-1918 political system (and a member of various coalitions), in 1938 the party was obliged to become part of the newly-created National Labour Party under the post-Munich system of "authoritarian democracy". Following the further dismantling of Czechoslovakia by Hitler in March 1939, the party went underground. It was a member of the government-in-exile in London during World War II, after which it participated in the Communist-dominated National Front, winning 37 of the 231 Czech seats in the May 1946 elections. The Social Democrats then came under mounting pressure from the Communists, who used the state security apparatus in a campaign to eliminate their main political rivals. Following a political crisis in February 1948, the ČSSD was forced to merge with the Communist Party and thereafter maintained its existence in exile.

Following the collapse of Communist rule in late 1989, the ČSSD was officially re-established in Czechoslovakia in March 1990, aspiring at that stage to be a "Czechoslovak" party appealing to both Czechs and Slovaks. It failed to secure representation in the June 1990 elections, after which its Czech and Slovak wings in effect became separate parties, although "Czechoslovak" remained its official descriptor. In the June 1992 elections the ČSSD won 16 seats in the 200-member Czech National Council (with 6.5% of the vote) and also secured representation in the Czech sections of both federal houses. It then mounted strong opposition to the proposed "velvet divorce" between Czechs and Slovaks, arguing in favour of a "confederal union", but eventually accepted the inevitability of the separation which duly came into effect at the beginning of 1993. At its first post-independence congress in February 1993, the party formally renamed itself the "Czech" SSD and elected a new leadership under Miloš Zeman. He declared his aim as being to provide a left-wing alternative to the neo-conservatism of the government in power, while at the same time ruling out co-operation with the →Communist Party of Bohemia and Moravia.

The ČSSD made a major advance in the 1996 parliamentary elections, winning 61 of the 200 lower house seats on a 26.4% vote share and becoming the second strongest party. It opted to give qualified external support to a new centre-right coalition headed by the →Civic Democratic Party (ODS), on the basis that privatization of the transport and energy sectors would be halted and that a Social Democrat would become chairman of the new lower house. Following the resignation of the government in November 1997, the ČSSD became the largest single party in early elections in June 1998, winning 74 of the lower house seats with 32.3% of the vote. Zeman therefore formed a minority ČSSD government, which was given external support by the ODS under a so-called "opposition agreement".

In March 1999 the Zeman government took the Czech Republic into NATO and in December secured official candidate status for European Union accession. It also con-

tinued the previous government's pro-market liberalization policies, although a deteriorating economic situation eroded its support, as did allegations of illicit ČSSD party financing. In partial Senate elections in November 2000 the ČSSD won only one seat (its representation in the 81-member upper chamber falling to 15), while in simultaneous regional elections its vote slumped to 14.7%.

In April 2001 Zeman vacated the party chairmanship and was succeeded by Vladimir Spidla, who distanced himself from the agreement with the ODS, arguing that the ČSSD should be "free and without commitment" in the parliamentary elections due in 2002. Zeman continued as Prime Minister, having been persuaded to remain in office by an ODS threat to withdraw its support if he were replaced by Spidla, who was regarded as too left-wing.

The ČSSD is a member party of the Socialist International.

Democratic Union
Demokratická Union (DEU)
Address. U Trativodu 358, Klánovice, 19014 Prague 9
Telephone. (+420–2) 2482–7029
Fax. (+420–2) 2482–7029
Email. deu@deu.cz
Website. www.deu.cz
Leadership. Ratibor Majzlík (chairman)

The right-wing DEU was founded in June 1994, backed by the *Český Deník* newspaper. It was critical of the then ruling →Civic Democratic Party (ODS) for emphasizing economic reform at the expense of law and order and was described by ODS Prime Minister Klaus as "a party of fundamentalist anti-Bolsheviks with no positive programme". The party won 2.8% of the vote and no lower house seats in 1996, although it returned one member to the Senate. In the 1998 lower house elections it again failed to secure representation, its vote falling to 1.4%.

In September 1999 the DEU joined the Coalition of Four opposition alliance with the →Freedom Union (US), the →Civic Democratic Alliance (ODA) and the →Christian Democratic Union–Czechoslovak People's Party (KDU-ČSL).

Freedom Union
Unie Svobody (US)
Address. Malostranské nám. 5, 11800 Prague 1
Telephone. (+420–2) 5701–1412
Fax. (+420–2) 5753–0102
Email. pavel.duchek@unie.cz
Website. www.unie.cz
Leadership. Hana Marvanová (chairperson); Ivan Pilip (first deputy chairman); Karel Kühnl (chairman of Chamber group); Pavel Duchek (general secretary)

The centre-right US was established in January 1998 by a breakaway group of the →Civic Democratic Party (ODS). Divisions within the ODS had intensified following the resignation in November 1997 of the government led by Václav Klaus, whose abrasive leadership style impelled a faction led by former Interior Minister Jan Ruml to form the new party. The new party attracted the support of 30 of the 69 ODS lower house deputies, including two of the ODS ministers in the post-Klaus interim government, who had accepted portfolios in defiance of a party instruction not to participate.

In early lower house elections in June 1998, the US retained only 19 seats, with an 8.6% vote share, and went into opposition to a minority government of the →Czech Social Democratic Party backed externally by the ODS. In opposition, the US in September 1999 formed a Coalition of Four with the →Civic Democratic Alliance (ODA), the →Christian Democratic Union–Czechoslovak People's Party (KDU-ČSL) and the →Democratic Union (DEU), announcing that the alliance would present a joint list of candidates and prospective ministerial team in the 2002 elections. In February 2000 Ruml was succeeded as party chairman by Karel Kühnl, a former Trade and Industry Minister. In the November 2000 partial Senate elections the FU advanced strongly within the opposition alliance, becoming the third largest party with 18 of the 81 seats.

As serious strains developed in the Coalition of Four, Kühnl was elected leader of the alliance in March 2001 to replace the original KDU-ČSL holder of the post. He therefore stood down as US chairman, being succeeded in June by Hana Marvanová, who became the first woman to lead a major Czech party.

Claiming a membership of 3,000, the US is an associate member of the European People's Party (EPP).

Republican Movement
Republikáni Miroslava Sládka (RMS)

Address. Senovázné nám. 6/III patro, 11000 Prague
Telephone. (+420–2) 2421–6893
Fax. (+420–2) 2421–6893
Email. m.zbela@seznam.cz
Website. www.republikani.cz
Leadership. Miroslav Sládek (chairman)

The far-right populist RMS is directly descended from the Association for the Republic–Czechoslovak Republican Party (SPR- RSČ), which was founded in February 1990 and subsequently campaigned for economic protectionism, drastic cuts in the state bureaucracy, military neutrality, non-participation in international organizations such as the IMF, rejection of restitution claims by Sudeten Germans expelled after World War II, measures against "unadaptable" minorities such as Gypsies and the reintroduction of capital punishment.

Obtaining its main support in northern Bohemia, the SPR-RSČ won 14 seats in the 200-member Czech National Council in June 1992 (with 6% of the vote); it also secured representation in both houses of the then Federal Assembly. At that stage the SPR-RSČ supported the preservation of Czechoslovakia and urged the recovery of the country's original 1918 borders, i.e. including Transcarpathian Ruthenia, which was annexed by the USSR in 1945 and today forms part of Ukraine. Following the inauguration of the independent Czech Republic in January 1993, the party experienced serious dissension within its parliamentary group, whose membership had fallen to six deputies by mid-1995 as a result of defections. Some of these were to the →Patriotic Republican Party launched in August 1995. In December 1995 party leader Miroslav Sládek received a suspended prison sentence for an assault on a policeman. In the 1996 lower house elections, however, the SPR-RSČ staged a recovery, winning 18 seats with 8% of the vote.

Sládek was again arrested in January 1998 for failing to appear in court on charges of inciting racial hatred, his sojourn in prison coinciding with his candidacy for the Czech presidency, in which he failed to progress to the second round of the parliamentary vote against incumbent Václav Havel. He was quickly acquitted on the incitement charges, but failed in a challenge to the validity of the presidential election. In May 1998 a physical attack on Sládek by Gypsies, over a speech with critical references to Gypsy life-style, sparked violent protests by party supporters. The SPR-RSČ subsequently supported a plan by a Czech town – which was eventually abandoned – to build a wall around a Gypsy neighbourhood to protect other citizens against their alleged criminality.

In the June 1998 lower house elections, the SPR-RS_ fell back to 3.9% of the vote and so failed to retain representation. In December 1999 the party was widely condemned for publishing a list of "Jews and Jewish half-breeds" in the political hierarchy. Having lost the state subsidy paid to represented parties, the SPR-RSČ was declared bankrupt in early 2001, following which the RMS was launched by Sládek as the successor party.

Other Parties

Civic National Movement (*Občanská Národne Hnuti, ONH*), launched in February 1996 by most of the deputies of the former Liberal National Social Party (LNSS), who had opposed the creation of the merged →Free Democrats–Liberal National Social Party the previous year.

Conservative Consensus Party (*Strana Konservativní Smlouvy, SKOS*), established in 1998 by a right-wing faction of the →Civic Democratic Alliance.
Address. Čímská 26, 12000 Prague 2
Telephone. (+420–2) 250223
Fax. (+420–2) 259424
Email. skos@skos.cz
Website. www.skos.cz

Countryside Party, founded in 1996 to articulate the concerns of the rural population.
Leadership. Jan Veleba (chairman)

Czech National Social Party (*Česká Strana Národně Sociální, CSNS*), right-wing formation.
Address. Londýnská 608/52, 12021 Prague 2
Telephone. (+420–2) 2251–4587
Fax. (+420–2) 2425–7637
Email. csns@mbox.vol.cz
Website. www.csns.cz
Leadership. Marie Machaté

Czech Right (*Česká Pravice, CP*), far-right party founded in 1993.
Address. Lublaňská 39, 12000 Prage 2
Email. cp-praha@email.cz
Website. www.ceskapravice.cz

Czechoslovak Communist Party (*Komunistická Strana Československa, KSČ*), formation advocating a return to pre-1989 political and economic arrangements, founded in 1995 by Miroslav Stepan on his release from prison for having, as Prague Communist Party boss in the late 1980s, ordered the security forces to break up pro-democracy demonstrations; barred from the 1996 elections because it could not pay the required deposits.
Email. ksc@ksc-uv.cz
Website. www.ksc-uv.cz
Leadership. Miroslav Stepan

European Democratic Party, founded in January 2000 by a former deputy of what became the far-right →Republican Movement, although it claims to have nothing in common with the latter.
Leadership. Pavel Maixner

Free Democrats–Liberal National Social Party (*Svobodní Demokraté–Liberálni Národně Sociální Strana, SD-LNSS*), formed in late 1995 as a merger of the SD and the LNSS, although most LNSS deputies later founded the →Civic National Movement. The LNSS had claimed descent from the National Socialist Party (founded in 1897), which had been a member of the post-war National Front, becoming the Czechoslovak Socialist Party (ČSS) on the Communist takeover in 1948, after which it had been a Front party. Unsuccessful in the 1990 elections, the ČSS had in 1991 joined the broader Liberal Social Union (LSU), which had won 16 Czech National Council seats in the 1992 elections but had thereafter suffered dissension, most of the ČSS component in June 1993 forming the centrist LNSS. The SD had derived from the liberal wing of the pro-democracy Civic Forum, which had become the Civic Movement (OH) following the secession of the →Civic Democratic Party in early 1991. After the OH had failed to secure representation in the 1992 elections, Jiří Dienstbier and his faction had in October 1993 launched the SD as a party. In the 1996 parliamentary elections the SD-LNSS achieved only 2.1% of the national vote.

Address. Republiky nám. 7, 11149 Prague 1

Telephone. (+420–2) 2422–3443

Fax. (+420–2) 2161–8554

Email. sdlsns@mbox.vol.cz

Leadership. Jiří Dienstbier (chairman)

Green Party (*Strana Zelených, SZ*), founded in 1989 and prominent in the "velvet revolution", but failed to win representation in the 1990 elections, and so for the 1992 elections joined the broader Liberal Social Union (LSU), which won 16 seats in the Czech National Council. The SZ opposed the conversion of the LSU into a unitary party and reverted to independent status in November 1993, but was barred from the 1996 elections because it could not pay the required deposits. The party is a member of the European Federation of Green Parties.

Address. Murmanská 13, 10000 Prague 10

Telephone/Fax. (+420–2) 736580

Email. miroslav_rokos@env.cz

Leadership. Jaroslav Vlček

Moravian Democratic Party, founded in Brno in 1997 as a merger of the Bohemian–Moravian Centre Union (ČMUS) and the Moravian National Party (MNS); argues that Moravians should be defined as a separate ethnic group.

Leadership. Ivan Drimal (chairman)

National Alliance, far-right formation; its leader was arrested in February 2000 on charges of inciting racial hatred.

Leadership. Vladimir Skoupy

National Social Bloc, alliance of far-right groupings founded in March 2001, including the →Patriotic Republican Party (VRS), the →National Alliance and

National Reistance; refused registration by the Interior Ministry.

Leadership. Jan Kopal

Party of Democratic Socialism (*Strana Demokratického Socialismu, SDS*), formed in 1998 as a merger of the Left Bloc and the Democratic Left Party.

Email. secret@sds.cz

Website. www.sds.cz

Leadership. Marie Stiborova

Patriotic Republican Party (*Vlástenecka Republikanska Strana, VRS*), far-right grouping founded in August 1995 as a merger of the National Democratic Unity (NDJ) and dissident members of what became the →Republican Movement.

Leadership. Rudolf Valenta (chairman)

Pensioners for a Secure Life (*Duchodci za Životní Jistoty, DZJ*), founded in December 1989 to promote the interests of pensioners in the post-communist era, obtained 3.8% of the vote in the 1992 Czech National Council elections, 3.1% in 1996 and 3.1% in 1998.

Address. Sudoměřská 32, 13000 Prague 3

Leadership. Josef Koniček (chairman)

Romany Civic Initiative (*Romanská Občanská Iniciativa, ROI*), a right-wing party promoting the interests of Gypsies in the Czech Republic.

Romany National Congress (*Romský Národní Kongres, RNK*), a left-wing party promoting the interests of Gypsies in the Czech Republic.

Socialist Alternative (*Socialistická Alternativa, SA*), Trotskyist grouping, Czech section of the Committee for a Workers' International.

Denmark

Capital: Copenhagen

Population: 5,250,000 (2000E)

Under its 1953 constitution the Kingdom of Denmark is a democratic, multi-party constitutional monarchy in which legislative power is vested in the unicameral *Folketing*, whose members are elected under a highly complex proportional system for a four-year term (subject to dissolution) by universal suffrage of those aged 18 years and above. Of the 179 *Folketing* members, 135 are elected by proportional representation in 17 metropolitan districts, with 40 additional seats being divided to achieve overall proportionality among parties that have secured at least 2 percent of the vote nationally. In addition, the Faroe Islands and Greenland are allotted two representatives each (see separate sections below). Denmark joined what became the European Union on Jan. 1, 1973, and elects 16 representatives to the European Parliament.

Public financial support for Danish parties falls into two categories. (1) Under Promulgation Act No 704 of Aug. 21, 1995, state funding is available (*a*) to parties represented in the *Folketing* in approximate proportion to their number of seats, and (*b*) to party organizations and independent candidates contesting national, regional or local elections on the basis of the number of votes received in the previous election (subject to a minimum requirement of 1,000 votes). Parties must not use income from one category of subsidy for expenditure in the other. The total amount available in this category in 2001 was Dkr77.5 million (about $9 million). (2) Under the rules of the *Folketing* as amended in December 1996, each party group is supported in its parliamentary work by (a) a basic payment, set at Dkr225,610 per month as from April 1, 2001, (*b*) an additional payment for each member of the group, set at Dkr35,323 per month as from April 1, 2001 (except that only a third of this sum, Dkr11,774, is payable where a group member is Speaker of the *Folketing* or a government minister). The total amount available under this category in 2001 was Dkr97.8 million (about $11 million).

Elections for the 175 metropolitan *Folketing* seats on March 11, 1998, resulted as follows: Social Democratic Party 63 seats (with 35.9% of the vote), Liberal Party (*Venstre*) 42 (24.0%), Conservative People's Party 16 (8.9%), Socialist People's Party 13 (7.6%), Danish People's Party 13 (7.4%), Centre Democrats 8 (4.3%), Radical Liberal Party 7 (3.9%), Red–Green Unity List 5 (2.7%), Christian People's Party 4 (2.5%), Progress Party 4 (2.4%). One of the two deputies elected from the Faroes joined the Conservative People's group and the other was a Faroese Social Democrat who remained independent; of the two Greenland deputies, one joined the Social Democratic group and the other the Liberal (*Venstre*) group.

Centre Democrats
Centrum-Demokraterne (CD)
Address. Ny Vestergade 7, DK-1471 Copenhagen K
Telephone. (+45–33) 127–115
Fax. (+45–33) 120–115
Email. matpost@centrumdemokraterne.dk
Website. www.centrumdemokraterne.dk
Leadership. Mimi Stilling Jakobsen (chairperson); Peter Duetoft (parliamentary group chairman); Yvonne Herløv Andersen (secretary-general)

The CD was established in November 1973 by right-wing dissidents of the →Social Democratic Party (SD) led by Erhard Jakobsen, who objected to the "increasingly leftist course" of the then SD government, particularly its plans for increased taxation. Favouring a mixed economy and rejecting "socialist experiments", the new party won 13 seats and 7.8% of the vote in the December 1973 elections, but fell back to three seats and 2.2% in 1975. Recovery in 1977 to 10 seats and 6.4% was followed by a further setback in the 1979 elections, in which the CD tally was six seats and 3.2%. The 1981 contest yielded the CD's best result to date (15 seats and 8.3%), with the result that in September 1982 the party entered a four-party non-socialist coalition headed by the →Conservative People's Party (KFP). Cut back to eight seats and 4.6% in 1984, the CD was the only coalition party to gain in the 1987 elections (to nine seats and 4.8%); it almost held its ground in the 1988 contest (nine seats and 4.7% vote) but went into opposition to a three-party coalition headed by the KFP. Under the new leadership of Mimi Jakobsen (a former Social Affairs Minister), the CD retained nine seats in the 1990 elections (with 5.1% of the vote).

Following the resignation of the centre-right coalition in January 1993, the CD joined a four-party centre-left administration headed by the SD. Strongly pro-European, the CD was a party to the "national compromise" which secured referendum approval of the Maastricht Treaty at the second attempt in May 1993. In the June 1994 European Parliament elections, the CD slumped to 0.9% and lost its two existing seats. It partially recovered to 2.8% and five seats in the September 1994 national elections, joining a three-party centre-left coalition again headed by the SD.

The CD withdrew from the ruling coalition in December 1996 in protest against a deal reached by the SD with the →Socialist People's Party and the →Red–Green Unity List in order to secure passage of the 1997 budget. Although it continued to give general external support to the government, in the March 1998 general election it lined up with the centre-right opposition and advanced to eight seats and a 4.3% vote share. It remained in opposition, while giving strong backing to the government's successful advocacy of a "yes" vote in the May 1998 referendum on the EU's Amsterdam Treaty. The CD again failed to win representation in the June 1999 elections to the European Parliament.

The CD was also part of the broad coalition which attempted to secure referendum approval in September 2000 for Danish membership of the euro single currency, the outcome being a decisive "no" vote by the electorate.

Christian People's Party
Kristeligt Folkeparti (KrFP)
Address. Allegade 24A/1, DK-2000 Frederiksberg
Telephone. (+45–33) 277–810
Fax. (+45–33) 213–116
Email. krf@ft.dk
Website. www.krf.dk
Leadership. Jann Sjursen (leader and parliamentary group chairman); Ib Algot Nielsen (secretary-general)

The KrFP was founded in April 1970 as an inter-denominational formation of Christian groups opposed to abortion on demand, pornography and the permissive society in general. The party achieved representation in the *Folketing* for the first time in 1973, winning seven seats and 4.0% of the vote. It advanced to nine seats and 5.3% in 1975 but lost ground in subsequent elections, taking only four seats and

2.3% in 1981. In September 1982 it was allocated two portfolios in a centre-right coalition headed by the →Conservative People's Party (KFP), but left the government after the 1988 elections, in which it just attained the 2% minimum required for representation and retained four seats. It again won four seats in the 1990 contest (on a 2.3% vote share) and in January 1993 was allocated two portfolios in a centre-left coalition headed by the →Social Democratic Party.

The KrFP slipped to 1.1% in the June 1994 European Parliament elections (insufficient for representation) and took only 1.8% in the September 1994 national elections, thus exiting from both the *Folketing* and the government. The party recovered to 2.5% in the March 1998 general election, enough to re-enter the *Folketing* with four seats. Although in opposition, the KrFP was part of the broad coalition which attempted to secure referendum approval in September 2000 for Danish membership of the euro single currency, the outcome being a decisive "no" vote by the electorate.

Claiming a membership of 6,500, the KrFP is affiliated to the Christian Democrat International and the European People's Party.

Conservative People's Party
Konservative Folkeparti (KFP)
Address. Nyhavn 4, Postboks 1515, DK-1020 Copenhagen K
Telephone. (+45–33) 134–140
Fax. (+45–33) 933–773
Email. konservative@konservative.dk
Website. www.konservative.dk
Leadership. Bendt Bendtsen (leader and parliamentary group chairman); Poul Andreassen (chairman); Jan Høgskilde (secretary-general)

The KFP was founded in February 1916 by progressive elements of the old *Hoejre* (Right) grouping that had been represented in the *Folketing* since 1849 but had lost its traditional dominance with the rise of the →Liberal Party (*Venstre*) and the →Social Democratic Party (SD). The new party abandoned the reactionary stance of the old *Hoejre*, adopting a programme featuring support for proportional representation and social reform. It provided parliamentary support for three *Venstre* governments in the 1920s but was in opposition from 1929 until joining a national unity coalition during World War II. After the war it maintained its pre-war electoral strength of 16–20% in most elections up to 1971 before falling to under 10% in the 1970s (and to a low of 5.5% and only 10 seats in 1975). It was in opposition to centre-left coalitions or minority SD governments for most of the period to 1982, the exceptional years being 1950–53, when it governed with the *Venstre*, and 1968–71, when it was in coalition with the →Radical Liberal Party (RV) and the *Venstre*. The KFP strongly backed Denmark's entry into the European Community in 1973 and also remained a staunch supporter of Danish membership of NATO.

Under the leadership of Poul Schlüter, the KFP recovered to 12.5% and 22 seats at the 1979 elections and to 14.5% and 26 seats in 1981, with the result that in September 1982 Schlüter became the first Conservative Prime Minister since 1901, heading a four-party centre-right coalition with the *Venstre*, the →Centre Democrats (CD) and the →Christian People's Party. Committed to reducing the role of the state, the Schlüter government was to remain in office for more than a decade, albeit with changes in its party composition in 1988 and 1990. A further KFP advance to a high of 23.4% and 42 seats in 1984 was followed by a decline to 20.8% and 38 seats in 1987 and to 19.3% and 35 seats in the 1988 snap elections, called by Schlüter after the government had been defeated on an opposition motion that visiting warships should be informed of Denmark's nuclear weapons ban. He was nevertheless able to form a new minority government, this time consisting of the KFP, the *Venstre* and the RV. The KFP fell back to 16.0% and 30 in the December 1990 elections, after which Schlüter was obliged to form a minority two-party coalition with the *Venstre* because the other centre-right parties declined to participate. In June 1992 the government was severely embarrassed when Danish voters disregarded its advice by narrowly rejecting the Maastricht Treaty on European Union.

The KFP participated in the seven-party "national compromise" of October 1992 establishing the terms of joint support for the Maastricht Treaty in a further referendum. Before it could be held, the "Tamilgate" scandal, relating to the exclusion of relatives of Tamil refugees in the late 1980s, unexpectedly brought about the downfall of the Schlüter government in January 1993 and the installation of a majority coalition (the first since 1971) headed by the SD. In opposition, the KFP in September 1993 elected Hans Engell, a former Defence and Justice Minister, to succeed Schlüter as party chair. The party won 17.7% of the vote in the June 1994 European balloting, increasing its representation from two to three seats. It slipped to 15.0% percent and 27 seats in the September 1994 national elections, remaining in opposition.

Engell was obliged to resign as KFP chair in February 1997 after being involved in a car accident and being found to be over the legal alcohol limit; he was replaced by Per Stig Møller (a former Environment Minister). The March 1998 general election resulted in a major setback for the party, which declined to 8.9% of the vote and 16 seats, losing votes to the new →Danish People's Party in particular. Møller was subsequently succeeded as party leader by Bendt Bendtsen. In the June 1999 European Parliament elections the KFP lost two of its three seats, winning only 8.6% of the vote. Although in opposition, the CD was part of the broad coalition which attempted to secure referendum approval in September 2000 for Danish membership of the euro single currency, the outcome being a decisive "no" vote by the electorate.

Claiming a membership of 25,000, the KFP is a member of the International Democrat Union and the European Democrat Union. Its European Parliament representative sits in the European People's Party/European Democrats group.

Danish People's Party
Dansk Folkeparti (DF)
Address. Christiansborg, DK-1240 Copenhagen K
Leadership. Pia Kjærsgaard (chairperson); Kristian Thulesen Dahl (parliamentary group chairperson); Steen Thomsen (secretary-general)
Telephone. (+45–33) 375–199
Fax. (+45–33) 375–191
Email. df@ft.dk
Website. www.danskfolkeparti.dk
The DF was launched in October 1995 by four disaffected deputies of the right-wing →Progress Party (FP), including Pia Kjærsgaard, who had been ousted as FP leader earlier in the year. The DF espoused the same policies as the FP but was regarded as being to the right of the parent party. Its overall objective is "to re-establish Denmark's independence and freedom to ensure the survival of the Danish nation and the Danish monarchy"; it opposes in particular the development of Denmark into a multi-ethnic society through immigration. It is also opposed to membership of the European Union (EU), arguing that European cooperation should be limited to free trade and protection of common natural assets.

After winning 6.8% of the vote in the November 1997 local elections, in its first general election in March 1998 the DF easily outpolled the rump FP, winning 13 seats with a 7.4% vote share. It unsuccessfully opposed approval of the EU's Amsterdam Treaty in the May 1998 referendum, taking some comfort from the size (44.9%) of the "no" vote. In the June 1999 European Parliament elections the DF won 5.8% of the vote and one of Denmark's 16 seats. Kjærsgaard was subsequently the effective leader of the successful

campaign against Danish membership of the euro single currency, which was decisively rejected by the electorate in a referendum in September 2000.

The party has a membership 4,000. Its representative in the European Parliament sits in the Union for a Europe of Nations group.

Freedom 2000
Frihed 2000
Address. Christiansborg, 1240 Copenhagen K
Telephone. (+45–33) 373–860
Fax. (+45–33) 151–399
Email. frihed@ft.dk
Leadership. Kirsten Jacobsen
Freedom 2000 was launched in late 1999 by the remaining four deputies of the populist →Progress Party (FP) following the decision of an FP congress to readmit controversial original FP leader Mogens Glistrup. The new grouping was active in the successful campaign against Danish membership of the euro single currency in the September 2000 referendum.

Liberal Party
Venstre (V)
Address. Søllerødvej 30, DK-2840 Holte
Telephone. (+45–45) 802–233
Fax. (+45–45) 803–830
Email. venstre@venstre.dk
Website. www.venstre.dk
Leadership. Anders Fogh Rasmussen (leader and parliamentary group chairman); Claus Hjort Frederiksen (secretary-general)
The *Venstre* (literally "Left", although the party has long opted for the rubric "Liberal") was founded in June 1870 as Denmark's first organized party, derived from the Friends of the Peasants (*Bondevennerne*) and drawing its main support from small independent farmers (and later from sections of the urban middle class) opposed to the conservatism and political hegemony of the old *Hoejre* (Right), forerunner of the present-day →Conservative People's Party (KFP). It became dominant in the then lower house by the 1880s but remained in opposition due to *Hoejre* control of the upper house. In 1901, however, what was then called the *Venstre* Reform Party formed a majority government under Johan Henrik Deuntzer, who was succeeded as Prime Minister by Jens Christian Christensen in 1905. The party was weakened in the latter year by the formation of the breakaway →Radical Liberal Party (RV) but recovered partially in 1910 when it reunited with the small Moderate *Venstre* faction under the simple title *Venstre*. The party remained dominant until the 1924 elections, when it was replaced as Denmark's leading political formation by the →Social Democratic Party (SD), although it was again in power in 1926–29.

In opposition through the 1930s, *Venstre* experienced electoral decline, to 17.8% of the vote in 1935 compared with a high of 47.9% in 1903. After participating in the World War II national unity government, it rose to 23.4% in 1945 and formed a minority government under Knut Kristensen. Despite improving to 28.0% in 1947, *Venstre* went into opposition until 1950, when it formed a coalition with the KFP under the premiership of Erik Eriksen, who oversaw the introduction of the 1953 constitution. It then remained in opposition for 15 years, during which it support declined from 25.1% in 1957 to 18.5% in 1968, when it entered a centre-right coalition with the RV and KFP. This coalition lasted until 1971, but the watershed December 1973 elections, yielding fragmentation of the party structure (and only 22 seats for the *Venstre* on a 12.3% vote share), resulted in a highly minority *Venstre* government under Poul Hartling. Despite almost doubling its support to 23.3% and 42 seats in 1975, the *Venstre* went into opposition and slumped to 12.0% and 21 seats at the 1977 elections.

In August 1978 the *Venstre* entered its first-ever formal

peace-time coalition with the SD, but this collapsed a year later, precipitating elections in which the *Venstre* obtained 12.5% and 22 seats. Having slipped to 11.3% and 21 seats in the 1981 elections, in September 1982 it joined a four-party centre-right government headed by Poul Schlüter of the KFP and also including the →Centre Democrats (CD) and the →Christian People's Party (KrFP). The KFP/*Venstre* tandem was to survive for over a decade, creating an all-time longevity record for a non-socialist government, although the CD and KrFP were replaced by the RV in 1998–90, after which the KFP and the *Venstre* formed a two-party coalition that lasted until January 1993. During this period *Venstre* electoral support improved to 12.1% and 22 seats in 1984, slipped to 10.5% and 19 seats in 1987, rose to 11.8% and 22 seats in 1988 and rose again to 15.8% and 29 seats in 1990.

As a pro-European party, the *Venstre* shared in the Schlüter government's embarrassment over the electorate's rejection of the EU's Maastricht Treaty in June 1992. In October 1992 it participated in the seven-party "national compromise" establishing the terms of joint support for the treaty in a second referendum. Before it was held, the Schlüter government resigned in January 1993 over the "Tamilgate" affair, so that the *Venstre* returned to opposition. Under the new leadership of Uffe Ellemann-Jensen (former Foreign Minister), the party headed the poll in the June 1994 European Parliament elections, winning 19.0% and four of Denmark's 16 seats. In September 1994 it was the principal victor in general elections, receiving its highest vote share (23.3%) for two decades and 42 seats. During the campaign Ellemann-Jensen controversially proposed the formation of a centre-right coalition that would for the first time include the populist →Progress Party. In the event, the party continued in opposition to another SD-led government.

Venstre repeated its 1994 success in the March 1998 national elections, again winning 42 seats with a slightly higher vote share of 24.0%. It remained in opposition, while giving strong backing to the SD-led government's successful advocacy of a "yes" vote in the May 1998 referendum on the EU's Amsterdam Treaty. In the June 1999 European Parliament elections *Venstre* headed the poll with 23.3%, increasing its representation from four to five seats. Although in opposition, *Venstre* was part of the broad coalition which attempted to secure referendum approval in September 2000 for Danish membership of the euro single currency, the outcome being a decisive "no" vote by the electorate.

Claiming a membership of some 84,000, the *Venstre* is a member party of the Liberal International. Its representatives in the European Parliament sit in the European Liberal, Democratic and Reformist (ELDR) group.

Progress Party
Fremskridtspartiet (FP)
Address. Christiansborg, DK-1240 Copenhagen K
Telephone. (+45–33) 374–699
Fax. (+45–33) 151–399
Email. fp@ft.dk
Website. www.frp.dk
Leadership. Per Larsen (chairman); Martin Ipsen (secretary-general)

The FP was launched in August 1972 by Mogens Glistrup, a tax lawyer, who advocated the abolition of income tax, the dismissal of most civil servants and a major reduction of the state's role in the economy. The resultant increase in consumer demand would, he envisaged, yield more revenue from value-added tax (VAT), sufficient to cover drastically reduced government expenditure. More idiosyncratically, he also urged the abolition of Denmark's defence forces and the replacement of the Defence Ministry by a telephone answering machine giving the message "we surrender" in Russian. The party caught a populist tide in the watershed 1973 general elections, contributing to the fragmentation of

the party system by winning 28 seats and 15.9% of the vote, so that it became the second strongest party in the *Folketing*. It fell back to 24 seats and 13.6% in 1975, recovered to 26 seats and 14.6% in 1977 and then declined progressively to 20 seats (11.0%) in 1979, 16 seats (8.9%) in 1981 and six seats (3.6%) in 1984.

Meanwhile, Glistrup's parliamentary immunity was regularly suspended so that he could face charges of tax fraud in what turned out to be the longest trial in Danish history. Finally convicted in 1983 and sentenced to three years' imprisonment, he was expelled from the *Folketing*, re-elected in the 1984 elections (on temporary release from prison) and again expelled soon afterwards and returned to prison (from which was released in March 1985). Meanwhile, the FP's slump in the 1984 elections had exacerbated internal party dissension over his leadership style, resulting in the election of a new leadership under Pia Kjærsgaard and the moderation of the FP's more controversial policies. In particular, it now endorsed Denmark's continued membership of NATO and the preservation of the welfare state. On the other hand, it took a strong anti-immigration stance, seeking to articulate growing public concern on the issue.

The FP advanced slightly in the 1987 elections (to nine seats and 4.8%), before becoming the main victor in the 1988 poll (rising to 16 seats and 9.0%). It fell back to 12 seats and 6.4% in the 1990 contest, prior to which Glistrup was expelled from the FP *Folketing* group for indiscipline and subsequently suspended from party membership. The FP was the only parliamentary party that opposed Danish ratification of EU's Maastricht Treaty in both the 1992 and the 1993 referendums, its lack of Euro-enthusiasm producing a slump in its vote to 2.9% in the June 1994 European Parliament elections. It recovered its 1990 share of 6.4% in the September 1994 national elections, although its representation slipped to 11 seats. During the campaign the →Liberal Party leader caused controversy by publicly envisaging the formal inclusion of the FP in a future centre-right coalition.

Internal divisions in the FP in 1995 resulted in the ousting of Pia Kjærsgaard as leader and her replacement by Kirsten Jacobsen, following which a dissident faction including four FP deputies broke away to form the →Danish People's Party (DF). The result was that the FP's vote slumped to 2.4% in the March 1998 general elections and its representation to four seats. In October 1999, however, the four FP deputies, including Jacobsen, resigned from the party after an FP congress had voted for the readmission of Glistrup. The four deputies formed the →Freedom 2000 grouping in the *Folketing*, so that the FP was left without parliamentary representation and was therefore required to re-register with the Interior Ministry if it wished to contest the next general elections.

Radical Liberal Party
Det Radikale Venstre (RV)
Address. Christiansborg, DK-1240 Copenhagen K
Telephone. (+45–33) 374–747
Fax. (+45–33) 137–251
Email. radikale@radikale.dk
Website. www.radikale.dk
Leadership. Johannes Lebech (chairman); Elisabeth Arnold (parliamentary group chairman); Anders Kloppenborg (secretary-general)

Preferring to be known in English by the inaccurate title "Social Liberal Party", the RV dates from 1905 as a left-wing splinter group of the historic →Liberal Party (*Venstre*) inspired by the example of the fiRadical Party of France. Its original Odense Programme called for Danish neutrality in war, constitutional reform (including universal adult suffrage), a secret ballot, democratic local elections, provision for referendums on major issues, progressive taxation and land reform. Progress towards these aims was achieved by all-RV governments that held office in 1909–10 and 1913–20 (under the premiership of Carl Theodor Zahle, and more especially by the 1929–40 coalition between the RV and the now dominant →Social Democratic Party (SD). Having participated in the World War II national unity government and the post-war all-party administration, the RV returned to coalition with the SD in 1957–64 (with the →Single-Tax Party participating in 1957–60). During this period the party share of the vote rose from 8.1% in 1945 to 8.6% in 1953 but slipped to 5.3% by 1964, in which year it won only 10 *Folketing* seats out of 175.

Having recovered to 7.3% and 13 seats in 1967, the RV made a major advance in January 1968, to 15.0% and 27 seats, under the leadership of Hilmar Baunsgaard, who became Prime Minister of a non-socialist coalition that also included the *Venstre* and the →Conservative People's Party (KFP). This lasted until 1971, when the RV slipped to a vote share of 14.3% (retaining 27 seats) and went into opposition; the next three elections also yielded major setbacks, to 11.2% and 20 seats in 1973, 7.1% and 13 seats in 1975, and 3.6% and six seats in 1977. Recovering to 5.4% and 10 seats in 1979, the RV slipped to 5.1% and nine seats in 1981 and remained outside the KFP-led centre-right coalition formed in September 1982. It improved to 5.5% and 10 seats in 1984 and to 6.2% and 11 seats in 1987, after which contest RV leader Niels Helveg Petersen rebuffed the SD's attempt to form a centre-left coalition and thereafter gave external support to a further centre-right government.

Having slipped to 5.6% and 10 seats in the 1988 elections, the RV accepted five cabinet posts in a new KFP-led coalition, but withdrew from participation in 1990 over its opposition to the latest austerity budget. In the December 1990 elections it slumped to a post-war low of 3.5% and seven seats, but nevertheless entered the SD-led centre-left coalition formed in January 1993, receiving three portfolios. In the June 1994 European Parliament balloting, the RV was the only government party to increase its vote share, to 8.5% (yielding one of the 16 seats). In the September 1994 national elections it scored 4.6% and increased its seat total to eight, thereafter joining another SD-led coalition that also included the →Centre Democrats (CD).

Following the exit of the CD in December 1996, the RV became the SD's only formal coalition partner. In the March 1998 national elections the RV lost some ground, winning seven seats on a 3.9% vote share. It nevertheless continued as the junior coalition party, receiving four portfolios out of 20 in the new SD-led minority government. In the June 1999 European Parliament elections the RV improved to 9.1% of the vote while again winning one seat.

The RV was part of the broad government/opposition coalition which attempted to secure referendum approval in September 2000 for Danish membership of the euro single currency, the outcome being a decisive "no" vote by the electorate. In somewhat belated acceptance of a share of responsibility for the defeat, RV Foreign Minister Niels Helveg Petersen resigned in December 2000.

Claiming a membership of 6,000, the RV is a member party of the Liberal International. Its representative in the European Parliament sits in the European Liberal, Democratic and Reformist (ELDR) group.

Red-Green Unity List
Enhedslisten-de Roed-Groenne (ELRG)

Address. Studiestræde 24, DK-1455 Copenhagen K
Telephone. (+45–33) 933–324
Fax. (+45–33) 320–372
Email. enhedslisten@enhedslisten.dk
Website. www.ehhedslisten.dk
Leadership. 21-member collective; Søren Kolstrup (parliamentary group chairperson); Keld Albrechtsen (secretary)
The ELRG was established in 1989 as an alliance of three parties of leftist and/or environmentalist orientation. Strongly opposed to Danish membership of NATO and the European Community (later Union), it was part of the campaign against Danish ratification of the Maastricht Treaty (successful in Denmark's first referendum in June 1992, but

unsuccessful in the second in May 1993). It achieved a breakthrough in the September 1994 general elections, winning 3.1% of the vote and six seats. Thereafter, its external support was important for the survival of the centre-left coalition government headed by the →Social Democratic Party (SD), notably in the passage of the 1997 budget.

The ELRG lost ground in the March 1998 national elections, slipping to 2.7% of the vote and five seats. It continued thereafter to give qualified external support to a new SD-led minority government, but was part of the left-right coalition which campaigned successfully against Danish membership of the euro in the September 2000 referendum.

Social Democratic Party
Socialdemokratiet (SD)

Address. Thorvaldsenvej 2, DK-1998 Frederiksberg C
Telephone. (+45–35) 391–522
Fax. (+45–35) 394–030
Email. socialdemokratiet@net.dialog.dk
Website. www.socialdemokratiet.dk
Leadership. Poul Nyrup Rasmussen (chairman); Ole Stavad & Lene Jensen (deputy chairpersons); Jan Petersen (parliamentary group chairman); Willy Stig Andersen (general secretary)
Founded in 1871 to represent the emerging industrial working class, the SD first won seats in the *Folketing* in 1884 and in 1913–20 supported a minority government of the →Radical Liberal Party (RV). It became the strongest parliamentary party (with 55 out of 148 seats) in 1924, in which year it formed its first government under the premiership of Thorvald Stauning. In opposition from 1926, the party returned to government in 1929 under Stauning, who headed a coalition with the RV until the German occupation in May 1940 and thereafter, until his death in May 1942, a national unity government. Having achieved its its highest voting support to date in the 1931 elections (46.1%), the SD was instrumental in the 1930s in introducing advanced welfare state legislation and other social reforms on the Scandinavian model.

The SD continued to be the dominant party after World War II, although it has never won an overall majority and has averaged about a third of the vote in recent elections. Stauning's successor as Prime Minister and SD leader, Vilhelm Buhl, headed the immediate post-war all-party coalition formed in May 1945, but the party lost support in the October 1945 elections and went into opposition. Talks with the Danish Communists on the creation of a broad Labour Party came to nothing. The SD returned to power in November 1947 as a minority government under Hans Hedtoft until his death in January 1955 and then under Hans Christian Hansen. In May 1957 the SD formed a majority coalition with the RV and the →Single-Tax Party, under the premiership of Hansen until his death in February 1960 and then under Viggo Kampmann. After improving to 42.1% and 76 seats in the November 1960 elections (its best post-war result), the party formed a two-party coalition with the RV, under Kampmann until he was succeeded as party leader and Prime Minister by Jens Otto Krag in September 1962.

Krag reverted to a minority SD government after the September 1964 elections (in which the party slipped to 41.9% but retained 76 seats); however, after losing ground in the next two elections, the party was in opposition from January 1968 until, following SD gains in the September 1971 elections (to 37.3% and 70 seats), Krag was able to form a new minority government the following month. Immediately after the October 1972 referendum decision in favour of European Community membership, Krag unexpectedly resigned in January 1973 and was succeeded by trade union leader Anker Jørgensen. Later that year the SD was weakened by the formation of the →Centre Democrats by a right-wing splinter group which claimed that the party was moving too far to the left. Heavy SD losses in the December 1973 elections (to 25.6% and 46 seats, its worst result in half a century) sent the party into opposition; but a partial recovery in the January 1975 contest (to 30.0% and 53 seats) resulted in an SD minority government under Jørgensen. Following a further SD recovery in the February 1977 elections (to 37.0% and 65 seats), Jørgensen in August 1978 negotiated the SD's first-ever formal coalition with the *Venstre* Liberals in peace-time. However, after another SD advance in the September 1979 elections (to 38.3% and 68 seats), Jørgensen formed an SD minority government.

The SD suffered a setback in the 1981 elections, falling to 59 seats and 32.9% of the vote. It nevertheless remained in office until September 1982, when Jørgensen resigned and was replaced by Denmark's first Prime Minister from the →Conservative People's Party since 1901. The SD lost further ground at the January 1984 and September 1987 elections (to 56 seats and 31.6%, then to 54 seats and 29.3%), by which time the party had experienced its longest period of opposition since the 1920s. After unsuccessfully seeking to form a coalition with the RV and the →Socialist People's Party (SFPP), Jørgensen resigned as SD chair after the 1987 elections and was succeeded (in November 1987) by Svend Auken. But a lacklustre SD performance in further elections in May 1988 (in which it slipped to 55 seats and 29.9%) kept the party in opposition. It improved sharply at the next contest in December 1990 (to 69 seats and 37.4%), but remained in opposition, with the eventual result that in April 1992 Auken was replaced as party chair by Poul Nyrup Rasmussen. Two months later the SD shared in the general embarrassment of the pro-European government parties when Danish voters narrowly rejected the Maastricht Treaty of the European Union (EU).

The SD participated in the seven-party "national compromise" of October 1992 establishing the terms of joint support for the Maastricht Treaty in a further referendum. Before it could be held, the "Tamilgate" scandal unexpectedly brought about the downfall of the centre-right coalition in January 1993 and the installation of a majority coalition (the first since 1971) headed by the SD and including the RV, the →Centre Democrats (CD) and the →Christian People's Party. The Maastricht Treaty was duly approved at the second time of asking in May 1993, but a significant minority of SD activists and voters remained in the "no" camp. The party's continuing difficulties over the EU were apparent in the June 1994 European Parliament elections, when the SD managed only 15.8% of the vote and three of the 16 Danish seats. In the September 1994 national elections, however, the party recovered to 34.6%, yielding 62 seats and enabling Rasmussen to form a three-party minority coalition with the RV and the CD.

The CD's resignation from the government in December 1996, in protest against an agreement between Rasmussen and the →Socialist People's Party and the →Red–Green Unity List ensuring passage of the 1997 budget, reduced the ruling coalition to two parties. Although it lost ground in the November 1997 local elections, in the March 1998 national elections the SD unexpectedly increased its vote share to 35.9% and its representation to 63 seats. Rasmussen accordingly formed another minority government in coalition with the RV. In the June 1999 European Parliament elections the SD posted its customary poor performance in such contests, again winning only three seats (with a 16.5% vote share).

Intense debate within the SD on whether Denmark should enter the single European currency eventually resulted in a majority decision in favour at the party's 2000 congress. Many SD supporters remained opposed, however, and contributed to the decisive majority against in the September 2000 referendum. Continuing in office despite this major setback, Rasmussen in December 2000 appointed five new ministers, including three relatively unknown Social Democrats, in an attempt to rejuvenate his government.

Claiming a membership of 100,000, the SD is a member party of the Socialist International. Its representatives in the European Parliament sit in the Party of European Socialists group.

Socialist People's Party
Socialistisk Folkeparti (SFP)

Address. Christiansborg, DK–1240 Copenhagen K
Telephone. (+45–33) 374–491
Fax. (+45–33) 147–010
Email. sf@sf.dk
Website. www.sf.dk
Leadership. Holger K. Nielsen (chairman); Aage Frandsen (parliamentary group chairman); Ole Hvas Kristiansen (secretary-general)

The SFP was founded in November 1958 by a dissident faction of the →Communist Party of Denmark (DKP) led by former DKP chair Aksel Larsen, following the latter's expulsion from the party for praising Titoism in Yugoslavia and criticizing the Soviet Union's suppression of the 1956 Hungarian Uprising. The new party advocated left-wing socialism independent of the Soviet Union, unilateral disarmament, Nordic co-operation, and opposition to NATO and to Danish accession to the European Community (EC).

The SFP won 11 seats and 6.1% of the vote at its first elections in 1960, fell back slightly in 1964 but advanced to 20 seats and 10.9% in 1966. Apart from the 1971 contest, the next five elections brought a gradual decline for the SFP, to a low of six seats and 3.9% in 1977, in part because of competition from the new →Left Socialists party, founded by SFP dissidents in 1967. In 1972 the SFP took a leading role in the unsuccessful "no" campaign in the Danish referendum on EC entry, acting in this as on other issues as an unofficial left wing of the →Social Democratic Party (SD). During the 1970s the SFP usually gave external support to the SD-led minority governments characteristic of the decade.

The four elections from 1979 yielded an SFP resurgence, to an all-time high of 27 seats and 14.6% in 1987, when it was the only party to make significant gains and became the third-strongest parliamentary party. It remained in opposition to the Schlüter centre-right government and lost ground in the 1988 contest, falling to 24 seats and 13.0% of the vote. SD gains in the 1990 elections further reduced the SFP tally, to 15 seats and 8.3%. The party campaigned on the "no" side in the June 1992 referendum in which Danish voters narrowly rejected the Maastricht Treaty of what became the European Union (EU), although it no longer advocated Denmark's withdrawal. In October 1992, after some agonizing, the KFP joined the seven-party "national compromise" setting new terms for approval of the treaty, which was given by voters at the second time of asking in May 1993.

In June 1994 the SFP won 8.6% of the vote in European Parliament elections, thus retaining the one seat it won in 1989. It declined to 13 seats and 7.3% in the September 1994 general elections, partly because of a rise in support for the new →Red-Green Unity List (ELRG), thereafter pledging conditional support for the reconstituted SD-led coalition. This support proved crucial in 1996 over the passage of the disputed 1997 budget, on the basis of a deal between the SD, the SFP and the ELGR which gave the two non-governmental parties a promise of increased social spending.

The SFP again won 13 seats in the March 1998 national elections, with a slightly increased vote share of 7.6%. and continued to give qualified support to another SD-led government. In the June 1999 European Parliament elections it retained its single seat with 7.1% of the vote. In 2000 the SFP was part of the left-right coalition which campaigned successfully against Danish membership of the euro in the September 2000 referendum.

With an official membership of 8,000, the SFP is a member of the New European Left Forum (NELF). Its European Parliament representative sits in the European United Left/Nordic Green Left group.

Other Parties and Movements

Communist Party of Denmark (*Danmarks Kommunistiske Parti, DKP*). Founded in 1919 and represented in the *Folketing* from 1932. It participated in the immediate post-war coalition government, winning 18 seats in 1945 but declined steadily thereafter to nil in 1960, having been weakened by the formation of the →Socialist People's Party. It re-entered the *Folketing* in 1973 with six seats, rising to seven in 1975 and 1977, but unrepresented since 1979.
Address. Studiesstræde 24/1, DK-1455 Copenhagen K
Telephone. (+45–33) 916–644
Fax. (+45–33) 320–372
Leadership. Mogens Høver (chairman)

Communist Party of Denmark–Marxist–Leninist (*Danmarks Kommunistiske Parti–Marxister–Leninister, DKP-ML*), formerly pro-Albanian formation.
Address. Griffenfeldsgade 26, DK-2200 Copenhagen N
Telephone. (+45–31) 356–069
Fax. (+45–35) 372–039
Email. dkp-ml@dkp-ml.dk
Website. www.dkp-ml.dk
Leadership. Jørgen Petersen

Danish Centre Party (*Dansk Center Parti, DCP*), deceptively named anti-immigration formation established in 1992, advocating a complete embargo on immigration and admittance of refugees.
Address. PB 150, DK-2880 Bagsværd
Telephone/Fax. (+45–44) 972–738
Email. dcp@post7.tele.dk
Website. home7.inet.tele.dk/dcp
Leadership. Per W. Johansson (chairman)

Democratic Renewal (*Demokratisk Fornyelse, DF*), electoral alliance of various left-wing and centrist groups opposed to membership of the European Union; won only 0.3% of the vote in 1998 general elections.
Address. Askevej 16, DK-3630 Jægerspris
Telephone/Fax. (+45–47) 500–692
Email. dem-forny@image.dk
Website. www.image.dk/~dem_for

Green Party (*Partiet de Grønne*), sub-titled **Realistic-Ecological Alternative** (*Oekoloisk-Realistik Alternativ*), founded in 1983, has remained small because of the strong environmentalist current in several mainstream parties and also because of the recent success of the →Red–Green Unity List; affiliated to the European Federation of Green Parties.
Address. Westend 15 st.th, DK-1661, Copenhagen V
Telephone. (+45–33) 253–339
Email. groenne@mail.danbbs.dk
Website. www.groenne.dk
Leadership. Anders Wamsler & Jean Thierry

International Socialists (*Internationale Socialister, IS*), Trotskyist formation linked to the International Socialist Tendency.
Address. PB 5113, DK-8100 Århus
Telephone. (+45–86) 193–024
Email. soc.revy@vip.cybercity.dk
Website. soc.revy.homepage.dk

June Movement (*Junibevægelsen, JB*), anti-EU formation named after the month of the initial Danish referendum rejection of the Maastricht Treaty; won 15.2% and two seats in the 1994 elections to the European Parliament, improving to 16.1% and three seats in the 1999 contest on a platform of vigorous opposition to any attempt to take Denmark into the single European currency; its MEPs sit in the Europe of Democracies and Diversities group at Strasbourg.
Address. Skindergade 29/1, DK-1159 Copenhagen K
Telephone. (+45–33) 930–046
Fax. (+45–33) 930–067
Email. juninet@inform-bbs.dk
Website. www.eusceptic.org/juninet
Leadership. Jens-Peter Bonde

Left Socialist Party (*Venstresocialisterne, VS*), founded in December 1967 by left-wing dissidents of the →Socialist People's Party (SFP), won four *Folketing* seats in 1968, lost them in 1971, regained them in 1975, reached high point of six seats in 1979, falling to five in 1981 and 1984, but weakened thereafter by factionalism and retro-defections to the SFP; unrepresented in the national parliament since 1987, much of its support having switched to the →Red-Green Unity List (with which it has allied in elections.)
Address. Griffenfeldsgade 41, DK-2200 Copenhagen N
Telephone/Fax. (+45–31) 350–608
Email. vs@venstresocialisterne.dk
Website. www.venstresocialisterne.dk

People's Movement against the European Union (*Folkesbevægelsen mod EF-Unionen*), founded to articulate rank-and-file anti-European feeling in officially pro-European parties, won 18.9% and four seats in the 1989 European Parliament elections, falling to 10.3% and two seats in 1994 (when it faced competition from the →June Movement) and to 7.3% and one seat in 1999; its MEP sits in the Europe of Democracies and Diversities group at Strasbourg.
Address. Sigurdsgade 39A, DK-2200 Copenhagen N
Telephone. (+45–35) 821–800
Fax. (+45–35) 821–806
Email. katte-ud@post1.tele.dk
Website. www.inform.dk/sturm/folkenet
Leadership. Lis Jensen & Ole Krarup

Schleswig Party (*Schleswigsche Partei*), founded in August 1920 following the incorporation of former German northern Schleswig into Denmark; representing the German minority, it had one *Folketing* seat until 1964 and again in 1973–79, latterly in alliance with the →Centre Democrats.
Address. Vestergade 30, DK-6200 Åbenrå
Telephone. (+45–74) 623–833
Fax. (+45–74) 627–939
Email. sp@post6.tele.dk
Website. www.bdn.dk/sp
Leadership. Peter Bieling (chairman)

Single-Tax Party, also known as the **Justice Party of Denmark** (*Danmarks Retsforbund*), founded in 1919 to propagate the theories of US economist Henry George, won between two and four *Folketing* seats in 1930s and 1940s, rising to 12 in 1950 but falling unevenly to nil in 1960, following participation in a coalition government headed by the →Social Democratic Party from 1957; re-entered *Folketing* in 1973 with five seats, lost them all in 1975, won six seats in 1977 and five in 1979, but has been unrepresented since 1981.
Address. Lyngbyvej 42, DK-2100 Copenhagen Ø
Telephone. (+45–39) 204–488
Fax. (+45–39) 204–450
Email. ref@post5.tele.dk
Website. www.retsforbundet.dk
Leadership. Mette Langdal Kristiansen (chairman)

Socialist Workers' Party (*Socialistisk Arbejderparti, SAP*), far-left grouping which has made little electoral impact.
Address. Nørre Allé 11A, PB 547, DK-2200 Copenhagen N
Telephone. (+45–31) 397–948
Fax. (+45–35) 373–217
Email. sap@sap-fi.dk
Website. www.sap-fi.dk

Danish Dependencies

Faroe Islands

Capital: Tórshavn

Population: 46,000 (2000E)

Under the 1993 Danish constitution the Faroe Islands are an internally self-governing part of the Kingdom of Denmark, whose government retains responsibility for their foreign affairs, defence, judiciary and monetary affairs. Executive power is formally vested in the Danish monarch, who is represented in Tórshavn by a High Commissioner, but actual authority for Faroese affairs (including fisheries) is exercised by a government (*Landsstyret* or *Landsstyrid*) headed by a Chief Minister (*Løgmadur* or *Lagmand*). Legislative authority is vested in a Faroes parliament (*Lagting* or *Løgting*), 27 of whose seats are filled by direct proportional election under universal adult suffrage and up to five more by distribution to party lists under an equalization system. Two representatives from the Faroes are elected to the *Folketing* in Copenhagen in Danish national elections. The Faroe Islands remained outside the European Community (later Union) when Denmark joined in 1973 but later signed a special trade agreement with the grouping.

Elections to the *Løgting* on April 30, 1998, resulted as follows: Republican Party 8 seats (with 23.8% of the vote), People's Party 8 (21.3%), Social Democratic Party 7 (21.9%), Union Party 6 (18.0%), Self-Government Party 2 (7.7%), Centre Party 1 (4.1%). The March 1998 elections to the Danish *Folketing* in the Faroes resulted in the return of candidates of the People's and Social Democratic parties.

Centre Party
Midflokkurin (Mfl)

Address. PO Box 3237, 110 Tórshavn

Email. jal@kambsdal.olivant.fo

Leadership. Tordur Niclasen (chairman)

The Mfl was founded in 1991 in opposition to the then coalition government of the →Social Democratic and →People's parties. It won two seats out of 32 in the July 1994 election (and continued in opposition) but failed to retain representation in the 1998 polling.

Christian People's Party/Faroes Progressive and Fishing Industry Party
Kristiligi Fólkaflokkurin/Framburds– og Fiskivinnuflokkurin (KF/FFF)

Address. Brekku 5, 700 Klaksvík

Telephone. (+298) 457–580

Fax. (+298) 457–581

Leadership. Rev. Niels Pauli Danielsen (chairman)

The KF/FFF was formed prior to the 1978 elections as an alliance of the centrist Progressive Party (which had been in coalition government in 1963–66) and centre-oriented fishing industry elements. Favouring increased self-government for the Faroes, it won two seats in 1978, 1980 and 1984, subsequently entering a centre-left coalition headed by the →Social Democratic Party. It again won two seats in 1988, switching to the resultant centre-right coalition headed by the →People's Party, but withdrawing in June 1989. It retained two seats in the 1990 and 1994 elections, but failed to win representation in 1998, when it took only 2.5% of the vote.

People's Party
Fólkaflokkurin (Fkfl)

Address. Árvegur, PO Box 208, Tórshavn

Email. jal@kambsdal.olivant.fo

Leadership. Anfínn Kallsberg (parliamentary leader); Óli Breckmann (chairman)

The moderate conservative and pro-autonomy Fkfl was founded in 1940 as a merger of a right-wing faction of the →Self-Government Party (Sjfl) and the small Commerce Party (*Vinnuflokkur*). It first entered a coalition government in 1950, with the →Union Party (Sbfl) until 1954 and thereafter with the Sjfl until 1958. In 1963–66 its then leader,

Jógvan Sundstein, headed a coalition with the →Republican Party (Tjfl), the →Christian People's Party/Progressive and Fishing Industry Party (KF/FFF) and the Sjfl. The party was again in opposition from 1966 to 1974, when it joined a centre-left coalition with the →Social Democratic Party (Jvfl) and the Tjfl, this alliance being continued after the 1978 election. In 1981 it entered a centre-right coalition with Sbfl and the Sjfl, becoming the second strongest parliamentary party in the 1984 elections with seven seats, but nevertheless going into opposition.

The Fkfl became the strongest party, with eight seats, in the 1988 election, after which Sundstein formed a centre-right coalition with the Tjfl, the Sjfl and the KF/FFF. This gave way to a Fkfl/Tjfl/Sbfl governing alliance in mid-1989, but the Fkfl's two new partners withdrew support in October 1990, precipitating an early election the following month in which the Fkfl slipped to seven seats. In January 1991 the party became the junior partner in a coalition with the Jvfl but withdrew in April 1993 over a fisheries policy disagreement. It declined to six seats in the July 1994 election, after which it remained in opposition.

The Fkfl again won one of the two Faroes seats in the Danish elections of March 1998, its deputy (Óli Breckmann) joining the metropolitan fiLiberal Party (*Venstre*) parliamentary group. In the April 1998 Faroes elections, the Fkfl advanced to eight seats with 21.3% of the vote. Accordingly, Anfinn Kallsberg of the Fkfl became Chief Minister of a coalition which also included the Tjfl and the Sjfl.

In February 2001 the Kallsberg government announced that it would call a referendum in May to seek popular endorsement for its plan to phase out the need for Danish subsidies over a 10-year period with a view to holding a further referendum in 2012 on declaring full independence. However, in the face of metropolitan displeasure, Kallsberg's Fkfl quickly withdrew its support for the plan, provoking a coalition crisis which was uneasily resolved in March by an agreement not to proceed with the referendum but to concentrate instead on laying the economic foundations of full sovereignty.

The Fkfl is affiliated to the International Democrat Union.

Republican Party
Tjódveldisflokkurin (Tjfl)

Address. Villingadalsvegi, 100 Tórshavn

Telephone. (+298) 314–412
Email. hoh@fl.fo
Leadership. Høgni Hoydal (chairman)

Its title meaning literally "Party for People's Government", the Tjfl was founded in 1948 as a left-wing party advocating secession from Denmark, citing as justification a 1946 plebiscite in which 48.7% had voted for independence and 47.2% for home rule under Danish sovereignty. Having won two seats in 1950, it improved sharply to six in 1954 and subsequently participated in centre-left coalitions in 1963–66, 1974–80 and 1985–88. It again won six seats in the 1988 election and joined a coalition headed by the →People's Party (Fkfl), but this finally collapsed in October 1990.

The Tjfl fell back to four seats in the November 1990 election and was in opposition until joining a coalition headed by the →Social Democratic Party in April 1993. It again won four seats in the July 1994 election, after which it went into opposition. It returned to government after advancing to eight seats (with 23.8% of the vote) in the April 1998 elections, joining a coalition headed by the Fkfl and also including the →Self-Government Party.

The Tjfl was the prime mover of the Kallsberg government's announcement in February 2001 that a referendum would be held in May on its plan to phase out dependence on Danish subsidies over a 10-year period and to hold a full independence referendum in 2012. It was therefore greatly displeased when Kallsberg's Fkfl quickly backed away from the plan, although it eventually agreed to remain in the coalition on the basis of an agreement to shelve the speedy referendum plan and to concentrate instead on laying the economic foundations of full sovereignty.

Self-Government Party
Sjálvstýrisflokkurin (Sjfl)

Address. Årvegur, PO Box 208, 110 Tórshavn
Email. spg@post.olivant.fo
Leadership. Helena Dam A. Neystabø (chairperson)

Also known in English as the Home-Rule Party, the Sjfl was founded in 1906 by the poet Joannes Patursson to campaign for real powers for the Faroes parliament (which then had a consultative role) and the preservation of the Faroese language. Opposing the pro-Danish line of the →Union Party (Sbfl), it won 51.7% of the popular vote in 1916 (but not a parliamentary majority) and 49.8% in 1918, when it obtained an absolute majority of seats for the first (and so far only) time. Following the defection of its left wing to the →Social Democratic Party (Jvfl) in 1928, a right-wing faction broke away in 1940 to join the →People's Party (Fkfl), leaving the rump Sjfl as a centrist party. Having fallen to 16.7% and four seats in 1940, the Sjfl was unrepresented from 1943 to 1946, when it regained two seats in an electoral alliance with the Jvfl.

From the granting of home rule to the Faroes in 1948, the party was a partner in coalition governments in 1948–50 and 1954–75 and was then opposition until until January 1981, when it joined a centre-right coalition with the →Union Party (Sbfl) and the Fkfl. Having slipped to one seat in 1966, the Sjfl recovered to two in 1974 and went up to three in 1980. After losing one seat in the 1984 election (on a slightly higher vote share), it entered a centre-left coalition headed by the Jvfl. After retaining two seats in the November 1988 election, it joined a centre-right coalition headed by the Fkfl but withdrew in June 1989. In early elections in November 1990 it moved back to three seats but remained in opposition until April 1993, when it joined another centre-left coalition.

The Sjfl slipped back to two seats in July 1994 (with 5.6% of the vote) but nevertheless joined a four-party coalition headed by the Sbfl. It continued in government after the April 1998 elections, in which it again won two seats (with 7.7% of the vote), joining a three-party coalition headed by the Fkfl and also including the Tjfl.

The Sjfl strongly backed the Kallsberg government's announcement in February 2001 that a referendum would be held in May on its plan to phase out dependence on Danish subsidies over a 10-year period and to hold a full independence referendum in 2012. It was therefore strongly critical of Kallsberg's Fkfl when it quickly reneged on the plan, although it agreed to remain in the coalition on the basis of an agreement to shelve the referendum plan and to concentrate instead on laying the economic foundations of full sovereignty.

Social Democratic Party
Javnadarflokkurin (Jvfl)

Address. Marinargø 3, 188 Hoyvëk
Telephone. (+298) 319–397
Fax. (+298) 319–397
Email. hps@hagstova.fo
Website. www.javnadarflokkurin.fo
Leadership. Jóannes Eidesgaard (chairman); Eydolvur Dimon (secretary-general)

Its Faroese title meaning "Equality Party", the Jvfl dates from 1925 and first gained representation in 1928, when it was strengthened by the adhesion of a splinter group of the →Self-Government Party (Sjfl). After making a breakthrough to six seats in 1936, it was a member of the first home rule government in 1948–50 and in 1958 became the strongest parliamentary party, winning eight seats out of 30 and forming a coalition with the Sjfl and the Union Party (Sbfl) under the premiership of Peter Mohr Dam. It was to retain a narrow plurality until 1978, although 27.6% was its highest vote share. In opposition from 1962, the Jvfl returned to government in 1966 and was continuously in office until 1980, providing the Chief Minister in 1966–68 and in 1970–80, latterly in the person of Atli Dam. After four years in opposition, the Jvfl again became the largest party in 1984, with eight seats out of 32, enabling Atli Dam to form a centre-left coalition with the Sjfl, the →Republican Party (Tjfl) and the →Christian People's Party/Progressive and Fishing Industry Party (KF/FFF).

A shift to the right in the 1988 election reduced the Jvfl to seven seats and consigned it to opposition. An early election in November 1990 restored the Jvfl to plurality status, with 10 seats, so that in January 1991 Atli Dam formed a two-party coalition with the →People's Party (Fkfl). In April 1993 Atli Dam was succeeded as Jvfl leader and Chief Minister by Marita Petersen, but in October 1993 the Fkfl withdrew from the government and was replaced by the Tjfl and the Sjfl. In the July 1994 election the Jvfl went down to a heavy defeat, winning only five seats (and 15.4% of the vote), partly because of competition from the new →Workers' Front (Vf). It nevertheless joined a new coalition headed by the Sbfl and including the Sjfl and the Vf.

The Jvfl went into opposition after the April 1998 elections, despite increasing its representation to seven seats on a 21.9% vote share. In the previous month's Danish elections, the Jvfl had won one of the two Faroes seats in the metropolitan legislature, although its representative (Jóannes Eidesgaard) did not formally join the Danish →→Social Democratic Party group. The party has a membership of 1,800.

Union Party
Sambandsflokkurin (Sbfl)

Address. Aarvegur, PO Box 208, Tórshavn
Email. edmund-j@post.olivant.fo
Leadership. Lisbeth L. Petersen (chairperson)

The conservative Sbfl was founded in 1906 in support of the maintenance of close relations between the islands and the Danish Crown and therefore in opposition in particular to the →Self-Government Party (Sjfl). It won 62.4% of the vote in its first election in 1906 and 73.3% in 1910, remaining the majority parliamentary party until 1918, when it was overtaken by the Sjfl. It recovered its dominance in the 1920s, but the advent of the →Social Democratic Party (Jvfl) in 1925 heralded increasing fragmentation of the party structure. In 1936 the Sbfl vote dropped sharply to 33.6%

and since 1943 the party has never exceeded a 30% share. Following the introduction of home rule in 1948, the Sbfl provided the Faroes' Chief Minister until 1958: Andreas Samuelsen headed a coalition of the Jvfl and the Sjfl in 1948-50, while Kristian Djurhuus led one with the People's Party (Fkfl) in 1950–54 and another with the Fkfl and the Sjfl in 1954–58. It continued in government in 1958–62, but went into opposition after the 1962 election, in which it won only six seats and 20.5% of the vote.

Although it remained at six seats in the 1966 election, it entered a coalition with the Jvfl and the Sjfl that lasted until 1974, with then party leader Pauli Ellefsen holding the premiership in 1968–70. Having slipped to five seats and 19.1% in the 1974 election, the Sbfl won a narrow plurality in 1978 (eight seats and 26.3% of the vote) but remained in opposition. It retained eight seats on a 23.9% vote share in the 1980 contest, following which Ellefsen formed a coalition with the Fkfl and the Sjfl that lasted until 1984. In the latter year it slipped to seven seats (and 21.2%) and reverted to opposition status, subsequently registering an identical electoral result in 1988. In June 1989 the Sbfl joined a coalition headed by the Fkfl and including the →Republican Party (Tjfl), but this collapsed in October 1990, causing an early election the following month in which the Sbfl won six seats.

After four years in opposition, the Sbfl became the largest party in the July 1994 election, with eight seats, and subsequently formed a coalition with the Jvfl, the Sjfl and the new →Workers' Front under the premiership of Sbfl leader Edmund Jønsen. The Sbfl again won one of the two Faroes seats in the March 1998 Danish elections, its deputy opting to join the Conservative People's Party parliamentary group in Copenhagen. In the April 1998 Faroes polling, the Sbfl fell back to six seats (with 18.0% of the vote) and returned to opposition status. In March 2001 Jønsen was replaced as party leader by Lisbeth L. Petersen, a former mayor of Tórshavn.

Workers' Front
Verkmannafylkingin (Vf)
Address. Árvegur, PO Box 208, 110 Tórshavn
Leadership. Óli Jacobsen (chair)
The Vf was founded in 1994 by left-wing dissidents of the →Social Democratic Party (Jvfl) in alliance with some trade union leaders unhappy with the recent performance of the Jvfl in government. In its first election in July 1994 the Vf won three seats (from 9.5% of the vote) and obtained one portfolio in a coalition government headed by the right-wing →Union Party and also including the Jvfl and the →Self-Government Party. Its government role ended at the April 1998 election, in which it slumped to 0.8% of the vote and no seats.

Greenland

Capital: Nuuk (Godthaab) **Population:** 56,000 (2000E)

The Arctic island of Greenland is a part of the Kingdom of Denmark but has had internal self-government since May 1979, as approved by referendum in January 1979 by 70.1% of participating voters. Greenland accordingly has its own 31-member parliament (*Landsting*), which is popularly elected by proportional representation, and a government (*Landsstyre*) with responsibility for internal economic and social affairs, while the Danish government retains responsibility for foreign affairs, defence and monetary policy. Greenland entered the European Community (later Union) in 1973 as part of Denmark, but withdrew with effect from Feb. 1, 1985, on the strength of a local referendum decision against membership in February 1982.

Elections to the *Landsting* on Feb. 16, 1999, resulted as follows: Forward (*Siumut*) 11 seats (with 35.3% of the vote), Community Party (*Atassut*) 8 (25.3%), Eskimo Brotherhood 7 (22.1%), Alliance of Candidates 4 (12.3%), others 1 (5.0%). The March 1998 elections to the Danish *Folketing* in Greenland again resulted in the return of candidates of the *Siumut* and *Atassut* parties.

Alliance of Candidates
Kattusseqatigiit
Kandidatforbundet
Address. c/o Landsting, 3900 Nuuk
Leadership. Anthon Frederiksen (chairman)
This pro-business and anti-independence grouping of independents won 12.3% of the vote and four seats (out of 31) in the February 1999 *Landsting* election, following which it formed part of the parliamentary opposition.

Centre Party
Akulliit Partiiat (AP)
Address. PO Box 456, 3900 Nuuk
Leadership. Bjarne Kreutzmann (chairman)
The liberal pro-market AP was formed prior to the 1991 Greenland election, in which it won two seats in the *Landsting*. It retained two seats in the March 1995 election and remained in opposition. It failed to gain representation in the February 1999 election.

Community Party
Atassut
Address. PO Box 399, 3900 Nuuk
Telephone. (+299) 323–366

Fax. (+299) 325–840
Email. rudo@greennet.gl
Website. www.atassut.gl
Leadership. Daniel Skifte (chairman); Otto Steenholdt (political vice-chairman); Erik H.K. Heilmann (organization vice-chairman); Godmann Filemonsen (secretary)
Describing itself as "Greenland's liberal party", the centrist *Atassut* was founded in 1978 and achieved official status as a political party in 1981 under the leadership of Lars Chemnitz, who was chair of the pre-autonomy Greenland council. In the April 1979 election preceding the move to autonomy it was defeated by the →Forward (*Siumut*) party and went into opposition, from where it campaigned in favour of Greenland remaining in the European Community in the 1982 referendum—unsuccessfully as it turned out. *Atassut* retained opposition status after the 1983 election despite winning a larger popular vote than Forward, which got the same number of seats. Chemnitz resigned the party leadership in March 1984 and *Atassut* lost ground in the June 1984 election, therefore remaining in opposition.

In the May 1987 election *Atassut* again overtook *Siumut* in popular vote terms but won the same number of seats (11) and therefore continued in opposition. Its status was not changed by the 1991 contest, in which it fell back to eight seats, but in March 1995 *Atassut* won 25.3% of the vote and 10 seats (out of 31) and accepted participation in a coalition headed by *Siumut*. However, *Atassut* slipped back to eight seats (and 25.3% of the vote) in the February 1999 *Landsting* elections, going into opposition to a coalition of *Siumut* and the →Eskimo Brotherhood.

Atassut has consistently returned one of Greenland's two members of the *Folketing* in Copenhagen, where its deputy usually sits in the parliamentary group of the Danish →→Liberal Party (*Venstre*).

Eskimo Brotherhood
Inuit Ataqatigiit (IA)
Address. PO Box 321, 3900 Nuuk
Telephone. (+299) 23702
Email. inuit.ataqatigiit@greennet.gl
Leadership. Josef Motzfeldt (chairman)
The IA was founded in 1978 by a group of Marxist–Leninists who had been active in the Young Greenland Council in Copenhagen and who opposed the home rule arrangements then being negotiated, advocating instead Greenland's "total independence from the capitalist colonial power". The new party also urged that Greenland citizenship should be restricted to those with at least one Eskimo parent and that the US military base at Thule should be closed. Having failed to persuade Greenlanders to vote against home rule in the January 1979 referendum, the IA failed to obtain representation in the April 1979 election, but was on the winning side in the 1982 referendum in which Greenlanders voted to leave the European Community. Having effectively absorbed the small Wage-Earners' Party (*Sulissartut*), the IA won two seats in the 1983 Greenland election. It increased to three seats in the next contest in 1984, when it joined a coalition government headed by the →Forward (*Siumut*) party.

The coalition collapsed in March 1987 after the then IA leader, Aqqaluk Lynge, had accused the *Siumut* Chief Minister of being "totally passive" in the face of the US government's enhancement of the Thule base. Having improved to four seats in the resultant May 1987 election, the IA joined another coalition with *Siumut* with increased ministerial responsibilities, but again withdrew in 1988. The IA moved up to five seats in the March 1991 election and again formed a coalition with *Siumut*, under a new Chief Minister. In the March 1995 election the IA made further progress, to six seats (out of 31) and 20.3% of the vote, but went into opposition after failing to persuade *Siumut* to take up its revived demand for complete independence for Greenland.

The IA gained further ground in the February 1999 *Landsting* election, winning seven seats and a vote share of 20.3%. Having moderated its pro-independence line, it joined a coalition government with *Siumut*, receiving two portfolios out of seven as well as the presidency of the *Landsting*.

Forward
Siumut
Address. PO Box 399, 3900 Nuuk
Telephone. (+299) 323–366
Fax. (+299) 325–840
Email. siumut@greennet.gl
Leadership. Jonathan Motzfeldt (chairman); Vittus Qujaukitsoq (secretary)
The socialist *Siumut* party was founded in July 1977, derived from earlier pro-autonomy groups and the political review *Siumut*. Having supported the autonomy arrangements approved by referendum in January 1979, *Siumut* won an absolute majority of 13 seats (out of 21) in the April 1979 election and formed Greenland's first home rule government under the premiership of Jonathan Motzfeldt. Opposed to Greenland's membership of the European Community, *Siumut* campaigned successfully for a vote in favour of withdrawal in the 1982 referendum.

In the April 1983 election the party slipped to 11 seats (out of 24) but continued as a minority government until another election in June 1984, when it again won 11 seats (out of 25) and formed a majority coalition with the small →Eskimo Brotherhood (IA). The coalition collapsed in March 1987, amid dissension over the status of the US military base at Thule, and *Siumut* retained 11 seats (out of 27) in the resultant May 1987 election, whereupon Motzfeldt sought to negotiate a "grand coalition" with the →Community (*Atassut*) party. This provoked opposition from within *Siumut*, the eventual outcome being a further left-wing coalition with the IA.

Triggered by allegations of corruption among government ministers, an early election in May 1991 resulted in *Siumut* again winning 11 seats (out of 27) and forming a new coalition with the IA, although Motzfeldt was obliged, in view of the scandal, to vacate the premiership and *Siumut* leadership in favour of Lars Emil Johansen. In the next election in March 1995 *Siumut* won 38.5% of the vote and 12 seats (out of 31), but attempts to reconstitute the *Siumut*/IA combination foundered on the IA's revived demand for complete independence for Greenland. The outcome was the formation of a "grand coalition" between *Siumut* and *Atassut* committed to maintaining Greenland's autonomous status.

Motzfeldt regained the *Siumut* leadership and the premiership in September 1997 when Johansen accepted appointment as deputy director of the state fisheries company. In the February 1999 *Landsting* election *Siumut* slipped to 11 seats and 35.3% of the vote. It nevertheless formed a coalition government with the IA (the latter having moderated its pro-independence aim) under the continued premiership of Motzfeldt.

An affiliate of the Socialist International, *Siumut* has consistently returned one of Greenland's two members of the *Folketing* in Copenhagen, where its deputy usually sits in the parliamentary group of the Danish →→Social Democratic Party.

Djibouti

Capital: Djibouti　　　　　　　　　　　　　　　　**Population**: 450,000 (2000E)

The Republic of Djibouti (formerly the French Territory of the Afars and the Issas) was ruled by President Hassan Gouled Aptidon from 1977 when the country gained independence until he stood down in 1999. The Popular Rally for Progress (RPP) was the ruling party in a single-party system from October 1981 until a referendum in September 1992 produced an overwhelming vote in favour of a multi-party constitution. Executive power is vested in the President who is elected for a six-year term. Legislative power is vested in a 65-member Chamber of Deputies (*Chambre des Députés*), which is elected for a five-year term. A total of four parties may compete for Chamber seats, although for the December 1992 poll only three were registered, one of which (the

National Democratic Party) withdrew before balloting began. Of the two that remained, the RPP eclipsed the Party of Democratic Renewal, taking all 65 seats.

In the presidential election on May 7, 1993, Hassan Gouled Aptidon (RPP) was re-elected for a fourth term of office, obtaining just over 60% of the vote. In further legislative elections on Dec. 19, 1997, the RPP in alliance with the Front for the Restoration of Unity and Democracy (FRUD) won all 65 seats with 78.6% of the vote. The opposition Party of Democratic Renewal (PRD) and National Democratic Party fielded candidates but failed to gain representation. In the presidential election on April 9, 1999, Ismail Omar Guelleh of the RPP succeeded his uncle and was elected as the country's second president.

Front for the Restoration of Unity and Democracy
Front pour la Restauration de l'Unité et de la Démocratie (FRUD)
Address. c/o *Chambre des Députés*, Djibouti
Leadership. Ali Mohamed Daoud (president); Ahmed Ougoureh Kifleh Ahmed (secretary-general)
The FRUD was formed in 1991 by the merger of three Afar groups: Action for the Revision of Order in Djibouti (*Action pour la Révision de l'Ordre à Djibouti*, AROD), the Front for the Restoration of Right and Equality (*Front pour la Restauration du Droit et l'Egalité*, FRDE) and the Djibouti Patriotic Resistance Front (*Front de la Résistance Patriotique de Djibouti*, FRPD). Advocating fair representation in government of Djibouti's different ethnic groups, the FRUD began an armed insurgency against the ruling regime in late 1991.

Factional divisions in the organization led in the first half of 1994 to the emergence of a new leadership, under Ali Mohamed Daoud, favouring negotiations with the government to end the civil war. This culminated in a peace agreement in December 1994, providing for an immediate ceasefire and revision of the constitution and of electoral lists before the next elections. It also provided for an alliance between the FRUD led by Daoud and the ruling →Popular Rally for Progress. The agreement, which led to the inclusion of two FRUD members in the government in 1995, was condemned by the faction of the ousted former FRUD leader, Ahmed Dini Ahmed, as a "betrayal" of the organization's aims. In April 1997, the pro-government faction of the FRUD convened its first party conference. Confirming its earlier power sharing agreement, it contested the December elections of that year with the RPP; it secured 11 of the 65 alliance seats and participated in the new government. The FRUD armed wing, which had split from the main party in 1994 and had launched a series of military attacks against the regime, signed a peace agreement with the government on May 12, 2001, apparently marking the end of Djibouti's civil war.

Party of Democratic Renewal
Parti du Renouveau Démocratique (PRD)
Address. BP 2198, Djibouti
Leadership. Abdullahi Hamareiteh (president); Maki Houmed Gaba (secretary-general)
The PRD was formed in September 1992 to succeed the Movement for Peace and Reconciliation, which had been launched six months earlier by Mohamed Djama Elabe. Advocating the establishment of democratic parliamentary government, the PRD was the only opposition party to take part in the 1992 legislative elections, but was not awarded any seats despite being credited with about a quarter of the vote. Djama Elabe was the runner-up in the 1993 presidential election, with a 22% share of the poll.

Hamareiteh was elected as the party's new president in May 1997 to succeed Djama Elabe, who had died in late 1996. The PRD failed to secure any seats in the December 1997 elections, although it polled around 19% of the vote. In 1999, the PRD backed the unsuccessful candidate of a coalition of opposition factions (Moussa Ahmed Idriss) in the presidential elections. The editor-in-chief of the party journal *Le Renouveau*, Daher Ahmed Farah, who had entered politics in 1992 and was a founding member of the PRD,

was sentenced to six months imprisonment in October 1999 for "spreading false news".

Popular Rally for Progress
Rassemblement Populaire pour le Progrès (RPP)
Address. c/o *Chambre des Députés*, Djibouti
Leadership. Ismael Omar Guelleh (chairman)
The RPP was set up in 1979, its main component being the African People's League for Independence (*Ligue Populaire Africaine pour l'Indépendance*, LPAI), which was a primarily Issa-supported organization prior to the country's accession to independence in 1977. The RPP was the ruling party under the single-party system from 1981, and was the first political group to be legalized under the pluralist constitution of 1992. Maintaining its grip on political power, the party took all the seats in the December 1992 elections to the Chamber of Deputies, and in the following year Hassan Gouled Aptidon was re-elected President of the Republic for a third six-year term.

In December 1994 the RPP signed a peace agreement with the →Front for the Restoration of Unity and Democracy (FRUD). The party retained power in the 1997 parliamentary elections, winning 54 of the 65 alliance seats and forming a coalition government with the FRUD. In February 1999 Gouled Aptidon announced his intention to retire from politics. The party named his nephew and chief of staff, Guelleh, as its presidential candidate for the April elections, and he was returned in the poll with a 74.1% share of the vote. Guelleh is reported to favour continuing Djibouti's traditionally strong ties with France and has played an important role in trying to reconcile the different factions in neighbouring Somalia.

National Democratic Party
Parti National Democratique (PND)
Leadership. Aden Robleh Awaleh (chairman)
The PND was founded in 1992 by Aden Robleh Awaleh, a former cabinet minister and vice-president of the ruling →Popular Rally for Progress (RPR) who, from exile, was active in anti-government groupings from 1986. The PND withdrew from the December 1992 legislative elections and subsequently appealed for the formation of a transitional government of national unity to supervise the implementation of democratic reforms. Robleh Awaleh came third in the May 1993 presidential election, attracting about 12% of the vote. In November 1995 he received a one-month suspended prison sentence for illegally organizing an opposition demonstration.

The PND participated, but failed to secure representation, in the 1997 legislative elections. Its presidential candidate, Moussa Ahmed Idriss (representing an opposition coalition which included the →Party of Democratic Renewal (PRD) and the Dini faction of the →Front for the Restoration of Unity and Democracy), stood alone against Guelleh of the RPR in the April 1999 presidential elections. He was defeated, attracting 25% of the vote.

Other Parties and Groups

Centrist and Democratic Reforms Party (*Parti Centriste et des Réformes Démocratiques, PCRD*), formed in late 1993 by a breakaway faction of the →Front for the Restoration of Unity and Democracy.
Leadership. Hassan Abdallah Watta (chairman)

Djibouti Democratic Union (*Union Démocratique Djiboutienne, UDD*), primarily Gadabursi (ethnic) party formed in January 1992.
Leadership. Mahdi Ibrahim God

Front for the Liberation of the Somali Coast (*Front pour la Libération de la Côte des Somalis, FLCS*), an Issa-supported group, urging that Djibouti be incorporated into a greater Somalia.
Leadership. Abdallah Waberi Khalif (chairman)

Group for Democracy and the Republic (*Groupe pour la Démocratie et la République, GDR*), formed in 1996 by a dissident faction of the →Popular Rally for Progress (RPP) which included 13 of the 65 members of the chamber of deputies. Party leader Bahdon Farah had opposed the 1994

peace agreement with the →Front for the Restoration of Unity and Democracy and the faction of the RPP supporting Ismael Omar Guelleh's candidacy for the presidency. He was dismissed from his positions as Minister of Justice and Islamic affairs and member of the RPP's executive committee, and was sentenced to six months imprisonment in 1996 for "insulting the head of state".
Leadership. Moumin Bahdon Farah

Movement for Unity and Democracy (*Mouvement pour l'Unité et la Démocratie, MUD*), launched in 1990 campaigning in favour of a pluralist democratic system. The party leader was an unsuccessful candidate in the 1993 presidential election, taking fourth place.
Leadership. Mohammed Moussa Ali Tourtour

Dominica

Capital: Roseau

Population: 72,000 (2000E)

The Commonwealth of Dominica gained its independence from the United Kingdom as a republic in 1978. The head of state is the President, who is elected by Parliament for not more than two five-year terms in office. The head of government is the Prime Minister. The legislature is the unicameral House of Assembly. Its 32 members comprise 21 members elected for five-year terms in single seat constituencies on the first past the post system, nine appointed senators, the Speaker and one ex-officio member.

There are three political parties, the Dominica Freedom Party (DFP), the Dominica Labour Party (DLP) and the United Workers' Party (UWP), each of which has had a period in government since independence. The DFP was in office from 1980–95, but lost power to the UWP in the June 1995 election, winning only five seats to the UWP's 11 despite taking a higher (35.8% to 34.4%) share of the vote. Further elections on Jan. 31, 2000, resulted in the DLP winning 10 seats with 43.1% of the vote, the UWP nine seats (43.3%) and the DFP two seats (13.6%). The following month the DLP formed a coalition government (the first since the establishment of ministerial government in 1956) with the DFP. Turnout in the election was 59.3%.

Dominica Freedom Party (DFP)
Address. 37 Great George Street, Roseau
Telephone/Fax. (+1–767) 448–2104
Email. dominicafree@hotmail.com
Leadership. Charles Savarin (leader)
The conservative DFP came to power, under the forceful leadership of its founder (later Dame) Eugenia Charles, the first woman Prime Minister in the Caribbean, in an overwhelming election victory in 1980 after a period of national political crisis following independence in 1978. The party then retained office, although with decreasing electoral majorities, until the June 1995 election (at which Charles retired from political life), when it won only five seats despite coming first in the popular vote.

The DFP took only two seats in the January 2000 election and entered a coalition government as minority partner with the →Dominica Labour Party, its one-time bitter rival. Former diplomat Charles Savarin has led the party since 1996. It is a member of the Caribbean Democrat Union.

Dominica Labour Party (DLP)
Address. 64 Cork Street, Roseau
Telephone/Fax. (+1–767) 448–8511
Email. jillian_charles@hotmail.com
Leadership. Pierre Charles (leader)
The centre-left (and formerly left-wing) DLP was in office at independence in 1978 but was subsequently weakened by internal schisms and lost power to the conservative →Dominica Freedom Party (DFP) in 1980. In 1981 the Dominican Defence Force was disbanded following its implication in a plot by supporters of former DLP Prime Minister Patrick John to overthrow the government. John was himself convicted in 1986 for his involvement and

served a prison term before being released in 1990 and returning to political life.

The DLP retained a minority position in successive elections from 1985 until January 2000, when it won the largest number of seats (10 of the 21) although polling slightly fewer votes than the governing →United Workers' Party(UWP), which took nine seats. DLP campaign themes in the 2000 election included criticism of the UWP government for corruption and alleged sale of passports to Mafia figures taking advantage of Dominica's lax financial regulation. A new government was formed under DLP leader (since 1992) Roosevelt (Rosie) Douglas, one of the 1970s generation of Caribbean political activists who had formerly cultivated links with Cuba, Libya and the Soviet Union and espoused the cause of radical national liberation movements worldwide. The new government had the support of the two members of the DFP, although the parties had in earlier decades been bitterly opposed.

Douglas died in office on Oct. 1, 2000, and was succeeded as Prime Minister and party leader by Pierre Charles.

The DLP is a consultative member of the Socialist International.

United Workers' Party (UWP)
Address. 37 Cork Street, Roseau
Telephone. (+1–767) 448–5051
Fax. (+1–767) 449–8448
Email. uwp@cwdom.dm
Leadership. Edison James (leader)
The UWP was established in 1988 and became the official opposition following the 1990 election when it came second to the →Dominica Freedom Party (DFP), winning six seats in the House of Assembly. In the June 1995 election the

UWP won 11 of the 21 elected seats (although polling fewer votes than the DFP) and formed the government with Edison James, a former leader of the banana growers' association, becoming Prime Minister. Under James the government sought to reduce Dominica's dependence on agriculture, especially bananas, and to promote financial services, although the pursuit of this policy led to allegations

of abuse of Dominica's light regulatory regime by criminals engaged in money laundering.

In the January 2000 elections, despite increasing its share of the vote to 43.3%, the UWP won only nine seats and lost office to a coalition of the →Dominica Labour Party (DLP) and the DFP.

Dominican Republic

Capital: Santo Domingo

Population: 8,500,000 (2000E)

A Spanish colony until 1821, the Dominican Republic was subjugated in 1822 by neighbouring Haiti before achieving its independence in 1844. Having been occupied by the United States from 1916 to 1924, the country was then dominated by Gen. Rafael Trujillo from 1930, when he overthrew the elected President, until his assassination in 1961. The United States again intervened militarily in 1965 to suppress a popular rebellion against a regime that had assumed power following a military coup in 1963. In 1966, following fresh elections, a new constitution was promulgated. Under its provisions, legislative power is exercised by a bicameral Congress of the Republic (*Congreso de la República*) consisting of a 30-member Senate (*Senado*) and a 149-member Chamber of Deputies (*Cámara de Diputados*). Members of both houses are elected for four years by universal adult suffrage. Executive power lies with the President, who is also elected by direct popular vote for four years.

Legislative elections held on May 16, 1998, saw the centre-left Dominican Revolutionary Party (PRD) take power from the centrist Dominican Liberation Party (PLD) with an absolute majority in both the Senate and the Chamber of Deputies. In presidential elections held on May 16, 2000, the PRD again defeated the incumbent PLD, with Hipólito Mejía Domínguez securing victory over defeated Danilo Medina Sánchez of the PLD and former President Joaquín Balaguer of the Christian Social Reform Party (PRSC).

Dominican Liberation Party
Partido de la Liberación Dominicana (PLD)
Address. Avda. Independencia 401, Santo Domingo
Telephone. (+1–809) 685–3540
Leadership. Danilo Medina Sánchez (leader)
Juan Bosch Gaviño, the founder of the →Dominican Revolutionary Party (PRD), led a breakaway group from that party to form the left-wing PLD during the 1974 election campaign. The PLD secured congressional representation in all elections from 1982, although in May 1994 it retained only 13 of the 44 seats in the Chamber of Deputies that it had won in the 1990 polling. An earlier serious factional split in 1992 had resulted in the defection of a large number of left-wing party members who subsequently formed the →Alliance for Democracy (APD). As the PLD presidential candidate, Bosch came third in the 1978, 1982 and 1986 elections, before running a very close second to incumbent President Balaguer in 1990. Having then come a distant third in the 1994 polling, he resigned as PLD president.

Bosch's replacement, Leonel Fernandez, proved more successful, wining a narrow victory against the PRD candidate in the 1996 presidential elections. The party's success was short-lived, however, since it lost heavily to the PRD in legislative and municipal elections held in May 1998. The defeat hinted at difficulties for Fernandez in maintaining his presidential hold, and the party chose to select another candidate, Danilo Medina Sánchez, to contest the May 2000 presidential election. The change had little effect and Medina Sánchez was defeated by the PRD candidate.

Dominican Revolutionary Party
Partido Revolucionario Dominicano (PRD)
Address. Avda. Bolívar, Casi esquina Dr Delgado, Santo Domingo
Telephone. (+1–809) 688–9735
Fax. (+1–809) 688–2753
Email. prd@partidos.com
Website. www.prd.partidos.com
Leadership. Hipólito Mejía Domínguez (leader); Hatuey

Decamps Jiménez (president); Rafael Subervi Bonilla (secretary-general)
The left-of-centre PRD was founded in 1939 by Juan Bosch Gaviño who, having been in exile throughout the Trujillo dictatorship, returned to win the presidential election in 1962. He was deposed in a military coup in mid-1963, and in 1965 the PRD led an insurrection against the new regime that resulted in armed intervention by the USA. Having lost the subsequent elections in 1966 to the →Social Christian Reformist Party (PRSC), the PRD remained in opposition for the following 12 years. During that period Bosch resigned to form the →Dominican Liberation Party (PLD).

In 1978 the PRD candidate, Silvestre Antonio Guzmán Fernandez, became President in the country's first peaceful and constitutional transfer of power. His party colleague, Jorge Salvador Blanco, was elected his successor in 1982 when the party also secured an absolute majority in both houses of Congress. During the Blanco regime the PRD experienced internal divisions between a pro-government bloc and rival centre-right and centre-left factions, led respectively by Jacobo Majluta Azar and José Fransisco Peña Gómez. Majluta registered his faction of the PRD (the →Liberal Party for Restructuring, PLE) as a separate political party in 1985, but nevertheless secured the PRD's nomination as presidential candidate in the 1986 contest (which he lost), while Peña Gómez succeeded him as PRD president.

In 1994 a revived PRD, in coalition with the Democratic Unity (UD), won 15 seats in the Senate and 57 in the Chamber of Deputies. Peña Gómez took second place by a very narrow margin in the presidential race-results, which prompted accusations by the PRD of widespread irregularities and led to the party boycotting Congress from August 1994. In the presidential elections of 1996 Peña Gómez, making his third bid for the presidency, was narrowly defeated by the PLD candidate, Leonel Fernandez.

In May 1998 the PRD swept to victory in legislative and municipal elections, despite the death of Peña Gómez a week before polling. Under new leader Hipólito Mejía Domínguez, the party won 83 seats in the newly-enlarged

149-seat Chamber of Deputies and 24 seats in the 30-member Senate. The PRD also took control of some 90% of the country's municipalities, including the capital, Santa Domingo. Mejía Domínguez went on to win the presidential elections of May 2000, as candidate of the PRD and six small allied parties. Despite winning less than an absolute majority in the first round of voting, his two challengers from the PLD and the PRSC withdrew from the race, making a second round unnecessary.

The PRD has been a member of the Socialist International since 1966.

Social Christian Reformist Party
Partido Reformista Social Cristiano (PRSC)
Address. Avenida San Cristobal, Ensanche, La Fe, Apdo 1332, Santo Domingo
Telephone. (+1–809) 682–9581
Fax. (+1–809) 567–6033
Leadership. Donald Reid Cabral (president); Federicdo Antun (secretary-general)
The centre-right PRSC was founded in 1964 by Joaquín Balaguer, who had been Vice-President and then President of the Republic (under the Trujillo dictatorship) between 1957 and 1962. He returned to presidential office in elections in 1966 (after the US military intervention of 1965), in which the PRSC also won a majority of seats in both houses of the new National Congress. Balaguer served three consecutive terms until his electoral defeat in 1978, when the PRSC became the main opposition party to the →Dominican Revolutionary Party (PRD). Having lost the 1982 elections, Balaguer narrowly regained the presidency and the PRSC won control of both congressional houses in the 1986 polls. In 1990 Balaguer retained office but the PRSC lost its majority in the Chamber of Deputies.

While most elections since the 1960s had been marked by accusations of fraud, the outcome in May 1994 sparked a political crisis. In the presidential poll Balaguer was awarded a disputed victory by a margin of less than 1% over his PRD rival, while the PRSC took 14 of the 30 Senate seats and 50 of the 120 seats in the Chamber of Deputies. Under the terms of an accord signed by all major parties in August 1994 to end the crisis, a fresh presidential election was to be held in November 1995 (subsequently rescheduled for May 1996 despite the opposition of the PRD) and re-election of a President to a consecutive term would be prohibited. With Balaguer barred from standing again, the PRSC nominated Jacinto Peynaldo as its presidential candidate. In the first round of the election in May 1996 Peynaldo trailed in third place with less than 18% of the vote and was eliminated from the second round run-off held at the end of June.

The PRSC, under Balaguer, was the main loser in the 1998 legislative elections, winning only two senate seats and 17 seats in the Chamber of Deputies. The party's decline continued in the May 2000 presidential election when Balaguer finished third, winning less than 25% of the vote. Balaguer was replaced as party president by former Foreign Minister Donald Reid Cabral.

The PRSC is affiliated to the Christian Democrat International and the International Democrat Union.

Other Parties

Dominican Communist Party (*Partido Comunista Dommicano, PCD*), formed in 1944 and outlawed from the early 1960s until 1977.

Independent Revolutionary Party (*Partido Revolucionario Independiente, PRI*), evolved from the →Liberal Party for Restructuring, registered as a separate political party in 1985; it formed part of the alliance headed by the victorious →Dominican Revolutionary Party in the 2000 presidential elections.

Liberal Party for Restructuring (*Partido Liberal por la Estructura, PLE*), centre-right party created in 1985 by Jacobo Majluta Azar as an offshoot of the →Dominican Revolutionary Party (PRD). An affiliate of the Liberal International.
Address. Av. Independencia No. 509 (Altos), Santa Domingo
Telephone. (+1–809) 688–1353
Fax. (+1–809) 685–0918
Leadership. Andres Van Der Host (secretary-general)

Quisqueyan Democratic Party (*Partido Quisqueyano Democrática, PQD*), founded in 1968 by Gen. Elías Wessin y Wessin, who had led the 1963 military which ousted the →Dominican Revolutionary Party (PRD) from office. Having long been allied with the →Social Christian Reformist Party, it backed the winning PRD candidate in the 2000 presidential elections.
Leadership. Pedro Berges (president)

East Timor

Capital: Dili

Population: 850,000 (2001E)

The Portuguese first settled in East Timor in 1633 and established it as a separate colony in 1896. In 1974 the new leftist government in Portugal announced that it would free all of its colonies, but in East Timor this provoked a civil war. The Revolutionary Front of Independent East Timor (Fretilin) took control of the capital, Dili, and declared independence in November 1975, but the prospect of an armed Marxist group in control of the enclave alarmed both the Indonesian and the US governments. Indonesian army "volunteers" invaded two days later, establishing a provisional government, which in May 1976 "requested" integration into Indonesia, though this effective annexation was never recognized internationally. Indonesia attempted to pacify the province whilst developing its economy. Nevertheless, Fretilin continued the struggle for over 20 years, at the cost of tens of thousands of lives on both sides.

After the collapse of the Suharto regime in Indonesia in May 1998, President B.J. Habibie unexpectedly declared his willingness to allow a referendum in East Timor on its status. The referendum was held under UN auspices on Aug. 30, 1999, and resulted in a 78.5% majority vote for independence. This triggered violent attacks on native East Timorese by settlers from other parts of Indonesia, sometimes with the connivance of the military. However, the outcome was reluctantly approved by the Indonesian House of Representatives on Oct. 20, 1999, and the province was transferred to a UN-backed interim administration.

On Aug. 30, 2001, 91% of eligible voters took part in elections to a Constituent Assembly of 88 members, of whom 75 were elected by proportional representation from national party lists and 13 from single-member constituencies corresponding to East Timor's 13 districts. Of the 16 parties which contested the elections, Fretilin won 55 seats (with 57.4% of the vote), the Democratic Party 7 (8.7%), the Social Democratic Party 6 (8.2%) and the Timorese Social Democratic Association 6 (7.8%), while five parties won two seats each and three parties one seat each. Fretilin thus fell just short of the two-thirds majority that would have enabled it to adopt a new constitution without other support. The Assembly was required to produce the constitution within three months, the expectation being that formal independence would be declared on April 1, 2002.

Democratic Party
Partido Democrático (PD)

Address. Rua Democracia No.1, Pantai Kelapa, Dili
Leadership. Fernando de Araujo

The PD was founded in early 2001 by a number of former activists of the →Revolutionary Front of Independent East Timor (Fretilin) as well as by some who had returned from abroad after the departure of Indonesian forces. It won seven seats in the August 2001 elections to the Constituent Assembly.

Revolutionary Front of Independent East Timor
Frente Revolucionária do Timor-Leste Independente (Fretilin)

Address. Rua dos Martires do Patria, West Dili
Leadership. Francisco Guterres-Lu Olo (president); Mari Alkatiri (secretary-general)

Fretilin was established in 1974 with a radical Marxist programme of social reform and created its own armed wing (Falintil). Its victory in the civil war following Portugal's withdrawal in 1974 provoked Indonesian intervention and the annexation of East Timor. Fretilin then led the resistance to Indonesian occupation, but from 1987 it moved towards a more inclusive strategy of national unity under its then leader, José Alexandre (Xanana) Gusmão. After his capture by the Indonesian authorities in 1992, a number of groups broke away from Fretilin.

The award of the 1996 Nobel Peace Prize to Fretilin overseas spokesman José Ramos-Horta heightened international awareness of the East Timor question. In April 1998 Fretilin joined with other pro-independence groups to form the National Council for Timorese Resistance (CNRT), of which Gusmão (then still in prison, but later released) was named president and Ramos-Horta vice-president. Following the collapse of the Suharto regime in May 1998, Fretilin spearheaded the campaign which produced an overwhelming pro-independence referendum vote in August 1999 followed by Indonesia's withdrawal. From July 2000 Fretilin representatives joined a joint UN–Timorese interim administration, Ramos-Horta becoming Foreign Minister in October.

With the conflict over, Fretilin turned to building up its party membership, claiming 150,000 members by mid-2001. Standing on a programme that called for democracy, pluralism and mutual toleration, Fretilin confirmed its political dominance in the August 2001 Constituent Assembly elections by winning 55 of the 88 seats.

Social Democratic Party
Partido Social Democrata (PSD)

Address. Apartado 312 Correios de Dili, Dili, Timor Loro Sae
Leadership. Mario Vargas Carrascalão

The PSD was launched in September 2000 at a founding conference attended by former members of the →Timorese Democratic Union (UDT) and also by José Alexandre (Xanana) Gusmão, the former leader of the →Revolutionary Front of Independent East Timor (Fretilin). The party projects itself as a moderate, centrist alternative to Fretilin and the UDT and argues that East Timor needs effective administration rather than mass movements. Advocating a government of national unity, the PSD won six Constituent Assembly seats in the August 2001 elections.

Timorese Democratic Union
União Democrática Timorense (UDT)

Address. Palapago Rua da India, Dili
Email. laclubar@iinet.net.au
Website. www.fitini.net/apps/lusonews/udt2
Leadership. João Viegas Carrascalão

Founded in 1974, the UDT originally consisted of former Portuguese colonial officials and members of local elites favouring looser ties with Portugal and eventual independence. Although strongly anti-communist, it joined with the Marxist-oriented →Revolutionary Front of Independent East Timor (Fretilin) to oppose integration with Indonesia. It later split with Fretilin and was forced to operate abroad during the 25-year Indonesian occupation.

In April 1998 the UDT joined with Fretilin and other pro-independence groups to form the National Council for Timorese Resistance (CNRT), which campaigned successfully for the withdrawal of the Indonesians. In the 2001 Constituent Assembly elections, it advocated a centralized, presidential system with election of local administrators and a role for village elders in solving local problems according to customary law. Having suffered a number of defections to the →Social Democratic Party, the UDT won only two seats in August 2001.

Timorese Nationalist Party
Partido Nacionalista Timorense (PNT)

Address. Matadauro – Petamakan, Dili
Leadership. Alianga Araujo

Founded in 1999, the PNT originally favoured the continuation of Indonesian status for East Timor, with broad autonomy to run its own affairs, although it accepted the overwhelming pro-independence verdict of the August 1999 referendum. In the August 2001 elections it won two seats in the Constituent Assembly.

Timorese Social Democratic Association
Associação Social-Democrata Timorense (ASDT)

Address. Avenida Direitos Humanos Lecidere, Dili
Leadership. Francisco Xavier do Amaral

The ASDT leader, Francisco Xavier do Amaral, was a founding figure in the →Revolutionary Front of Independent East Timor (Fretilin) and was briefly President of East Timor in 1975. Eventually expelled from the Fretilin leadership after disagreements over tactics, he was later captured by the Indonesians and spent 22 years in jail. In the August 2001 Constituent Assembly elections, the ASDT campaigned using the old Fretilin flag to win support in the countryside, especially in the highlands around Turiscai. It obtained six seats, following which Do Amaral said that he would stand for the post of President.

Other Parties

Association of Timorese Heroes (*Klibur Oan Timor Asuwain, KOTA*), originally established in 1974 as the Popular Association of Monarchists of Timor, whose leader at first accepted integration into Indonesia. Reconstituted in 2000, KOTA stands for traditional Timorese values and is primarily an association of traditional monarchical families, although it accepts universal human rights and a multi-party democracy. It won two seats in August 2001.
Leadership. Leao Pedro dos Reis

Christian Democratic Party (*Partido Democrata Cristão, PDC*), established in August 2000 after a split in the →Timor Christian Democratic Party. It won two seats in August 2001.
Leadership. Antonio Ximenes

Liberal Party (*Partai Liberal, PL*), won one seat in August 2001.
Leadership. Armando Jose-Dourado da Silva

Timor Christian Democratic Party (*Partido Democrata-Cristão de Timor, UDC/PDC*, a combination of two Christian parties which have co-operated, split and recombined since their founding in 2000. It won one seat in August 2001.
Leadership. Vicente da Silva Guterres

Timor People's Party (*Partido do Povo do Timor, PPT*), established in May 2000 with some support from local monarchical families and also local pro-Indonesian militias seeking East Timor's return to Indonesia. It won two seats in August 2001.
Leadership. Jacob Xavier

Timor Socialist Party (*Partido Socialista de Timor, PST*), founded in the 1990s by a student-based splinter group of the →Revolutionary Front of Independent East Timor (Fretilin). Advocating a socialist, classless society, it won one seat in 2001.
Leadership. Pedro Martires da Costa

Ecuador

Capital: Quito

Population: 12,900,000 (2000E)

The Republic of Ecuador achieved independence from Spain in 1822 as part of Gran Colombia and became a separate republic in 1830. Its first 120 years were marked by frequent changes of government, particularly the period from 1925 to 1948, during which 22 heads of state held office. In 1963 the Liberal government of President José María Velasco Ibarra was toppled by a military coup. Velasco was reinstalled in 1968 for a fifth term and from 1970 assumed dictatorial powers. He was ousted by the military in 1972 and a civilian democratic government was not restored until 1979.

Under the 1979 constitution Ecuador has an executive President. The President is directly elected, together with a Vice-President, for a four-year term and is precluded from seeking re-election. If no candidate wins an absolute majority, there follows a run-off election between the two best-placed candidates. The President appoints the Cabinet and the governors of Ecuador's 20 provinces, including the Galapagos Islands. Legislative power is exercised by the unicameral National Congress (*Congreso Nacional*), which is elected for a four-year term on a national basis. It sits for a 60-day period from Aug. 10 of every year, although special sessions may be called. Congress is required by the constitution to set up four full-time legislative commissions to consider draft laws when the House is in recess. Under a set of new electoral rules approved in 1998, the number of seats in the Congress was increased from 82 to 121 and mid-term elections were abolished.

Presidential elections held in May and July 1996 were won by Abdalá Bucaram Ortiz of the populist Ecuadorian Roldosist Party (PRE). After only nine months in power, however, Bucaram was removed from office by the National Congress on grounds of mental incapacity. Fabián Alarcon Rivera, hitherto Speaker, was appointed by the National Congress as interim President for an 18-month period. In fresh elections held on May 31 and July 12, 1998, Quito mayor Jamil Mahuad Witt of the centre-left Popular Democracy (DP) was elected as the new President. In the midst of a prolonged economic and political crisis, and after repeated calls for his resignation, President Mahuad was ousted in a bloodless coup in January 2000. After an unsuccessful attempt at installing a civilian-military junta, Mahuad was replaced by Vice-President Alvaro Noboa Ponton.

No single party won an overall majority in elections to the National Congress held on May 31, 1998, but the DP emerged with the largest number of seats (33), followed closely by the centre-right Social Christian Party (PSC) with 28 and the PRE with 22.

Alfarist Radical Front
Frente Radical Alfarista (FRA)
Address. c/o Congreso Nacional, Palacio Legislativo, Piedrahita y 6 de Diciembre, Quito
Leadership. Fabián Alarcón Rivera (leader)
Founded in 1972 by dissidents from the →Radical Liberal Party (PLR), the centre-left FRA was named after the leader of the 1895 Liberal Revolution, Eloy Alfaro. Although the party is small (it won only two seats in the 1998 legislative elections), it has played a major role in Ecuadorian politics in recent years. In February 1997 the party's leader and the then Speaker of the National Congress, Fabián Alarcón Rivera, was appointed as interim President for an 18-month period after President Bucaram was declared unfit to serve.

Democratic Left
Izquierda Democrática (ID)
Address. Polonia 161, entre Vancouver y Eloy Alfaro, Quito
Telephone. (+593–2) 564436
Fax. (+593–2) 569295
Leadership. Rodrigo Borja Cevallos (leader)
Founded in 1970, the ID is a social democratic party in orientation but in office has proved to be rather conservative and neo-liberal in its economic policies. The party was formed by a faction of the →Radical Liberal Party (PLR) led by Rodrigo Borja Cevallos, together with some independents and dissident members of the →Ecuadorian Socialist Party (PSE).

The ID gained power in 1988, Borja winning the presidential election and the party gaining the largest number of seats in Congress. Borja's first task was to deal with Ecuador's economic problems, which he did by implementing highly unpopular austerity measures. Although modest in comparison to economic shock therapy in other Latin American countries, they lost the ID the 1990 mid-term legislative elections. In 1991 the party absorbed the left-wing *Alfaro Vive, Carajo!* (AVC) guerrilla group. The ID's candidate in the 1992 presidential poll, former Congress Speaker Raul Baca Carbo, had close links with the unpopular Borja government and consequently came a poor fourth.

The party again performed badly in the 1996 elections, making little progress in the presidential poll and winning only three legislative seats. However, it enjoyed an upsurge in support in the 1998 poll, when Borja Cevallos stood as the party's candidate and finished third, gaining over 16% of the vote. In the legislative elections the party won 17 seats. In regional and local elections held in May 2000, the ID candidate, Gen. (retd) Francisco Moncayo Gallegos, was the winner in the contest for the mayoralty of Quito. An ID Congress member, Moncayo was alleged to have been instrumental in the January 2000 coup against President Mahuad. However, he enjoyed great popularity as a result of his role in the brief war with Peru.

The ID is a member party of the Socialist International.

Democratic Popular Movement
Movimiento Popular Democrático (MPD)
Address. c/o Congreso Nacional, Palacio Legislativo, Piedrahita y 6 de Diciembre, Quito
Leadership. Maria Eugenia Lima Garzón (1998 presidential candidate)

The leftist MPD has had some limited electoral success, winning a small number of legislative seats (two in the 1998 elections) and fielding candidates in the presidential contests. In the 1998 presidential election, the MPD candidate, Maria Eugenia Lima Garzón, was eliminated in the first round of voting, gaining 2.4% of the vote.

Jaime Hurtado González, the party's founder and leader, and presidential candidate in the 1980s, was assassinated outside the National Congress building in Quito in February 1999. One of those arrested after the killing was reported to have claimed that the assassination had been ordered by right-wing Colombian paramilitaries in reprisal for Hurtado's alleged support for left-wing Colombian guerrillas.

Ecuadorian Conservative Party
Partido Conservador Ecuatoriano (PCE)
Address. Wilson 578, Quito
Telephone. (+593-2) 505061
Leadership. Sexto Durán-Ballén Córdovez (leader)

Dating from 1855, the right-wing PCE is Ecuador's oldest extant political party. It was founded by Gabriel García Moreno, who was assassinated in 1875 after ruling the country as a dictator for 15 years. The party has traditionally represented the country's oligarchy, the church and the army, and its ideology has remained basically unchanged despite major reorganizations, most recently in 1995, when it incorporated the Republican Unity Party (PUR) led by Sexto Durán-Ballén, who had served as President from 1992 to 1996. With the incorporation of the PUR, Durán-Ballén became PCE leader of the PCE, but the party's fortunes diminished and it managed to win only two seats in the 1996 and the 1998 legislative elections.

Ecuadorian Roldosist Party
Partido Roldosista Ecuatoriano (PRE)
Address. c/o Congreso Nacional, Palacio Legislativo, Piedrahita y 6 de Diciembre, Quito
Leadership. Abdalá Bucaram Ortiz

The PRE was founded in 1982 by former Olympic hurdler Abdalá Bucaram Ortiz and was named after his brother-in-law, Jaime Roldos Aguilera, who served as President from 1979 until his death in 1981. The party started as a movement within Roldos's Concentration of Popular Forces (PCD), but registered as a party in its own right after Roldos's death.

The PRE's strong opposition to the post-1988 Borja government of the →Democratic Left (ID) paid dividends in the 1990 legislative elections, in which the PRE increased its representation to 13 seats. The party joined forces with the →Social Christian Party (PSC) and, as the dominant congressional bloc, caused the Borja government serious problems. Bucaram was selected as PRE candidate for the May 1992 presidential election, despite fears that his past adverse comments about the army might result in a military coup if he were elected. In the event, he came third with 20.7% of the vote and the party won 13 seats in the accompanying congressional elections.

The 1996 presidential election was notable for Bucaram's populist campaigning style. Bucaram, who eventually won the election in a second round of voting, adopted the nickname *El Loco* ("madman") and campaigned under the slogan "Vote for the madman, vote for the clown". He made numerous populist pledges, including the provision of low-cost housing to 200,000 poor families and the extension of social security benefits to poor peasant families. However, once in power, Bucaram adopted unpopular free-market policies designed to tackle the country's large budget deficit, including rises of up to 300 per cent in basic utility prices. Charges of political nepotism and allegations of gross corruption fuelled cross-party demands for Bucaram's resignation and culminated in violent nationwide strikes and protests in early 1997. In February 1997 the National Congress declared Bucaram unfit to remain in office and he left the country, accusing the military of intervening to oust him.

The PRE initially nominated Marco Proaño as its next presidential candidate, but a party convention in Panama in January 1998 opted for the exiled Bucaram. His stand-in in the elections in mid-1998 was Alvaro Noboa Pontín, who came second in the first round with 26.5% of the vote and lost the run-off to Jamil Mahuad Witt of the →Popular Democracy (DP). In concurrent legislative elections the PRE won 22 seats, becoming the third largest party in Congress. Following the ousting of President Mahuad in a military coup in January 2000, replacement Gustavo Noboa Bejarano (DP) appointed a government which included members of the PRE and the →Social Christian Party (PSC).

Pachakutik Plurinational United Movement—New Country
Movimiento Unidad Plurinacional Pachakutik—Nuevo País (MUPP-NP)
Address. c/o Congreso Nacional, Palacio Legislativo, Piedrahita y 6 de Diciembre, Quito
Leadership. Freddy Ehlers Zurita

The MUPP-NP is an indigenous anti-establishment formation founded by television journalist Freddy Ehlers, who contested the 1996 presidential elections on an environmentalist and anti-corruption platform and came third in the first round with 21% of the vote. In the concurrent congressional elections his movement won eight seats. In the mid-1998 elections Ehlers slipped to fourth place in the presidential contest with 14.3% and the MUPP-NP to six congressional seats.

Popular Democracy–Christian Democratic Union
Democracia Popular–Unión Demócrata Cristiana (DP-UDC or DP)
Address. C/ Pradera n. 30–58 y San Salvador, Casilla 17–012300, Quito
Telephone. (+593-2) 900968
Fax. (+593-2) 555567
Email. dp@interactive.net.ec
Leadership. Ramiro Rivera-Molina (president); Pedro Salas Montalvo (secretary-general)

The centre-left DP has consistently campaigned on the issues of communal socialism, democracy and Latin American nationalism. The party had its origins in the

Christian Democratic Party (PDC), formed in 1964, which merged with the progressive faction of the →Ecuadorian Conservative Party (PCE) led by Julio César Trujillo to form the DP in 1978.

In 1979 Osvaldo Hurtado Larrea (formerly PDC leader) was elected Vice-President to President Jaime Roldós Aguilera of the Concentration of Popular Forces (CFP) and assumed the presidency after the latter's death in a plane crash in 1981. Hurtado's DP government became unpopular with the left for his policy of reducing state spending and for austerity measures introduced in 1983, but also with the right, which opposed any state intervention in the running of the economy. DP presidential candidate Trujillo was accordingly defeated in the 1984 elections.

Having backed the successful presidential candidate of the →Democratic Left (ID) in 1988, the DP withdrew from the alliance in late 1989, following disagreements over vegetable oil price rises imposed by the government. This decision saved the DP from suffering the fate of the ID (whose seats were nearly halved) in the 1990 mid-term congressional elections, in which the party retained its seven seats. In the 1992 elections, however, DP presidential candidate Vladimiro Alvarez Grau received a negligible vote and the party's representation was reduced to five seats (which fell to four in the 1994 legislative polls).

The DP performed better in 1996, when it won 12 seats in the legislature and its candidate in the presidential poll, Rodrigo Paz, gained 13.5% of the total vote. This advance led on to a major success in the mid-1998 elections, in which the DP candidate, Quito mayor Jamil Mahuad Witt, won the presidential poll (with 35.3% in the first round and 51.3% in the second) and the party gained the largest number of seats (33) in the National Congress. However, triumph soon turned to disaster for the party. In the midst of a prolonged economic and political crisis, and after repeated calls for his resignation, Mahuad was ousted in a bloodless coup in January 2000 and replaced by Vice-President Alvaro Noboa Ponton of the PRE.

The DP is a member of the Christian Democrat International and the Christian Democrat Organization of America.

Social Christian Party
Partido Social Cristiano (PSC)

Address. Carrion 548 y Reina Victoria, Casilla 9454, Quito
Telephone. (+593–2) 568560
Fax. (+593–2) 568562
Leadership. Jaime Nebot Saadi (president)

The PSC was formed in 1951 (as the Social Christian Movement) to support Camilo Ponce Enríquez, who went on to serve as President in 1956-60. The party adopted its present name in 1967 and continued to operate during the 1972–79 military dictatorship, but went through a period of crisis after Ponce's death in 1976. In the 1988 elections the PSC's presidential candidate, Sexto Durán-Ballén, came third with around 15% of the vote and the party was reduced to only six deputies in the National Congress. (Durán-Ballén went on to form the Republican Unity Party, which was eventually incorporated into the →Ecuadorian Conservative Party, and served as President from 1992 to 1996.)

The party had more success in the June 1990 mid-term elections, winning 16 seats, making it the largest party in Congress. The PSC then entered into a parliamentary alliance with the →Ecuadorian Roldosist Party (PRE), establishing joint control of Congress. Jaime Nebot Saadi was the PSC presidential candidate in the 1992 elections, coming second to Durán-Ballén in the first round with 26.2% of the vote before losing the run-off. In the simul-

taneous congressional elections the PSC won 21 seats, making it the largest party bloc.

The PSC was again the only conspicuous winner in the 1994 polls with 26 seats, which increased to 27 in 1996, eight more than its nearest rival, the PRE. However, Nebot Saadi was less successful in the 1996 presidential poll, again losing over two rounds, this time to the PRE's Abdalá Bucaram Ortiz. In the run-up to the 1998 presidential elections Nebot Saadi announced that he would not contest the poll, in which the party did not present a candidate. Despite Nebot Saadi's withdrawal, the PSC performed well in the congressional elections, winning 28 seats, only five less than the →Popular Democracy (DP), the overall winner. Initially the party offered support to President Mahuad Witt (DP), but in March 1999 it announced its refusal to endorse the President's controversial austerity programme and eventually backed the campaign against him. Following the ousting of President Mahuad in a military coup in January 2000, replacement Gustavo Noboa Bejarano appointed a government which included PSC representatives.

Other Parties and Movements

Confederation of Ecuadorian Indigenous Nationalities (*Confederación de Nacionalidades Indígenas del Ecuador, CONAIE*), the country's main indigenous peoples' organization. It has campaigned for the return of traditional community-held lands, the payment by oil companies of compensation to tribes for environmental damage and for the recognition of Quechua as an official Ecuadorian language. In January 2000 CONAIE played a key role in the ousting of President Jamil Mahuad Witt (→Popular Democracy) by mobilizing thousands of Indians who, with the acquiescence of the army, occupied Quito and other provincial capitals. In early 2001 CONAIE, alongside trade unions and civic groups, organized a "great national mobilization" which secured a reversal in government policy on fuel taxation.
Leadership. Luis Macas (president)

Independent Movement for an Authentic Republic (*Movimiento Independiente para una República Auténtica, MIRA*), created in 1996 by Rosalía Arteaga, who in 1996–97 served as Vice-President under President Bucaram Ortiz of the →Ecuadorian Roldosist Party. During the turmoil which accompanied Bucaram's downfall in early 1997, Arteaga briefly held the presidency for a few days, before it passed to Congress Speaker Fabián Alarcon Rivera. One of two women who contested the 1998 presidential election, Arteaga came fifth with only 5.2%, while MIRA failed to win any congressional seats.
Leadership. Rosalía Arteaga Serrano de Fernández de Córdova

Movement of Ecuadorian Forces (*Movimiento Fuerza Ecuador, MFE*), contested the 1998 legislative election but failed to win a seat. The MFE was accorded observer status of the Liberal International at the organization's 2000 congress in Ottawa.
Address. Luis Urdaneta 204 y Cordova, Guayaquil
Telephone. (+593–4) 568863
Fax. (+593–4) 5666291
Email. info@fuerzaecuador.org
Website. www.fuerzaecuador.org
Leadership. Humberto X. Mata (president); Ivan Baquizero (secretary-general)

Egypt

Capital: Cairo   **Population**: 69,536,644 (2001E)

The Arab Republic of Egypt achieved full independence in 1936, initially as a monarchy, which was overthrown in 1952. There were several experiments with single-party structures, the last and most durable being the Arab Socialist Union (ASU), effectively a platform for the late President Gamal Abdel Nasser. Under Nasser's successor, Anwar Sadat, a limited multi-party system evolved from 1976 which has been dominated by the National Democratic Party (NDP). Under the 1971 constitution, legislative power is exercised by the unicameral People's Assembly (*Majlis al-Shaab*) of 444 elective and 10 appointed members, which is elected for a five-year term by universal adult suffrage (of those aged 18 years and over). The Assembly nominates the President, who is confirmed by popular referendum for a six-year term. The President then appoints a Council of Ministers. In addition, there is an advisory Consultative Council (*Shura*). Two-thirds of its 210 members are popularly elected; the rest are appointed by the President.

In elections to the People's Assembly on Nov. 29 and Dec. 6, 1995, the NDP was officially stated to have won 317 of the 444 elective seats, "independents" 114, the New Wafd Party 6, the National Progressive Unionist Party 5, the Liberal Socialist Party 1 and the Nasserite Party 1. Of the 114 "independent" deputies, 99 quickly declared their allegiance to the NDP. A further 10 members of the Assembly were appointed by the President.

In a national referendum on Oct. 4, 1993, Mohammed Hosni Mubarak of the NDP, the sole candidate, was endorsed for a third six-year presidential term by 94.9% of valid votes cast. In October–November 2000, following an even larger presidential victory in 1999, Egypt held People's Assembly elections in which the NDP won a commanding 353 seats. Another 35 "independents" subsequently joined the party in the Assembly. The New Wafd Party, National Progressive Unionist Party and Nasserites won seven, six and three seats respectively.

However, the NDP's victory came only after initial reports of significant opposition gains, subsequently denied by the government. There were allegations of irregularities, despite the presence of judges inside polling stations for the first time. Protests continued into 2001, especially after the widespread arrest of Islamist candidates in April, prior to the *Shura* Council elections of May.

Liberal Socialist Party (LSP)
Hizb al-Ahrar al-Ishtiraki
Address. c/o Majlis al-Shaab, Cairo
Leadership. (still unresolved following the death of former leader Mustapha Kamal Murad in 1998)
A small party that emerged in 1976 from the right wing of the then ruling Arab Socialist Union, the LSP promotes private enterprise within the Egyptian economy. The party's representation in the People's Assembly fell progressively from 12 seats to none in elections between 1976 and 1984. It then allied itself with the stronger →Socialist Labour Party (SLP) - which also unofficially included the →Muslim Brotherhood (MB) - and saw three of its Assembly candidates elected in 1987. The LSP boycotted polls in 1990, and subsequently discontinued its alliance with the SLP and the MB. It won one seat in the 1995 Assembly elections, and one in 2000.

National Democratic Party (NDP)
Hizb al-Wataniyh al-Dimuqratiyah
Address. Corniche al-Nil Street, Cairo
Telephone. (+20–2) 575–7450
Fax. (+20–2) 360–7681
Leadership. Mohammed Hosni Mubarak (chairman); Dr Yusuf Amin Wali (secretary-general)
The NDP was organized by President Anwar Sadat in July 1978 as the party of government in succession to the Arab Socialist Union (ASU). The latter party, seen as the creature of the late President Nasser, had been dissolved in 1977. Its three constituent "forums", representing left, right and centre, were incorporated into the NDP in October 1978. That same month Sadat instituted a National Development Bank to finance the NDP's various development projects. The new party, which derived its legacy from the long defunct National Party founded in 1907, was to be a broad-based centrist force favouring a mixed economy. The NDP confirmed its dominance with an overwhelming majority at

the 1979 Assembly elections and in all subsequent polls, though the opposition claims the electoral system is biased in its favour.

After Sadat's assassination in October 1981, Vice-President Hosni Mubarak became president of both the country and the ruling party. Twice the NDP was ruled to have abused the constitution, via its slate system of elections, in 1987 and 1990, and on both occasions the Assembly had to be dissolved. Mubarak has won four consecutive presidential elections, most recently in 1999, by overwhelming majorities. Critics have accused NDP representatives of being supine and rubber-stamping executive decisions although legislators have played a role in unearthing corruption and highlighting social problems.

After the October–November 2000 Assembly elections, the NDP was announced to have won 353 seats, up from 318 previously. A further 35 "independents" later joined the NDP. Widespread protests erupted following allegations of rigged polls. Initially numerous candidates from the NDP's official list had apparently suffered defeat and only "corrective" recounts and run-off polls, claimed opponents, explained the magnitude of the NDP's victory. Human rights groups and Egyptian lawyers criticized security forces for bullying voters into supporting the NDP. Mubarak was blamed for curtailing non-NDP campaigning; banning critical publications; and arresting several candidates. The NDP for its part claimed the elections were the "cleanest yet". In 2001 Gamal Mubarak, son of the President, began publicly recruiting youth for the NDP, prompting rumours that he was being groomed to succeed his father.

The NDP is an affiliate of the Socialist International.

National Progressive Unionist Party (NPUP)
Hizb al-Tagammu al-Wataniyah al-Taqaddumi al-Wahdawi
Address. 1 Karim al-Dawla Street, Talaat Harb, Cairo
Telephone. (+20–2) 575–9281

Fax. (+20–2) 578–6298
Leadership. Rifaat El Said (secretary-general)
The NPUP was created in 1976 by chairman Khaled Mohieddin from the left-wing component of the Arab Socialist Union. It advocated state ownership of industry and the exclusion of foreign investment. The NPUP claims to have suffered harassment by the government, particularly in the late 1970s because of its antipathy (alone among the main parties) towards the Egyptian–Israeli peace process. Having failed to win any seats in the elections of 1979, 1984 and 1987, the party shunned the electoral boycott by other opposition parties in 1990, and secured six seats in the Assembly.

The NPUP led domestic opposition to the decision to participate in the US-led coalition that fought Iraq in the 1991 Gulf war. The party also opposed the passage of legislation in 1992 aimed primarily at combating Islamic fundamentalists, which gave the authorities greater internal security powers (in addition to those under emergency laws in force since 1981). The NPUP won five seats in the 1995 legislative elections, and six in the 2000 elections. NPUP politburo chief, Dr El Said, formerly spent 14 years as a political prisoner, but is currently a member of the *Shura* Council. The party fielded women and Copts amongst its 40 candidates.

New Wafd Party (NWP)
Hizb al-Wafd al-Gadid
Address. 1 Bolis Hanna Street, Dokki, Cairo
Telephone. (+20–2) 348–0830
Fax. (+20–2) 360–2007
Website. www.alwafd.org
Leadership. Naaman Gomaa (chairman)
The original Wafd (Delegation) had been a popular liberal and nationalist movement in the 1920s, and was pivotal in the early years of Egyptian independence, after 1936. However, it was banned after the 1952 revolution, despite its opposition to the now deposed King Farouk, because of its association with British interests. The Wafd re-emerged as the NWP in February 1978 under its veteran leader, Fouad Serageddin. In 1981 he led opposition to Egypt's peace treaty with Israel. After a prolonged legal struggle the NWP won the right to contest Assembly elections in October 1983. In alliance with a number of Islamic groups, most notably the →Muslim Brotherhood, the NWP won 58 seats with 15 per cent of the vote in May 1984, so becoming the only opposition party with parliamentary representation. Although strengthened by absorbing the small National Front Party led by Mahmoud al-Qadi, the NWP lost 23 of its seats in the 1987 election, the Muslim Brotherhood having entered into a de facto coalition with the →Socialist Labour Party (SLP) and →Liberal Socialist Party (LSP). Together with other opposition parties that favoured constitutional reform, the NWP boycotted the 1990 Assembly elections, although party members running as independents retained at least 14 seats.

The NWP was the only opposition party to support President Mubarak's commitment of troops to Saudi Arabia during the Gulf crisis of 1990–91, a position which prompted widespread internal dissension and the defection of an influential leading member, Naaman Gomaa. The party was officially credited with six seats in the Assembly elections of late 1995. Deserters decreased the tally to four in 1997. Increasingly, the NWP acquired an Islamist tinge and criticized governmental corruption. Serageddin said the government had rigged the 1995 elections, undermined peaceful opposition, and thereby had lent succour to militant foes like the →Islamic Group. Within the party, a new generation chafed at the NWP's "ossified" ancient leadership. Some even deserted to the NDP in local elections.

Gomaa was subsequently rehabilitated, and in August 2000, following Seraguddin's death at 91, he defeated the latter's brother, deputy party leader and reputed Mubarak ally, Yassin, to became head of the NWP. Gomaa's triumph raised hopes that he would rehabilitate the party. But with little time to plan a decisive campaign, his party gained just seven seats in the election of 2000. Even so, it was again Egypt's largest opposition party.

Socialist Labour Party (SLP)
Hizb al-Amal al-Ishtiraki
Address. 313 Port Said Street, Sayyida Zeinab, Cairo
Telephone. (+20–2) 390–9261
Fax. (+20–2) 390–0283
Leadership. Ibrahim Shukri (chairman); Adel Hussain (secretary-general)
The SLP was officially organized in November 1978 to provide "loyal and constructive opposition" to the ruling →National Democratic Party (NDP). While affirming the need for Islamic precepts to serve as the basis of Egyptian legislation, the party advocated a democratic regime with a more equal sharing of wealth between urban and rural areas. Although the largest opposition party after the 1979 elections, the SLP lost ground to the benefit of the →New Wafd Party in the early 1980s, failing to secure any elective Assembly seats in May 1984. In the 1987 elections, however, it joined an alliance that became the principal opposition force. The SLP, →Liberal Socialist Party (LSP), and others on a joint list which unofficially included candidates of the (formally proscribed) →Muslim Brotherhood, won 60 seats (20 of which the SLP held in its own right). The SLP boycotted the 1990 Assembly election, claiming that President Mubarak's government was insufficiently committed to democracy, although eight party members reportedly won seats as independents.

In the build-up to the 1991 Gulf war, the SLP was a vocal critic of the government's alignment with the US-led coalition against Iraq. This campaign led to judicial action against party members for inciting unrest. Anti-government articles in the party newspaper in 1993–94 led to the brief detention of several SLP members and accusations of defamation against the party chairman, Shukri. Amidst growing restraints on forces both liberal and Islamist, the SLP was formally suspended in May 2000, and Adel Hussain, charged with "working against national unity". Simultaneously, Ahmed Idris and Hamdi Ahmed claimed to have toppled the venerable Shukri as party boss.

Other Parties

Centre Party (*Al Wasat*), led by Abul Ella Madi, launched in early 1996 by a youthful faction of the →Muslim Brotherhood. It included some Christian Copts as well as Muslims. Governmental refusal to recognize the party was seen as a favour to ageing Brotherhood leaders.

Nasserite Party (NP), or Nasserite Arab Democratic Party, led by Diaeddin Dawood, has experienced a revival in recent years. In 2000 the party won three seats, compared with one seat won under the former leadership of Farid Abdel Karim in 1995. Refused legalization in 1990 because it allegedly advocated a return to totalitarianism, in late 2000 the NP exploited nostalgia for the old hero of pan-Arabism, and seemed to provide a home for those who distrust both Israel and Islamic militants in equal measure.

National Accord Party, founded in March 2000, the first new party to win a licence in 22 years and providing a home for malcontents from other opposition parties.

Illegal Groups

Egyptian Communist Party (*Hizb al-Shuyui al-Misri*), has been banned since 1925, subsequently experiencing numerous ideological schisms and breakaways which have yielded many splinter groups.

Holy War (*Jihad*), a secret organization of militant Muslims who split from the →Muslim Brotherhood in the late 1970s because of the latter's objection to the use of violence. The group was blamed for the assassination of President Sadat in 1981. In 1998 the group allied itself to the terrorist cell network headed by the renegade Afghan-based Saudi, Osama bin Laden. But this move generated a split between more cautious figures, and the group's leader, Dr Ayman al (Zawahiri), one of Bin Laden's closest colleague. *Jihad* figures were accused of involvement in the bombing of US embassies in east Africa, in August 1998. *Jihad* reputedly lacks the mass support of the →Islamic Group. Its political offshoot, the *Sharia* (Islamic Law) Party, has yet to be recognized.

Islamic Group (*Gamaa i-Islami*), emerged in the 1970s as the student wing of the →Muslim Brotherhood, subsequently breaking away and aligning (until the mid-1980s) with →Holy War (*Jihad*) in seeking to overthrow the government. A loose-knit, but very militant umbrella organization for many smaller groups, it has been accused of spearheading attacks on the security forces, government officials and tourists since 1992. Militants affiliated with the group were blamed for 900 deaths from 1992–95. The spiritual leader of the Islamic Group is believed to be Sheikh Omar Abdel Rahman, a blind theologian. Egyptian authorities still seek his extradition from detention in the United States, where he was charged with being behind the bombing of the World Trade Centre in 1993. In June 1994 it claimed responsibility for a failed attempt on the life of President Mubarak in Addis Ababa and in November 1997 *Gamaa* was blamed for a massacre of 57 tourists in Luxor. However, in March 1998 its leaders announced a truce in their six-year terror campaign, following a concerted government campaign to arrest members and freeze its assets. Later that year, party officials tried to distance themselves

from the Saudi-born terrorist chief, Osama bin Laden, with whom they had formerly associated. *Gamaa* now backs the Islamist Reform Party, but it lacks official recognition.

Muslim Brotherhood (*Ikhwan al-Muslimin*), established in 1928 to promote the creation of a pan-Arab Islamic state, and declared an illegal organization in 1954. Nasser executed its leading ideologist, Sayid Qutb, in the 1960s. Sadat, however, nurtured unofficial ties with the movement and, although still technically banned, the Brotherhood has enjoyed de facto recognition since entering into coalition politics under President Mubarak. It secured indirect Assembly representation in 1984 by running a number of its candidates under →New Wafd Party auspices, and in the 1987 elections it joined forces with the →Socialist Labour Party and →Liberal Socialist Party, winning 37 of the coalition's 60 seats.

The Brotherhood boycotted the 1990 elections along with other opposition parties, but is still thought to have the largest following and financial resources among Egypt's Islamic organizations, despite the emergence of more radical groups, like the →Islamic Group (*Gamaa*) and →Holy War (*Jihad*). It has 5,000 local offices throughout Egypt, has much influence over professional syndicates, and runs extensive charity and finance networks. Nonetheless, in 1995 fears at Islamic violence inspired an unexpected crackdown on even the moderate *Ikhwan*. Frustrated at domination by an ageing *ulama* (Muslim priesthood) many prominent younger Brothers resigned en masse in 1996.

The movement's spiritual leader is Mustafa Mashhur, who succeeded Hamid Abu al-Nasr following the latter's death in January 1996. Maamoun al-Hudaiby is its secretary-general and chief public spokesman; he stood for elections to the district of Doqqi and Agouza in 2000, but failed to win, claiming polling irregularities.

El Salvador

Capital: San Salvador

Population: 6,120,000 (2000E)

The Republic of El Salvador was ruled by Spain until 1821 and gained full independence in 1839. Throughout its history, military dictatorships have often either ruled directly or dominated the civilian administrations nominally in power, frequently intervening in the electoral process to choose a President suitable to the requirements of the current dictatorship and of the country's powerful oligarchy.

Under the 1983 constitution, legislative power is vested in a unicameral Legislative Assembly (*Asamblea Legislativa*), enlarged to 84 seats in 1991. Executive power rests with the President, who appoints the Council of Ministers and is assisted by a Vice President. Every two years the legislature appoints three substitute Vice-Presidents to assume the presidency in the case of the Vice-President being unable to do so. The President and Vice-President are elected nationally by universal adult suffrage for a five-year term and may not stand for immediate re-election. The members of the Legislative Assembly are elected for three-year terms. Suffrage is universal for nationals over 18 years of age, except for members of the armed forces, who are not permitted to vote. Elections are regulated by the electoral law of 1961, which established the Electoral Council as a supervisory body for all elections.

The most recent presidential elections held on March 7, 1999, resulted in victory for Francisco Flores Pérez of the Nationalist Republican Alliance (Arena). At the time of his election, Flores's party narrowly held most seats in the Legislative Assembly after elections in 1997 had given Arena 28 seats against 27 for the Farabundo Marti National Liberation Front (FMLN). However, the former left-wing guerrillas of the FMLN gained the upper hand in the legislative elections of March 12, 2000, winning 31 seats compared with 29 for Arena, while the National Conciliation Party took 13 and three other parties 11. Arena nonetheless retained control of the Assembly through a right-wing coalition.

Christian Democratic Party
Partido Demócrata Cristiano (PDC)
Address. 3ra Calle Poniente No.924, San Salvador
Telephone. (+503) 281–9251

Fax. (+503) 281–9271
Leadership. René Aguiluz (secretary-general)
Founded in 1960 by José Napoleón Duarte, the PDC originally claimed to be seeking a "third way" between capital-

ism and communism. However, years of co-habitation with the military during the 1980s shifted the party to the right, especially in the late 1980s, when it called for the "re-privatization" of the economy.

Although the PDC contested legislative and presidential elections in 1964 and 1967 respectively, it was not until the 1970s that it made a significant political impact. In 1972 and 1977 the PDC led an opposition electoral alliance, the National Opposition Union (UNO), backing Duarte's candidacy for the presidency. Duarte was elected President in 1972 but was forced to flee the country following a military coup. He returned from exile in 1979 to join the "government junta" formed after the overthrow of the Romero military regime and in December was appointed President, the first civilian to hold the post in almost 50 years.

The PDC participated in two more national junta governments until 1982, relying on a tacit pact with the military. Right-wing parties controlled the legislature following the 1982 elections, but the PDC's 24 seats legitimized its participation in a government of national unity. Duarte's victory in the presidential elections of March 1984 was widely believed to have been reliant on US assistance. The outcome, however, ensured that the existing "unity Cabinet" was replaced by a PDC one. The party consolidated its hold on power in the March 1985 elections in which it won 33 Assembly seats and gained control of the majority of local councils.

The Duarte government was involved in intermittent efforts to negotiate a peace settlement with the →Farabundo Marti National Liberation Front (FMLN), but was constrained by hardliners in the military high command opposed to any major concessions. It retained the support of the US administration under President Ronald Reagan, whose aid financed the quadrupling of the army and an intensification of the civil war against the guerrillas. A serious political split over the PDC presidential nomination for the 1989 elections debilitated the party and led to the PDC's loss of control of the Legislative Assembly in 1988, when it won only 25 seats.

Fidel Chávez Mena then shifted the party appreciably to the right by advocating liberal economic policies, but was comfortably defeated in the first round of the 1989 presidential elections by Alfredo Cristiani Burkard of the →Republican Nationalist Alliance (Arena). In elections to an enlarged 84-seat Assembly in March 1991, the PDC won 26 seats, coming second to Arena. In the run-up to the 1994 presidential elections there were two leading PDC factions sparring for the party's nomination, which eventually went again to Chávez Mena rather than his main rival, Abraham Rodríguez. However, the PDC candidate finished third in the national poll, while the battle between the two competing factions finally came to a head with dissident *abrahamistas* (supporters of Rodríguez) breaking away to form the →Renewal Social Christian Movement.

Support for the PDC has dwindled in recent years. The party won only seven Assembly seats in 1997 and slipped further to six seats in March 2000. Likewise, PDC presidential candidate Rodolfo Antonio Parker Soto only managed to finish a distant fourth in the elections of March 1999, with less than 6% of the vote.

The PDC is affiliated to the Christian Democrat International and the Christian Democrat Organization of America.

Farabundo Marti National Liberation Front
Frente Farabundo Martí para la Liberación Nacional (FMLN)

Address. 29 Cl Pte. Pje. + 1613 Col. Layco, San Salvador
Telephone. (+503) 260–4382
Leadership. Fabio Castillo (co-ordinador general)
Founded in 1980, the FMLN took its name from a communist leader of the 1932 peasant revolt and was originally a hard left guerrilla organization with the Democratic Revolutionary Front (FDR) as its political arm. FMLN guer-

rillas launched a general offensive in January 1981, during which they secured strongholds in many areas. However, from the mid-1980s onwards, the FMLN was almost as active on the diplomatic front as it was militarily, proposing various power-sharing solutions to end the civil war. The FMLN sought to make the country ungovernable so long as the ruling →Nationalist Republican Alliance (Arena) resisted a negotiated settlement. To this end it launched large-scale military offensives in May and November 1990, both of which penetrated into the capital, San Salvador, to strengthen its position in UN-sponsored peace talks with the government. A peace agreement was signed in January 1992. Then, in May 1992, the FMLN announced that it intended to form itself into a political party. The party was recognized by the Supreme Electoral Court in December 1992, by which time the leadership had effectively abandoned the FMLN's original Marxist–Leninist orientation and embraced democratic socialism.

At its first national convention in September 1993, the FMLN endorsed Rubén Ignacio Zamora Rivas of the Democratic Convergence (CD)—later part of the →United Democratic Centre—as its 1994 presidential candidate. In the event, Zamora came second, with some 26% of the vote, while in its first legislative elections in March 1994 the FMLN won 21 seats (against Arena's 39). The candidacy of Zamora exacerbated already existing internal tensions, and in December 1994 a majority of two of the FMLN's constituent groups left the Front to form the →Democratic Party.

In the 1997 legislative elections the FMLN improved to 27 seats (compared with 28 for Arena), also winning 100 of the 262 municipalities it contested, including San Salvador. It suffered a setback in the March 1999 presidential elections when its candidate, Facundo Guardado, was defeated by Francisco Flores of Arena, taking only 29% of the vote after appearing to have a good chance of winning. Guardado resigned from the Front's national co-ordinating body in the aftermath of the defeat.

The FMLN had greater success in legislative elections in March 2000, winning 31 seats (against Arena's 29) with 35% of the vote. The Front was helped by a pre-election promise made by the new FMLN mayor of San Salvador, Hector Silva, to co-operate with business and avoid new taxes. However, despite gaining the largest number of seats in the Assembly, the Front remained in opposition because of Arena's ability to forge an alliance with other right-wing parties.

Nationalist Republican Alliance
Alianza Republicana Nacionalista (Arena)

Address. Prolongación Cl Arce No. 2423. Ent 45 y 47 Av. Nte. San Salvador
Telephone. (+503) 260–4400
Fax. (+503) 260–5918
Leadership. Alfredo Cristiani Burkard (president)
Arena was founded in 1981 by Roberto D'Aubuisson Arrieta, a former major and once head of the intelligence section of the notoriously brutal National Guard. This complemented his involvement during the 1970s in the National Democratic Organization (Orden), a mass-based paramilitary organization said to be linked to the security forces and the White Warriors Union, one of several right-wing death squads.

Arena quickly became a leading political force, winning 19 seats in the 1982 elections to the legislature, of which D'Aubuisson was elected president. D'Aubuisson was accused of personally organizing political killings from an office in the Assembly, the most notorious being the assassination in March 1980 of Monsignor Oscar Arnulfo Romero, Archbishop of San Salvador and a fierce critic of state violence.

Having been shunned by the 1977–81 US Democratic administration of Jimmy Carter, D'Aubuisson was rehabilitated by the succeeding Republican administration of

Ronald Reagan as part of its anti-communist cold war stance towards Central America. However, D'Aubuisson's continued association with the death squads meant that the USA did not endorse his candidacy for President in 1984 but instead supported, and some said "engineered", the victory of José Napoleón Duarte of the →Christian Democratic Party. The defeat provoked the first split in Arena, D'Aubuisson's vice-presidential running-mate Hugo Barrera forming a breakaway party in May 1985.

Eager for increased influence and respectability, Arena's September 1985 national general assembly accepted D'Aubuisson's resignation as secretary-general and elected him as honorary life president. Under the new leadership of Alfredo Cristiani Burkard, Arena presented a more moderate image, especially to the USA, and won the 1988 presidential elections on a programme that offered the prospect of national reconciliation. In the March 1991 legislative elections, the party lost its overall majority in the Legislative Assembly; although it remained the country's largest party, the result encouraged moderate elements to pursue a course of political consensus. Tentative peace negotiations with the →Farabundo Marti National Liberation Front (FMLN), which hardline elements in both the army and Arena tried to sabotage, began in April 1990 under UN auspices; a peace treaty was formally signed in January 1992 and a ceasefire established in February 1992. Before dying of throat cancer in February 1992, D'Aubuisson adopted an increasingly "pragmatic" approach to the peace process and was judged to have played a crucial role behind the scenes in keeping Arena's most fundamentalist anti-communist factions in line behind Cristiani.

The party's legislative representation was unchanged in 1994, when Arena candidate Armando Calderón Sol was the comfortable victor in presidential elections. In 1997 Arena lost considerable ground to the FMLN and only managed to defeat it in legislative elections by a margin of one seat. The party retained the presidency in March 1999, when Francisco Guillermo Flores Pérez easily defeated the FMLN candidate with 51.4% of the vote. However, Arena faced further difficulties in the 2000 legislative elections, winning 29 seats against 31 for the FMLN. Analysts believed that the party lost some popular support because of fears about rising crime and its continued espousal of free-market policies. Despite losing first place to the FMLN in the poll, Arena managed to retain control of the Assembly through the support of other right-wing parties.

National Conciliation Party
Partido de Conciliación Nacional (PCN)

Address. 15 Av. Nte y 3a Cl Pte. No. 244. , San Salvador
Telephone. (+503) 221–3752
Leadership. Ciro Cruz Zepeda Peña (secretary-general)
The direct successor of the Revolutionary Party of Democratic Unification, the right-wing PCN was founded in 1961 as a social reform party and was in power from 1961 to 1979 until a coup overthrew President Carlos Humberto Romero in October 1979. The party was then a vehicle for a succession of fraudulently elected military Presidents, supported by the elite families, and also used patronage to maintain the loyalty of civilian officials.

In the 1982 elections the PCN obtained 14 seats in the 60-seat Constituent Assembly and received four Cabinet posts in a government of national unity, despite the party's strong anti-reformist bias and remaining close ties with the military. The party, however, split in the same year, with its right wing, including nine Assembly delegates, forming the Authentic Institutional Party (PAISA). In 1985, the PCN, as a junior partner in a alliance with the →Nationalist Republican Alliance (Arena) party, won 12 seats in the 1985 elections, a short-lived partnership ending when the party expelled three leaders who had colluded with the Arena to get the elections declared void.

In 1987, in an attempt at political rehabilitation, the PCN claimed to have rediscovered its "social democratic" roots

and opposed the →Christian Democrat Party (PDC) government's austerity package, including a war tax. The manoeuvre produced scant reward, the party winning only seven seats in the March 1988 legislative elections and its candidate in the 1989 presidential election received a modest 4.9% of the vote. In July 1989 the party temporarily joined an alliance with the PDC and the Democratic Convergence (CD), claiming to be interested in promoting dialogues with the →Farabundo Marti National Liberation Front (FMLN).

In the lead-up to the March 1991 legislative elections, the PCN had clear problems deciding where to locate itself on the political spectrum, one leader claiming that the party was "to the left of Arena and to the right of the PDC". It chose not to ally itself with Arena and came third after the PDC, winning 9% of the vote and nine seats. In 1994, despite having developed links with Arena, support for the PCN slumped and it won only four seats in the Assembly. The party's performance improved in 1997, when it won 11 seats, which increased to 14 in 2000, making it the third most powerful force in the legislature. In the 1999 presidential poll, the party's candidate, Rafael Hernán Contreras, won less than 4% of valid votes.

United Democratic Centre
Centro Demócratico Unido (CDU)

Address. c/o Asamblea Legislativa, Palacio Legislativo, Centro de Gobierno, AP 2682 San Salvador
Leadership. Rubén Ignacio Zamora Rivas; Ana Guadeloupe Martinez
The social democratic CDU was formed prior to the 1999 presidential elections through a merger of the Democratic Convergence (CD), the Social Democrat Party (PSD) and the Popular Laborist Party (PPL). The CD, which had founded in 1987 as an umbrella organisation of Marxist parties and professional and labour organizations, made up the bulk of the newly-formed CDU. In the 1999 presidential election, the CDU's candidate (and former CD leader), Rubén Ignacio Zamora Rivas, finished third with 7.4% of the vote. The party won three Assembly seats in elections held in March 2000.

Other Parties

Democratic Party (*Partido Democrata, PD*), centre-left party formed in 1995 by Joaquín Villalobos, a former guerrilla leader, with the avowed aim of capturing the political centre, modernizing national institutions and consolidating democratic structures. The party was largely composed of members of two former constituent groups of the →Farabundo Martí National Liberation Front (FMLN)—the Peoples' Renewal Expression (ERP) and the National Resistance (RN)— which had left the Front in 1994. At its formation the PD had the support of seven members of the Assembly, five of whom offered immediate vital support to efforts by the right-wing →National Republican Alliance (Arena) government to increase VAT. The PD fought the 1997 legislative elections in alliance with the →Christian Democratic Party (PDC) and won three seats, but lost them in 2000. The PD has observer membership of the Socialist International.
Address. Urb Médica, Blvd. Héctor Silva + 128, San Salvador
Fax. (+503) 225–3166
Leadership. Jorge Meléndez (president)

Democratic Republican League (*Liga Republicana Demócratica, LIDER*), whose leader won 1.6% of the vote in the March 1999 presidential election.
Leadership. Salvador Nelson Garcia

Liberal Democratic Party (*Partido Liberal Demócratico, PLD*), won 1.3% of the vote and no seats in the March 2000 legislative election.

Address. Cl El Progreso, Pje El Rosal No. 11. Col. El Rosal, San Salvador
Telephone. (+503) 224–2143
Leadership. Kirio Waldo Salgado Mina (president)

National Action Party (*Partido Accion Nacional, PAN*), won 3.7% of the vote and two Assembly seats in the March 2000 elections.
Address. 3ra. Avenida Norte No. 320. Locales 5B y 6B, San Salvador
Telephone. (+503) 281–1776
Leadership. Horacio Ríos (leader); Gustavo Rogelio Salinas (secretary-general)

Party of the United People and the New Deal (*Partido de la Gente Unida y el Trato Nuevo, PUNTO*), whose leader

won only 0.36% of the vote in the March 1999 presidential election.
Leadership. Francisco Ayala de Paz

Social Christian Union (*Union Social Cristiana, USC*), derived from a 1994 left-wing breakaway group of the Christian Democratic Party. In the 1999 presidential election the party supported Facundo Guardado, the losing candidate of the →Farabundo Martí National Liberation Front (FMLN). In the 2000 Assembly elections it won 1.9% of the vote and no seats. The party is affiliated to the Christian Democrat International and the Christian Democrat Organization of America.
Address. 12 Cl Pte. y 31 Av. Sur Col. Flor Blanca
Telephone. (+503) 222–0571
Leadership. Carlos Abraham Rodríguez (president)

Equatorial Guinea

Capital: Malabo

Population: 474,000 (2000E)

The Republic of Equatorial Guinea gained independence from Spain in 1968. The current President, Brig.-Gen. Teodoro Obiang Nguema Mbasogo, seized power from the dictatorship of Francisco Macias Nguema in a coup in 1979. Ruling through a Supreme Military Council (composed of both military and civilians from December 1981), the regime banned all political parties until mid-1987, when the President announced the formation of a single "party of government" called the Democratic Party of Equatorial Guinea (PDGE). Constitutional amendments, approved by referendum in 1982, extended the President's term of office for a further seven years, and provided for the holding of presidential and legislative elections in a gradual transition from military to civilian rule. President Obiang Nguema secured another seven-year term when he was elected unopposed in June 1989. A new constitution, providing for the introduction of multi-party politics, was adopted by referendum in November 1991. It also provided for the separation of powers between the President and Prime Minister, and gave the President protection from impeachment, prosecution and subpoena before, during and after his term of office. The constitution also provides for a unicameral House of People's Representatives (*Cámara de Representantes del Pueblo*) of 80 members who are directly elected for a five-year term by universal adult suffrage.

The first multi-party legislative elections, held on Nov. 2, 1993, but boycotted by some opposition parties, resulted in the PDGE winning 68 seats, the Social Democratic Convergence 6, the Social Democratic Union 5 and the Liberal Democratic Convention 1. In presidential elections on Feb. 25, 1996, President Obiang Nguema was re-elected with 99% of the vote, in a contest described by opposition groups and international observers as "a farce". In 1998 the Government passed a new electoral law to mandate the replacement of open voting by secret ballot but prohibiting coalitions between political parties in future elections.

Further legislative elections held on March 7, 1999 (which had been postponed in November 1998) gave the PDGE an increased majority with 75 seats. Unlike in the previous poll, the main opposition parties fielded candidates; the Popular Union (UP) gained four seats and the Social Democratic Convergence (CPDS) one seat. However, the opposition parties protested during the campaign against electoral irregularities and have refused to take up their new seats in parliament calling for the results to be annulled.

Democratic Party of Equatorial Guinea
Partido Democrático de Guinea Ecuatorial (PDGE)
Address. c/o Cámara de Representantes del Pueblo, Malabo
Leadership. Brig.-Gen. Teodoro Obiang Nguema Mbasogo (chairman)
The PDGE was launched as the sole legal political party by President Obiang Nguema in October 1987. Shortly afterwards, a law was passed requiring all wage earners and public employees to contribute 3% of their income to the new government party. In response to increasing pressure for greater pluralism, party delegates at an extraordinary congress in August 1991 urged the regime to establish a framework for the legalization of other political parties. A new constitution, approved in November 1991, abolished the PDGE's sole party status and legislation permitting the formation of other parties, although very restrictive in its application, was adopted in early 1992.

The party maintained its dominance in the legislative elections in November 1993, taking 68 of the 80 seats, and was the only party represented in the government appointed

the following month. In October 1994 two prominent members of the PDGE resigned from the party in protest against the government's alleged human rights violations and its obstruction of the democratic process. The official results giving the PDGE victory in the September 1995 municipal elections were contested by the opposition, as was the official outcome of the presidential elections in February 1996 giving Obiang Nguema 99% of the vote.

In April 1997 the government and 13 opposition parties agreed a new national pact for holding elections which provided for the creation of a multiparty electoral commission and an observance commission to monitor compliance. However, the 1999 legislative elections were held amid opposition claims that the government did not abide by the provisions, that its candidates were arrested and harassed and that electoral malpractice was rife. The PDGE increased its parliamentary majority by seven seats, claiming 85.5% of the vote. It also won power in all 30 municipal councils in May 2000, according to official results of the elections which were marked by a low voter turnout following a boycott call by the opposition parties.

Popular Union
Unión Popular (UP)

Address. C/Kenia s/n Apdo. 587, Malabo
Leadership. Andrés-Moisés Mba Ada (leader); Fabian Nsue Nguema (secretary-general).

The UP was legally recognized in 1992. As a member of the Joint Opposition Platform (POC, formed in 1992 but dissolved in 1996), it boycotted the November 1993 legislative elections but participated in the March 1999 poll, securing four seats with 6.45% of the vote. The UP rejected the election results, alleging irregularities in procedure; it refused to join the new administration or to take part in the May 2000 municipal elections.

The UP has observer status with the Christian Democrat International.

Progress Party of Equatorial Guinea
Partido del Progreso de Guinea Ecuatorial (PPGE)

Address. C/Mongomo No 15 Puerta No 3, Apdo. 486, Malabo
Telephone. (+240) 94665
Leadership. Leoncio Conten May (leader); José Luis Jones (secretary-general)

The PPGE was formed by Severo Mota Nsa, a former minister, in exile in Spain in 1983. He and other PPGE leaders returned to Equatorial Guinea in 1988, apparently expecting reconciliation with the ruling regime. However, a petition for legal recognition of the party was denied by the government. This was followed by a further period of exile for Moto and brief imprisonment for José Luis Jones on coup plot charges. Moto returned again in May 1992, and the following October the PPGE was granted legal recognition. The PPGE became a prominent member of the Joint Opposition Platform (POC) and was one of the POC parties that boycotted the November 1993 legislative elections.

In April 1995 Mota and others were convicted and sentenced by a military court on charges related to an alleged coup plot. However, they were all unexpectedly pardoned by President Obiang Nguema in August of that year. In June 1997, the PPGE was declared illegal by presidential decree, following allegations of a planned coup in which Moto Nsa was apparently involved. He became a political refugee in Spain and was subsequently convicted of treason *in absentia* and sentenced to 101 years' imprisonment in August. The party split into factions, for and against Mota, and some members defected to the →Democratic Party of Equatorial Guinea (PDGE). The ban was still in force at the time of the 1999 elections, from which the party was excluded.

The PPGE is an affiliate of the Christian Democrat International.

Social Democratic Convergence
Convergencia para la Democracia Social (CPDS)

Address. c/o Cámara de Representantes del Pueblo, Malabo
Leadership. Placido Miko Abogo (secretary-general)

The CPDS was formed in 1984 in Paris by two opposition groups, of which the Democratic Movement for the Liberation of Equatorial Guinea (*Reunión Democrática para la Liberación de Guinea Ecuatorial*, RDLGE) led by Manuel Rubén Ndongo had in March 1983 announced the creation of a provisional government-in-exile. The CPDS was active within Equatorial Guinea from 1991 onwards in pressing for democratization, and was legally recognized in February 1993. The party did not join the boycott of the November 1993 elections and secured six seats in the House of People's Representatives.

In the 1999 legislative elections, the CPDS retained only a single seat with 5.3% of the vote. With other opposition parties, it formally demanded the annulment of the poll and refused to take up its seat alleging fraud during the voting. Miko Abogo also complained that there were insufficient numbers of international observers to monitor polling procedures. The party did not participate in the municipal elections in 2000.

The CPDS is a full member of the Socialist International.

Other Parties

Coordinating Board of the Joint Opposition (*Coordinadora de la Oposición Conjunta, CODE*), established in 1999 to represent opposition groups exiled in Spain.
Leadership. Joaquin Elema Borengue

Democratic National Union (*Unión Democrática Nacional, UDENA*), affiliated to the Liberal International.
Leadership. Pedro Bueriberi Bokesa (president)

Democratic Social Union (*Unión Democráta Social, UDS*), formerly an opposition grouping based in Gabon. Having achieved legal recognition in October 1992, the UDS won five seats in the November 1993 legislative elections but none in the 1999 polling.
Leadership. Carmelo Modu Akuse (secretary-general)

Movement for the Self-determination of the Island of Bioko (*Movimiento para la Autodeterminación de la Isla de Bioko, MAIB*), a secessionist movement founded in 1993 to represent Bioko's ethnic minority Bubi population.

Eritrea

Capital: Asmara   **Population**: 4,136,000 (2000E)

A former Italian colony, Eritrea was a British protectorate from 1941 to 1952, when it became federated with Ethiopia by decision of the United Nations. It was annexed by Ethiopia in 1962. Following the fall of the government of Mengistu Haile Mariam in Ethiopia in 1991, Eritrea functioned as an autonomous region with the Eritrean People's Liberation Front (EPLF), now the People's Front for Democracy and Justice (PFDJ), establishing a provisional government. The Republic of Eritrea was declared in May 1993 following a referendum, bringing to an end a 30-year struggle for independence. A transitional government was established to administer the country for a maximum of four years pending the drafting of a constitution and multi-party elections. Legislative power was vested in a unicameral National Assembly, comprising 75 members of the central committee of the PFDJ, plus (from March 1994) an equal number of members elected by PDFJ regional committees. The National Assembly elected the President, who was in turn its Chairman. Executive power was vested in a State Council appointed and chaired by the President.

In May 1997 a Constituent Assembly, comprising the 150 members of the current National Assembly and 377 representatives of regional assemblies and Eritreans living outside the country, adopted a draft constitution.

Under this a President would be popularly elected for a maximum of two 5-year terms, while a popularly elected legislature would have powers to revoke the President's mandate by a two-thirds majority vote. Political "pluralism" was authorized on a "conditional" basis with a view to holding elections (and thereby bringing the new constitution into force) in 1998. Pending the elections, legislative power was vested in a transitional National Assembly comprising the 75 members of the PDFJ central committee, 60 regional members of the former Constituent Assembly and 15 representatives of Eritreans living outside the country. The presidency and the executive continued to function on the basis of existing transitional arrangements. The holding of elections in 1998 was precluded by the outbreak of a two-year border war with Ethiopia, and it was not until October 2000 that the transitional National Assembly set a new target date of December 2001 for the elections. Regulations governing political parties were to be drafted by a committee of the transitional National Assembly.

People's Front for Democracy and Justice (PFDJ)

Address. PO Box 1081, Asmara
Leadership. Issaias Afewerki (chairman); Gen. Alamin Mohamed Said (secretary-general)

The PFDJ's predecessor, the Eritrean People's Liberation Front (EPLF), was originally founded in 1970 as a left-wing breakaway group from the traditionalist →Eritrean Liberation Front, in pursuit of Eritrean independence. It latterly moved away from a Marxist stance. For much of its pre-independence existence the EPLF controlled large areas of the Eritrean countryside. By 1989 it claimed to control 90 per cent of the province, completing its dominance thereafter with the fall of the Mengistu regime in 1991. The EPLF converted itself from a national liberation movement into a political party, taking the PFDJ designation, at a congress in February 1994. The 75 members of the central committee of the PFDJ constituted the core membership of the transitional National Assembly set up to exercise legislative power pending the finalization of a timetable for holding multi-party elections. The transitional legislature was responsible for electing the President of Eritrea (an office held by Issaias Afewerki throughout the transitional period).

Other Groups

Democratic Movement for the Liberation of Eritrea (DMLE), an organization opposed to the →People's Front for Democracy and Justice (PFDJ).
Leadership. Hamid Turky

Eritrean Islamic Jihad (EIJ), a radical opposition group.
Leadership. Sheikh Mohamed Arafa

Eritrean Liberation Front (ELF), mainly Muslim and formed in the late 1950s to pursue Eritrean autonomy. It initiated anti-Ethiopian guerrilla activity in the early 1960s, but its influence later declined as it was increasingly marginalized by the breakaway Eritrean People's Liberation Front (which later became the →People's Front for Democracy and Justice). Now split into numerous factions, the ELF opposed the PDFJ transitional government of Eritrea.

Estonia

Capital: Tallinn

Population: 1,380,000 (2000E)

The full sovereignty of the Republic of Estonia was declared on Aug. 20, 1991 (and recognized by the USSR State Council on Sept. 6, 1991), following the Estonian legislature's repudiation in March 1990 of the absorption of Estonia by the USSR in August 1940. A new constitution approved by referendum in June 1992 provided for a parliamentary system combined with a strong presidency. The President is elected for a five-year term by secret ballot of members of the legislature. In the absence of the required two-thirds majority after three voting rounds, the President is elected by a special assembly of parliamentary deputies and local council representatives. The President nominates the Prime Minister, who forms the Council of Ministers. The government must command the support of the 101-member unicameral Parliament (*Riigikogu*), itself popularly elected for a four-year term by a system of proportional representation of parties which obtain at least 5% of the vote. Under constitutional amendments adopted in November 1998, parties may not contest elections in alliances, although joint lists of candidates are permissible. The franchise is vested in those possessing Estonian citizenship.

Parliamentary elections held on March 7, 1999, resulted as follows: Estonian Centre Party (EKe) 28 seats (with 23.4% of the vote), Fatherland Union (IML) 18 (16.1%), Estonian Reform Party (ER) 18 (15.9%), Moderates 17 (15.2%), Estonian Coalition Party (EK) 7 (7.6%), Estonian Rural People's Party (EME) 7 (7.3%), United People's Party of Estonia (EÜR) 6 (6.1%). In mid-2000 the EME merged into the new Estonian People's Union (ERL).

Estonian Centre Party
Eesti Keskerakond (EKe)

Address. PO Box 3737, Tallinn 10158
Telephone. (+372–6) 273460
Fax. (+372–6) 273461
Email. keskerakond@keskerakond.ee
Website. www.keskerakond.ee
Leadership. Edgar Savisaar (chairman); Toomas Varek (parliamentary group chairman); Küllo Arjakas (secretary-general)

The populist EKe was founded in October 1991, being an offshoot of the Estonian Popular Front (*Eestimaa Rahvarinne*, ER) which had spearheaded the post-1988 independence movement but had split into various parties after independence was achieved. As ER leader, Edgar Savisaar had been Prime Minister from April 1990 to January 1992, having previously been chairman of the Estonian branch of the Soviet-era Planning Committee (Gosplan). The EKe used the ER designation in the

September 1992 parliamentary and presidential elections, winning 15 seats (with 12.2% of the vote) and achieving third place (with 23.7%) for its presidential candidate, Rein Taagepera, in the popular balloting which then applied. The EKe absorbed the Estonian Entrepreneurs' Party (*Eesti Ettevtjate Erakond*, EEE) prior to the March 1995 parliamentary elections, in which it won 16 seats with 14.2% of the vote. In April 1995 it joined a coalition government with the Coalition and Rural People's Union (headed by the →Estonian Coalition Party, EK), Savisaar becoming Minister of Internal Affairs.

The dismissal of Savisaar in October 1995 for alleged involvement in phone-tapping (of which he was later cleared) resulted in the collapse of the government and the exclusion of the EKe from the succeeding coalition. Savisaar was replaced as EKe leader by Andra Veidemann and announced his retirement from politics. In early 1996, however, he became leader of an anti-Veidemann faction and was re-elected leader of the party in March. Veidemann and her supporters responded by forming the breakaway →Progressive Party (AP), which was joined by seven of the 16 EKe deputies.

Having absorbed the small Green Party in June 1998, the EKe entered into talks with the →Estonian Rural People's Party (EME) on a ruling coalition after the March 1999 parliamentary elections. Campaigning on a populist platform designed to appeal to voters disenchanted with the free-market economy, the EKe advanced strongly to become the largest party 28 seats and 23.4% of the vote). However, the fact that the EME won only seven seats meant that an EKe-EME government was not feasible. The EKe therefore continued in opposition, to a precarious coalition led by the →Fatherland Union (IL).

In August 2001 the Liberal International announced that it had rejected the EKe's latest application for membership on the grounds that the conduct of Savisaar "does not always conform to liberal principles".

Estonian Coalition Party
Eesti Koonderakond (EK)

Address. Tulika 19, Tallinn 10613
Telephone. (+372–6) 505113
Fax. (+372–6) 505114
Email. koondera@delfi.ee
Website. www.koonderakond.ee
Leadership. Märt Kubo (chairman); Mart Siimann (parliamentary group chairman); Juhan Hindov (secretary-general)
The centrist urban-based EK was founded in December 1991, its then effective leader, Tiit Vähi, becoming caretaker Prime Minister in January 1992. In the September 1992 parliamentary elections the party was part of the nationalist Secure Home coalition, which formed the main parliamentary opposition until 1995. The EK headed the Coalition and Rural People's Union (KMÜ) in the March 1995 parliamentary elections, winning 18 of the alliance's 41 seats. The following month Vähi became Prime Minister of a coalition government between the KMÜ and the →Estonian Centre Party (EKe).

A government crisis in October 1995 resulted in the departure of the EKe and its replacement by the →Estonian Reform Party (ER), under the continued premiership of Vähi. He remained in office after the ER also withdrew from the government in November 1996, but finally resigned in February 1997. He was succeeded as Prime Minister and EK chairman by Märt Siimann, who led the party to a major defeat in the March 1999 parliamentary elections. The EK won only seven seats (with 7.6% of the vote) and went into opposition. In May 1999 Siimann was replaced as party chairman by Märt Kubo, who faced falling support for a party which appeared to have failed to reconcile its broadly pro-market line with its caution on the dismantling of the state-controlled economy.

With a membership of just over 1,000, the EK is a member of the Liberal International.

Estonian People's Union
Eestimaa Rahvaliit (ERL)

Address. Marja 4d, Tallinn 10617
Telephone. (+372–6) 112909
Fax. (+372–6) 112908
Email. erl@erl.ee
Website. www.erl.ee
Leadership. Villu Reiljan (chairman); Arnold Rüütel (honorary chairman); Mai Treial & Ants Kaarma (deputy chairpersons); Lea Kiivit (secretary-general)
The ERL was founded in June 2000 as a merger of the Estonian Rural People's Party (EME), the country's largest agrarian formation, with the small Estonian Rural Union (EM) and the Estonian Pensioners' and Families' League (EPPL). These three parties had each gained representation in the 1995 parliamentary elections as components of the victorious Coalition and Rural People's Union (KMÜ), but only the EME had continued to be represented after the 1999 elections.

The EME was founded in September 1994 on the initiative of Arnold Rüütel, who as Chairman of the Estonian Supreme Soviet had supported moves to throw off Soviet rule and had become independent Estonia's first head of state. Rüütel had subsequently headed the popular poll in the September 1992 presidential elections as the Secure Home candidate, winning 42.2% of the vote, but had been narrowly defeated in the decisive legislative balloting. The EME formed the KMÜ alliance with the →Estonian Coalition Party (EK) for the 1995 elections, bringing agrarian support to the alliance. Having won nine seats, it joined a coalition government headed by the EK. In February 1996 the EME was weakened by two defections from its parliamentary group, but it made its presence felt in government by opposing what it regarded as over-hasty pro-market reforms. In the run-up to the March 1999 elections the EME and the →Estonian Centre Party (EKe) drew up plans to form a post-election government. However, despite the EKe's major advance, the EME retained only seven seats (with 7.3% of the vote), so that an EKe-EME coalition was not feasible.

Founded in March 1991, the EM had contested the 1992 parliamentary elections as part of the Secure Home coalition and had won eight seats in the 1995 elections as part of the KMÜ. The EPPL was derived from the Estonian Democratic Justice Union/Pensioners' League (EDO/PÜ) and had won six seats in 1995.

A congress of the new ERL in Tallinn in June 2001 elected honorary chairman Rüütel as the party's candidate in the forthcoming presidential elections. ERL chairman Villu Reiljan, a former Environment Minister, directed fierce criticism at the government headed by the →Fatherland Union, calling for its resignation.

Estonian Reform Party
Eesti Reformierakond (ER)

Address. Tõnismägi 3a-15, Tallinn 10119
Telephone. (+372–6) 408740
Email. info@reform.ee
Website. www.reform.ee
Leadership. Siim Kallas (chairman); Toomas Savi (parliamentary group chairman); Eero Tohver (secretary-general)
The centre-right pro-market ER was launched by Siim Kallas in late 1994 after he had helped, as president of the Bank of Estonia, to bring about the downfall of Prime Minister Mart Laar (of the Pro Patria National Coalition, later the →Fatherland Union) but had then failed to secure parliamentary endorsement as Laar's successor in the premiership. The ER incorporated the Estonian Liberal Democratic Party (*Eesti Liberaaldemokraatlik Partei*, ELDP) led by Paul-Eerik Rummo, which had contested the 1992 elections as part of the winning Pro Patria coalition but had withdrawn from the latter in June 1994 in protest against Maar's leadership style.

Using the unofficial designation "Liberals", the ER took

second place in the March 1995 parliamentary elections, winning 19 seats and 16.2% of the vote. Having thus effectively become leader of the opposition, Kallas resigned from his central bank post. Six months later, in November 1995, he became Deputy Premier and Foreign Minister when the ER joined a new government coalition headed by the →Estonian Coalition Party and including five other ER ministers. In late 1996, however, the ER left the government, while continuing to give it qualified external support.

In the March 1999 parliamentary elections the ER slipped to 18 seats with 15.9% of the vote. It nevertheless joined a centre-right coalition headed by the Fatherland Union in which Kallas obtained the finance portfolio and four other ER ministers were appointed. Despite an ongoing court case against him over alleged financial impropriety, Kallas was re-elected ER chairman in May 1999. He was again re-elected in May 2001, at a party congress which also elected ER parliamentary group chairman Toomas Vilosius as the party's candidate in the forthcoming presidential elections.

With an official membership of some 2,000, the ER is a member of the Liberal International.

Estonian Social Democratic Labour Party
Eesti Sotsiaalemokraatlik Tööpartei (ESDT)
Address. PO Box 4102, Tallinn 10111
Telephone. (+372–6) 493965
Fax. (+372–6) 472147
Leadership. Tiit Toomsalu (chairman)
The ESDT was established in 1992 as the Estonian Democratic Labour Party (EDT) by elements of the former ruling Estonian Communist Party, now proclaiming a democratic socialist orientation. Having unsuccessfully contested the 1995 elections within the Justice (*Õiglus*) alliance, the EDT became the ESDT in December 1997. In the March 1999 parliamentary elections it won two seats on the list of the →United People's Party of Estonia (EÜRP).

Fatherland Union
Isamaaliit (IML)
Address. Endla 4a/VI Korrus, Tallinn 10142
Telephone. (+372–6) 263325
Fax. (+372–6) 263324
Email. isamaaliit@isamaaliit.ee
Website. www.isamaaliit.ee
Leadership. Mart Laar (chairman); Trunne Kelam (vice-chairman); Andres Ammas (secretary-general)
The centre-right IML was founded in December 1995 as a merger of the Fatherland (or "Pro Patria") National Coalition (*Rahvuslik Koonderakond Isamaa*, RKI) and the Estonian National Independence Party (*Eesti Rahvusliku Sõtumatuse Partei*, ERSP). Then the dominant government formations, these two parties had contested the March 1995 elections in alliance but had retained only eight seats with 7.9% of the vote, thereafter going into opposition.

The RKI had been formed in early 1992 as an alliance of several Christian democratic and other centre-right parties seeking to make a decisive break with the Soviet era. Led by Mart Laar, it won an indecisive plurality of 29 seats in the September 1992 elections (with 22% of the vote), its deputies combining the following month with those of the ERSP and others to elect Lennart Meri as President despite his having come second in the popular balloting with 29.8% of the vote. Laar then engineered the conversion of the RKI into a unitary formation and was named to head a coalition government. But he was eventually ousted as Prime Minister in September 1994, in part because of his self-confessed "dictatorial" methods.

The ERSP had been founded in August 1988, being then the only organized non-communist party in the whole of the USSR. Although centrist in orientation, it was consistently more anti-communist than other pro-independence formations, declining to participate in the 1990 Estonian Supreme Soviet elections and instead organizing the alternative "Congress of Estonia". Following independence in 1991,

the ERSP became Estonia's strongest party, but was eclipsed by the RKI in the September 1992 elections, when the then ERSP chair, Lagle Parek, took fourth place in the presidential contest with only 4.3% of the vote. Thereafter the ERSP became a junior coalition partner in the government headed by the RKI.

In the March 1999 parliamentary elections the IML took second place, winning 18 seats with 16.1% of the vote. The resultant constellation of forces meant that Laar was able to form a three-party centre-right coalition with the →Moderates and the →Estonian Reform Party, the new government commanding 53 of the 101 parliamentary seats. In April 2001 an IML congress elected Peeter Tulviste, chairman of the Tartu city council, as the party's candidate in the forthcoming presidential elections.

The IML is a member of the International Democrat Union and the Christian Democrat International.

Moderates
Mõõdukad
Address. Valli 4, Tallinn 10148
Telephone. (+372–6) 207980
Fax. (+372–6) 207988
Email. moodukad@moodukad.ee
Website. www.moodukad.ee
Leadership. Andres Tarand (chairman); Toomas-Hendrik Ilves, Ivari Padar & Katrin Saks (deputy chairpersons); Tõnu Köiv (secretary-general)
Mõõdukad was launched in 1990 as an electoral alliance of the Estonian Rural Centre Party (EMK) and the Estonian Social Democratic Party (ESDP). The EMK had been founded in 1990 to represent small farmers who favoured transition to a market economy and the restoration of pre-war property rights. Re-established in 1990, the ESDP was descended from the historic Social Democratic Party founded in 1905 (when Estonia was part of the Russian Empire) and was maintained in exile during the post-1945 Soviet era.

The alliance won 12 seats in the 1992 parliamentary elections, becoming a member of the resultant government headed by the Pro Patria National Coalition (later the →Fatherland Union). It was therefore closely associated with the radical pro-market policies pursued by the 1992-95 government and with resultant rising unemployment and high inflation. Its punishment in the March 1995 elections, in which it was endorsed by then Prime Minister Andres Tarand (EMK), was a slump to only six seats in aggregate (with 6% of the vote). The response of the partners was to merge under the *Mõõdukad* title in April 1996, with Tarand becoming chairman.

In the March 1999 parliamentary elections the Moderates recovered strongly to 17 seats on a 15.2% vote share, becoming the progressive wing of a new centre-right coalition government headed by the Fatherland Union and also including the →Estonian Reform Party. Having failed to obtain the premiership, Tarand became chairman of the coalition's co-ordinating council. In May 1999 the Moderates absorbed the People's Party (*Rahvaerakond*), which had been formed in 1998 as a merger of the Estonian Farmers' Party (ETRE) and the right-wing Republican and Conservative People's Party (*Parempoolsed*).

The party inherited the ESDP's full membership of the Socialist International.

United People's Party of Estonia
Eestimaa Ühendatud Rahvapartei (EÜRP)
Address. Estonia pst 3/5, Tallinn 10143
Email. eurp@stv.ee
Website. www.stv.ee/~eurp
Leadership. Viktor Andreyev (chairman)
The EÜRP is the main party of the estimated 30% of Estonia's population who were, or are descended from, Soviet-era settlers, mainly from Russia. For the 1995 parliamentary elections the EÜRP joined with the →Russian

Party of Estonia (VEE) and the →Russian Unity Party (RUP) in the Our Home is Estonia (*Meie Kodu on Eestimaa*, MKE) alliance. This strongly opposed the 1993 Estonian citizenship law defining ethnic Russians and other Soviet-era settlers as foreigners and setting exacting conditions for their naturalization. The fact that only Estonian citizens were entitled to vote resulted in the alliance obtaining only 5.9% of the vote and six seats. The resultant parliamentary group was called the Russian Faction, which quickly split into at least two sub-factions and was dissolved in December 1996, before being revived in June 1998.

The EÜRP contested the March 1999 parliamentary elections in a bloc with the RUP and the (ex-Communist) →Estonian Social Democratic Labour Party (ESDT), the outcome again being six seats (on a 6.1% vote share). The personality clashes that had kept the VEE out of the bloc appeared to be resolved later in 1999. In May 2000 the EÜRP parliamentary faction outraged most Estonian parties by signing a co-operation agreement with the →→Fatherland–All Russia group in the Russian Duma, confirming among other things the parties' joint opposition to Estonian membership of NATO.

Other Parties

Estonian Blue Party (*Eesti Sinine Erakond, ESE*), also known as the Democrats, unsuccessful in the 1995 and 1999 elections, winning 1.6% in the latter contest.
Leadership. Neeme Kuningas

Estonian Christian People's Party (*Eesti Kristlik Rahvapartei, EKRP*), Christian democratic formation which won 2.4% of the vote in the March 1999 parliamentary elections.
Address. Nava 51, Tallinn 10152
Telephone. (+372–6) 688490
Fax. (+372–6) 688491
Email. ekrpkesk@uninet.ee
Website. home.uninet.ee/~ekrpkesk

Estonian Greens (*Eesti Rohelised, ER*), founded in 1991, won one legislative seat in 1992, but failed to win representation in 1995 as part of the Fourth Force (*Neljas Jud*, NJ) coalition with the →Estonian Royalist Party.
Leadership. Jüri Liim

Estonian Home (*Eesti Kodu*), formed part of the unsuccessful right-wing alliance Better Estonia and Estonian Citizens (*Parem Eesti ja Eesti Kodanik*) in the 1995 elections.
Leadership. Kalju Poldvere (chairman)

Estonian National Party (*Eesti Rahvuslik Erakond*), formed part of the unsuccessful right-wing alliance Better Estonia and Estonian Citizens (*Parem Eesti ja Eesti Kodanik*) in the 1995 elections.
Leadership. Elmut Laane (chairman)

Estonian National Progressive Party (*Eesti Rahvuslik Eduerakond*), formed part of the unsuccessful right-wing alliance Better Estonia and Estonian Citizens (*Parem Eesti ja Eesti Kodanik*) in the 1995 elections.
Leadership. Ants Erm (chairman)

Estonian National Protection Party (*Eesti Rahva Jäägerpartei*), formed part of the unsuccessful right-wing alliance Better Estonia and Estonian Citizens (*Parem Eesti ja Eesti Kodanik*) in the 1995 elections.
Leadership. Asso Kommer (chairman)

Estonian Royalist Party (*Eesti Rojalistlik Partei, ERP*), founded in 1989, won eight legislative seats in 1992 but lost them all in 1995 standing as part of the Fourth Force (*Neljas Jud*, NJ) alliance with the →Estonian Greens. Seeking a candidate to head an Estonian constitutional monarchy, the party at one stage proposed Prince Edward of England, before endorsing a Swedish prince with better credentials.
Address. PO Box 300, Tartu 2400
Telephone. (+372–7) 432986
Fax. (+372–7) 431466
Leadership. Kalle Kulbok (chairman)

Farmers' Assembly (*Põllumeeste Kogu, PK*), founded in 1992, was a component of the victorious Coalition and Rural People's Union in the March 1995 elections, in which its candidates stood under the banner of the →Estonian Rural People's Party, with which it formed a joint parliamentary group. In February 1996, however, the two PK deputies withdrew their support from the government (effectively becoming independents) on the grounds that it had given insufficient attention to the needs of farmers. The PK won only 0.5% of the vote in the 1999 parliamentary elections.
Address. PO Box 543, Tallinn 10111
Leadership. Eldur Parder

Party for Legal Justice (*Õigusliku Tasakaalu Erakond, OTE*), led by contested the 1995 elections within the unsuccessful Justice (*Õiglus*) alliance, which also included what became the →Estonian Social Democratic Labour Party.
Address. Nunne 8, Tallinn 10111
Leadership. Peeter Tedre (chairman)

Progressive Party (*Arengupartei, AP*), launched in May 1996 by a dissident faction of the →Estonian Centre Party (EKe) led by Andra Veidemann, who had replaced Edgar Savisaar as EKe leader in October 1995 on the party's exit from government. She had then faced internal opposition orchestrated by Savisaar, who had been re-elected EKe leader in March 1996, whereupon she and six other EKe deputies founded the AP, which was identified as being to the right of the parent party. It joined the ruling coalition led by the →Estonian Coalition Party. Facing the probable loss of their seats, Veidemann and the other AP deputies opted for inclusion on the list of the Estonian Rural People's Party (later the →Estonian People's Union) in the March 1999 parliamentary elections, and were promptly expelled from the AP, which won only 0.4% of the vote.

Russian Party of Estonia (*Vene Erakond Eestis, VEE*), seeking to represent Estonia's substantial ethnic Russian minority, won 2% of the vote in the 1999 parliamentary elections.
Leadership. Nikolai Maspanov (chairman)

Russian Unity Party (RUP), contested the 1999 parliamentary elections in alliance with the →United People's Party of Estonia.
Leadership. Igor Sedashev (chairman)

Ethiopia

Capital: Addis Ababa　　　　　　　　　　　　　　　　　**Population**: 64,117,500 (2000E)

What is now the Federal Democratic Republic of Ethiopia was a monarchy under the Emperor Haile Selassie until the 1974 revolution, after which there was military rule until the introduction of the 1987 constitution proclaiming the People's Democratic Republic of Ethiopia. Rebel forces under the Ethiopian People's Revolutionary Democratic Front (EPRDF) took control of Addis Adaba in May 1991, and Lt.-Col. Mengistu Haile Mariam, who had come to power after an internal struggle within the military leadership in 1977, fled the country. In July 1991 an 87-member Council of Representatives, elected at a multi-party conference, confirmed the leader of the EPRDF, Meles Zenawi, as transitional President. In December 1994 a new constitution was adopted, restructuring Ethiopia into nine ethnically-based states (each with a popularly elected legislature) and providing for a system of national government centred on a bicameral federal parliament. This comprises a directly elected House of People's Representatives with a maximum of 550 members and an upper House of the Federation whose members are elected by the state legislatures. The maximum interval between legislative elections is 5 years. The federal President (ceremonial head of state) is elected by a two-thirds majority of both houses of the federal parliament for a 6-year term (renewable once); candidates are nominated by the House of People's Representatives. A presidential candidate who is a member of parliament must resign from parliament if elected President. The federal Prime Minister (leader of the majority party in the House of People's Representatives) is head of the executive branch, chairman of the Council of Ministers and commander-in-chief of the armed forces.

In elections to the House of People's Representatives held on May 5, 1995, but boycotted by many opposition parties, the EPRDF won a landslide victory, consolidating its hold on power. In August 1995 the Federal Democratic Republic of Ethiopia was proclaimed. Elections for federal and state legislatures were held on May 14, 2000, two days after the launching of a major Ethiopian offensive in the current border war with Eritrea. Although the 2000 elections were contested by several opposition parties and many independent candidates, more than half of the seats in the House of People's Representatives were won by unopposed EPRDF or EPRDF-affiliated candidates. On completion of the federal elections (including some re-run and postponed contests) the House of People's Representatives was made up of 481 members of the EPRDF's main constituent organizations, 37 members of groupings loosely affiliated to (or informally supportive of) the EPRDF, 16 members of parties opposed to the EPRDF, and 13 members elected as independents. The incumbent Prime Minister, Meles Zenawi, was formally confirmed in office in October 2000.

The introduction of Ethiopia's new constitutional structures in 1995 tended both to stimulate the formation of new political parties and movements (in a country already notable for the large number of very small parties) and to ensure that the vast majority of them would play little or no part in federal politics. The following selective listing includes parties, groupings and resistance movements of some current significance in Ethiopian national politics.

All Amhara People's Organization (AAPO)
Address. c/o House of People's Representatives, Addis Ababa
Leadership. Kegnazmatch Neguea Tibeb
The AAPO was established in 1991 to defend the rights of the Amhara people, which it believed were best served by a unitary Ethiopian state rather than the federation advocated by the →Ethiopian People's Revolutionary Democratic Front (and implemented in the 1995 constitution). The AAPO's then leader was jailed from 1994 to 1998, having been convicted of incitement to armed insurrection for making statements which he claimed were within his right to free speech. The AAPO boycotted the 1995 federal elections but contested those of 2000 in order to retain its party registration (which would otherwise have been withdrawn). It fielded 17 candidates for the House of People's Representatives and won one seat in Addis Ababa.

Amhara National Democratic Movement (ANDM)
Address. c/o House of People's Representatives, Addis Ababa
Leadership. Adisu Legese (secretary-general)
Amhara National Democratic Movement is the name adopted in 1994 by the former Ethiopian People's Democratic Movement (EPDM), founded in 1980. The EPDM was one of the two original components of the →Ethiopian People's Revolutionary Democratic Front (EPRDF) set up in May 1988, its forces having emerged as a military element in the anti-Mengistu insurgency in the mid-1980s, particularly in Wollo province. The party's change of name in 1994 reflected its standing as the EPRDF constituent party in areas of predominantly Amharic ethnicity. In the 2000 federal elections the ANDM fielded candidates for 134 of the 138 seats allocated to Amhara state in the House of People's Representatives. All 134 candidates were elected. The party also won 11 seats in Addis Ababa.

Council of Alternative Forces for Peace and Democracy in Ethiopia (CAFPDE)
Address. c/o House of People's Representatives, Addis Ababa
Leadership. Beyene Petros (chairman)
The CAFPDE was formed in 1993 but was unable to contest the 1995 elections because it was not granted official registration until mid-1996. Chaired by Beyene Petros and including his →Southern Ethiopia People's Democratic Coalition among its constituent groupings, it sought to bring together political parties and organizations based on a variety of interests, as well as bodies representing professional groups, to campaign on a pro-human rights and economic liberalization agenda. Originally comprising 30 organizations and groupings, the CAFPDE was reduced to a coalition of five small groupings following a split in December 1999. Beyene Petros successfully contested the 2000 federal

elections as a CAFPDE candidate in a constituency where a new election was held on June 25 after annulment of the May 14 result by the National Electoral Board (which had upheld claims that the conduct of the May elections in this and 13 other southern Ethiopian constituencies was "undemocratic and not free"). No other CAFPDE candidates were elected (although several other members of parties in the coalition were elected to represent their own parties).

Ethiopian Democratic Party (EDP)

Address. c/o House of People's Representatives, Addis Ababa

Leadership. Lidetu Ayalew (secretary-general)

The EDP was formed in 1998 following a split in the →All Amhara People's Organization. It fielded 15 candidates for the federal House of People's Representatives in May 2000, winning two seats in Addis Ababa. Its policies included land reforms to benefit peasant farmers. EDP party members (including candidates in current local government elections) were among those targeted by the security forces in May 2001 in a campaign against "political activists" following the violent suppression of student demonstrations in Addis Ababa.

Ethiopian People's Revolutionary Democratic Front (EPRDF)

Address. c/o House of People's Representatives, Addis Ababa

Leadership. Meles Zenawi (chairman)

The EPRDF was set up in May 1988 at the initiative of the →Tigre People's Liberation Front (TPLF), in alliance with the Ethiopian People's Democratic Movement (later renamed the →Amhara National Democratic Movement, ANDM). The EPRDF's third full member was the →Oromo People's Democratic Organization (OPDO), a party formed on the initiative of the TPLF in 1990 after the →Oromo Liberation Front (OLF) had refused to join the EPRDF. Although the TPLF had long subscribed to Marxist-Leninist ideology, an EPRDF congress in early 1991 endorsed an expansion of private enterprise and the introduction of market mechanisms in small-scale agriculture. While advocating a united federal Ethiopia, the congress also accepted Eritrea's right to self-determination.

In military co-operation with the OLF and the Eritrean People's Liberation Front (which subsequently set up the first government of independent Eritrea, renaming itself the fiPeople's Front for Democracy and Justice), the EPRDF led the march on Addis Adaba which toppled the Mengistu regime in May 1991. Meles Zenawi became interim President of the transitional government which oversaw the drafting and introduction of a new federal constitution. Already the largest grouping in the interim Council of Representatives formed in July 1991 (where its member parties had 32 of the 87 seats), the EPRDF created an extensive network of affiliated parties and groupings throughout most of Ethiopia. In November 1993 a total of 17 EPRDF affiliates in southern Ethiopia formed the →Southern Ethiopian People's Democratic Front (SEPDF), which became the EPRDF's fourth full member.

The EPRDF and its affiliates won an overwhelming majority when elections were held under a new federal constitution in 1995, easily retaining power in 2000. The numbers of federal seats won by each full member of the EPRDF in the 2000 legislative elections were TPLF 40, SEPDF 114, ANDM 145 and OPDO 182. Within the EPRDF's general council (the highest policy-making body) each full member has a fixed entitlement of 20 seats.

The long tradition of TPLF dominance within the EPRDF appeared to be under threat in early 2001 when Meles Zenawi's leadership was challenged by a dissident faction of the TPLF central committee. According to some reports from Ethiopia, leaders of the SEPDF, ANDM and OPDO did not come out in support of Meles Zenawi until it was clear that his faction had prevailed within his own party.

According to political analysts, Ethiopia's 1998-2000 border war with Eritrea had reinforced cross-party Ethiopian nationalist sentiments within the EPRDF, a development which tended to undermine the TPLF's influence in joint policy-making forums.

Hadiya National Democratic Organization (HNDO)

Address. c/o House of People's Representatives, Addis Ababa

Leadership. Beyene Petros (president)

The HNDO, founded in 1991, is a regionally-based party associated with several wider alliances promoted by its leader, Beyene Petros (a professor at Addis Ababa university). His outspoken criticisms of government encroachments on human rights and political freedoms made him one of the most prominent opposition figures in Ethiopian parliamentary politics in 2001. The HNDO won 5 seats in the federal House of People's Representatives in 2000, although Beyene Petros himself stood in a neighbouring constituency as a candidate of the →Council of Alternative Forces for Peace and Democracy in Ethiopia. All the HNDO deputies were, like Beyene Petros himself, returned in new elections held on June 25 after the annulment of the May 14 results by the National Electoral Board.

Oromo Liberation Front (OLF)

Leadership. Daoud Ibsa Gudina (chairman)

Formed in 1975, the OLF operated through different branches with little central leadership, making a minor contribution to the military struggle against the Mengistu regime compared with the contributions of Eritrean forces or the →Tigre People's Liberation Front (TPLF). Mutual antipathy between the OLF and TPLF led to the creation, under the latter's auspices, of the rival →Oromo People's Democratic Organization (OPDO) in 1990. Initially committed to an independent Oromo state, the OLF said in June 1991 that it would support substantial regional autonomy within a federal Ethiopia, and in August 1991 it accepted four ministerial posts in the transitional government headed by Meles Zenawi of the →Ethiopian People's Revolutionary Democratic Front (EPRDF).

Clashes between members of the OLF and members of OPDO (an EPRDF member-party) during the run-up to elections led to a final break with the EPRDF in 1992, after which the OLF went into armed opposition to the Government, carrying out low-level guerrilla operations and advocating boycotts of all elections. The OLF also clashed with rival Oromo rebel groups (some of which had come into being through splits in the OLF).

In July 2000 the OLF held a meeting with three other groups (United Oromo Liberation Front, Oromo Liberation Council and Islamic Front for the Liberation of Oromia) to discuss joint action against the Ethiopian Government, which had ignored a peace proposal put forward by the OLF in February 2000.

Oromo National Congress (ONC)

Address. c/o House of People's Representatives, Addis Ababa

Leadership. Merera Gudina (president)

The ONC, founded in 1996 by a member of Addis Ababa university's political science faculty, exists to oppose the →Oromo People's Democratic Organization through legitimate electoral channels (in contrast to the armed opposition of the →Oromo Liberation Front and other resistance movements, which the ONC condemns). It fielded 36 candidates in the 2000 federal elections and won one seat in the federal House of People's Representatives.

Oromo People's Democratic Organization (OPDO)

Address. c/o House of People's Representatives, Addis Ababa

Leadership. Kuma Demeksa (secretary-general)

The OPDO was set up in 1990 under the direction of the

→Tigre People's Liberation Front (TPLF) as the Oromo ethnic element in the →Ethiopian People's Revolutionary Democratic Front (EPRDF). Its creation was regarded as a hostile act by the major Oromo organization active at that time, the →Oromo Liberation Front (OLF), which had itself refused to join the EPRDF. A member of the OPDO, Negasso Gidado, was elected President (ceremonial head of state) of Ethiopia in August 1995. In the 2000 elections to the federal House of People's Representatives the OPDO won a total of 182 seats, including 173 of the 178 federal seats in Oromia state.

Somali People's Democratic Party (SPDP)

Address. c/o House of People's Representatives, Addis Ababa

Leadership. Mahmud Dirir Gidi (chairman)

The SPDP, a party supportive of the ruling →Ethiopian People's Revolutionary Democratic Front and represented in the federal government, was formed in 1998 through the merger of the Ogaden National Liberation Front and the Ethiopian Somali Democratic League (an 11-party alliance). In the 2000 elections in the Somali state of Ethiopia, the SPDP won 19 of the state's 23 seats in the federal House of People's Representatives (the remaining four going to independents) and 148 of the 168 seats in the State Council.

Southern Ethiopia People's Democratic Coalition (SEPDC)

Address. c/o House of People's Representatives, Addis Ababa

Leadership. Beyene Petros (chairman)

The SEPDC was founded in 1992 as a multi-party coalition under the leadership of Beyene Petros, president of the →Hadiya National Democratic Organization. Having attained a peak membership of 14 parties, it split in 1993, retaining as members several parties which were prepared to accept exclusion from the transitional Council of Representatives over a current political dispute. Strongly critical of the EPRDF government's record in office (and of the authorities' conduct of the elections), the SEPDC won three seats in the federal House of People's Representatives in 2000.

Southern Ethiopian People's Democratic Front (SEDPF)

Address. c/o House of People's Representatives, Addis Ababa

Leadership. Abate Kisho (secretary-general)

The SEPDF was created in November 1993 on the initiative of the →Ethiopian People's Revolutionary Democratic Front (EPRDF) to provide a joint platform within the EPRDF for a number of small parties representing different groups in the ethnically diverse south of Ethiopia. In terms of the state boundaries adopted in 1995, the SEPDF's heartland is the Southern Nations, Nationalities and Peoples (SNNP) state, the federation's third most populous state

after Oromia and Amhara. Each of 17 parties or groupings of parties within the SEPDF contests elections under its own name as the local representative of the EPRDF line on core policy issues. There is an SEPDF parliamentary group in the federal legislature and an SEPDF party hierarchy whose senior figures participate in EPRDF decision-making. In the 2000 federal elections SEPDF member parties won 112 of the SNNP state's 123 seats in the House of People's Representatives, plus two of the Addis Ababa seats. Several of the smallest SEPDF member-parties (e.g. the Konso People's Democratic Organization) won one seat each, having each fielded one candidate. The largest component of the SEPDF (the Walayta, Gamo-Gofa, Dawro and Konta Peoples' Democratic Organization) fielded 33 candidates and won 30 seats.

Tigre People's Liberation Front (TPLF)

Leadership. Meles Zenawi (chairman)

Originally formed as a Marxist-Leninist party in 1975, the TPLF pursued a separatist goal for Tigre Province until the late 1980s. It then moderated its ideological stance and its objective became an overall change of regime in a federally structured Ethiopia. Having achieved dominance over Tigre province through its military insurgency, the TPLF initiated the establishment of the →Ethiopian People's Revolutionary Democratic Front in 1988, precipitating the overthrow of the Mengistu regime in May 1991 and the assumption of power in the name of the EPRDF by TPLF chairman, Meles Zenawi. As the leader of the EPRDF (the majority group in the House of People's Representatives), Meles Zenawi became the first federal Prime Minister (executive head of government) under the new constitution introduced in 1995. He was reappointed to the premiership after the legislative elections of 2000. Although the TPLF (with 40 federal seats in 2000, including all 38 in Tigre state) is the EPRDF component with the smallest parliamentary group, it has always been the dominant political force within the wider grouping.

A major split occurred in the TPLF's central committee in early 2001 after a "hard-line" faction led by the party's deputy chairman, Tewolde Wolde-Mariam, accused Meles Zenawi and his closest advisers of embracing capitalist values, kowtowing to the USA and abandoning the TPLF's original aim of creating a "popular revolutionary democracy". Meles Zenawi was also attacked for the terms on which a border war with Eritrea had been ended in late 2000 (and in particular for agreeing to the deployment of UN peace-keepers). Tewolde Wolde-Mariam and 11 other dissident members of the 30-member TPLF central committee were expelled from the party after they refused to appear at an EPRDF general council meeting in March 2001 to explain their views (for which they had already been suspended from the TPLF). Nine of the dissidents were subsequently deprived of their parliamentary seats (on the basis of voters' petitions to the National Electoral Board) and by-elections were ordered to be held in July 2001.

Fiji

Capital: Suva

Population: 790,000 (2000E)

Formerly a British colony, Fiji became an independent state within the Commonwealth in 1970. The moderate Alliance Party, defending the constitutional and legal rights of the indigenous Fijian (Melanesian–Polynesian) population, ruled the country from independence until its defeat in the general election of April 1987 (after which it effectively ceased to operate). A new government was formed from a coalition of the Fiji Labour Party (FLP) and the National Federation Party (NFP), which largely drew support from the population of Indian descent. In May 1987 a military coup was staged by Lt.-Col. Sitiveni Rabuka. Although civilian government was subsequently restored with the establishment of an interim administration, Rabuka staged a second coup in September 1987. The following month he announced that the 1970 constitution had been revoked and declared

Fiji a republic. The British sovereign ceased to be the head of state upon the resignation of the Governor-General, and Fiji's membership of the Commonwealth lapsed. The country was returned nominally to civilian rule in December 1987 when the former Governor-General accepted the presidency of the republic and a Fijian-dominated Cabinet (including Rabuka as Minister for Home Affairs) was appointed.

A new constitution, promulgated in 1990, guaranteed the political dominance of the indigenous Fijian community within a bicameral parliament. In 1995, however, a Constitutional Review Commission (CRC) was set up, the eventual result being the 1997 constitution, which prescribes a parliamentary structure and electoral system properly reflecting the multi-ethnic nature of Fijian society. It provides for a bicameral Parliament consisting of (i) a 32-member Senate *(Seniti),* appointed by the President on the recommendation of the Great Council of Chiefs and the political parties, with 23 seats being reserved for ethnic Fijians and nine for Indians and other groups; and (ii) a 71-member House of Representatives *(Vale)* elected for a five-year term. The House has 46 "communal" seats (23 reserved for indigenous Fijians, 19 for Indo-Fijians, three for other ethnic groups and one for the inhabitants of Rotuma) and 25 seats "open" to all races but filled from single-member constituencies. The head of state is the President, who is appointed by the Great Council of Chiefs for a five-year term. The head of government is the Prime Minister, who is appointed by the President subject to parliamentary approval and who himself appoints the Cabinet.

The 1999 general elections brought the FLP back to office in a coalition with two indigenous Fijian parties which was headed by Mahendra Chaudhry, who thus became the first Fijian Prime Minister of Indian descent. In May 2000 the Chaudhry government was overthrown in a civilian coup led by George Speight, who claimed that indigenous Fijian interests were under threat. Two months later the army intervened to install an interim administration headed by Laisenia Qarase of the new National Unity Party (SDL). General elections on Aug. 25 and Sept. 2, 2001, were contested by some 20 parties and resulted in the SDL becoming the largest party in the House of Representatives with 31 seats. The FLP won 27 seats, the Conservative Alliance (MV) 6, the New Labour Unity Party (NLUP) 2, the National Federation Party (NFP) 1, the United General Party (UGP) 1 and independents 2. The resultant government was a coalition headed by the SDL and including the MV and a member of the NLUP.

Conservative Alliance
Matanitu Vanua (MV)
Address. PO Box 1694, Nasea Labasa
Telephone. (+679) 362560
Leadership. Rakuita Vakalalabure (leader)
The MV consists of supporters of the May 2000 coup. Amongst its members are coup leader George Speight and several others who had been imprisoned with him on Nukulau island, off Suva, due to their involvement. The party has an extremist nationalist ideology that indigenous Fijians must have total control of political power. It advocates amendment of the 1997 constitution to provide more protection for indigenous Fijian rights. Its supporters are largely rural people from Tailevu and Cakaudrove provinces.

The MV won six seats in the 2001 elections, its successful candidates including Speight. The party was included in the new coalition government, being allocated two ministerial posts.

Fiji Labour Party (FLP)
Address. PO Box 2162, Suva
Telephone. (+679) 308602
Fax. (+679) 307829
Leadership. Mahendra Chaudhry (general secretary)
The FLP was formed in 1985 as a multi-racial party, although it has drawn most of its support from the Indo-Fijian community. It came to power briefly, in coalition with the →National Federation Party (NFP), in the April 1987 general elections, but this government was overthrown the following month in a military coup. In 1991 the FLP broke with the NFP over the former's decision (which was ultimately reversed) to boycott the 1992 general elections. Of the 13 (Indian-reserved) seats gained by the FLP in the 1992 elections, only seven were retained in the balloting in February 1994.

In the May 1999 general elections the FLP won all the Indian seats (open and communal) and an overall total of 34 out of 71 seats in the House of Representatives. This enabled the FLP to form the new government in a coalition arrangement which included the →Fijian Association Party and the →General Voters' Party, with Mahendra Chaudhry becoming Fiji's first Indo-Fijian Prime Minister. He was quickly accused of pro-Indian nepotism and of being anti-

Fijian in his policies. In May 2000 the government was overthrown in a Fijian nationalist civilian coup, Chaudhry being among those held hostage for nearly two months. Following his release and the installation of an interim government, Chaudhry insisted that he was the legal Prime Minister. He obtained an Appeal Court ruling to that effect in March 2001 and was reinstated, but was immediately dismissed by the President so that new elections could be held.

In the election run-up the FLP experienced internal divisions, resulting in the departure of deputy party leader Tupeni Baba to form the →New Labour Unity Party. In the August-September 2001 balloting the FLP fell back to 27 seats and became the principal opposition to a coalition government headed by the →National Unity Party (SDL), after the SDL had refused to entertain the FLP's conditions for joining the government. The FLP subsequently challenged the constitutional legitimacy of the new government in court.

The FLP is a consultative member of the Socialist International.

National Federation Party (NFP)
Address. PO Box 4399, Samabula, Suva
Telephone. (+679) 385916
Fax. (+679) 381991
Leadership. Attar Singh (leader)
Formed in the 1960s, the NFP is the oldest political party in Fiji, deriving its support predominantly from the Indo-Fijian community. It was the main opposition party following independence in 1970, but came to power in a coalition with the →Fiji Labour Party (FLP) following the April 1987 elections. The new government was promptly ousted in a military coup the following month. The alliance with the FLP ended in 1991 when the NFP voted not to join the FLP in its decision (which was subsequently reversed) to boycott the 1992 general elections. Having won 14 of the 27 seats reserved for Indo-Fijians in that election, the NFP increased its representation to 20 seats in the February 1994 polling.

In the 1999 elections the NFP failed to win representation, losing all of its seats to Labour, with the result that then leader Jai Ram Reddy resigned. The party regained a single seat in the 2001 elections, opting to be part of the opposition despite being approached to join the new coalition headed by the →National Unity Party.

National Unity Party
Soqosoqo Duavata ni Lewenivanua (SDL)

Address. 28 Tuisowaqa Road, Namadi Heights, Suva
Telephone. (+679) 314609
Fax. (+679) 314491
Leadership. Laisenia Qarase (leader)

The SDL was formed in May 2001 by members of the interim government installed under the premiership of Laisenia Qarase, after the eventually abortive coup by indigenous Fijian militants in May 2000. The party has a multi-racial stance with considerable support amongst business people of all ethnic groups, while also aiming to promote the business interests of indigenous Fijians. Although a new party, the SDL attracted impressive support in the August-September 2001 elections, especially among indigenous Fijians, winning 31 seats to become the largest in parliament.

Qarase was sworn in as Prime Minister on Sept. 9, 2001, at the head of a 20-member Cabinet which included 15 SDL members, two from the →Conservative Alliance, one from the →New Labour Unity Party and two independents. The new coalition was predominantly drawn from indigenous Fijians, whilst the opposition led by the →Fiji Labour Party was mainly Indo-Fijian.

New Labour Unity Party (NLUP)

Address. PO Box 1258, Suva
Telephone. (+679) 370511
Fax. (+679) 370511
Leadership. Tupeni Baba (leader)

Formed in April 2001, the NLUP is a breakaway from the →Fiji Labour Party (FLP) by a faction which had been dissatisfied with the leadership style of Labour leader Mahendra Chaudhry. The party has a multi-racial base and believes in national unification of all ethnic groups through dialogue. Its significant Indian and Fijian following yielded two seats in the 2001 elections, although party leader Tupeni Baba failed to be re-elected. One of the victorious NLUP candidates accepted a post in the new government headed by the →National Unity Party, whereas the other decided not to. This caused friction within the party, the member who joined the government being threatened with expulsion from the party.

United General Party (UGP)

Address. PO Box 9403, Nadi Airport
Telephone. (+679) 312866
Fax. (+679) 303052
Leadership. Mick Beddoes (leader)

The UGP is a breakaway from the →General Voters' Party (GVP), representing "general" voters from ethnic groups other than indigenous Fijians and Indo-Fijians (i.e. Europeans, Chinese and various Pacific islanders). Whereas the GVP failed to win representation in the 2001 elections, the UGP gained one seat and became part of the opposition.

Other Parties

Fijian Association Party (FAP), formed prior to the 1994 elections by a breakaway faction of the →Fijian Political Party (SVT). It was part of the ruling coalition headed by the →Fiji Labour Party after the 1999 elections, but was weakened by a split. The rump FAP had no success in the 2001 elections, party leader and former Deputy Premier Kuini Speed losing her seat.
Address. PO Box 633, Suva

Telephone/Fax. (+679) 307282
Leadership. Kuini Speed

Fijian Political Party (*Soqosoqo ni Vakavulewa ni Taukei, SVT*), launched in 1991 with the aim of uniting indigenous Fijians, headed in the 1990s by Sitiveni Rabuka, who had led two military coups in 1987. The party won majorities in the 1992 and 1994 elections, forming coalition governments under Rabuka's premiership. It was in opposition from the 1999 elections until the May 2000 coup, being weakened subsequently by the defection of a faction to the →National Unity Party. The failure of the rump SVT in the 2001 elections was attributed to indigenous Fijians' rejection of its "moderate" multi-racialism.
Address. PO Box 2259, Suva
Telephone. (+679) 308300
Fax. (+679) 300717
Leadership. Filipe Bole

General Voters' Party (GVP), formed in 1990, representing those not belonging to either the indigenous Fijian or ethnic Indian communities (i.e. Europeans, Chinese and Pacific islanders). It won five seats in the 1992 elections (and four in 1994), participating in a government led by the →Fijian Political Party until withdrawing in 1995. It again held office following the 1999 elections until the May 2000 coup. Weakened by breakaways such as that producing the →United General Party, it failed to win any seats in the 2001 elections.
Address. PO Box 482, Government Buildings, Suva
Telephone. (+679) 305811
Fax. (+679) 314095
Leadership. John Sanday

Nationalist Vanua Tako Lavo Party (NVTLP), a revamped version of the original Fijian Nationalist Party, which used to advocate the repatriation of Indo-Fijians to India. The NVTLP won a seat in a 1997 by-election and two seats in the 1999 elections. It broke up into factions over the 2000 coup, some supporting it and others not, and failed to win representation in 2001.
Address. PO Box 323, Suva
Leadership. Watisoni Butadroka

Party of National Unity (PANU), formed in 1998, with a multi-racial philosophy, based in western Fiji. It was set up by western chiefs unhappy with the distribution of state resources to the area producing the large sugar and tourism revenues. Presenting a similar programme to →Protector of Fiji, it was unsuccessful in the 2001 elections.
Address. PO Box 4106, Lautoka
Telephone. (+679) 665559
Leadership. Meli Bogileka

Protector of Fiji (*Bai Kei Viti, BKV*), formed in early 2001, dominated by indigenous Fijians from the western part of Fiji, for whom it advocates a fair distribution of resources. Despite having some high-profile political figures, it won no seats in 2001.
Address. PO Box 7260, Lautoka
Telephone. (+679) 668859
Leadership. Tevita Momoidonu & Apisai Tora

Finland

Capital: Helsinki

Population: 5,200,000 (2000E)

Under its 1919 constitution as amended, the Republic of Finland is a democratic parliamentary state with a President elected for a six-year term by universal adult suffrage in two rounds of voting if no candidate obtains an absolute majority in the first. The President has considerable executive powers (particularly in the foreign policy sphere) and appoints a Council of Minister under a Prime Minister which must enjoy the confidence of the 200-member unicameral Diet (Eduskunta) elected for a four-year term by universal adult suffrage. Parliamentary elections are held under a system of proportional representation in 15 electoral districts, with the number of seats being allocated according to the most recent population census figures. One of the electoral districts is formed by the autonomous Åland Islands (inhabited mainly by ethnic Swedes), which return one deputy to the Finnish Diet. Finland joined what became the European Union on Jan. 1, 1995, and elects 16 members of the European Parliament.

The state contributes to the financing of the national and international activities of political parties represented in the Diet in proportion to their number of seats. In 2001 the total amount available was FMk64.2 million (about $10.3 million), of which, for example, the Finnish Social Democratic Party was allocated FMk17.9 million (about $2.6 million).

Parliamentary elections on March 21, 1999, resulted as follows: Finnish Social Democratic Party 51 seats (with 22.9% of the vote), Centre Party of Finland 48 (22.4%), National Coalition 46 (21.0%), Left Alliance 20 (10.9%), Swedish People's Party 12 (5.1%), Green Union 11 (7.5%), Finnish Christian Union 10 (4.2%), Reform Group 1 (1.1%), True Finns Party 1 (1.0%).

Presidential elections held on Jan. 16 and Feb. 6, 2000, resulted in the candidate of the Finnish Social Democratic Party, Tarja Halonen, being elected with 51.6% of the second-round vote.

Centre Party of Finland
Suomen Keskusta (KESK)

Address. Pursimiehenkatu 15, 00150 Helsinki
Telephone. (+358-9) 172–721
Fax. (+358-9) 653–589
Email. keskusta@keskusta.fi
Website. www.keskusta.fi
Leadership. Esko Aho (chairman); Mauri Pekkarinen (parliamentary group chairman); Eero Lankia (secretary-general)

The Centre Party was founded in 1906 as the Agrarian Union, committed to improving the lot of Finland's large rural population and also to national independence, social justice and democracy. Its chief ideologue was Santeri Alkio (1862–1930), who wrote the first detailed Agrarian programme. Following Finland's declaration of independence in 1917, the Agrarians were part of the successful opposition to right-wing attempts to install a monarchy, while welcoming the victory of the anti-Bolshevik Whites in the 1918 civil war. On the declaration of a republic in 1919, the party increased its electoral support to 19.7% and began its long career in government. Of the 63 governments formed since independence, 48 have included the Agrarian/Centre Party, which has provided the Prime Minister on 20 occasions, as well as three Presidents, namely Lauri Kristian Relander (1925–32), Kyösti Kallio (1937–40) and Urho Kekkonen (1956–81).

The Agrarians reached an inter-war electoral peak of 27.3% in 1930, but were usually the second party after the →Finnish Social Democratic Party (SSDP), with which they formed a "red-green" coalition from 1937. The Agrarians subsequently shared government responsibility for Finland's hostilities with the USSR in 1939–40 and 1941–44, resulting in the loss of a tenth of Finnish territory. Under the leadership of V.J. Sukselainen, the party took 21.4% of the vote in the 1945 elections and became the third largest party in the Diet. Rising to 24.2% in 1948, it became the largest parliamentary party and retained this status in the 1951 and 1954 elections. Kekkonen held the premiership in five out of the seven governments formed between 1950 and

1956. Elected President in 1956, he was to complete four consecutive terms before resigning during his fifth (in October 1981) because of ill-health. His main contribution in the foreign policy sphere was to refine the so-called "Paasikivi-Kekkonen line", involving preferential relations with the USSR in the context of neutrality and non-alignment. By this strategy, he hoped to secure the return of the Finnish territories ceded during World War II, but faced a firm Soviet refusal to consider territorial change.

The Agrarians fell back to third position in the 1958 elections and were weakened by the formation in 1959 of the Finnish Rural Party (SMP) by right-wing Agrarian dissidents (→True Finns Party). They nevertheless continued to play a pivotal role in successive coalitions and in 1962 recovered a Diet plurality, winning 53 seats and 23.0% of the vote. In November 1963 Ahti Karjalainen (Agrarian) formed the first non-socialist government since World War II, the other participants being the conservative →National Coalition (KOK), together with what became the →Liberal People's Party (LKP) and the →Swedish People's Party (RKP/SFP). It resigned the following month and was eventually succeeded in September 1964 by one of the same party composition but headed by the Agrarian leader, Johannes Virolainen. In 1965 the Agrarians followed the Scandinavian trend by changing their name to Centre Party, aiming to broaden their support beyond the declining rural population. In the 1996 elections, however, the party slipped to 49 seats and 21.2% and joined a centre-left coalition headed by the SSDP. Because of competition from the SMP, KESK lost further ground in the next two elections, falling to 37 seats and 17.1% in 1970 and to 35 seats and 16.4% in 1972. Karjalainen was nevertheless again Prime Minister in 1970-71 and the party participated in subsequent centre-left combinations.

Having recovered to 39 seats and 17.6% in 1975, KESK provided the Prime Minister (Martti Miettunen) of centre-left coalitions in office until 1977, when it switched to a subordinate ministerial role. It slipped back to 36 seats and 17.3% in the 1979 elections (which it fought in alliance with the LKP), thereafter participating in SSDP-led coalitions until 1987. In 1980 Paavo Väyrynen was elected KESK chairman at the age of 34. In 1982 the LKP became a constituent organization of KESK, which inched up to 38 seats and 17.6% in the 1983 elections. In 1986 the LKP reverted to independent status; but its support remained with KESK, which improved to 40 seats and 17.6% (again) in the 1987 elections, after which the party had the unusual experience of being in opposition for a whole parliamentary term. Its reward in the 1991 elections was a surge to a plurality of 55 seats and 24.8%, enabling it to form a centre-right coalition with KOK, the RKP/SFP and the →Finnish Christian Union (SKL), with new KESK leader Esko Aho (37) becoming the youngest Prime Minister in Finnish history.

Contending with deepening economic recession, the Aho government also faced dissent within the coalition parties on its aim of accession to the European Union (EU), not least within KESK itself. An additional farm support package served to defuse opposition to the entry terms in KESK rural ranks, and accession was duly approved in the October 1994 referendum, although not before the anti-EU SKL had withdrawn from the coalition. Meanwhile, former KESK leader Väyrynen had been placed third in the first round of presidential elections in January 1994, winning only 19.5 of the vote. In the March 1995 legislative elections, moreover, KESK was the main loser, falling to 44 seats and 19.9%, and went into opposition to a five-party coalition headed by the SSDP.

KESK made a comeback in the October 1996 European Parliament elections, heading the poll with 24.4% (which gave it four of Finland's 16 seats) on a platform of opposition to further European integration. In the March 1999 national elections KESK advanced to 48 seats (on a 22.4% vote share) but remained in opposition to another SSDP-led coalition. In the June 1999 European Parliament elections KESK slipped to 21.3% of the vote but again won four seats.

Standing as the KESK candidate in the January–February 2000 presidential elections, Aho came second in the first round with 34.4% of the vote, but was narrowly defeated by the SSDP nominee in the second in a 48.4% to 51.6% split.

With an official membership of 270,000, KESK is an affiliate of the Liberal International. Its European Parliament representatives sit in the European Liberal, Democratic and Reformist group.

Finnish Christian Union
Suomen Kristillinen Liitto (SKL)

Address. Mannerheimintie 40D, 00100 Helsinki
Telephone. (+358–9) 3488–2200
Fax. (+358-9) 3488–2228
Email. skl@skl.fi
Website. www.skl.fi
Leadership. C.P. Bjarne Kallis (chairman); Jouko Jääskeläinen (parliamentary group chairman); Milla Kalliomaa (secretary)

The SKL is an evangelical party founded in 1958 to propagate Christian values in public life and to resist secularization. It won its first Diet seat in 1970 on a 1.1% vote share, advancing to four seats and 2.5% in 1972 and to nine seats and 3.3% in 1975, when it benefited from the electoral slump of the Finnish Rural Party (SMP) (→True Finns Party). After SKL candidate Raino Westerholm had won a respectable 9% of the vote in the 1978 presidential elections, the party retained nine seats on a 4.8% vote share in the 1979 Diet elections. It slipped back to three seats and 3.0% in 1983, while in 1987 its reduced share of 2.6% gave it five seats on the strength of local electoral alliances with the →Centre Party of Finland (KESK) and the →Liberal People's Party (LKP). It advanced again in 1991, to eight seats and 3.1%, and opted for its first taste of government, joining a non-socialist coalition headed by KESK and including the conservative →National Coalition and the →Swedish People's Party.

Opposed to Finnish accession to the European Union (as supported by its coalition partners), the SKL withdrew from the government in June 1994. In the March 1995 Diet elections the SKL slipped to seven seats and 3.0% of the vote, remaining in opposition and subsequently losing one deputy to KESK. It revived to 10 seats and 4.2% in the March 1999 elections, but again continued in opposition. A vote share of 2.4% in the June 1999 European Parliament elections gave the SKL one seat.

With an official membership of 16,500, the SKL is affiliated to the Christian Democrat International. Its representative in the European Parliament sits in the European People's Party/European Democrats group.

Finnish Social Democratic Party
Suomen Sosiaalidemokraattinen Puolue (SSDP)

Address. Saariniemenkatu 6, 00530 Helsinki
Telephone. (+358–9) 478–988
Fax. (+358-9) 712–752
Email. palaute@sdp.fi
Website. www.sdp.fi
Leadership. Paavo Lipponen (chairman); Antero Kekkonen & Liisa Jaakonsaari (deputy chairpersons); Antti Kalliomäki (parliamentary group chairman); Kari Laitinen (general secretary)

The party was founded in 1899 as the Finnish Workers' Party to represent the growing ranks of organized labour as well as landless labourers, adopting its present name in 1903, when Finland was still part of the Russian Empire. The advent of universal suffrage in 1906 enabled the SSDP to become the largest parliamentary party (with 37% of the vote in that year), but its reforms were blocked by the Tsar. Following Finland's declaration of independence in 1917, radical Social Democrats fought on the losing Red side in the 1918 civil war (and later founded the →Finnish Communist Party), whereas the non-revolutionary majority led by Vainö Tanner made its peace with the victorious Whites and embarked on a reformist path in the independent Finnish Republic declared in 1919. Despite electoral competition from Communist-front formations and the powerful Agrarians, the Social Democrats were usually the strongest party in the inter-war period, but managed only one period of minority government (in 1926–27) before entering a "red-green" coalition with the Agrarians in 1937. The SSDP vote rose to 39.8% in 1939, whereupon Tanner not only backed Finland's losing popular cause in the 1939–40 Winter War with the USSR but also supported Finnish participation in Nazi Germany's invasion of the USSR in 1941 with the aim of recovering lost territory. The SSDP leadership rejected adhesion to the Communist-led Finnish People's Democratic League (SKDL) formed in 1944, but many pro-Soviet party sections defected to the new organization. Finland's defeat in 1944, combined with post-war Soviet regional ascendancy, resulted in Tanner being imprisoned in 1946–48 for wartime pro-German activities.

Having won only 25.1% of the vote in the 1945 elections, the SSDP remained in a coalition government with the SKDL and the Agrarians (later called the →Centre Party, KESK), but internal strife between pro-Soviet left and anti-communist right was to fester for more than two decades. With its vote share remaining stable at around 26% in successive elections, the party participated in coalition governments in 1951 and 1954–57, the latter a centre-left combination with the Agrarians. In the 1956 presidential elections Karl-August Fagerholm of the SSDP was narrowly defeated by Urho Kekkonen (Agrarian). In 1957 Fagerholm was also defeated (by one vote) for the SSDP chair, the victor being a rehabilitated Tanner, whose return provoked a new phase of internal party strife. In the 1958 elections the SSDP lost its customary status as the biggest parliamentary party (and declined further in 1962). In 1959 left-wing dissidents broke away to form what became the Social Democratic League of Workers and Smallholders (TPSL), which won seven seats in the 1966 election in alliance with the SKDL. But the same contest yielded a major recovery for the SSDP to 27.2% of the vote, well ahead of its rivals.

Moreover, the TPSL failed to win seats in the 1970 and 1972 contests, while successive SSDP-led centre-left coalitions – under Rafael Paasio (who had succeeded the 82-year-old Tanner as party leader in 1963), Mauno Koivisto and Kalevi Sorsa – confirmed the ascendancy of the SSDP's moderate wing. The party headed the poll in all four elections of the 1970s, but had fallen to 23.9% of the vote by 1979.

In January 1982 Koivisto was elected President of Finland as the SSDP candidate and a new centre-left coalition was formed under Sorsa's premiership. A strong SSDP advance in the 1983 elections, to 26.7%, enabled Sorsa to form another government embracing KESK, the Finnish Rural Party (SMP) (→True Finns Party) and the →Swedish People's Party (RKP/SFP). The March 1987 elections produced a setback for the SSDP, to 24.1% and 56 seats, only just ahead of the conservative →National Coalition (KOK), which became the lead party in a new coalition surprisingly including the SSDP. At the 34th SSDP congress in June 1987 Sorsa was succeeded as party chairman by Pertti Paasio (son of Rafael). The same congress adopted a new programme which defined the party's six central aims as being a world of cooperation, peace and freedom; coexistence with nature; the transfer of power from capital owners to working people; a shift from representative democracy to "an active civil state"; a culturally equal society; and a vigorous process of social reform. In February 1988 President Koivisto was elected to a second six-year term as candidate of the SSDP.

The March 1991 elections ended a quarter-century of continuous SSDP government office, the party slipping to 22.1% and 48 seats and going into opposition to a centre-right coalition. Having replaced Paasio as SSDP chairman in November 1991, Ulf Sundqvist (an ethnic Swede) himself resigned the leadership in February 1993 over allegations of financial impropriety in his previous post as executive director of the STS-Bank. He was succeeded by Paavo Lipponen, who steered the party into supporting Finnish accession to the European Union in the October 1994 referendum, although rank-and-file SSDP opposition was considerable. In March 1995 Lipponen led the party to a major victory in legislative elections, its vote share rising to a post-1945 high of 28.3%, which yielded 63 seats out of 200. In April 1995 Lipponen formed a five-party "rainbow" coalition that included KOK, the RKP/SFP, the →Left Alliance and the →Green Union. Meanwhile, in Finland's first direct presidential elections in January–February 1994, SSDP candidate Martti Ahtisaari had won a second-round victory with 53.9% of the vote, having headed the first-round voting with 25.9%.

In the first direct Finnish elections to the European Parliament in October 1996, the SSDP fell back to 21.5% of the vote and four of the 16 seats, appearing to be damaged by the government's decision to take Finland into the EU's exchange rate mechanism. Further buffeted by events, the party recovered only slightly in the March 1999 national elections, to a 22.9% vote share and 51 seats, 12 less than in 1995. It nevertheless remained the largest party, forming a new coalition government of the same parties with Lipponen continuing as Prime Minister. In the June 1999 Euro-elections the SDDP was relegated to third place, with only 17.8% of the vote and three seats.

The SSDP nominated Foreign Minister Tarja Halonen as its candidate in the January–February 2000 presidential elections. She headed the first-round voting with 40% and narrowly triumphed in the second with 51.6%, becoming Finland's first female head of state.

With an official membership of 72,000, the SSDP is a member of the Socialist International. Its representatives in the European Parliament sit in the Party of European Socialists group.

Green Union
Vihreä Liitto (VL or VIHR)

Address. Eerikinkatu 24/A7, 00100 Helsinki
Telephone. (+358–9) 693–3877
Fax. (+358–9) 693–3799
Email. vihreat@vihrealiitto.fi
Website. www.vihrealiitto.fi
Leadership. Satu Hassi (chairman); Ulla Anttila (parliamentary group chairman); Ari Heikkinen (secretary)

The VL was formed in February 1987 as a cooperative body for various existing local and national environmentalist organizations, the latter including the Green Parliamentary Group (*Vihreä Eduskuntaryhmä*), which had won two seats in 1983. Presenting a mainstream environmentalist platform, the Greens increased to four seats in the March 1987 elections and to 10 in March 1991. They fell back to nine seats on a 6.5% vote share in March 1995 but nevertheless took ministerial office for the first time the following month, when Pekka Haavisto became Environment Minister in a five-party "rainbow" coalition headed by the →Finnish Social Democratic Party (SSDP).

Bolstered by its government status and despite being fundamentally "Eurosceptic", the VL advanced to 7.6% in the October 1996 direct elections to the European Parliament, taking one of the 16 seats. In the March 1999 national elections it won 7.5% of the vote and 11 seats, subsequently joining a new SSDP-led coalition in which it took two portfolios. In the June 1999 European Parliament elections the VL made a major advance to 13.4% of the vote and two seats. In the first round of presidential elections in January 2000, however, VL candidate Heidi Hautala, a member of the European Parliament, came in fifth place with only 3.3% of the vote.

The VL is affiliated to the European Federation of Green Parties. Its two members of the European Parliament sit in the Greens/European Free Alliance group.

Left Alliance
Vasemmistoliitto (VAS)
Vänsterförbundet

Address. Siltasaarenkatu 6, 00530 Helsinki
Telephone. (+358–9) 774–741
Fax. (+358–9) 7747–4200
Email. vas@vasemmistoliitto.fi
Website. www.vasemmistoliitto.fi
Leadership. Suvi-Anne Siimes (chairman); Outi Ojala (parliamentary group chairman); Ralf Sund (secretary)

VAS was launched in April 1990 at a Helsinki congress of representatives of the leading Communist and left-socialist groups, who took cognizance of the collapse of East European communism then in progress. Following the congress, the →Finnish Communist Party (SKP) and its electoral front organization, the Finnish People's Democratic League (*Suomen Kansan Demokraattinen Liitto*, SKDL), voted to disband in favour of the new party, which adopted a left-socialist programme and declared its opposition to Finnish membership of the European Community, later Union (EC/EU), as favoured by most other parties.

The SKP had been founded in 1918 by the pro-Bolshevik wing of the →Finnish Social Democratic Party (SSDP) and had remained banned until 1944, when Finland accepted its second military defeat in five years by the USSR. Reflecting Moscow's new influence in internal Finnish affairs, the SKDL front was created in 1944 and established a sizeable electoral constituency, winning 23.5% of the vote in 1945, becoming the largest parliamentary party in 1958-62 and participating in various centre-left coalitions until 1982. Meanwhile, the SKP had in 1969 split into majority "revisionist" and minority "Stalinist" wings, the latter being formally ousted from the party in 1984 and two years later launching its own Democratic Alternative (*Demokraattinen Vaihtoehto*, DEVA) electoral front, which achieved little more than to weaken the SKDL, whose electoral support slumped to 9.4% in 1987 against 4.2% for DEVA.

In its first general elections in March 1991, VAS won 10.2% of the vote and 19 seats, thereafter forming part of the opposition to the 1991–95 centre-right government. It was prominent in the unsuccessful "no" campaign in the October 1994 referendum on EU accession, acting as a focus for considerable anti-EU sentiment among SSDP activists. In a substantial swing to the left in the March 1995 parliamentary elections, VAS advanced to 11.2% and 22 seats, subsequently being allocated two portfolios in a five-party "rainbow" coalition headed by the SSDP and also including the conservative →National Coalition, the →Swedish People's Party and the →Green Union.

The VAS won 10.5% of the vote and two seats in the European Parliament elections in October 1996. In the March 1999 national elections it took 10.9% of the vote, slipping to 20 seats. It nevertheless continued in a new SSDP-led coalition of the same composition. In the June 1999 European Parliament elections the VAS slipped to 9.1% and was reduced to one seat.

The VAS has an official membership of 14,000 and is a member of the New European Left Forum (NELF). Its representative in the European Parliament sits in the European United Left/Nordic Green Left group.

Liberal People's Party
Liberaalinen Kansanpuolue (LKP)
Address. Frederikinkatu 58A/6, 00100 Helsinki
Telephone. (+358–0) 440227
Fax. (+358–0) 440771
Email. liberal@liberaalit.fi
Website. www.liberaalit.fi
Leadership. Altti Majava (chairman); Kaarina Talola (general secretary)

The LKP was launched in 1965 as a merger of the Finnish People's Party (*Suomen Kansanpuolue*, SKP) and the Liberal Union (*Vapaamielisten Liitto*, VL), both descended from the pre-independence liberal movement by way of the National Progressive Party (*Kansallinen Edistyspuolue*), which had a significant following in the inter-war years (and provided two Finnish Presidents). Post-war divisions and electoral weakness led in 1950 to the formation of the SKP, which recovered some support and participated in various coalition governments in the 1950s and early 1960s. The more conservative VL, dating from 1951, obtained negligible electoral support prior to the 1965 merger creating the LKP.

The LKP won nine seats and 6.5% of the vote in 1966, but its support gradually declined in subsequent elections, to four seats and 3.7% in 1979. During this period it participated in many coalition governments of the centre-left parties. At a national congress in June 1982, the LKP voted to become a constituent group of the much larger →Centre Party of Finland (KESK), while retaining its own identity. However, an unhappy experience in the 1983 elections impelled the LKP to resume independent status in June 1986, whereafter it won only 1.0% of the vote in 1987 and failed to gain representation. It was no more successful in 1991 and 1995 (when its share of the vote was 0.6%). For the 1999 elections it was allied with the →Young Finns Party, which had won two seats in 1995; but the alliance failed to win representation.

With an official membership of 3,000, the LKP is a member party of the Liberal International.

National Coalition
Kansallinen Kokoomus (KK/KOK)
Address. Kansakoulukuja 3, 00100 Helsinki
Telephone. (+358–9) 69381
Fax. (+358–9) 694–3736
Email. kokoomus@kokoomus.fi
Website. www.kokoomus.fi
Leadership. Sauli Niinistö (chairman); Ben Zyskowicz (parliamentary group chairman); Maija Perho (secretary-general)

The moderate conservative KOK was founded in December 1918 following the victory of the anti-Bolshevik Whites in the civil war that ensued after the end of Russian rule. Although monarchist in sympathy, the new party reconciled itself with the republic declared in 1919 and participated in several inter-war coalitions, averaging around 15% of the vote. In the early 1930s it gravitated towards the semi-fascist Lapua rural movement, but KOK leader J.K. Paasikivi later broke with the far right. KOK participated in all five governments in office from 1939 to 1944 (providing the Prime Minister on two occasions) and thus shared responsibility for the conduct of the 1939–40 Winter War against the USSR and for Finland's participation in Nazi Germany's invasion of the USSR in 1941.

KOK was in opposition to successive centre-left coalitions from 1944 to 1958, its vote share fluctuating from a high of 17.3% in 1948 to a low of 12.8% in 1954. On the other hand, Paasikivi served in the powerful post of President from 1946 to 1956 and was instrumental in establishing a consensus on Finland's post-war policy of good relations with the USSR, as continued by his successor, Urho Kekkonen of what became the →Centre Party (KESK), and therefore known as the "Paasikivi-Kekkonen line". Between 1958 and 1966 KOK participated in several coalition governments, including the first completely non-socialist administration since the war, formed in 1963 and headed by KESK. Having slipped to 13.8% in the 1966 elections, KOK reverted to opposition status and was to remain out of office for over two decades. Under the successive chairmanships of Juhta Rihtniemi (1965-71) and Harri Holkeri (1971-79), the party moved to a more centrist position, notably by endorsing the "Paasikivi-Kekkonen line". One consequence was the departure of traditionalist elements in 1973 to join the →Constitutional Party of the Right. But KOK compensated by attracting additional support in the centre, rising steadily to 22.1% of the vote in 1983 and establishing itself as the second strongest party after the →Finnish Social Democratic Party (SSDP).

KOK made another advance in the 1987 elections (to 23.1% and 53 seats) and proceeded to form a four-party coalition with the SSDP, the →Swedish People's Party (RKP/SFP) and the Finnish Rural Party (SMP) (→True Finns Party), with Holkeri becoming Finland's first KOK Prime Minister since 1944. The coalition was weakened by the withdrawal of the SMP in August 1990 and also faced sharply deteriorating economic conditions. In the March 1991 elections KOK slipped to 19.3% and 40 seats (the third largest contingent) and was obliged to accept a subordinate role in a four-party non-socialist coalition headed by KESK and also including the RKP/SFP and the →Finnish Christian Union (SKL). In presidential elections in January 1994 the KOK candidate, Raimo Ilaskivi, came in fourth place in the first round with 15.2% of the vote. KOK strongly backed Finland's accession to the European Union, although internal strains were apparent when Deputy Prime Minister Pertti Salolainen resigned as KOK chairman in June 1994 after some party members had criticized his role in the accession negotiations.

The general elections of March 1995 brought a further setback to KOK, which fell to 17.9% and 39 seats. It nevertheless opted to join a "rainbow" coalition headed by the SSDP and also including the RKP/SFP, the →Left Alliance and the →Green Union. The party advanced to 20.2% of the vote and four seats in the October 1996 European Parliament elections and to 21.0% and 46 seats in the March 1999 national elections, after which it joined another SSDP-led coalition government. In the June 1999 European Parliament elections KOK won 25.3% of the vote, retaining its four seats. In the first round of presidential elections in January 2000, KOK candidate Riitta Uosukainen, the parliamentary Speaker, came in third place with 12.8% of the vote.

With an official membership of 50,000, KOK is affiliated to the Christian Democrat International and the International

Democrat Union. Its representatives in the European Parliament are members of the European People's Party/European Democrats group.

Reform Group
Remonttiryhma (REM)

Address. Mannerheimintie 40A, 00100 Helsinki
Telephone. (+358–9) 414–3352
Fax. (+358–9) 645–379
Email. risto.kuisma@eduskunta.fi
Leadership. Risto Kuisma (chairman); Seija Lahti (secretary)

The REM was launched in 1997 by veteran trade union activist and member of parliament Risto Kuisma, who defected from the →Finnish Social Democratic Party and initially joined the →Young Finns but soon accused the latter of elitism and founded his own party. Describing itself as "the movement of people who want change", the REM stands for full employment and a radical reduction in income tax. In the March 1999 parliamentary elections it won 1.1% of the vote and one seat.

Swedish People's Party
Svenska Folkpartiet (SFP)
Ruotsalainen Kansanpuolue (RKP)

Address. Gräsviksgatan 14, PO Box 282, 00181 Helsinki
Telephone. (+358–0) 694–2322
Fax. (+358–0) 693–1968
Email. sfp@sfp.fi
Website. www.sfp.fi
Leadership. Jan-Erik Enestam (chairman); Ulla-Maj Wideroos (parliamentary group chairman); Peter Heinström (secretary)

The RKP/SFP was founded in 1906, when Finland was still a duchy of the Russian Empire, to represent the political and social interests of the ethnic Swedish population, which was then economically dominant. Being ethnically based, the party has traditionally encompassed a wide spectrum of ideological preferences, although it is usually characterized as centrist with progressive leanings. Its share of the overall vote has shown a gradual decline over recent decades (from 8.4% in 1945 to 5.1% in 1999), in line with the falling proportion of ethnic Swedes in the population. However, its post-war representation in the Diet has remained rather more constant (the 1999 tally being 12 seats, compared with a high of 15 in 1951 and a low of 10 in the elections of the 1970s). The RKP/SFP's parliamentary contingent customarily includes the single deputy returned by the ethnic Swedish inhabitants of the autonomous Åland Islands, where the main local parties, modelled on those of Sweden, form the Ålands Coalition for Finnish national elections.

The RKP/SFP has been in government more often than it has been in opposition, having participated in about two-thirds of all Finnish coalitions formed since 1906, including centre-left, centre-right and ideologically-mixed combinations. The pattern after 1945 was RKP/SFP participation in successive centre-left coalitions headed by the →Finnish Social Democratic Party (SSDP) or the →Centre Party (KESK), although in 1963–66 it was a member of the first entirely non-socialist governments since the war. Subsequent centre-left combinations also included the RKP/SFP as a pivotal member, while in 1987 it joined a four-party coalition headed by the conservative →National Coalition (KOK) and also including the SSDP and the Finnish Rural Party (SMP) (→True Finns Party). Having slipped from 13 to 12 seats in the 1991 elections, the RKP/SFP joined another non-socialist coalition, this time headed by KESK and including KOK and the →Finnish Christian Union.

For the January–February 1994 presidential elections the RKP/SFP candidate was Defence Minister Elisabeth Rehn, who surprised many (given her Swedish ethnicity and gender) by taking second place in the first round, with 22% of the vote. Going forward to the second round, she was defeated by the SSDP candidate but won 46.1% of the vote. The RKP/SFP supported Finland's accession to the European Union (as approved in the October 1994 referendum) and was allocated one of Finland's 16 seats in the European Parliament. Having retained 12 seats in the March 1995 parliamentary elections, it accepted two portfolios in a five-party "rainbow" coalition headed by the SSDP and also including KOK, the →Left Alliance and the →Green Union.

In the October 1996 direct elections to the European Parliament the RKP/SFP retained its single seat with 5.8% of the vote. In the March 1999 national elections it again won 12 seats (with 5.1% of the vote) and opted to join another five-party coalition headed by the SSDP. In the June 1999 European Parliament elections it advanced to 6.8%, retaining its single seat. Rehn was again the party's candidate in the January–February 2000 presidential elections, but this time she managed only fourth place in the first round with 7.9% of the vote.

With an official membership of 40,000, the RKP/SFP is affiliated to both the International Democrat Union and the Liberal International. Its representative in the European Parliament sits in the European Liberal, Democratic and Reformist group.

True Finns Party
Perussuomlaiset (PS)

Address. Mannerheimintie 40B, 00100 Helsinki
Telephone. (+358–9) 454–0411
Fax. (+358–9) 454–0466
Email. timo.soini@eduskunta.fi
Leadership. Timo Soini (chairman); Rolf (Fred) Sormo (secretary)

The PS was founded prior to the 1999 elections as successor to the Finnish Rural Party (SMP), following serious internal disputes in the latter. The SMP had been derived from the Finnish Smallholders' Party, which was launched in 1959 by a dissident faction of what later became the →Centre Party of Finland (KESK). Led by the charismatic Veikko Vannamo, the breakaway party took an anti-establishment, "Poujadist" line, defending the rights of "forgotten Finland" and claiming that the parent party had neglected the interests of small farmers and small businessmen. Renamed the SMP after obtaining negligible support in the 1962 and 1966 elections, the party came to prominence in 1968 when Vennamo won over 11% in challenging incumbent Urho Kekkonen (KESK) for the presidency. It achieved a breakthrough in the 1970 parliamentary elections, winning 10.5% and 18 seats (mainly as the expense of KESK), and retained 18 seats in 1972, although it support slipped to 9.2%.

The SMP was then weakened by splits arising from criticism of Vennamo's authoritarian leadership style and right-wing opposition to his willingness to co-operate with parties of the left. In the 1975 elections the rump SMP slumped to two seats and 3.6%, recovering only partially to seven seats and 4.5% in 1979, in which year Vennamo stood down as leader and was succeeded by his son Pekka. The 1983 elections yielded another breakthrough for the SMP, which won 17 seats and 9.7% of the vote and thereafter entered government for the first time as part of a coalition headed by the →Finnish Social Democratic Party (SSDP) and including KESK and the →Swedish People's Party (RKP/SFP). In the 1984 municipal elections the SMP obtained over 600 council seats.

The SMP fell back to nine seats and 6.3% in the 1987 elections but nevertheless joined a four-party coalition headed by the conservative →National Coalition and including the SSDP and the RKP/SFP. It withdrew from the coalition in August 1990 in protest against new pension proposals, but lost further support to a resurgent KESK in the 1991 elections, falling to seven seats and 4.8% and remaining outside the resultant non-socialist coalition headed by KESK. Having been part of the unsuccessful opposition to Finnish accession to the European Union, the SMP almost disappeared from the Diet in the March 1995 elections, winning only one seat on a 1.3% vote share.

A period of internal division followed, culminating in the creation of PS as the successor party. In the March 1999 elections the PS just managed to retain one seat, winning only 1% of the vote. The same percentage was obtained by PS candidate Ilkka Hakalehto in the first round of the 2000 presidential elections.

Other Parties

Communist Workers' Party (*Kommunistinen Työväenpuolue, KTP*), founded in 1988 by a Stalinist faction of the Democratic Alternative (later part of the →Left Alliance). It contested the 1991, 1995 and 1999 elections under the slogan "For Peace and Socialism", winning 0.2% and 0.1% of the vote respectively.
Address. PL 93, Vantaa
Telephone. (+358-9) 857-1022
Fax. (+358-9) 857-3097
Email. ktp@kaapeli.fi
Website. www.kaapeli.fi
Leadership. Timo Lahdenmäki & Heikki Männikö

Ecological Party (*Ekologinen Puolue, EP*). Founded in 1990 as a populist formation aiming to provide a "non-ideological" alternative to the left-leaning →Green Union; failed to win representation in the 1991 Diet elections, but secured one seat on a 0.3% vote share in March 1995, losing it in 1999 with only 0.4%.
Address. Mannerheimintie 40A, 00100 Helsinki
Telephone. (+358-9) 432-3566
Fax. (+358-9) 432-2717
Leadership. Pertti (Veltto) Virtanen (chairman)

Finnish Communist Party (*Suomen Kommunistinen Puolue, SKP*). Re-launched in 1997 as self-declared successor to the historic SKP, in opposition to the participation of the →Left Alliance in a "neo-liberal" government; won 0.8% of the vote in both the 1995 and 1999 elections; contested 1996 Euro-elections on joint list with →Communist Workers' Party and other leftist groups.
Address. Petter Wetterintie 1A, 6 krs, 00810 Helsinki
Telephone. (+358-9) 5840-0350
Fax. (+358-9) 5840-0355
Email. skp@skp.fi
Website. www.skp.fi
Leadership. Yrjö Hakanen (chairman); Arto Viitaniemi (general secretary)

Finnish Pensioners' Party (*Suomen Eläkeläisten Puolue, SEP*), launched in 1986 but has had minimal electoral impact, winning 0.1% of the vote in 1995 and 0.2% in 1999.
Leadership. Erkki Pulli & Saara Mölsä

League for a Free Finland (*Vapaan Suomen Liitto, VSL*), right-wing nationalist formation which won 1% of the vote in 1995 and 0.4% in 1999.

Patriotic National Alliance (*Isänmaallinen Kansallis-Litto, IKL*), right-wing formation seeking to stimulate Finnish patriotism.
Address. PL 22, 61801 Kauhajoki
Fax. (+358-6) 231-1747
Email. ikl@kauhajoki.fi
Website. kauhajoki.fi/~ikl
Leadership. Ajan Suunta

Pensioners for the People (*Elakeläiset Kansan Asialla, EKA*), senior citizens' grouping, won only 0.2% in the 1999 elections.

Socialist League (*Sosialistiliitto, SL*), Trotskyist formation, contested 1999 elections as part of "Change 99" (*Muutos 99*) alliance in order to agitate against parliamentary politics.
Address. PO Box 288, 00171 Helsinki
Telephone. (+358-9) 278-2244
Email. sl.org@saunalahti.fi
Website. www.dlc.fi/~sosliitto
Leadership. Juhani Lohikoski

Young Finns Party (*Nuorsuomalainen Puolue, NSP*), also known as the "Progessive Finnish Party". Founded in 1994 as a radical pro-market party arguing that Finland needed a deregulated economy to compete in the European Union following accession at the beginning of 1995. It won two seats and 2.8% in the 1995 parliamentary elections, but failed to retain representation in 1999 on a joint list with the →Liberal People's Party.
Address. Lönnrotinkatu 32A, 00180 Helsinki
Telephone. (+358-9) 685-6211
Fax. (+358-9) 685-6233
Email. nuorsuom@nuorsuom.fi
Website. www.nuorsuom.fi
Leadership. Risto E.J. Penttilä (chairman)

France

Capital: Paris

Population: 58,500,000 (2000E)

The French Republic has one of the world's most developed multi-party systems that is perpetually fluid but essentially unchanging in its broad ideological structure. Under the 1982 constitution of the Fifth Republic as amended, an executive President, who appoints the Prime Minister, is elected by universal suffrage of citizens above the age of 18 years, the requirement being an absolute majority of the votes cast either in the first round of voting or, if necessary, in a second. In September 2000 referendum approval was given to a reduction of the presidential term from seven to five years with effect from the 2002 elections. Legislative authority is vested in a bicameral Parliament (*Parlement*) consisting of (i) a 321-seat Senate (*Sénat*) whose members are indirectly elected for a nine-year term (a third being renewed every three years), 309 by electoral colleges of national and local elected representatives in the metropolitan and overseas departments/territories and 12 by the *Conseil Supérieur des Français de l'Étranger* to represent French citizens living abroad; and (ii) a 577-member National Assembly (*Assemblée Nationale*) directly elected for a maximum five-year term by universal adult suffrage. For the March 1986 Assembly elections the then Socialist-led government introduced a system of department-based proportional representation for the first time under the Fifth Republic; however, the incoming centre-right administration enacted legislation providing for a return to the previous system of majority voting in two rounds in single-member constituencies. France was a founder member of what is now the European Union and elects 87 members to the European Parliament.

Under laws enacted in March 1988 and January 1990, state funding is payable to (i) political parties with parliamentary representation, in proportion to the size of their respective groups; (ii) all accredited presidential candidates (with the two reaching the second round receiving additional sums), according to a complex formula for the reimbursement of varying proportions of the ceilings set for campaign expenses; and (iii) Assembly election candidates who receive at least 5% of the first-round vote, at a rate equivalent to 10% of the applicable expenses ceilings. The total amount disbursed in 1990 under category (i) was FF260,267,857 (about $51 million), of which, for example, the Socialist Party, then substantially the largest Assembly party, received FF95,530,134 (about $18.8 million).

National Assembly elections held on May 25 and June 1, 1997, resulted as follows: Socialist Party (PS) 241 seats (with 23.5% of the first-round vote), Rally for the Republic (RPR) 134 (15.7%), Union for French Democracy (UDF) 108 (14.2%), French Communist Party (PCF), 38 (9.9%), Left Radical Party (PRG) 12 (1.5%), various Greens 7 (6.8%), National Front (FN) 1 (14.9%), various left 21 (2.8%), various right 14 (6.6%), independents and others 1 (4.0%).

Presidential elections on April 23 and May 7, 1995, resulted in Jacques Chirac of the RPR being elected in the second round with 52.6% of the votes cast, against 47.4% for the PS candidate.

Citizens' Movement
Mouvement des Citoyens (MDC)

Address. 9 rue du Faubourg-Poissonnière, 75009 Paris
Telephone. (+33–1) 4483–8300
Fax. (+33–1) 4483–8320
Email. info@mdc-france.org
Website. www.mdc-france.org
Leadership. George Sarre (president); Paul Loridant (secretary-general)

The MDC was launched in 1993 by former →Socialist Party (PS) minister Jean-Pierre Chevènement on a platform of opposition to the Maastricht Treaty and further European integration. In the 1994 European Parliament elections Chevènement headed the "Alternative Politics" (*L'Autre Politique*) list, winning 2.5% of the vote and no seats. Having won a National Assembly by-election in December 1995, the MDC contested the mid-1997 Assembly elections in alliance with the PS, winning seven seats in its own right and subsequently joining the new PS-led coalition government, in which Chevènement became Interior Minister (and stood down from the MDC leadership). The MDC deputies in the Assembly joined the Radical, Citizen and Green group headed by the →Left Radical Party (PRG), while in the Senate the MDC secretary-general, Paul Loridant, sits in the Communist, Republican and Citizen group headed by the →French Communist Party. The MDC was part of the PS-headed list for the June 1999 European Parliament elections (with the PRG), taking two of the 22 seats won by the list.

Chevènement got into difficulties in May 2000 when he criticised German proposals for a federal Europe by contending that Germany had "an ethnic concept of nationhood", was still aspiring to creating "a Germanic Holy Roman Empire" and had still not recovered from "the aberration of Nazism". In August 2000 he resigned from the government (for the third time in his political career) in protest against a new plan for Corsican autonomy, claiming in May 2001, when it was adopted by the National Assembly, that the plan was "a time-bomb" which would lead to the "territorial fragmentation" of France.

Together with the PS and PRG members, the MDC representatives in the European Parliament sit in the Party of European Socialists group. The party is a member of the New European Left Forum (NELF).

French Communist Party
Parti Communiste Français (PCF)

Address. 2 place du Colonel Fabien, 75019 Paris
Telephone. (+33–1) 4040–1212
Fax. (+33–1) 4040–1356
Email. pcf@pcf.fr
Website. www.pcft.fr
Leadership. Robert Hue (president); Marie-George Buffet (national secretary); Alain Bocquet (Assembly group chairman); Hélène Luc (Senate group chairman)

The PCF came into being in December 1920 when a majority of delegates at the Tours congress of the →Socialist Party (then the SFIO) voted to join the Soviet-run Communist International (Comintern), whereas the anti-Bolshevik minority opted to maintain the SFIO. From 1921 to 1933 the PCF pursued a hardline policy of class war and opposition to all "bourgeois" parties, including the SFIO. From 1934, however, it gave priority to the struggle against fascism and supported (without joining) the 1936–38 Popular Front government headed by the Socialists. The PCF approved the August 1939 non-aggression pact between Nazi Germany and the USSR, but reverted to anti-fascist mode following the German invasion of the USSR in June 1941, its activists subsequently playing a prominent role in the French Resistance. The party joined the post-liberation government formed by Gen. de Gaulle in 1944, although it was denied any powerful portfolios. With the onset of the Cold War, it was excluded from the 1947 government headed by Paul Ramadier (SFIO) and was to remain in opposition for 34 years.

Strongly based in the General Confederation of Labour (the largest trade union body), the PCF outvoted the SFIO in most elections under the Fourth Republic, winning 25–29% of the vote. Having opposed the creation of the Fifth Republic in 1958, the PCF saw its vote fall to 18.9% in Assembly elections later that year but recovered to 20–22% in the contests of the 1960s and 1970s. In December 1966 the then PCF leader, Waldeck Rochet, signed an agreement with the Socialist-led Federation of the Democratic and Socialist Left (FGDS) providing for reciprocal voting support in the March 1967 Assembly elections. The arrangement resulted in PCF representation almost doubling, to 73 seats, although this tally was reduced to 34 in elections held in June 1968 in the aftermath of the "May events" that nearly toppled President de Gaulle. The PCF repudiated the Soviet-led military intervention that suppressed the 1968 "Prague Spring" in Czechoslovakia, although it remained in most respects an orthodox Marxist–Leninist party aligned to Moscow and opposed to French membership of NATO and the European Community. In 1969 the Communist presidential candidate, Jacques Duclos, came third in the first round, with 21.3% of the vote.

Following the election of François Mitterrand as leader of the new Socialist Party (PS) in 1971, the following year the PCF signed a common programme with the PS and the Left Radical Movement (MRG), now the →Left Radical Party. The union yielded major left-wing gains in the March 1973 Assembly elections, which restored Communist representation to 73 seats. From 1974, however, serious strains developed within the alliance, not least because the steady growth of PS strength was viewed by the PCF as imperilling the union's equilibrium and as encouraging the Socialists to revert to a centre-left strategy. At its 22nd congress in February 1976 the PCF repudiated the thesis of the dictatorship of the proletariat and came out in favour of a specifically French model of socialism. The party nevertheless kept its distance from the revisionist "Eurocommunist" line then being advanced by the Italian Communists. Mainly because of PS and MRG resistance to further PCF nationalization proposals, no agreement was reached on a revised common programme for the March 1978 Assembly elections, in which the PCF presented its own manifesto. Second-round reciprocal support nevertheless applied, with the result that the PCF rose to 86 seats amid a left-wing advance that fell short of an overall majority.

The PCF candidate in the watershed May 1981 presidential elections was the then party leader, Georges Marchais, who obtained 15.4% of the first-round vote, whereafter the PCF swung behind Mitterrand in the second round and contributed to the PS leader's victory. In the resultant Assembly elections of June 1981, second-round support arrangements among the left-wing parties yielded most benefit to the Socialists, who won an absolute majority, while the PCF fell to 44 seats. The French Communists nevertheless entered government for the first time since 1947, obtaining four portfolios in the new PS-led administration. But strains quickly developed between the PS and PCF in government, notably over the latter's refusal to condemn the imposition of martial law in Poland and its opposition to the deployment of new US nuclear missiles in Europe. In the European Parliament elections of June 1984 the PCF took only 11.2% of the vote, less than in any national election since 1932. When Laurent Fabius of the PS formed a new government in July 1984, the Communists refused to participate, on the grounds that he was equivocal on giving priority to economic expansion and job-creation. In September 1984 the PCF deputies broke with the PS-led Assembly majority and voted against the government for the first time in the budget debate of December 1984.

At the PCF congress of February 1985 the party leadership under Marchais firmly resisted the demand of a "renovator" group for changes in policy and for greater internal party democracy. The Assembly elections of March 1986 produced a further setback for the PCF, which slipped to 35 seats and 9.8% of the vote, in part because some of its working-class support in city suburbs with a high immigrant population switched to the far-right →National Front (FN). Further internal strains and defections served to harden the Marchais line, which prevailed at the PCF conference in Nanterre in June 1987, when hardliner André Lajoinie was adopted as PCF presidential candidate. Prior to its 26th congress in December 1987, the PCF central committee expelled Pierre Juquin for having announced his presidential candidacy as a Communist "renovator". In the first round of the April–May 1988 presidential contest that saw the re-election of Mitterrand, Lajoinie recorded the PCF's lowest-ever national vote share (6.8%), while Juquin got 2.1%. In the June 1988 Assembly elections the PCF recovered somewhat to 11.3% in the first round, but slipped to representation of 27 seats.

Still resisting pressure for change in the PCF, Marchais responded to the collapse of East European communism in 1989-90 and of the USSR in 1991 by claiming that he had been "duped" by his erstwhile comrades in that part of the world. The party suffered a further setback, to 9.2% of the first-round vote, in the March 1993 Assembly elections which brought the right back to governmental power, but displayed resilience in its strongholds by retaining 23 seats. Avowedly because of ill-health, Marchais formally vacated the PCF leadership at the party's 28th congress in January 1994 and was succeeded by Robert Hue, who was assigned the title "national secretary" as part of a decision to abandon "democratic centralism" in party decision-making. The Communist list won only 6.9% of the vote in the June 1994 European Parliament elections (and seven of the 87 French

seats). In the April–May 1995 presidential elections, Hue took fifth place in the first round with 8.6% of the vote, whereupon the PCF backed the unsuccessful candidacy of Lionel Jospin (PS) in the second round.

In a high-profile Assembly by-election for a Marseilles constituency in October 1996, the PCF candidate defeated an FN challenge on the strength of second-round backing from centre-left parties. For the mid-1997 Assembly elections the PCF issued a joint declaration of policy objectives with the PS, but the two parties confined their electoral cooperation to mutual second-round support. The PCF shared in the victory of the left, winning 38 seats and a first-round vote share of 9.9%, and subsequently accepting portfolios in a Socialist-led coalition government. In the June 1999 European Parliament elections the PCF list slipped to six seats on a vote share of 6.8%, two of the elected candidates being "independents".

In 2000 the PCF became caught up in the wave of corruption allegations buffeting French parties, being accused of benefiting from the system of kickbacks for public contracts allegedly run by the →Rally for the Republic (RPR) in Paris when Jacques Chirac was mayor in 1977–95. In October 2000, moreover, Hue and 19 others went on trial in Paris on charges related to an alleged slush fund operated by the PCF in the early 1990s. Hue denied the charges, contending that the party had always been entirely financed by members' dues, levies on PCF parliamentarians' salaries and May Day sales of lillies of the valley (the party's official flower). In late October 2000 the trial was adjourned *sine die* after defence lawyers had challenged the impartiality of the judge.

The PCF fared badly in countrywide local council elections in March 2001, losing many seats and being ousted from control in about a dozen of its former strongholds. Calls for withdrawal from the government in advance of the 2002 elections were resisted by the leadership, which saw no alternative to continued co-operation with the PS. In October 2001 Hue was succeeded as national secretary by youth Minister Marie-George Buffet.

The PCF members of the European Parliament sit in the European United Left/Nordic Green Left group. The party is a member of the New European Left Forum (NELF).

The Greens
Les Verts
Address. 107 ave Parmentier, 75011 Paris
Telephone. (+33–1) 4355–1001
Fax. (+33–1) 4355–1615
Email. verts@verts.imaginet.fr
Website. www.verts.imaginet.fr
Leadership. Dominique Voynet (national secretary); Alain Lipietz (2002 presidential candidate); Marie-Anne Isler Béguin, Martine Billard, Denis Baupin & Stéphane Pocrain (spokespersons)
The Greens were organized as a unified mainstream environmentalist party in January 1984, officially embracing the suffix Ecologist Confederation–Ecologist Party (*Confédération Écologiste–Parti Écologiste*). This cumbersome nomenclature reflected the complexities of the movement's evolution since it fielded René Dumont for the presidency in 1974 and received 1.3% of the first-round vote. In the 1978 Assembly elections the earlier movement presented 200 candidates under the banner *Écologie 78*, winning 2.1% of the vote, while the *Écologie Europe* list took 4.4% in the 1979 European Parliament elections. Encouraged by that relative success, the movement in February 1980 joined with other groups to create the *Mouvement d'Écologie Politique* (MEP), which in 1981 backed the presidential candidacy of Brice Lalonde, then leader of Friends of the Earth and later founder of →Ecology Generation (GE). As Ecology Today (*Aujourd'hui l'Ecologie*), the MEP presented 82 candidates in the 1981 Assembly elections, winning 1.2% of the first-round vote (and no seats). In November 1982 the MEP became a political party called

Les Verts-Parti Écologiste (VPE), which won some 6% of the overall vote in the 1983 municipal elections and elected several dozen councillors. The adoption of the longer title referred to above occurred at a Clichy congress (in January 1984) which achieved a merger of the VPE with various other environmentalist group.

Standing as *Les Verts-Europe Écologie*, the formation again failed to win representation in the 1984 European Parliament elections, when its vote fell to 3.4%, and was no more successful in the 1986 Assembly elections, when it managed only 1.1% of the first-round vote. Subsequent internal divisions were reflected in the rejection by a Paris general assembly in September 1986 of a policy paper presented by the movement's four spokesmen urging rapprochement with like-minded groups. Four new spokesmen were elected from among the "fundamentalist" wing, one of whom, Antoine Waechter, stood in the 1988 presidential elections, winning 3.8% of the first-round vote. The Greens declined to present official candidates for the June 1988 Assembly elections in protest against the return to constituency-based polling as opposed to the proportional system used in 1986. Returning to the electoral fray, they polled strongly in the 1989 European Parliament elections on a joint list with other groups, winning 10.6% of the vote and nine seats.

The 1993 Assembly elections yielded a 4% first-round vote for the Greens but no seats, despite an agreement with the GE not to run competing candidates. At their annual conference in November 1993 the Greens moved sharply to the left, electing Dominique Voynet as 1995 presidential candidate, while the disaffected Waechter later broke away to form the →Independent Ecological Movement. Standing separately in the 1994 European Parliament elections, neither the Greens nor the GE gained sufficient support to win seats. Standing as the sole Green candidate in the 1995 presidential contest, Voynet was placed eighth of nine candidates, with 3.3% of the vote.

For the mid-1997 Assembly elections the Greens presented 455 candidates, 29 of whom were backed by the →Socialist Party (PS) while the Greens agreed to support PS candidates in 70 constituencies. The outcome was a breakthrough for the Greens, to seven Assembly seats on the strength of a first-round vote of 6.8% achieved in alliance with other groups. The Greens thereupon joined the new PS-led coalition government, in which Voynet became Minister of the Environment. Its Assembly deputies joined the Radical, Citizen and Green group headed by the →Left Radical Party. In the June 1999 European Parliament elections the Greens advanced strongly to 9.7% of the vote, taking nine of the 87 French seats, the leader of the list being the 1968-vintage revolutionary Daniel Cohn-Bendit.

In the March 2001 municipal and local council elections, the Greens played a key role in securing the election of the PS candidate as mayor of Paris, their 12.3% share of the first-round vote being swung behind the Socialists in the second round. In June 2001 the party selected Alain Lipietz, a former Maoist, as its candidate in the 2002 presidential elections. The following month Voynet left the government to take over the party leadership, being replaced as Environment Minister by Yves Cochet, a former Green MEP. In October 2001 the controversial Lipietz was dropped as presidential candidate and replaced by Noël Mamère.

The French Greens are affiliated to the European Federation of Green Parties. Their representatives in the European Parliament sit in the Greens/European Free Alliance group.

Hunting, Fishing, Nature, Traditions
Chasse, Pêche, Nature, Traditions (CPNT)

Address. 245 blvd de la Paix, 64000 Pau
Telephone. (+33–5) 5914–7171
Fax. (+34–5) 5914–7172
Email. cpnt@cpnt.asso.fr

Website. www.cpnt.asso.fr
Leadership. Jean Saint-Josse (president); Michel Raymond (secretary-general)

The CPNT movement advocates the protection and furtherance of traditional countryside pursuits and maintenance of the rural way of life and values. Opposed to further European integration, it contested the 1994 European Parliament elections without success (taking 3.9% of the vote), but made a breakthrough in the 1999 contest, winning 6.8% and six seats.

The CPNT members of the European Parliament sit in the Europe of Democracies and Diversities group.

Left Radical Party
Parti Radical de Gauche (PRG)

Address. 13 rue Duroc Paris
Telephone. (+33–1) 4566–6768
Fax. (+33–1) 4566–4793
Email. prg-nat@club-internet.fr
Website. www.radical-gauche.org
Leadership. Jean-Michel Baylet (president); Roger-Gérard Schwartzenberg (Assembly group chairman)

The PRG is the current rubric of what was the Left Radical Movement (MRG) until 1996, following a succession of name changes that were disputed in the courts. The MRG had originated in July 1972 as a left-wing faction of the historic →Radical Party which endorsed the common programme issued the previous month by the →Socialist Party (PS) and the →French Communist Party (PCF), whereas the Radical majority then led by Jean-Jacques Servan-Schreiber declined to join the new Union of the Left. Initially organized as the Radical-Socialist Study and Action Group, the left-wing faction was expelled in October 1972 and contested the March 1973 Assembly elections on a joint list with the PS called the *Union de la Gauche Socialiste et Démocrate*, taking 11 of the 100 seats won by the alliance. The faction formally constituted itself as the MRG in December 1973 under the presidency of Robert Fabre, taking as its watchword the famous Radical slogan "*Pas d'ennemi à gauche*" ("No enemy to the left").

In contentious negotiations on revision of the common programme for the March 1978 Assembly elections, the MRG caused the first formal breakdown of talks in September 1977, when Fabre rejected the extensive nationalization programme demanded by the PCF. In the 1988 elections the MRG presented its own policy platform which differed from those of the PS and PCF in important respects; but the electoral alliance with the PS was maintained, and reciprocal support arrangements between the PS/MRG and the PCF again came into play in the second round. The result was that the MRG took 10 of the 113 seats won by the PS/MRG alliance. Immediately after the polling, Fabre repudiated the original common programme of the left and resigned the MRG presidency. He was succeeded by Michel Crépeau, who favoured the continuation of left-wing union, whereas the MRG right advocated reversion to a centre-left orientation and eventually, for the most part, rejoined the parent Radical Party or other centre-left groupings.

Crépeau stood as the MRG candidate in the first round of the 1981 presidential elections, winning only 2.2% of the vote. In the second round the MRG backed François Mitterrand of the PS, whose victory resulted in the appointment of a left-wing government in which Crépeau obtained a ministerial portfolio. In the June 1981 Assembly elections the MRG increased its seat tally to 14 by virtue of a further alliance with the victorious PS. Thereafter, the MRG participated in the PS-led government throughout its five-year tenure, while regularly seeking to assert its distinct political identity. In the 1984 European Parliament elections, for example, it was the principal component of a centre-left/ecological list called *Entente Radicale Écologiste pour les États-Unis d'Europe*, which secured 3.3% of the vote and no seats. The MRG also contested the 1986 Assembly elections in its own right (the move to proportional representation obviating the need for a joint list with the PS), but mustered only 0.4% of the total vote and two seats. The party nevertheless maintained a significant presence in local and regional government.

In opposition in 1986–88, the MRG experienced much internal agonizing about whether to maintain its leftward orientation or to turn to the centre. In the event, it was again allied with the PS in the 1988 Assembly elections held after the re-election of Mitterrand to the presidency. With majority voting by constituency having been reinstated, the MRG obtained nine seats and was allocated three ministerial posts in the resultant PS-led coalition. It remained in government for the next five years, but had little success in its attempts to build a "second force" within the then "presidential majority". In the March 1993 Assembly elections the MRG shared in the heavy defeat of its Socialist allies, although left-wing voting discipline and the MRG's resilience in its remaining strongholds enabled the party to retain six seats with a first-round vote share of 0.9%.

Again in opposition, the MRG was temporarily strengthened by the adhesion of controversial businessman Bernard Tapie, who had served two brief spells as a minister in 1992-93 and had been elected as a "presidential majority" candidate in the 1993 Assembly elections. In the June 1994 European Parliament elections Tapie headed the MRG's *Énergie Radical* list, which won 13 seats on an impressive vote share of 12.1%, while the PS under the new leadership of Michel Rocard performed so badly that Rocard had to resign. Having backed Rocard's efforts to build a broader social democratic party, the MRG was much less enthusiastic about his left-wing successor, Henri Emmanuelli, and initially announced that its leader, Jean-François Hory, would contest the 1995 presidential elections with the aim of rallying the centre-left opposition. In the event, the selection of Lionel Jospin as the PS candidate served to restore the PS/MRG axis, in that Hory withdrew his candidacy and the MRG contributed to Jospin's powerful, albeit losing, performance in the presidential contest. Shortly after the second-round polling (in May 1995), the MRG's "Tapie era" finally ended when the former tycoon (by now bankrupt) was sentenced to a prison term after being convicted of attempted match-fixing when he owned Marseilles football club.

Hory resigned as MRG president in October 1995 and was succeeded by Jean-Michel Baylet in January 1996, when a party congress also elected six vice-presidents. These included the former Socialist minister, Bernard Kouchner, whose Reunite (*Réunir*) grouping, founded in November 1994, was merged into the MRG. With a view to sharpening its public image, the party decided to adopt the one-word title "Radical" for campaigning purposes, thereby creating much scope for confusion as between it and the historic Radical Party. In March 1996 a Paris court ordered it to revert to the MRG name within four months. It then opted for the title "Radical Socialist Party" (PRS), under which name it won 12 seats in the mid-1997 Assembly elections in alliance in many constituencies with the PS. In then joined the new PS-led coalition government, receiving one portfolio.

The party was subsequently told by a court that its PRS title was also unlawful because of potential confusion, so that in January 1998 it almost reverted to its original name by becoming the "Left Radical Party" (PRG). In the June 1999 European Parliament elections the party was part of a joint list with the PS and the →Citizens' Movement, the list heading the poll with 22% of the vote and 22 seats, of which the PRG took two.

Liberal Democracy
Démocratie Libérale (LD)
Address. 105 rue de l'Université 75007 Paris
Telephone. (+33–1) 4062–3030
Fax. (+33–1) 4062–3040
Email. info@democratie-liberale.asso.fr

Website. www.democratie-liberale.asso.fr
Leadership. Alain Madelin (president); José Rossi (Assembly group chairman); Laurent Dominati (secretary-general)

The liberal conservative LD was launched following the mid-1997 Assembly elections as successor to the Republican Party (*Parti Républicain*, PR), adopting the suffix "Independent Republicans and Republicans". The PR had been formed in May 1977 as a merger of the National Federation of Independent Republicans (*Fédération Nationale des Républicains Indépendants*, FNRI), the Social and Liberal Generation (*Génération Sociale et Libérale*, GSL), Act for the Future (*Agir pour l'Avenir*) and various support committees which had backed Valéry Giscard d'Estaing in his successful bid for the presidency in 1974. The PR's social liberal and strongly pro-European orientation was closely based on the theses advanced by Giscard d'Estaing his 1977 book *Démocratie Française.*

The FNRI had been established in June 1966 by Giscard d'Estaing as leader of a modernizing faction that had broken away from the →National Centre of Independents and Peasants (CNIP) in 1962 in order to be able to criticize government policy while remaining part of the ruling "majority". On founding the FNRI Giscard d'Estaing himself left the government of Georges Pompidou (although other FNRI representatives continued to participate) and led the new party to significant advances in the 1967 and 1968 Assembly elections (to 42 and 61 seats respectively) on the basis of his celebrated "*oui, mais*" ("yes, but") line of qualified support for the Gaullist-led government. In April 1969 Giscard d'Estaing effectively supported the winning "no" side in the constitutional referendum which yielded the resignation of President de Gaulle, whereupon the FNRI backed the victorious Pompidou in the June 1969 presidential elections. The FNRI leader then resumed his former post as Economy and Finance Minister, retaining it in successive Gaullist-led governments under the Pompidou presidency, while the FNRI slipped to 55 seats in the 1973 Assembly elections.

Following Pompidou's death in office in April 1974, Giscard d'Estaing was elected President in May as candidate of the FNRI and other centrist formations, taking second place in the first round (with 32.9% of the vote) and winning a narrow 50.7% victory in the run-off against François Mitterrand of the →Socialist Party (PS). He proceeded to appoint Jacques Chirac (Gaullist) to head a government with strong centrist representation, including his principal FNRI lieutenant, Michel Poniatowski, at the powerful Interior Ministry. Growing strains between the Giscardian and Gaullist wings of the "majority" from 1975 resulted in Chirac's resignation in August 1976 and his replacement by a non-Gaullist (Raymond Barre), whereafter Chirac relaunched the Gaullist party as the →Rally for the Republic (RPR). The superior organization of the new RPR over the FNRI and other centrist parties (and the challenge to presidential authority which the RPR represented) was highlighted in March 1977 when Chirac defeated a candidate backed by the President in elections for the important post of mayor of Paris.

Seeking to build an effective counterweight to the RPR for the 1978 Assembly elections, the new PR participated in the formation of the broader Union for French Democracy (UDF), winning 71 of the 124 UDF seats. PR representatives took prominent portfolios in the reconstituted Barre government, but suffered from association with scandals such as the De Broglie affair. In 1981 the PR and the rest of the UDF endorsed Giscard d'Estaing's re-election bid, although the President chose to stand as a "citizen-candidate" without specific party attribution. Following his narrow defeat by Mitterrand in the second round, the PR shared in the decimation of the UDF in the June 1981 Assembly elections, retaining only 32 seats. After five years in opposition, however, the PR shared in the centre-right's victory in the March 1986 Assembly elections, winning 59 seats in its own right and accordingly taking a prominent role in the resultant centre-right "cohabitation" government headed by Chirac of the RPR.

In mid-1987 the then PR president and government minister, François Léotard, disappointed Chirac by announcing that the PR would not support the RPR leader in the first round of the 1988 presidential elections, but rather would put up its own candidate. After speculation that Léotard would run himself, in September 1987 the PR gave its backing to Barre (not a PR member). However, the former Prime Minister managed only third place in the first round of voting in April 1988 (with 16.5%) and was eliminated, whereafter the PR backed Chirac in his losing contest with Mitterrand in the second round. In the June 1988 Assembly elections the PR shared in the defeat of the centre-right alliance, although its individual seat tally of 58 out of 129 for the UDF showed electoral resilience. The PR was then in opposition for five years, during which it established itself as the organizational core of UDF, although the traditional reluctance of the centrist parties to develop party structures outside parliament continued to be apparent.

In the landslide victory of the RPR/UDF alliance in the March 1993 Assembly elections, the PR took 104 of the 213 seats won by the UDF and was accordingly allocated important portfolios in the new centre-right "cohabitation" government headed by Edouard Balladur of the RPR. The PR was subsequently tainted by a series of corruption scandals that necessitated the resignations of several of its ministers, including in October 1994 the then PR president Gérard Longuet, amid allegations of irregular party financing activities. The February 1994 murder of PR deputy Yann Piat (once a member of the far-right →National Front) added to the party's poor public image. The decision of Giscard d'Estaing (by now heading the UDF) not to contest the 1995 presidential elections deprived the PR of its obvious candidate, with the result that the party opted for Balladur as the more centrist of the two RPR contenders. After Balladur had been eliminated in the first round, the PR supported the victorious candidacy of Chirac in the second, being rewarded with a strong ministerial presence in the resultant centre-right government. In June 1995 François Léotard was elected to resume the PR presidency in succession to Longuet.

The PR shared in the defeat of the centre-right in the mid-1997 Assembly elections, whereupon the party converted itself into the DL under the leadership of former Finance Minister Alain Madelin, embracing a more free-market economic policy. In the new Assembly the 44-strong Liberal Democracy and Independents group was separate from the UDF. In May 1998 a DL convention decided that the party should formally withdraw from the UDF and instead become an autonomous component of the "Alliance" umbrella organization which the RPR and UDF had created that month (→New Union for French Democracy).

In the June 1999 European Parliament elections the DL opted to stand on a joint list with the RPR and other groups, but the result was a disappointing third place yielding 12.8% of the vote and 12 seats, of which the DL took four. The RPR-DL members of the European Parliament sit in the European People's Party/European Democrats group.

National Centre of Independents and Peasants
Centre National des Indépendants et Paysans (CNIP)

Address. 146 rue de l'Université, 75007 Paris
Telephone. (+33–1) 4062–6364
Fax. (+33–1) 4556–0263
Leadership. Jean Perrin (president); Annick du Roscoat (secretary-general)

The CNIP is derived from the *Centre National des Indépendants* (CNI), which was formed in July 1948 on the initiative of Roger Duchet and René Coty and quickly succeeded in federating most independent parliamentarians of the moderate right. The CNI became the CNIP in January 1949 when it absorbed the small peasant-based *Parti Républicaine de la Liberté*. Between 1951 and 1962 the CNIP took part in various coalition governments, with party members Antoine Pinay being Prime Minister in 1952 and Coty serving as President in 1952–59. In July 1954 the CNIP was joined by Gaullist dissidents of the *Action Républicaine et Sociale* who had supported the Pinay government. In 1958 the CNIP supported the return to power of Gen. de Gaulle and the creation of the Fifth Republic, reaching its electoral peak in the November 1958 Assembly elections, in which it won 22% of the vote and 132 seats. One of these was filled by Jean-Marie Le Pen, who was later to become leader of the far-right →National Front (FN).

The CNIP's influence declined in the 1960s. Deeply divided over de Gaulle's policy of withdrawal from Algeria, it finally broke with him in October 1962. In Assembly elections the following month it lost almost all its representation, as its outgoing deputies either were defeated or transferred to the "majority" camp as Independent Republicans (later the nucleus of the Republican Party, now →Liberal Democracy). In 1967–68 the CNIP was in alliance with Jean Lecanuet's *Centre Démocrate*, but proposals for a formal merger came to nothing. Although nominally an opposition leader during this period, CNIP honorary president Pinay declined invitations to stand against de Gaulle and Georges Pompidou in the presidential elections of 1965 and 1969 respectively. In 1974 the CNIP supported the successful presidential candidacy of Valéry Giscard d'Estaing (Independent Republican) and thereafter became one of the four main parties of the "presidential majority", being represented from 1976 in successive governments headed by Raymond Barre.

The CNIP contested the March 1978 Assembly elections in alliance with other non-Gaullist "majority" parties (winning nine seats), although it did not join the →Union for French Democracy formed on the eve of the poll. Having backed Giscard d'Estaing's unsuccessful re-election bid in 1981, the CNIP was reduced to five seats by the Socialist landslide in the June 1981 Assembly elections, despite an electoral pact with the other centre-right parties. Another pact for the 1986 Assembly elections brought the CNIP a similar level of representation as a component of the victorious centre-right front, although its influence was further eroded by the Socialist victory in the 1988 presidential and Assembly elections. Through this period the CNIP maintained a significance presence in the Senate, where its representatives sat in broader centre-right groups. Continuance of the relationship in the 1993 Assembly elections was impaired by the CNIP's public support for the anti-immigration policies of the FN. However, both in that contest and in the 1997 Assembly elections successful "various right" candidates included a number of CNIP adherents.

National Front
Front National (FN)

Address. 4 rue Vauguyon, 92210 Saint Cloud
Telephone. (+33–1) 4112–1018
Fax. (+33–1) 4112–1086
Email. contact@front-nat.fr
Website. www.front-nat.fr
Leadership. Jean-Marie Le Pen (president); Jean-Claude Martínez (vice-president); Bruno Gollnisch (secretary-general)

The right-wing populist FN was founded in October 1972 on an anti-immigration, law and order, and strongly pro-market platform, bringing together various groups and personalities of the far right. The party has consistently denied that it is racist, pointing to the presence of French Afro-Caribbeans in its ranks and claiming that it welcomes non-whites provided they fully embrace French culture and civilization. Its founder and leader, Le Pen, had served in the elite Parachute Regiment and had been a National Assembly deputy in 1956–62, initially as a member of the *Union de Défense des Commerçants et Artisans* (UDCA) led by Pierre Poujade and later under the auspices of the →National

Centre of Independents and Peasants (CNIP), and had been closely identified with the *Algérie Française* movement. The FN made little impact in the 1970s, winning only 2.5% of the vote in the 1973 Assembly elections and 3% in 1978, while Le Pen took only 0.7% in the first round of the 1974 presidential contest and was unable to stand in 1981 because he could not obtain the required sponsorship of at least 500 national or local elected representatives.

The return to national power of the left in 1981 and increasing public concern about immigration yielded a surge of support for the FN, which successfully repackaged itself as a legitimate force on the right of the centre-right opposition. This approach brought the first far-right electoral success in 25 years when, in the March 1983 municipal elections, an FN candidate was returned to one of the new district councils in the Paris region, while later in the year the then FN secretary-general, Jean-Pierre Stirbois, won 16.7% of the first-round vote in a local by-election in Dreux, thus bringing about a second-round alliance between the FN and the Gaullist →Rally for the Republic (RPR). The FN's major breakthrough came in the European Parliament elections of June 1984, when to the surprise of many observers it won 10.9% of the French vote and 10 seats. In the March 1985 regional elections it slipped to 8.7% of the first-round vote, and was weakend in late 1985 by a split which produced the rival *Front d'Opposition Nationale*. However, in the March 1986 Assembly elections (held under proportional representation), it secured 35 of the 577 seats, winning some 2.7 million votes (9.7%), many of them in working-class areas of high immigrant population where previously the →French Communist Party (PCF) had held sway. As a result of simultaneous regional elections, several RPR regional presidents were elected or re-elected with FN support.

Although the FN initially decided to support Jacques Chirac (then RPR Prime Minister) in the 1988 presidential elections, in May 1986 it withdrew its backing because of Chirac's insistence on abandoning proportional representation for Assembly elections. In January 1987 Le Pen announced his own presidential candidacy, thereby generating dissension within the RPR between those who rejected any co-operation with the far right and those who recognized that the centre-right candidate might need FN backing in the second round. In September 1987 Le Pen caused a major controversy when he publicly referred to Nazi extermination camps as a "detail" of the history of World War II, although he later expressed regret for the remark. The episode did him little damage in the 1988 presidential elections, in which he took fourth place in the first round with 14.4% of the vote (and declined to give endorsement to Chirac in the second). However, in Assembly elections in June 1988 (for which constituency-based majority voting again applied), the FN lost all but one of its seats despite achieving a first-round vote share of 9.7%. The successful FN candidate was Yann Piat (in the Var), but she was expelled from the FN in October 1988, whereafter she joined the Republican Party (and was assassinated in 1994) (→Liberal Democracy).

The FN regained an Assembly seat in a by-election for Dreux in December 1989, when Marie-France Stirbois (widow of Jean-Pierre, who had died in a car crash in November 1988) won 61.3% of the second-round vote. Le Pen acclaimed the result as demonstrating public support for the FN's opposition to immigration and to "French decadence", and called for the repatriation of all foreigners who had come to France since 1974. While not opposing French membership of the European Union (EU), the FN strongly endorsed the old Gaullist concept of a "Europe of nation states" and therefore was part of the opposition to the EU's Maastricht Treaty on ever closer union, which obtained wafer-thin referendum endorsement by French voters in September 1992. In the March 1993 Assembly elections, the FN failed to win representation, despite a national first-round vote share of 12.4% and an election campaign in

which the "respectable" centre-right parties took up many of the FN's concerns about immigration and the rule of law.

In the June 1994 European Parliament elections the FN slipped back to 10.5% (winning 11 of the 87 French seats). In the 1995 presidential elections, however, Le Pen took fourth place in the first round with an all-time FN electoral high of 15.0% (4,573,202 votes). He again declined to give endorsement to Chirac of the RPR in the second round, announcing that he would cast a blank ballot in protest against "a detestable choice between two left-wing candidates". The FN continued its advance in municipal elections in June 1995, trebling its complement of councillors to 1,075 and winning control of three substantial southern towns (Toulon, Orange and Marignane). According to a post-election statement by Le Pen, the FN would apply "national preference" in the municipalities under its control, so that immigrants and foreigners would no longer get equal treatment in the allocation of subsidized housing, welfare benefits and public-sector jobs.

In February 1997 the FN narrowly won a high-profile mayoral by-election in Vitrolles, near Marseilles, and the following month gained more publicity when its 10th congress in Strasbourg attracted a major protest demonstration backed by the →Socialist Party (PS) and the PCF. In the mid-1997 National Assembly elections the NF advanced to 14.9% of the first-round vote, but returned only one deputy (from Toulon). It lost even this seat in a May 1998 by-election (called because the NF deputy had infringed party finance rules in the 1997 contest) and failed to regain it in a further by-election in September 1998 (called because of ballot irregularities in the first). There was evidence in these and other electoral contests that moderate conservative voters were prepared to combine with the left in unofficial "republican fronts" to defeat the FN.

In November 1998 a Versailles appeal court disqualified Le Pen from elective office for a year and confirmed a suspended three-month sentence imposed on the FN leader for assaulting a PS candidate in the 1997 Assembly elections. The affair contributed to deepening internal divisions, which came to a head in January 1999 when deputy leader and chief ideologue Bruno Mégret was elected leader of the "National Front–National Movement" (FN-*Mouvement National*, FN-MN) at a conference held in Marignane after some 17,000 of the 40,000 FN members had signed a petition in favour of a leadership election. Le Pen boycotted the conference and also dismissed Mégret's claim that he now led the authentic FN. The dispute between the two was about political strategy rather than ideology, in that Le Pen opposed any alliances with other parties, whereas Mégret favoured pragmatic electoral pacts with centre-right formations. Le Pen appeared to be losing the struggle when in March 1999 the influential FN mayor of Toulon declared his support for Mégret. However, in May a Paris court banned the Mégret faction from "usurping" the FN name and logo, with the result that it assumed the title →National Republican Movement (MNR) and Le Pen continued as leader of the FN.

Headed by Le Pen, the FN list in the June 1999 European Parliament elections easily outpolled the MNR, although it took only 5.7% of the vote and elected five MEPs, who were numbered among the "unattached" contingent when the new Parliament assembled. In February 2000 Le Pen's disqualification from public office was at last applied to his seat on the Provence-Alpes-Côte d'Azur regional council, while two months later the French government banned him from sitting in the European Parliament. Le Pen lost appeals against this decision in October 2000, whereupon European Parliament president Nicole Fontaine (France) ordered his exclusion. In January 2001, however, the European Court of Justice ruled that Fontaine had acted illegally in relying on French legal decisions to exclude Le Pen, who therefore regained his seat.

The FN suffered a major setback in the March 2001 local council elections, losing control of Toulon and surrendering many seats to centre-right/left second-round alliances. Nevertheless, in June 2001 Le Pen confirmed that he would contest the 2002 presidential elections and that the FN would field candidates for all 577 seats in the subsequent National Assembly elections.

National Republican Movement
Mouvement National Républicain (MNR)

Address. 15 rue de Cronstadt, 75015 Paris
Telephone. (+33–1) 5656–6434
Fax. (+33–1) 5656–5247
Email. m-n-r@m-n-r.com
Website. www.m-n-r.com
Leadership. Bruno Mégret (president); Serge Martínez (vice-president); Franck Timmermans (secretary-general)
The MNR was founded in 1999 by a dissident faction of the radical right-wing →National Front (FN) led by Bruno Mégret, the FN deputy leader and chief ideologue, who had come into serious conflict with FN leader Jean-Marie Le Pen over political strategy. Whereas Le Pen opposed any alliances between the FN and other parties, Mégret favoured pragmatic electoral pacts with centre-right formations. After some 17,000 of the 40,000 FN members had signed a petition in favour of a leadership election conference, and Le Pen had opted to ignore the petition, a conference of the dissident faction in Marignane in January 1999 elected Mégret as leader of the "National Front–National Movement". Having boycotted the conference, Le Pen dismissed Mégret's claim that he now led the authentic FN.

The breakaway party was strengthened when in March 1999 the influential FN mayor of Toulon declared his support for it. However, in May a Paris court banned the Mégret faction from "usurping" the FN name and logo, with the result that it assumed the title National Republican Movement (MNR). In the June 1999 European Parliament elections the Mégret list was easily outpolled by the rump FN, winning only 3.3% of the vote and no seats.

New Union for French Democracy
Nouvelle Union pour la Démocratie Française (NUDF)

Address. 133bis rue de l'Université, 75014 Paris
Telephone. (+33–1) 5359–2000
Fax. (+33–1) 5359–2059
Email. internet@udf.org
Website. www.nouvelle-udf.org
Leadership. François Bayrou (president); Hervé de Charette (president delegate); Philippe Douste-Blazy (Assembly group chairman); Pierre-André Wiltzer (secretary-general)
The "New" UDF was launched in 1999 following a UDF congress decision in November 1998 that the UDF constituent parties would formally combine into a unified organization and therefore cease to exist independently. The centre-right UDF had been created in February 1978 as an electoral alliance of the non-Gaullist "majority" (i.e. then ruling) parties, namely (i) what was then called the Republican Party (PR), which in 1997 became →Liberal Democracy and in May 1998 left the UDF; (ii) the Radical Party; (iii) what was then called the Centre of Social Democrats (CDS) and in 1995 become the Democratic Force (FD); (iv) what later became the Social Democratic Party (PSD); and (v) the *Clubs Perspectives et Réalités*, which in 1995 became the Popular Party for French Democracy (PPDF).

Of the original UDF components, the **Radical Party** was by far the oldest, having been founded in 1901 from pre-existing Radical groups sharing a commitment to anti-clericalism and the separation of Church and State. Its full title, rarely used under the Fifth Republic, was Radical Republican and Radical-Socialist Party (*Parti Républicain Radical et Radical-Socialiste*, PRRRS), reflecting the Radicals' history as the mainstay of the Third Republic (1871–1940) and their frequent cooperation with the left-wing parties under both the Third and Fourth Republics. The party was also often referred to as the *Parti Valoisien* after

its headquarters address in Paris, from where it provided many Prime Ministers up to and after World War I, including Georges Clemenceau in 1906–09 and 1917–19. Its celebrated slogan was "*Pas d'ennemi à gauche*" ("No enemy to the left"), on which basis it participated in the anti-fascist Popular Front government formed in 1936 under the leadership of what was then the SFIO and much later became the →Socialist Party (PS). Despite a post-war electoral decline, the Radicals remained a focal point in the frequent coalition building of the Fourth Republic until its demise in 1958, providing the Prime Ministers of no less than 12 governments.

Traditionally eschewing rigid structures, the Radical Party suffered a series of splits in 1954–56, when Pierre Mendès-France moved the party to the left and tried to impose more internal discipline. By late 1958 Mendès-France and his left-wing followers had become the minority and subsequently broke away to participate in the formation of the Unified Socialist Party (PSU), part of which later joined the PS. During the first decade of the Fifth Republic (1958–68) the rump Radicals under the leadership of René Billères participated in moves towards union of the non-Communist left, joining the Federation of the Democratic and Socialist Left (FGDS) in 1965 and participating in the FGDS advance in the 1967 Assembly elections. After the May 1968 political and social crisis, however, Maurice Faure moved the party back to a centrist posture, which was consolidated following the election of Jean-Jacques Servan-Schreiber to the party presidency in 1971. The Radical majority's refusal to subscribe to a new union of the left involving the Socialists and the →French Communist Party (PCF) caused the exit of the left-wing minority in 1972 to form what became the Left Radical Movement (MRG), now called the →Left Radical Party (PRG).

In the 1974 presidential elections the Radicals backed the successful candidacy of Valéry Giscard d'Estaing (Independent Republican), but only after the first round and in return for specific policy commitments. Under the Giscard d'Estaing presidency the Radicals were included in successive centre-right coalitions, although their initial return to government was controversial: appointed Minister of Reforms, Servan-Schreiber was dismissed within a fortnight for criticizing the proposed resumption of French nuclear tests in the Pacific. Pursuing attempts to forge greater unity among the smaller centrist and centre-left parties, the Radicals in July 1977 absorbed the Movement of Social Liberals (*Mouvement des Sociaux Libéraux*, MSL), which had been formed earlier in the year by Gaullist dissidents led by Olivier Stirn.

The forerunner of the **Democratic Force** (*Force Démocrate*, FD) was the centrist, Christian democratic and pro-European Centre of Social Democrats (*Centre des Sociaux Démocrates*, CSD) founded in May 1976, although its constituent elements had their roots in a 19th-century movement aimed at reconciling Catholics with the Third Republic (1871–1940). After World War II these forces were represented by the Popular Republican Movement (*Mouvement Républicain Populaire*, MRP) led by Georges Bidault and other wartime resistance leaders, which was the strongest parliamentary party until the 1951 elections and took part in most Fourth Republic governments until its demise in 1958. Bidault was himself Prime Minister in 1946 and 1949–50; other MRP premiers were Robert Schuman (1947–48) and Pierre Pflimlin (1958). The immediate antecedents of the CDS were the Democratic Centre (*Centre Démocrate*, CD) and the Democracy and Progress Centre (*Centre Démocratie et Progrès*, CDP), both of which emerged under the Fifth Republic.

The CD had been launched in March 1966 by Jean Lecanuet, who had scored 15.9% in the 1965 presidential elections. In the 1969 contest most CD elements had backed Alain Poher (who received 23.3% in the first round and 41.8% in the second), although some had supported the successful Gaullist candidate, Georges Pompidou, thus abandoning the previous centrist policy of acting as a balancing force between the right-wing "majority" parties and the left-wing opposition. The CDP had been founded after the 1969 elections by centrist supporters of President Pompidou, notably Jacques Duhamel, Joseph Fontanet and René Pleven. In the 1973 Assembly elections the CD and the CDP had returned 24 and 34 deputies respectively, the former as part of the Reformers' Movement (created in 1971 by various centrist groups then outside the government "majority") and the latter in alliance with the ruling Gaullists and Independent Republicans. In the first round of the 1974 presidential elections the CDP had supported Jacques Chaban-Delmas (Gaullist) and the CD Giscard d'Estaing, but both parties had contributed to the victory of the latter in the second round. Both parties had joined the resultant centre-right government headed by Jacques Chirac and had been prominent in further moves towards greater cohesion of the centre, notably the six-party Federation of Reformers created in June 1975, prior to the launching of the CDS in May 1976 under the presidency of Lecanuet.

The forerunner of the **Popular Party for French Democracy** (*Parti Populaire pour la Démocratie Française*, PPDF) was the Perspectives and Realities Clubs (*Clubs Perspectives et Réalités*, CPR) grouping founded in 1965 by Jean-Pierre Fourcade, which had acted as a think tank for the UDF as a whole, providing a political home for centrist intellectuals reluctant to join a traditional political party. Many of its leading members were associated with the Republican Party component of the UDF (→Liberal Democracy), notably its chair from 1982 to 1984, Jean-François Deniau, who had been a minister and European commissioner under the Giscard d'Estaing presidency (1974–81). Having lost the French presidency in 1981, Giscard d'Estaing himself took the chairmanship of the CPR until 1989.

The **Social Democratic Party** (*Parti Social-Démocrate*, PSD) had been established in December 1973 as the Movement of Democratic Socialists of France (*Mouvement des Démocrates Socialistes de France*, MDSF) by a faction of the PS opposed to the common programme issued by the PS and PCF in 1972. Claiming to enshrine the authentic socialist tradition of Jean Jaurès and Léon Blum, the MDSF advocated centrist unity and joined both the Reformers' Movement and the Federation of Reformers in the mid-1970s. The first MDSF vice-president, Émile Muller, won 0.7% of the vote in the first round of the 1974 presidential elections, whereafter the MDSF backed the successful candidacy of Giscard d'Estaing in the second. The MDSF transformed itself into the PSD in October 1982, at the same time absorbing some other social democratic elements.

The decision of the above parties to create the Union for French Democracy (Union pour la Démocratie Française, UDF) a month before the March 1978 Assembly elections was inspired in part by the decision of the (Gaullist) RPR to withdraw from first-round electoral pacts with the PR and CDS on the grounds that negotiation by these two parties of separate first-round agreements with the Radicals (the most left-wing of the "majority" parties) had violated the terms of the RPR/PR/CDS agreement. The UDF was backed from the outset by President Giscard d'Estaing (after whose 1977 book *Démocratie Française* the alliance was named) and by his Prime Minister, Raymond Barre. Its creation therefore heightened tensions between the Giscardian and Gaullist wings of the "majority", the former viewing it as an attempt to engineer electoral superiority. In the 1978 elections the UDF parties won increased aggregate representation of 124 seats (compared with 154 for the RPR), assisted by the operation of reciprocal voting support arrangements with the RPR in the second round. The elected UDF deputies included 71 from the PR, 35 from the CDS, seven Radicals and four from the MDSF. Immediately after polling the UDF council formally elevated the alliance to the status of a federation of its constituent parties, under the presidency of Jean Lecanuet (leader of the CDS). In the June 1979 elec-

tions to the European Parliament the strongly pro-European UDF list (*Union pour la France en Europe*) came top of the poll with 27.6%.

The UDF was the mainstay of Giscard d'Estaing's bid for a second presidential term in 1981 as a "citizen-candidate" rather than as the nominee of any party. Following his narrow second-round defeat by François Mitterrand (PS), the UDF formed an electoral alliance with the RPR for the June 1981 Assembly elections, called the *Union pour la Majorité Nouvelle* (UMN) and providing for single first-round candidates in 385 of the 474 metropolitan constituencies as well as reciprocal voting support for the best-placed second-round candidate in the others. The UDF nevertheless shared in the rout of the centre-right by the PS, winning 19.2% of the first-round vote and retaining only 63 Assembly seats, of which the PR took 32, the CDS 25 and the Radicals two. It therefore went into opposition for the next five years, the UMN alliance lapsing in 1983.

In April 1985 the UDF signed a new cooperation agreement with the RPR, with which it drew up a joint manifesto for the March 1986 Assembly elections (in which proportional representation applied). Presenting some candidates jointly with the RPR and others in its own right, the UDF played its part in the defeat of the PS-led government, increasing its representation to 131 seats out 577, the PR remaining the strongest UDF component with 59 seats. In the succeeding centre-right coalition headed by the RPR, the UDF parties received 17 ministerial posts out of 41. But the fragility of the ruling coalition became apparent in 1987 when the PR leader, François Léotard, announced that he would not support the RPR leader (and Prime Minister), Jacques Chirac, in the first round of the 1988 presidential elections. When it was announced in September 1987 that Barre (a centrist without formal party affiliation) would be a candidate, the PR and other UDF components declared their support for him. In the event, Barre came in third place in the first round in April 1988 with 16.5% of the vote, whereupon the UDF gave second-round support to Chirac in his unsuccessful attempt to deny Mitterrand a second term.

New Assembly elections held in June 1988 (by constituency-based majority voting) were contested by the UDF in an alliance with the RPR called the *Union du Rassemblement et du Centre* (URC). The centre-right parties lost their majority but the UDF showed resilience, for the first time returning more deputies (129) than the RPR (127), the UDF contingent including 58 PR, 49 CDS, three Radical and three PSD deputies. Immediately after the elections Giscard d'Estaing replaced Lecanuet as president of the UDF. In opposition over the next five years, most of the UDF contested the 1989 European elections on a joint list with the RPR (winning 28.9% of the vote and 26 seats), whilst the CDS presented an independent list which took 8.4% and seven seats. In June 1990 the UDF and RPR announced the creation of the *Union pour la France* (UPF), amid much talk about the need for a unified party. In reality, the UDF and the RPR continued their long struggle for supremacy on the centre-right, with the added ingredient of resumed rivalry between Giscard d'Estaing and Chirac. Also divisive was the Maastricht Treaty on European union, which was fully supported by the UDF, whereas important sections of the RPR campaigned for a "no" vote in the September 1992 referendum that yielded a narrow majority for French ratification.

As widely anticipated, the Assembly elections of March 1993 produced a landslide victory for the UDF/RPR alliance, which won 80% of the seats on a 40% first-round vote share. Crucially, the RPR emerged with 247 of the 577 seats, against 213 for the UDF parties, thus effectively dashing Giscard d'Estaing's further presidential ambitions. The PR remained dominant in the UDF elected contingent, taking 104 seats compared with 57 for the CDS (which had declined to give automatic support to better-placed centre-right candidates in the second round). The UDF parties were allocated important portfolios in the new "cohabitation" government headed by Edouard Balladur of the RPR, and in the European Parliament elections of June 1994 Giscard d'Estaing headed another joint UDF/RPR list (this time including the CDS), which slipped to 25.6%, giving it 28 seats.

The UDF was weakened by a series of corruption scandals which yielded the resignations of several ministers in 1994, with the result that both Giscard d'Estaing and Barre announced that they would not stand in the 1995 presidential elections. In the absence of a candidate from their own ranks, most UDF components initially supported Balladur as the more centrist of the two RPR contenders. After Balladur had been eliminated in the first round, however, the UDF officially swung behind the victorious candidacy of Chirac in the second, being rewarded with a strong ministerial presence in the resultant centre-right government headed by Alain Juppé of the RPR. In an apparent reconciliation of their longstanding personal rivalry, Giscard d'Estaing was invited to give "elder statesman" advice to the newly-installed President Chirac.

In July 1995 the CPR grouping converted itself into the PPDF under the leadership of Hervé de Charette and Jean-Pierre Raffarin, while in November 1995 the CDS became the FD under the leadership of François Bayrou. Both new creations remained under the UDF umbrella.

Giscard d'Estaing stood down as UDF leader in March 1996 (to devote himself to founding a centrist think tank) and indicated his preference that the succession should go to Alain Madelin (then of the PPDF, formerly a vice-president of the PR and subsequently leader of Liberal Democracy), who had the previous August been dismissed as Economy and Finance Minister after failing to persuade Prime Minister Juppé of the need for drastic measures to curb the budget deficit. However, UDF constituents preferred the PR leader, François Léotard, who secured 57.4% of delegates' vote at a national council meeting in Lyon. Thereafter, the growing influence of the far-right →National Front (FN) became an increasingly divisive issue, with some UDF elements being prepared to support left-wing candidates to defeat the FN, while the UDF leadership declined to give specific endorsement to anti-FN "republican fronts".

The UDF shared in the defeat of the centre-right in the mid-1997 Assembly elections, its aggregate representation falling to 108 seats following a first-round vote share of only 14.2%. Consigned to opposition, the UDF also lost ground in the March 1998 regional elections, following which five UDF politicians were elected as regional assembly presidents on the strength of FN support. Two of these subsequently stood down under pressure, but the other three were expelled from the UDF, with the result that one of them, Charles Millon, launched what later became the →Liberal Christian Right. In May 1998 the UDF and the RPR set up the "Alliance" as a joint umbrella organization, whereupon Liberal Democracy (successor to the PR) formally withdrew from the UDF and opted instead to become an autonomous component of the Alliance.

Mired in a party financing scandal, Léotard was in September 1998 succeeded as president of the UDF by François Bayrou, leader of Democratic Force (now the largest UDF component). At a congress in Lille in November 1998 the remaining UDF formations decided that they would cease to have separate existences and would instead combine into a unitary party. Bayrou resisted RPR pressure for another joint list for the June 1999 Euro-elections, opting for a separate UDF slate, which took 9.3% of the vote and only nine seats. The UDF then resorted to the time-honoured marketing stratagem of adding "New" to its title, so that it became "*La Nouvelle* UDF".

Memories of old scandals were revived in March 2000 when three former ministers, Pierre Méhaignerie, Jacques Barrot and Bernard Bosson, were fined and give suspended prison sentences after being convicted of illegal funding of the CDS (before it became the FD). Evidence also emerged in 2000 that the old UDF had been implicated in the system of kickbacks for public contracts allegedly run by the RPR in Paris when Chirac was mayor in 1977–95. Nevertheless, the combined forces of the NUDF and the RPR outpolled the ruling coalition parties in the March 2001 local council elections, winning 46.9% of the first-round vote. At the same time, NUDF parliamentary forces maintained their independence of the RPR by ensuring the passage in April 2001 of a government proposal that the 2002 presidential elections should precede Assembly elections rather then follow them, thereby probably reducing Chirac's chances of being re-elected.

The NUDF is a member of the International Democrat Union and the European Democrat Union; through the FD it is also affiliated to the Christian Democrat International. The NUDF members of the European Parliament sit in the European People's Party/European Democrats group.

Rally for France and the Independence of Europe
Rassemblement pour la France et l'Indépendance de l'Europe (RPF-IE)

Address. 159 ave Charles de Gaulle, 92521 Neuilly-sur-Seine
Telephone. (+33–1) 5562–2424
Fax. (+33–1) 5562–2435
Email. rpf@rpf-ie.org
Website. www.rpf-ie.org
Leadership. Charles Pasqua (president): Jean-Jacques Guillet (secretary-general)

Opposed to further European integration, the RPF-IE was formally established as a political party in November 1999, following the success of the RPF-IE list in the June 1999 European Parliament elections. It united the Rally for France (RPF), launched by former Gaullist Interior Minister Charles Pasqua in June 1998 as a breakaway from the →Rally for the Republic (RPR), and the Movement for France (*Mouvement pour la France*, MPF) led by Philippe de Villiers.

The MPF had been formed in November 1994 as the successor to The Other Europe (*L'Autre Europe*), which had been created to contest the June 1994 European Parliament elections, principally on the initiative of the French-British financier, Sir James Goldsmith. Opposed to the Maastricht process of closer EU economic and monetary union, it also condemned the 1993 GATT world trade liberalization agreement, arguing that Western Europe needed to protect its industry and employment levels from Asian competition based on cheap labour. In the 1994 European poll, The Other Europe list obtained 12.4% of the vote and 13 of the 87 French seats. In the 1995 presidential elections, MPF leader de Villiers (a former member of the →New Union for French Democracy) was placed seventh out of nine first-round candidates, winning 4.7% of the vote.

In the June 1999 Euro-elections the RPF-IE list took second place, ahead of the RPR, winning 13.1% of the vote and 13 seats on a platform of opposition to further European integration and enlargement. In late 1999 the new formation numbered five Assembly members and six senators among its adherents. By mid-2000, however, policy and personal differences between Pasqua and de Villiers had caused the withdrawal of the latter, who in January 2001 told magistrates investigating an arms trafficking affair that Pasqua had received illegal funds via the company at the centre of the scandal. On being placed under criminal investigation in April 2001, Pasqua dismissed the allegations as "trumped-up rubbish" and as "an attempt to destabilize democracy".

The 13 RPF-IE members of the European Parliament sit in the Union for a Europe of Nations group.

Rally for the Republic
Rassemblement pour la République (RPR)

Address. 123 rue de Lille, 75007 Paris
Telephone. (+33–1) 4955–6300
Fax. (+33–1) 4551–4479
Email. webmaster@rpr.org

Website. www.rpr.asso.fr

Leadership. Michèle Alliot-Marie (president); Jean-Louis Debré (Assembly group chairman)

Although established under its present name in December 1976, the broadly conservative RPR is directly descended from the *Rassemblement du Peuple Français* (RPF) established in April 1947 by Gen. Charles de Gaulle, who had been head of the London-based Free French forces during World War II and then Prime Minister of the first post-liberation government (1944–46). Formed with the central objective of returning de Gaulle to power, the RPF became the strongest Assembly party in 1951 (with 118 seats), but was weakened in 1952 by the creation of the dissident *Action Républicaine et Sociale* (ARS). When members of the rump RPF accepted ministerial posts in 1953, de Gaulle severed his links with the party, which was dissolved as a parliamentary group. Gaullist deputies then created the *Union des Républicains d'Action Sociale* (URAS), which became the *Centre National des Républicains Sociaux* (CNRS) in February 1954. Following de Gaulle's return to power in mid-1958 amid the collapse of the Fourth Republic, the movement was reconstituted for the November 1958 Assembly elections as the *Union pour la Nouvelle République* (UNR), which won a plurality of 188 seats. Inducted as President of the Fifth Republic in January 1959, de Gaulle appointed Michel Debré (UNR) as his Prime Minister.

Under the right-oriented Debré premiership a left-wing Gaullist faction formed the *Union Démocratique du Travail* (UDT), which was reunited with the UNR following the replacement of Debré by the technocratic Georges Pompidou in April 1962. In the November 1962 Assembly elections the UNR-UDT increased its dominance by winning 219 seats. In December 1965 de Gaulle won popular election for a second presidential term, comfortably defeating left-wing candidate François Mitterrand in the second round with 55.2% of the vote. For the March 1976 Assembly elections the UNR-UDT adopted the title *Union des Démocrates pour la Cinquième République* (UDCR), which slipped to 200 seats and henceforth relied on Valéry Giscard d'Estaing's Independent Republicans for a parliamentary majority. In November 1967 the UDCR title was formally adopted by the party, which at the same time absorbed a faction of the (Christian democratic) *Mouvement Républicain Populaire* (MRP) and other groups further to the left. In the wake of the May 1968 national crisis, the Gaullists registered a landslide victory in Assembly elections in June, winning 292 seats under the designation *Union pour la Défense de la République* and continuing in office under the reformist premiership of Maurice Couve de Murville. The new parliamentary group preferred the slightly different title *Union des Démocrates pour la République* (UDR), which was subsequently applied to the party as a whole.

De Gaulle resigned in April 1969 after unexpectedly being denied referendum approval of constitutional and regional reform proposals. He was succeeded in June elections by Pompidou, who won a comfortable 57.6% victory over a centrist candidate in the second round. The new Gaullist Prime Minister was Jacques Chaban-Delmas, seen as representative of the UDR's modernist wing, but corruption charges and other difficulties resulted in his replacement by the orthodox Pierre Messmer in July 1972. In the Assembly elections of March 1973 the UDR slumped to 183 seats, but Messmer continued as Prime Minister at the head of a coalition with centrist parties. Pompidou's death in office in April 1974 precipitated presidential elections in May, when Chaban-Delmas as the UDR candidate was eliminated in the first round (with only 14.6% of the vote). Many Gaullist voters preferred the more dynamic Giscard d'Estaing (Independent Republican), who won a narrow second-round victory over Mitterrand and proceeded to appoint Jacques Chirac (UDR) to head a government with strong centrist representation. Increasing strains between President and Prime Minister yielded Chirac's resignation in August 1976, whereupon the Gaullists ceased to hold the premiership but continued as part of the ruling coalition. In December 1976 Chirac engineered the conversion of the UDR into the RPR, which became his power base in increasingly acrimonious competition between the Gaullist and Giscardian wings of the "majority". In March 1977 Chirac was elected mayor of Paris, defeating the centrist candidate backed by the President.

After Chirac had failed to create a "majority" alliance for the March 1978 Assembly elections, the RPR slipped to 154 seats, against 124 for the new Union for French Democracy (UDF), grouping the Giscardian centrist parties (→New Union for French Democracy, NUDF). In the June 1979 European Parliament elections the RPR list (called *Défense des Intérêts de la France*, reflecting traditional Gaullist doubts about the European idea) managed only 16.3% (and fourth place) as against the UDF's 27.6%. In the 1981 presidential elections, moreover, Chirac took a poor third place in the first round (with 18% of the vote) and was eliminated; although he said that he would personally vote for Giscard d'Estaing in the second round in May, his failure to urge RPR supporters to do likewise was seen as contributing to the incumbent's narrow defeat by Mitterrand. In the resultant Assembly elections in June the RPR shared in the centre-right's decimation by the →Socialist Party (PS), slumping to 88 seats notwithstanding the presentation of single centre-right candidates in over three-quarters of the metropolitan constituencies under the banner of the *Union pour la Majorité Nouvelle* (UMN).

In opposition from 1981 to 1986, the RPR launched an internal modernization and rejuvenation programme, with Chirac bringing forward a new generation of leaders more favourable to European integration and more in tune with the changing social composition of France. On the basis of a declaration signed in April 1985, the RPR and the UDF presented a joint manifesto in the March 1986 Assembly elections as well as single candidates for many seats. In the resultant centre-right victory, the RPR emerged with 155 deputies in the new 577-seat Assembly elected by proportional representation, ahead of the UDF, so that Chirac was again appointed Prime Minister of a coalition government in which the RPR held 21 posts and the UDF parties 17. During the ensuing two years of "cohabitation" between a Socialist President and a Gaullist Prime Minister, the RPR experienced internal divisions about how to respond to the growing strength of the far-right →National Front (FN) led by Jean-Marie Le Pen, with some Gaullists rejecting any links with the FN and others arguing that the party could not be ignored, especially since the FN was making inroads into RPR support. The debate intensified in January 1987 when Le Pen announced his own candidacy in the 1988 presidential elections, having previously indicated that the FN would support Chirac. After some equivocation, the RPR leader announced in May 1987 that there would be no national alliance between the RPR and the FN, while not prohibiting the informal RPR/FN voting co-operation that was already a factor in some localities and regions.

In his second tilt at the presidency in April-May 1988, Chirac took second place in the first round (with 19.9% of the vote) and thus went forward to the second against Mitterrand, losing to the incumbent by 45.98% to 54.02%. The relatively wide margin of the RPR candidate's defeat was attributed in part to the refusal of Le Pen to instruct his four million first-round supporters to vote for Chirac in the second. Assembly elections in June 1988 (held by constituency-based majority voting) were contested by the RPR in an alliance with the UDF called the *Union du Rassemblement et du Centre* (URC), but not only did the centre-right parties lose their majority but also the RPR for the first time returned fewer deputies (127) than the UDF (129). In opposition over the next five years, the RPR and UDF contested the 1989 European Parliament on a joint list (winning 28.9% of the vote) and in June 1990 announced the creation of yet another alliance, called the *Union pour la France* (UPF), amid much talk about the need for a unified party in the next legislative elections and a single presidential candidate. In reality, the RPR and the UDF continued their long struggle for supremacy on the centre-right, with the added spice of resumed personal rivalry between Chirac and Giscard d'Estaing. Also divisive in this period was the Maastricht Treaty on European union, which was supported wholeheartedly by the UDF, whereas important sections of the RPR (although not Chirac himself) campaigned for a "no" vote in the September 1992 referendum that yielded a very narrow majority for French ratification.

As widely forecast, the Assembly elections of March 1993 produced a landslide victory for the RPR/UDF alliance, which won 80% of the seats on a 39.5% first-round vote share. Crucially, the RPR emerged with 247 of the 577 seats (and 20.4% of the first-round vote), against 213 (and 19.1%) for the UDF parties, so that Chirac was able to nominate the new Prime Minister. His choice fell on Edouard Balladur, a former RPR Finance Minister and supposedly a Chirac loyalist, who was charged with running the government while the RPR leader concentrated on mounting a third attempt on the presidency. A leading RPR campaigner against the Maastricht Treaty, Philippe Séguin, was elected president of the National Assembly in April 1993. In the event, Balladur became so popular as Prime Minister that he was persuaded to renege on a pledge not to enter the presidential race. The upshot was that both Chirac and Balladur contested the 1995 elections, with the latter securing backing from within the UDF (which did not put up a candidate). Meanwhile, the RPR/UDF alliance was maintained for the June 1994 European Parliament elections, in which their combined vote slipped to 25.6%, yielding 28 of the 87 French seats.

After a slow start, Chirac's campaigning skills and command of the powerful RPR party machine, plus a late-breaking phone-tapping scandal in which Balladur was implicated, took the RPR leader to second place in the first round of the presidential balloting in April 1995 (with 20.8% of the vote), behind the Socialist candidate but ahead of Balladur (18.6%). Chirac therefore went into the second round in May and was at last victorious with 52.6% of the vote, despite again being denied second-round endorsement by the FN. Pledging himself to restoring "social cohesion", Chirac named Foreign Minister Alain Juppé (who had been the new President's campaign manager in his role as RPR secretary-general) to head a new coalition government maintaining approximate balance between the RPR and the UDF. At a party congress in October 1995 Juppé was formally elected to the RPR presidency in succession to Chirac, receiving 93% of the ballots in an uncontested election.

Damaged by corruption allegations in 1996, the RPR also experienced internal divisions on how the party should respond to the growing strength of the FN. Although the RPR leadership opposed any political cooperation with the FN, it declined to give formal backing to anti-FN "republican fronts" with the centre and left, despite narrowly defeating the FN in a mayoral by-election in Dreux in November 1996 on the strength of left-wing support. In an Assembly by-election in Vitrolles, near Marseilles, in February 1997 Juppé urged first-round RPR voters "to face up to their responsibilities" in the second, but the contest was won by the FN candidate. Meanwhile, an RPR national council meeting had approved an age-limit of 75 years for candidates in the next Assembly elections and of 70 thereafter; it had also declared its opposition to French-style "multiple mandates" often held by politicians and decided that in future party list elections at least one-third of RPR candidates with a chance of being elected would be women.

Despite the Juppé government's unpopularity, Chirac unexpectedly called early Assembly elections for May-June 1997. A general rout for the centre-right, in which the RPR slumped to 134 seats and a first-round vote share of 15.7%, resulted in Chirac having to accept "cohabitation" with a Socialist-led government. It also resulted in Juppé's immediate resignation as RPR president, in which post he was succeeded by Séguin at a special party congress in July. Séguin declared that the RPR should neither demonize the FN nor form tactical alliances with it, but should rather seek to appeal to most FN voters who were "neither fascists nor opposed to democracy". In regional elections in March 1998 the RPR/UDF were again outpolled by the left, though only narrowly. An injunction from both the RPR and UDF leaderships that their regional parties should not make deals with the FN to secure regional presidencies was observed by RPR federations (but not by the UDF).

Having failed to persuade a party conference that the RPR should shorten its name to "*Le Rassemblement*", Séguin was buffeted in early 1998 by further corruption cases involving RPR politicians in Paris and elsewhere. In April 1998 dissident RPR members of the Paris city council launched the →PARIS formation, in protest against the alleged corruption of the RPR administration. In the same month RPR members of the Assembly staged a surprise walk-out before a vote to approve French participation in the single European currency (euro), contending that their action did not indicate disapproval of the euro but opposition to the government's economic policies. In May 1998 RPR and UDF agreed to form a loose umbrella organization called the "Alliance". However, the RPR was weakened in June 1998 by the launching of a new movement by former Gaullist Interior Minister Charles Pasqua opposed to further European integration and enlargement. In February 1999 efforts by Séguin to persuade the UDF as a whole to present a joint list under his leadership in the forthcoming Euroelections came to nought, amid much acrimony on both sides. In April 1999 Séguin unexpectedly resigned as RPR president, claiming that his authority had been undermined by Chirac. RPR secretary-general Nicolas Sarkozy became acting president and led the party in the June 1999 Euroelections, in which the RPR presented a joint list with former UDF component →Liberal Democracy (DL) which also included →Civil Society and →Ecology Generation. The list was relegated to third place with 12.8% of the vote and 12 of the 87 seats (of which the RPR took six), being outpolled by Pasqua's new →Rally for France and the Independence of Europe (RPF-IE).

Sarkozy immediately resigned as RPR acting president and in September 1999 also vacated the post of secretary-general, asserting that he would not seek the party presidency. A divisive leadership contest resulted in the election in early December of former Sports Minister Michèle Alliot-Marie as RPR president. A pro-European, Alliot-Marie easily defeated Chirac-backed candidate Jean-Paul Delevoye in the runoff balloting, to become the first woman leader of a major French party.

Alliot-Marie immediately faced a deluge of new evidence about a system of kickbacks for public contracts allegedly run by the RPR in Paris when Chirac was mayor in 1977–95 and about vote-rigging and other illegal practices under his successor, Jean Tiberi, aided and abetted by his redoubtable wife, Xavière Tiberi. As investigations ground on, Jean Tiberi was expelled from the RPR in October 2000 for refusing to accept the nomination of party elder Philippe Séguin as the RPR mayoral candidate in Paris. He took his revenge in the March 2001 municipal elections, running as an independent and winning 14% of the first-round vote, thus reducing Séguin to 26% and second place against the PS candidate. Although Tiberi gave unenthusiastic backing to Séguin in the second round, the PS candidate triumphed and the right lost control of the capital for the first time since 1871. In the rest of the country, however, the RPR and its allies in what was now the NUDF polled strongly, obtaining 46.9% of the first-round vote against 44.9% for the ruling coalition parties and winning control of 318 of the 583 larger towns, a net gain of 40.

The Paris corruption scandal deepened in April 2001 when the investigating magistrate concluded that there was plausible evidence of Chirac's past involvement in illegal activities and, in view of the President's immunity from prosecution in the courts, invited parliament to institute impeachment proceedings. Chirac continued to make robust denials of any wrongdoing, but came under further intense pressure in June 2001 over new disclosures about large cash payments made by him in 1992–95 for holidays for himself and members of his family. The President again denied any impropriety and claimed that the PS and its supporters in the judiciary were seeking to damage his prospects of re-election in 2002.

Claiming a membership of some 400,000, the RPR is a member of the International Democrat Union and of the European Democrat Union. Its representatives in the European Parliament sit in the European People's Party/European Democrats group.

Socialist Party
Parti Socialiste (PS)

Address. 10 rue de Solférino, 75333 Paris 07
Telephone. (+33–1) 4556–7700
Fax. (+33–1) 4556–7953
Email. infops@parti-socialiste.fr
Website. www.parti-socialiste.fr
Leadership. Lionel Jospin (political leader); Françoisl Hollande (first secretary)

The party was founded in April 1905 as the French Section of the Workers' International (*Section Française de l'Internationale Ouvrière*, SFIO), being a merger of the Socialist Party of France (inspired by Jules Guesde) and the French Socialist Party (led by Jean Jaurès). The SFIO sought to rally pre-1914 labour opposition to war within the Second International, but a majority of the party regarded World War I as one of French national defence (one notable exception being Jaurès, who was assassinated in July 1914 by a nationalist fanatic). At its December 1920 congress in Tours the SFIO was split when a majority of delegates voted for membership of the Communist International (Comintern) and thus founded the →French Communist Party (PCF), while the minority maintained the SFIO as a non-revolutionary party. Having supported →Radical Party administrations from 1924, the SFIO became the largest party in the 1936 elections under the leadership of Léon Blum, who formed a Popular Front government with the Radicals, supported externally by the PCF. In opposition from 1938, the "reconstituted" SFIO went underground following the French surrender to Nazi Germany in 1940; it played an active part in the resistamce and also participated in the Algiers Committee set up by Gen. Charles de Gaulle as leader of the Free French.

Following the liberation of France in 1944, the SFIO joined a provisional government headed by de Gaulle, becoming the third largest Assembly party in the 1945 elections with 139 seats, behind the PCF and the (Christian democratic) Popular Republican Movement, and retaining this ranking in both 1946 elections, although its representation fell to 93 seats. Eschewing alliance with the PCF in favour of centre-left cooperation, the SFIO headed the first two Fourth Republic governments (under Blum in 1946–47 and Paul Ramadier in 1947), instituting an extensive nationalization programme. In 1947 Vincent Auriol of the SFIO was elected President of France, and in the 1951 Assembly elections the SFIO recovered to 104 seats. Although it fell back to 95 seats in the 1956 elections, in 1956–57 the then SFIO leader, Guy Mollet, was Prime Minister of the Fourth Republic's longest-lasting government, playing a major role in the creation of the European Economic Community. However, internal dissension and defections over the role of the Mollet government in the 1956 Suez crisis and over the SFIO's support for the retention of French sovereignty in Algeria were intensified by the participation of Mollet and other SFIO ministers in the national unity government formed by de Gaulle on the collapse of the Fourth Republic in mid-1958. In Assembly elections in November 1958 the

SFIO slumped to 40 seats, following which the party leadership supported the installation of de Gaulle as President of the Fifth Republic. The SFIO nevertheless refused to participate in the Gaullist-led government formed in January 1959 and was to remain in opposition for over two decades.

Having recovered somewhat to 66 seats in the 1962 Assembly elections, the SFIO in September 1965 joined with the Radicals and the small Convention of Republican Institutions (CIR) to form the Federation of the Democratic and Socialist Left (*Fédération de la Gauche Démocratique et Socialiste*, FGDS). Elected president of the FGDS was the CIR leader, François Mitterrand, who as leader of the former Democratic and Social Union of the Resistance (*Union Démocratique et Sociale de la Résistance*, UDSR) had participated in successive Fourth Republic governments and had opposed Gen. de Gaulle's return to power in 1958. As candidate of the FGDS, and supported by the PCF and other left-wing formations, Mitterrand took de Gaulle to the second round in the 1965 presidential elections (held by direct suffrage), winning 44.8% of the vote. In the 1967 Assembly elections the FGDS benefited from a second-round support pact with the PCF, winning a total of 121 seats. However, in further elections held in June 1968 in the wake of the May "events" the FGDS retained only 57 seats, amid a landslide to the Gaullists. This defeat heightened disagreements among the FGDS constituent groupings, in light of which Mitterrand resigned from the presidency in November 1968, shortly before the Radicals decided against joining a unified party based on the FGDS.

Notwithstanding the effective collapse of the FGDS, the SFIO pursued the goal of a broader "new" socialist party on the basis of a merger with Mitterrand's CIR and the Union of Clubs for the Renewal of the Left (*Union des Clubs pour le Renouveau de la Gauche*, UCRG). On the eve of the May 1969 presidential elections an intended founding congress of the new party was held at Alfortville, but the CIR refused to back the presidential candidacy of SFIO right-winger Gaston Defferre (mayor of Marseilles), who went on to score an ignominious 5% of the vote in the first round. Subsequently, the CIR did not participate when a new Socialist Party was proclaimed at the Issy-les-Moulineaux congress of July 1969, as a merger of the SFIO and the UCRG, whose leader, Alain Savary, was elected PS first secretary (and Mollet bowed out after 23 years as SFIO leader). However, renewed efforts to bring the CIR into the new party reached a successful conclusion in June 1971 with the holding of a "congress of socialist unity" at Epinay, with Mitterrand being elected first secretary of the enlarged PS.

Under Mitterrand's leadership, the PS adopted a strategy of "union of the left", signing a common programme with the PCF and the Left Radical Movement (MRG) (→Left Radical Party) in June 1972 which featured wide-ranging nationalization plans. On the basis of the programme, the left made major gains in the Assembly elections of March 1973, when the PS and the MRG (standing as the Union of the Socialist and Democratic Left) jointly returned 102 deputies, including 89 Socialists. The following year Mitterrand contested presidential elections as the agreed candidate of virtually the entire left in both rounds of voting, but was narrowly defeated by Valéry Giscard d'Estaing (Independent Republican) in the second round, receiving 49.2% of the vote. In 1975 the PS was further enlarged when it was joined by the minority wing of the Unified Socialist Party (*Parti Socialiste Unifié*, PSU) led by Michel Rocard and also by a "third component" consisting mainly of affiliated members of the Socialist-led CFDT trade union federation. However, the steady growth of PS strength engendered serious strains in the party's alliance with the PCF, culminating in the failure of the left to agree on a revised common programme for the March 1978 Assembly elections. In that contest reciprocal support arrangements were operated by the left-wing parties in the second round, but the PS tally of 103 seats (plus 10 for the MRG) was disappointing, even though the PS could claim to have become the strongest single party with around 23% of the first-round vote.

Standing as the PS candidate in the May 1981 presidential elections, Mitterrand obtained 25.9% in the first round, which was also contested by PCF and MRG candidates; backed by the entire left in the second round, he defeated incumbent Giscard d'Estaing by 51.8% to 48.2%, thus becoming President at his third attempt. Assembly elections in June 1981 gave the Socialists their first-ever absolute majority, of 285 seats out of 491. The new PS-led government, which included MRG and PCF ministers, was headed by Pierre Mauroy, while Lionel Jospin succeeded Mitterrand as PS first secretary. The Mauroy government proceeded to implement extensive nationalization measures, but was quickly obliged to abandon plans for state-led economic expansion in the interests of containing inflation and preventing currency depreciation. The PCF withdrew from the government in July 1984 when Mauroy was replaced as Prime Minister by Laurent Fabius, who faced considerable unrest in the party and country over the government's switch to orthodox economic policies. In the Assembly elections of March 1986 (held under proportional representation) the PS lost its absolute majority, although it remained the largest party with 206 seats and 31.6% of the vote. It accordingly went into opposition to a centre-right coalition headed by Jacques Chirac of the (Gaullist) →Rally for the Republic (RPR), with whom President Mitterrand was obliged to govern in uneasy political "cohabitation".

In opposition, the PS undertook a reassessment of its economic policies, including its traditional commitment to state ownership, and advocated a broad alliance of "progressive" forces against the centre-right. But the party's relations with the PCF remained badly strained, not least because of the growing influence of the "moderate" PS faction led by Rocard, who favoured realignment towards the centre. In the 1988 presidential elections Mitterrand was opposed in the first round by two Communist candidates (one official) as well as by Chirac for the RPR and Raymond Barre for the centrist Union for French Democracy (UDF, →New Union for French Democracy, NUDF). He headed the poll with 34.1% of the vote, whereupon all the left-wing parties backed him in the second round, in which he easily defeated Chirac by 54.01% to 45.98%. In new Assembly elections in June 1988 (for which constituency-based majority voting was reinstated), the PS increased its representation to 260 seats out of 577, short of an overall majority but sufficient to underpin a PS-led government headed by Rocard that included the MRG and independent centrists. Immediately after the presidential contest, former Prime Minister Mauroy succeeded Jospin as PS first secretary.

Legislative setbacks and disagreements with Mitterrand provoked Rocard's resignation in May 1991 and his replacement by Édith Cresson (PS), who became France's first woman Prime Minister. She failed to stem plummeting support for the government and was replaced in April 1992 by Pierre Bérégovoy, a Mitterrand loyalist and hitherto Finance Minister. In January 1992, moreover, former Prime Minister Fabius, also a Mitterrand loyalist, was elected to succeed Mauroy as PS first secretary, following an extraordinary party congress in December 1991 at which delegates had accepted that only free-market policies could achieve economic growth. The Bérégovoy government had some success in restoring stability, and in September 1992 secured referendum approval of the controversial Maastricht Treaty on European union, albeit by a very narrow majority. But public disquiet at continuing economic recession was aggravated by a series of corruption and other scandals involving prominent PS politicians.

The PS went down to a widely-predicted heavy defeat in the March 1993 Assembly elections, retaining only 54 seats on a 17.6% first-round vote share and going into opposition to another "cohabitation" government of the centre-right. In

the immediate aftermath, Rocard took over the PS leadership from Fabius and embarked upon an attempt to convert the party into a broader-based social democratic formation oriented towards the centre. However, unresolved internal party divisions contributed to a poor performance in the June 1994 European Parliament elections, in which the PS list managed only 14.5% (and 15 of the 87 French seats), compared with 23.6% in the 1989 contest. Rocard immediately resigned as party leader and was succeeded by Henri Emmanuelli, a former National Assembly president identified with the traditional PS left. Straitened financial circumstances were highlighted by the sale of the PS headquarters building in Paris, while the implication of PS officials in further corruption cases added to the party's problems in the run-up to the 1995 presidential elections.

An attempt to draft the outgoing president of the European Commission, Jacques Delors, as the PS presidential candidate was rebuffed by Delors himself in December 1994. In February 1995 a special PS congress in Paris endorsed former party leader Jospin as presidential candidate, on the basis of a primary election among party members in which the former Education Minister had easily defeated Emmanuelli, winning 66% of the votes. Closely supported by Delors, Jospin confounded the pundits by mounting an impressive presidential campaign and heading the first-round voting in April 1995, with 23.3% of the vote. He was defeated by Chirac of the RPR in the second round, but his tally of 47.4% as the candidate of the left served to restore Socialist morale after two years of turmoil. In June 1995 Jospin replaced Emmanuelli as PS first secretary and declared his intention to carry out a complete reform of party structures and policies before the next Assembly elections. The previous month Emmanuelli had received a suspended one-year prison sentence for receiving illicit campaign contributions as PS treasurer in the 1980s. Seven months after leaving office, Mitterrand died in January 1996 at the age of 79.

In late 1996 the PS national council decided that women candidates would be presented in at least 30% of constituencies in the next Assembly elections. In April 1997 the PS issued a joint declaration with the PCF setting a 35-hour week (with no loss of wages) and a halt to major privatizations as central objectives of a left-wing government, although the two parties made no formal electoral pact. In contrast, the PS entered into agreements with both the Left Radicals and the →Greens not to oppose a number of their candidates in the first round of voting. The outcome of the polling in May-June 1997 gave the PS a large relative majority of 241 seats (on a first-round vote share of 23.5%) and the left as a whole an overall majority. Facing a period of "cohabitation" with the Chirac presidency, Jospin formed a coalition government dominated by the PS and also including the PCF, the Greens, the Left Radicals and the →Citizens' Movement (MDC) led by former PS minister Jean-Pierre Chevènement.

From January 1998 the Elf-Aquitaine affair, centring on financial corruption allegations against former PS Foreign Minister Roland Dumas (then the president of the Constitutional Council), caused increasing embarrassment for the party. The PS-led government, and Jospin in particular, nevertheless retained a high popularity rating, despite continuing high unemployment, as it implemented key policies such as the 35-hour week. The PS and its allies outpolled the centre-right in regional elections in March 1998, and the following month the government secured parliamentary approval for French entry into the single European currency, relying on centre-right votes to counter PCF and MDC opposition. In May 1998 PS candidate Odette Casanova narrowly prevented the far-right →National Front (FN) from regaining its single Assembly seat in Toulon, on the strength of second-round support from the centre-right parties. She repeated the feat in September 1998 when the by-election had to be re-run.

The PS contested the June 1999 European Parliament

elections in alliance with the Left Radicals and the MDC, their joint list heading the poll with 22% of the vote and 22 of the 87 French seats, of which the PS took 18. For the elections the PS had subscribed to a joint manifesto of EU Socialist parties which had sought to bridge the gap between the pro-market "third way" line of the British →→Labour Party and the continental preference for the social market economy. In a speech to EU Socialists in October 1999, however, Jospin distanced the PS from the Anglo-Saxon model, asserting that "the market economy does not find harmony of its own accord" and that "it needs rules".

In 2000 the PS was tarnished by new disclosures about its involvement in corrupt party funding in Paris allegedly orchestrated by the RPR when Chirac was mayor in 1977–95. It also faced the embarrassment in early 2001 of the trial of Dumas, his former mistress and five others in the Elf corruption case, which exposed some of the web of illegal payments by the company at home and abroad, notably under the Mitterrand presidency and often at his instigation. The trial did not prevent a PS senator, Bertrand Delanoë, being elected mayor of Paris in local elections in March 2001, bringing the left to power in the capital for the first time since the 1871 Commune. But the PS and the other government parties fared poorly elsewhere in the country, being outvoted by the centre-right parties by 46.9% to 44.9%, while several PS ministers failed in mayoral candidacies.

The conviction of Dumas and four other defendants in the Elf trial in May 2001 led to further difficulties for the PS. On bail pending his appeal, Dumas the following month told the press that two senior ministers in the current government, Foreign Minister Hubert Védrine and Employment and Solidarity Minister Elisabeth Guigou, had been complicit, as Mitterrand aides in the 1990s, in Elf's illicit payments practices. Both ministers denied any impropriety. Also in June 2001, Prime Minister Jospin was forced to admit that he had been a committed Trotskyist before joining the PS in 1971, although he did not respond to press claims that he had been an "entryist" and had remained a member of what became the →International Communist Party (PCI) at least until the mid-1970s. Jospin had previously denied reports of his radical past, so that his image of integrity suffered a blow in advance of his expected candidacy in the 2002 presidential elections.

The PS is a member party of the Socialist International. Its representatives in the European Parliament sit in the Party of European Socialists group.

Workers' Struggle
Lutte Ouvrière (LO)

Address. BP 233, 75865 Paris 18
Leadership. Arlette Laguiller & François Duborg (spokespersons)

Descended from a Trotskyist group which in 1940 rejected membership of the French Committees for the Fourth International, the LO was founded in June 1968 as the direct successor to *Voix Ouvrière* following the banning of the latter and other student-based Trotskyist organizations in the wake of the May 1968 "events". It contested the 1973 Assembly elections jointly with the Communist League (itself later succeeded by the →Revolutionary Communist League, LCR), but the two groups put up separate candidates in the 1974 presidential elections, in which Arlette Laguiller of the LO won 2.3% in the first round. Having failed to return any of its 470 candidates in the 1978 Assembly elections on a platform that featured robust condemnation of the common programme of the mainstream left, the LO reverted to alliance with the LCR for the 1979 European Parliament elections, their joint list (*Pour les États-Unis Socialistes d'Europe*) winning 3.1% of the vote but no seats.

Laguiller again won 2.3% in the first round of the 1981 presidential contest and all 158 LO candidates were again unsuccessful in the ensuing Assembly elections. Standing on its own, the LO slipped to 2.1% in the 1984 Euro-elec-

tions, while Laguiller managed only 1.99% in the first round of the 1988 presidential contest and her party failed to win representation in either the 1988 or the 1993 Assembly elections. In her fourth presidential bid in 1995, however, Laguiller had her best result to date, winning 1,616,566 votes (5.3%) in the first round. The LO again won no seats in the mid-1997 Assembly elections, its candidates being credited with about 2% of the first-round vote.

For the June 1999 European Parliament elections the LO entered into a new alliance with the LCR on a platform of opposition to a "capitalist Europe" and in favour of a "Europe for workers". Headed by Laguiller, the joint list achieved an electoral breakthrough, winning 5.2% of the vote and five seats, three of which were taken by the LO. In June 2001 Laguiller was named as the LO candidate for the 2002 presidential elections, which would be her fifth campaign.

The LO/LCR representatives in the European Parliament are members of the European United Left/Nordic Green Left group.

Other National Parties

Anarchist Federation (*Fédération Anarchiste*), umbrella organization of local anarchist cells, rejects electoral politics, has occasionally been linked with acts of violence by extremist groups.

Bonapartist Party (*Parti Bonapartiste, PB*), founded in 1993 to promote the ideas and achievements of Emperor Napoleon Bonaparte.
Leadership. Emmanuel Johans

Civil Society (*Société Civile, SC*), centre-right formation allied with →Rally for the Republic in June 1999 European Parliament elections, returning one representative (Christine de Veyrac), who joined the European People's Party/European Democrats group.
Leadership. Christine de Veyrac

Convention for a Progressive Alternative (*Convention pour une Alternative Progressiste, CAP*), left-wing ecologist movement.
Address. 17-19 rue des Envierges, 75020 Paris
Telephone. (+33–1) 4462–9791
Fax. (+34–1) 4462–9792
Website. www.perso.hol.fr/~cap
Leadership. Gilbert Wasserman

Ecology Generation (*Génération Écologie, GE*), established in 1990 by Brice Lalonde, a presidential candidate for Friends of the Earth (*Amis de la Terre*) and other groups in 1981 (when he received 3.9% of the first-round vote) and subsequently Environment Minister in the 1991–92 government led by Édith Cresson of the →Socialist Party (PS). Then more sympathetic to the Socialists than the rival →Greens, the GE nonetheless refused to enter the subsequent Bérégovoy administration headed by the PS. The GE won 7% of the vote at the March 1992 regional elections, before slipping to less than 1% in the 1993 Assembly elections, despite a reciprocal support agreement with the Greens. Contesting the June 1994 European Parliament poll as an independent list, the GE recovered to just over 2% of the vote, without winning a seat. Following the victory of Jacques Chirac of the →Rally for the Republic (RPR) in the April-May 1995 presidential elections, a former GE member, Corinne Lepage, accepted appointment as Environment Minister in the new centre-right government. In the mid-1997 Assembly elections the GE again failed to win representation, but in the June 1999 European Parliament elections the GE won one seat on the list headed by the RPR, its representative joining the European People's Party/European Democrats group.

Address. 22 rue Daguerre, 75014 Paris
Telephone. (+33–1) 4427–1166
Fax. (+33–1) 4327–0555

Federalist Party (*Parti Fédéraliste, PF*), advocates creation of a federal European state.
Address. 18 place du 8 Septembre, BP 76222, 25015 Besançon 6
Telephone/Fax. (+33–3) 8121–3233
Email. pfed.allen@wanadoo.fr
Website. www.dalmatia.net/parti-federaliste
Leadership. Jean-Philippe Allenbach

Federation for a New Solidarity (*Fédération pour une Nouvelle Solidarité, FNS*), a rightist formation derived from the European Labour Party (*Parti Ouvrier Européen,* POE), created by Argentine-born Jacques Chéminade to support his candidacy in the 1995 presidential elections, in which he finished last of nine first-round candidates, with only 0.3% of the vote.
Leadership. Jacques Chéminade

French and European Nationalist *Party (Parti Nationaliste Français et Européen, PNFE),* a far-right group.
Leadership. Claude Cornilleau

French Nationalist Party (*Parti Nationaliste Français, PNF*), far-right grouping formed in 1983 by a faction of the →National Front opposed to the leadership of Jean-Marie Le Pen.

French Royalist Movement (*Mouvement Royaliste Français, MRF*), anti-left grouping aiming to restore a French monarchy.
Leadership. Jean de Beauregard

Independent Ecological Movement (*Mouvement Ecologiste Indépendant, MEI*), formed by Antoine Waechter, the 1988 presidential candidate of the →Greens, from which he broke away in 1993; critical of the Greens' participation in the post-1997 government headed by the →Socialist Party; Waechter headed an MEI list for the 1999 European Parliament elections which obtained 267,853 votes (1.5%) without winning a seat.
Address. 7 rue du Vertbois, 75003 Paris
Telephone. (+33–1) 4027–8536
Fax. (+34–1) 4027–8544
Email. mei@novomundi.com
Website. www.novomundi.com/mei
Leadership. Antoine Waechter

Internationalist Communist Party (*Parti Communiste Internationaliste, PCI*), Trotskyist grouping founded in 1944, subsequently undergoing various name changes, broke with Fourth International in 1952 and helped to found the rival Fourth International–International Centre of Reconstruction, embraced electoral politics in the 1980s, with minimal impact.
Address. 87 rue du Faubourg Saint-Denis, 75010 Paris
Telephone. (+33–1) 4801–8820
Leadership. Pierre Lambert & Daniel Gluckstein

Liberal Christian Right (*Droite Libérale Chrétienne, DLC*), led by former Defence Minister Charles Millon. Launched at a Paris conference in November 1999 on the basis of "The Right" (*La Droite*) created by Millon in April 1998 following his expulsion from the UDF (→New Union for French Democracy) for having accepted →National Front (FN) support to secure re-election as president of the Rhône-Alpes regional council. Claiming a membership of 20,000, the DLC aspires to become the French equivalent of Germany's Christian Democratic/Social Union (CDU/CSU).

Address. 21 rue de Bourgogne, 75007 Paris
Telephone. (+33–1) 5359–5300
Email. La-Droite@wanadoo.fr
Website. www.la-droite.org
Leadership. Charles Millon (president)

Liberal Party for the Economy, Regions and Environment (*Parti Libéral pour l'Économie, la Région et l'Environment, PLERE*), founded after the 1997 Assembly elections in opposition to the "false right" of the outgoing government and the new left-wing coalition.
Address. 61 rue Falguière, 75015 Paris
Telephone. (+33–1) 4320–9498
Fax. (+33–1) 4320–6560
Email. arbidou@micronet.fr
Website. persoweb.francenet.fr/~arbidou

Modern France (*France Moderne, FM*), political association headed by Alain Juppé, former Prime Minister and former leader of the →Rally for the Republic (RPR), aiming to provide "dynamic opposition" to the post-1997 left-wing government and supportive of President Chirac's aim to be re-elected in 2002
Address. 10 rue Royale, 75008 Paris
Telephone. (+33–1) 4296–8586
Website. www.france-moderne.asso.fr
Leadership. Alain Juppé (president)

Movement of Communist Renovators (*Mouvement des Rénovateurs Communistes, MRC*), a reformist splinter group of the →French Communist Party.
Leadership. Claude Llabrès

Movement of Democrats (*Mouvement des Démocrates, MdD*), founded in 1974 by former Gaullist Foreign Minister Michel Jobert, backed →Socialist Party candidate François Mitterrand in 1981 presidential election.
Address. 96 ave de Nantes, 86000 Poitiers
Telephone. (+33–5) 4988–8035
Fax. (+33–5) 4988–9143
Leadership. Michel Jobert (president)

National Restoration (*Restauration Nationale, RN*), right-wing pro-monarchy formation supporting the claim of the Count of Paris, weakened in 1971 by a breakaway that led to the creation of →New Royalist Action.
Leadership. Guy Steinbach (president)

New Royalist Action (*Nouvelle Action Royaliste, NAR*), founded in 1971 as a splinter group of →National Restoration, advocating the restoration of a progressive monarchy.
Address. 17 rue des Petits-Champs, 75001 Paris
Telephone. (+33–1) 4297–4257
Website. www.mygale.org/10/francesc/royaliste
Leadership. Bertrand Renouvin & Yvan Aumont

Red and Green Alternatives (*Alternatifs Rouge et Verte, ARV*). Founded in November 1989 as a merger of the rump Unified Socialist Party (*Parti Socialiste Unifié,* PSU) and the New Left (*Nouvelle Gauche,* NG), espousing anarcho-syndicalism, internationalism, environmentalism and feminism; dating from 1960, the PSU had remained in existence when a minority faction led by Michel Rocard had joined the →Socialist Party in 1975, while the NG had been founded in 1987 by an expelled "renovator" of the →French Communist Party, Pierre Juquin, who won 2.1% in the 1988 presidential elections.
Address. 40 rue de Malte, 75011 Paris
Telephone. (+33–1) 4357–4480
Fax. (+33–1) 4357–6450
Email. alternatifs@wanadoo.fr
Website. perso.wanadoo.fr/alternatifs

Reformers' Movement (*Mouvement des Réformateurs,*

MdR), founded in 1992 as a new centre-left formation aligned with the →Socialist Party, taking the name of the main centrist umbrella organization of the 1970s; sought to attract centrist voters from what became the →New Union for French Democracy in subsequent elections.
Address. 7 rue de Villersexel, 75007 Paris
Telephone. (+33–1) 4544–6150
Leadership. Jean-Pierre Soisson (president)

Revolutionary Communist League (*Ligue Communiste Révolutionnaire, LCR*), a Trotskyist party founded in 1973 as successor to the Communist League, as whose candidate Alain Krivine won 1.1% of the vote in the 1969 presidential elections; contested Assembly and European elections of the 1970s in alliance with the →Workers' Struggle (LO), which became the stronger of the two. Krivine on his own won 0.4% in the 1974 presidential contest, while in 1988 the LCR backed Pierre Juquin of the New Left (which later joined the →Red and Green Alternative. Having contributed to LO leader Arlette Laguiller's 5.3% first-round vote in the 1995 presidential elections, the LCR joined with the LO in the June 1999 Euro-elections, their joint list winning 5.2% and five seats, Krivine being elected as one of two successful LCR candidates, who joined the European United Left/Nordic Green Left group.
Address. 2 rue Richard Lenoir, 93198 Montreuil
Telephone. (+33–1) 4870–4230
Fax. (+33–1) 4859–2328
Leadership. Alain Krivine

Social and Democratic Renewal (*Rénovation Sociale et Démocratique, RSD*), centre-left formation founded in 1997.
Email. info@rsd.org
Website. www.rsd.org
Leadership. Jean-Louis Laurence

Workers' Party (*Parti des Travailleurs, PT*), extreme left-wing grouping.
Address. 87 rue du Faubourg Saint-Denis, 75010 Paris
Telephone. (+33–1) 4801–8829
Leadership. Yannick Giou

Regional Parties

ALSACE-LORRAINE
Alsace-Lorraine National Forum (*Nationalforum Elsass-Lothringen/Forum Nationaliste d'Alsace-Lorraine*), based in the German-speaking population of Alsace-Lorraine.
Email. geraldmueller@nfel.org
Website. www.geocities.com/~bfel
Leadership. Gerald Müller

Union of the Alsatian People (*Union du Peuple Alsacien/Elsass Volksunion, UPA/EVU*), political movement favouring autonomy for Alsace within the European Union.
Address. BP 75, 67402 Illkirch Graffenstaden
Fax. (+33–3) 8907–9024
Website. www.multimania.com/elsassnet

BRITTANY
Breton Democratic Union (*Unvaniezh Demokratel Breizh/Union Démocratique Bretonne, UDB*), left-oriented party founded in 1964 in quest of complete autonomy for Brittany in the French Republic and European Union by non-violent means; has obtained representation on most main city councils in Brittany, including Nantes, Rennes, Lorient and Saint-Malo, but remains a regional minority party; a member of Democratic Party of the Peoples of Europe–European Free Alliance.
Address. BP 203, 56102 Lorient, Brittany
Telephone/Fax. (+33–2) 9784–8523
Email. christian_guyonvarch@yahoo.fr
Website. www.geocities.com/CapitolHill/2177
Leadership. Christian Guyonvarc'h

Party for the Organization of a Free Brittany (*Parti pour l'Organisation d'une Bretagne Libre, POBL*), proclaiming "the inalienable right of the Breton people freely to rule itself and to become independent again".
Address. BP 4518, 22045 Saint-Brieuc 2
Email. pobl@wordnet.fr
Website. rafale.wordnet.net/~pobl

CORSICA
Corsican Nation (*Corsica Nazione, CN*), electoral coalition of nationalist movements, with linked trade union and social organizations, which claims to have won around 20% of vote in recent Corsican regional elections; highly critical of Corsican autonomy plan adopted by French National Assembly in May 2001.
Address. c/o Assemblée de Corse, BP 215, 20187 Ajaccio Cedex 1
Website. www.corsica-nazione.com
Leadership. P. Andreucci

Independence (*Indipendenza*), separatist political formation founded in May 2001 from a merger of *A Cuncolta Indipendentista*, the political wing of the banned Front for the National Liberation of Corsica–Historic Wing (FLNC-CH), with three other hardline groups (*Corsica Viva, Associu per a Suvranita* and *U Collettivu Naziunale*). Although *A Cuncolta* had been weakened by the arrest of several leaders in 1996–97 on terrorism charges, the FLNC-CH was believed to have become the largest faction of the FLNC following the latter's signature of a ceasefire in December 1999. The new Independence grouping declared that nationalist violence "is given legitimacy by the aggressive line taken by the French state" and vowed to contest the next Corsican elections within the →Corsican Nation alliance on a platform of opposition to the autonomy plan approved by the French National Assembly in May 2001.

National Presence (*Presenza Naziunale*), nationalist formation, whose leader François Santoni in July 2001 called for the release of all Corsican political prisoners held on mainland France and for an alternative to the "government lies" enshrined in the autonomy plan for the island. In August 2001 Santoni was murdered in Corsica by unidentified gunmen.

Union of the Corsican People (*Unione di u Populu Corsu, UPC*), legal pro-autonomy party which has obtained minority representation in the Corsican regional assembly, sometimes in alliance with more militant nationalist groups.
Address. BP 165, 20293 Bastia, Corsica
Telephone. (+33–4) 9532–2787
Fax. (+33–4) 9531–6490

NORMANDY
Normandy Movement (*Mouvement Normand, MN*), formation advocating a self-governing Normandy within the European Union.
Address. Le Gab, Les Bruyères, 27290 Écaquelon
Email. mouvement.normand@wanadoo.fr

Party for Independent Normandy (*Parti pour la Normandie Indépendante, PNI*), seeks an independent Normandy with its political capital at Caen, its industrial capital at Le Havre and its military capital at Cherbourg, to which end it has set up a "provisional government".
Website. www.multimania.com/pni
Leadership. Jérémy Lefèvre & Sylvain Bion

OCCITANIA
Occitania Party (*Partit Occitan, POC*), founded in Toulouse in 1987 to seek "self-government" for the region of southern France where Occitan is spoken; won up to 1.8% of the vote in southern constituencies in 1997 Assembly elections.
Address. Sant Ostian, 43260 St Julien Chapteuil

Telephone/Fax. (+33–4) 7157–6413
Email. poc@multimania.com/poc
Website. www.multimania.com/poc
Leadership. Gustave Alirol

SAVOY

Savoy League (*Ligue Savoisienne/Liga de Saboya, LS*), founded in 1995 with aim of reversing French annexation of Savoy in 1860 and re-establishing it as a sovereign independent state; its secretary-general is a regional concillor.
Address. 2 ave de la Mavéria, 74940 Annecy le Vieux, Savoy
Telephone. (+33–4) 5009–8713
Fax. (+33–4) 5009–9580
Email. ligue@savoie.com
Website. www.ligue-savoie.org
Leadership. Patrice Abeille (secretary-general)

Overseas Departments

Under decentralization legislation enacted in 1982 by the then Socialist-led government in Paris, the four French overseas departments (*départements d'outre-me*, DOM) of French Guiana, Guadeloupe, Martinique and Réunion each have the additional status of a region of France. Each therefore has a regional council (*conseil régional*) that is directly elected for a six-year term from party lists by proportional representation and has increased powers as compared with the previous indirectly-elected bodies. At the same time, the traditional departmental council (*conseil général*) remained in being in each overseas department, these bodies also being directly elected for a six-year term but by majority voting over two rounds in constituent cantons. Each overseas department elects representatives to the National Assembly and the Senate in Paris according to the procedures applicable in metropolitan France (the precise number depending on size of population) and the DOM electorates also participate in French elections to the European Parliament. Political parties active in the overseas departments include local sections of metropolitan parties as well as a number of formations specific to particular departments.

French Guiana

Situated on the northern South American littoral between Suriname and Brazil, French Guiana (*capital*: Cayenne; *population*: 155,000) has been under French control since the 17th century and a recognized French possession since 1817, being accorded departmental status in 1946. Elections to the 31-member regional council on March 15, 1998, resulted as follows: Guianese Socialist Party 11 seats, Rally for the Republic 6, Walawari 2, others 12.

Democratic Socialist Union (*Union Socialiste Démocratique, USD*), small left-of-centre formation.
Leadership. Théodore Roumillac

Guianese Democratic Action (*Action Démocratique Guyanaise, ADG*), left-wing pro-independence party founded c.1981, represented in the regional council in 1986-92 and subsequently in the departmental council, of which Lecante became president.
Address. ave d'Estrées, Cayenne
Leadership. André Lecante

Guianese Democratic Forces (*Forces Démocratiques Guyanaises, FDG*), founded in 1989 by a dissident faction of the →Guianese Socialist Party, became second-largest party in the regional council in 1992 but lost ground sharply

in May 1998, though Othily was re-elected to the French Senate in September 1998.
Leadership. Georges Othily

Guianese National Popular Party (*Parti National Populaire Guyanais, PNPG*), leftist party founded in 1985, supportive of independence for French Guiana, was represented in the regional council in the 1980s.
Address. BP 265, Cayenne
Leadership. José Dorcy

Guianese Socialist Party (*Parti Socialiste Guyanais, PSG*), founded in 1956, consistently the strongest party in the department, for long led by Elie Castor, once officially the departmental section of the metropolitan →→Socialist Party, now autonomous and supportive of autonomy for French Guiana leading to full independence; won 16 regional council seats in 1992, subsequently providing the presidents of both the regional council and the general council, although it lost its National Assembly seat to an independent leftist in 1993; slipped to 11 regional council seats in March 1998 and to five out of 19 departmental council seats, Karam being nevertheless re-elected to the council presidency, whereas Stéphan Phinéra-Horth of the PSG lost the departmental council presidency.
Address. 1 cité Césaire, Cayenne
Leadership. Antoine Karam

Movement for Decolonization and Social Emancipation (*Mouvement pour la Décolonisation et l'Émancipation Sociale, MDES*), advocates independence for French Guiana.
Leadership. Maurice Pindard

New Union for French Democracy (*Nouvelle Union pour la Démocratie Française, NUDF*), departmental section of the metropolitan party, has made little electoral impact despite essaying alliances with the local →Rally for the Republic.
Leadership. R. Chow-Chine

Rally for the Republic (*Rassemblement pour la République, RPR*), departmental section of the metropolitan RPR, supports the constitutional status quo, took a distant third place in the 1992 regional council elections, but retained its National Assembly seat in 1993 and 1997; advanced to six seats in the 1998 regional council elections.
Address. 84 ave Léopold Héder, Cayenne
Leadership. Roland Ho-Wen-Sze

Socialist Party (*Parti Socialiste, PS*), departmental section of the metropolitan party, but eclipsed locally by the autonomous →Guianese Socialist Party.
Leadership. Pierre Ribardière

Walawari, left-wing movement emphasizing non-French aspects of departmental society, won two regional council seats in 1998.
Leadership. Christiane Taubira-Delannon

Guadeloupe

A group of islands located in the Caribbean south-east of Puerto Rico, Guadeloupe (*capital*: Basse-Terre; *population*: 430,000) has been a French possession since the 17th century and was annexed in 1815. Elections to the 41-member regional council on March 15, 1998, resulted as follows: Guadeloupe Objective (OG) 25 seats, Socialist Party 12, Guadeloupe Communist Party 2, various right 2.

Guadeloupe Communist Party (*Parti Communiste Guadeloupéen, PCG*), founded in 1944 as the departmental section of the →→French Communist Party, became independent in 1958, for long favoured retention of departmental status, moved to cautious support for eventual independence in the 1980s as it steadily lost former electoral dominance; weakened by the formation of the →Guadeloupe Progressive Democratic Party, it managed only fifth place in the 1992 regional council elections with three seats and slipped to two in 1998.

Address. 119 rue Vatable, Pointe-à-Pitre
Leadership. Christian Céleste

Guadeloupe Progressive Democratic Party (*Parti Progressiste Démocratique Guadeloupéen, PPDG*), founded in 1991 by dissident members of the →Guadeloupe Communist Party (PCG) and others, outpolled the PCG in the 1992 regional council elections but took only fourth place; despite retaining a National Assembly seat in mid-1997, it lost its representation in the regional council in 1998, although Lubeth was elected president of the departmental council.

Leadership. Marcellin Lubeth & Ernest Moutoussamy

New Union for French Democracy (*Nouvelle Union pour la Démocratie Française, NUDR*), departmental section of the centre-right metropolitan formation; after serious strains in the 1980s it resumed alliance with the →Rally for the Republic for the 1992 regional council elections, participating in the eventual victory of the →Guadeloupe Objective alliance and its further triumph in 1998.

Leadership. Marcel Esdras

Popular Movement for an Independent Guadeloupe (*Konvwa pou Liberayson Nasyon Gwadloup/Mouvement Populaire pour une Guadeloupe Indépendante, KLNG/MPGI*), founded in 1982 as a radical pro-independence movement, later handicapped by the imprisonment in 1985 of then leader Luc Reinette, who was implicated in violent activities (and who later escaped).

Leadership. Simone Faisans-Renac

Popular Union for the Liberation of Guadeloupe (*Union Populaire pour la Libération de la Guadeloupe, UPLG*), founded in 1978 as a semi-underground pro-independence movement, later operating legally in favour of greater autonomy, took a poor sixth place in the 1992 regional council elections.

Leadership. Roland Thesaurus

Rally for the Republic (*Rassemblement pour la République, RPR*), departmental federation of the metropolitan party, supportive of French status, suffered electorally from the defection of the RPR regional council president to the Union for French Democracy in 1986 (→→New Union for French Democracy), but recovered in 1992 as the leading component of the →Guadeloupe Objective (OG) alliance, which won a narrow overall majority in re-run elections in January 1993, although the party took only one of Guadeloupe's four National Assembly seats in 1993 and 1997; the RPR-led GO won an overall majority of 25 regional council seats in March 1998, Michaux-Chevry being re-elected council president.

Address. 1 rue Baudot, Basse-Terre
Leadership. Lucette Michaux-Chevry & Aldo Blaise

Socialist Party (*Parti Socialiste, PS*), departmental federation of the metropolitan party, held the presidency of the regional council from 1986, but was split into two factions for the 1992 elections, the main party winning nine seats and a dissident group led by Dominique Larifla seven; went into regional council opposition after the December 1993 re-run election, but returned one National Assembly deputy (out of four) in March 1993 and retained its dominance of the general council in March 1994 elections; won 12 seats in the 1998 regional council elections.

Address. rés. Collinette 801, Grand Camp, Les Abymes
Leadership. Georges Louisor

Martinique

Located in the Caribbean, Martinique (*capital*: Fort-de-France; *population*: 400,000) came under French control in the 17th century and was annexed in 1790, achieving departmental status in 1946. Elections to the 41-member regional council on March 15, 1998, resulted as follows: Independent Martinique Movement 13, Martinique Progressive Party 7, Rally for the Republic 6, Martinique Forces of Progress 5, Martinique Socialist Party 3, others 7.

Independent Martinique Movement (*Mouvement Indépendantiste Martiniquais, MIM*), pro-independence formation that once aimed to seize power through revolution, obtained increasing support through the 1980s, taking second place in the 1992 regional council election campaigning as the Martinique Patriots (*Patriotes Martiniquais*); after Marie-Jeanne had been returned to the French National Assembly in 1997, the MIM headed the poll with 13 seats in 1998 regional council elections, Marie-Jeanne being elected president.

Address. Mairie de Rivière-Pilote, Martinique
Leadership. Alfred Marie-Jeanne

Martinique Communist Party (*Parti Communiste Martiniquais, PCM*), founded in 1957 when the departmental federation of the fiFrench Communist Party split and the socialist pro-autonomy →Martinique Progressive Party (PPM) was formed; the PCM itself later favoured autonomy, especially after its pro-independence wing broke away in 1984; from 1974 co-operated with the PPM and other left-wing parties, often in government in the department; shared in the electoral decline of French communism in the 1980s, taking fourth place in the 1992 regional council election standing as For a Martinique of Labour; left-wing voting discipline secured the election of Émile Capgras of the PCM as council president, but he lost the post following the further PCM decline in the 1998 regional elections.

Address. rue Émile Zola, Fort-de-France
Leadership. Georges Erichot

Martinique Forces of Progress (*Forces Martiniquaises de Progrès, FMP*), successor to the departmental federation of the centre-left metropolitan →→New Union for French Democracy (NUDF); as the UDF, had been junior partner to the →Rally for the Republic (RPR), their combined forces consistently proving inferior to those of the Martinique left, as after the 1992 regional council elections, in which the RPR/UDF Union for a Martinique of Progress list won the most seats but remained in opposition; the UDF took one of the four Martinique seats in the 1993 French National Assembly elections but lost it in 1997, before winning five seats in the March 1998 regional council elections.

Martinique Progressive Party (*Parti Progressiste Martinique, PPM*), founded in 1957 by a splinter group of the →Martinique Communist Party, eventually overtaking the parent party, Césaire being elected president of the first directly-elected regional council in 1983, retaining the post in 1986; dissension between the PPM pro-autonomy and pro-independence wings weakened the party thereafter, third place being achieved in the 1992 regional council elections; won one of Martinique's four National Assembly seats in 1993 and 1997, as well as holding both departmental seats in French Senate; slipped to seven seats in 1998 regional council elections, but Claude Lise of the PPM was re-elected president of departmental council.

Address. rue André Aliker, Fort-de-France
Leadership. Aimé Césaire & Camille Darsières

Martinique Socialist Party (*Parti Martiniquais Socialiste, PMS*), won three seats in 1998 regional council elections.

Leadership. Louis Joseph Dogué & Ernest Wan Ajouhu

Rally for the Republic (*Rassemblement pour la République, RPR*), departmental federation of the metropolitan party and of similar conservative persuasion, formerly the strongest single party in Martinique but usually in opposition to left-wing alliances; allied with the Union for French Democracy (UDF) in the 1992 regional council elections, their Union for a Martinique of Progress list winning a substantial plurality, although not enough to obtain the council presidency; won two of the department's four National Assembly seats in 1993 and 1997 but slipped to six seats in the 1998 regional council elections standing independently of the UDF (→Martinique Forces of Progress).
Leadership. Anicet Turinay & Pierre Petit

Socialist Federation of Martinique (*Fédération Socialiste de Martinique, FSM*), departmental section of the metropolitan fiSocialist Party, but consistently surpassed electorally by other left-wing parties, securing a poor fifth place for its New Socialist Generation list in the 1992 regional contest and declining further in 1998.
Address. cité la Meynard, 97200 Fort-de-France
Leadership. Jean Crusol

Socialist Revolution Group (*Groupe Révolution Socialiste, GRS*), pro-independence Trotskyist formation founded in 1973, has made little electoral impact despite seeking to build a regional alliance against "colonialist represssion".
Leadership. Gilbert Pago

Réunion

The Indian Ocean island of Réunion (*capital*: Saint-Denis; *population*: 700,000) has been a French possession since the 17th century and an overseas department since 1946. Elections to the 45-member regional council on March 15, 1998, resulted as follows: New Union for French Democracy 8 seats, Réunion Communist Party 7, Socialist Party 6, FreeDOM 5, Rally for the Republic 4, various right 15.

FreeDOM, led by Camille Sudre (formerly a member of the →Socialist Party) and Marguerite (Margie) Sudre, pro-autonomy but conservative movement whose use of English in its title has raised eyebrows in Paris; polled strongly in the 1991 general council and 1992 regional council elections, Camille Sudre (a medical doctor and well-known pirate broadcaster) being elected president of the latter body but later being obliged to face new elections in 1993 because of illegal broadcasts; again returned as the largest single party, FreeDOM secured the election of Margie Sudre (wife of Camille) as regional council president, to which post she added that of metropolitan State Secretary for Francophone Affairs following the advent of a centre-right government in Paris in 1995; in some disarray after the defeat of the metropolitan centre-right in mid-1997, FreeDOM candidates retained only five seats in the 1998 regional council elections.
Leadership. Camille Sudre & Marguerite (Margie) Sudre

Left Radical Party (*Parti des Radicaux de Gauche, PRG*), departmental section of the metropolitan party, supportive of independence for Réunion (unlike the other main left-wing parties).
Leadership. Jean-Marie Finck

Movement for the Independence of Réunion (*Mouvement pour l'Indépendance de la Réunion, MIR*), pro-autonomy formation dating from 1981.

National Front (*Front National, FN*), departmental section of the radical right-wing metropolitan party.
Leadership. Alix Morel

New Union for French Democracy (*Nouvelle Union pour la Démocratie Française, NUDF*), departmental section of the centre-right metropolitan formation, favouring retention of French status, has been allied with the larger →Rally for the Republic (RPR) in recent elections; won eight regional council seats in March 1998, when Poudroux was elected president of the departmental council with some left-wing support.
Leadership. Gilbert Gérard & Jean-Luc Poudroux

Rally for the Republic (*Rassemblement pour la République, RPR*), departmental section of the conservative metropolitan party, favouring retention of French status, for long the leading electoral formation in alliance with what became the →New Union for French Democracy (NUDF), but in local opposition in the 1980s to the combined forces of the left; lost ground in the 1992 and 1993 regional council elections to the new →FreeDOM movement, and to the left in the 1994 general council elections; returned one of Réunion's five National Assembly deputies in 1993 and 1997; won four regional council seats in 1998.
Address. BP 11, 97400 Saint-Denis
Leadership. André-Maurice Pihouée & Tony Manglou

Réunion Communist Party (*Parti Communiste Réunionnaise, PCR*), founded as an autonomous party in 1959 by the departmental branch of the fiFrench Communist Party, disavowed pro-Soviet orthodoxy of metropolitan party, has consistently been the leading left-wing electoral force in Réunion, supporting the successful →Socialist Party (PS) candidate for general council president in 1994; returned one of Réunion's five National Assembly deputies in 1993 and three in 1997; allied with the PS and some conservative elements in the *Rassemblement* for the 1998 regional council elections, it slipped from nine to seven seats, but Vergès (also a metropolitan senator) became council president.
Address. 21bis rue de l'Est, Saint-Denis
Leadership. Paul Vergès & Elie Hoarau

Socialist Party (*Parti Socialiste, PS*), departmental federation of the metropolitan fiSocialist Party, supports retention of departmental status, consistently allied with the stronger →Réunion Communist Party (PCR) against the departmental right, Payet being elected general council president in 1994 with PCR support; returned one of Réunion's five National Assembly deputies in 1993 and 1997; won six seats in March 1998 regional council elections, allied with the PCR and some conservative elements in the *Rassemblement*.
Address. 85 rue d'Après, Saint-Denis
Leadership. Jean-Claude Fruteau & Christophe Payet

Overseas Territories and Collectivities

The French overseas territories (*territoires d'outre-mer*, TOM), namely French Polynesia, the French Southern and Antarctic Territories (with no permanent population), New Caledonia and the Wallis & Futuna Islands, are regarded as integral parts of the French Republic under present arrangements, the three with permanent populations electing representatives to the National Assembly and Senate in Paris and also participating in French elections to the European Parliament. They differ from the overseas departments in that their representative body is the territorial assembly (*assemblée territoriale*) elected by universal adult suffrage) and that they have a greater, although varying, degree of internal autonomy. Also covered below are the two French overseas territorial collectivities (*collectivités territoriales*), namely Mayotte and St Pierre & Miquelon, whose status is explained in the relevant introductions.

French Polynesia

French Polynesia (*capital*: Papeete, Tahiti; *population*: 220,000) consists of some 120 South Pacific islands, including Tahiti, which became a French protectorate in 1847 and a colony in 1860, with the other island groups being annexed later in the 19th century. The territory includes the former French nuclear testing site of Mururoa Atoll. Elections to the 49-member territorial assembly on May 7, 2001, resulted in the People's Front/Rally for the Republic winning 29 seats, the Liberation Front of Polynesia 13 and New Star 7.

Autonomous Patriotic Party (*Pupu Here Ai'a Te Nuina'a Ia Ora*), pro-autonomy rural party formed in 1965, contested 1991 assembly elections as part of the Polynesian Union, by the end of the year joining the territorial government; won one of the two French Polynesia seats in the National Assembly in 1993 but lost it in 1997.
Address. BP 3195, Papeete, Tahiti

Liberation Front of Polynesia (*Tavini Huiraatira/Front de Libération de la Polynésie, FLP*), main pro-independence movement, won four seats in 1991 assembly elections, advancing strongly to 10 in May 1996 and to 13 in May 2001, but remaining in opposition.
Leadership. Oscar Temaru

New Land (*Ai'a Api*), centrist pro-autonomy party founded in 1982, was briefly in territorial government with the →People's Front in 1991, having taken third place in that year's territorial elections; retained five seats in 1996 territorial elections, party leader Émile Vernaudon being elected to the French National Assembly in mid-1997 with support from the People's Front; failed to win representation in May 2001 territorial elections.
Address. BP 11055, Mahina, Tahiti
Leadership. Émile Vernaudon

New Star (*Fe'tia Api*), won one seat in May 1996 territorial assembly elections, improving to seven in May 2001.
Leadership. Boris Léontieff

People's Front (*Tahoeraa Huiraatira, TH*), territorial branch of the metropolitan fiRally for the Republic (RPR), founded in 1971 as a merger of various groups; under assorted names led the territorial government through most of the 1970s and early 1980s, in opposition from 1986, but returned to office under Gaston Flosse on winning a plurality in 1991, first with the support of →New Land and then backed by the →Autonomous Patriotic Party (also linked with the RPR), whose leader became president of the territorial assembly. Flosse survived a 1992 conviction for illegal use of authority, being re-elected to the French National Assembly in 1993 and in 1998 to the Senate. The TH gained overall majorities in the May 1996 and May 2001 territorial elections, so that Flosse remained head of government into the 21st century, despite a further conviction for corruption in November 1999.
Address. BP 471, Papeete, Tahiti
Leadership. Gaston Flosse (president)

Power to the People (*Ia Mana Te Nunaa*), leftist pro-independence party founded in 1976, represented in the territorial assembly in the 1980s.
Address. BP 1223, Papeete, Tahiti
Leadership. Jacques Drollet

Rally of Liberals (*Rassemblement des Libéraux/Pupu Taina*), linked to the metropolitan fiNew Union of French Democracy, favouring the retention of French status.
Address. BP 169, Papeete, Tahiti
Leadership. Michel Law

Te Henua Enata Kotoa, won one territorial assembly seat in May 1996.
Leadership. Lucien Kimitete

Te Tiaraama, founded in 1987 by a faction of the →People's Front, contested the 1991 territorial elections as part of the Polynesian Union headed by the →Autonomist Patriotic Party.
Leadership. Alexandre Léontieff

True Path (*Te Avel'a Mau*), won one territorial assembly seat in May 1996.
Leadership. Tinomana Ebb

Mayotte

The Indian Ocean island of Mayotte or Mahoré (*capital*: Dzaoudzi; *population*: 132,000) has been a French possession since the mid-19th century, remaining such when the other Comoro Islands declared independence from France in 1975. In two referendums in 1976 its mainly Christian population opted for maintenance of the French connection rather than incorporation into the Muslim-dominated Comoros, being granted the special status of "territorial collectivity" pending possible elevation to that of a French overseas department. The island's representative body is its 19-member general council. Elections in March 1997 gave the Mahoré People's Movement 8 seats, the Mahoré Rally for the Republic (RMPR) 5, the Socialist Party 1, various right 5.

Mahoré People's Movement (*Mouvement Populaire Mahorais, MPM*), led by Younoussa Bamana (president of the Mayotte general council) and Marcel Henry (member of the French Senate), articulated majority resistance to incorporation into a Comoro state in the mid-1970s, favouring permanent overseas departmental status; dominant in the local general council, although the party's 1994 overall majority was reduced to a plurality in March 1997 by-elections.
Leadership. Younoussa Bamana & Marcel Henry

New Union for French Democracy (*Nouvelle Union pour la Démocratie Française, NUDF*), local section of the centre-right metropolitan formation, unrepresented in the island's general council, but has returned Mayotte's National Assembly deputy in recent elections.
Leadership. Henri Jean-Baptiste

Party for the Mahoran Democratic Rally (*Parti pour le Rassemblement Démocratique des Mahorais, PRDM*), founded in 1978, favours Mayotte's incorporation into the Comoro Republic, finding little local support for this aim.
Leadership. Daroueche Maoulida

Mahoré Rally for the Republic (*Rassemblement Mahorais pour la République, RPR*), local federation of the conservative metropolitan party, favouring departmental status, rose to five seats in the general council in March 1997 by-elections.
Leadership. Mansour Kamardine

Socialist Party (*Parti Socialiste, PS*), local branch of the metropolitan PS.

New Caledonia

The New Caledonia archipelago of Pacific islands (*capital*: Nouméa; *population*: 200,000) has been a French possession since 1853. In recent years local politics have been dominated by a demand for the severance of the French connection by groups representing indigenous Melanesians

(Kanaks), forming about 45% of the population, and the equally insistent demand of French and other settler groups that French status should be retained. Under complex and frequently changing arrangements instituted to accommodate local aspirations, there are currently three autonomous provincial assemblies (North, South and Loyalty Islands), whose members make up an overall territorial congress. In a November 1998 referendum New Caledonian voters gave 71.9% approval to an accord between the French government and the main territorial parties providing for a gradual transfer of powers to local bodies and for a referendum on independence within 15 to 20 years.

Elections on May 9, 1999, resulted in the 54 seats in the territorial congress becoming distributed as follows: Rally for Caledonia in the Republic 24, Kanak Socialist National Liberation Front 18, Federation of Pro-independence Coordinating Committees 4, National Front 4, Kanak Socialist Liberation 1, others 3.

A New Caledonia for All (*Une Nouvelle Calédonie pour Tous, NCPT*), founded in 1995 to support retention of French status on the basis of reconciliation of competing aspirations, took second place in South province elections of July 1995 and third place overall.
Leadership. Didier Leroux

Caledonia Tomorrow (*Calédonie Demain, CD*), right-wing grouping created by dissidents of the →Rally for Caledonia in the Republic and the →National Front.
Leadership. Bernard Marant

Caledonian Generation (*Génération Calédonienne, GC*), founded in 1995 to rally the younger generation in opposition to corruption.
Leadership. Jean Renaud Posap

Develop Together to Construct the Future (*Développer Ensemble pour Construire l'Avenir, DEPCA*), pro-reconciliation grouping that won two seats in North province in 1995.

Federation for a New Caledonian Society (*Fédération pour une Nouvelle Société Calédonienne, FNSC*), founded in 1979 as moderate pro-autonomy alliance of Caledonian Republican Party (PRC), Democratic Union (UD), New Caledonian Union (UNC) and Wallis and Futuna Movement (MWF).
Leadership. Jean-Pierre Aïfa

Federation of Pro-independence Co-ordinating Committees (*Fédération des Comités de la Coopération pour l'Indépendance, FCCI*), founded in 1998 by a dissident group of the →Kanak Socialist National Liberation Front (FLNKS), won four seats in the May 1999 territorial congress elections, opting to join a coalition government headed by the →Rally for Caledonia in the Republic (RPCR) and including the FLNKS.
Leadership. Raphael Mapou & Léopold Jorédie

Front for the Development of the Loyalty Islands (*Front pour le Développement des Îles Loyautés, FDIL*), won one seat in Loyalty Islands province in 1995 elections.

Kanak Socialist Liberation (*Libération Kanak Socialiste, LKS*), led by Nidoïsh Naisseline, pro-independence Melanesian grouping based in the Loyalty Islands, where it won one seat in 1995 on a list called Kanak Future, retaining the seat in 1999.

Kanak Socialist National Liberation Front (*Front de Libération Nationale Kanak Socialiste, FLNKS*), established in 1984 by radical elements of a pre-existing Independence Front, including the Caledonian Union (UC) and Kanak Liberation Party (PALIKA); prominent in pro-independence

agitation in late 1980s and early 1990s, it helped to secure the restoration of New Caledonia to UN list of non-self-governing territories in 1986. The Front accepted the 1988 proposals of Socialist government in Paris for New Caledonia to be divided into three autonomous regions (two dominated by Kanaks), but the assassination in 1989 of then FLNKS leader Jean-Marie Tjibaou and his deputy by a Kanak militant demonstrated the perils of compromise. The FLNKS won pluralities in the North and Loyalty Islands provinces in the 1995 elections, but the dominance of the →Rally for Caledonia in the Republic (RPCR) in the populous South province confined the FLNKS to second place in the territorial congress. It gave quaified support to the 1998 Nouméa devolution accord and again took a strong second place in the May 1999 territorial elections, opting to join a coalition government headed by the RPCR.
Leadership. Déwé Gorodey, Rock Wamytan & Paul Neaoutyine

National Front (*Front National, FN*), territorial section of radical right-wing metropolitan party, won two South province seats in 1995.
Leadership. Guy George

National Union for Independence (*Union Nationale pour l'Indépendance, UNI*), pro-independence competitor of the →Kanak Socialist National Liberation Front in North province, where it won five seats in July 1995 elections.

Oceanic Union (*Union Océanienne, UO*), conservative formation founded in 1989, based in community originating from Wallis and Futuna Islands.
Leadership. Michel Hema

Popular Congress of the Kanak People (*Congrès Populaire du Peuple Kanak, CPPK*), pro-independence grouping founded in 1992 as successor to United Kanak Liberation Front (*Front Uni de Libération Kanak, FULK*), which had been associated with numerous acts of violence and had rejected 1988 accord with Paris government establishing provincial structure.
Leadership. Yann Céléné Uregeï

Provisional Committee for the Defence of Republican Principles of French New Caledonia (*Comité Provisoire pour la Défense des Principes Républicains de la Nouvelle Calédonie Française, CPDPRNCF*), founded in September 1998 by pro-French elements opposed to the constitutional accord approved by referendum two months later.

Rally for Caledonia in France (*Rassemblement pour une Calédonie dans la France, RCF*), strongly supportive of French status, won two South province seats in 1995.

Rally for Caledonia in the Republic (*Rassemblement pour la Calédonie dans la République, RPCR*), territorial section of the conservative metropolitan fiRally for the Republic, allied with local branches of component parties of centre-right New Union for French Democracy, represents both *caldoches* (established settlers) and *métros* (recent immigrants), favours retention of French status, has consistently been the leading electoral force, providing not only the territorial congress president but also the islands' representatives in the French National Assembly and Senate. It remained dominant in the May 1999 territorial congress elections, assembling majority support for the election of Jean Leques (RPCR) as New Caledonia's first President under the 1998 devolution accord. Leques resigned in March 2001, however, and was succeeded the following month by Pierre Frogier at the head of a coalition which again included the pro-independence →Kanak Socialist National Liberation Front (FLNKS) as well as the →Federation of Pro-independence Co-ordinating Committees (FCCI).

Address. BP 306, Nouméa
Leadership. Pierre Frogier

United Kanak Liberation Front (*Front Uni de Libération Kanak, FULK*), activist wing of the Melanesian liberation movement, associated with numerous acts of violence, rejected 1988 accord with Paris government establishing provincial structure; in 1992 launched Popular Congress of the Kanak People (*Congrès Populaire du Peuple Kanak, CPPK*) in quest for complete independence for New Caledonia.
Leadership. Yann Céléné Uregei

St Pierre & Miquelon

St Pierre & Miquelon consists of eight islands off the Canadian Newfoundland coast (*capital*: Saint-Pierre; *population*: 6,750) that have been French possessions since the 17th century and have a population of French stock. Their elevation in 1976 from the status of overseas territory to that of overseas department generated a local campaign for reversion to territorial status with special elements, leading to legislation in 1984 converting the islands into an overseas territorial collectivity with effect from June 1985. Under these arrangements the islands' 19-member general council is the principal representative body, its members also serving as the territorial assembly. Elections to the general council on March 19 and 26, 2000, resulted in the Socialist Party list winning 12 seats, the New Union for French Democracy list 5 and the Cape of the Future list 2.

Cape of the Future (*Cap sur l'Avenir*), local branch of the metropolitan →→Left Radical Party (PRG), won only two seats in the 2000 general council elections, although it took 34% of the first-round vote.
Leadership. Annick Girardi

New Union for French Democracy (*Nouvelle Union pour la Démocratie Française, NUDF*), local section of centre-right metropolitan formation. For long overshadowed electorally by the local →Socialist Party, it turned the tables in March 1994 with its Archipelago Tomorrow (*Archipel Demain*) list in St Pierre, which together with the allied Miquelon Objectives (*Objectifs Miquelonnais*) list won 15 of the 19 council/assembly seats; elected president of the council, leader Gérard Crignon resigned in June 1996 and was succeeded by Bernard Le Soavec, defined politically as "various right". In the 2000 elections Archipelago Tomorrow, now also designated Forward St Pierre (*En Avant St Pierre*, retained only five seats with 29% of the first-round vote. The NUDF has held the islands' National Assembly seat since 1986, Crignon being the deputy.
Leadership. Gérard Grignon

Rally for the Republic (*Rassemblement pour la République, RPR*), local section of conservative metropolitan formation, participated in 1994 in the victorious Archipelago Tomorrow coalition, which lost power in 2000. Reux retained the islands' seat in French Senate in 1998.
Leadership. Victor Reux

Socialist Party (*Parti Socialiste, PS*), local section of the metropolitan fiSocialist Party, for long the majority party in the general council, led the successful campaign against departmental status. In March 1994 its St Pierre & Miquelon 2000 list in St Pierre and the allied Future Miquelon (*Miquelon Avenir*) list led by Jean de Lizarraga won only four general council/territorial assembly seats and went into opposition. It returned to power in the March 2000 elections using the designation Together to Build (*Ensemble pour Construire*), winning 12 of the 19 seats with 37% of the first-round vote.
Address. 2 rue Sœur Césarine, 97500 St Pierre & Miquelon
Leadership. Marc Plantagenest & Karine Claireaux

Wallis & Futuna Islands

Situated in the Pacific Ocean north of Fiji and west of Western Samoa, the Wallis & Futuna Islands (*capital*: Mata-Utu; *population*: 15,000) became a French protectorate in 1842 but were never formally annexed. The islands are governed by a French administrator assisted by a 20-member territorial assembly elected by universal adult suffrage for a five-year term. There are also three traditional kingships, of Wallis, Sigave and Alo, exercising limited local powers. Assembly elections on March 16, 1997, and by-elections on Sept. 6, 1998, resulted in the Rally for the Republic holding 11 seats and leftists and independents 9.

Left Radical Party (*Parti des Radicaux de Gauche, PRG*), territorial section of the centre-left metropolitan party, held the islands' seat in the French National Assembly until 1997.
Leadership. Kamilo Gata

New Union for French Democracy (*Nouvelle Union pour la Démocratie Française, NUDF*), territorial section of metropolitan centre-right party, known locally as *Luakaetahi.*

Rally for the Republic (*Rassemblement pour la République, RPR*), territorial section of the conservative metropolitan formation, dominant in recent territorial elections. Victor Brial of the RPR was elected president of territorial assembly following the March 1997 elections and also won the islands' National Assembly seat later that year; the RPR's 1997 tally of 14 assembly seats was reduced to 11 in September 1998 by-elections called because of irregularities in 11 constituencies.
Leadership. Clovis Logologofolau & Victor Brial

Union for Wallis and Futuna (*Union pour Wallis et Futuna, UWF*), alliance of Bright Future (*Taumu'a Lelei*) led by Soane Mani Uhila and the Local Popular Union (*Union Populaire Locale*, UPL) founded in 1985 by Falakiko Gata (hitherto a member of the territorial →New Union for French Democracy and before that of the territorial →Rally for the Republic).
Leadership. Soane Mani Uhila & Falakiko Gata

Gabon

Capital: Libreville

Population: 1,208,000 (2000E)

The Gabonese Republic achieved independence from France in 1960. Executive power is vested in the President, who is elected for a seven-year term and who appoints the Prime Minister and the Council of Ministers. Legislative power is vested in the bicameral parliament, which comprises the 120-member National Assembly

(*Assemblée Nationale*) with a term of five years and the 91-member Senate (*Sénat*) which is elected for a six-year term in single member constituencies by local and departmental councillors. The Gabonese Democratic Party (PDG) was the only legal political party from 1968 to 1990, when a national conference in March–April approved the introduction of a pluralist system and opposition parties were legalized.

In multi-party legislative elections held in September-November 1990 the PDG retained an overall majority in the National Assembly, although seven opposition parties gained representation. The results of the elections in five constituencies were subsequently annulled, and by-elections were held in March 1991 resulting in a redistribution of seats mainly in favour of the ruling party.

The re-election of Omar Bongo as President for the fourth time in December 1993 was disputed by the opposition and resulted in months of political unrest. An agreement between the government and opposition was negotiated in Paris in September 1994 whereby a transitional coalition government was to be installed, with local government elections scheduled to take place in 12 months and legislative elections six months later; also, the electoral code was to be revised. In October 1994 a new government was appointed in which six portfolios were allocated to opposition parties. In a referendum in July 1995, voters overwhelmingly approved the full implementation of the constitutional changes envisaged in the Paris Accords. Municipal elections were held on Oct. 20, 1996, in which the PDG gained a majority, although the opposition parties did well in Gabon's economic capital, Port-Gentil, and northern cities. The polling dates were rescheduled several times for the legislative elections in 1996 owing to organizational difficulties, such as the failure to revise electoral registers in time. Following two rounds of voting on Dec. 15 and 29, the PDG maintained its absolute majority with a total of 85 seats. Elections to the new Senate took place on Jan. 26 and Feb. 9, 1997; the PDG won 54 of the 91 seats while the opposition Rally of Woodcutters came second with 20 seats.

On April 18, 1997, the National Assembly passed a constitutional amendment extending the presidential term from five to seven years and creating the position of Vice-President to be appointed by the Head of State. In the presidential elections on Dec. 6, 1998, President Bongo was re-elected in a single round of voting with 66.6% of the vote against a divided opposition of eight candidates. Although opposition discontent was high as the parties claimed intimidation and alleged electoral malpractice, in contrast to 1993 there was no serious civil disorder following the election.

African Forum for Reconstruction
Forum Africain pour la Réconstruction (FAR)
Address. c/o Assemblée Nationale, Libreville
The FAR was created in early 1992 by an alliance of the following three formations: the Movement for National Regeneration–Originals (*Mouvement de Redressement National*, MORENA-*Originels*), the original MORENA faction which won seven seats in the 1990 legislative elections; the Gabonese Socialist Union (*Union Socialiste Gabonais*, USG), led by Serge Mba Bekale, which initially won four seats in the 1990 elections but subsequently lost one in the March 1991 by-elections; and the Gabonese Socialist Party (*Parti Socialiste Gabonais*, PSG), an extra-parliamentary party. MORENA had been set up in 1981 in clandestine opposition to the then single-party Bongo regime. By early 1990 the party had given rise to dissident factions, the most important of which was what later became the →Rally of Woodcutters. In the December 1993 presidential elections, PSG leader Léon Mboyebi polled less than 2% of the votes cast. In the 1996 National Assembly elections, the USG won two seats and the Movement for National Regeneration-Originals one seat.

Gabonese Democratic Party
Parti Démocratique Gabonais (PDG)
Address. BP 268, Libreville
Telephone. (+241) 703121
Fax. (+241) 703146
Leadership. Omar Bongo; Simplice Guedet Manzela (secretary-general)
Founded by Omar Bongo in 1968, the PDG was the ruling and sole legal party until early 1990, when a national political conference, convened in the light of growing pressure for democratization and widespread unrest, resulted in the acceptance by the President of a multi-party system. In the legislative elections in the latter part of 1990, the PDG won a majority with 63 seats (subsequently increased to 66 seats following the by-elections in March 1991). In December 1993 Bongo was re-elected as President, despite opposition claims of irregularities, with just over 51% of the vote. In the December 1996 National Assembly elections the PDG

increased its majority by winning 85 seats, although some of its candidates had been defeated by opposition mayors in several major cities in the municipal elections a few months earlier. The party was also predominant in the Senate elections in 1997, winning over half of the seats.

President Bongo was re-elected for a fifth consecutive term of office in 1998 and is one the longest serving presidents in sub-Saharan Africa.

Gabonese People's Union
Union du Peuple Gabonais (UPG)
Address. c/o Assemblée Nationale, Libreville
Leadership. Pierre Mamboundou (chairman)
The UPG was founded in 1989 in France as an opposition party whose leader, Pierre Mamboundou, was allowed to return from exile in November 1993 but was prevented from contesting the presidential elections the following month. The party secured a single seat in the 1996 elections to the National Assembly. Mamboundou was in second place in the 1998 presidential election with 16.5% of the vote; he represented an alliance of five smaller opposition parties, the High Council of the Resistance (Haut Conseil de la Resistance, HCR,) which was originally launched by Fr Paul M'ba Abessole of the →Rally of Woodcutters against President Bongo in the aftermath of the 1993 election.

Gabonese Progress Party
Parti Gabonais du Progrès (PGP)
Address. c/o Assemblée Nationale, Libreville
Leadership. Pierre-Louis Agondjo-Okawe (president); Anselme Nzoghe (secretary-general)
Established as an opposition party in early 1990, the PGP won 18 seats in the National Assembly in the legislative elections later that year – a total subsequently increased to 19 following the March 1991 by-elections. Party leader Pierre-Louis Agondjo-Okawe contested the presidential election in December 1993 but, despite achieving third place, gained less than 5% of the votes cast. In December 1996, the PGP came second in the National Assembly elections, although its total number of seats was halved; it secured four seats in the 1997 senatorial elections.

The PGP is a consultative member of the Socialist International.

Rally of Woodcutters
Rassemblement des Bûcherons

Address. c/o Assemblée Nationale, Libreville
Leadership. Fr Paul M'Ba Abessole (leader); Vincent Moulengui Boukosso (secretary-general)

The party name was adopted in February 1991 by what had been the Woodcutters (*Bûcherons*) faction of the Movement for National Regeneration (MORENA) in an effort to more clearly distinguish itself from the parent organization (the original rump of which later joined the →African Forum for Reconstruction). The formation emerged from the 1990 legislative elections as the largest single opposition party, initially with 20 of the 120 seats. Despite its success, the party accused the government of electoral fraud and called for the holding of fresh elections under international supervision. The party boycotted the March 1991 by-elections that led to a reduction in its representation to 17 seats.

In the December 1993 presidential election Fr M'Ba Abessole was the runner-up to President Bongo, securing 26.5% of the votes cast – a result disputed by the opposition on the grounds of alleged electoral malpractice by the government. He subsequently successfully united the main opposition parties into an alliance, the High Resistance Council (*Haut Conseil de la Résistance*, HCR).

In the 1996 municipal elections, the party secured a majority of the seats in Libreville (where Abessole was elected mayor) but was returned with only seven seats in the legislative elections. In the 1997 Senate polling, it came second to the PDG with 20 seats. Before the 1998 presidential election, divisions within the leadership led to a split in the party and the expulsion of its secretary general Pierre-André Kombila Koumba. He was elected to lead a dissident faction within the party and stood as a rival presidential candidate taking fourth place with less than 2% of the vote. M'Ba Abessole, as the official candidate, came third in the election with 13.4% of the vote.

The Woodcutters are associated with the International Democrat Union through the Democrat Union of Africa.

Republican and Democratic Alliance
Alliance Démocratique et Républicaine (ADERE)

Address. c/o Assemblée Nationale, Libreville
Leadership. Mboumbou Ngoma (president; Didjob Divungui-Di-N'Dingue (secretary-general)

Divungui-Di-N'Dingue was an unsuccessful candidate in the 1993 presidential election. ADERE secured one seat in the 1996 National Assembly polling and three seats in the 1997 senatorial elections. Divungui-Di-N'Dingue was appointed to the new position of Vice-President in 1997; he was required to deputize for President Bongo, but with no power of succession.

Other Parties

Circle for Renovation and Progress (*Cercle pour le Renouveau et le Progrès, CRP*), obtained one seat in the 1990 and 1996 National Assembly elections.

Circle of Liberal Reformers (*Cercle des Liberaux Reformateurs, CLR*), formed in late 1992 by a breakaway faction of three members (including a former minister) of the →Gabonese Democratic Party (PDG). It secured two seats in the National Assembly elections in 1996 and one seat in the Senate elections in 1997.
Leadership. Jean-Boniface Assele

Congress for Democracy and Justice (*Congrès pour la Démocratie et la Justice, CJD*), secured one seat in the 1996 National Assembly elections.
Leadership. Jules Bourdes Ogouliguende (president)

Rally for Democracy and Progress (*Rassemblement pour la Démocratie et le Progrès, RDP*), secured one seat in both the 1996 National Assembly elections and the 1997 senatorial elections.
Leadership. Pierre Emboni (president)

Social Democratic Party (*Parti Social-Démocrate, PSD*), formed in 1991. The party leader, who is an economist and former minister, contested the December 1993 presidential election, achieving fourth place but attracting less than 4% of the votes cast. In the December 1998 election he came fifth polling less than 1% of the vote.
Leadership. Pierre Claver Maganga-Moussavou

The Gambia

Capital: Banjul

Population: 1,367,000 (2000E)

Gambia achieved independence from Britain in 1965 and became a republic in 1970. Under the 1970 constitution, executive power was vested in the President, elected by universal suffrage for a five-year term. Legislative power was vested in a unicameral 50-member House of Representatives, comprising 36 members directly for a five-year term, five indirectly elected chiefs, eight non-voting members and the Attorney-General. In July 1994 Sir Dawda Kairaba Jawara, then President of the Republic and leader of the ruling People's Progressive Party (PPP), was overthrown in a bloodless coup by young army officers led by Capt. Yahya Jammeh, who became head of state. An Armed Forces Provisional Ruling Council (AFRPC) was established, the constitution suspended, the House of Representatives dissolved and all political activity banned. Two failed coup attempts against the new regime were reported in November 1994 and January 1995.

A new constitution was approved in a referendum held in August 1996, after which the members of the AFRPC retired from the armed forces and Yahya Jammeh announced his intention to stand for the presidency as the candidate of a newly formed Alliance for Patriotic Reorientation and Construction (APRC). The PPP was banned from contesting the forthcoming presidential and legislative elections, as were the two other parties that had held seats in the pre-coup parliament, while all holders of elective office in the 30 years preceding the 1994 coup were declared ineligible to stand in the elections. Yahya Jammeh (one of four candidates to stand) won the September 1996 presidential election with 55.7% of the vote and was inaugurated for a five-year term as President in the following month.

In January 1997 the APRC won 33 seats in the first elections to a newly created 49-seat unicameral legislature (the National Assembly). Of the remaining elective seats 7 were won by the United Democratic Party (UDP), two by the National Reconciliation Party (NRP), one by the People's Democratic Organization for Independence and Socialism (PDOIS) and two by independent candidates. The other four members of the Assembly were nominated by the President in accordance with the provisions of the new constitution (which took full effect from January 1997), the Assembly being required to select its Speaker and Deputy Speaker from among these nominees.

Alliance for Patriotic Reorientation and Construction (APRC)

Address. GAMSTAR Building, Banjul
Leadership. Yahya Jammeh (chairman)
The ARRC was formed in 1996 to support Yahya Jammeh's campaign in the forthcoming election to restore a civilian presidency; the leader of the 1994 military coup had previously been associated with the July 22 Movement (officially a non-political organization). The presidential election held on Sept. 26, 1996, was won by Jammeh with 55.7% of the vote after a campaign in which the three other candidates suffered many obvious disadvantages (including lack of coverage by the state-owned media). In National Assembly elections held on Jan. 2, 1997, the APRC (the only party with the means to stand in all 45 constituencies) won 33 seats, five of them unopposed, with 52% of the national vote.

National Reconciliation Party (NRP)

Leadership. Hamat N.K. Bah
The NRP was founded in 1996. Its leader, Hamat N.K. Bah, came third in the presidential election of Sept. 26, 1996, with 5.5% of the vote. The NRP won two National Assembly seats, with 2% of the national vote, in the legislative elections of Jan. 2, 1997, having fielded candidates in five constituencies.

People's Democratic Organization for Independence and Socialism (PDOIS)

Leadership. Halifa Sallah, Sam Sarr, Sidia Jatta (leaders)
The PDOIS, a radical socialist grouping, was formed in 1986. Sidia Jatta, who had been an unsuccessful presidential candidate in 1992, came fourth in the September 1996 presidential election, with 2.8% of the vote. The PDOIS won one National Assembly seat in the January 1997 legislative elections, having contested 17 constituencies and won 8% of the total national vote.

United Democratic Party (UDP)

Address. 16 Ecowas Ave., Banjul
Telephone. (+220) 227442
Fax. (+220) 223894
Email. info@udpgambia.org
Website. www.udpgambia.org
Leadership. Col. (retd) Sam Sillah (president); Ousainou Darboe (leader)
The UDP was formed in 1996 by a prominent human rights lawyer, Ousainou Darboe, whose associates included some former members of pre-1994 parliamentary parties. Darboe was the runner-up in the September 1996 presidential election, winning 35.8% of the vote. UDP candidates stood in 34 constituencies in the January 1997 National Assembly elections, in which the party won 7 seats with 34% of the total national vote. Col. (retd) Sam Sillah, who became party president in March 2000, was seen as a future UDP candidate for the presidency of the country.

The UDP is associated with the International Democrat Union through the Democrat Union of Africa.

Other Parties

Gambia People's Party (GPP), a socialist party established in 1986 by a dissident faction of former →People's Progressive Party members. In the 1992 elections the party secured two seats in the House of Representatives, its leader finishing a distant third in the presidential vote. The GPP was banned from contesting the 1996 and 1997 elections.

National Convention Party (NCP), formed in 1975, advocated social reform and a more equitable distribution of national wealth. In the 1992 elections the party won 6 legislative seats, and its candidate came second in the presidential poll with 22 per cent of the votes cast. The NCP was banned from contesting the 1996 and 1997 elections.

People's Democratic Party (PDP), launched in 1991 and advocating agricultural self-sufficiency, mass education and development of the country's infrastructure. Its president was an unsuccessful candidate in the 1992 presidential election.
Leadership. Momodou Lamin Bojang (president)

People's Progressive Party (PPP), founded in 1958 under British colonial rule. The moderate centre-left PPP held a dominant position as the ruling party between independence in 1965 and July 1994. In the legislative and presidential elections in April 1992 the party won 25 of the 36 directly elected seats in the House of Representatives and its then leader, Sir Dawda Kairaba Jawara, was elected for a sixth term of office with over 58 per cent of the votes cast. After the 1994 military coup Jawara fled the country. The PPP was banned from contesting the 1996 and 1997 elections.

Georgia

Capital: Tbilisi

Population: 5,000,000 (2000E)

The Republic of Georgia replaced the Georgian Soviet Socialist Republic in August 1990 and declared independence from the USSR in April 1991, achieving full sovereignty on the demise of the USSR in December 1991, although it did not join the Commonwealth of Independent States (CIS) until March 1994. A new constitution promulgated in October 1995 renamed the country Georgia and provided for an executive President, who is directly elected for a five-year term (once renewable) by universal adult suffrage and who appoints and presides over a Council of Ministers. The constitution provides for a bicameral parliament when the country's territorial integrity is restored. In the interim legislative authority is vested in a unicameral parliament elected for a four-year term and consisting of 150 deputies returned by a system of proportional representation subject to a 7% threshold and a further 85 elected from single-member constituencies by simple plurality. The 7% threshold was established in advance of the 1999 parliamentary elections, after 11 parties and blocs had surpassed the previous 5% barrier in the 1995 elections. The constitution maintains the autonomous status under Georgian sovereignty of Abkhazia, South Ossetia and Adzharia (each containing either a dominant or a significant Muslim population), this provision being specifically rejected by the parliament of the self-proclaimed sovereign republic of Abkhazia.

In legislative elections on Oct. 31 and Nov. 14, 1999, the Citizens' Union of Georgia (SMK) won 132 seats (with 41.7% of the proportional vote), the All-Georgian Union for Revival 58 (25.2%), Industry Will Save Georgia 15 (7.1%), the Labour Party 2 (6.7%) and independents 16. In addition, 12 Abkhazia deputies elected in 1992 continued to sit in the legislature. In presidential elections held on April 9, 2000, Eduard Shevardnadze of the SMK was re-elected for a third term with the support of 79.8% of those voting.

All-Georgian Union for Revival
Sruliad Sakartvelos Aghordzinebis Kavshiri (SSAK)

Address. 7 Gogebashvili Street, Batumi
Telephone. (+995–222) 76500
Leadership. Aslan Abashidze (chairman)

Founded in 1992 to represent Muslims in the autonomous republic of Adzharia, the SSAK contested the 1992 elections within the broad-based Peace Bloc (which won a narrow plurality). Standing on its own, the party came in third place in the 1995 parliamentary elections, winning a 6.8% vote share and a total of 31 seats. The party subsequently urged the creation of a free economic zone in Batumi, the capital of Adzharia, of which SSAK leader Aslan Abashidze was President.

In July 1999 the SSAK established the "Batumi Alliance" with the →Union of Georgian Traditionalists (KTK), the →Socialist Party of Georgia (SSP), the →People's Party, the 21st Century group of supporters of former President Zviad Gamsakhurdia and a faction descended from the former ruling Georgian Communist Party (GCP) led by Dzhumber Patiashvili. A former GCP first secretary, Patiashvili had come second in the 1995 presidential election with 19.5% of the vote. In the October–November 1999 parliamentary elections, the SSAK and allied parties came in second place with 58 seats on a 25.2% vote share and so became the principal opposition to the ruling →Citizens' Union of Georgia (SMK). In February 2000 Abashidze vacated his parliamentary seat, fearing an attempt on his life by Georgian security agents.

Abashidze opted at the last minute not to run against SMK incumbent Eduard Shevardnadze in the April 2000 presidential election, in which the main opposition mantle was again taken by Patiashvili. Despite being endorsed by Yevgenii Dzhughashvili, Stalin's grandson and leader of the →People's Patriotic Union of Georgia, Patiashvili again came a distant second with only 16.7% of the vote.

Citizens' Union of Georgia
Sakartvelos Mokalaketa Kavshiri (SMK)

Address. 4 Marshal Gelovani Street, Tbilisi
Telephone. (+995–32) 384787
Leadership. Revaz Adamia (parliamentary group chairman); Mikhail Machavariani (general secretary)

The SMK was established in November 1993 by President Eduard Shevardnadze, who had come to power in March 1992 with the assistance of a Military Council which had ousted Zviad Gamsakhurdia two months earlier. Under Soviet rule Shevardnadze had been first secretary of the Georgian Communist Party for 13 years until being appointed USSR Foreign Minister and a full CPSU politburo member in 1985; a leading reformer and close associate of Mikhail Gorbachev, he had resigned from both posts in 1990, warning that the USSR was in danger of becoming a dictatorship. Shevardnadze told the SMK's founding congress that the formation would be an alliance of parties retaining their individual policy programmes, but would act together on legislative issues.

The SMK quickly attracted other pro-democracy and pro-market formations into its ranks. In November 1995 Shevardnadze was re-elected President with 76.8% of the popular vote, while in concurrent legislative elections the SMK became the dominant party in the new Assembly with 107 out of 231 seats filled. The party increased its advantage in the 1999 parliamentary elections, winning 132 seats filled (with 41.7% of the vote) on a platform promising an improvement in economic conditions, wage increases and assured payment of state pensions.

In the April 2000 presidential election, which was boycotted by the leader of the main opposition →All-Georgian Union for Revival (SSAK), Shevardnadze again identified the improvement of economic and social conditions as his primary aim and was re-elected with a further overwhelming majority of 79.8% of those voting. The new SMK government was headed by Georgi Arsenishvili, who said that its external priorities would be admittance to the European Union and NATO.

Following the presidential election, a number of SMK and allied deputies, including the 12-strong Abkhazeti Bloc representing ethnic Georgian refugees from Abkhazia, resigned from the SMK parliamentary group in protest against government policy decisions. In October 2000 some of the defectors formed what became the →New Right Party. In September 2001 Shevardnadze resigned from the SMK chairmanship, acknowledging the validity of the longstanding opposition contention that the post was incompatible with being President.

The SMK is an observer member of the Socialist International.

Industry Will Save Georgia (IWSG)
Mretsveloba Gadaarchens Sakartvelos

Address. c/o Sakartvelos Parlamenti, ul. Rustaveli, Tbilisi
Leadership. Giorgi Topadze (chairman)

The pro-business IWSG, which uses the initials of its English title, was launched in advance of the 1999 parliamentary elections by brewery owner Giorgi Topadze, who maintained that government taxation policies were damaging Georgian business and forcing dependence of foreign aid. He called for tax reductions and import controls until a stable economy was established. Allied in the elections with the ultra-nationalist Georgia First movement and the Movement for Georgian Statehood, the IWSG won 15 seats with a 7.1% vote share. Its group of deputies adopted the name Entrepreneurs and opted to steer a middle course between opposition and supporting the government of the →Citizens' Union of Georgia.

Labour Party
Shromis

Address. c/o Sakartvelos Parlamenti, ul. Rustaveli, Tbilisi
Leadership. Shalva Natelashvili (chairman)

Founded in 1995, *Shromis* did unexpectedly well in local elections in 1998, winning 9% of the vote. Advocating protection of the socially weak, the creation of a middle class and Georgian membership of Western organizations, the party just failed to surmount the 7% barrier to proportional representation in the October-November 1999 parliamentary elections but won two constituency seats. It claimed that its failure in the proportional balloting was due to vote-rigging by the ruling →Citizens' Union of George (SMK). In February 2000 *Shromis* joined the new "Freedom and Democracy" bloc of some 25 mainly extra-parliamentary opposition parties, which urged a boycott of the April 2000 presidential elections.

National Democratic Alliance
Erovnul Demokratiuli Aliansi (EDA)

Address. 21 Rustaveli Street, 380008 Tbilisi
Telephone. (+995–32) 990453
Fax. (+995–32) 999616
Leadership. Irina Sarishvili-Chanturia (leader); Ivane (Mamuka) Giorgadze (political secretary)
The EDA is dominated by the National Democratic Party (EDP), which is descended from a pre-Soviet party of the same name and was re-established in 1988 as a pro-independence grouping with a Christian democratic orientation and favouring restoration of the monarchy as a means of national unification. Allied with the secular Democratic Party, the EDP won 32.6% of the vote in the 1990 republican elections; after independence, however, it took only 12 seats in the 1992 parliamentary elections. Having initially supported Shevardnadze's assumption of power in March 1992, the EDP became critical of his policy of rapprochement with Moscow and also opposed Georgian accession to the Commonwealth of Independent States (CIS) in March 1994.

In December 1994 EDP leader Georgi Chanturia was assassinated when gunmen opened fire on his car in Tbilisi, the EDP subsequently blaming "Russian imperialist forces" and organized criminals for the murder. Chanturia's wife, Irina Sarishvili (a former Deputy Prime Minister), was seriously injured in the attack, but recovered sufficiently to assume leadership of the EDP. In the November 1995 legislative elections the EDP came in second place, winning 7.9% of the proportional vote and 31 seats. In January 1996 the EDP deputies failed in their bid to block ratification of the 1994 friendship treaty with Russia.

For the 1999 parliamentary elections, the EDP established the EDA bloc with the Republican Party and the National Party of Entrepreneurs, but its "Third Way" list won only 4.5% of the proportional vote and no seats.

The EDP is affiliated to the Christian Democrat International.

Socialist Party of Georgia
Sakartvelos Sotsialisturi Partia (SSP)

Address. 41 Leselidze Street, Tbilisi
Telephone. (+995–32) 983367
Leadership. Vakhtang Rcheulishvili (chairman)
The SSP was founded in 1995 on a moderate left-wing programme and joined with the dominant →Citizens' Union of Georgia (SMK) in endorsing the candidacy of Eduard Shevardnadze in the November 1995 presidential election. In the simultaneous parliamentary contest the SSP, with 3.8% of the vote, failed to achieve the 5% minimum required for proportional representation but won four constituency seats. In July 1999 the SSP joined the opposition "Batumi Alliance" headed by the →All-Georgian Union for Revival (SSAK), securing 12 seats within the bloc in the October-November 1999 parliamentary elections.

Thought to be the largest left-of-centre party in Georgia, and claiming a membership of 60,000, the SSP initiated the creation of the Black Sea Assembly of Left-Centre Parties, grouping 12 kindred formations.

Union of Georgian Traditionalists
Kartvel Traditsionalistta Kavshiri (KTK)

Address. c/o Sakartvelos Parlamenti, Tbilisi
Leadership. Akaki Asatiani (chairman)
Advocating the restoration of the Georgian monarchy, the KTK won seven seats in the 1992 parliamentary elections. It

failed to cross the 5% proportional threshold then in force in the 1995 elections (winning 4.2% of the vote), but returned two constituency-based deputies. In July 1999 the KTK joined the opposition "Batumi Alliance" headed by the →All-Georgian Union for Revival (SSAK), securing representation within the bloc in the October–November 1999 parliamentary elections.

Other Parties and Alliances

Agrarian Party of Georgia (*Sakartvelos Agraruli Partia, SAP*), founded in 1994 under the leadership of Roin Liparteliani, who came last in the 1995 presidential elections with 0.4% of the vote.

Christian Democratic Union of Georgia, affiliated to the Christian Democrat International, a strong advocate of private ownership and political pluralism; formed part of October 11 Bloc in the 1992 legislative elections.
Leadership. Irakli Shengelaya

Communist Party of Georgia, one of several self-proclaimed successors to the former ruling party; its chairman failed to secure inclusion on the 2000 presidential election ballot paper.
Leadership. Ivane Tsiklauri (chairman)

David Aghmashenebeli ("the Builder") Party, whose leader was nominated for the 2000 presidential elections but could not meet the registration requirements.
Leadership. Loin Lipartelian

Democratic Georgia Union (*Demokratiuli Sakartvelo, DS*), pro-market party which in the 1992 parliamentary elections formed part of the conservative Peace Bloc (which won 29 seats); failed to secure representation in later elections.
Leadership. Eldar Shengelaya

Georgia Greens, member of European Federation of Green Parties.
Address. 182 Aghmashenebeli Ave, 380012 Tbilisi
Telephone. (+995–32) 952033
Fax. (+995–32) 351674
Email. gagreens@greens.org.ge

Georgian Agrarian Union (*Sakartvelos Agraruli Kavshiri, SAP*), in the 1992 parliamentary elections formed part of the conservative Peace Bloc (which won 29 seats); failed to secure representation in later elections.

Georgian Independent Social Democratic Party, formed in 1999 by a dissident faction of the Georgian Social Democratic Party.
Leadership. David Lomidze (chairman)

Georgian Monarchists' Party (*Sakartvelos Monarchistuli Partia, SMP*), in the 1992 parliamentary elections formed part of the conservative Peace Bloc (which won 29 seats); failed to secure representation in later elections.
Leadership. Temur Zhorzholiani

Georgian National Independence Party, played a leading role in the struggle for independence in 1991, but lost influence subsequently.
Leadership. Irakliy Tsereteli

Georgian Social Democratic Party (*Sakartvelos Sotsial-Demokratiuli Partia, SSDP*), descended from a pre-Soviet Menshevik grouping (founded in 1893) which was dissolved in 1921 after the republic had been incorporated into the USSR. Revived in 1990, the party adopted a cautious approach to the independence issue, supporting the abortive new Union Treaty proposed by Soviet leader Mikhail Gorbachev in 1991. Following independence, the SSDP won only two seats in the October 1992 parliamentary elections and subsequently aligned itself with President Shevardnadze's →Citizens' Union of Georgia. In 1999 the SSDP was weakened by the formation of the breakaway →Georgian Independent Social Democratic Party.

Address. 2 Tskhra Aprilis Street, 380018 Tbilisi
Telephone. (+995–32) 999550
Fax. (+995–32) 987389
Leadership. Yemal Kakhiashvili (secretary-general)

Green Party of Georgia (*Sakartvelos Mtsvaneta Partia*, SMP), originating in 1988 as a section of the All-Georgian Rustaveli Society, an anti-Soviet cultural formation then headed by Tengiz Sigua, who later founded the →National Liberation Front. As in other parts of the then USSR, concern for environmental questions in Georgia had been equivalent to being against the centralized Soviet regime. The Greens won 11 seats in the October 1992 legislative elections, subsequently becoming part of the ruling →Citizens' Union of Georgia in 1993, but later opting for independent opposition. Having failed to win representation in the 1999 parliamentary elections, in February 2000 the SMP joined the new "Freedom and Democracy" bloc of some 25 mainly extra-parliamentary opposition parties, which urged a boycott of the April 2000 presidential elections.

Address. 182 Davit Aghmashenebeli Ave., 380012 Tbilisi
Leadership. Zurab Zhvania

Ilia Chavchavadze Society, founded in 1987, named after an aristocratic Georgian nationalist of the late Tsarist period, won seven seats in the 1992 elections, but none in later elections. It tried and failed to nominate Gia Chkhikvadze for the 2000 presidential elections.

Leadership. Tamara Chkheidze

Lion All-Georgian Political Association (*Lemi Sruliad Sakartvelos Politikuri Gaertianeba*), founded in 1989, based in the mountain district of Svaneti, advocating the transfer of resources to that region. It won one seat in the 1995 parliamentary elections.

Leadership. Akaki Gasviani (chairman)

Mdzleveli National Political Union, for which architect Avtandil Djoglidze contested the 2000 presidential election, winning only 0.1%.

National Ideology Party, whose leader was nominated for the 2000 presidential elections but withdrew before polling and endorsed Eduard Shevardnadze of the →Citizens' Union of Georgia.

National Independence Party (*Erovnuli Damoukideblobis Partia, EDP*), founded in 1988, obtained 32.6% of the vote in the last Soviet-era elections in 1990, but declined to four seats in October 1992 and one in 1995 and 1999. In 2000 the party joined the "Freedom and Democracy" opposition bloc of extra-parliamentary parties.

Leadership. Irakli Tsereteli

National Liberation Front (*Erovnuli Gantavisuplebis Pronti, EGP*), founded in 1993 by Tengiz Sigua (a former head of state) and Tengiz Kitovani, who had both been instrumental in overthrowing the Gamsakhurdia regime in January 1992 but had fallen out with President Shevardnadze after his return to power in March 1992, being opposed to any concessions to Abkhazian separatism. In February 1994 it was announced that Kitovani's *Mkhedrioni* (Horsemen) paramilitary force had been dissolved and incorporated into the regular Georgian army. In January 1995, however, Kitovani mustered a 350-strong EGP force which marched to "liberate" Abkhazia before being intercepted by government troops. The episode resulted in Kitovani being arrested and the EGP banned. A further crackdown on the *Mkhedrioni* followed the assassination attempt of President Shevardnadze in August 1995.

Leadership. Tengiz Sigua & Tengiz Kitovani

New Communist Party, registered in June 2001 under the chairmanship of Yevgenii Dzhughashvili (grandson of Josef Stalin), who in 1999 had launched the broader →People's Patriotic Union of Georgia.

Leadership. Yevgenii Dzhughashvili (chairman)

New Right Party, formed as the New Faction in October 2000 by dissidents of the →Citizens' Union of Georgia, renamed in June 2001.

Leadership. David Gamkrelidze (chairman)

Party for the Liberation of Abkhazia, advocating the return of Abkhazia to Georgian control, aligned with the ruling →Citizens' Union of Georgia.

Leadership. Tamaz Nadareishvili

People's Party (*Sakhalkho Partia, SP*, formed in 1996 by a breakaway faction of the →National Democratic Alliance. In July 1999 the SP joined the opposition "Batumi Alliance" headed by the →All-Georgian Union for Revival (SSAK), but contested the October–November 1999 parliamentary elections in alliance with the national Didgori grouping, winning 4.1% of the vote and no seats. A member of the Christian Democrat International.

Leadership. Mamuka Giorgadze (chairman)

People's Patriotic Union of Georgia, pro-Russian formation launched in August 1999 as an alliance of several left-wing parties under the leadership of Stalin's grandson, a former colonel in the Soviet army; backed the unsuccessful candidate of the →All-Georgian Union for Revival in April 2000 presidential elections.

Leadership. Yevgenii Dzhughashvili (chairman)

Progressive Party of Georgia, whose chairman won 0.1% in the 2000 presidential elections on a platform of rejecting imported economic and economic models.

Leadership. Vazha Zhghenti (chairman)

Reformers' Union of Georgia–National Concord (*Sakartvelos Reformatorta Kavshiri–Erovnuli Tankhmoba, SRK-ET*), liberal centrist party dating from the foundation of the SRK in 1993 under the leadership of Bakur Gulua (a Deputy Premier). Standing on a platform of pro-market reform and close relations with Russia in the 1995 elections, the broader SRK-ET included the Sportsmen's Union of Georgia (*Sakartvelos Sportsmenta Kavshiri*, SSK) led by Edisher Machaidze and the Kolkheti Georgian Citizens' Political Association (*Sakartvelos Mokalaketa Politikuri Gaertianeba Kolkheti*) led by Miron Subeliani. The alliance took only 2.9% of the vote in the party list section but won two single-member seats.

Leadership. Bakur Gulua (chairman)

Union for a Law-Governed State (*Sakhelmtsipoebriv Samartlebrivi Gaertianeba, SSG*), founded in August 1995 on a centrist platform, the SSG won one constituency seat in the parliamentary elections towards the end of the year. Its leader was chairman of the previous legislature's legal committee.

Leadership. Shalva Natelashvili (chairman)

Union of Georgian Nationalists, tried and failed to nominate philologist Gia Mamaladze for the 2000 presidential elections.

Union of Social Justice of Georgia (*Sakartvelos Sotsialuri Samartlianobis Kavshiri, SSSK*), in the 1992 parliamentary elections formed part of the conservative Peace Bloc (which won 29 seats); failed to secure representation in later elections.

United Communist Party of Georgia (*Sakartvelos Ertiani Komunisturi Partia, SEKP*), launched in mid-1994 as an attempted merger of various factions claiming descent from the Soviet-era Georgian Communist Party (GCP). As the ruling party during the Soviet era, the GCP had been less enmeshed in corruption and abuse of power than its counterparts in other Soviet republics. It had nevertheless been dissolved in August 1991 in the wake of the failed hardliners' coup in Moscow, and its leaders had shifted their support to other parties. Following independence, Communist organizational structures were maintained by the Communist Workers' Party and the Alliance of Communists of Georgia. Despite the creation of the SEKP, unity of former GCP elements proved difficult to achieve. Standing on a conservative/nationalist platform, SEKP leader Maj.-Gen. Panteleimon Giorgadze came fourth in the November 1995 presidential elections with only 0.5% of the vote. In the parliamentary elections a list called the "United Communists and Social Democrats" failed to win representation, as did a "United Communist Party (Stalin) and Workers' Union" list in 1999, its vote being only 1.4%. The SEKP candidate in the 2000 presidential elections, Kartos Gharibashvili, managed only 0.3%. A party congress in December 2000 called for the rehabilitation of Stalin as "the most gifted political leader of the 20th century".
Address. 45 Chodrishvili Street, Tbilisi
Telephone/Fax. (+995–32) 953216
Leadership. Maj.-Gen. Panteleimon Giorgadze (first secretary)

United Republican Party (*Gaertianebuli Respublikuri Partia, GRP*), founded in 1995 as a merger of the Georgian Popular Front (GPF), the Charter 1991 Party and the Republican Party. The GPF had been launched by Nodar Natadze in 1989 to work toward "a free and democratic society and the restoration of Georgia's complete state independence", its leader heading the parliamentary group which opposed President Gamsakhurdia prior to his ejection in January 1992. In the October 1992 legislative elections the GPF had formed part of the October 11 Bloc (which won 27 seats), subsequently giving qualified support to President Shevardnadze. In the 1995 parliamentary elections the GRP failed to surmount the then applicable 5% barrier for proportional seats, but won one constituency seat. It later joined in opposition demands for the withdrawal of Russian troops from Georgian territory (including Abkhazia). It failed to win representation in the 1999 elections and in February 2000 joined the multi-party "Freedom and Democracy" opposition bloc.
Leadership. Nodar Natadze (chairman)

Unity Bloc (*Ertoba*), formed in 1992 under the leadership of Mikheil Naneishvili, encompassing the Liberal Democratic Party (*Liberalur Demokratiuli Partia*, LDP) and the All-Georgian Party of Peace and Freedom (*Sruliad Sakartvelos Mshvidobisa da Tavisuplebis Partia*, SSMTP); the alliance won 14 seats in the October 1992 parliamentary elections, but none in subsequent contests.

Workers' Union of Georgia, contested the 1999 parliamentary elections on an unsuccessful joint list with the →United Communist Party of Georgia.
Leadership. Vakhtang Gabunia (chairman)

Germany

Capital: Berlin **Population:** 83,000,000 (2000E)

The Federal Republic of Germany (FRG) was established in 1949 in the three Western zones of post-World War II occupation (British, US and French), achieving full sovereignty in May 1955. The FRG's Basic Law (constitution) defined it as "a democratic and social federal state" with a bicameral parliament consisting of (i) a lower house (*Bundestag*) directly elected for a four-year term by universal adult suffrage, and (ii) an upper house (*Bundesrat*) indirectly constituted by representatives of the legislatures of the FRG's constituent states (*Länder*). Executive power was vested in the federal government headed by a Chancellor elected by the *Bundestag*, while the largely ceremonial President (head of state) is elected for a five-year term by a Federal Assembly (*Bundesversammlung*) made up of the *Bundestag* deputies plus an equal number of delegates nominated by the *Länder* parliaments. The reunification of Germany in October 1990 was achieved by the FRG's absorption of the five eastern *Länder* (Brandenberg, Mecklenburg-West Pomerania, Saxony, Saxony-Anhalt and Thuringia) of the former Soviet-occupied and Communist-ruled German Democratic Republic, and also of Berlin (previously under four-power administration). The post-1990 FRG thus consists of 16 *Länder*, with a federal structure still governed by the 1949 Basic Law, under which each *Land* has a parliament exercising substantial powers in the economic and social fields. The FRG was a founder member of what is now the European Union, its membership being extended to the five eastern *Länder* at reunification. Germany elects 99 members of the European Parliament.

The *Bundestag* is formed by a combination of direct elections from 328 single-member constituencies and the proportional allocation of a theoretically equal number of seats to party lists according to their share of the vote. Proportional seats are only allocated to parties winning at least 5% of the national vote or to those returning three deputies directly in any one electoral district (i.e. *Land*). In the 1994 *Bundestag* elections the 328 directly-elected seats were supplemented by 344 proportional seats (for a total complement of 672), the 16 additional "supraproportional" mandates being required to achieve overall proportionality.

In 1954 Germany became the first West European country to introduce direct public funding of political parties. Under legislation enacted in July 1967, political parties are defined as being a constitutionally necessary element of a free democratic order and as contributing to the formation of the national political will, by influencing public opinion, encouraging participation in public life and training citizens for public office. On these grounds, state funding is granted to political parties or independent candidates obtaining at least 0.5% of the national party-list vote or 10% in any electoral district, payable retrospectively in the next electoral period. Under an amendment to the 1967 law effective from January 1994, parties and independent candidates are entitled to annual payments for each vote received in federal, state and European Parliament elections, at a rate of DM1.30 up to 5 million votes and DM1 for each additional vote above that figure. They are also allocated DM0.50 to match every DM1 that they receive from members' contributions or donations, although the total amount of state aid may not exceed a party's income from such sources in the previous year. In 2000 the global sum available in state aid to parties was capped at DM245 million (about $116 million), the parties' share being calculated in proportion to their entitlement if the above rules had been fully applied, so that the Social Democratic Party of Germany obtained DM93,432,647 (about $44 million) and the Christian Democratic Union DM79,524,889 (about $37 million). Separate state aid is paid to foundations associated with the main parties, although such bodies must maintain their organizational independence and not use such funding for party political purposes.

Elections to the *Bundestag* on Sept. 27, 1998, resulted as follows: Social Democratic Party of Germany (SPD) 298 seats (40.9% of the vote), Christian Democratic Union (CDU) 198 (28.4%), Christian Social Union (CSU) 47 (6.7%), Alliance 90/The Greens 47 (6.7%), Free Democratic Party (FDP) 43 (6.2%), Party of Democratic Socialism (PDS) 36 (5.1%).

Each of the 16 *Länder* has its own parliament (*Landtag*, or *Bürgerschaft* in the case of Bremen and Hamburg), elected for a four- or five-year term, the most recent results being as follows:

Baden-Württemberg (March 25, 2001) – CDU 63, SPD 45, FDP 10, Greens 10
Bavaria (Sept. 13, 1998) – CSU 123, SPD 67, Greens 14
Berlin (Oct. 21, 2001) – SPD 44, CDU 35, PDS 33, FDP 15, Greens 14
Brandenburg (Sept. 5, 1999) – SPD 37, CDU 25, PDS 22, German People's Union 5
Bremen (June 6, 1999) – SPD 47, CDU 42, Greens 10, German People's Union 1
Hamburg (Sept. 23, 2001) – SPD 46, CDU 33, Law and Order Offensive Party 25, Greens 11, FDP 6
Hesse (Feb. 7, 1999) – CDU 50, SPD 46, Greens 8, FDP 6
Lower Saxony (March 1, 1998) – SPD 83, CDU 62, Greens 12
Mecklenburg-West Pomerania (Sept. 27, 1998) – SPD 27, CDU 24, PDS 20
North Rhine–Westphalia (May 14, 2000) – SPD 102, CDU 88, FDP 24, Greens 17
Rhineland-Palatinate (March 25, 2001) – SPD 49, CDU 38, FDP 8, Greens 6
Saarland (Sept. 5, 1999) – CDU 26, SPD 25
Saxony (Sept. 19, 1999) – CDU 76, PDS 30, SPD 14
Saxony-Anhalt (April 26, 1998) – SPD 47, CDU 28, PDS 25, German People's Union 16
Schleswig-Holstein (Feb. 27, 2000) – SPD 41, CDU 33, FDP 7, Greens 5, South Schleswig Voters' Union 3
Thuringia (Sept. 12, 1999) – CDU 49, PDS 21, SPD 18

Alliance 90/The Greens
Bündnis 90/Die Grünen

Address. Platz vor dem Neuen Tor 1, 10115 Berlin
Telephone. (+49–30) 284–420
Fax. (+49–30) 2844–2210
Email. info@gruene.de
Website. www.gruene.de
Leadership. Fritz Kuhn & Claudia Roth (co-chairpersons); Kerstin Müller & Rezzo Schlauch (parliamentary group leaders); Reinhard Bütikofer (general secretary)

The Greens first emerged in West Germany in the 1970s at state and local level. A number of these disparate groups came together at a Frankfurt conference in March 1979 to form the Alternative Political Union, The Greens (*Sonstige Politische Vereinigung, Die Grünen*), which was given a federal structure under the rubric The Greens at a Karlsrühe congress in January 1980. A programme adopted in March 1980 called for a worldwide ban on nuclear energy and on chemical and biological weapons, the non-deployment of nuclear missiles in Europe, unilateral disarmament by West Germany, the dismantling of NATO and the Warsaw Pact, and the creation of a demilitarized zone in Europe. It also advocated the dismantling of large economic concerns into smaller units, a 35-hour week and recognition of the absolute right of workers to withdraw their labour.

Having taken only 1.5% of the vote in the 1980 federal elections, the Greens broke through to representation in 1983, winning 5.6% and 27 lower house seats. They progressed to 8.2% in the 1984 European Parliament elections and to 8.3% in the 1987 federal elections, winning 42 seats. Prominent in the Greens' rise was Petra Kelly, whose charismatic leadership attracted national publicity and acclaim. However, opposition within the party to "personality politics" contributed to her departure from the joint leadership in April 1984. (Some years later, in October 1992, Kelly and her partner, former army general turned pacifist Gert Bastian, were found dead in their Bonn apartment; according to the German police, Kelly had been shot by Bastian, who had then killed himself.)

Divisions also surfaced between the Greens' "realist" wing (*Realos*), favouring co-operation with the →Social Democratic Party of Germany (SPD), and the "fundamentalists" (*Fundis*), who rejected any compromises with other formations. In December 1985 the "realist" Greens of Hesse joined a coalition government with the SPD (the first such experience for both parties), but this collapsed in February 1987 after the Green environment minister, Joschka Fischer, had unsuccessfully demanded that the state government should halt plutonium processing at a plant near Frankfurt. The Hesse experience strengthened the "fundamentalist" wing at the Greens' annual congress in May 1987, when it obtained eight of the party's 11 executive seats. By 1989, however, the *Realos* had regained the initiative, in alliance with a "Fresh Start" (*Aufbruch*) group led by Antje Vollmer which had sought to mediate between the contending factions.

In late 1989 a Green Party (*Grüne Partei*) was launched in East Germany, being at that stage opposed to German reunification. It joined with the Independent Women's League (*Unabhängige Frauenbund*) in contesting the March 1990 *Volkskammer* elections, winning 2.2% of the vote and eight seats. Unwilling to join forces with the West German Greens, the eastern Greens instead joined Alliance 90, which had been founded in February 1990 by a number of East German grassroots organizations, including the New Forum (*Neues Forum*) and Democracy Now (*Demokratie Jetzt*), on a platform urging "restructuring" of the GDR along democratic socialist lines, rather than German unification or the importation of capitalism. In the all-German *Bundestag* elections of December 1990 Alliance 90 secured eight seats by surmounting the 5% threshold in the former GDR, even though its overall national vote was only 1.2%. In contrast, the western Greens, with an overall 3.9% share, failed to retain representation.

With German reunification a fact, the western Greens and Alliance 90 gradually resolved their differences, until parallel congresses in Hannover in January 1993 voted to unite under the official name Alliance 90 but with the suffix "The

Greens" being retained for identification purposes. The merger was formalized at a Leipzig congress in May 1983. The Greens' Mannheim congress in February 1994 opted in principle for a "red-green" coalition with the Social Democrats at federal level, although without modifying policies (such as opposition to NATO membership) that were unacceptable to the SPD leadership. In the June 1994 European Parliament elections the Green list took third place with a 10.1% vote share, winning 12 of the 99 German seats. In the October 1994 *Bundestag* elections the Greens achieved a further federal advance, to 7.3% and 49 seats. The new parliamentary arithmetic precluded a coalition with the SPD, but the Green presence was acknowledged by the election of a Green deputy (Antje Vollmer) as one of the *Bundestag*'s four vice-presidents.

In 1995 the Greens registered significant advances in *Länder* elections in Hesse (February), North Rhine–Westphalia and Bremen (May) and Berlin (October), winning a vote share of 10–13% in the four contests. At a Green party conference in Bremen in December 1995, a majority of delegates endorsed the party's traditional opposition to any external military role for Germany, although an unprecedented 38% backed a motion by Joschka Fischer (by now a leading Green deputy in the *Bundestag*) to the effect that German troops could be deployed on UN peacekeeping missions. Further divisions were in evidence at the Greens' March 1998 congress, where delegates responded to Fischer's appeal for "discipline and realism" by calling for Germany's withdrawal from the NATO-led peacekeeping force in Bosnia and by adopting a raft of radical proposals, including the trebling of the price of petrol over a 10-year period.

Ousted from the Saxony-Anhalt parliament in April 1998, the Greens also lost ground in the federal elections in September, slipping to 6.7% of the vote and 47 seats. It nevertheless entered into Germany's first "red-green" federal coalition (in which Fischer became Foreign Minister and Vice-Chancellor, Jürgen Trittin Environment Minister and Andrea Fischer Health Minister), on the basis of a pact with the SPD which included commitments to "ecological tax reform" and withdrawal from nuclear power generation. Strains quickly appeared in the coalition, notably over the SPD's insistence on a 20-year time-span for the phasing-out of nuclear plants. A Green congress in Leipzig in December 1998 approved the lifting of the party ban on members holding both public and party offices and set up a 30-member council to defuse internal policy disputes. But it rebuffed a proposal that the Greens should have a recognized chairperson, so that Fischer's aim of establishing a "normal" organizational structure for the party remained unrealized at that stage. On the other hand, at Fischer's urging, a special Green conference in Bielefeld in May 1999 defeated by 444 votes to 318 a proposal from the party's pacifist wing that the Green ministers should not support the NATO military action against Yugoslavia over Kosovo, thus effectively backing the deployment of German troops outside the NATO area.

In the June 1999 European Parliament elections the Greens fell back to 6.4% of the vote, losing five of their 12 seats. They also lost ground in a series of state elections in 1999-2000, being eliminated from the Saarland parliament in September 1999 and losing ground in the Schleswig-Holstein state elections in February 2000 and in North Rhine–Westphalia in May. The following month a party conference in Münster at last opted for a leadership structure akin to those of other parties, electing Renate Künast and Fritz Kuhn as co-chairpersons. In January 2001 Künast was elevated to the federal government as Minister of Consumer Protection, Nutrition and Agriculture, amidst the onset of "mad cow disease" (BSE) in Germany. She and the Greens got some credit for articulating public concern about BSE, but the bad election results continued in March 2001, when the Green vote fell from 12% to 7.7% in Baden-Württemberg and from 7% to 5.2% in Rhineland-Palatinate.

The Greens' electoral problems in 2000-01 were related to activists' disenchantment with compromises made by the

party in government, notably its agreement to the resumption of German nuclear waste transportation. Also of concern within the party was the content of a federal government agreement to phase out nuclear power generation in Germany by 2021. Although the accord was hailed by Green ministers as the most dramatic abandonment of nuclear power by any major country, many in the party disliked the long phasing-out period and feared that the agreement might never be implemented. Among the wider electorate, the Greens were damaged in early 2001 by revelations about Fischer's youthful career as a militant street-fighter in Frankfurt in the 1970s, not so much by the facts of his radical past but more by his admission that he had not been honest about it.

In June 2001 the Greens came to office in Berlin, joining a coalition with the SPD pending early elections. In late 2001 the Greens participated in state-level coalition governments with the SPD in Berlin, North Rhine–Westphalia and Schleswig-Holstein.

With an official membership of about 50,000 the German Greens are affiliated to the European Federation of Green Parties. The party's representatives in the European Parliament are members of the Greens/European Free Alliance group.

Christian Democratic Union
Christlich-Demokratische Union (CDU)

Address. Klingelhöferstrasse 8, 10785 Berlin
Telephone. (+49–30) 220–700
Fax. (+49–30) 220–70111
Email. post@cdu.de
Website. www.cdu.de
Leadership. Angela Merkel (chairperson); Friedrich Merz (parliamentary group leader); Laurenz Meyer (secretary-general)

The moderate conservative CDU was established in October 1950 as a federal organization uniting autonomous groups of Christian Democrats (both Catholic and Protestant) which had re-emerged in all parts of Germany after World War II, descended in part from the Centre Party founded in the 19th century and prominent in the pre-Hitler Wiemar Republic. Following a strong showing in the first *Länder* elections held in West Germany in 1947, an alliance of these groups, including the →Christian Social Union (CSU) of Bavaria, had become the strongest element in the first *Bundestag* elections in 1949 under the leadership of Konrad Adenauer, who became the first West German Chancellor. On the formation of the CDU in 1950, the CSU remained a separate though allied party in Bavaria, and has generally been regarded as the more right-wing of the two.

The CDU remained in government until 1969, presiding over the blossoming of the "German economic miracle" under the successive chancellorships of Adenauer (until 1963), Ludwig Erhard (1963–66) and Kurt-Georg Kiesinger (until 1969). From 1959, moreover, Heinrich Lübke of the CDU served two five-year terms in the federal presidency. During this period the CDU/CSU tandem was in coalition with the →Free Democratic Party (FDP) until 1957, governed with an absolute *Bundestag* majority until 1961, returned to a coalition with the FDP in 1961–66 and then formed a "grand coalition" with the →Social Democratic Party of Germany (SPD). Having slipped to 46.1% in the 1969 elections, the CDU/CSU went into opposition to an SPD/FDP coalition that was to endure until 1982. The CDU/CSU share of the vote fell to 44.9% in 1972, rose to 48.6% in 1976 and then fell to 44.5% in 1980, when a joint electoral list was headed by Franz-Josef Strauss of the CSU, who had threatened a rupture with the CDU unless he was accepted as the alliance's Chancellor-candidate. Meanwhile, Karl Carstens of the CDU had been elected President of West Germany in May 1979.

The FDP's desertion of the SPD-led coalition in October 1982 enabled the CDU/CSU to form a new government with the FDP under the leadership of Helmut Kohl. In *Bundestag* elections in March 1983 the CDU advanced strongly to

38.2% and 191 seats (and the CSU also gained ground), so that the CDU/CSU/FDP coalition continued in office. In May 1984 Richard von Weizsäcker of the CDU, a former mayor of West Berlin, was elected to succeed Carstens as President. In the January 1987 lower house elections the CDU declined to 34.5% and 174 seats (and the CSU also lost ground), but gains by the FDP enabled Kohl to continue as Chancellor with the same coalition partners. Criticism of Kohl's leadership surfaced at the CDU's congress of November 1987, when he was re-elected chairman (as the only candidate) by his lowest-ever number of delegates' votes. In the June 1989 European Parliament elections the CDU slipped to 29.5% of the national vote.

Confidence in Kohl's leadership was restored by his performance as government leader through the process of German reunification in 1990, after which his position in the CDU was unassailable. In the all-German elections of December 1990 the CDU won 36.7% of the vote overall and took 268 seats in the enlarged 662-member *Bundestag*. Although the combined CDU/CSU share of the vote was the lowest since 1949, an SPD decline enabled Kohl to form a further CDU/CSU/FDP coalition. In the 1990 contest the CDU was confirmed as the strongest party in the eastern *Länder*, although it later lost ground because the Kohl government was blamed for the problems of economic transition. As a dedicated pro-European party, the CDU strongly supported German ratification of the Maastricht Treaty on European union (which was finally completed in October 1993); it also backed moves to amend the German constitution so that German forces could be deployed on UN-approved peacekeeping missions outside the NATO area. In May 1994 Roman Herzog of the CDU was elected President, while in the following month's European Parliament elections the CDU registered 32.0% of the vote, winning 39 of the 99 German seats.

In the October 1994 *Bundestag* elections the CDU slipped to 34.2% and 244 seats (out of 672), sufficient to underpin a further CDU/CSU/FDP coalition under the continued chancellorship of Kohl (who was re-elected CDU chairman in November 1994 with over 94% of delegates' votes at a special congress). However, CDU setbacks in *Länder* elections in 1993–94 meant that the SPD established a majority in the indirectly-elected *Bundesrat* (federal upper house). Further setbacks followed in state elections, but Kohl nevertheless announced in April 1997 that he would stand for a fifth term as Chancellor. He was confirmed as the CDU (and CSU) candidate at a party congress in October 1997, when he at last designated CDU/CSU parliamentary leader Wolfgang Schäuble as his preferred successor.

The September 1998 *Bundestag* elections produced a widely-predicted defeat for Kohl and the CDU, whose vote share fell sharply to 28.2% and seat total to 198, with the result that it went into opposition after 17 years of continuous power. In November 1998 Kohl was succeeded as CDU chairman by Schäuble, who was elected unopposed. In the June 1999 European Parliament elections the CDU advanced strongly to 39.3% of the vote and 43 of the 99 German seats. State elections in 1999 also produced some notable successes for the CDU, as the party orchestrated a nationwide campaign against government plans to abolish Germany's 100-year-old law restricting the right of citizenship to those with German blood.

The CDU was tainted from late 1999 by a major funding scandal surrounding its receipt under Kohl's leadership of large secret donations, apparently in return for favours granted by the CDU-led government. Criminal and parliamentary investigations were launched into such illegal funding, the tentacles of which spread to several CDU state parties. One much-publicized allegation was that the CDU's 1994 election campaign had been largely financed by a "commission" from the French Elf-Aquitaine oil company (then state-owned), paid on the orders of President François Mitterrand (a close friend of Kohl's) for assistance in Elf's purchase of an East German oil refinery. Kohl admitted that

the CDU had operated a secret slush fund under his leadership, but denied any personal corruption and also doggedly refused to name contributors to the fund, saying that he had given his word of honour to keep them secret.

Accepting responsibility for mishandling the scandal, Schäuble resigned as CDU chairman in February 2000 and was succeeded in April by secretary-general Angela Merkel, a Protestant from East Germany who had been an active Communist in her youth. Meanwhile, the CDU had been punished in state elections in Schleswig-Holstein, losing ground in a contest it had been expected to win. Merkel set about repairing the party's image but quickly came into conflict with her successor as secretary-general (and effectively deputy leader), Ruprecht Polenz. The ousting of Polenz in October 2000 and his replacement by Laurenz Meyer appeared to strengthen Merkel, although the following month both she and Schäuble were fiercely criticized by Kohl in his memoirs for trying to discredit him. The CDU was also accused of being racist for proposing in November 2000 that immigrants should accept Germany's "guiding culture" (*Leitkultur*) by learning German and embracing German traditions and law, including equality for women.

The funding scandal rumbled on in early 2001, amidst complex court battles over fines imposed on the CDU by the *Bundestag* Speaker for its past financial transgressions. In February 2001 Kohl agreed to a deal with the public prosecutors under which he paid a DM300,000 fine in return for the dropping of criminal investigations against him. But he continued to face a slow-moving parliamentary inquiry, and in May 2001 criminal charges were filed against former CDU Interior Minister Manfred Kanther and two others for alleged financial improprieties in Hesse.

Meanwhile, state elections in Baden-Württemberg in March 2001 had brought some relief to the CDU, whose vote share rose from 41.4% to 44.8%, in part because of a collapse in support for the far-right →Republicans. But simultaneous polling in Rhineland-Palatinate produced another setback for the CDU, while in June 2001 the CDU was forced into opposition in Berlin amidst revelations of financial incompetence and corruption in the city-state CDU. In late 2001 the CDU governed alone in Saarland, Saxony and Thuringia; it was in coalition with the FDP in Baden-Württemberg and Hesse, with the FDP and the →Law and Order Offensive Party in Hamburg and with the SPD in Brandenburg and Bremen.

With an official membership of 635,000, the CDU is a member of the Christian Democrat International and the International Democrat Union. Its European Parliament representatives sit in the European People's Party/European Democrats group.

Christian Social Union
Christlich-Soziale Union (CSU)

Address. Franz-Josef-Strauss-Haus, Nymphenburger Strasse 64-66, 80335 Munich
Telephone. (+49–89) 1243–0
Fax. (+49–89) 1243–299
Email. landesleitung@csu-bayern.de
Website. www.csu.de
Leadership. Edmund Stoiber (chairman); Michael Glos (federal parliamentary group leader); Alois Glück (Bavarian parliamentary group leader); Thomas Goppel (general secretary)

The CSU was established in Bavaria in January 1946 by various Catholic and Protestant political groups with the aim of rebuilding the economy on the basis of private initiative and property ownership and of restoring the rule of law in a federal Germany. Led by Josef Müller, it won an absolute majority in the first Bavarian *Landtag* elections in December 1946 (with 52.3% of the vote), although the emergence of the separatist →Bavaria Party in the 1950 elections reduced the CSU to a relative majority, obliging it to form a coalition with the state →Social Democratic Party of Germany (SPD). The CSU continued in being on the formation of the →Christian Democratic Union (CDU) in October 1950, it being agreed that the CSU would be the CDU's sister party in Bavaria and that neither would oppose the other at elections. While both parties have espoused essentially the same policies, the CSU is generally reckoned to be more conservative than the CDU. It is also less enthusiastic than the CDU leadership about plans for European monetary union and favours retention of the Deutsche Mark for the foreseeable future rather than German participation in a single European currency.

The post-war CSU/SPD coalition in Bavaria lasted until 1954, when the CSU went into opposition to a four-party government headed by the SPD. Under the leadership of Hanns Seidel, the CSU returned to office in 1957 at the head of a three-party coalition and in 1962 regained an absolute majority in the Bavarian *Landtag*, which it has held ever since. Seidel was succeeded as CSU leader by Franz-Josef Strauss in 1961 and as Bavarian minister-president by Alfons Goppel, who held office from 1962 until 1978. Strauss became the CSU's dominant figure in the CDU-led federal government, serving as Defence Minister from 1956 until being forced to resign in 1963 over the *Spiegel* affair. He returned to government as Finance Minister in the 1966–69 "grand coalition" between the CDU, the CSU and the SPD, but in 1978 opted to become head of the CSU government of Bavaria. Strauss was the unsuccessful CDU/CSU candidate for the chancellorship in the 1980 *Bundestag* elections, in which the CSU vote slipped to 10.3% (from 10.6% in 1976) and its seat total to 52.

Having been in federal opposition since 1969, the CSU returned to government in 1982 as part of a coalition headed by the CDU and including the →Free Democratic Party (FDP). In the 1983 *Bundestag* elections that confirmed the coalition in power the CSU improved to 10.6% and 53 seats, although two CSU deputies later departed to join the far-right →Republicans. In the 1987 elections the CSU slipped to 9.8% and 49 seats but continued its participation in the federal government. Strauss died in October 1988 and was succeeded as CSU leader by Theo Waigel and as Bavarian minister-president by Max Streibl. In the June 1989 European Parliament elections the CSU list took 8.2% of the overall West German vote. In Bavarian state elections in October 1990 the CSU maintained its absolute majority, winning 54.9% of the vote and 127 of the 204 seats.

As Germany moved towards reunification in 1990 the →German Social Union (DSU) was set up in the re-established eastern *Länder* as a would-be sister party of the CSU. However, in the all-German *Bundestag* elections of December 1990 the DSU made minimal impact, while the percentage vote of the Bavaria-based CSU inevitably fell, to 7.1% (8.8% in western Germany), yielding 51 seats out of 662 and enabling the CSU to continue as part of the federal coalition. In the June 1994 European Parliament elections the CSU list took 6.8% and eight of the 99 German seats, while in the Bavarian *Landtag* elections of September 1994 the party won its customary overall majority, although its seat total slipped to 120 and its vote share to 52.8%. The party therefore suffered little from a corruption scandal which had caused the resignation of Steibl as Bavarian minister-president in May 1993 and his replacement by Edmund Stoiber.

The CSU improved its vote share slightly to 7.3% in the October 1994 *Bundestag* elections (although its representation fell to 50 seats) and obtained three portfolios in the re-formed CDU/CSU/FDP federal coalition. In February 1998 it suffered a major defeat when a Bavarian referendum yielded an overwhelming majority in favour of abolition of the state's second chamber, despite CSU advice to the contrary.

The party shared in the federal coalition's defeat in September 1998, slipping to 6.7% of the national vote and to 47 *Bundestag* seats, but retained its overall majority in that month's Bavarian state elections, winning 123 seats on a vote share of 52.9%. Having announced his resignation

after the elections, Waigel was succeeded as CSU chairman by Stoiber in January 1999. The party improved to 9.4% of the vote in the June 1999 European Parliament elections, taking 10 seats.

With an official membership of 177,170, the CSU is affiliated to the Christian Democrat International and the International Democrat Union. Its representatives in the European Parliament sit in the European People's Party/European Democrats group.

Free Democratic Party–The Liberals
Freie Demokratische Partei (FDP)–Die Liberalen
Address. Thomas-Dehler-Haus, Reinhardtstrasse 14, 10117 Berlin
Telephone. (+49–30) 284–9580
Fax. (+49–30) 2849–5822
Email. fdp-point@fdp.de
Website. www.fdp.de
Leadership. Guido Westerwelle (chairman); Wolfgang Gerhardt (parliamentary group leader); Cornelia Pieper (secretary-general)

Strongly based in the farming community, the centrist and secular FDP was founded in December 1948 at a conference in Heppenheim (near Heidelberg) as a fusion of various liberal and democratic *Länder* organizations descended from the German State Party (*Deutsche Staatspartei*) and the more right-wing German People's Party (*Deutsche Volkspartei*, DVP) of the Weimar Republic (1918–33), and more distantly from the People's Party (*Volkspartei*) founded in 1866. The DVP had been revived in Baden-Württemberg in 1945 under the leadership of Reinhold Maier (who became the state's first premier and was later FDP leader in 1957–60) and Theodor Heuss (who became the first FDP leader and was then West Germany's first President, from 1949 until 1959). An attempt in 1947 to create an all-German liberal party had foundered on the opposition of the East German Communists to the participation of the Berlin-based Liberal Democratic Party (LDP), whose enforced support for socialism impelled prominent members, notably Hans-Dietrich Genscher, to flee to the West to join the FDP.

The FDP secured representation in the first West German *Bundestag* elected in 1949, with an 11.9% vote share, and joined a coalition government headed by what became the →Christian Democratic Union (CDU) and also including the Bavarian →Christian Social Union (CSU). It slipped to 9.5% in the 1953 elections and was in opposition in 1956–61, declining further to 7.7% of the vote in the 1957 federal elections. A major advance in 1961, to 12.8%, brought it back to office in a new coalition with the CDU/CSU that lasted until 1966, when the FDP again went into opposition, this time to a "grand coalition" of the CDU/CSU and the →Social Democratic Party of Germany (SPD). Having declined to 9.5% in the 1965 elections, FDP fell back sharply to 5.8% in 1969, but nevertheless joined a centre-left coalition with the SPD. Having succeeded Erich Mende as FDP chairman in 1968, Walter Scheel served as Vice-Chancellor and Foreign Minister from 1969 until being elected West German President in 1974. During this period opposition within the party to the government's *Ostpolitik* caused several FDP deputies, including Mende, to desert to the opposition Christian Democrats. Scheel was succeeded in his party and government posts by Genscher, under whose leadership the FDP slipped to 7.9% in the 1976 elections (from 8.4% in 1972), before recovering to 10.6% in 1980.

The SPD/FDP federal coalition finally collapsed in September 1982 when the Free Democratic ministers resigned rather than accept the proposed 1983 budget deficit. The following month the party joined a coalition with the CDU/CSU, this switch to the right causing internal dissension and the exit of some FDP left-wingers. The party slumped to 6.9% in the 1983 federal elections and failed to secure representation in the 1984 European Parliament contest, its problems including the steady decline of its traditional farming constituency. The election of Martin Bangemann as FDP chairman in 1985 in succession to Genscher (who nevertheless remained Foreign Minister) resulted in the party taking a more conservative tack, on which basis it revived to 9.1% in the 1987 *Bundestag* elections and continued its coalition with the CDU/CSU. In 1988 Bangemann opted to become a European commissioner and was succeeded as FDP chairman by Count Otto Lambsdorff, who won a tight party election despite having been forced to resign from the government in 1984 after being convicted of illegal party financing activities. Having recovered some ground in state elections in the late 1980s, the FDP regained representation in the European Parliament in 1989 (winning 5.6% of the German vote).

On the collapse of Communist rule in East Germany, an eastern FDP sister party was formally established in February 1990. In the East German elections of March 1990 this party was part of the League of Free Democrats (together with the Communist-era LDP under new leadership and the German Forum Party), which took a 5.3% vote share. On the reunification of Germany in October 1990 these eastern elements were effectively merged into the western FDP, enabling the party to make a major advance in the all-German *Bundestag* elections in December 1990, to 11.0% of the overall vote and 79 seats out of 662. Maintaining its federal coalition with the CDU/CSU, the FDP showed electoral buoyancy in 1991 but encountered new difficulties following Genscher's resignation from the government in April 1992, as highlighted by the enforced resignation in January 1993 of the FDP Vice-Chancellor and Economics Minister, Jürgen Möllemann, over a corruption scandal.

In June 1993 Genscher's successor as Foreign Minister, Klaus Kinkel, replaced Lambsdorff as FDP chairman, but he failed to halt a series of electoral failures at state level, while the party slumped to 4.1% in the June 1994 Euro-elections and thus failed to win any seats. Kinkel obtained a reprieve when the FDP unexpectedly retained a *Bundestag* presence in the October 1994 federal elections, winning 47 out of 672 seats on a 6.9% vote share. Despite previous strains over issues such as overseas German troop deployment (which the FDP opposed), the party opted to continue the federal coalition with the CDU/CSU and was rewarded with further electoral failures in Bremen and North Rhine–Westphalia in May 1995, whereupon Kinkel vacated the FDP leadership while remaining Foreign Minister. Elected as his successor at a special party congress in June 1995, Wolfgang Gerhardt distanced himself from Chancellor Kohl on various policy issues, but a further FDP failure in Berlin elections in October 1995 served to intensify internal divisions on the party's future course. In December 1995 the FDP Justice Minister, Sabine Leutheusser-Schnarrenberger, resigned after her party colleagues had backed a government plan to institute electronic surveillance of suspected criminals.

After relaunching itself with a more right-wing orientation in January 1996, the FDP polled strongly in state elections in Baden-Württemberg, Rhineland-Palatinate and Schleswig-Holstein in March, winning representation in all three contests. A party congress in June 1996 confirmed the shift to the right, adopting a new programme which placed less emphasis on civil liberties than previous texts. The FDP shared in the defeat of the ruling coalition in the September 1998 federal elections, slipping to 6.3% of the vote and 43 seats.

In opposition, the FDP again failed to secure European representation in June 1999, winning only 3.0% of the national vote, and also fared moderately in state elections in 1999. It gained ground in Schleswig-Holstein in February 2000 and then had a major success in North Rhine–Westphalia in May, returning to the state parliament with 9.8% of the vote. Nevertheless, increasing criticism of Gerhardt resulted in his resignation as party chairman in January 2001 and his replacement by Guido Westerwelle,

Gerhardt becoming parliamentary group leader. Hitherto FDP secretary-general, Westerwelle quickly announced the termination of the party's longstanding centre-right alignment with the CDU, declaring that the FDP would contest the 2001 federal elections "on its own" with its options open.

The FDP lost ground in state elections in Baden-Württemberg and Rhineland-Palatinate in March 2001, although it remained well above the 5% barrier in each state. In late 2001 the FDP held office in Baden-Württemberg and Hesse (in coalition with the CDU), in Rhineland-Palatinate (in coalition with the SPD), in Hamburg (in coalition with the CDU and the →Law and Order Offensive Party) and in Berlin (in coalition with the SPD and the Greens).

Having an official membership of 63,500, the FDP is a member party of the Liberal International and of the European Liberal, Democratic and Reformist Party (ELDR).

German People's Union
Deutsche Volksunion (DVU)

Address. Postfach 600464, 81204 Munich
Telephone. (+49–89) 896–0850
Fax. (+49-89) 834–1534
Email. info@dvu.net
Website. www.dvu.net
Leadership. Gerhard Frey (chairman)

The extreme right-wing DVU claims not to be a neo-fascist party but has been prominent in anti-foreigner and anti-immigration agitation, contending that the majority of Germans want a "racially pure" country. In 1987 Frey launched a DVU/List D movement (the D signifying *Deutschland* as an electoral alliance which included elements of the →National Democratic Party of Germany and which won one seat in the Bremen state elections of September 1987. In January 1990 the DVU participated in the creation of the →German Social Union in East Germany, although with minimal lasting electoral impact. Following unification the DVU increased its Bremen representation to six seats in 1991 (with 6.2% of the vote) and also won six seats in Schleswig-Holstein in 1992 (with 6.3%).

The DVU backed the unsuccessful →Republicans in the October 1994 federal elections in the wake of reports that the two groups might overcome their longstanding rivalry for the far-right vote. In the May 1995 Bremen elections the DVU declined to 2.5% and lost its representation in the state assembly. It also failed to retain any seats in the Schleswig-Holstein state election on March 1996, taking only 4.3% of the vote. It had more success in the depressed eastern state of Saxony-Anhalt in April 1998, producing the best post-war performance for a far-right party by winning 12.9% of the vote and 16 of the 116 seats.

The DVU obtained only 1.2% of the vote standing in its own right in the September 1998 federal elections; but it returned to the Bremen state parliament in June 1999, winning only 3% of the vote but being awarded one seat because its vote in Bremerhaven was 6%. In September 1999 it returned five members in elections in Brandenburg, giving it representation in three state parliaments.

Law and Order Offensive Party
Partei Rechtsstaatlicher Offensive (PRO, Schill Partei)

Address. Postfach 203138, 20221 Hamburg
Telephone. (+49–40) 2368–6001
Fax. (+49–40) 2368–6003
Email. pro@planet-interkom.de
Leadership. Ronald Barnabas Schill (chairman); Mario Mettbach (first deputy chairman)

The populist PRO was launched in July 2000 by Ronald Schill, a former Hamburg judge who had achieved notoriety for his robust views on law and order, which included support for the death penalty and the castration of sex offenders. Known in the press as the "black sheriff" or "judge merciless" for handing down severe sentences for relatively minor offences, Schill had been dismissed from the

Hamburg bench in 1997 for advocating the restoration of capital punishment for "bestial" murders and contract killings. As leader of the new PRO, he accused the government then in power in Hamburg of failing to deal with the city's spiralling crime rate, claiming that it was ten times higher than that of Munich and closely related to the recent influx of large numbers of immigrants.

The PRO's campaign for the September 2001 elections in Hamburg was boosted by the discovery that three of the suspected perpetrators of the terrorist attacks on the USA on Sept. 11 had lived for a time in Hamburg, whose authorities were accused by Schill of having provided "the best conditions for their work". The results showed that in its first electoral contest the PRO had won 19.4% of the vote and 25 of the 121 seats in the Hamburg parliament, drawing votes in particular from previous supporters of the far-right →German People's Union (DVU). After the elections the PRO joined a coalition with the →Christian Democratic Union and the →Free Democratic Party which ended 44 years of government by the →Social Democratic Party of Germany in Hamburg. Schill became the state interior minister.

Party of Democratic Socialism
Partei der Demokratischen Sozialismus (PDS)

Address. Karl-Liebknecht-Haus, Kleine Alexanderstrasse 28, 10178 Berlin
Telephone. (+49–30) 240–090
Fax. (+49–30) 241–1046
Email. pdspv@pds-online.de
Website. www.pds-online.de
Leadership. Gabrielle Zimmer (chairperson); Roland Claus (parliamentary leader); Wolfgang Gehrcke (general secretary)

The PDS was established under its present name in February 1990 amid the collapse of Communist rule in East Germany, being descended from the former ruling Socialist Unity Party of Germany (*Sozialistische Einheitspartei Deutschlands*, SED), although it sought to throw off this provenance by espousing a commitment to multi-party democracy. The SED itself had been created in April 1946 as an enforced merger of the East German →Social Democratic Party of Germany (SPD) with the dominant Soviet-backed Communist Party of Germany (*Kommunistische Partei Deutschlands*, KPD). The KPD had been founded in December 1918 by the left-wing minority of the SPD and other leftist elements and had played an important opposition role in the inter-war Weimar Republic, usually in conflict with the SPD, until being outlawed on the advent to power of Hitler's Nazi regime in 1933. During the Third Reich many German Communists had taken refuge in Moscow, returning to Germany at the end of World War II to assume power in the eastern Soviet-occupied zone.

In what became the German Democratic Republic (GDR), the SED was effectively the sole ruling party for over four decades, operating through the familiar device of a National Front that included four other "democratic" parties supportive of socialism, namely the Christian Democratic Union, the Democratic Farmers' Party, the Liberal Democratic Party and the National Democratic Party. Walter Ulbricht was elected SED leader in 1950, in which year several leading party members were expelled in the wake of Yugoslavia's break with the Cominform; other were purged in consequence of the major anti-government uprising in East Berlin in 1953. Some of these expellees were rehabilitated in 1956, but further purges followed the Hungarian Uprising later that year. Economic difficulties and the nationalization of agriculture served to increase the exodus of East Germans to the West, to staunch which the authorities erected the Berlin Wall in 1961, extending it along the entire length of the border with West Germany. In August 1968 East German troops participated in the Soviet-led military intervention that crushed the "Prague Spring" in Czechoslovakia.

In May 1971 Ulbricht was replaced as SED leader by Erich Honecker, under whom East Germany normalized its relations with West Germany in 1972 and became a UN member in 1974. In the 1980s Honecker maintained rigid orthodoxy, showing no enthusiasm for the post-1985 reform policies of Mikhail Gorbachev in the USSR. In 1989, however, a rising tide of protest and renewed flight of East German citizens to the West via Hungary resulted in Honecker being replaced in October by Egon Krenz, who himself resigned in December after the historic opening of the Berlin Wall on Nov. 9 had unleashed irresistible pressure for change. Later in December an emergency SED congress abandoned Marxism, added the suffix "Party of Democratic Socialism" to the party's name and elected Gregor Gysi as chairman. A government of "national responsibility" appointed in February 1990 contained a minority of Communists for the first time in East Germany's history, although Hans Modrow of the SED-PDS retained the premiership. Having dropped the SED component from its name, the PDS polled better than expected in multi-party elections in March 1990 (winning 16.4% of the vote), assisted by the personal standing of Modrow. It nevertheless went into opposition to a broad coalition of parties committed to German reunification.

In the all-German *Bundestag* elections of December 1990 the PDS won only 2.4% of the overall vote but scored 11.1% in the eastern *Länder* and was therefore allocated 17 of the 662 seats by virtue of the separate application of the 5% theshold rule to the two parts of Germany. Thereafter the PDS suffered from a tide of disclosures about the evils of the former SED regime, but retained a substantial following among easterners disadvantaged by rapid economic and social change. In February 1993 Gysi was succeeded as PDS chairman by Lothar Bisky, under whom the party polled strongly in elections in the eastern *Länder* in 1993–94. Although the PDS failed to win representation in the June 1994 Euro-elections, in the October 1994 federal elections it increased its national vote share to 4.4% and its eastern share to around 18%, being allocated 30 *Bundestag* seats from the proportional pool by virtue of having returned three candidates in a single electoral district (Berlin).

In January 1995 a PDS congress voted in favour of a "left-wing democratic" programme and voted down the party's Stalinist faction led by Sarah Wagenknecht. In June 1995 the PDS received a financial boost when an independent commission agreed that it could retain a proportion of the former SED's assets. In Berlin legislative elections in October 1995 the PDS advanced to 14.6% of the vote (giving it 34 of the 206 seats), mainly at the expense of the SPD. Whereas the SPD's then leader, Rudolf Scharping, had consistently rejected any co-operation with the PDS, his successor elected in November 1995, Oskar Lafontaine, envisaged building a broad progressive front, including the PDS, to challenge the Kohl government in the next federal elections. The PDS was the only major party to oppose the proposed merger of Berlin and Brandenburg, which voters of the latter rejected in a referendum in May 1996.

Having polled strongly in Saxony-Anhalt in April 1998 (winning 19.6% and 25 seats), the PDS for the first time surmounted the national 5% barrier in the September 1998 federal elections, winning 5.1% of the vote and 36 seats. In simultaneous state elections in Mecklenburg–West Pomerania, moreover, the PDS advanced to 25.5% and 20 seats, on the strength of which it entered government for the first time in the new Germany, as junior coalition partner to the SPD. Having become a supporter of European integration, the PDS entered the European Parliament for the first time in June 1999, winning a 5.8% vote share and six seats. It then registered major advances in eastern state elections, benefiting from the unpopularity of the SPD-led federal coalition and continuing high unemployment in eastern Germany. In polling in Thuringia and Saxony in September 1999 it pushed the SPD into third place by taking, respectively, 21.4% and 22.2% of the vote. In the Berlin elections in October 1999 the PDS won 17.7% and 33 seats. The party was also strengthened in the *Bundestag* by the defection of a left-wing SPD deputy in late 1999, with the result that PDS representation increased to 37 seats.

The PDS moved to a new leadership generation in October 2000, electing Gabrielle Zimmer (45), PDS parliamentary leader in Thuringia, as chairperson in succession to Bisky, while Roland Claus replaced Gysi as federal parliamentary leader. Though a former Communist official, Zimmer was identified with the PDS reformist wing and in April 2001 issued a new strategy document envisaging the party's participation in government and co-operation with the SPD to bring about social change. The SPD immediately rejected such co-operation, but in June 2001 the collapse of the Berlin coalition government of the →Christian Democratic Union (CDU) and the SPD gave the PDS the opportunity to provide the necessary external support to the succeeding minority coalition of the SPD and the Greens.

The PDS members of the European Parliament sit in the European United Left/Nordic Green Left group. The party has an official membership of 90,000.

The Republicans
Die Republikaner

Address. Schmidt-Ott-Strasse 10/A, 12165 Berlin
Telephone. (+49–30) 7909–8310
Fax. (+49–30) 7909–8315
Email. republikaner-bgs@t-online.de
Website. www.rep.de
Leadership. Rolf Schlierer (federal chairman)

The far-right anti-immigration Republicans were established as a party in November 1983 by two former *Bundestag* deputies of the Bavarian →Christian Social Union (CSU) who had criticized the alleged dictatorial style of the then CSU leader, Franz Josef Strauss, particularly as regards the latter's involvement in developing relations with East Germany in contravention of CSU policy. Standing for German reunification, lower business taxes and restrictions on foreigners, the new party was also joined by the small Citizens' Party (*Bürgerpartei*) of Baden-Württemberg. Having won only 3% in their first electoral contest, for the Bavarian *Landtag* in 1986, the Republicans did not contest the 1987 federal elections. Under the leadership of former SS officer Franz Schönhuber, however, the party won 7.5% and 11 seats in the January 1989 Berlin legislative elections. It also did well in the June 1989 European Parliament elections, winning 7.1% and six seats (on a platform of opposition to European integration).

Amid the progression to reunification in 1990, the Republicans' electoral appeal waned. They obtained less than 2% in state elections in North Rhine-Westphalia and Lower Saxony in May 1990, whereupon Schönhuber was briefly ousted from the party chairmanship, recovering the post in July. In the December 1990 all-German elections the party managed only 2.1% (and no seats), while in simultaneous polling it lost its representation in Berlin, falling to 3.1%. The party made a comeback in the Baden-Württemberg state elections in April 1992, winning 10.9% of the vote and 15 seats. In May 1993, moreover, it secured *Bundestag* representation for the first time when it was joined by a right-wing deputy of the →Christian Democratic Union (CDU), Rudolf Krause. In June 1994, however, it failed to retain its European Parliament seats (falling to a 3.9% vote share), while in the October 1994 *Bundestag* elections the Republicans won only 1.9% (and no seats). Prior to the federal polling Schönhuber was again deposed as leader, officially because of an unauthorized meeting with the leader of the →German People's Union, but also because of his negative media image.

In state elections in March 1996, the Republicans again polled strongly in Baden–Württemberg, winning 9.1% and 14 seats, while in Rhineland–Palatinate they improved to 3.5%, without gaining representation. In the September 1998 federal elections, however, the Republicans managed

only 1.8% of the vote, subsequently falling back to 1.7% in the June 1999 European Parliament elections. In March 2001 the party lost its representation in Baden-Württemberg, slumping to only 4.4% of the vote.

Social Democratic Party of Germany
Sozialdemokratische Partei Deutschlands (SPD)

Address. Willy-Brandt-Haus, Wilhelmstrasse 140, 10963 Berlin
Telephone. (+49–30) 259–910
Fax. (+49–30) 2599–1720
Email. parteivorstand@spd.de
Website. www.spd.de
Leadership. Gerhard Schröder (chairman); Rudolf Scharping, Renate Schmidt, Wolfgang Thierse and Heidemarie Wieczorek-Zeul (deputy chairpersonss); Peter Struck (parliamentary group leader); Franz Müntefering (secretary-general)

The origins of the SPD lie in the reformist General Association of German Workers (*Allgemeiner Deutscher Arbeiterverein*, ADA) founded by Ferdinand Lassalle in 1863 and the Social Democratic Labour Party (*Sozialdemokratische Arbeiterpartei*, SDAP) founded by the Marxists Wilhelm Liebknecht and August Bebel in 1869. In 1875 these two forerunners merged to form the Socialist Labour Party of Germany (*Sozialistische Arbeiterpartei Deutschlands*, SAPD), which was outlawed from 1878 under Chancellor Bismarck's anti-socialist laws. Relegalized in 1890, the SAPD became the SPD at the 1891 Erfurt congress, when the party reaffirmed its Marxist belief in inevitable socialist revolution, although in practice it was already following the reformist line advocated by Eduard Bernstein. Representing the rapidly expanding industrial working class and benefiting from universal manhood suffrage, the SAPD became the largest party in the *Reichstag* in 1912, although it played no part in Germany's unrepresentative government before 1914.

Ideological divisions within the SPD were intensified by World War I, during which the party split into a "majority" reformist wing supportive of the German war effort and the anti-war "Independent Social Democrats" led by Liebknecht and Rosa Luxemburg. Most of the latter faction joined the Communist Party of Germany founded in December 1918, while the main SPD became a key supporter of the post-war Weimar Republic, of which party leader Friedrich Ebert was the first Chancellor and the first President (from 1919 to 1925). SPD participation in most Weimar coalition governments was accompanied by theoretical criticism of capitalism, notably in the Heidelberg Programme of 1925, but thereafter the party was identified as a defender of the status quo against Soviet-backed Bolshevism on the left and the rising tide of fascism on the right. In the July 1932 elections the SPD was overtaken as the largest party by Hitler's National Socialist German Workers' Party (the Nazis), the latter winning 37.4% and the SPD 24.3%. In further elections in November 1932 the Nazis fell back to 33.2% and the SPD to 20.7%, while the Communists increased from 14.3% to 17%. Nevertheless, Hitler was appointed Chancellor in January 1933 and was granted emergency powers following the burning of the *Reichstag* the following month. In new elections in March 1933 the Nazis won 43.9% against 18.3% for the SPD and 12.1% for the Communists, whereupon an enabling act approved by the non-Nazi centre-right parties (but not by the SPD) gave Hitler absolute power to ban his political opponents, including the SPD.

After World War II the SPD was re-established in both the Western and the Soviet occupation zones, headed in the former by Kurt Schumacher and in the latter by Otto Grotewohl. The East German SPD was quickly constrained to merge with the Communists in the Socialist Unity Party of Germany (SED), founded in April 1946. In the first elections to the West German *Bundestag* in August 1949 the SPD came a close second to the Christian Democrats, with a 29.2% vote share, and was the principal opposition party until 1966, under the leadership of Schumacher until his death in 1952, then of Erich Ollenhauer and from 1958 of Willy Brandt (the mayor of West Berlin). During this opposition phase, the SPD's federal vote slipped to 28.8% in 1953 but then rose steadily, to 31.8% in 1957, 36.2% in 1961 and 39.3% in 1965. Faced with the evidence of West Germany's economic miracle of the 1950s, the SPD in 1959 adopted its celebrated Godesberg Programme, which jettisoned Marxist theory, embraced private ownership within the context of an equitable social order and industrial co-determination (*Mitbestimmung*), and reversed the party's previous opposition to NATO and the European Community.

In October 1966 the SPD entered a West German federal government for the first time, in a coalition headed by the →Christian Democratic Union (CDU) and the Bavarian →Christian Social Union (CSU). Brandt became Vice-Chancellor and Foreign Minister, in which capacity he pursued an *Ostpolitik* seeking normalization of relations with the Communist-ruled East European states, including East Germany. In March 1969 Gustav Heinemann became West Germany's first SPD President, elected with the backing of the →Free Democratic Party (FDP). In the September 1969 federal elections the SPD at last broke the 40% barrier, winning 42.7% of the vote and forming a centre-left coalition with the FDP. Brandt became West German Chancellor and led the SPD to a further advance in the 1972 *Bundestag* elections, to a post-war high of 45.8% of the vote. Brandt continued as head of an SPD/FDP coalition until 1974, when the discovery that a close aide was an East German spy forced him to resign. He was succeeded as Chancellor by Helmut Schmidt (although Brandt remained SPD chair) and the SPD/FDP coalition under Schmidt's leadership continued in power through the 1976 and 1980 federal elections, in which the SPD vote was 42.6% and 42.9% respectively.

The SPD/FDP government finally collapsed in September 1982, when the FDP withdrew and opted to join a coalition headed by the CDU/CSU. The SPD remained in opposition after the March 1983 and January 1987 *Bundestag* elections, in which its support fell back to 38.2% and 37.0% respectively, eroded in particular by the advancing Greens. Brandt finally resigned as SPD chairman in March 1987, when the party objected to his appointment of a non-SPD Greek lady as his spokesperson. He was succeeded by Hans-Jochen Vogel, a prominent SPD moderate, who launched a major reappraisal of the party's basic policy programme, although without achieving a definitive resolution of the vexed question of whether the SPD should formally commit to a future federal coalition with the Greens. In the latter context, however, the "red–green" coalition formed in 1985 between the SPD and the Greens in the state of Hesse set a trend of co-operation between the SPD and what was later named the →Alliance 90/The Greens.

The sudden collapse of East European communism from late 1989 caught the opposition SPD on the back foot, with the result that it tended to follow in the wake of events leading to German reunification in October 1990. Launched in October 1989, an East German SPD led by Ibrahim Böhme won 21.9% of the vote in multi-party elections in March 1990 and joined an eastern "grand coalition" government. Böhme quickly resigned on being found to have been a Stasi agent and was succeeded by Markus Meckel (then East German Foreign Minister), who was himself replaced by Wolfgang Thierse in June 1990. In September 1990 the East and West German SPDs were merged, but the party found it difficult to recover its pre-war strength in the east. Oskar Lafontaine was the SPD's Chancellor-candidate in the December 1990 all-German *Bundestag* elections, in which the party won only 33.5% of the overall vote (35.7% in the western *Länder*, 24.3% in the east), which yielded 239 of the 662 seats.

The SPD therefore continued in opposition and Vogel

immediately resigned as SPD chairman, being succeeded by Björn Engholm, then premier of Schleswig-Holstein. In November 1992 a special SPD conference endorsed a leadership recommendation that the party should give qualified backing to government-proposed constitutional amendments which would end the automatic right of entry to asylum-seekers and would allow German forces to be deployed outside the NATO area on UN-approved peace-keeping missions. Damaged by the revival of an old political scandal, Engholm resigned as SPD leader in May 1993 and was succeeded by Rudolf Scharping (then premier of Rhineland-Palatinate). In the June 1994 European Parliament elections the SPD slipped to 32.2% of the vote (from 37.3% in 1989) and won 40 of the 99 German seats. Scharping then led the SPD to its fourth successive federal election defeat in October 1994, although its share of the vote improved to 36.4% and its representation in the *Bundestag* rose to 252 seats out of 672. Concurrent SPD advances at state level gave it a majority in the *Bundesrat* (upper house), although in May 1995 the party lost ground in North Rhine-Westphalia and Bremen, and in October went down to a heavy defeat in Berlin (once an SPD stronghold).

In November 1995 an SPD conference in Mannheim elected Oskar Lafontaine (then premier of Saarland) as SPD chairman in succession to Scharping, who remained the SPD leader in the *Bundestag*. Located ideologically on the SPD left, Lafontaine had opposed the Maastricht Treaty on European union, on the grounds that it contained inadequate provisions for real political union, and was also an advocate of a political alliance between the SPD, the Greens and the (ex-communist) →Party of Democratic Socialism (PDS). He took the SPD into a stance of opposition to any speedy adoption of a single European currency and to the automatic granting of citizenship to ethnic German immigrants from Russia. The party suffered further setbacks in three state elections in March 1996 and also lost ground in Hamburg in September 1997.

In March 1998 the SPD executive elected Gerhard Schröder, an ideological pragmatist who had just won a third term as minister-president of Lower Saxony, as the party's Chancellor-candidate in preference to Lafontaine, who continued as party chairman. Gains for the SPD in Saxony-Anhalt in April were followed by a significant advance in the September 1998 federal elections, in which the SPD vote increased to 40.9% and its *Bundestag* representation to 298 seats. The following month Schröder formed an historic "red-green" federal coalition with the Greens, on the basis of a government programme setting the fight against unemployment as the main priority and also including Green objectives such as an "ecological tax reform" and the phasing-out of nuclear power generation.

SPD-Green strains quickly developed on the nuclear and other issues, but more damage was done to the government by divisions between Schröder and Finance Minister Lafontaine, the former advocating a "New Middle" (*Neue Mitte*) course, the latter preferring a traditional social democratic line. In March 1999 Lafontaine resigned from the government and also as SPD chairman, following a major disagreement with the Chancellor, who was elected as SPD party leader in April. The following month Johannes Rau (former SPD minister-president of North Rhine–Westphalia) was elected as President of Germany by 690 votes in the 1,338-member Federal Assembly.

In European Parliament elections in June 1999 the SPD slipped to 30.7% of the vote, losing seven of its 40 seats. Amid growing public disquiet about the federal government's performance, state elections in September–October 1999 saw the SPD being relegated to third place in Saxony and Thuringia, being ousted from power in Saarland and losing ground in Brandenburg and Berlin. The losses meant that the SPD-led federal government commanded only 26 out of 69 votes in the *Bundesrat* (the upper legislative house representing the states).

The SPD's negative electoral trend was reversed in Schleswig-Holstein in February 2000, partly because of the funding scandal then besetting the CDU. It also remained dominant in North Rhine–Westphalia in May, although its vote share fell by over 3%. Despite much criticism of SPD ministers over the outbreak of "mad cow disease" (BSE) in Germany in November 2000 and darkening economic clouds, the SPD continued its electoral recovery in Baden-Württemberg and Rhineland–Palatinate in March 2001, its 8% advance in the former being attributed to glamorous state SPD leader Ute Vogt, who at 36 was the youngest lead candidate of any major party in modern German history. In June 2001, moreover, the CDU-SPD coalition in Berlin was replaced by one led by the SPD and including the Greens, dependant on the external support of the PDS. The new SPD mayor of Berlin, Klaus Wowereit, became the first prominent German politician to announce that he was a homosexual. In late 2001 the SPD was in sole control in Lower Saxony and Saxony-Anhalt; in coalition with the Greens in North Rhine–Westphalia and Schleswig-Holstein; in coalition with the Greens and FDP in Berlin; in coalition with the CDU in Brandenburg and Bremen; in coalition with the FDP in Rhineland–Palatinate; and in coalition with the PDS in Mecklenburg-West Pomerania.

With an official membership of 800,000, the SPD is a member party of the Socialist International. Its European Parliament representatives sit in the Party of European Socialists group.

South Schleswig Voters' Union
Südschleswigscher Wählerverband (SSW)
Sydslesvigsk Vaelgerforening (SSV)
Address. Schiffbrücke 42, 24939 Flensburg
Telephone. (+49–461) 1440–8310
Fax. (+49–461) 1440–8313
Email. info@ssw-sh.de
Website. www.ssw-sh.de
Leadership. Gerda Eichhorn (chairperson); Anke Spoorendonk (parliamentary group leader); Dieter Lenz (secretary-general)
The SSW was founded in 1948 to represent the ethnic Danish minority in the northern state of Schleswig-Holstein and has a current membership of 4,500. Enjoying exemption from the 5% threshold rule in state elections, the party won one seat in the 1992 Schleswig-Holstein elections with 1.9% of the vote, increasing to two seats in 1996 with 2.5%. It made further progress in the February 2000 elections, receiving 60,367 votes (4.1%) and being allocated three of the 89 seats in the state legislature.

Other Parties

Some 80 other parties are officially registered in Germany. The following selection focuses on those that have obtained a degree of support in recent federal, state or European Parliament elections.

Anarchist Pogo Party of Germany (*Anarchistische Pogo Partei Deutschland, APPD*), leftist alternative formation in whose title "Pogo" signifies "wild and mindless dance"; won 0.1% of the vote in 1998 federal elections.
Address. Zenettistrasse 49, 80337 Munich
Email. kontakt@appd.de
Website. www.appd.de
Leadership. Markus Gäthke in association with the "The Unknown Ape" (*Der Unbekannte Affe*)

Animal Rights Party (*Tierschutzpartei, TP*), won 0.3% in 1998 federal elections and 0.7% in 1999 Euro-elections.
Address. Frankfurter Strasse 7, 65825 Schwalbach
Telephone. (+49–6796) 888–007
Fax. (+49–6196) 889–7306
Website. www.tierschutzpartei.de
Leadership. Gisela Bulla

Bavaria Party (*Bayernpartei, BP*), founded in 1946 to seek the restoration of an independent Bavarian state, represented in the *Bundestag* in 1949–53 (but not since) and influential in the Bavarian *Landtag* until the mid-1960s, won 0.1% in 1994 and 1998 federal elections and 0.1% in 1999 Euro-elections.
Address. Unter Weidenstrasse 14, 81543 Munich
Telephone. (+49–89) 651–8051
Fax. (+49–89) 654–259
Email. bayernpart@aol.com
Leadership. Dorn Hubert (chairman)

Car-Drivers' Party of Germany (*Autofahrer Partei Deutschlands, APD*), promotes drivers' rights and citizens' interests, won 0.7% of national vote in 1994 European elections, falling to 0.4% in 1999.
Address. Emilstrasse 71A, 44869 Bochum
Telephone/Fax. (+49–2327) 59391
Email. apdberlin@aol.com
Leadership. Dr E. Hörber (chairman)

Car Taxpayers' Party (*Automobile Steuerzahler Partei, ASP*), another drivers' rights party, founded in 1993, won 0.1% in 1999 European elections.
Address. Georg-Knorr-Strasse 25B, 85662 Hohenbrunn
Telephone. (+49–8102) 6836
Fax. (+49–8102) 72129
Email. info@as-partei.de
Website. www.as-partei.de
Leadership. Bernd Bräuer (chairman)

Chance 2000, won 0.1% in 1998 federal elections.
Address. Eckenheimer Landstrasse 160, 60318 Frankfurt
Telephone. (+49–69) 597–4575
Fax. (+49–69) 9552–0199
Email. chance2000@freunde.de
Website. www.chance2000.com
Leadership. Alexander Karschnia, Matthias Riedel & Herbert Rusche

Christian Middle (*Christliche Mitte, CM*), won 0.2% in 1994 European elections, falling to 0.1% in 1999.
Address. Lippstädter Strasse 42, 59329 Liesborn
Telephone. (+49–2523) 8388
Fax. (+49–2523) 6138
Email. christliche-mitte@t-online.de

Citizens' Rights Solidarity Movement (*Bürgerrechtsbewegung Solidarität, BüSo*), inspired by maverick US campaigner Lyndon H. LaRouche, won 0.1% in 1994 European elections and less than 0.1% in 1998 federal and 1999 European elections.
Address. Postfach 3366, 55023 Mainz
Telephone. (+49–6131) 237–384
Fax. (+49–6131) 237–387
Email. info@bueso.de
Website. www.bueso.de
Leadership. Helga Zepp-LaRouche

Democratic Party of Germany (*Demokratische Partei Deutschlands, DPD*), founded in October 1995 to represent foreigners in Germany and to oppose racism, based in the two-million-strong Turkish immigrant community (most of whom do not have German citizenship and are therefore not entitled to vote); won negligible vote in 1998 federal elections.
Address. Denkendorfer Straase 2, 71636 Ludwigsburg
Telephone. (+49–7156) 959–688
Fax. (+49–7156) 959–698
Leadership. Nuri Yaman

Ecological Democratic Party (*Ökologisch–Demokratische Partei, ÖDP*), standing for sustainable development and protection of the environment, won 0.4% in both the 1990

and 1994 federal elections, rising to 0.8% in 1994 Euro-elections, but slipping to 0.2% in 1998 federal elections and 0.4% in June 1999 Euro-elections, when it had some 300 municipal councillors; current membership is 6,730.
Address. Bohnesmühlgasse 5, 97070 Würzburg
Telephone. (+49–931) 40486
Fax. (+49–931) 404–8629
Email. geschaeftsstelle@oedp.de
Website. www.oedp.de
Leadership. Uwe Dolata (chairman); Claudius Moseler (secretary-general)

Family Party of Germany (*Familienpartei Deutschlands, FPD*), won 0.1% in 1998 federal elections and less than 0.1% in 1999 Euro-elections.
Address. Postfach 4122, 66376 St Ingbert
Telephone. (+49–6894) 4209
Fax. (+49–6894) 382–362
Email. familien.partei@t-online.de

Feminist Party (*Feministische Partei, FP*), campaigns as "Women" (Die Frauen), won 0.1% in 1998 federal elections and 0.4% in 1999 Euro-elections.
Address. Hausdorffstrasse 99, 53129 Bonn
Telephone. (+49–228) 231–455
Fax. (+49–228) 235–529
Email. w-pomper@t-online.de

German Communist Party (*Deutsche Kommunistische Partei, DKP*), founded in West Germany in 1969 some 13 years after the banning of its predecessor, for long led by Herbert Mies, had close links with the then ruling Socialist Unity Party of East Germany, but lost any impetus on the collapse of the East German regime in 1989; Mies resigned in October 1989 and was replaced by a four-member council at the party's 10th congress in March 1990; won negligible vote in 1994 and 1998 federal elections.
Address. Hoffnungstrasse 18, 45127 Essen
Telephone. (+49–201) 225–148;
Fax. (+49–201) 202–467;
Email. dkp.pv@t-online.de

German Social Union (*Deutscher Sozialer Union, DSU*), launched in East Germany in January 1990 as an umbrella organization of 12 conservative groups including the far-right →German People's Union, then allied with the →Christian Social Union (CSU) of West Germany; won only 0.2% in December 1990; its decision in April 1993 to campaign throughout Germany caused a breach with the CSU; won negligible vote in 1994 and 1998 federal elections.
Address. Zur Wetterwarte 27/127, 01109 Dresden
Telephone. (+49–351) 886–4487
Fax. (+49–351) 886–4486
Email. dsu@dotexpress.com
Leadership. Roberto Rink (chairman)

The Greys (*Die Grauen*), also known as the Grey Panthers, formerly a pensioners' group within the West German Greens, became a separate party in mid-1989 to represent the interests of older citizens; won 0.8% of the federal vote in 1990, 0.5% in 1994 and 0.3% in 1998, recovering to 0.4% in 1999 Euro-elections.
Address. Kothener Strasse 1-5, 42285 Wuppertal
Telephone. (+49–202) 280–700
Fax. (+49–202) 280–7070
Email. grauepanther@t-online.de
Leadership. Trude Unruh

Instead of a Party (*Unabhängen Statt Partei, SP*), set up in July 1993 to promote "a different kind of politics", including a reduction in government bureaucracy, the introduction of popular referendums and more voting according to conviction rather than by party discipline; main founder and lawyer Markus Ernst Wegner had previously been a member of the →Christian Democratic Union (CDU) and attracted support not only from Hamburg CDU branches but also from other parties; in 1993 Hamburg elections the SP won 5.6% of the vote and eight seats (out of 121) and entered into a "co-operation" agreement with the new minority government of the →Social Democratic Party of Germany; obtained only 0.01% of the vote in 1994 federal elections and lost its Hamburg seats in 1997.
Address. Postfach 600247, 22202 Hamburg
Telephone/Fax. (+49–40) 5149–1661
Leadership. Markus Ernst Wegner & Mike Bashford

Islamic Party of Germany (*Islamische Partei Deutschlands, IPD*), based in Germany's Muslim immigrant communities.
Address. Bereiteranger 11, 81541 Munich
Telephone. (+49–89) 6511–5190
Fax. (+49–89) 6511–5195
Email. ipd_info@fireball.de
Leadership. Sulaiman Hani

Marxist-Leninist Party of Germany (*Marxistisch-Leninistische Partei Deutschlands, MLPD*), Maoist formation whose belief in Marxist–Leninist precepts has survived their collapse in European countries where they were once practised.
Address. Kostrasse 8, 45899 Gelsenkirchen
Telephone. (+49–209) 951–940
Fax. (+49–209) 951–9460
Email. mlpd_zk@compuserve.com
Website. www.mlpd.de
Leadership. Stefan Engel

National Democratic Party of Germany (*National-demokratische Partei Deutschlands, NPD*), far-right formation founded in 1964, reached a high of 4.3% in 1969 federal elections and won seats in several state parliaments in the late 1960s; the party declined thereafter, being supplanted by the →Republicans on the radical right. In April 1995 then leader Günter Deckert received a prison sentence for incitement to racial hatred and other offences. The party won 0.3% in 1998 federal elections and 0.4% in 1999 Euro-elections, becoming the most prominent far-right formation. In late 2000 the federal government applied to the Constitutional Court for the party to be banned.
Address. Postfach 103528, 70030 Stuttgart
Telephone. (+49–711) 610–605
Fax. (+49–711) 611–716
Email. pressenpd@aol.de
Leadership. Udo Voigt (chairman)

New Liberal Party Pro-Deutschmark (*Neue Liberale Partei Pro-Deutsche Mark, NLP Pro-DM*), free-market movement opposed to German participation in the single European currency, won 0.9% in 1998 federal elections.
Address. Tiergartenstrasse 17, 40237 Düsseldorf
Telephone/Fax. (+49–721) 567–458

Party of Bible-Believing Christians (*Partei der Bibeltreuen Christen, PBC*), won vote share of 0.1% in 1994 and 1998 federal elections and 0.3% in 1999 Euro-elections.
Address. Postfach 410810, 76208 Karlsrühe
Telephone. (+49–721) 495–596
Fax. (+49–721) 494–125
Email. pbc.de@t-online.de

Party of the Unemployed and Socially Excluded (*Partei der Arbeitslosen und Sozial Schwachen, PASS*), won 0.4% in 1994 European elections and 0.3% in 1999, rising to 0.5% in October 1999 Berlin state elections.
Address. Babelsberger Strasse 5, 10715 Berlin
Telephone. (+49–30) 853–8104
Fax. (+49–30) 834–4695

Email. bund@passpartei.de
Website. passpartei.de
Leadership. Andreas Lüdecke (Berlin) & Herbert Schleiermacher (Hesse)

Work for Bremen (*Arbeit für Bremen, AfB*), a left-wing splinter group of the →Social Democratic Party of

Germany, formed prior to the May 1995 state elections, in which it won 10.7% and 12 seats, losing them all in 1999.
Address. Sögestrasse 43, 28195 Bremen
Telephone. (+49–421) 320–707
Fax. (+49–421) 320–708
Email. roland2801@aol.de

Ghana

Capital: Accra

Population: 19,533,500 (2000E)

The Republic of Ghana achieved independence from Britain in 1957. Since the overthrow of the country's first President, Kwame Nkrumah, in 1966, Ghana has experienced several long periods of military rule. The most recent military regime, dating back to December 1981, relinquished power in January 1993 under a civilian constitution approved in a referendum in April 1992. The constitution provides for a directly elected 200-member House of Parliament and an advisory Council of State with 25 members appointed by the President. The ban on the operation of political associations imposed in 1982 was lifted in May 1992. Presidential and legislative elections were held in November and December 1992 respectively, as a prelude to the inauguration of the Fourth Republic in January 1993. Flt.-Lt. (retd) Jerry Rawlings, who had come to power as a result of the coup in December 1981, was elected President with over 58% of the votes cast. His National Democratic Congress (NDC) also won an overwhelming victory in the simultaneous legislative polls, which were boycotted by the opposition parties.

In December 1996 Rawlings was re-elected President with 57% of the votes cast, while the NDC won 133 of the 200 parliamentary seats in the same month's legislative elections. Having served two four-year terms, Rawlings was ineligible to stand in the December 2000 presidential election, which was won by John Kufuor of the New Patriotic Party (NPP) with 57% in the second round, while the NDC candidate, Vice-President John Atta Mills, won 43%. The NPP won 100 seats in the December 2000 legislative elections, as against 92 for the NDC; of the remaining seats, three were won by the People's National Convention (PNC), one by the Convention People's Party (CPP) and four by independents.

Convention People's Party (CPP)
Address. c/o Parliament House, Accra
Leadership. Abubakar Alhassan (chairman); Nii Noi Duwuona (secretary-general)
The name Convention People's Party – associated historically with the late Kwame Nkrumah, Ghana's first President – was adopted prior to the 2000 election campaign by the party hitherto known as the Convention Party (CP). The CP was itself formed in 1998 through the merger of the People's Convention Party (PCP), which had won five seats in the 1996 parliamentary elections, and the National Convention Party (NCP), which had ceased to serve as junior coalition partner of the then ruling →National Democratic Congress in 1995 and had been refused permission to contest the 1996 elections on the grounds that it had not followed correct nomination procedures.

Having fielded 35 candidates, the CPP won one seat in the December 2000 parliamentary elections. Its presidential candidate, George Hagan, was placed fourth with 1.8% of the first-round vote.

National Democratic Congress (NDC)
Address. c/o Parliament House, Accra
Leadership. Flt.-Lt. (retd) Jerry John Rawlings (life chairman); Huudu Yahaya (secretary-general)
The NDC was launched formally in June 1992, following the legalization of political parties, as a coalition of pro-government organizations. Opposition groups charged the NDC with intimidation during the presidential election in November 1992, won by Flt.-Lt. Rawlings, and staged a boycott of the legislative elections the following month. Consequently, the NDC won 189 of the 200 parliamentary seats, with another nine seats going to its electoral allies (among which the National Convention Party became a junior coalition partner of the NDC until 1995). In 1996

Rawlings was re-elected President with a virtually unchanged share of the vote, but the NDC's parliamentary strength was reduced to 133 seats after a campaign contested by the opposition parties. The post of "life chairman" of the NDC was created for Rawlings at a party congress in December 1998.

In December 2000 Rawlings was ineligible to stand for re-election as President, having served two terms, and abided by the constitution. The incumbent Vice-President, John Atta Mills, stood for election as NDC presidential candidate but was defeated by John Kufuor of the →New Patriotic Party (NPP). The NDC (92 seats) was also defeated by the NPP (100 seats) in the simultaneous parliamentary election.

New Patriotic Party (NPP)
Address. Private Mail Bag, Accra-North, Accra
Telephone. (+233-21) 227951
Fax. (+233-21) 224418
Email. npp@africaonline.com.gh
Website. www.nppghana.com
Leadership. John Kufuor (leader); Samuel Odoi-Sykes (chairman); Daniel Botwe (secretary-general)
The NPP announced its formation in June 1992, advocating the protection of human rights and the strengthening of democracy. Its candidate in the November 1992 presidential election, Albert Adu Boahen, was the closest challenger to Jerry Rawlings of the →National Democratic Congress (NDC), polling just over 30% of the votes cast. The NPP boycotted the December 1992 legislative elections. In December 1996 the NPP's John Kufuor (whose candidacy was also supported by the People's Convention Party) won 39.8% of the vote in the presidential election, while the NPP won 60 seats in the parliamentary elections.

In the December 2000 presidential election, Kufuor

defeated John Atta Mills, the NDC candidate, his share of the vote rising from 48.3% in the first-round ballot to 57% in the second round. In simultaneous parliamentary elections the NPP increased its strength to 100 seats (half the membership of the House). President Kufuor, who had accused the NDC of inefficient management of the public sector, was committed to enlarging the role of the private sector as part of a programme of free-market reforms.

The NPP is associated with the International Democrat Union through the Democrat Union of Africa.

People's National Convention (PNC)
Address. c/o Parliament House, Accra
Leadership. Edward Mahama (chairman)
The PNC was founded in 1992 by former President Hilla Limann, who was placed third in that year's presidential election. The PNC won one seat in the 1996 parliamentary election and three seats in the December 2000 election. Its presidential candidate, Edward Mahama, received 3% of the vote in 1996 and 2.5% in 2000.

Other Parties

Democratic People's Party (DPP), founded in 1992. The DPP supported the →National Democratic Congress (NDC) candidate in the 1992, 1996 and 2000 presidential elections. It is affiliated to the NDC through the →Progressive Alliance.
Leadership. Daniel K.C. Markin (chairman)

EGLE (Every Ghanaian Living Everywhere) Party, evolved from a pro-Rawlings organization, the Eagle Club, formed in 1991, and won one seat in the 1992 legislative elections. EGLE supported the →National Democratic Congress (NDC) candidate in the 1992, 1996 and 2000 presidential elections. It is affiliated to the NDC through the →Progressive Alliance.

Great Consolidated People's Party (GCPP), contested the December 2000 presidential election, in which its candidate, Daniel Lartey, won 1% of the first-round vote.

National Reform Party (NRP), founded in 1999 by former members of the →National Democratic Congress. Its candidate at the 2000 presidential election, Augustus Goosie Tanoh, won 1.2% of the first-round vote.

Progressive Alliance (PA), electoral alliance through which the →Democratic People's Party and the →EGLE Party gave their formal support to the →National Democratic Congress in the 1992, 1996 and 2000 elections.

United Ghana Movement (UGM), founded in 1996. Its leader came last (with 0.3% of the first-round vote) in the 2000 presidential election.
Leadership. Charles Wereko-Brobby

Greece

Capital: Athens

Population: 10,500,000 (2000E)

Officially called the Hellenic Republic, Greece is a parliamentary democracy with a largely ceremonial President as head of state, elected by vote of the parliamentary deputies for a five-year term. Predominant executive power resides in the Prime Minister and members of the Cabinet, who must enjoy the confidence of the 300-member unicameral Parliament (*Vouli*). The latter is elected for a four-year term by universal adult suffrage under a system of proportional representation based on electoral constituencies returning between one and 26 deputies depending on their population size. Voting is compulsory for citizens aged 18 years and over (unless they are ill or incapacitated). By-elections are held to fill any vacancies, except during the final year of a parliamentary term. Political parties are required by the 1975 constitution to "serve the free functioning of democratic government".

State financing of political parties dates from 1984 and is currently regulated by a 1996 law providing for ordinary and electoral funding. Ordinary funding is allocated annually and from 1998 has been equivalent to 1.02% of annual state revenue (reduced in that year by 15% from the previous proportion), while electoral funding is allocated in years of national and/or European Parliament elections and is currently equivalent to 0.425% of annual state revenue. Parties are also eligible for financial aid equivalent to 0.085% of state revenue for their research and educational activities. Of the available funds, 85% is allocated to parties or coalitions represented in the Greek Parliament in proportion to their share of the vote, 5% in equal shares to parties or coalitions which obtain representation in the European Parliament and 10% in equal shares between parties or coalitions presenting candidates in 70% of constituencies and obtaining at least 3% of the national vote. The total amount allocated in ordinary and research/educational funding of parties in 2001 was 13,923 million drachmas (about $37 million), while election expenses funding was 4,656 million drachmas in 2000.

Parliamentary elections held on April 9, 2000, resulted as follows: Pan-Hellenic Socialist Movement 158 seats (with 43.8% of the vote), New Democracy 125 (42.7%), Communist Party of Greece 11 (5.5%), Coalition of the Left and Progress 6 (3.2%).

Coalition of the Left and Progress
Synaspismos tis Aristeras kai tis Proodou
Address. Plateia Eleftherias 1, 10553 Athens
Telephone. (+30–1) 337–8400
Fax. (+30–1) 321–9914; 321–7003
Email. intrelations@syn.gr
Website. www.syn.gr
Leadership. Nicos Constantopoulos (president); Stergios Pitsiorlas (secretariat co-ordinator)

Synaspismos was created prior to the June 1989 general elections as an alliance of the orthodox →Communist Party of Greece (KKE) "exterior", the Greek Left Party (*Elleniki Aristera*, EAR) and a number of minor leftist formations. The EAR had been launched in April 1987 by the majority wing of the KKE "interior", itself founded in 1968 by resident Communists opposed to the pro-Soviet orthodoxy of the exiled leadership of the KKE, which became known as the "exterior" party. Following the restoration of democracy in 1974, the Eurocommunist KKE "interior" had been part of the United Democratic Left (EDA), then including the KKE "exterior", and had won two of the EDA's eight seats in the November 1974 elections. In 1977 it had obtained one of the two seats won by an Alliance of Progressive and Left Forces (the precursor of *Synaspismos*), but had failed to win representation in 1981, before regaining one seat in 1985, when its share of the vote was 1.8%. In the 1984 European Parliament elections the KKE "interior" had again won one seat, on a 3.4% vote share.

Reuniting many of the Greek Communist factions, *Synaspismos* polled strongly in the June 1989 national elections, winning 28 seats out of 300 and 13.1% of the vote. In concurrent European Parliament elections a *Synaspismos* list won four of the 24 Greek seats with 14.3% of the vote. However, the decision of the *Synaspismos* leadership to join a temporary coalition government with the conservative →New Democracy (ND) generated rank-and-file unrest, with the result that the alliance fell back to 21 seats and 11.0% in the November 1989 elections. The subsequent participation of *Synaspismos* in another temporary coalition, this time with ND and the →Pan-Hellenic Socialist Movement (PASOK), was also controversial, and the alliance slipped again in the April 1990 elections, to 19 seats and 10.2% of the vote. The upshot was that in February 1991 the orthodox faction regained control of the KKE "exterior", which in June 1991 withdrew from *Synaspismos* and expelled elements that opted to remain in the alliance. The following month the prominent Communist reformer Maria Damanaki was re-elected *Synaspismos* chair.

In opposition to an ND government, *Synaspismos* endeavoured to transform itself into a unified party, to which end the EAR was dissolved in June 1992. However, the local organizational strength of the KKE (now the sole Communist Party) proved decisive in the October 1993 general election victory of PASOK, in which *Synaspismos* failed to win representation (on a 2.9% vote share), whereas the KKE won nine seats. Damanaki thereupon resigned as *Synaspismos* leader and was succeeded by Nicos Constantopoulos. In the June 1994 European Parliament elections *Synaspismos* recovered to 6.3% (only narrowly behind the KKE) and took two of the 25 Greek seats.

Benefiting from disenchantment among some PASOK voters with the incumbent government, *Synaspismos* returned to the Greek parliament in the September 1996 elections, winning 5.1% of the vote and 10 seats. In opposition to a further PASOK government and economic austerity measures in preparation for entry into the single European currency, *Synaspismos* polled strongly in local elections in October 1998. In the June 1999 European Parliament elections it again won two seats, on a 5.2% vote share. But the party slipped to 3.2% of the vote in the April 2000 parliamentary elections, being reduced to six seats.

The *Synaspismos* members of the European Parliament sit in the European United Left/Nordic Green left group, as do the KKE representatives. The party is a member of the New European Left Forum (NELF).

Communist Party of Greece
Kommounistiko Komma Elladas (KKE)

Address. Leoforos Irakliou 145, 14231 Athens
Telephone. (+30–1) 259–2111
Fax. (+30–1) 259–2298
Email. cpg@kke.gr
Website. www.kke.gr
Leadership. Aleka Papariga (general secretary); Harilaos Florakis (honorary president)

For long known as the "exterior" Communist Party because many of activists were forced into exile after World War II, the present KKE is directly descended from the Socialist Workers' Party of Greece (SEKE) founded in November 1918, which joined the Communist International (Comintern) in 1924 and changed its name to KKE. The party secured its first parliamentary representation in 1926

and in 1936 held the balance of power between the Monarchists and the Liberals, the resultant deadlock provoking a military coup by Gen. Metaxas in August 1936, following which all political parties were banned. During World War II popular resistance to the occupying Axis powers was organized by the Communists in the National Liberation Front (EAM) and the guerrilla Greek People's Liberation Army (ELAS), which gained control of the countryside. Following the liberation, however, ELAS was suppressed by British (and later US) troops after civil war had broken out between the Communists and centre-right forces favouring restoration of the monarchy. The KKE was officially banned in July 1947 and by 1949 had been defeated, its leadership and thousands of members fleeing to Communist-ruled countries.

The banned KKE became the dominant force within the Democratic Party (which won 9.7% of the vote in 1950) and then within the legal United Democratic Left (EDA), which won 10.4% of the vote in 1951, rising to 24.4% and 79 seats in 1958, before falling back to 11.8% and 22 seats in the the 1964 elections won by the centre-left Centre Union. During this period the KKE remained an orthodox Marxist-Leninist party whose pro-Soviet line was unaffected by the suppression of the Hungarian Uprising in 1956. In 1967–74 the KKE took a leading role in the opposition to the Greek military junta, but factional conflict not only within the exiled party but also between it and Communist forces in Greece culminated in a decision by the latter in February 1968 to form an independent "interior" KKE. The "exterior" KKE's support for the Soviet-led suppression of the Czechoslovak "Prague Spring" later in 1968 and the gravitation of the KKE "interior" towards reformist Eurocommunism served to widen the ideological gap between the two factions. Accused of prime responsibility for the split, the KKE "exterior" leader, Constantine Kolliyannis, was replaced by Harislaos Florakis in 1973.

Legalized after the fall of the military regime, the KKE "exterior" contested the November 1974 elections as part of the EDA, which also included the "interior" Communists, winning five of the EDA's eights seats. Standing on its own in subsequent elections, the KKE "exterior" advanced to 11 seats in 1977 (with 9.4% of the vote) and to 13 in 1981 (10.9%), when it also secured three of the 24 Greek seats in the European Parliament (with a 12.8% vote share). After its overtures for representation in the new government of the →Pan-Hellenic Socialist Movement (PASOK) had been rejected, the KKE "exterior" subsequently adopted a critical attitude towards PASOK, accusing it of betraying its election promises, notably its pledge to take Greece out of the European Community and NATO. For its part, the PASOK government allowed tens of thousands of KKE supporters, exiled since the late 1940s, to return to Greece.

Concurrently, the party's rigid pro-Moscow orthodoxy, which included support for the Soviet intervention in Afghanistan, caused some internal dissension and defections. In the 1984 Euro-elections the KKE "exterior" vote slipped to 11.6% (although it again won three seats), while in the June 1985 national elections it achieved 9.9% of the vote and 12 seats. On the latter occasion the deputies elected on the KKE "exterior" list included a former PASOK Finance Minister and nominees of the Agrarian Party (AKE) and the United Socialist Alliance of Greece (ESPE), the latter launched by PASOK dissidents in 1984. In the October 1986 municipal elections the KKE "exterior" withheld crucial second-round support from PASOK candidates, thus ensuring their defeat in Athens, Piraeus and Salonika (the three largest cities).

Influenced by the formation of the Greek Left Party (EAR) by the KKE "interior" the previous month, the 12th congress of the KKE "exterior" in May 1987 issued a call for a new left-wing alliance committed to socialism. The eventual result was the →Coalition of the Left and Progress (*Synaspismos*) between the KKE "exterior", the EAR (including the KKE "interior") and other groups, the alliance winning 28 seats in the June 1989 general elections on a 13.1% vote share. In simultaneous European Parliament elections a joint Communist list won 14.3% and four seats. However, the subsequent participation of *Synaspismos* in two temporary governments, the first with the conservative →New Democracy (ND) and the second with ND and PASOK (after further elections in November 1989 in which *Synaspismos* slipped to 21 seats and 11.0%), generated unrest in the KKE "exterior", leading to some defections. The party remained in *Synaspismos* for the April 1990 elections, in which the alliance fell back to 19 seats and 10.2% of the vote. However, the 13th KKE "exterior" congress in February 1991 resulted in the party's orthodox wing narrowly gaining control and in the election as general secretary of Aleka Papariga, who in June 1991 took the party out of *Synaspismos*. By then the "exterior" suffix was no longer required as an identifier, in that the "interior" party had ceased to be a distinct formation.

Having opted for independence, the KKE experienced further internal turmoil, involving the expulsion or departure of various elements that preferred the reformist line of *Synaspismos*. In the October 1993 elections, however, the KKE retained appreciable support, winning 4.5% of the vote and nine seats, whereas *Synaspismos* failed to obtain representation. In the June 1994 Euro-elections the KKE advanced to 6.3%, taking two of the 25 Greek seats, and thereafter maintained a critical stance on the policies of the PASOK government. In the September 1996 general elections the KKE advanced to 5.6% of the vote and 11 seats, remaining in opposition to a further PASOK administration.

In the June 1999 European Parliament elections the KKE won an additional seat on the strength of a vote share of 8.7%. In the April 2000 national elections, the party virtually retained its position, again winning 11 seats, this time with 5.5% of the vote.

The three KKE representatives in the European Parliament sit in the European United Left/Nordic Green left group, as do the *Synaspismos* representatives.

Democratic Social Movement
Dimokratiko Kinoniko Kinima (DIKKI)

Address. Odos Xalkokondili 9, 10677 Athens
Telephone. (+30–1) 380–1712
Fax. (+30–1) 383–9047
Email. dikki@otenet.gr
Website. www.dikki.gr
Leadership. Dimitris Tsovolas (president)

DIKKI originated in 1995 in a breakaway from the ruling →Pan-Hellenic Socialist Movement (PASOK) opposed in particular to the government's policy of participating in closer European Union integration and of preparing Greece for membership of the single European currency by austerity measures. In the September 1996 general elections DIKKI achieved 4.4% of the popular vote and won nine parliamentary seats.

In the June 1999 European Parliament elections, DIKKI advanced to 6.8%, taking two of the 25 Greek seats. But it failed to repeat this success in the April 2000 national elections, winning only 2.7% of the vote and therefore failing to retain representation.

The DIKKI members of the European Parliament sit in the European United Left/Nordic Green Left group.

New Democracy
Nea Dimokratia (ND)

Address. Odos Rigillis 18, 10674 Athens
Telephone. (+30–1) 729071–79
Fax. (+30–1) 725–1491
Email. valinak@otenet.gr
Website. www.nd.gr
Leadership. Costas Karamanlis (president); Dimitrios Sioufas (parliamentary spokesman); Evaggelos Meimarakis (secretary-general)

The moderate conservative ND was founded in October 1974 by Constantine Karamanlis, who had been Prime Minister in 1956–63 as leader of the National Radical Union (ERE) and had opposed the colonels' regime of 1967–74 from exile in Paris. The new party won an absolute majority in the November 1974 elections, securing 220 of the 300 seats on a 54.4% vote share. It was confirmed in power in the November 1977 elections, although it slipped to 172 seats and 41.8% of the vote, with Karamanlis continuing as Prime Minister until being elected President in May 1980, when he was succeeded as government and party leader by George Rallis. In January 1981 a key ND policy aim was achieved when Greece became a member of the European Community, but in the October 1981 elections the party was heavily defeated by the →Pan-Hellenic Socialist Movement (PASOK), retaining only 115 seats and 35.9% of the vote.

In the wake of ND's 1981 defeat Rallis was ousted as leader and replaced by right-winger Evangelos Averoff-Tossizza, but the latter resigned in August 1984 following the ND's poor showing in the European Parliament elections two months earlier. He was succeeded by the moderate Constantine Mitsotakis, who led ND to another election defeat in June 1985, although it improved to 126 seats and 40.8% of the vote. Mitsotakis's leadership then came under strong criticism from "new right" elements led by Constantine Stephanopoulos, who in September 1985 broke away to form the Democratic Renewal Party (DIANA). Mitsotakis reasserted his authority at a February 1986 ND congress, when "new right" policy theses were rejected, and in October 1986 the party made significant gains in municipal elections, taking control from PASOK in the three largest cities (Athens, Piraeus and Salonkia). Nevertheless, internal strains resurfaced in May 1987 when Rallis resigned from the party in protest against the earlier expulsion of his son-in-law for criticizing the ND leadership for its alleged departure from the policies of Karamanlis.

ND won a relative majority of 145 seats in the June 1989 general elections, the parliamentary arithmetic obliging it to form a temporary coalition with the →Coalition of the Left and Progress (*Synaspismos*). Another election in November 1989 produced another stalemate, with ND representation edging up to 148 seats (on a 46.2% vote share), so that a temporary three-party coalition of ND, PASOK and *Synaspismos* representatives plus non-party technocrats was formed. Yet more general elections in April 1990 gave ND exactly half the seats (150) with 46.9% of the vote, so that Mitsotakis was able to form a single-party government with the external support of the single DIANA deputy. In May 1990 Karamanlis was returned for another term as President, securing parliamentary election as the ND candidate although at 82 he was no longer a party politician.

Amid a deteriorating economic situation, the Mitsotakis government experienced growing internal rifts in 1992–93, culminating in the formation of the breakaway →Political Spring (PA) in June 1993. Deprived of a parliamentary majority, Mitsotakis resigned in September 1993, precipitating early elections in October, in which ND was heavily defeated by PASOK, falling to 111 seats and 39.3% of the vote. Mitsotakis immediately resigned as ND leader and was succeeded by Miltiades Evert, who had been dismissed from the ND government in October 1991 for criticizing its free-market policies. ND took second place in the June 1994 European Parliament elections, winning 32.7% of the vote and nine of the 25 Greek seats, one of which went to the singer Nana Mouskouri despite (or perhaps because of) her self-admitted ignorance of politics. In October 1994 the ND candidate registered a notable victory in the Athens mayoral contest, while remaining much weaker than PASOK in local government.

In January 1995 the Greek parliament voted to drop phone-tapping and various corruption charges against Mitsotakis arising from his term as Prime Minister; the former ND leader complained that the decision denied him the opportunity of proving his innocence in court. In March 1995 the ND candidate, Athanasios Tsaldaris, failed to secure parliamentary election as President, being defeated by Constantine Stephanopoulos, who was nominated by the PA (and backed by PASOK in the interests of avoiding a general election), having disbanded his DIANA party following its failure in the 1994 Euro-elections.

In the September 1996 general elections the ND failed to fulfill expectations that it would oust the PASOK government, winning only 108 seats and 38.2% of the vote. Evert speedily announced his resignation as leader, but secured re-election in October after a power-struggle in which Mitsotakis had advanced the claims of his daughter, former Culture Minister Dora Bakoyiannis. Evert's victory was short-lived, however, because in March 1997 he was replaced by Costas Karamanlis (nephew of the ND founder), who at 40 became the youngest ever leader of a major Greek political party. His election was seen as drastic action by a party fearing marginalization and concerned at having lost business community support to PASOK.

Under new leadership, ND made a strong showing in the October 1998 local elections, retaining the mayorships of Athens and Salonika, although it was potentially weakened by the launching in May 1999 of the →Liberals by a former ND deputy. The ND won 36.0% of the vote in the June 1999 European Parliament elections, thus overtaking PASOK, although its representation remained at nine seats. In the April 2000 national elections, the party narrowly failed to oust PASOK from power, advancing to 42.7% of the vote and 125 seats.

With an official membership of 400,000, ND is a member party of the Christian Democrat International, the International Democrat Union and the European Democrat Union. Its members of the European Parliament sit in the European People's Party/European Democrats group.

Pan-Hellenic Socialist Movement
Panellenio Sosialistiko Kinema (PASOK)

Address. Odos Charilaou Tricoupi 50, 10680 Athens
Telephone. (+30–1) 368–4037
Fax. (+30–1) 368–4042
Email. pasok@pasok.gr
Website. www.pasok.gr
Leadership. Costas Simitis (president); Costas Skandalidis (general secretary)

PASOK was founded in 1974, being derived from the Pan-Hellenic Liberation Movement (PAK) created by Andreas Papandreou in 1968 to oppose the military dictatorship which held power in Greece from 1967 to mid-1974. Having worked in the USA as an economics professor (and become a US citizen), Papandreou had returned to Greece in 1959 and had held ministerial office in pre-1967 Centre Union governments headed by his father George. Briefly imprisoned after the 1967 colonels' coup, he had been allowed to go into exile and had founded PAK, becoming convinced of the need for an unequivocally socialist party that would follow a "third road" distinct from West European social democracy and East European communism. According to Papandreou, the absence of a socialist tradition in Greece meant that PASOK had its roots in the wartime resistance and in the post-war National Liberation Front (EAM), which had been Communist-led, with a later centre-left admixture deriving from the Centre Union. PASOK was originally committed to the socialization of key economic sectors and also to withdrawal from the then European Community (EC) and NATO, but was later to revise such policies when it came into government.

PASOK emerged from the November 1974 elections as the third strongest party, with 12 of 300 seats and 13.6% of the vote. In the November 1977 elections it became the strongest opposition party, with 93 seats and 25.3%, and in October 1981 it won an absolute majority of 170 seats (with 48.1% of the vote) and formed its first government under Papandreou's premiership. Four years later, in June 1985, PASOK was returned for a second term, although with its representation reduced to 161 seats on a 45.8% vote share.

Prior to the 1985 contest, the PASOK candidate, Christos Sartzetakis, had been elected President in acrimonious parliamentary balloting in March. In office, PASOK experienced considerable internal divisions over the government's foreign and economic policies, including a new five-year agreement signed in September 1983 allowing US bases to remain in Greece, the dropping of opposition to EC and NATO membership, and the introduction of an economic austerity programme in 1985. Various critics of the leadership were expelled from PASOK in the 1980s and a number of breakaway groups were formed, although none had any enduring impact. In the October 1986 municipal elections PASOK suffered sharp reverses, losing the three largest cities to the conservative →New Democracy (ND), although it remained by far the strongest party at local level.

In the June 1989 parliamentary elections PASOK was damaged by the Koskotas affair, involving financial malpractice in the Bank of Crete, and by Papandreou's extramarital affair with a young air hostess called Dimitra Liani, with whom he later contracted his third marriage. The party's representation slumped to 125 seats (on a 39.2% vote share) and it went into opposition to a temporary coalition between ND and the →Coalition of the Left and Progress (*Synaspismos*). Further elections in November 1989 produced another statemate, with PASOK improving slightly to 128 seats and 40.7% of the vote, well behind ND, although the latter's lack of an overall majority dictated the formation of another temporary coalition, this time of the three main parties (but not including their leaders). Meanwhile, Papandreou had been indicted on corruption charges arising from the Koskotas affair. Greece's third general elections in less than a year, held in April 1990, broke the deadlock, with PASOK slipping to 123 seats and 38.6% and going into opposition to an ND government.

Continuing divisions within PASOK were highlighted during its second congress in September 1990, when Papandreou's nominee for the new post of party general secretary, Akis Tsochatzopoulos, was approved by a bare one-vote majority. Papandreou nevertheless remained unchallenged as PASOK leader, and in January 1992 was finally acquitted of the various corruption charges against him. In the October 1993 elections PASOK stood on a manifesto which jettisoned much of the left-wing rhetoric of the 1980s and instead professed a "social democratic" identity, supportive of EC and NATO membership and of good relations with the USA. It won an overall majority of 170 seats (on a 46.9% vote share) and returned to government with Papandreou once again Prime Minister. Also reappointed (as Minister of Culture) was the famous actress and 1967–74 pro-democracy campaigner Melina Mercouri, although she was to die in office in March 1994. In the June 1994 European Parliament elections PASOK headed the poll, winning 37.6% of the vote and 10 of the 25 Greek seats. In October 1994 PASOK maintained its dominance in local elections, although losing the Athens mayoral contest to an ND candidate.

Growing unrest within PASOK over the ageing Papandreou's continued leadership and the undisguised political ambitions of his wife Dimitra developed into a full-scale succession struggle when the Prime Minister fell seriously ill in November 1995. Papandreou eventually resigned in January 1996 and was succeeded as PASOK political leader and Prime Minister by Costas Simitis, who defeated acting Prime Minister Apostolos Tsokhatzopoulos in a runoff ballot of PASOK deputies by 86 votes to 75. Simitis had resigned from the government in September 1995 in protest against alleged sabotage of his reform plans by the PASOK hierarchy. Following the death of Papandreou on June 22, 1996, Simitis prevailed over strong internal opposition by securing election to the PASOK presidency at a special party congress at the end of the month.

Simitis consolidated his position in the September 1996 general elections, rather unexpectedly securing a further mandate for PASOK, which won 162 seats on a 41.5% vote share. Nevertheless, his government's economic austerity measures to prepare Greece for the single European currency were resisted by the PASOK "old guard", three of whose members were expelled from the parliamentary group in December 1997 for opposing the 1998 budget. Early in 1998, moreover, 10 PASOK deputies voted against a government bill aimed at cutting the deficits of many public-sector enterprises.

Having lost ground in the October 1998 local elections, PASOK was relegated to second place in the June 1999 European Parliament elections, obtaining only 32.9% of the vote and nine seats. The party nevertheless narrowly retained power in the April 2000 national elections, winning 158 seats with 43.8% of the vote.

PASOK is a member party of the Socialist International. Its representatives in the European Parliament sit in the Party of European Socialists group.

Other Parties

Communist Party of Greece–Renovating Left (*Kommunistiko Komma Ellados–Ananeotiki Aristera, KKE-AA*), led by Yiannis Banias, created in 1987 by a minority faction of the "interior" Communist Party opposed to the majority's decision to join a broader Greek Left Party (which later became part of the →Coalition of the Left and Progress).

Green Party (*Prassini Politiki, PP*), pro-environment formation that has made minimal electoral impact, affiliated to European Federation of Green Parties.
Address. Kolokotroni 31, 10562 Athens
Telephone. (+30–1) 251–1304
Fax. (+30–1) 322–4344

Hellenic Front (*Elliniko Metopo, EM*), right-wing party founded in 1994, seeking to promote Greek national interests.
Address. Kolokotroni 11, 10562 Athens
Telephone. (+30–1) 325–1054
Fax. (+30–1) 325–1521
Email. elliniko@metopo.gr
Website. www.metopo.gr
Leadership. Makis Voridis (president)

Hellenic Liberal Party, mainstream liberal formation led by the grandson of former Prime Minister Eleftherios Venizelos (1864–1936), from whose historic Liberal Party (founded 1910) the present party claims direct descent.
Address. Vissarionos 1, 10672 Athens
Telephone. (+30–1) 360–6111
Leadership. Nikitas Venizelos

Hellenic Women's Party (*Komma Ellinidon Gynaikon, KEG*), founded in 1998, aiming to promote the political, economic and social rights of women.
Address. Rostan 37, Ano Patisia, 11141 Athens
Telephone. (+30–1) 202–1828
Fax. (+30–1) 223–5823
Email. emmanecon@vip.gr
Leadership. Emmanuel Economakis

Hellenism Party (*Komma Ellinismou*, KE), pan-Hellenic formation founded in 1981, affiliated to the Hellenic World Unification Movement.

Address. Dimakapoulos 24, 11145 Athens
Telephone. (+30–1) 228–0820
Fax. (+30–1) 201–1162
Email. komhellin@yahoo.com
Website. www.komma-ellinismou.gr
Leadership. Sotirios Sofianopoulos (president)

The Liberals (*Oi Fileleftheroi*), launched in April 1999 by Stephanos Manos, a former National Economic and Finance Minister who had been expelled from →New Democracy (ND) in 1998 for not following the party line of opposition to legislation tabled by the government of the →Pan-Hellenic Socialist Movement (PASOK) aimed at making state enterprises more competitive. Calling for fundamental reforms to prepare Greece for the 21st century, the new formation was the latest attempt to create a modern political party that could claim the mantle of the historic Greek Liberal Party of Eleftherios Venizelos (1864–1936).
Address. Anastasiou Tsocha 15–17, 11521 Athens
Telephone. (+30–1) 645–5070
Fax. (+30–1) 645–8946
Email. liberals@otenet.gr
Website. www.liberals.gr
Leadership. Stephanos Manos (president); Aristotelis Aivaliotis (secretary-general)

National Political Union (*Ethniki Politiki Enosis, EPEN*), far-right party founded in 1984, at first led by ex-Col. George Papadopoulos (military dictator in 1967–73), held one European Parliament seat in 1984–89.
Leadership. Chryssanthos Dimitriades

Political Spring (*Politiki Anixi, PA*), right-wing populist party established in June 1993 by Antonis Samaras, a dissident member of the then ruling →New Democracy (ND) who had been dismissed as Foreign Minister in April 1992 because of his hardline opposition to the recognition of the ex-Yugoslav republic of Macedonia under that name. The new party attracted three other ND deputies into defection, so that the government lost its narrow parliamentary majority and was forced to resign. In early general elections in October 1993 Samaras (42) campaigned for an end to rule by the "dinosaurs" of ND and the →Pan-Hellenic Socialist Movement (PASOK), winning 10 seats with a vote share of 4.9%, becoming part of the parliamentary opposition to the new PASOK government. In the European Parliament elections of June 1994 the PA advanced to 8.7% of the vote, giving it two of the 25 Greek seats, and in March 1995 it successfully nominated the veteran conservative politician Constantine Stephanopoulos as President. But it failed to retain representation in the September 1996 national elections (winning only 2.9% of the vote) and the June 1999 Euro-elections (2.3% of the vote)

Union of the Democratic Centre (*Enosi Dimokratikou Kentrou, EDIK*), centre-left formation founded in 1974 as a merger of pre-1967 parties (including the Centre Union), won 60 seats in 1974, 15 in 1977 and none in 1981 (suffering from the left-right polarization of Greek politics); its leader was elected a deputy in 1985 with the backing of the →Pan-Hellenic Socialist Movement.
Leadership. Ioannis G. Zighdis

Grenada

Capital: St George's

Population: 89,000 (2000E)

A former British dependency, Grenada became a fully independent member of the Commonwealth in 1974. In 1979 the elected Grenada United Labour Party (GULP) government, headed by Sir Eric Gairy, was overthrown in a coup staged by the Marxist New Jewel Movement. This established a People's Revolutionary Government under the leadership of Maurice Bishop. Factional conflict within the regime led to the murder of Bishop in October 1983, prompting US–Caribbean military intervention. Following this the New National Party (NNP) came to power at a general election in December 1984, and a phased withdrawal of US forces was completed by June 1985. The NNP has since then been in government other than in 1990-1995.

The head of state is the British sovereign, represented by a Governor-General. The head of government is the Prime Minister. Parliament comprises a 13-member Senate and a 15-member House of Representatives. Members of the House of Representatives are elected on the Westminster model for five-year terms by simple majority in single-member constituencies. Senators are appointed by the Governor-General: seven are appointed on the advice of the Prime Minister; three on the advice of the Leader of the Opposition; and three on the advice of the Prime Minister after the Prime Minister has consulted organizations or interests which he believes should be represented.

Politics tend to be fractious with a history of fluid allegiances and short-lived personality-based political formations. In a general election in January 1999, the New National Party (NNP) of Prime Minister Keith Mitchell retained power, winning all 15 seats in the House. The votes cast were: NNP 25,850, National Democratic Congress (NDC) 10,337, Grenada United Labour Party/United Labour (GULP/UL) 4,998, Maurice Bishop Patriotic Movement (MBPM) 252, Good Old Democracy (GOD) 69.

Grenada United Labour Party (GULP)
Leadership. Hubert Prudhomme (generally regarded as leader)

The conservative GULP was formed in 1950, held office for periods in the colonial era, and led Grenada to independence in 1974, with its leader Eric Gairy becoming Prime Minister. Gairy was overthrown by the New Jewel Movement coup in 1979 and went into exile, returning in 1984 following the US-led intervention. Subsequent efforts to re-establish the GULP as a significant force were unsuccessful, however, and it won only two seats at elections in 1995 and none in 2000. Gairy died in 1997 and the party has subsequently been beset by factional divisions, with former Deputy Prime Minister Hubert Prudhomme and prominent lawyer Jerry Seales leading opposing factions.

National Democratic Congress (NDC)
Leadership. Tillman Thomas (leader)

The centrist NDC was launched in 1987 by former →New National Party (NNP) minister George Brizan. Brizan's successor as leader, Nicholas Brathwaite, became Prime Minister after the 1990 election. Brizan returned to replace Brathwaite as NDC leader in 1994 and as Prime Minister in February 1995. In the June 1995 general election the party retained only five seats and moved into opposition. In the January 1999 election it took 24.9% of the vote, but lost all its seats. Brizan subsequently stepped down as party leader and was reported to have accepted a job as adviser to the victorious NNP. In October 2000 Tillman Thomas was elected party leader; in May 2001 his deputy, Livingstone Nelson, resigned saying that the party was not being forceful enough in opposing the NNP.

New National Party (NNP)
Address. PO Box 393, Lucas Street, St George's
Telephone. (+1–473) 440–1875
Fax. (+1–473) 440–1876
Leadership. Keith Mitchell (leader)

The NNP was created in August 1984 by the merger of the conservative Grenada National Party (GNP), led by Herbert Blaize; the centrist National Democratic Party (NDP), formed earlier in 1984 and then led by George Brizan; and the right-wing Grenada Democratic Movement (GDM), dating from 1983 and led by Francis Alexis. The GNP, which had been set up in 1956, held a majority of the elective seats in the colonial legislature from 1957 to 1961 and from 1962 to 1967, when Blaize was Chief Minister. In the December 1984 general election the NNP won 14 of the 15 seats, and Blaize became Prime Minister. However, the party subsequently suffered internal divisions and in April 1987 Brizan and Alexis left the government and moved into opposition. In January 1989 Keith Mitchell defeated Prime Minister Blaize for the party leadership, prompting the latter to form his own National Party (Blaize died in office in December 1989).

The NNP won only two seats in the 1990 general election but came to power in the June 1995 election, when it won eight seats. The NNP lost its majority in Parliament as a result of the resignation in November 1998 of Foreign Minister Raphael Fletcher, precipitating an early general election in January 1999. Capitalizing on buoyant economic conditions and falling unemployment, the Mitchell government went on to win a sweeping victory, taking 62% of the vote and winning all 15 seats.

The NNP is an associate member of the International Democrat Union and a member of its regional organization, the Caribbean Democrat Union.

224

Guatemala

Capital: Guatemala City

Population: 10,828,000 (2000E)

Guatemala's modern political history has been very unstable. For a brief period after 1944 Guatemala enjoyed democratic government, until in 1955 the United States sponsored the overthrow of a reformist government led by Col. Jacobo Arbenz. Three separate constitutions have been promulgated since then, but for much of the period the country has been under direct or disguised military rule. There have been four successful military coups (1957, 1963, 1982 and 1983) and two failed coups (in May and December 1988). In 1960, encouraged by the example of the Cuban revolution, insurgency broke out, although it took nearly 30 years and the loss of more than 100,000 lives before left-wing guerrillas formed a united front to challenge the monopoly on power held by a small ruling class and the military. Peace talks aimed at national reconciliation, the expansion of democracy, the ending of gross human rights abuses and demilitarization, began between the government, moderate sections of the army and the guerrillas in the early 1990s. Under an agreement signed in 1996 the guerrilla front was converted into a legal political party and contested the 1999 elections.

Under its 1985 constitution, which came into effect in January 1986, the Republic of Guatemala has a unicameral Congress (*Congreso de la República*) elected for a four-year term. Since 1999 the Congress has had 113 members, 91 of whom are directly elected and 22 chosen by party list on a proportional representation basis. Executive authority resides in the President, who is also elected for a four-year term and may not be re-elected. If in a presidential election none of the candidates secures an absolute majority, a second round between the two leading candidates takes place. The President is assisted by a Vice-President and an appointed Cabinet. Voting is compulsory for those 18 years of age and older who can read and write but is optional for illiterates from the same age group. Non-voting is punishable by a small fine. The police and military personnel on active duty are not allowed to vote.

On Jan. 14, 2000, Alfonso Antonio Portillo Cabrera of the Guatemalan Republican Front (FRG) took office as President. He had led the ballot in the first round of presidential elections held on Nov. 7, 1999, with 47.8% of the vote and had been elected in the second round on Dec. 26 with 68.3% against 31.7% for Oscar Berger Perdomo of the National Advancement Party (PAN). Elections to the unicameral Congress on Nov. 7, 2000, were won by the FRG with 63 of the 113 seats. The PAN won 37 seats, the New Nation alliance of the Guatemalan National Revolutionary Unity and Authentic Integral Development (URNG-DIA) 9, the Guatemalan Christian Democratic Party (DCG) 2, the Democratic Union/Green Party coalition (UD/LOV) 1 and the Progressive Liberation Party (PLP) 1.

Democratic Union
Union Democrática (UD)

Address. Av. Reforma 12-01, zona 10, nivel 13, of. 4, Guatemala City

Telephone. (+502–2) 331–8573

Email. chea@infovia.com.gt

Leadership. José Luis Chea Urruela

The conservative UD was launched prior to the 1994 general elections and campaigned on a platform of being a party with no historical baggage. However, it won only one congressional seat, which it retained at the 1995 and 1999 elections. In 1995 its presidential candidate, José Chea, won 3.5% of the votes cast. In 1999 the party ran in association with the →Green Organization (LOV), but their joint candidate for the presidency, José Enrique Asturias Rudeke, obtained only 1.1% of the vote.

Guatemalan Christian Democratic Party
Democracia Cristiana Guatemalteca (DCG)

Address. Av. Elena 20-66 Zona 3, Guatemala City

Telephone. (+502–2) 251–7804

Fax. (+502–2) 254–1385

Leadership. Mario Vinicio Cerezo Arévalo (secretary-general)

Founded in August 1955, the DCG is a centre-right party which, despite its reformist rhetoric, has been decidedly conservative when in office. The party came out of an anticommunist tradition and was founded with the help of the Roman Catholic Church in the belief that a Christian approach to politics would prevent the left coming to power. The DCG's initial policy was to oppose violence and pro-

mote social justice through direct church assistance, while at the same time closing ranks with the right-wing →National Liberation Movement (MLN). These internal contradictions came to a head during the regime of Col. Enrique Peralta Azurdia (1963–1966), when an anti-communist faction accepted 10 seats in Congress while the majority of the party campaigned in opposition for basic social welfare and army reforms. After the expulsion of the right-wing faction, the DCG gained considerable support from students, trade unionists and rural communities during the unrest and repression of the 1960s.

Following attacks by right-wing paramilitaries and the murder of several of its leaders, the DCG went underground in June 1980 but re-emerged for the 1982 election campaign as a partner of the National Renewal Party (PNR) in the National Opposition Union (UNO). The alliance won three seats in Congress and the PNR presidential candidate came third with 15.6%. The DCG initially supported the 1982 coup led by Efrain Ríos Montt, who promised to put an end to violence and corruption, but distanced itself from the regime when it became an open dictatorship.

Widely seen as the party least involved in repression and corruption and the one most likely to promote social reforms, the DCG won the most seats (20 out of 88) in the 1984 Constituent Assembly elections heralding a return to civilian rule. This paved the way for the party's resounding victory in the late 1985 elections, in which Mario Vinicio Cerezo Arévalo was elected President and the DCG secured a majority in Congress. The Cerezo government disappointed many of its original supporters by pursuing conservative policies. It nevertheless experienced three coup attempts and a number of coup plots by the extreme right and sections of the army between 1987 and 1989.

For the November 1990 elections the DCG attempted to restore its progressive image by forging an alliance with the Democratic Convergence (DC), but the deteriorating economy and allegations of corruption against party leaders strengthened general disillusionment. The party mustered only 27 seats in the November 1990 congressional elections, while Alfonso Cabrera, who was unable to campaign because of illness, came third in the presidential contest with 17.3% of the votes. In the 1994 elections, moreover, the party's representation fell to 13 seats.

After the party had joined a National Front alliance with the →Union of the National Centre and the Social Democratic Party in April 1995, a number of disgruntled DCG deputies resigned their party membership and set up an independent bloc in Congress. In the November 1995 congressional elections the rump DCG's representation fell to three seats, of which only two were retained in November 1999.

The DCG is a member of the Christian Democrat International and the Christian Democrat Organization of America.

Guatemalan Republican Front
Erente Republicano Guatemalteco (FRG)

Address. 3 Calle 5–50, zona 1, Guatemala City
Telephone. (+502–2) 238–2756
Leadership. Alfonso Antonio Portillo Cabrera

The authoritarian right-wing FRG was formed in the late 1980s as a vehicle for former President Gen. (retd.) Efrain Ríos Montt, who had staged a military coup in 1982, assumed dictatorial powers and fought a vicious counter-insurgency campaign before himself being ousted in 1983. The FRG was a key participant in the 1990 "No Sell-Out Platform" *(Plataforma No Venta,* PNV) alliance which included the Democratic Institutionalist Party (PID) and the National Unity Front (FUN). The alliance was de-registered after the 1990 poll on the ground that former heads of state who had participated in coups were banned from running for the presidency.

The FRG was similarly affected by this ban, but in the 1994 legislative contest staged an impressive recovery, winning 32 of the available seats, a result which gained Montt the presidency of Congress. The former President's wife, Teresa Sosa de Ríos, was initially chosen as the FRG's 1995 presidential election candidate but, on being ruled out on constitutional grounds, was replaced by Alfonso Antonio Portillo Cabrera, a populist who admitted to having killed two people in self-defence in 1982. He secured 22.1% in the first round but was defeated in the run-off in January 1996, while the FRG won 21 seats in the legislative elections.

As the principal opposition to the post-1996 administration of the →National Advancement Party (PAN), the FRG benefited from doubts about the peace agreement ending 36 years of civil war and also from deteriorating economic and social conditions. In the November–December 1999 elections, Portillo swept to a convincing victory in the presidential contest, winning 47.8% in the first round and 68.3% in the runoff against a PAN candidate. In the concurrent congressional elections the FRG won an absolute majority of 63 of the 113 seats.

Guatemalan National Revolutionary Unity
Unidad Revolucionaria Nacional Guatemalteca (URNG)

Address. 11 Av. 11–56 zona 2, Guatemala City
Telephone. (+502–2) 254–05–72, 334–28–08/09
Email. prensaurng@guate.net
Leadership. Alvaro Colom Caballeros; Raúl Molina Mejía

The URNG was founded in 1979 as an umbrella organization of the various left-wing guerrilla groups in order to present a unified front against army offensives. The framework for a central military command was set up in early 1982, but until the late 1980s the individual member groups continued to operate separately. The new period of civilian rule that began in 1986 encouraged the guerrillas to seek an agreement that would allow the URNG to enter the political mainstream. Semi-official peace talks with the National Reconciliation Commission (CNR), made up of representatives from Guatemalan political parties and of "notable citizens", started in Norway in March 1990 and resulted in the Oslo Accords, which set a rough timetable for formal peace negotiations. A major breakthrough came in talks in Mexico City in April 1991, attended for the first time by representatives of the Guatemalan armed forces. Three months later a framework peace agreement was agreed, although a definitive accord was not achieved until 1996.

In 1995, for the first time in its history, the URNG urged Guatemalans to participate in national elections in support of so-called "alternative candidates", although such candidates were wisely not named. In the 1999 elections the URNG ran jointly with →Authentic Integral Development (DIA). The DIA-URNG candidate for the presidency, Alvaro Colom Caballeros, came third with 12.3% of the votes cast, while the grouping obtained a modest nine seats in Congress.

National Advancement Party
Partido de Avanzada Nacional (PAN)

Address. 7 Av. 10–38, zona 9, Guatemala City
Telephone. (+502–2) 334–1702
Leadership. Alvaro Enrique Arzú Irigoyen (president); Luis Flores (secretary-general)

Founded in 1989, the centre-right PAN is currently the second force in Guatemalan politics after the right-wing →Guatemalan Republican Front (FRG). The party's founder, Alvaro Arzú Irigoyen, gained his reputation as an efficient administrator during his years as mayor of Guatemala City (1985–90). He resigned from the mayoral post to contest the 1990 presidential elections (with support from the business community and the US government), coming fourth in the first round with 17.3% of the vote, whilst the PAN obtained 12 seats in concurrent congressional elections. A PAN member, Oscar Berger Perdomo, was elected mayor of Guatemala City with 34% of the vote.

Having given second-round support to the victorious 1990 presidential candidate, Jorge Serrano Elías of the →Solidarity Action Movement (MAS), Arzú was named as Foreign Minister in the new government and the PAN was also given the communications, transport and public works portfolios. However, it became clear during the Mexico peace talks with the →Guatemalan National Revolutionary Unity (URNG) guerrillas in May 1991, to which Arzú was not invited, that President Serrano would not allow him a major role in government. Arzú resigned as Foreign Minister in September 1991 in protest at Serrano's decision to establish diplomatic relations with Belize, sovereignty over which had long been claimed by Guatemala.

Following the deposition of Serrano in a military coup in June 1993, PAN representatives were included in new national unity government appointed to serve until fresh elections could be held. In congressional elections in August 1994 the PAN was runner-up to the FRG, winning 24 seats to the FRG's 32. It turned the tables in the November 1995 elections, however, by obtaining an overall majority of 43 seats in Congress, while Arzú headed the first-round presidential poll with 36.6% and went on to defeat the FRG candidate in the run-of contest in January 1996 with 51.2% of the vote.

President Arzú moved quickly to sign a definitive peace agreement ending the civil war, overriding familiar reservations from the authoritarian right and the military. But his administration gradually lost popular support, as it failed to make much impact on intractable economic and social problems. The outcome was defeat for the PAN in the 1999 November elections, in which its presidential candidate, Oscar Berger Perdomo, came a poor second to the FRG contender (with only 31.7% of the second-round vote) and the party's representation in an enlarged Congress was reduced to 37 seats out of 113.

Progressive Liberation Party
Partido Libertador Progresista (PLP)
Address. 5a Calle 9–28, zona 2, Guatemala City
Telephone. (+502–2) 232–5548
Email. plp@intelnet.net.gt
Leadership. Aciscio Valladares Molina (1999 presidential candidate)

The moderate conservative PLP was founded to support the 1995 presidential candidacy of Aciscio Valladares Molina, who secured 5.2% of the votes cast in the first round, while the party failed to gain representation in Congress. Valladares stood again in the November 1999 presidential elections, his vote slipping to 3.1%, but the PLP won one seat in Congress.

Other Parties and Movements

Authentic Integral Development (*Desarrollo Integral Auténtico, DIA*), left-wing group which first presented candidates in 1995, when it secured 3.3% in the legislative elections and won no seats. It ran in alliance with →Guatemalan National Revolutionary Unity (URNG) in the 1999 elections.
Address. 12 Calle 2–18, zona 1, Guatemala City
Telephone. (+502–2) 232–8044
Email. morlain@guate.net

Green Organization (*La Organización Verde, LOV*), environmentalist grouping which contested the 1999 elections in alliance with the →Democratic Union (UD).
Address. 5 Calle A 0–64, zona 3, Guatemala City
Telephone. (+502–2) 230–3946

National Liberation Movement (*Movimiento de Liberación Nacional, MLN*), extreme right-wing party founded in 1960 by Mario Sandóval Alarcón in opposition to negotiations with guerrilla groups, successor of the National Democratic Movement (MDN) which, with US backing, overthrew the reformist Arbenz government in 1954. The MLN staged the 1963 coup led by Col. Peralta Azurdia and formed a government which was itself overthrown in 1964. The party held the presidency under Col. Carlos Araña Osorio (1970–74) and Gen. Kjell Laugerud (1974–78), at the height of activity by MLN-linked death squads. The MLN became less influential in the 1980s and from 1990 backed peace talks with the →Guatemalan National Revolutionary Unity Movement (URNG). Its congressional representation declined steadily in the 1990s to zero in 1999, when its presidential candidate, Carlos Humberto Pérez Rodríguez, obtained 0.6% of the vote.

New Guatemala Democratic Front (*Frente Democrático de Nueva Guatemala, FDNG*), moderate left-wing alliance whose presidential candidate, Jorge Luis González del Valle, obtained 7.7% of the vote in 1995, when the party won six seats in Congress. In the 1999 elections, however, the party polled only 1.1% of the presidential vote and lost its congressional representation.
Leadership. Ana Catalina Soberanis Reyes (1999 presidential candidate)

Union of the National Centre (*Union del Centro Nacional, UCN*), founded in 1983 by Jorge Carpio Nicolle, a newspaper publisher, who came second in the 1985 presidential elections with 31.6%, while his party gained 22 congressional seats and headed the opposition. The UCN advanced strongly to 41 of 116 seats in 1990, when Carpio was again narrowly defeated for the presidency. His assassination in July 1993 was largely responsible for the collapse of UCN congressional representation in the 1990s. In 1999 its presidential candidate, Danilo Julián Roca Barillas, gained only 1% of the vote and the party won no seats in Congress.
Leadership. Edmond Mulet (secretary-general)

Guinea

Capital: Conakry

Population: 7,466,000 (2000E)

The Republic of Guinea gained independence from France in 1958. The first President, Ahmed Sekou Touré, dominated the political stage for the next quarter of a century, pursuing a policy of socialist revolution and internal suppression. After his death in March 1984, the armed forces staged a coup, forming a Military Committee for National Recovery (CMRN) under the leadership of Maj.-Gen. Lansana Conté. The 1982 constitution was suspended after the takeover, as was the Democratic Party of Guinea, which had been the ruling and sole legal political party. A new constitution was approved by referendum in December 1990; in early 1991 the CMRN was dissolved and a mixed military and civilian Transitional Committee of National Recovery was set up as the country's legislative body. In April 1992 legislation providing for the legalization of political parties came into effect.

President Conté was confirmed in office in December 1993 in Guinea's first multi-party elections. In legislative elections in June 1995, the Party of Unity and Progress, led by the President, won a majority of the seats in the new 114-seat National Assembly (*Assemblée Nationale*). Some 850 candidates representing 21 out of 46 legalized parties participated in the elections. Opposition parties challenged the results, claiming electoral malpractice, and announced that they would boycott the new parliament.

In December 1998 President Conté won his second five-year mandate by a larger majority, winning about 56% of the vote. Legislative elections were due to take place in November 2000 but were postponed due to internal security concerns.

Democratic Party of Guinea–African Democratic Rally
Parti Démocratique de Guinée–Rassemblement
Démocratique Africain (PDG-RDA)

Address. c/o Assemblée Nationale, Conakry
Leadership. Ismael Mohamed Gassim Gushein

President Touré's former ruling Democratic Party of

Guinea, which had been dissolved in 1984, was revived in 1992 as the PDG-RDA. Following the 1993 presidential election, in which the PDG-RDA leader, Ismael Mohamed Gassim Gushein, secured less than 1% of the vote, the party split, with dissidents forming the Democratic Party of Guinea (PDG-AST) under the leadership of Marcel Cros. Each faction won one National Assembly seat in the 1995 legislative elections.

Party of Unity and Progress
Parti de l'Unité et le Progrès (PUP)
Address. c/o President's Office, Conakry
Leadership. Maj.-Gen. Lansana Conté (leader)
Acting as the core of an informal coalition supporting the ruling regime, the PUP nominated Maj.-Gen. Conté as its candidate for the December 1993 presidential poll, in which he won nearly 52% of the votes cast. In the 1995 legislative elections the PUP won an absolute majority with 71 seats. In December 1998 Conté won his second five-year presidential term, securing about 56% of the vote.

Rally of the Guinean People
Rassemblement du Peuple Guinéen (RPG)
Address. c/o Assemblée Nationale, Conakry
Leadership. Alpha Condé, Tidiane Cisse (leaders)
The RPG leader, Alpha Condé, had been a prominent exiled opponent of former President Touré and the subsequent military regime until his eventual return to Guinea in May 1991. The RPG was one of the first parties registered under the new parties law in 1992. In the December 1993 presidential election, Condé took second place with a 19.5% share of the vote. In the 1995 legislative elections, the RPG won the most seats among the opposition parties with 19. Condé again contested the presidential elections in December 1998, but achieved only third place with 16.6% of the vote. He was arrested and detained after the poll, and eventually sentenced in September 2000 to five years' imprisonment, in what was widely criticized as a show trial. In May 2001 he was unexpectedly released.

The RPG is a consultative member of the Socialist International.

Union for the New Republic
Union pour la Nouvelle République (UNR)
Address. c/o Assemblée Nationale, Conakry
Leadership. Mamadou Boye Ba (leader)
Party leader and presidential candidate, Mamadou Boye Ba, took third place in the December 1993 ballot with just over 13% of the vote. The UNR won nine seats in the 1995 elections to the National Assembly. In September 1998 the UNR absorbed the Party of Renewal and Progress (*Parti pour le Renouveau et le Progrès*, PRP) led by Siradiou Diallo, which had won nine seats in the 1995 legislative elections. Mamadou Boye Ba stood in the December 1998 presidential elections as the joint candidate, coming second with 24.6% of the vote.

Other Parties

Democratic Opposition Coordination (*Coordination de l'Opposition Démocratique, CODEM*), an umbrella anti-Conté grouping which proposes to field a joint candidate in the presidential elections scheduled for 2003.

Djama Party (*Parti Djama*), secured one seat in the National Assembly poll in 1995.
Leadership. Mohamed Mansour Kaba

Guinean People's Party (*Parti du Peuple de Guinée, PPG*), contested the December 1998 presidential elections, but party leader Tolno won less than 1% of the vote to claim fifth place.
Leadership. Charles Pascal Tolno

National Union for Prosperity in Guinea (*Union Nationale pour la Prospérité de la Guinée, UNPG*), formed in August 1993, gaining two seats in the June 1995 legislative elections.

Union for the Progress of Guinea (*Union pour le Progrès de Guinée, UPG*), contested the 1993 and 1998 presidential elections but with minimal impact.
Leadership. Jean-Marie Doré

Guinea-Bissau

Capital: Bissau

Population: 1,286,000 (2000E)

The Republic of Guinea-Bissau achieved independence from Portugal in 1974. Its first President, Luis Cabral, was overthrown in a coup in 1980 by the present head of state, Brig.-Gen. João Bernardo Vieira. The African Party for the Independence of Guinea and Cape Verde (PAIGC) continued to be the sole ruling party after the 1980 coup, although the Cape Verde branch broke away from the Guinea-Bissau branch in 1981. In a constitution adopted in 1984 Guinea-Bissau was declared to be an anti-colonialist and anti-imperialist republic and a state of revolutionary national democracy, with the PAIGC as the leading force in society and the state. In January 1991 the PAIGC formally approved the introduction of multi-party democracy, and in May legislation legalizing political activity by opposition parties was adopted. The first political parties were recognized in November 1991. The revised constitution provided for the direct election of the President and a National People's Assembly (*Assembléia Nacional Popular*).

Multi-party legislative elections took place in July 1994, resulting in victory for the PAIGC, which secured an absolute majority of seats. In presidential elections, which were conducted over two rounds in July and August 1994, President Vieira was returned to office, with just over 52% of the vote in the second ballot.

In June 1998 an army rebellion led by Gen. Ansumane Mane (who had been dismissed as chief of staff the previous February) plunged the country into crisis. Troops from neighbouring Senegal and Guinea were called in to help the forces loyal to President Vieira. Following prolonged fighting and efforts at mediation, a peace accord was reached on Nov. 1, 1998. This provided for the withdrawal of foreign troops, the deployment of a West African ceasefire monitoring group and the holding of elections. Following a further outbreak of hostilities, a new government of national unity was sworn in Feb. 20, 1999. However, on May 7, President Vieira was ousted from power by the rebel military junta led by Gen. Mane. National People's Assembly president Malam Baca

Sanha was appointed acting President of the Republic pending fresh elections, and the government of national unity remained in office. Vieira was allowed to leave the country in June for medical treatment abroad.

In July 1999 constitutional amendments were adopted, limiting the holding of presidential office to two five-year terms, abolishing the death sentence and stipulating that the holders of principal state posts be Guinea-Bissau nationals born of Guinea-Bissau parents.

Presidential and legislative elections were held on Nov. 28, 1999. The presidential poll required a second round of voting on Jan. 16, 2000, resulting in a victory (with 72% of the vote) for Koumba Yalla of the Social Renewal Party (PRS) over Malam Baca Sanha of the PAIGC. In the National People's Assembly elections, the PRS emerged as the largest party with 38 seats, while the Guinea-Bissau Resistance–Bafata Movement (RMB-MB) won 28, the PAIGC 24 and other parties 12.

African Party for the Independence of Guinea and Cape Verde
Partido Africano da Indepêndencia da Guiné e Cabo Verde (PAIGC)
Address. CP 106, Bissau
Leadership. Francisco Benante (president)
The PAIGC was founded in 1956 and engaged in armed struggle against Portuguese colonial rule from the early 1960s. From independence in 1974 it was the sole and ruling party. It had been initially a joint Guinea-Bissau and Cape Verde organization with a bi-national leadership, but the Cape Verde branch broke away from the mainland organization following the November 1980 coup in Guinea-Bissau. While retaining a leftist stance, the PAIGC at the beginning of the 1990s endorsed the establishment of a new multi-party system. In legislative elections in July 1994 the PAIGC won 62 of the 100 seats in the National People's Assembly, with 46% of the votes cast. The simultaneous presidential polls produced no outright winner in the first round, but incumbent President Vieira was returned in the second round run-off against the →Social Renewal Party candidate in August.

In June 1998 the authority of the PAIGC government was challenged by an army rebellion. Troops from neighbouring Senegal and Guinea were called to help the forces loyal to President Vieira. Despite ceasefires and mediation efforts, the ensuing year-long civil war led to Vieira's overthrow in May 1999 by the rebel military junta. National People's Assembly president Malam Baca Sanha was appointed acting President of the Republic pending fresh elections, and the government of national unity which had been appointed the previous February remained in office. Vieira was allowed to leave the country in June for medical treatment abroad. In September 1999 he was expelled from the PAIGC and Francisco Benante assumed the party presidency.

In legislative elections held on Nov. 28, 1999, the PAIGC won only 24 of the 102 National People's Assembly seats, while in the second round of presidential elections on Jan. 16, 2000, PAIGC candidate Malam Baca Sanha lost decisively to Kumba Yalla of the →Social Renewal Party (PRS).

Front of Struggle for the Liberation of Guinea
Frente da Luta para a Liberaçao da Guiné (FLING)
Leadership. François Kankoila Mendy
The FLING claims to trace its organization back to the initiation of armed struggle against Portuguese colonial rule, opposing the unification of Cape Verde with the mainland. In 1981 it was announced that it had been dissolved into the ruling →African Party for the Independence of Guinea and Cape Verde, although remnants of the organization continued to be active in exile. It was legalized in its present form in May 1992. FLING won a single seat in the 1994 legislative elections; its leader contested the presidential poll, but achieved less than 3% of the first ballot vote.

Guinea-Bissau Resistance–Bafata Movement
Resistência da Guiné-Bissau–Movimento Bafatá (RGB-MB)
Address. c/o Assembléia Nacional Popular, Bissau

Leadership. Helder Vaz Lopes (chairman)
Founded in Portugal in 1986 and legalized in December 1991, the party came second to the ruling →African Party for the Independence of Guinea and Cape Verde in the 1994 legislative elections, winning 19 seats. In the November 1999 elections, the RCB-MB gained 28 seats, becoming the second largest party in the National People's Assembly. Its candidate in the presidential poll held at the same time was eliminated after the first ballot, taking third place with 8.2% of the vote.

National Union for Democracy and Progress
União Nacional para a Democracia e o Progresso (UNDP)
Address. c/o Assembléia Nacional Popular, Bissau
Leadership. Abubacar Baldé
The UNDP was formed in April 1998 by Abubacar Baldé, a former Interior Minister. Standing in the first round of the November 1999 presidential elections, he took sixth place with 5.4% of the vote. In the legislative polling at the same time, the UNDP secured one National People's Assembly seat.

Social Democratic Front
Frente Democrática Social (FDS)
Address. c/o Assembléia Nacional Popular, Bissau
Leadership. Rafael Barbosa
The FDS was among the first groups to emerge openly in opposition to the Vieira regime, and was the first to announce its formation as an opposition party. It was legalized in December 1991. Party leader Barbosa had been one of the founders of the PAIGC, but was subsequently purged and imprisoned before being formally amnestied in 1987. Factional strife within the FDS has led to several defections by members to launch other groups, including the →United Social Democratic Party and the →Social Renewal Party. In the November 1999 legislative elections, the FDS won one seat in the National People's Assembly.

Social Renewal Party
Partido para a Renovação Social (PRS)
Address. c/o Assembléia Nacional Popular, Bissau
The PRS was set up in January 1992 by defectors from the →Social Democratic Front, and was legalized the following October. In the 1994 legislative elections it secured 12 seats in the National People's Assembly. Having come second to President Vieira in the first round of the presidential poll, the then party leader Yalla was narrowly defeated in the second round run-off with nearly 48% of the vote, despite being endorsed by all opposition parties.

Following the military overthrow of the Vieira regime, presidential and legislative elections were held in November 1999. The PRS emerged as the largest single party in the National People's Assembly with 38 of the 102 seats, and Koumba Yalla headed the first ballot of the presidential poll with almost 39% of the vote. In the second round of voting in January 2000, Yalla decisively beat the PAIGC candidate and was inaugurated as President of the Republic in February. He resigned as PRS chairman in May 2000.

Union for Change
União para a Mudança (UM)
Address. c/o Assembléia Nacional Popular, Bissau
The UM was set up as an opposition coalition to contest the July 1994 elections. It won six seats in the National People's Assembly, but its presidential candidate, Bubakar Djalo, attracted less than 3% of the vote in the first ballot. Reconstituted in 1995, the UM comprises the →Democratic Front, the →Democratic Party of Progress, the →Party of Renovation and Development, the →Social Democratic Front and the →United Democratic Movement. In the November 1999 elections the UM won three seats in the National People's Assembly.

Other Parties

Democratic Alliance (*Aliança Democrática, AD*), won four seats in the National People's Assembly in the November 1999 legislative elections.

Democratic Front (*Frente Democrática, FD*), left-of-centre party formed in 1990, initially refused legalization in August 1991, but then granted legal status (the first opposition party to be registered) in November 1991.
Leadership. Marcelino Batista

Democratic Party of Progress (*Partido Democrático do Progresso, PDP*), launched in December 1991 and granted legal status in August 1992.
Leadership. Amine Michel Saad

Guinea-Bissau League for Ecological Protection (*Liga da Guiné-Bissau para a Protecção da Ecologia, LIPE*), an environmentalist party dating from 1993.
Leadership. Alhaje Bubakar Djalo

Guinean Civic Forum (*Foro Cívico da Guiné, FCG*), whose candidate for the 1994 presidential election, Antonieta Rosa Gomes, won 1.8% of the vote.

Party of Democratic Convergence (*Partido da Convergência Democrática, PCD*), won 5.3% of the votes cast in the 1994 legislative polls but no seats; its candidate took fourth place in the first ballot of the presidential election.

Party of Renovation and Development (*Partido da Renovação e Desenvolvimento, PRD*), legalized in October 1992 and initially known as the "Group of 121", formed by dissidents of the ruling →African Party for the Independence of Guinea and Cape Verde who advocated more rapid democratization.
Leadership. Manuel Rambout Barcelos

Social Democratic Party (*Partido Social Democrático, PSD*), reported as formed by dissidents of the →Guinea-Bissau Resistance–Bafata Movement, the PSD contested the November 1999 legislative elections, winning three seats.

Socialist Alliance of Guinea-Bissau (*Aliança Socialista da Guiné-Bissau, ASG*), formed in May 2000 by a former chairman of the national human rights league.
Leadership. Fernando Gomes

United Democratic Movement (*Movimento da Unidade Democrática, MUDE*), legalized in August 1992.
Leadership. Filinto Vaz Martins

United Social Democratic Party (*Partido Unido Social Democrático, PUSD*), formed by a splinter group of the →Social Democratic Front in July 1991. Its then leader, Vitor Saude Maria, had earlier been a Prime Minister under the Vieira regime until March 1984 when he left the ruling →African Party for the Independence of Guinea and Cape Verde. The party won no seats in the National People's Assembly in 1994, and its candidate secured only 2% of the vote in the presidential election.

Guyana

Capital: Georgetown   **Population:** 850,000 (2000E)

Guyana (formerly British Guiana) became independent in 1966 and the Co-operative Republic of Guyana was formally proclaimed within the Commonwealth in 1970. Under the 1980 constitution legislative power is held by the 65-member unicameral National Assembly elected for five years by universal suffrage on the basis of proportional representation. Executive power is held by the President and his government. The President appoints a First Vice-President and Prime Minister (who must be an elected member of the National Assembly) and a Cabinet which may include non-elected members and is collectively responsible to the legislature.

The victory of the incumbent People's Progressive Party/Civic (PPP/C) in the December 1997 general elections gave rise to a major political crisis, as the opposition People's National Congress (PNC) disputed their validity amidst violent conflict between supporters of the mainly Indo-Guyanese PPP/C and the predominantly Afro-Caribbean PNC. In January 1998 the two sides signed the CARICOM-brokered Herdmanston Accord, which succeeded in restoring an uneasy peace, although the PNC continued its legal challenge to the elections. Under the accord, a widely representative commission drew up proposals resulting in the passage of the Constitution (Amendment) Act 2000 establishing a permanent Elections Commission to be responsible for the fair conduct of elections. Also passed was the Elections Laws (Amendment) Act 2000, under which 25 of the 65 Assembly members would be elected in 10 geographical regions and the other 40 "national top-up" seats would be allocated proportionally to party lists, headed by the presidential candidate of each party, according to percentage share of the national vote. Under the legislation, at least a third of the candidates on party lists must be women.

In new elections held on March 19, 2001, the PPP/C headed the poll with 52.9% of the vote, so that incumbent President Bharrat Jagdeo was re-elected and the party took 34 of the Assembly seats. The PNC-Reform obtained 41.8% and 27 seats and three small parties the remaining four seats. Although declared transparent and fair by a number of local and international observers, the elections were followed by some violent protests.

Guyana Action Party–Working People's Alliance (GAP–WPA)

Address. Rodney House, 80 Croal Street, Georgetown
Telephone. (+592–2) 253679
Fax. (+592–2) 253679
Website. www.saxakali.com/wpa
Leadership. Paul Hardy (leader, GAP); Rupert Roopnaraine (leader, WPA)

The WPA was formed in the mid-1970s as an alliance of left-wing groups that included the African Society for Cultural Relations with Independent Africa (ASCRIA), Indian Political Revolutionary Associates (IPRA), *Ratoon* (a student group) and the Working People's Vanguard Party (which left before the WPA constituted itself as a political party in 1979). In 1980 one of its leaders, Walter Rodney, was killed by a bomb explosion, an incident blamed in some quarters on supporters of the ruling →People's National Congress (PNC). Having boycotted the 1980 elections, the WPA won one seat in 1985 and two in 1992. The WPA contested the 1997 elections jointly with the Guyana Labour Party in the Alliance for Guyana, which won one Assembly seat.

The WPA contested the March 2001 elections on a joint list with the Guyana Action Party (GAP), which seeks to represent the country's marginalized Amerindian and other hinterland communities. It was agreed that the GAP would field a presidential candidate (Paul Hardy), while the WPA would field a prime ministerial candidate (Rupert Roopnaraine). Having campaigned for a government of national unity, the GAP-WPA alliance came in third position with 2.4% of the vote and two Assembly seats.

The WPA is a consultative member of the Socialist International.

People's National Congress/Reform (PNC/R)

Address. Congress Place, Sophia, PO Box 10330, Georgetown
Telephone. (+592–2) 257850
Email. pnc@guyana-pnc.org
Website. www.guyana-pnc.org
Leadership. Hugh Desmond Hoyte (leader); Robert Corbin (chairman); Oscar E. Clarke (general secretary)

The PNC was founded in 1957 by Forbes Burnham, formerly chairman of the →People's Progressive Party (PPP), following an open split between Burnham and PPP leader Cheddi Jagan. The PNC was the main opposition party after the 1957 and 1961 elections, but in 1964, after a change in the electoral system, it joined →The United Force (TUF) in a coalition government which led British Guiana to independence in 1966. Drawing most of its support from the African-descended population, the party won all elections until 1992, although these contests were widely regarded as rigged in the party's favour.

The PNC initially followed a moderate socialist line with emphasis on co-operative principles, before taking a swing to the left in the 1970s and early 1980s. It adopted a more pragmatic approach under the leadership of Hugh Desmond Hoyte, who took over the country's presidency and the party leadership on Burnham's death in 1985. The party experienced severe internal divisions prior to the 1992 elections, in which it lost power to the PPP, winning 27 Assembly seats with 43.6% of the vote. In 1994 a new party constitution was adopted which ceased to refer to the PNC as a socialist movement.

The PNC was also declared the loser of the December 1997 general elections, in which it took 26 Assembly seats and 35% of the vote. The party staged protests against the outcome and there were violent disturbances and attacks on Indian-owned businesses. Tension was reduced by CARICOM mediation but the PNC continued its legal challenge to the election outcome, securing High Court rulings in January 2001 that it had been illegitimate, although the judge also found that she had no powers to remove the President or his government from office.

Meanwhile, in December 2000 the PNC had formed an alliance with the Reform Group, a political interest group led by Jerome Khan and Stanley Ming and drawing its membership from younger professionals and the business class and with an international network in the Guyanese diaspora. Also including the People's Unity Party (PUP) led by Peter Ramsaroop, the alliance took the name PNC/Reform, the letters of the suffix denoting its main policy principles as follows: R - racial harmony, religious tolerance, rebirth and renewal; E - economic revitalization, prosperity and sustainability; F - financial integrity, financial transparency and vision; O - one people, one nation, one destiny; R - rule of law; M - multiculturalism, multi-ethnicism and modernization.

Contesting the March 2001 general elections as a unitary party under Hoyte's leadership, the PNC/R achieved an increased vote share of 41.8% but failed to unseat the ruling PPP/C, its representation in the new Assembly being 27 seats (14 national and 13 geographical). Amidst renewed clashes with PPP supporters, the PNC/R again disputed the results but its court challenge failed to prevent the installation of a further PPP/C administration. In May 2001 the PNC/R recognized the legitimacy of the government, on the basis of an agreement with the PPP/C that an ethnic relations commission would be created and voter registration procedures reviewed. It reserved the right, however, to challenge aspects of the recent elections in the courts.

People's Progressive Party/Civic (PPP/Civic)

Address. Freedom House, 41 Robb Street, Georgetown
Telephone. (+592–2) 272095
Fax. (+592–2) 272096
Email. ppp@guyana.net.gy
Website. www.pppcivic.org
Leadership. Bharrat Jagdeo (leader); Sam Hinds (Prime Minister); Donald Ramotar (general secretary)

The left-wing PPP, which was formed by Cheddi Jagan in 1950 from an earlier Political Affairs Committee, started as an anti-colonial party speaking for the lower social classes. It has since drawn its support mainly from the majority ethnic Asian–Indian community. In 1957 the PPP gained an absolute majority in the Assembly and Jagan became the first Chief Minister. In 1961, when internal autonomy had been conceded by the British authorities, the party again won a majority and Jagan was appointed Prime Minister. In the 1964 elections, held under a British-imposed proportional representation system, the PPP won the most votes but less than half of the Assembly seats, thereby losing power to the coalition headed by the →People's National Congress (PNC).

In 1969 the PPP began its formal transformation into a Marxist–Leninist party, Jagan being designated to the new post of "general secretary", which he retained until his death in 1997. After boycotting the National Assembly for over a year in protest at the rigged 1973 elections, the PPP in mid-1975 offered the PNC government its "critical support" in light of the PNC's perceived move towards a socialist path. The party nevertheless denounced the further election victories of the PNC in 1980 and 1985 as fraudulent. Following the collapse of communism in Europe, in 1990 the PPP effectively abandoned its previous Marxist–Leninist line and instead declared its support for a market-oriented economy based on collaboration between the state, private and co-operative sectors.

Prior to the delayed general elections eventually held in October 1992, the PPP became the PPP/Civic, having sought to broaden its appeal by bringing together the Civic group of prominent non-party people from various ethnic and ideological backgrounds. The strategy was successful, in that the party returned to power with 52.3% of the vote and 35 Assembly seats. Cheddi Jagan was accordingly sworn in for a five-year term as President and a PPP/C government was installed.

Cheddi Jagan died in office in March 1997 and was succeeded temporarily by the Prime Minister and Vice-President, Sam Hinds, who quickly stood down to allow his predecessor's widow, Janet Jagan, to become President. An American Jew by origin and active in the party since its inception, Janet Jagan led the PPP/C in the general elections held in December 1997, in which the party was again declared the winner with 48% of the vote and 36 Assembly seats, amidst claims of widespread fraud. Janet Jagan stepped down in August 1999 on grounds of ill-health and was succeeded as President by Bharrat Jagdeo, hitherto Second Vice-President. In the March 2001 elections the PPP/C retained power, winning 52.9% of the vote and 34 Assembly seats (23 national and 11 geographical). Amidst yet another major confrontation with what was now the PNC/Reform, President Jagdeo appointed a new PPP/C-dominated government headed by Sam Hinds and including a representative of →The United Force (TUF).

Rise, Organize and Rebuild (ROAR)

Address. 186 Parafield, Leonora, West Coast Demerara, PO Box 101409
Telephone. (+592–268) 2452
Email. guyroar@hotmail.com
Website. www.jaiag.com/roar
Leadership. Ravindra Dev (leader)
ROAR was formed in January 1999 in West Coast Demerara to protest against the murder of 30 people of Indian descent during the previous year and also in response to what the party's leadership perceived to have been silence following anti-Indian riots in January 1998. Despite this genesis, the movement evolved into a political party claiming to be national with the aim of creating a multi-ethnic society. Campaigning on a platform of social and economic improvements, equal opportunities in the civil service, judiciary, police and army, and an end to corruption and ethnic divisions, the party won 0.9% of the vote in the March 2001 elections and was allocated one National Assembly seat.

The United Force (TUF)

Address. 96 Robb & New Garden Streets, Georgetown
Telephone. (+592–2) 262596
Fax. (+592–2) 252973
Email. manzoornadir@yahoo.com
Website. tuf.homestead.com
Leadership. Manzoor Nadir (leader)
The conservative TUF was formed in 1961. Advocating racial integration and a mixed economy, it has historically drawn much of its support from the white, Amerindian and other minority communities. The party joined a coalition government with the →People's National Congress (PNC) in 1964 but withdrew in 1968 in protest at the enfranchisement of the many emigrant Guyanese. In the first post-independence elections in 1968, TUF representation fell to four Assembly seats. It failed to win any seats in the 1973 election but was credited with two seats in both the 1980 and 1985 polls.

TUF retained only one Assembly seat in the 1992, 1997 and 2001 elections, winning 0.7% of the vote in the last contest. Its leader was nevertheless appointed to the new government formed by the →People's Progressive Party/Civic, being allocated the trade, tourism and industry portfolio.

Other Parties

Guyana Democratic Party (GDP), formed in 1997 by Asgar Ally, who had been Finance Minister in the 1992–1997 administration of the →People's Progressive Party/Civic. Capitalist in orientation, the party promised to give entrepreneurs confidence to invest in Guyana as well as to develop the infrastructure of the country in order to encourage capital inflows into areas such as manufacturing, tourism and agriculture. The party won one Assembly seat in 1997 but none in 2001, when its share of the vote was 0.34%.
Address. (+592–2) 261119
Fax. (+592–2) 256894
Leadership. Asgar Ally (leader)

Justice For All Party (JFAP), claiming to speak for the poor and marginalized, founded by TV channel owner and campaigning broadcaster C.N. Sharma. Contesting the 2001 elections only in the Georgetown region on a platform of lowering the cost of living and a resolution of ethnic problems, it took 0.71% of the vote and no seats.
Address. 73 Robb & Wellington Streets, Lacytown, Georgetown
Telephone. (+592–2) 265462
Fax. (+592–2) 273050
Email. sharma@guyana.net.gy
Leadership. Chandra Narine Sharma (leader)

National Front Alliance (NFA), opposed to racial politics, won only 0.11% of the vote in the 2001 elections.
Leadership. Keith Scott

Haiti

Capital: Port-au-Prince

Population: 6,900,000 (2000E)

The Republic of Haiti became independent from France in 1804. Between 1957 and 1986 its rulers were President for Life François "Papa Doc" Duvalier and, from 1971, his son Jean-Claude. The latter years of Jean-Claude "Baby Doc" Duvalier's rule were marked by prolonged popular unrest, and he fled abroad in February 1986. A new constitution, which was drawn up in late 1986 and overwhelmingly approved in a referendum in March 1987, provided for a bicameral legislature made up of a 27-member Senate (*Sénat*) and a Chamber of Deputies (*Chambre des Deputés*) of at least 70 members (currently 82). Repeated military intervention, however, prevented the creation of stable civilian government.

Jean-Bertrand Aristide was elected as President for the first time in 1990, but was toppled by a violent military coup in 1991, the result of which was reversed by a US military intervention in 1994.

Aristide handed over power to his elected successor, René Préval, in 1996. However, Aristide won the next presidential election held on Nov. 26, 2000, with 91.8% of the vote and was inaugurated in February 2001. Elections to the Chamber of Deputies and partial elections to the Senate were held in three stages on May 21, July 30 and Nov. 26, 2000, resulting in an overwhelming victory for Aristide's Lavalas Family.

Christian National Movement
Mouvement Chrétien National (Mochrena)

Address. c/o Chambre des Deputés, Port-au-Prince

Also known as the Christian Movement to Build a New Haiti (*Mouvement Chrétien pour Bâtir une Nouvelle Haïti*) and dating from 1991, Mochrena won three seats in the 2000 elections to the Chamber of Deputies, making it the largest party in the Chamber after the ruling →Lavalas Family.

Lavalas Family
Fanmi Lavalas (FL)

Address. c/o Chambre des Deputés, Port-au-Prince

Leadership. Jean-Bertrand Aristide (leader)

The pro-Aristide, centrist Lavalas (variously translated as "waterfall", "flood" or "avalanche") Family emerged in the late 1990s when the Lavalas Political Organization (OPL) split into two main factions. The division had its roots in the presidency of René Préval. Soon after his inauguration as President in February 1996, Préval saw his support base within the OPL erode, as he failed to push ahead with his main policy objective, a market-based restructuring of the economy. Resistance to Préval's reforms came from within the OPL, including Aristide himself. Aristide's criticism of Préval resulted in the split of the OPL into two new, and opposing, political entities, the Lavalas Family (headed by Aristide) and the →Organization of Struggling People, headed by the former OPL leader Gérard Pierre-Charles. Despite the split, Aristide's faction emerged victorious from the 2000 legislative elections, winning all but a few seats in both houses. Aristide went on to an overwhelming victory in the presidential election held in late 2000 and replaced Préval as President in February 2001.

Open the Gates Party
Parti Louvri Barye (PLB)

Address. c/o Chambre des Deputés, Port-au-Prince

The PLB was formed in 1992 as a pro-Aristide party, its co-founder Matine Remilien being killed shortly afterwards after being arrested by the military for fly-posting photographs of Aristide. In the 2000 legislative elections, the party won two seats in the Chamber of Deputies and one seat in the Senate.

Organization of Struggling People
Organisation de Peuple en Lutte (OPL)

Address. c/o Chambre des Deputés, Port-au-Prince

Leadership. Gérard Pierre-Charles

The OPL emerged from a split within the pro-Aristide Lavalas Political Organization (OPL) in the late 1990s. At this time Aristide himself created the →Lavalas Family, whilst his erstwhile supporter, and OPL leader, Gérard Pierre-Charles, formed the Organization of Struggling People, which retained the OPL acronym. The OPL contested the 2000 legislative elections as the main opposition party, but managed to win only one seat in the Chamber of Deputies. In late 2000 the OPL united with other opposition groups in the Democratic Convergence to press for an annulment of the election results.

The OPL has observer status in the Socialist International.

Other Parties and Alliances

Confederation of Democratic Unity (*Kovansyon Inite Demokratik, KID*), opposition grouping opposed to the rule of Aristide and the →Lavalas Family.

Leadership. Evans Paul

Consultation Group, member of the opposition →Democratic Convergence which has pressed for the annulment of the 2000 legislative and presidential elections. Leading members include Evans Paul, Victor Benolt and Fred Biutus.

Democratic Convergence (*Convergence Démocratique, CD*), a loose coalition of opposition parties and groups, which pressed, unsuccessfully, for the annulment of the 2000 legislative and presidential elections, won by the →Lavalas Family and Jean-Bertrand Aristide. The coalition included leading figures from the →Organization of Struggling People, the →Consultation Group and the →Progressive Democratic and National Reunion.

Koodinasyon Resistans Grandans (Korega-Eskanp), won one seat in the Chamber of Deputies during the 2000 elections.

Leadership. Joachim Samedi

Mobilization for National Development (*Mobilisation pour le Développment National, MDN*), centre-right party founded in 1986 and which claims to be the country's first legal political party; latterly opposed to Aristide and the →Lavalas Family.

Website. www.mdnhaiti.org

Leadership. Hubert de Ronceray (president)

Movement for the Installation of Democracy in Haiti (*Mouvement pour l'Instauration de la Démocratie en Haïti, MIDH*), centre-right party founded in 1986 by Marc Bazin, who had briefly served as Finance Minister in a Duvalier cabinet. The party has opposed the ruling →Lavalas Family in recent years.

Leadership. Marc Bazin (leader)

Party of the National Congress of Democratic Movements (*Pati Kongre Nasyonal Mouvman Demokratik Yo, KONAKOM*), social democratic party founded in 1987 by delegates from an array of political groups, trade unions, peasants' and students' organizations, and human rights associations. The party is a member of the opposition →Consultation Group and is a full member of the Socialist International.

Leadership. Victor Benoît (general secretary)

Progressive Democratic and National Rally (*Rassemblement Démocratique Progressiste et National, RDPN*), Christian democratic party, a member of the opposition →Democratic Convergence which has pressed for the annulment of the 2000 legislative and presidential elections. The RDPN is a member of the Christian Democrat International and of the Christian Democratic Organization of America.

Address. 234 Route de Delmas, BP 1199, Port-au-Prince

Telephone. (+509) 363313

Fax. (+509) 383982

Leadership. Leslie Manigat (president)

Revolutionary Progressive Nationalist Party (*Parti Nationaliste Progressiste Révolutionnaire, PANPRA*), social democratic party formed in 1986, a member of the Socialist International.

Leadership. Serge Gilles (leader)

Space of Concerted Action
Espace de Concertation

Address. c/o Chambre des Deputés, Port-au-Prince

Founded in 1999, this party won one seat in the Chamber of Deputies during the 2000 elections.

Honduras

Capital: Tegucigalpa

Population: 6,250,000 (2000E)

The Republic of Honduras gained its independence from Spain in 1821 and was a member of the United Provinces of Central America until 1838. The country was ruled by the conservative National Party of Honduras (PNH) from 1933 to 1957, a period which also marked the political ascendancy of the army. In an interlude of civilian government, a series of moderate social and political reforms were introduced by the Liberal Party of Honduras (PLH), in office from 1957 to 1963, which included a programme of land reform and the establishment of the state social security system. The military then ruled from 1963 to 1980, except for a short period under PNH government in 1971-72, before the PLH returned to power in 1980 although with the military still wielding great influence. The PLH won the presidential election of 1985, but lost power to the PNH in November 1989.

Under its 1982 constitution, Honduras has a unicameral National Congress (*Congreso Nacional*) and executive power rests with the President, who is elected for a four-year non-renewable term by a simple majority of votes. The 128-member National Congress is elected for a four-year term on the basis of proportional representation, voting being compulsory for those aged between 18 and 60.

The most recent decade has been dominated by the PLH. In presidential elections held on Nov. 28, 1993, Carlos Roberto Reina of the PLH emerged as the winner with 52.4% of the vote. Simultaneous congressional elections were also won by the PLH. The PLH enjoyed a similar margin of victory in presidential elections held on Nov. 30, 1997, with its candidate, Carlos Flores Facussé, receiving 52.7% of the vote against 42.7% for the PNH's Alba Nora Gúnera. In simultaneous congressional elections the PLH won 67 seats (with 49.5% of the vote), the PNH 55 (41.6%), the National Innovation and Unity Party–Social Democracy 3 (4.1%), the Christian Democratic Party of Honduras 2 (2.6%) and the Democratic Unification Party 1 (2.1%).

Christian Democratic Party of Honduras
Partido Demócrata Cristiano de Honduras (PDCH)

Address. Colonia San Carlos, 2da. Av. Atrás de los Castaños No.204, AP 1387, Tegucigalpa DC
Telephone. (+504) 323139
Fax. (+504) 326060
Leadership. Arturo Corrales Álvarez (president and 1997 and 2001 presidential candidate)

Founded in 1980, the PDCH is a Christian democratic party with both progressive and conservative wings. The party has not fared well in presidential and legislative elections, receiving less than 2% in presidential races and no more than two seats in the Assembly. It has not, however, been without political significance, joining with other parties in the 1980s in promoting Honduran neutrality in regional conflicts. In the early 1990s, moreover, a member of the PDCH served as a member of the government of the →National Party of Honduras as Head of the National Agrarian Institute (INA), an agency in charge of agrarian reform. For the presidential elections due in November 2001 the PDCH again nominated Arturo Corrales Álvarez, who beat off a challenge from former party president Marco Orlando Iriate.

The party is a member of the Christian Democrat International and the Christian Democrat Organization of America.

Democratic Unification Party
Partido de Unificación Democrática (PUD)

Address. c/o Congreso Nacional, Palacio Legislativo, AP 595, Tegucigalpa
Leadership. Matías Fúnez Valladares

The PUD was launched in 1993 as the political wing of a number of former elements of the *Movimiento Revolucionario Hondureño* (MRH), a clandestine guerrilla alliance. The MRH was itself formed in 1983 as an umbrella organization in an attempt to co-ordinate the efforts of the militant left. The aim was a force under one command to conduct a guerrilla war and to play an active part in the event of a regionalization of the Central America crisis. Founding members included the Communist Party of Honduras, the Social Action Party of Honduras, the Central American Workers' Revolutionary Party (PRTC), the Lorenzo Zelaya Popular Revolutionary Forces (FPR-LZ, founded by students at the National Autonomous University in 1980-81), the Revolutionary Unity Movement (MUR), the Cinchonero Popular Liberation Movement (MPL Cinchoneros) and the Morazanista Front for the Liberation of Honduras (FMLH).

As tensions eased throughout the region, all member groups of the MRH (originally known as the *Directorio Nacional Unificado–Movimiento de Unidad Revolucionario*, DNU-MUR) took advantage of a general amnesty in June 1991, although some rebels made it known that they intended to continue fighting. The group was banned from democratic participation until 1997, when its presidential candidate, Matías Fúnez Valladares, won 1.2% of the vote and the party's 2.6% of the popular vote ensured one seat in the National Congress.

Liberal Party of Honduras
Partido Liberal de Honduras (PLH)

Address. Col. Miramontes, Atrás del Supermercado, 'La Colonia' no. 1, Tegucigalpa DC
Telephone. (+504) 320520
Fax. (+504) 320797
Leadership Carlos Flores Facussé (President of Honduras); Rafael Pineda Ponce (2001 presidential candidate)

Founded in 1890 and therefore the country's oldest party, the PLH has both conservative and progressive wings, both of which have tended to be conservative in office. In recent times, the party held power from 1957–63 before being deposed by the military, an experience which did not prevent it, in 1980, from being the main force in an interim government under the then military President Gen. Policarpo Paz Garcia. Since 1970 the PLH has been, in effect, a coalition of disparate tendencies, each with its own leadership and structure, overlaying the traditional divide between the conservative rural and the more reformist urban wings of the party.

The PLH won elections in November 1981, gaining an absolute majority in the legislature. Its leader from 1979, Roberto Suazo Córdova, a pro-US right-winger and head of the conservative *rodista* faction of the party, was installed as President in January 1982, formally ending 18 years of almost uninterrupted military rule, although the armed forces retained extensive legal and de facto powers. In January 1983 the PLH almost lost its legislative majority when Suazo Córdova's *rodistas* clashed with the Popular Liberal Alliance (ALIPO) faction of the party, led by the brothers Carlos Roberto Reina and Jorge Arturo Reina, who were subsequently driven out and in February 1984 established the Revolutionary Democratic Liberal Movement (MLDR or M-Lider). The *rodistas* in turn split in 1985, with competing factions backing Oscar Mejía Arellano and José Azcona del Hoyo for the presidency. Azcona had resigned from Suazo Córdova's government in 1983 and subsequently accused the regime of corruption.

Azcona won the presidency in November 1985 in alliance with ALIPO, having agreed a power-sharing national unity pact with the →National Party of Honduras (PNH), the second since 1971, giving the PNH two cabinet posts and control of the Supreme Court and other important political and administrative posts. While President Azcona's government was preoccupied with issues arising from the Nicaraguan conflict, not least the presence in the country of some 20,000 US-backed right-wing *contra* rebels, a battle for the PLH presidential nomination ensued, which was eventually won in December 1988 by Carlos Flores Facussé, a former minister in the Suazo Córdova government who had forged a surprise alliance with the dissident M-Lider. Although Flores Facussé lost the 1989 presidential election, the party received two posts in the new PNH cabinet.

More recent times have seen Liberal domination. Carlos Reina won handsomely in the presidential elections of 1993 against former Supreme Court president Oswaldo Ramos of the PNH, while in legislative balloting the Liberals again defeated the Nationalists by 71 seats to 55. In the November 1997 presidential elections Flores Facussé was again the PLH candidate and was elected with 52.7% of the vote, while the Liberals also won 67 National Congress seats to the National Party's 55.

The battle for the PLH presidential nomination for the November 2001 elections was eventually won by Rafael Pineda Ponce. The diversity of the party was reflected in the six other candidates in contention, namely Víctor Sierra Corea (of the M-Lider faction), Esteban Handal Pérez (*Nueva Generácion*), Vera Rubí (*Siglo XXI*), Manuel Zelaya (*Movimiento Esperanza Liberal*), Jaime Rosenthal Oliva (*Jaimistas*) and Tito Livio Sierra (*Reforma y Justicia*).

The PLH is a full member of the Liberal International.

National Innovation and Unity Party–Social Democracy
Partido de Innovación Nacional y Unidad–Social Democrácia (PINU-SD)
Address. AP 105, 29 Avenida de Comayagüela 912, Tegucigalpa
Telephone. (+504) 371357
Leadership. Olban Valladares Ordoñez (president and 1997 presidential candidate)
Founded in 1970 the PINU describes itself as social democratic in orientation. The party, whose support comes mainly from professionals and some rural workers' groups, was not afforded legal recognition until 1978. In 1981 it secured only 2.5% of the vote and three of the 82 seats in the National Assembly, one of which was won by Lulin Mendez, the first *campesino* (peasant) leader ever to sit in the legislature. It has enjoyed mixed fortunes since, faring relatively well in the 1997 elections, in which party leader Olban Valladares Ordoñez received over 2% to finish third in the presidential race and the party also secured three seats in the National Congress.

National Party of Honduras
Partido Nacional de Honduras (PNH)
Address. Paseo Obelisco, Camayagüela MDC, AP 3300, Tegucigalpa
Telephone. (+504) 323066
Fax. (+504) 385275
Leadership. Porfirio Loba Sosa (president); Ricardo Maduro (2001 presidential candidate)
Founded in 1923, the PNH is a traditionally conservative party which now promotes neo-liberal economic measures. Traditionally the party of large landowners, the party has also been closely identified with the military. It held power from 1933 to 1957, including under the dictatorship of Gen. Tiburcio Carías Andino (1939–49), and in 1971–72 and 1985-87, when it participated with the →Liberal Party of Honduras (PLH) in short-lived national unity governments.

The PNH, like the PLH, comprises various factions, including the Movement for Nationalist Democratization (MDN), the Movement for Unity and Change (MUC) and the Nationalist Labour Tendency (TNL). The PLH government of 1981-85 encouraged PNH infighting by using the then PLH-dominated Supreme Court and the National Electoral Tribunal (TEN) to support the pro-government MUC in its claim to control the party. This decision was reversed in 1985 by the military, which supported the accession to power of the newly-created MONARCA faction led by Rafael Leonardo Callejas. MONARCA won all 63 of the PNH's 134 seats in the 1985 general election, and as part of the subsequent national unity government, in which it held the foreign affairs and labour portfolios, forced the PLH to give it control of the Supreme Court, the TEN and an important role in the administration of the legislature.

Callejas was the unopposed PNH candidate in the 1989 presidential elections, which he won comfortably. On taking office, his government restored relations with the IMF and other creditors and implemented a package of IMF-approved neo-liberal economic measures. These included the wholesale dismissal of thousands of public sector workers (many of whom were PLH supporters), the privatization of state-owned agencies, the abolition of price controls on basic essentials and the devaluation of the currency. The measures caused widespread social unrest throughout 1990–91, despite Callejas' periodic promises to increase social sector spending. Anti-government protest was increasingly repressed by the security forces, leading to international protests at the high level of systematic human rights abuses.

The PNH lost the 1993 presidential elections under the candidature of former Supreme Court president Oswaldo Ramos Soto. Following this defeat, internal divisions within the party intensified, so that by the end of 1995 there were eight distinct factions, the most important being the *Oswaldista* and *Roma* movements. Such disunity partially explained why the 1997 PNH presidential candidate, Alba Nora Gúnera, was so easily defeated (42.7% to 52.8%) by her PLN opponent. The party nevertheless maintained a substantial presence in the National Congress, winning 55 seats with 41.6% of the vote.

In the run-up to the November 2001 elections, Ricardo Maduro of the *Movimiento Arriba Honduras* faction was eventually, after some debate about his eligibility, chosen as the party's nominee for the presidency. The other contenders were Carlos Kattán (*Nueva Estrella*), Héctor René Fonseca (*Patria Nueva*) and Elías Asfura (*Avance*).

The party is a member of the International Democrat Union, the Christian Democrat International and the Christian Democrat Organization of America.

Hungary

Capital: Budapest   **Population:** 10,250,000 (2000E)

After four decades of communist rule in the People's Republic of Hungary, in January 1989 the National Assembly legalized freedom of assembly and association. A month later the then ruling Hungarian Socialist Workers' Party (MSMP) approved the formation of independent parties, some of which had begun organizing on an informal basis the previous year. In September formal sanction was given to multi-party participation in national elections, the People's Republic giving way the following month to the revived Hungarian Republic. The President as head of state is indirectly elected for a five-year term by the unicameral National Assembly (*Országgyülés*), which is elected for a four-year term by universal adult suffrage in two rounds of voting, its 386 members including eight providing ethnic minority representation. The complex electoral system involves the election of 176 deputies from single-member constituencies, 152 from 20 multi-member constituencies by a form of proportional representation of parties which obtain at least 5% of the vote, and 58 from national party lists to ensure overall proportional representation.

Hungarian parties receive central budget funding for their election campaign expenses, proportionally to the number of candidates presented (with independent candidates receiving the same as one party candidate). Under the electoral law in force for the 1998 parliamentary elections, each party was allowed to spend a maximum of 386 million forints (about $2 million), i.e. Ft1 million per candidate. Additional state subsidies are available to parties represented in the National Assembly in proportion to their number of seats.

The Assembly elections of May 10 and 24, 1998, resulted as follows: Federation of Young Democrats–Hungarian Civic Party 147 seats (with 38.3% of the vote), Hungarian Socialist Party 134 (34.7%), Independent Party of Smallholders, Agrarian Workers and Citizens 48 (12.4%), Alliance of Free Democrats 24 (6.2%), Hungarian Democratic Forum 18 (4.4%), Hungarian Justice and Life Party 14 (3.6), others 1.

Alliance of Free Democrats
Szabad Demokraták Szövetsége (SzDSz)

Address. 6 Mérleg utca, 1051 Budapest V
Telephone. (+36–1) 117–6911
Fax. (+36–1) 118–7944
Email. intldept@mail.datanet.hu
Website. www.szdsz.hu
Leadership. Gábor Demszky (president); István Szent-Ivanyi (parliamentary group leader); András Keszthelyi (chief of staff); Csaba Szabady (managing director)

The centrist SzDSz began life in March 1988 as the Network of Free Initiatives, representing the centre-left "urban" rather than the "populist" strand in the opposition, many of its members being lapsed Marxists. The grouping was reorganized as a political party in November 1988 and held its first general assembly in March 1989. It won 91 Assembly seats in 1990 on a vote share of 21.4%, becoming the leading opposition party of the post-communist era. Factional strife between "pragmatists" and "ideologues" appeared to be healed in November 1992 by the election of Iván Peto as party president.

Despite hopes of a major breakthrough, the party slipped to 70 seats in the May 1994 Assembly elections, its first-round voting share falling to 19.8%. It opted to join a centre-left coalition with the →Hungarian Socialist Party (MSzP), its presidential nominee, Arpád Göncz, being elected President of Hungary by the Assembly in June 1995. Tarnished by corruption allegations, Peto resigned as SzDSz president in April 1997 and was succeeded the following month by Gábor Kuncze, then Interior Minister and Deputy Prime Minister.

The SzDSz was the biggest loser in the defeat of the government parties in the May 1998 Assembly elections, falling to 24 seats (with only 6.2% of the vote) and going into opposition. Kuncze was quickly replaced as party president by Bálint Magyar, who was in turn replaced in December 2000 by Gábor Demszky, the mayor of Budapest. However, Demszky resigned in June 2001, on the grounds that he had not been supported in his efforts to establish an independent liberal line for the party. Gábor Kuncze returned to the lead-ership and quickly entered into a mutual support pact with the MSzP for the 2002 parliamentary elections.

The SzDSz is affiliated to the Liberal International.

Federation of Young Democrats–Hungarian Civic Party
Fiatal Demokraták Szövetsége–Magyar Polgári Párt (FIDESz-MPP)

Address. 28 Lenday utca, 1062 Budapest VI
Telephonr. (+36–1) 269–5353
Fax. (+36–1) 269–5343
Email. sajto@fidesz.hu
Website. www.fidesz.hu
Leadership. Viktor Orbán (political leader); Zoltán Pokorni (chairman); József Szájer (parliamentary leader), János Ader (general secretary)

Then known simply as the Federation of Young Democrats, this moderate right-wing grouping came in fifth place in the 1990 Assembly elections, winning only 20 of 378 elective seats on a 7.0% vote share, although later that year it won elections for mayor in nine of the country's largest cities. In the May 1994 general elections, its national representation declined further to 20 seats and it remained an opposition party. A 35-year age limit on membership was abandoned in April 1993, paving the way for the adoption of the FIDESz-MPP designation two years later.

The FIDESz-MPP was strengthened in 1997 and early 1998 by its absorption of part of the →Christian Democratic People's Party (KDNP). Benefiting from public disenchant-ment with the ruling coalition headed by the →Hungarian Socialist Party (MSzP), the FIDESz-MPP achieved a major advance in the May 1998 Assembly elections, winning 147 seats on a 38.3% vote share. As chairman of the largest party, Viktor Orbán unexpectedly opted to form a right-wing coalition with the →Independent Party of Smallholders, Agrarian Workers and Citizens (FKgP) and the →Hungarian Democratic Forum (MDF), the FIDESz-MPP being allocated 12 of the 17 ministerial posts. The new government took Hungary into NATO in March 1999 and set accession to the European Union as its key objective.

In January 2000 a FIDESz congress decided to divide the

236

party chairmanship from the premiership and elected Secret Services Minister László Kövér to the party post. However, having come under criticism for his aggressive style, Kövér stood down in March 2001 and was replaced by Zoltán Pokorni, the Education Minister. The party then entered into talks with the MDF on forming an alliance in the next parliamentary elections.

Having previously been an affiliate of the Liberal International, FIDESz in September 2000 opted to join the Christian Democrat International by becoming an associate member of the European People's Party. It is also affiliated to the European Democrat Union.

Hungarian Democratic Forum
Magyar Demokrata Fórum (MDF)

Address. 3 Bem József tér., 1027 Budapest II
Telephone (+36–1) 212–4601
Fax. (+36–1) 156–8522
Email. kulugy@freemail.c3.hu
Website. www.mdf.hu
Leadership. Ibolya David (chairperson)

A centre-right party of populist/nationalist orientation, the MDF was founded in September 1988 with the avowed purpose of "building a bridge between the state and society". It held its first national conference in Budapest in March 1989, when it demanded that Hungary should again become "an independent democratic country of European culture". In the April 1990 Assembly election the party won a plurality of 165 of 378 elective seats, on a first-round vote of 24.7%. The result was an MDF-led coalition headed by József Antall, also including the →Christian Democratic People's Party (KDNP) and the →Independent Party of Smallholders, Agrarian Workers and Citizens (FKgP).

In January 1993 Antall survived a challenge to his MDF leadership from the party's nationalist right, led by István Csurka. In early June Csurka and three parliamentary colleagues were expelled from the party, promptly forming the →Hungarian Justice and Life Party. Antall died in December 1993 and was succeeded, on a temporary basis, by Sandor Lezsák, who was named chairman of the MDF executive committee in February 1994, after resigning from the party chairmanship in favour of the then Defence Minister, Lajos Für.

The May 1994 Assembly elections delivered a major rebuff to the MDF, which slumped to 37 seats on a vote share of only 11.7% and went into opposition. As a result, Lezsák withdrew completely from the leadership at the beginning of June, being succeeded by former Finance Minister Iván Szabo as parliamentary leader. On being confirmed as MDF chairman in September, Für ruled out a merger with the KDNP "for the time being". Various problems contributed to Für's decision early in 1996 to vacate the leadership, which returned to Lezsák, who faced major opposition within the party. An anti-Lezsák group immediately formed the breakaway →Hungarian Democratic People's Party, the rump MDF being reduced to some 20 Assembly members.

Notwithstanding an alliance with the →Federation of Young Democrats–Hungarian Civic Party (FIDESz-MPP) in the May 1998 elections, the MDF declined further to 18 seats and 4.4% of the vote. It was nevertheless included in the new three-party right-wing coalition government headed by the FIDESz-MPP and including the FKgP. In January 1999 Lezsák was finally ousted as MDF leader by Ibolya David, the Justice Minister, who in February 2000 launched the "Right Hand of Peace 2000" alliance of assorted right-wing groups with the aim of recovering lost support for the MDF. In mid-2001 the MDF entered into negotiations with the FIDESz-MPP on a mutual support pact for the 2002 parliamentary elections.

The MDF is affiliated to both the International Democrat Union and the Christian Democrat International, being also an associate member of the European People's Party.

Hungarian Justice and Life Party
Magyar Igazság es Elet Párt (MIEP)

Address. 3 Akadémia utca, 1054 Budapest V
Telephone. (+36–1) 268–5199
Fax. (+36–1) 268–5197
Email. istvan.csurka@miep.parlament.hu
Website. www.miep.hu
Leadership. István Csurka (chairman)

The extreme right-wing MIEP was launched in June 1993 by dissidents of the then ruling →Hungarian Democratic Forum (MDF) after István Csurka had unsuccessfully challenged József Antall for the MDF leadership. Openly anti-semitic, the party contends that national revival is being thwarted by a "Jewish–Bolshevik–liberal conspiracy" and advocates the restoration of Hungary's pre-1914 borders, starting with the annexation of the majority ethnic Hungarian province of Vojvodina in Yugoslavia. The party's original Assembly contingent of about 10 deputies fell to none when it secured only 1.6% of the vote in the May 1994 Assembly elections. It regained representation in the May 1998 elections, winning 14 seats with 3.6% of the vote.

Alone among the parliamentary parties, the MIEP in February 1999 voted against Hungary's accession to NATO. In September 2000 Csurka demanded that a referendum should be held before Hungary joined the European Union. In speeches in mid-2001, Csurka declared the MIEP's willingness to join a "genuinely right-wing" government with the →Federation of Young Democrats–Hungarian Civic Party (FIDESz-MPP) after the 2002 parliamentary elections.

Hungarian Socialist Party
Magyar Szocialista Párt (MSzP)

Address. 26 Köztársaság tér., 1081 Budapest
Telephone. (+36–1) 210–0068
Fax. (+36–1) 210–0011
Email. info@mszp.hu
Website. www.mszp.hu
Leadership. László Kovács (chairman); Katalin Szili (deputy chairperson); Sándor Nagy (parliamentary group leader); György Jánosi (chairman of national board); Peter Medgyessy (candidate for Prime Minister)

The MSP is the successor to the former ruling (Communist) Hungarian Socialist Workers' Party (MSMP), which had been created under an earlier designation by the June 1948 merger of Hungary's Communist and Social Democratic parties. The original Hungarian Communist Party was founded in November 1918 and took a leading role in the short-lived Republic of Councils (soviets) declared in Hungary in March 1919, its leading activists going underground during the succeeding "White Terror" and Horthy dictatorship. Many prominent Communists took refuge in Moscow, and towards the end of World War II (during which Hungary was allied to the Axis powers) the entry into Hungary of Soviet forces was followed by the establishment of a provisional government comprising Communists, Smallholders, Social Democrats and the National Peasant Party. Although the Smallholders obtained an absolute majority (57%) in elections held in November 1945, the coalition was continued, with a Communist as Interior Minister. Two years later, in the elections of August 1947, the Communists emerged as the strongest single party with 22% of the vote), ahead of the Smallholders, while the combined share of the Communists, Social Democrats and National Peasant Party was 45%. Under the leadership of Mátyás Rákosi, the Communists then effectively eliminated their coalition partners as independent political forces and in June 1948 the Social Democratic Party was merged with the Communist Party to form the Hungarian Workers' Party (HWP), many Social Democrats who opposed the merger going into exile.

In elections held in May 1949 the HWP presented an unopposed joint list with four other parties called the People's Independence Front (PIF); of the 402 elective seats in parliament, over 70% were allotted to the HWP. In August 1949 a new constitution was adopted similar to those of other East European "people's democracies". In the elections of May 1953 the HWP was the only party to be mentioned in the manifesto of the PIF, which in October 1954 was replaced by the broader-based Patriotic People's Front *(Hazafiás Népfront)*. Meanwhile, former Social Democrats had been gradually eliminated from the HWP leadership and purges were conducted by the Rakosi "Muscovites" against the "home Communists", notably László Rajk, who was executed in October 1949 after a show trial, and János Kádár, who spent several years in prison.

Following Stalin's death in March 1953, Rakosi resigned from the premiership (although continuing as party leader), in which post he was succeeded in July 1953 by Imre Nagy. He embarked on a "new course" economic policy involving the halting of compulsory collectivization, greater emphasis on the production of consumer goods, the release of political prisoners and greater cultural freedom. However, in early 1955 the HWP central committee condemned the new policies as "right-wing" and "opportunist", with the result that Nagy was removed from the premiership and dismissed from his party posts in April 1955.

Following Nikita Khrushchev's denunciation of Stalin at the 20th congress of the Soviet Communist Party in February 1956, Rakosi was obliged to resign from the Hungarian party leadership in July 1956. Thereafter, widespread opposition built up to Rakosi's successor, Ernö Gerö (another hard-liner), culminating in the reappointment of Nagy to the premiership in October 1956 amid violent clashes between Hungarian demonstrators and Soviet forces, which were then withdrawn from the country. Nagy announced a new programme, including free elections, Hungary's withdrawal from the Warsaw Pact and a policy of permanent neutrality, and formed a national coalition administration including non-Communist representatives.

Gerö was succeeded as party secretary by Kádár, who initially supported Nagy's programme but who in early November 1956 formed an alternative "revolutionary workers' and peasants' government". At the invitation of the latter, Soviet forces then returned in strength and crushed Hungarian resistance over several days of heavy fighting. Nagy and his associates were executed as traitors and Kádár was confirmed as leader of the party, which was reconstituted as the Hungarian Socialist Workers' Party (MSzWP). After a period of severe reprisals, Kádár instituted a policy of reconciliation and limited liberalization, which was only partly tarnished by Hungary's participation in the Soviet-led intervention in Czechoslovakia in 1968.

Economic, social and cultural liberalization was followed in 1983 by a partial democratization of the political process, involving in particular a choice of candidates in national and local elections, although still within a framework of MSzWP supremacy. These and other Hungarian initiatives were specifically acknowledged by the new post-1985 Soviet Communist Party leadership as having furnished some guidelines for the Soviet Union's own reform programme under Mikhail Gorbachev.

As communist rule began to collapse in Eastern Europe, an extraordinary party congress of the MSzMP in October 1989 renounced Marxism in favour of democratic socialism, adopted its current name and appointed Rezsö Nyers to the newly-created post of presidium chairman. Chosen to succeed Nyers in May 1990, Gyula Horn led the party to an overall majority in the May 1994 Assembly elections, with a tally of 209 seats on a 32.6% vote share. Nevertheless, mainly for purposes of international respectability, Horn brought the centrist →Alliance of Free Democrats (SzDSz) into a new coalition.

Speedily becoming unpopular for its economic austerity measures, the MSzP-led government was also troubled by various corruption scandals and by deep dissension within the party. In the May 1998 Assembly elections, it fell back to second place with 134 seats, although its share of the vote increased slightly to 34.7%. The party went into opposition and in September 1998 Horn was succeeded as chairman by former Foreign Minister László Kovács.

MSzP deputies backed the entry of Hungary into NATO in March 1999 and also formed part of the consensus in favour of accession to the European Union. A party congress in October 1999 resolved that at least 20% of MSzP elected bodies must be under 35 and/or women. The next party congress in November 2000 re-elected Kovács as chairman and elected Katalin Szili to the new post of deputy chairman, while in December Sándor Nagy succeeded Kovács as MSzP parliamentary group leader. In mid-2001 the MSzP entered into a mutual support pact with the SzDSz for the 2002 parliamentary elections, for which it nominated former Finance Minister Peter Medgyessy as its prime ministerial candidate.

With a membership of 35,000, the MSzP is a full member party of the Socialist International and an associate member of the Party of European Socialists.

Independent Party of Smallholders, Agrarian Workers and Citizens
Független Kisgazda, Földmunkas és Polgári Párt (FKgP)

Address. 24 Belgrád rakpárt, 1056 Budapest V
Telephone. (+36–1) 318–2855
Fax. (+36–1) 318–1824
Email. fkgpczp@matavnet.hu
Website. www.fkgp.hu
Leadership. József Torgyán (chairman)

Advocating the return of collectivized land to former owners, the FKgP was founded in November 1989 as a revival of the party which had emerged as the best supported in Hungary's first post-war election in 1945. Deep internal divisions on the desirability and extent of reparations for property lost during the Communist era came to a head in December 1989. A group of dissidents led by Imre Boros resigned from the FKgP to form the National Smallholders' and Bourgeois Party, which developed no taste for life on the outside and rejoined the parent party in August 1991. Meanwhile, the FKgP had won 44 seats and 11.7% of the vote in the 1990 Assembly elections and had joined a centre-right coalition government headed the →Hungarian Democratic Forum (MDF).

In February 1992 FKgP leader József Torgyán announced that the party was withdrawing from the government coalition because the MDF had denied it an opportunity to influence policy. This decision was accompanied by the expulsion of 33 of the FKgP's 45 Assembly deputies, who launched the →United Smallholders' Party–Historical Section (EKP-TT) in order to support the MDF-led Antall government. In the May 1994 general elections the rump party recovered somewhat by winning 26 seats on an 8.9% vote share. It then experienced a surge in popular support in the polls, as expressions of extreme nationalist sentiment emanated from Torgyán.

The party then became embroiled in fierce conflict over government moves to produce a new constitution to replace the much-amended communist-era text. One FKgP proposal was that the President should be directly elected, with enhanced powers, on the expiry of the five-year term of Arpád Göncz of the →Alliance of Free Democrats (SzDSz) in August 1995. Seeking to force a referendum, the FKP collected well over the number required for a popular consultation, but the then ruling →Hungarian Socialist Party (MSzP) contended that such a change would generate political instability. As a consequence of a split in the MDF in March 1996, the FKgP became the largest single opposition party in the Assembly, although it was weakened in late 1997 another split resulting in the formation of the →New Federation.

Allied with the rump →Christian Democratic People's Party (KDNP) in the May 1998 Assembly elections, the

FKgP advanced strongly to 48 seats (with 13.2% of the vote) and joined the subsequent centre-right government headed by the →Federation of Young Democrats–Hungarian Civic Party (FIDESz-MPP). By late 2000, however, the party was again beset by chronic internal dissension, centring on hostility to Torgyán's continued leadership and allegations that he had been guilty of various improprieties as Agriculture Minister since 1998. Torgyán resigned from the government in February 2001, but stubbornly refused to vacate the FKgP leadership, despite a stream of defections and the formation of at least three alternative Freeholders' parties. A special congress in Cegled in May re-elected Torgyán as chairman, but dissidents in Budapest simultaneously elected Zsolt Lanyi to the same position. Torgyán was then expelled from the FKgP parliamentary group, but promptly obtained a court ruling that the expulsion was illegal. In June 2001, claiming that his enemies wanted to assassinate him, Torgyán also obtained a Supreme Court ruling that he was still the legal FKgP chairman. The following month two recent FKgP breakaway factions joined with the older EKP-TT to announce that a new Freeholders' party would be formed if Torgyán had not resigned by September 2001.

The FKgP is affiliated to the Christian Democrat International, an associate member of the European People's Party and a member of the European Democrat Union.

Other Parties

Agrarian Union (*Agrárszövetsége, ASz*), founded in December 1989 as a merger of leftist agrarian groups opposed to the land privatization policies of the →Independent Party of Smallholders, Agrarian Workers and Citizens (FKgP). It was allocated one Assembly seat in May 1994 on the basis of a 2.1% vote share; contested 1998 elections in alliance with →Hungarian Socialist Party.
Address. 10 Arany János u., Budapest V
Telephone. (+36–1) 131–0953
Fax. (+36–1) 111–2663
Leadership. Jozsef Solymosy (chairman)

Alliance for Eastern Hungary, launched in early 2000 by two deputies, one previously of the Federation of →Young Democrats–Hungarian Civic Party (FIDESz–MPP) and the other of the →Hungarian Justice and Life Party (MIEP), to promote the interests of the "neglected" population of the eastern party of the country.
Leadership. Sándor Cseh & Attila Szábo

Christian Democratic People's Party (*Kereszténydemokrata Néppárt, KDNP*), centre-right formation claiming to be a revival of the Popular Democratic Party, the leading opposition formation in the immediate post-World War II period. The party won 21 Assembly seats in 1990 on a 6.5% vote share, joining a three-party coalition government headed by the →Hungarian Democratic Forum (MDF). Avoiding the MDF's rout in the 1994 elections, the KDNP improved to 22 seats with 7.1% of the vote, but was weakened in 1997-98 by defections to the →Federation of Young Democrats–Hungarian Civic Party (FIDESz–MPP). The rump KDNP won only 2.6% in the 1998 elections and no seats. In June 2001 György Giczy resigned as party chairman.
Address. 5 Nagy Jenö u., 1126 Budapest XII
Telephone. (+36–1) 201–8389
Fax. (+36–1) 202–0405
Email. btivadar@freemail.hu
Website. www.kdnp.hu
Leadership. Tivadar Bartók (secretary-general)

Green Alternative (*Zöld Alternativa, ZA*), dating from 1989, took only 0.4% of the vote in 1990 and half of that in 1994; member of European Federation of Green Parties.

Address. 29 Vadász utca, 1053 Budapest
Telephone/Fax. (+36-1) 353-0100
Email. dunadrop@mail.elender.hu
Leadership. György Droppa

Hungarian Democratic People's Party (*Magyar Demokrata Néppárt, MDNP*), launched in March 1996 by Iván Szabo after he had been rebuffed in a challenge for the presidency of the →Hungarian Democratic Forum, of which he was then leader in the National Assembly. The new party attracted over a dozen centre-leaning MDF deputies, but none were re-elected on the MDNP ticket in 1998. In April 2001 the MDNP resolved to form an alliance with the →Liberal Citizens' Alliance, also known as the Entrepreneurs' Party.
Leadership. Erzsebet Pusztai (chairwoman)

Hungarian Independence Party (*Magyar Függetlenség Pártja, MFP*), right-wing formation launched in April 1989 as a revival of a post-war group of the same name.
Address. 97 Arany János utca, 7400 Kaposvár
Leadership. Tibor Hornyak

Hungarian People's Party (*Magyar Néppárt, MNP*), centrist grouping founded in 1989 as successor to pre-war National Peasant Party (*Nemzeti Parasztpárt, NPP*), which title it uses as a suffix; won less than 1% of the vote in 1990 and failed to present any candidates in 1994 and 1998.
Address. 61 Baross utca, 1082 Budapest VIII
Leadership. János Marton

Hungarian Romany Alliance, formed in June 2001 for the 2002 parliamentary elections by the Roma Unity Party, the Roma Party in Hungary, the Interest Association of Gypsy Organizations in Hungary and the Hungarian Roma Civil Rights Movement.
Leadership. Pal Ruva

Hungarian Social Democratic Party (*Magyarországi Szociáldemokrata Párt, MSzDP*), revival of the party forced to merge with Hungary's Communist Party in 1948; split in 1989 into "historic" and "renewal" wings, reunited in October 1993; secured less than 1% in the 1994 and 1998 general elections; a consultative member of the Socialist International whereas the (ex-communist) →Hungarian Socialist Party is a full member.
Address. 76 Dohány u., 1074 Budapest VII
Leadership. László Kapolyi (chairman)

Hungarian Welfare Alliance (*Magyar Népjóleti Szövetség, MNSz*), extreme right-wing grouping led by a Hungarian-born Australian citizen, successor to the World National Party for People's Power (VNP.
Leadership. Albert Szabo (chairman)

Liberal Citizens' Alliance (*Liberális Polgári Szövetség, LPSz*), launched in 1989 as the Entrepreneurs' Party to promote a market economy and low taxation for the country's emerging entrepreneurs. It adopted its present name in June 1990 but failed to secure representation in the 1990 elections. It was credited with one constituency seat in 1994 and none in 1998. In April 2001 the LPSz resolved to form an alliance with the →Hungarian Democratic People's Party.
Leadership. József Ekes (chairman)

National Democratic Party (*Nemzeti Demokrata Párt, NDP*), small radical right-wing formation.
Leadership. Vincze János (chairman)
Email. ndp@mail.datanet.hu
Website. www.datanet.hu/ndp

New Federation (*Uj Szöevetség, USz*), founded in late 1997 by a splinter group of the →Independent Party of Smallholders, Agrarian Workers and Citizens (FKgP) opposed to the leadership of József Törgyán; failed to win representation in 1998 elections.

Leadership. Agnes Nagy Maczo (chairperson)

Party of the Republic (*Köztársaság Párt, KP*), founded in 1992 on the initiative of János Palotas, a colourful entrepreneur who had been elected to the Assembly in 1990 as a candidate of the →Hungarian Democratic Forum (MDF) but had quickly become alienated from that party. The KP won only 2.5% of the national vote in the May 1994 Assembly elections, but was allocated one seat by virtue of a local alliance with the MDF.

Address. 8 Szentkirály utca, 1088 Budapest VIII
Telephone. (+36–1) 138–3744
Fax. (+36–1) 138–4642
Leadership. János Palotas (chairman)

United Smallholders' Party–Historical Section (*Egyesült Kisgazda Párt–Töténelmi Tagozat, EKP-TT*), launched as a result of the February 1992 decision of the leadership of the →Independent Party of Smallholders, Agrarian Workers and Citizens (FKgP) to leave the government coalition, this move being opposed by three-quarters of the 44 FKgP Assembly deputies. Claiming to represent continuity with established FKgP policies, the EKP-TT remained a part of the then ruling coalition headed by the →Hungarian Democratic Forum, but failed to secure representation in May 1994 or May 1998.

Address. 34 Jókai utca, 1065 Budapest VI
Telephone. (+36–1) 132–2900
Leadership. János Szabo (chairman)

Workers' Party (*Munkáspárt, MP*), derived from pro-reform decisions taken at the October 1989 congress of the then ruling Hungarian Socialist Workers' Party (MSzMP), when hardline Communists opposed to conversion into the →Hungarian Socialist Party launched the "János Kádár Society" as the "legal heir" to the MSzMP. Using the MSzMP title, it won only 3.7% in 1990 (and no seats). Having adopted the present name prior to the 1994 election, it slipped to 3.3%. It recovered to 4.1% in 1998, but still won no seats.

Address. 61 Baross utca, 1082 Budapest
Telephone. (+36–1) 334–2721
Email. hir@hungary.cc
Website. www.munkaspart.hu
Leadership. Gyula Thürmer (chairman)

Iceland

Capital: Reykjavík   **Population:** 270,000 (2000E)

The Republic of Iceland was established in 1944 (having previously been a Danish possession), with a democratic parliamentary system of government. Under the 1944 constitution as amended, the President is directly elected as head of state for a four-year term (renewable without restriction), although real executive power resides in the cabinet headed by the Prime Minister. Legislative authority is vested in the unicameral parliament (*Althing*) of 63 members, also elected for four years (subject to dissolution) by a mixed system of proportional and direct representation. The *Althing* divides itself by election into an Upper House (*Efri Deild*) of a third of its members and a Lower House (*Nedri Deild*) of the remaining two-thirds.

Icelandic parties are eligible for subventions from state funds, to finance research on political questions, in proportion to the number of *Althing* seats held plus one. In 2001 the total available was IKr46.7 million (about $460,000), of which, for example, the Independence Party received IKr17.8 million. Furthermore, parties holding seats in the *Althing* are also eligible for state funds to finance their general operations in proportion to votes received at the last parliamentary election. In 2001 the total paid out in this category was IKr164 million (about $1.6 million), of which, for example, the Progressive Party received IKr30.3 million.

Elections to the *Althing* on May 8, 1999, resulted as follows: Independence Party 26 seats (with 40.7% of the vote), Social Democratic Alliance (*Samfylkingin*, consisting of the People's Alliance, the Social Democratic Party and the Women's Alliance) 17 (26.8%), Progressive Party 12 (18.4%), Left–Green Alliance 6 (9.1%), Liberal Party 2 (4.2%). By agreement of the parties, Olafur Ragnar Grímsson of the People's Alliance was reinstalled for a second term as President on Aug. 1, 2000, without an election, having first been elected on June 29, 1996, with 40.9% of the popular vote.

Independence Party (IP)
Sjálfstædisflokkurinn
Address. Háaleitisbraut 1, 105 Reykjavík
Telephone. (+354) 515–1700
Fax. (+354) 515–1717
Email. xd@xd.is
Website. www.xd.is
Leadership. Davíd Oddsson (chairman); Geir H. Haarde (vice-chairman); Sigrídur Anna Thórdardóttir (parliamentary group leader); Kjartan Gunnarsson (secretary-general)
The IP is a liberal conservative party, advocating Iceland's continued membership of NATO and the retention of the existing US military base in Iceland. It was established in 1929 by a merger of conservative and liberal groups favouring Iceland's independence from Denmark (achieved in 1944). Having consistently been the strongest party in the *Althing* (although never with an absolute majority), it has taken part in numerous coalition govemments: with the →Social Democratic Party (SDP) and a Communist-led left-wing front in 1944–46; with the →Progressive Party (PP) and the SDP in 1947–49; with the PP in 1950–56; with the SDP in 1959–71; and with the PP in 1974–78 and 1983–87. Meanwhile, in 1980–83 dissident IP deputies had participated in a coalition with the PP and the →People's Alliance (PA).

In the April 1987 elections the IP suffered a major setback (principally because of the impact of a breakaway Citizens' Party), winning only 27.2% of the vote and 18 of 63 seats (as against 38.7% and 23 of 60 seats in 1983). It nevertheless continued in government at the head of a "grand coalition" with the PP and the SDP, with the IP leader, Thorsteinn Pálsson becoming at 39 Iceland's youngest-ever Prime Minister.

Pálsson stepped down as Prime Minister in September

1988 because of a dispute over economic policy, being succeeded as party chairman in March 1991 by Davíd Oddsson, who formed a government following an election in which the IP consolidated its position as the largest party, rising from 18 to 26 seats. Only one of these was lost in the 1995 election, in which the IP took 37.1% of the vote. However, because of losses by its SDP coalition partner, it opted to form a new centre-right coalition with the PP in order to ensure parliamentary stability and majority government.

Despite vociferous opposition from the left-wing parties, especially after the PA, the SDP and the →Women's Alliance formed an electoral front in mid-1998, the IP-led government gained credit for strong economic growth and low inflation in the May 1999 parliamentary elections. The IP itself advanced to 26 seats and 40.7% of the vote, so that Oddsson was able to form a new centre-right coalition with the PP.

The IP is affiliated to the International Democrat Union and the European Democrat Party.

Left-Green Alliance
Vinstrihreyfing-Grænt Frambod

Address. c/o Althing, v/Austurvöll, 150 Reykjavík
Email. vg@vg.is
Website. www.vg.is
Leadership. Steingrímur Sigfússon (chairman); Ögmundur Jónasson (parliamentary group leader)
The Left-Green Alliance was launched in 1998s by factions of the →People's Alliance (PA) and the →Women's Alliance opposed to the creation by those parties of the United Left (*Samfylkingin*) alliance. In the May 1999 parliamentary elections the Left–Green Alliance helped to ensure the defeat of *Samfylkingin* by winning six seats with 9.1% share of the vote.

Liberal Party (LP)
Frjáslyndi Flokkurin

Address. Einimelur 9, 107 Reykjavík
Telephone. (+354) 562–4515
Fax. (+354) 563–0780
Email. xf@xf.is
Website. www.xf.is
Leadership. Sverrir Hemannsson (chairman); Gudjón A. Kristinsson (parliamentary group leader)
The LP was established in 1998 by Sverrir Hemannson, a former director of the National Bank of Iceland and a former government minister associated with the →Independence Party. In the May 1999 parliamentary elections, the new formation won two seats with 4.2% of the vote. By mid-2001 the party had some 4,000 members.

Progressive Party (PP)
Framsóknarflokkurinn

Address. Hverfisgata 33, 101 Reykjavík
Telephone. (+354) 540–4300
Fax. (+354) 540–4301
Email. framsokn@framsokn.is
Website. www.framsokn.is
Leadership. Halldór Ásgrímsson (leader); Siv Fridleifsdóttir (chairperson); Kristinn H. Gunnarsson (parliamentary group leader); Arni Magnusson (secretary-general)
The PP's principal aim is to safeguard the Icelandic nation's economic and cultural independence on the basis of a democratic and parliamentary system, with emphasis on the freedom of the individual. The party also stands for basing the national economy on private initiative, with state intervention remaining exceptional. The party has favoured Iceland's continued membership of NATO but has called for the withdrawal of NATO forces from the country.

The party was established in 1916 to represent farming and fishing interests and the co-operative movement in these sectors. Usually the second largest party in the *Althing,* the PP has taken part in various coalition governments: with the →Independence Party (IP) and the →Social Democratic Party (SDP) in 1946-49; with the IP in 1950–56; with the SDP and the People's Alliance (PA) in 1956–58; with the PA and the Union of Liberals and Leftists in 1971–74; with the IP in 1974–78; with the SDP and the PA in 1978–79; with the PA and dissident IP members in 1980–83; with the IP in 1983-87; with the IP and the SDP in 1987–91; and with the IP since 1995.

The 1983–87 period of coalition with the IP resulted in both parties losing ground in the April 1987 elections, in which PP slipped from 14 to 13 seats, although its share of vote increased from 8.5% to 18.9%. Three months later the PP entered a "grand coalition" headed by the IP and also including the Social Democrats. Upon the resignation of the IP Prime Minister in September 1988, then PP leader Steingrímur Hermannsson formed a new government which included the IP and the SDP.

The PP went into opposition following the election of April 1991, at which its parliamentary representation was unchanged. It returned to government after the 1995 contest, in which it advanced to 23.3% of the vote, as the junior partner in a centre-right coalition with the IP.

The PP has a current membership of 8,150 and is a member party of the Liberal International.

Social Democratic Alliance (SDA)
Samfylkingin

Address. Austurstr—ti 14, 101 Reykjavík
Telephone. (+354) 551–1660
Fax. (+354) 563–0745
Email. bgs@althingi.is
Website. www.samfylking.is
Leadership. Össur Skarphédinsson (chairman); Margret Frímannsdóttir (vice-chairperson); Bryndís Hlödversdóttir (parliamentary group leader); Björgvin G. Sigurdsson (secretary-general)
The SDA was launched in mid-1998 initially as an electoral front of the People's Alliance (*Althydubandalagid*), the Social Democratic Party (*Althduflokkurinn*) and the Women's Alliance (*Samtök um Kvennalista*) and was converted into a unitary party in May 2000 following the defeat of the front in the May 1999 parliamentary elections.

The **People's Alliance (PA)** had its origins in the formation of the Communist Party of Iceland in 1930 following a split in the Social Democratic Party (SDP). Having joined the Comintern, the Icelandic Communists first obtained representation in the *Althing* in 1937 (with three seats). Although a proposal for reunification was rejected by the SDP in 1938, left-wing Social Democrats joined with the Communists to form the United People's Party–Socialist Party (SA–SF), which left the Comintern and in 1942 won seven parliamentary seats. When Iceland became independent in 1944, the SA–SF entered a coalition government with the SDP and →Independence Party (IP), but withdrew in 1946 mainly over its opposition to a US military presence in Iceland.

For the 1956 elections, the SA–SF combined with the small National Defence Party and a left-wing faction of the SDP to form the People's Alliance, which won eight seats and joined a coalition with the SDP and the →Progressive Party (PP) which lasted until 1958. Having been essentially an electoral alliance, the PA converted itself into a single political party in 1968, whereupon the non-Marxist section broke away to form the (now defunct) Union of Liberals and Leftists, claiming that the PA had become "the Communist Party under another name". At the same time, the PA denounced the Soviet-led military intervention in Czechoslovakia and thereafter adopted a "Eurocommunist" orientation. Strongly based in the trade union movement, it described itself as a party of "leftists who want to defend and strengthen the independence of the Iceland people, protect the interests of the working class, and ensure progress at all levels in the country on the basis of democratic socialism and co-operation". It also advocated Iceland's withdrawal from NATO and the closure of the US military base.

After winning 10 seats in the 1971 elections, the PA joined a coalition with the PP and the Union of Liberals and Leftists, which resigned in 1974. The PA won 14 seats in the 1978 elections and formed a coalition with the PP and the SDP. After new elections the following year, in which its representation fell to 11 seats, the party entered a coalition with the PP and dissident IP members early in 1980. However, it fell back to 10 seats in 1983 and went into opposition. In the April 1987 elections the PA was for the first time overtaken in terms of votes and representation by the SDP and remained in opposition.

The PA's representation in the *Althing* rose to nine seats in 1991, this level being maintained in 1995 on a slightly reduced vote share of 14.3%. The party remained in opposition through both elections, being active in the opposition to government economic austerity measures. Former Finance Minister Ólafur Ragnar Grímsson vacated the PA leadership in late 1995 in order to stand for the Icelandic presidency, to which in June 1996 he was elected by a comfortable relative majority over three other candidates.

Founded in 1916 by the trade unions, the **Social Democratic Party (SDP)** became organizationally independent in 1940 but was weakened by the defection of its left-wing faction to the Communist-dominated United People's Party-Socialist Party (later the PA). Over the following three decades the SDP remained the fourth strongest party in a stable four-party system, usually polling around 15% in general elections, and participated in five coalition governments, the longest-lived being one with the →Independence Party (IP) in 1959–71; it also briefly formed a minority SDP government In 1958–59.

Amid decreasing political stability in the 1970s and early 1980s, the SDP experienced shifting fortunes and was mostly in opposition, although it participated in a centre-left coalition in 1978–79 and then formed another interim minority government. Competition from short-lived alternative social democratic parties resulted in electoral setbacks for the SDP, notably in 1983 when the impact of a left-wing dissident Social Democratic Federation reduced the SDP to only six seats and 11.7% of the vote.

Under the new leadership of Jón Baldvin Hannibalsson, however, the SDP was reinvigorated, as well as strengthened by the return of most of the Federation dissidents in 1986. In the April 1987 elections its share of the vote increased to 15.2% and its representation to 10 seats (out of 63), giving it the status of third-strongest party, ahead of the PA for the first time. The SDP thereupon entered a "grand coalition" headed by the IP and also including the →Progressive Party (PP).

The SDP retained 10 seats in the 1991 elections, after which it joined a coalition with the IP. Internal party unrest over government austerity measures culminated in June 1994 in an unsuccessful challenge to the leadership of Hannibalsson (then Foreign Minister) by his deputy, Jóhanna Sigurdardottir (then Social Affairs Ministers), who promptly formed the breakaway People's Movement (PM). In the 1995 *Althing* elections the SDP fell back to fourth place, winning only 11.4% of the vote (and going into opposition), directly damaged by the PM's garnering of an impressive 7.2% vote share and four seats under the campaigning name "Awakening of the Nation".

The **Women's Alliance (WA)** had been launched in March 1983 as an explicitly feminist party, believing the improvement of the condition of women to be "imperative" and also that "the experience, values and perspectives of women are urgently needed to influence the decision-making processes of our society". Rejecting classification on the left/right spectrum and boasting a collective and rotating leadership the Alliance also advocated decentralization of local and national government, the transfer of economic and administrative power to the people, an end to the arms race and the abolition of all military alliances.

Possibly given additional credibility by the fact that Iceland elected a woman President in 1980, the WA was successful in its first general election contest in April 1983, winning 5.5% of the vote and three of the 60 *Althing* seats. It made further significant progress in the April 1987 elections, when it took 10.1% of the vote and doubled its representation to six seats (out of 63). In post-election coalition negotiations with other parties, the WA refused to compromise on its policy principles and accordingly remained in opposition.

The WA fell back to five seats in the 1991 *Althing* elections, remaining in opposition. More evidence of the ebbing of the feminist tide came in the 1995 elections, when the WA slipped further to three seats on a 4.9% vote share, apparently losing support to the new People's Movement under the charismatic female leadership of Jóhanna Sigurdardottir, formerly deputy leader of the →Social Democratic Party (SDP). In the June 1996 presidential election, however, WA candidate Gudrun Agnarsdottir won an impressive 26% of the vote.

In the post-1995 parliament, the SDP, PM, PA and WA deputies found themselves co-operating closely in opposition to the centre-right government of the IP and the PP. In due course Sigurdardottir and her followers returned to the SDP fold and were influential in the SDP's decision to enter the SDA, its first-ever formal alliance with the PA. The WA also joined, overcoming its previous resistance to left/right labels. The policy compromises involved in alliance agreement resulted in significant factions of both the PA and the WA defecting to the →Left–Green Alliance.

To secure the alliance, the PA moderated its opposition to NATO membership and the US military presence in Iceland, while the pro-European SDP agreed that a *Samfylkingin* government would not seek to join the EU in the next parliamentary term. Instead, the focus would be on improving the social services and introducing family-friendly measures. However, policy differences between the component formations were exposed in the run-up to the May 1999 parliamentary elections, in which the alliance won only 17 seats and 26.8% of the vote, well below the aggregate performance of its component parties in 1995. The alliance therefore remained in opposition to a further centre-right coalition of the IP and the PP.

The SDA inherited the SDP's full membership of the Socialist International.

India

Capital: New Delhi

Population: 1,000,027,000 (2001E)

The Republic of India gained independence from the United Kingdom in 1947, when the sub-continent was divided into the new states of India and Pakistan. It is a secular and democratic republic, comprising 28 self-governing states and seven union territories. The head of state is the President, who is elected for a five-year term by an electoral college consisting of elected members of the upper and lower houses of parliament (respectively the *Rajya Sabha* and the *Lok Sabha*) and of state legislative assemblies. The President appoints a Prime Minister (the head of government) and, on the latter's advice, a Council of Ministers, all of whom are responsible to parliament. Most of the 245 members of the *Rajya Sabha* are indirectly elected by the state assemblies (one-third being replaced every two years), while all but two of the 545 members of the *Lok Sabha* are directly elected for a five-year term by universal adult suffrage. Legislative responsibility is divided between the Union and the states, the former possessing exclusive powers to make laws in the realm of foreign affairs, defence, citizenship and overseas trade.

At the general election of April–May 1996, the Hindu nationalist *Bharatiya Janata* Party (BJP) was returned with the largest number of seats (161) and invited by the President to form a government. However, it experienced great difficulty in securing coalition partners and lasted only 13 days. The Indian National Congress – Congress (I) also having tried and failed to form an administration, the mantle of government eventually fell upon a United Front (UF) consisting of a loose alliance of 13 broadly leftist and regional organizations dominated by three national parties, namely the *Janata Dal* (JD), the Communist Party of India–Marxist (CPI-M) and the Communist Party of India (CPI). It also included the All-India Forward Bloc, the All-India Indira Congress–*Tiwari*, the Assam People's Council, the Dravidian Progressive Federation (DMK), the Karnataka Congress Party, the *Madhya Pradesh Vikas* Congress, the *Maharastrawadi Gomantak*, the Revolutionary Socialist Party, the *Samajwadi* Party, the *Tamil Maanila* Congress and the *Telugu Desam* Party–*Naidu*. Altogether, the UF could still only amass about 180 seats and was kept in office by the support of Congress (I) from the back benches. It elected as its first leader (who then became Prime Minister) H.D. Deve Gowda of the JD. But, within a year, he was ousted by pressure from the Congress (I) in favour of I.K. Gujral, also from the JD. In December 1997, the Congress (I) entirely withdrew its support and the UF government fell.

At the general election of March 1998, the BJP was again returned as the largest single party in the *Lok Sabha* (with 180 seats) and this time succeeded in constructing a coalition government under the leadership of Prime Minister Atal Behari Vajpayee. Its principal sources of support were the *Samata* Party, the *Shiv Sena*, the All-India Dravidian Progressive Federation (AIADMK), the All-India *Trinamool* Congress and the *Telugu Desam* Party–*Naidu*. However, its overall majority was always small and, in April 1999 following the withdrawal of the AIADMK, it fell. The Congress (I) then attempted, but again failed, to put together another coalition. To spare the country the costs of a second general election within a year (and a third within three), President K.R. Narayanan made use of a constitutional provision putting parliament into recess and allowing Vajpayee's cabinet to continue as an interim administration for six months.

In preparation for the next general election, which was held in October 1999, the BJP drew its would-be coalition partners into a National Democratic Alliance (NDA), which presented a collective identity at the polls while allowing each of its constituent parties also to stand in its own right. In comparison to Vajpayee's 1998–99 coalition, the AIADMK was replaced by its local rival in Tamil Nadu politics, the Dravidian Progressive Federation (DMK) and included several fractions of the JD which, in common with the former UF, was then breaking apart. In all, 24 parties stood at the election under the NDA's banner. The BJP was, again, returned as the largest single party in the *Lok Sabha* with 182 seats. But, with the experience of the NDA behind him, Vajpayee had little difficulty in forming a more substantial coalition government. At the time of its taking office, this government commanded an overall majority of about 30 seats. Since then, its size has waxed and waned as coalition partners (and aspirants) have come, gone and returned. As of August 2001, it was thought to possess a comfortable majority of about 35 seats.

Meanwhile, the opposition to it has further fragmented. The Congress (I) suffered a disastrous result at the 1996 election, losing nearly half its seats and returning only 140 members. Since then, and in spite of the efforts of the new leader Sonia Gandhi to revive it, it has undergone further splits and decline. In 1998, it won only 119 seats and, in 1999, just 112. Its attempts to co-ordinate the general opposition to the BJP have also failed and have exacerbated tensions with the remnants of the UF. But the UF parties, themselves, have faired little better. The JD has broken apart into a series of different, and frequently hostile, parties based on regional and personal connections. Although the communist parties retain their own regional followings, their impact on national politics has weakened and, in 2001, the CPI–M even lost its accredited status as a 'national' party with the Election Commission of India.

All-India Dravidian Progressive Federation
All-India Anna Dravida Munnetra Kazhagam
(AIADMK)
Address. 275 Awai Shanmugam Salai, Royapettah, Madras 600014
Leadership. Jayalalitha Jayaram (leader)
The AIADMK, which reflects Tamil nationalist sentiment, was formed in 1972 by a breakaway faction of the →Dravidian Progressive Federation (DMK), and became one of the dominant regional parties in Tamil Nadu state from 1977. It held power in the state from 1977 to 1989 and from 1991 to 1996 and was re-elected in 2001. Its principal regional rival, the →Dravidian Progressive Federation (DMK), held power in the interim. The party's leader, former film-star Jayalalitha Jayaram, is a highly controversial figure and was banned from standing in the 2001 regional elections following convictions for corruption. Nonetheless, her party swept the polls in a landslide victory

and she was appointed chief minister. In all-India politics, the AIADMK has shifted in alliance between the →*Bharatiya Janata* Party (whose coalition government it supported in 1998-99) and the →Indian National Congress-Congress (I) with which it was allied by 2001. In the October 1999 general election, the AIADMK won 10 seats to the *Lok Sabha* (all in Tamil Nadu) and also, as of August 2001, held 6 seats in the *Rajya Sabha*.

All-India Trinamool Congress (AITC)
Address. 30-B, Harish Chatterjee Street, Calcutta 600026
Email. Gbasu@trinamool.org
Website. www.trinamool.org
Leadership. Mamata Banerjee (parliamentary chair)
The Trinamool Congress originated in 1997 as a break away from the West Bengal organization of the →Indian National Congress – Congress (I) under the leadership of Mamata Banerjee and in opposition to the local alliance of the

Congress (I) with Communists. It was renamed as the All-India Trinamool Congress in 1998 although predominantly based in West Bengal. It won seven seats in the *Lok Sabha* at the 1998 general election and eight in 1999 (all of them in West Bengal). The AITC supported the ruling federal coalition governments headed by the →*Bharatiya Janata* Party (BJP) from 1998 with Banerjee serving as Railways Minister; however, the party resigned from the federal government and re-formed an alliance with the Congress (I) to fight the West Bengal state legislature elections in May 2001. It in turn resigned from this alliance and re-joined the →National Democratic Alliance in August 2001. As at August 2001, the AITC was without a seat in the *Rajya Sabha*.

Bahujan Samaj Party (BSP)

Address. 12 Gurudwara, Rakabganj Road, New Delhi 110001
Website. www.dalitstan.org/bahujan
Leadership. Kanshi Ram and Mayawati Kumari (leaders)
The BSP represents India's Harijans or "untouchables". Following the 1993 state elections in Uttar Pradesh, the party joined a governing coalition led by the →*Samajwadi* Party. It then withdrew from the coalition in June 1995 and formed a new government itself, with the aid of opposition parties. However, on the resignation of the BSP chief minister in October 1995, President's rule was imposed in the state. Since the restoration of the State Assembly in 1996, it has twice formed brief administrations supported by the →*Bharatiya Janata* Party (BJP). However, it does not support the BJP-led federal coalition government and sits on the opposition benches. In the October 1999 general election, it won 14 seats (all of them from Uttar Pradesh) in the *Lok Sabha* and it holds 4 *Rajya Sabha* seats. The BSP is also represented in the Punjab and Madhya Pradesh legislative assemblies.

Bharatiya Janata Party (BJP)

Address. 11 Ashoka Road, New Delhi 110001
Email. Bjpco@bjp.org
Website. www.bjp.org
Leadership. Atal Behari Vajpayee (parliamentary leader and Prime Minister)
The *Bharatiya Janata* ("Indian People's") Party was formed in 1980 as a breakaway group from the →*Janata* Party, establishing itself as a radical, right-wing Hindu nationalist organization influenced by the Hindu social-cultural organization the *Rashtriya Swayamsevak Sangh*. Its influence as a national party rose dramatically in the 1989 general election, when it won 88 *Lok Sabha* seats (compared with only two in 1984), becoming the third largest party. Having increased its legislative representation to 119 seats in 1991, it became the main opposition to the →Indian National Congress–Congress (I) government. It was associated in this period with many actions by militant Hindus opposed to Muslim influence and establishments in the "Hindu belt" of central-northern India.

In the April–May 1996 general election the BJP emerged for the first time as the largest single party, winning at least 161 seats and commanding the support of about another 35 *Lok Sabha* deputies from other parties. In mid-May party leader Vajpayee was invited to form a new BJP minority federal government (including →*Shiv Sena* representation); however, his administration could not muster sufficient parliamentary support to secure a vote of confidence, with the result that his government resigned after only 13 days in office. But, following the March 1998 election in which it was again returned as the largest single party (with 180 seats), the party did succeed in cobbling together a coalition government under Vajpayee's leadership with the support of a number of smaller regional parties. In April 1999, this coalition was defeated in parliament but subsequently stayed in office for a full six months as an 'interim' government before a new general election was held. Prior to the

October 1999 election, the party built a series of electoral alliances with other parties and stood as part of a →National Democratic Alliance (NDA). The NDA was victorious (with the BJP winning 182 seats in a total of 19 states and territories) and Vajpayee reconstructed his coalition government on its basis. As of August 2001 the BJP also formed the administration (either as the governing party or in coalition) in seven states and held 49 seats in the *Rajya Sabha*. In national office the BJP has moderated its earlier extreme Hindu nationalism and has also aligned itself with a continuation of the policies of gradual economic liberalization adopted but largely unfulfilled by the previous Congress Party administration.

Biju Janata Dal (BJD)

Address. Naveen Nivas, Aerodrom Gate, Bhubaneswar 75109, Orissa
Leadership. Naveen Patnaik (president)
The majority section of the →*Janata Dal* (JD) in Orissa, organized around long-time Orissa chief minister Biju Patnaik. Having broken away from the main JD it won nine seats in the *Lok Sabha* in 1998 and 10 in 1999. It supported the 1998-99 federal coalition government headed by the →*Bharatiya Janata* Party (BJP) and was a founder member of the →National Democratic Alliance; currently it is the ruling party in Orissa state and, as at August 2001, held three seats in the *Rajya Sabha*.

Communist Party of India (CPI)

Address. Ajay Bhavan, 15 Kotla Marg, New Delhi 110002
Telephone. (+91–11) 323-5546
Fax. (+91–11) 323-5543
Email. Cpi@cpofindia.org
Website. www.cpofindia.org
Leadership. A.B. Bardhan (general secretary)
Founded in 1925, the CPI split in 1964 when the rival →Communist Party of India–Marxist (CPI–M) was formed. From the end of the 1970s the CPI maintained a policy of opposition to the political dominance of the →Indian National Congress–Congress (I), working closely with the CPI–M and other left-wing parties. In the general election of April–May 1996 the CPI won 12 seats in the *Lok Sabha* (compared with 13 in 1991) and became an important component within the →United Front (UF) government (1996-98). However, it fared badly in the 1998 and 1999 general elections, winning nine seats at the first and only four at the second (three of them in West Bengal). As of August 2001 the party held six seats in the *Rajya Sabha* and participated in the Left Front coalition governing in West Bengal.

Communist Party of India–Marxist (CPI-M)

Address. AK Gopalan Bhavan, 27–29 Bhai Vir Singh Marg, New Delhi 110001
Telephone. (+91–11) 334–4918
Fax. (+91–11) 374–7483
Email. Cpim@vsnl.com
Website. www.cpim.org
Leadership. Harkishan Singh Surjit (general secretary)
The CPI-M was created in 1964 by dissident members of the →Communist Party of India (CPI) favouring a more radical leftist line. Originally pro-Chinese, the party declared its independence of China in 1968. Although claiming to be a national party, the CPI–M's main support has traditionally come from West Bengal, Kerala and Tripura. This distinctly regional bias in 2001 led the Election Commission of India to de-recognize it as a national party. In the 1996 general election the CPI–M secured 32 seats in the *Lok Sabha* (having won 35 in 1991) and supported the →United Front (UF) alliance government (1996–98) from the back benches. In the 1999 general elections the party won 32 seats, of which 21 were in West Bengal and eight in Kerala, but found itself in opposition to the ruling coalition led by the →*Bharatiya Janata* Party. In state assembly elections in May 2001, the CPI–M retained power (as part of the Left

Front government) in West Bengal but lost it (as part of a defeated leftist coalition) in Kerala. As at August 2001, it also held 14 seats in the *Rajya Sabha*.

Dravidian Progressive Federation
Dravida Munnetra Kazhagam (DMK)
Address. Anna Arivalayam 268–269, Anna Salai, Teynampet, Madras 600018, Tamil Nadu
Website. www.thedmk.org
Leadership. M. Karunanidhi (president)

A Tamil nationalist party founded in 1949, the DMK urges full autonomy for the state of Tamil Nadu within the Indian Union and opposes the retention of Hindi as an official language. In 1977 it lost power in Tamil Nadu to the →All-India Dravidian Progressive Federation (AIADMK), which had earlier broken away from the parent party. The rump DMK was briefly returned as the ruling party from 1989 until 1991, but after a period of President's rule its AIADMK rival was swept back to power with a large majority in the state legislature. Assisted by various government scandals and a split in the Tamil Nadu →Indian National Congress–Congress (I) which produced the pro-DMK →Tamil Maanila Congress, the DMK turned the tables in the 1996 state elections, winning 172 seats and forming a government on May 13 under veteran leader Muthuvel Karunanidhi. But it was then swept out of power again in May 2001 when the AIADMK secured a landslide victory.

Having won no seats in the *Lok Sabha* in the 1991 general election, the DMK returned 17 representatives from Tamil Nadu constituencies in the April–May 1996 national poll and joined the →United Front federal government (1996-98). In the 1998 general election, it won six seats and sat with the opposition to the ruling coalition led by the →Bharatiya Janata Party (BJP). However, for the general election of October 1999, it joined the →National Democratic Alliance led by the BJP and, on winning 12 seats, became a key member of the new BJP-led coalition. As of August 2001, the DMK held nine seats in the *Rajya Sabha*.

Indian National Congress–Congress (I)
Address. 24 Akbar Road, New Delhi 110001
Telephone. (+91–11) 301–9606
Fax. (+91–11) 301–7701
Leadership. Sonia Gandhi (president)

The Indian National Congress, dating from 1885 and traditionally committed to democracy, socialism and secularism, has been India's ruling formation for most of the period since it led India to independence in 1947 under Jawaharlal (Pandit) Nehru. In 1969, three years after Nehru's daughter, Indira Gandhi, had acceded to the leadership, the party split into two groups when an anti-Gandhi conservative faction – the Indian National Congress-Organization (INC-O) – became India's first recognized opposition party. Having aroused widespread opposition by governing under emergency powers from 1975, the Congress government was defeated in the March 1977 general elections, going into opposition for the first time since independence. Further splits resulted in Gandhi forming the mainstream Congress (I), which returned to power with an overwhelming majority in the elections of early 1980. Her new government's more pro-market orientation contributed to the formation of the breakaway →Indian National Congress (Socialist) in 1981. In July 1981 the Supreme Court ruled that Congress (I) was the authentic heir of the historic Congress party, although the Congress (I) designation continued in universal usage.

Indira Gandhi was assassinated by Sikh militants in October 1984 and was succeeded as Prime Minister and party leader by her son, Rajiv Gandhi. Rajiv led the party to a convincing general election victory in 1984–85. However, substantial opposition to his leadership subsequently developed, leading to expulsions and resignations from the party, including the exit of V.P. Singh, who in 1987 formed the

Jan Morcha anti-corruption movement which heralded the establishment of the opposition →*Janata Dal*. As a result of the November 1989 general elections, Congress (I) was forced into opposition by a National Front alliance dominated by *Janata Dal*.

During the next election campaign, Rajiv was assassinated by Sri Lankan Tamil militants in May 1991, but Congress (I) regained power and formed a government under the premiership of the party's new president, P.V. Narasimha Rao. By early 1996, however, Rao's administration was deeply unpopular, its political standing having been badly damaged by alleged involvement in the country's largest corruption scandal and by related ministerial resignations. In the April–May 1996 elections Congress (I) returned only 140 members to the *Lok Sabha*, representing a loss of nearly half of its previous representation. Having manouevred to deny a parliamentary vote of confidence to the minority government formed in May by its principal electoral rival, the →*Bharatiya Janata* Party (BJP), Congress (I) gave its tacit support to the →United Front administration inaugurated in June. However, early in 1998 it withdrew this support, precipitating a general election in which its *Lok Sabha* base contracted further (to 119 seats). A consequence of this election was the emergence of Sonia Gandhi (the Italian-born widow of Rajiv Gandhi) as the party's new leader. In April 1999, she helped to bring down the ruling BJP-led coalition but was unable to form an alternative coalition government under her own leadership. Further splits within the party followed (leading to the formation of the →Nationalist Congress Party) and, at the October 1999 general election, its representation was further reduced to 112 seats. Its support base remains the most geographically spread of Indian parties, however, the party holding seats in a total of 21 states and territories. In spite of its recent decline in national politics, Congress (I) has maintained a vigorous presence in the local politics of many of the regional states, where governments or coalitions under its leadership alternate in power with those headed either by the BJP and its coalition partners or by erstwhile United Front parties. As of August 2001, Congress (I) held or shared power in eleven states. It also held 57 *Rajya Sabha* seats.

Janata Dal–United (JDU)
Address. Sardar Patel Bhawan, 7 Jantar Mantar Road, New Delhi 110001
Leadership. Devendra Prasad (Yadav)

The *Janata Dal* ("People's Party") was formed in 1988 as a merger of the *Jan Morcha* ("Popular Front") dissident faction of the →Indian National Congress–Congress (I), the *Lok Dal* and other outgrowths of the old →*Janata* Party. It advocates non-alignment, the eradication of poverty, unemployment and wide disparities in wealth, and protection of minorities. The JD contested the 1989 general election as the dominant component of an opposition →National Front, winning 141 of the Front's 144 seats. With the support of the →*Bharatiya Janata* Party (BJP) and the communist parties, the National Front formed a fragile new government, ousting Congress (I) from power.

A split in the JD in late 1990 resulted in the creation of the breakaway *Janata Dal* (S), which subsequently evolved into the →*Samajwadi* Party. This instability led to an early general election in 1991, in which the official JD won only 55 *Lok Sabha* seats and Congress (I) was returned to power. A further party split in 1994 saw the establishment of a separate parliamentary group, which subsequently adopted the →*Samata* Party designation.

For the April–May 1996 general elections the JD was the largest constituent in a leftist →United Front (UF), but was itself reduced to some 45 seats in the *Lok Sabha*. Following the elections, the Front commanded the support of about 180 lower house deputies, so that it was eventually able to form a new government under the premiership of H.D. Deve Gowda of the JD. In 1997, Gowda was replaced by I.K.

Gujral, also of the JD. But the UF government fell early in December 1997, when the Congress (I) withdrew its back bench support and, subsequently, the JD has suffered further disintegration. Breakaway factions include the →*Biju Janata Dal* (Orissa), the →*Rashtriya Janata Dal* (Bihar) and the *Lok Jan Shakti Party* (Karnataka). The rump of the JD – now called the *Janata Dal*–United (JDU) – secured six *Lok Sabha* seats in the 1999 general election and, as of August 2001, also held six *Rajya Sabha* seats.

Janata Dal is an observer member of the Socialist International

National Democratic Alliance (NDA)

A loose cross-party 'front', the NDA was formed in June 1999 around the core of the multi-party coalition, headed by the →*Bharatiya Janata* Party (BJP), which had provided the federal government between March 1998 and April 1999. Its purpose was to offer a coherent platform for the general election of October 1999. Its principal constituents, besides the BJP, were: the →*Telugu Desam* Party (TDP), the →Dravidian Progressive Federation (DMK), the →*Shiv Sena*, the →*Biju Janata Dal* (BJD), *the* →All-India *Trinamool* Congress (AITC), the →*Shiromani Akali Dal* (SAD), the →*Lok Shakti* Party and the →*Samata* Party. In all, 24 parties stood under the NDA banner and were successful, gaining an overall majority of about 30 seats in the *Lok Sabha* and forming a new federal government under the leadership of Atal Behari Vajpayee of the BJP.

Revolutionary Socialist Party (RSP)

Address. 37 Ripon Street (Muzaffar Ahmed Sarani), Calcutta 700016, West Bengal
Leadership. T.J Chandrachoodan (general secretary)
In the general elections of April–May 1996 the Marxist–Leninist RSP won five seats in the *Lok Sabha*, all from West Bengal, as part of the →United Front (UF) alliance, but did not join the subsequent UF government. At both the 1998 and 1999 elections, its representation was reduced to three seats (all from West Bengal). As of August 2001, it held three seats in the *Rajya Sabha* and enjoyed representation in a number of state legislative assemblies, including West Bengal, Tripura and Kerala.

Samajwadi Party (SP)

Address. 18 Copernicus Lane, New Delhi 110001
Leadership. Mulayam Singh Yadav (leader)
Inaugurated at a convention in 1992, the SP, whose strength lies in Uttar Pradesh although it has contested elections in some other states, derives from a dissident faction of the →*Janata Dal* (JD). Following the 1993 state elections in Uttar Pradesh, the SP formed a governing coalition with the →*Bahujan Samaj* Party (BSP). However, the coalition collapsed in June 1995 and President's rule was imposed in the state the following October pending fresh elections. In the general elections of April–May 1996 the SP won 17 *Lok Sabha* seats and was allocated the defence portfolio in the new administration. Since the 1998 and 1999 elections, where it won 20 and 26 seats respectively (all of them from Uttar Pradesh), it has taken a leading role on the opposition benches. However, its relations with other opposition parties (most notably the →Indian National Congress – Congress (I) and the BSP) have been fraught. As of August 2001, it held eight seats in the *Rajya Sabha*.

Samata Party

Address. 220 Vitthalbhai Patel House, Rafi Marg, New Delhi 110001
Leadership. George Fernandes (president)
The *Samata* ("Equality") Party derives from a factional split in the →*Janata Dal* (JD) in early 1994, its president being a veteran socialist and trade union leader. The new grouping contested the general elections of April–May 1996, winning six *Lok Sabha* seats in the state of Bihar, but surprisingly was not part of the victorious →United Front alliance.

Following the 1998 election, where it won 12 seats, the party joined the ruling coalition headed by the →*Bharatiya Janata* Party (BJP) and party-leader George Fernandes accepted the defence portfolio. In the 1999 election, the *Samata* Party stood as a member of →National Democratic Alliance headed by the BJP. It again won 12 *Lok Sabha* seats and Fernandes resumed as Defence Minister although, in March 2001, he was obliged to resign following a defence contracts scandal (being re-appointed in October 2001). As of August 2001, the *Samata* Party held one *Rajya Sabha* seat.

Shiromani Akali Dal (SAD)

Address. House No. 256, Sector 9-C, Chandigarth
Leadership. Prakash Singh Badal (president)
The SAD is the main political organization of India's Sikh community, which is concentrated in Punjab. In support of its demands for Sikh self-determination, the SAD became increasingly militant in the early 1980s and has since been subject to factional rivalry and division. In the general elections of April–May 1996 the party won eight of Punjab's 13 *Lok Sabha* seats. In the 1998 elections, it again won eight seats and supported the ruling coalition led by the →*Bharatiya Janata* Party (BJP). Perhaps as a result, it suffered severely in the elections of October 1999 and was reduced to two seats. In the *Rajya Sabha*, the party currently holds five seats.

Shiv Sena

Address. Shivsena Bhavan, Gadkari Chowk, Dadar, Bombay 400028
Website. www.shivsena.org
Leadership. Bal Thackeray (president)
Founded in 1967 and based in Maharashtra state, *Shiv Sena* is a right-wing Hindu communalist party allied to the →*Bharatiya Janata* Party (BJP) at state government and federal parliamentary levels. In the general elections of April–May 1996 the party won 15 seats in the *Lok Sabha* and supported the subsequent short-lived BJP federal administration. In the 1998 election, its representation was reduced to six seats but it became part of the ruling BJP-led coalition government. In the 1999 election, it recovered to 15 seats (all in Maharashtra) as part of the victorious BJP-led →National Democratic Alliance. Between 1995 and 2000, it governed Maharashtra state in alliance with the BJP. As at August 2001 it held five seats in the *Rajya Sabha*.

Tamil Maanila Congress (TMC)

Address. Satyamurthy Bhavan, General Platters Road, Madras 600002, Tamil Nadu
Leadership. G.K. Vasan (leader)
The TMC is a breakaway faction of the →Indian National Congress–Congress (I) in Tamil Nadu. Its leaders were formally expelled from the parent party in April 1996, prior to the general election in which the TMC secured 20 of Tamil Nadu's 39 seats in the *Lok Sabha*. At state level it was allied with the victorious →Dravidian Progressive Federation (DMK), winning 39 legislative assembly seats in its own right. The party was a leading component of the →United Front federal government inaugurated in June 1996, being awarded the finance portfolio and four other posts in the new administration. However, it faired poorly in the 1998 election, when it was reduced to three seats, and even worse in the 1999 election, when it failed to win any seats. It also broke its alliance with the DMK, when the latter moved to support the National Democratic Alliance headed by the →*Bharatiya Janata* Party in 1999, and re-allied with the →All-India Dravidian Progressive Federation (AIADMK). As of August 2001, it held three seats in the *Rajya Sabha*.

Telugu Desam Party (TDP)

Address. Telugu Desam Party Office, House No. 3–5–837, Sultan Manzil, Hyderguda, Hyderabad 500029, Andhra Pradesh

Website. www.tdparty.org
Leadership. N. Chandrababu Naidu (president)
Founded in 1982 as an Andhra Pradesh-based leftist party by N.T. Rama Rao, the TDP was the ruling party in the state from 1983 to 1989. In 1994 it regained power from the →Indian National Congress–Congress (I) in a convincing victory in the state elections, Rao becoming chief minister again. Political divisions within the party resulted in a split in 1995 between those state assembly deputies supporting Rao and those supporting Chandrababu Naidu (Rao's son-in-law). In August Rao resigned the premiership and was replaced by Naidu in September. On Rao's death in January 1996, leadership of his faction was taken over by his wife, Lakshmi Parvati. In the general election of April–May 1996, the TDP–Naidu faction won 16 seats in the *Lok Sabha* (and the Parvati faction none), being allocated four posts in the subsequent →United Front federal government formed in June 1996. At the 1998 general election, the party (over which Naidu had by now established firm leadership) won 12 seats and supported the BJP-led federal government from the back benches. In the 1999 election, the TDP not only triumphed by winning 29 seats (all in Andhra Pradesh) but, in simultaneous polls to the state legislative assembly, was returned to government with an enhanced majority. For the general election, it remained allied to the BJP as part of the →National Democratic Alliance (NDA) but, once again, refused to accept portfolios in the NDA's new federal government. Party leader Chandrababu Naidu has established a reputation as one of the principal proponents of liberal economic reform in India and as the chief minister of one of the country's most economically-dynamic states, where the 'cyber-revolution' has been particularly strong. As at August 2001, the TDP held 11 seats in the *Rajya Sabha*.

United Front (UF)
Address. c/o *Lok Sabha*, New Delhi 110001
Officially called the National Front–Left Front for the April–May 1996 general elections, the UF consisted of a loose alliance of 13 broadly leftist and regional organizations dominated by three national parties, namely the →*Janata Dal* (JD), the →Communist Party of India–Marxist (CPI-M) and the →Communist Party of India (CPI). It also included the →All-India Forward Bloc, the All-India Indira Congress–*Tiwari*, the →Assam People's Council, the →Dravidian Progressive Federation (DMK), the →Karnataka Congress Party, the →*Madhya Pradesh Vikas* Congress, the →*Maharastrawadi Gomantak*, the →Revolutionary Socialist Party, the →*Samajwadi* Party, the →*Tamil Maanila* Congress and the →*Telugu Desam* Party–*Naidu*.

Upon the demise of the short-lived post-election government of the →*Bharatiya Janata* Party at the end of May 1996, the UF parties, with the support of about 180 members in the *Lok Sabha* and the acquiescence of the →Indian National Congress–Congress (I) deputies, formed a new federal administration under the premiership of Deve Gowda (JD) which won a parliamentary vote of confidence the following month. The CPI–M opted not to take ministerial portfolios, while continuing to be a member of the Front, which advocated the preservation of national unity, social and economic equality, and commitment to secularism and federalism. However, after its government fell early in 1998 when the Congress Party withdrew its support, the UF fell apart. Most its constituent parties faired badly in the elections of 1998 and 1999 and many of them suffered internal splits. Occasionally invoked as the basis of a 'third' political front – in juxtaposition to those led by the BJP and the Congress Party – the UF, as at August 2001, had been reduced to a shadow existence.

Other Parties

India has a great profusion of political parties. The following have had an impact at state or national level.

All-India Forward Bloc (AIFB), based mainly in West Bengal, where it is a constituent of the Left Front state administration led by the →Communist Party of India-Marxist. In the general election of October 1999 the party won two *Lok Sabha* seats (both in West Bengal) but it is without a seat in the *Rajya Sabha*.
Address. 28 Gurudwara Rakab Ganj Road, New Delhi 110001
Leadership. Debabrata Biswas (general secretary)

All-India Majlis-e-Ittehadul Muslimeen (AIMEIM), a Muslim-based party led by Sultan Salahuddin Owaisi that secured representation in the *Lok Sabha* in a 1994 by-election; declared its support for the →United Front central government inaugurated in June 1996; retained its single seat in the 1998 and 1999 general elections.

Assam People's Council (*Asom Gana Parishad, AGP*), won power in Assam in 1985, the year of its foundation. However, in 1989 the federal government imposed President's rule in the state as a result of the activities of separatist groups. The party was subsequently defeated by the →Indian National Congress–Congress (I) in fresh state elections in 1991. It emerged from the April-May 1996 general election with five *Lok Sabha* seats (having won only two in 1991) and obtained two ministerial posts in the →United Front national government inaugurated in June 1996. In simultaneous state elections, an AGP-led alliance secured a majority in the Assam legislative assembly, regaining power from Congress (I). However, it failed to retain any of its *Lok Sabha* seats at the 1998 and 1999 general elections and, in May 2001, lost power to Congress (I) in the state. The AGP holds 2 seats in the *Rajya Sabha*.
Address. Gopinath Bordoloi Road, Guwahati 781001, Assam
Leadership. Prafullo Kumar Mohanta (president)

Autonomous State Demand Committee (ASDC), secured representation in the *Lok Sabha* in a 1994 by-election and retained it in the 1996 and 1998 general elections; however, was defeated in 1999. As of August 2001, the ASDC held one seat in the *Rajya Sabha*.
Address. Head Quarter-Diphu, Karbi Anglong 782460, Assam
Leadership. Jayanta Rongpi (general secretary)

Communist Party of India (Marxist-Leninist) Liberation (CPI–ML), founded in 1969 by revolutionaries expelled from the →Communist Party of India-Marxist (CPI–M), with which it then engaged in a bitter and bloody struggle, particularly in West Bengal. Retains Marxist–Leninist positions advocating a "revolutionary democratic front". Failed to gain national representation until in won a single *Lok Sabha* seat at the 1999 general election.
Address. U-90, Shakarpur, Delhi 110 092
Telephone. (+91–11) 222–1067
Fax. (+91–11) 221 8248
Website. www.cpiml.org

Haryana Vikas Party (HVP), returned three *Lok Sabha* members from Haryana constituencies in April–May 1996 and supported the short-lived government of the →*Bharatiya Janata* Party; suffered internal split in 1997 and returned just one member to the *Lok Sabha* at the 1998 and 1999 general elections.
Address. Kothi No. 136/22, Sonipat Road, Rohtak, Haryana
Leadership. Bansi Lal (president)

Hill State People's Democratic Party (HSPDP), advocating the preservation of the distinct identity of the tribal peo-

ples of Meghalaya state and the protection of their interests within the Indian Union; without a seat in the *Lok Sabha*.
Address. Kench's Trace, Laban, Shillong 793004, Meghalaya
Leadership. H.S. Lyngdoh (president)

Himachal Vikas Congress, state party in Himachal Pradesh that held one seat in the *Lok Sabha* following the 1999 elections.
Address. Samkhetar Bazar, Mandi 175001, Himachal Pradesh
Leadership. Sukh Ram (president)

Indian National Lok Dal, won five seats in the *Lok Sabha* in 1999 elections.
Address. 100 Lodhi Estate, New Delhi
Leadership. Om Parkash Chautala (president)

Indian Union Muslim League (IUML), a remnant of the pre-independence Muslim League, aiming to represent the interests of the Muslim ethnic and religious minority; has attracted support mainly in southern India, particularly in Kerala state.

Jammu and Kashmir National Conference (JKNC), a state-based party, opposed to Hindu communalism and advocating the maintenance of Jammu and Kashmir's status as an integral part of the Indian Union but with internal autonomy and self-government. It was the dominant party in Kashmir for most of the period from independence until 1990, when communal violence led to the imposition of President's rule in the state. Constitutional government was restored in 1996 with the JKNC winning a majority of seats and forming a government in the State Legislative Assembly although on the basis of a tiny voter turnout. The party won three *Lok Sabha* seats at the 1998 general election and four at the 1999 polls. It supported the federal coalition governments led by the →*Bharatiya Janata* Party (BJP) after both elections but withdrew its backing in 2000 following a dispute over Kashmir policy. As of August 2001, it held three *Rajya Sabha* seats.
Address. Sher-e-Kashmir Bhavan, Residency Road, Jammu
Leadership. Farooq Abdullah

Janata Party (JP), in power at the federal level from March 1977 until January 1980, after which it fragmented and the rump party's influence declined. It is currently unrepresented in the *Lok Sabha*.
Address. AB-13, Mathura Road, New Delhi 110001
Leadership. Subramanian Swamy (president)

Jharkhand Mukti Morcha (JMM), founded in 1980 to represent the interests of the tribal people of the state of Bihar, where it won about 5% of the seats in the 1995 legislative assembly; also represented in the Orissa state assembly. It won a handful of seats in 1996 general elections to the *Lok Sabha* but lost them at the 1998 and 1999 polls. Nonetheless, JMM pressure was significant in achieving the creation of a new Jharkhand regional state – carved out of Bihar and Orissa – in 2000, where it currently heads a coalition government. As at August 2001, the JMM held one seat in the *Rajya Sabha*.
Address. Bariatu Road, Ranchi 834008, Bihar
Leadership. Shibu Soren (president)

Karnataka Congress Party (KCP), an autonomous state party that won one *Lok Sabha* seat in 1996 as part of the →United Front coalition, but subsequently lost it.

Kerala Congress (KC), a participant in the Left Democratic Front coalition government, headed by the →Communist Party of India-Marxist (CPI–M), which came to power in Kerala in May 1996 following state elections but was defeated in 2001. However, the KC won one *Lok Sabha* seat in the 1998 general election and retained it in 1999, while a breakaway faction (the →Kerala Congress–M) also won a seat in 1999. As of August 2001, the KC held one *Rajya Sabha* seat.
Address. State Committee Office, Near Star Theatre Junction, Kottayam South, Kerala
Leadership. Eapan Varghese (chairman)

Kerala Congress–M, a breakaway from the →Kerala Congress; won one seat in 1999 elections to the *Lok Sabha*.
Address. State Committee Office, Near Fire Station, Kottayam, Kerala
Leadership. C.F. Thomas (chairman)

Lok Shakti, broke away from the Karnataka cadre of the *Janata Dal* (JD) under the leadership of R.K. Hegde in 1998; won three seats in the *Lok Sabha* at the 1998 general election and supported the federal coalition government led by the →*Bharatiya Janata* Party with Hegde serving as Commerce Minister. Hegde led a section of the party into the →Janata Dal (United) and →National Democratic Alliance in July 1999 and won four seats at the 1999 election. The residual *Lok Shakti* was de-recognized as a state party in Karnataka and Nagaland by the Election Commission in September 2000.

Madhya Pradesh Vikas Congress (MPVC), formed early in 1996 by Madhya Pradesh dissidents of the →Indian National Congress–Congress (I), won two lower house seats in the subsequent general elections, declared support for the →United Front government inaugurated in June 1996, but was defeated in 1998 and 1999.

Maharashtrawadi Gomantak Party (MGP), a Hindu-dominated party that has long competed for control of the Goan legislative assembly with the →Indian National Congress–Congress (I). Won one *Lok Sabha* seat in 1996 as part of the →United Front coalition but was unsuccessful in 1998 and 1999 elections.
Address. c/o Baban A. Naik, "Anant" Dada Vaidya Road, Panaji 403001, Goa
Leadership. Surendra Sirsat (president)

Manipur People's Party (MPP), a state level party that holds no seats in the *Lok Sabha*.
Address. People's Road, Imphal 795001, Manipur

Manipur State Congress Party (MSCP), broke away from the →Indian National Congress-Congress (I) in 1997; won one *Lok Sabha* seat at the 1998 general election and retained it in 1999.
Address. Babupara, Imphal 795001, Manipur

Mizo National Front (MNF), legalized in 1986 (upon the conferment of statehood on Mizoram), having earlier waged an underground campaign for national self-determination. Has failed to win any seats to the *Lok Sabha*.

Marumalarchi Dravidian Progressive Federation (MDMK), a breakaway faction of the →Dravidian Progressive Federation (DMK). It allied with the →All-India Dravidian Progressive Federation (AIADMK) for the 1998 general election, winning three seats in the *Lok Sabha* and supporting the federal coalition government headed by the →*Bharatiya Janata* Party (BJP). It broke with the AIADMK to join the DMK for the 1999 general election where it stood as part of the →National Democratic Alliance and won four seats (all in Tamil Nadu); left the DMK to stand independently in the 2001 Tamil Nadu state elections. Unrepresented in the *Rajya Sabha*.
Address. "Thayagam", No. 141, Rukmani Lakshmi Pathi Salai, Egmore, Madras 600008, Tamil Nadu
Leadership. Thiru Vaiko (president)

Nationalist Congress Party (NCP) broke away from the main →Indian National Congress – Congress (I) in 1999 under the direction of Sharad Pawar and P.A. Sangma in protest at the party leadership of Sonia Gandhi. It has its main base in Pawar's home state of Maharashtra where it took six of the eight *Lok Sabha* seats it won in the 1999 general election. It has tried to revive the non-Congress (I) forces of opposition, especially in association with the →*Samajwadi* Party; however, the NCP was forced to re-ally with the Congress (I) in Maharashtra in order to form a coalition government to displace the previously ruling combine of →*Shiv Sena* and the →*Bharatiya Janata* Party. As of August 2001, the NCP held one seat in the *Rajya Sabha*.
Address. 10 Bishambhar Das Marg, New Delhi 110001
Leadership. Sharad Pawar (president)

Pattali Makkal Katchi (PMK), a party of the large Vanniya caste which is prominent in north Tamil Nadu; vigorously led by Dr S. Ramdoss, the PMK broke its long term association with the →Dravidian Progressive Federation (DMK) to stand independently at the 1998 general election where it won three seats in the *Lok Sabha* and joined the federal coalition government headed by the →*Bharatiya Janata* Party (BJP) in association with the →All India Dravidian Progressive Party (AIADMK). It broke its connection to the AIADMK when the latter resigned from the federal government and re-aligned itself with the DMK for the 1999 general election, joining the →National Democratic Alliance (NDA) and winning five *Lok Sabha* seats (all in Tamil Nadu); however, it deserted the DMK again to stand independently at the Tamil Nadu state legislature elections of May 2001. As at August 2001, the PMK held no seat in the *Rajya Sabha*.
Address. 63, Nattu Muthu Naiken Street, Vanniya Teynampet, Madras 60001

Peasants' and Workers' Party of India (PWPI), a Marxist party led by Dajiba Desai, operates primarily in the state of Maharashtra. The PWPI won one Lok Sabha seat in the 1998 general election and retained it in 1999.

Rashtriya Janata Dal (RJD), a breakaway faction of the →*Janata Dal* (JD) formed in 1998 around erstwhile JD leader Laloo Prasad Yadav and having its main base in Bihar. The breakaway was fomented by Yadav's indictment for corruption and subsequent forced resignation as Bihar chief minister; however, the party then installed his wife, Rabri Devi, in his place and continued to govern the state. In the 1998 general election, the RJD won 17 seats in the *Lok Sabha* and, in 1999, seven (all in Bihar). As at August 2001, it held 10 seats in the *Rajya Sabha*.
Address. 2 Moti Lal Nehru Place, Akbar Road, New Delhi 110011
Leadership. Laloo Prasad Yadav

Republican Party of India (RPI), committed to the egalitarian aims and objectives set out in the preamble to the 1950 Indian constitution; won four *Lok Sabha* seats at the 1998 general election but lost them all in 1999. As of August 2001, the RPI held one *Rajya Sabha* seat.
Address. Satpuda, Malabar Hill, Bombay
Leadership. R.S. Gavai (president)

Sikkim Democratic Front (SDF), a moderate regionalist party that became the ruling party in Sikkim in December 1994. In the April–May 1996 general election the party won Sikkim's single *Lok Sabha* seat, which it retained in the 1998 and 1999 elections.
Address. Upper Deorali, Gongtok, East Sikkim
Email. Sdf@sikkim.org
Website. www.sikkiminfo.com
Leadership. Pawan Kumar Chamling (president)

Sikkim Revolutionary Forum (*Sikkim Sangram Parishad (SSP)*) The SSP lost its majority in the Sikkim legislature to the →Sikkim Democratic Front (SDF) in state elections in December 1994. In the April-May 1996 general election the party also lost Sikkim's single *Lok Sabha* seat to the SDF.
Address. Sangram Bhavan, Jewan Theeng Marg, Gangtok, Sikkim
Leadership. Nar Bahadur Bhandari (president)

Indonesia

Capital: Jakarta

Population: 224,784,210 (2000E)

The Republic of Indonesia, comprising mainly some 13,700 islands, was known until 1949 as the Netherlands East Indies. It has the largest Muslim population in the world, but the 1945 provisional constitution enshrined the principle of *pancasila*, enjoining monotheism, humanitarianism, national unity, democracy by consensus and social justice. Following a brief period as a federation, Indonesia became a unitary state in 1950. A brief period of parliamentary politics ensued, but this led to increasing disorder, with the result that in 1959 the 1945 constitution was re-enacted by presidential decree. Still in force, it specifies that the President is head of state and government, elected for a five-year term by the Consultative Assembly (*Majelis Permusyarwaratan Rakyat*) consisting principally of the 500 members of the legislative House of Representatives (*Dewan Perwakilan Rakyat*). Under amendments introduced in 1999, the other 200 Assembly members are government appointees, delegates of the regional assemblies and representatives of parties and groups (appointed in proportion to their elective seats in the House of Representatives). Of the 500 members of the House, 462 are currently elected for a five-year term by direct universal adult suffrage, the remaining 38 being appointed from the armed forces by the President. Having numbered 75 prior to 1999, these military places are to be phased out entirely at some undetermined point in the future.

After 1959 President Sukarno "guided" democracy, but in 1965 he lost power following an abortive coup by the Indonesian Communist Party (PKI). He was replaced by Gen. Suharto, who established a military-backed "New Order" regime which lasted until 1998. Indonesian society became increasingly urban, better educated and more sophisticated. In 1976 Indonesia annexed East Timor following the withdrawal of Portuguese troops, although anti-Indonesian protests there ultimately forced a referendum in 1999 in which the people voted for independence (see under East Timor). Suharto's regime was brought down by the 1997 Asian financial crisis, which served as a catalyst for pent-up popular discontent over his authoritarian rule and the corruption associated with his family.

Suharto was replaced in May 1998 by his Vice-President, B.J. Habibie, who quickly lifted restrictions on the formation of political parties and called elections to the House of Representatives for June 1999. Whereas under Suharto there had been only three approved political formations, some 150 parties now sought registration and 48 were approved to present candidates because they met the requirement of having branches in at least half the districts of at least nine out of the 27 (effectively 26) provinces/special regions. The basic political cleavage is over religion, i.e. Islamic values versus others, and from 1999 this degenerated into inter-communal violence in various parts of the country.

The results of the polling on June 7, 1999, showed that the three Suharto-era parties had won the most seats among 19 parties which obtained representation (13 with less than 10 seats each), as follows: Indonesian Democratic Party–Struggle (PDI-K) 154 seats (with 37.4% of the vote), Golkar Party 120 (20.9%), United Development Party 58 (10.7%), National Awakening Party (PKB) 51 (17.4%), National Mandate Party 35 (7.3%), Crescent Star Party 14 (1.8%), Justice Party 6 (1.3%), Justice and Unity Party 6 (0.9%), Nahdlatul Ummat Party 3 (0.6%), Indonesian Democratic Party 3 (0.4%), Love the Nation Democratic Party 3 (0.3%), People's Sovereignty Party 2 (0.3%), seven other parties 1 seat each. Inside the new legislature the parties grouped themselves into 11 factions.

In post-election negotiations between delegates to the Consultative Assembly, the liberal-minded Muslim cleric Abdurahman Wahid (popularly known as Gus Dur) of the PKB surprisingly emerged as President in October 1999. In August 2001, however, the Assembly succeeded at the second attempt in impeaching him for corruption. He was replaced by his Vice-President, Megawati Sukarnoputri, the daughter of ex-President Sukarno and leader of the PDI–P.

Crescent Star Party
Partai Bulan Bintang (PBB)
Address. Jalan Kramat VI/14A, Jakarta Pusat 10450
Fax. (+62–21) 310–6739
Leadership. Yusril Ilza Mahendra (chairman)
Founded in July 1998, the PBB claims to be the successor to the Masyumi Party banned under the Suharto regime. It is one of the more conservative Islamic parties and wants a state "based on Islamic principles", without acknowledging *pancasila*. It accepts the need for parliamentary activity and advocates extensive decentralization. Its main support is in the outer islands, especially among urban Muslims. It won 14 seats in 1999.

Golkar Party
Partai Golongan Karya (Golkar)
Address. Jalan Anggrek Nelly Murni, Slipi, Jakarta 11480
Telephone. (+62–21) 530–2222
Website. www.golkar.net
Leadership. Akbar Tanjung (chairman)
Originally formed in 1964, Golkar became a government-sponsored amalgamation of groups representing farmers, fishermen and the professions, and including members of the Indonesian armed forces. It was the dominant political force under Suharto's military regime, for which it provided a civilian basis. His fall was an enormous challenge. In July 1998 Golkar removed him as leader and issued an apology for wrongdoings in the past. The party then repositioned itself as a secular-nationalist party. It remained the party with the most resources, although since Suharto's fall its offices round the country have frequently been ransacked.

In the 1999 elections it won 120 seats, with most of its support coming from the outer islands. This made it the second largest party, and Akbar Tanjung became Speaker of the legislature. Golkar representatives helped to elect Abdurahman Wahid of the →National Awakening Party as President in October 1999, albeit after considerable hesitation. As President Wahid's support declined, Golkar representatives were active in urging impeachment.

Indonesian Democratic Party
Partai Demokrasi Indonesia (PDI)
Address. Jalan Denpasar Raya Blok C3 No.4, Jakarta Selatan
Telephone. (+62–21) 520–1630
Fax. (+62–21) 520–1631
Leadership. Budi Hardjono (chairman)
The present PDI is the rump of the pro-*pancasila* party founded in 1973 as a merger of three nationalist and two Christian-based parties, as part of the Suharto government's move to consolidate the party system. As one of the three parties authorized in that era, it advocated the restoration of full civilian rule but remained largely supportive of the Suharto regime, usually obtaining around 15% of the electoral vote. Eclipsed by →Indonesian Democratic Party-Struggle from the mid-1990s, the PDI won three seats in 1999.

Indonesian Democratic Party–Struggle
Partai Demokrasi Indonesia (PDI–P)
Address. Jalan Lenteng Agung 99, Jakarta Selatan 12610
Telephone. (+62–21) 780–6020
Fax. (+62–21) 780–2824
Leadership. Megawati Sukarnoputri (chairperson)
The PDI–P is derived from the original →Indonesian Democratic Party (PDI), which in 1994 chose Megawati Sukarnoputri (the daughter of former President Sukarno) as its leader. When Suharto prevented her re-election in 1996, she formed the rival PDI–P, thus marginalizing the old PDI. Strong in all 26 provinces, the PDI–P called for the restoration of trust in officials, the market and the judicial system. In the late 1990s Megawati was very robust in defending the integrity of Indonesia and enjoyed support amongst the military. Part of the party's image remained that of being closer to "Christian" than to Muslim values.

Although the PDI–P won most seats (154) in the 1999 legislative elections, Megawati failed to be elected President by the Consultative Assembly, amidst grumblings from Muslims that a woman should not hold the post. Instead she accepted the vice-presidency. For the first year she loyally supported President Wahid of the →National Awakening Party, but relations gradually deteriorated, so that the PDI–P supported his impeachment. She became President in August 2001.

Justice Party
Partai Keadilan (PK)
Address. Jalan Mampang Prapatan Raya No.98 D–E–F, Jakarta Selatan
Telephone. (+62–21) 799–5425
Fax. (+62–21) 799–5433
Leadership. Nur Mahmudi Ismail (chairman)
The Muslim-based PK was founded in July 1998, seeking to appeal to educated young Muslims, especially women, and advocating morality above capitalism and materialism. Drawing particular support in the outer islands, it won six seats in the 1999 legislative elections.

Justice and Unity Party
Partai Keadilan dan Persatuan (PKP)
Address. Jalan Raya Cilandak No.32, Jakarta Selatan
Telephone. (+62–21) 780–7653
Leadership. Edi Sudrajat (chairman)
Standing for *pancasila* values, the PKP was founded in December 1998 by a number of disillusioned former officials and officers of the Suharto regime. Party leader Edi Sudrajat, a former general, had failed to become the →Golkar Party leader after Suharto's fall. The party won six seats in the 1999 elections.

National Awakening Party
Partai Kebangkitan Bangsa (PKB)
Address. Jalan Kalibata Timur 24B, Jakarta Selatan
Telephone. (+62–21) 7919–0920
Fax. (+62–21) 7919–3486
Leadership. Matori Abdul Jalil (chairman); Abdurahman Wahid (chairman of NU)
Formed in 1998, the party is effectively led by Abdurahman Wahid (popularly known as Gus Dur) and so is close to the largest Muslim organization, the *Nahdlatul Ulama* (NU), of which he is the head. Having 30 million members, the NU is associated with more conservative Sunni values and is especially strong in Java, but is moderate, committed to the principles of democracy, and (albeit with some qualification) accepts *pancasila* as the basis of authority in Indonesia. It also accepts the importance of the Chinese community for the Indonesian economy.

Its chief appeal being for national reconciliation, the PKB won 51 seats in the June 1999 elections, making it the fourth party in the new legislature. Skilful manoeuvring with the other parties led to Wahid's election as President in October 1999. As President, Wahid attempted to accommodate the separatist movements in various parts of the country that came to the fore after Suharto's fall. However, his eccentric and sometimes aloof style of governing increasingly undermined his support and in August 2001 the Assembly succeeded at the second attempt in impeaching him for corruption. He was replaced by Vice-President Megawati Sukarnoputri, the leader of the →Indonesian Democratic Party–Struggle.

National Mandate Party
Partai Amanat Nasional (PAN)
Address. Jalan H. Nawi 15, Radio Dalam, Jakarta Selatan
Telephone. (+62–21) 7279–4535
Fax. (+62–21) 726–8695
Leadership. Amien Rais (chairman)
Founded in 1998, the moderate Islamic PAN accepts *pancasila* principles as the sole basis of the Indonesian state. Party leader Amien Rais has a doctorate in political science from the University of Chicago and was a strident and courageous opponent of the Suharto regime. Until 1998 he chaired the *Muhammadiyah*, the second largest Muslim organization with 28 million members, which aggressively advocates Islamic values in society but also supports modernization. The national leadership of PAN, however, is explicitly non-religious and includes many Christian and secular activists.

The party's economic policy has a nationalist orientation, although in the 1999 elections Rais tried to present himself as moderate and liberal. His party did less well than expected, winning only 35 seats, but he negotiated his election as Speaker of the Consultative Assembly and played a crucial role in the successful impeachment of President Wahid in August 2001.

United Development Party
Partai Persatuan Pembangunan (PPP)
Address. Jalan Diponegoro 60, Jakarta 10310
Telephone. (+62–21) 336338
Email. dpp@ppp.or.id
Website. www.ppp.or.id
Leadership. Hamzah Haz (president)

The PPP, like the →Indonesian Democratic Party (PDI), was created in 1973 as a result of the Suharto regime's pressure on political organizations to "simplify" the party system. Four Islamic groups merged initially to form the party, although the *Nahdlatul Ulama* (NU) faction withdrew in 1984, after which support for the PPP fell considerably. After the departure of Suharto in 1998, however, the party recovered support as a moderate reformist Islamic party. Whilst President Suharto had required it to accept *pancasila* as the basis of state authority, it has since revived its demands that government policy should always conform to the principles of Islam, calling for more benefits to be given to the people and for economic democracy.

Despite the alignment of the NU with the new →National Awakening Party (PKB), the PPP did surprisingly well in the 1999 elections, becoming the third-largest party in the legislature with 58 seats (including 19 obtained from vote-sharing arrangements with five small Islamic parties).

Other Parties

Christian Catholic Indonesia (*Kristen Katolik Indonesia, KKI*), a member of the Christian Democrat International.
Address. Djalan Kramat V 18/A, Jakarta
Leadership. Ben Mang Reng Say

Independence Vanguard Party (*Partai IPKI, PIPKI*), originally founded in 1954 and revived in September 1998, committed to pancasila values and national unity. It won one seat in 1999.
Address. Gedung Joang DHN 45 Lt. 2, Jalan Menteng Raya No.31, Jakarta Pusat 10340
Telephone/Fax. (+62–21) 314–1382
Leadership. Mayjen R. Soeprapto

Indonesian National Party Front Marhaenis (*Partai Nasional Indonesia Front Marhaenis, PNIFM*), originally founded in 1927, re-established in 1998 to advocate global reconciliation based on the values of *pancasila* and Marhaenism. It won one seat in 1999.
Address. Jalan Cikini Raya N.48, Jakarta Pusat
Telephone. (+62–21) 314–1223
Leadership. H. Probotusedjo

Indonesian National Party Massa Marhaenis (*Partai Nasional Indonesia Massa Marhaenis, PNIMM*), also originally founded in 1927 and re-established in 1998. It won one seat in 1999.
Address. Tanjung Duren Barat Green Vile No.1, Jakarta 11510
Telephone. (+62–21) 567–2429
Fax. (+62–21) 569–7187
Leadership. Bachtar Oscha Chalik

Indonesian United Islam Party (*Partai Syarikat Islam Indonesia, PSII*), an Islamic party originally established in 1912; it was revived in 1998 and won one seat in 1999.
Address. Jalan Taman Amir Hamzah No.2, Jakarta Pusat 10320
Telephone/Fax. (+62–21) 390–4101
Leadership. Taufiq Rusjdi Tjokroaminoto

Indonesian Unity in Diversity Party (*Partai Bhinneka Tunggal Ika Indonesia, PBI*), founded in June 1998 and won one seat in 1999.
Address. Jalan K.H. Hasyim Ashari No. 33C, Jakarta 11110
Telephone. (+62–21) 631–4888
Fax. (+62–21) 631–6889
Leadership. Nurdin Purnomo

Love the Nation Democratic Party (*Partai Demokrasi Kasih Bangsa, PDKB*), founded in August 1998, the *pancasila*-oriented PDKB won three seats in 1999.
Address. Kompleks Widuri Indah Blok A-4, Jalan Palmerah Barat 353, Jakarta Barat 12210

Telephone. (+62–21) 533–0973
Email. pdkb@pdkb.or.id
Website. www.pdkb.or.id
Leadership. Manasse Malo

Nahdlatul Ummat Party (*Partai Nahdlatul Ummat, PNU*), a rival of the →National Awakening Party (PKB) for the support of members of the *Nahdlatul Ulama*. It won three seats in 1999.
Address. Jalan Cipinang Cempedak IV No.1, Jatinegara, Jakarta 13340
Telephone. (+62–21) 857–1736
Fax. (+62–21) 421–2701
Leadership. Sjukron Ma'mun

Muslim Community Awakening Party (*Partai Kebangkitan Umat, PKU*), founded in September 1998, aims to reconcile Muslim and *pancasila* values. It won one seat in 1999.
Address. Jalan Dr. Saharjo 204A, Jakarta 12870,

Telephone. (+62–21) 835–7310
Fax. (+62–21) 830–8769
Leadership. K.H. Yusuf Hasyim

People's Sovereignty Party (*Partai Daulat Rakyat, PDR*), founded in January 1999, won two seats in the 1999 election.
Address. Jalan Cimandiri 24, Cikini, Jakarta Pusat 10330
Telephone. (+62–21) 31907232
Fax. (+62–21) 31907231/3102174
Leadership. H. Abdul Latief Burhan

Unity Party (*Partai Persatuan, PP*), an Islamic party founded in January 1999. It won one seat in the elections.
Address. Jalan Cidodol Raya 40, Kebayoran Lama, Jakarta 12220
Telephone. (+62–21) 725–6979
Fax. (+62–21) 722–7407
Leadership. H. Jailani Naro

Iran

Capital: Tehran

Population: 65,600,000 (2000E)

The Islamic Republic of Iran was proclaimed in 1979 after the overthrow of the monarchy. Overall authority is exercised by the *Wali Faqih*, the country's spiritual leader. The state President and the 290-member legislature, the *Majlis-e-Shoura-e-Islami* (Islamic Consultative Assembly), are elected by universal suffrage every four years on a non-party basis. The *Majlis* approves the appointment of all members of the Council of Ministers and may request their resignation. The post of Prime Minister was formally abolished in July 1989. An Assembly of Experts is elected, also by universal suffrage, to decide issues such as succession to the position of *Wali Faqih*. It is composed entirely of clerics. Ayatollah Ruhollah Khomeini, Iran's *Wali Faqih* since 1979, died in June 1989, and the Assembly of Experts elected Ayatollah Sayed Ali Khamenei as his successor. A 12-member Council of Constitutional Guardians made up of experts in Koranic law and up to six civil lawyers supervises elections and examines legislation adopted by the *Majlis* to ensure its conformity to the principles of religious law and the constitution.

In June 2001 Seyyed Mohammed Khatami was re-elected President for a second successive four-year term. A general election held in February and May 2000 strengthened the position of supporters of Khatami's reformist policies (espousing economic and political liberalization and openness in foreign relations).

Article 26 of the Iranian constitution permits the formation of parties, societies, political or professional associations and Islamic or other religious societies of recognized minorities. The law on activities of parties and political groups was approved in 1981 by the Majlis, but its enforcement was postponed until 1989. According to Article 10 of the Parties Law, a commission comprising representatives of the State Prosecutor General, political judicial council, the Interior Ministry and two *Majlis* deputies are delegated with the responsibility of issuing operating permits for parties and supervising them. Before the inauguration of President Khatami in 1997, some 39 parties, political societies and associations received permits from the Article 10 Commission of the Interior Ministry. By January 2000, the number had risen to 103. Despite this, the number of significant and active political parties and groups in Iran hardly exceeds a dozen.

Executives of Construction Party (ECP)
Hezbe Kargozarane Sazandegi Iran
Leadership. Hussein Marashi (acting secretary general)
Formed in 1997 by senior aides of the former President Akbar Hashemi Rafsanjani, the ECP is moderate in orientation and has supported the policies of President Khatami. Former Tehran mayor Gholam Hussein Karbaschi served as secretary general of the ECP until his imprisonment in May 1999 on corruption charges; *Majlis* deputy Hussein Marashi replaced him as acting secretary general. Other senior members of the ECP include Ataollah Mohajerani (former Minister of Islamic Culture and Guidance) and Mohsen Nourbakhsh (governor of the Central Bank of Iran).

Freedom Movement of Iran (FMI)
Nehzate Azadie Iran
Leadership. Ebrahim Yazdi
The FMI was formed in 1962 by a number of dissident clergy (including Ayatollah Seyed Mahmoud Taleqani and Muslim

intellectuals such as Mahdi Bazargan and Yadollah Sahabi. Political and religious activities of the FMI before the 1979 Islamic Revolution led to the imprisonment of a number of its members. After the Islamic Revolution, Ayatollah Khomenei appointed Bazargan, the then FMI leader, to form the first government of the Islamic Republic of Iran; Bazargan's government did not last long, resigning after the occupation of the US embassy in Tehran. After the death of Mahdi Bazargan in 1994, Ebrahim Yazdi was elected as secretary general of the FMI. The Movement has failed to obtain an operating permit from the Interior Ministry's Parties Commission and for this reason has been deprived of an official presence in a number of gatherings. The FMI has not been given permission to publish a newspaper as its official organ. It has supported the reformist policies of President Khatami.

Islamic Assembly of Women (IAW)
Majma'e Eslamie Banovan
Leadership. Fatemeh Karroubi

The IAW has similar objectives to the →Islamic Republic of Iran Women's Society (IRIWS).

Islamic Coalition Association (ICA)
Jamiate Moutalefeye Eslami
Leadership. Habibollah Asgar-Owladi (secretary general)
The conservative ICA is among the oldest parties in Iran, with origins among religious groups opposed to the last Shah and supporting Ayatollah Khomeini. The ICA reduced its activities after the victory of the Islamic Revolution and most of its members joined the (now dissolved) Islamic Republic Party (IRP). It was revived in 1988 to "coordinate the faithful" in pursuit of pure Islam.

Islamic Iran Partnership Front (IIPF)
Jebheye Mosharekate Irane Eslami
Leadership. Mohsen Mirdamadi (secretary general)
Formed in 1998 by supporters of President Khatami's administration. Prominent members of the Front include Mohammad Reza Khatami (President Khatami's brother), Saeed Hajjarian (former political advisor to President Khatami and member of Tehran City Council), Abbas Abdi (journalist), Mohammad Reza Aref (First Vice President), Habibollah Bitaraf (Energy Minister) and Hussein Nasiri (presidential advisor and secretary of the High Council of Free Trade Zones).

Islamic Iran Solidarity Party
Hezbe Hambastegie Irane Eslami
Leadership. Mohammad Reza Rah-Chamani (secretary general)
Formed after the 1997 election victory of President Khatami to support his reformist plans. The party includes a number of *Majlis* deputies.

Islamic Republic of Iran Women's Society (IRIWS)
Jamiate Zanane Jomhurie Eslamie Iran
Leadership. Zahra Mostafavi (secretary general)
Assists the "intellectual, cultural and scientific promotion of women in line with Islamic ideals". The IRIWS is active, like many other parties, at the time of elections and seldom enters into political, social and cultural debates and dialogue at other times. Its secretary general is Zahra Mostafavi, daughter of Ayatollah Khomeini. During the past two elections, it has supported the candidacy of President Khatami.

Islamic Revolution Mujahedin Organization (IRMO)
Sazemane Mojahedine Enqelabe Eslami
Leadership. Mohammad Salamati
A staunch supporter of President Khatami, the IRMO was formed immediately after the formation of the Islamic Republic in 1979 through the coalition of seven underground and semi-secret organizations. As a result of internal disputes at the beginning of the Iraq-Iran war, the IRMO suspended its activities until the end of the war.

Islamic Society of Engineers (ISE)
Jame'e Eslami Mohandesin
This is a society of technocrats formed at the end of the Iran-Iraqi war (1988) with the objective of "elevating the Islamic, political, scientific and technical knowledge of the Muslim people of Iran, defending major freedoms such as freedom of expression and gatherings, as well as continued campaign against foreign cultural agents whether Eastern or Western materialism." Prominent members of the ISE include former Energy Minister and *Majlis* member Hassan Ghafori-Fard and the managing director of the *Resalat* daily and *Majlis* member Morteza Nabavi.

Militant Clergy Association (MCA)
Jame'e Rouhaniyate Mobarez
Leadership. Mohammad Reza Mahdavi Kani (secretary general); Seyed Reza Taqavi (spokesman)
This is a conservative political clerical grouping with a prominent membership, including former President Ali Akbar Hashemi Rafsanjani, Mohammad Emami Kashani (former member of the Council of Guardians and substitute leader of Tehran Friday prayers) and Mohammad Yazdi (the former head of the judiciary). The MCA has not obtained a formal permit from the Interior Minister for political activities.

Militant Clerics League (MCL)
Majma'e Rouhanioune Mobarez
Leadership. Mahdi Karroubi (secretary general)
This is a breakaway faction of the →Militant Clergy Association (MCA), formed by members of the late Ayatollah Khomeini's office. The MCL's stated goals include: safeguarding the bases and objectives of Islam; campaigning against global arrogance; spreading Imam Khomeini's attitudes, and explaining the historical status of the sacred institution of the clergy. The reformist MCL supports political and cultural development policies and is among the major supporters of President Khatami.

Zainab Society (ZS)
Jame'e Zainab
Leadership. Maryam Behrouzi
Society for Iranian women whose objective is to "expand genuine Islamic culture and eliminate deviations, eclecticisms and imported culture from among women." The ZS usually follows the policies of the conservative →Militant Clergy Association (MCA).

Illegal parties and organizations

Organizations in exile include the following.

Communist Party of Iran, established in 1979 as an alternative to the pro-Soviet stance of the →Party of the Masses (*Tudeh*).
Email. Cpi@cpiran.org
Website. www.cpiran.org

Democratic Party of Iranian Kurdistan (PDKI), founded in 1945. Successive general secretaries of the party were assassinated by Iranian agents, in 1989 and 1992. Gained observer status with the Socialist International in 1996.
Address. BP 102-75623 Paris, Cedex 3, France
Email. Pdkiran@club-internet.fr
Website. www.pdk-iran.org

National Movement of Iranian Resistance, two of whose leaders – Abdol-Rahman Boroumand and former Prime Minister Dr Shapour Bakhtiar – were assassinated in 1991, apparently by Iranian agents.
Email. Iran_resistance@hotmail.com

National Resistance Council, established in October 1981 in France by Abolhassan Bani-Sadr (deposed as President of Iran earlier that year) and the Council's current leader, Massoud Rajavi of the *Mujaheddin-e-Khalq*. Bani-Sadr left the Council in 1984 because of his objection to Rajavi's growing links with the Iraqi government. The Council in 1993 nominated prominent woman political figure Maryam Rajavi to become president of Iran in a transitional period prior to elections following the overthrow of the current regime and says it favours a democratic, pluralist, market-based society freed of religious fundamentalism and respecting women's rights.
Website. www.iran-e-azad.org

Party of the Masses (Tudeh), historic left-wing Iranian party, communist and traditionally pro-Soviet from its formation in 1941. Having been banned in 1949, the party came into the open in 1979 but was banned again in 1983 by the Islamic regime.
Address. Postfach 100644, 10566 Berlin, Germany
Email. Mardom@tudehpartyiran.org
Website. www.tudehpartyiran.org

Iraq

Capital: Baghdad

Population: 22,680,000 (2000E)

The Republic of Iraq was declared in 1958 following the overthrow of the monarchy. Since 1979 power has been concentrated in the hands of President Saddam Hussein, his family and close associates. The President appoints the Revolutionary Command Council (RCC), which formally elects the President by a two-thirds majority from among its own members, and the Council of Ministers. Legislative authority is shared between the RCC and the 250-member National Assembly, the latter elected by universal adult suffrage under a system of proportional representation. A leading role is also played by the 17-member "regional command" of the dominant *Baath* Arab Socialist Party, which itself dominates the broader state-sponsored National Progressive Patriotic Front (NPPF).

In 1991 Saddam nominally ended de facto one-party rule by the *Baath* Party by approving a measure authorizing the creation of political parties outside the NPPF framework. However, there have been no reports of the formation of such groups in areas under government control. A national referendum in October 1995 approved a further seven-year term of office for President Saddam. In May 1994 Saddam had assumed the additional post of Prime Minister. Elections to 220 seats in the National Assembly were held in March 2000. The *Baath* Party won 165 seats and a further 55 seats were won by "independent" candidates. A further 30 "independents" had been appointed by the government to represent the Kurdish controlled areas of Sulaymaniyah, Arbil and Dohuk.

Since the Gulf War and Kurdish uprising of 1991 the central government has been unable to enforce control in the northern area of Iraqi Kurdistan, which is effectively protected from Iraqi attack by a US-led coalition. In this area a Kurdistan National Assembly was elected in May 1992. One hundred seats allocated to the Kurds were divided equally between the Kurdistan Democratic Party (KDP), which took 44.5% of the vote, and the Patriotic Union of Kurdistan (PUK), which took 44.3% of the vote. Five seats were allocated to representatives of the Assyrian minority while the Turkmen minority (which had been allocated ten seats) did not participate. The KDP and PUK subsequently formed a coalition administration (the Kurdistan Regional Government) but this collapsed when military conflict broke out between the KDP and PUK in 1994, leading to an effective partitioning of the region between KDP and PUK forces. A peace accord between the parties was agreed in Washington in September 1998, stabilizing the situation. However, although the Washington Accord laid out a timetable for the creation of a unified regional government and elections to a regional assembly within nine months, as of late 2001 no such elections had taken place and the de facto partition of the region continued with both sides referring to their administrations as the Kurdistan Regional Government.

Baath Arab Socialist Party
Hizb al-Baath al-Arabi al-Ishtiraki

Address. PO Box 6012, al-Mansour, Baghdad
Leadership. Saddam Hussein (secretary general of regional command)

The *Baath* (Renaissance) stands for secular pan-Arabism, socialism, anti-imperialism and anti-Zionism. It is historically (but now only theoretically) a regional party of which the Iraqi party is one "regional command", others being in Lebanon and Syria. Founded originally in Syria in the latter part of the 1940s, the *Baath* has held power in Iraq since July 1968, when it was the leading force in the Revolutionary Command Council (RCC) which overthrew the Aref military regime. The party had previously been part of the group that overthrew the dictatorship of President Kassem in February 1953, but was then itself deposed in a military coup in November of the same year.

In 1973 the *Baath* was instrumental in setting up an umbrella National Progressive Front with the aim of securing the co-operation of other political forces. This organization was renamed the →National Progressive Patriotic Front following the outbreak of war with Iran in 1980. Saddam Hussein has held the party leadership (as well as the Iraqi presidency) since 1979. There have been periodic purges in which critics of his leadership have been removed.

At the 12th regional congress of the *Baath* held in Baghdad in May 2001 Saddam's younger son, Qusai Hussein, was elected as a new member of the Iraq Command (the party's leadership body), his first official party post. Qusai was subsequently named as one of two deputy commanders of the party's influential military branch. The election of Qusai to the Iraq Command strengthened speculation that he was being groomed to succeed his father as President.

National Progressive Patriotic Front (NPPF)

Address. c/o National Assembly, Baghdad
Leadership. Naim Haddad (secretary general)

Formed in 1973 as the National Progressive Front (the addition of the word Patriotic in the early 1980s indicating the need for national solidarity in the war with Iran), this *Baath*-dominated organization serves in practice as little more than a mechanism for compiling and endorsing lists of electoral candidates.

Illegal Opposition Groups

There are numerous illegal organizations opposing the Saddam regime, including parties in exile and those in control of Iraqi Kurdistan.

Assyrian Democratic Movement (Zowaa), originating in 1979 to oppose the persecution of (non-Arab Christian) Assyrians in their homeland of Bet-Nahrein (northern Iraq); it participates in the →Iraqi National Congress and has built relations with the de facto Kurdish authorities in Kurd controlled areas of northern Iraq.
Website. www.atour.com/adm

Assyrian National Congress (ANC), based in the USA and led by Sargon Dadesho, an umbrella for several Assyrian organizations including the →Bet-Nahrein Democratic Party; favours an independent Assyrian homeland in northern Iraq and is in opposition to the →Assyrian Democratic Movement.

Assyrian Progressive Nationalist Party (APNP), founded in 1990 and calling for a "greater Mesopotamia" including non-Iraqi territories.
Website. www.leb.net/tigris/anp

Bet-Nahrein Democratic Party (BNDP), based in the USA and calling for an autonomous Assyrian state in northern Iraq. Supports the →Assyrian National Congress.
Website. www.bndp.net

Constitutional Monarchy Movement, calls for the restoration of the Hashemite monarchy overthrown in 1958 and backs the claim to the throne of London-based Sharif Ali Bin al-Hussain, who participates in the leadership of the →Iraqi National Congress.
Website. www.iraqcmm.org

Iraqi Communist Party (ICP), allied with the Kurdistan Communist Party-Iraq; opposes both Saddam and intervention in Iraq by "imperialists". Held its seventh national congress in August 2001 in Iraqi Kurdistan.
Address. BM Al-Tarik, London WC1N 3XX, United Kingdom
Fax. (+44-20) 7419 2552
Email. Iraq@iraqcp.org
Website. www.iraqcp.org
Leadership. Hameed Mousa (secretary)

Iraqi National Congress (INC), launched in 1992, aiming to unite the various Kurdish, Sunni and Shia factions of the opposition. The founders committed themselves to the overthrow of President Saddam Hussein and the establishment of a federal system permitting a substantial degree of ethnic autonomy without partition of the country. The retention of the current borders of Iraq has remained a principle of the INC. A seven man leadership group elected in New York in November 1999 included Ayad Allawi (Iraqi National Accord); Riyad al-Yawar (independent); Sharif Ali Bin al-Hussain (→Constitutional Monarchy Movement); Ahmed Chalabi (independent); Shaikh Mohammed Mohammed Ali (independent); Latif Rashid (→Patriotic Union of Kurdistan); and Hoshiar Zebari (→Kurdistan Democratic Party). The USA has given backing and financial support to the INC as the voice of the Iraqi opposition, but is reported to have concerns that the INC lacks common objectives and has no base in the dominant Sunni Muslim population on which the Iraqi regime is founded. Kurdish political leaders have also been reported as reluctant to engage in "adventurism" in respect of Iraq as a whole that might endanger their own de facto autonomy in northern Iraq. The INC has its headquarters in Salahuddin (Arbil province) in Iraqi Kurdistan with its external base in London.
Email. Pressoffice@inc.org.uk
Website. www.inc.org.uk

Kurdistan Democratic Party (KDP), founded in 1946, became the leading Kurdish political organization and controlled the largest rebel force during the unsuccessful 1991 uprising against Saddam Hussein. Took 50 seats in the Kurdistan National Assembly elected in 1992, participating on a 50/50 basis in a coalition government with the →Patriotic Union of Kurdistan (PUK) before the two organizations engaged in military conflict in 1994–98, in which the KDP received Iraqi and Turkish military support. As a result of the conflict Iraqi Kurdistan is effectively partitioned by the KDP and PUK with the KDP governing its area (the provinces of Arbil and Duhok, with a population of about 2 million) from Arbil city. It leads a coalition government that also includes members of the →Iraqi Communist Party, the Assyrian Movement, the Independent Work Party of Kurdistan, the Islamic Union and independents. It now participates with the PUK in the →Iraqi National Congress. It favours self-determination for Iraqi Kurds in the context of the preservation of a unified, federalist Iraq.
Website. www.kdp.pp.se
Leadership. Massoud Barzani (president)

Patriotic Union of Kurdistan (PUK), a rival to the →Kurdistan Democratic Party (KDP), from which it originated as a breakaway in 1975, and led by Jalal Talabani since its foundation. Took 50 seats in the Kurdistan National Assembly elected in 1992 in Iraqi Kurdistan and joined with the KDP in government but engaged in bitter military conflict with the KDP from 1994–98. Governs an area of Iraqi Kurdistan with 1.5 million people from its base in Sulaymaniyah as the leading force in the Kurdistan Democratic Alliance, which also includes the Kurdistan Toilers Party, the Kurdistan Social Democratic Party, the Islamic Movement and the Kurdistan Conservative Party. Participates in the →Iraqi National Congress. Seeks self-determination for the Kurds within a unified Iraq and describes itself as social democratic although it has traditionally had diverse ideological currents.
Email. Puk@puk.org
Website. www.puk.org
Leadership. Jalal Talabani (general secretary)

Supreme Council of the Islamic Revolution of Iraq (SCIRI), also known as the Supreme Assembly of the Islamic Revolution of Iraq, SAIRI), formed in 1982 by Shia Muslim opponents of the Sunni-based ruling regime. It has carried out periodic military attacks from its bases in Iran. It is close to Iran and does not participate in the →Iraqi National Congress.

Turkmen People's Party, representing the 2.5 million Turkmen minority, who inhabit areas of northern and central Iraq now effectively partitioned between Iraqi controlled areas and Kurd controlled areas in the north.
Website. www.angelfire.com/tn/halk
Leadership. Necdet Kocak (leader)

Ireland

Capital: Dublin   **Population:** 3,700,000 (2000E)

The Irish Republic's 1937 constitution expressly stated that it applied to the whole of Ireland (Éire), not just to the 26 counties actually comprising the Republic, and was therefore seen as containing an implicit territorial claim to the six counties of Northern Ireland under UK sovereignty. However, following the signature of the Good Friday Agreement on Northern Ireland in April 1998, constitutional amendments approved by referendum in the Republic on May 22, 1998, formally enshrined the principle of popular consent to any change in the status of the North. These amendments were promulgated on Dec. 2, 1999, on the establishment of a power-sharing executive in the North and the inauguration of a consultative North-South Ministerial Council (see United Kingdom, Northern Ireland, chapter).

The Irish parliament (*Oireachtas*) consists of (i) the President (*Uachtarán na hÉireann*) directly elected for a seven-year term (once renewable); (ii) a 166-member lower house (*Dáil Éireann*) elected by universal adult suffrage for a five-year term); and (iii) a 60-member indirectly-elected Senate (*Seanad*), including 11 prime ministerial appointees, with power to delay, but not to veto, lower house legislation. The cabinet, which is responsible to the *Dáil*, is headed by a Prime Minister (*Taoiseach*), who is the leader of the majority party or coalition. Members of the *Dáil* are elected by the single transferable vote (STV) version of proportional representation, from multi-member constituencies. Ireland joined what became the European Union in 1973 and elects 15 members of the European Parliament.

Under legislation governing the remuneration of public representatives as revised in 2001, leaders of parties with one or more elected representative in the *Dáil* or Senate receive annual payments from state funds at a rate of between IR£38,234 and IR£15,297 per deputy and between IR£25,000 and IR£12,500 per senator, the rate tapering the more representatives a party has. These amounts, which are for parliamentary activities such as research, policy formation, training and administration, are reduced by a third for parties in government. Under the 1997 Electoral Act there is a separate scheme under which registered parties receiving over 2% of first-preference votes in a general election share IR£1 million proportionately to the size of their vote. In addition, parties' election expenses are reimbursed by the state up to a maximum of IR£5,000 for each candidate who receives at least a quarter of the quota of votes required for election at any stage of the count.

Elections to the *Dáil* on June 6, 1997, resulted as follows: *Fianna Fáil* 77 seats (with 39.3% of first-preference votes), *Fine Gael* 54 (27.9%), Labour Party 17 (10.4%), Progressive Democrats 4 (4.7%), Democratic Left 4 (2.5%), Green Party 2 (2.8%), *Sinn Féin* 1 (2.5%), Socialist Party 1 (0.7%), Independent *Fianna Fáil* 1, others 5. (In January 1999 the Democratic Left merged into the Labour Party.) In presidential elections held on Oct. 30, 1997, Mary McAleese (*Fianna Fáil*) was elected for a seven-year term with 45.2% of the vote in the first count and 58.7% in the second.

Fianna Fáil

Address. 65-66 Lower Mount Street, Dublin 2
Telephone. (+353–1) 676–1551
Fax. (+353–1) 678–5690
Email. fiannafail@iol.ie
Website. www.fiannafail.ie
Leadership. Bertie Ahern (president); Rory O'Hanlon (parliamentary chairman); Martin Mackin (general secretary)

Republican, nationalist and populist, *Fianna Fáil* seeks the peaceful reunification by consent of Ireland, national self-sufficiency, social justice and the preservation of the Irish language and culture. It strongly supports the European Union's common agricultural policy but opposes any extension of the powers of the European Parliament. It favours nuclear disarmament and wants all of Ireland to be a nuclear-free zone.

Fianna Fáil (literally "Soldiers of Destiny" but officially known in English as the Republican Party) was founded in 1926 by Éamon de Valera. He was the sole surviving leader of the 1916 rebellion as well as the leading opponent of the 1921 treaty with Britain. It boycotted the Free State *Dáil* (because of a required oath of allegiance to the British monarchy) until 1927; in 1932 it came to power in general elections. De Valera then became *Taoiseach* (and was President of Ireland from 1959 until his death in 1973).

Fianna Fáil remained in government until 1948, introducing the autonomist (and strongly Catholic) constitution of 1937 and maintaining neutrality during World War II, at the end of which De Valera outraged many in Britain and the USA by sending a message of condolence to Germany on the death of Hitler. The party was again in power in 1951–54, 1957–73, 1977–81 and in 1982. Charles Haughey became party leader and *Taoiseach* in 1979, his ministerial career having survived gun-running allegations in 1970. *Fianna Fáil* maintained its status as usually the largest in the *Dáil*, although only once (in 1965) secured an overall majority. It returned 75 TDs in the November 1982 elections (with 47.3% of the vote) and 81 in 1987 (with 44.1%), when Haughey returned as Prime Minister.

In the June 1989 elections FF parliamentary strength was reduced to 77 seats. The result was the first really serious political impasse in independent Ireland's history. It was resolved by Haughey agreeing the following month to the inclusion of the →Progressive Democrats (PDs) in *Fianna Fáil*'s first-ever experience of coalition government. Subsequently, the FF deputy leader and Defence Minister, Brian Lenihan, began as favourite to win the November 1990 presidential election, but lost public confidence when he was dismissed from the government a month before voting over a scandal, the consequence being that he was heavily defeated by Mary Robinson, the nominee of the →Labour Party.

Haughey finally bowed out in January 1992, being succeeded as *Fianna Fáil* leader and therefore as Prime Minister by his old party adversary, Albert Reynolds. In November 1992 the party experienced its poorest election result since World War II (its *Dáil* representation falling to 68 seats and its first-preference vote to 39.1%), but Reynolds managed to entice the resurgent Labour Party into a majority coalition. Less than two years later, however, the coalition collapsed over the affair of an allegedly paedophile Catholic priest, which forced Reynolds's resignation in November 1994. *Fianna Fáil* then went into opposition to a three-party coalition headed by →Fine Gael, although it remained the largest parliamentary party under the new leadership of Bertie Ahern.

Fianna Fáil returned to power after the June 1997 elections, in which it recovered to 77 *Dáil* seats, while improving only marginally, to 39.3%, in first-preference votes. As incoming *Taoiseach*, Ahern formed a minority coalition with the →Progressive Democrats (PDs), his government being dependent on independents for a parliamentary majority. He quickly lost his Foreign Minister, Ray Burke, who resigned in October 1997 after being named in a financial corruption case. In the same month, however, *Fianna Fáil* candidate Mary McAleese was elected Irish President with 58.7% of the vote on the second count.

Ahern played a major role in the conclusion of the potentially historic Good Friday Agreement in Northern Ireland in April 1998 and the following month successfully recommended resultant constitutional revisions to Republic voters, involving formal acceptance that Irish unity could only be achieved by consent of the people north and south of the border. At the same time, the Ahern government secured popular endorsement for the EU's Amsterdam Treaty. The surfacing in February 1999 of another alleged financial corruption case damaged *Fianna Fáil* in the June

1999 European Parliament elections, in which the party slipped from seven to six of the 15 Irish seats, on a vote share of 38.6%.

Corruption allegations continued to dog *Fianna Fáil* in 2000–01. In April 2000 Ahern was forced to deny receiving an illicit payment from a property developer in 1989. Two months later FF backbench TD Liam Lawlor resigned from the party rather than co-operate with an internal corruption inquiry. In January 2001 Lawlor was imprisoned for a week for refusing to co-operate with a judicial inquiry. The government nevertheless continued to get credit for the country's rapidly expanding economy and was only slightly dented when Irish voters in June 2001 rejected its recommendation that the EU's Nice Treaty should be ratified.

The *Fianna Fáil* members of the European Parliament sit in the Union for a Europe of Nations group, the largest component of which is the French "Eurosceptic" Rally for France and the Independence of Europe.

Fine Gael

Address. 51 Upper Mount Street, Dublin 2
Telephone (+353–1) 619–8444
Fax. (+353–1) 662–5046
Email. finegael@finegael.com
Website. www.finegael.com
Leadership. Michael Noonan (leader); Jim Mitchell (deputy leader); Phil Hogan (*Dáil* group chairman); Tom Curran (general secretary)

Of Christian democratic orientation, *Fine Gael* advocates free enterprise, social justice, decentralization, reconciliation with the North, participatory democracy, tax equity and the improvement of education and welfare provision. It also supports an active Irish role in strengthening the European Union and the constructive use of Irish neutrality in addressing international issues such as peace, disarmament, human rights and self-determination for peoples.

Fine Gael (literally "Tribe of the Gael", but officially known in English as the United Ireland Party) was created in 1933 by the merger of *Cumann na nGaedheal* (Society of the Gaels), the ruling party of the Irish Free State in 1923-32, with the Centre Party and the fascist Blueshirt Movement of Gen. Eoin O'Duffy, who briefly led the new party. Although it was the main party in favour of the treaty which established the state, *Fine Gael* supported the 1949 declaration of a republic and has since retained nationalist ideals. Since the 1970s the party has been involved in efforts to make Irish society more pluralistic, supporting the lifting of the constitutional prohibitions on divorce and abortion.

The party ruled through coalitions when it was in power in the post-war decades, all involving the →Labour Party, heading governments in 1948–51, 1954–57, 1973–77, 1981–82 and 1982–87, latterly under the premiership of Garret FitzGerald, who became *Fine Gael* leader in 1977. In the February 1987 elections, however, *Fine Gael* was reduced to 27.1% and 51 *Dáil* seats (from 37.3% and 70 seats in November 1982), which resulted in the resignation of FitzGerald. The new *Fine Gael* leader, Alan Dukes, maintained the party's strong commitment to the 1985 Anglo-Irish Agreement whereby the Republic's government recognized the partition of Ireland but secured a consultative role in the administration of the North.

In the June 1989 elections *Fine Gael* increased its parliamentary representation to 55, but remained in opposition. In November 1990 Dukes resigned as party leader and was replaced by his more right-leaning deputy, John Bruton. In the November 1992 *Dáil* elections *Fine Gael* slumped to 45 seats and 24.5% of first-preference votes, its worst showing since 1948. Nevertheless, a political crisis in late 1994 resulted in the resignation of the →*Fianna Fáil* Prime Minister and enabled Bruton to form a three-party coalition government with Labour and the Democratic Left. Meanwhile, *Fine Gael* had taken 24.3% of the vote and four seats in the June 1994 European Parliament elections.

In the June 1997 *Dáil* elections *Fine Gael* recovered to 54 seats and 27.9% of first-preference votes but went into opposition to a centre-right coalition headed by *Fianna Fáil*. In the June 1999 European Parliament elections *Fine Gael* improved slightly to 24.5% of the vote, again taking four of Ireland's 15 seats. Opposition to Bruton's continued leadership mounted in 2000, culminating in his defeat in a confidence vote in the parliamentary party in January 2001. He was succeeded the following month by the instigator of the vote, former Justice Minister Michael Noonan.

With an official membership of 23,000, *Fine Gael* is affiliated to the Christian Democrat International. Its members of the European Parliament sit in the European People's Party/European Democrats group.

Green Party
Comhaontas Glas

Address. 5A Upper Fownes Street, Dublin 2
Telephone. (+353–1) 679–0012
Fax. (£353–1) 679–7168
Email. info@greenparty.ie
Website. www.greenparty.ie
Leadership. John Gormley & Trevor Sargent (parliamentary representatives); Heidi Bedell (national co-ordinator)

The Green Party stands internationally for a globally-sustainable economic system and the redistribution of resources to the world's poor, and nationally for political, economic and social decisions to be taken at the lowest possible level and the promotion of workers' co-operatives and small family businesses. The party was established as the Ecology Party of Ireland (EPI) in December 1981 with support from what became the UK fiGreen Party and from members of anti-nuclear and environmental protection groups in Ireland. It became the Green Alliance in 1983 and the Green Party in 1987.

The party won its first *Dáil* seat in the June 1989 election, retaining it in 1992. Like other Green parties in the European Union, it made a greater impact in the June 1994 European Parliament elections, winning two of Ireland's 15 seats with 7.9% of the vote. The party improved to two seats in the June 1997 national elections (taking 2.8% of first-preference votes), one of its successful candidates, John Gormley, having in 1994 become Dublin's first Green lord mayor. The Greens again won two seats in the June 1999 European Parliament elections, although the party's vote share slipped to 6.7%.

Whilst supporting Irish membership of the European Union, the Greens were prominent in the successful opposition to Ireland's ratification of the EU's Nice Treaty in a referendum held in June 2001. The party's objections focused on a perceived threat of the creation of an unaccountable EU super-state under the treaty.

The Green Party is affiliated to the European Federation of Green Parties. Its representatives in the European Parliament sit in the Greens/European Free Alliance group.

Labour Party
Páirtí Lucht Oibre

Address. 17 Ely Place, Dublin 2
Telephone. (+353–1) 661–2615
Fax. (+353–1) 661–2640
Email. head_office@labour.ie
Website. www.labour.ie
Leadership. Ruairí Quinn (leader); Proinsías de Rossa (president); Ray Kavanagh (general secretary)

The social democratic Labour Party seeks the peaceful transformation of Irish society into a socialist republic. It calls for the resolution of economic problems by means which will not impoverish weaker sections of society, favouring public-sector job creation and taxation equity between wage-earners and the self-employed, especially farmers. It advocates the reunification of Ireland by consent, as well as the maintenance of strict Irish neutrality in international relations and the furtherance of Ireland's membership of the European Union.

Founded in 1912 by James Connolly and Jim Larkin, the Labour Party was the main opposition party in the *Dáil* of the Irish Free State in 1922–26, becoming independent of the Irish trade unions in 1930. It supported the →*Fianna Fáil* minority government under Éamon de Valera in 1932–33 but opposed the 1937 constitution, while supporting its main effect, which was to create a republic outside the British Empire. The party participated in coalition governments in 1948–51 with four other parties, in 1954–57 with →*Fine Gael* and a farmers' party, and with *Fine Gael* alone in 1973–77, 1981–82 and 1982–87, providing the *Tánaiste* (Deputy Prime Minister) in these governments.

A Labour conference decided in 1986 to end its participation in coalitions, which had been consistently opposed by its left wing and which had resulted in a steady loss of electoral support (from 17% in 1969 to 9.1% in 1982 and to 6.5% in 1987). The party accordingly withdrew from government in early 1987 in opposition to proposed cuts in the health budget, thus precipitating general elections in which it dropped to 12 seats (from 16 in 1982). Labour's recovery began at the June 1989 elections, when it increased its *Dáil* representation from 12 to 15 seats. The following year it joined with the →Workers' Party in backing the successful presidential candidacy of Mary Robinson, who had twice been a Labour parliamentary candidate but was no longer a party member.

In the November 1992 elections Labour achieved its best election result to date, more than doubling its *Dáil* representation to 33 seats (from 19.3% of first-preference votes) after a campaign focusing on the shortcomings of the *Fianna Fáil* government. Nevertheless, in January 1993 the party entered into a majority coalition with FF, which lasted until November 1994, when Labour ministers took exception to *Fianna Fáil* conduct in the case of a Catholic priest accused of paedophilia. The party promptly rediscovered its sympathies with *Fine Gael*, joining a three-party coalition that also included the small Democratic Left party. Meanwhile, Labour had won one of Ireland's 15 European Parliament seats in June 1994 with 11.0% of the vote.

The Labour Party was punished in the June 1997 national elections, being reduced to 17 seats and 10.4% of first-preference votes and remaining in opposition. In October 1997 Labour candidate Adi Roche came a poor fourth in presidential election, with only 6.9% of the vote. The following month Spring resigned as Labour leader and was succeeded by Ruairí Quinn, hitherto deputy leader.

Seeking to strengthen its political base, the Labour Party in January 1999 effectively absorbed the Democratic Left (DL), whose leader became president of the combined party, while Quinn was confirmed as leader. The DL had been launched by a reformist faction of the Marxist →Workers' Party in 1992 and had won four seats in that year's *Dáil* elections, retaining them in 1997. The new Labour Party's representation in the lower chamber was therefore 21 seats. Nevertheless, the enlarged party fared badly in the June 1999 European Parliament elections, taking only 8.8% of the vote, although retaining its single seat.

The Labour Party is a member of the Socialist International. Its member of the European Parliament sits in the Party of European Socialists group.

Progressive Democrats (PDs)
An Partí Daonlathaoh
Address. 25 South Frederick Street, Dublin 2
Telephone. (+353–1) 679–4399
Fax. (+353–1) 679–4757
Email. info@progressivedemocrats.ie
Website. www.progressivedemocrats.ie
Leadership. Mary Harney (parliamentary leader); John Higgins (general secretary)
The PDs are a centre-right grouping calling for reduced government spending, privatization, a secular state and acceptance of the reality of the partition of Ireland. The party was founded in December 1985 under the leadership of former

cabinet minister Desmond O'Malley following a split in the then opposition →*Fianna Fáil* which led four TDs to break away. The PDs campaigned mainly for fiscal responsibility, to which end they supported what they regarded as "essential and balanced" measures by successive governments, while opposing those seen as "ill-thought-out and unjust". In its first electoral test in February 1987, the party secured 11.8% of the vote and 14 seats in the *Dáil*, thus displacing the →Labour Party as the third strongest parliamentary formation.

The PDs then experienced a loss of momentum, falling to only six seats at the 1989 election, after which the party opted to join a coalition government headed by *Fianna Fáil*. Its withdrawal three years later precipitated the November 1992 *Dáil* elections, in which PD representation rose to 10 seats, but the party remained in opposition. O'Malley resigned as PD leader in October 1993 and was succeeded by the first female head of a significant Irish party, Mary Harney.

In the June 1997 national elections the PDs slumped to only four seats and opted to join a coalition led by *Fianna Fáil* in which it was awarded one post, Harney becoming Ireland's first-ever woman Deputy Prime Minister. In the June 1999 European Parliament elections the PDs failed to gain representation.

Sinn Féin (SF)
Address. 44 Parnell Square, Dublin 1
Telephone. (+353–1) 872–6100
Fax. (+353–1) 873–3074
Email. sinnfein@iol.ie
Website. www.sinnfein.ie
Leadership. Gerry Adams (president)
Republican, revolutionary and nationalist, *Sinn Féin* (literally "Ourselves") supports the Irish Republican Army (IRA) campaign in Northern Ireland and seeks the establishment of a unitary democratic socialist state. The party was founded in 1905 by Arthur Griffith and was radicalized by the popular impact of the 1916 rebellion in Dublin. In 1918 it won (but did not take up) 72 of the 105 Irish seats in the UK House of Commons; instead, it set up the *Dáil* in Dublin, whereupon Northern loyalists organized resistance to Irish independence.

After a three-year guerrilla war the 1922 Treaty partitioned Ireland into the autonomous Irish Free State in 26 counties and British-ruled Northern Ireland in the other six. The anti-treaty *Sinn Féin* under Éamon de Valera supported the IRA in a subsequent civil war with Free State forces. De Valera left *Sinn Féin* in 1926 to form →*Fianna Fáil*, following which *Sinn Féin* was left on the margins of Irish politics, supporting IRA campaigns conducted mainly in Britain and on the Northern border. *Sinn Féin* won (but did not take up) four seats in the *Dáil* in 1957 but lost them in 1961.

The movement split in 1969-70, the left wing evolving into the →Workers' Party, while the nationalist faction became known as Provisional *Sinn Féin* and had as its military wing the Provisional IRA ("the Provos"). By the 1980s *Sinn Féin* had become involved in community and electoral politics in the South, winning some local council seats, although not in the *Dáil*. In 1986 the party ended its policy of non-participation in the *Dáil*. The policy change proved to be somewhat academic, since *Sinn Féin* continued to be signally unsuccessful in Irish Republic elections, winning no seats in 1987, 1989 or 1992. In the June 1997 contest, however, it returned one member to the *Dáil*, winning 2.5% of first-preference votes overall. In the June 1999 European Parliament elections *Sinn Féin* doubled its vote share to 6.3%, but failed to win a seat.

Whilst supporting Irish membership of the European Union, *Sinn Féin* was prominent in the successful opposition to Ireland's ratification of the EU's Nice Treaty in a referendum held in June 2001. Its objections focused on a perceived threat to Irish neutrality under the treaty and the possibility that Ireland might be drawn into military alliance with the United Kingdom.

Socialist Party (SP)
Address. 141 Thomas Street, Dublin 8
Telephone. (+353–1) 677–2686
Email. dublinsp@clubi.ie
Website. www.socialistparty/net
Leadership. Joe Higgins (leader)
The SP was formed prior to the June 1997 national elections as a party seeking "to fight for the interests of working-class people" and contending that the →Labour Party and the Democratic Left had "embraced the dictates of the market". Opposed to the EU's Maastricht Treaty and Irish participation in the single European currency, the SP returned Joe Higgins as its sole member of the *Dáil*.

Other Parties

Christian Solidarity Party (CSP) (*Comhar Críostaí*), founded in 1994; fielded eight candidates in 1997 elections, winning 0.5% of first-preference votes but no seats.
Address. 52 Foxrock Ave, Dublin 18
Telephone. (+353–1) 289–1040
Fax. (+353–1) 289–1042
Email. comharcriostai@tinet.ie
Leadership. Patrick D. Smyth

Communist Party of Ireland (CPI), all-Ireland formation founded in 1921 by Roddy Connolly, reestablished in 1933, split during the World War II over a 1941 decision to suspend activities in the Republic with reunification of its southern and northern elements not occurring until 1970; staunchly pro-Soviet right up to the demise of the USSR (though harbouring a reformist minority), it has never won a *Dáil* seat and has only limited industrial influence.
Address. 43 East Essex Street, Dubblin 2
Telephone/Fax. (+353–1) 671–1943
Leadership. James Stewart (general secretary); Eugene McCartan (chairman)

National Party (NP), conservative formation founded in 1995, committed to traditional Irish values and culture, stressing the importance of the family; fielded 16 candidates in 1997 elections, taking 1.1% of first-preference votes but no seats.
Address. 41 Dalysfort Road, Salthill, Co. Galway
Telephone. (+353–61) 364–172

Website. wwwcastletown.com/national
Leadership. Nora Bennis

People of Ireland Party (*Muintir na hÉireann*), an anti-abortion formation founded in 1995, led by a local councillor who had been a →Green Party member.
Address. 58 The Palms, Roebuck Road, Dundrum, Dublin 14
Telephone/Fax. (353–1) 283–1484
Email. muintir@indigo.ie
Website. aoife.indigo.ie/~muintir
Leadership. Richard Greene

Socialist Workers' Party (SWP), leftist formation rejecting what it sees as the revisionism of the →Labour Party and the Democratic Left; nominated four candidates in 1997 elections, winning 0.1% of first-preference votes.
Address. PO Box 1648, Dublin 8
Telephone. (+353–1) 872–2682
Email. swp@clubi.ie
Website. www.clubi.ie/swp

The Workers' Party (WP) (*Pairtí na nOibrí*), standing for a united democratic socialist Irish republic; claims descent from the historic →*Sinn Féin* following the 1969-70 split producing the Official IRA/*Sinn Féin* and the Provisionals, the former disbanding as an active military organization and from 1971 pursuing a parliamentary strategy; called *Sinn Féin* The Workers' Party from 1977, it adopted its present name in 1982, having returned one *Dáil* member in 1981; rising to four seats in 1987, the party advanced to seven seats in 1989, although six of these deputies, including leader Proinsías de Rossa, resigned after their proposal to abandon Leninism in favour of democratic socialism had been narrowly rejected at a party conference, the result being the Democratic Left (now merged into the Labour Party); the rump WP failed to secure parliamentary representation in November 1992 and June 1997 elections, nominating seven candidates in the latter and winning 0.4% of first-preference votes.
Address. 23 Hill Street, Dublin 1
Telephone. (+353–1) 874–0716
Fax. (+353–1) 874–8702
Email. pqloc@indigo.ie
Website. www.workers-party.org
Leadership. Pat Quearney (general secretary); Tom French (president)

Israel

Capital: Jerusalem (not recognized by UN)   **Population**: 5,840,000 (2000E)

The State of Israel declared its independence in 1948, following the end of the British mandate to administer what was then Palestine. The existence of numerous parties within a proportional representation system has meant that no one party has ever secured an overall parliamentary majority. In consequence, the country has been governed by a succession of coalitions. Israel's unicameral 120-seat parliament (*Knesset*) is elected for a maximum term of four years, although several early elections have been called in recent years. The *Knesset* in turn elects the President (a largely ceremonial role) as the constitutional head of state for a five-year renewable term.

Constitutional changes enacted in 1992 provided for the direct election of the Prime Minister (the head of government) with effect from the 1996 general elections. Voters therefore had two ballots, one for the prime ministerial contest and the other for the party election. A two-thirds *Knesset* majority was now required to remove a Prime Minister. In early 2001 the *Knesset* overturned this system, and reverted to the original single poll system. However, this change will not take effect until the next election, scheduled for 2003.

In elections on May 29, 1996, Binyamin Netanyahu (*Likud*) won the prime ministerial contest with 50.4% of the vote against 49.5% for Shimon Peres of the Israel Labour Party (ILP). Simultaneous elections to the 14th *Knesset* resulted in the ILP winning 34 seats and *Likud* 32. Remaining seats were shared between nine smaller parties. Despite *Likud's* poor *Knesset* tally, Netanyahu's direct mandate empowered him to head a *Likud*-led coalition government.

A successful vote of no confidence led to new parliamentary and prime ministerial elections on May 17, 1999. Ehud Barak, the new leader of the ILP, defeated Netanyahu in the prime ministerial polls, taking 56% of the votes cast. In the *Knesset* elections, results were as follows: the ILP (competing as One Israel) won 26 seats, *Likud* 19, *Shas* 17, and *Meretz* 10. In addition, *Yisrael Ba'aliya, Shinui* and the Centre Party won 6 each, the National Religious Party, United Torah Judaism and the United Arab List, 5 each; National Union and *Yisrael Beitenu*, 4 each; the Democratic Front for Peace and Equality 3; and *Balad* and One Nation, 2 each. Barak headed a broad-based ILP-led government, and the *Likud* went into opposition.

Internal political problems, exacerbated by the failure of the Oslo peace process and outbreak of a second Palestinian *intifada*, prompted new prime ministerial elections on Feb. 6, 2001. Ariel Sharon, leader of the *Likud*, defeated the incumbent Prime Minister, Ehud Barak, by 62.4% to 37.6%. No simultaneous *Knesset* elections were held. Ariel Sharon subsequently led a "government of national unity", including *Likud*, the ILP, and several other parties. *Meretz* currently heads the opposition.

Note. For political movements in the Gaza Strip and West Bank, see separate section on Palestinian Entity.

Balad

Leadership. Azmi Bishara (leader)

Formed in 1996 *Balad*, which means "homeland" in Arabic, won five seats in elections that year, when it ran jointly with the →Democratic Front for Peace and Equality. In 1999 party leader Bishara became the first Arab to stand in Israeli prime ministerial elections, although he withdrew after negotiations with the eventual winner, →Israel Labour Party leader Ehud Barak. The party subsequently won two seats in the *Knesset* poll. It demands that Israel redefine itself as a state of all its citizens, rather than a Jewish state. In June 2001 Bishara was indicted for allegedly incendiary anti-Israeli remarks made on a visit to Damascus.

Democratic Front for Peace and Equality
Hadash

Address. PO Box 26205, 3 Rehov Hashikma, Tel Aviv
Telephone. (+972–3) 827492
Leadership. Mohammed Barakei (leader)

The largely Arab-supported *Hadash* party was established in its present form prior to the 1987 elections, its main component being the pro-Soviet New Communist Party (*Rakah*). *Hadash* maintained close ties with the →→Palestine Liberation Organization, despite an official ban on such relations prior to 1993. It won three seats in the 1992 elections, subsequently lending its support to, though not officially joining, Rabin's →Israel Labour Party- led coalition. In 1996 *Hadash* gained five *Knesset* seats, running on a joint ticket with →*Balad*. In 1999 its tally declined to three seats, to the benefit of the →United Arab List.

Israel Labour Party (ILP)
Mifleget Avoda Hayisraelit

Address. PO Box 3263, Tel Aviv 69302
Telephone. (+972–3) 527–2315
Fax. (+972–3) 527–1744
Leadership. Shimon Peres (acting chairman)

The ILP is a Zionist and democratic socialist party, which supports territorial compromise as a means of achieving peace with Israel's Arab neighbours. It was formally established in 1968 through a merger of the *Mapai* Labour Party (the mainstay of coalition governments since 1948) and two other factions (*Rafi* and *Achdut Ha'avoda*). Its unbroken hold on power ended with the electoral defeat of 1977. The party remained in opposition to →*Likud*-led coalitions. After the 1984 elections, neither of the opposing political blocs commanded a parliamentary majority. The ILP thereupon became a partner in a 'rotating premiership' national unity coalition with *Likud*.

Following the 1988 elections the ILP formed another national unity coalition with *Likud*, but this collapsed in 1990. In February 1992 the former Labour Prime Minister, Yitzhak Rabin, regained the party leadership from Shimon Peres. In *Knesset* elections in June the ILP emerged as the largest party with 44 seats, and Rabin became Prime Minister. He led the subsequent ILP-dominated government which negotiated the historic peace agreement between

Israel and the Palestine Liberation Organization in September 1993, until his assassination by a right-wing Jewish fanatic in November 1995. He was succeeded as party chair and Prime Minister by Peres, who continued the Middle East peace process. In April 1996 an ILP convention accepted the principle of creating a Palestinian state. In elections the following month, however, Peres narrowly lost the prime ministerial contest to the *Likud* leader. In the separate *Knesset* poll the ILP slumped to 34 seats and went into opposition, although it remained the largest single party in the assembly.

Ehud Barak, a former military Chief of Staff regarded as a protégé of the late Rabin, succeeded Peres as party chairman in June 1997, and became Leader of the Opposition. Shortly before the elections of 1999, the ILP created and headed a new alliance called →One Israel. Barak defeated *Likud* leader Netanyahu in the prime ministerial polls, receiving 56% of the votes cast. In the accompanying *Knesset* elections, however, One Israel won just 26 seats (of which 23 belonged to the ILP, 11 less than it had in 1996).

Barak formed a broad coalition government that included →*Meretz*, religious groups, the →National Religious Party and →*Shas*. Barak fulfilled his promise to withdraw Israeli troops from southern Lebanon (achieved in May 2000). However, his administration was blighted by infighting between *Shas* and *Meretz*, hopes of peace with Syria were dashed, and negotiations with the Palestinians at Camp David collapsed in July 2000, leading to the outbreak of a second *intifada* in September. Faced with crumbling support, Barak called for new elections. *Knesset* members vetoed holding a parliamentary poll, and Barak was further undermined by a bid to unseat him by former party leader, Shimon Peres. On Feb. 6, 2001, in prime ministerial elections, Barak lost badly to Ariel Sharon, who set up an ILP-*Likud*-dominated "national coalition government".

After initial confusion, Barak resigned and handed over temporary party leadership to Peres, now Sharon's Foreign Minister. One Israel disbanded, and →*Gesher* returned to *Likud*. Within the ILP, former *Knesset* Speaker Avraham Burg was declared the winner in a September 2001 vote for a new leader, defeating Defence Minister Binyamin Ben-Eliezer, although the result was disputed.

The ILP is a member party of the Socialist International.

Likud

Address. 38 Rehov King George, Tel Aviv 61231
Telephone. (+972–3) 563–0666
Fax. (+972–3) 528–2901
Website. www.likud.org.il
Leadership. Ariel Sharon (leader)

Its title meaning "consolidation" or "unity", *Likud* is identified with the claim to indivisible sovereignty over the whole of the biblical Land of Israel (including the West Bank and Gaza). Economically, its constituent groups favour a liberal and free enterprise philosophy. The bloc was formed in 1973, under the leadership of Menachem Begin, as a parliamentary alliance between *Herut* (Freedom), the

Liberal Party of Israel, the *Laam* (For the Nation) grouping, and the *Ahdut* faction. On coming to power in 1977, *Likud* was joined by Ariel Sharon's *Shlomzion* group, while two further groups were absorbed prior to the 1988 elections.

The *Likud*-dominated governments of 1977–84, first under Begin and then under Yitzhak Shamir, saw an historic peace agreement signed with Egypt (and the return of Sinai captured by Israel in 1967) and the Israeli invasion of Lebanon in 1982. Having reached an all-time high of 48 seats in 1981, *Likud* fell back to 41 seats in the 1984 elections and was obliged to enter into a "rotating premiership" arrangement with the →Israel Labour Party (ILP). This national unity coalition was continued after a further *Likud* decline in the 1988 poll (to 39 seats), until finally breaking down in 1990. The subsequent Shamir government survived with the help of small right-wing parties. This factor probably hastened *Likud's* electoral defeat in June 1992, when its representation fell to 32 seats.

In March 1993 the youthful and telegenic Binyamin Netanyahu was elected leader of *Likud* in succession to Shamir. His acrimonious relationship with his leadership rival, David Levi, led to a split in early 1996. Levi formed the →*Gesher* party, though it later rejoined an electoral alliance with *Likud* and →*Tzomet*. Backed by all of the secular and religious right, Netanyahu narrowly defeated Peres in the May 1996 direct elections for the premiership, although in the simultaneous *Knesset* contest *Likud* and its allies remained at 32 seats. Netanyahu formed a coalition which included representatives of→*Shas*, the →National Religious Party, →*Yisrael Ba-Aliya* and →Third Way.

The new administration vowed to "slow down" the Oslo peace process, but in time Netanyahu had to acknowledge it as a fait accompli. He weathered Palestinian unrest in 1996, signed an accord on Hebron in 1998, and the Wye River Agreement in 1999. But senior *Likud* figures accused him of secrecy, procrastination, fraud, divisiveness and remoteness, and began to resign from his cabinet.

In the May 1999 elections, Netanyahu was beaten by ILP leader Ehud Barak. *Likud* dropped 11 seats to 19 in the Knesset poll, putting it just two ahead of the third party, *Shas*. Netanyahu immediately resigned as leader of *Likud*, and was replaced by the former general and outgoing Foreign Minister Ariel Sharon. Although initially regarded as a spent force and caretaker leader, Sharon succeeded in rebuilding *Likud's* damaged party institutions. His controversial visit to Jerusalem's Temple Mount was widely blamed for igniting the second Palestinian uprising. In late 2000, rebuffing a return bid by Netanyahu, Sharon led opposition to Barak's failing policies and defeated him convincingly at prime ministerial polls the following February. Currently *Likud* and the ILP lead a broad-based coalition government, with the greatest number of ministers in Israel's history.

Meretz

Address. c/o Knesset, Jerusalem
Website. www.meretz.israel.net
Leadership. Yosi Sarid (leader)
Meretz (meaning "vitality" or "power") was formed in early 1992 as an alliance of three parties of the left. Two of these are the Civil Rights and Peace Movement (*Ratz*) led by Shulamit Aloni (a former member of the →Israel Labour Party) and →*Shinui* (Change). The third, possibly dominant, component consists of the United Workers' Party (*Mapam*), a socialist Zionist bloc with strong support in the Kibbutz movement. Originally founded in 1948, *Mapam* was subsumed within the →Israel Labour Party (ILP) from 1969 until 1984, when it left the alignment, objecting to ILP participation in a coalition government with *Likud*.

The *Meretz* alliance stands for civil rights, equal status for women, electoral reform and religious pluralism. It also advocates a phased peace settlement with the Palestinians and Israel's Arab neighbours by way of interim agreements, and was the first Zionist party to accept the idea of a

Palestinian state. In the 1992 *Knesset* elections *Meretz* secured 12 seats and thereafter served as a coalition partner in an ILP-led government. In February 1996 Yosi Sarid, then Environment Minister, ousted Aloni as *Meretz* leader. The formation's representation slipped to nine seats in the May elections, after which it went into opposition and bitterly criticized Prime Minister Netanyahu's record in implementing the peace process.

Meretz gained 10 seats in the 1999 elections, making it the fourth largest party. One of its new representatives was the first Arab woman in the *Knesset*. *Meretz* joined a broad coalition led by the ILP, which was now constituted as →One Israel. Following the election of Ariel Sharon as Prime Minister in February 2001, and the ILP's decision to join a coalition government with →*Likud*, *Meretz* became the chief party of opposition.

Meretz inherited *Mapam's* membership of the Socialist International.

National Religious Party (NRP)
Hamiflaga Hadatit Leumit (Mafdal)

Address. 166 Ibn Gavirol Street, Kastel Building, Tel Aviv
Telephone. (+972–3) 544–2151
Fax. (+972–3) 546–8942
Leadership. Yitzhak Levy (leader)
The NRP was founded in 1956 and favours adherence to Jewish religion and tradition, although in a more accommodating way than the ultra-orthodox parties. Having participated in governments headed by the →Israel Labour Party up to 1977, the party was represented in →*Likud*-led coalitions from 1986. During this period its young guard was closely associated with the pro-settler →*Gush Emunim* lobby. The NRP went into opposition following the June 1992 elections, in which it secured six *Knesset* seats, but returned to government (with two portfolios) after increasing its representation to nine seats in May 1996. In 1999 its tally of seats fell to five. Factors seen as involved in this decline include the death of its charismatic former chief, Zevulun Hammer and the desertion of religious Sephardic voters to →*Shas*. Although the NRP served under Barak, it surprised many by choosing to oppose Ariel Sharon in March 2001.

National Union (NU)

Address. c/o Knesset, Jerusalem
The newly formed National Union won four seats in the 1999 elections. A coalition of three far-right wing parties, two of its seats went to members of *Moledet* (Homeland), a secular ultra-Zionist party led by Gen. Rechavam Ze'evi and founded in 1992. A third seat gained in 1999 went to Binyamin Begin, son of former Prime Minister Menachem Begin, and head of *Herut Ha-Hadasha* (a breakaway from *Likud*). *Tekumah* (Rebirth) forms the third component of the union. NU leader Ze'evi was assassinated on Oct. 17, 2001.

Shas (Sephardic Torah Guardians)
Shomrei Torah Sephardim

Address. Beit Abodi, Rehov Hahida, Bene Baraq
Telephone. (+972–3) 579776
Leadership. Eli Yishai (acting political leader); Aryeh Deri (official political leader); Rabbi Ovadiah Yosef (spiritual leader)
Shas is an ultra-orthodox religious party, formed in 1984 as a splinter group from *Agudat Yisrael* (which later became part of the →United Torah Judaism). It derives most of its support from members of Israel's large Sephardic (Oriental Jewish) community. Just prior to the 1992 legislative elections, Rabbi Yosef, former Sephardic Chief Rabbi of Israel, displaced Rabbi Eliezer Menachem Shacéh as spiritual leader of the party. This was regarded as a sign of renewed Oriental Jewish confidence (Shach was head of the Ashkenazi Lithuanian *yeshiva*, or seminary, network).

Shas retained its six seats in the 1992 elections and, although previously allied with the right-wing bloc in the *Knesset*, it joined the coalition formed by the →Israel Labour Party and →*Meretz* in July of that year. However, it withdrew from the government in September 1993 after a clash over educational policy with the secular *Meretz*, and announced its formal return to opposition status in February 1995. *Shas* increased its representation to 10 seats in the May 1996 elections. It was subsequently allocated two portfolios in the new government headed by →*Likud*.

In 1999 *Shas* increased its representation to 17 seats (just two short of *Likud*), confounding predictions that it had reached its maximum strength. Analysts suggested that many secular voters opted for *Shas* for reasons of ethnic pride or resentment at an Ashkenazi-dominated polity, rather than for purely religious reasons. Its political genius, Aryeh Deri, is currently serving a prison sentence for corruption - a *cause célèbre* that animates *Shas* voters.

All *Shas* MKs are male and obey the political edicts of a Council of Sages. Critics say the party's *El Ha-Ma'ayan* school and social network, largely for poorer Sephardim, acts like a state within a state. *Shas* also has support from some traditionally minded Arab voters. *Shas* deserted its alliance with *Likud* to serve under Ehud Barak. It garnered several important ministerial positions, but clashed again with *Meretz*. After March 2001 it joined the Sharon government and holds key social portfolios. Recent inopportune anti-Arab and anti-Ashkenazi remarks by spiritual leader, Rabbi Ovadiah Yosef, may cost the party in future polls.

Shinui

Address. 100 Hashmona'im Street, Tel Aviv
Telephone. (+972–3) 5620118
Email. shinui@shinui.org.il
Website. www.shinui.org.il
Leadership. Yosef "Tommy" Lapid (leader)
Shinui ("change") claims to be Israel's only truly liberal party. Founded in 1974, and subject to numerous splits and mergers, it advocated free enterprise, and under Amnon Rubinstein formed one of the constituent groups of →*Meretz*. One *Knesset* representative defected after 1996 to recreate an independent *Shinui*. Then in 1999 Tommy Lapid, a Holocaust survivor and notoriously acidic television interrogator, took over the party, and increased its seat tally to six. This "new" *Shinui* had one main aim - strident opposition to orthodox fundamentalism. Although hitherto regarded as left-wing, *Shinui* proved sceptical about chances for peace with Palestinians. Unlike fellow secularists in *Meretz*, it refused to serve alongside the religious →*Shas* in the Ehud Barak administration of 1999–2001.

Shinui is a member of the Liberal International.

United Arab List (UAL)
Ra'am

Address. c/o Knesset, Jerusalem
Leadership. Abdul Malik Dahamshe
The UAL was created in early 1996 as a coalition between the leftist Arab Democratic Party (ADP), itself founded in 1988 by Abd al-Wahab Darawshah, and the Islamic Movement of Israel, whose radical wing is affiliated with *Hamas*. *Ra'am* is committed to a Palestinian state with east Jerusalem as its capital, the dismantling of Jewish settlements in the occupied territories, and civil equality between Arab and Jewish citizens of Israel. The UAL won four seats in the 1996 *Knesset* elections (the ADP having won two *Knesset* seats in 1992) and five in 1999, making it the largest non-Zionist and Arab-backed party in Israel.

United Torah Judaism (UTJ)

Address. c/o Knesset, Jerusalem
Leadership. Meir Porush, Rabbi Avraham Ravitz (leaders)
United Torah Judaism was formed before the 1992 elections as a coalition of the ultra-orthodox *Agudat Yisrael* (originally established in 1912) and *Degel Hatora* (Flag of the Torah), together with two smaller formations (*Poale Agudat Yisrael* and *Moria*). The UTJ won four seats in 1992 and again in 1996, and five seats in 1999. Its policy is described as non- or even anti-Zionist, rendering it distinct from the →National Religious Party. However, in recent years it has appeared more lukewarm about the Oslo peace process. It opposes conscription of *haredim* (ultra-orthodox Jews) and the admission to Israel of Jews from non-orthodox communities. The UTJ is part of the current Sharon government.

Yisrael Ba-Aliya

Address. c/o Knesset, Jerusalem
Leadership. Natan Sharansky (leader); Yuli Edelstein (deputy leader)
Founded in 1992 with considerable support from Israel's 900,000-strong Russian Jewish immigrant community, *Yisrael Ba-aliya* (Movement for Immigration and Israel) achieved a high profile through the media skills of Natan Sharansky. The former dissident and political prisoner (then called Anatoly Shcharansky) had immigrated to Israel under a Soviet-Western exchange of 1986. Initially Sharansky supported →*Likud,* but in June 1995 he launched his new party, so as to advocate a higher government priority for the absorption of immigrants, and limited Palestinian autonomy. It won seven seats in the May 1996 *Knesset* elections and was awarded two portfolios in the subsequent *Likud*-led coalition government. Sharansky became Industry and Trade Minister and Yuli Edelstein Absorption Minister. The party fell to six seats in 1999, with some voters deserting to a rival party, →*Yisrael Beitenu*. Nonetheless, Sharansky's party stayed in the →Israel Labour Party-led coalition after 1999, and the *Likud*-led coalition after 2001, in which he serves as Deputy Prime Minister.

Yisrael Beitenu

Address. c/o Knesset, Jerusalem
Website. www.beytenu.org.il
Leadership. Avigdor Lieberman (leader)
Founded in 1999 by the director-general of the office of former Prime Minister Binyamin Netanyahu, *Yisrael Beitenu* (Our Israel) is a largely secular right-wing party backed by immigrants from the former Soviet Union. It criticizes Israel's legal system, and won four seats in its first elections, eating into support from its main rival, →*Yisrael Ba-Aliya*. It currently shares a joint front with the →National Union and is part of the current government.

Other Parties and Movements

Centre Party, founded prior to the 1996 elections by former mayor of Tel Aviv Roni Milo on an anti-orthodox platform. He was joined by prominent deserters from →*Likud*, including former Defence Minister Yitzhak Mordechai and Dan Meridor. A popular national figure, Mordechai became party leader, but withdrew his candidacy for the prime ministerial elections as support began to wane. The party won six seats in the 1999 *Knesset* elections, but failed in its promise to "break the mould" in Israeli politics. Many members returned to their former parties. However, as of August 2001, and under the leadership of the moderate pro-peace Meridor, it joined the Sharon government.

Gesher, or "bridge", began as a faction within →*Likud* in 1993. It became a separate party in February 1996, headed by the Moroccan-born David Levi, a former →*Likud* Foreign Minister who was defeated by Binyamin Netanyahu in a leadership contest in 1993. *Gesher* drew support from Sephardim (Oriental Jews), backed major social programmes, and contested the May 1996 *Knesset* elections in alliance with *Likud* and →*Tzomet*. But in 1998 Levi clashed with Netanyahu and again led *Gesher* MKs out of *Likud*. Prior to the 1999 Knesset elections, Gesher joined →One Israel. It gained two seats, out of a total alliance tally of 25. In August 2000 *Gesher* broke with the →Israel Labour Party concerning concessions over Jerusalem. In 2001 it rejoined *Likud*. →*Shas*, not Gesher, has won the bulk of disgruntled Sephardic *Likud* voters.

Gush Emunim ("Bloc of the Faithful") was formed in 1974 as a pressure group for Jewish settlers in the occupied territories. It had links to the right wing of the →National Religious Party and the now defunct *Tehiya* and *Morasha* parties. Under the leadership of Daniella Weiss it established unauthorized settlements via an arm called *Amarna*. The group split into radical and comparatively moderate groups in 1984, following revelations of ties between some members and the terrorist Jewish Underground. Rabbi Benny Elon created a "second generation" group called simply *Emunim*. Radical members deserted to →*Kach*, while the *Yesha* Council now carries out many of the less ideological, municipal functions of the original body.

Kach ("Thus"), a right-wing religious nationalist and racist party founded by US Jew Rabbi Meir Kahane, who was assassinated in New York in 1990. The party wants to expel all Arabs from Israel and the occupied territories, and eradicate Israeli democracy in favour of a Jewish theocracy. *Kach* was banned in 1994 after one follower massacred Muslim worshipers in Hebron. It still operates clandestinely, especially in certain Jewish settlements. Yigal Amir, assassin of Prime Minister Yitzhak Rabin, belonged to a group affiliated with *Kach*. It is unclear who *Kach's* current leader is, although the name of Noam Federman is often mentioned. *Kach* is associated with extremist offshoots like *Ateret Ha-Cohenim* (Crown of the Priests), Temple Mount Faithful, *Zo Artzeinu* (This is Our Land) and Committee for Safety on the Roads.

Kahane Lives (*Kahane Chai*), a right-wing religious nationalist party named after Rabbi Meir Kahane. It split from →*Kach* after Kahane's assassination in 1990, and was led by Rabbi Binyamin Zeev Kahane (son of the late leader). The party advocates the expulsion of all Arabs from Israel and the occupied territories. It was banned in 1994, along with *Kach*. In December 1999 Palestinian gunmen killed the younger Rabbi Kahane during the second *intifada*.

Meimad, a moderate religious Zionist grouping, it won no seats in 1992, but won a single seat within the →One Israel list in 1999. Its leader since 1996 and sole representative, Rabbi Michael Melchior, was Minister for Diaspora Affairs after 1999, and Deputy Foreign Minister in 2001.

One Israel (*Yisrael Ehad*) was formed in 1999 as an electoral union between the →Israel Labour Party (ILP), →*Gesher* and →*Meimad*. The ILP was the dominant partner, and ILP leader, Prime Minister Ehud Barak, became its head. One Israel's *Knesset* seats were allocated as follows: 23 for ILP, 2 for *Gesher* and 1 for *Meimad*. Following Barak's electoral defeat in 2001, the union effectively came asunder. *Gesher* returned to its original home in the →*Likud*, while the ILP reconstituted itself in its former, more familiar guise.

One Nation, an offshoot of the →Israel Labour Party, led by Amir Peretz, former head of the *Histadrut* labour confederation, it espouses a stronger socialist policy than the ILP, and has two *Knesset* seats.

Peace Now, a pressure group calling originally for withdrawal from Lebanon in the early 1980s, subsequently opposed to settlement of the territories, and favouring more determined peace policies.

Progressive List for Peace (PLP), a Jewish–Arab movement dating from the early 1980s and led by Muhammad Miari; it lost its small *Knesset* representation in 1992.

Third Way (*Derech Hashlishi*), founded and led by Avigdor Kahalani, an offshoot of the →Israel Labour Party, it opposed Israeli withdrawal from the Golan Heights. It won four seats in 1996, and joined the →*Likud*-led government, but failed to win a seat in 1999.

Tzomet, meaning "crossroads", a right-wing, nationalist secular group that won eight *Knesset* seats in 1992, but suffered repeated splits and failed to win a seat in 1999.

Italy

Capital: Rome

Population: 58,000,000 (2000E)

Under its 1948 constitution, Italy is "a democratic republic founded on work", with a system of parliamentary democracy. The head of state is the President, who is elected for a seven-year term by an electoral college of the two houses of parliament (plus delegates named by the regional assemblies) and who appoints the Prime Minister and, on the latter's recommendation, other ministers. The President has the important power of being able to dissolve parliament at any time except in the last six months of its full term. Legislative authority and government accountability are vested in a legislature of two houses with equal powers, namely (i) the upper 315-member Senate of the Republic (*Senato della Repubblica*), whose members are directly elected for a five-year term on a regional basis, except that life senators (numbering 11 in mid-2001) may be appointed by the President; and (ii) the lower 630-member Chamber of Deputies (*Camera dei Deputati*), which is also directly elected for a five-year term subject to dissolution. Under electoral system modifications approved by referendum in April 1993, proportional representation by share of vote gave way to a predominantly "first-past-the-post" system for both houses. In the case of the Chamber, 475 of its 630 members are elected by plurality voting in constituencies and the other 155 by a system of proportional representation, subject to a requirement that at least 4% of the national vote must be won to obtain seats. A founder member of what is now the European Union, Italy elects 87 members of the European Parliament.

Italian parties have been eligible for state financial subventions since a referendum on the issue in 1976 produced a 56.4% majority in favour of parties being subsidized from public funds. There are two state funds on which parties can draw, one relating to campaign expenses in an election year and the other for defraying ongoing organizational costs. From the first fund some Lit30,000 million (about $19 million) was distributed to parties which won at least one parliamentary seat in 1996. From the second fund a total of some Lit110,000 million (about $67 million) was payable in 1998, about three-quarters being allocated to parties in proportion to their seat totals, just under a quarter equally to parties that presented candidates in at least two-thirds of constituencies in the most recent election, and 2% equally to all represented parties.

The established post-war party structure came under increasing challenge in the 1980s, before effectively disintegrating in the early 1990s amid a torrent of scandals, mostly concerning illegal party financing and other graft. The party establishments reacted by creating new party names and alliances, thus giving a new facade to Italian party politics whilst maintaining underlying orientations.

Elections to the Chamber on May 13, 2001, resulted as follows: House of Freedom 368 seats (with 49.4% of the proportional vote), Olive Tree 242 (35.0%), Communist Refoundation Party (PRC) 11 (5.0%), South Tyrol People's Party (SVP) 8, others 1. In the simultaneous Senate elections, the House of Freedom won 177 seats (42.5%), Olive Tree 125 (38.7%), the SVP 5 (0.9%), the PRC 3 (5.0%), European Democracy 2 (3.2%), Italy of Values 1, Autonomous Lombardy Alliance 1, Valdostan Union 1.

Party Alliances

House of Freedom
Casa delle Libertà
Address. c/o Camera dei Deputati, Piazza Montecitorio, 00186 Rome
Leadership. Silvio Berlusconi

The *Casa delle Libertà* was the campaigning title adopted for the May 2001 parliamentary elections by the right-wing parties previously linked in the Freedom Alliance (*Polo delle Libertà*, PL). The main participating parties were →*Forza Italia* (FI), the →National Alliance (AN), the →Northern League (LN), the →New Italian Socialist Party (NPSI), the →Christian Democratic Centre (CCD) and the →United Christian Democrats (CDU). Of these, the CCD and the CDU maintained a bilateral alliance called →White Flower.

The previous PL had been formed for the March 1994 general elections, winning a 43% vote share and coming to power under the premiership of Silvio Berlusconi. The alliance quickly experienced dissension, which resulted in the exit of the LN in December 1994 and the resultant collapse of the PL government. The PL structure remained largely in place for the April 1996 general elections, although personal rivalry and public disputation between Berlusconi and AN leader Gianfranco Fini did the alliance little good at the polls. Although the PL's overall share of the proportional vote rose to some 44%, about 10% higher than that obtained by the centre-left →Olive Tree parties, the latter's relative majority of seats meant that the PL parties became the principal opposition to succeeding governments dominated by the →Democrats of the Left.

Campaigning on a pledge to "revolutionize" Italy's governmental system, the *Casa delle Libertà* swept to a decisive victory in the bitterly contested May 2001 elections, winning 368 seats out of 630 seats in the Chamber (with 49.6% of the proportional vote) and 177 of the 315 elective Senate seats. The following month Berlusconi was sworn in for his second term as Prime Minister, forming Italy's 59th government since World War II. It included nine FI ministers, five from the AN, three from the LN, two Christian Democrats and five independents.

La Margherita
Address. c/o Camera dei Deputati, Piazza Montecitorio, 00186 Rome
Leadership. Francesco Rutelli (president); Pierluigi Castagnetti (Chamber group chairman); Willer Bordon (Senate group chairman)

La Margherita (daisy flower in English) was formed for the May 2001 parliamentary elections by the centrist formations within the broader centre-left →Olive Tree (*Ulivo*) alliance, namely the →Italian Popular Party (PPI), the →Democrats, →Italian Renewal (RI) and the →Democratic Union for Europe (UDeuR). *La Margherita*'s leader in the campaign, was Francesco Rutelli of the Democrats, who also headed the overall *Ulivo* alliance. In the confusing Italian tradition,

La Margherita also styled itself as Democracy and Liberty (*Democrazia è Libertà*, DL).

The outcome was a heavy defeat for the *Ulivo* government parties, although within the alliance *La Margherita* formations polled strongly, winning 14.5% of the centre-left's 38.7% share of the proportional vote in the Chamber elections. *La Margherita*'s group in the new Chamber had 84 members and its Senate group 41 members. In July 2001 Rutelli was confirmed as president of a complex constituent committee of representatives of members of the alliance, its aim being to make the DL–*La Margherita* a more cohesive structure.

Olive Tree
Ulivo
Address. c/o Camera dei Deputati, Piazza Montecitorio, 00186 Rome
Email. info@perlulivo.it
Website. www.perlulivo.it
Leadership. Francesco Rutelli

The centre-left *Ulivo* alliance dates from July 1995, when a Rome conference of the main centre-left parties endorsed economics professor Romano Prodi, then of the liberal wing of the Christian democratic →Italian Popular Party (PPI) and later leader of the →Democrats, as their standard-bearer in the forthcoming general elections. Aiming to reverse the victory of the right-wing parties in the 1994 elections, the alliance drew up a programme of constitutional and economic reform, including a commitment to preparing Italy for participation in the single European currency (euro). In the April 1996 Chamber elections the *Ulivo* parties won 34.8% of the proportional vote, well behind the right-wing Freedom Alliance, but dominated polling for the 475 directly elective seats, ending up with a relative majority of 284 seats. Prodi accordingly formed an Olive Tree minority government, dependent on external parliamentary support from the →Communist Refoundation Party (PRC).

The Prodi administration succeeded in manœuvring Italy into being accepted as founder participation in the euro (from Jan. 1, 1999), but its constitutional reform proposals made little progress in face of right-wing opposition. The government also upset the PRC with its economic austerity measures, the constant aggravation on that score culminating in the PRC's withdrawal of support and the ousting of Prodi in October 1998. His defeat was largely engineered by the →Democrats of the Left (DS), the strongest *Ulivo* party, whose leader, Massimo D'Alema, became Prime Minister of a new centre-left coalition tilted more to the left and including the then non-*Ulivo* →Party of Italian Communists (PdCI).

In October 1999 leaders of the main *Ulivo* parties declared their support for "the relaunching of the spirit of the Olive Tree and its opening to new political forces, all in support of the D'Alema government". This did not prevent D'Alema's resignation in April 2000 after the centre-left had been heavily defeated in regional elections. The new government was headed by former Prime Minister

(1992–93) and outgoing Treasury and Budget Minister Giuliano Amato (non-party), but included representatives of all of the *Ulivo* parties. The new government quickly failed to secure referendum approval in May 2000 for seven constitutional changes, including one to abolish the remaining element of proportional representation.

Amato gained credit for successful economic stewardship, but announced in September 2000 that he would not lead the centre-left in the 2001 parliamentary elections. The following month a Milan conference of *Ulivo* parties endorsed Francesco Rutelli, the popular mayor of Rome, as the alliance's prime ministerial candidate. Rutelli's own power base within *Ulivo* was the centrist →*Margherita* alliance, embracing the Democrats, the PPI, →Italian Renewal (RI) and the →Democratic Union for Europe (UDeuR). But the more left-wing DS remained dominant in the *Ulivo*, which also included the radical →Sunflower alliance (of the →Green Federation and the →Italian Democratic Socialists) as well as the previously distant PdCI and a faction of the regional →South Tyrol People's Party (SVP).

Despite Rutelli's popular appeal, the *Ulivo* alliance went down to heavy defeat at the hands of the right-wing →House of Freedom alliance in the May 2001 parliamentary elections, winning only 242 of the 630 Chamber seats (with 35% of the proportional vote) and 125 of the 315 elective seats in the Senate (with 38.7%). However the centre-left took some consolation from its success in simultaneous mayoral elections in retaining control of Rome, Turin and Naples.

Sunflower
Il Girasole
Address. c/o Camera dei Deputati, Piazza Montecitorio, 00186 Rome
Leadership. collective
Il Girasole was formed for the May 2001 parliamentary elections by the →Green Federation and the →Italian Democratic Socialists, as a sub-grouping within the overarching →Olive Tree (*Ulivo*) alliance of centre-left parties. The sub-grouping shared in *Ulivo*'s decisive defeat, winning only 2.2% of the proportional vote in the Chamber elections.

White Flower
Biancofiore
Address. c/o Camera dei Deputati, Piazza Montecitorio, 00186 Rome
Leadership. Pier Ferdinando Casini (CCD) & Rocco Buttiglione (CDU); Luca Volonte' (Chamber group chairman); Francesco D'Onofrio (Senate group chairman)
Biancofiore was formed for the May 2001 parliamentary elections by the →Christian Democratic Centre (CCD) and the →United Christian Democrats (CDU), as a sub-grouping within the overarching →House of Freedom alliance of right-wing parties. The sub-grouping shared in the House of Freedom's decisive victory, winning 3.2% of the proportional vote in the Chamber elections. The CCD–CDU *Biancofiore* group in the new Chamber had 40 members and the Senate group 29 members.

National Parties

Christian Democratic Centre
Centro Cristiana Democratica (CCD)
Address. Via Due Macelli 66, 00187 Rome
Telephone. (+39–6) 697–9100
Fax. (+39–6) 679–1586
Email. infoccd@ccd.it
Website. www.ccd.it
Leadership. Pier Ferdinando Casini (president)
The CCD was established by a right-wing group of the former ruling Christian Democratic Party when the majority wing of the latter opted to become the →Italian Popular Party in January 1994. As a member of the victorious Freedom Alliance (PL) coalition in the March 1994 election, the CCD was allocated one portfolio in the short-lived first government of Silvio Berlusconi of →*Forza Italia* (FI). Remaining part of the PL, it contested the April 1996 parliamentary elections in close alliance with the →United Christian Democrats (CDU), their joint list taking a 5.8% vote share and both parties going into opposition.

The CCD broke with the PL in February 1998, aligning itself instead with the new Democratic Union for the Republic (later the →Democratic Union for Europe, UDeuR) led by former President Francesco Cossiga, which in October 1998 joined the centre-left →Olive Tree (*Ulivo*) government headed by the →Democrats of the Left. In the June 1999 European Parliament elections the CCD took two of Italy's 87 seats on a vote share of 2.6%.

Whereas the UDeuR remained within the *Ulivo* alliance for the 2001 parliamentary elections, the CCD and UDI opted to rejoin the right-wing camp, now called the →House of Freedom, and formed the →White Flower mini-alliance within the broader alliance. Having contributed to the defeat of the centre-left, the CCD was allocated one portfolio in the resultant second Berlusconi government. Party leader Pier Ferdinando Casini was elected president of the new Chamber of Deputies.

The CCD is a member of the Christian Democrat International. Its representatives in the European Parliament sit in the European People's Party/European Democrats group.

Communist Refoundation Party
Partito della Rifondazione Comunista (PRC)
Address. Viale Policlinico 131, 00161 Rome
Telephone. (+39–6) 4418–2286
Fax. (+39–6) 4423–9490
Email. esteri.prc@rifondazione.it
Website. www.rifondazione.it
Leadership. Fausto Bertinotti (secretary-general); Francesco Giordano (Chamber group chairman); Luigi Malabarba (Senate group chairman)
The PRC came into being at a session held in Rome in February 1991 of dissident members of the Italian Communist Party (PCI) opposed to the latter's majority preference for conversion into the Democratic Party of the Left (PDS), renamed the →Democrats of the Left (DS) in 1998. After legal proceedings, the PRC was awarded the right to use the traditional hammer and sickle symbol of the PCI and was formally launched at a Rome conference in May 1991. Having won 5.6% of the vote in the 1992 general elections, the PRC advanced to 6.0% in 1994, when it was part of the left-wing Progressive Alliance (AP) headed by the PDS. Subsequently distancing itself from the AP, the PRC contested the June 1994 European Parliament elections on a joint list with other ex-PCI elements, winning 6.1% of the vote and five seats, while the April–May 1995 regional elections yielded an 8.4% vote share.

In June 1995 the PRC was weakened by the defection of 14 of its 35 lower house deputies in protest at the alleged "isolationism" of the party leadership, the defectors becoming the Unitary Communists (*Comunisti Unitari*), most of whom later joined the DS. Undeterred, the rump PRC contested the April 1996 parliamentary elections independently and increased its vote share to 8.6%, which restored its Chamber representation to 35 seats. Although it had, by mutual agreement, remained outside the centre-left →Olive Tree alliance, the PRC opted to give qualified parliamentary backing to the Olive Tree minority government of Romano Prodi.

After the PRC had polled strongly in local elections in April–May 1997, persistent strains over PRC opposition to government economic policies eventually resulted in the collapse of the Prodi government in October 1998 and its replacement by a majority coalition headed by the DS. Now deprived of its leverage in parliament, the PRC was also weakened by the concurrent launching of the →Party of Italian Communists (PdCI) under the leadership of Armando Cossutta, until then president of the PRC.

The fourth national PRC congress in Rimini in March 1999 reaffirmed the party's "class opposition to the centre-left, now and forever". Standing alone in the June 1999 European elections, the PRC slipped to 4.3% of the vote and four seats. In the May 2001 parliamentary elections it recovered slightly to 5% of the proportional vote, taking 11 Chamber seats and three in the Senate.

The PRC's representatives in the European Parliament sit in the European United Left/Nordic Green Left group and the party is also a member of the New European Left Forum (NELF).

Democratic Union for Europe
Unione Democratica per l'Europa (UDeuR)

Address. Piazza de Gesù 46, 00186 Rome
Telephone. (+39–6) 67751
Email. info@udr.org
Website. www.udr.org
Leadership. Francesco Cossiga (president); Rocco Buttiglione (co-ordinator)

The centre-right UDeuR began life as the Democratic Union for the Republic (UDR), which was launched in February 1998 by Francesco Cossiga, who had been elected President of Italy in 1985 as candidate of the then Christian Democratic Party (now the →Italian Popular Party). The UDR initiative was endorsed by the →Christian Democratic Centre (CCD) and the →United Christian Democrats (CDU), which thereby distanced themselves from the Freedom Alliance of conservative parties. In October 1998 the UDR joined the new →Olive Tree alliance headed by the →Democrats of the Left, receiving three cabinet portfolios.

For the June 1999 European elections, the UDR used the UDeuR title, winning 1.6% of the vote and one of Italy's 87 seats. The party then adopted the UDeuR label as its official title, under the new leadership of Irene Pivetti, a former Chamber president who had been expelled from the →Northern League in 1996. Whereas the CCD and CDU reverted to right-wing alignment within the →House of Freedom, the UDeuR remained within the Olive Tree alliance for the May 2001 parliamentary elections as part of the →*Margherita* sub-grouping. It therefore shared in the centre-left's defeat. In July 2001 Pivetti became a member of a constituent *Margherita* executive committee.

The UDeuR member of the European Parliament sits in the European People's Party/European Democrats group.

The Democrats
I Democratici

Address. Piazza SS Apostoli 73, 00187 Rome
Telephone. (+39–6) 695–191
Fax. (+39–6) 6978–1764
Email. sede@democraticiperlulivo.it
Website. www.democraticiperlulivo.it
Leadership. Arturo Parisi (executive president)

This grouping was launched in February 1999 by Romano Prodi, formerly of the →Italian Popular Party (PPI), who had been Prime Minister of the centre-left →Olive Tree coalition government formed after the June 1996 elections but who had been ousted in October 1998 and replaced by Massimo D'Alema of the →Democrats of the Left (DS). Described by Prodi as intended to strengthen the centre-left, the new initiative was seen as the former Prime Minister's attempt to redress the balance in the Olive Tree alliance back to the centre and to counter the new dominance of the DS. Groupings backing the new party included the →Network Movement for Democracy (*La Rete*); the →Italy of Values, movement formed by Antonio Di Pietro following his exit from the Prodi government in November 1996 in contentious circumstances; and the Hundred Cities for a New Italy (*Centocittá per un Italia Nuova*) movement of mayors, environmentalists and voluntary groups.

A joint list put forward by the "Democrats for the New Olive Tree" and *La Rete* in the June 1999 European elections won seven of Italy's 87 seats with 7.7% of the vote. Some doubt was then cast on the Democrats' future by Prodi's appointment as President of the European Commission and his resultant withdrawal from Italian party politics. However, under the new chairmanship of Arturo Parisi, the Democrats remained a strong Olive Tree component and provided the alliance's leader in the person of Francesco Rutelli, the popular mayor of Rome, who had entered politics in 1983 as a member the →Radical Party and had later joined the →Green Federation, before switching to the Democrats in 1999.

The Democrats were the leading party in the →*Margherita* centrist wing of the Olive Tree alliance in the May 2001 parliamentary elections, sharing in the centre-left's defeat by the right-wing →House of Freedom. In opposition, the Democrats participated in moves to solidify *La Margherita*, which was also styled Democracy and Liberty (*Democrazia è Libertà*, DL). In July 2001 Parisi became a member of a constituent DL-*Margherita* executive committee under Rutelli's presidency.

The Democrats' representatives in the European Parliament are members of the European Liberal, Democratic and Reformist (ELDR) group.

Democrats of the Left
Democratici di Sinistra (DS)

Address. Via delle Botteghe Oscure 4, 00186 Rome
Telephone. (+39–6) 6830–7666
Fax. (+39–6) 679–8376
Email. posta@democraticidisinistra.it
Website. www.democraticidisinistra.it
Leadership. Massimo D'Alema (president); Luciano Violante (Chamber group chairman); Gavino Angius (Senate group chairman)

The DS is directly descended organizationally, but not ideologically, from the Italian Communist Party (*Partito Comunista Italiano*, PCI), which voted at a March 1990 extraordinary congress to abandon the traditional name of the PCI. Adoption of "Democratic Party of the Left" (PDS) as the party's name followed in February 1991, at a final congress (*ultimo congresso*) of the PCI. A further change in February 1998, when the party was joined by most of the Unitary Communists (*Comunisti Unitari*) who had defected from the →Communist Refoundation Party in 1995, produced the shortened DS title.

Formed as a result of the split in the Italian Socialist Party (→Italian Democratic Socialists, SDI) at the 1921 Livorno congress, the PCI went underground during the Mussolini period, its then leader, Palmiro Togliatti, escaping to Moscow, where he worked for the Comintern until his return to Italy in 1944. In the early 1940s the PCI played a leading role in the struggle against the fascist regime and the German Nazi occupation forces. Under Togliatti's leadership the PCI participated in the post-war coalition government until being excluded in May 1947, after which it mounted a violent campaign of political and industrial opposition. Following the decisive election victory of the Christian Democrats in April 1948 the PCI took the road of democratic opposition and subsequently developed into the largest and most influential non-ruling Communist party in Europe. Throughout the post-war period the PCI was consistently the second strongest party (after the Christian Democrats) in terms of both votes and seats in parliament.

From 1975 the PCI governed a large number of regions, provinces and municipalities (particularly in the "red belt" of Emilia-Romagna, Umbria and Tuscany), usually in coalition with other left-wing parties. At national level, the PCI's claims for admission to government responsibility were resisted, although following the sharp increase in the party's vote in the June 1976 elections (to over 34%) successive Christian Democrat-led governments accepted parliamentary support from the PCI, initially through abstention and subsequently, from March 1978, on the basis of the PCI being included in the official parliamentary majority. The PCI withdrew from this arrangement in January 1979 and reverted to a position of full opposition; in the elections of that year its vote share fell to 30.4%.

In 1980 the PCI adopted a new "democratic alternative" strategy based on an alliance with the Socialists, but the latter remained committed to centre-left coalitions. In the 1983 general elections the PCI again lost ground, winning 198 seats and 29.9% of the vote, although in the June 1984 European Parliament elections it emerged as the largest party for the first time in its history, winning 33.3% of the vote. Under the new leadership of Alessandro Natta (who had succeeded Enrico Berlinguer on the latter's death in June 1984), the PCI was strengthened in November 1984 by absorbing the Party of Proletarian Unity for Communism (originally founded in 1972). However, it lost ground in the May 1985 regional and local elections (surrendering Rome to the Christian Democrats) and suffered a further setback in the June 1987 general elections, when its Chamber representation fell to 177 seats and its share of the vote to 26.6%.

In June 1988 Natta was succeeded as PCI leader by Achille Occhetto, who promised a "new course" for Italian communism. This process turned out to be the abandonment of much of the traditional party line and the transformation of the PCI into the PDS in February 1991, with a democratic socialist orientation. Having won 16.1% of the national vote in the 1992 elections, the PDS advanced to 20.4% in the March 1994 contest, although it failed to make the hoped-for breakthrough to political power as a member of the left-wing Progressive Alliance. In the June 1994 European Parliament elections PDS support slipped to 19.1%, which gave the party 16 seats. This setback precipitated the resignation of Occhetto as general secretary and the succession of Massimo D'Alema. In late 1994 and April-May 1995 the PDS made major advances in local and regional elections, on the latter occasion heading the poll with 24.6% of the vote.

In July 1995 the PDS took the momentous decision to enter a structured centre-left alliance, called the →Olive Tree (*Ulivo*) movement, which registered a major victory in the April 1996 parliamentary elections. The PDS secured 21.1% of the vote and 156 seats in its own right, being awarded nine posts in the resultant centre-left coalition of Romano Prodi. D'Alema and his renamed DS were the main political beneficiaries of the collapse of the Prodi government in October 1998, the DS leader becoming Prime Minister of new centre-left coalition. Following D'Alema's appointment, he was succeeded as DS national secretary by former Deputy Prime Minister Walter Veltroni.

The DS slipped to 17.4% of the vote and 15 seats in the June 1999 European elections. It also shared in the centre-left's heavy defeat in regional elections in April 2000, which resulted in D'Alema's resignation and the appointment of Giuliano Amato as non-party Prime Minister of a further *Ulivo* government in which the DS remained dominant. In July 2000 the party newspaper *L'Umanità*, famous in PCI days, was closed down for financial reasons. In October 2000 the DS supported the selection of Francesco Rutelli, then mayor of Rome and a member of the centrist →Democrats, as the *Ulivo* standard-bearer in the May 2001 parliamentary elections. The party shared in *Ulivo*'s defeat by the right-wing →House of Freedom, its own proportional vote in the Chamber elections slipping to 16.6% within *Ulivo*'s 35% share. The DS group in the new Chamber had 136 members and its Senate group 65 members.

A consolation for the DS was the election of Veltroni as Rutelli's successor as mayor of Rome, also in May 2001. Veltroni resigned as DS national secretary on June 1, whereupon an 11-member interim collegial leadership was set up under the presidency of D'Alema pending the election of a new national secretary at a party congress in November 2001.

The DS representatives in the European Parliament sit in the Party of European Socialists group, the party having been admitted to the Socialist International in 1992.

European Democracy
Democrazia Europea (DE
Address. Corso Vittorio Emanuele 326, 00186 Rome
Telephone. (+39–6) 687–2543
Fax. (+39–6) 6821–4906
Website. www.sergiodantoni.it
Leadership. Sergio D'Antoni (president)
The centrist DE seeks to end the political "blockage" caused by "false bi-polarism" between right and left. It contested the May 2001 elections independently, winning 2.4% of the proportional vote for the Chamber (and no seats) and 3.2% in the Senate contest, which yielded two upper house seats.

Federation of Liberals
Federazione dei Liberali (FdL)
Address. Via Laurina 20, 00187 Rome
Telephone. (+39–6) 3211–0200
Website. www.luda.it/~liberali
Leadership. Valerio Zanone (president); Raffaello Morelli (political secretary)
The FLI acts as the umbrella body of liberalism in Italy following the effective demise of the historic Italian Liberal Party (*Partito Liberale Italiano*, PLI) amid the party corruption scandals of the early 1990s. The PLI had its roots in the 19th-century liberal movement of Count Camillo di Cavour, the diplomatic architect of Italian unification. After World War II the party's representation in the Chamber of Deputies rose to a high of 39 seats in 1963 but declined unevenly in the 1970s and 1980s, during which it participated in successive centre-left governments.

In the April 1996 parliamentary elections the Liberal remnants formed part of the Democratic Union, itself a member of the victorious →Olive Tree alliance of centre-left parties. In the June 1999 European elections a joint list of the Liberals and the →Italian Republican Party (PRI) won 0.5% of the vote and one of the 87 Italian seats. The list's representative in the European Parliament joined the European Liberal, Democratic and Reformist group.

Forza Italia (FI)
Address. Via dell'Umiltà 36, 00100 Rome
Telephone. (+39–6) 67311
Fax. (+39–6) 5994–1315
Email. lettere@forza-italia.it
Website. www.forza-italia.it
Leadership. Silvio Berlusconi (president); Elio Vito (Chamber group chairman); Renato Giuseppe (Schifani) (Senate group chairman); Claudio Scajola (national co-ordinator)
The FI was launched in January 1994, its Italian title being variously translated into English as "Go Italy!" and "Come On Italy!", as being the English equivalent of the traditional chant of supporters of the Italian football team which provided the party's title. The FI was created by Berlusconi, Italy's most powerful media tycoon (and owner of the leading Milan football club), who identified the prevention of an electoral victory by the ex-Communist Democratic Party of the Left (PDS), later renamed →Democrats of the Left (DS), as the new formation's principal objective. To this end, it organized the right-wing Freedom Alliance (PL), which secured an absolute parliamentary majority of 366 seats in the March 1994 general elections and accordingly formed a new government.

In the June 1994 European Parliament elections the PL won a narrow majority of 44 of Italy's 87 seats, 27 of which were credited to the FI on a vote share of 30.6%. However, growing strains between the coalition parties culminated in the collapse and ejection of the Berlusconi government in December 1994 as a result of the withdrawal of the →Northern League (LN). There followed strong FI pressure for fresh general elections, despite disappointing local election results for the party in late 1994 and April–May 1995. Berlusconi had greater success in a multiple referendum exercise in June 1995, when there were majorities for propositions effectively maintaining the dominance of his media interests. But the FI leader was increasingly tainted by financial corruption allegations in the run-up to the April 1996 general elections, in which the FI remained at 21% within a reduced PL alliance and the centre-left →Olive Tree alliance came to power.

In opposition, the FI was damaged by further court proceedings against Berlusconi, while the PL was weakened in February 1998 by defections to what became the →Democratic Union for Europe (UDeuR). Nevertheless, in April 1998 Berlusconi was formally elected FI president, whilst in June 1998 the FI achieved wider respectability by being accepted as a member of the European People's Party group in the European Parliament, having previously been part of the Union for a Europe of Nations group. Although he had been convicted several times (without going to prison), Berlusconi's acquittal in March 1999 on a tax fraud charge helped the FI to head the poll again in the June 1999 European elections, in which it took 25.2% of the vote and 22 seats.

For the May 2001 parliamentary elections the PL became the →House of Freedom, under the leadership of Berlusconi, who promised that an FI-led government would introduce a large tax cut, higher minimum pensions, lower unemployment, more public works and better policing of urban areas. Despite still having charges pending against him, he achieved a decisive victory, the alliance winning 368 of the 630 Chamber seats and 177 seats in the Senate. Of the alliance's overall vote share of 45.4%, the FI took 29.4%, its group in the new Chamber having 178 members and its Senate group numbering 82. The following month Berlusconi was sworn in for his second term as Prime Minister, forming Italy's 59th government since World War II.

The FI representatives in the European Parliament sit in the European People's Party/European Democrats group. The FI is also a member party of the European Democrat Union.

Green Federation
Federazione dei Verdi

Address. Via Salandra 6, 00187 Rome
Telephone. (+39–6) 420–3061
Fax. (+39–6) 4200–4600
Email. notizie@verdi.it
Website. www.verdi.it
Leadership. Grazia Francescato (president); Stefano Bocco (Chamber group chairman)

The Italian Greens were founded as a national electoral movement at a constituent assembly held in Florence in December 1984. The formation won some 1.8% of the vote overall in regional and local elections in May 1985, when it was backed by the →Radical Party, and made a significant breakthrough in the July 1987 general elections, winning 2.5% of the vote and returning 13 Chamber deputies and one member of the Senate.

The Greens improved further in 1992, winning four Senate and 16 Chamber seats on a vote share of 2.8%. For the 1994 general elections the Greens joined the Progressive Alliance, headed by what later became the →Democrats of the Left (DS), their vote share slipping to 2.7%. In a recovery in the June 1994 European Parliament elections, the Greens won three seats on a 3.2% vote share. Joining the centre-left →Olive Tree alliance for the April 1996 parliamentary elections, the Greens won 2.5% of the proportional vote and had the satisfaction of seeing party member Edo Ronchi appointed Environment Minister in the new Olive Tree government. He was joined by Laura Balbo as Equal Opportunities Minister when a new coalition was formed in October 1998 under the leadership of the DS.

Damaged by the rival appeal of the Emma Bonino List (→Radical Party) in the June 1999 European elections, the Greens slipped to 1.8% of the vote and two seats. In January 2000 a party conference in Chianciano established a more formal leadership structure, electing Grazia Francescato as president. For the May 2001 parliamentary elections the Greens formed the →Sunflower (*Il Girasole*) sub-alliance with the →Italian Democratic Socialists within the Olive Tree alliance. The sub-grouping shared in Olive Tree's heavy defeat, winning only 2.2% of the proportional vote in the Chamber elections. The Greens had seven deputies in the new Chamber and 10 members of the new Senate.

The Italian Greens are members of the European Federation of Green Parties. The party's representatives in the European Parliament sit in the Greens/European Free Alliance group.

Italian Democratic Socialists
Socialisti Democratici Italiani (SDI)

Address. Piazza San Lorenzo in Lucina 26, 00186 Rome
Telephone. (+39–6) 6830–7666
Fax. (+39–6) 6830–7659
Email. socialisti@socialisti.org
Website. www.socialisti.org
Leadership. Enrico Boselli (president); Roberto Villetti & Gianfranco Schietroma (vice-presidents)

The SDI resulted from the merger in 1998 of the Italian Socialists (SI), a designation adopted by the historic Italian Socialist Party (*Partito Socialista Italiano*, PSI) in 1994, and the Italian Democratic Socialist Party (*Partito Socialista Democratico Italiano*, PSDI), which itself had derived from a left–right split in the PSI in 1947.

Founded in 1892, the PSI had first split at its Livorno congress in 1921 when a pro-Bolshevik group broke away to form the Italian Communist Party (→Democrats of the Left, DS). At the Rome congress in January 1947 Giuseppe Saragat's right-wing PSI faction, opposed to the majority Pietro Nenni wing's policy of alliance with the Communists, broke away to form the Workers' Socialist Party (PSLI), which in 1952 merged with other factions to become the PSDI. Whereas the Democratic Socialists took part in successive coalitions in 1947-63 headed by the Christian Democrats (→Italian Popular Party, PPI), the rump PSI remained in opposition, its Chamber representation rising to 87 seats in 1963.

Following the 1963 "opening to the left", the PSI repeatedly co-operated with the dominant Christian Democrats, either by joining coalition governments or by giving external support. The PSI and PSDI signed a reunification agreement in 1966, a combined PSI/PSDI list called the *Partito Socialista Unificato* winning 91 Chamber seats in 1968. The following year, however, the merger attempt broke down and the two parties re-established their separate identities, although both usually continued to be part of the centre-left majority. Having resigned from the Fanfani government, the PSI advanced from 62 to 73 seats in the June 1983 Chamber elections, with the result that party leader Bettino Craxi formed Italy's first-ever Socialist-led government, based on a coalition with the Christian Democrats, the PSDI and two other parties.

The Craxi administration lasted an unprecedented four years, eventually resigning in March 1987 over a dispute with the Christian Democrats about the application of a rotation pact under which a Christian Democrat was to take over the premiership early in 1987. In the June 1987 elections the PSI gained further ground, to 94 seats and 14.3% of the vote, subsequently joining a further five-party coalition headed by the Christian Democrats and including the PSDI (which declined from 23 to 17 seats and 3% in 1987). In the April 1992 elections the PSI slipped to 92 seats and 13.6% of the popular vote, but remained in the government coalition, as did the PSDI, which had won 17 seats and 2.7%.

Craxi then came under judicial investigation on numerous charges of financial corruption and illegal party funding, with the consequence that he resigned as PSI leader in February 1993, having served 17 years in the post. In the wake of charges against many other PSI representatives, the party slumped to 2.2% in the March 1994 Chamber elections, in which the PSDI failed to win any Chamber seats at all. Some PSI elements contested the elections under the banner of the Democratic Alliance, doing the same in the European Parliament elections in June 1994, in which the PSI and PSDI managed only one seat each. The following month Craxi received a long prison sentence, and still faced other charges, along with several dozen other former PSI officials.

Seeking to recover its former constituency, the PSI transformed itself into the SI in November 1994, believing that dropping the discredited descriptor "party" from its title would improve its public image. In the April 1996 parliamentary elections the SI and the PSDI were both components of the victorious →Olive Tree alliance, in close alliance with the new →Italian Renewal formation. Reunification of the SI and PSDI was finally accomplished in 1998, the resultant SDI obtaining one portfolio in the government formed in October 1998 by Massimo D'Alema of the DS.

In the June 1999 European elections the SDI won only two seats with 2.1% of the vote. For the May 2001 parliamentary elections the SDI joined the →Sunflower (*Il Girasole*) sub-alliance with the →Green Federation within the Olive Tree alliance. The sub-grouping shared in Olive Tree's heavy defeat, winning only 2.2% of the proportional vote in the Chamber elections. The SDI elected nine deputies to the new Chamber.

The SDI representatives in the European Parliament sit in the Party of European Socialists group. The SDI inherited the Socialist International membership held by both the PSI and the PSDI.

Italian Popular Party
Partito Popolare Italiano (PPI)

Address. Piazza de Gesù 46, 00186 Rome
Telephone. (+39–6) 67751
Fax. (+39–6) 6775–3951
Email. ppidirnaz@pronet.it
Website. www.popolari.it
Leadership. Pierluigi Castagnetti (national secretary)

The PPI is the successor to the post-war Christian Democratic Party (DC), for long Italy's dominant formation, which in January 1994, beset by corruption scandals, reverted to the PPI title of an earlier age. The PPI had been founded by Don Luigi Sturzo before World War I and had functioned as Italy's Catholic party until the rise of fascism in 1922. It was revived as the DC towards the end of World War II, taking part in January 1944 in the first congress of (six) democratic parties for over 20 years (in Bari). The post-war DC leader, Alcide De Gasperi, was Prime Minister from December 1945 until August 1953, overseeing the post-war reconstruction programme and Italy's participation in the creation of what later became the European Union. The party continued in office thereafter, either as the sole government party or in coalition, at first with Liberals and Democratic Socialists, and later also with Republicans and Socialists under the post-1962 "opening to the left" *(apertura a sinistra)*. The DC was consistently returned as the largest parliamentary party until the 1990s.

A pivotal DC leader from the early 1970s was Giulio Andreotti, who formed seven governments between 1972 and 1991. The DC then became a leading victim of the political corruption cases which resulted in a meltdown of the Italian party system, the most prominent DC casualty being Andreotti himself, who was accused of maintaining links with the Mafia (and later brought to trial on such charges, although eventually acquitted). The party slumped to a post-war low of 29.7% and 206 seats in the April 1992 parliamentary elections, being obliged therefore to cede the premiership to a Socialist, although it remained a government party.

The DC's plummeting fortunes were revealed in local elections in June 1993, when only one of 47 DC candidates prevailed in mayoral contests. Having reverted to the historical PPI name in January 1994, the party contested the March 1994 general elections as part of a centrist alliance called the Pact for Italy (*Patto per l'Italia*, PI), which had been launched in January by Mario Segni, leader of the →Segni Pact. As the leading component of the PI, the PPI won only 11.1% of the vote in the March 1994 general election, slipping further to 10% in the June elections to the European Parliament, in which the party took only eight of Italy's 87 seats.

In opposition, the PPI experienced deep divisions over whether to form an alliance with Silvio Berlusconi's then ruling Freedom Alliance. The controversy resulted in an open split in March 1995, when the anti-Berlusconi "Democratic" wing elected Gerardo Bianco as PPI leader in the absence of the previously dominant right-wing faction, which disputed the election's legitimacy. In local elections in April–May 1995 the two factions competed separately, the "Democrats" winning 6% and the pro-Berlusconi faction 3%. In July 1995 the pro-Berlusconi faction finally broke away, forming the →United Christian Democrats, while the rump PPI became the second-largest component of the victorious centre-left →Olive Tree alliance in the April 1996 general elections, its list of candidates featuring Olive Tree leader Romano Prodi. The PPI accordingly obtained substantial representation in the resultant Prodi government and also, following the collapse of the latter in October 1998, in the succeeding coalition headed by the →Democrats of the Left.

Weakened by Prodi's formation of the →Democrats in February 1999, the PPI slumped to 4.3% of the vote and four seats in the June 1999 European Parliament elections. For the May 2001 parliamentary elections the PPI was part of the →*Margherita* centrist wing of the Olive Tree alliance headed by Francesco Rutelli of the Democrats, sharing in the centre-left's defeat by the right-wing →House of Freedom. But it took some comfort from the centre-left's strong showing in the May 2001 mayoral elections, securing the election of former PPI Interior Minister Rosa Russo Jervolino as the first female mayor of Naples. PPI leader Pierluigi Castagnetti was elected president of the *Margherita* group in the new Chamber and in July 2001 became a member of a constituent *Margherita* executive committee under Rutelli's presidency.

The PPI representatives in the European Parliament sit in the European People's Party/European Democrats group. The party is also a member of the Christian Democrat International and the International Democrat Union.

Italian Republican Party
Partito Repubblicano Italiano (PRI)

Address. Corso Vittorio Emanuele II 326, 00186 Rome
Telephone. (+39–6) 683–4037
Fax. (+39–6) 654–2990
Website. www.pri.it
Leadership. Francesco Nucara (national co-ordinator)

Founded as such in 1894, the PRI has its origins in the *Fiovine Italia* of 1831, who as republicans fought, under the leadership of Giuseppe Mazzini, for national unity and independence. The party's still-influential daily newspaper, *La Voce Repubblicana*, was founded in 1921. The PRI was dissolved by the Facist regime and reconstituted in 1943, taking part in the Resistance. Under the republican constitution introduced in January 1948 the PRI was a partner in numerous coalition governments led by Christian Democrats from 1948 to 1981.

In June 1981 the then PRI leader, Giovanni Spadolini, became the first non-Christian Democrat to head an Italian government since the war, forming a five-party centre-left Cabinet which lasted until November 1982. Thereafter the PRI continued its participation in centre-left coalitions until going into opposition in April 1991.

Then a PRI member, Antonio Maccanico accepted the post of Cabinet Secretary in the Ciampi government formed in May 1993, although the party itself remained in opposition. Having won 4.4% of the national vote in 1992, the PRI contested the March 1994 poll as a member of the Democratic Alliance (AD), and thus also of the broader Progressive Alliance (AP). In the June 1994 European balloting a specifically PRI list secured 0.7% of the vote, its one seat going to Giorgio La Malfa. Having resigned the party leadership in 1988 and been reinstated in January 1994, La Malfa again resigned in October 1994 and was again reinstated in March 1995.

The PRI contested the April 1996 general elections within Maccanico's new (and short-lived) Democratic Union, and therefore as part of the victorious →Olive Tree alliance of centre-left parties. In the resultant Prodi coalition government Maccanico became Minister of Posts and Telecommunications, but was not reappointed when Prodi gave way in October 1998 to a more left-tilted coalition headed by the →Democrats of the Left (DS).

The PRI contested the June 1999 European elections on a joint list with the Liberals (Federation of Italian Liberals) which obtained 0.5% of the vote and one seat. It was taken by PRI member Luciana Sbarbati), who in the European Liberal, Democratic and Reformist group. In July 2001 the long-time PRI secretary, Giorgio La Malfa, resigned from the post.

Italian Renewal
Rinnovamento Italiano (RI)

Address. Via di Ripetta 142, 00186Rome
Telephone. (+39–6) 6880–8380
Fax. (+39–6) 6880–8480
Email. informa@rinnovamento.it
Website. www.rinnovamento.it
Leadership. Lamberto Dini (president); Pino Pisicchio (national co-ordinator); Italo Tanoni (national secretary)
The formation of the RI was announced by Prof. Dini in February 1996, a month after the fall of his year-old government of technocrats. The new formation formed part of the victorious →Olive Tree alliance in the April 1996 elections, obtaining three posts in the resultant government of Romano Prodi, in which Dini became Foreign Minister. He retained the post in the succeeding coalition headed by the →Democrats of the Left (DS) formed in October 1998.

The RI won one of Italy 87 seats in the June 1999 European elections with a 1.1% vote share. The following year Dini's high society wife, Donatella Dini, caused embarrassment for her husband by becoming the subject of tax evasion and business corruption investigations. For the May 2001 parliamentary elections the RI was part of the →*Margherita* centrist wing of the Olive Tree alliance headed by Francesco Rutelli of the →Democrats, sharing in the centre-left's defeat by the right-wing →House of Freedom. In July 2001 Dini became a member of a constituent *Margherita* executive committee under Rutelli's presidency.

The RI representative in the European Parliament sits in the European People's Party/European Democrats group.

Italy of Values
Italia dei Valori (IdV)

Address. Piazza S. Eustachio 83, 00186 Rome
Telephone. (+39–6) 6706–4009
Fax. (+39–6) 6706–3797
Email. adpietro@tin.it
Website. www.antoniodipietro.org
Leadership. Antonio Di Pietro (president)
The IdV was launched in 1999 by Antonio Di Pietro, who as a magistrate in Milan had achieved fame in the early 1990s for his "cleans hands" anti-corruption investigations which had helped to bring down Italy's old business and political elite. He had joined the →Olive Tree government in May 1996 as Public Works Minister but had resigned six months later in protest against the launching of an investigation—later ruled to be illegitimate—into his own alleged corruption. In November 1997 he had been elected to the Senate in a by-election, standing for the →Democrats of the Left (DS), but had gravitated to the →Democrats after forming the IdV, being elected to the European Parliament in June 1999 on the Democrats' list.

Contesting the May 2001 parliamentary elections independently as the *Lista di Pietro Italia dei Valori*, the party won 3.9% of the proportional vote for the Chamber (and no seats) and 3.4% in the Senate contest, which yielded one upper house seat.

In the European Parliament Di Pietro sits in the European Liberal, Democratic and Reformist (ELDR) group, to which the IdV was formally admitted in December 2000.

National Alliance
Alleanza Nazionale (AN)

Address. Via della Scrofa 39, 00186 Rome
Telephone. (+39–6) 6880–3014
Fax. (+39–6) 654–8256
Email. uffintan@tin.it
Website. www.alleanza-nazionale.it
Leadership. Gianfranco Fini (president); Ignazio La Russa (Chamber group chairman); Domenico Nania (Senate group chairman)
The radical right-wing AN is the direct descendant of the post-war Italian Social Movement (MSI), which was founded in 1946 as a successor to the outlawed Fascist Party of the late dictator Benito Mussolini. The MSI first contested parliamentary elections in 1948, winning six seats in the Chamber of Deputies. Between 1953 and 1972 its representation in the Chamber fluctuated between 29 and 24 members. It contested the 1972 general elections in an alliance *(Destra Nazionale,* DN) with the Italian Democratic Party of Monarchical Unity, the joint list winning 56 seats in the Chamber. The two parties formally merged as the MSI-DN in January 1973, but in the 1976 elections the new party obtained only 35 seats in the Chamber.

The MSI-DN did not rule out the use of violence in its activities, and its extremist members were involved in numerous clashes and other acts of violence, which were not approved by the party as a whole. In December 1976 a total of 26 MSI-DN parliamentarians (17 deputies and nine senators) broke away from the party to form a group known as *Democrazia Nazionale* (DN), which was led by Ernesto De Marzio. It repudiated all fascist tendencies and announced that it would support the Christian Democrats. However, in the 1979 elections this group won no seats, while the rump MSI-DN retained 30 seats in the Chamber of Deputies.

In the 1983 elections the party made significant gains both at national and at regional and provincial level, gaining 42 seats in the Chamber of Deputies (with 6.8% of the vote). In the June 1987 elections, however, it slipped back to 35 seats (5.9% of the vote). The party's veteran leader, Giorgio Almirante (who had been a member of Mussolini's government), retired in December 1987 and was succeeded by Gianfranco Fini, regarded as a representative of the young "new face" of the party. Meanwhile, the party had decided in October 1987 to mount an active campaign in South Tyrol/Bolzano in support of the Italian speaking minority and against the political aspirations of the German-speaking majority.

In the 1992 parliamentary elections the MSI-DN slipped to 34 Chamber seats and 5.4% of the vote, one of the party's successful candidates in Naples being Alessandra Mussolini, grand-daughter of the former dictator. It then sought to capitalize on the massive corruption scandals that engulfed the centre-left parties so long in government. The AN designation was used by the MSI-DN from January 1994 as part of a strategy to attract support from former Christian Democrats and other right-wing groups, including Italian monarchists, and the party joined the Freedom Alliance (PL) of conservative parties headed by Silvio

Berlusconi's new →*Forza Italia* party, becoming the leading force in the PL's southern arm, designated the Good Government Alliance (*Polo del Buon Governo*). In the March 1994 elections the AN advanced strongly to 13.5% of the proportional vote as part of the PL, its support being concentrated in southern Italy. Six AN ministers were included in the Berlusconi government appointed in May 1994. In the following month's European Parliament elections the AN won 12.5% of the vote and 11 seats.

The party's first post-war experience of national office ended with the collapse of the Berlusconi government in December 1994. The following month the AN title was officially adopted at a Rome congress which also decided to delete most references to fascism in basic AN policy documents. Thereafter party spokesmen became even more insistent in rejecting the "neo-fascist" label commonly appended by the media and others, especially since a hardline minority which saw no discredit in the term "fascist" had in effect broken away by forming what became the →Tricolour Flame Social Movement.

The regional elections of April–May 1995 showed a modest increase in the AN vote to 14.1%, which rose appreciably to 15.7% in the April 1996 general elections, for which the AN remained within the PL alliance, winning 91 Chamber seats in its own right. In the 1996 contest Fini added to his reputation as a keen debater and effective campaigner, rather overshadowing Berlusconi. In opposition to a centre-left →Olive Tree government, the AN in March 1998 relaunched itself as a "modern, open right-wing party" in which fascist ideology was said to have no place, adopting the ladybird on its new logo. In the June 1999 European elections the AN was allied with the →Segni Pact, but the joint list secured only 10.3% of the vote and nine seats.

In the May 2001 parliamentary elections the AN remained in the right-wing alliance, now called the →House of Freedom, participating in its decisive victory. Of the alliance's overall vote share of 45.4%, the AN took 12%, its group in the new Chamber having 99 members and its Senate group numbering 45. The following month five AN ministers were appointed to the second Berlusconi government, including Fini as Deputy Prime Minister.

The AN's representatives in the European Parliament sit in the Union for a Europe of Nations group.

Network Movement for Democracy
Movimento per la Democrazia La Rete (MpD–La Rete)
Address. Lungotevere Marzio 3, 00186 Rome
Telephone. (+39–6) 6830–0447
Fax. (+39–6) 6830–0446
Website. www.larete.it
Leadership. Leoluca Orlando
This anti-Mafia movement was founded as *La Rete* (The Network) at Palermo, Sicily, in 1991 and became the city's leading party in the 1992 general elections, winning three Senate and 12 Chamber seats. As a member of the left-wing Popular Alliance in the March 1994 elections it won 1.9% of the national vote. In the June European Parliament poll it obtained one seat on a 1.1% vote share. By now also using the MpD label, the party contested the April 1996 general elections as part of the victorious →Olive Tree alliance.

In February 1999 *La Rete* backed the launching of the →Democrats to strengthen the centre within the centre-left. A joint list of the two formations won 7.7% and seven seats in the June 1999 European elections.

New Italian Socialist Party
Nuovo Partito Socialista Italiano (NPSI)
Address. c/o Camera dei Deputati, Piazza Montecitorio, 00186 Rome
Telephone. (+39–6) 6920–2275
Fax. (+39–6) 6992–5181
Email. bobocra@tiscalinet.it
Website. www.socialisti.net
Leadership. Bobo Craxi (national secretary); Gianni De Michelis (secretary); Claudio Martelli (secretary)
The NPSI was formed prior to the May 2001 parliamentary elections by a dissident faction of the →Italian Democratic Socialists (SDI) which rejected the SDI's participation in the centre-left →Olive Tree alliance. As part of the right-wing →House of Freedom alliance, the NPSI contributed 0.9% of its 49.4% share of the proportional vote for the Chamber, securing three seats in the lower house.

Northern League
Lega Nord (LN)
Address. Via Arbe 63, 20125 Milan
Telephone. (+39–2) 607–0379
Fax. (+39–2) 6680–2766
Email. info@leganord.org
Website. www.leganord.org
Leadership. Umberto Bossi (federal secretary); Stefano Stefani (federal president); Alessandro Ce' (Chamber group chairman); Francesco Moro (Senate group chairman)
The Northern League (LN) "for the independence of Padania" originated in February 1991 as a federation of the Lombardy League (*Lega Lombarda*, LL) and fraternal parties in Emilia-Romagna, Liguria, Piedmont, Tuscany and Venice. The LL had been launched in 1979, named after a 12th-century federation of northern Italian cities. It had achieved prominence in the 1980s as the most conspicuous of several regional groups to challenge the authority of the government in Rome, in particular its use of public revenues from the rich north to aid the impoverished south. Adopting the same stance, the LN called at its foundation for a move to a federal system with substantial regional autonomy in most areas except defence and foreign policy. More fundamentally, the eventual LN objective was the full independence of the lands north of the Po, which it called "Padania". Party leaders subsequently denied that the LN's attitude to southern Italians was tantamount to racism but made no apology for the League's advocacy of a strong anti-immigration policy, including resolute action against illegal immigrants and against criminality in immigrant communities.

Having won 8.7% of the national vote and 55 Chamber seats in the 1992 elections, the LN made political capital out of popular disgust over the bribery and corruption scandals engulfing Italy's political establishment, winning a record 40% of the vote in the Milan mayoral election of June 1993. For the March 1994 parliamentary elections the LN was part of the victorious right-wing Freedom Alliance (PL), winning 8.4% of the national vote and joining a PL government headed by Silvio Berlusconi of →*Forza Italia*. In June 1994 the LN won six European Parliament seats on a 6.6% vote share.

In December 1994 the LN brought about the collapse of the Berlusconi government by withdrawing from it, because of chronic policy and personality clashes with other PL components, notably between LN leader Umberto Bossi and Berlusconi. Contesting the April 1996 general elections independently, the LN increased its share of the national vote to 10.1%, taking 59 Chamber seats, and became the strongest single party in northern Italy. In opposition to the resultant centre-left →Olive Tree government in Rome, the League convened a "parliament" in Mantua in May 1996, when Bossi reasserted the League's secessionist objective and announced the creation of a "Committee for the Liberation of Padania" to act as a "provisional government". However, such schemes received a rebuff in local elections the following month, when the LN polled poorly throughout "Padania" and managed only third place in Mantua, seat of its "parliament". Bossi also came under criticism by moderates within the LN, responding in August 1996 by expelling their leader, former Chamber president Irene Pivetti (who later became leader of the →Democratic Union for Europe).

Also in August 1996, Bossi came under pressure from local investigating magistrates, who requested the Rome parliament to lift his parliamentary immunity so that he could face charges of inciting political violence at LN rallies in the north. Contending that he was not answerable to judges of "colonial Italy", Bossi in September 1996 led a three-day march along the River Po culminating in a Venice rally and the declaration of the independent "Republic of Padania". An accompanying "transitional constitution" provided that the declaration would not come into effect for up to 12 months, during which the LN "provisional government" would negotiate a "treaty of agreed separation" with the Rome government. Bossi announced at the same time that a "national guard" would be set up to protect "Padania's interests". The reaction in Rome was that the government "will not be troubled by political projects that have no roots in the past and no future", whilst police raided the NL headquarters in Milan to search for evidence of the party's alleged unconstitutional activities.

The third LN congress in February 1997 featured some moderation of the party's demand for speedy independence, with Bossi now calling for "consensual secession". Local elections in April-May 1997 were disappointing for the LN and an unofficial referendum organized by the party on May 25, when 99% of participants were said to have supported independence for "Padania", was dismissed by the government as a political stunt. Nevertheless, in October 1997 the LN proceeded to organize "elections" for a 200-member "constituent assembly of the Republic of Padania". The body held its inaugural meeting in November, when the guests included Russian nationalist leader Vladimir Zhirinovsky of the fiLiberal Democratic Party of Russia.

In January 1998 a Bergamo court gave Bossi a one-year prison sentence and fined him Lit170 million after he had been convicted of inciting criminal acts at an LN rally in 1995. In July 1998, moreover, Bossi and another NL leader were given suspended sentences of seven and eight months respectively for offenses committed in a clash with police in 1996. In the June 1999 European elections the LN slipped to 4.5% of the national vote and from six seats to four.

Bossi and Berlusconi achieved sufficient resolution of their differences in 2000 for the LN to re-join the right-wing front, now called the →House of Freedom. In November 2000 Bossi derided claims by the centre-left government that the return of the LN to government would provoke a crisis with the European Union akin to the one caused by the advent of the →→Freedom Party of Austria to power in Vienna. In the May 2001 parliamentary elections the LN participated in a right-wing victory, although its contribution to the alliance's 45.4% vote share in the Chamber elections was only 3.9%. Having 30 members in the new Chamber and 17 in the Senate, the LN was allocated three portfolios in the second Berlusconi government.

The LN representatives in the European Parliament are not attached to any political group.

Party of Italian Communists
Partito dei Comunisti Italiani (PdCI)

Address. Corso Vittorio Emanuele II 209, 00186 Rome
Telephone. (+39–6) 686–271
Fax. (+39–6) 6862–7230
Email. direzionenazionale@comunisti-italiani.it
Website. www.comunisti-italiani.it
Leadership. Armando Cossutta (president)

The PdCI was formally launched in October 1998 under the leadership of Armando Cossutta, until then president of the →Communist Refoundation Party (PRC). The new party grouped elements deriving from the historic Italian Communist Party (PCI) in its "Eurocommunist" later phase who rejected the PCI's transformation into the left-of-centre →Democrats of the Left (DS) but who also opposed the "unreconstructed" line of the PRC. On its formation, the PdCI joined the new →Olive Tree coalition government headed by Massimo D'Alema of the DS, receiving two cabinet portfolios.

In the June 1999 European Parliament elections the PdCI

won two of Italy's 87 seats with a vote share of 2.0%. It remained within the Olive Tree fold for the May 2001 parliamentary elections, thereby sharing in the defeat of the centre-left by the right-wing →House of Freedom alliance. With a vote share of 1.7%, the PdCI obtained 10 seats in the new Chamber.

The two PdCI representatives in the European Parliament joined the European United Left/Nordic Green Left group.

Radical Party
Partito Radicale (PR)

Address. Via di Torre Argentina 76, 00186 Rome
Telephone. (+39–6) 689–791
Fax. (+39–6) 880–5396
Email. radical.party@radicalparty.org
Website. www.radicalparty.org
Leadership. Marco Pannella (president); Emma Bonino (leader of Radical MEPs)

The PR was founded in December 1955 on a platform of non-violence, anti-militarism, human and civil rights, and the construction of a "socialist and democratic society". It has also campaigned for women's and homosexual rights, against nuclear energy and against "extermination by famine" in the Third World. Originally formed by a left-wing faction of the Italian Liberal Party, the PR became concerned with civil rights from 1962. It sponsored the legalization of divorce in 1970 and subsequently campaigned against the use of the referendum to change the law. It successfully supported legislation on conscientious objection, the lowering of the age of majority to 18 years, more liberal laws on drug offences and family relations, and the partial legalization of abortion. The Radicals were the first Italian party to have a woman secretary (in 1977–78).

Having obtained four Chamber seats in 1976, the Radicals achieved a significant success in the 1979 elections, in which they won 18 seats in the Chamber and two in the Senate. After slipping to 11 Chamber seats in 1983, the party advanced to 13 in 1987, its new deputies including Ilona Staller, a famous Hungarian-born pornographic film actress better known as Cicciolina. In January 1988 a Radical congress in Bologna decided that the party would not take part in any future Italian elections.

Meanwhile, in November 1979 the then PR secretary-general, Jean Fabre (a French national), had been sentenced by a Paris court to a month in prison for evading conscription. More serious was the 30-year prison sentence passed in 1984 on a PR deputy, Antonio Negri, following his conviction for complicity in terrorist acts, although he and seven others were acquitted in January 1986 of being "moral leaders" of extremist groups such as the Red Brigades.

Marco Pannella's return to the PR leadership in 1992 served to end the electoral non-participation policy and also shifted the party to the right. Contesting the March 1994 elections as part of the Freedom Alliance headed by →*Forza Italia*, the PR presented a "Pannella List" but won no seats in its own right. Running as "Pannella Reformers" in the June 1994 European Parliament elections, it won two seats with a 2.1% vote share. In June 1995 referendum approval was given to three out of four proposals presented by the PR leader with the aim of restricting trade union powers.

The PR again presented a "Pannella List" in the June 1996 national elections, failing to win representation in the Chamber (with 1.9% of the proportional vote) but returning one member to the Senate. It contested the June 1999 European elections as the "Emma Bonino List", headed by the popular former European commissioner, which secured 8.5% of the national vote and seven of Italy's 87 seats. One of those elected was Pannella (then 70), who in November 1999 was given a four-month prison sentence for distributing marijuana to draw attention to what he called "the absurdity of the law".

The PR remained independent of the main alliances in the May 2001 parliamentary elections, presenting a "Pannella-Bonino List" which won 2.3% of the vote for the Chamber and 2% of the Senate election vote, but no seats in either case. During the campaign Bonino staged a six-day hunger strike in protest against media bias and the non-coverage of smaller parties.

The Radical/Bonino representatives in the European Parliament are among the "non-attached" contingent. The PR has spawned the Transnational Radical Party, with members in 43 countries.

Segni Pact
Patto Segni (PS)

Address. Via Belsiana 100, 00187 Rome
Telephone. (+39–6) 6994–1838
Fax. (+39–6) 6994–1840
Email. patto.segni@pattosegni.it
Website. www.pattosegni.it
Leadership. Mario Segni

The PS leader, Mario Segni, had been a leading anti-corruption campaigner within the then Christian Democratic Party (later the →Italian Popular Party, PPI), until breaking away in 1992 to advocate reform of the Italian political system. For the March 1994 general elections he launched the Pact for Italy, drawing in the PPI to assume the dominant role. Having received only 4.6% of the national vote on that occasion, the PS fell back to 3.3% in the June 1994 European Parliament elections, in which it won three seats.

Segni was an initial supporter of the centre-left →Olive Tree alliance in 1995, but withdrew before the April 1996 general elections, which his party did not contest. He then launched a grass-roots movement for political reform (*Comitatidi Base per la Costituente*, COBAC), calling for the election of a constituent assembly to write a new constitution. In the June 1999 European elections the Segni Pact was allied with the right-wing →National Alliance (AN), their joint list winning 10.3% of the vote and nine of Italy's 87 seats.

The AN/PS representatives in the European Parliament sit in the Union for a Europe of Nations group.

Tricolour Flame Social Movement
Movimiento Sociale Fiamma Tricolore (MSFT)

Address. Via Simone De Saint Bon 89, 00195 Rome
Telephone. (+39–6) 370–1756
Fax. (+39–6) 372–0376
Email. fiamma@msifiammatric.it
Website. www.msifiammatric.it
Leadership. Pino Rauti (national secretary); Manlio Sargenti (honorary president)

The MSFT originated in the opposition of a minority pro-fascism faction of the former Italian Social Movement–National Right (MSI-DN) to the party's decision in January 1995 to convert itself into the →National Alliance (AN). Having made little impact in the 1996 general elections, the splinter group adopted the "Tricolour Flame" logo and won one of Italy's 87 seats in the June 1999 European elections, receiving 1.6% of the vote. In the May 2001 parliamentary elections, the MSFT won around 1% of the proportional vote, without gaining representation in either the Chamber or the Senate.

The MSFT representative in the European Parliament is a member of the "non-attached" group.

United Christian Democrats
Cristiani Democratici Uniti (CDU)

Address. Piazza del Gesù 46, 00146 Rome
Telephone. (+39–6) 6775–3265
Fax. (+39–6) 6775–3267
Email. cdu@axnet.it
Website. www.axnet.it/cdu
Leadership. Rocco Buttiglione (president)

The CDU was launched in July 1995 by a right-wing minority group of the →Italian Popular Party (the former Christian Democratic Party) which favoured participation in the Freedom Alliance (PL) rather than the centre-left →Olive Tree alliance. As part of the PL, the CDU contested the proportional section of the April 1996 parliamentary elections in close co-operation with the →Christian Democratic Centre (CCD), their joint list securing 5.8% of the vote. In the June 1999 European Parliament elections the CDU list obtained 2.1% of the vote and elected two candidates.

After a brief flirtation with the Olive Tree via the →Democratic Union for Europe, UDeuR), both the CDU and the CCD were in the right-wing camp, now called the →House of Freedom, in the May 2001 parliamentary elections, for which they formed the →White Flower mini-alliance. Having contributed to the defeat of the centre-left, the CDU was allocated one portfolio in the resultant second Berlusconi government.

The CDU representatives in the European Parliament sit in the European People's Party/European Democrats group. The CDU is also affiliated to the Christian Democrat International and the European Democrat Union.

Regional Parties

Emilia and Romagna Freedom (*Libertà Emilia & Rumagna, LER*), founded in 1999 as successor to Emilian Freedom/Emilia Nation (*Libertà Emiliana/Nazione Emilia*), itself dating from a 1994 breakaway by an Emilian faction of the →Northern League opposed to the latter's participation in the Freedom Alliance; a centre-left liberal formation, the LER seeks self-government for Emilia-Romagna within a European Union of historic regions; has one councillor in Sandiano and contested 1999 Euro-elections jointly with →Sardinian Action Party. The LER is a member of the Democratic Party of the Peoples of Europe–European Free Alliance.
Address. Corso Vallisneri 17v, Scandiano, Reggio Emilia
Telephone/Fax. (+39–522) 981–254
Email. matteoincerti@hotmail.com
Website. utenti.tripod.it/libertaemiliana
Leadership. Manuela Pilosio (president); Farouk Ramadan (co-ordinator)

Autonomous Lombardy Alliance (*Aleanza Lombardia Autonoma, ALA*), seeks to articulate aspirations to self-government in Italy's border regions in the Alps; includes the Lombard Alpine League (Lega Alpina Lombarda, LAL), which won one Senate seat in March 1994 and 0.3% of the vote in the June 1994 European elections. In the May 2001 parliamentary elections the ALA won one Senate seat

North-Eastern Union (*Unione Nord-Est*), advocating autonomy for the historic lands of Lombardy and Venezia within a "Europe of regions".
Address. Via Rella 1/4, 17100 Savona
Telephone. (+39–198) 485–032
Fax. (+39–198) 487–352
Email. alpazur@geocities.com
Website. www.geocities/capitolhill/3004

Romagna Autonomy Movement (*Movimento per l'Autonomia della Romagna, MAR*), founded in 1991, advocating self-government for the Romagna region of central Italy.
Address. Via C. Battisti 149, 47023 Cesena
Telephone. (+39–547) 20876
Email. mar@cyberforli.it
Website. mbox.cyberforli.it/mar
Leadership. Lorenzo Cappelli & Stefano Servadei

Sardinian Action Party (*Partito Sardo d'Azione, PsdA*), favouring autonomy for the island of Sardinia, took four Chamber seats in 1996 elections as part of →Olive Tree Movement, strongly represented in Sardinian regional council; member of Democratic Party of the Peoples of Europe–European Free Alliance.

Address. Via Roma 231, 09100 Cagliari
Telephone. (+39–70) 657–599
Fax. (+39–70) 657–779
Email. psdaz@sol.dada.it
Website. www.mediamundi.it/partidus

Sicilian Action Party (*Partito Siciliano d'Azione, PsdA*), seeking the full implementation of Sicily's regional statute.
Address. Via Malta 10, 93100 Caltanissetta
Telephone. (+39–934) 592–470
Fax. (+39–934) 459–796
Email. euratolo@tin.it
Website. www.sicilianet.it/partitosiciliano
Leadership. Nino Italico Amico

Two Sicilies (*Due Sicilie*), movement seeking autonomy for the area once covered by the Kingdom of the Two Sicilies and the creation of a "new Europe" based on historic regions.
Email. info@duesicilie.org
Website. www.duesicilie.org

South Tyrol People's Party (*Südtiroler Volkspartei, SVP*), Christian democratic party of the German-speaking population of Bolzano/Bozen province (South Tyrol). From 1948 onwards it consistently held three seats in the Italian Chamber of Deputies, and from 1979 one directly elective seat in the European Parliament. The party's struggle for equal rights for the German-speaking and Ladin-speaking population of South Tyrol led to Austro-Italian agreements on the status of the province in 1969–71 and a new statute for the Trentino–Alto Adige region in 1971. The SVP became the strongest party in the South Tyrol *Landtag* and the second strongest in the regional council of Trentino–Alto Adige, winning 22 seats out of 70 in November 1983. Normally securing representation in the Rome parliament thereafter, the SVP again won one seat in the June 1994 European Parliament elections. For the April 1996 general elections the SVP was part of the victorious centre-left →Olive Tree Movement. The SVP is affiliated to the European Democrat Union.
Address. Brennerstrasse 7/A, 39100 Bozen/Bolzano
Telephone (+39–471) 304–000
Fax. (+39–471) 972–666
Email. info@svpartei.org
Website. www.svpartei.org
Leadership. Siegfried Brugger (president); Luis Durnwalder (provincial government head); Thomas Widmann (general secretary)

Union for South Tyrol (*Union für Südtirol, UfS*), deriving from the radical Fatherland Union (*Heimatbund*), advocates a South Tyrol "free state" able to opt for union with Austria; has challenged the regional dominance of the →South Tyrol People's Party in seeking enhanced rights for the German-speaking majority; member of Democratic Party of the Peoples of Europe–European Free Alliance.
Address. Garibaldistrasse 6, 39100 Bozen/Bolzano
Telephone. (+39–471) 975–696
Fax. (+39–471) 978–559
Email. union@unionfs.com
Website. www.unionfs.com
Leadership. Eva Klotz & Andreas Pöder

Southern League (*Lega Meridionale, LM*), a *Mezzogiorno* formation, won 0.7% in June 1994 European Parliament elections.

For Trieste (*Per Trieste*), founded in opposition to the 1975 Osimo Treaty settling the Trieste territorial dispute between Italy and the then Yugoslavia, autonomist group advocating special status for Trieste within the special statute region of Friuli–Venezia Giulia.
Leadership. Manlio Cecovini

Valdostan Union (*Union Valdôtaine/Unione Valdostana, UV*), pro-autonomy grouping founded in 1945 to further the

interests of the French-speaking minority in the special statute region of Val d'Aosta, represented in the regional assembly from 1959, winning 17 of 35 seats (40.1% of vote) in May 1998 elections; usually represented in the national parliament, retaining one Chamber and one Senate seat in 1999.
Address. Ave des Maquisards, 11100 Aoste
Telephone. (+39–165) 235–181
Fax. (+39–165) 364–289
Email. peuple@aostanet.com
Website. www.unionvaldotaine.org
Leadership. August Rollandin

Venetian Republic League (*Liga Veneta Repubblica*), also known as Venetians for Europe (*Veneti d'Europa*), seeks the restoration of the historic Republic of Venice (which fell in 1797) within a region-based European Union; has six representatives in Veneto regional council.
Address. c/o Consiglio Regionale Veneto, Venice
Email. venetideuropa@consiglio.regione.veneto.it
Website. www.consiglio.regione.veneto.it/gruppipolitici/lvr
Leadership. Ettore Beggiato

Other Parties

Fascism and Liberty Movement (*Movimento Fascismo e Libertà, MFL*), far-right grouping founded in 1991.
Address. Piazza Chiaradia 9, Milan
Telephone. (+39–2) 5681–4233
Fax. (+39–2) 5681–5402
Leadership. Giorgio Pisano

Italian Marxist-Leninist Party (*Partito Marxista-Leninista Italiano, PMLI*), Maoist formation founded in 1977 from earlier grouping dating from 1969, advocates abstention in all elections.
Address. Via Gioberti 101, 50121 Florence
Telephone/Fax. (+39–55) 234–7272
Email. pmli@dada.it
Website. www.dadacase.com/pmli
Leadership. Giovanni Scuderi (general secretary)

Italian Monarchist Movement (*Movimento Monarchico Italiano, MMI*), seeks the restoration of the monarchy to cement national unity and territorial integrity; opposed to all regional separatism. The MMI has backed recent parliamentary moves to end the constitutional ban on Prince Victor Emanuel (son of Italy's last king, who reigned for 27 days in 1946) setting foot on Italian soil.
Address. Via Roma 108, 97100 Ragusa
Telephone/Fax. (+39–932) 245–075
Email. movimento.monarchico@monarchici.org
Website. www.monarchici.org
Leadership. Francesco Garofalo Modica

Monarchist Alliance (*Alleanza Monarchica, AM*), umbrella organization for a number of pro-monarchy groupings.
Address. Via Mercanti 30/C, 10121 Turin
Telephone. (+39–11) 540–720
Email. anmitaly@geocities.com
Website. www.geocities.com/anmitaly

National Front (*Fronte Nazionale, FN*), radical right-wing formation modelled on the National Front of France.
Email. info@frontenazionale.org
Website. www.frontenazionale.org

Pensioners' Party (*Partito Pensionati, PP*), created to oppose any reduction in Italy's generous pension provisions, especially for civil servants; won 0.7% in the June 1999 European elections, its one seat going to party leader Carlo Fatuzzo, who joined the European People's Party/European Democrats group.
Leadership. Carlo Fatuzzo

Jamaica

Capital: Kingston

Population: 2,650,000 (2000E)

A former British dependency, Jamaica became a fully independent member of the Commonwealth in 1962. The head of state is the British sovereign, represented by a Governor-General. The head of government is the Prime Minister, who is formally appointed by the Governor-General. There is a bicameral parliament. The House of Representatives has 60 members, who are elected on the Westminster model for five-year terms by simple majority in single seat constituencies. The Senate has 21 members, of whom 13 are normally appointed on the advice of the Prime Minister and eight on that of the Leader of the Opposition.

The Jamaica Labour Party (JLP) and the People's National Party (PNP) have dominated Jamaican politics since the first elections under adult suffrage in 1944, with no third party ever establishing a substantial position. The PNP has been in power since 1989, being re-elected most recently on Dec. 18, 1997, when it won 50 seats against the 10 won by the JLP.

There is a long-standing tradition of rival armed gangs, especially in Kingston, supporting the two main parties and deriving patronage from them, with some neighbourhoods in Kingston being virtual "no go" areas for political opponents. In July 2001 there was an upsurge in violence between gangs linked to the parties, resulting in 25 fatalities.

Jamaica Labour Party (JLP)
Address. JLP Information Centre, 5 Pawsey Place, Kingston 5
Telephone. (+1–876) 754–7213
Fax. (+1–876) 754–7214
Email. jlp@colis.com
Website. www.thejlp.com
Leadership. Edward Seaga (leader)

The JLP is a conservative party with a free market orientation. Founded in 1943 by Alexander Bustamante as the political wing of the Bustamante Industrial Trade Union (BITU), the JLP was the ruling party from 1944 to 1955 and from 1962 (when it led Jamaica to independence) to 1972. The 1970s saw a sharp polarization in Jamaican politics, with the →People's National Party (PNP), in government from 1972, adopting leftist policies that were bitterly opposed by the JLP. Political violence in the run-up to the 1980 election, in which the JLP won back power, resulted in several hundred deaths.

From 1980 JLP Prime Minister Edward Seaga reversed the PNP's previous programme of state control of the economy. He also improved relations with the United States, severing diplomatic relations with Cuba in October 1981 and backing the US-led intervention in Grenada in October 1983. In December 1983 the JLP won all 60 seats after the PNP boycotted the elections. The JLP lost office in 1989, however, and has since been in opposition, winning only eight (of the 60) seats in the House in elections in 1993 and ten in 1997.

Notwithstanding three successive election defeats, Seaga has survived as party leader (a position he has held since 1974) despite periods of internal dissension. In July 2001 Seaga charged that police raids on JLP strongholds in Kingston, which precipitated widespread violence, were intended to strengthen the PNP's position ahead of elections due by 2002.

The JLP is a member of the Caribbean Democrat Union, a regional organization of the International Democrat Union.

People's National Party (PNP)
Address. 89 Old Hope Road, Kingston 6
Telephone. (+1–876) 927–7520
Fax. (+1–876) 927–4389
Email. pnp@pnp.org.jm
Website. www.pnp.org.jm
Leadership. Percival J. Patterson (leader)

The PNP was founded in 1938 by Norman Manley, who led the party until 1969. It first held office, in the pre-independence period, from 1955–62. Norman Manley was succeeded by his son, Michael Manley, who became Prime Minister following the PNP's first post-independence electoral success in February 1972. The subsequent Manley government adopted radical socialist policies, nationalizing key enterprises and building ties with Cuba. According to the →Jamaica Labour Party (JLP) the 1970s saw a "wave of terror" against its supporters, including wholesale "partisan cleansing" of JLP neighbourhoods by gangs linked to the PNP. JLP officials were detained under emergency powers in the run-up to the 1976 election in which the PNP retained power. The run-up to the 1980 elections, against a background of economic crisis, was marked by widespread violence and loss of life, and the PNP was defeated 51–9 by the JLP.

The PNP boycotted elections in December 1983, but then returned to power (winning 45–15) in February 1989, Manley abandoning the PNP's 1970s policies and instead continuing the programme of market deregulation and privatization adopted by the JLP. Manley stood down as leader for health reasons in March 1992 and was succeeded by Percival J. Patterson, under whom the party won 52 of the 60 House seats in elections in March 1993.

Despite economic contraction in 1996–97, high unemployment, a series of scandals, and rampant drug-related crime giving Jamaica one of the highest murder rates in the world, the PNP was re-elected with 50 seats in December 1997.

The PNP is an affiliate of the Socialist International.

Other Parties

National Democratic Movement (NDM). Founded by Bruce Golding in October 1995 following his resignation as chairman of the →Jamaica Labour Party. The NDM subsequently called for sweeping reform of Jamaican society and politics, pledging to tackle issues such as corruption in government and public contracts, police brutality and paramilitarism, judicial inefficiency, rotten prisons and bureaucratic negligence. It won no seats in the 1997 general election, however. Golding stood down as leader after a poor by-election result in March 2001.
Address. NDM House, 3 Easton Avenue, Kingston 5
Email. mail@ndmjamaica.org
Website. www.ndmjamaica.org

Japan

Capital: Tokyo   **Population**: 126.92 million (2000)

Under its constitution adopted in 1947, Japan is a constitutional monarchy with the hereditary Emperor as head of state. Legislative authority is vested in a popularly-elected bicameral Diet (*Kokkai*), which is composed of (i) an upper House of Councillors (*Sangiin*), whose 247 members are elected for six years, half being due for re-election every three years; and (ii) a lower House of Representatives (*Shugiin*) of 480 members elected for up to four years, 300 from single-member constituencies and 180 by proportional representation from party lists in 11 electoral districts. The single-member constituencies for the lower house were introduced under legislation enacted in 1994 with the aim of reducing the prevalence of "money politics" in election campaign funding. Under the previous system all members had been elected in multi-member electoral districts, with resultant competition not only between parties but also between candidates from the same party. Electoral success had therefore become increasingly dependent on a candidate's ability to attract funding.

Under the new legislation, corporate and other private donations to individual politicians for electoral purposes were banned (after a five-year transitional period) and provision made for annual state subsidies to be paid to individual parties according to their Diet representation and percentage share of the vote in the most recent election. One effect of the availability of such annual subsidies has been to encourage groups to break away from existing parties and to form new ones.

The Liberal Democratic Party (LDP) was in office from its formation in 1955 until 1993 when, undermined by a series of scandals and splits, it lost control of the lower house for the first time and gave way to a coalition of seven former opposition parties. Since then Japan has had a succession of coalition or minority governments, against a background of constant flux and realignment in the party structure. The LDP regained the premiership in January 1996 and re-established its legislative dominance in the October 1996 lower house elections, thereafter forming a one-party government until bringing in the Liberal Party in January 1999 and the New Komeito Party in October 1999. In April 2000 the Liberals were replaced by the New Conservative Party in a new three-party coalition headed by Yoshiro Mori of the LDP.

Elections to the House of Representatives on June 25, 2000, resulted as follows: LDP 233 seats (with 41.0% of the constituency vote and 28.3% of the proportional vote), Democratic Party of Japan 127 (27.6%/25.1%), New Komeito Party 31 (2.0%/13.0%), Liberal Party 22 (3.4%/11.0%), Japan Communist Party 20 (12.1%/11.2%), Social Democratic Party of Japan 19 (3.8%/9.4%), New Conservative Party 7 (2.0%/0.4%), Independents' Group 5 (1.1%/0.3%), Liberal League 1 (1.8%/1.1%), independents 15. The LDP, New Komeito and New Conservative coalition partners lost 38 seats in aggregate but retained a comfortable overall majority, so that a new three-party coalition was formed under the continued premiership of Mori. In April 2001, however, Mori was succeeded as LDP leader and Prime Minister by Junichiro Koizumi. Elections to the House of Councillors on July 29, 2001, resulted in the three coalition parties commanding an aggregate overall majority of 164 of the 247 seats.

Democratic Party of Japan (DPJ)
Nihon Minshuto
Address. 1-11-1, Nagata-cho, Chiyoda-ku, Tokyo 100-0014
Telephone. (+81–3) 3595–9988
Fax. (+81–3) 3595–9961
Email. info@dpj.or.jp
Website. www.dpj.or.jp
Leadership. Yukio Hatoyama (chairman); Naoto Kan (secretary-general)

The DPJ was founded in September 1996 principally by breakaway factions of the →New Party Harbinger (*Sakigake*) and the →Social Democratic Party of Japan (SDJP). The new party's leaders were the popular Health Minister, Naoto Kan, and former *Sakigake* secretary-general Yukio Hatoyama, whose grandfather, former Prime Minister Ichiro Hatoyama, had been leader of the historic Democratic Party before the creation of the →Liberal Democratic Party (LDP) in 1955. The new party came third behind the LDP and the New Frontier Party (*Shinshinto*) in the October 1996 lower house elections, winning 52 of the 500 seats, mostly at the expense of the SDJP and the rump of *Sakigake*.

In opposition to LDP-led governments, the DPJ in 1998 absorbed various smaller groupings resulting from the disintegration of *Shinshinto*, becoming the strongest opposition force in the Diet. In September 1999 Hatoyama, hitherto DPJ secretary-general, replaced Kan as party chairman, the latter assuming Hatoyama's previous post. Two months later Hatoyama was sued by the →New Komeito Party for claiming that its deputies had been bribed to join a coalition government with the LDP.

The DPJ advanced strongly in the June 2000 lower house elections, consolidating its position as second party by winning 127 of the 480 seats. It remained in opposition, being again outwitted by the LDP in its search for coalition partners to form a government. In the July 2001 upper house elections DPJ gains increased the party's representation to 59 seats out of 247.

Japan Communist Party (JCP)
Nihon Kyosanto
Address. 4-26-7, Sendagaya, Shibuya-ku, Tokyo 151.
Telephone. (+81–3) 3403–6111
Fax. (+81–3) 3740–0767
Email. info@jcp.or.jp
Website. www.jcp.or.jp
Leadership. Tetsuzo Fuwa (central committee chairperson); Kazuo Shii (executive committee chairperson); Tadayoshi Ichida (head of secretariat)

Founded in 1922 but not legalized until 1945, the JCP has in recent decades presented itself as a democratic party independent of external influences, following its own programme of "scientific socialism" (having abandoned the theory of the dictatorship of the proletariat in 1976). Its share of the vote in the 1980s was consistently some 9% and its lower house representation around 30 seats. Although it lost ground after the collapse of the Soviet Union, it subsequently recovered some support because of its image of being free of corruption.

Having won 15 seats in the 1993 lower house elections, the JCP adopted a democratic socialist orientation for the 1996 contest, advancing to 26 seats by attracting support from former voters of the →Social Democratic Party of Japan. In June 1998 the JCP normalized relations with the fiCommunist Party of China, having broken contacts in 1966. In the June 2000 lower house elections, the JCP fell back to 20 seats, and the party also held 20 upper house seats after the July 2001 elections.

Liberal Democratic Party (LDP)
Jiyu-Minshuto
Address. 1–11–23, Nagata-cho, Chiyoda-ku, Tokyo 100
Telephone. (+81–3) 3581–6211
Fax. (+81–3) 3503–4180
Email. ldp@hq.jimin.or.jp
Website. www.jimin.or.jp
Leadership. Junichiro Koizumi (president); Taku Yamasaki (secretary-general)
The conservative LDP favours private enterprise, a continuing close relationship with the United States and an expansion of Japanese interests in Asia. It has also strongly protected the interests of farmers, rural areas being disproportionately well represented in the Diet. It was formed in 1955 by a merger of the Liberal and Democratic parties. Both of these constituent elements had contained factions based around individuals, and this characteristic became an enduring feature of the LDP and its leadership succession. These factions remain strong because they raise their own funds, separate from those of the party itself.

The LDP remained the ruling party until 1993 when, weakened by corruption scandals and defections, it was forced from office at the general election in July, retaining only 223 of the 511 seats with less than 37% of the vote. In June 1994, however, the party returned to government in an unlikely coalition with the →Social Democratic Party of Japan (SDPJ), which provided the Prime Minister, and the →New Party Harbinger (*Sakigake*). In January 1996 the new LDP president, Ryutaro Hashimoto, regained the premiership for the party, in continued coalition with the SDPJ and *Sakigake*. In the October 1996 lower house elections the LDP won enough seats (239 out of 500) to be able to form a government on its own, with the external support of the SDPJ and *Sakigake* until June 1998, although by late 1997 the LDP commanded a majority on its own due to defections.

Hashimoto survived in office until July 1998, when the LDP again failed to win a majority in the upper house, and was replaced as LDP president and Prime Minister by Keizo Obuchi. Amidst deepening economic recession, Obuchi brought the new →Liberal Party (*Jiyuto*) into the government in January 1999, expanding the coalition to the →New Komeito Party in October 1999. Obuchi suffered a fatal stroke in April 2000 and was succeeded by Yoshiro Mori, hitherto LDP secretary-general, who formed a new three-party coalition in which *Jiyuto* was replaced by the →New Conservative Party (*Hoshuto*).

In general elections to the House of Representatives in June 2000, the LDP slipped to 233 seats out of 480 and the three coalition parties collectively lost ground, while retaining a clear majority. In addition, 10 members of the new lower house who had been elected as independents after being refused the LDP ticket formed the 21st Century Club, five being admitted to the LDP's Kato faction even though they were not party members. Their aim was to be allowed to join or rejoin the LDP.

The extremely unpopular Mori was forced to resign in April 2001 and was succeeded as LDP president and Prime Minister by the maverick former Health Minister, Junichiro Koizumi, who had stood aside from Mori's faction to run an independent campaign. Offering a new style of politics and radical reforms after years of economic stagnation, he obtained overwhelming grass-roots LDP backing and was then elected with the support of 51% of the LDP Diet members. The party's reward was unexpected success in upper house elections in July 2001, when the LDP increased its representation to 110 seats out of 247.

Liberal Party
Jiyuto
Address. 2–2–12, Akasaka, Kokusai Kogyo Akasaka Building, Minato-ku, Tokyo 107
Telephone. (+81–3) 5562–7112
Fax. (+81–3) 5562–7122
Website. www.jiyuto.or.jp
Leadership. Ichiro Ozawa (president); Hirohisa Fujii (secretary-general)
The *Jiyuto* party was founded in January 1998 by Ichiro Ozawa, who claimed that it would be true to the principles of the historic Liberal Party, which had merged into the →Liberal Democratic Party (LDP) in 1955. Ozawa had previously been LDP secretary-general until resigning in 1993 to set up, firstly, the Japan Renewal Party (*Shinseito*) and in 1994 the New Frontier Party (*Shinshinto*). The latter had become the largest opposition party in the 1996 elections but had disintegrated by the end of 1997, in part because of Ozawa's autocratic leadership.

The two chief principles of the *Jiyuto* platform are a more normal foreign policy, including possible Japanese participation in international military operations under UN control, and large-scale deregulation of the economy. In January 1999 the party (with 39 seats in the lower house) joined a government coalition with the LDP. However, strains developed after the coalition was extended to the →New Komeito Party in October 1999, while Ozawa's power-broking political style continued to antagonize his own supporters. In April 2000 *Jiyuto* was badly damaged when about half of its lower house members defected to form the →New Conservative Party, which was then brought into the LDP government in place of *Jiyuto*. In the June 2000 lower house elections *Jiyuto* won only 22 seats, while upper house elections in July 2001 left it with eight seats.

Jiyuto is an observer member of the Liberal International.

New Conservative Party
Hoshuto
Address. c/o Shugiin, 1–7–1 Nagat-cho, Chiyoda-ku, Tokyo
Email. info@hoshutoh.com
Website. www.hostutoh.com
Leadership. Chikage Ogi (chairperson)
The *Hoshuto* party was formed in April 2000 by defectors from the →Liberal Party (*Jiyuto*) and was almost immediately invited into the coalition government headed by the →Liberal Democratic Party (LDP), whereas what remained of the parent party went into opposition. One of only two main parties with a woman leader (who obtained a ministerial post), *Hoshuto* stressed the need for educational reform and modernization of the constitution. In the June 2000 elections its representation in the lower house fell from 25 to seven seats, but the party remained in the government coalition. Chikage Ogi retained her seat in the July 2001 upper house elections, following which *Jiyuto* held five seats.

New Komeito Party
Address. 17 Minamo-Moto-machi, Shinjuku-ku, Tokyo 160-0012
Telephone. (+81–3) 5562–7111
Fax. (+81–3) 3353–9746
Email. info@komei.or.jp
Website. www.komei.or.jp

Leadership. Takenori Kanzaki (leader); Tetsuzo Fuyushiba (secretary-general)

The New Komeito ("Clean Government") Party dates in its latest incarnation from the merger in November 1998 of the Komei New Party (*Komeishinto*) and the New Peace Party (*Shinto Heiwa*).

The original Komeito had been established in 1964 as a political party associated with the *Soka Gakkai* Buddhist organization, following a centrist ideology based on respect for humanity, universal peace and probity in public life. Four members were ministers in the short-lived Hosokawa and Hata coalition governments formed after the →Liberal Democratic Party (LDP) temporarily lost its dominance in 1993. In December 1994 Komeito split into two groups, half joining the New Frontier Party (*Shinshinto*) and the other half forming *Komeishinto*. The failure to defeat the LDP in the 1996 lower house elections provoked further realignment leading to the collapse of *Shinshinto* in late 1997 and the emergence of *Shinto Heiwa* as one of the successor parties.

In October 1999 New Komeito opted to join the LDP-led coalition government of Keizo Obuchi, justifying its change of heart by claiming that the public at large was tired of party politicking and that its opposition had been to the old corrupt LDP. As a government party, it won a disappointing 31 seats in the June 2000 lower house elections, while the July 2001 upper house elections resulted in the party having 23 seats.

Social Democratic Party of Japan (SDPJ)
Shakai Minshuto Zenkoku Rengo

Address. 1–8–1 Nagata-cho, Chiyoda-ku, Tokyo 100–8909
Telephone. (+81–3) 3580–1171
Fax. (+81–3) 3506–9080
Leadership. Takako Doi (chairperson)

Founded in 1945, the party was known in English until 1991 and in Japanese until 1996 as the Japan Socialist Party (JSP). It was briefly in power in 1947-8 as part of a broad coalition but thereafter perpetually in opposition until 1993. A radical party platform was adopted in the mid-1960s (advocating non-alignment, a non-aggression pact among the great powers and a democratic transition from capitalism to socialism), but from the mid-1980s the party began to abandon much of its Marxist ideology in favour of democratic socialism on the West European model. This process was accelerated by the party's heavy defeat in the 1986 lower house elections, following which Takako Doi was elected party leader for the first time, becoming the first woman to head a major Japanese party, although she resigned after another setback for the SDPJ in the 1991 local elections.

In the July 1993 lower house elections, the SDPJ's representation fell sharply from 136 to 70 seats, but it remained the second largest formation after the →Liberal Democratic Party (LDP) and was subsequently a partner in several coalitions excluding the hitherto-dominant LDP. Then SDPJ leader Tomiichi Murayama became Prime Minister in June 1994 and, although previously the leader of the party's left-wing faction, overturned some of the party's deepest principles by accepting the constitutionality of the Self-Defence Forces and the Japan–US Security Treaty, as well as accepting nuclear electric power stations already in operation.

Murayama resigned as Prime Minister in January 1996 and was replaced by the LDP leader, although the SDPJ accepted six posts in the new government. In the same month an SDPJ convention formally approved the change of the party's Japanese name to Social Democratic Party and adopted a new platform incorporating social democratic aims and values in place of the leftist orientation which the party had maintained on paper but had repudiated in practice. Badly weakened by defections to the →New Socialist Party and the →Democratic Party of Japan, the SDPJ won only 15 seats in the October 1996 lower house elections, after which it gave external support to a new LDP government.

With the party in crisis, Takako Doi returned to the leadership in January 1998 and withdrew support from the ruling coalition later in the year. In the June 2000 lower house elections the SDPJ improved marginally to 19 seats, but partial elections for the upper house in July 2001 reduced the party's representation to an all-time low of eight seats.

The SDPJ is a member of the Socialist International.

Other Parties

Independents' Group (*Muzoshoku-no-kai*), former LDP members who split away in the mid-1990s, previously known as the Councillors' Club (*Sangiin*). The group won five lower house seats in 2000 and since 1998 has held four seats in the upper house, where it forms a loose bloc with the →Democratic Party of Japan.
Leadership. Motoo Shiina

Liberal League (*Jiyu Rengo*), founded in December 1995, its platform focusing on medical and welfare issues, reducing the size of central government and a foreign policy more independent of the USA. Originally including two members in each house, it lost one lower house seat in 2000 and lost its upper house representation in 2001 (despite fielding 47 candidates, many of them celebrities).
Address. c/o Shugiin, 1–7–1 Nagat-cho, Chiyoda-ku, Tokyo
Website. www.jiyuren.or.jp
Leadership. Torao Tokuda (chairman); Ichiji Ishii (secretary-general)

New Party Harbinger (*Sakigake*), founded in June 1993 by a faction of the →Liberal Democratic Party (LDP); won 13 lower house seats in 1993 and joined two non-LDP coalitions, before becoming a junior government partner to the LDP in mid-1994. Most of the party having joined the new →Democratic Party of Japan, the rump *Sakigake* slumped to two lower house seats in 1996 and to zero in 2000, although it held one upper house seat after the 2001 elections.
Leadership. Tenzo Okumura

New Socialist Party (*Shin Shakai To*), founded in March 1996 by a left-wing faction of the →Social Democratic Party of Japan opposed to its gravitation to the centre. It lost its small Diet representation in the 1996 and 1998 elections and failed to regain it in 2001–01.
Email. *honbu@sinsyakai.or.jp*
Website. *www.sinsyakai.or.jp*
Leadership. Osamu Tatabe (chairman)

Jordan

Capital: Amman   **Population**: 4,312,000

The Hashemite Kingdom of Jordan attained independence in 1946. It is a constitutional monarchy in which the King, as head of state, appoints a Prime Minister, who in turn selects a Council of Ministers in consultation with the monarch. The Council is responsible to the bicameral National Assembly (*Majlis al-Umma*). This comprises the 80-member lower House of Representatives (*Majlis al-Nuwwab*) (which is elected for a four-year term, in single-seat constituencies) and the upper House of Notables (*Majlis al-Ayaan*), whose 40 members are appointed by the King. In April 1992 King Hussein ibn Talal formally abolished all martial law provisions introduced after the 1967 Arab–Israeli War (in which Israel had occupied the West Bank of the Jordan). In July 1992 legislation was passed lifting the ban on political parties and some 26 parties were registered by 1997, with a rationalization in June 1997, when nine centrist parties united as the National Constitutional Party. Under current regulations, parties are not allowed to receive funding from abroad and are required to undertake to work within the constitution.

The first parliamentary elections in 22 years were held in November 1989. Multi-party elections to the House of Representatives were held on Nov. 8, 1993. With the exception of the Islamic Action Front (IAF), most political parties had a low profile in the elections and the majority of candidates elected were independents. Indeed, the percentage of MPs having party affiliations dropped from 42% in the 11th House to 20% in 1993. The IAF boycotted the polls of Nov. 4, 1997, leading non-partisans to outnumber party MPs by 75 to just five. Turnout was 45.45%.

Following the death of King Hussein, his eldest son was sworn in as King Abdullah II on 7th February 1999. Both houses of parliament pledged their loyalty to the new monarch. Constitutional debate continued about electoral reform, with the government favouring the present first-past-the-post system and opposition forces preferring proportional representation.

Municipal elections held on July 14, 1999 resulted in gains for the Islamist tendency. In April 2001 King Abdullah used his royal prerogative to extend the term of the lower house by two years, elections having been due later in the year. It was reported that the King feared an electoral backlash, as a result of anger about the new *Intifada* on the West Bank and Jordan's own ailing economy. However, on June 16 the King dissolved the Assembly, thus paving the way for new elections expected in July 2002. A new draft electoral law appeared shortly thereafter, endorsing the creation of another 24 seats in densely populated areas (the present demarcation being said to favor tribal rural areas over the largely Palestinian cities).

Arab Islamic Democratic Movement
Haraki al-Arabiyya al-Islamiyya al-Dimaqrati (Du'a)
Leadership. Yusuf Abu Bakr (secretary-general)
The party is a liberal Islamist grouping, highly critical of the →Islamic Action Front's "regressive" interpretation of the Koran. It aims to reinforce the relationship between Muslims and Christians, and includes women and Christians on its executive committee. It won no seats in 1997, and faces a challenge from the →Muslim Centre Party, formed in July 2001.

Communist Party of Jordan
Hizb al-Shuyui al-Urduni
Leadership. Yaqub Zayadin (secretary-general)
Address. Umm Utheina, Dammam Street, Amman
Banned since 1957, the Communist Party applied for legal status in October 1992. Authorization was initially denied, but granted in early 1993 on the condition that the phraseology of party philosophy was amended to agree with constitutional stipulations. The organization stands for Arab nationalism combined with Marxist–Leninist ideology. It won no seats in 1997.

Future Party
Hizb al-Mustaqbal
Address. Al-Jaheth Street, Building No 66, Amman
Leadership. Vacant.
Recognized in late 1992, this conservative pan-Arab party is a strong proponent of Palestinian rights and opposed normalization of relations with Israel. In the 1993 elections it won one seat in the House of Representatives, though none in 1997. Its venerated former secretary-general Suliman Arrar died in 1998. The party joined the →Popular Participation Bloc in May 1999, prior to municipal elections in July.

Islamic Action Front (IAF)
Jabhat al-'Amal al-Islami
Address. Amman, Abdali district, Building no. 6
Leadership. Abdel Latif Arabiyat (secretary-general)
The IAF, a broad-based Islamic coalition but dominated by the Muslim Brotherhood, was formed and registered in late 1992. It advocates the establishment of a *sharia*-based

Islamic state, with the retention of the monarchy, and advocates the equal rights of women with men. The Front is generally perceived as hostile to peace talks with Israel. More extreme members blame Israel and Jews for spreading corruption in Jordan. Sometimes IAF members are co-opted into government, but always hold domestic portfolios, never foreign policy. Their pragmatism in office has often surprised critics.

Generally, the IAF fulfills the role of an opposition. Although critical of foreign influence in Jordan, it has an understanding with Jordan's Royal Family. The IAF supports national institutions as long as the Hashemites - who are regarded as descended from the Prophet Mohammed - adhere to Islamic values. In the November 1993 elections to the House of Representatives, the IAF emerged as by far the largest single party with 16 seats. In municipal elections in July 1995, however, the IAF was heavily defeated as traditional tribal leaders won majorities in most constituencies.

Abdel Latif Arabiyat replaced the veteran moderate, Ishaq Farhan, a former Minister of Education and Islamic *Awqaf* (Endowments), as party leader in the late 1990s. Farhan remained head of the party's consultative council. Abdul Majid al-Zuneibat, leader of the Muslim Brotherhood, increasingly speaks on the IAF's behalf. The party boycotted the 1997 elections, citing 'discriminatory' electoral laws. Others suggested that the IAF feared losing support (the number of Islamist MPs had already fallen from 28 in 1989 to 17 in 1993), resented the ineffectiveness of parliament, or deliberately sought to undermine the legitimacy of Jordan's nascent democratic institutions.

Sources within the IAF expressed regret that they failed to enter the →Popular Participation Bloc, a 13-party opposition bloc formed in May 1999. Nonetheless, the IAF did contest municipal elections in July 1999, and scored particularly well in urban areas with high Palestinian populations, like Zarka, Irbid and Ruseifeh. Some 80% of declared IAF candidates won seats, tapping popular unease with Jordan's economic and social malaise. More than half of IAF members who campaigned as independents won seats. Government sources took some comfort from the low turnout, and the IAF's poorer showing in the capital, Amman. Jordan's expulsion of leaders of the Palestinian *Hamas* movement in late 1999 appeared to engender a split within the Muslim Brotherhood's leading *shura* council, seen as unsettling the IAF itself.

Jordanian Arab Democratic Party (JADP)
Hizb al-Arabi al-Dimaqrati al-Urduni
Leadership. Muniz Razzaz (secretary-general)
Most members of the leftist JADP are former *Baath*-ists and pan-Arabists. The party was recognized in July 1993 and gained two seats in the House of Representatives the following November. The two elected members subsequently joined a broadly leftist parliamentary bloc of leftists, known as the Progressive Democratic Coalition.

Jordanian Arab Socialist Baath Party (JASBP)
Hizb al-Baath al-Arabi al-Ishtiraki al-Urduni
Leadership. Taysir Homsi (secretary-general)
Initially denied legal status because of apparent ties with its Iraqi counterpart, the party was legalized in January 1993, following assurances of its independence and a change of name from the *Baath* Arab Socialist Party in Jordan to the JASBP. Its ideology is described as extreme leftist. One member was returned to the House of Representatives in the 1993 elections, and one in 1997.

Jordanian People's Democratic Party
Hizb al-Shaab al-Dimaqrati (Hashd)
Leadership. Salim al-Nahhas (secretary-general)
The leftist *Hashd* was set up in 1989 by the Jordanian wing of the →→Democratic Front for the Liberation of Palestine, a component of the Palestine Liberation Organization (PLO). It was recognized in January 1993 after initial concerns over its independence, and won one seat in the elections the following November. In 1999 the *Hashd* joined the 13-party opposition →Popular Participation Bloc.

Jordanian Peace Party
Leadership. Dr Shaher Khreis (secretary-general)
Created in June 1996 as a faction supporting improved relations with the former enemy, Israel, the Peace Party failed to win seats in 1997.

Jordanian Progressive Democratic Party
Hizb al-Taqaddumi al-Dimaqrati al-Urduni
Address. c/o Majlis al-Nuwwab, Amman
Leadership. Ali Abd al-Aziz Amer (secretary-general)
The party was originally formed as a merger of three leftist groups—the Jordanian Democratic Party, the Jordanian Party for Progress, under Fawaz Hamid Zo'bi (which later withdrew, and was known as the →Freedom Party) and the Palestinian Communist Labour Party Organization. It was the first leftist party to attain legal status (in mid-January 1993), and secured one seat in the November 1993 elections. The secretary-general and several other party figures are former members of the Palestinian National Council, as well as of the →→Democratic Front for the Liberation of Palestine.

Jordanian Socialist Democratic Party (JSDP)
Hizb al-Dimaqrati al-Ishtiraki al-Urduni
Leadership. Isa Madanat (secretary-general)
Established by former members of the →Communist Party of Jordan, the leftist JSDP achieved legal status in January 1993 despite refusing a government request to delete the word 'socialism' from its party platform. In 1997 the party lost its one member elected in 1993.

National Constitutional Party (NCP)
Address. c/o Majlis al-Nuwwab, Amman
Leadership. Abd al-Hadi al-Majali (secretary-general)
The NCP was created as a merger between nine centrist parties in 1997, and is in effect a successor to the Jordanian Pledge Party, *Hizb al-Ahd al-Urduni*, which was also led by al-Majali. One of the prime movers behind the alignment was Abd al-Salam al-Majali, a relative of

the Pledge Party leader and the then Prime Minister of Jordan.

The NCP also incorporates the Jordanian National Alliance Party (JNA, or *Hizb al-Tajammu al-Watani*) led by Mijhem Haditha al-Khreisha, Popular Unionist Party (*Hizb al-Wihda al-Shabiyya*) led by Talal Haroun Ismail al-Ramahi, the Progress and Justice Party (*Hizb al-Taqaddumi wa al-Adl*) led by Mohammed Ali Farid al-Sa'ad, and Reawakening Party (*Hizb Al-Yaqtha*) led by Abdul Raouf Rawabdeh. Other parties included the United Arab Democratic Party (*Hizb al-Wahdawi al-Arabi al-Dimaqrati* also known as The Promise, *Al-Wa'd*) led by Anis Muasher, the Homeland Party (*Hizb al-Watan*) led by Hakam Khair, the Jordanian Arab People's Party led by Abdul Khaleq Shatat, and the Jordanian Popular Movement Party (*Hizb al-Wihda al-Shabiyya al-Dimaqrati al-Urduni*) led by Musa al-Ma'aytah.

The Jordanian Pledge Party itself was recognized in December 1992. It supported political pluralism, democracy and a free market economy, and emphasized a clear distinction between the Jordanian and Palestinian political entities. Two members were elected to the House of Representatives in 1993. Afterwards, Pledge aligned itself with a group of independent deputies in a National Action Front.

The larger 1997 merger broadened the identity of the resultant NCP. For instance, the JNA (with four members elected in 1993) added strength amongst southern tribal leaders, and *Wa'd* advocated the need to attract foreign investment. Meanwhile the Jordanian Popular Movement Party, which represented Jordanian supporters of the fiPopular Front for the Liberation of Palestine, brought a leftist hue to the otherwise conservative coalition.

In the 1997 elections, the NCP became the largest single party in the *Majlis*, although with only two MPs (the same tally as Pledge had held on its own in 1993). One member of the NCP, Abdul Raouf Rawabdeh, formerly head of the Reawakening Party (*Al-Yaqtha*) was appointed Prime Minister of Jordan in March 1999 by the newly appointed King.

Other Parties

Arab Baath Party for Progress (*Hizb al-Baath al-Arabi al-Taqaddumi*), a leftist and pro-Syrian grouping legalized in April 1993, led by Mahmud al-Maayta.

Arab Democratic Front, created on Sept. 30, 2000, by two former Prime Ministers of Jordan, Ahmed Ubaydat and Tahir Masri. It favors bolstering Jordan's civil society and democratic institutions, and appears to have received Royal sanction to pursue pan-Arab ties. Ubaydat became head of the Senate in April 2001. The Front's two leaders led a high profile visit to Iraq in May 2001.

Freedom Party (*Hizb al-Huriyya*), led by Fawaz Hamid al-Zobi, a former member of the →Communist Party of Jordan, reported to be "trying to combine Marxist ideology with Islamic tradition and nationalist thinking"; legalized in February 1993.

Jordanian Arab Dawn Party, licensed on November 29, 1999.

Jordanian Arab Partisans' Party (*Hizb al-Ansar al-Arabi al-Urduni*), led by Muhammed Faysal al-Majali, legalized in December 1995.

Muslim Centre Party, founded by Bassam Emoush in July 2001. Many of its members are former ministers and deputies, including moderate dissidents from the →Muslim Brotherhood and →Islamic Action Front. Emoush himself had been forced to leave the Brotherhood because he flouted a boycott and stood in elections in 1997.

New Generations Party, led by Zahi Kasim, licensed in October 2000.

Popular Participation Bloc, an alliance of 13 opposition leftist, *Baath*-ist and pan-Arab parties. Created in May 1999, shortly after King Abdullah II came to power, it tried but failed to incorporate members of the →Islamic Action Front, after much negotiation. The following parties joined the Bloc: →Jordanian People's Democratic Party (*Hashd*), →Arab *Baath* Party for Progress, the →Jordanian Arab *Baath* Socialist Party, the →Communist Party of Jordan, the Arab Land Party, →Future Party (*al-Mustaqbal*), Progressive Party, the National Democratic Movement, National Action Party (*Al Haq*, led by Mohammed Zo'bi), the Arab Constitutional Front (led by Milhem Tell), the Popular Unity Party, *Al Ansar* (led by Mohammed Majali), and *Al Ahrar* (led by Ahmad Zo'bi).

Kazakhstan

Capital: Astana

Population: 15,000,000 (2001E)

A constituent republic of the USSR for over half a century, Kazakhstan was one of the last group of Soviet republics to declare independence, on Dec. 16, 1991, on the eve of the demise of the Soviet Union. Later that month Kazakhstan joined the newly formed Commonwealth of Independent States. Nationwide, though uncontested, presidential elections were held in the immediate aftermath of independence. Nursultan Nazarbayev (formerly First Party Secretary of the Communist Party of Kazakhstan), won a landslide victory; he was confirmed in office for a five-year term. The first post-Soviet constitution was adopted in January 1993 and subsequently underwent several modifications. In 1995 the presidential term was extended by referendum until 2000. A new constitution was approved by referendum on Aug. 30, 1995. This provided for an executive President with substantial authority, popularly elected for a five-year term, with powers to appoint the Prime Minister and other ministers, and likewise to dissolve the legislature.

Further constitutional changes were introduced in October 1998. These included the abolition of the maximum age limit for presidential candidates (formerly set at 65 years of age); extension of the term of office of the elected President to seven years; extension of the term of office of deputies from four to six years; and removal of the need to have a minimum of 50% of the electorate participating in the poll. At the same time, a decree was issued confirming that presidential elections would be brought forward to January 1999 (a year earlier than required by law). Although these elections were contested, Nursultan Nazarbayev was again the winner, gaining 79.78% of the vote; There was strong international criticism of the election proceedings, which were felt to have been overly biased in favour of the incumbent President. In June 2000 a bill was passed granting Nazarbayev extraordinary powers and privileges after the expiry in 2006 of his current term of office; opposition leaders sharply criticized this move, on the ground that it amounted to life presidency.

The supreme legislative body is the bicameral *Kenges*, consisting of a Senate (*Senat*) of 39 members (32 elected by local government bodies and seven appointed by the President) and a 77-member Assembly (*Majlis*) directly elected on the basis of a mixed system of 67 single-seat constituencies and 10 "national list" seats decided by proportional representation for parties. Ten parties took part in *Majlis* elections on Oct. 10 and 24, 1999, the conduct of which was strongly criticized by the OSCE's Office for Democratic Institutions and Human Rights (ODIHR) for mismanagement and obstruction on the part of the authorities. The ODIHR's final report published in January 2000 gave the results as follows: Fatherland Party (*Otan*) 24 seats (with 30.9% of the national list vote), Civic Party 11 (11.2%), Communist Party of Kazakhstan 3 (17.8%), Agrarian Party 3 (12.6%), People's Congress of Kazakhstan 1 (2.8%), Republican People's Party of Kazakhstan 1, pro-government independents 20, non-party "business" 10, others/unknown 4.

Agrarian Party (AP)
Address. c/o Kenges, Astana
Leadership. Erkin Ramazdanov
The AP was founded in Astana in January 1999 with the aim of providing support for Kazakhs engaged in agricultural production, grouping workers' unions and agricultural co-operatives. Generally centrist and supportive of President Nazarbayev, the party won three seats in the October 1999 *Majlis* elections, being officially credited with 12.6% of the national list vote.

Civic Party (CP)
Address. c/o Kenges, Astana
Leadership. Rahmet Mukyshev (chairman); Azat Perushayev (first secretary)
A pro-presidential party, representing workers in the metallurgy industry, the CP ran an energetic, high-profile campaign during the October 1999 *Majlis* elections, nominating some 30 candidates. Nine of these were successful in constituency contests and two were elected in the proportional section (with 11.2% of the national list vote), so that the party became the second strongest in the new legislature.

Communist Party of Kazakhstan
Kommunisticheskaya Partiya Kazakhstana (KPK)
Address. c/o Kenges, Astana
Leadership. Serikbolsyn Abdildin (chairman)
The KPK was maintained in being when a faction of the old ruling party opposed its conversion into the →Socialist Party of Kazakhstan in September 1991; it eventually achieved legal registration in March 1994. The party advocated close economic ties with other ex-Soviet republics, retention of state ownership of strategic sectors of the economy, universal welfare provision and equality of ethnic groups. The KPK won two seats in the parliamentary elections of late 1995–early 1996.

By the late 1990s the party was broadly social democratic in orientation and represented the main opposition to the government. In the January 1999 presidential elections, party leader Serikbolsyn Abdildin was runner-up to the incumbent, winning 11.7% of the vote. In the October 1999 *Majlis* elections the KPK nominated over 20 candidates, two of whom were elected to national list seats and one in a constituency contest. Official sources gave its share of the popular vote as 17.8%, but independent exit polls estimated that it had won around 28%, more than any other party.

Fatherland Party
Otan

Address. c/o Kenges, Astana
Leadership. Sergei Tereshchenko (chairman)
The *Otan* party was founded in Almaty in March 1999 by presidential supporters, espousing a social democratic stance. The chairmanship was first offered to President Nazarbayev, but he declined on constitutional grounds; the post was then offered to former Prime Minister Sergei Tereshchenko, who accepted. The new party incorporated a number of other organizations, including the People's Unity Party of Kazakhstan (SNEK), the Kazakhstan 20–30 Movement and the Democratic Movement of Kazakhstan. It rapidly became the dominant party in the country, closely associated with the government and all levels of the administration.

In the October 1999 parliamentary elections, *Otan* fielded the largest number of candidates (some 60 in all) and won the largest number of seats, 20 in constituency contests and four in the national list section. Its share of the proportional vote was officially given as 30.9%, but independent exit polls put its true vote much lower.

People's Congress of Kazakhstan
Narodnyi Kongress Kazakhstana (NKK)

Address. c/o Kenges, Astana
Leadership. Olzhas Suleymenov (chairman)
The NKK was founded in October 1991, deriving from a well-supported anti-nuclear movement and smaller intellectual groups; it included ecological and internationalist aims in its platform. The party initially appeared to have the backing of President Nazarbayev, and so attracted support in the state bureaucracy. Gravitating to opposition, the party won nine seats in the 1994 election. In August 1995 its chairman was appointed as Kazakhstan's ambassador to Italy. It subsequently lost much of its popular support. In the October 1999 *Majlis* elections, it fielded four candidates, one of whom was elected.

Republican People's Party of Kazakhstan
Respublikanskoye Narodnoye Partiya Kazakhstana (RNPK)

Address. c/o Kenges, Astana
Leadership. Akezhan Kazhegeldin (chairman)
Founded in early 1999 by former Prime Minister Akezhan Kazhegeldin as an opposition party, the RNPK espoused a platform that included such aims as the building of a law-based society, a socially oriented market economy and the observance of civic freedom and human rights. The party has suffered severe harassment from government officials. It was allowed to participate in the October 1999 *Majlis* elections, but withdrew its candidates from the party list section on the eve of the election, on the grounds that its leader had been denied registration. It did contest eight constituency seats, winning one.

Other Groupings

Alash National Freedom Party (*Partiya Natsionalynoi Svobody Alash*), founded on the eve of independence and named after a legendary founder of the Kazakh nation. An extreme xenophobic, Islamist grouping, it enjoyed a brief period of popular support in the early 1990s, but was later marginalized. It subsequently revived in a more moderate form and fielded two candidates in the October 1999 *Majlis* elections, without success.
Leadership. Aron Atabek and Rashid Nutushev

Alliance for the Unity and Salvation of the Ethnic Peoples of Kazakhstan, founded in April 2000, with the intention of promoting ethnic harmony.
Leadership. Zhaksibay Bazilbayev

Association of Russian and Slavic Organizations, representing the interests of the Slav population; sometimes forms a tactical alliance with the →Republican People's Party of Kazakhstan known as the Republican Bloc.

Citizen Democratic Party (*Azamat*), founded in April 1996 as an opposition alliance that called for a government of "honest and competent" people. It was the first opposition formation and included eminent public figures from the bureaucracy and the intelligentsia. By 1998 it was close to disintegration, but was relaunched as a political party, moderately oppositional in character, in April 1999. It nominated some 30 candidates in the October 1999 *Majlis* elections, but did not win any seats.
Leadership. Galym Abylsiitov (chairman)

December National Democratic Party (*Natsionalnaya Demokraticheskaya Partiya–Jeltogsan, NDP-Jeltoqsan*), founded in 1990 as a pro-independence movement, named after the month of anti-government riots in the capital in 1986 (in the Soviet era). A nationalist movement, *Jeltoqsan* advocates close links with Turkey and Iran, and in 1992 announced the sending of party volunteers to assist Azerbaijan in its conflict with Armenia. In 1995 its leader was prominent in the opposition to the presidential constitution adopted in August.
Leadership. Hasen Kozhakhmetov

Freedom Civil Movement of Kazakhstan (*Grazhdanskoye Dvizhenie Kazakhstana–Azat, GDK-Azat*), nationalist formation founded in 1990 to promote Kazakhstan's independence, but soon losing ground to other political forces. In October 1992 it joined with the →December National Democratic Party and the →Republican Party of Kazakhstan to form the Republican Party *Azat*, but the merger quickly broke down over policy and personal differences. By the late 1990s it was moribund.
Leadership. Mikhail Isinaliyev

Generation (*Pokoleniye*), movement seeking to represent the interests of pensioners; sometimes forms alliances with other political parties such as the →Citizen Democratic Party (*Azamat*).
Leadership. Irina Savostina

Kazakhstan Revival Party, small pro-presidential party, it nominated 10 candidates in the October 1999 elections to the *Majlis*, but failed to win any seats.

My Kazakhstan, founded in September 2001 under the leadership of a nephew of President Nazarbayev.
Leadership. Qayrat Satybaldy

Orleu Movement, opposition movement founded in February 1999, sometimes loosely allied with the →Republican People's Party of Kazakhstan in the Republican Bloc. It failed to qualify for participation in the October 1999 *Majlis* elections.
Leadership. Seydahmet Kuttykadam

Republican Party of Labour, small relatively new centrist party, formed on the basis of the Republican Engineering Academy. It fielded six candidates in the October 1999 *Majlis* elections, but failed to win any seats.

Republican People's Slavic Movement–Harmony (*Respublikanskoye Obshestvennoye Slavyanskoye Dvizhenie–Lad*, founded in mid-1993, becoming the largest ethnic Russian movement in Kazakhstan, also drawing support from other Russian-speaking groups such as Tatars, Germans and Koreans. Advocating close relations with Russia, dual citizenship for ethnic Russians and equal status for the Russian language, it won four seats in the 1994 elections but did not participate in the October 1999 contest.

Russian Centre (*Rossiiskyi Tsentrum*), grouping based in the ethnic Russian community, denied registration for the 1995 elections.

Socialist Party of Kazakhstan (*Sotsialisticheskaya Partiya Kazakhstana, SPK*), formed a month after the abortive hardline coup in Moscow in August 1991 as would-be successor to the then ruling →Communist Party of Kazakhstan (KPK), adopting a programme of political pluralism and cautious economic reform. President Nazarbayev (the former first party secretary of the KPK) withdrew from the SPK in December 1991 and subsequently launched the People's Unity Party of Kazakhstan (SNEK) as the government party (→Fatherland Party). The SPK then took on the role of an opposition party. It won eight seats in the 1994 legislative elections but was not credited with any in December 1995. In April 1996 SPK leader Petr Svoik, a former head of the State Committee on Prices and Anti-Monopoly Measures, became a co-chairman of the new →Citizen Democratic Party (*Azamat*), although the SPK retained its individual identity. It sought to contest the October 1999 parliamentary elections, but was deemed ineligible on the grounds that Svoik formed part of the leadership of a different party, namely *Azamat*).

Leadership. Petr Svoik(chairman)

Kenya

Capital: Nairobi

Population: 30,340,000 (2000E)

Kenya achieved independence from the United Kingdom in 1963 and was proclaimed a republic the following year. In 1964 the ruling Kenya African National Union (KANU) became effectively the sole legal party, and it was not until December 1991 that President Daniel arap Moi, faced with increasing internal and external pressure, approved constitutional amendments establishing a multi-party system. The central legislative authority is the unicameral National Assembly, with 210 directly-elected representatives, 12 nominated members and two ex-officio members (Speaker and Attorney General). It has a maximum term of five years. Executive power is vested in the President, Vice-President and Cabinet. Both the Vice-President and the Cabinet are appointed by the President, who is elected for a five-year term by universal adult suffrage. The winning presidential candidate must have received at least 25% of the votes cast in at least five of the eight provinces of Kenya.

In a presidential election held on Dec. 29, 1997, Daniel arap Moi, the candidate of KANU, was re-elected for his fifth successive term of office with 40.6% of the votes cast in a 15-way contest (this being a record number of candidates in a Kenyan presidential election). President Moi subsequently stated that this would be his final term as President. In legislative elections held on Dec. 29, 1997, the 210 elective seats were distributed as follows: KANU 107, Democratic Party (DP) 39, National Development Party (NDP) 21, Forum for the Restoration of Democracy—Kenya (FORD-Kenya) 17, Social Democratic Party (SDP) 15, Safina 5, Forum for the Restoration of Democracy for the People (FORD-People) 3, Kenya Social Congress 1, Forum for the Restoration of Democracy—Asili (FORD-Asili) 1, Shirikisho Party of Kenya (SPK) 1. The party distribution of the 12 nominated Assembly seats was as follows: KANU 6, DP 2, NPP 1, FORD-Kenya 1, SDP 1, Safina 1.

Democratic Party (DP)

Address. PO Box 53695, Nairobi
Telephone. (+254–2) 573595
Email. dpkenya@wananchi.net
Website. www.dp-kenya.org
Leadership. Mwai Kibaki (national chairman)

The DP emerged at the beginning of 1992 as a result of the departure of former →Kenya African National Union members from the ruling party to join the opposition. Its leader, Mwai Kibaki, who had been a longstanding government figure until his resignation in December 1991, attacked widespread official corruption and declared the new party's commitment to democracy, open government and free enterprise. In the December 1992 elections, which were denounced as rigged and fraudulent by the opposition, Kibaki took third place in the presidential balloting with almost 20% of the votes cast, while DP candidates secured 23 seats in the National Assembly.

In the December 1997 presidential election Kibaki was the runner-up with 31.5% of the vote. The High Court dismissed a subsequent petition by Kibaki challenging the validity of the election result. The DP won 39 seats in the December 1997 legislative elections, making it the largest opposition party in the National Assembly.

The DP is associated with the International Democrat Union through its membership of the Democrat Union of Africa.

Forum for the Restoration of Democracy-Asili (FORD-Asili)

Address. PO Box 75695, Nairobi
Leadership. Martin Shikuku

FORD was formed by prominent opposition politicians in August 1991, attracting immediate government hostility. The most high-profile figure at that stage was Oginga Odinga, a Vice-President of Kenya in the 1960s and a former member of the ruling →Kenya African National Union (KANU). The government's repressive response to the FORD pro-democracy campaign drew international condemnation, threatening Kenya's relations with crucial aid donors. The party was registered immediately following the regime's acceptance of multi-partyism at the end of 1991. From mid-1992, however, FORD was weakened by mounting internal divisions and rivalry over the selection of the party's presidential election candidate; this resulted in a split into two opposing factions—FORD-Asili under Kenneth Matiba and →FORD-Kenya led by Odinga—which were registered as separate political parties in October 1992.

In the December 1992 elections, in which the party claimed that gross irregularities took place, Matiba finished second to President Moi with 26% of the vote, while FORD-Asili candidates won 31 seats in the National Assembly (although one representative subsequently defected to KANU in June 1993). Divisions within FORD-Asili emerged in November 1994 when the party's national executive committee reportedly suspended Matiba for six months. Further internal turmoil ensued, with new party officers appointed in March 1996 failing to obtain support from their predecessors. Matiba subsequently formed a separate party, →FORD-People.

In the December 1997 presidential election, Martin Shikuku received less than 1% of the vote, while FORD-Asili won only one seat in the simultaneous legislative elections.

Forum for the Restoration of Democracy for the People (FORD-People)

Address. c/o National Assembly, Nairobi
Leadership. Kimani wa Nyoike (chairman)
Founded in 1997 by Kenneth Matiba, a former leader of the →Forum for the Restoration of Democracy for the People-Asili, following a split in that party. FORD-People won three seats in the December 1997 legislative elections.

Forum for the Restoration of Democracy-Kenya (FORD-Kenya)

Address. PO Box 57449, Nairobi
Telephone. (+254–2) 570361
Leadership. Kijana Wamalwa (chairman)
FORD-Kenya was one of the two main rival elements to emerge from the original FORD opposition movement. The party was registered in October 1992, initially under the leadership of Oginga Odinga, who achieved fourth place in the presidential election of December 1992, with almost 17.5% of the votes cast. In the simultaneous legislative elections FORD-Kenya tied for second place with →FORD-Asili, winning 31 National Assembly seats. FORD-Kenya subsequently joined an opposition alliance to challenge the validity of the election results. In June 1993 Odinga assumed the leadership of the official opposition in the National Assembly. However, in January of the following year he died and was succeeded as chairman of FORD-Kenya by Kijana Wamalwa, hitherto the party's vice-president.

In June 1995 secretary-general Munyua Waiyaki resigned his party membership, subsequently joining the →United Patriotic Party of Kenya. At the end of November 1995 it was reported that Wamalwa had been ousted as chairman of FORD-Kenya by Raila Odinga (a son of the late leader), reflecting factional rivalries within the party. However, the following month the High Court confirmed Wamalwa as party chairman, restraining Odinga from taking over the leadership. Odinga subsequently joined the →National Development Party (NDP).

In the December 1997 presidential election Wamalwa was placed fourth, with 8.4% of the vote. In the simultaneous legislative elections FORD-Kenya won 17 Assembly seats, placing it behind the NDP (21 seats) but substantially ahead of FORD-Asili (one seat) and its offshoot FORD-People (3 seats).

Kenya African National Union (KANU)

Address. PO Box 72394, Nairobi
Telephone. (+254–2) 332389
Email. info@kanu-kenya.org
Website. www.kanu-kenya.org
Leadership. Daniel arap Moi (national chairman); Joseph Kamotho (secretary-general)
KANU was established in 1960 espousing centralized government, "African socialism" and racial harmony. It has been the ruling party since 1964, and between 1982 and 1991 its status as the sole legal political organization was embodied in the constitution. Daniel arap Moi succeeded Jomo Kenyatta as President and party leader in 1978. In December 1990, following President Moi's lead, KANU delegates voted to retain the one-party system. However, the sustained pro-democracy campaign and international pressure for reform made this position increasingly untenable,

and in December 1991 the party endorsed Moi's abrupt decision to introduce multi-partyism. KANU subsequently suffered a number of defections to new opposition parties.

In the December 1992 elections, Moi retained the presidency with just over 36% of the votes cast, the opposition vote having been split between the leaders of three opposition parties. In the legislative elections KANU faced strong opposition attacks on government corruption. The party retained power with 100 of the elective National Assembly seats, although many sitting KANU members were defeated, including 15 cabinet ministers.

In December 1997 Moi was re-elected President with 40.6% of the vote, while KANU won 107 seats in the National Assembly, where it was subsequently supported by the →National Development Party.

Kenya Social Congress (KSC)

Address. PO Box 55318, Nairobi
Leadership. George Anyona (leader)
Founded and legalized in 1992, the KSC secured one seat in the 1992 and 1997 legislative elections.

National Development Party (NDP)

Address. PO Box 78810, Nairobi
Telephone. (+254–2) 716352
Fax. (+254–2) 716354
Website. www.arcc.or.ke/ndp
Leadership. Raila Odinga (leader); Sospeter Ojaamong (secretary-general)
Formed in 1994, the NDP appointed Raila Odinga (once a contender for the leadership of the →Forum for the Restoration of Democracy-Kenya) as its leader in May 1997. In the December 1997 presidential election, Odinga was placed third, receiving over 11% of the vote. In the simultaneous legislative elections, the NDP was also placed third, winning 21 seats in the National Assembly. Odinga subsequently aligned the NDP with the ruling →Kenya African National Union (KANU) and himself chaired a parliamentary commission on constitutional reform whose report (tabled in April 2000) was rejected by the main opposition parties.

In June 2001 the NDP's policy of "co-operation" with the government moved closer to full coalition (although this term was not used) when Odinga and another NDP member were appointed to senior ministerial office. Two other NDP members became assistant ministers, while virtually all of the party's backbenchers moved to sit alongside the KANU members of the National Assembly.

Safina

Address. PO Box 135, Nairobi
Leadership. Farah Ma'alim (chairman); Mwandawiro Mghanga (secretary-general)
In May 1995 the internationally recognized conservationist and palaeontologist, Richard Leakey, announced that he was joining Paul Muite and other members of the Mwangaza Trust (the charitable status of which had been revoked by the government in January 1995) in the formation of a new opposition party. The following month the party name, Safina ("Noah's Ark"), was announced and an application for registration was made. Despite not gaining its registration until November 1997, Safina won five seats in the following month's National Assembly elections after campaigning on an anti-corruption and pro-human rights platform. In July 1999 Leakey was subsequently appointed head of the civil service and secretary to the Cabinet (with responsibility for combating corruption), but resigned from this post in March 2001.

Shirikisho Party of Kenya (SPK)

Address. PO Box 70421, Nairobi
Leadership. Rashid Suleiman Shakombo
The SPK, based in Kenya's Coast province, won one seat in the December 1997 legislative elections. It has advocated a

federal system of government in Kenya. The party was embroiled in a series of leadership disputes in 1998–99.

Social Democratic Party (SDP)
Address. PO Box 55845, Nairobi
Telephone. (+254–2) 260309

Leadership. Charity Kuluki Ngilu (chairperson); Apollo Lugano Njonjo (secretary-general)

Founded in 1992, the SDP won 15 seats in the December 1997 National Assembly elections. Its candidate was placed fifth (with 7.8% of the vote) in the simultaneous presidential election.

Kiribati

Capital: Tarawa

Population: 80,000 (2000E)

Kiribati (the former UK protectorate of the Gilbert Islands) became an independent republic in 1979. Under the constitution, legislative power is vested in a unicameral 41-seat House of Assembly (Maneaba ni Maungatabu). This consists of 39 popularly elected members, one nominated representative of the displaced Banaban community (resident since the 1950s in Fiji because of the environmental degradation of their island by phosphate mining), and the Attorney General (as an ex-officio member, unless already elected). An executive President (the Beretitenti), who is popularly elected from amongst members of the Assembly, governs with the assistance of an appointed Cabinet and is empowered to dissolve the Assembly and to call general elections. Both President and Assembly serve a four-year term.

Traditionally there have been no formally organized political parties in Kiribati. In recent elections, however, loose associations have been formed in response to specific issues or in support of particular individuals. In Assembly elections held on Sept. 23 and 30, 1998, two such groupings, the Maneaban Te Mauri (MTM) and the Boulokanto Koaava (BK), secured 14 and 11 seats respectively, the other 14 elective seats being won by independents. Presidential elections held on Nov. 27, 1998, resulted in the re-election of Teburoro Tito of the MTM with 52.3% of the vote.

Boulokanto Koaava (BK)
Address. c/o Maneaba ni Maungatabu, Tarawa
Leadership. Harry Tong

Rendered as "Pillars of Truth" or "Supporters of Truth", the BK grouping won 11 of the 39 elective seats in the September 1998 Assembly elections. In presidential elections two months later, BK leader Harry Tong was runner-up with an impressive 45.8% of the vote.

Maneaban Te Mauri (MTM)
Address. c/o Maneaba ni Maungatabu, Tarawa
Leadership. Teburoro Tito

Its title being variously translated as "Protect the Maneaba", "Blessings of the Meeting House" or simply "Good Luck", the MTM emerged in the mid-1990s as the supporting group of President Teburoro Tito. Tito had been elected in 1994 with the backing of a Protestant-oriented Christian Democratic Party (CDP), defeating incumbent Teatao Teannaki, whose supporters were grouped in the National Progressive Party (NPD). The CDP subsequently coalesced with the NPD to become the MTM, which won 14 of the 39 elective seats in the September 1998 Assembly elections and backed Tito's successful re-election bid two months later.

North Korea

Capital: Pyongyang

Population: 22,082,000 (2000E)

Liberated in 1945 from Japanese colonial rule, the Korean peninsula was occupied by Soviet troops in the north and by US forces in the south. In 1948 separate states were established on either side of the 38th parallel (the north becoming the Democratic People's Republic of Korea, commonly known as North Korea), each of which reflected the ideology of its respective super-power and each of which claimed jurisdiction over the entire peninsula. In 1950 the communist North invaded the South and was resisted by US-led United Nations forces. The Korean War was ended by an armistice in 1953, with the ceasefire line (which became the new *de facto* border) straddling the 38th parallel.

Under North Korea's 1972 constitution as amended in 1998, the highest state organ is the unicameral Supreme People's Assembly (SPA), whose 687 members are elected every five years, while the SPA Presidium acts for the SPA between its full sessions. The highest executive body, elected by the SPA, is the 10-member National Defence Committee (NDC), whose chairman holds "the highest office of the state", although the chairman of the SPA Presidium represents the state on formal occasions and receives the credentials of foreign emissaries. The SPA also elects the Prime Minister and Cabinet.

Actual political control is exercised by the communist Korean Workers' Party (KWP), which was dominated by Kim Il Sung, as KWP general secretary and head of state, until his death in July 1994. Also known as the "Great Leader", Kim was the object of an extravagant personality cult and spent his last two decades in power preparing the way for the succession of his son, Kim Jong Il (known as the "Dear Leader"). More than three years after his father's death, Kim Jong Il was in October 1997 formally named as KWP general secretary. In September 1998 he was re-elected chairman of the NDC and thus as de facto head of state under the 1998 constitutional amendments.

Elections to the SPA were last held on July 26, 1998, from a single list of KWP or KWP-approved candidates

Korean Workers' Party (KWP)
Chosun No-dong Dang
Address. c/o Supreme People's Assembly, Pyongyang
Leadership. Kim Jong Il (general secretary)
Originating at the end of World War II, the KWP became the sole ruling force in the Democratic People's Republic of Korea established in 1948 and has since maintained control of all political activity within the state. Under Kim Il Sung's undisputed leadership, the party adhered to the concept of *Juche* (variously defined as involving political independence, economic self-reliance and national self-defence) as the ideological foundation for North Korean communism.

Having in 1961 again recognized the Communist Party of the Soviet Union as the "vanguard of the world communist movement", the KWP moved to a pro-Chinese line from 1963 and later to an independent stance on the ideological competition between Moscow and Beijing. The sixth KWP congress in Pyongyang in October 1980 resulted in the election of a five-member politburo presidium as the party's new supreme body. No congress has been held since then (and three of the five presidium members have died and one has been dismissed without being replaced).

The rapid post-1989 collapse of communism in Eastern Europe and of the Soviet Union itself in 1991 did not appear to shake the KWP's certainty about its right to rule. With communist regimes becoming an endangered species, the KWP inevitably drew closer to China. But there was no inclination in Pyongyang to follow the Chinese lead in combining communist rule with economic liberalization, and little sympathy in Beijing for North Korea's problems. The result was that North Korea remained in isolated backwardness, amidst increasing economic hardship for its people.

The death of Kim Il Sung in July 1994 generated much external expectation that the forces of political reform would be unleashed in North Korea. In the event, nothing changed in the system of KWP rule, at least on the surface. Long

groomed for the succession to his father, Kim Jong Il was at last named as KWP general secretary in October 1997 and a year later was confirmed as head of state. Constitutional amendments introduced in 1998 provided for a very limited move to a market economy, without appreciable effect as the country descended into famine conditions in the late 1990s. In June 2000 Kim Jong Il received the South Korean President in Pyongyang for the first North-South talks since 1948; but there was no sign of any North Korean readiness to abandon its one-party system or to move towards Korean reunification.

Approved Formations

In North Korea's system of one-party rule, the Democratic Front for the Reunification of the Fatherland is an umbrella body for the ruling →Korean Workers' Party (KWP) and two minor political parties (below), together with several mass working people's organizations.

Chondoist Chongu Party
Chondogyo Chong-u-dang
Leadership. Yu Mi Yong (chairwoman)
Descended from an anti-Japanese religious nationalist movement of the pre-war period, this party enjoyed a measure of independence until the Korean War, following which it became a subservient appendage of the ruling KWP.

Korean Social Democratic Party (KSDP)
Choson Sahoeminj-u-dang
Leadership. Kim Pyong Sik (chairman)
Founded as the Democratic Party in 1945, the KSDP initially attracted substantial middle-class and peasant support until its original leaders either fled to the South or were liquidated in 1946. Since then it has been under the effective control of the KWP.

South Korea

Capital: Seoul

Population: 47,470,969 (2000E)

Liberated in 1945 from Japanese colonial rule, the south of the Korean peninsula was occupied by United States troops and the north by Soviet forces. In 1948 separate states were established on either side of the 38th parallel (the south becoming the Republic of Korea), each reflecting the ideology of its respective protecting power and each claiming jurisdiction over the entire peninsula. In 1950 South Korea was invaded by the communist North, but was saved from defeat by US-led United Nations military intervention. The Korean War was ended by an armistice in 1953, with the ceasefire line (which became the *de facto* border) straddling the 38th parallel.

There were frequent constitutional revisions as South Korea evolved through five republics between 1948 and 1987, brief experiments with democracy being invariably undermined by military intervention in the political process. The Sixth Republic was proclaimed in February 1988, following a revision of the constitution the previous October after massive popular unrest. Under this instrument, executive power is held by the President, who is popularly elected for a single five-year term and who governs with the assistance of an appointed State Council (Cabinet) led by a Prime Minister. Legislative authority rests with a unicameral National Assembly (*Kuk Hoe*), serving a four-year term. The number of Assembly seats was reduced from 299 to 273 for the 2000 elections, 227 being filled by constituency-based direct election and 46 on the basis of proportional representation.

In presidential elections held on Dec. 18, 1997, amidst a major economic and financial crisis, longstanding opposition figure Kim Dae Jung, running as candidate of the National Congress for New Politics (NCNP), won a narrow victory with 40.3% of the vote against 38.7% for Lee Hoi Chang of the Grand National Party (GNP). In January 2000 the NCNP was renamed the Millennium Democratic Party (MDP). In elections to the National Assembly on April 13, 2000, the GNP won 133 seats (with 39.0% of the vote), the MDP 115 (35.9%), the United Liberal Democrats 17 (9.8%), the Democratic People's Party 2 (3.7%), the New Korea Party of Hope 1 (0.4%) and independents 5.

Democratic People's Party (DPP)
Minkook Dang
Address. c/o Kuk Hoe, Yeongdongpo-gu, Seoul
Telephone. (+82–2) 784–1114
Leadership. Kim Yoon Hwan (president)

The DPP was formed in February 2000 by dissident Assembly members of the opposition →Grand National Party (GNP) associated with former President Kim Young Sam (1993–98) and aggrieved that they had been excluded from the GNP list of candidates for the April 2000 elections. Also including defectors from the ruling →Millennium Democratic Party, the new party retained only two seats in the Assembly elections. Following the appointment of DPP leader Kim Yoon Hwan as Minister of Foreign Affairs and Trade in March 2001, the DPP opted for formal membership of the MDP-led government coalition.

Grand National Party (GNP)
Hannara Dang
Address. 17-7 Yoido-dong, Yongdeungpo-ku, Seoul 150–874
Telephone. (+82–2) 3786–3371
Fax. (+82–2) 3786–3610
Email. jylsej@yahoo.com
Website. www.hannara.or.kr
Leadership. Lee Hoi Chang (chairman)

The GNP was created in December 1997 as a merger of the New Korea Party (NKP) and the Democratic Party (DP) to back the presidential candidacy of Lee Hoi Chang in the elections of that month.

The NKP was the successor to the Democratic Liberal Party (DLP), which had been launched in 1990 as a merger of then President Roh Tae Woo's Democratic Justice Party with Kim Jong Pil's New Democratic Republican Party and Kim Young Sam's Reunification Democratic Party. As the DLP candidate, Kim Young Sam had been elected President in December 1992 with about 42% of the vote. In early 1995, after a dispute with President Kim, Kim Jong Pil had resigned as DLP chairman, subsequently forming the →United Liberal Democrats (ULD). The DLP's change of name to NKP in December 1995 had been seen as an attempted break with the legacy of corruption that had enveloped former senior party figures. It had yielded some benefit in the April 1996 legislative elections, in which the NKP had consolidated its position as substantially the largest party with 139 seats out of 299.

The DP had been launched in 1990 mainly by dissident members of the Reunification Democratic Party opposed to the creation of the DLP and in September 1991 had absorbed the New Democratic Party led by Kim Dae Jung, who was the unsuccessful DP candidate in the 1992 presidential elections. The DP had then been the principal opposition party until September 1995, when a majority of its Assembly members had defected to Kim Dae Jung's new National Congress for New Politics (NCNP), later renamed the →Millennium Democratic Party (MDP). In the 1996 Assembly elections the rump DP had retained only 15 seats.

The NKP-DP merger to create the GNP on the eve of the December 1997 presidential elections was an attempt to counter an earlier split in the NKP arising from the selection of Lee Hoi Chang as the NKP candidate. The selection had for the first time been made in open voting at a party convention (rather than by presidential nomination), but the losing contender, Rhee In Je, had refused to accept the decision and had formed the breakaway New People's Party (NPP) to support his own presidential campaign. In the event, this split enabled NCNP candidate Kim Dae Jung to win the contest with 40.3% of the vote against 38.7% for Lee Hoi Chang and 19.2% for Rhee.

The GNP formed the main opposition to the post-1998 administration of Kim Dae Jung, which made the customary use of incumbency in power to consolidate its support in the Assembly at the expense of the GNP. In the April 2000 Assembly elections, however, the GNP retained its status as the largest party by winning 133 of the 273 seats.

The GNP is a member party of the International Democrat Union.

Millennium Democratic Party (MDP)
Minju Dang
Address. Kisan Building, 15 Yeoeuido-dong, Youngdeungpo-ku, Seoul 150–101
Telephone. (+82–2) 784–7007
Fax. (+82–2) 784–8095
Email. minjoo@minjoo.or.kr
Website. www.minjoo.or.kr
Leadership. Kim Dae Jung (leader); Han Gwang Ok (chairman); Rhee In Je (campaign manager)

The MDP was launched in January 2000 as successor to the National Congress for New Politics (NCNP) to support the administration of President Kim Dae Jung, who had been elected as the NCNP candidate in December 1997.

The NCNP had been inaugurated in September 1995 following Kim Dae Jung's return to politics. He had been a major opposition figure in the 1980s, but had been defeated in the 1992 presidential elections by Kim Young Sam (→Grand National Party, GNP) as candidate of the Democratic Party (DP). The new NCNP had attracted sufficient DP defectors to become the largest opposition group in the Assembly but had won only 79 seats out of 299 in the 1996 elections and had thus remained in opposition. In the December 1997 presidential elections, however, Kim Dae Jong won with 40.3% of the vote against 38.7% for the GNP candidate and 19.2% for Rhee In Je of the New People's Party (NPP), a GNP splinter group.

Inaugurated in February 1998, Kim Dae Jung formed a coalition government between the NCNP and the United Liberal Democrats (ULD), with a ULD Prime Minister, also drawing sufficient support from the NPP and GNP defectors to ensure a working Assembly majority. On the launching of the new MDP in January 2000, Rhee was appointed as its campaign manager, thus obtaining a base for another presidential bid in 2002. Despite the name change and the benefits of presidential incumbency, the MCP failed to become the largest party in the April 2000 Assembly elections, in which its representation rose to 115 seats out of 273. The renewal of the MCP-ULD coalition strengthened the government's Assembly position, which was further improved when the →Democratic People's Party joined the government in April 2001.

United Liberal Democrats (ULD)
Jayu Minju Yonmaeng
Address. Insan Building, 103-4 Shinsoo-dong, Seoul 121–110
Telephone. (+82–2) 701–3355
Fax. (+82–2) 707–1637
Email. jamin@jamin.or.kr
Website. www.jamin.or.kr
Leadership. Kim Jong Pil (honorary president); Lee Han Dong (president)

The conservative ULD was established in March 1995 by Kim Jong Pil and other defectors from the then ruling Democratic Liberal Party (→Grand National Party, GNP). Having its chief regional base is Chungchong province, it became the third largest party with 50 seats in the April 1996 Assembly elections. In December 1997 the ULD backed the successful presidential candidacy of Kim Dae Jung of what later became the →Millennium Democratic Party (MDP) on the understanding that South Korea would move to a more parliamentary system and that Kim Jong Pil would be appointed Prime Minister.

Kim Jong Pil resigned the premiership at the beginning of 2000 and in February took the ULD out of the government in preparation for the April 2000 Assembly elections. It suffered a serious setback, however, winning only 17 seats, whereupon Kim Jong Pil resigned as ULD chairman. He was replaced by Lee Han Dong, who took the ULD back into coalition with the MDP and was appointed Prime

Minister in August 2000. The ULD remained committed to a more parliamentary form of government, but neither the MDP nor the main opposition GNP showed any enthusiasm for the idea.

Other Parties

Democratic Labour Party (DLP), founded in January 2000 on an anti-capitalist and pro-unification platform, its president having won 1.2% of the vote in the 1997 presidential elections as "People's Victory 21" candidate. The DLP also took 1.2% in the 2000 Assembly elections.

Email. jjagal@yahoo.co.kr
Website. www.kdlp.org
Leadership. Kwon Young Ghil (president)

New Korea Party of Hope (NKPH), won one constituency seat and 0.4% of the vote in the 2000 Assembly elections.

Youth Progress Party, left-wing formation which took 0.7% of the vote but no seats in the 2000 Assembly elections.

Kuwait

Capital: Kuwait City

Population: 2,238,000 (2000E)

Kuwait is an hereditary monarchy governed by the Amir, who is chosen by and from the royal family. He appoints the Prime Minister and the Council of Ministers. The 1962 constitution provides for an elected legislature. However, following the dissolution of the National Assembly in 1986, Amir Jabir al-Sabah ruled by decree without reference to any legislative body until 1990, when a National Council (partly elected and partly appointed) was created. In August 1990 Kuwait was invaded and occupied by Iraq. Following Kuwait's liberation from Iraqi annexation by US-led coalition forces in the Gulf War, a new National Assembly *(Majlis al-Umma)* superseded the old Council in 1992. The Assembly has some veto rights and consists of 50 members elected for a four-year term by direct (but very restricted) adult male suffrage and 25 appointed by the Amir. No political parties as such have been authorized in Kuwait and Assembly candidates stand as independents. Nevertheless, several political "tendencies" have functioned since the October 1992 Assembly elections, some in opposition to the government. A decree issued by Amir Jabir in May 1999 specified that women would have the vote and be eligible for public office from 2003. However, the Assembly's rejection of the decree in November 1999 and a Constitutional Court ruling against female enfranchisement in January 2001 made it uncertain whether the changes would be implemented as decreed.

The 1992 Assembly elections produced Kuwait's first legislative opposition majority, encompassing liberal and Islamist groupings. The next Assembly balloting in October 1996 resulted in pro-government members becoming the largest single bloc, although opposition groups continued to be strong. Tensions between the opposition and the government, headed by Crown Prince Saad al-Abdullah al-Sabah since 1978, culminated in the dissolution of the Assembly in May 1999 when the government was threatened with defeat in a no-confidence vote. Early elections on July 3, 1999, resulted in a strong showing for liberal and Islamist opposition candidates, whereupon the government resigned. Its successor was again headed by Crown Prince Saad, but showed many changes seen as taking account of opposition criticism of government economic and social policy. Further major ministerial changes were made in a new government formed by Crown Prince Saad in February 2001.

Islamic Constitutional Movement, a moderate Sunni Muslim grouping enjoying support from merchants and professionals, and deriving influence from *diwaniyat*, private weekly meetings held in the homes of prominent families. Having gained representation in the 1992 Assembly elections, the grouping returned four adherents in 1996 and five in 1999. It has usually formed part of the opposition to the government.
Leadership. Ismael al-Shatti

Islamic National Coalition, drawing support from the Shia community, who make up about a quarter of the Kuwaiti population.

Islamic Popular Movement, a small conservative Sunni Muslim faction, also known as the *Salafiyoun* (roughly "founding fathers"); three members were elected to the Assembly in 1996 and two in 1999.

Islamic Popular Scientific Movement, returned one member in both the 1996 and the 1999 Assembly elections.

Kuwait Democratic Forum, a loose pro-reform grouping which encompasses secular liberals and pan-Arabist Nasserists. It has been represented in the Assembly since 1992, two members being elected in 1996 and three in 1999.
Leadership. Yousef Naser Salah al-Shaiji

Kyrgyzstan

Capital: Bishkek   **Population:** 4,800,000 (2001E)

Having been a constituent republic of the USSR since December 1936, the independent Republic of Kyrgyzstan was proclaimed in August 1991; it became a sovereign member of the Commonwealth of Independent States in December 1991. Under the post-Soviet constitution of May 1993, as amended significantly by referendum in February 1996, the President is popularly elected for a five-year term and appoints and dismisses the Prime Minister (subject to parliamentary endorsement). The Soviet-era unicameral legislature was replaced in 1995 by a bicameral Supreme Council (*Zhorgorku Kenesh*), consisting of (i) a Legislative Assembly (*Myizam Chygaruu Jyiyny*) of 60 members directly elected for a five-year term, 45 in single-member constituencies and 15 from national party lists on a proportional basis subject to a 5% threshold; and (ii) a People's Representative Assembly (*El Okuldor Jyiyny*) of 45 members, also directly elected for a five-year term from single-member constituencies.

Legislative elections held on Feb. 20 and March 12, 2000, were contested by 11 of the 27 registered parties (most of the prominent opposition formations being barred on minor technicalities), although a large majority of the 420 candidates for the two chambers stood as independents. The conduct of the elections was strongly criticized by the OSCE's Office for Democratic Institutions and Human Rights (ODIHR) as unfair to opposition parties and there were many allegations of vote falsification. Confused and disputed results indicated that the vast majority of successful constituency candidates were non-partisans. The allocation of the 15 national list seats in the Legislative Assembly was as follows: Party of Communists of Kyrgyzstan (PKK) 5 (with 27.7% of the vote), Union of Democratic Forces (SDS) 4 (18.6%), Democratic Party of the Women of Kyrgyzstan 2 (12.7%), Political Party of War Veterans in Afghanistan 2 (8.0%), Socialist Party–Fatherland (*Ata-Meken*) 1 (6.5%), My Country Political Party (*Moya Strana*) 1 (5.0%). Of these, the PKK, the SDS, *Ata-Meken* and *Moya Strana* also won constituency seats, as did the Agrarian Labour Party of Kyrgyzstan, the People's Party and the Progressive-Democratic Party of Free Kyrgyzstan.

In July 1998 the Constitutional Court ruled that President Askar Akayev, who had been re-elected for a five-year term with around 72% of the vote in December 1995, was eligible to stand again in 2000, rejecting the opinion of many opposition leaders that this would amount to seeking a third term, which was not permitted under the constitution. Akayev was duly re-elected on Oct. 29, 2000, gaining 74.4% of the vote against five other candidates. Several nominees were excluded on technicalities, such as allegedly failing the obligatory Kyrgyz language test. There were again allegations of widespread ballot-rigging from Kyrgyz commentators as well as international observers.

Agrarian Labour Party of Kyrgyzstan
Agrarno-Trudovnaya Partiya Kyrgyzstana (ATPK)
Address. 120 Kievskaya Street, Bishkek
Telephone. (+996–3312) 215508
Leadership. Usun Sydykov (chairman)
The ATPK was founded in June 1995 to represent agro-industrial workers. In the February 2000 parliamentary elections it gained 2.5% of the vote and so failed to win any national list seats. However, it won at least one of the constituency contests. In March 2001 the ATPK became a component of a newly-formed People's Patriotic Movement of nine opposition parties.

Democratic Movement of Kyrgyzstan
Demokraticheskoye Dvizhenie Kyrgystana (DDK)
Address. 205 Abdymomunova Street, Bishkek
Telephone. (+996–3312) 277205
Leadership. E.A. Sarybayev (chairman)
Founded in May 1990, the DDK originally served as an umbrella for a number of pro-democracy and pro-independence groups, including the Mutual Help Movement (*Ashar*), Truth (*Aqi*) and the Osh Region Union (*Osh Aymaghi*). Following Kyrgyzstan's declaration of independence from the Soviet Union in August 1991, several components broke away to launch independent formations, leaving the rump DDK with a more nationalist identity. The DDK backed the election of Askar Akayev to the presidency in October 1991, but later withdrew its support because it opposed his policies of equal rights for all ethnic groups. The DDK formally constituted itself as a political party in June 1993.

Although enjoying considerable popular support, the

DDK was excluded from the February 2000 parliamentary elections on the grounds of alleged irregularities in its congress earlier that year.

Democratic Party of the Women of Kyrgyzstan
Demokraticheskaya Partiya Zhenshchin Kyrgyzstana (PDZK)
Address. 145 Baitik Batyr Street, Bishkek
Telephone. (+996–3312) 271681
Leadership. Tokon A. Shailiyeva (chairperson)
Founded in 1994 to encourage the participation of women in politics, the PDZK won the third largest share of the popular vote in the February 2000 parliamentary elections, gaining 12.7% and securing two seats. In August 2000, however, the Bishkek city court ruled that the party should forfeit these seats on the grounds of technical irregularities.

Dignity
Ar-Namys
Address. 60 Isanova Street, Bishkek
Leadership. Feliks Kulov (chairman)
The moderate centrist *Ar-Namys* was founded in autumn 1999 by former Vice-President Feliks Kulov, a former mayor of Bishkek, and quickly established itself as the main opposition party. It was harassed by the government in the run-up to the February 2000 parliamentary elections, which it was not allowed to contest because it had existed for less than a year. The leadership therefore took the decision to merge, at least temporarily, with the →Democratic Movement of Kyrgyzstan (DDK). However, the DDK was also excluded from the elections, so that Kulov stood as an

independent in a constituency contest. Although he headed the poll in the first round, he was defeated in the run-off in contested circumstances.

Quickly arrested, Kulov was tried on charges of abuse of authority when he was National Security Minister in 1997–98. Although he was acquitted in August 2000, the case was reopened by the authorities, who in January 2001 secured Kulov's conviction and sentencing to seven years' imprisonment. Meanwhile, *Ar-Namys* had backed the unsuccessful candidate of the →Socialist Party–Fatherland in the October 2000 presidential elections, on the understanding that if he had won Kulov would have become Prime Minister.

In February 2001 further charges were brought against Kulov, who was now in prison, related to his tenure of a regional governorship in 1995. The following month *Ar-Namys* became a leading component of a newly-formed People's Patriotic Movement of nine opposition parties.

My Country Political Party
Politicheskaya Partiya Moya Strana (MS)
Address. 110 Tynystanova Street, Bishkek
Leadership. J.O. Otorbayev (chairman)
Moya Strana was founded in January 1999 as a party broadly supportive of President Akayev. It contested the February 2000 parliamentary elections, winning 5.0% of the popular vote and securing one national list seat and at least three constituency seats.

Party of Communists of Kyrgyzstan
Partiya Kommunistov Kyrgyzstana (PKK)
Address. 31–6 Erkindik Blvd., Bishkek
Telephone. (+996–3312) 225685
Leadership. Absamat Masaliyev (first secretary)
The PKK was launched in June 1992 as the successor to the former ruling Kyrgyz Communist Party, which had been disbanded in August 1991. Registered in September 1992, the PKK attracted significant support and won representation in the February 1995 general elections. In 1999, amidst accusations of corruption and nepotism, the PKK experienced an internal split; this resulted in the formation of a small splinter group, the →Communist Party of Kyrgyzstan. Nevertheless, in the February 2000 parliamentary elections the PKK won more votes than any other party (27.7%), securing five national list seats and at least one constituency seat. In March 2001 the PKK became a component of a newly-formed People's Patriotic Movement of nine opposition parties.

People's Party
El (Bei Becharalai)
Address. 63 Razzakova Street, Bishkek
Telephone. (+996–3312) 264984
Leadership. Melis Eshimanov (chairman)
This party was formed in 1995 to represent disaffected intellectuals and students and by 2000 had become one of the largest opposition formations in Kyrgyzstan. The party was denied registration for the national list section of the February 2000 parliamentary elections and several of its nominees for constituency seats, including the then party chairman, Daniyar Usenov, were excluded from participation on administrative technicalities. However, at least two candidates associated with the party were successful in constituency contests. In March 2001 El became a component of a newly-formed People's Patriotic Movement of nine opposition parties.

Political Party of War Veterans in Afghanistan
Politicheskaya Partiya Veteranov Vojny v Afganistane (PPVVA)
Address. 4/A Chui pr., Bishkek
Leadership. A.D. Tashtanbekov (chairman)
Previously called the Democratic Party of Economic Unity, the PPVVA has an even longer full title encompassing an aspiration to represent veterans from other conflicts apart

from Afghanistan. Classified as a "pro-presidential" party, it won 8.0% of the popular vote and two national list seats in the February 2000 parliamentary elections.

Progressive-Democratic Party of Free Kyrgyzstan
Progressivno-Demokraticheskaya Partiya Erkin Kyrgyzstan (ErK)
Address. 205 Kirova Street, Bishkek
Telephone. (+996–3312) 277107
Leadership. Bakir Uulu Tursunbai (chairman)
The ErK (an acronym meaning "Will") was founded in 1991 as a splinter group of the →Democratic Movement of Kyrgyzstan on a platform of moderate nationalism and support for a liberal market economy. It was weakened in 1992 by the secession of the more nationalist *Ata-Meken* group (→Socialist Party–Fatherland), after which its attempts to build a pro-democracy alliance made little progress. The party has suffered frequent harassment from the government. In 1996 its founder, Topchubek Turgunaliyev (a former rector of the Bishkek Humanities University), was charged with defaming the honour of the President and imprisoned for four years (whereupon Amnesty International adopted him as a prisoner of conscience). He was released in November 1998 on parole.

ErK contested the February 2000 elections, in which it took 4.2% of the proportional vote and therefore failed to win national list representation, although at least one ErK candidate was successful in the constituency contests. The party was further weakened in May 2000 by the formation of the breakaway →Freedom party under Turgunaliyev's leadership.

Socialist Party–Fatherland
Socialisticheskaya Partiya Ata-Meken
Address. 64 Erkindik Blvd., Bishkek
Telephone. (+996–3312) 271779
Leadership. Omurbek Tekebayev (chairman)
Ata-Meken was founded in 1992 by a splinter nationalist faction of the →Progressive-Democratic Party of Free Kyrgyzstan. In the February 2000 parliamentary elections it gained 6.5% of the proportional vote and was allocated one national list seat, while at least one *Ata-Meken* candidate won a constituency seat. In the October 2000 presidential elections party leader Omurbek Tekebayev came second to the incumbent with 13.9% of the vote, having received backing from Honour (*Ar-Namys*) and other opposition parties. In March 2001 *Ata-Meken* became a leading component of a newly-formed People's Patriotic Movement of nine opposition parties.

Union of Democratic Forces
Soyuz Demokraticheskikh Sil (SDS)
Address. c/o Zhorgorku Kenesh, Bishkek
Leadership. Chingiz Aitmatov (leader)
Strongly pro-presidential in orientation, the SDS came second to the →Party of Communists of Kyrgyzstan in the February 2000 parliamentary elections, winning 18.6% of the vote and gaining four national list seats. It also won some eight constituency seats.

Other Parties

Agrarian Party of Kyrgyzstan, founded in 1993. In the February parliamentary 2000 elections it formed alliances with smaller parties and gained 2.4% of the vote but no seats.
Address. 96 Kievskaya Street, Bishkek
Leadership. Erkin Aliyev (chairman)

Banner National Revival Party (*Partiya Natsionalnogo Vozrozhdeniya Asaba*), named after a Kyrgyz military banner and launched in November 1991 by a nationalist faction of the →Democratic Movement of Kyrgyzstan, In the

February 2000 parliamentary elections it gained 1.5% of the vote but no seats.
Address. 26 Chui pr., Bishkek
Leadership. Chaprashty Bazarbayev (chairman)

Communist Party of Kyrgyzstan (*Kommunist Partiya Kyrgyzstana, KPK*), formed in August 1999 by a dissident faction of the →Party of Communists of Kyrgyzstan (PKK) which claimed that the PKK leader had failed to combat corruption.
Address. 241/12 Panfilova Street, Bishkek
Leadership. Klara Adzhibekova (chairperson)

Freedom (*Erkindik*), founded in May 2000 by a splinter group of the →Progressive-Democratic Party of Free Kyrgyzstan (ErK). In September 2000 the new party's chairman (the original founder of ErK) received a 16-year prison sentence (later reduced to 10 years) on being convicted of the "ideological leadership" of an assassination plot against President Akayev. He was granted clemency in September 2001.

Address. 115 Chamgarak Street, Bishkek
Leadership. Topchubek Turgunaliyev (chairman)

Justice (*Adilet*), also known as the Kyrgyzstan Republican Party, founded in November 1999 by leading scholars and political activists, including former Prime Minister Apas Jumagulov. Its aims are to promote "constructive cooperation" with other parties, a more equal distribution of power among state institutions and the development of the business sector. It formed part of the →Union of Democratic Forces in the 2000 parliamentary elections.
Leadership. Yuruslam Toichubekov (chairman)

Party of Spiritual Renaissance (*Manas-El*), advocating the unity of the Kyrgyz people, won 1.5% of the vote in the February 2000 elections.
Address. 4 Balyk-Kumar Street, Orto-Sai
Leadership. O.V. Zubkov (chairman)

Laos

Capital: Viang Chan (Vientiane)　　　　　　　　　　　　　　　　　　　　**Population:** 5,100,000 (2000E)

The Lao People's Democratic Republic (LPDR) was proclaimed on Dec. 20, 1975, bringing to an end the six-century-old Lao monarchy and installing in its place a communist regime modeled on those of the Soviet Union and the Democratic Republic of Vietnam. The victory of the Lao revolutionary movement (the *Pathet Lao*) climaxed a "30-year struggle" waged first against French colonialism, then against the government of the independent Kingdom of Laos. The structure of the new regime comprised the President (the head of state), the Council of Ministers presided over by the Prime Minister, and the Supreme People's Assembly (SPA), nominally the supreme law-making body, but in reality little more than a rubber-stamp parliament for legislation already decided upon by the leadership of the Lao People's Revolutionary Party (LPRP). All political power is exercised by the LPRP, the sole legal political organization.

The original Supreme People's Assembly was a nominated body and the first elections for the SPA were not held until 1989. The first task of the newly-elected 79-member SPA was to ratify the constitution of the LPDR, which was eventually promulgated in August 1991. Under its terms, the SPA was renamed the National Assembly (*Sapha Heng Xat*). The constitution spelled out the powers of the President, the government and the National Assembly. The only mention of the LPRP is in Article 1, which defines Laos as a "people's democratic state" under the leadership of the LPRP, as the "leading nucleus" of the political system. Members of the National Assembly are elected for five-year terms by all Lao citizens over the age of 18 years. The Assembly in turn elects the President, who appoints, with the endorsement of the National Assembly, the Prime Minister and ministers forming the government (also for a five-year period).

New elections for an expanded 85-member National Assembly were held under the terms of the new constitution on 20 December 1992. All 154 candidates who contested the election had been approved by the Lao Front for National Construction (LFNC), the broad umbrella organization of regional, social and even religious groups that in 1979 succeeded the Lao Patriotic Front (LPF). The LFNC is organized at the local, regional, provincial and national levels and is theoretically open to all Lao, party and non-party members alike. Its three principal tasks are to unify all ethnic groups, raise political consciousness, and mobilize the people to develop the national economy. Like the LPF before it, the LFNC remains under the close control of the LPRP.

The first President of the LPDR was Prince Souphanouvong. In August 1991, for reasons of ill-health, he was replaced by Kaison Phomvihan, who was concurrently leader of the LPRP. When Kaison died in November 1992, Nouhak Phoumsavan became state President. Nouhak retired in 1998 to make way for Gen. Khamtai Siphandon, who like Kaison added the state presidency to the presidency of the LPRP.

Elections took place on Dec. 21, 1997, for 99 seats in an enlarged National Assembly, held in accordance with the provisions of the Electoral Law passed in April 1997. Of the 159 candidates, all vetted by the LFNC, only four were not members of the LPRP. Of these four candidates, only one was elected. Voting is for a slate of candidates within 18 multi-member constituencies representing 16 provinces, one "special zone" (Xaisombun) and one municipality (Viang Chan). Members elected represented the three broad ethnic groups in the country: ethnic Lao and upland Tai (70), Austroasiatic-speaking tribal minorities (18) and Hmong-Mien and Sino-Tibetan speakers from northern Laos (11).

Lao People's Revolutionary Party (LPRP)
Phak Paxaxon Pativat Lao
Address. PO Box 662, Viang Chan
Telephone. (+856–21) 413515
Fax. (+856–21) 413513
Leadership. Gen. Khamtai Siphandon (president); Gen. Saman Vignaket, Gen. Choummali Xainyason, Thongsing Thammavong, Gen. Osakan Thammatheva, Bounnyang Vorachit, Gen. Sisavat Keobounphanh, Gen. Asang Laoly, Bouasone Bouphavanh, Thongloun Sisoulith & Maj.-Gen. Douangchay Phichit (other members of politburo)

The LPRP traces its origins back to the Indochinese Communist Party (ICP), founded in 1930 by Ho Chi Minh. The first two Lao members joined in 1935, but in 1951 the ICP was wound up to make way for national parties in Vietnam, Cambodia and Laos. A small nucleus of Lao communists formed the Lao People's Party (LPP) in March 1955, renamed the LPRP at its second party congress in 1972. By that time the party's membership had climbed to around 21,000. Throughout the "30-year struggle", successively the clandestine ICP, LPP and LPRP constituted the leading force directing the Lao Patriotic Front (LPF) and the Lao revolutionary movement (*Pathet Lao*). On three occasions (in 1957, 1962 and 1973) the LPF entered into coalition government with moderate neutralist and right-wing parties, until such time as the LPRP was able to rule alone. Upon its seizure of power in 1975, all other political parties were banned.

The LPRP has a structure similar to other communist parties. From its founding the party was led by its secretary-general, Kaison Phomvihan. At the fifth party congress in 1991, the secretary-general was re-designated president of the party. Upon Kaison's death in November 1992, Khamtai Siphandon became party president. The party leader presides over a political bureau (politburo) of between seven and 11 members elected by the central committee, whose membership has doubled in size from the original 27 to the present 53 members. Until its abolition in 1991, a small secretariat ran the day-to-day business of the party. Since then this task has been handled by the office of the party president and by the politburo.

The LPRP is poorly represented in many of the country's 11,500 villages, but has cells in all district towns and provincial capitals. It is also well represented in the Lao People's Army and in the bureaucracy. The party is organized on the basis of democratic centralism, with lower levels electing representatives to higher levels. Every five years the party elects representatives from throughout the country to the party congress. The central committee and political bureau are elected at the party congress, from among representatives to the congress.

At the sixth party congress in March 1996, the Lao People's Army powerfully increased its representation on the central committee, and especially on the politburo. Of the nine politburo members, six were serving or former generals and one was a former colonel. Gen. Sisavath Keobounphan was appointed as the country's first Vice-President. At the seventh party congress held in March 2001, army representation on the politburo was increased to eight out of eleven members. Following the congress, the National Assembly endorsed Gen. Khamtai Siphandon as state President, Gen. Choummali Xainyason as Vice-President, and former colonel Bounnyang Vorachit as Prime Minister presiding over a reshuffled ministry.

Dissident Groups

Since the seizure of power by the →Lao People's Revolutionary Party and declaration of the Lao People's Democratic Republic in December 1975, various organizations have been formed by anti-communist Lao who fled abroad. Some of these were short-lived; all supported more or less ineffective guerrilla operations mounted out of Thailand (and briefly China in the early 1980s). Broadly speaking, guerrilla operations fell into two groups. In northern Laos members of the Hmong ethnic minority who had previously been recruited to fight the US Central Intelligence Agency's "secret war" kept up their opposition to the new regime; while in the south guerrilla operations were mounted by ethnic Lao. In 1980 dissident groups formed the **United National Front for the Liberation of the Lao People,** though cooperation between Lao and Hmong was never close.

By the late 1980s, as Thai policy towards Laos changed from antagonism to economic co-operation, Thai authorities withdrew their support for Lao resistance movements. Resolution of the problem of Cambodia in the early 1990s, and particularly the return of Sihanouk as King, gave the Lao diaspora (primarily located in the United States, France, Australia and Canada) renewed hope for international support for restoration of the Lao monarchy. Ineffective armed struggle largely gave way to political agitation, though an organization known simply as the **Lao National Resistance** continued to function. A broad political front was formed called the **Movement for Democracy in Laos (MDL)**. Within this movement, political activists formed the **Laos Democracy Party,** with the elderly former Royal Lao government minister Inpeng Suryadhay as president, and the **Lao Liberal Democratic Party,** with Somnuk Phongsouvanh as president. The MDL has held a series of conferences in the USA of Lao representatives abroad. It supports the claim of Prince Soulivong Savang to the Lao throne. The Prince is the eldest son of the former Crown Prince of Laos, Vong Savang, who died under *Pathet Lao* imprisonment in 1980.

Latvia

Capital: Riga

Population: 2,370,000 (2000E)

Independent from 1920, Latvia was effectively annexed by the Soviet Union in August 1940 but repudiated its Soviet status in May 1990 and gained Soviet endorsement of its resumption of sovereignty in September 1991 as the Republic of Latvia. Reactivated in 1990, Latvia's 1922 constitution was fully restored in 1993, confirming the Republic as a parliamentary democracy in which the sovereign power of the people is exercised through a directly elected unicameral Parliament (*Saeima*). The head of state is the President, who is elected for a four-year term by the *Saeima*, an absolute majority of the total complement of 100 deputies being required. The appointment and continuance in office of the Prime Minister and other ministers is also subject to the *Saeima*'s consent. Members of the *Saeima* are elected from five electoral districts for a four-year term by universal, equal, direct, secret and non-compulsory suffrage of those aged 18 and over, on the basis of proportional representation but subject to at least 5% of the vote being obtained by a party.

Elections to the *Saeima* on 3 October 1998, resulted as follows: People's Party (TP), 24 seats (with 21.2% of the vote), Latvia's Way (LC) 21 (18.1%), Fatherland and Freedom–Latvian National Conservative Party (TB-LNNK) 17 (14.7%), National Harmony Party 16 (14.1%), Latvian Social Democratic Union (LSDA) 14 (12.8%), New Party (JP) 8 (7.3%). The LSDA became the Latvian Social Democratic Workers' Party (LSDSP) in May 1999, while the JP became the New Christian Party (JKP) in January 2001.

Fatherland and Freedom–Latvian National Conservative Party
Tevzemei un Brvibai–Latvijas Nacionala Konservativa Partija (TB–LNNK)

Address. Kaleju iela 10, Riga 1050
Telephone. (+371) 708–7273
Fax. (+371) 708–7268
Email. tb@tb.lv
Website. www.tb.lv
Leadership. Mâris Grinblats (chairman); Vladimirs Makarovs & Janis Straume (deputy chairmen); Vents Balodis (*Saeima* group chairman); Juris Saratovs (secretary-general)

The right-wing TB–LNNK was formed in June 1997 as a merger of the TB and the LNNK, intended to consolidate popular support for the right. However, some LNNK members rejected the merger and defected to the new →Latvian National Reform Party.

Of the two components, the TB was itself an alliance of several groups of the far right, reportedly in contact with right-wing extremists in Germany, and was viewed as being descended from the party of the *Waffen SS* at the time of the German occupation during World War II. The TB won 5.4% of the vote and six seats in the 1993 parliamentary elections, this tally rising to 11.9% and 14 seats in the 1995 elections. It thus became the strongest single party within the National Bloc alliance of conservative parties founded in September 1994. After the TB leader, Mâris Grinblats, had tried and failed to build a viable coalition government, the party joined a broad centre-right coalition headed by a non-party Prime Minister, with Grinblats becoming a Deputy Prime Minister and Education Minister.

The LNNK was founded in 1988 as the Latvian National Independence Movement (*Latvijas Nacionala Neatkaribas Kustiba*, LNNK), retaining the LNNK abbreviation when it became the Latvian National Conservative Party in June 1994. Ultra-nationalist and anti-Russian, the party wanted welfare benefits to be limited to ethnic Latvians and that no more than 25% of non-Latvians should be accorded Latvian citizenship. In the 1993 general elections the party won 15 seats on a 13.6% vote share; but its image was tarnished by association with the campaign rhetoric of a far-right party member of German origin, Joahims Zigerists, who was later expelled from the LNNK and formed the →Popular Movement for Latvia-Zigerists Party. On the President's invitation, Andrejs Krastiņš (then the LNNK associate chairman) attempted to form a right-wing government in August 1994, but was rebuffed by the *Saeima*. The LNNK was also a member of the opposition National Bloc launched in September 1994. However, for the autumn 1995 parliamentary elections it formed an unlikely alliance with the →Latvian Green Party, winning eight seats on a 6.3% vote share. It subsequently joined a broad centre-right coalition government under a non-party Prime Minister, in which Krastiņš (by now LNNK chairman) became a Deputy Prime Minister and Defence Minister.

Immediately after the TB–LNNK merger, the party in August 1997 successfully nominated Guntars Krasts as Prime Minister of a reconstituted centre-right coalition. In the October 1998 parliamentary elections, however, the TB–LNNK won only 17 of the 100 seats on a 14.7% vote share, well below combined vote of the component parties in 1995. The party also failed to get popular endorsement in a simultaneous referendum for its attempt to block recent legislation liberalizing Latvia's naturalization laws. It nevertheless joined a new centre-right coalition headed by

→Latvia's Way (LC), continuing in government when the →People's Party obtained the premiership in July 1999 and also when it reverted to the LC in April 2000.

Latvia's Way
Latvijas Ceļš (LC)

Address. Jauniela iela 25-29, Riga 1050
Telephone. (+371) 722–4162
Fax. (+371) 782–1121
Email. lc@lc.lv
Website. www.lc.lv
Leadership. Andris Berzins (leader); Andrejs Pantelejevs (chairman); Kristiana Libane (*Saeima* group chairperson)

The LC originated as an association of well-known pro-independence personalities, sponsored by the World Federation of Free Latvians and the influential Club 21 network, who came together prior to the 1993 parliamentary elections. Although evincing a centre-right political stance and a liberal-conservative socio-economic approach, the party was viewed by many Latvians as rooted in the ways of the Soviet era because of the earlier careers of many of its leading members. Nevertheless, its pivotal parliamentary position enabled it to lead successive post-independence coalition governments, its 32.4% vote share in 1993 making it the largest party in the *Saeima*, with 36 seats.

Paying the democratic penalty for government incumbency in difficult times, the LC slumped to 17 seats and 14.6% in the 1995 elections, although it continued in government in a broad centre-right coalition in which the *Saimnieks* Democratic Party (→Latvian Democratic Party) had the dominant position, with Maris Gailis of the LC becoming a Deputy Prime Minister and Environment and Regional Development Minister.

In the October 1998 elections the LC recovered somewhat to 21 seats and 18.1% of the vote, so that the LC's Vilis Kristopans became Prime Minister of a new centre-right coalition government. In July 1999 the LC surrendered the premiership to the →People's Party but recovered it in April 2000 in the person of Andris Berzins, the mayor of Riga, who became head of Latvia's ninth government in a decade of independence.

The LC is a member party of the Liberal International.

Latvian Democratic Party
Latvijas Demokratiska Partija (LDP)

Address. Maza Monetu iela 3, Riga 1050
Telephone. (+371) 728–7739
Fax. (+371) 728–8211
Email. ldp@ldp.lv
Website. www.ldp.lv
Leadership. Andris Ameriks (chairman)

The LDP is descended from the pre-war Democratic Centre Party (*Demokratiska Centra Partija*, DCP), which was relaunched in 1992 and won five seats on a 4.8% vote share in 1993. The DCP subsequently became the Democratic Party before merging with another group in 1994 under the *Saimnieks* Democratic Party (DPS) label, a Latvian term denoting a traditional source of authority (usually rendered in English as "Master"). Taking a pro-market position on economic issues and exhibiting a moderate national policy orientation, *Saimnieks* became the largest single party with 15.1% of the vote and 19 seats in the 1995 general elections. After an attempt by party chairman Ziedonis Čevers to form a coalition including the far-right →Popular Movement for Latvia–Zigerists Party had been thwarted by presidential opposition, *Saimnieks* settled for participation, as the strongest party, in a broad centre-right coalition headed by a non-party Prime Minister.

Subsequent tensions between *Saimnieks* and its coalition partners were apparent in the party's decision to nominate Ilga Kreituse (DPS Speaker of the *Saeima*) as its presidential candidate in 1996, in opposition to incumbent Guntis Ulmanis of the →Latvian Farmers' Union. In the parliamentary voting in June 1996, Kreituse was runner-up with 25 votes. The following month *Saimnieks* was strengthened by an agreement that it would absorb the small Republican Party (led by Andris Plotnieks) and by the decision of two deputies of the →National Harmony Party (TSP) to defect to its ranks. But it was weakened in early 1997 by a row over the irregular funding practices of then Finance Minister Aivars Kreituss, who was expelled from the party and who launched the rival →Labour Party. Shortly afterwards *Saimnieks* lost more adherents to the new →Latvian National Reform Party.

Saimnieks withdrew from the government coalition in April 1998, but was still punished in the October 1998 parliamentary elections, its vote share slumping to 1.6%, so that it failed to retain representation. Ćevers thereupon resigned as chairman and in December 1999 the party opted to drop the *Saimnieks* label and to become simply the Latvian Democratic Party (LDP).

Latvian Social Democratic Workers' Party
Latvijas Socialdemokratiska Stradnieku Partija (LSDSP)

Address. Bruninieku iela 29–31, Riga 1001
Telephone. (+371) 227–4039
Fax. (+371) 227–7319
Email. lsdsp@lis.lv
Website. www.lsdsp.lv
Leadership: Juris Bojars (chairman); Egils Baldzens (*Saeima* group chairman); Valdis Lauskis (general secretary)

Having been Latvia's leading party in the 1920s, the LSDSP was re-established in 1989 after 50 years' existence in exile. It fared badly in early post-independence elections, not least because social democratic forces were split. In October 1997 it joined with the (ex-communist) Latvian Social Democratic Party (LSDP) to launch the Latvian Social Democratic Union (LSDA), which in the October 1998 elections advanced strongly to 14 seats on a 12.8% vote share. In February 1999 the LSDA undertook to give qualified support to the incumbent centre-right coalition headed by →Latvia's Way. In May 1999 the LSDA components opted for collective reversion to the historic LSDSP designation.

The LSDSP is a member party of the Socialist International.

Latvian Socialist Party
Latvijas Socialistiska Partija (LSP)

Address. Burtnieku iela 23, Riga 1006
Telephone. (+371) 755–5535
Fax. (+371) 755–5535
Website. www.vide.lv/lsp
Leadership. Alfréds Rubiks (chairman)

The LSP was created in 1994 as successor to the Equal Rights Party (commonly known as Equality), which had been founded in 1993 to represent the interests of the non-Latvian population and had advocated the adoption of Russian as Latvia's second official language. At the time of the June 1993 general elections, the party's most prominent figure, Alfréds Rubiks (a former member of the Politburo of the USSR Communist Party), was in prison awaiting trial for supporting the abortive August 1991 coup by hardliners in Moscow. The party won seven seats on a 5.8% vote share, although Rubik's credentials as an elected deputy were rejected by the new *Saeima*.

In July 1995 Rubiks was sentenced to eight years' imprisonment for conspiring to overthrow the government in 1991. He was nevertheless placed at the head of the candidates'

list of the new LSP for the autumn 1995 elections, in which the party won five seats on a 5.6% vote share. Still in prison, Rubiks was a candidate in the June 1996 *Saeima* elections for a new President, receiving five votes. Following his release in late 1997, he was elected chairman of the LSP, shortly after the party's five deputies had formed a parliamentary alliance with the →National Harmony Party (TSP).

For the October 1998 elections the LSP joined an alliance with the TSP and two ethnic Russian groupings called "For Human Rights in a United Latvia", but it failed to secure registration in time to run under that label. The alliance's candidates therefore stood under the TSP banner, winning 16 seats on a 14.1% vote share and becoming the largest component of the opposition to the succeeding centre-right coalition. The LSP itself took four seats.

National Harmony Party
Tautas Saskanas Partija (TSP)

Address. Lačpleša iela 60, Riga 1010
Telephone (+371) 728–9913
Fax. (+371) 728–1619
Leadership. Janis Jurkans (chairman and parliamentary leader)

The TSP consists of the residue of the Harmony for Latvia–Rebirth (*Saskana Latvijai–Atdzimana*) grouping following a split in 1994 which led to the creation of the now defunct Political Union of Economists. It won six seats on a 5.6% vote share in the autumn 1995 elections, on a platform advocating harmony between Latvians and non-Latvians with guaranteed rights for minorities. In July 1996 the TSP *Saeima* contingent was reduced to four (one below the number required for official recognition as a group) by the decision of two members to join the *Saimnieks* Democratic Party (→Latvian Democratic Party). However, it was strengthened in September 1997 by a parliamentary alliance with the five-strong →Latvian Socialist Party (LSP) group led by Alfreds Rubiks, who had been leader of the Soviet-era Latvian Communist Party.

For the October 1998 elections the TSP created an alliance called "For Equal Rights in a United Latvia", which included the LSP and two ethnic Russian groupings, but failed to secure registration in time to run under that label. The alliance's candidates therefore stood under the TSP banner, winning 16 seats on a 14.1% vote share and becoming the largest component of the opposition to the succeeding centre-right coalition.

By late 2000 serious divisions had developed within the TSP-led alliance over the LSP's advocacy of civil disobedience by ethnic Russians against language law regulations.

New Christian Party
Jauna Kristigo Partija (JKP)

Address. c/o Saeima, 11 Jēkaba, Riga 1811
Email. tatjanaj@saeima.lv
Leadership. Guntis Dislers (chairman); Ingrida Udre (*Saeima* group chairperson)

The centre–left JKP was founded as the New Party (JP) in March 1998 and renamed in January 2001. Popular composer Raimond Pauls was principal founder and first chairman of the JP, which drew support from the upwardly-mobile young for its pro-market, pro-Western policies combined with an inclusive approach to ethnic Russians (provided they learnt Latvian). In the October 1998 parliamentary elections, however, the JP won only eight of the 100 seats (with 7.3% of the vote), being upstaged by the even newer →People's Party (TP). It nevertheless became the most junior partner in a centre-right coalition government headed by →Latvia's Way.

In February 2001 the JP withdrew from the government, claiming that it had failed to honour pledges to introduce new laws on pensions and property taxes. The following month the JP transformed itself into the JKP, with clergyman Guntis Dislers as chairman, in what was seen as a move to attract support from existing Christian democratic parties.

People's Party
Tautas Partija (TP)
Address. c/o Saeima, 11 Jëkaba, Riga 1811
Telephone. (+371) 708–7222
Fax. (+371) 708–7289
Email. tautpart@saeima.lv
Website. www.tautaspartija.lv
Leadership. Andris Skéle leader); Andris Díçle (chairman); Vineta Muizniece (*Saeima* group chairperson); Karlis Greiškalns (general secretary)

The centre-right TP was officially launched in May 1998 by Andris Skéle, a former businessman who had been non-party Prime Minister in 1995–97 attempting to lead a series of fractious centre-right coalitions. Advocating family values and national regeneration in the October 1998 parliamentary elections, the TP emerged as narrowly the largest party, winning 24 of the 100 seats on a 21.2% vote share. It nevertheless went into opposition to a coalition headed by →Latvia's Way (LC), until July 1999, when Skéle returned to the premiership at the head of majority centre-right coalition. Skéle was forced to resign in April 2000 over a paedophilia scandal (later being cleared of allegations against him personally), whereupon the TP again became a junior partner in a coalition headed by the LC.

The TP is an associate member of the European People's Party.

Popular Movement for Latvia–Zigerists Party
Tautas Kustiba Latvijai–Zigerists Partija (TKL-ZP)
Address. Gertrudes iela 64, Riga
Telephone. (+371) 721–6762
Leadership. Joahims Zigerists (chairman)

The radical right-wing TKL–ZP, commonly referred to as *Latvijai*, was founded in 1995 by Joahims Zigerists, who had been elected to the *Saeima* in 1993 as a candidate of the Latvian National Conservative Party (LNNK) (→Fatherland and Freedom) but had later been expelled from the LNNK after a court conviction in Germany for incitement to racial hatred. Zigerists had been born and brought up in Germany (as Joachim Siegerist) but claimed Latvian nationality through his father, an ethnic German who had fled from Latvia as the Red Army approached at the end of World War II. In August 1995 Zigerists was expelled from the *Saeima* for poor attendance and was also barred from standing in the autumn 1995 general elections because of his inability to speak much Latvian. His party nevertheless took an impressive third place, winning 14.9% of the vote and 16 *Saeima* seats. A post-election move by the *Saimnieks* Democratic Party to draw the TKL–ZP into a government coalition was successfully resisted by President Ulmanis.

In *Saeima* elections for the state presidency in June 1996, the TKL–ZP candidate, Imants Liepa, took third place with 14 votes. In the same month the TKL–ZP parliamentary group was weakened by the departure of six deputies on the grounds that the party had become "undemocratic". Further defections followed. In the October 1998 parliamentary elections the party won only 1.7% of the vote and therefore no seats.

Other Parties

There were some 50 other registered parties in Latvia as at mid-2001. The following listing focuses on those which contested the 1998 parliamentary elections.

Christian People's Party (*Kristigo Tautas Partija, KTP*), formed in February 1996 as successor to the residue of the Latvian Popular Front (*Latvijas Tautas Fronte*, LTF), which had led Latvia's independence campaign but had failed to win seats in the 1993 and 1995 elections.
Leadership. Uldis Augstkalns

Labour Party (*Darba Partija, DP*), launched in March 1997 by Aivars Kreituss and his wife Ilga Kreituse after he had been expelled from the *Saimnieks* Democratic Party (→Latvian Democratic Party) and she had resigned, thereby quickly losing the speakership of the *Saeima*. Favouring retention of a state economic role, the DP contested the 1999 elections in alliance with the →Latvian Christian Democratic Union and the →Latvian Green Party, their vote share of only 2.3% yielding no seats.
Leadership. Aivars Kreituss (chairman)

Latvian Christian Democratic Union (*Latvijas Kristigo Demokratu Savieniba, LKDS*), founded in March 1991 and descended from pre-war parties of similar orientation that had substantial parliamentary representation. Having won six seats and 5% of the vote in 1993, the LKDS was allied with the →Latvian Farmers' Union in the autumn 1995 elections, in which the alliance took eight seats and 6.3% of the vote, subsequently participating in government at junior level. In the 1998 elections the LKDS was allied with the →Labour Party and the →Latvian Green Party, the alliance winning 2.3% of the vote. The LKDS is affiliated to the Christian Democrat International.
Address. 28 Jekaba iela, Riga 1811
Telephone. (+371) 732–3534
Fax. (+371) 783–0333
Leadership. Talavs Jundzis (chairman)

Latvian Farmers' Union (*Latvijas Zemnieku Savieniba, LZS*), the modern descendant of a similarly-named organization founded in 1917 and prominent in the inter-war period until banned in 1934. The party is primarily devoted to defending rural interests, taking a somewhat conservative position on the nationality issue. It won 12 seats in the June 1993 general elections (with 10.6% of the vote), following which Guntis Ulmanis (a former chairman of the Latvian Supreme Soviet) was the successful LZS candidate in the July parliamentary election of a new President. For the autumn 1995 elections the LZS entered into alliance with the →Latvian Christian Democratic Union and the Democratic Party of Latgale, winning eight seats on a 6.3% vote share. It subsequently joined a broad centre-right coalition government under a non-party Prime Minister and in June 1996 Ulmanis was re-elected President with the backing of most of the coalition parties, serving until mid-1999. In the 1998 parliamentary elections the LZS slumped to 2.5% of the vote, ceasing to be represented.
Address. 2 Republikas laukums, Riga 1010
Telephone. (+371) 732–7163
Leadership. Augusts Brigmanis (chairman)

Latvian Green Party (*Latvijas Zala Partija, LZP*), founded in 1990, captured only 1.2% of the vote and no seats in the 1993 election, although a Green became Minister of State for the Environment in the new government headed by →Latvia's Way. The Greens also obtained representation at junior ministerial level in the broad centre-right coalition government formed after the 1995 elections, which it had contested in alliance with the Latvian National Conservative Party. The Greens contested the 1998 elections in alliance with the →Labour Party and the →Latvian Christian Democratic Union, their 2.3% vote share yielding no seats.
Address. Kalnciema iela 30, Riga 1046
Telephone. (+371) 761–2626
Fax. (+371) 761–4927
Leadership. Indulis Emsis

Latvian National Reform Party (*Latvijas Nacionala Reformu Partija, LNRP*), launched in mid-1997 by then EU Affairs Minister Aleksandrs Kirsteins, hitherto a member of →Fatherland and Freedom–Latvian National Conservative Party, with the aim of accelerating Latvia's preparations for EU and NATO membership. It failed to make any impact in the 1998 elections.
Leadership. Aleksandrs Kirsteins (chairman)

Latvian Unity Party (*Latvijas Vienibas Partija, LVP*), established in 1994 by a group of orthodox Communists opposed to rapid economic and social change. Its 7.1% and eight seats in the 1995 parliamentary elections gave it a pivotal role in the formation of a broadly conservative coalition. Appointed a Deputy Prime Minister and Agriculture Minister, LVP leader Alberis Kauls lasted only eight months, being forced to resign in May 1996 over his persistent criticism of the coalition's agricultural policy and being replaced by LVP deputy leader Roberts Dilba. The party failed to win representation in 1998.

Leadership. Alberis Kauls (chairman)

Lebanon

Capital: Beirut

Population: 4,079,000 (2000)

The Republic of Lebanon gained independence from France in 1944. A "National Covenant", agreed in 1943, determined that power should be allocated between the country's main religious communities on the basis of their relative numerical strength according to a (disputed) 1932 census. The President is by convention a Maronite Christian, the Prime Minister a Sunni Muslim and the Speaker of the unicameral National Assembly (*Majlis al-Umma/Assemblée Nationale*) a Shia Muslim. Between 1975 and 1990 civil war caused immense damage to Lebanon. Rooted in traditional inter-communal rivalries and exacerbated by foreign political and military interventions, the conflict undermined central government authority and enhanced the power of contending militias and paramilitary factions.

Constitutional amendments were approved in September 1990, within the framework of the 1989 Taif Accord. Designed to restore civil peace, the Accord upgraded the executive powers of the (Sunni) Prime Minister and the Cabinet, gave greater powers to the (Shia) Speaker, and reduced the powers of the (Maronite) President. A 1992 electoral law added 20 seats in the National Assembly, to achieve equal representation of Christian and Muslim communities, rather than the previous ratio of 6:5 in favour of the Christians. Few Palestinians are Lebanese citizens and accordingly, although they make up about 10% of the population, they are barred from national politics.

The subsequent return of relative peace to most of Lebanon, with a strong Syrian military presence and the disarming of militia groups, enabled general elections to be held for the first time in 20 years. Several militias reconstituted themselves as political parties. However, communal allegiances tended to persist, despite calls for national unity.

Voting for the 128-member Assembly was conducted in stages between August and October 1992. Thirty-four seats were reserved for Maronite Christians (despite the Christian parties' boycott), 27 for Sunnis and 27 for Shias. Remaining seats were shared among smaller religious denominations (Greek Orthodox, Greek Catholics, Druzes, Armenian Orthodox, Armenian Catholics, Alaouites and Protestants). Most Christian parties refused to participate, so Syrian nominees made up the numbers. New elections were held in 1996 and again in 2000. Meanwhile, Lebanon held local elections for the first time in 35 years, in 1998. However, polling did not take place in the south, where fighting still simmered between *Hizballah* and Israel's allies.

The National Assembly elected Elias Hrawi as President for a six-year term in November 1989, artificially extended by two years in 1995. In November 1998, former army chief Emile Lahoud replaced him as president. Greater power, though, resided in the construction magnate, Rafiq Hariri, who took office as Prime Minister in 1992.

Lebanese political parties maintain their independent structure, but at election time they reformulate themselves as electoral blocs or lists divided by region. (The six electoral districts or *muhafazat* were originally North Lebanon, Beirut, Mount Lebanon, Beka', Nabatiyya and South Lebanon; some were later subdivided, resulting in the current 14 *muhafazat*). This approach, overseen by Syria, forces politicians to draw support from outside their usual ethno-religious support base. The correlation between parties and lists is not distinct and anti-Syrian dissidents charge that both "government" and "opposition" blocs are dominated by Damascus.

Given the weakness of political parties, powerful figures tend to command the allegiance of looser blocs of MPs. After he took office in 1992, Prime Minister Hariri counted on the loyalty of up to 40 MPs and the Speaker, Nabi Berri, on some 25 MPs. Together, Hrawi, Hariri and Berri were referred to as "the troika". More Christians participated in the 1996 elections, but many still accused Syria of bribing voters, rigging lists and manipulating constituency boundaries to divide Christian power bases.

In 1998 Hariri lost power to Salem al-Hoss amidst economic turmoil and allegations of corruption but was re-elected Prime Minister after elections on August 27 and September 3, 2000. The departure of Israeli troops from southern Lebanon in March 2000 prompted calls for 35,000 Syrian troops to leave the rest of the country.

Lists that participated in the 2000 elections

The following lists won seats in the 2000 elections to the 128-member National Assembly, in addition to which 20 non-partisans were elected.

Resistance and Development, formed mainly by the rival Shia parties, →*Hizballah* and →*Amal,* and led by Nabi Berri, it took 23 seats in 2000 and forms the largest bloc in the Assembly. *Hizballah*'s attempt to run independently in 1996 were reportedly quashed by Syrian fiat. In 2000 the bloc dominated the polls in South Lebanon and Nabatieh.

Al-Karamah (Dignity), a combination of three electoral

lists in Beirut, allied with Rafiq Hariri, it won 18 out of 19 possible seats, thus displacing rival lists led by sitting Prime Minister Salim al-Hoss. 106 out of 128 Assembly members subsequently supported a new Hariri administration.

Baalbeck-Hermel al Ii'tilafiah (Baalbeck-Hermel Coalition), the →Progressive Socialist Party leader Walid Jumblatt led this bloc, also backed by →Hizballah. It won nine out of 10 allocated seats in this mostly Shia area.

Al Jabhar Al Nidal Al Watani (National Defence Front, JNW), took 8 seats.

Wahdal al Jabal (Mountain Union, WJ), won 7 seats.

Ii'tilafiah (Coalition), contesting a northern district dominated by the anti-Syrian Christian Samir Geagea, this list won 6 out of 11 seats.

Al-Karal (Decision), took 6 seats in West Beka'.

Al Kitla Al Chaabi-Elias Shaft (People's Front-Elias Shaft), took 5 seats.

Al Wifah Al Matni (Metn Accord, WM), this list represents the Interior Minister Michel Murr and took 5 seats.

Al Karamah wah Tajdid (Dignity and Renewal, KT), led by Suleiman Franjieh and Najib Mikati, this list won 5 seats, eating into support for Omar Karami in his Tripoli and Zaghorta fiefdom.

Al Karal al Chaabi (Popular Decision), this list headed by Fouad Turk staged an opposition upset in Zahle, taking 3 seats.

Al Wifac wal Tajdid (Consensus and Renewal), based in the Baabda-Aley district of Mount Lebanon, led by Wajdi Mrad and Talal Arslan, Druze rival to the →Progressive Socialist Party's Walid Jumblatt; took 3 seats.

Al Irada al Chaabia (Popular Will), took 3 seats.

Al Karamah al Wataniyah (National Dignity), took 2 seats, supporting Omar Karami in Tripoli and Zaghorta.

Al Tawafoc al Watani (National Understanding), won 1 seat.

Al Kitla al Chaabi-Fouad el Turk (People's Front – Fouad Turk, KC-T), won 1 seat.

Lubnan (Lebanon), won 1 seat.

Al Huriya (Freedom), won 1 seat

Political Parties

Amal
Leadership. Nabi Berri
Amal ("Hope") was founded by Imam Musa Sadr, a charismatic Iranian-educated Shia preacher, as a political adjunct to his Movement of the Downtrodden. Nabi Berri assumed the leadership after Imam Sadr "disappeared" in Libya in 1978. Although a part of the Muslim leftist and Palestinian Alliance in the post-1975 civil war, *Amal* subsequently focused more on its own Shia constituents, and clashed during the 1980s with other Muslims, Palestinians, and the Christian right. Increasingly the leadership aligned itself with Syria. It also adopted a more secular orientation, and fought for the Shia turf with its religiously zealous rival, the Iranian-backed →*Hizballah*.

In October 1992, following legislative elections in which *Amal* made an impressive showing in the south, Berri was elected as Speaker of the National Assembly. Contesting the 2000 elections together with the rival *Hizballah*, *Amal* helped secure their joint →Resistance and Development Bloc a solid 23-seat presence in the National Assembly.

Baath Arab Socialist Party (BASP)
Hizb al-Baath al-Arabi al-Ishtiraki
Leadership. Abd al-Majid Rafii (secretary-general of pro-Iraqi wing); Abdullah al-Amin (secretary-general of pro-Syrian wing)
Originally established as the Lebanese regional command of the pan-Arab *Baath* ("Renaissance"), the BASP soon split into competing pro-Iraqi and pro-Syrian factions. Neither wing enjoys the strength of the party in Iraq or Syria. After civil war began in 1975 the BASP joined the left-wing National Movement, and in 1984 joined a new Muslim leftist National Democratic Front. The pro-Syrian wing has eclipsed the pro-Iraqi element, thanks in part to the presence of Syrian forces in Lebanon.

Hizballah
Leadership. Sheikh Sa'id Hassan Nasrallah (secretary-general); Sheikh Naim Qassem (deputy secretary-general)
Hizballah (or *Hezbollah*), meaning "Party of God" in Arabic, began as a militant, pro-Iranian Shia Muslim group in 1982, opposed to both Israel and the West. Affiliated groups were involved in numerous kidnappings, suicide bombings and other violence. In the 1980s *Hizballah* fought against its pro-Syrian and more secular Shia rival, →*Amal*. Meanwhile *Hizballah's* armed wing, *Al Moqawama al Islamia* (The Islamic Resistance) fought Israel and her allies, the South Lebanese Army (SLA). A cross-border strike by Israeli forces in February 1992 killed *Hizballah* secretary-general, Abbas Musawi.

Hizballah survived a massive Israeli attack called Operation Grapes of Wrath in April 1996, and was forced to negotiate indirectly with the old enemy. Sporadic fighting continued regardless and eventually Israeli forces were persuaded to vacate their "southern security zone" in March 2000. This was hailed as a victory for Lebanon as a whole and *Hizballah* in particular. However, the triumph raised questions over whether *Hizballah* would now at last disarm, as other militias had done. Also, its evident reluctance to surrender control of the south to the National Army, and its pledge to prosecute defeated SLA officers for treason, worried Beirut.

Beyond the battle zone, *Hizballah* grew into a more broad-based, populist group. Enjoying generous sponsorship from its Iranian supporters, its widespread health and welfare facilities operated as alternatives to Lebanon's still weak state institutions, especially in its three strongholds: the south, Beqa' Valley and West Beirut.

Musawi's death exacerbated an internal power struggle, with the more pragmatic Sheikh Hassan Nasrallah triumphing over Hassan Tufayli to become secretary-general in 1992. In the late 1990s Tufayli set up a breakaway group in the Beqa' Valley, which clashed with *Hizballah*. Tufayli supporters failed to win much support against the parent party in the 2000 elections in Baalbek. Sheikh Mohammed Fadlallah remained the group's spiritual mentor throughout. *Hizballah* also began building alliances with Christian groups, partly allaying earlier fears that it was seeking to institute an Islamic *shari'a* state over all of Lebanon.

While not supporting the Taif Accord, the group accepted it as a "bridge to a internal peace" and non-sectarianism. *Hizballah* first participated as a political party in the 1992 elections, contributing, with *Amal,* to a significant Shia representation in the National Assembly. The two parties contested the 1996 elections jointly, as the →Resistance and Development Bloc; in 2000, the Bloc won 23 seats in the National Assembly, of which nine belonged to *Hizballah*. Relations between Hariri and *Hizballah* cooled as cross-border raids mounted since 1998. However, *Hizballah's* national prestige rose after Israel's departure in 2000, and Nasrallah was unanimously re-elected leader in August 2001.

Lebanese Forces Party (LFP)
Website. www.lebanese-forces.org

The Lebanese Forces (LFP) began as a wing of the →Phalangist militia, but under the leadership of Samir Geagea constituted itself as a party in its own right in 1990, opposed to the Taif Accord. In March 1994 the government proscribed the LFP. Geagea was arrested the following month in connection with the assassination in 1990 of Dany Chamoun, leader of the →National Liberal Party, and was sentenced to life imprisonment in June 1995. In 1998 some 300 LFP officials won seats in municipal elections, and in 1999 the LFP in the "diaspora" established a temporary political council under Dr. Joseph Gebeily.

National Bloc
Kutla Al-Wataniyah
Leadership. Carlos Edde

A conservative Maronite Christian party founded in 1943 by a former President, Emile Edde, the National Bloc opposed basic changes in Lebanon's traditional power structure, and seeks to exclude the military from politics. It was one of the few political movements not to run a militia during the civil war. Raymond Edde led the Bloc from 1949 until his death in Parisian exile in 2000. His nephew and successor, Carlos Edde, advocates more "co-ordination" with Syria, and backed Jumblatt's list in the Chouf during the 2000 elections.

National Liberal Party
Hizb al-Ahrar alWatani
Parti National Liberal (PNL)
Address. rue du Liban, Beirut
Leadership. Dory Chamoun

Founded in 1958 by Camille Chamoun at the end of his term as President of Lebanon, the PNL lost ascendancy among Maronite Christians to its Phalangist Party rivals in the late 1970s. Having assumed the party leadership from his father in the mid-1980s, Dany Chamoun was assassinated in 1990 (for which murder the then →Phalangist militia leader was convicted in June 1995). He was succeeded by his brother, Dory, in May 1991. The party has pressed for the withdrawal of Syrian forces from the country and has argued that a federal system is the only way to preserve a single Lebanese state. The PNL boycotted the polls in 1992, 1996 and 2000.

Phalangist Party
Kata'eb
Leadership. Georges Saade (party president)

The Phalangist Party is a right-wing, originally quasi-fascist Maronite Christian organization, founded in 1936 by Pierre Gemayel. He dominated its affairs until his death in 1984. Gemayel was succeeded as party leader by his vice-president, Elie Karameh, who was replaced by the present leader in 1986. From the early 1970s the party built up militias to counter the growing strength and militancy of Lebanese Muslim leftists and Palestinian groups. Phalangists spearheaded the Christian side in clashes leading to the outbreak of civil war in 1975 and, following subsequent rivalry with the →National Liberal Party (PLN), emerged at the end of the decade as the dominant Christian formation. From 1982 to 1988 the Phalangist's pro-American leader Amin Gemayel was Lebanon's President.

Georges Saade helped negotiate the Taif Accord on national reconciliation in 1989. However, the party backed the Maronite Christian boycott of the 1992 elections, demanding that Syrian troops withdraw from Lebanon before it would contest seats. It participated in 1996 polls, but cried foul when it lost out to Syrian-backed candidates.

Progressive Socialist Party (PSP)
Hizb al-Taqaddumi al-Ishtiraki
Parti Socialiste Progressiste (PSP)
Address. PO Box 11–2893–1107–2120, Beirut
Telephone. (+961–1) 303455
Fax. (+961–1) 301231
Email. secretary@psp.org.lb
Website. www.psp.org.lb
Leadership. Walid Jumblatt (president); Sharif Fayad (general secretary)

Founded in 1949, the PSP draws most support from the Druze, a Muslim sub-sect, and advocates democratic socialism. Following the outbreak of civil war in 1975, the PSP helped create the National Movement of Muslim leftists and Palestinians against the →Phalangists and other right-wing Christian formations. Walid Jumblatt assumed the leadership on the assassination of his father Kamal in 1977. He has fended off threats from the rival Arslan family. The PSP fought against the Israeli invasions of 1978 and 1982. It then consolidated control of the Chouf Mountains, the Druze heartland. It created a separate civil administration there, yet never fulfilled its threat to secede from Lebanon altogether.

The PSP also became increasingly hostile to the Shia →Amal movement, with which PSP forces engaged in heavy fighting in 1987. The party participated in the 1992 National Assembly elections (in which Druze candidates achieved eight seats), and subsequent elections in 1996 and 2000. Its leader has served as a minister in successive governments, and was responsible for repatriating refugees uprooted by the 16-year civil war. In 2001 Jumblatt marked a new departure by forging a joint Druze-Christian front against Syrian "occupation" with the Maronite Patriarch, Nasrallah Sfeir.

The PSP is a member party of the Socialist International.

Other Groupings

Ahbash (officially, the Society of Islamic Philanthropic Projects) is a quasi-political Sufi grouping popular amongst Sunnis, but regarded as a Syrian front by foes.

Free National Current (FNC) (*Al-Tayyar al Watani*), represents supporters of the popular Gen. Michel Aoun, who acted as Prime Minister until ousted by the Syrians in 1990 and is currently in exile in Paris. In his absence, Nadim Lteifacts as the FNC's national co-ordinator. The FNC took part in municipal elections in 1998 and has organized street demonstrations against the Syrian troop presence since April 2000. It claims support across sectarian divisions, and favours a national unity government.
Website. www.generalaoun.org

Islamic Unification Movement (*Tawhid Islami*), a Sunni Muslim group with a religious orientation, formed in Tripoli in 1982, led by Sheikh Said Shaban until his death in 1998.

Lebanese Christian Democratic Union (*Union Chrétienne Démocrate Libanaise,* UCDL), a member of the Christian Democrat International.
Address. 23 Benoit Barakat Street, Jabre Building 3rd Floor, Badaro, Beirut
Telephone. (+961–1 386444
Fax. (+961–1) 383 583
Email. george@lawjabre.com
Leadership. George Jabre

Lebanese Communist Party (*Hizb Al-Shuyui Al-Lubnani*), dates from 1924 but was legalized only in 1970; primarily Christian during the first 50 years of its existence (drawing support from the Greek Orthodox community in particular), the party participated in leftist Muslim fronts in the post-1975 civil war, although it often clashed with the Shia →Amal movement; party secretary-general Faruq Dahruj narrowly failed to win a seat in West Beka' in the 2000 elections.

Address. POB 633, rue Al-Hout, Beirut

Website. www.communistparty-lb.org

Leadership. Faruq Dahruj (secretary-general)

Syrian Social National Party (*Parti Socialiste Nationaliste Syrien, PSNS*), organized in 1932 and banned between 1962 and 1969. Led by Dawoud Baz, it advocates a "Greater Syria" embracing Lebanon, Syria, Iraq, Jordan and Palestine.

Website. www.ssnp.com

Waad Party, formed in 1991 by breakaway members of the →Lebanese Forces militia and led by Elie Hobeika, a Syrian loyalist and ex-minister, formerly allied to Israel. Hobeika was accused of carrying out the Sabra and Chatilla massacre of 1982. In 1996 his "list" carried the constituency of South Metn, amidst allegations of ballot-stuffing.

Lesotho

Capital: Maseru

Population: 2,143,000 (2000E)

The Kingdom of Lesotho became an independent hereditary monarchy in 1966. Between 1970, when the constitution was suspended, and the beginning of 1986 the country was ruled by a Council of Ministers headed by Chief Leabua Jonathan, and the power of the King was considerably eroded. In January 1986 the armed forces staged a bloodless coup, executive and legislative powers being conferred upon the King, although a Military Council became the effective ruling body. In March 1986 all political activity was banned. In March 1990 the chairman of the Military Council removed executive and legislative powers from King Moshoeshoe II, who went into exile. His son, Letsie III, was elected King by an assembly of chiefs.

Following changes in the military leadership in April 1991 a new constitution was instituted, providing for the re-establishment of a bicameral parliament consisting of a directly-elected National Assembly and a Senate made up of chiefs and nominated members. Executive power is vested in the Prime Minister, as leader of the majority parliamentary party, and the Cabinet appointed by the Prime Minister. In multi-party elections held in March 1993 the Basotho Congress Party (BCP) won all the seats in the National Assembly. The following month the BCP leader, Ntsu Mokhehle, was sworn in as Prime Minister and the Military Council was dissolved.

In August 1994 King Letsie III suspended the constitution, dissolving the National Assembly and dismissing the BCP government, and attempted to install a non-elected transitional council. However, following the intervention of South Africa and other regional powers, then agreed to restore the elected government. Following Letsie's voluntary abdication, Moshoeshoe II was restored to the throne in January 1995 but was killed in a car accident in January 1996. Letsie III then returned to the throne, having given a formal undertaking not to involve the monarchy in politics. In 1997 the Prime Minister and 37 other members of the National Assembly resigned from the BCP and formed a new party, the Lesotho Congress for Democracy (LCD), which became the party of government.

At the next legislative elections, on May 23, 1998, the voting age was lowered from 21 to 18 years and the number of seats in the National Assembly was increased to 80, elected from single-member constituencies by majority vote. The LCD, with 60.7% of the vote, won 79 seats, while the Basotho National Party, with 24.5%, won only one seat. The outcome led to widespread protests, and in September 1998 the government invited South African and Botswanan troops into Lesotho to counter a perceived danger of a military coup. In December 1998 a multi-party Interim Political Authority, backed by expert international mediators, was set up to draft a new electoral system for Lesotho and in particular to address opposition calls for the introduction of an element of proportional representation. Following several postponements of target election dates, Lesotho's electoral authorities said in March 2001 that they did not expect the process of voter registration to be completed before the end of January 2002.

Basotho Congress Party (BCP)

Address. POB 111, Maseru

Leadership. Molapo Qhobela (leader)

The BCP was formed as a pan-Africanist and left-wing party in the early 1950s. Its refusal to co-operate with the government of Chief Jonathan following the suspension of the 1970 constitution led to a factional split. One wing of the party, led by Gerard Ramoreboli, accepted seats in an appointed interim National Assembly. The main branch, led from exile by Ntsu Mokhehle, continued to oppose the Jonathan regime, launching numerous armed attacks on progovernment targets, allegedly with South African support. Mokhehle was allowed by the Military Council to return to Lesotho in the late 1980s. The BCP won a landslide victory in the multi-party elections in March 1993, securing all 65 seats in the National Assembly, and the military regime

relinquished power to a civilian government headed by Mokhehle.

In June 1997, after a long period of bitter rivalry between different factions of the party, Mokhehle resigned from the BCP and formed the →Lesotho Congress for Democracy with the backing of 37 other members of the National Assembly. Molapo Qhobela, who had been dismissed from Mokhehle's Cabinet in May 1996, was elected as the new leader of the BCP and thus became the leader of the official opposition in the National Assembly. In the general election of May 1998 the BCP failed to win any seats.

Basotho National Party (BNP)

Address. POB 124, Maseru

Leadership. Justin Metsing Lekhanya (leader)

The BNP was founded in the late 1950s as the Basutoland

National Party (changing its name at independence in 1966) by Chief Leabua Jonathan, who was Prime Minister from 1965 until the military coup in January 1986. During his premiership Chief Jonathan wrested executive control from the King, suspending the 1970 constitution and increasing his power over the country. Following the overthrow of the BNP government, supporters of Chief Jonathan (who died in 1987) were barred from political activity. With the legalization of political parties in May 1991, the BNP emerged as one of the leading parties. However, this was not reflected in the results of the March 1993 legislative polls, prompting BNP accusations of electoral malpractice by the Basotho Congress Party.

In the May 1998 general elections the BNP received 24.5% of the total vote but won only one seat in the National Assembly. The BNP subsequently led a campaign for the introduction of full proportional representation, modelled on the system currently used in neighbouring South Africa.

The BNP is associated with the International Democrat Union through its membership of the Democrat Union of Africa.

Lesotho Congress for Democracy (LCD)
Address. c/o National Assembly, PO Box 190, Maseru 100
Leadership. Bethuel Pathalitha Mosisili (leader); Phebe Motebang (chairman)
The LCD was formed in June 1997 by Lesotho's then Prime Minister, Ntsu Mokhehle, when he resigned from the →Basotho Congress Party (BCP). He chose to retain his seat in the National Assembly (as did 37 other sitting BCP members who joined the LCD) and the LCD became the party of government for the remainder of the current leg-islative term. In February 1998 Mokhehle was succeeded as LCD leader by Pathalitha Mosisili, who led the party to victory in the May 1998 general election, when it gained 60.7% of the vote and won 79 of the 80 seats in an enlarged National Assembly. As Prime Minister, Mosisili came under intense pressure to hold fresh elections under a more representative voting system, and he agreed in December 1998 to the establishment of an Interim Political Authority to oversee arrangements for the next elections.

Other Parties

Communist Party of Lesotho (CPL), set up in the early 1960s, operating legally until it was banned in 1970. This ban was only partially lifted in 1984, and not until 1992 did the party begin operating in the open. The CPL has drawn its support mainly from Basotho migrant workers in South Africa.
Address. POB 441, Maseru
Leadership. Mokhafisi Kena (secretary-general)

Kopanang Basotho Party (KBP), launched in 1992 to campaign against what it terms repressive and discriminatory laws against women in Lesotho.
Address. Lithoteng Private Centre, PB 133, Maseru
Leadership. Limakatso Ntakatsana (leader)

Progressive National Party (PNP), established in 1995 following a split in the →Basotho National Party.
Leadership. Chief Peete Nkoebe Peete (leader)

Liberia

Capital: Monrovia

Population: 3,164,000 (2000E)

The Republic of Liberia, an independent state from 1847, was founded by freed black slaves from the USA. In September 1990 Gen. Samuel Kanyon Doe, who had seized power in a military coup in 1980 and had been elected President in 1985, was deposed and killed as rival rebel groups struggled with government forces for control. The Economic Community of West African States (ECOWAS), which had sent a peace-keeping force to Liberia in August 1990, backed the nomination of Amos Sawyer as Interim President, and in January 1991 an Interim Government of National Unity (IGNU) was appointed. Civil war, however, continued.

In July 1993 a UN-sponsored peace agreement was signed by the IGNU, the National Patriotic Front of Liberia (NPFL) and the United Liberation Movement for Democracy in Liberia (ULIMO). It provided for a ceasefire, the encampment of troops and the formation of a transitional civilian administration. A five-member Council of State and 35-member Transitional Legislative Assembly were installed in March 1994, while the National Transitional Government met for the first time two months later. As a result of further peace talks involving all the main factions, it was agreed in December 1994 that a new Council of State should be appointed which would hand over to an elected government on Jan. 1, 1996, following multi-party elections in November 1995. However, negotiations on the composition of the Council were stalled until August 1995 when a new peace accord was brokered. In September the Council was inaugurated, a new 16-member transitional government was formed and elections were rescheduled for August 1996. However, further heavy fighting erupted in Monrovia in April 1996, and it was not until February 1997 that ECOWAS was able to announce a new target election date of May 1997. The main faction leaders, having formally disbanded their military organizations (some of which were reconstituted as political parties), resigned from the Council of State in order to stand for the presidency.

After further delay, elections were finally held on July 19, 1997. The former NPFL leader, Charles Taylor, standing as the candidate of the National Patriotic Party (NPP), won 75.3% of the votes cast in a 13-way contest for the presidency (seven of the longer established political parties having failed to agree on a joint presidential candidate). Under Liberia's 1986 constitution, the President is elected for a six-year term of office (renewable once) as head of state, head of executive government and commander-in-chief of the armed forces. President Taylor assumed office on Aug. 2, 1997. Legislative elections were held on July 19, 1997, for a 64-member House of Representatives (term of office 6 years) and a 26-member Senate (term of office 9 years). The distribution of seats in the House of Representatives was as follows: NPP 49, Unity Party (UP) 7, All Liberian Coalition Party (ALCOP) 3, Alliance of Political Parties (the Liberian Action Party and the Liberian Unification Party) 2, United People's Party (UPP) 2, Liberian People's Party (LPP) 1. In the Senate, the NPP won 21 seats, the UP 3 and the

ALCOP 2. The legislature played a marginal role under the Taylor presidency, many sessions of the House of Representatives being abandoned for want of a quorum.

A group of 11 parties agreed in November 2000 to form an alliance called Collaborating Political Parties with the aim of mounting a joint campaign in the elections due to be held in 2003. The parties involved were the UP, ALCOP, the Liberian Action Party, the UPP, the LPP, the National Democratic Party of Liberia, the Free Democratic Party, the Liberia National Union, the People's Progressive Party, the People's Democratic Party of Liberia and the Reformation Alliance Party.

All Liberia Coalition Party (ALCOP)

Address. c/o House of Representatives, Capitol Building, Monrovia
Leadership. Lusinee Kamara (leader)
The ALCOP was founded in 1997 by elements of the former armed faction ULIMO-K (the wing of the United Liberation Movement of Liberia for Democracy led by Alhaji G.V. Kromah). Alhaji Kromah won 4% of the vote in the 1997 presidential election. In the legislative elections ALCOP won three seats in the House of Representatives and two seats in the Senate. Alhaji Kromah left the country in 1998 after his dismissal as head of a national reconciliation commission.

Liberian Action Party (LAP)

Address. c/o House of Representatives, Capitol Building, Monrovia
Leadership. Cletus Wotorson (leader)
Founded in 1984, the LAP fought the 1997 elections as part of the Alliance of Political Parties, comprising also the →Liberian Unification Party. The Alliance won two seats in the House of Representatives, while its joint candidate received 2.6% of the vote in the presidential election.

Liberian People's Party (LPP)

Address. c/o House of Representatives, Capitol Building, Monrovia
Leadership. Togba-Nah Tipoteh (leader)
Formed in 1984 by former members of the Movement for Justice in Africa, the LPP won one seat in the House of Representatives in July 1997. Its leader received 1.6% of the vote in the presidential election.

National Patriotic Party (NPP)

Address. c/o House of Representatives, Capitol Building, Monrovia
Leadership. Charles Ghankay Taylor (leader); Christian Herbert (secretary-general)
The NPP was founded in 1997 by members of the former armed faction, the National Patriotic Front of Liberia (NPFL), whose leader, Charles Taylor, had launched the armed rebellion that led to the collapse of the Doe regime in September 1990 and embroiled the country in protracted civil war. Charles Taylor won the 1997 presidential election with 75.3% of the vote, while the NPP won 49 of the 64 seats in the House of Representatives and 21 of the 26 seats in the Senate.

United People's Party (UPP)

Address. c/o House of Representatives, Capitol Building, Monrovia
Leadership. Gabriel Bacchus Matthews (chairman)
The UPP was founded in 1984 by former members of the Progressive People's Party (in opposition prior to the 1980 military coup). It won two seats in the House of Representatives in July 1997, when its candidate received 2.5% of the vote in the presidential election.

Unity Party (UP)

Address. c/o House of Representatives, Capitol Building, Monrovia
Leadership. Charles Clarke (leader)
Founded in 1984, the Unity Party was the runner-up in the July 1997 elections, winning seven seats in the House of Representatives and three seats in the Senate. Its presidential candidate, Ellen Johnson-Sirleaf (a senior official of a United Nations Agency), received 9.6% of the vote in the presidential election.

Other Parties

Free Democratic Party (FDP), contested the 1997 legislative elections. Its presidential candidate received 0.3% of the vote.

Liberia National Union (LINU), contested the 1997 legislative elections. Its presidential candidate received 1% of the vote.
Leadership. Henry Moniba (chairman)

Liberian Unification Party (LUP), formed in 1984. The LUP fought the 1997 elections as part of the Alliance of Political Parties, comprising also the →Liberian Action Party (LAP).

National Democratic Party of Liberia (NDPL), founded in 1997 by members of the former armed faction, the Liberia Peace Council. In the July 1997 elections the NDPL received 1.3% of the presidential vote and won no seats in the legislature.
Leadership. Isaac Dakinah (leader)

National Reformation Party (NRP), contested the 1997 legislative elections. Its presidential candidate received 0.5% of the vote.

New Democratic Alternative for Liberia Movement, also known as New Deal, was launched in January 2000 with a radical anti-corruption programme. Its offices were ransacked by members of the security forces in March 2000.

People's Democratic Party of Liberia (PDPL), contested the 1997 legislative elections. Its presidential candidate received 0.5% of the vote.

People's Progressive Party (PPP), contested the 1997 legislative elections. Its presidential candidate received 0.3% of the vote.
Leadership. Chea Cheapoo (chairman)

Reformation Alliance Party (RAP), contested the 1997 legislative elections. Its presidential candidate received 0.3% of the vote.
Leadership. Henry Boimah Fainbulleh (chairman)

Libya

Capital: Tripoli

Population: 5,100,000 (2000E)

Libya achieved independence in 1951 under a monarchy which was subsequently overthrown in 1969 by a military coup led by Col. Moamer al Kadhafi. Kadhafi himself is referred to as "the leader of the revolution", wielding considerable power but holding no official post. Initial moves by the regime towards a party structure were superseded when the 1977 constitution of the Socialist People's Libyan Arab *Jamahiriyah* was introduced. Officially, under the constitution, authority is vested in the Libyan people, with local "basic people's congresses" forming an indirect electoral base for the General People's Congress (the legislature), which is serviced by a Secretariat and which appoints the General People's Committee (broadly equivalent to a Council of Ministers). There are no political parties and no opposition groups have been able to emerge within the country itself.

Islamic opposition

In the 1990s, there was an upsurge of Islamist opposition to the Kadhafi regime. Such opposition remains fragmented and has suffered at the hands of the regime's security apparatus. The Islamic Liberation Party and the Muslim Brotherhood are among the groups that have caused anxiety for the regime. The Islamic Liberation Party's platform attacks the paralysis and corruption of the state and advocates a progressive agenda of equitable redistribution of wealth. The party's endorsement of armed resistance and its successful recruitment of students from the universities and military academies has made it an important source of opposition. Although long prosecuted by the regime, the Muslim Brotherhood has also experienced a revival. The Islamic Martyrs' Movement and the Libyan Islamic Group are said to have memberships including Libyan veterans of the Afghan war who are disenchanted with their limited economic prospects. The level of Islamist violence reached a new degree of intensity in the latter half of the 1990s, particularly in central and eastern Libya where there were reports of frequent clashes between the security forces and the Islamists.

Exile organization

National Front for the Salvation of Libya (NFSL), the main expatriate opposition to the Kadhafi regime. It was formed in Sudan in 1981 with the goal of ending Kadhafi's rule, and the establishment of "a constitutional and democratically elected government in Libya". It operates out of Egypt and the USA.
Website. www.nfsl-libya.com

Liechtenstein

Capital: Vaduz

Population: 32,000 (2000E)

The Principality of Liechtenstein is an hereditary monarchy in the male line which has maintained an independent existence since the Middle Ages under a system which is still feudal in many legal respects, although the country is essentially a parliamentary democracy. Under its constitution of 1921, the Prince exercises legislative power jointly with a unicameral Diet (*Landtag*) of 25 members, who are elected every four years by universal adult suffrage under a proportional representation system based in the Principality's two constituencies and subject to a minimum requirement that 8% of the vote must be obtained. The Chief of Government is appointed by the sovereign from the majority party or group in the Diet.

Having been introduced for most local elections in 1977, female suffrage at national level was narrowly approved by referendum in July 1984 (of male voters), the first elections in which women could vote being held in February 1986.

In *Landtag* elections on Feb. 9 and 11, 2001, the Progressive Citizen's Party in Liechtenstein (FBPL) won 13 seats (with 49.9% of the vote), the Fatherland Union (VU) 11 (41.3%) and the Free List 1 (8.8%). Having been in opposition since 1997, the FBPL formed a new government on April 5, 2001.

Fatherland Union
Vaterländischen Union (VU)
Address. Fürst-Franz-Josef-Strasse 13, 9490 Vaduz
Telephone. (1423) 236–1616
Fax. (141–75) 236–1617
Email. gs@vu-online.li
Website. www.vu-online.li
Leadership. Heinz Frommelt (chairman); Peter Kranz (general secretary)
Considered the more liberal of the two major parties, the VU favours a constitutional monarchy, democracy and social progress. It was founded at the end of World War I as the People's Party (Volkspartei, VP), which attracted substantial working-class support (particularly among returning emigrant workers) for its programme of economic union with Switzerland and a constitution according rights to the people. After winning a majority in the 1918 elections, the party formed the government in 1918–28 and implemented many of the aforementioned policies.

In 1936 the VP merged with the Heimatdienst movement

to create the VU, which served as the junior coalition partner of the →Progressive Citizens' Party in Liechtenstein (FBPL) from 1938 to 1970, when it became the senior partner. It lost its coalition seniority to the FBPL in 1974 but regained it in 1978, holding the government leadership until the elections of February 1993, when the FBPL gained the advantage. However, unprecedented second elections the same year re-established the VU as the leading government party under the premiership of Mario Frick.

The VU again won 13 of the 25 Landtag seats in early 1997 elections, whereas the FBPL lost one and opted to end the 39-year-old coalition, going into opposition to a VU government headed by Frick. The VU was therefore solely accountable for subsequent difficulties, including the naming of Liechtenstein as a "harmful tax haven" by the OECD and strains with Prince Hans-Adam over his demand for constitutional changes to give more power to the citizenry, which the VU saw as an increase in royal prerogatives at the expense of parliament. The party paid the price in the February 2001 elections, retaining only 11 Landtag seats and going into opposition to a majority government of the FBPL.

The VU is a member party of the European section of the International Democrat Union (as is the FBPL).

Free List
Freie Liste (FL)
Address. Im Bretscha 4, Postfach 177, 9494 Schaan
Email. fliste@lie-net.li
Website. www.freieliste.li
Leadership. Pepo Frick, Karin Jenny & René Hasler (executive members)

The environmentalist and social democratic FL was formed prior to the 1986 elections, in which it mounted the first third-party challenge to the then ruling coalition parties since 1974 but narrowly failed to secure the 8% vote share necessary for parliamentary representation. The FL again fell short in 1989, in part because 3.2% of the vote went to a new Liechtenstein Non-Party List (which quickly became defunct). Its breakthrough came in the February 1993 elections, when it won two seats, although it was reduced to one

in the second 1993 elections in October. The FL again won two seats in the 1997 elections, becoming a vigorous critic of the →Fatherland Union government in the next parliamentary term. In the 2001 elections, however, the party fell back to one seat.

The FL has links with the European Federation of Green Parties.

Progressive Citizens' Party in Liechtenstein
Fortschrittliche Bürgerpartei in Liechtenstein (FBPL)
Address. Aeulestrasse 56, 9490 Vaduz
Telephone. (1423) 237–7940
Fax. (1423) 237–7949
Email. marcus.vogt@fbp.li
Website. www.fbpl.li
Leadership. Otmar Hasler (leader); Ernst Walch (chairman); Marcus Vogt (secretary)

Founded in 1918 as the conservative Citizens' Party (Bürgerpartei), what subsequently became the FBPL held a majority of Diet seats from 1928 to 1970 and in 1974–78 and therefore headed the government in those periods. From 1938 it participated with the →Fatherland Union (VU) in long-serving government coalition, being the junior partner in 1970–74 and from 1978 until it regained the premiership in the elections of February 1993. However, the incoming FBPL Chief of Government, Markus Büchel, quickly alienated his own party and in September 1993 lost a confidence vote tabled by the FBPL itself. Further general elections in October, in which the FBPL list was headed by Josef Biedermann, reduced the FBPL to junior status in the ruling coalition.

In the 1997 Landtag elections the FBPL lost one of its 11 seats and unexpectedly decided to go into opposition to the VU, thus ending Europe's longest-lasting coalition government. Its reward in the February 2001 elections was a major advance (by local standards) from 10 to 13 seats with just short of half the popular vote. The FBPL accordingly formed a new single-party government under the premiership of Otmar Hasler.

The FBPL is a member party of the European section of the International Democrat Union (as is the VU).

Lithuania

Capital: Vilnius

Population: 3,491,000 (2001E)

The Republic of Lithuania was independent from the end of World War I until being absorbed by the Soviet Union in August 1940, an action that was repudiated by the Lithuanian legislature in March 1990, following which the country's full independence was recognized by the USSR State Council in September 1991. Lithuania's 1992 constitution provides for an executive President who is directly elected for a five-year term and who appoints the Prime Minister and other ministers, subject to parliamentary approval. Legislative authority is vested in a Parliament (*Seimas*) of 141 members serving a four-year term, of whom 71 are elected from constituencies by majority voting and 70 by proportional representation. Under changes to the electoral law given parliamentary approval in June 1996, the threshold for obtaining proportional seats was raised from 4% to 5% (and previous concessions on the threshold rule for minority parties were abolished), while voters became entitled to record a preference for individual candidates on party lists.

Under legislation enacted in 1999, Lithuanian parties became eligible for annual state funding if they receive at least 3% of the vote in the most recent national and/or local elections. Allocated in proportion to representation and support obtained, the total sum available is set at a ceiling of 0.1% of budgeted government expenditure each year.

In presidential elections held in two rounds on Dec. 21, 1997, and Jan. 4, 1998, an independent candidate endorsed by the Homeland Union–Lithuanian Conservatives (TS–LK), Valdus Adamkus, was elected with 50.3% of the second-round vote, against 49.7% for independent left-wing candidate Arturas Paulauskas. Parliamentary elections on Oct. 8, 2000, resulted in the Brazauskas Social Democratic Coalition, consisting mainly of the Lithuanian Democratic Labour Party (LDDP) and the Lithuanian Social Democratic Party (LSDP), winning 51 seats (with 31.1% of the vote), the Lithuanian Liberal Union (LLS) 34 (17.3%), the New Union–Social Liberals (NS–SL) 29 (19.6%), the TS–LK 9 (8.6%), the Lithuanian Peasants' Party 4 (4.1%), the

Lithuanian Christian Democratic Party 2 (3.1%), the Lithuanian Centre Union (LCS) 2 (3.1%) and the Lithuanian Polish Union 2 (1.9%), with five other lists obtaining one seat each and three independents being elected.

The first outcome of the October 2000 parliamentary elections was a coalition government headed by the LLS and including the NS–SL and the LCS. In January 2001 the LDDP and LSDP merged under the historic LSDP title. Following the collapse of the LLS-led government in June 2001, a coalition of the LSDP and the NS–SL was installed in July.

Homeland Union–Lithuanian Conservatives
Tevynes Sajunga–Lietuvos Konservatoriai (TS-LK)
Address. 15 Gedimino pr., Vilnius 2000
Telephone. (+370–2) 396450
Fax. (+370–2) 396450
Email. rupetr@lrs.lt
Website. www.tslk.lt
Leadership. Vytautas Landsbergis (chairman); Jurgis Razma (executive secretary)
The centre-right TS–LK was launched in May 1993 as successor to the remnants of the Lithuanian Reform Movement (*Sajudis*), which had spearheaded Lithuania's independence campaign. Under the leadership of Vytautas Landsbergis, the broadly-based *Sajudis* had been the leading formation in the 1990 elections, but in the face of economic adversity had suffered a heavy defeat in 1992, winning only 20% of the popular vote. Boosted by the unpopularity of the post-1992 left-wing government, the TS–LK won an overall majority of 70 seats in the 1996 parliamentary elections, opting to form a centre-right coalition with the →Lithuanian Christian Democrats (LKD) and the →Lithuanian Centre Union (LCS) under the premiership of Gediminas Vagnorius. However, in direct presidential elections in late 1997 and early 1998, Landsbergis came a poor third in the first round with only 15.7%, following which the TS–LK backed the narrow second-round winner, Valdas Adamkus (non-party).

In May 1999 Vagnorius was succeeded as Prime Minister by Rolandas Paksas, then the TS–LK mayor of Vilnius, but growing divisions between the coalition partners resulted in his replacement in October 1999 by Andrius Kubilius. Splits within the TS–LK followed, including the defection of Paksas to the →Lithuanian Liberal Union and the formation of the →Moderate Conservative Union by Vagnorius. In the parliamentary elections of October 2000 the rump party was reduced to nine seats and went into opposition.

The TS–LK is a member of the European Democrat Union.

Lithuanian Centre Union
Lietuvos Centro Sajunga (LCS)
Address. Literatu 8, Vilnius 2001
Telephone. (+370–2) 224095
Fax. (+370–2) 223790
Email. info@lcs.lt
Website. www.lcs.lt
Leadership. Kestutis Glaveckas (chairman); Ruta Rutkelyte (secretary-general)
Registered in 1993, the pro-market LCS won 13 seats in the 1996 parliamentary elections, becoming a junior partner in a centre-right government headed by the →Homeland Union–Lithuanian Conservatives (TS–LK). It was punished for the government's unpopularity in the October 2000 elections, retaining only two seats and 2.9% of the vote. The party nevertheless became part of the succeeding centre-right coalition supporting a government headed by the →Lithuanian Liberal Union (LLS), until its collapse in June 2001.

Having a membership of 3,200, the LCS is an observer member of the Liberal International.

Lithuanian Christian Democrats
Lietuvos Krikščionys Demokratai (LKD)
Address. Pylimo 36/2, Vilnius 2001
Telephone. (+370–2) 626126

Fax. (+370–2) 227387
Email. lkdp@takas.lt
Website. www.lkdp.lt
Leadership. Kazys Bobelis (chairman); Algirdas Saudargas & Edvardas Pabarcius (deputy chairmen); Petras Gražulis (executive board chairman)
The LKD came into being in May 2001 as a merger of the Lithuanian Christian Democratic Party (LKDP) and the Lithuanian Christian Democratic Union (LKDU), healing a split dating from 1992 in an attempt to restore Christian Democratic electoral fortunes.

The LKDP had been launched in 1989 as the revival of a pre-Soviet party dating from 1905, adopting a classic Christian democratic programme advocating a social market economy and Lithuanian membership of Western institutions. The breakaway LKDU was formed prior to the 1992 parliamentary elections, in which the LKDP came third with 18 seats and 12.2% of the vote, achieved in co-operation with *Sajudis* (later the →Homeland Union–Lithuanian Conservatives, TS–LK) and other groups, while the LKDU won one seat. Both parties were in opposition until the 1996 elections, in which the LKDP fell back to 16 seats and 10% of the vote but became the second-largest party, while the LKDU retained its single mandate. The LKDP then joined a centre-right coalition government headed by the TS–LK. In the 1997 presidential elections the LKDU leader, Kazys Bobelis, came fifth with 4% of the vote.

Tensions in coalition relations from mid-1999 were accompanied by further factional strife in LKDP ranks, resulting in the formation of the →Modern Christian Democratic Union (MKDS). In the October 2000 parliamentary elections the rump LKDP slumped to two seats and 3.1% of the vote, going into opposition, while the LKDU and the MKDS won one seat each.

The reunification of the LKDP and LKDU was achieved at a joint conference in Vilnius in May 2001, with Bobelis being elected chairman of the new KDS and former LKDP leader Algirdas Saudargas becoming one of two deputy chairmen. A small faction of the LKDP led by Alfonsas Svarinskas declined to join the merged party.

The LKD is a member of the Christian Democrat International and an associate member of the European People's Party.

Lithuanian Liberal Union
Lietuvos Liberalu Sajunga (LLS)
Address. A. Jakoto 9, Vilnius 2001
Telephone. (+370–2) 313264
Fax. (+370–2) 791910
Email. lls@lls.lt
Website. www.lls.lt
Leadership. Eugenijus Gentvilas (acting chairman)
The LLS was founded in November 1990 by pro-independence activists at Vilnius University and elsewhere. It failed to gain representation in the 1992 elections and won only one seat in 1996, but in December 1999 was greatly strengthened by the adhesion of a breakaway faction of the →Homeland Union–Lithuanian Conservatives (TS–LK) led by former Prime Minister Rolandas Paksas, who became LLS chairman.

In the October 2000 parliamentary elections the LLS achieved a major advance, to 34 seats on a 17.3% vote share. Paksas was therefore able to form a centrist majority coalition government embracing the LLS, the →New Union–Social Liberals and the →Lithuanian Centre Union

(LCS). In June 2001, however, the government collapsed over differences on privatization policy and the LLS went into opposition to a government headed by the →Lithuanian Social Democratic Party. Paksas resigned as LLS chairman in September 2001.

The LLS is a member of the Liberal International.

Lithuanian Peasants' Party
Lietuvos Valstiečiu Partija (LVP)
Address. Blindziu 17, Vilnius 2000
Telephone. (+370–2) 725268
Leadership. Ramunas Karbauskis (chairman)
Dating from 1905 and revived in 1990 as Lithuania's principal agrarian party, the LVP adopted its present name in 1994. Having won one seat in the 1996 legislative elections, the party polled strongly in local elections in March 2000, before advancing to four national seats (with 4.1% of the vote) in the October 2000 elections.

Lithuanian Polish Union
Lietuvos Lenku Sajunga (LLS)
Address. 40 Didžioji, Vilnius 2001
Telephone. (+370–2) 223388
Leadership. Valdemar Tomasevski (chairman)
Founded in 1992 to represent Lithuania's ethnic Poles (about 8% of the total population), the LLS seeks the "national rebirth" of Lithuanian Poles through the promotion of Polish education but stresses its commitment to the Lithuanian state. Having won four *Seimas* seats in 1992 with a 2.1% vote share, it contested subsequent elections as the Lithuanian Poles' Electoral Action (LLRA), falling to one seat in 1996 but recovering to two in October 2000 with 1.9% of the vote.

Lithuanian Social Democratic Party
Lietuvos Socialdemokratu Partija (LSDP)
Address. Barboros Radvilaites 1, Vilnius 2000
Telephone/Fax. (+370–2) 615420
Email. gekirk@lrs.lt
Website. www.lsdp.lt
Leadership. Algirdas Brazauskas (chairman)
The LSDP is directly descended from the original LSDP founded in 1896 and was relaunched in January 2001 as a merger of the (ex-communist) Lithuanian Democratic Labour Party (LDDP) and the post-independence LSDP.

Prominent in the inter-war period of independence, the LSDP was revived in 1989 with a social democratic platform on the West European model. Having formed part of the broad pro-independence movement under the umbrella of *Sajudis* (later the →Homeland Union–Lithuanian Conservatives), the party contested the 1992 parliamentary elections independently, winning eight seats with 5.9% of the vote) and subsequently forming part of the parliamentary opposition to the ruling LDDP. The LDDP had been launched in December 1990 by a pro-reform and pro-independence faction of the Lithuanian Communist Party (LCP) following a constitutional revision revoking its monopoly of power (the LCP being banned in August 1991 and its property confiscated). It had registered an unexpected victory in the 1992 parliamentary elections, winning an overall majority of seats with 42.6% of the vote on a platform of gradual transition to a market economy. The LDDP leader, Algirdas Brazauskas, was accordingly elected chairman of the *Seimas* and thus head of state, in which capacity he received popular endorsement in presidential elections in February 1993.

Damaged by government financial scandals and internal feuding, the LDDP was heavily defeated in the October 1996 parliamentary elections, retaining only 12 seats and 10% of the vote, whereas the LSDP advanced to 12 seats and 7%. The LSDP candidate, Vytenis Andriukaitis, came fourth with 5.7% of the vote in the first round of presidential elections in December 1997. However, the LSDP and the LDDP mounted increasingly effective joint opposition

to the post-1996 centre-right government headed by the →Homeland Union–Lithuanian Conservatives (TS–LK) and contested the October 2000 parliamentary elections within the "Brazauskas Social Democratic Coalition", which also included the small →New Democracy Party (NDP) and the →Lithuanian Russian Union (LRS). The alliance became substantially the largest bloc, winning 51 of the 141 seats with 31.1% of the vote.

Outmanoeuvred in the subsequent inter-party negotiations, the LSDP and LDDP went into opposition to a centrist coalition government headed by the →Lithuanian Liberal Union (LLS). The two parties formally merged at a Vilnius congress in January 2001, Brazauskas being elected chairman of the unified party, which adopted the historic LSDP name to signify the reunification of the Lithuanian left after 80 years of division. Following the collapse of the government coalition in June 2001, the LSDP came to power in July, with Brazauskas becoming Prime Minister of a new majority coalition with the →New Union–Social Liberals.

The LSDP is a member of the Socialist International.

New Democracy Party
Naujosios Demokratijos Partija (NDP)
Address. Jakšto 9–22, Vilnius 2001
Telephone/Fax. (+370–2) 615613
Email. ndpartija@takas.lt
Website. www.5ci.lt/ndmp
Leadership. Kazimira Danute Prunskiene
The leader of the centre-left NDP, Kazimira Danute Prunskiene, was Prime Minister in 1990–91 as Lithuania regained its independence, having then been a member of the Lithuanian Communist Party. After leaving office, she had rejected a Supreme Court ruling of 1992 that in the Soviet era she had collaborated with the KGB as head of the Lithuanian Women's Association. Elected to the *Seimas* in 1996 as candidate of the Lithuanian Women's Party (LMP), she was re-elected in 2000 for the NDP, which won two seats within the alliance headed by what became the →Lithuanian Social Democratic Party.

New Union–Social Liberals
Naujoji Sajunga–Socialliberalai (NS-SL)
Address. Mickevičiaus 14, Vilnius 2004
Telephone. (+370–2) 791664
Fax. (370–2) 791653
Email. centras@nsajunga.lt
Website. www.nsajunga.lt
Leadership. Arturas Paulauskas (chairman)
The centrist NS-SL was launched in April 1998 by Arturas Paulauskas, a former public prosecutor who, standing as an independent, had narrowly lost the presidential elections in December 1997 and February 1998, taking a commanding lead in the first round with 44.7% but narrowly losing in the second to the candidate backed by the →Homeland Union–Lithuanian Conservatives. The NS-SL polled strongly in its first parliamentary elections in October 2000, winning 29 seats on a 19.6% vote share. NS-SL leader Arturas Paulauskas was elected president of the new *Seimas* and the party became a leading component of the resultant centrist coalition headed by the →Lithuanian Liberal Union (LLS). It continued in government on the formation in July 2001 of a centre-left coalition headed by the →Lithuanian Social Democratic Party.

Other Parties

Lithuanian Freedom Union (*Lietuvos Laisves Sajunga*, *LLS*), right-wing formation which won one seat in the 2000 parliamentary elections with 1.3% of the vote.
Leadership. Vytautas Sustauskas

Lithuanian National Party (*Lietuviu Nacionaline Partija*,

LNP), right-wing formation which won one parliamentary seat in 1996 under the "Young Lithuania" (*Jaunoji Lietuva*, JL) banner and retained it in 2000 in the Young Lithuania–New Nationalists (*Naujuju Tautininku*, NT)–Political Prisoners' Union (*Politiniu Kaliniu Sajunga*, PKS) alliance, which took 1.2% of the vote.
Leadership. Stanislovas Buskevicius

Lithuanian National Union (*Lietuviu Tautininku Sajunga, LTS*), right-wing party launched in April 1989 as a revival of a leading inter-war party of the same name. The LTS 1992 election list, which incorporated the Lithuanian Independence Party, won four seats, but the party was reduced to one seat in 1996 and none in 2000, when its vote share was 0.9%. The LTS leader took 0.4% of the 1997 presidential election vote.
Leadership. Rimantas Smetona

Lithuanian People's Union (*Lietuvos Liaudies Sajunga*, LLS), contested the 2000 parliamentary election under the slogan "For the Fair Lithuania" (*Už Teisinga Lietuva*), obtaining 1.5% of the vote but no seats.
Leadership. Julius Veselka

Lithuanian Russian Union (*Lietuvos Rusu Sajunga, LRS*), party representing the Russian minority, whose leader was elected to the *Seimas* in 2000 within the alliance headed by what became the unified →Lithuanian Social Democratic Party.
Leadership. Sergejus Dmitrijevas

Lithuanian Social Democracy Party 2000 (*Lietuvos Partija Socialdemokratija 2000, SD-2000*), founded in opposition to the alliance between the →Lithuanian Social Democratic Party and the (ex-communist) Lithuanian Democratic Labour Party; won 0.5% of the vote in the 2000 elections.
Leadership. Rimantas Dagys

Moderate Conservative Union (*Nuosaikiuju Konservatoriu Sajunga*, NKS), splinter group of the →Homeland Union–Lithuanian Conservatives, won one seat in the 2000 *Seimas* elections with 2% of the vote.
Leadership. Gediminas Vagnorius (chairman)

Modern Christian Democratic Union, (*Moderniuju Krikščioniu Demokratu Sajunga*, MKDS), breakaway party from what became the →Lithuanian Christian Democrats, won one seat in the 2000 parliamentary elections.
Leadership. Algis Kaseta

Luxembourg

Capital: Luxembourg-Ville

Population: 405,000 (2000E)

Fully independent since 1867, the Grand Duchy of Luxembourg is, under its 1868 constitution as amended, a constitutional hereditary monarchy in which the head of state (the Grand Duke) exercises executive power through a government headed by a Prime Minister and accountable to the legislature. The latter is the Chamber of Deputies (*Chambre des Députés*), whose 60 members are elected for a five-year term by citizens aged 18 and over (voting being compulsory). A system of proportional representation is based on four electoral districts, in which each voter has the same number of votes as there are seats and may cast them all for a single party list or may select candidates of more than one party. There is also an advisory Council of State, whose 21 members are appointed for life, seven directly by the Grand Duke and the other 14 by him on the recommendation of the Council itself or of the Chamber of Deputies. A founder member of what became the European Union, Luxembourg elects six members of the European Parliament.

Since political parties in Luxembourg do not have a legal personality, there is no law providing for state funding of parties. However, groups represented in the Chamber of Deputies receive subsidies from public funds according to their size for the purposes of financing their parliamentary activities. Parties also have the benefit of certain free postal services during election campaigns.

Elections to the Chamber on 13 June, 1999, resulted as follows: Christian Social People's Party 19 seats (with 30.1% of the vote), Democratic Party 15 (22.4%), Luxembourg Socialist Workers' Party 13 (22.3%), Action Committee for Democracy and Justice 7 (11.3%), The Greens 5 (9.1%), The Left 1 (3.3%).

Action Committee for Democracy and Justice
Aktiounskomitee fir Demokratie a Gerechtegkeet (ADR)
Comité d'Action pour la Démocratie et la Justice (CADJ)
Address. BP 365, L-4004 Esch sur Alzette
Telephone. (+352) 463–742
Fax. (+352) 463–745
Email. adr@chd.lu
Website. www.adr.lu
Leadership. Robert (Roby) Mehlen (president); Fernand Greisen (secretary-general)
The ADR was launched in March 1987 as the "Five-Sixths Action Committee" to campaign for universal entitlement to pensions worth five-sixths of final salary. Benefiting from the increasing number of pensioners on electoral rolls, the right-leaning formation won four Chamber seats in the 1989 elections and five in 1994. In the June 1999 elections it advanced to seven seats, with a vote share of 10.5%, but failed to gain representation in simultaneous elections for the European Parliament, in which it won 8.99% of the vote.

Christian Social People's Party
Chrëschtlech-Sozial Volkspartei (CSV)
Parti Chrétien Social (PCS)
Address. 4 rue de l'Eau, BP 826, L-2018 Luxembourg
Telephone. (+352) 225–731
Fax. (+352) 472–716
Email. csv@csv.lu
Website. www.csv.lu
Leadership. Erna Hennicot-Schoepges (president); Lucien Weiler (Chamber group chairman); Claude Wiseler (secretary-general)
Committed to the promotion of "a policy of solidarity and

social progress under the guidance of Christian and humanist principles" and the preservation of the constitutional status quo, the CSV has long been Luxembourg's strongest party, drawing its support from the conservative middle class, Catholic workers and the farming community. The party is a keen proponent of European economic and monetary union via the European Union (EU), with the proviso that Luxembourg's special banking secrecy laws must be maintained against any EU encroachment. Founded as the *Parti de la Droite*, the CSV adopted its present name in December 1914. Since 1919 the party has taken part in coalition government with various other parties and has supplied Prime Ministers as follows: Émile Reuter (1919–25), Joseph Bech (1926–37), Pierre Dupong (1937–53), Joseph Bech (1953–58), Pierre Frieden (1958–59), Pierre Werner (1959–74 and 1979–84), Jacques Santer (1984–94) and Jean-Claude Juncker (from 1995).

The party formed a coalition with the →Luxembourg Socialist Workers' Party (LSAP) following the June 1984 elections, prior to which it had been in coalition with the →Democratic Party. Its share of the vote in June 1984 was 34.9%, while in simultaneous elections to the European Parliament it retained three of Luxembourg's six seats. In the June 1994 elections the CSV's Chamber representation fell back to 21 seats (with 31.4% of the vote), while in simultaneous European elections it lost one of its three seats. Having formed another coalition with the LSAP, CSV Prime Minister Jacques Santer was unexpectedly appointed president of the European Commission from January 1995, being succeeded as head of the Luxembourg government and CSV leader by Juncker, hitherto Finance Minister.

In the June 1999 elections the CSV slipped further to 19 seats (and 30.1% of the vote) but remained the biggest Chamber party, so that Juncker was able to form a new coalition government, this time with the DP. In simultaneous European elections, the CSV again won two of Luxembourg's six seats, with a vote share of 31.7%. One of the CSV seats was taken by Santer, who had resigned as European Commission president in March 1999, together with his fellow commissioners, after an inquiry set up by the European Parliament had found evidence of corruption and fraud in the Commission.

The CSV is a member of the Christian Democrat International and the International Democrat Union. Its two representatives in the European Parliament sit in the European People's Party/European Democrats group.

Democratic Party
Demokratesch Partei (DP)
Parti Démocratique (PD)

Address. 46 Grand'rue, L-1660 Luxembourg
Telephone. (+352) 221–021
Fax. (+352) 221–013
Email. dp@dp.lu
Website. www.dp.lu
Leadership. Lydie Polfer (president); Henri Grethen (secretary-general)

Dating from the origins of parliamentary democracy in Luxembourg in the 1840s, the DP became an established party in the 19th century, unsuccessfully resisting the introduction of universal suffrage and suffering a major defeat in 1919 in consequence. After a process of adaptation, the party became one of the three major national parties represented in the post-1945 Chamber, taking part in many coalition governments: in the national unity administration of 1945–47; in coalition with the →Christian Social People's Party (CSV) in 1947–51 (when the PD was known as the *Groupement Patriotique et Démocratique*) and in 1959–64 and 1968–74; with the →Luxembourg Socialist Workers' Party (LSAP) in 1974–79; and with the CSV again in 1979–84.

In the June 1984 elections the DP slipped to 14 seats (and from 21.3 to 18.7% of the vote) and went into opposition to a coalition of the CSV and LSAP. At the same time, it retained one of Luxembourg's six seats in the European Parliament. The DP remained in opposition after the 1989 elections, in which it fell back to 11 seats, and also after 1994 elections, in which it improved 12 seats, taking 18.9% of the vote. It retained its European Parliament seat on both occasions.

By Luxembourg standards the June 1999 elections brought a breakthrough for the DP, to the status of second-strongest Chamber party with 15 seats, from a 22.4% vote share. It accordingly returned to government after 15 years in opposition, taking half of the portfolios in a new coalition headed by the CSV, with Lydie Polfer of the DP becoming Deputy Prime Minister. In the simultaneous European elections, the DP retained its single seat with a 20.5% vote share.

The DP is affiliated to the Liberal International, its member of the European Parliament sitting in the European Liberal, Democratic and Reformist group.

The Greens
Déi Gréng
Les Verts

Address. BP 454, L-2014 Luxembourg
Telephone. (+352) 463–740
Fax. (+352) 463–741
Email. greng@greng.lu
Website. www.greng.lu
Leadership. Marthy Thull & Carlo De Toffoli (spokespersons); Abbès Jacoby & Félix Braz (joint secretaries)

The organized Greens date from June 1983, when a number of individuals and groups, including former Socialists, founded the Green Alternative (*Di Gráng Alternativ/Parti Vert Alternatif*, GA/PVA). The new party won two seats and 5.2% of the vote in the June 1984 national elections, while in European Parliament elections the same month it achieved 6.1% without winning representation. In accordance with the rotation principle established by the German Greens (Alliance 90/The Greens Party), the party's two elected deputies were replaced by alternatives half way through the parliamentary term. The GA/PVA again won two seats in the 1989 elections, before making a major advance in the 1994 contest, to five seats. Concurrent elections to the European Parliament were contested jointly with the less radical Green Ecologist Initiative List (*Gréng Lëscht Ekologesch Initiativ/Initiative Vert Écologiste*, GLEI/IVE), the alliance achieving 10.9% of the vote and one of the Grand Duchy's six seats.

A long-contemplated merger between the GA/PVA and most of the GLEI/IVE was eventually consummated in advance of the June 1999 elections, although the Greens' then representative in the European Parliament launched the separate →Green and Liberal Alliance. In the elections the Greens retained five seats, although their vote share slipped to 9.1%. In the simultaneous European elections the Greens took 10.7% of the vote and again won one seat, the party's representative joining the Greens/European Free Alliance group. The party is also affiliated to the European Federation of Green Parties.

The Left
Déi Lénk
La Gauche

Address. BP 817, L-2018 Luxembourg
Telephone. (+352) 2620–2072
Fax. (+352) 2620–2073
Email. sekretariat@dei-lenk.lu
Website. www.dei-lenk.lu
Leadership. Aloyse Bisdorff (Chamber deputy); Fred Heyar (administrative secretary)

This grouping, which does not like to be called a political party, was launched prior to the June 1999 elections by leftist groups and individuals and with the backing of the →Communist Party of Luxembourg, which had failed to win parliamentary representation in 1994. The new formation achieved 3.3% of the vote and won one Chamber seat, while taking only 2.8% in the simultaneous European Parliament elections. The grouping has a 45-member national co-ordination committee with no declared leaders.

Luxembourg Socialist Workers' Party
Lëtzebuerger Sozialistesch Arbechterpartei (LSAP)
Parti Ouvrier Socialiste Luxembourgeois (POSL)

Address. 16 rue de Crécy, L-1364 Luxembourg
Telephone. (+352) 455–991
Fax. (+352) 456–575
Email. info@lsap.lu
Website. www.lsap.lu
Leadership. Jean Asselborn (president); Paul Bach (secretary-general)

Founded in 1902 as the Luxembourg Social Democratic Party, the party made little initial progress because of the qualified franchise. After a minority had broken away in 1921 to form the →Communist Party of Luxembourg, the party first took part in government from the end of 1937, after which the Socialist ministers laid the basis for modern social legislation. During the Nazi occupation the party was dismembered, but after World War II it re-emerged under its present name and took part in a government of national union until 1947, when it returned to opposition. Following renewed government participation in 1951–59 and 1964–68, the party was defeated in the 1968 legislative elections, after which it was temporarily weakened by the formation of the breakaway Social Democratic Party (which later became defunct).

A reconstructed LSAP made gains in the 1974 elections, after which it joined a coalition government with the →Democratic Party (DP). It returned to opposition after losing ground in the June 1979 elections, but returned to government (in coalition with the →Christian Social People's Party, CSV) after making a major advance in the June 1984 national elections, in which it rose from 14 to 21 seats and from 24.3 to 33.6% of the vote. In European Parliament elections the same month the LSAP retained two of the six Luxembourg seats. The LSAP won 18 seats (25.5% of the vote) in a smaller Chamber in 1989 and slipped to 17 (24.8%) in 1994, retaining two European Parliament seats on both occasions and continuing as the junior coalition partner.

The LSAP was the principal loser in the June 1999 elections, falling to third place in the Chamber behind the CSV and the DP, winning only 13 seats on a slightly reduced vote share of 24.3%. In simultaneous European elections, the LSAP retained two seats with 23.6% of the vote.

The LSAP is a member party of the Socialist International, its two representatives in the European Parliament being members of the Party of European Socialists group.

Other Parties

Communist Party of Luxembourg (*Kommunistesch Partei vu Letzeburg/Parti Communiste Luxembourgeois, KPL/PCL*), formed as a result of a split in the →Luxembourg Socialist Workers' Party (LSAP) at the 1921 Differdange congress. It first obtained a Chamber seat in 1934 but the result was annulled by the Chamber majority (though a proposal to ban the party was defeated in a referendum in 1937). The party was represented in the Chamber from 1945, its number of seats fluctuating between three in 1954–64 and six in 1968–74, and declining to two in 1979. It took part in the national unity government of 1945–47, after which it went into opposition, but co-operated with the LSAP at local level. In the June 1979 elections the KPL obtained 5.8% of the vote (compared with 10.4% in 1974), while in 1984 its share fell to 5.0%. The KPL's representation fell to a single seat in the 1989 elections, while the death in 1990 of veteran leader René Urbany (son of the party's previous leader) was a further blow. Having in 1994 experienced its first post-war failure to win Chamber representation, the party did not contest the 1999 elections directly, instead backing the →Left list, which won one seat.
Address. 16 rue Christophe Plantin, L-2339 Luxembourg
Telephone. (+352) 492–095
Fax. (+352) 496–920
Leadership. Aloyse Bisdorff (president)

Green and Liberal Alliance (*Gréng a Liberal Allianz, GaL*), centrist ecology party led by Jup Weber, who had been elected to the European Parliament in 1994 but who opposed the subsequent merger which created the →Greens (and also backed Jacques Santer prior to his resignation as European Commission president in March 1999. The GaL failed to gain representation in the June 1999 elections, winning only 1.1% of the vote for the Chamber and 1.8 in the European contest.
Email. info@gal.lu
Website. www.gal.lu
Leadership. Jup Weber

Taxpayers' Party (*De Steierzueler*), middle-class formation advocating lower state expenditure, won 0.4% of the vote in the 1999 national elections.

Third Age Party (*Partei vum 3. Alter*), aspiring to represent the interests of pensioners, more centrist than the right-inclined →Action Committee for Democracy and Justice, won 0.1% of the vote in the 1999 national elections.

Macedonia

Capital: Skopje

Population: 2,000,000 (2000E)

A former constituent republic of the Socialist Federal Republic of Yugoslavia, Macedonia declared independence under its November 1991 constitution, as approved by referendum two months earlier. The constitution defines Macedonia as a democratic, pluralist state based on citizenship, not ethnicity, and specifically rules out any territorial claims on neighbouring countries. It provides for an executive President who is directly elected for a five-year term and a Cabinet, headed by a Prime Minister, accountable to the legislature. The latter is the unicameral Assembly (*Sobranje*) of 120 members, who are elected for a four-year term by those aged 18 and over, 85 in single-member constituencies and 35 by proportional representation subject to a 5% threshold.

The objection of Greece to the new state being called "Macedonia"—the name of a northern Greek province harking back to ancient Macedon, the founder state of post-classical Greece—blocked the new country's admission to the United Nations until April 1993, under the interim designation "Former Yugoslav Republic of

Macedonia" (FYROM). An agreement of September 1995 on related issues concerning Macedonia's flag and constitution left the basic dispute on the "Macedonia" name unresolved, so the FYROM designation remained the country's name under international law as at mid-2001.

Macedonia's third post-independence Assembly elections were held on Oct. 18 and Nov. 1, 1998, and resulted in an alliance of the Internal Macedonian Revolutionary Organization–Democratic Party for Macedonian National Unity (VMRO–DMPNE) and the Democratic Alternative (DA) winning 59 seats (with 38.8% of the proportional vote), the Social Democratic Union of Macedonia (SDSM) 29 (25.1%), an alliance of the Party for Democratic Prosperity (PDP) and the Democratic Party of Albanians (DPA) 25 (19.3%), an alliance of the Liberal Democratic Party (LDP) and the Democratic Party of Macedonia (DPM) 4 (7.0%), and an alliance of the Socialist Party of Macedonia and the Roma Union of Macedonia (SRM) 3 (4.7%). In presidential elections on Oct. 31 and Nov. 14 (with a partial re-run on Dec. 5, 1999), Boris Trajkovski of the VMRO–DMPNE was elected with 52.9% of the second-round vote, defeating Tito Petkovski of the SDSM.

The post-1998 three-party coalition government of the VMRO–DMPNE, the DA and the DPA was reduced to two-party status by the withdrawal of the DA in November 2000. Further government and party realignments were generated by the onset in February 2001 of armed insurrection by ethnic Albanian militants who claimed that the mainly Muslim Albanians were oppressed by the Christian Slav majority. The formation of a six-party government of national unity in May 2001 was followed by the deployment in August of NATO troops charged with overseeing a ceasefire and the surrender of weapons, as intensive efforts were made to find agreement on new constitutional and political arrangements that would bridge the widening gulf between the two sides.

Democratic Alternative
Demokratska Alternativa (DA)

Address. c/o Sobranje, Skopje 91000
Telephone. (+389–2) 362–713
Fax. (+389–2) 363-089
Website. www.da.org.mk
Leadership. Vasil Tupurkovski (chairman)

The centrist pro-market DA was founded in March 1998 by Vasil Tupurkovski, who had been the Macedonian member of the federal Yugoslav presidency in the last phase of communist rule. Seeking to appeal to all ethnic groups, the party formed the "For Change" alliance with the nationalist →Internal Macedonian Revolutionary Organization–Democratic Party for Macedonian National Unity (VMRO–DPMNE) in the autumn 1998 parliamentary elections, contributing to the victory of the alliance by winning 13 of its 59 seats and 10.7% of its 28.1% vote share. Five DA members were appointed to the resultant coalition government headed by the VMRO–DPMNE and also including the ethnic Albanian →Democratic Party of Albanians (DPA). The DA Foreign Minister, Aleksandar Dimitrov, was closely involved in Macedonia's controversial decision in January 1999 to recognize Taiwan (which was reversed in June 2001).

Initial plans that Tupurkovski would be the joint candidate of the main ruling parties in the 1999 presidential elections foundered on chronic disagreements between the DA and the VMRO–DPMNE. Running as the DA candidate, Tupurkovski obtained only 16% of the first-round vote and was therefore eliminated. Divisions in the ruling coalition intensified thereafter, resulting in the DA's withdrawal from the government in November 2000, although some DA deputies supported the successor administration

As Macedonia descended into civil war between Slavs and ethnic Albanians from February 2001, DA dissidents broke away to establish →New Democracy (ND). Neither faction was included in the government of national unity formed in May 2001.

Democratic Party of Albanians
Demokratska Partija na Albancite (DPA)

Address. Maršal Tito 2, Tetovo 94000
Telephone. (+389–94) 31534
Email. arben@pdsh.org
Website. www.pdsh.org
Leadership. Arben Xhaferi (chairman); Iliaz Halimi (deputy chairman)

One of several parties representing ethnic Albanians (consisting of about 25% of the population), the DPA was founded in mid-1997 by a merger of factions of the →Party for Democratic Prosperity (PDP) opposed to the PDP's participation in government. The new formation contested the autumn 1998 elections in partial alliance with the PDP, winning 11 seats (compared with 14 for the PDP), and then unexpectedly opted to join a coalition government headed by the Slav nationalist →Internal Macedonian Revolutionary Organization–Democratic Party for Macedonian National Unity (VMRO–DPMNE), whereas the PDP went into opposition.

In the 1999 presidential elections the DPA candidate was Muharem Nexhipi, who came fourth in the first round with 14.9% of the vote, against 4.2% for the PDP contender. Despite this apparent vote of confidence from ethnic Albanians, the DPA's government participation came under increasing criticism from its supporters as inter-ethnic civil war broke out in 2001. The government of national unity formed in May 2001 included both DPA and PDP representatives, the result being that militant anti-government factions broke away from both parties.

Internal Macedonian Revolutionary
Organization–Democratic Party for Macedonian
National Unity
Vnatrešna Makedonska Revolucionerna
Organizacija–Demokratska Partija za Makedonsko
Nacionalno Edinstvo (VMRO–DPMNE)

Address. Macedonia 17A, 91000 Skopje
Telephone. (+389–2) 124244
Fax. (+389–2) 124336
Email. info@vmro-dpmne.org.mk
Website. www.vmro-dpmne.org.mk
Leadership. Ljupčo Georgievski (chairman)

The nationalist VMRO was named after an historic movement founded in 1893 by Goce Delčev, which had fought for independence from Ottoman Turkish rule. The DPMNE, established by Macedonian migrant workers in Sweden, merged with the VMRO in June 1990 to create a party describing itself as being of the "democratic centre" and favouring a revival of Macedonian cultural identity. The VMRO–DPMNE became the largest single party in the 1990 Assembly elections (with 38 seats) and formed the core of the resultant "government of experts" which asserted Macedonia's independence. However, a mid-1992 government crisis resulted in the party going into opposition, from where it failed to gain representation in the 1994 legislative elections. Party leader Ljupčo Georgievski was the runner-up in simultaneous presidential elections, receiving 21.6% of the vote. In October 1995 the VMRO–DPMNE condemned an assassination attempt on President Kiro Gligorov (of the →Social Democratic Union of Macedonia, SDSM), but was suspected in some quarters of having been involved, in light of its fierce criticism of concessions made by the government to obtain recognition of the state by Greece.

In revived opposition to the post-1994 government headed by the SDSM, the VMRO–DPMNE allied with the new pro-business →Democratic Alternative (DA) for the autumn 1998 legislative elections. The alliance emerged as the largest grouping, with 59 of the 120 seats, forming a coalition government under the premiership of Georgievski. In addition to the DA, the government also embraced the →Democratic Party of Albanians (DPA), despite the clash between the VMRO–DPMNE's Slav nationalism and the DPA's concern for ethnic Albanian rights. The VMRO–DPMNE consolidated its authority in the late 1999 presidential elections, in which party candidate Boris Trajkovski was elected with 52.9% of the second round vote. However, internal dissension resulted in the formation in April 2000 of a breakaway VMRO under the leadership of former Finance Minister Boris Zmejkovski.

The DA's withdrawal from the government in November 2000 left the remaining VMRO–DPMNE/DPA coalition dependent on DA dissidents and the small →Liberal Party of Macedonia for a parliamentary majority. Greater difficulties ensued from early 2001, when an armed insurrection by ethnic Albanian militants in northern Macedonia called forth demands from the VMRO–DPMNE's natural Slav nationalist constituency for a vigorous response, whereas the government came under intense Western pressure to make concessions. The pressure resulted in the formation in May 2001 of a six-party government of national unity, under the continued premiership of Georgievski and including not only the DPA but also the more militant ethnic Albanian →Party for Democratic Prosperity. The new government agreed to the supposedly temporary deployment of NATO troops in Macedonia in August; but the VMRO–DPMNE as a party remained strongly opposed to constitutional concessions to the ethnic Albanians.

Liberal Democratic Party
Liberalno-Demokratskata Partija (LDP)
Address. Partizanski odredi 89, 91000 Skopje
Telephone. (+389–2) 363675
Fax. (+389–2) 363099
Email. contact@ldp.org.mk
Website. www.ldp.org.mk
Leadership. Risto Penov (president); Jovan Manasievski & Angelka Peeva (vice-presidents); Vlado Popovski (secretary)
The centrist pro-market LDP was created in January 1997 as a merger of the →Liberal Party of Macedonia (LPM) and the Democratic Party of Macedonia (DPM). However, the LDP's failure to restore Liberal fortunes in subsequent elections impelled former LPM elements to restore the party as a separate formation in 2000, leaving the LDP as effectively the successor to the DPM.

The DPM had been founded in 1993 on the initiative of Petar Gošev, who had been a member of the communist-era Macedonian presidency and had later headed the →Social Democratic Union of Macedonia (SDSM). In the mid-1992 government crisis he had refused to become Prime Minister of an SDSM-led coalition and had spent a year in the political wilderness before setting up the DPM, which drew in four minor parties. In the 1994 Assembly elections, however, the DPM had won only one seat (while the LPM had taken 29).

In the 1998 Assembly elections the merged LDP polled disastrously, retaining only four seats with 7% of the proportional vote. Gošev accordingly resigned as president and was succeeded in March 1999 by Risto Penov, the mayor of Skopje. In the late 1999 presidential elections, LDP candidate Stojan Andov managed only fifth place with 11.2% of the first-round vote, although he quickly obtained some compensation by being elected for his second term as Assembly Speaker. He then failed in a bid for the LDP presidency, whereupon in early 2000 he and his supporters broke away to re-establish the LPM. Both parties were included in the government of national unity appointed in May 2001.

The LDP, which has an official membership of 35,000, is affiliated to the Liberal International.

Liberal Party of Macedonia
Liberalnata Partija na Makedonija (LPM)
Address. c/o Sobranje, Oktomvri 11, 91000 Skopje
Website. www.liberalna.org.mk
Leadership. Stojan Andov (president)
The LPM was originally founded in 1989 as the Alliance of Reform Forces of Macedonia (SRSM), which was an affiliate of the federal Alliance of Yugoslav Reform Forces (SRSJ). In the 1990 elections it was allied in some areas with the Young Democratic Progressive Party (MDPS), which it later absorbed. The alliance won only six seats in 1990, but SRSM representatives were included in the resultant coalition government. In 1992 the SRSM adopted the name Reform Forces of Macedonia–Liberal Party and used the shorter LPM designation in the 1994 elections, when as part of the Union for Macedonia it won 29 Assembly seats and continued to be a component of the government coalition headed by the →Social Democratic Union of Macedonia (SDSM). However, increasing dissension with the SDSM culminated in the LPM being dropped from the government in February 1996, whereupon party leader Stojan Andov resigned as Speaker of the Assembly (and was later accused by the SDSM of financial corruption).

In January 1997 the LPM merged with the Democratic Party of Macedonia to form the →Liberal Democratic Party (LDP). However, after the LDP had polled dismally in the 1998 parliamentary elections, LDP candidate Stojan Andov was relegated to fifth place with 11.2% of the first-round vote in the late 1999 presidential elections. Having regained the Assembly chairmanship in December 1999, Andov then sought the LDP presidency. When he failed, he and his supporters broke away in early 2000 to re-establish the LPM, which gave external support to the centre-right government headed by the →Internal Macedonian Revolutionary Organization–Democratic Party for Macedonian National Unity (VMRO-DPMNE). The LPM and the LDP were both included in the government of national unity appointed in May 2001.

Party for Democratic Prosperity
Partija za Demokratski Prosperitet (PDP)
Partia per Prosperitet Demokratik (PPD)
Address. 62 Karaorman, 94000 Tetovo
Telephone. (+389–94) 25709
Leadership. Ymer Ymeri (chairman); Qemal Musliu & Shpetim Pollozhani (deputy chairmen); Mahi Nesimi (secretary-general)
The PDP is the main party of Macedonia's ethnic Albanians, constituting about a quarter of the country's population, organizing only in areas with substantial Albanian population. Subsequent to the 1990 election (in which it won 25 seats) it absorbed the smaller ethnic Albanian National Democratic Party (NDP) led by Ilijas Halili. After joining a coalition government headed by what became the →Social Democratic Union of Macedonia (SDSM) in 1992, the PDP underwent a split in February 1994 between pro-government moderates led by Dzeladin Murati and anti-government Albanian nationalists led by Halili, who opted to re-establish the NDP as an independent party.

Claiming to be the "party of continuity", the rump PDP came into sharp conflict with its government coalition partners in mid-1994 over the conviction of a group of alleged Albanian separatists, including PDP honorary president Mithat Emini, on subversion charges. The party fell back sharply to 10 seats in the 1994 Assembly elections but continued to be a member of the government headed by the SDSM. From February to July 1995 its deputies boycotted the Assembly in protest against a new law banning the use of Albanian in official identity documentation. This phase was marked by the defection of another anti-government PDP faction to form the Party for Democratic Prosperity of Albanians in Macedonia (PDPSM).

PDP deputies boycotted the Assembly for six months in 1995 in protest against a new law banning the use of Albanian in official identity documentation; but this action failed to prevent the defection of another anti-government PDP faction and the formation in mid-1997 of the →Democratic Party of Albanians (DPA) as a merger of anti-PDP ethnic Albanian groupings, including the NDP and the PDPSM. Nevertheless, the PDP contested the autumn 1998 Assembly elections in partial alliance with the PDA, winning 14 seats (against 11 for the PDA), thereafter going into opposition, whereas the PDA opted to join the new government headed by the Slav nationalist →Internal Macedonian Revolutionary Organization–Democratic Party for Macedonian National Unity (VMRO–DPMNE). In the presidential elections of late 1999, PDP candidate Muhamed Halili won only 4.4% of the first-round vote (while the PDA nominee obtained 14.9%).

The PDP's pre-1998 status as the leading ethnic Albanian party was further eroded by the onset of ethnic strife in Macedonia in early 2001 and by the formation in March 2001 of a revived NDP by militant ethnic Albanians. Under heavy Western diplomatic pressure, the PDP joined the six-party national unity government formed in May 2001; but the gulf between PDP prescriptions for improving the status of ethnic Albanians and those of the Slav parties remained wide.

Social Democratic Union of Macedonia
Socijaldemokratski Sojuz na Makedonija (SDSM)
Address. Biháćka 8, 91000 Skopje
Telephone. (+389–2) 321-371
Fax. (+389–2) 221-071
Email. contact@sdsm.org.mk
Website. www.sdsm.org.mk
Leadership. Branko Crvenkovski (chairman)
The SDSM describes itself as standing in the "European democratic tradition", favouring an effective market economy and the "transformation" of property relations and a multi-cultural society. It is directly descended from the former ruling League of Communists of Macedonia (SKM), which in 1989 attempted a relaunch by adding "Party of Democratic Change" (*Partija za Demokratska Preobrazba*, PDP) to its title. Under the SKM-PDP designation it came second in the 1990 Assembly elections, with 31 seats; but its nominee, Kiro Gligorov, was elected head of state by the Assembly in January 1991 and the renamed SDSM became the leading component of a coalition government formed in mid-1992.

In 1994 the SDSM was confirmed in power in both presidential and Assembly elections (winning 58 seats in the latter), heading the Union of Macedonia (SM) alliance with the →Liberal Party of Macedonia (LPM) and the →Socialist Party of Macedonia. Reappointed SDSM Prime Minister in December 1994 at the head of a coalition of the SM parties and the ethnic Albanian →Party for Democratic Prosperity, Branko Crvenkovski carried out a major government reshuffle in February 1996 in which the LPM ceased to be a member of the ruling coalition.

The SDSM lost power in the parliamentary elections of late 1998, retaining only 29 seats on a 25.1% vote share and going into opposition to a government headed by the →Internal Macedonian Revolutionary Organization–Democratic Party for Macedonian National Unity (VMRO–DPMNE). In the late 1999 presidential elections, moreover, SDSM candidate Tito Petkovski, after leading in the first round with 33.2%, was defeated in the second by the VMRO-DPMNE nominee. In May 2000 the SDSM formed an opposition alliance with the →Liberal Democratic Party and other centrist elements.

In the face of insurrection by ethnic Albanians in northern Macedonia, the SDSM joined the six-party government of national unity formed in May 2001. Amidst escalating inter-ethnic conflict, the SDSM thereafter made common cause with the VMRO-DPMNE and other "Macedonian bloc" parties in opposition to ethnic Albanian demands for radical constitutional change.

The SDSM is an observer member of the Socialist International.

Socialist Party of Macedonia
Socijalistika Partija na Makedonija (SPM)
Address. Ilindenska bb, 91000 Skopje
Telephone. (+389–2) 228–015
Fax. (+389–2) 220–025
Leadership. Ljubisav Ivanov (chairman)
Previously known as the Socialist Alliance–Socialist Party of Macedonia and registered in September 1990, the SPM is the successor to the Macedonian branch of the Socialist Alliance of the Working People of Yugoslavia, the front organization of the communist era. For the 1990 elections the SPM formed an alliance with the →Party for the Total Emancipation of Romanies in Macedonia (PCERM), winning four Assembly seats on a platform advocating the creation of a "politically free, economically effective, ecologically responsible and socially just state". In the 1994 contest it formed part of the victorious Union of Macedonia headed by the →Social Democratic Union of Macedonia (SDSM), doubling its representation to eight seats and being included in the resultant government.

In the 1998 parliamentary elections the SPM reverted to an alliance with the PCERM which included four other ethnic minority parties and was called the Movement for Cultural Tolerance and Civic Co-operation. The joint list won 4.7% of the proportional vote, thus falling below the 5% threshold, but the SPM won two constituency seats.

Other Parties

Democratic Party of Turks in Macedonia (*Demokratska Partija na Turcite vo Makedonija, DPTM*), based in Macedonia's small ethnic Turk community. The DPTM contested the 1994 Assembly elections in alliance with the →Party for Democratic Action, winning one seat. In 1998 it was part of a broader alliance headed by the →Socialist Party of Macedonia but failed to retain representation.
Leadership. Erdogan Sarach

Democratic Progressive Party of Romanies in Macedonia (*Demokratska Progresivna Partija na Romite od Makedonija, DPPRM*), seeking to promote the interests of the estimated 65,000 Roma (Gypsies) in Macedonia, contested the 1998 elections unsuccessfully in alliance with the →Socialist Party of Macedonia.

Party for Democratic Action (*Partija za Demokratska Akcija, PDA*), Muslim-based party using the suffix "Islamic Path" (*Islamska Svetba*), allied with the →Democratic Party of Turks in Macedonia in the 1994 elections and with the →Socialist Party of Macedonia in 1998.
Leadership. Mazlam Kenan

Party for the Total Emancipation of Romanies in Macedonia (*Partija za Celosna Emancipacija na Romite vo Makedonija, PCERM*), won one Assembly seat in 1990 in alliance with the →Socialist Party of Macedonia, retaining it in 1994 but losing it in 1998.
Leadership. Faik Abdić

Union of Roma of Macedonia (*Sojuz no Romite od Makedonija, SRM*), another formation representing Macedonia's Gypsies, won one Assembly seat in 1998 in alliance with the →Socialist Party of Macedonia.

Madagascar

Capital: Antananarivo

Population: 15,500,000 (2000E)

The Republic of Madagascar became fully independent from France in 1960. Post-independence politics were dominated by President Philibert Tsiranana and his Malagasy Social Democratic Party until 1972, when the military took control. In 1975 Didier Ratsiraka assumed the presidency, his regime retaining power until a new multiparty constitution heralded a decisive opposition victory in presidential and legislative elections in 1993. The constitution, which had been approved by national referendum in August 1992, was amended and also endorsed by referendum in March 1998. The amendments strengthened presidential powers and introduced provincial autonomy. The President, directly elected as head of state for a five-year term, appoints the Prime Minister and Council of Ministers. The bicameral legislature consists of (i) the Senate (*Sénat*) as the upper house, two-thirds of whose 90 members are indirectly elected by an electoral college representing the autonomous provinces and a third nominated by the President; and (ii) the National Assembly (*Assemblée Nationale*), whose 150 members are directly elected for a four-term from 82 single-member and 34 dual-member constituencies.

Presidential elections in November 1992 and February 1993 resulted in Albert Zafy, representing an alliance of opposition forces launched in 1991, defeating the incumbent President Ratsiraka, taking nearly 67% of the vote in the second round. In legislative elections in June 1993 political groupings supporting President Zafy secured a majority in the National Assembly with over 70 of the 138 seats contested. The following three years were characterized by a series of power struggles between the President and the Assembly, leading in September 1996 to Zafy's impeachment. In subsequent presidential elections held on Nov. 3 and Dec. 29, 1996, Zafy was narrowly defeated by Ratsiraka, who took 50.7% of the second-round vote. President Ratsiraka consolidated his position in 1998 with the strengthening of presidential powers in a constitutional referendum on March 15. In National Assembly elections on May 17, 1998, Ratsiraka's Association for the Rebirth of Madagascar (AREMA) won 63 of the 150 seats and predominantly pro-Ratsiraka independent candidates 32.

Action, Truth, Development and Harmony
Asa, Fahamarinana, Fampandrosoana, Arinda (AFFA)

Address. c/o Assemblée Nationale, Antananarivo
Leadership. Albert Zafy

AFFA was established in 1998 by former President Zafy (1993-96) in opposition to President Ratsiraka and his →Association for the Rebirth of Madagascar (AREMA). In the May 1998 elections AFFA won six seats in the National Assembly, one of them going to Zafy.

Association for the Rebirth of Madagascar
Association pour la Renaissance de Madagascar (AREMA)
Andry sy Riana Enti-Manavotra an'i Madagasikara (AREMA)

Address. c/o Assemblée Nationale, Antananarivo
Leadership. Didier Ratsiraka; Pierrot Rajaonarivelo (secretary-general)

Launched by Ratsiraka in 1976 (and also known variously as the Vanguard of the Malagasy Revolution and the Vanguard for Economic and Social Recovery), AREMA was the dominant element of a coalition front, known as the National Front for the Defence of the Revolution (FNDR), within which all political formations were required to conduct their activity. From March 1990, however, participation in the FNDR ceased to be obligatory for political parties. In elections in 1993, Ratsiraka lost the presidency to Albert Zafy and AREMA lost its dominance in the National Assembly.

Ratsiraka made a come-back in 1996, being re-elected to the presidency, while AREMA emerged from the 1998 Assembly elections as by far the largest single party with 63 of the 150 seats, with some 60 of the other seats being won by pro-Ratsiraka parties or independents. In indirect Senate elections in March 2001 AREMA took 49 of the 60 elective seats.

Congress Party for Madagascar Independence-Renewal
Parti du Congrès pour l'Indépendance de Madagascar–Renouveau
Antoky Kongresy Fahaleonvantenani Madagaskar (AKFM)–Fanavaozana

Address. c/o Assemblée Nationale, Antananarivo
Leadership. Rev. Richard Andriamanjato

The AKFM–*Fanavaozana* was launched by a breakaway faction of the left-wing Congress Party for Madagascar Independence (AKFM) in 1989. A pro-Zafy group, it took five seats in the 1993 legislative elections, while the pro-Ratsiraka AKFM rump won none. Andriamanjato took fifth place, with 4.9% of the vote, in the first round of the 1996 presidential elections. In the 1998 Assembly elections, the AKFM–*Fanavaozana* won three seats.

Judged by One's Work
Ny Asa Vita no Ifampitsanara (AVI)

Address. c/o Assemblée Nationale, Antananarivo
Leadership. Norbert Ratsirahonana

Promoting human rights and hard work, the AVI was founded in 1997 and secured 14 seats in the May 1998 legislative elections to become the third largest party in the National Assembly. Party leader Ratsirahonana had earlier gained 10.1% of the first-round vote in the 1996 presidential elections.

Leader–Fanilo

Address. c/o Assemblée Nationale, Antananarivo
Leadership. Herizo Razafimahaleo

Founded in 1993 as a pro-Ratsiraka party, *Fanilo* returned 13 deputies to the National Assembly in the 1993 elections. Party leader Razafimahaleo came third in the first round of the 1996 presidential elections with 15.1% of the vote. In the May 1998 legislative elections, *Fanilo* won 16 seats to become the second largest party in the Assembly.

Movement for the Progress of Madagascar
Mouvement pour le Progrès de Madagascar
Mpitolona ho'amin'ny Fanjakan'ny Madinika (MFM)
Address. c/o Assemblée Nationale, Antananarivo
Leadership. Manandafy Rakotonirina
The MFN was formed in 1972 as the Movement for Proletarian Power, originally with radical left-wing credentials but latterly with an increasingly liberal outlook. A significant opposition group by the end of the 1980s, it was the second largest party in the National Assembly following legislative elections in 1989. Party leader Rakotonirina, who stood as a first-round presidential candidate in November 1992 (taking third place with just over 10% of the vote), supported the victorious Albert Zafy in the second round. However, following the June 1993 legislative elections, in which it won 15 Assembly seats, the party went into opposition. In the May 1998 Assembly polling, the MFM's representation fell to three seats.

Rally for Socialism and Democracy
Rassemblement pour le Socialisme et la Démocratie (RPSD)
Address. c/o Assemblée Nationale, Antananarivo
Leadership. Evariste Marson
The RPSD leader came fourth in the first round of the presidential elections in November 1992 with 4.6% of the vote. The party switched allegiance to the winner, Albert Zafy, in the second round, but later, having won eight National Assembly seats in the June 1993 elections, went into opposition. In the May 1998 Assembly elections the RPSD increased its representation to 11 seats.

Other Parties

Action and Reflexion Group for the Development of Madagascar (*Groupe de Réflexion et d'Action pour le Développement de Madagascar, GRAD/Iloafo*), an anti-Ratsiraka party, the GRAD/*Iloafa* won a single seat in both the 1993 and the 1998 Assembly elections.
Leadership. Tovananahary Rabetsitonta

Confederation of Civil Societies for Development–Fihaonana (*Confédération des Societés pour le Développement–Fihaonana*), a pro-Zafy formation which won eight seats in the 1993 legislative elections, but fell to a single seat in 1998.
Leadership. Guy Razanamasy

Malawi

Capital: Lilongwe

Population: 10,385,850 (2000E)

The former British protectorate of Nyasaland achieved independence as Malawi in 1964, becoming a one-party republic under a new constitution two years later. The authoritarian regime of President Hastings Banda and his Malawi Congress Party (MCP) retained power from that time until widespread popular protest in the early 1990s led to constitutional amendments introducing multi-party democracy in 1993. An interim constitution, drafted by a National Consultative Council and approved in May 1994, provided for a directly elected executive President and a 177-member National Assembly, both serving five-year terms. The constitution was formally promulgated in May 1995 at the end of its review period. The size of the Assembly, which is elected from single-member constituencies, was increased to 193 members in 1999. A constitutional provision for the creation of an indirectly elected Senate as an upper chamber was repealed by the required two-thirds majority of the Assembly in January 2001.

Multi-party legislative and presidential elections in May 1994 resulted in victory for the United Democratic Front (UDF) and its leader, Bakili Muluzi, whose government initially included representatives of other former opposition parties. In presidential elections held on June 15, 1999, Muluzi was re-elected, winning 51.4% of the vote in a five-way contest. In simultaneous elections for the National Assembly, the UDF won 93 seats (with 47.3% of the vote), the MCP 66 (33.8%), the Alliance for Democracy (AFORD) 29 (10.6%) and independents 4. The postponed election for the remaining seat was later won by the UDF. The four independent MPs were all former UDF members who decided to vote with the UDF in the Assembly, thus giving that party a slim working majority.

Alliance for Democracy (AFORD)
Address. Private Bag 28, Lilongwe
Telephone. (+265) 743166
Fax. (+265) 743170
Leadership. Chakufwa Chihana (president)
AFORD was launched in September 1992 to secure democratic reforms in Malawi. Later that year the government declared membership of the group illegal, and its leader was subsequently imprisoned until mid-1993, when the party was legalized. In March 1993 AFORD absorbed the membership of the former Malawi Freedom Movement, an organization founded by Orton Chirwa, who had been a minister in the Banda regime in the 1970s before being arrested and imprisoned for treason in 1981.

In the multi-party legislative elections in May 1994, AFORD won 36 seats. In the presidential poll, Chakufwa Chihana came third with 18.6% of the votes cast. Subsequent talks to bring AFORD into the coalition government led by the →United Democratic Front (UDF) broke down, and in June 1994 the party declared that it had signed a memorandum of understanding with the defeated →Malawi Congress Party (MCP). However, in September 1994, Chihana and five other AFORD politicians joined the Cabinet, and the party's alliance with the MCP was terminated the following January.

In July 1995 AFORD's ties with the UDF were strengthened by the signature of a formal coalition agreement. In May 1996 Chihana resigned as Second Vice-President and Minister of Irrigation in order to spend more time on party work, and in June 1996 AFORD terminated the coalition agreement. Several AFORD ministers who refused to resign from the Cabinet were dismissed from AFORD's national executive. They remained in the Cabinet as independent members of the Assembly, rejecting demands from AFORD and the MCP that they should resign their Assembly seats and seek formal re-election as independents.

AFORD contested the June 1999 presidential and legislative elections in alliance with the MCP. Chihana was the vice-presidential running-mate of the MCP candidate, who came second in the election. AFORD won 29 Assembly seats (all but one in the northern region) and subsequently co-operated with the MCP (66 seats) in mounting an ultimately unsuccessful legal challenge to the election results in certain constituencies won by the UDP.

Malawi Congress Party (MCP)

Address. Private Bag 388, Lilongwe 3
Telephone. (+265) 783322
Leadership. Gwanda Chakuamba (president); John Tembo (vice-president)

Under the leadership of Hastings Banda, the traditionalist and conservative MCP was the sole legal party from 1966 until 1993, when multi-party democracy was introduced in the wake of growing popular demands for political reform. The MCP lost power in May 1994, coming second in the Assembly elections with 56 seats, while Dr Banda was defeated in the presidential election by the →United Democratic Front (UDF) candidate, winning only 33.6% of the vote.

An alliance between the MCP and the →Alliance for Democracy (AFORD), which had been announced in June 1994, was ended by AFORD in January 1995. However, a subsequent coalition agreement between AFORD and the UDF (now the effective party of government) was short-lived, and AFORD entered into a new alliance with the MCP. In the campaign for the June 1999 elections, the MCP accused the UDF government of abetting corruption and failing to deliver on its economic and social promises. In the presidential contest, MCP president Gwanda Chakuamba was runner-up with 44.3% of the vote, while the MCP won 66 Assembly seats (most of them in the central region) and became the official opposition to the UDF government, supported by AFORD.

After two MCP deputies had defected to the UDF in May 2000, opposing factions of the MCP organized rival party conventions in August 2000. One re-elected Chakuamba as party president, while the other elected John Tembo (the MCP vice-president) to the same post. Litigation to resolve the leadership issue resulted in a court ruling that Chakuamba remained the legal party president. Pending an appeal, Tembo organized a meeting in Lilongwe in June 2001 at which 37 of the 41 MCP district chairmen called on Chakuamba to stand down and declared their support for Tembo.

The MCP is associated with the International Democrat Union through its membership of the Democrat Union of Africa.

United Democratic Front (UDF)

Address. PO Box 5946, Limbe
Telephone. (+265) 651275
Fax. (+265) 645725
Email. udf@malawi.net
Website. www.udf.malawi.net
Leadership. Bakili Muluzi (president); Reid Katenga-Kaunda (secretary-general)

The UDF was formed in 1992 by former officials of the →Malawi Congress Party (MCP) to campaign for a multi-party democracy, and emerged from the elections in May 1994 as the leading political force. The party won 85 Assembly seats and party leader Bakili Muluzi secured the presidency with 47.3% of the votes cast. UDF members predominated in subsequent governments, a coalition agreement with the →Alliance for Democracy (AFORD) proving to be short-lived. As the ruling party, the UDF claimed to be promoting human rights after the repression of the Banda era and to be working for economic improvement in the face of harsh global conditions.

In the June 1999 elections President Muluzi was returned to office with an absolute majority (51.4%), an outcome that was unsuccessfully challenged in the courts by the MCP and AFORD. The UDF narrowly failed to win an overall majority in the National Assembly, but with a final tally of 94 of the 193 seats (80% of them in the southern region) was able to form a minority UDF government with the support of independent members.

During 2000 UDF party unity came under increasing strain, while the Muluzi government became subject to allegations of economic mismanagement, corruption and nepotism. In November 2000 President Muluzi dismissed several senior ministers, one of whom, Brown Mpinganjira, was subsequently acquitted of corruption charges. Claiming that his dismissal had been politically motivated, Mpinganjira announced in early 2001 the establishment of a "pressure group" called the National Democratic Alliance (NDA), which gained some support from disaffected UDF Assembly members, who left the governing party to sit as independents. The new pressure group was strongly opposed to President Muluzi's reported intention to seek re-election for a third presidential term. The UDF government responded by securing the passage in June 2001 of a law specifying that the seat of any Assembly member defecting to another party would be declared vacant.

The UDF is a member party of the Liberal International.

Other Parties

The 1999 parliamentary elections were contested unsuccessfully by eight other parties, of which the three below also presented presidential candidates.

Congress for National Unity (CNU), received 0.51% of the vote in the 1999 presidential election for its candidate, Daniel Nkhumbwe.

Malawi Democratic Party (MDP), performed poorly in the 1994 elections, attracting less than 1% in both the legislative and presidential contests. In 1999 the party's presidential candidate, Kamulepo Kalua, came third with 1.43% of the vote.
Leadership. Kamulepo Kalua

United Party (UP), founded in 1997. The UP candidate in the 1999 presidential election, Bingu wa Mutharika, received 0.46% of the vote.

Malaysia

Capital: Kuala Lumpur

Population: 22,000,000 (2000E)

The Federation of Malaysia consists of the 11 states of Peninsular Malaysia and the two states of Sarawak and Sabah situated on the northern coast of the island of Kalimantan (Borneo). It gained independence from the United Kingdom in 1957, subsequently merging with the self-governing state of Singapore and the former British crown colonies of Sarawak and Sabah in 1963. Singapore's inclusion was terminated in 1965. The constitution codifies a federal system of government under an elective constitutional monarchy. The nine hereditary Malay rulers of Peninsular Malaysia (but not the heads of the states of Malacca, Penang, Sarawak and Sabah) elect a Supreme Head of State (*Yang di-Pertuan Agong*) every five years from among their own number. The *Yang di-Pertuan Agong* then gives sanction to a Cabinet headed by a Prime Minister. The bicameral legislature consists of an appointed Senate (*Dewan Negara*) and a fully elected (by universal adult suffrage) 193-member House of Representatives (*Dewan Rakyat*). Each state has its own constitution and a unicameral state assembly which shares power with the federal parliament.

The major political force in Malaysia is the National Front (*Barisan Nasional*), a coalition of 13 parties representing the country's major ethnic groups (Malay, Chinese and Indian). In elections to the House of Representatives on Nov. 28–29, 1999, the BN alliance, dominated by the United Malays National Organization (UMNO), was returned to power with 148 seats. The other 45 seats were distributed as follows: Pan-Malaysian Islamic Party (PAS) 27, Democratic Action Party 10, National Justice Party (PKN) 5, United Sabah Party (PBS) 3. In concurrent elections for the 11 state assemblies of Peninsular Malaysia, the BN won nine.

National Front
Barisan Nasional (BN)
Address. Suite 1 & 2, 8th Floor, Menara Dato' Onn, World Trade Center, Jalan Tun Ismail, 50480 Kuala Lumpur
Telephone. (+60–3) 292–0384
Fax. (+60–3) 293–4743
Email. info@bn.org.my
Website. www.bn.org.my
Leadership. Dato' Datuk Sri Mohammed Rahmat (secretary-general)
The BN is the governing multi-ethnic coalition, comprising 13 parties (each described below) in 2001. Launched in 1973, the BN superseded the earlier Alliance Party, which had been founded in 1952 and held power from independence in 1957. The coalition contests state and federal elections as a single political body, with candidates of the constituent parties agreeing not to stand against each other. It has remained in power since its foundation, winning a majority of seats in 10 consecutive general elections. In the 1999 federal elections, the BN won 148 of the 193 seats in the House of Representatives. In simultaneous elections to the 11 state assemblies of Peninsular Malaysia, the BN won in all states except Kelantan and Terengganu. It continued to control the state governments of Sabah and Sarawak.

National Front Parties

Liberal Democratic Party (LDP)
Parti Liberal Demokratik
Address. Level 2, Lot 1, Jasaga Bldg., Leboh Dua, PO Box 1125, 90712 Sandakan, Sabah.
Telephone. (+60–89) 271888
Fax. (+60–89) 288278
Leadership. Datuk Chong Kah Kiet (president)
The LDP is an ethnic Chinese-dominated party based in Sabah. It joined the federal National Front (BN) in 1991 and won one parliamentary seat in the 1999 election. Under the BN's rotational scheme, the LDP leader, Datuk Chong Kah Kiet, is the current chief minister of Sabah.

Malaysian Chinese Association (MCA)
Persatuan China Malaysia
Address. Wisma MCA, 8th Floor, 163 Jalan Ampang, PO Box 10626, 50720 Kuala Lumpur
Telephone. (+60–3) 261–8044
Fax. (+60–3) 263–5715
Email. info@mca.org.my
Website. www.mca.org.my
Leadership. Datuk Seri Dr Ling Liong Sik (president)
The MCA was formed in 1949 to support the interests of the Chinese community in Malaysia, though it is most closely associated with Chinese business interests. In 1969 the party withdrew from the →National Front (BN) in protest against the government's response to communal rioting in which many Chinese were killed, with the result that the MCA was abandoned by much of its mass constituency. However, it

rejoined the reformed BN prior to the 1982 federal elections, thereafter making an important contribution to successive BN electoral victories.

In the 1995 elections the MCA increased its parliamentary representation from 18 to 30 seats, retaining 29 in 1999 and helping to offset the decline of the →United Malays National Organization (UMNO). However, the party continued to experience factional strains between its English-educated leadership, seeking accommodation with the UMNO, and Chinese-educated cadres with a more assertive stand on Chinese interests in language and culture. In May 2000 MCA leader Ling Liong Sik resigned as federal Transport Minister amidst complaints that the party had obtained insufficient senior posts after the 1999 elections.

Malaysian Indian Congress (MIC)
Kongres India Se-Malaysia
Address. Menara Manickavasagam, 6th Floor 1 Jalan Rahmat, Off Jala Off Jalan Tun Ismail, 50350 Kuala Lumpur
Telephone. (+60–3) 442–4377
Fax. (+60–3) 442–7236
Email. michq@mic.org.my
Website. www.mic.org
Leadership. Dato Seri S. Samy Vellu (president)
The MIC, founded in the mid-1940s, is the main representative of the ethnic Indian community in Malaysia. It joined what became the →National Front (BN) in the mid-1950s and has remained a steadfast member ever since. Although Malaysia's Indian community forms a majority in none of the country's 193 constituencies, the MIC was allocated seven seats to contest in the 1999 federal elections, and was successful in all of them.

Malaysian People's Movement Party
Parti Gerakan Rakyat Malaysia (PGRM, Gerakan)
Address. No. 8, Jalan Pudu Hulu, Cheras, 56100 Kuala Lumpur
Telephone. (+60–3) 987-6868
Fax. (+60–3) 987–8866
Email. pgrmhq@pgrmhq.po.my
Website. www.gerakan.org.my
Leadership. Dato Seri Dr Lim Keng Yaik (president)
Founded in 1968 and mainly based in Penang, *Gerakan* is a social democratic party that attracts most of its support from Chinese intellectuals and the middle class, competing for that constituency with the opposition →Democratic Action Party. Unlike other →National Front (BN) parties, however, it claims to be non-communal in its membership recruitment and ideology. The party won six seats in the 1999 federal elections as part of the BN.

People's Progressive Party (PPP)
Address. 27–29A Jalan Maharajalela, 50150 Kuala Lumpur
Telephone. (+60–3) 244–1922
Fax. (+60–3) 244–2041
Website. www.jaring.my/ppp

Leadership. Datuk M. Kayveas (president)

Founded in the mid-1950s and centred in Ipoh, the nominally left-wing PPP was originally based in the local Chinese community but today draws most of its support from lower-caste Indians. Although a member of the →National Front (BN) since the mid-1970s, it has not held a federal lower house seat for many years. Its president, however, holds an appointed seat in the Senate and has been attempting to revitalize the party as the "New" (*Baru*) PPP.

Sabah Progressive Party (SAPP)
Parti Maju Sabah

Address. Level 2, Lot 23, Bornion Centre, Luyang, 88300 Kota Kinabalu, Sabah

Telephone. (+60–88) 242107

Fax. (+60–88) 248188

Email. sapp@po.jaring.my

Website. www.jaring.my/sapp

Leadership. Datuk Yong Teck Lee (leader)

The SAPP was set up in 1994 as a breakaway group from the →Sabah United Party, being a predominantly ethnic Chinese party within the →National Front (BN). In 1996 its leader, Yong Teck Lee, was appointed Sabah chief minister under the state BN's two-year rotational scheme. The SAPP contested the 1999 federal elections under the BN banner and won two parliamentary seats.

Sarawak National Action Party (SNAP)
Parti Kebangsaan Sarawak

Address. Lot 304-5 Mei-jun Bldg., No. 1, Rubber Rd, PO Box 2960, 93758 Kuching, Sarawak

Telephone. (+60–82) 254244

Fax. (+60–82) 253562

Leadership. Datuk Amar James Wong Kim Min (president)

Supported largely by the Iban population (ethnic Dayaks) of Sarawak, the SNAP is a member not only of the federal →National Front (BN) but also of the BN in Sarawak, where it has participated in dominant BN coalitions. The SNAP won four parliamentary seats in the 1999 federal election.

Sarawak Native People's Party
Parti Bansa Dayak Sarawak (PBDS)

Address. No. 622, Jalan Kedandi, Tabuan Jaya, PO Box 2148, 93742 Kuching, Sarawak

Telephone. (+60–82) 363734

Fax. (+60–82) 363734

Leadership. Datuk Amar Leo Moggie Anak Irok (president)

The PBDS was set up in 1983 by a breakaway group of the →Sarawak National Action Party (SNAP). The following year it was accepted as a →National Front (BN) partner and formed a state coalition government with the SNAP, the →United Traditional Bumiputra Party and the →Sarawak United People's Party. In 1987, having been dismissed from the state (but not the federal) BN coalition, the PBDS emerged from state elections as the largest single party with 15 seats. However, its presence in state politics was sharply eroded in subsequent elections. The PBDS rejoined the BN in 1994. In the 1999 federal elections, the party won six lower house seats.

Sarawak United People's Party (SUPP)
Parti Rakyat Bersatu Sarawak

Address. 7 Jalan Tan Sri Datuk Ong Kee Hui, PO Box 454, 93710 Kuching, Sarawak

Telephone. (+60–82) 246999

Fax. (+60–82) 256510

Email. secretariat@supp.com.my

Website. www.supp.org.my

Leadership. Datuk Amar George Chan Hong Nam (president); Datuk Sim Kheng Hui (secretary-general)

The traditionally Chinese-based SUPP is a member not only of the ruling →National Front (BN) at the federal level but also of the Sarawak BN, as part of which it has gained significant representation in the state assembly. The SUPP won eight parliamentary seats in the 1999 federal elections.

United Malays National Organization (UMNO)
Pertubuhan Kebangsaan Melayu Bersatu

Address. Menara Dato' Onn, 38th Floor, Putra World Trade Center, Jalan Tun Dr Ismail, 50480 Kuala Lumpur

Telephone. (+60–3) 442–9511

Fax. (+60–3) 441–2358

Email. info@umno.org.my

Website. www.umno.org.my

Leadership. Dato' Seri Mahathir bin Mohamad (president); Abdullah Ahmed Badawi (vice-president)

Founded in 1946, the UMNO supports the interests of the numerically dominant Malay community, while also promoting the right of all Malaysians to participate in the political, economic, and cultural life of the nation. The party has been the dominant political organization since independence in 1957, and it is the leading component of the ruling →National Front (BN). It has been led since 1981 by Mahathir bin Mohamad, who succeeded Datuk Hussein bin Onn as UMNO president and Prime Minister.

Following an economic recession in the mid-1980s, the UMNO experienced intense internal conflict, with Prime Minister Mahathir only narrowly defeating a challenge for the party presidency by one of his key ministers, Tengku Razaleigh Hamzah. The intra-party strife culminated in 1988 in the organization of the "New" UMNO (UMNO–*Baru*) by the pro-Mahathir faction, while Razaleigh and his dissident supporters formed the rival "Spirit of '46" party. Despite this period of discord, Mahathir led the party (under its original name) to another federal election success in 1990, and he was subsequently reconfirmed as party president.

In the 1995 federal elections, the UMNO secured 88 of the BN's 162 seats in the House of Representatives. The rival "Spirit of '46" was dissolved in the following year. In the wake of the East Asian economic crisis of 1997-98, fierce rivalry erupted between Mahathir and his heir-presumptive, Anwar Ibrahim, who was dismissed as Deputy Prime Minister and Finance Minister in September 1998. Anwar was then arrested on various criminal charges widely seen as politically inspired, resulting in April 1999 in his receiving a nine-year prison sentence for corruption and a further six-year term in August 2000 for sodomy. Anwar's wife responded by launching the anti-Mahathir →National Justice Party (PKN) in April 1999.

That the Anwar affair had damaged the UMNO among its Malay constituency was confirmed by the 1999 federal elections. Although the BN alliance retained a clear majority, the UMNO fell from 88 to 71 seats, less than the total representation gained by its coalition partners. It was also defeated by the →Pan-Malaysian Islamic Party (PAS) in concurrent state elections in Kelantan and Terengganu. Nevertheless, Mahathir was re-elected as UMNO president in May 2000 (a putative challenge by veteran rival Razaleigh Hamzah having come to nothing), while in November 2000 the UMNO supreme council successfully resisted grass-roots calls for more internal party democracy.

Pressure on Mahathir intensified in June 2001 when his long-standing ally, Daim Zainuddin, resigned as Finance Minister and UMNO treasurer following allegations of impropriety. At the annual UMNO congress later in the month, however, the Prime Minister dismissed criticism of his leadership and warned that if it did not cease the opposition could win the elections due in 2004.

United Pasok Momogun Kadazandusun Organization (UPKO)

Address. c/o Sabah State Assembly, Kota Kinabalu

Telephone. (+60–88) 718182

Fax. (+60–88) 71870

Leadership. Datuk Bernard Dompok

The UPKO was formed from the Sabah Democratic Party,

which in turn had been organized by defectors from the →Sabah United Party (PBS) in 1994. It draws support from non-Muslim indigenous groups in Sabah, complementing the appeal of the →United Malays National Organization (UMNO) to indigenous Muslims. The UPKO leader, Bernard Dompok, served as Sabah's chief minister in 1998-2000 under the unique two-year rotational scheme operated by the →National Front (BN). Running under the BN banner in the 1999 federal elections, the UPKO won three parliamentary seats.

United Sabah People's Party
Parti Bersatu Rakyat Sabah (PBRS)

Address. PO Box 20148, Luyang, 88761 Kota Kinabalu, Sabah
Telephone. (+60–88) 269282
Fax. (+60–88) 269282
Leadership. Datuk Joseph Kurup (leader)
The PBRS was formed in 1994 by a breakaway faction of the →Sabah United Party and is a member of the ruling →National Front (BN). Like →United Pasok Momogun Kadazandusun Organization (UPKO), it draws support from non-Muslim indigenous groups within Sabah. Its leader, Joseph Kurup, contested the 1999 federal elections under the BN banner, but was unsuccessful.

United Traditional Bumiputra Party
Parti Pesaka Bumiputra Bersatu (PBB)

Address. Lot 401, Jalan Bako, PO Box 1953, 93400 Kuching, Sarawak
Telephone. (+60–82) 448299
Fax. (+60–82) 448294
Leadership. Tan Sri Datuk Patinggi Amar Haji Abdul Taib Mahmud (president)
A member of the federal →National Front (BN), the PBB is also the dominant partner in the ruling coalition in Sarawak state, together with the →Sarawak United People's Party, the →Sarawak National Action Party and the →Sarawak Native People's Party. In the 1999 federal election, the PBB won 10 parliamentary seats, helping to sweep the state for the BN.

Main Non-Front Parties

Democratic Action Party (DAP)
Parti Tindakan Demokratik

Address. 24 Jalan 20/9, 46300 Petaling Jaya, Selangor
Telephone. (+60–3) 7957–8022
Fax. (+60–3) 7957–5718
Email. dap.malaysia@pobox.com
Website. www.malaysia.net/dap
Leadership. Kerk Kim Hock (secretary-general); Lim Kit Siang (president)
The DAP was founded in 1966 as the Malaysian offshoot of the →→People's Action Party (PAP) of Singapore and is a predominantly Chinese party with a democratic socialist orientation. Contesting its first general elections in May 1969 in alliance with the →Malaysian People's Movement Party (*Gerakan*), it made a political breakthrough for non-Malays, winning 13 federal and 31 state assembly seats. However, this success precipitated a wave of serious communal violence and the detention of leading DAP members, including then leader Lim Kit Siang. Thereafter the DAP's activities were circumscribed by various internal security measures. It nevertheless remained the main opposition party at the national level during the 1970s and 1980s, although its representation in the House of Representatives dropped sharply in the April 1995 federal elections from 20 seats to nine.

In the 1999 federal elections, the DAP co-operated with the →Pan-Malaysian Islamic Party (PAS) under the umbrella of the Alternative Front (*Barisan Alternatif*, BA). However, many Chinese were fearful of the PAS commitment to an Islamic state, with the result that the DAP won only 10 parliamentary seats, while the PAS advanced to 27 seats and replaced the DAP as the main opposition party. Having lost his own parliamentary seat, Lim Kit Siang was replaced as DAP secretary-general (leader) by Kerk Kim Hock, becoming party president.

Growing strains in the DAP's alliance with the PAS came to a head over the massive terrorist attack on the USA in September 2001. After the PAS had publicly backed resistance by Muslims to any resultant US-led attack on an Islamic state, the DAP formally withdrew from the BA and reiterated its commitment to a secular Malaysia.

The DAP is a member of the Socialist International.

National Justice Party
Parti Keadilan Nasional (PKN, Keadilan)

Address. No. 101 & 201, Block A, Pusat Dagangan Phileo Damansara II, No. 15, Jalan 16/11, off Jalan Damansara, 46350 Petaling Jaya, Selangor
Telephone. (+60–3) 7954–0469
Fax. (+60–3) 7954–0419
Email. webmaster@partikeadilan.org
Website. www.partikeadilan.org
Leadership. Datin Wan Azizah Wan Ismail (president); Tian Chua (vice-president)
The PKN was launched in April 1999 by Wan Azizah Wan Ismail following the prosecution of her husband, former Deputy Prime Minister Anwar Ibrahim, and his expulsion from the ruling →United Malays National Organization (UMNO). The party began as a pressure group geared principally to winning Anwar's release, but evolved quickly into a political party bridging the gulf between the →Pan-Malaysian Islamic Party (PAS) and the →Democratic Action Party (DAP) within the opposition Alternative Front (*Barisan Alternatif*, BA). Officially non-communal but drawing most of its support from middle-class Malays, the PKN failed to make the hoped-for impact in the 1999 federal elections. Although Wan Azizah successfully defended her husband's seat in Penang, her party won only five seats in total.

The second trial of Anwar and his conviction for sodomy in August 2000 were accompanied by government-backed crackdowns on PKN activists, some of whom were enticed back into the UMNO fold. In November 2000, however, the PKN delivered a shock federal by-election defeat on the government in Kedah state, drawing support from ethnic Chinese voters. Wan Azizah's rejection in January 2001 of an invitation to talks on national unity with Prime Minister Mahathir was followed by further anti-PKN actions by the authorities. In June 2001 a PKN conference gave approval in principle to a merger with the small but venerable People's Party of Malaysia (*Parti Rakyat Malaysia*), to form a new party tentatively christened the People's National Justice Party (*Parti Rakyat Keadilan Nasional*).

Pan-Malaysian Islamic Party
Parti Islam se-Malaysia (PAS)

Address. Markaz Tarbiyyah PAS Pusat, Lorong Haji Hassan, off Jalan Batu Geliga, Taman Melawar, 68100 Batu Caves, Selangor
Telephone. (+60–3) 689–5612
Fax. (+60–3) 688–9520
Email. webmaster@parti-pas.org
Website. www.jaring.my.pas
Leadership. Datuk Fadzil Nor (president); Datuk Haji Nik Abdul Aziz Nik Mat (spiritual leader)
Founded in the early 1950s, the revivalist PAS seeks the establishment of an Islamic state and society. It joined the ruling →National Front (BN) in 1973, but returned to opposition four years later. Contesting the 1990 and 1995 elections as part of the Muslim Unity Movement (formed in 1989 as a loose opposition alliance), the PAS won seven seats in the federal House of Representatives on both occasions. In the 1990 state assembly elections, the party won control of Kelantan, its stronghold, enabling Datuk Haji Nik

Abdul Aziz Nik Mat to form a PAS government in coalition with the "Spirit of '46" splinter group of the United Malays National Organization (UMNO).

For the 1999 elections the PAS joined a more deeply integrated opposition coalition called the Alternative Front (*Barisan Alternatif*, BA), including the →Democratic Action Party (DAP) and the →National Justice Party (PKN). The PAS greatly increased its representation in the federal parliament to 27 seats, also retaining control of Kelantan and winning enough seats to form a new state government in Terengganu under the chief ministership of Datuk Haji Abdul Hadi Awang. As a result of the elections, the PAS president, Datuk Fadzil Noor, became leader of the opposition in the federal parliament.

In June 2000 the PAS leadership rejected rank-and-file calls for the lifting of the party's ban on women standing as PAS election candidates. On the other hand, in June 2001 Lolo Mohamad Ghazali became the first woman to be elected to the PAS central committee. In September 2001 the PAS reaction to the suspected Islamic terrorist attacks on New York and Washington, particularly calls by Nik Abdul Aziz Nik Mat for Muslim opposition to any US-led retaliatory attack on an Islamic state, caused the DAP to withdraw from the BA.

Sabah United Party
Parti Bersatu Sabah (PBS)
Address. Block M, Lot 4, 2nd & 3rd Floor, Donggongan Newtownship, Penamapng, Sabah
Telephone. (+60–8) 871–4891
Fax. (+60–8) 871–8067
Email. pbshq@pbs-sabah.org
Website. www.pbs-sabah.org
Leadership. Datuk Joseph Pairin Kitingan (president)
The PBS was founded in 1985 by dissidents from the Sabah People's Union (Berjaya) and won a majority of state assembly seats that year, drawing most of its support from non-Muslim indigenous groups. The PBS was admitted to the federal →National Front (BN) in 1986, but its relations with dominant →United Malays National Organization (UMNO) remained strained. Just days before the 1990 federal elections the PBS withdrew from the BN and went into the opposition, prompting the UMNO to set up its Sabah branch. The PBS suffered damaging defections in early 1994, forcing it to relinquish the state government to the BN. The party contested the 1999 federal elections as an opposition party, winning three parliamentary seats.

Maldives

Capital: Male   **Population:** 301,450 (2000E)

There are no political parties in the Republic of Maldives, a former British protectorate until independence in 1965. There is a 50-member legislature (the People's *Majlis),* 42 members of which are elected for five years, with the remaining eight appointed by the President. The People's *Majlis* designates the President for a five-year term, but the action must be confirmed by popular referendum. The President appoints, and presides over, the Cabinet.

President Mamoun Abdul Gayoom first took office in 1978. His re-election for a fifth term was confirmed in October 1998 after he won an overwhelming majority of votes cast in a national referendum. Non-party elections to the People's *Majlis* were held in November 1999.

Mali

Capital: Bamako   **Population:** 10,700,000 (2000E)

Mali was under French rule until it achieved independence with Senegal as the Federation of Mali in June 1960. The Federation, formed the previous year, was dissolved in August 1960 when Senegal withdrew, the title of the Republic of Mali then being adopted. Following a coup in 1968, the country was ruled until 1991 by a Military Committee for National Liberation with Gen. Moussa Traoré as executive President, head of state and government, and (from 1979) secretary-general of the sole legal political party, the Mali People's Democratic Union. In March 1991 the regime was overthrown in a coup and replaced by a transitional military civilian administration (the Transition Committee for the Salvation of the People, CTSP). A new constitution establishing multi-party rule was approved in a referendum in January 1992. It provides for a directly elected executive President, with a five-year term of office, and a National Assembly *(Assemblée Nationale)* of 129 members (13 of whom represent the interests of Malians resident abroad), who also serve for five years. In January 1997, a new Electoral Code was adopted which, inter alia, raised the number of National Assembly seats to 147.

In multi-party legislative elections held over two rounds in July and August 1997 the →Alliance for Democracy in Mali (ADEMA), in power since 1992, secured an overwhelming majority in the National Assembly. (A first round of polling had taken place in April, but the results of this vote had been annulled by the Constitutional Court because of "serious irregularities".) The elections were characterized by a low turnout in both rounds of voting and by violence in which at least two people were killed. A presidential election held in May 1997 resulted in the re-election of incumbent President Alpha Oumar Konare, the leader of ADEMA.

MALTA

Alliance for Democracy in Mali
Alliance pour la Démocratie au Mali (ADEMA)
Address. BP 1791, Bamako
Leadership. Alpha Oumar Konare (leader)
ADEMA was a principal element in the pro-democracy campaign launched in 1990 against the Moussa Traoré regime and was represented in the Transition Committee (CTSP) set up after the March 1991 coup. In March–April 1992 it gained control of the legislature in multi-party elections and Konare won the presidential ballot. In the 1997 legislative elections ADEMA won 129 of the 147 seats in the National Assembly. ADEMA faced little co-ordinated opposition during the campaign as a boycott organized by parties grouped within the main opposition alliance was implemented. In the May 1997 presidential election Konare was re-elected with 95.9 per cent of the votes cast. His share of the poll was such that the second round of the election, scheduled for May 25, was rendered unnecessary. However, Konare's victory was achieved in the face of an almost total boycott of the poll by other candidates. His only opponent was Mamadou Maribatrou Diaby of the →Party for Unity, Progress and Democracy (PUDP).

ADEMA is a full member of the Socialist International.

Convention for Progress and the People
Convention pour le Progrès et la Peuple (COPP)
Address. c/o Assemblée Nationale, BP 284, Bamako
The COPP won a single seat in the 1997 elections to the National Assembly.

Democracy and Justice Party
Parti pour la Démocratie et la Justice (PDJ)
Address. c/o Assemblée Nationale, BP 284, Bamako
The PDJ won a single seat in the 1997 elections to the National Assembly.

Democratic and Social Convention
Convention Démocratique et Sociale (CDS)
Address. c/o Assemblée Nationale, BP 284, Bamako
The CDS secured the largest vote of any opposition party during the 1997 legislative elections, winning four seats in the National Assembly. Following the election, senior CDS legislators entered into negotiations with the ruling →Alliance for Democracy in Mali (ADEMA) concerning the possibility of forming a broad based ruling coalition. However, ADEMA's strength in the National Assembly left the CDS isolated and the coalition negotiations ended without agreement.

National Democratic Rally
Rassemblement National Démocratique (RND)
Address. c/o Assemblée Nationale, BP 284, Bamako
The RND won a single seat in the 1997 elections to the National Assembly.

Party for Democracy and Progress
Parti pour la Démocratie et le Progrès (PDP)
Address. BP 1823, Bamako
Leadership. Idrissa Traoré (leader)
In the 1997 legislative elections the PDP retained the two seats it had won in the 1992 elections.

Party for National Renewal
Parti pour le Rénouvellement National (PARENA)
Address. c/o Assemblée Nationale, BP 284, Bamako
In the 1997 elections to the National Assembly PARENA won eight seats and entered into an informal coalition agreement with the →Alliance for Democracy in Mali (ADEMA). During the campaign PARENA had publicly allied itself with ADEMA and had supported President Konare's candidacy during the presidential elections.

Party for Unity, Progress and Democracy
Parti pour l'Unité, Progrès et Démocratie (PUDP)
Address. c/o Assemblée Nationale, BP 284, Bamako
Leadership. Mamadou Maribatrou Diaby
The PUDP failed to secure any seats in the 1997 legislative elections. Party leader Diaby opposed President Konare of the Alliance for Democracy in Mali (ADEMA) in the presidential election held in May 1997. Diaby had been one of nine opposition leaders who had said that they would boycott the presidential contest in protest over the earlier annulment of legislative elections. In the event, Diaby secured only 4.1 per cent of the votes cast and was the sole opponent to Konare.

Union for Democracy and Development
Union pour la Démocratie et le Développement (UDD)
Address. c/o Assemblée Nationale, BP 284, Bamako
Leadership. Moussa Balla Coulibaly
The UDD was formed in April 1991 and won two seats in the 1997 National Assembly elections.

Other Parties

The following parties boycotted the legislative and presidential elections of 1997. The party leaders were all arrested in the aftermath of the elections and faced charges related to violent incidents reported during the election campaign.

Movement for Independence, Renewal and African Integration (*Mouvement pour Indépendance, Renouvellement et Africain Intégration, MIRAI*)
Leadership. Mohammed Lamine Traore

National Congress for Democratic Initiative (*Congrès Nationale pour la Initiative Démocratie CNID*)
Leadership. Mountaga Tall

Rally for Democracy and Progress (*Rassemblement pour la Démocratie et le Progrès RDP*)
Leadership. Almamy Sylla

Union of Democratic and Popular Forces (*Union des Démocratiques et Populaires Forces UDPF*)
Leadership. Youssouf Traore

Malta

Capital: Valletta

Population: 385,000 (2000E)

Malta was granted independence from Britain in 1964 as a member of the Commonwealth and declared itself a Republic in 1974. Its 1964 constitution as amended in 1974 defines Malta as a parliamentary democracy, with a largely ceremonial President elected for a five-year term by the legislature. Executive power resides in the

Cabinet headed by the Prime Minister, chosen from and responsible to the unicameral House of Representatives of 65 members elected for a five-year term (subject to dissolution) by universal suffrage of those aged 18 and over. Members are returned from multi-seat electoral divisions by proportional representation, a degree of overall proportionality being ensured under a 1987 constitutional amendment which specifies that a party winning a majority of the popular vote should be awarded "bonus" seats if such are needed to give it a parliamentary majority. Another amendment adopted at the same time, also by agreement between the two main parties, gave constitutional force to Malta's status as a neutral state.

Elections to the House of Representatives on Sept. 5, 1998, resulted as follows: Nationalist Party 35 seats (51.81% of the vote), Malta Labour Party 30 (46.97%).

Malta Labour Party (MLP)
Partit tal-Haddiema

Address. Centra Nazzjonali Laburista, Triq Milend, Hamrun HMR 02
Telephone. (+356) 249900
Fax. (+356) 244204
Email. jimmy.magro@mlp.org.mt
Website. www.mlp.org.mt
Leadership. Alfred Sant (leader); Emanuel Cuschieri (president); Jimmy Magro (secretary-general)

The MLP was founded in 1920 as a trade union party and played an important role in the 1921–30 period of internal self-government. In the first elections to a Maltese Legislative Assembly held in October 1947 under a new constitution restoring self-government, the MLP, then led by Paul Boffa, won 24 out of the Assembly's 40 seats. A government formed by Boffa was in office until September 1950. In October 1949, however, the MLP was split, with Boffa founding a (moderate) Independent Labour Party, which gained 11 seats in the 1950 Assembly elections, seven (as the Malta Workers' Party) in 1951 and three in 1953, whereafter it contested no further elections.

The MLP first gained a majority of seats (23 out of 40) in the Assembly in 1955 and was thereafter in power under Dom Mintoff until 1958, when his government resigned over a dispute with Britain on Malta's constitutional future. In the 1962 general election the MLP was defeated, gaining only 16 out of 42 seats in parliament, after the Roman Catholic Church hierarchy had called on the electorate not to vote Labour. It was not returned to power until 1971 (under Mintoff's leadership) when it won 28 out of the 55 seats in the House of Representatives. In May 1978 the party was officially amalgamated with the General Workers' Union.

Returned to power with an increased majority of 34 out of 65 seats in 1976, the MLP achieved the same result in the December 1981 elections, but came under severe criticism from the opposition →Nationalist Party (NP) for achieving a parliamentary majority on the strength of fewer popular votes than the NP. After a lengthy constitutional crisis, during which the Nationalists boycotted the House of Representatives for 15 months, the constitution was amended so that a party winning a majority of votes would if necessary be given additional seats to enable it to govern. This happened in the May 1987 elections, when the MLP retained 34 seats to the NP's 31, but the latter won 50.9% of the votes and was therefore allocated four additional seats. Labour thus went into opposition under Karmenu Mifsud Bonnici (who had succeeded Mintoff in December 1984).

The MLP's decline continued in the 1992 general elections, to 46.5% of the vote, so that it remained in opposition and Mifsud Bonnici gave way to Alfred Sant as party leader. The latter initiated a modernization of Labour's programme and organization (including completing a palatial new party headquarters), while maintaining the party's policy of clear neutrality in international relations and opposition to membership of the European Union (EU).

The MLP returned to power under Sant's leadership in early elections in October 1996, winning 50.7% of the vote and thus being allocated a one-seat overall majority of 35 seats. The new Labour government immediately suspended Malta's participation in NATO's Partnership for Peace (agreed by the previous NP government) and halted moves towards EU accession. Responding to worsening economic conditions in 1997, the government introduced spending cuts and austerity measures which provoked fierce trade union opposition and also caused former leader Mintoff, still a member of the House, to give up the party whip. Effectively without a majority, Sant called new elections in September 1998 in which the MLP was decisively defeated, being reduced to 47% of the vote and 30 seats. In opposition again, the MLP vigorously opposed the new NP government's opening of fast-track negotiations for EU accession in 1999.

The MLP is a member party of the Socialist International.

Nationalist Party (NP)
Partit Nazzjonalista (PN)

Address. Dar Centrali, Triq Herbert Ganado, Pietà
Telephone. (+356) 243641
Fax. (+356) 242886
Website. www.pn.org.mt
Leadership. Edward Fenech Adami (leader); Lawrence Gonzi (deputy leader); Joe Saliba (secretary-general)

Dating from 1880, the NP has its origins in the wave of nationalism which swept Europe in the 19th century and it fought successfully for Malta's self-government and later independence. Between 1887 and 1903, when Malta had representative government, the party held all elective seats in the Council of Government. After a period of colonial rule representative government was reintroduced in 1921 and the party held a majority of seats until 1927, when the Constitutional Party and the →Malta Labour Party (MLP) formed an alliance. When the NP regained a majority in 1933, the self-government constitution was revoked.

During World War II several leaders of the party were detained or exiled, but from 1950 to 1955 the party was in government in coalition with the Workers' Party. It later held office from 1962 to 1971, during which period Malta became independent in 1964 under the premiership of Giorgio Borg Olivier.

The party was narrowly defeated by the MLP in 1971 and again in 1976. In the elections of December 1981 the party gained 50.9% of the vote but only a minority of seats in the House of Representatives. The party subsequently started a civil disobedience campaign and boycotted sessions of the House until March 1983. However, following constitutional amendments ensuring proportionality between votes obtained and representation, the NP obtained a majority in May 1987 (31 elective seats and four "bonus" seats) and formed a government under Edward Fenech Adami.

The NP retained a majority in the February 1992 general elections and therefore continued in office. The NP government's main priority externally was to expedite Malta's application to become a full member of the European Union (submitted in 1990). It also signed up for NATO's Partnership for Peace programme in 1995, while pledging to uphold the 1987 constitutional guarantee of neutrality. However, Fenech Adami unwisely called early elections in October 1996 in which the MLP regained a narrow 35–34 ascendancy in the House of Representatives.

The Labour government's chronic problems resulted in

further elections being held in September 1998, when Fenech Adami led the NP back to power with a decisive 51.8% vote share and a 35–30 majority in the House. In 1999 the new government embarked upon fast-track negotiations for EU accession, undertaking to hold a referendum on membership when the negotiations were completed.

The NP is affiliated to the Christian Democrat International and is an associate member of the European People's Party. It is also a member of the International Democrat Union.

Other Parties

Communist Party of Malta (*Partit Komunista Malti, PKM*), founded in 1969 as an orthodox pro-Soviet party by former members of the →Malta Labour Party, to which it gave unofficial support in the Mintoff era by not contesting

elections. The party achieved minimal support in subsequent elections.
Leadership. Anthony Vassallo (general secretary)

Democratic Alternative (*Alternattiva Demokratika*, AD), environmentalist party formed prior to 1992 elections, in which it obtained 1.7% of the vote and no seats. After slipping to 1.5% in 1996, it contested the 1998 elections on a joint list with the →Social Justice Alliance which took 1.2% of the vote. The AD belongs to the European Federation of Green Parties.
Leadership. Wenzu Mintoff (chairman); Harry Vassallo (secretary-general)

Social Justice Alliance (*Alleanza Gustizzja Socijal, AGS*), progressive grouping which contested the 1998 elections on a joint list with the →Democratic Alternative.

Marshall Islands

Capital: Dalap-Uliga-Darrit (Majuro)

Population: 57,000 (2000E)

The Marshall Islands consist of a double chain of atolls in the Pacific region of Micronesia. From 1947, as part of the UN Trust Territory of the Pacific, they were administered by the United States. In 1979 a new constitution was adopted, and in 1982 the Republic of the Marshall Islands signed a compact of free association (implemented in 1986) under which the United States recognized the territory as a fully sovereign and independent state, while retaining authority in regard to defence. In December 1990 the UN Security Council approved the termination of the Trusteeship in relation to the Marshall Islands, and the country joined the UN the following year.

The Marshall Islands have a 12-member Council of Chiefs (the *Iroij*), composed of traditional leaders, with consultative authority on matters relating to custom. Legislative authority resides in a 33-member legislature (the *Nitijela*), which is elected for four years and which chooses a President from among its members. The President is both head of state and head of government and appoints the Cabinet.

President Amata Kabua was returned to office for a fifth successive term in November 1995, having been chosen by members of the new *Nitijela* elected earlier that month. Following his death in December 1996, he was succeeded by his cousin, Imata Kabua. In the traditional absence of political parties, presidential and opposition forces were at that stage aligned in loose informal groupings. However, further elections to the *Nitijela* on Nov. 22, 1999, marked the emergence of the country's first recognizable party, the United Democratic Party (UDP), which won 18 of the 33 seats and in January 2000 secured the election of Kessai Note to replace Imata Kabua as President.

United Democratic Party (UDP)
Address. c/o Nitijela, Dalap-Uliga-Darrit, Majuro Atoll
Leadership. Kessai Note
The UDP emerged from the *Ralik-Ratak* grouping formed in 1991 under the leadership of Tony DeBrum in opposition to President Amata Kabua, whose own supporters were associated with the Our Islands (*Ailin Kein Ad*) movement chaired by the President. Following the 1995 elections to the *Nitijela*, its newly-elected Speaker, Kessai Note, became the

leader of anti-Kabua forces and stood unsuccessfully for the presidency following Amata Kabua's death in December 1996. In the November 1999 elections to the *Nitijela*, Note's supporters adopted the UDF designation and became the majority grouping with 18 seats. The resultant election of Note as President in January 2000 was the first time that a sitting government had been voted out of office since the Marshall Islands became independent.

Mauritania

Capital: Nouakchot

Population: 2,670,000 (2000E)

The Islamic Republic of Mauritania achieved independence from France in 1960 as a one party state under the Mauritanian People's Party. Following a military coup in 1978, the constitution was suspended and the legislature and former government and ruling party were dissolved. The Military Council of National Salvation (CMSN), headed from 1984 by the Armed Forces Chief of Staff Col. Moaouia Ould Sid' Ahmed Taya, ruled until 1992.

Mauritania was affected to some degree by the movement to greater political pluralism apparent in much of Africa in the early 1990s. In July 1991 a new constitution was approved, providing for the election of a President by universal suffrage for a six-year term and for the appointment of a Prime Minister. Legislative power was vested in a 79-member National Assembly (*Assemblée Nationale*) directly elected for five years, and a 56-member Senate, indirectly elected for a six-year term. At the same time legislation allowing the formation of political parties was approved by the CMSN. Taya's Democratic and Social Republican Party (PRDS) won an overwhelming victory in multi-party elections held in March 1992, Taya having also won the presidential election in January 1992. Further legislative elections were held over two rounds in October 1996, with the PRDS taking 71 of the seats in the National Assembly. Other seats were taken by non-partisans with Action for Change (AC) winning the only seat won by any party opposed to the government although, following allegations of electoral fraud by the Union of Democratic Forces (UFD), the second round had been largely boycotted by opposition parties. The PRDS also maintained control of the Senate, taking 52 of the 56 seats (with one other held by an independent and three representing Mauritanians abroad) when indirect elections were held in April 2000.

Multi-party presidential elections were held in late 1997 when President Taya was returned to office for a further term with more than 90 per cent of the votes cast, defeating four other candidates.

Action for Change
Action pour Changement (AC)
Address. c/o Assemblée Nationale, Nouakchott
Leadership. Messaoud Duid Boulkueil
Formed in August 1995, the AC did not join the opposition boycott of the 1996 National Assembly elections and secured one seat, the only seat taken by a party other than the →Democratic and Social Republican Party.

Democratic and Social Republican Party
Parti Républicain Démocratique et Social (PRDS)
Address. c/o Assemblée Nationale, Nouakchott
The centre-left PRDS was formed following the legalization of multi-partyism in 1991 as a vehicle for Moaouia Ould Sid' Ahmed Taya, who had headed the ruling military council since 1984. It won 67 of the 79 seats in elections to the new National Assembly in March 1992, retaining power in October 1996 elections when it won 71 seats. The PRDS has maintained an overwhelming majority in the indirectly elected Senate since success in the inaugural election of 1992.

Mauritanian Renewal Party
Parti Mauritanien pour le Rénouvellement (PMR)
Leadership. Moulaye al-Hassan Ould Jeydid (leader)
Registered in 1991, the centrist PMR failed to secure any electoral success in the 1996 lower house elections. Jeydid stood as a candidate in the 1997 presidential election and finished in third place with less than 1 per cent of the vote.

National Vanguard Party
Parti Nationale de l'Avant-Garde (PNAG)
Leadership. Khattri Ould Jiddou
Legalized in late 1991, the PNAG failed to secure any seats in the 1996 National Assembly election. In December 1997, however, PNAG leader Jiddou was appointed to the government as Minister of Culture and Islamic Orientation.

Rally for Democracy and National Unity
Rassemblement pour la Démocratie et l'Unité Nationale (RDUN)
Leadership. Ahmed Mokhtar Sidi Baba (leader)
The centre-right RDUN failed to win any seats in the first round of the 1996 legislative elections and subsequently joined other parties in boycotting the second round.

Socialist and Democratic Popular Union
Union Populaire Socialiste et Démocratique (UPSD)
Leadership. Mohammed Mahmoud Ould Mah (leader)

Legalized in 1991, the UPSD contested the December 1997 presidential election, but party leader, Ould Mah, came fourth in the poll with only 0.7 per cent of the votes cast. The party had boycotted the October 1996 legislative elections.

Umina Party
Leadership. Ould Sidi Yayia (leader)
An influential Islamic fundamentalist organization, Umina was formed in 1991 but was prevented from registering as a political party because of the constitutional ban on parties based on religion.

Union for Democracy and Progress
Union pour la Démocratie et le Progrès (UDP)
Leadership. Hamdi Ould Mouknass (president)
The UDP was legalized in 1993, its ranks reportedly including former prominent members of the →Union of Democratic Forces.

Union of Democratic Forces
Union des Forces Démocratiques (UFD)
Leadership. Ahmed Ould Daddah (leader)
Legalized in October 1991 and generally considered the strongest opposition formation, the UFD organized the boycott of the October 1996 legislative elections. The move followed the publication of results from the first round of voting in which the →Democratic and Social Republican Party (PRDS) had secured 61 seats. UFD leader Daddah accused the government of tampering with the voters' register to exclude opposition supporters and called on all parties to boycott the second round of voting.

Other Parties

In April 2001 the Interior Ministry legalized six new political parties. They were the **Mauritanian Liberal Democrats**, led by Mustapha Ould Lemrabet; the **Third Generation**, led by Lebat Ould Jeh; the **Democratic Alliance**, led by Mohammed Ould Taleb Othman; the **Mauritanian Labour Party**, led by Mohammed Hafid Ould Denna; the **New Mauritanian Renewal Party**, led by Atiq Ould Attia and the **Alliance for Justice and Democracy**, led by Kabeh Abdoulaye.

Mauritius

Capital: Port Louis

Population: 1,186,000 (2000E)

A former British colony, Mauritius achieved independence in 1968. The British monarch remained as head of state until the country became a republic in March 1992. The post of President is a largely ceremonial role, executive power being vested in the Prime Minister who is leader of the majority parliamentary party. The President, elected for a five-year term by the National Assembly, appoints the Council of Ministers on the recommendation of the Prime Minister. There is a unicameral National Assembly, 62 of whose members are elected by universal adult suffrage for a term of five years from single-member constituencies, while up to eight additional seats are allocated by the independent Electoral Supervisory Commission under a "best loser" system.

General elections on Sept. 11, 2000, were won by an alliance led by the Mauritian Militant Movement (MMM) and the Militant Socialist Movement (MSM), which took 54 of the 60 Mauritius elective seats with 51.7% of the vote. The six remaining seats and 36.6% of the vote went to an alliance led by the Labour Party and the Xavier-Luc Duval Militant Movment (PMXD), while the Organization of the People of Rodrigues (OPR) retained the two Rodrigues elective seats. Four "best loser" seats were allocated to the MSM/MMM alliance, two to the Labour/PMXD alliance (one of these to the PMXD leader, who had failed to retain his elective seat) and two to the Rodrigues Movement. Minor parties within the MSM/MMM alliance included the Republican Movement and the rump of the Mauritian Social Democratic Party, each of which won one elective seat.

Cassam Uteem (a former MMM minister) was elected President of Mauritius by the National Assembly in June 1992 and re-elected June 1997. An August 2000 pre-election pact between the leaders of the MSM and the MMM envisaged an extension of President Uteem's current term (due to end in June 2002) until September 2003, at which point the MSM's Sir Anerood Jugnauth (appointed Prime Minister in September 2000) would become President, while the premiership would pass from him to the MMM's Paul Bérenger (appointed Deputy Prime Minister in September 2000).

Labour Party
Parti Travailliste
Address. 7 Guy Rozement Square, Port Louis
Telephone. (+230) 212–6691
Fax. (+230) 670–0720
Email. labour@intnet.mu
Website. www.labour.intnet.mu
Leadership. Navinchandra Ramgoolam (leader); Sarat Dutt Lallah (secretary general)
The Labour Party led Mauritius to independence in 1968 under the premiership of Sir Seewoosagur Ramgoolam but lost all of its elective seats in 1982. Recovering some ground in the 1983 contest, it was a constituent of the subsequent governing coalitions led by the →Militant Socialist Movement (MSM). In September 1990 it moved into opposition as a consequence of an electoral alliance forged between the MSM and the →Mauritian Militant Movement (MMM) to promote constitutional measures that would allow Mauritius to become a republic. The Labour Party contested the 1991 general election in an opposition alliance with the →Mauritian Social Democratic Party (PMSD), but won only a handful of seats.

In April 1994 the Labour Party signed an electoral pact with the MMM, and in the December 1995 general election this alliance defeated the ruling coalition, taking all the elective seats for the main island. Labour leader Navinchandra Ramgoolam (son of Sir Seewoosagur) was sworn in as the country's new Prime Minister at the end of December. He stated that his Labour/MMM coalition government would continue the pro-market economic policies of its predecessor but with more emphasis on equal opportunities and welfare for the poor.

Holding 35 seats, the Labour Party governed alone after the ending of its coalition with the MMM in 1997, although in September 1999 it backed the successful by-election campaign of Xavier-Luc Duval, who had formed the Mauritian Party of Xavier-Luc Duval (PMXD) breakaway faction of the PMSD and who joined the government the following month. The September 2000 general election was called against a background of corruption scandals involving Labour Party ministers. It resulted in the defeat (by an MSM/MMM alliance) of Labour and its current electoral allies, which retained only six elective and two "best loser" seats in the new National Assembly.

The Labour Party is a full member of the Socialist International.

Mauritian Militant Movement
Mouvement Militant Mauricien (MMM)
Address. 21 Poudrière Street, Port Louis
Telephone. (+230) 212 6553
Fax. (+230) 208 9939
Leadership. Paul Bérenger (leader); Ahmed Jeewah (chairman); Ivan Collendavelloo (general secretary)
The socialist MMM was founded in 1969 with a substantial trade union following. Briefly in government from 1982, the party split in 1983 when the then MMM president and Prime Minister, Sir Aneerood Jugnauth, was expelled from the party and thereupon formed the →Militant Socialist Movement (MSM). In the 1991 general election an alliance of the MMM, the MSM and the Democratic Labour Movement won a large parliamentary majority, and the MMM gained substantial representation in the new coalition government which transformed the country into a republic in 1992. Disputes between the MMM and the MSM during 1993 led to the dismissal of the MMM leader, Paul Bérenger, from the Council of Ministers and the subsequent departure, in mid-1994, of the pro-coalition faction within the party to form the →Mauritian Militant Renaissance. In April 1994 the MMM signed an electoral pact with the Labour Party, and in the December 1995 general election this alliance ousted the ruling coalition.

In June 1997 Bérenger was dismissed from the Labour government led by Navinchandra Ramgoolam, of whose policies he had become an increasingly outspoken critic, after which he took the MMM into opposition for the remainder of the current parliament. The MMM entered into an "informal" alliance with the MSM in February 1999, subsequently concluding a detailed agreement in August 2000 when a general election was called. Pursuant to this agreement, the substantial MSM/MMM victory in September 2000 was followed by Bérenger's appointment as Deputy Prime Minister in the government formed by Sir Anerood

323

MAURITIUS

Jugnauth, who had given an undertaking to relinquish the premiership in Bérenger's favour in September 2003.

Mauritian Social Democratic Party
Parti Mauricien Social-Démocrate (PMSD)
Address. c/o National Assembly, Port Louis
Leadership. Maurice Allet (leader); Hervé Duval (honorary president); Mamade Kodabaccus (secretary-general)

The conservative PMSD originated in the pre-independence period, mainly representing the French-speaking and Creole middle classes. Under the leadership of Gaëtan Duval, the party increased its representation to 23 seats in 1967 and took part in the 1969–73 national unity government led by the →Labour Party, with Duval as External Affairs Minister. Its departure in December 1973 was because of Labour opposition to Duval's policy of dialogue with South Africa. The PMSD was again in coalition with Labour in 1976–82, while from 1983 until 1988 it was a junior member of coalition headed by the alliance of Labour and the →Militant Socialist Movement (MSM).

Although the PMSD fought the 1991 election in an opposition alliance with Labour, it agreed to enter the governing coalition led by the MSM in February 1995, one of its ministerial appointees being Sir Gaëtan Duval's son, Xavier-Luc Duval, who had succeeded his father as PMSD party leader. Opposition to this move from within the party led to Xavier-Luc Duval's departure from the government and the subsequent reversion to his father of the party leadership. Tarred by the government's unpopularity and despite standing as the "Gaëtan Duval Party", the PMSD failed to win an elective seat in the December 1995 contest, although Sir Gaëtan was awarded the party's "best loser" seat.

On Sir Gaëtan Duval's death in May 1996, his brother, Hervé Duval, took over the party leadership and became its representative in the National Assembly. The leadership was subsequently regained by Xavier-Luc Duval as the party became increasingly polarized into a faction loyal to him and a faction loyal to his uncle, who claimed to represent the so-called "true blue" traditions of the party. The Hervé Duval faction came to be identified with the designation PMSD (and therefore effectively with the full party name), while Xavier-Luc began to use the designation PMXD, standing for the →Xavier-Luc Duval Mauritian Party, notably in political situations where there was direct confrontation between the two factions. Hervé Duval was elected leader of the PMSD at a congress organized by his faction in January 1999, but stepped down in favour of Maurice Allet later in the year. This faction of the PMSD fought the 2000 election as an ally of the MSM/MMM, its only successful candidate being Maurice Allet. Allet was confirmed unopposed as leader at the next party congress in May 2001, the party executive having refused to allow the nomination of Ghislaine Henry (sister of Hervé Duval), who was seen as an advocate of reunification with the PMXD.

Militant Socialist Movement
Mouvement Socialiste Militant (MSM)
Address. Sun Trust Building, 31 Edith Cavell Street, Port Louis
Telephone. (+230) 212 8787
Fax. (+230) 208 9517
Website. www.msmsun.com
Leadership. Sir Aneerood Jugnauth (leader); Joe Lesjondard (president); Nando Bohde (secretary)

Formed in 1983 by Sir Aneerood Jugnauth, following his expulsion from the →Mauritian Militant Movement, the MSM was the dominant party in subsequent coalition governments until the general election in December 1995 when, in alliance with the Mauritian Militant Renaissance, it failed to retain any seats in the National Assembly. In 1999 the MSM prepared the ground for a long-term alliance with the MMM, and in September 2000 (having returned to power as the head of an MSM/MMM coalition) Sir Aneerood Jugnauth appointed the MMM leader, Paul Bérenger, as his Deputy

Prime Minister on the understanding that Bérenger would take over the premiership after three years.

Organization of the People of Rodrigues
Organisation du Peuple Rodriguais (OPR)
Address. c/o National Assembly, Port Louis
Leadership. Louis Serge Clair (leader)

Representing the interests of the people of the island of Rodrigues, the OPR has consistently held the two elective seats for Rodrigues in the National Assembly and has been included in most post-independence government coalitions.

Xavier-Luc Duval Mauritian Party
Parti Mauricien Xavier-Luc Duval (PMXD)
Address. c/o National Assembly, Port Louis
Leadership. Charles Gaëtan Xavier-Luc Duval

The designation PMXD came into use in the late 1990s to distinguish the faction of the →Mauritian Social Democratic Party (PMSD) led by Xavier-Luc Duval following a rift within that party. He won a parliamentary by-election as PMXD candidate in October 1999, subsequently serving as a minister in the →Labour Party government of Navinchandra Ramgoolam. The PMXD fought the September 2000 general election as an ally of the Labour Party, but failed to win any elective seats. Its leader was, however, allocated a "best loser" seat in the new Assembly.

Other Parties

Democratic Union of Mauritius, member of the Christian Democrat and People's Parties International; unrepresented in the legislature.
Address. 105 Chancery House, Port Louis
Telephone. (+230) 212 0252
Fax. (+230) 212 8799
Leadership. Guy Ollivry (president); Rossind Bowwarbe (secretary general)

Hizbullah, an Islamic fundamentalist formation that obtained sufficient support in the December 1995 elections to be awarded one "best loser" seat.
Leadership. Cehl Mohamed Fakeemeeah (leader)

Mauritian Militant Socialist Movement (*Mouvement Militant Socialiste Mauricien*), supported the Labour Party in the 2000 general election campaign, but failed to win any seats.
Leadership. Madun Dulloo (leader)

Rally for Reform (*Rassemblement pour la Réforme, RPR*), supported the Labour Party in the 2000 general election campaign, but failed to win any seats.
Leadership. Sheila Bappoo (leader)

Republican Movement (*Mouvement Républicain*), founded in 1996 and won one seat in the 2000 general election, having given its support to the winning MMM/MSM alliance. In May 2001 the party instructed its sole Assembly member, Sunil Dowarkasing, to switch his support from the ruling coalition to the official opposition, a move which seemed likely to lead to his leaving the Republican Movement to sit as an independent.
Leadership. Rama Valayden (leader)

Rodrigues Movement (*Mouvement Rodriguais*), founded in 1992 to represent the interests of Rodrigues island, competing with the →Organization of the People of Rodrigues; was allocated two "best loser" seats in the National Assembly following the 1995 and 2000 general elections.
Leadership. Nicholas Von Mally (leader)

Socialist Workers' Party (*Parti Socialiste Ouvrier, PSO*), founded in 1997 with a Marxist–Leninist programme.
Leadership. Didier Edmond (general secretary)

Mexico

Capital: Mexico City

Population: 101,000,000 (2000E)

Mexico achieved independence from Spain in 1821. The iron rule of Porfirio Díaz, President from 1876 to 1911 (known as the *Porfiriato*), except for the period 1880-84, ended the political instability of earlier years but precipitated the violent revolution of 1910–20 which produced such leaders as Emiliano Zapata and Francisco "Pancho" Villa. From 1929 one party, renamed the Institutional Revolutionary Party (PRI) in 1946, inherited the mantle of the revolution and held power until 2000.

Under the 1917 constitution (as amended) a bicameral Congress is made up of a 128-member Senate, elected every six years (two directly from each state plus two under a complicated proportional representation mechanism), and a 500-member federal Chamber of Deputies. Executive power rests with the President, who appoints a Cabinet. State governors, state legislators and the head of the Federal District are elected directly. As with national elections, executive positions are elected under a first past the post system whereas legislators are elected under proportional representation.

The President is elected for a six-year term, known as the *sexenio*, as are the senators. The 500 deputies are elected every three years. Each state has its own constitution and is administered by a governor, who is elected for a six-year term. All elections, both national and state, are held on the basis of universal adult suffrage. All Mexican citizens 18 years of age and older are required to vote, although the law is rarely enforced.

The PRI finally lost its tenure of power when Vicente Fox Quesada, as the candidate of a coalition of parties whose main component was the conservative National Action Party (PAN), defeated Francisco Labastida Ochoa of the PRI in the July 2000 presidential election by a margin of 42.5% to 36.1%. The candidate of the leftist Party of the Democratic Revolution (PRD), Cuauhtémoc Cárdenas was in third place, taking 16.6%. This outcome came at the end of a long period in which the PRI's share of the vote in presidential elections had been in decline, falling from 95% in 1976 to 74% in 1982, 51% in 1988, and 50% in 1994. One factor in this decline is that elections have become increasingly fair and vigorously contested with the PRI and PAN competing as the two main parties.

Legislative elections in July 2000 left no party in overall control. Competing as part of the Alliance for Change formed for the election, the PAN took 218 seats in the Chamber of Deputies, with its junior partner in the Alliance, the Green Ecologist Party of Mexico (PVEM) taking 5 seats. The PRI, standing independently, won 209 seats, while the Alliance for Mexico, a coalition of left-leaning parties, took 68 seats; of these 53 were won by the Party of the Democratic Revolution (PRD), nine by the Labour Party (PT) and two each by the Convergence for Democracy (CD), the Socialist Alliance Party (PAS) and the Nationalist Society Party (PSN). The Senate contests resulted as follows: PRI 60 seats, PAN 46, PRD 15, PVEM 5, PT 1, CD 1.

Institutional Revolutionary Party
Partido Revolucionario Institucional (PRI)
Address. Insurgentes Norte 59, 06350 Mexico DF
Website. www.pri.org.mx
Leadership. Dulce Maria Sauri Riancho (president); Rodolfo Echeverría Ruiz (secretary-general)

The PRI was founded in 1929 as the National Revolutionary Party. It was renamed the Party of the Mexican Revolution in 1938 before becoming the Institutional Revolutionary Party (PRI) in 1946. The party inherited a populist and symbolic tradition from the 1910–20 Mexican Revolution which gave it room to manoeuvre in practice, uniting disparate political tendencies from socialism and social democracy through to right-wing conservatism. Its current belief in a market-led economy and the conservatism of its foreign policy, points to a clear move to the right.

Of the many PRI Presidents, the most radical and most influential was probably Gen. Lázaro Cárdenas (1934-40). His re-organization of the party led to it becoming a huge network for social control and patronage, incorporating labour and peasant unions and popular organizations for civil servants, professional groups and the army. Cárdenas nationalized the oil industry in 1938 and introduced significant land reforms through the *ejido* common land system.

The authoritarian face of the party was shown most forcibly during the presidencies of Gustavo Díaz Ordaz (1964–70) and Luis Echeverría Alvárez (1970–76), when student unrest was violently repressed. Rhetorically Díaz

Ordaz was associated with the right and Echeverría with the left, but they were both repressive presidents. President José López Portillo (1976–82) headed another authoritarian regime but in foreign policy it supported the 1979 Nicaraguan revolution and permitted the legalization of several left-wing parties.

President Miguel de la Madrid (1982–88), from the right of the party, had to deal with the severe economic consequences of a debt crisis that hit all of Latin America in 1982. He adopted some ambitious market-oriented reforms. Internal unrest also surfaced within the PRI as dissidents in the Critical Current faction (*Corriente Crítica*) and the Movement for Democratic Change (*Movimiento por el Cambio Democrático*, MCD) objected to the lack of internal democracy and the continuation of the *dedazo* system whereby the President hand-picked election candidates and delegates to the PRI's national assembly.

The 1988 election victory of President Carlos Salinas de Gortari, by the smallest margin in the PRI's history, was one of the most controversial ever, opposition leaders being united in their claims that the PRI had been involved in widespread fraud. In the past, there had not been enough democratic competition to make fraud necessary, but by 1988 there were the first signs of competitive democracy taking root. In July 1989 the PRI conceded victory to the →National Action Party candidate in the governorship election in Baja California, its first electoral defeat in 60 years.

The Salinas administration set out to improve the country's image and continue with the policy of market-oriented reform and gradual democratization. Salinas initiated an ambitious programme to deregulate and liberalize the economy and privatize the state sector, most notably re-privatizing state banks nationalized in 1982. Negotiations were also begun in 1990 to conclude a North American Free Trade Agreement (NAFTA) with the USA and Canada. Mexico's entry into the NAFTA in January 1994 became the centre piece of the government's strategy to modernize the country and extricate it from a decade of debt-ridden stagnation.

In 1994 Salinas chose Donaldo Colosio to be his replacement, much to the disappointment of Manuel Camacho Solís who had expected the nomination (and went on to found the →Party of the Democratic Centre). However, Colosio was murdered in March 1994, and Ernesto Zedillo Ponce de Leon, who had been Education Minister under Salinas, was nominated in his place. Zedillo was elected to the presidency in August 1994, and pledged to continue with the Salinas government's policies. However in December 1994 financial crisis returned as the Mexican government bungled a devaluation and once more nearly defaulted on its debts. This contributed to PRI unpopularity, and the party lost control of the Chamber of Deputies in the mid-term 1997 elections.

Zedillo gave up the right to choose his own successor as presidential candidate, and instead organized a primary election within the party. The two main candidates for the nomination were Francisco Labastida Ochoa and Roberto Madrazo Pintado. Labastida won the nomination but in July 2000 presidential election went down to defeat at the hands of Vicente Fox of the National Action Party. In the July 2000 legislative elections, the PRI came second (with 209 seats) to the PAN (218), while remaining in first place in the Senate (although without an overall majority), with 60 seats to the 46 held by the PAN. Since 2000 the policy of allowing party activists to choose the main candidates has continued although with some significant local variations.

The PRI is a consultative member of the Socialist International.

National Action Party
Partido Acción Nacional (PAN)
Address. Angel Urraza 812, Del Valle, 03109 Mexico DF
Telephone. (+52–5) 559–6300
Email. Pan@pan.org.mx
Website. www.pan.org.mex
Leadership. Vicente Fox Quesada (president of Mexico); Luis Felipe Bravo Mena (president of the party)
Founded in 1939, the PAN is a conservative social Christian party. It has close associations with the Roman Catholic Church, and also with some of the business community.

Since its founding, the party has been the major opposition grouping and has stood against the →Institutional Revolutionary Party (PRI) in congressional elections since 1943 and most presidential elections since 1952. Internal disputes prevented it from presenting a presidential candidate in 1976. Its fortunes have been on a slowly rising trend since 1982.

Together with the →Authentic Party of the Mexican Revolution (PARM), the PAN was long regarded as a fairly benign opposition permitted to win a limited number of seats in order to give a pluralist credibility to a monolithic system dominated by the PRI. However, the bank nationalization of 1982 led to the PAN taking a much more militantly oppositional line than it had earlier. During 1984–86, PAN supporters accused the PRI of blatant electoral fraud and were involved in numerous and occasionally violent protests, mainly in the relatively prosperous northern states from which the party drew much of its support. In July 1989, the party inflicted the first electoral defeat on the PRI in 60 years when the PAN candidate won the governorship of the state of Baja California Norte. In the August 1991 congressional elections, however, the PAN's representation in the Congress was cut from 102 to 89 seats.

In the August 1994 presidential election, the PAN came second to the PRI with 25.9% of the popular vote whilst also taking the party's chamber representation above its 1991 level by winning 119 seats. It also took 25 seats in the newly enlarged Senate.

In July 1997 the PAN together with the →Party of the Democratic Revolution (PRD) were able to deny the PRI overall control of the Senate. The PAN continued to perform generally well in state governorship elections after 1997 despite surprisingly losing the governorship of Chihuahua in 1998. Ahead of the 2000 elections, it nominated businessman Vicente Fox as its presidential candidate although Fox ran at the head of an alliance ('Alliance for Change') that included some minor parties. He ended PRI control of the presidency and the party also won more seats (218) in the Chamber of Deputies than did the PRI (209), although the PAN with 46 seats remained in second place in the Senate.

The PAN is a member of the Christian Democrat International.

Party of the Democratic Revolution
Partido de la Revolución Democrática (PRD)
Address. Centro de Cómputo PRD, Durango 338, Col Roma, CP 06700, Mexico DF
Website. www.cen-prd.org.mx
Leadership. Amalia Garcia (president); Cuauhtémoc Cárdenas Solorzano (presidential candidate)
The PRD originated from a split in the →Institutional Revolutionary Party (PRI) that developed during 1986–87 over the free market policies being followed by the government. Cuauhtémoc Cárdenas, the son of former President Lázaro Cárdenas (1934–40) and the leader of the Democratic Current faction within the PRI, was expelled from the party in 1987. He then brought together several parties to form an electoral coalition, the National Democratic Front (*Frente Democrático Nacional,* FDN), to back his candidacy in the July 1988 presidential election. These included the →Authentic Party of the Mexican Revolution (PARM), the Popular Socialist Party (PPS), the Mexican Socialist Party (PMS), the right-wing Mexican Democratic Party (PDM) and the Socialist Workers' Party (*Partido Socialista de los Trabajadores,* PST).

The FDN claimed that the subsequent PRI victory was a "massive fraud", Cárdenas contending that he had won a clear majority. The FDN parties, however, still managed to stun the PRI by taking over 31% of the vote and receiving between them a total of 139 seats in the Congress owing to a low direct vote being boosted by seats awarded by proportional representation.

Of the FDN parties, only the PMS merged into the newly-formed PRD in October 1988 and the FDN itself became effectively defunct. The PRD emerged as the most important party on the left, with a few minor fringe parties continuing to operate independently.

The PRD never again reached the high point that it achieved in 1988, although it did continue to maintain an electoral presence of some significance. In the August 1994 presidential elections, Cárdenas received 16.6% of the vote while PRD representation in the Chamber rose to 71 seats and to eight in the enlarged Senate. It then benefited from the economic recession that hit Mexico during 1995-97 by winning the first ever elections for the mayoralty of Mexico City and by winning enough seats in elections for the Senate to be able, in alliance with the →National Action Party (PAN), to deny an automatic majority to the PRI.

In the 2000 presidential election Cárdenas, backed by the Alliance for Mexico (involving mainly the PRD but also some minor parties), took 16.6% of the vote. In the legislative elections the PRD won 53 seats in the Chamber of Deputies and 15 in the Senate, maintaining its position as the third force in Mexican politics.

The PRD is a full member party of the Socialist International.

Other Parties

In addition to the following national parties there are also a number of purely local political parties that occasionally contest local and regional elections, usually as a flag of convenience for a well-known individual.

Authentic Party of the Mexican Revolution (*Partido Auténtico de la Revolución Mexicana, PARM*) was founded in 1954. It is led by Porfirio Muñoz Ledo, who withdrew his candidacy in the 2000 presidential election to support Vicente Fox of the →National Action Party. Notwithstanding this move, he still received 0.4% of the vote. Although the PARM is very weak, and has no seats in the Congress, Porfirio Muñoz Ledo is a well-known figure on the Mexican political scene.
Website. www.parm.org.mx

Democratic Convergence (DC) (*Convergencia por la Democracia*), founded in 1999 and formed part of the left-leaning coalition led by the →Party of the Democratic Revolution in the 2000 elections; won two seats in the Chamber of Deputies.
Address. Louisiana 113, Col. Napoles, CP 03810 Mexico DF
Telephone. (152–5) 543–8557

Green Ecologist Party of Mexico (*Partido Verde Ecologista de Mexico, PVEM*), entered the political arena in 1987; its 1994 presidential candidate obtained 0.9% of the vote; in the 2000 elections it competed as part of the Alliance for Change led by the →National Action Party and won five seats in the Chamber of Deputies.
Address. Medicina No. 74 esq. AV. Copilco, Universidad, Deleg. Coyoacán, CP 04360 Mexico DF
Website. www.pvem.org.mx

Labour Party (*Partido del Trabajo, PT*), founded before the 1991 congressional elections; in 2000 it ran as part of the Alliance for Mexico led by the →Party of the Democratic Revolution, and won nine seats in the Chamber of Deputies.

Address. Cuauhtémoc 47, Colonia Roma, CP 06700, Mexico DF
Telephone. (+52–5) 525 8419
Email. pt@pt.org.mx
Website. www.pt.org.mx

Nationalist Society Party (*Partido de la Sociedad Nacionalista, PSN*), founded in 1999 and joined the Alliance for Mexico coalition led by the →Party of the Democratic Revolution in the 2000 elections, in which it won two seats in the Chamber of Deputies.
Address. Adolfo Priento 428, Col. Del Valle, CP 03100 Mexico DF
Website. www.psn.org.mx

Party of the Democratic Centre ((*Partido de Centro Democrático, PCD*) was founded by Manuel Camacho Solís for whom it served as a personal vehicle; Camacho was a close ally of Salinas, but left the →Institutional Revolutionary Party in 1994 in disappointment at not being selected for the presidential nomination. He ran for president in 2000 and received 0.6% of the vote. The PCD failed to win a seat in Congress.

Social Alliance Party (*Partido Alianza Social, PAS*), founded in 1999 and joined the Alliance for Mexico coalition led by the →Party of the Democratic Revolution in the 2000 elections, in which it won two seats in the Chamber of Deputies.
Address. Edison 89, Col. Tabacalera, CP 06030 Mexico DF
Telephone. (+52–5) 566–5361
Website. www.pas.org.mx

Social Democracy (*Democracia Social, DS*)), is largely the personal vehicle of a widely-respected Mexican politician, Gilberto Rincón Gallardo. He is associated with the left and was formerly a senior figure in the Mexican Socialist Party (PMS). In 2000 he won 1.6% of the presidential vote, but his party failed to secure any congressional representation.

Federated States of Micronesia

Capital: Palikir

Population: 118,000 (2000E)

The Federated States of Micronesia (FSM), consisting of more than 600 islands, occupies the archipelago of the Caroline Islands in the western Pacific Ocean. From 1947, as part of the UN Trust Territory of the Pacific, they were administered by the United States. In 1979 a new constitution was adopted, and in 1982 the FSM signed a compact of free association (implemented in 1986) under which the United States recognized the territory as a fully sovereign and independent state, while retaining authority in regard to defence. In December 1990 the UN Security Council approved the termination of the Trusteeship in relation to the FSM, and the republic joined the UN the following year.

The four constituent states of the FSM are the island groups of Chuuk (formerly Truk), Kosrae, Pohnpei and Yap, each of which have elected governors and legislatures. Federal authority is vested in a President who is elected by the unicameral federal Congress from among its members together with a Vice-President. The Congress has 14 senators, of whom four "at large" members (one from each state) are elected for a four-year term and the other 10 for a two-year term. There are no formal political parties in the FSM.

Following congressional elections on March 2, 1999, Leo Falcam was elected President on May 12, 1999, in succession to Jacob Nena. Further congressional elections were held on March 6, 2001.

Moldova

Capital: Chişinău   **Population:** 4,400,000 (2000E)

The Moldavian Soviet Socialist Republic declared independence from the USSR in August 1991 as the Republic of Moldova, becoming a sovereign member of the Commonwealth of Independent States (CIS) in December 1991. Under its 1994 constitution as amended in 2000, Moldova is a "parliamentary republic" in which supreme authority is vested in the unicameral Parliament (*Parlamentul*) of 101 members, who are elected by universal adult suffrage for a four-year term by a system of proportional representation requiring lists to obtain at least 6% of the vote to gain representation. The head of state is the President, who is elected by the Parliament for a four-year term (having been directly elected for a five-year term before 2000). Executive authority is exercised by the Prime Minister and the Council of Ministers, subject to approval by the Parliament. Under the constitution special autonomous status is conferred on the Transdnestria and Gagauz regions, respectively of predominantly ethnic Russian and ethnic Turk population.

Parliamentary elections on Feb. 25, 2001, resulted as follows: Communist Party of the Moldovan Republic 71 seats (with 49.9% of the vote), Braghis Alliance 19 (13.4%), Christian Democratic People's Party 11 (8.3%).

Braghis Alliance
Alianţa Braghis (AB)
Address. c/o Parlamentul, Blvd. Stefan cel Mare 105, Chişinău
Leadership. Dumitru Braghis (chairman)
The centre-left AB bloc was founded in January 2001 under the leadership of Dumitru Braghis, who had been Prime Minister of a mainly technocratic government since December 1999. It reflected disenchantment with factionalism in the centre-right parties which had been dominant since the 1998 elections. Members of the AB included the New Force Social-Political Movement (*Miscarea Social-Politica Forta Noua*, MSPFN), the Hope Movement of Professionals (*Miscarea Profesionistilor Speranta-Nadejda*), the Centrist Union of Moldova (*Uniunea Centrista din Moldova*, UCM), the Ant Social Democratic Party (*Partidul Democratiei Sociale Furnica*, PDSF), the Socialist Party of Moldova (*Partidul Socialist din Moldova*, PSM) and the Labour Union (*Uniunea Muncii*, UM).

In the February 2001 parliamentary elections the AB took a distant second place to the →Communist Party of the Moldovan Republic, winning 19 of the 101 seats and 13.4% of the vote. It subsequently rejected a PCRM proposal that it should join a new government, Braghis stating that the grouping would advocate its policies from a stance of opposition.

Christian Democratic People's Party
Partidul Popular Creştin-Democrat (PPCD)
Address. Str. Nicolae Iorga 5, Chişinău
Telephone. (+373–2) 238–666
Fax. (+373–2) 234–480
Email. magic@cni.md
Website. ppcd.dnt.md
Leadership. Iurie Roşca (chairman); Sergiu Burca & Vlad Cubreacov (deputy chairmen); Ion Neagu (secretary-general)
The centre-right PPCD was founded in 1992 as the Christian Democratic People's Front (FPCD), itself the successor of the radical pan-Romanian wing of the Popular Front of Moldova, which had been the dominant political grouping during the collapse of Soviet rule in mid-1991. Calling Moldova by the historic name Bessarabia, the FPCD saw independence as the first step towards the "sacred goal" of reunification with Romania. Under the new leadership of Iurie Roşca, the FPCD shared in the defeat of pro-Romanian parties in the first multi-party elections in February 1994, winning nine seats on a vote share of 7.5%.

Having backed the unsuccessful re-election bid of Mircea Snegur in the late 1996 direct presidential elections, the FPCD was in June 1997 a founder component of the Democratic Convention of Moldova (CDM), which included Snegur's Party of Revival and Accord of Moldova (PRCM). In the March 1998 legislative elections the CDM won only 26 seats with 19.2% of the vote and was outpolled by the revived →Communist Party of the Moldovan Republic (PCRM); but the CDM and other centre-right formations were able to form a coalition government which included FPCD representation.

The FPCD broke with the CDM and the centre-right coalition in March 1999 when it joined the PCRM in voting against the installation of Ion Sturza as Prime Minister. In opposition, the FPCD in December 1999 changed its name to Christian Democratic People's Party (PPCD) and adopted a new basic programme calling for "integration within a Europe of nations and the fulfilment of national unity" (instead of its previous advocacy of "the national unity of all Romanians in Romania and Moldova").

In early parliamentary elections in February 2001, in which the PCRM obtained a landslide majority, the PPCD was one of only two other parties to gain representation, winning 11 seats with 8.3% of the vote.

The PCD is a member of the Christian Democrat International.

Communist Party of the Moldovan Republic
Partidul Comunistilor din Republica Moldova (PCRM)
Address. Str. M. Dosoftei 118, Chişinău 2073
Telephone. (+373–2) 248–384
Fax. (+373–2) 233–673
Leadership. Vladimir Voronin (chairman); Victor Stepaniuk (parliamentary group chairman)
The PCRM obtained registration in 1994 as effectively the successor to the Soviet-era Communist Party, which had been banned in August 1991. Although not legalized in time for the 1994 parliamentary elections, the PCRM subsequently attracted defectors from other parties and formed the Popular Patriotic Forces front to support the candidacy of party leader Vladimir Voronin in the 1996 direct presidential elections. He came third in the first round with 10.3% of the vote, whereupon the party backed the victorious Petru Lucinschi in the second and was rewarded with two ministerial posts in the resultant coalition government.

In its first parliamentary elections in March 1998 the PCRM advocated "the rebirth of a socialist society and became the strongest single party with 40 seats and 30.1% of the vote, but went into opposition to a centre-right coalition. In one of a series of subsequent government crises, Voronin was in late 1999 nominated by President Lucinschi to take over the premiership, but he failed to obtain sufficient parliamentary support.

The PCRM exacted revenge in early parliamentary elections in February 2001, winning a landslide victory with 71 of the 101 seats with 49.9% of the vote. In early April Voronin was elected President of Moldova by the new Parliament, but the party opted for an independent businessman, Vasile Tarlev, as Prime Minister, heading a largely PCRM government committed to a strong state role in the economy and the re-establishment of close ties with Russia. Later in April the new President was re-elected PCRM chairman, after the Constitutional Court had ruled that the two posts were not incompatible.

Other Parties and Alliances

Democratic Agrarian Party of Moldova (*Partidul Democrat Agrar din Moldova, PDAM*), founded in 1991 by Soviet-era agrarian forces. Favouring continued Moldovan independence and participation in CIS economic structures, it won a narrow overall parliamentary majority in 1994, with 43.2% of the popular vote. However, weakened by splits and new parties formations, it won only 1.2% of the vote in 2001.
Address. Bdul Stefan cel Mare 162, et. 4, Chişinău
Telephone. (+373–2) 246144
Leadership. Dumitru Motpan (chairman)

Democratic Forum of Moldova (*Forum Democatice din Moldova, FDM*), formed in May 2001 as an alliance of seven non-parliamentary parties which had failed to surmount the 6% hurdle in the February elections, namely (i) the **Party of Revival and Accord** (*Partidul Renaşterii si Concilierii din Moldova, PRCM*) led by Mircea Snegur, which won 5.7%; (ii) the **Democratic Party of Moldova** (*Partidul Democrat din Moldova, PDM*) led by Dumitru Diacov, which won 5.1%; (iii) the **National Liberal Party**

(*Partidul National Liberal, PNL*) led by Mircea Rusu, which took 2.8%; (iv) the **Social Democratic Party of Moldova** (*Partidul Social Democrat din Moldova, PSDM*) led by Nantoi Oazu, an observer member of the Socialist International, which obtained 2.5%; (v) the **Christian Democratic National Peasants' Party** (*Partidul National Tărănesc Creştin Democrat, PNTCD*) led by Valeriu Muravschi, which won 1.7%; (vi) the **Social-Political Movement for Order and Justice** (*Mişcare Social-Politică Pentru Ordine şi Dreptate, MSPOD*) led by Vyacheslav Untila, which obtained 1.5%; and (vii) the **Party of Democratic Forces** (*Partidul Fortelor Democratice, PFD*) led by Valeriu Matei, which took 1.2%. Disagreements immediately surfaced on the extent to which the FDM would be a federation of parties or a unitary organization, as some parties within it initiated bilateral merger talks.

Motherland Social-Political Movement (*Mişeare Social-Politică Plai Natal, MSPPN*), contested the 2001 elections in alliance with the National Youth League of Moldova, winning only 1.6% of the vote.

Transdnestria and Gagauz Parties

Dignity (*Demnitatea*), also known as the Left-Bank Democratic Movement (*Mişcarea Democratică din Stînga Nistrului*), anti-separatist Transdnestria formation.

Union of Patriotic Forces, leading Transdnestria separatist movement, led by Igor Smirnov (president of "Dnestr Republic") and Vasily Yakovlev.

Democratic Party of the Gagauz, led by G. Savostin.

Motherland Party (*Vatan*), the leading ethnic Turkish formation in the Gagauz region, led by Stepan Topol and Andrei Cheshmeji.

Monaco

Capital: Monaco-Ville **Population:** 33,000 (2000E)

The Principality of Monaco is an hereditary monarchy dating from the 13th century in which constitutional limitations on the monarch's powers have been in force since 1911. The 1962 constitution vests executive authority in the Prince, who governs through a Minister of State selected from a list of three French civil servants submitted by the French government, assisted by government councillors and palace personnel. Legislative authority is vested in the Prince and the National Council (*Conseil National*) of 18 members, who are elected by citizens aged 21 and over for a five-year term. There are no formal political parties in Monaco, although informal groupings have been formed to contest recent elections. In National Council elections on Feb. 1 and 8, 1998, the National and Democratic Union (UND) won all 18 seats.

National and Democratic Union (*Union Nationale et Démocratique, UND*), formed in 1962 as a merger of the National Union of Independents (*Union Nationale des Indépendants*) and the National Democratic Entente (*Entente Nationale Démocratique*). It won all 18 National Council seats in the elections of 1968, 1978, 1983 and 1988,

before being superseded by more politically focused lists in 1993. It returned to electoral dominance in 1998.

National Union for the Future of Monaco (*Union Nationale pour l'Avenir de Monaco, UNAM*), contested the 1998 National Council elections, but failed to win a seat.

Mongolia

Capital: Ulan Bator   **Population:** 2,382,500 (2000)

Mongolia was, prior to January 1992, called the Mongolian People's Republic (MPR). The MPR had been proclaimed in the Constitution adopted in November 1924 by the first Great *Hural* (national assembly), following the decision of the (communist) Mongolian People's Revolutionary Party (MPRP) to pursue "non-capitalist development", making the country the first Soviet satellite.

The collapse of communist regimes abroad and the growth of the popular democratic movement at home forced the old MPRP leaders out of office in March 1990 and obliged the new ones to give up the MPRP's monopoly of power. In April the People's Great *Hural* voted to remove from the preamble of the 1960 Constitution the passage defining the MPRP's role as the "guiding and directing force of society and the state". In May it passed a law legalizing political parties, and amended the 1960 Constitution to institute the post of President and set up a 50-member standing legislature called the State Little *Hural*. The MPRP, having secured victory in the first multi-party elections in July 1990, was awarded 31 seats in the State Little *Hural* on the basis of proportional representation.

In February 1992 a new constitution entered into force, emphasizing human and civil rights and permitting all forms of ownership. It proclaimed Mongolia an independent sovereign republic with a directly elected legislature and directly elected President. The members of the unicameral 76-seat Mongolian Great *Hural* are elected for a four-year term by all citizens over 18 years of age. The majority party in the Great *Hural* nominates the Prime Minister, whose appointment is supported by the President and approved by the Great *Hural*. The Prime Minister nominates his Cabinet, whose members are approved by the Great *Hural* individually.

The Great *Hural* elections on June 28, 1992 were won by the MPRP with 71 seats. Four years later, however, elections on June 30, 1996, resulted in the defeat of the MPRP by the Mongolian National Democratic Party (MNDP) and Mongolian Social Democratic Party (MSDP), whose Democratic Alliance won 50 seats, but left the MPRP with sufficient seats to prevent the Democratic Alliance forming a quorum. At the next elections on July 2, 2000 the MPRP returned to power, winning 72 of the 76 seats in the *Hural*. Three parties (the newly formed Civil Courage Party, the MNDP and the Mongolian Democratic New Socialist Party, MDNSP) won one seat each with the remaining seat going to a non-partisan. In December 2000 several opposition parties, including the MNDP and the MSDP, merged to form the Democratic Party.

The first direct presidential election was held on June 6, 1993, resulting in victory for the incumbent, Punsalmaagiyn Ochirbat, who received 57.8% of the vote, defeating the MPRP candidate, Lodongiyn Tudev. Ochirbat had been elected President by the People's Great *Hural* in 1990 as a representative of the ruling MPRP, but was rejected by the MPRP in April 1993 and adopted by the opposition. In the second presidential election, held on May 18, 1997, President Ochirbat was beaten by the MPRP candidate, Natsagiyn Bagabandi, who received 60.8% of the vote.

The third presidential election, held on May 20, 2001, resulted in victory for President Bagabandi, who took 57.9% of the vote. Radnaasumbereliyn Gonchigdorj, standing for the Democratic Party, took 36.6% of the vote and Luvsandambyn Dashnyam, candidate of the Civil Courage Party, 3.6%.

Civil Courage Party (CCP)

Address. Post Office Box 49, Ulan Bator 13
Telephone. (+976–11) 312649
Fax. (+976–11) 328243
Leadership. Sanjaasurengiyn Oyuun (president)
The CCP was created in March 2000 by dissident Mongolian Great *Hural* members of the Mongolian National Democratic Party, led by Sanjaasurengiyn Oyuun, sister of Sanjaasurengiyn Zorig, the Minister of Infrastructure Development murdered in 1998, one of the founders of Mongolia's democracy movement. The party is also sometimes called the Citizens' Will Party. Oyuun is the CCP's only member of the Mongolian Great *Hural* elected in July 2000. In November 2000 the For Mongolia Party and the Regional Development Party merged with the CCP. The party's May 2001 presidential candidate, Luvsandambyn Dashnyam, took 3.6% of the vote.

Democratic Party (DP)

Address. Chingisiyn Orgon Choloo 1, Ulan Bator
Telephone. (+976–11) 324221
Fax. (+976–11) 325170
Email. mndp@mongol.net

Leadership. Dambyn Dorligjav (chairman)
The DP was created in December 2000 on the amalgamation of five parties, the Mongolian National Democratic Party (MNDP), Mongolian Social Democratic Party (MSDP), Mongolian Democratic Party (MDP), Mongolian Democratic Renewal Party (MDRP), and the Mongolian Believers' Democratic Party (MBDP). The DP National Advisory Council comprises two members representing each of the 76 Mongolian Great *Hural* constituencies, plus former party leaders and prime ministers, and has standing committees on policy issues similar to those of the Great *Hural*. The DP has two members in the Mongolian Great *Hural* elected in July 2000: ex-Prime Minister Janlavyn Narantsatsralt, who stood for the MNDP, and Lamjavyn Gundalay, who was an independent but joined the DP. Radnaasumbereliyn Gonchigdorj, the DP's presidential candidate in May 2001, came second with 36.6% of the vote.

The DP is an associate member of the International Democrat Union.

Mongolian Democratic New Socialist Party (MDNSP)

Address. Post Office Box 44, Ulan Bator 49
Telephone. (+976–11) 453176

Fax. (+976–11) 453178
Leadership. Badarchiyn Erdenebat (chairman)
The MDNSP was founded in December 1998 by Badarchiyn Erdenebat, a businessman, founder of the Erel company. Erdenebat is the party's only member of the Mongolian Great *Hural* elected in July 2000. Since the election, the MDNSP has tended to support the →Mongolian People's Revolutionary Party, backing its nominee for the 2001 presidential election.

Mongolian People's Revolutionary Party (MPRP)

Address. Baga Toyruu 37, Ulan Bator 11
Telephone. (+976–11) 323245
Fax. (+976–11) 320368
Leadership. Nambaryn Enhbayar (chairman)
Founded in 1921 as the Mongolian People's Party, the MPRP was the country's only authorized political formation from 1924 until 1990. During that time it was organized along communist lines with a tightly centralized structure, its policies reflecting its close links with the Comintern and Soviet Communist Party. In March 1990, the ruling MPRP Politburo headed by Jambyn Batmonh were replaced by new leaders headed by the former trade union chairman Gombojavyn Ochirbat. In April an extraordinary MPRP congress approved separation of the powers of party and state, and the first multi-party elections were held in July, which the MPRP won.

Following the adoption of the country's new Constitution in February 1992, the MPRP adopted a new programme in which it redefined itself as a parliamentary party standing for national democracy and pledged to implement the Constitution. Aiming for continuity, it abandoned "outdated" Marxist–Leninist concepts, but promised to build "humane socialism" in Mongolia. On this basis it won the multi-party elections of June 1992. The party lost office in the elections of June 1996 but returned to power in July 2000, winning 72 of the 76 seats in the Great Hural. Former party chairman Natsagiyn Bagabandi was elected President of Mongolia in 1997 and re-elected in May 2001. The current party chairman (since 1997), Nambaryn Enhbayar, has been Prime Minister since 2000.

The MPRP has observer status with the Socialist International.

Other Parties

Mongolian Green Party, organized in 1990 as the political wing of the Mongolian Alliance of Greens. For the July 2000 election the party was in an unsuccessful alliance with the →Civil Courage Party, and in January 2001 its chairman, Davaagiyn Basandorj, signed a long-term electoral cooperation agreement with the →Democratic Party.

Mongolian People's Party, formed in 1991 to forestall plans by the restructured →Mongolian People's Revolutionary Party (MPRP) to revert to its original name. A faction of the party merged with the MPRP in March 1999, but the party's independence was reasserted in April 2000. The party did not participate in the July 2000 election, although the chairman, Lama Dorligjavyn Baasan, stood as an independent.

Mongolian Republican Party, formed in 1997 on the basis of the Mongolian Capitalists' Party under the chairmanship of Bazarsadyn Jargalsayhan, a businessman, founder of the Buyan company. Having failed to win any seats in the July 2000 election, in 2001 the party was contemplating a merger with the →Civil Courage Party.

Mongolian United Heritage Party, formed in 1993 by an amalgamation of four small groups supporting small business and private ownership. For the July 2000 election the party joined an unsuccessful alliance which won no seats. The party, also sometimes called the Mongolian Traditional United Party, split in December 2000, when several leaders deserted it to join the new →Democratic Party, but chairman Urjingiyn Hurelbaatar remained in place.

Morocco

Capital: Rabat

Population: 30,100,000 (2000E)

The Kingdom of Morocco was established in 1957 (the former French and Spanish protectorates having joined together as an independent sultanate the previous year). It became a constitutional monarchy under the 1962 constitution, with the Prime Minister and Cabinet appointed by the King. King Mohammed VI ascended the throne in July 1999, following the death of his father, King Hassan II.

A national referendum held in September 1996 approved constitutional amendments providing for the introduction of a bicameral legislature. This comprises a 325-member Assembly of Representatives (*Majlis al-Nuwab*), the lower house, elected for a five year term in multi-seat constituencies and a 270-member Assembly of Councillors (*Majlis al-Mustasharin*), elected for a nine year term by local councils (162 seats), professional chambers (91 seats) and wage-earners (27 seats).

Elections to the Assembly of Representatives were held in November 1997. The opposition left-nationalist *Koutla* group of parties won 102 of the 325 seats, of which 57 went to the country's largest left-wing party, the Socialist Union of Popular Forces (USFP). The Independence Party (*Istiqlal*), the other major *Koutla* partner, won 32 seats, compared with the 51 that it had held in the outgoing legislature. The pro-government, right-wing, *Wifaq* grouping secured 100 seats, of which a half were won by the Constitutional Union (UC). A number of centre parties won 97 seats between them.

Indirect elections were held to the Assembly of Councillors in December 1997. The pro-government *Wifaq* bloc and the centre parties emerged as clear winners, gaining a total of 166 seats. The opposition left-nationalist *Koutla* bloc won only 44 seats.

In early 1998 Abderrahmane el-Yousifi, the veteran leader of the USFP, was appointed as the new Prime Minister. Yousifi's Cabinet comprised ministers from the *Koutla* bloc (the USFP, *Istiqlal*, and the Party of Renewal and Progress), centre parties (the National Rally of Independents and the National Popular Movement), the Front of Democratic Forces, the Socialist Democratic Party (PSD) and a number of independents.

Action Party
Parti de l'Action (PA)
Address. 113 Avenue Allal ben Abdellah, Rabat
Telephone. (+212–7) 206661
Leadership. Mohammed el-Idrissi (national secretary)
This is a liberal party, formed in 1974 to advocate democracy and progress. The PA contested the 1997 legislative elections, winning two seats in the lower house and 13 seats in the upper house. The party did not join the ruling coalition formed in 1998.

Constitutional and Democratic Popular Movement
Mouvement Populaire Constitutionnel et Démocratique (MPCD)
Address. 352 Bld Mohamed V, Rabat
Telephone. (+212–7) 734601
Leadership. Abdelkarim Khatib (secretary-general)
This moderate Islamist party was formed in the late 1960s as a breakaway group from the →Popular Movement. In the 1997 legislative elections the party won nine seats in the lower chamber, the Assembly of Representatives. The party did not join the coalition government led by Abderrahmane el-Yousifi, leader of the →Socialist Union of Popular Forces (USFP), and is a member of the opposition.

In May 1999 MPCD member Abdelilah Ben Kirane won a seat in the Assembly of Representatives in a by-election at Sale, near the capital, Rabat. Ben Kirane defeated the candidate of the USFP, the dominant member of the ruling coalition. Ben Kirane was regarded as a firebrand from Morocco's Islamist youth movement in the 1970s, and his victory sent shock waves through the political establishment.

Constitutional Union
Union Constitutionelle (UC)
Address. 158 Avenue des FAR, Casablanca
Telephone. (+212–2) 313630
Fax. (+212–2) 441141
Founded in 1983 and supporting the constitutional status quo, the centre-right UC became the dominant element in the government coalition formed after the 1984 elections, participating in the National Entente of pro-government parties. In the 1993 parliamentary elections the party's representation in the legislature fell significantly to 54 seats. The UC contested the 1997 elections as the main member of the pro-government, right-wing *Wifaq* group and secured 50 seats in the lower chamber and 28 seats in the upper chamber. After the elections the UC became the main opposition party.

Democratic and Social Movement
Mouvement Démocratique et Social (MDS)
Address. 471 Avenue Mohamed V, Rabat
Telephone. (+212–7) 709110
Leadership. Mahmoud Archane (secretary-general)
Formed in 1996, the centrist MDS performed well in the 1997 elections, wining 32 seats in the lower house and 33 seats in the upper house. The party did not join the coalition government led by Abderrahmane el-Yousifi, leader of the Socialist Union of Popular Forces (USFP), and is a member of the opposition.

Democratic Party for Independence
Parti Démocratique pour l'Indépendance (PDI)
Address. c/o Chambre des Représentants, B.P. 432, Rabat
Leadership. Thami el-Ouazzani (leader)
Established in the 1940s, this small party contested the 1997 legislative elections, winning one seat in the lower house and four seats in the upper house. The party is not a member of the ruling coalition.

Front of Democratic Forces
Parti du Front des Forces Démocratiques (FFD)
Address. 13 Bld Tarik Ibnou Ziad, Rabat

Telephone. (+212–7) 661623
Leadership. Thami Khyari (secretary-general)
Formed in 1997, the FFD contested the legislative elections held at the end of that year, winning nine seats in the Assembly of Representatives (the lower house) and 12 seats in the Assembly of Councillors (the upper house). The FFD subsequently joined the ruling coalition headed by Abderrahmane el-Yousifi, leader of the →Socialist Union of Popular Forces (USFP), and the party secretary general (Thami Khyari) has served as Minister Delegate for Fisheries and Minister of Health.

Independence Party
Parti de l'Istiqlal (Istiqlal)
Address. 4 Avenue Ibn Toumert, Bab El Had, Rabat
Telephone. (+212–7) 730951
Fax. (+212–7) 725354
Leadership. Abbas El Fassi (secretary-general)
The party was founded in 1943 and was the leading political force prior to Moroccan independence. Originally a firm supporter of the monarchy, it has adopted a reformist and critical stance, stressing the need for better living standards and equal rights for all Moroccans. A member of the left-nationalist *Koutla* group of parties, *Istiqlal* won 32 seats in elections to the Assembly of Representatives held in November 1997 and 21 seats in indirect elections to the upper house (the Assembly of Councillors) held the following month. The party is a member of the coalition government formed in early 1998 by →Socialist Union of Popular Forces (USFP) leader Abderrahmane el-Yousifi.

National Democratic Party
Parti National Démocrate (PND)
Address. 18 rue de Tunis, Hassan, Rabat
Telephone. (+212–7) 732127
Fax. (+212–7) 720170
Leadership. Mohammed Arsalane al-Jadidi (secretary-general)
The PND, established in 1981 by disaffected members of the →National Rally of Independents, was one of the smaller parties in the centre-right coalition government formed after the 1984 parliamentary elections. As a National Entente party, it maintained its legislative representation in the 1993 elections, winning 24 seats. The PND contested the 1997 elections as a member of the pro-government, right wing *Wifaq* group (alongside the →Constitutional Union and the →Popular Movement) and secured 10 seats in the lower chamber and 21 seats in the upper chamber. After the elections the PND became an opposition party.

National Popular Movement
Mouvement National Populaire (MNP)
Address. Avenue Imam Malik, Rue El Madani Belhoussni, Souissi Rabat
Telephone. (+212–7) 753623
Fax. (+212–7) 759761
Leadership. Mahjoubi Aherdane (leader)
The National Popular Movement was set up in 1991 by Mahjoubi Aherdane, former leader of the →Popular Movement. Contesting the 1993 elections as a National Entente party, the MNP won 25 seats in the legislature. In the 1997 legislative elections, the party won 19 seats in the lower house and 15 seats in the upper house. The party joined the coalition government of Abderrahmane el-Yousifi formed in early 1998 and was given a small number of portfolios.

National Rally of Independents
Rassemblement National des Indépendants (RNI)
Address. 6, Rue Laos, Avenue Hassan II, Rabat
Telephone. (+212–7) 721420
Fax. (+212–7) 733824
Leadership. Ahmed Osman (president)
Essentially a political vehicle for the late King Hassan, the

332

royalist RNI was established in 1978 to give cohesion to the group of independents which was then numerically dominant in the legislature. Even after a number of independents had defected to the →National Democratic Party in 1981, the RNI was able to emerge as the second strongest party after the 1984 legislative elections, continuing its government participation. Its parliamentary representation fell to 41 seats in the 1993 elections, but in elections to the Assembly of Representatives (the lower house of the newly-created bicameral legislature) held in November 1997, the party won 46 seats. The RNI emerged as the largest party (with 42 seats) in the new second chamber, the Assembly of Representatives, indirectly elected in December 1997. In early 1998 the party joined the coalition government led by Abderrahmane el-Yousifi, leader of the →Socialist Union of Popular Forces.

Organization of Democratic and Popular Action
Organisation de l' Action Démocratique et Populaire (OADP)
Address. 29 Avenue Lalla Yacout, Appt No 1, BP 15797, Casablanca
Telephone. (+212–2) 278442
Fax. (+212–2) 278442
Leadership. Mohamed Bensaid Ait Idder (secretary-general)
The left-wing OADP was formed in 1983. Although the party contested the 1997 legislative elections as a member of the left-nationalist *Koutla* group, winning four seats in the lower house, the Assembly of Representatives, it did not join the coalition government led by Abderrahmane el-Yousifi, leader of the →Socialist Union of Popular Forces.

Party of Renewal and Progress
Parti du Renouveau et du Progrès (PRP)
Address. 4 Rue ibn Zakour, Quartier des Oranges, Rabat
Telephone. (+212–7) 208672
Fax. (+212–7) 208674
Leadership. Ismail Alaoui (secretary-general)
Recognized in 1974 (as the Party of Progress and Socialism, until it changed its name in 1994), the party was the successor to the banned Moroccan Communist Party. It advocates nationalization and democracy as part of its left-wing orientation, and joined in the formation of the opposition Democratic Bloc in 1992. The party contested the 1997 legislative elections as part of the left-nationalist *Koutla* group (alongside the →Socialist Union of Popular Forces (USPF), the →Independence Party and the →Organization of Democratic and Popular Action) and gained nine seats in the lower house and seven seats in the upper house. In early 1998 the party joined the coalition government led by Abderrahmane el-Yousifi, leader of the USPF. The PRP leader, Ismail Alaoui was appointed as Minister of National Education; he was shifted to Agriculture in a reshuffle carried out in September 2000.

Popular Movement
Mouvement Populaire (MP)
Address. 66 Rue Patrice Lumumba, Rabat
Telephone. (+212–7) 767320

Fax. (+212–7) 767537
Leadership. Mohammed Laensar (secretary-general)
The centre-right MP was set up in 1957, its support coming principally from the Berber population. It has been a participant in government coalitions from the early 1960s. The party's founder, Mahjoubi Aherdane, was ousted as MP secretary general in 1986 and later set up the breakaway →National Popular Movement. Contesting the 1997 elections as a member of the right-wing *Wifaq* bloc, the MP secured 40 seats in the Assembly of Representatives (the lower house) and 27 seats in the Assembly of Councillors (the upper house). The MP did not join the coalition government formed after the elections and is a member of the opposition.

Reform and Development
Parti de Réforme et Développement (PRD)
Leadership. Abderrahmane El Cohen (leader).
Formed in June 2001 by former members of the →National Rally of Independents.

Socialist Democratic Party
Parti Socialiste Démocratique (PSD)
Address. 43 Rue Abou Fariss Al Marini, Rabat
Telephone. (+212–7) 208571
Fax. (+212–7) 208573
Leadership. Aissa Ouardighi (secretary-general)
Founded in 1996, the PSD contested the 1997 legislative elections and won five seats in the Assembly of Representatives (the lower house) and four seats in the Assembly of Councillors (the upper house). In early 1998 the PSD joined the ruling coalition headed by Abderrahmane el-Yousifi, leader of the →Socialist Union of Popular Forces (USFP).

Socialist Union of Popular Forces
Union Socialiste des Forces Populaires (USFP)
Address. 17 rue Oued Souss, Agdal, Rabat
Telephone. (+212–7) 773902
Fax. (+212–7) 773901
Website. www.usfp.ma
Leadership. Abderrahmane el-Yousifi (first secretary)
Originally the Rabat section of the National Union of Popular Forces, and temporarily suspended by the government in 1973, the party was formed separately with its current name the following year. The social democratic USFP has close links with the Democratic Confederation of Labour (CDT) trade union centre. The USFP fought elections to the Assembly of Representatives (the lower house of the bicameral legislature) held in November 1997 as part of the opposition left-nationalist *Koutla* group of parties. The *Koutla* parties won 102 of the 325 seats, of which 57 went to the USFP. However, in indirect elections to the upper house (the Assembly of Councillors) held the following month, the USFP won only 16 of the 270 seats. In early 1998 USFP leader Abderrahmane el-Yousifi was appointed as the new Prime Minister at the head of a coalition government that included a large number of USFP members.
The USPF is an affiliate of the Socialist International.

Mozambique

Capital: Maputo

Population: 19,105,000 (2000E)

The Republic of Mozambique gained independence from Portugal in June 1975 after a 10-year armed struggle by the Front for the Liberation of Mozambique (FRELIMO). A one-party system was established with FRELIMO as the sole legal party, but a continuing rebellion was waged against the regime by the anti-communist Mozambique National Resistance (RENAMO). After FRELIMO had in 1989 abandoned Marxist–Leninist ideology in favour of democratic socialism, the following year a new constitution came into effect heralding a multi-party system, direct elections and a free market economy. Under the constitution, the President was to be elected by universal adult suffrage for a five-year period, and might be re-elected on only two consecutive occasions. Legislative authority was to be vested in the Assembly of the Republic (*Assembléia da República*), similarly elected for a five-year term.

Negotiations between the FRELIMO government and RENAMO to end the protracted civil war culminated in the signing of a peace accord in October 1992. Because of delays in the implementation of the peace plan, presidential and legislative elections did not take place until October 1994. These resulted in victory for incumbent President Joaquim Chissano and for FRELIMO, which won 129 of the 250 seats in the Assembly, against 112 for RENAMO and nine for the Democratic Union. Eleven of the 14 groups contesting the Assembly elections failed to win representation.

The presidential election held on Dec. 3–5, 1999, was won by the FRELIMO incumbent, Joaquim Chissano, who received 52.3% of the votes, as against 47.7% for the RENAMO leader, Afonso Dhlakama, whose candidacy was supported by an alliance of RENAMO with a group of opposition parties styled RENAMO–Electoral Union (RENAMO–UE). The RENAMO–UE alliance also presented a joint list of candidates in the December 1999 legislative election, in which FRELIMO won 133 Assembly seats with 48.5% of the vote, while RENAMO-UE won the remaining 117 seats with 38.8% of the vote. The validity of the 1999 election results (strongly challenged by RENAMO) was upheld by the Mozambique Supreme Court and by international monitors. Opposition members took up their seats in the new Assembly but boycotted its proceedings to protest against the election results. The RENAMO–UE coalition continued to function as a single opposition bloc, within which RENAMO itself reportedly had 99 seats and its junior partners 18 seats.

Democratic Renewal Party
Partido Renovador Democrático (PRD)
Address. c/o União Eleitoral, Assembléia da República, CP 1516, Maputo
Leadership. Maneca Daniel (president)
The PRD obtained legal status in 1994. It won no seats in that year's legislative elections. It fought the 1999 elections as part of the RENAMO-UE alliance, led by the main opposition party →Mozambique National Resistance (RENAMO).

Front for the Liberation of Mozambique
Frente de Libertação de Moçambique (FRELIMO)
Address. Rua Pereira do Lago 3, Maputo
Telephone. (+258–1) 490181
Leadership. Joaquim Chissano (president)
FRELIMO was founded in 1962 by the merger of three nationalist organizations. It fought against Portuguese rule from 1964 until 1974, when agreement on independence was reached, thereafter assuming the status of the sole legal party until 1990. Although initially committed to a Marxist-Leninist ideology, FRELIMO abandoned the doctrine in 1989 (subsequently embracing democratic socialism), at the same time calling for a negotiated settlement with the Mozambique National Resistance (RENAMO), against which it had been fighting a protracted civil war. In the October 1994 elections, consequent upon the peace process dating from the 1992 accord, FRELIMO retained power. President Chissano won the presidential election with 53% of the votes cast, while the party secured 129 of the 250 seats in the Assembly of the Republic. In December 1999 Chissano was re-elected with a virtually unchanged share of the vote (52.3%), while the party increased its representation in the Assembly to 133 seats.

FRELIMO is a full member party of the Socialist International.

Independent Alliance of Mozambique
Aliança Independente de Moçambique (ALIMO)
Address. c/o União Eleitoral, Assembléia da República, CP 1516, Maputo
Leadership. Ernesto Sergio (secretary-general)
Founded in 1998, ALIMO fought the 1999 elections as part of the RENAMO-UE alliance, led by the main opposition party →Mozambique National Resistance (RENAMO).

Mozambique National Movement
Movimento Nacionalista Moçambicano (MONAMO)
Address. Av Mao Tse Tung 230, 1st Floor, Maputo
Telephone. (+258–1) 422781
Leadership. Maximo Dias (secretary-general)
The social democratic MONAMO, founded in 1992, fought the 1999 elections as part of the RENAMO-UE alliance, led by the main opposition party →Mozambique National Resistance (RENAMO).

Mozambique National Resistance
Resistência Nacional de Moçambique (RENAMO)
Address. Av Ahmed Sekou Toure 657, Maputo
Telephone. (+258–1) 422617
Leadership. Afonso Dhlakama (president); João Alexandre (secretary-general)
Reportedly with foreign support, RENAMO was in military conflict with the →Front for the Liberation of Mozambique (FRELIMO) government from 1976 until the peace process launched by the October 1992 accord. It registered as a political party in August 1994, and was the principal opponent and the runner-up to FRELIMO in the elections the following October. Afonso Dhlakama was the closest contender after FRELIMO's Chissano for the presidency, winning almost 34% of the vote, while RENAMO candidates secured 112 seats in the Assembly of the Republic. RENAMO fought the December 1999 presidential and legislative elections in an alliance (RENAMO–UE) with eight small parties. Dhlakama (as the sole opposition candidate) won 47.7% of the vote for the presidency, to which FRELIMO's Joaquim Chissano was re-elected. The RENAMO–UE alliance won 117 seats in the Assembly, of which 99 were reportedly allocated to RENAMO and 18 to its allies. The outcome of the 1999 elections was strongly contested by RENAMO, which threatened to set up "parallel governments" in the six provinces where RENAMO–UE had won a majority of the votes cast. Following violent clashes between police and opposition supporters in the previous month, Dhlakana met with President Chissano in December 2000 (their first meeting since the elections) to discuss ways of reducing political tensions.

RENAMO is a member party of the Chrtistian Democrat International.

National Convention Party
(Partido de Convenção Nacional, PCN)
Address. c/o União Eleitoral, Assembléia da República, CP 1516, Maputo
Leadership. Lutero Simango (chairman); Gabriel Mabunda (secretary-general)
The PCN, which obtained legal status in 1992, favours free-market economics, support for agriculture and respect for

human rights. Having failed to win any seats in the 1994 Assembly elections, it fought the 1999 elections as part of the RENAMO–UE alliance, led by the main opposition party →Mozambique National Resistance (RENAMO).

National Unity Party
Partido de Unidade Nacional (PUN)
Address. c/o União Eleitoral, Assembléia da República, CP 1516, Maputo
Formed in 1995 and registered in 1997, the PUN fought the 1999 elections as part of the RENAMO–UE alliance, led by the main opposition party →Mozambique National Resistance (RENAMO).

Patriotic Action Front
Frente de Ação Patriotica (FAP)
Address. c/o União Eleitoral, Assembléia da República, CP 1516, Maputo
Leadership. João Palaço (president); Raul da Conceição (secretary-general)
Founded in 1991, the FAP fought the 1999 elections as part of the RENAMO–UE alliance, led by the main opposition party →Mozambique National Resistance (RENAMO).

Popular Party of Mozambique
Partido Popular de Moçambique (PPM)
Address. c/o União Eleitoral, Assembléia da República, CP 1516, Maputo
The PPM fought the 1999 elections as part of the RENAMO–UE alliance, led by the main opposition party →Mozambique National Resistance (RENAMO).

United Front of Mozambique
Frente Unida de Moçambique (FUMO)
Address. Av Mao Tse-tung 230, Maputo
Leadership. José Samo Gudo (secretary-general)
In the 1994 elections FUMO (which won no seats) advocated the defence of human rights, the privatization of all state-owned companies, a market economy and denationalization of land. The party fought the 1999 elections as part of the RENAMO–UE alliance, led by the main opposition party →Mozambique National Resistance (RENAMO).

Other Parties

Democratic Liberal Party of Mozambique (*Partido Democrático Liberal de Moçambique, PADELIMO*), founded in 1998. PADELIMO failed to win any seats in the 1999 Assembly elections, in which it received less than 1% of the vote.
Leadership. Joaquim José Nyota (president)

Democratic Party of Mozambique (*Partido Democrático de Moçambique, PADEMO*), legally recognized in June 1993 and strongly federalist in outlook, PADEMO secured less than 1% of the vote in the 1994 Assembly elections, while its candidate in the presidential contest was a distant third. It fought the 1999 Assembly elections as part of the Mozambique Opposition Union (UMO) coalition, which received 1.5% of the vote and failed to win any seats.
Leadership. Wehia Ripua (president)

Green Party of Mozambique (*Partido Verde de Moçambique, PVM*), founded in 1997.
Leadership. Armando Sapembe

Independent Party of Mozambique (*Partido Independente de Moçambique, PIMO*), an Islamically oriented party, founded in 1994, which gives priority in its policies to moral education and peace, land privatization and job creation for demobilized soldiers. It won just over 1% of the vote in both

the presidential and legislative polls in 1994 and less than 1% in the 1999 legislative elections.
Leadership. Yaqub Sibindy (president)

Labour Party (*Partido Trabalhista, PT*), formed in 1993. Decentralist and mildly socialist, the party came last in the 1994 legislative elections. It received 2.7% of the vote and won no seats in the 1999 elections.
Leadership. Miguel Mabote (president)

Liberal and Democratic Party of Mozambique (*Partido Liberal e Democrático de Moçambique, PALMO*), founded in 1990. PALMO has been particularly critical of what it regards as the economic domination of the country by the non-indigenous population. The party fought the 1994 Assembly elections as a coalition member of the Democratic Union, which won nine seats. In the 1999 Assembly elections PALMO received 2.47% of the vote and won no seats.
Leadership. Martins Bilal (chairman); Antonio Muedo (secretary-general)

Mozambican National Union (*União Nacional Moçambicana, UNAMO*), formed in 1987 by a breakaway faction of the →Mozambique National Resistance (RENAMO). A federalist and social democratic organization, it was the first opposition party to be granted legal status. It won no seats in the 1994 legislative elections, while its presidential candidate received less than 3% of the vote. It fought the 1999 Assembly elections as part of the Mozambique Opposition Union (UMO) coalition, which received 1.5% of the vote and failed to win any seats.
Leadership. Carlos Reis (president)

National Democratic Party (*Partido Nacional Democrático, PANADE*), legalized in 1993. Supports a market economy, better education and training, and incentives to private investment. It contested the 1994 Assembly elections as a coalition member of the Democratic Union, which won nine seats. In the 1999 Assembly elections the Democratic Union (now comprising PANADE and the →National Party of Mozambique) received 1.48% of the vote and won no seats.
Leadership. Jose Massinga (leader)

National Party of Mozambique (*Partido Nacional de Moçambique, PANAMO*), joined with the →Liberal and Democratic Party of Mozambique and the →National Democratic Party (PANADE) to contest the 1994 elections as a constituent of the Democratic Union alliance, which won nine seats. In the 1999 elections the Democratic Union (now comprising only PANAMO and PANADE) received 1.48% of the vote and won no seats.
Leadership. Marcos Juma (president)

National Workers' and Peasants' Party (*Partido Nacional dos Operários e Camponêses, PANAOC*), founded in 1998. In the 1999 elections it received less than 1% of the vote and won no seats
Leadership. Armando Gil Sueia

Progressive Liberal Party of Mozambique (*Partido de Progresso Liberal de Moçambique, PPLM*), founded in 1993, received less than 1% of the vote and won no seats in the 1999 Assembly elections.
Leadership. Neves Pinto Serrano

Social, Liberal and Democratic Party (*Partido Social, Liberal e Democrático, SOL*), formed by a breakaway faction of the →Liberal and Democratic Party of Mozambique and legally recognized in 1993, SOL campaigned on a platform of equality, a market economy and decentralization, taking fifth place in the 1994 Assembly elections with nearly 1.7% of the vote but no seats. In the 1999 elections it received 2% of the vote and won no seats.
Leadership. Casimiro Nhamithambo (president)

Myanmar (Burma)

Capital: Yangon (Rangoon)   **Population**: 52,000,000 (2000E)

The Union of Myanmar (formally the Union of Burma) achieved independence from the United Kingdom in 1948, with a Westminster-style parliamentary democracy. The government was led by a broad-based coalition, the Anti-Fascist People's Freedom League (AFPFL), until a military coup in 1962. The Revolutionary Council, led by General Ne Win, established a socialist state and banned all political parties except for the newly formed Burma Socialist Programme Party (BSPP). Initially established as a cadre party, the BSPP was expanded into a mass organization, controlled by retired military officers, and took over state leadership from the Revolutionary Council in 1974. In July 1988, economic strife and political demonstrations led to the announcement by Ne Win, then chairman of the BSPP, that multi-party elections would be held. This failed to appease political dissent, and on Sept. 18, 1988 a military coup brought the State Law and Order Restoration Council (SLORC) to power.

SLORC maintained that it was a transitional body and it allowed political parties to register and campaign for an election held on May 27, 1990. Over 200 parties were registered and 93 contested the election. However, when the main opposition party, the National League for Democracy (NLD) won around 60% of the vote, SLORC refused to let a parliament convene. It has since maintained that the purpose of the election was to elect delegates to draft a new constitution at a National Convention, which was formed in January 1993. Only seven of the political parties (but including the NLD) that won seats in the election were invited to take part. Other participants included members of former insurgent organizations that had reached ceasefire agreements with the government, and representatives of social groups chosen by SLORC. Some of the participants denounced the National Convention as a sham, and it has not formally met since the NLD withdrew at the end of 1995. The process of drafting a constitution, according to official sources, is being continued by the National Convention Convening Committee (NCCC).

Although the NLD and some other parties have not been de-registered, their operations have been severely restricted and many members have been imprisoned for attempting to carry out political activities. The repression eased somewhat after the NLD and the State Peace and Development Council (SPDC), as the re-organized SLORC was renamed in 1997, entered into confidence-building talks in October 2000.

Since 1989, eighteen insurgent organizations have reached ceasefire agreements with the government, and remain as political entities in their areas with varying degrees of autonomy.

National League for Democracy (NLD)
Address. 97B West Shwegondine Road, Bahan Township, Yangon
Leadership. U Aung Shwe (chairman), Daw Aung San Suu Kyi (general secretary), U Tin Oo (vice-chairman)
The NLD was formed soon after the September 1988 military coup as a broad-based coalition to unite the opposition. Daw Aung San Suu Kyi, the daughter of the father of Burmese independence, became general secretary and figurehead of the NLD. Both she and party chairman U Tin Oo were placed under house arrest in July 1989 but in transitional elections in May 1990 the NLD won 392 of the 485 contested seats. The result proved meaningless as the SLORC arrested NLD leaders and failed to convene a Constitutent Assembly. In October 1991 Suu Kyi was awarded the Nobel Peace Prize. During 1991–92 the regime took steps to annul the election of numerous NLD Assembly members and to effect the expulsion of Suu Kyi from the party.

From January 1993 the NLD participated in a National Convention, formed to draft a new constitution. In March 1995 U Tin Oo was released from prison and in July 1995, in the face of international pressure, the regime unexpectedly freed Suu Kyi from house arrest and she was reinstated as the general secretary of the NLD in October 1995. In November 1995 the NLD withdrew from the National Convention and was formally expelled for non-attendance. In an effort to highlight the military's continued refusal to convene the parliament elected in 1990 (although many of the elected MPs were imprisoned, in exile or deceased), the NLD formed a ten-member Committee Representing the People's Parliament, in September 1998. The party has survived despite long periods of house arrest

of its leaders, imprisonment of many members, and the shutting down of many of its offices. However this repression has slightly eased since the NLD and the regime entered into confidence-building talks in October 2000. By September 2001, over 200 political prisoners had been released, and several NLD party offices in Yangon permitted to reopen.

National Unity Party (NUP)
Leadership. U Than Kyaw, chairman
The National Unity Party was formed as a successor to the former ruling Burma Socialist Programme Party (BSPP) to contest the 1990 election. It inherited the former party lists, and was given considerable government backing and extra privileges in the election campaign, but won only ten seats. After the election, the NUP faded into obscurity, as civil servants were not permitted to join political parties.

Shan Nationalities League for Democracy (SNLD)
Leadership. U Khun Tun Oo, chairman
Formed to unite Shan ethnic nationalities within a democratic system, the SNLD in 1990 won 23 seats in Shan state, in the northeast of the country, and gained the second largest number of elected representatives after the NLD.

Other Parties

The following ethnically based parties participated in the National Convention, but have not had an active role to play since the last meeting in 1996: **Khami National Solidarity Organisation (KNSO); Lahu National Development Party (LNDU); Shan State Kokang Democratic Party (SSKDP); Union Pa-O National Organization (UPNO)**

Other Political Organizations

National Coalition Government of the Union of Burma (NCGUB), formed by elected MPs who fled to the Thai-Burmese border in 1990 as a government-in-exile. It was formed within an umbrella organisation, the National Council of the Union of Burma, which was an alliance of armed ethnic organizations, the National Democratic Front, and the Democratic Alliance of Burma. However, these alliances have been weakened as some of the groups entered ceasefire agreements with the government, and following the capture by government forces of the headquarters at Manerplaw in 1995. The NCGUB's primary role is advocacy in international organizations such as the United Nations General Assembly.
Address. NCGUB Information Office, 815 15th Street, NW, Suite 910, Washington DC 20005, USA
Telephone. (+1–202) 393–7342

Fax. (+1–202) 393–7343
Email. ncgub@ncgub.net
Website. www.ncgub.net
Leadership. Dr Sein Win ("prime minister")

Union Solidarity and Development Association (USDA), formed in September 1993 as a mass social organization to promote national unity. It is hierarchically structured, with an executive committee at the top and associations parallel to each level of government. Often compared by observers to Indonesia's Golkar, it offers the only path other than the military for social mobility, and membership is vital to promotion in the civil service and to educational opportunities. Members are groomed for leadership in political, economic and social fields, and are obliged to show support for the government in staged mass rallies.
Leadership. Senior General Than Shwe (patron), U Than Aung (secretary-general)

Namibia

Capital: Windhoek

Population: 1,771,000 (2000E)

Having been under South African control from 1915, the Republic of Namibia achieved independence in March 1990. South Africa's mandate to rule the territory was terminated by the United Nations in 1966, but it continued its occupation until final agreement was reached at the end of 1988 on the implementation of a UN-sponsored independence plan. Under the 1990 multi-party constitution, executive power is vested in the President and the Cabinet. The President, as head of state and government, is directly elected by universal adult suffrage, and must receive more than 50% of the votes cast. One person may not hold the office of President for more than two five-year terms. The legislature consists of the National Assembly and the National Council. The National Assembly, with a five-year mandate, has 72 directly-elected members and up to six non-voting members nominated by the President. The indirectly-elected and mainly advisory National Council, consisting of two members from each region, has a six-year term of office.

The first post-independence presidential and legislative elections were held on Dec. 7–8, 1994, resulting in incumbent President Sam Nujoma of the South West Africa People's Organization of Namibia (SWAPO) being returned for a second term and SWAPO winning 53 seats in the National Assembly (this being a sufficiently large majority to pass constitutional amendment bills). In 1998 the constitution was amended to permit the current incumbent (as an exceptional case) to stand for a third five-year presidential term. Following regional council elections held in December 1998, SWAPO increased its representation in the 26-member National Council from 19 to 22 members. Voting for the presidency and the National Assembly took place on Nov. 30 and Dec. 1, 1999. President Nujoma was re-elected with 76.8% of the vote in a four-way presidential contest, while SWAPO won 55 of the elective Assembly seats with 76.1% of the vote.

Congress of Democrats (CoD)
Address. PO Box 40905, Ausspannplatz, Windhoek
Telephone. (+264–61) 256954
Fax. (+264–61) 256980
Email. codemo@mweb.com.na
Website. www.cod.org.na
Leadership. Benjamin Ulenga (leader); Ignatius Nkotongo Shixwameni (secretary-general)
The CoD was formed in March 1999 by a former senior official of the →South West Africa People's Organization of Namibia (SWAPO), Benjamin Ulenga, who had resigned his post as Namibian high commissioner in London in protest against SWAPO's 1998 decision to amend the constitution to allow President Nujoma to stand for a third term of office. The CoD's campaign against various aspects of Nujoma's record in office prompted several government policy initiatives in 1999 to address the problems of certain aggrieved groups (notably unemployed ex-combatants). In the November–December 1999 elections, Ulenga was runner-up to Nujoma in the presidential contest, winning 10.5% of the vote, while the CoD won 7 elective seats in the National Assembly with 9.9% of the vote. Observers agreed that the CoD's support at the election came not from former

SWAPO voters but from opposition voters who had previously supported the →Democratic Turnhalle Alliance of Namibia (DTA), the official opposition party in the previous Assembly. Although the CoD won a slightly higher share of the popular vote in the 1999 Assembly elections, the DTA (which also won 7 seats) entered into a coalition with the →United Democratic Front to form the official opposition in the new Assembly.

Democratic Turnhalle Alliance of Namibia (DTA)
Address. PO Box 173, Windhoek
Telephone. (+264–61) 238530
Fax. (+264–61) 226494
Website. www.democratafrica.org/namibia/dta
Leadership. Katuutire Kaura (president); Johan de Waal (chairman)
Founded in 1977 as a multiracial coalition, the DTA was the majority political formation in the South African-appointed transitional government prior to independence and was supported by South Africa. Following Constituent Assembly elections in 1989 (organized under the UN-sponsored independence plan) it became the main opposition grouping. Having been revamped as a single party in November 1991,

the DTA contested the legislative and presidential elections in 1994, focusing on the issues of unemployment, rising crime and corruption. In the presidential poll, the DTA candidate came second to incumbent President Nujoma of the →South West Africa People's Organization of Namibia (SWAPO) with nearly 24% of the votes cast. In the National Assembly elections the party secured 15 seats with a 20.8% vote share, trailing SWAPO by a considerable margin. In the 1999 elections, the DTA candidate came third in the presidential contest, with 9.6% of the vote, while the party won 7 Assembly seats with 9.5% of the vote. In April 2000 the DTA entered into a coalition with the →United Democratic Front to form the official opposition in the National Assembly.

The DTA is an associate member of the International Democrat Union and a member of its regional associate, the Democrat Union of Africa.

Monitor Action Group (MAG)
Address. PO Box 80808, Olympia, Windhoek
Leadership. Kosie Pretorius
The MAG, set up during 1994 by the former leader of the predominantly white Action Christian National (ACN), defines itself as a pressure group for "principle politics" rather than a political party as such. It aims to promote "a Christian outlook and standpoint" and advocates the removal of the "secular concept" from the Namibian constitution. In the elections to the National Assembly in December 1994 the MAG won a single seat, which it retained in the 1999 elections.

South West Africa People's Organization of Namibia (SWAPO)
Address. PO Box 1071, Windhoek
Telephone. (+264–61) 238364
Fax. (+264–61) 232368
Website. www.swapo.org.na
Leadership. Samuel Daniel Nujoma (president); Hifikepunye Pohamba (secretary-general)
SWAPO was established in 1958 as the Ovamboland People's Organization, adopting its present name in 1968. It was the principal liberation movement in the pre-independence period, having launched an armed struggle in 1966.

From 1973 it was recognized by the UN General Assembly as "the authentic representative of the people of Namibia". In the pre-independence Constituent Assembly elections in 1989, SWAPO won a majority. In February 1990 the Assembly adopted the new constitution and elected SWAPO leader Sam Nujoma to be Namibia's first President. Following independence, SWAPO formed the government, advocating national reconciliation, economic development, and an improvement in the basic conditions of life for the majority.

In December 1991 SWAPO held its first congress since its inception. The constitution and political programme were amended to transform SWAPO from a liberation movement into a mass political party. In the December 1994 elections Nujoma retained the presidency, winning just over 76% of the vote, while SWAPO candidates secured 53 of the 72 elective seats in the National Assembly. This was a sufficient majority to amend the constitution framed by the Constituent Assembly in the run-up to independence. In 1998 the constitution was amended to allow Nujoma (as an exceptional case) to stand for a third presidential term. Nujoma was re-elected President in December 1999 with 76.8% of the vote, while SWAPO won 55 elective Assembly seats with 76.1% of the vote.

United Democratic Front (UDF)
Address. POB 20037, Windhoek
Telephone. (+264–61) 230683
Fax. (+264–61) 237175
Leadership. Justus Garoeb (president); Eric Biwa (national chairman)
Founded as a centrist alliance of eight ethnic parties, the UDF won four seats in the 1989 Constituent Assembly elections, subsequently reorganizing itself as a unitary party in October 1993. Although in third place in the December 1994 legislative poll, the party attracted only 2.7% of the vote and won only two National Assembly seats. In the 1999 elections it retained two Assembly seats (with 2.9% of the vote), while its presidential candidate received the lowest share of the vote (3%). In April 2000 the UDF went into coalition with the →Democratic Turnhalle Alliance of Namibia to form the official opposition in the National Assembly.

Nauru

Capital: Domaneab   **Population:** 11,500 (2000E)

Nauru achieved independence in 1968, having previously been a UN Trust Territory administered by Australia. Under the constitution, legislative power is vested in an 18-member unicameral Parliament, directly elected for up to three years, which selects a President from among its members. The President, who is head of state, governs with the assistance of an appointed Cabinet.

Nauru's first President, Hammer DeRoburt, dominated the island's politics until 1989, when he was succeeded by Bernard Dowiyogo, who served six mostly consecutive terms until being replaced by René Harris in March 2001. The political process tends to operate on family rather than party lines, although members of the legislature have from time to time grouped themselves into informal parties. Most recently, supporters of Dowiyogo have been identified as the Democratic Party and those of Harris as the Nauru Party.

Nepal

Capital: Kathmandu   **Population:** 24,000,000 (2000E)

Following the overthrow of the ruling Rana family in a popular revolt in 1950, the King of Nepal resumed an active political role. In 1959 the country's first constitution was promulgated and a parliament was elected.

However, at the end of the following year the King dissolved parliament and dismissed the government. All political parties were banned in 1961 and for the next 30 years Nepal experienced direct rule by the monarchy, although a tiered, party-less system of *panchayat* (council) democracy was introduced under a new constitution in 1962.

In February 1990 a series of peaceful demonstrations in support of the restoration of democracy and human rights escalated into full-scale confrontation with the government. The following April the ban on political parties was rescinded, restrictions on the press lifted and constitutional reform promised. A new constitution guaranteeing parliamentary government and a constitutional monarchy was proclaimed in November 1990. It provides for a bicameral legislature comprising a popularly-elected 205-member House of Representatives *(Pratinidhi Sabha)* and a National Council *(Rashtriya Sabha)* of 60 members, of whom 10 are nominees of the King, 35 are elected by the House of Representatives and 15 are elected by an electoral college.

The first multi-party general election was held in May 1991 and resulted in a victory for the Nepali Congress Party (NCP). In further elections on Nov. 15, 1994, the United Communist Party of Nepal (UCPN) became the largest party with 88 seats against 83 for the NCP, with the National Democratic Party (RPP) winning 20, the Nepal Workers' and Peasants' Party 4, the Nepal Goodwill Council (NSP) 3 and independents 7. The UCPN leader, Man Mohan Adhikari, was accordingly sworn in as the country's first communist Prime Minister at the end of the month.

A political crisis arose in June 1995 when Adhikari recommended the dissolution of parliament by King Birendra and a fresh general election, apparently to avoid losing an imminent vote of no confidence. The Prime Minister's decision, and his appointment as head of a caretaker government pending elections scheduled for November, were challenged by opposition parties which, in August, won a ruling from the Supreme Court reinstating the existing parliament. In September Adhikari resigned after losing a parliamentary vote of no confidence and was replaced as Prime Minister by Sher Bahadur Deuba of the NCP. A new coalition government led by the NCP and including the RPP and the NSP then took office.

However, Deuba's government fell in March 1997 to be replaced by one headed by Lokendra Bahadur Chand of the RPP, who split his party and formed a coalition with the NCP, the NSP and also the UCPN. But, in October 1997, Chand was forced to resign after losing a no-confidence motion in the *Pratinidhi Sabha*. He was replaced as Prime Minister by Surya Bahadur Thapa, who headed the other faction of the RPP and drew support from the NCP and the NSP. However, this combination also proved short-lived. In March 1998, the UCPN split, leaving the NCP as the largest party in parliament. In April 1998, NCP leader Girija Prasad Koirala was invited to take office at the head of a minority administration, which lasted only until December when Koirala was re-appointed to head a coalition government between the NCP and the majority faction of the UCPN.

A new general election in May 1999 finally changed the awkward composition of the previous *Pratinidhi Sabha*. The NCP was returned with 110 of the 205 seats and formed a majority government under Krishna Prasad Bhattarai, who was a rival of Koirala for the party's leadership. The rump of the main UCPN won 68 seats, while the new communist breakaway group, the Communist Party of Nepal–Marxist–Leninist (CPN–ML), failed to win any. The RPP (Thapa) took 11 seats and the RPP (Chand) was left seatless. The NSP gained 5 seats, as did the National People's Front (RJM), which had stood in the original 1991 election but had split in 1993. However, Bhattarai's government lasted only until March 2000 when it was overthrown by an internal coup inside the NCP, restoring Koirala to the party leadership and the Prime Minister's office. But Koirala, himself, faced mounting party dissidence, having to re-shuffle his cabinet no fewer than 9 times in 15 months, and eventually fell victim to the circumstances surrounding the assassination of King Birendra in June 2001. In July, he was replaced as Prime Minister of the NCP government by Sher Bahadur Deuba.

Meanwhile, from 1993, dissident factions within the old United People's Front (SJMN), which had played a pivotal role in the 1990 campaign for democracy, had begun to contemplate armed resistance to the constitutional state. A "Maoist" strategy was put into force in 1996, which was strengthened in 1998 when many former members of the (now-split) UCPN became attracted to it. Maoist guerrilla groups, of which the most prominent is the Nepal Communist Party–Maoist (NCP–M), led by "Comrade Prachand" (Kamal Pushpa Dahal), now effectively control considerable stretches of rural territory where the writ of the government does not run.

National Democratic Party
Rashtriya Prajatantra Party (RPP)
Address. c/o House of Representatives, Kathmandu
Leadership. Lokendra Bahadur Chand, Surya Bahadur Thapa (leaders)
The right-wing, monarchist RPP is composed of two principal factions, led by former Prime Ministers Chand and Thapa respectively. In the November 1994 elections the party secured 20 seats in the House of Representatives, joining the NCP-led coalition government which replaced the communist administration in September 1995. But, in March 1997, Chand bid for the prime ministership himself, seeking to draw the communists into a new coalition. This precipitated a deeper split in the RPP and, in October 1997 he was displaced in office by Thapa at the head of a new coalition excluding the communists. However, this government was also short-lived and fell in March 1998. At the 1999 general election, the two factions stood independently,

the Thapa group winning 14 seats in the *Pratinidhi Sabha* and the Chand group none.

Nepal Goodwill Council
Nepal Sadhbhavana Parishad (NSP)
Address. c/o House of Representatives, Kathmandu
Leadership. Gajendra Narayan Singh (president); Hridayesh Tripathi (general secretary)
This small party promotes the rights of the Madhesiya Indian community of the Terai region of Nepal. In November 1994 it won three seats in the elections to the House of Representatives. Its president was awarded a portfolio in the NCP-led coalition government formed in September 1995. It also supported a series of subsequent coalition governments and, in the 1999 general election, won five seats.

Nepal Workers' and Peasants' Party
Nepal Mazdoor Kisan Party (NMKP)

Address. c/o House of Representatives, Kathmandu
Leadership. Narayan Man Bijukche (chairman)

The pro-Chinese communist NWPP won four seats in the House of Representatives in the 1994 elections but only one in 1999, with 0.6% of the vote.

Nepali Congress Party (NCP)

Address. Central Office, Teku, Kathmandu
Telephone. (+977–1) 227748
Fax. (+977–1) 227747
Email. ncparty@mos.com.np
Website. www.nepalicongress.org.np
Leadership. Girija Prasad Koirala (president); Sushil Koirala (general secretary)

Founded in the late 1940s as Nepal's wing of the →→Indian National Congress, with a socialist but pro-monarchist orientation, the NCP came to government in 1959 but was ejected by the monarch a year later and banned along with other political parties from 1961. Over the following two decades many NCP activists were detained or restricted, while the exiled leadership campaigned for the restoration of democracy. The party achieved a measure of official acceptance through the 1980s, although various moves to reach a political accord with the King were inconclusive amid periodic repressive action by the authorities.

Following the widespread popular agitation that began in early 1990, the NCP president was appointed by the King to lead a coalition government pending multi-party elections in May 1991, in which the NCP won an overall majority of 110 seats. In further elections to the House of Representatives in November 1994 (brought about by a vote of no confidence in the NCP government), the party won only 83 of the 205 seats and relinquished power to the →United Communist Party of Nepal (UCPN). However, following the resignation of the UCPN administration in September 1995, the NCP formed a new coalition under the premiership of Sher Dahadur Deuba. This was displaced in March 1997 by two short-lived coalitions led by the →National Democratic Party (RPP) in which the NCP participated. From March 1998 to May 1999, the NCP headed a series of minority and coalition governments under the leadership of Girija Prasad Koirala. At the May 1999 general election, the party won 110 of the 205 seats in the House of Representatives and, to July 2001, had formed three successive majority governments: first, under Krishna Prasad Bhattarai, then under Koirala and then under Deuba again. Internecine feuds between these three leaders has been a dominant feature of the party since the restoration of full democracy in 1991.

The NCP is a member party of the Socialist International.

United Communist Party of Nepal (UCPN)

Address. POB 5471, Kathmandu.
Telephone. (+977–1) 223639
Leadership. Man Mohan Adhikari (leader)

The UCPN was formed in early 1991 by the merger of the Marxist and Marxist–Leninist factions of the Communist Party of Nepal. In the May 1991 elections it won the second highest number of seats (69) in the House of Representatives, thereby becoming the official opposition. Although the party was left short of a workable majority in the November 1994 elections (from which it emerged as the largest party with 88 seats), the UCPN leader, Man Mohan Adhikari, was invited to form a new government. However, his controversial efforts to maintain his administration ended with his resignation as Prime Minister in September 1995 and the party's return to opposition status. Between March and October 1997, the party supported the coalition government led by Lokendra Bahadur Chand of the →National Democratic Party (RPP). But this precipitated a major split in March 1998 when the Communist Party of Nepal–Marxist–Leninist (CPN–ML) left the main branch of the party. In the general election of May 1999, the UCPN won 68 seats and the CPN–ML, although polling 6.4% of the vote, none.

Other Parties

Communist Party of Nepal–Maoist (CPN–M), a communist faction led by 'Comrade Prachand' (Kamal Pushpa Dahal) which is organizing an armed insurrection against the state.

National People's Council *(Rashtriya Janata Parishad, RJP),* formed in 1992 by Maitrika Prasad Koirala and Kirti Nidhi Dista, both former Prime Ministers seeking a non-radical alternative to the →Nepali Congress Party. In the 1999 general election, as the Rashtriya Janata Morcha, RJM, it won five seats in the House of Representatives.

United People's Front–Nepal (SJMN), a leftist movement which participated in the campaign for democracy in 1990 and won nine seats in the *Pratinidhi Sabha* at the 1991 election. However, it split in 1993 over the issue of whether to work within the constitution or to raise armed resistance against it. A small group has continued to follow the parliamentary path and won one seat at the 1999 election. But the majority faction, informed by leading ideologue Baburam Bhattarai, has gravitated towards the insurrectionist politics of the →Communist Party of Nepal–Maoist.

Netherlands

Capital: Amsterdam

Population: 15,750,000 (2000E)

The Kingdom of the Netherlands (consisting of the Netherlands in Europe and the Caribbean territories of Aruba and the Netherlands Antilles) is a constitutional and hereditary monarchy whose two non-European parts enjoy full autonomy in internal affairs (see next section). Under its 1815 constitution as amended, the Netherlands in Europe has a multi-party parliamentary system of government employing proportional representation to reflect the country's religious and social diversity. Executive authority is exercised on behalf of the monarch by a Prime Minister and other ministers, who are accountable to the States-General *(Staten-Generaal)*. The latter consists of (i) the 75-member First Chamber *(Eerste Kamer)* elected by the members of the country's 12 provincial councils for a four-year term; and (ii) the 150-member Second Chamber *(Tweede Kamer)*, also elected for a four-term but by universal suffrage of those aged 18 and over by a system of "pure" proportional representation with no minimum percentage threshold requirement. A founder member of what is now the European Union, the Netherlands elects 31 members of the European Parliament.

While political parties in the Netherlands have traditionally relied on members' subscriptions and donations, since 1972 state funding has been available for policy research and educational foundations attached to parties represented in the Second Chamber. Parties also receive certain concessions to defray expenses during election campaigns, including a limited amount of free media access.

Elections to the Second Chamber on May 6, 1998, resulted as follows: Labour Party 45 seats (with 29.0% of the vote), People's Party for Freedom and Democracy 38 (24.7%), Christian Democratic Appeal 29 (18.4%), Democrats 66 14 (9.0%), Green Left 11 (7.3%), Socialist Party 5 (3.5%), Reformational Political Federation 3 (2.0%), Reformed Political Party 3 (1.8%), Reformed Political Association 2 (1.3%).

Christian Democratic Appeal
Christen-Democratisch Appèl (CDA)

Address. Dr Kuyperstraat 5, 2514 BA The Hague
Telephone. (+31–70) 342–4888
Fax. (+31–70) 364–3417
Email. bureau@cda.nl
Website. www.cda.nl
Leadership. M.L.A. van Rij (chairman); Cees Bremmer (general secretary); Bert de Vries (parliamentary party leader)

The right-of-centre Christian-inspired CDA was founded in April 1975 as a federation of (i) the Anti-Revolutionary Party *(Anti-Revolutionaire Partij*, ARP) founded in 1878 by Abraham Kuyper; (ii) the Christian Historic Union *(Christelijk Historische Unie*, CHU*)* established by ARP dissidents in 1908; and (iii) the Catholic People's Party *(Katholieke Volkspartij*, KVP*)* dating from 1928 and renamed in 1945. The new CDA formation represented an attempt by these confessional parties to reverse the steady decline in their vote since 1945. The CDA was constituted as a unified party in October 1980, after a five-year preparatory phase. It gained 49 seats in the Second Chamber in 1977, 47 in 1981 and 45 in 1982.

From 1977 the CDA headed several coalition governments: with the →People's Party for Freedom and Democracy (VVD) until September 1981, with the →Labour Party and the →Democrats 66 (D66) until May 1982, with D66 only until November 1982, and with the VVD after that under Ruud Lubbers. Having slipped from 48 to 45 Second Chamber seats in the September 1982 elections, the CDA subsequently experienced some internal dissension over the government's economic and defence policies. Nevertheless, in May 1986 it staged a sharp recovery, to 54 seats, and continued in government with the VVD.

The CDA retained 54 seats in the 1989 Second Chamber elections (with 35.3% of the vote), after which it formed a centre-left coalition with the PvdA, under the continued premiership of Lubbers, who became the Netherlands' longest-serving post-war Prime Minister. In advance of the May 1994 election, however, Rubbers announced his retirement from Dutch politics, with the result that the CDA campaigned under the new leadership of Elco Brinkman, amid difficult economic and social conditions. The outcome was that the party suffered its worst-ever electoral defeat, losing a third of its 1989 support and slumping to 22.2% and 34 seats, three less than the PvdA. The CDA recovered somewhat in the June 1994 European Parliament elections, to 30.8%, which yielded 10 of the 31 Dutch seats; nevertheless, Brinkman resigned as CDA leader in August 1994, as the party went into opposition to a PvdA-led coalition.

The CDA lost even more ground in the May 1998 general elections, winning only 18.4% of the vote for the Second Chamber and falling to 29 seats. It therefore remained in opposition to another PvdA-led coalition. In the June 1999 European elections the party slipped to 26.9% of the national vote, losing one of the 10 seats it held previously. Jaap de Hoop Scheffer resigned as party leader in parliament at the end of September 2001 saying he lacked support from party leaders for him to head the 2002 election campaign.

The CDA is a member of the Christian Democrat International. Its representatives in the European Parliament sit in the European People's Party/European Democrats group.

Democrats 66
Democraten 66 (D66)

Address. PO Box 660, 2501 CR The Hague
Telephone. (+31–70) 356–6066
Fax. (+31–70) 364–1917
Email. info@d66.nl
Website. www.d66.nl
Leadership. Thom de Graaf (leader); Gerard Schouw (chairman); Willem Steetskamp (general secretary)

D66 was founded in 1966 as a left-of-centre progressive non-socialist party with "a commitment to change inspired by a sense of responsibility for the future", favouring pragmatism over ideology and strongly libertarian in inclination. Long-term leader Hans van Mierlo recorded that both liberalism and socialism were sources of inspiration for D66, both movements having "taken responsibility for a part of the whole truth" but then having erected their part into "the whole truth", so that false antetheses had been engendered, such as liberty against equality, individual against community and the free market against state control.

D66 won seven seats in the Second Chamber in 1967 and 11 in 1971, but only six seats in 1973 and eight in 1977. In 1981 the party increased its electoral support significantly, gaining over 11% of the vote and 17 seats in the Second Chamber. A downward trend reappeared in 1982, when the party was reduced to six seats. However, in May 1986 it recovered to nine seats and 6.1 % of the votes. D66 has usually regarded the →Labour Party (PvdA) as its most obvious partner for participation in government. It took part in a coalition government with the PvdA (and three other parties) in 1973-77, but subsequently joined in coalition with the →Christian Democratic Appeal (CDA) in 1982. This last experience of government was seen as contributing to the party's setback in the September 1982 elections, in light of which Jan Terlouw resigned as leader and was eventually replaced by his predecessor, Hans van Mierlo.

D66's lower house representation rose from nine seats in 1986 to 12 in 1989, the latter tally being doubled to 24 in a major advance in May 1994 on a vote share of 15.5%, on the basis of which the party joined a coalition government with the PvdA and the →People's Party for Freedom and Democracy (VVD). In the June 1994 European Parliament elections D66 slipped back to 11.7%, taking four of the 31 Dutch seats. A key condition of D66 participation in the government was that the constitution should be amended to make provision for "corrective referendums" in which parliamentary legislation on some subjects could be overturned by the people. After VVD ministers had opposed the proposal and Labour had expressed doubts, the version given cabinet approval in October 1995 excluded more subjects from referendum correction than D66 had originally proposed.

The May 1998 general elections delivered a major setback to D66, which slumped to 9.0% of the vote and 14 seats. The party nevertheless joined a further coalition with the PvdA and VVD. The November 1998 D66 conference in Gouda adopted a proposal by a group of young activists called "Upheaval" *(Opschudding)* that the party should officially identify itself as a "social liberal" formation, a committee being set up to draft a new mission statement to that effect. In the June 1999 European elections the D66 vote was halved, to 5.8%, and its representation reduced from four to two seats.

With an official membership of 12,000, D66 is a member

party of the Liberal International. Its representatives in the European Parliament sit in the European Liberal, Democratic and Reformist group.

Green Left
GroenLinks (GL)
Address. PO Box 8008, 3503 RA Utrecht
Telephone. (+31–30) 239–9900
Fax. (+31–30) 230–0342
Email. info@groenlinks.nl
Website. www.groenlinks.nl
Leadership. Mirjam de Rijk (chairman); Paul Rosenmuller (parliamentary leader)
The GL was founded prior to the 1989 Second Chamber elections as an alliance of the Evangelical People's Party (*Evangelische Volkspartij*, EVP), the Radical Political Party (*Politieke Partij Radikalen*, PPR), the Pacifist Socialist Party (*Pacifistisch Socialistische Partij*, PSP) and the Communist Party of the Netherlands (*Communistische Partij van Nederland*, CPN). It became a unitary party in 1991, when each of its constituent groups voted to disband.

Of the component parties, the EVP had been formed in 1978 and had held one seat in the 1982-86 Second Chamber. The PPR had been founded in 1968 by a left-wing faction of the Catholic People's Party (later the mainstay of the →Christian Democratic Appeal), had won seven seats in 1972 and had participated in a centre-left coalition in 1973–77. The PSP had dated from 1957 and had won between one and four seats in subsequent elections. The CPN had been founded in 1918 by left-wing Social Democrats, had held 10 seats in post-1945 Second Chamber but had steadily declined to zero representation in 1986.

Having won six seats and 4.1% of the vote in its first general election contest in 1989, the GL slipped to five seats and 3.5% in May 1994. In the following month's European Parliament elections it recovered slightly to 3.7%, retaining one of the two seats it had won in 1989. It registered major gains in the May 1998 national elections, more than doubling its vote share to 7.3% and its Second Chamber representation to 11 seats. It continued its advance in the June 1999 European elections, winning 11.9% of the vote and four seats.

With an official membership of 14,000, the GL is affiliated to the European Federation of Green Parties. Its representatives in the European Parliament sit in the Greens/European Free Alliance group.

Labour Party
Partij van de Arbeid (PvdA)
Address. Herengracht 54, 1000 BH Amsterdam
Telephone. (+31–20) 551–2155
Fax. (+31–20) 551–2250
Email. pvda@pvda.nl
Website. www.pvda.nl
Leadership. Willem (Wim) Kok (leader); Ad Melkert (parliamentary leader); Marijke van Hees (chairperson); Annie Brouwer-Korf (general secretary)
The PvdA was founded in 1946 as the post-war successor to the Social Democratic Workers' Party, founded in 1894 by P.J. Troelstra and other dissidents of the Social Democratic Union (created by F.D. Nieuwenhuis in 1881). From its establishment in 1946 as a broader-based party including many former Liberals, the PvdA engaged in the reconstruction of the Netherlands after the German occupation. Its leader, Willem Drees, was Prime Minister of a Labour-Catholic coalition government from 1948 to 1958, whereafter the PvdA was in opposition for 15 years—except briefly in 1965–66, when it took part in a coalition government with the Catholic People's Party (KVP) and the Anti-Revolutionary Party (ARP). The PvdA was weakened in 1970 by a right-wing breakaway by followers of Dr Willem Drees (son of the former Prime Minister), who formed the Democratic Socialists 1970 (DS-70) party. Although DS-70 gained eight seats in the 1971 elections, thereafter its rep-

resentation declined and the party was dissolved in January 1983.

In 1971 and 1972 the PvdA contested elections on a joint programme with the →Democrats 66 (D66) and the Radical Political Party, and in 1973 it formed a coalition government with these parties and also the KVP and the ARP, with the then PvdA leader, Joop den Uyl, becoming Prime Minister. This was the first Dutch government with a left-wing majority of ministers. However, after the 1977 elections, in which the PvdA increased its seats in the Second Chamber from 43 to 53, the party went into opposition to a centre-right government led by the →Christian Democratic Appeal (CDA). From September 1981 to May 1982 the party took part in a coalition government with the CDA and D66. The PvdA was then in opposition, despite achieving a significant advance in the May 1986 Second Chamber elections, from 47 to 52 seats. Following those elections, Wim Kok (hitherto leader of the Netherlands Trade Union Confederation) became PvdA leader in succession to den Uyl (who died in December 1987).

Although it fell back to 49 seats on a 31.9% vote share, the PvdA returned to government after the 1989 elections, as junior coalition partner to the CDA. In August 1991 Marjanne Sint resigned as PvdA chairperson because of the party's acceptance of cuts in the state social security system, introduced by the CDA–PvdA coalition. In the May 1994 lower house elections the PvdA slipped again, to 24.0% and 37 seats, but overtook the CDA as the largest party and therefore became the senior partner in a new three-party coalition, this time with the →People's Party for Freedom and Democracy (PVV) and D66. In the June 1994 elections to the European Parliament, support for Labour declined further, to 22.9%, giving it eight of the Netherlands' 31 seats.

Helped by the popularity of Prime Minister Kok, the PvdA staged a major recovery in the May 1998 general elections, winning 45 seats on a 29.0% vote share. Kok accordingly formed a further coalition with the PVV and D66. In the June 1999 European elections, however, the PvdA declined to 20.1% of the vote, its representation falling from eight to six seats.

In August 2001 Kok announced that he would not be a candidate for the premiership after the general elections due in May 2002 and would stand down from the PvdA leadership in advance of the elections. His designated successor was Ad Melkert, the party's parliamentary leader.

With an official membership of 60,000, the PvdA is a member party of the Socialist International. Its European Parliament representatives sit in the Party of European Socialists group.

People's Party for Freedom and Democracy
Volkspartij voor Vrijheid en Democratie (VVD)
Address. Koninginnegracht 57, PO Box 30836, 2500 GL The Hague
Telephone. (+31–70) 361–3061
Fax. (+31–70) 360–8276
Email. alg.sec@vvd.nl
Website. www.vvd.nl
Leadership. Frits Bolkestein (leader); Hans F. Dijkstal (parliamentary leader); Willem Hoekzema (chairman); Jan Korff (general secretary)
Founded in 1948, the VVD is descended from the group of Liberals led by J.R. Thorbecke who inspired the introduction of constitutional rule in 1848. Organized as the Liberal Union from 1885, the Dutch Liberals (like their counterparts elsewhere in Europe) lost influence as the move to universal suffrage produced increasing electoral competition on the left, with the result that after World War II many Liberals joined the new →Labour Party. However, other Liberal elements under the leadership of P.J. Oud founded the VVD, which remained in opposition to Labour–Catholic coalitions until 1959, when an electoral advance enabled the party to join a coalition with the Catholics.

After languishing electorally in the 1960s, the VVD made steady advances in the 1970s under the leadership of Hans Wiegel, winning 28 seats in the Second Chamber in 1977 and joining a coalition headed by the new →Christian Democratic Appeal (CDA). Reduced to 26 seats in 1981, the VVD went into opposition, but under the new leadership of Ed Nijpels made a big advance to 36 seats the following year and joined a further coalition with the CDA. This was continued after the 1986 elections, although the VVD slipped back to 27 seats and from 23.1 to 17.4% of the vote.

The VVD lost ground in both the 1986 and the 1989 elections, on the latter occasion going into opposition for the first time since 1982. In the May 1994 contest, however, the VVD made a major advance by Dutch standards, from 14.6 to 19.9% of the vote, while the June European Parliament elections gave it a 17.9% tally and six of the 31 Dutch seats. In August 1994 the VVD returned to government, joining a coalition with the PvdA and →Democrats 66 (D66). In provincial elections in March 1995 the VVD struck a popular chord with its tough policy prescriptions on immigration and asylum seekers, overtaking the CDA as the strongest party at provincial level and therefore increasing its representation in the First Chamber to 23 seats. Within the national government, VVD ministers urged cuts in government spending to reduce the deficit to the Maastricht criterion for participation in a single European currency, thereby coming into conflict with the PvdA, which preferred to raise taxes.

In the May 1994 national elections the VVD overtook the CDA as the second-strongest party, winning 24.7% of the vote and 38 Second Chamber seats and subsequently joining a further coalition with the PvdA and D66. In the June 1999 European elections, moreover, it advanced to 19.7% and retained six seats.

The VVD is a member of the Liberal International. Its European Parliament representatives sit in the European Liberal, Democratic and Reformist group.

Reformational Political Federation
Reformatorische Politieke Federatie (RPF)

Address. PO Box 302, 8070 AH Nunspeet
Telephone. (+31–341) 256744
Fax. (+31–341) 260348
Email. rpf@rpf.nl
Website. www.rpf.nl
Leadership. A. van den Berg (chairman); Leen C. van Dijke (parliamentary leader); A.L. Langius (secretary)
Founded in March 1975, the RPF seeks a reformation of political and social life in accordance with the Bible and Calvinistic tradition and creed. The party was formed by the National Evangelical Association, dissenters from the Anti-Revolutionary Party (ARP) and the Associations of Reformed (Calvinist) Voters. It won two seats in the Second Chamber in 1981 and again in 1982, when it also obtained 10 seats in provincial elections and about 100 in municipal elections. In 1986 it was reduced to one seat, which it retained in 1989, but trebled this tally in May 1994 on a 1.8% vote share. For the following month's European Parliament elections the RPF presented a joint list with the →Reformed Political Association (GPV) and the →Reformed Political Party (SGP), which took a 7.8% vote share and elected two members (neither from the RPF).

The RPF improved to 2.0% in the May 1998 national elections, retaining three Second Chamber seats. In the June 1999 European Parliament elections it again presented a joint list with the GPV and SGP, which improved to 8.7% of the vote and three seats, one of which went to the RPF. All three representatives joined the Europe of Democracies and Diversities group.

Reformed Political Association
Gereformeerd Politiek Verbond (GPV)

Address. Berkweg 46, PO Box 439, 3800 AK Amersfoort
Telephone. (+31–33) 461–3546

Fax. (+31-33) 461-0132
Email. bureau@gpv.nl
Website. www.gpv.nl
Leadership. S.J.C. Cnossen (chairman); Gert J. Schutte (parliamentary leader)
On its creation in April 1948, the founders of the GPV claimed to represent the continuation of the ideas of the Dutch national Calvinists of the 16th and 17th centuries, but on the basis of recognition of the separation of church and state and of spiritual and fundamental freedoms. Before World War II the Anti-Revolutionary Party had claimed to represent these ideas, but the founders of the GPV objected to the "partly liberal and partly socialistic" tendencies which they believed to be developing in that party.

Having won one Second Chamber seat in 1986, the GPV recovered to two seats in 1989 and retained them in the 1994 and 1998 elections, with 1.3% of the vote in each contest. In the 1994 and 1999 European Parliament elections the GPV presented a joint list with the →Reformational Political Federation (RPF) and the →Reformed Political Party (SGV), which took 7.8% of the vote and two seats in 1994, rising to 8.7% and three seats in 1999, one for each constituent party. All three representatives joined the Europe of Democracies and Diversities group. The GPV has an official membership of 13,912.

Reformed Political Party
Staatkundig Gereformeerde Partij (SGP)

Address. Laan van Meerdervoort 165, 2517 AZ The Hague
Telephone. (+31–70) 345–6226
Fax. (+31–70) 365–5959
Email. partijbureau@sgp.nl
Website. www.sgp.nl
Leadership. Bastiaan Johannis (B.J.) van der Vlies (parliamentary leader); Rev. D.J. Budding (president-minister); W. Kolijn (president-general); W. van 't Hul (secretary-general)
Founded in 1918, the right-wing Calvinist SGP bases its political and social outlook on its interpretation of the Bible. It advocates strong law enforcement, including the use of the death penalty, and is opposed to supranational government on the grounds that it would expose the Netherlands to corrupting influences. It has consistently attracted somewhat under 2% of the vote, which gave it three Second Chamber seats through the 1980s, slipping to two in May 1994 on a vote share of 1.7%. For the following month's European Parliament elections the SGP presented a joint list with the →Reformed Political Association (GPV) and the →Reformational Political Federation (RPF), which took a 7.8% vote share and two seats (one for the SGP and one for the GPV).

The SGP improved to 1.8% of the vote in the May 1998 national elections, sufficient to increase its Second Chamber representation to three seats. In the June 1999 European Parliament elections it again presented a joint list with the GPV and RPF, which improved to 8.7% of the vote and three seats, one of which went to the SGP. All three representatives joined the Europe of Democracies and Diversities group. The SGP has an official membership of 25,500.

Socialist Party
Socialistische Partiji (SP)

Address. Vijverhofstraat 65, 3032 SC Rotterdam
Telephone. (+31–10) 243–5555
Fax. (+31–10) 243–5566
Email. sp@sp.nl
Website. www.sp.nl
Leadership. Jan Marijnissen (chairman and parliamentary leader); Tiny Kox (general secretary)
The left-wing SP derives from a Maxist–Leninist party founded in 1971 and has latterly obtained electoral support from former adherents of the Communist Party of the Netherlands, which disbanded in 1991 to become part of the

→Green Left. The SP increased its vote share from 0.4% in 1989 to 1.3% in the May 1994 Second Chamber elections, returning two deputies.

Contending in the May 1998 elections that the incumbent coalition led by the →Labour Party had done little to alleviate poverty and had allowed wealth differentials to grow, the SP almost trebled its vote, to 3.5%, and won five Second Chamber seats. It registered a further advance in the June 1999 European Parliament elections, taking 5.0% of the vote and winning its first seat. Its representative joined the European United Left/Nordic Green Left group. The party has an official membership of 26,000.

Other Parties

55+ Union (*Unie 55+*), one of several Dutch pensioners' parties, being more inclined to radicalism than the →General Union of the Elderly (AOV); obtained 0.9% of the vote and one Second Chamber seat in the May 1994 elections, but a joint list with the AOV in May 1998 won only 0.5% and no seats.
Address. PO Box 111, 7450 AC Holten
Telephone. (+31–548) 362422
Fax. (+31–548) 363422
Leadership. Bert Leerks (chairman)

Centre Democrats (*Centrumdemocraten, CD*), radical right-wing party created in 1986 by the majority "moderate" wing of the Centre Party (CP). Established on an anti-immigration platform mainly by former members of the ultra-nationalist Dutch People's Union (NVU), the CP had succeeded in attracting significant support among white working-class voters in inner city areas with heavy immigrant concentrations. In the 1982 Second Chamber elections it had obtained over 68,000 votes (0.8%) and one seat, while in the 1984 local elections it won 10% of the vote in Rotterdam and eight seats on the city council. Violent incidents occurred at several CP meetings prior to the May 1986 Second Chamber elections, in which the party failed to secure representation. Eight days before polling the CP had been declared bankrupt by a Dutch court after failing to pay a fine of 50,000 guilders imposed for forgery of election nominations. Re-emerging as the CD, the party regained one Second Chamber seat in 1989 and advanced to three seats in May 1994, winning 2.5% of the vote. It slumped to 0.6% in May 1998 and failed to win a seat.
Address. PO Box 84, 2501 CB The Hague
Telephone. (+31–70) 346–9264
Leadership. Hans Janmaat (chairman)

Dutch Middle Class Party (*Nederlandse Middenstands Partij, NMP*), conservative formation founded in 1970, won 0.3% in 1998 lower house elections.
Address. PO Box 285, 1250 AG Laren
Email. info@nmp.nl
Website. www.nmp.nl
Leadership. Martin Dessing (chairman)

European Party (*Europese Partij, EP*), founded in 1998 to advocate "global subsidiarity" and "democratic European governance" for its citizens and to oppose the "wasteful bureaucracy" of the present European Union.
Address. PO Box 136, 2501 CC The Hague
Telephone. (+31–10) 213–6218
Email. info@europeanparty.org

Website. www.europeanparty.org
Leadership. Kees Nieuwenkamp & Roel Nieuwenkamp

Frisian National Party (*Fryske Nasjonale Partij, FNP*), founded in 1962 to seek autonomy for northern province of Friesland within a federal Europe; affiliated to Democratic Party of the Peoples of Europe–European Free Alliance.
Address. Obrechtstrjitte 32, 8916 EN Ljouwert
Telephone. (+31–58) 213–1422
Fax. (+31–58) 213–1420
Email. fnp@eboa.com
Website. www.eboa.com/fnp
Leadership. Rindert Straatsma (chairman)

General Union of the Elderly (*Algemeen Ouderen Verbond, AOV*), pledged to opposing cuts in the state pension and other benefits for the elderly; won 3.6% of the vote in the May 1994 Second Chamber elections, giving it six seats, but then damaged by internal dispute, which resulted in three deputies breaking away or being expelled from the group; a joint list with →55+ Union in May 1998 won only 0.5% and no seats.
Address. Louis Kookenweg 12, 5624 KW Eindhoven
Telephone. (+31–40) 433–961
Fax. (+31–40) 124765
Leadership. Martin Batenburg & W.J. Verkerk

The Greens (*De Groenen*), founded in 1984 as a conservative church-oriented environmentalist party, opposed to leftist radicalism of →Green Left; won one upper house seat in March 1995 but failed to gain lower house representation in 1994 or 1998, its vote share in the latter contest being 0.2%; member of European Federation of Green Parties.
Address. PO Box 6192, 2001 HD Haarlem
Telephone. (+31–23) 542-7370
Fax. (+31–23) 514–4176
Email. info@degroenen.nl
Website. www.degroenen.nl
Leadership. Ron van Wonderen

Netherlands Mobile (*Nederland Mobiel*), conservative pro-motorist party founded in 1997, won 0.5% in 1998 lower house elections.
Address. PO Box 65712, 2506 EA The Hague
Website. www.nederland-mobiel.nl
Leadership. J.H.van Laar & Alphen aan de Rijn

New Dutch Communist Party (*Nieuwe Communistische Partij Nederland, NCPN*), leftist formation.
Address. Donker Curtiusstraat 7/325, 1051 JL Amsterdam
Telephone. (+31–20) 682–5019
Fax. (+31–20) 682–8276
Email. 106057.1021@compuserve.com
Website. www.ncpn.nl

Political Party of the Elderly (*Politieke Partij voor Ouderen, PPO*), contested 1998 elections as Seniors 2000 (*Senioren 2000*), winning only 0.4% of vote.
Leadership. K. Blokker (chairman)

Socialist Workers' Party (*Socialistiese Arbeiderspartij, SAP*), Trotskyist formation founded in 1974.
Address. Sint Jacobstraat 10–20, 1012 NC Amsterdam
Telephone. (+31–20) 625–9272
Fax. (+31–20) 620–3774
Leadership. H.E.W. Lindelauff

344

Netherlands Dependencies

The Kingdom of the Netherlands incorporates two Caribbean territories which became Dutch possessions in the 17th century, namely Aruba and the Netherlands Antilles, both of which exercise full autonomy in domestic affairs and have flourishing multi-party systems. Unlike those in French dependencies in the same region, political parties in Aruba and the Netherlands Antilles have little direct connection with or derivation from metropolitan parties.

Aruba

Capital: Oranjestad   **Population:** 78,000 (2000E)

Located off the north-east coast of Venezuela, the island of Aruba was part of the Netherlands Antilles until it secured self-government (*status aparte*) on Jan. 1, 1986. It has an appointed Governor representing the Dutch sovereign and a 21-member legislature (*Staten*) elected for a four-year term, to which the Prime Minister and Council of Ministers are accountable for their executive authority (which excludes external relations and defence). Elections to the *Staten* on Sept. 28, 2001, resulted as follows: People's Electoral Movement 12 seats (with 52.4% of the vote), Aruban People's Party 6 (26.7%), Aruban Patriotic Party 2 (9.6%), Aruban Liberal Organization 1 (5.7%).

Aruban Liberal Organization
Organisacion Liberal Arubano (OLA)
Address. c/o Staten, Oranjestad
Leadership. Glenbert F. Croes
Founded in 1991, the moderate OLA won two seats in the 1994 elections and joined a coalition headed by the →Aruban People's Party (AVP). It withdrew from the government in September 1997 but again won only two seats in the resultant December 1997 elections and re-joined the AVP in office. It fell back to one seat in the September 2001 elections and went into opposition.

Aruban Patriotic Party
Partido Patriótico Arubano (PPA)
Address. c/o Staten, Oranjestad
Leadership. Benedict (Benny) J.M. Nisbett
The PPA was founded in 1949 and later became an anti-independence grouping. It won two seats in the 1985 elections and joined an Aruban home rule government headed by the →Aruban People's Party (1986–89) and then a coalition headed by →People's Electoral Movement (1989–93). It was reduced to one seat in the 1993 elections and was unrepresented in 1994–2001, but returned to the *Staten* in September 2001 with two seats.

Aruban People's Party
Arubaanse Volkspartij (AVP)
Address. Ave Alo Tromp 57, Oranjestad
Telephone. (+297) 26326
Fax. (+297) 37870
Leadership. Jan Henrik (Henny) A. Eman (leader); Robertico Croes (chairman); Mito Croes (secretary-general)
The AVP was founded by Henny Eman in 1942 and long advocated separation from Netherlands Antilles (but not full independence). On the achievement of home rule in 1986, Eman became Prime Minister of Aruba. It was in opposition from 1989 until 1994 when it formed a coalition with →Aruban Liberal Organization (OLA).

The AVP/OLA coalition collapsed in acrimony in September 1997, but was revived after the December elections, in which the AVP retained 10 seats. This government almost served its full term, but was defeated by the →People's Electoral Movement (MEP) in elections in September 2001, with the AVP retaining only six seats.

The AVP is affiliated to the Christian Democrat International and the Christian Democrat Organization of America.

People's Electoral Movement
Movimento Electoral di Pueblo (MEP)
Address. Santa Cruz 74D, Oranjestad
Telephone. (+297) 854495
Fax. (+297) 850768
Email. mep@setarnet.aw
Website. www.setarnet.aw/organisationpage/mep
Leadership. Nelson Orlando Oduber (chairman)
The MEP was founded in 1971 by Gilberto (Betico) François Croes and became the leading advocate of Aruba's separation from Netherlands Antilles and eventual full independence, not least so that Aruba would have full benefit from offshore oil reserves. In opposition on the achievement of separate status in 1986, the MEP returned to power after the 1989 elections under Nelson Oduber, who became head of a coalition government which included the →Aruban Patriotic Party. The MEP then back-tracked on the aim of full independence in 1996, instead accepting continued Dutch sovereignty. The government collapsed in 1994, causing new elections in which the MEP took second place (with nine of 21 seats) and went into opposition to a coalition headed by the →Aruban People's Party.

The MEP remained at nine seats in the December 1997 elections and continued in opposition. In September 2001, however, Oduber led it back to power with an absolute majority of 12 seats.

The MEP is a member party of the Socialist International.

Other Parties

Aruban Democratic Alliance (*Aliansa Democratico Arubana, ADA*), won 3.5% of the vote in its first elections in 2001, but failed to achieve representation.
Leadership. Robert Frederick Wever

National Democratic Action (*Acción Democratico Nacional, ADN*), founded in 1985 and a member of the first post-separation coalition in 1986–89 headed by the →Aruban People's Party. It was in a coalition headed by the →People's Electoral Movement in 1989–94, meanwhile winning only one seat in the 1993 elections, which it lost in 1994. The ADN took 2.4% of the vote in 1997 and 1.1% in 2001.

Leadership. Pedro Pablo Kelly

Netherlands Antilles

Capital: Willemstad (Curaçao)

Population: 202,000 (2000E)

Consisting of the Caribbean islands of Curaçao, Bonaire, St Maarten, St Eustatius (or Statia) and Saba, the Netherlands Antilles have an appointed Governor representing the Dutch sovereign and a 22-member legislature (*Staten*), to which the Prime Minister and Council of Ministers are responsible. The *Staten* members are elected for a four-year term subject to dissolution, 14 from Curaçao, three each from Bonaire and St Maarten and one each from St Eustatius and Saba. In a referendum in St Maarten in June 2000, nearly 70% of voters approved proposals for St Maarten to leave the Netherlands Antilles and to become an autonomous territory within the Kingdom of the Netherlands.

Producing the customary wide distribution of seats between the parties, most of which exist in one island only, elections to the *Staten* on Jan. 30, 1998, resulted as follows: Restructured Antilles Party 4 seats (with 18.9% of the vote), National People's Party 3 (14.9%), Labour Party People's Crusade 3 (13.9%), Workers' Liberation Front of May 30 2 (10.4%), New Antilles Movement 2 (8.4%), Democratic Party-St Maarten 2 (5.3%), Democratic Party-Bonaire 2 (2.8%), four other parties 4. *Note*. The foreign-language party names given below are thought to be those most commonly used of the Spanish, Dutch and Papiamento (local dialect) versions.

Democratic Party-Bonaire
Democratische Partij-Bonaire (DP-B)
Address. 13A Kaya America, PO Box 294, Kralendijk, Bonaire
Leadership. Laurenso A. (Jopie) Abraham (leader)
The centrist DP-B was founded in 1954 as an autonomous island party linked with other Antilles Democratic parties. It won control of the Bonaire council in 1984 and two *Staten* seats in 1985, joining the Antilles coalition headed by the →New Antilles Movement (MAN). The party failed to win representation in the 1990 *Staten* elections, but regained two seats in 1994 and joined a coalition headed by the →Restructured Antilles Party (PAR). In April 1995 its again won control of the Bonaire council with five of the nine seats.

The DP-B retained two *Staten* seats in the January 1998 elections and joined the government eventually formed by the →National People's Party (PNR), with party leader Jopie Abraham becoming Second Deputy Prime Minister. He lost that status (but retained his ministerial portfolios) when the PAR regained the premiership in November 1999.

Democratic Party–St Martin
Democratische Partij–Sint Maarten (DP–SM)
Address. PO Box 414, Philipsburg, St Maarten
Leadership. Sarah Wescott-Williams
The centrist DP–SM is based in the English-speaking community of St Maarten and has participated in successive Antilles governments, as well as usually having strong representation in the St Maarten council. Having two *Staten* seats in 1990, the party was weakened thereafter by splits and corruption allegations against its then leaders and was reduced to one seat in 1994. Under the new leadership of Sarah Wescott-Williams, the DP–SM recovered to two seats in 1998 and held two portfolios in the 1998-99 Antilles government headed by the →National People's Party (PNR).

In elections to the St Maarten council in May 1999 the DP–SM won seven of the 11 seats and formed the territory's first-ever non-coalition government. In a referendum in June 2000 the government secured nearly 70% backing for its proposal that St Maarten should leave the Netherlands Antilles and become an autonomous territory within the Kingdom of the Netherlands.

Labour Party People's Crusade
Partido Laboral Krusada Popular (PLKP)
Address. Schouwburgweg 44, Willemstad, Curaçao
Telephone. (+599–9) 737–0644
Fax. (+599–9) 737–0831
Website. www.cur.net/krusado
Leadership. Errol A. Cova (leader)
The Curaçao-based PLKP was launched in 1997 with trade union backing and won three *Staten* seats its first elections in January 1998, opting to join a six-party centre-left government headed by the →National People's Party (PNP). The party also polled strongly in Curaçao council elections in May 1999, winning four seats.

National People's Party
Partido Nashonal di Pueblo (PNP)
Address. Penstraat 24, Willemstad, Curaçao
Telephone. (+599–9) 462–3544
Fax. (+599–9) 461–4491
Email. scamelia@pnp.an
Leadership. Suzanne (Suzi) Camelia-Römer (leader); Dudley Lucia (secretary-general)
Founded in 1948, the Christian democratic Curaçao-based PNP provided the Netherland Antilles' first woman Prime Minister in 1984–85, when a coalition was headed by then leader Maria Liberia-Peters. She returned to the premiership in 1988 but resigned over the defeat in a November 1993 referendum of the PNP's proposal that Curaçao should seek Aruba-style separate status. The party was reduced from seven to three *Staten* seats in 1994 elections, being outpolled by the new →Restructured Antilles Party (PAR). The PNP again won three *Staten* seats in the January 1998 elections, following which new leader Suzi Camelia-Römer eventually became Prime Minister of a six-party coalition. This collapsed in November 1999, whereupon Camelia-Römer became Deputy Prime Minister with responsibility for economic policy in a new coalition headed by the PAR. Meanwhile, in elections to the Curaçao council in May 1999, the PNP had advanced from four seats to five.

The PNP is affiliated to the Christian Democrat International and the Christian Democrat Organization of America.

New Antilles Movement
Movimentu Antiá Nobo (MAN)
Address. Landhuis Morgenster, Willemstad, Curaçao
Telephone. (+599–9) 468–4781
Leadership. Kenneth Gijsbertha (leader)
The Curaçao-based centre-left MAN was founded in the 1970s by a non-Marxist faction of the →Workers' Liberation

346

Front of May 30. Under the leadership of Dominico F. Martina it headed Antilles coalition governments in 1982–84 and 1985–88 but was reduced to two *Staten* seats in 1990. It again won two seats in 1994, when it joined a coalition headed by the →Restructured Antilles Party (PAR), but went into opposition after failing to improve on its two-seat tally in 1998. The MAN has participated in several recent Curaçao governments, although its representation in the island's council fell from six seats to two in May 1999.

The MAN is a member party of the Socialist International.

Restructured Antilles Party
Partido Antiá Restrukturá (PAR)

Address. Fokkerweg 26/3, Willemstad, Curaçao
Telephone. (+599–9) 465–2566
Fax. (+599–9) 465–2622
Leadership. Miguel A. Pourier (president); Pedro J. Atacho (secretary-general)

The Christian social Curaçao-based PAR was founded in 1993 and became the leading Antilles party in the 1994 elections with eight seats, so that Miguel Pourier became Prime Minister of a government coalition with five other parties. It slumped to four seats in the January 1998 *Staten* elections, leaving it as still the largest single party but unable to form a new majority coalition. It therefore went into opposition to a government headed by the →National People's Party (PNP), until a crisis in November 1999 enabled Pourier to regain the premiership at the head of a broad-based coalition. Meanwhile, in Curaçao council elections in May 1999, the PAR had slipped from six to five seats, although it had remained the largest single party.

Workers' Liberation Front of May 30
Frente Obrero Liberashon 30 di Mei (FOL)

Address. Mayaguanaweg 16, Willemstad, Curaçao
Telephone. (+599–9) 461–8105
Email. agodett@fol.an
Leadership. Anthony Godett (leader)

The Curaçao-based pro-independence FOL was founded in 1969 and held one *Staten* seat in 1985–90. Having moderated its original Marxist ideology, it regained representation in 1998, winning two seats in alliance with the Independent Social (*Soshal Independiente*) grouping formed by dissidents of the →National People's Party (PNP). The party then opted to join a six-party government headed by the PNP. The FOL won four Curaçao council seats in May 1999.

Other Parties

Bonaire Patriotic Union (*Unión Patriótico Bonairiano, UPB*), represented in the *Staten* since 1977, won one seat in 1985, three in 1990 and one in 1994 and 1998. Affiliated to the Christian Democrat International and the Christian Democrat Organization of America.
Address. Kaya Hulanda 26, Kralendijk, Bonaire
Telephone. (+599–7) 8906
Fax. (+599–7) 5447
Leadership. Ramon Booi

Democratic Party–St Eustatius (DPSE), was the dominant party on mainly Catholic St Eustatius until 1998, when it lost the island's single *Staten* seat to the →St Eustatius Alliance (SEA). It was also defeated by the SEA in the May 1999 island council elections, retaining only two of the five seats.
Leadership. Julian Woodley

Saba Democratic Labour Movement (SDLM), became ruling party on mainly English-speaking Saba in May 1995, winning three of the five island council seats; was reduced to one seat in 1999 and went into opposition to the →Windward Islands People's Movement.
Leadership. Steve Hassell

St Eustatius Alliance (SEA), won the single St Eustatius *Staten* seat in 1998, having been strengthened by defectors from the previously dominant →Democratic Party–St Eustatius (DPSE). It also took three of the five island council seats in May 1999.
Leadership. Kenneth van Putten

St Maarten Patriotic Alliance (SPA), founded in 1990 in opposition to the then dominant →Democratic Party–St Maarten. It became the leading St Maarten party in the 1991 island council elections and won two Antilles seats in 1994, joining a coalition headed by the →Restructured Antilles Party. It was reduced to a single *Staten* seat in 1998, despite being allied with the →Serious Alternative People's Party. The same alliance lost its dominant position in the St Maarten council elections of May 1999, retaining only three of the 11 seats.
Address. Frontstraat 69, Philipsburg, St Maarten
Telephone. (+599–5) 31064
Fax. (+599–5) 31065
Leadership. Vance James Jr

Serious Alternative People's Party (SAPP), won one seat on St Maaarten island council in May 1995, entering an island coalition with →Democratic Party-St Maarten. It was allied with the →St Maarten Patriotic Alliance (SPA) in both the 1998 *Staten* and 1999 island council elections, unproductively in both contests.
Leadership. Julian Rollocks

Windward Islands People's Movement (WIPM), based in mainly English-speaking and Catholic Saba and St Eustatius (Statia). It was the dominant party in Saba until 1995 and has won Saba's single *Staten* seat in the last four general elections, joining a broad-based coalition government after the 1998 contest. It returned to power in Saba in the May 1999 council elections, winning four of the five seats. The party is affiliated to the Christian Democrat International and the Christian Democrat Organization of America.
Address. The Level 211, Av. Windwardside, Saba
Telephone. (+599–4) 2244
Leadership. Will Johnston (president)

New Zealand

Capital: Wellington

Population: 3,850,000 (2001)

New Zealand is a constitutional monarchy in which the British monarch is sovereign and the Governor-General exercises the powers of appointed representative. The unicameral parliament has 120 members, seven of whom represent Maori territorial units, and is elected for three years. Although the Prime Minister and cabinet are at the apex of the political system, parliament is the ultimate source of democratic accountability. As a result, the tenure of any government is dependent upon its ability to retain the confidence of parliament.

347

From the 1930s New Zealand politics had a two party character with the conservative National Party and the Labour Party alternating in government. Even when the two-party vote dropped, plurality voting effectively ensured that the two major parties maintained a stranglehold on parliamentary and executive power. Beginning in the late 1970s, electoral support for the two major parties began to decline, from an average of 95% per cent in the post-World War II period to 70% per cent in 1993. The radical economic and welfare policies of successive Labour (1984–90) and National (1990–93) governments provoked deep divisions within party ranks and brought about the formation of a number of splinter parties. By 1992 a five-party Alliance had emerged, mostly from the left flank of Labour, and in 1993 the New Zealand First party was formed from the populist and nationalist wing of the National Party. The gradual transition to a more fragmented multi-party system was completed by the electorate's decision, which took effect in 1996, to replace the plurality voting system with proportional representation.

As a result of a general election on Nov. 27, 1999 a total of seven parties held seats in the new parliament, as follows: New Zealand Labour Party 49 (with 38.7% of the vote), New Zealand National Party 39 (30.5%), Alliance 10 (7.7%), ACT New Zealand 9 (7.0%), Green Party of Aotearoa 7 (5.2%), New Zealand First Party 5 (4.3%), United New Zealand 1 (6.5%). The Labour Party subsequently formed a minority coalition government with the Alliance Party.

ACT New Zealand

Address. PO Box 99651, Newmarket, Auckland
Telephone. (+64–4) 523–0470
Fax. (+64–9) 523–0472
Email. info@voteact.org.nz
Website. www.act.org.nz
Leadership. Richard Prebble (leader); Sarah Judd (president); Bruce Howat (chief executive)
The ACT Party was formed in 1994 as the political instrument of a right-wing pressure group, the Association of Consumers and Taxpayers. Its founding leader, Roger Douglas, was Labour's Minister of Finance during the 1980s. ACT's core beliefs include the maximization of 'individual freedom and choice, personal responsibility, respect for the rule of law, and the protection of the life, liberty and property of each and every citizen'. At various times it has advocated the abolition of personal income tax, fewer MPs and ministers, and the introduction of a voucher system for health and education. At the 1996 election the party won 6.1% of the vote and eight seats. Between 1998 and 1999 its support was crucial to the survival of the minority →New Zealand National Party government. It is an extremely well funded party, with substantial business donations, and appeals to tactical voters who view the small party as an integral part of any future centre-right coalition. In 1999 it won 7% of the vote and nine parliamentary seats.

The Alliance

Address. PO Box 2948, Wellington
Fax. (+64–9) 361–2562
Email. inforequest@alliance.org.nz
Website. www.alliance.org.nz
Leadership. Jim Anderton (leader); Matt McCarten (president); Gerard Hehir (general secretary)
In 1991, four minor parties formed an electoral alliance with a view to putting up one candidate per constituency, thereby improving their chances of electoral success under the former first-past-the-post voting system. Although drawn from quite diverse social and ideological traditions, the four parties were united in their opposition to the free market policies of the two major parties.

New Labour was formed from the left wing of Labour in 1989. As well as attracting 5% of the vote at the 1990 election, its leader, Jim Anderton, a former Labour MP and party president, held on to his parliamentary seat. A second party, the **Democrats**, was the oldest third party in New Zealand, having been formed in 1953 as the Social Credit Political League. As a monetary reform movement, it appealed to small business people and farmers. Despite contesting all seats at every election, it elected only four MPs. A third party, *Mana Motuhake*, was established as a predominantly Maori political grouping in 1979 aimed at improving the economic, social and cultural conditions of New Zealand's indigenous people (who make up approximately 15% of the population). Another founding member of the Alliance was the →**Green Party**, although it broke away in 1999. In 1992 a fifth party, the **Liberal Party**, joined the Alliance. Unlike the other Alliance parties, the Liberals were a breakaway movement from the →New Zealand National Party.

The Alliance's most successful election performance was in 1993, when it attracted 18% of the vote. However, because the 1993 election was conducted under the rules of first-past-the-post, the five-party grouping gained only two parliamentary seats. Since then its vote has progressively declined, from 10% in 1996 to 8% in 1999 but with the Alliance winning 13 and 10 seats respectively. Although the parties of the Alliance retain separate organizations, with the departure of the Greens and the Liberals (the latter party was wound up in 1999) pressure has mounted to conflate the various small groupings into a single Alliance organisation.

Green Party of Aotearoa (New Zealand)

Address. PO Box 11 652, Wellington
Fax. (+64-4) 801–5104
Email. greenparty@greens.org.nz
Website. www.greens.org.nz
Leadership. Jeanette Fitzsimons and Rod Donald (co-leaders); Margaret O'Brien and David Clendon (co-convenors); Craig Palmer (general secretary)
The Green Party's precursor, the Values Party, was formed in 1972. Values contested several elections, with little electoral success, before evolving into an environmental pressure group. In late 1989 the Values Party was officially disbanded. This left the way open in 1990 for the creation of the Green Party. Although its focus was the environment, the new party adopted the same post-materialist or 'quality-of-life' issues that had characterised Values. In recent years, for example, the party has been a vocal critic of economic globalization, genetically modified plants and food, and the logging of native forests. Only months after its formation, the Greens attracted 7% of the vote at the 1990 election. As a member of the third party grouping→The Alliance, the party had three MPs elected at the 1996 election. However, tensions over policy priorities and organizational strategies, together with a growing confidence that the Greens had the electoral potential to go it alone, caused a break with the third party grouping in early 1999. It is the only parliamentary party to disclose its membership figures (2,800) and has relations with federations of green parties worldwide.

New Zealand First Party

Address. Private Box 1574, Wellington

Telephone. (+64–4) 470–6688
Fax. (+64–4) 499–0569
Email. nzfirst@parliament.govt.nz
Website. www.nzfirst.org.nz
Leadership. Winston Peters (leader); Doug Woolerton (president); Graham Harding (secretary general)

New Zealand First was established in 1993 as the political vehicle of a prominent Maori politician, Winston Peters. The former →New Zealand National Party MP's criticism of that party's neo-liberal agenda led to his dismissal from cabinet in 1991 and expulsion from the party caucus the following year. New Zealand First made its mark as a populist movement, adopting strong nationalistic policies on such issues as immigration and foreign investment. At the 1993 election it received 8.4% of the vote nationwide. Following the 1996 election, in which its 13.4% share of the vote gave it the balance of power, New Zealand First formed a coalition with its former National Party adversary. On the collapse of the coalition in 1998, nine of New Zealand First's 17 MPs broke away from the party and continued to support the government. At the 1999 election New Zealand First received only 4.3% of the vote and five parliamentary seats.

New Zealand Labour Party

Address. PO Box 784, Wellington
Telephone. (+64–4) 384–7649
Fax. (+64–4) 384–8060
Email. labour.party@parliament.govt.nz
Website. www.labour.org.nz
Leadership. Helen Clark (leader); Mike Williams (president); Mike Smith (general secretary)

The Labour Party is the oldest of New Zealand's political parties, having been formed in 1916. During its first period in office from 1935–49 it introduced legislation creating a comprehensive welfare state. From 1949–84 the party was in opposition to the →New Zealand National Party other than for terms in 1957–60 and 1972–75. During a second significant period of reform, between 1984 and 1990, under Prime Minister David Lange, Labour faced the consequences of deep-seated economic stagnation caused in good measure by loss of traditional markets for the agricultural commodities that were the bedrock of the economy. The new Labour programme reversed previous socialist and protectionist policies and instead included a commitment to economic deregulation, the ending of subsidies to the manufacturing and agricultural sectors, privatization of state-owned assets, encouragement of multi-national investment, and a more targeted system of welfare. Paradoxically it also introduced a system of compulsory trade union membership of a sort not seen in any other Western country. Whilst pursuing a largely neo-conservative economic agenda, Labour adopted a liberal position on such social issues as homosexual law reform and pay equity for women. Internationally, Labour's most prominent initiative was its ban on nuclear-powered and armed ships, a decision that led to the cancellation of New Zealand's ANZUS defence treaty with the United States.

Labour's economic reforms sparked conflict between the party's left and right wings, both in government and in the wider party. In 1989, following a public disagreement between the Finance Minister, Roger Douglas, and the Prime Minister, David Lange, over the cabinet's decision to introduce a flat 23% rate of income tax, Lange tendered his resignation. The following year, a group of Labour activists broke away to form a new left-wing party, which they named New Labour. Despite having had three Prime Ministers in as many years (Lange 1984-89; Geoffrey Palmer 1989-90; and Mike Moore 1990), Labour was unable to stem the growing tide of defections. At the 1990 election the National Party was returned to power with a landslide majority.

Following Labour's 1993 election defeat, its second in succession, Helen Clark replaced Moore as party leader. Despite its modest 28% share of the vote at the 1996 election, Labour was widely expected to lead the first coalition government under proportional representation. Instead, the third party holding the balance of power (→New Zealand First) surprised almost everyone, including its own supporters, by choosing to go into government with its former adversary, National. During the next three years, the Labour leader established the basis for a workable coalition arrangement with the →Alliance. In the November 1999 election Labour emerged as the largest party with 49 seats and it then formed a minority government with the Alliance (which had won 10 seats), the Alliance being given four seats in the 20-seat cabinet. Under Clark's prime ministership, Labour attempted to broaden its appeal as the party of "middle New Zealand" by pursuing a 'Third Way' agenda based on a commitment to conservative economic principles, individual responsibility, and moderate social welfare reform. At the same time it criticized "excesses" in neo-liberalism and market deregulation under the previous National administration.

The Labour Party is a member party of the Socialist International.

New Zealand National Party

Address. PO Box 1155, Wellington
Telephone. (+64–4) 472–5211
Fax. (+64–4) 478–1622
Email. hq@national.org.nz
Web. www.national.org.nz
Leadership. Jenny Shipley (leader); Michelle Boag (president); David Major (chief executive)

The National Party was a product of the merger of two conservative parties, Reform and United, in 1936. In fulfilment of the claim implicit in its title of representing the interests of all major segments of the New Zealand community, for most of the post-war period National was the party of government (1949–57; 1960–72; 1975–84; 1990–99). As a pragmatic party of a mildly conservative hue, the early National Party was able to persuade voters that in an era of plentiful job opportunities and high living standards it was the party best equipped to provide a balance between the goals of individual liberty, free enterprise, and welfare.

When National returned to power in 1990, Prime Minister Jim Bolger and Finance Minister Ruth Richardson intensified the process of economic liberalization begun by the →New Zealand Labour Party while in office from 1984 in response to the country's worsening economic position. National carried out deregulation of the labour market (scrapping the system of compulsory trade union membership enacted by Labour in 1984), sharp reductions in government spending, and repayment of overseas debt through such methods as the selective privatization of state-owned assets. The impact of these policies resulted in an attrition of party members, especially those on fixed retirement incomes. In 1992 two National MPs defected to form an anti-free-market party, which later joined the →Alliance, and the following year a former National cabinet minister and Maori MP, Winston Peters, established the →New Zealand First Party.

Following National's modest but nonetheless winning performance at the 1993 election (when it took 35% of the vote, compared with 34.7% for Labour and a combined total of 30.3% for the minor parties), the Prime Minister signalled a return to a more moderate policy agenda. The success of the 1993 electoral referendum, together with the precariousness of his one-seat parliamentary majority, prompted Bolger to introduce a number of changes, including relieving Richardson of her finance portfolio, suspending several key privatization plans, and introducing a more measured and gradual approach to welfare reform. Following yet more defections from National's parliamentary ranks, Bolger entered into a coalition arrangement with a new centre party, the →United Party, in February 1996. Although National lost further ground at the 1996 election, declining to a 33.8% share of the vote, New Zealand First's decision to go into coalition with the National Party provided National with its third successive term in government.

The National/New Zealand First coalition was unpopular from the time of its formation, even among the two parties' own voters. At the end of 1997, Jenny Shipley replaced Bolger as Prime Minister, a move intended to strengthen National's hand in its dealings with New Zealand First. The following year Shipley expelled Peters, who was the Deputy Prime Minister and Treasurer, from the cabinet. Although National was able to retain power with the help of the →ACT Party and a small group of minor party defectors, notably from New Zealand First, it trailed Labour in the opinion polls from the time of the coalition's break-up. In the November 1999 election its share of the vote (30.5%) plummeted to its lowest since National was established in 1936.

The National Party is a member of the International Democrat Union and the Asia-Pacific Democrat Union

United Future New Zealand
Address. PO Box 13–236, Wellington
Telephone. (+64-4) 471–9410
Fax. (+64-4) 499–7266
Email. peter.Dunne@parliament.govt.nz
Web. www.united.nz.org.nz
Leadership. Peter Dunne (leader); Anthony Walton (deputy leader); Ian Tulloch (president); Murray Smith (general secretary)
The party was formed as the United Party in 1995 with the defection of seven MPs from the →New Zealand National Party and the →New Zealand Labour Party. As a centre party, it propped up the National government by taking a seat in cabinet in the final months leading up to the 1996 election. Although it received less than 1% of the vote at both the 1996 and 1999 elections, it was able to retain one seat by virtue of Peter Dunne's victory in the affluent Wellington constituency of Ohariu-Belmont. In 2000 the party merged with a Christian party, Future New Zealand, to become United Future New Zealand.

New Zealand's Associated Territories
Cook Islands

Capital: Avarua (on Rarotonga)

Population: 20,400 (2000E)

The Cook Islands became a self-governing territory in free association with New Zealand in August 1965. Although New Zealand takes responsibility for foreign affairs and defence, it acts in consultation with the Cook Islands government. The head of state is the British monarch, and the parliament is a unicameral body of 25 members. At the last five-yearly election, which was held in June 1999, the Democratic Alliance Party took 11 seats, the Cook Islands Party 10 and the New Alliance Party 4. The Cook Islands Party, which had been in government for ten years under the premiership of Geoffrey A. Henry, was replaced by a coalition of its two rivals. The leader of the Democratic Alliance Party leader, Dr Terepai Maoate, became both Prime Minister and Finance Minister.

Cook Islands Party
Address. Parliament Buildings, Rarotonga
Leadership. Joe Williams (leader)
Long the dominant party in Cook Island politics (at the 1994 election it won 20 of 25 seats), the Cook Islands Party lost popularity after the government declared bankruptcy and introduced a number of austerity measures from 1996. These included a reduction by two-thirds in the size of the public service, salary cuts for those civil servants who remained, and the privatization of a number of state-owned assets. It lost office in the 1999 elections.

Democratic Alliance Party
Address. PO Box 492, Rarotonga
Leadership. Terepai Maoate (leader and Prime Minister)
In the 1999 election campaign the Democratic Alliance Party accused the governing →Cook Islands Party of economic mismanagement and promised a range of reforms,

including reduced government intervention in the economy, increased welfare payments to children and the elderly, and a referendum on reducing the size and cost of parliament. Following the election it formed a coalition government with the →New Alliance Party. Conflict between the Prime Minister, Dr Maoate, and his deputy Prime Minister, New Alliance leader Norman George, led to the latter's dismissal in July 2001.

New Alliance Party
Address. Parliament Buildings, Rarotonga
Leadership. Norman George (leader)
Before forming a government with the →Democratic Alliance Party in 1999, this small centre party was in coalition with the →Cook Islands Party. By August 2001, discussions were underway over a possible merger of the New Alliance and Democratic Alliance Parties.

Other Territories

New Zealand's other associated territories include **Niue**, with a population of 2,500. Since 1974 Niue has had self-government in free association with New Zealand. There is a local Assembly but the political system is not based on formal party organizations. The **Ross Dependency**, in Antarctica, has no permanent population. In **Tokelau**, which has a population of 1,500, executive authority is exercised by an administrator appointed by New Zealand; the territory's national representative body is the General *Fono*, but there are no political parties.

Nicaragua

Capital: Managua

Population: 4,800,000 (2000E)

The Republic of Nicaragua achieved independence in 1838 but was subject to US military intervention in 1912–25 and 1927–33. The country was subsequently left in the control of the Somoza family until the overthrow of the right-wing dictatorship of Gen. Anastasio Somoza Debayle by a popular revolutionary movement, the Sandinista National Liberation Front *(Frente Sandinista de Liberación Nacional,* FSLN) in 1979. Far-reaching economic and social reforms were introduced despite attempts by conservative groups and US-backed right-wing *contra* rebels to destabilize the government. The FSLN won the presidential and legislative elections in 1984, the first to be held in the country since 1974, but lost subsequent elections held in 1990 and 1996.

War fatigue among the population and a decade of economic austerity were instrumental factors in the FSLN's unexpected and heavy electoral defeat in 1990. Although the FSLN remained the country's largest party, a right-wing alliance won on a platform that promised to end the civil war, promote national reconciliation and attract foreign aid and investment. Arnoldo Alemàn Lacayo, the candidate of the Liberal Alliance (AL, the main opposition to the FSLN), won the next presidential election held in October 1996. Alemàn won 51% of the vote, easily defeating ex-President Daniel Ortega Saavedra of the FSLN, who took less than 38% of the vote. The AL also won the legislative poll held at the same time, gaining 42 seats in the National Assembly, against 37 seats for the FSLN. With the support of other conservatives, the Alliance patched together an absolute majority in the legislature.

Under the 1987 constitution, executive power rests with the President, who is head of state and commander-in-chief of the Defence and Security Forces and governs with the assistance of a Vice President and an appointed Cabinet. Amendments to the constitution approved in 1995 reduced the presidential term from six to five years and barred the President from serving more than two consecutive terms. A unicameral National Assembly is made up of 90 representatives (each with an alternative representative), who are directly elected for a five-year term by a system of proportional representation. Additional seats (currently three) are allotted to losing presidential candidates who have obtained the required national quotient to be elected to the Assembly. Further constitutional reforms signed into law in 2000 reduced the percentage of votes required to elect a president without the need for a run-off, from 45% of the total to 35%.

Central American Unionist Party
Partido Unionista Centro Americana (PUCA)
Address. Costado Oeste Hotel Intercontinental, 2 c. al Norte, Managua
Leadership. Blanca Rojas Echaverry
A member of the ruling →Liberal Alliance which won the 1996 legislative elections.

Christian Social Union Party
Partido Unidad Social Cristiana (PUSC)
Address. De la Iglesia de Santa Ana 2 Cuadras al Oeste, Managua
Telephone. (+505–2) 24772
Centre-right party and a member of the →Nicaraguan Democratic Movement Alliance (MDNA) formed in 2000 to contest the 2001 presidential and legislative elections.

The PUSC is a member of the Christian Democrat and People's Parties International.

Conservative Party of Nicaragua
Partido Conservador de Nicaragua (PCN)
Address. Costado Sur de la Diplotienda, Managua
Leadership. Fernando Aguero Rocha (president)
The PCN was formed in 1992 when the Democratic Conservative Party of Nicaragua (PCDN) entered into a merger with the much smaller Conservative Social Party (PSC) and the Conservative Party of Labour (PCL). (Launched in 1979, the PCDN had been a right-wing party formed by three factions of the traditional Conservative Party, which had been the main legal opposition during the Somoza era). In the 1996 presidential election the party's

candidate, Noel José Vidaurre, finished forth, winning just over 2% of the vote. The party won three National Assembly seats in legislative elections held at the same time. The party is a member of the →Nicaraguan Democratic Movement Alliance (MDNA) formed in 2000 to contest the 2001 presidential and legislative elections.

Conservatives for Democracy
Conservadores por la Democracia (CD)
Address: c/o Asamblea Nacional, Managua
Member of the ruling →Liberal Alliance which won the 1996 legislative elections.

Constitutional Liberal Party
Partido Liberal Constitucionalista de Nicaragua (PLC)
Address. Apartado Postal 4569, Managua
Telephone. (+505–2) 781754
Fax. (+505–2) 781800
Email. plc@ibw.com.ni
Website. www.partidoliberal.org
Leadership. Leopoldo Navarro Bermudez (president)
The PLC is the principal rival to the →Sandinista National Liberation Front and headed the government from 1996. Formed in 1968, the PLC gained parliamentary representation for the first time in 1990 as part of the victorious National Opposition Union (UNO) alliance. In 1994 the PLC created a new coalition, the →Liberal Alliance (AL), to support the forthcoming presidential bid of the party's leader, Arnoldo Alemàn Lacayo. Not only did Alemàn win the 1996 election, but the AL, dominated by the PLC, also managed to win control of the legislature. In mid-1998 the

party held a convention at which Leopoldo Navarro, hitherto the party secretary-general, was elected as party president in place of Alemàn.

The PLC is a member of the Liberal International.

Independent Liberal Party
Partido Liberal Independiente (PLI)

Address. Cuidad Jardin, H-4 Calle Principal, Managua
Telephone. (+505–2) 443556
Fax. (+505–2) 480012
Leadership. Virgilio Godoy Reyes

The PLI was founded in 1946 by a dissident faction of Somoza's National Liberal Party who were opposed to the extension of the dictatorship's powers and who subsequently boycotted rigged elections. It welcomed the 1979 revolution and joined both the Revolutionary Patriotic Front and the Council of State. Party leader Virgilio Godoy Reyes served as Minister of Labour in the Sandinista-led government. Opposed to restrictions placed on campaign activities, it called for a boycott of the 1984 elections shortly before the poll but won nine seats in the National Constituent Assembly. In 1985 the PLI joined other centre-right opposition groups in the externally based Nicaraguan Democratic Co-ordinator (CON) alliance in campaigning for new elections, a ceasefire in the civil war and the de-politicization of the army, a general amnesty and the return of lands seized by the Sandinistas to their original owners.

The party refused to sign the 1987 constitution and joined the National Opposition Union (UNO) alliance of parties which won the 1990 presidential election, Godoy becoming Vice-President. The PLI did not to join the →Liberal Alliance (AL), preferring to remain in the Opposition Political Alliance (APO). The party performed poorly in the 1996 elections, winning only one seat in the National Assembly. It is a member of the →Patriotic Movement (MP) alliance formed in 1998 to contest the 2001 presidential and legislative elections.

Independent Liberal Party for National Unity
Partido Liberal Independiente de Unidad Nacional (PLIUN)

This is a liberal conservative party founded in 1988 by a group of defectors from the →Independent Liberal Party led by Eduardo Coronado Perez. It is a member of the ruling →Liberal Alliance which won the 1996 legislative elections.

Liberal Alliance
Alianza Liberal (AL)

Leadership. Arnoldo Alemàn Lacayo

This conservative and centrist alliance was founded in late 1994 to support the successful presidential bid of Arnoldo Alemàn Lacayo in October 1996. The member parties of the AL also managed to gain control of the National Assembly in legislative elections held at the same time, winning 42 of the Assembly's 93 seats before forging an absolute majority with the support of other conservatives. The main member of the AL is the →Constitutional Liberal Party. Other members are the →Neo-Liberal Party (PALI); the →Independent Liberal Party for National Unity (PLIUN); the →Central American Unionist Party (PUCA); →Conservatives for Democracy (CD); and →Liberal Convergence (CL).

Liberal Convergence
Convergencia Liberal (CL)

Address. c/o Asamblea Nacional, Managua

Member of the ruling →Liberal Alliance which won the 1996 legislative elections.

Liberal Democratic Party
Partido Liberal Demócrata (PLD)

Leadership. José Antonio Alvarado

The PLD was founded in July 2000 by José Antonio Alvarado following his dismissal as Defence Minister in the →Constitutional Liberal Party (PLC)-led government. In December 2000 the Supreme Electoral Council (CSE) refused recognition to the PLD.

Movement for a New Alternative
Movimiento Nueva Alternativa (MNA)

Centre-right party and a member of the →Patriotic Movement alliance.

National Conservative Party
Partido Nacional Conservador (PNC)

Leadership. Silviano Matamoros Lacayo

Formed in 1990, the right-wing PNC was a member of the National Opposition Coalition (UNO) that came to power in 1990. It contested the 1996 elections alone, and won one seat in the National Assembly. The PNC is affiliated to the Americas Democrat Union.

National Opposition Union '96 Alliance
Union Nacional Opositora '96 Alianza (UNO '96 Alliance)

The UNO '96 Alliance consisted of remnants of the National Opposition Union (UNO) which had won both the legislative and presidential election of 1990. By the time of the next election in 1996, UNO had been eclipsed as the main centre-right coalition and, in the legislative poll, managed to win only 0.6% of the vote and one National Assembly seat.

National Project
Proyecto Nacional (Pronal)

Address. c/o Asamblea Nacional, Managua
Leadership. Antonio Lacayo Oyanguren

Pronal was launched in April 1995 as a presidential vehicle for the group's leader, Antonio Lacayo Oyanguren, being in effect a working coalition of most of the Centre Group together with the →Nicaraguan Social Christian Party, the Social Democratic Party and the →Nicaraguan Democratic Movement. A son-in-law and close adviser to the then President Violeta Barrios de Chamorro, Lacayo resigned from the government in 1995 specifically to fight the election. However, Lacayo was constitutionally barred as a relative of the outgoing President from standing for the presidency himself and the party was represented instead by Benjamin Lanzas, who failed to make an impact. In the legislative elections, Pronal managed to win two National Assembly seats. The party is a member of the →Nicaraguan Democratic Movement Alliance (MDNA) formed in 2000 to contest the 2001 presidential and legislative elections.

National Unity Party
Partido Unidad Nacional (PUN)

Leadership. Gen. Joaquín Cuadra Lacayo

The PUN was founded by the former commander-in-chief of the army, Gen. Joaquín Cuadra Lacayo, in June 2000. In January 2001 the Supreme Electoral Council (CSE), refused it registration as a political party, effectively barring Gen. Cuadra from the 2001 presidential election.

Neo-Liberal Party
Partido Neo-Liberal (PALI)

PALI is a member of the ruling →Liberal Alliance which won the 1996 legislative elections.

Nicaraguan Democratic Movement
Movimiento Democrático Nicaragüense (MDN)

Leadership. Roberto Urroz Castillo

A small, left-of-centre party formed in 1978, the MDN was initially a backer of the Sandinistas then moving over to the *contra* side under the leadership of Alfonso Robelo Callejas. In 1995 it became a member of the →National Project (Pronal) alliance of parties, but in 1998 it joined the →Patriotic Movement alliance and two years later it formed another alliance, the →Nicaraguan Democratic Movement Alliance (MDNA) to contest the 2001 presidential and legislative elections.

Nicaraguan Democratic Movement Alliance
Movimiento Democrático Nicaragüense Alianza (MDNA)

Formed in 2000 to contest the 2001 presidential and legislative elections, the alliance consists of the following parties: the →Nicaraguan Democratic Movement (MDN); the →Party of the Nicaraguan Christian Road (PCCN); the →Sandinista Renewal Movement (MRS); the →Conservative Party of Nicaragua; the →Christian Social Union Party (PUSC); and the →National Project (Pronal).

Nicaraguan Popular Party
Partido Popular Nicaragüense (PPN)

Leadership. Alvaro Ramirez

The centrist PPN was created in 1999 by Alvaro Ramirez, a former member of the →Sandinista National Liberation Front (FSLN), who had unsuccessfully challenged Daniel Ortega for the party's candidacy in the 1996 presidential election.

Nicaraguan Resistance Party
Partido de la Resistencia Nicaragüense (PRN)

Address. Optica Nicaragüense, 100 varas al Lago, Managua
Telephone. (+505–2) 668098

The PRN was formed in late 1992 by former *contra* commanders. In the 1996 legislative elections the party managed to win 1.2% of the vote and one seat in the National Assembly. The PRN is a member of the →Patriotic Movement, an alliance formed in 1998 to contest elections in 2001.

Nicaraguan Social Christian Party
Partido Social Cristiano Nicaragüense (PSCN)

Address. Cindad Jardin, P. Maria, 1 calle al Lago, Managua
Telephone. (+505–2) 22026
Leadership. Germán Alfaro Ocambo (president)

Founded in 1957 and opposed to the Somoza dictatorship, the PSCN survived splits in 1976 and 1979. After the 1979 revolution it joined the Council of State, from which it resigned in November 1980. In 1981 it was a founder member of the Nicaraguan Democratic Co-ordinator (CDN), a right-wing coalition of parties opposed to the Sandinistas. In the 1990 elections, the PSCN joined the UNO opposition alliance, winning a single seat in association with an electoral ally, the Yatama, a right-wing *contra* rebel organization formed in 1987 from indigenous Atlantic coast political rebel groups. The Yatama disbanded along with other *contra* groups in mid-1990. Prior to the 1996 elections, the party joined the National Project alliance, which won two seats in the National Assembly.

Party of the Nicaraguan Christian Road
Partido Camino Cristiano Nicaragüense (PCCN)

Address. c/o Asamblea Nacional, Managua
Leadership. Antonio Asorno Molina

The Christian, right-wing PCCN won 3.7% of the vote and four National Assembly seats in the 1996 legislative elections. The party's candidate in the 1996 presidential elections, Guillermo Osorno, finished a distant third, winning some 4% of the vote. The party is a member of the →Nicaraguan Democratic Movement Alliance (MDNA) formed in 2000 to contest the 2001 presidential and legislative elections.

Patriotic Movement
Movimiento Patria (MP)

An alliance formed in 1998 to contest the 2001 presidential and legislative elections, the centrist MP consists of the following parties: the →Popular Conservative Alliance (APC), the →Movement for a New Alternative (MNA), the →Independent Liberal Party (PLI) and the →Nicaraguan Resistance Party (PRN). The following parties were members of the MP alliance in 1998, but went on to join the →Nicaraguan Democratic Movement Alliance (MDNA) in 2000: the →Nicaraguan Democratic Movement (MDN); the →Christian Social Union Party (PUSC); and the →Conservative Party of Nicaragua (PCN).

Popular Conservative Alliance
Alianza Popular Conservadora (APC)

Leadership. Eduardo Paladino Cabrera

Centre-right party and a member of the →Patriotic Movement alliance.

Sandinista National Liberation Front
Frente Sandinista de Liberación Nacional (FSLN)

Address. Costado Oeste, Parque El Calmen, Managua
Telephone. (+505–2) 660845
Fax. (+505–2) 661560
Email. fsln@fsln.org.ni
Website. www.fsln.org.ni
Leadership. Daniel Ortega Saavedra (secretary-general)

The FSLN was founded in 1961 and is named after the national hero Augusto César Sandino. It was founded by a small group of intellectuals, including former Nicaraguan Socialist Party (PSN) member Carlos Fonseca Amador and Tomás Borge Martínez, and began guerrilla activity against the US-backed Somoza regime in 1963. After suffering a series of defeats, it abandoned all military activity from 1970 to the end of 1974.

Fonseca, the FSLN's leading theoretician, was killed in 1976, and after 1975 disagreements on strategy split the movement into three factions. The Protracted People's War (GPP) group, led by Borge, favoured the creation of "liberated zones" on the Chinese and Vietnamese model, which would provide bases from which to attack towns. The Proletarian Tendency (PT), led by Jaime Wheelock, maintained that the FSLN should concentrate on winning the support of the urban working class. The "third way" group *(terceristas),* led by Daniel Ortega Saavedra, advocated a combination of an armed offensive and broad political alliances with other opposition organizations, which would lead to a general insurrection.

A synthesis of all three strategies was finally agreed upon but with the *terceristas* the dominant tendency, and in March 1979 a national directorate was formed, consisting of the three main leaders of each faction. After intensified fighting, the Somoza regime was overthrown in the popular revolution of July 1979.

The FSLN's decisive role in the overthrow of the Somoza dictatorship inevitably made it the dominant political force after the revolution, although it shared power initially with anti-Somoza forces in the FSLN-led Patriotic Revolutionary Front (FPR) and with elements of the conservative middle class, in a Council of State. This Council was superseded in 1984 when Daniel Ortega was elected President and the FSLN secured a clear majority in a new National Assembly.

Half the national budget came to be devoted to the war against US-backed right-wing *contra* rebels who had initiated in 1981 a guerrilla war to destabilize the government. US trade and investment embargoes led to greater reliance on Soviet-bloc aid until 1987, when the Soviet Union began to scale down its oil supplies. In 1987, the emphatic opposition of the FSLN to direct negotiations with the *contras* was modified when it welcomed peace plans devised by the Contadora group and by President Arias of Costa Rica which took shape in the Guatemala region peace accords. The Sandinistas made major concessions to their critics in the hope of achieving peace, including an end to the state of emergency; a readiness to talk to the contras; an amnesty of prisoners; and an end to bans on the media. In December 1989, the FSLN signed a regional agreement calling for the demobilization of the Salvadoran guerrillas in the expectation that other governments would finally act to dismantle *contra* camps in Honduras.

After their surprise defeat in the 1990 presidential and legislative elections, the Sandinistas vowed to defend the "fundamental conquests of the revolution", such as nationalization of banks and foreign trade, state farms and the rights and freedoms contained in the 1987 constitution. After the elections, however, the FSLN lost both its discipline and unity. Grass-root members became increasingly alienated from the leadership, which was criticized for collaborating too much with the Chamorro government in the name of a responsible opposition. This gulf deepened when the leadership interposed itself between the centre-right government and the mass Sandinista organizations during 1990 strikes against cuts in jobs and services. Accusations that the FSLN leadership had personally benefited from laws allowing for the disposal of state property and land before the Sandinistas relinquished power (known locally as the *pinata* after a children's game where everyone rushes to grab what they can) also left their mark on rank-and-file supporters. However, when right-wing parties in the National Assembly in June 1991 repealed the laws which had also given land to *campesinos* (peasants), all 39 FSLN delegates withdrew from the Assembly indefinitely. Sandinista mass organizations rallied to their defence and in September President Chamorro partially vetoed the Assembly's decision.

Following an extraordinary party congress in May 1994, three distinct factions emerged within the FSLN: an "orthodox" faction headed by Ortega; a moderate 'renewalist' faction headed by former Nicaraguan Vice President Sergio Ramírez Mercado; and a centrist 'unity' grouping headed by Henry Ruiz Hernández. At the congress, the Ortega faction proved victorious, although Ramírez gained for himself the role of Ortega's alternate. Ramírez was ousted from this post by Ortega in September 1994 at which point the FSLN delegation elected a moderate, Dora María Téllez, as its new leader rather than Ortega. In early 1995 the disagreement came to a head with Ramírez, Téllez and 75% of the Sandinista legislative delegation withdrawing from the FSLN to form a new party, the →Sandinista Renewal Movement (MRS).

In the presidential election of October 1996, Ortega was defeated by Arnoldo Alemàn Lacayo, candidate of the →Liberal Alliance (AL). Ortega polled some 38% of the vote, against 51% for Alemàn. The AL was also successful in the accompanying legislative poll, winning 42 seats against 37 for the FSLN, which did, however, manage to fend off the threat from the MRS, which won only one seat. Following the election, the FSLN staged protests in Managua against alleged electoral irregularities, but the results stood and the Sandinistas remained in opposition.

Ortega was re-elected by an overwhelming majority as secretary general of the FSLN at a party congress in May 1998. In municipal elections held in November 2000, the FSLN won 49 municipalities (against 97 for the AL), including 11 important departmental capitals (its mayoral candidate was elected in Managua), compared with the five won by the AL.

The FSLN is a member party of the Socialist International.

Sandinista Renewal Movement
Movimiento de Renovación Sandinista (MRS)
Address. lc Tienda Katty, Abaja, Apdo 24, Managua
Telephone. (+505–2) 780279
Fax. (+505–2) 780268
Leadership. Sergio Ramírez Mercado
At an extraordinary party congress of the →Sandinista National Liberation Front (FSLN) in May 1994, the Daniel Ortega faction within the party proved dominant, at the expense of Sergio Ramírez Mercado in particular. He was ousted by Ortega in September 1994, at which point the FSLN membership elected the moderate Dora María Téllez as its new leader rather than Ortega. In January 1995 the disagreement came to a head with Ramírez, Téllez and three-quarters of the Sandinista Assembly deputies withdrawing from the FSLN to form a new party, the MRS. However, the party performed poorly in the 1996 legislative elections, winning only 1.3% of the vote and one seat in the National Assembly. The party is a member of the →Nicaraguan Democratic Movement Alliance (MDNA) alliance formed in 2000 to contest the 2001 presidential and legislative elections.

Workers' and Peasants' Nicaraguan Unity
Unidad Nicaragüense Obreros Campesinos (Unidad)
Address. c/o Asamblea Nacional, Managua
Left wing party which won less than 1% of the vote and one National Assembly seat in the 1996 legislative elections.

Niger

Capital: Niamey　　　　　　　　　　　　　　　　**Population**: 10,080,000 (2000E)

The Republic of Niger attained independence from France in 1960. Following a coup in 1974, the military took control and set up a Supreme Military Council, under Lt.-Col. Seyni Kountché, which ruled the country for the next 15 years. After Kountché's death in 1987, the Council appointed Brig. Ali Saibou as his successor. The National Movement for a Society of Development-*Nassara (Mouvement National pour une Société de Développement* (MNSD–*Nassara*) was formed as the sole legal political party in August 1988 with Saibou as its chairman. In May 1989 Saibou was named as head of the country's new ruling body, a joint military-civilian Higher Council for National Orientation, which superseded the Supreme Military Council. A national conference held between July and November 1991 suspended the constitution, took over executive authority from Saibou and then appointed a transitional Prime Minister. In a referendum in December 1992, voters approved a new multi-party constitution. This provided for a directly elected President with a five-year term (once renewable) and for a similarly elected 83-member National Assembly (*Assemblée Nationale*), also with a five-year mandate.

In April 1999, President Ibrahim Bare Mainassara, who had overthrown President Mahamane Ousmane in a military coup in 1996, was himself deposed in an army coup led by Maj. Douada Mallam Wanke. The National Assembly, last elected in November 1996, was then dissolved and a National Reconciliation Council, led by Wanke, took power for the transitional period leading to the return of civilian rule. In July 1999 a new Constitution introducing a balance of powers between the President, Prime Minister and legislature was approved by popular referendum, and promulgated shortly thereafter.

Multi-party legislative and presidential elections held in October and November 1999 were won by the MNSD. Final results gave an absolute majority to the MNSD in combination with its ally the Democratic and Social

Convention *Rahama* (CDS–*Rahama*), which obtained 38 and 17 seats respectively. A grouping of opposition parties, led by the centre-left Niger Party for Democracy and Socialism *Tarayya* (PNDS) secured the remaining 28 seats. The presidential race was won by the MNSD candidate Tandja Mamadou, a retired army colonel, who defeated former Prime Minister Mahamadou Issoufou of PNDS. Wanke relinquished power in December 1999 and Mamadou was sworn in for a five-year term.

Democratic and Social Convention–Rahama
Convention Démocratique et Social–Rahama (CDS)

Address. c/o Assemblée Nationale, BP 12234, Place de la Concertation, Niamey

Leadership. Mahamane Ousmane (leader)

A former member party of the Alliance of Forces for Change (AFC) coalition, the CDS–*Rahama* won 22 seats in the February 1993 legislative elections, and party leader Ousmane secured the presidency of the country in March 1993 (he was, however, overthrow in a military coup in 1996). In the January 1995 National Assembly elections the party increased its number of seats to 24. However, other AFC parties did not secure sufficient additional seats to retain the coalition's majority over the →National Movement for a Society of Development-*Nassara* (MNSD) and its allies. In the legislative elections of October 1999 the CDS–*Rahama* secured the second largest share of seats in the National Assembly with 17 legislators elected, and entered into an informal coalition with the MNSD. In the first round of voting in the October 1999 presidential elections Ousmane was placed third, with only a 0.2% margin between himself and →Niger Party for Democracy and Socialism-*Tarayya* (PNDS) candidate Mahamadou Issoufou.

National Movement for a Society of Development-Nassara
Mouvement National pour une Société de Développement (MNSD)

Address. c/o Assemblée Nationale, BP 12234, Place de la Concertation, Niamey

Leadership. Tandja Mamadou (chairman); Hama Amadou (secretary general)

The MNSD was formed by the military regime in 1988 as the sole legal political party. Although the MNSD won 29 seats in the February 1993 legislative elections the formation of the Alliance of Forces for Change (AFC) coalition relegated it to minority status. In the January 1995 elections the MNSD again won 29 seats, securing, with other opposition parties, a three-seat majority over AFC members. In October 1999 the MNSD secured the largest share of seats in the National Assembly, with some 38 legislators elected, and became the senior partner in an informal ruling coalition with the →Democratic and Social Convention-*Rahama*. In the presidential election also held in late 1999, the MNDS leader Mamadou secured 59.9% of the vote and defeated former Prime Minister Issoufou of the →Niger Party for Democracy and Socialism *Tarayya*.

Niger Alliance for Democracy and Social Progress–Zaman Lahiya
Alliance Nigérienne pour la Démocratie et le Progrès Social–Zaman Lahiya (ANDPS-Zaman Lahiya)

Address. c/o Assemblée Nationale, BP 12234, Place de la Concertation, Niamey

Leadership. Moumouni Djermakoye (leader)

A former member of the Alliance of Forces for Change (AFC) coalition the ANDPS–*Zaman Lahiya* won 11 seats in the 1993 legislative elections but its representation fell to nine seats in the 1995 elections. In the legislative elections of October 1999 the ANDPS–*Zaman Lahiya* secured four seats in the National Assembly.

Niger Party for Democracy and Socialism–Tarayya
Parti Nigérien pour la Démocratie et le Socialisme (PNDS)

Address. c/o Assemblée Nationale, BP 12234, Place de la Concertation, Niamey

Leadership. Mahamadou Issoufou (secretary general)

PNDS secretary general Issoufou was appointed Prime Minister after elections in early 1993, holding the post until September 1994, when the party withdrew from the ruling Alliance of Forces for Change. This move led to early legislative elections in January 1995, in which the party took third place with 12 seats. In the legislative elections of October 1999 the centre-left PNDS secured 16 seats in the National Assembly and formed the main opposition to the →National Movement for a Society of Development-*Nassara* (MNSD). In the second round of voting in the presidential election in November 1999 Issoufou polled 40.1% of the vote, but was defeated by the MNSD candidate, Tandja Mamadou.

The PNDS is a consultative member of the Socialist International.

Rally for Democracy and Progress–Djamaa
Rassemblement pour la Démocratie et le Progrès (RDP)

Address. c/o Assemblée Nationale, BP 12234, Place de la Concertation, Niamey

The RDP–*Djamaa* was the largest political force in the defunct Convergence for the Republic (CPR), a 15-member grouping of political parties formed in August 1998 to support President Mainassara. In the legislative elections of October 1999 the RDP–*Djamaa* secured eight seats in the National Assembly.

Nigeria

Capital: Abuja **Population:** 123,337,500 (2000E)

Nigeria attained independence from the United Kingdom in 1960, becoming a federal republic within the Commonwealth in 1963. A series of coups have punctuated the post-independence politics of the country, resulting in long periods of military rule. Having come to power in 1985, the regime of Gen. Ibrahim Babangida promised a return to pluralist politics by 1992. The handover was delayed, although in 1989 two political parties were created by the regime, namely the Social Democratic Party (SDP) to represent centre-left opinion and the National Republican Convention (NRC) to represent the conservative spectrum, with no regional, religious or tribal politics being permissible. In presidential elections eventually held on June 12, 1993, the SDP candidate, Moshood Abiola, was widely believed to have defeated the NRC candidate, but the regime aborted the contest amid legal wrangling. In August 1993 Babangida stepped down as President, transferring power to a non-elected Interim National Government under Chief Ernest Shonekan. The term of office of the new administration was to run until the end of March 1994, during which time fresh presidential elections were to be organized. However, in November 1993 Defence Minister Gen. Sani Abacha seized power in a bloodless coup. The existing organs of the state were dissolved and political activity was prohibited. The two official political parties created in 1989 were proscribed. At the same time, a Provisional Ruling Council (PRC) was established with Gen. Abacha as chairman.

A government-sponsored National Constitutional Conference (NCC), inaugurated in June 1994 to consider the political future of the country, proposed in December that military rule should continue until Jan. 1, 1996. In April 1995, however, as it formally adopted a draft constitution, the NCC declared that a transition to civilian rule could not be achieved within that time. In June 1995 Abacha lifted the ban on political activity, and then announced in October 1995 that the military government would remain in office for a further three years. He asserted that by October 1998 democratic reforms would be completed in readiness for elections. A law on the formation of political parties was introduced in June 1996, under which 15 parties applied for official registration. Five applications were approved and 10 rejected, the unsuccessful organizations being dissolved by decree. In May 1997 United Action for Democracy (UAD), an alliance of 22 pro-democracy and human rights organizations, was formed to put pressure on Abacha to step down and allow a transitional government of national unity to oversee the restoration of elected institutions. Abacha, however, emerged as a candidate for the civilian presidency, and secured nomination as the sole "consensus candidate" of all five legal political parties at special party conventions organized (with government funding) in April 1998. The UAD responded by calling for a boycott of legislative elections held in the same month.

In June 1998 Abacha died and was succeeded as head of state by Gen. Abdulsalam Abubakar, whose pledge to continue with Abacha's programme prompted further protests by the UAD. In the following month the new regime released the detained 1993 election candidate, Moshood Abiola, whose subsequent death prompted violent anti-government protests. Gen. Abububakar then abandoned the Abacha programme and adopted a new timetable for a return to civilian rule by May 1999. The results of the elections that had already been held were annulled, the five legal political parties were dissolved, existing electoral institutions were superseded by new supervisory bodies, a civilian element was introduced into the transitional government, and there were releases of political detainees and invitations to opposition activists to engage in dialogue with the transitional authorities. In October 1998 an independent national electoral commission considered registration applications from 29 political parties, of which nine were provisionally approved. Municipal council elections were held in December 1998 in which three parties received sufficiently large shares of the vote (and a sufficiently wide geographical spread of their vote) to qualify for registration to contest the forthcoming state and federal elections.

Elections to the 36 state legislatures were held on Jan. 9, 1999, after which two of the three registered parties, the All People's Party (APP) and the Alliance for Democracy (AD), agreed to mount a joint campaign in the federal elections. The presidential election, held on Feb. 27, 1999, was won by the People's Democratic Party (PDP) candidate, Gen. (retd) Olusegun Obasanjo, who received 62.8% of the vote as against 37.2% for Olu Falae, the joint candidate of the AD and the APP. President Obasanjo was inaugurated on May 29, 1999, bringing into effect a federal constitution broadly based on the 1979 constitution (drawn up when Obasanjo had presided over a previous transition to civilian rule). The President is head of state, chief executive of the federation and commander-in-chief of the federal armed forces. The presidential term is four years, and the successful candidate is required to win at least 25% of the popular vote in at least two-thirds of the states of the federation. The President's nominees for appointment to ministerial office are subject to confirmation by the Senate.

The President and both houses of the National Assembly are directly elected by universal adult suffrage, with a voting age of 18 years. In National Assembly elections held on Feb. 20, 1999 (and completed by a subsequent by-election), the party shares of the 360 seats in the House of Representatives were PDP 221, APP 70 and AD 69, while the 109 seats in the Senate were distributed PDP 67, APP 23 and AD 19. The term of both houses of the federal legislature is four years. Legislation may originate in either house. A bill returned to the National Assembly with presidential assent withheld may be voted into law by a two-thirds majority of each house.

The PDP, APP and AD (each of which had been formed by a diverse range of interest groups) remained Nigeria's only registered national parties in mid-2001 at the mid-point of the first electoral term under the new constitution. All three parties had by this point experienced acrimonious leadership contests—the outcome of an AD dispute in late 2000 being decided by the intervention of the independent national electoral commission (INEC)—and the three leaders in place in mid-2001 did not support calls for the early registration of new national parties. The case for new registrations was put forward by numerous pressure groups and unregistered parties, and there were many calls for a clarification of the constitutional position of INEC. Groups campaigning for the registration of new parties in 2001 included the National Progressive Forum (one of whose members was the former presidential candidate, Olu Falae) and Democratic Alternative (which in March 2001 sought to challenge INEC's registration policy in the federal high court).

All People's Party (APP)

Address. c/o House of Representatives, PMB 141, Abuja
Leadership. Alhaji Yusuf Garba Ali (national chairman); George Moghalu (national secretary)

The APP was established in 1998 by a number of groupings which had formerly participated in the Abacha regime's programme for the reintroduction of civilian rule. In the January 1999 state elections its best results were achieved in central and some northern areas of Nigeria. In a development that was subsequently revealed to be rooted in factional rivalries over the selection of a candidate from within the APP, the party agreed to support the presidential candidate of the →Alliance for Democracy (AD) in the February 1999 federal elections. The presidential election was won by the candidate of the →People's Democratic Party (PDP), while in the legislative elections the APP was the runner-up to the PDP in terms of the overall number of seats won. In the aftermath of the elections the organizers of the APP's presidential candidate selection process came under fierce criticism from rival factions of the party. This conflict was resolved in December 1999 by the holding (on the initiative of the APP's state governors and National Assembly members) of a party convention which elected a new national leadership acceptable to all sections of the party.

Alliance for Democracy (AD)

Address. Abeokuta Street, Area 8, Garki, Abuja
Telephone. (+234–9) 2345463
Email. info@alliancefordemocracy.org
Website. www.afrikontakt.com/alliance
Leadership. Alhaji Adamu Ahmed Abdulkadir (national chairman)
Founded in late 1998, the AD was the most radical of the three parties that won registration to contest the Nigerian elections of January and February 1999. Many of its founders had previously been associated with the National Democratic Coalition (NADECO), a grouping of human rights activists, civilian politicians and retired military officers which was formed in May 1994 to campaign for the resignation of the Abacha regime and a rapid return to democratic government. After the state election results of Jan. 9, 1999, confirmed the AD's position as the strongest party in the south-western part of Nigeria, the AD agreed to ally itself with the →All People's Party (APP, whose best results were in other areas) in the forthcoming federal election campaign. The AD's Olu Falae was selected as the alliance's joint presidential candidate, with the APP's Umaru Shinkafi as his running mate for the vice-presidency. The AD won one fewer seats than the APP in the legislative elections of Feb. 20, 1999, but the overall winner of these elections was the →People's Democratic Party (PDP), which gained an absolute majority of seats in each chamber. The presidential election of February 1999 was also decisively won by the PDP candidate, with 62.8% of the vote, compared with 37.2% for Falae. Alhaji Adamu Ahmed

Abdulkadir was elected national chairman of the AD at a party convention held on Nov. 1, 2000, in the presence of observers from the independent national electoral commission. The electoral commission rejected as illegitimate a rival AD meeting's election of Yusuf Mamman to the same post (which he had previously held on an interim basis).

People's Democratic Party (PDP)

Address. c/o House of Representatives, PMB 141, Abuja
Leadership. Barnabas Gemade (national chairman)
The PDP was founded in August 1998 by a broad range of political interest groups, represented principally by 34 former senior political figures who had come forward earlier in 1998 to challenge the legality of Sani Abacha's bid to secure the civilian presidency of Nigeria. At least nine established groupings were brought into the new party as it sought to build a nationwide presence. In the January 1998 state elections the PDP's only area of significant weakness was the south-west (where the →Alliance for Democracy predominated), while in parts of northern and central Nigeria the PDP was challenged with some success by the →All People's Party. The PDP's candidate for the federal presidency, Gen. (retd) Olusegun Obasanjo, a native of the south-west, was a former detainee of the Abacha regime and a strong supporter of Nigerian federalism. In February 1999 Obasanjo was elected President with 62.8% of the vote, defeating the joint candidate of the two other parties, while the PDP won substantial majorities in the Senate and House of Representatives. This did not, however, guarantee the easy passage of legislation supported by the President, as the broadly-based and ideologically unfocused PDP proved to be notably lacking in party discipline. Barnabas Gemade, elected party chairman in November 1999, faced dissent from several sections of the membership, and in mid-2001 his unsuccessful rival in the chairmanship election, Sunday Awoniyi, was one of five members of the board of trustees to be expelled from the PDP for "anti-party activities". Also expelled were three national executive committee members who had taken legal action to challenge their earlier suspension from office.

Norway

Capital: Oslo

Population: 4,500,000 (2000E)

Norway achieved independence from Sweden in 1905 on the basis of the 1814 Eidsvold Convention, which as subsequently amended provides for a constitutional and hereditary monarchy, with the monarch exercising authority through a Council of State (government) headed by a Prime Minister. The government is accountable to the legislature (*Storting*) of 165 members, who are elected for a four-year term by universal suffrage of citizens aged 18 and over on the basis of proportional representation in 19 electoral districts. The *Storting* divides itself by election into an upper house (*Lagting*) of a quarter of its members and a lower house (*Odelsting*) of the remaining three-quarters, with each house being required to consider and vote on legislative proposals. In the event of a disagreement between the houses, a bill requires approval by a majority of two-thirds of the *Storting* as a whole. An important feature of the constitution is that the *Storting* cannot be dissolved between elections and that any vacancies are filled from party lists rather than by-elections. If the government falls on a vote of no confidence, the leader of the opposition party holding the highest number of seats is asked to form a new government.

Norwegian political parties receive funds from the public purse in proportion to their electoral support, to be used in connection with their political education work and parliamentary activities. The total amount allocated in 2000 was NOK230,899,000 (about US$26 million), of which some 80% was received by party organizations and the balance by party groups in the *Storting*. Under current rules for the latter disbursements, each party represented receives a basic annual sum of NOK886,000 as well as a supplement of NOK196,000 for each elected member. Opposition parties with five or more deputies receive an additional NOK886,000 and those with three or four deputies an additional NOK443,000.

Parliamentary elections on Sept. 10, 2001, resulted as follows: Norwegian Labour Party 43 seats (with 24.4% of the vote), Conservative Party 38 (21.2%), Progress Party 26 (14.7%), Socialist Left Party 23 (12.5%), Christian People's Party 22 (12.4%), Centre Party 10 (5.6%), Liberal Party 2 (3.9%), Coastal Party 1 (1.7%). On

Oct. 17, 2001, Jens Stoltenberg (Labour) stood down as Prime Minister to allow the formation of a minority right-of-centre coalition government under Kjell Magne Bondevik comprising Bondevik's Christian People's Party, the Conservative Party and the Liberals and which the Progress Party said it would support.

Centre Party
Senterpartiet (SP)
Address. PB 6734, St Olavs plass, 0130 Oslo
Telephone. (147) 2298–9600
Fax. (147) 2220–6915
Email. epost@senterpartiet.no
Leadership. Anne Enger Lahnstein (chairperson); Odd Roger Enoksen (parliamentary leader)

Originating from the agrarian trade union, the party was founded in 1920 as the Agrarian Party with the object of gaining greater political and parliamentary influence for those working in rural occupations and raising them to the level of other occupations. Since 1931, when co-operation with the agrarian trade union was ended, the party has been independent and has worked for society in general, changing its name to Centre Party in 1959, thus emphasizing its position between the right-wing and left-wing parties.

In 1931–33 the party formed a minority government. After unsuccessful efforts to work with the Conservatives and Liberal parties, the party, in 1935, entered into a "crisis compromise" with the →Norwegian Labour Party (DNA), which was then in power for 30 years. In 1963 the party entered into a brief minority coalition with other non-socialist parties; from 1965 to 1971 it headed a majority non-socialist government; and in 1972–73 it participated in a minority government with the →Liberal Party (*Venstre*) and the →Christian People's Party (KrF).

The SP was in opposition to minority Labour governments from 1973 to September 1981, when it gave its general support to a minority →Conservative Party administration. In June 1983 it entered a majority three-party centre-right government headed by the Conservatives, which continued until, in May 1986, it was replaced by a further minority Labour administration. Meanwhile, the SP had won 12 seats and 6.7% of the vote in the September 1985 elections, as against its earlier high-point of 20 seats and 11% in 1973.

Having slipped from 12 to 11 seats in the 1989 elections (on a 6.5% vote share), the SP joined another centre-right coalition headed by the Conservatives but withdrew in October 1990 in protest against government policy on foreign financial interests. This caused the coalition's collapse and the formation of a minority Labour government in November 1990 to which the SP gave qualified parliamentary support. Campaigning on a strongly anti-EU platform, the SP made major gains in the September 1993 elections, overtaking the Conservatives by increasing its representation to 32 seats on a 16.7% vote share (a post-war high). It subsequently played a prominent role in the successful "no" campaign in the November 1994 referendum on EU accession.

With the EU issue resolved for the foreseeable future, the SP slumped to 11 seats and 7.9% of the vote in the September 1997 elections, but was nevertheless included in a minority government with the KrF and *Venstre*. This government resigned in March 2000 after losing a vote of confidence and was replaced by a minority Labour administration. In the September 2001 elections the SP slipped further to 10 seats and 5.6% of the vote.

Christian People's Party
Kristelig Folkeparti (KrF)
Address. Øvre Slottsgate 18–20, 0105 Oslo
Telephone. (+47) 2310–2800
Fax. (+47) 2310–2810
Email. krf@krf.no
Website. www.krf.no
Leadership. Valgerd Svarstad Haugland (leader); Einar

Steensnæs (first deputy leader); Odd Anders With (second deputy leader)

Founded in 1933 as a non-socialist Christian-oriented formation, the KrF returned its first member to the *Storting* in 1933, followed by two in 1936, and became established at national level by 1939. Having won eight seats in 1945, it steadily increased its parliamentary representation, winning 22 seats in 1977 and thus becoming the country's third strongest party (although in 1981 it retained only 15 seats). It took part in majority coalition governments in 1965-71 (with the →Conservative, →Liberal and →Centre parties) and in a minority coalition government with the Centre and Liberal parties in 1972–73 under the premiership of Lars Korvald of the KrF. In June 1983 it entered a centre-right government with the Conservatives and the Centre Party, but went into opposition in May 1986 to a minority administration of the →Norwegian Labour Party. In the September 1985 elections the party had won 16 seats and 8.3% of the vote, retaining its position as the third strongest formation.

The KrF fell back to 14 seats in the 1989 elections (8.5%), after which it joined a centre-right coalition with the Conservative and Centre parties that lasted only a year. It fell again to 13 seats (7.9%) in the September 1993 contest, its advocacy of the popular cause of opposition to EU membership doing it little good, as non-socialist voters of that persuasion opted for the Centre Party.

The KrF advanced strongly to 25 seats and a vote share of 13.7% in the September 1997 elections, as a result of which Kjell Magne Bondevik of the KrF, a Lutheran priest, was appointed Prime Minister of a government which included the Centre and Liberal parties but which commanded only 42 of the 165 *Storting* seats. The strains of office induced depression in Bondevik, who took a month's sick leave in September 1998. He soldiered on until March 2000, when his government lost a confidence vote on its opposition to two new gas-fired power stations and was replaced by a minority Labour administration. In the September 2001 elections the KrF slipped to fourth place with 22 seats and 12.4% of the vote, failing to benefit from a big swing against Labour. However, on Oct. 17, Labour Prime Minister Jens Stoltenberg stood down and Bondevik returned to office as leader of a right-of-centre coalition. Bondevik was seen as having gained popularity for the openness with which he had dealt with his problems with depression.

The KrF is a member of the Christian Democrat International and an observer member of the European People's Party.

Coastal Party
Kystpartiet (KP)
Address. c/o Stortinget, Karl Johansgt. 22, 0026 Oslo
Website. www.kystpartiet.no
Leadership. Steinar Bastesen (chairman)

The KP was founded to represent the interests of the whaling industry and fishermen in northern Norway, with particular reference to the continuing international hostility to whaling as practiced by Norway. The party broke through to parliamentary representation in the September 1997 elections, when its chairman won a *Storting* seat in Nordland county with 0.4% of the national vote. It retained the seat in the September 2001 elections, increasing its national vote share to 1.7%.

Conservative Party
Høyre (H)
Address. Stortingsgaten 20, PB 1536 Vika, 0117 Oslo

Telephone. (+47) 2282–9000
Fax. (+47) 2282–9080
Email. hoyre@hoyre.no
Website. www.hoyre.no
Leadership. Jan Petersen (chairman); Eirik O.H. Moen (secretary-general)

Since its foundation in 1884 the Conservative Party has participated in many governments, most of them coalitions with other non-socialist parties. Having commanded half of the electorate in its early days, the party declined to around 20% in the years before World War II, since when its support has fluctuated from well under 20% to around 30%. On the basis of the substantial gains in the September 1981 elections, then Conservative leader Kåre Willoch formed a one-party minority administration, which was transformed into a three-party government in June 1983 when the →Centre and →Christian People's parties accepted cabinet membership. However, this government fell in April 1986 and was replaced by a minority administration of the →Norwegian Labour Party. In August 1986 Willoch was succeeded as party leader by Rolf Presthus, but the latter died unexpectedly in January 1988 and was succeeded by Jan. P. Syse.

Although the party's representation declined to 37 seats in 1989 (on a 22.2% vote share), Syse succeeded in forming a minority centre-right coalition with the Centre and Christian People's parties. This collapsed a year later upon the withdrawal of the Centre Party, giving way to another minority Labour government. In the September 1993 *Storting* elections the Conservatives slumped to 28 seats (and 16.9%), being damaged by their strong advocacy of Norwegian membership of the European Union (EU). The party accordingly remained in opposition under the new leadership of Jan Petersen.

The party's decline continued in the 1997 elections, to an all-time low of 14.3% and 23 seats. In the September 2001 contest, however, the unpopularity of the incumbent Labour government enabled the Conservatives to recover to 38 seats (the second largest tally) and 21.2% of the vote. In October a new government was formed with Kjell Magne Bondevik of the Christian People's Party returning as Prime Minister while the Conservatives took the key portfolios of foreign affairs (Jan Petersen) and finance (Per-Kristian Foss).

The Conservative Party is affiliated to the International Democrat Union and is an associate member of the European People's Party.

Liberal Party
Venstre (V)

Address. Møllergt. 16, 0179 Oslo
Telephone. (+47) 2240–4350
Fax. (+47) 2240–4351
Email. venstre@venstre.no
Website. www.venstre.no
Leadership. Lars Sponheim (leader); Aud Folkestad (first deputy leader); Gunnar Kvassheim (second deputy leader)

Founded in 1884, *Venstre* held 23 seats in the *Storting* in 1936, but its parliamentary representation after World War II was consistently lower, its 21 seats in 1949 being reduced to 14 by 1961, though rising to 18 in 1965. Of its 13 members elected in 1973, a majority supported the projected entry of Norway into what is today the European Union. After entry had been rejected in the referendum of September 1972, the anti-membership minority participated in a coalition government with the →Christian People's and →Centre parties, while the pro-European Liberals formed the breakaway Liberal People's Party (DLF).

The rump *Venstre* was thus left with only four seats in the *Storting,* this number being reduced to two in September 1973. It retained two seats in 1977 and 1981, but failed to secure representation in 1985, when its share of the vote fell to 3.1%. In June 1988 the DLF rejoined the parent party, which nevertheless failed to regain *Storting* representation in 1989, when its vote share was 3.2%.

A partial Liberal comeback began in the September 1993

elections, in which the party took one seat with 3.6% of the vote. It continued in the September 1997 legislative polling, which yielded six seats (with 4.5% of the vote) and resulted in the party joining a minority government with the Christian People's and Centre parties. However, following the collapse of this government in March 2000, *Venstre* fell back to two seats and 3.9% in the September 2001 parliamentary elections. It subsequently joined the right-of-centre coalition government formed by Christian People's Party leader Kjell Magne Bondevik.

Venstre is a member of the Liberal International.

Norwegian Labour Party
Det Norske Arbeiderparti (DNA)

Address. PB 8734 Youngstorget, 0028 Oslo
Telephone. (+47) 2294–0600
Fax. (+47) 2294–0601
Email. dna@dna.no
Website. www.dna.no
Leadership. Jens Stoltenberg (parliamentary leader); Thorbjørn Jagland (chairman); Solveig Torsvik (general secretary)

Descended from a rural socialist movement of the mid-19th century, the DNA was established in 1887 amid a rapid growth of urban trade unionism in the 1880s. In 1904 the party won four seats in the *Storting* and by 1915 it had 62,000 members and the support of over 30% of the electorate. In 1918 the party leadership was taken over by the left wing, largely under the influence of the Russian revolution, but disagreements ensued over whether to join the Third International (Comintern). In 1921 anti-Bolshevik dissenters formed the Social Democratic Party, while the →Communist Party was formed in 1923 by part of the Labour left. In 1927, however, a reunified Labour Party (including the Social Democrats and some Communists) obtained 36.8% of the electoral vote, thus becoming the strongest party.

After a short-lived first Labour minority government in 1927, the party won 40% of the vote in 1933 and two years later formed its second government. Under the German occupation during World War II the party was illegal and its leaders went into exile or were sent to German concentration camps. At the end of the war Labour leader Einar Gerhardsen formed a broad coalition government, but in October 1945 Labour obtained a parliamentary majority and remained in office until 1965 except for a brief interval in 1963. The party was again in power from 1971 to 1972, when the government headed by Trygve Bratteli resigned on being defeated in a referendum which rejected Norway's membership of what is now the European Union (EU).

During the 1973–81 period the party formed a series of minority governments, but went into opposition following a setback in the September 1981 elections. However, the →Conservative-led non-socialist coalition collapsed in April 1986 and was replaced by a further minority Labour government under Gro Harlem Brundtland. Meanwhile, the DNA had won 71 seats and 41.2% of the vote in September 1985, an improvement on its 27.1% share in 1981 but significantly below the levels regularly obtained up to 1969. The DNA went in opposition after the September 1989 elections, in which it lost eight seats. A year later, however, Brundtland formed her third minority government, with the parliamentary backing of the →Centre Party.

In November 1992, following the death of her son, Brundtland resigned the DNA chairmanship, while continuing as Prime Minister. Her successor in the party post was Thorbjørn Jagland, hitherto general secretary. In the September 1993 elections Labour rose to 67 seats on a 36.9% vote share, so that Brundtland formed her fourth minority government. In June 1994 delegates at a special party conference decided by a two-to-one majority to support Norwegian accession to EU in the forthcoming national referendum, although substantial rank-and-file opposition to membership contributed to the decisive 52.2% "no" vote in

November 1994. Unlike her Labour predecessor in 1972, and despite having strongly advocated a "yes" vote, Brundtland did not resign over an acknowledged major defeat. Instead, she stressed the need for continuity and for negotiations to clarify Norway's relationship with the EU as a non-member.

Brundtland eventually vacated the premiership in October 1996, being succeeded by Jagland, who was quickly beset by several scandals involving senior Labour figures. In the September 1997 elections the DNA fell back to 65 seats and 35.1%, whereupon Jagland honoured his pre-election pledge not to continue as Prime Minister if Labour lost ground. Nominally in opposition over the next two-and-a-half years to a minority coalition headed by the →Christian People's Party, the DNA exerted substantial external influence on the government's budgetary and other policies.

In February 2000 Jagland was replaced as DNA parliamentary leader by Jens Stoltenberg, a former Foreign Minister, who the following month moved to bring down the government and to become, at 41, Norway's youngest-ever Prime Minister, heading yet another minority Labour administration. Despite being compared to Tony Blair of the →→Labour Party in Britain, Stoltenberg had even less success than Jagland in the popularity stakes, amidst mounting public opposition to high taxation combined with deteriorating public services. In the September 2001 elections Labour lost support both to the centre-right and to the →Socialist Left Party, slumping to an 80-year low of 24.4% and 43 seats. In the aftermath of the election Stoltenberg stood down as Prime Minister on Oct. 17 and a right-of-centre government took office.

The DNA is a member party of the Socialist International.

Progress Party
Fremskrittspartiet (FrP)
Address. PB 8903 Youngstorget, 0028 Oslo
Telephone. (+47) 2313–5400
Fax. (+47) 2242–5401
Email. frp@frp.no
Website. www.frp.no
Leadership. Carl Ivar Hagen (chairman and parliamentary leader); Siv Jensen (first deputy chairperson); John I. Alvheim (second deputy chairperson); Geir Mo (secretary-general)

The right-wing populist FrP was established in April 1973 as Anders Lange's Party for a Strong Reduction in Taxation and Public Intervention, its founder being a well-known dog-kennel owner who had become a national celebrity as a result of his political comments in a dog-breeding magazine. Following Lange's death in 1974, the party took its present name in January 1977. Having never exceeded four *Storting* seats in previous contests, the FrP became the third strongest parliamentary party in the 1989 elections, winning 22 seats and 13.0% of the vote but was excluded from the resultant government formed by the traditional centre-right parties.

In the 1993 elections the FrP experienced a major reverse, winning only 10 seats and 6.3% of the vote. It recovered strongly in 1997, becoming the second-strongest parliamentary party after the →Norwegian Labour Party with 25 seats and a 15.3% vote share. It nevertheless continued to be treated as a pariah by the other centre-right parties, notwithstanding some calls in the →Conservative Party in particular for it to be accepted as a potential coalition partner. During the next parliamentary term the FrP, in opposition to successive centrist and Labour minority governments, was by early 2001 heading polls of voting intentions. However, the party was damaged by the enforced resignation in February 2001 of deputy leader and heir apparent Terje Sœvines over rape allegations. In the September 2001 elections, although the FrP improved from 25 to 26 seats, its vote slipped to 14.7% and it fell back to third place behind Labour and the resurgent Conservatives.

It said it would support the new coalition government formed in October 2001 by the →Christian People's, Conservative and →Liberal parties.

Socialist Left Party
Sosialistisk Venstreparti (SV)
Address. Storgata 45, 0185 Oslo
Telephone. (+47) 2193–3300
Fax. (+47) 2193–3301
Email. post@sv.no
Website. www.sv.no
Leadership. Kristin Halvorsen (leader); Øystein Djupedal & Inge Ryan (deputy leaders); Bård Vegar Solhjell (secretary)

The SV was founded in March 1975 as the unitary successor to the Socialist Electoral Alliance, linking the →Communist Party of Norway, the Socialist People's Party and the Left Social Democratic Organization. In the 1973 elections the Alliance had won 16 seats in the *Storting* (with 11.2% of the vote) on a strongly socialist economic and social platform which also included opposition to Norwegian membership of NATO and what later became the European Union. On the conversion of the Alliance into the SV, the Communist Party decided not to merge into the new party.

The SV won only two seats in the 1977 parliamentary elections, but progressed to four seats in 1981 and to six in 1985. It made a major advance in 1989, to 17 seats on a vote share of 10.1%, but fell back to 13 seats (7.9%) in 1993. It subsequently played a prominent part in the successful campaign against Norwegian accession to the EU, but got no reward in the 1997 parliamentary elections, in which it declined further to nine seats and 6% of the vote.

The unpopularity of the minority government of the →Norwegian Labour Party formed in March 2000 yielded substantial benefit to the SV in the September 2001 elections, in which the party increased its representation to 23 seats from a vote share of 12.5%.

Other Parties

Communist Party of Norway (*Norges Kommunistiske Parti, NKP*), founded in 1923 by left-wing faction of the →Norwegian Labour Party (DNA); was influential during and after World War II, winning 11 parliamentary seats in 1945, but declining in the 1950s and ceasing to be represented from 1961. In 1973 the party joined the Socialist Election Alliance, which won 16 seats in that year's elections, but it declined to join the successor →Socialist Left Party. Having polled 0.2% in 1985, the NKP was allied with the Red Electoral Alliance in 1989 without success and did not contest the 1993 elections. It polled 0.1% in 1997 and presented no candidates in 2001.
Address. Helgesens gt. 21, 0553 Oslo
Telephone. (+47) 2271–6044
Fax. (+47) 2271–7907
Email. nkp@nkp.no
Website. www.nkp.no
Leadership. Zafer Gözet (chairman)

Green Party of Norway (*Miljøpartiet de Grønne*), founded in October 1988 from earlier groups, has won some local representation but none nationally, in part because environmental issues are promoted by major formations, notably the →Socialist Left Party; affiliated to the European Federation of Green Parties.
Address. PB 9124 Grønland, 0133 Oslo
Telephone. (+47) 2242–9758
Fax. (+47) 2266–0122
Email. gronne@gronne.no
Website. www.gronne.no
Leadership. Lisa Fröyland (female spokesperson); Jan Bojer Vindheim (male spokesperson); Snorre Sletvold (secretary)

Pensioners' Party (*Pensjonistpartiet, Pp*), founded in 1985 and active in the pensioners' cause in recent elections, polling 0.7% in 2001.

Address. Landstads gt. 30, 3210 Sandefjord
Telephone. (+47) 3346–7319
Website. www.pensjonistpartiet.no
Leadership. Finn Moe Johannesen (chairman)

The Political Party (*Det Politiske Parti, DPP*), founded in October 2000 and advocating "total democracy" in which the people would vote via the Internet on every issue before parliament and the government would always abide by the electorate's decision. The party took 0.7% of the vote in 2001.

Address. PB 2736 St Hanshaugen, 0131 Oslo
Telephone. (+47) 2323–4503
Fax. (+47) 2323–4501
Email. sekretariat@dpp.no
Website. www.dpp.no
Leadership. Atle Antonsen & Johan Golden

Red Electoral Alliance (*Rød Valgallianse, RV*)**,** derived from the electoral front of the (Maoist) Workers' Communist Party (founded in 1972), later attracted independent socialists and left-wing members of the →Norwegian Labour Party. It was allied with the →Communist Party of Norway in the 1989 elections, failing to make an impact. Standing on its own in 1993 it won one seat (on a 1.1% vote share), but lost it in 1997 even though it vote increased to 1.7%. It polled 1.2% in 2001 without regaining representation.

Address. 27 Osterhausgt., 0183 Oslo
Telephone. (+47) 2298–9050
Fax. (+47) 2298–9055
Email. rv@rv.no
Website. www.rv.no
Leadership. Aslak Sira Myhre

Oman

Capital: Muscat   **Population**: 2,533,400 (2000E)

The Sultanate of Oman is ruled by decree, with the Sultan taking the advice of an appointed Cabinet and Consultative Council (*Majlis al-Shura*). Qaboos bin Said has served as Sultan since he deposed his father in a palace coup in 1970. Elections to the Consultative Council were last held in September 2000. A total of 597 candidates stood for the 82 seats available. Two women were amongst the winning candidates. There are no recognized political parties.

Pakistan

Capital: Islamabad   **Population**: 160,000,000 (2001E)

The Islamic Republic of Pakistan was proclaimed in March 1956, Pakistan having been granted independence as a Commonwealth dominion following the partition of the British Indian Empire in August 1947. The constitution promulgated in 1973 provided for a parliamentary system with a bicameral federal legislature (*Majlis-e-Shoora*) consisting of a 237-member National Assembly, to serve a five-year term and in which 217 seats (207 Muslim and 10 non-Muslim) are directly elected and 20 reserved for women, and an 87-member upper house (Senate), half of whose members are elected every three years for a six-year term. The President, who is elected by the federal legislature for a (renewable) term of five years, is empowered under the constitution to dismiss the Prime Minister and dissolve parliament. In practice military governments have largely dominated the political stage since independence.

Gen. Zia ul-Haq came to power in a coup in 1977 in which he overthrew the Pakistan People's Party (PPP) government of Zulfiquar Ali Bhutto. Zia was killed in an air crash in August 1988 and subsequent elections resulted in victory for the PPP with Bhutto's daughter, Benazir Bhutto, becoming Prime Minister. Her government was dismissed by President Ghulam Ishaq Khan in August 1990. Fresh elections in October 1990 resulted in victory for the right-wing Islamic Democratic Alliance (IDA) headed by Mian Mohammad Nawaz Sharif, who formed a coalition administration. Subsequently, the IDA fell into disarray, and political paralysis led to the resignations of both President Khan and Prime Minister Nawaz Sharif in July 1993. As a result of further National Assembly elections held on Oct. 9, 1993, the PPP returned to power as the largest single party.

The new PPP government led by Prime Minister Benazir Bhutto survived until Nov. 5, 1996, when it was dismissed by President Farooq Leghari. The country was facing multiple economic, political, judicial and constitutional crises amidst widespread allegations of corruption against her cabinet and the Bhutto family, especially Benazir's husband, Asif Ali Zadari. In new elections held in February 1997, the Pakistan Muslim League-Nawaz (PML(N)), led by Nawaz Sharif, took power, winning 135 seats in the National Assembly. The PPP, in considerable disarray and suffering public opprobrium, took just 19 seats. Of the other parties, the *Muhajir* National Movement (MQM(A)) strengthened its position winning 12 seats and the *Awami* National Party (ANP) took 9. Among the Islamist groups, the Assembly of Islamic Clergy (JUI) increased its representation to two seats but the Pakistan Islamic Assembly (JI) and Assembly of Pakistani Clergy (JUP) boycotted the polls. A major feature of the election was the very low level of voter turn out (28%), which considerably qualified the scale of Nawaz Sharif's triumph.

In provincial elections held at the same time, the PML(N) also swept the board in Punjab winning 211 out of 231 seats, and, in Sindh, it took 15 seats which, in association with the 28 won by the MQM(A), enabled it to displace the dominance of the PPP, which captured only 36 seats. In North-West Frontier Province, the ANP, with 31 seats, closely matched the PML(N)'s 33, and in Baluchistan, the regionalist Baluchistan National Party (BNP) (10 seats) did well alongside the Islamist JUI (7 seats).

Nawaz Sharif formed a new government based on the PML(N) which, however, rapidly proved controversial. He attempted to use his dominant position in the National Assembly to concentrate power in his own hands, first, over his party and, second, over the other institutions of the state. This provoked further splits within the PML and led to a series of constitutional crises involving the Supreme Court, the office of the President and, finally, the army. In October 1999, after being forced by international pressure to withdraw support for an army-backed guerrilla incursion into Indian-held Kashmir, he attempted to remove the Commander-in-Chief of the Armed Forces, General Pervez Musharraf, but was instead overthrown himself in a military coup. Musharraf then suspended the constitution in order to impose direct military rule. In 2000, his coup was ratified by the Supreme Court on the understanding that it was temporary and that he would restore a democratic constitution by October 2002. Responding to this understanding, in April–May 2001 Musharraf organized elections to local councils and municipalities but on a basis which prohibited the operation of political parties. In July 2001, he also declared himself President for three years and dissolved the National Assembly, the Senate and the provincial assemblies (all of which had been in recess since October 1999) with a view to restructuring them for new elections to be held within the specified time period.

Awami National Party (ANP)

Leadership. Ajmal Khattak (president)

The ANP was formed in 1986 by merger of a number of left-wing groups. Having won six National Assembly seats in the 1990 elections, the ANP secured only three in the October 1993 polls. The party held one ministerial appointment in the →Pakistan People's Party (PPP)-led government. In the general election of February 1997, it increased its representation to nine seats in the National Assembly and 31 in its regional stronghold in the North-West Frontier Province assembly.

Muhajir National Movement
Muhajir Qaumi Mahaz (MQM)

Leadership. Altaf Hussain (leader of main faction)
Address. Nine Zero, 494/8 Azizabad, Federal B Area, Karachi

Founded in 1981, the MQM advocates the recognition of Urdu-speaking Muslim migrants to Pakistan (*Muhajirs*), who came mostly from India at the time of partition, as the "fifth nationality" of the country. The party won 15 seats in the National Assembly elections in 1990 and was represented in the Sharif coalition government until its withdrawal in mid-1992. Divided into two main factions, the MQM did not contest the National Assembly in the 1993 elections, but retained substantial support in the Sindh province assembly poll. MQM militants and the government held talks during 1995 in an attempt to end serious fighting and civil disorder in areas of Sindh, especially in Karachi. Little progress was made, however, and the death toll in 1995 approached 2,000. Renewed violence in December 1995 followed the discovery on the outskirts of Karachi of the bullet-riddled bodies of two relatives of the main MQM leader, Altaf Hussain. By then the MQM was split into at least two factions. However, the fall of Benazir Bhutto's government in November 1996 revived its fortunes, especially those of the MQM(A) led by Altaf Hussain. At the general election of February 1997, it won 12 seats in the National Assembly and 28 in the Sindh provincial assembly. By contrast, the other faction, MQM (Haqiqi), which was widely seen as a creature of the army and secret service, did poorly. The MQM(A) used its strengthened assembly positions to pursue a policy of co-operation with the →Pakistan Muslim League (Nawaz) government of Prime Minister Nawaz Sharif until its fall in October 1999.

Pakistan Islamic Assembly
Jamaat-e-Islami-e-Pakistan (JI)

Address. Mansura, Multan Road, Lahore
Telephone. (+92–42) 54195204
Fax. (+92–42) 5419505

Email. jipmedia@jamaat.org
Website. www.jamaat.org
Leadership. Qazi Hussain Ahmad (president); Syed Munawwar Hasan (secretary-general)

The JI (or JIP) is an Islamist party founded in 1941. It participated in the formation of the Islamic Democratic Alliance (IDA) in 1988 and in the 1990 elections won eight National Assembly seats. However, in May 1992 the party withdrew from the IDA, alleging that the alliance had failed to implement the process of Islamization that had been part of its election manifesto. In 1993 it was instrumental in launching the Pakistan Islamic Front (PIF), which contested the October 1993 elections and won three National Assembly seats. It endorsed the presidential dismissal of the →Pakistan People's Party government and dissolution of the National Assembly in 1996 but boycotted the general election of 1997. In October 2001 it organized protests against US military action in Afghanistan with leader Qazi Hussain Ahmad predicting that Gen. Musharraf's continued support for the USA would lead to his downfall and the installation of an Islamic regime in Pakistan. Numerous JI activists were reported to have been arrested.

Pakistan Muslim League (PML)

Leadership. Javed Hashmi (acting president of Nawaz group); Hamid Nasir Chattha (leader of Junejo group); Mian Azhar (leader of *Quaid-I-Azam* or Like-Minded group)

The PML was established in 1962 as the successor to the pre-independence All-India Muslim League. It has long been beset by factional rivalries and divisions. By 1995, the PML(N) (Nawaz group) was the largest factional element, headed by former Prime Minister Nawaz Sharif, who had been instrumental in the formation of the Islamic Democratic Alliance, which had won the 1990 federal elections. Following the October 1993 elections, in which it secured 73 National Assembly seats, the PML(N) formed the core of the parliamentary opposition to the →Pakistan People's Party (PPP) administration. The PML(J) (Junejo group), headed by Hamid Nasir Chatta, won six seats in the 1993 federal polling and joined the PPP-led government in coalition. By contrast, in the 1997 elections the PML(N) won 135 National Assembly seats and formed a new government under Nawaz Sharif, while the PML(J) failed to retain a single seat and was reduced to a representation of just five members across the provincial assemblies of Punjab, North-West Frontier Province and Baluchistan. However, the PML(N) itself then began to split: first, in reaction to Nawaz Sharif's attempts to impose a personal dictatorship and, subsequently, following Sharif's displacement by a military coup. A PML(Q) (*Quaid-I-Azam*), or PML(LM) (Like-Minded) group, has emerged under the leadership of Mian Azhar to offer broad support to General Musharraf's new government. Since Nawaz Sharif's trial, conviction and exile, effective leadership of the PML(N) has passed to Javed Hashmi as acting president.

Pakistan People's Party (PPP)

Address. Zardari House-8, Street 19, Sector F-8/2, Islamabad

Email. ppp@comsats.net.pk

Website. www.ppp.org.pk

Leadership. Benazir Bhutto (chairperson); Jahangir Badar (general secretary)

The PPP was formed in 1967, advocating Islamic socialism, democracy and a non-aligned foreign policy. A PPP government was overthrown in a coup in 1977 led by Gen. Zia ul-Haq and the party's founder, Zulfiquar Ali Bhutto, was executed in 1979 by the military regime. The party leadership was then assumed by his widow, Begum Nasrat, and by his daughter, Benazir. In the November 1988 National Assembly elections, held after Gen. Zia's death in a plane crash, the PPP became the largest single party (although without an overall majority) and Benazir Bhutto was designated Prime Minister. The party lost power with the dismissal of her government in August 1990, after which, in elections the following October, its legislative strength was more than halved. In 1992 the party formally abandoned its previous state socialist programme in favour of building a social market economy. The party returned to power in the October 1993 elections, winning 89 of 206 contested National Assembly seats and assuming control (by April 1994) of three of the country's four provincial assemblies. In a presidential election in November 1993, the federal parliamentary deputies elected Farooq Leghari, the PPP nominee.

In December 1993 the PPP hierarchy ousted the Prime Minister's mother as party co-chair, reflecting the estrangement between Benazir and both her mother and her brother, Murtaza Bhutto, who announced the formation of a breakaway faction of the PPP, the PPP(SB), in March 1995. However, Murtaza was assassinated in 1996 and although his wife attempted to sustain his faction it did poorly at the elections of 1997, winning only one seat in the National Assembly and two in the Sindh provincial assembly. Meanwhile, following the dismissal of Benazir Bhutto's government by President Leghari in November 1996, the main PPP also went into decline. In the 1997 elections, it retained only 19 of the 98 National Assembly seats that it had won in 1993 and saw its representation in the Sindh provincial assembly reduced to a minority 36 seats. After her indictment for corruption later in 1997, Benazir Bhutto also left the country and subsequently has attempted to maintain her leadership from abroad. Following press speculation that the Musharraf government was negotiating with senior PPP officials for the party to drop Bhutto as leader, she announced in early September 2001 that she intended to lead the party in the elections promised for 2002.

Following the terrorist attacks in the USA of Sept. 11, 2001, the PPP called on the Musharraf government to distance itself from the Taleban and create a government of national consensus.

The PPP is a consultative member of the Socialist International.

Other Parties

Assembly of Islamic Clergy (*Jamiat-ul-Ulema-e-Islam, JUI*), Islamist formation that won six National Assembly seats in the 1990 elections, failed to retain any in 1993 but won back two in 1997; it also won seven seats in the Baluchistan provincial assembly and one in the North-West Frontier province assembly in 1997. Seen as having close links with the Taleban in Afghanistan; following the commencement of US-led hostilities against the Taleban regime in October 2001 it organized demonstrations hostile to the Musharraf government's pro-US position.

Assembly of Pakistani Clergy (*Jamiat-ul-Ulema-e-Pakistan, JUP*), a progressive Sunni Muslim formation led by Maulana Shah Ahmed Noorani Siddiqui, which was represented in the Sharif coalition government following the October 1990 elections; failed to gain representation in 1993 and boycotted the polls in 1997.

Baluchistan National Party (BNP), regionalist party that won three seats in the February 1997 National Assembly elections.

Islami Jamhoori Mahaz (IJM), won four seats in October 1993 Assembly elections but retained none of them in February 1997.

Jamhoori Wattan Party (JWP), won two seats in October 1993 Assembly elections, which it retained in 1997 when it also won eight seats in the Baluchistian provincial assembly.

Justice Movement (JM), founded in April 1996 by Imran Khan, the former Pakistan cricket captain, who declared that its aim was to "bring about a change in the country by demanding justice, honesty, decency and self-respect". His party proved a failure at the polls of February 1997, winning no seats in either the National Assembly or the Punjab provincial assembly.

National People's Party (NPP), formed in 1986 by a breakaway faction from the →Pakistan People's Party (PPP), the NPP was a member of the Sharif coalition government from 1990 until its expulsion in March 1992. Won one seat in both the 1993 and 1997 elections.

Leadership. Ghulam Mustafa Jatoi (chair)

Pakhtoon Khawa Milli Awami Party (PKMAP), won three seats in October 1993 Assembly elections; failed to retain any of them in February 1997 but took two seats in the North-West Frontier Province assembly.

Sindh National Front (SNF), led by Mumtaz Ali Bhutto (an uncle of the former Prime Minister), advocating broad autonomy for the four provinces of Pakistan; won one seat in the Sind provincial assembly in 1997.

Palau

Capital: Koror

Population: 17,500 (2000E)

The Republic of Palau (also known as Belau) consists of a chain of islands and islets in the western Pacific Ocean. From 1947, as part of the UN Trust Territory of the Pacific, they were administered by the United States. At the beginning of 1981 a popularly approved constitution came into force which prohibited the stationing of US nuclear weapons and the storage of nuclear waste in Palau. However, the following year Palau and the United States signed a compact of free association under which the US granted internal sovereignty and economic aid in return for continuing control of Palau's defence. From 1983 onwards, a succession of referendums to override the constitutional ban on the transit and storage of nuclear materials and enable the compact to come into effect failed to gain the required 75% majority. In 1992 the approval requirement was lowered to that of a simple majority, and in a referendum the following year the compact was accepted. On Oct. 1, 1994, Palau became a sovereign and independent state, and the UN Trust Territory of the Pacific was terminated.

Under the 1981 constitution, executive authority is vested in a President, who is directly elected for a four-year term. Legislative authority is exercised by the National Congress (*Olbiil era Kelulau*), a bicameral body consisting of a 16-member House of Delegates (one member from each of Palau's constituent states) and a 14-member Senate. The constitution also provides for a Council of Chiefs to advise the President on matters relating to tribal laws and customs. There are no formal political parties, although two broad tendencies emerged during the pre-independence constitutional dispute, namely the Coalition for Open, Honest and Just Government, which opposed the compact of free association, and the *Ta Belau* Party, which defended it. More recently an opposition Palau National Party has been formed.

In the most recent presidential election on Nov. 7, 2000, the incumbent Vice-President, Tommy Remengesau, was elected with 52% of the vote against 48% for Senator Sandra Pierantozzi.

Palestinian Entity

Government centre: Ramallah and Gaza City

Population: 2,783,084 (1997)

Of the Arab territories captured by Israel in the Six-Day War of 1967, the Gaza Strip, the West Bank and East Jerusalem contained a substantial Palestinian Arab population. The Palestine Liberation Organization (PLO), founded in 1964, subsequently led resistance to Israeli occupation and increasing Jewish settlement of these areas. Following the *intifada* revolt, which began in December 1987, a peace process started in October 1991, which indirectly resulted in a declaration of principles (DOP) on interim Palestinian self-rule, in September 1993. The PLO now agreed to renounce terrorism and recognize Israel's right to exist within secure borders. For its part, Israel recognized the PLO as "the legitimate representative of the Palestinian people". The DOP also established a timetable for progress towards a final settlement.

By early 1996, the Israeli military had withdrawn from most of the Gaza Strip and most Arab towns and villages in the West Bank, though Jewish settlements remained under Israeli military protection. The accord also transferred many powers to a PLO-dominated Palestine National Authority (PNA) and mandated elections for an 88-member Palestinian Legislative Council (PLC) and for a President. On Jan. 20, 1996, over 750,000 voters out of an electorate of 1,013,235 participated in these dual ballot elections. PLO chairman, Yassir Arafat, was returned as President by an overwhelming majority against one other candidate. His *Fatah* grouping and allies (mainly independent candidates) won a decisive majority in the Palestinian Council, and PLO factions began developing into political movements. However, "rejectionist" groups both within and outside the PLO refused to take part, notably the Islamic Resistance Movement (*Hamas*), while opposition forces alleged that Arafat's government was ignoring the PLC.

The right took power in Israel in May 1996 and initially halted Israeli withdrawal from the West Bank. Labour's victory in Israel's 1999 elections suggested that the peace process might resume. However, the collapse of talks on "final status issues" at Camp David in the USA, in July 2000, increased popular Palestinian frustration, and a new *intifada* (uprising) erupted in October 2000. Israeli politicians—notably after February 2001, new Prime Minister Ariel Sharon—accused Arafat of fomenting revolt, and retaliated against PNA institutions.

Al-Fatah
Website. www.fateh.net

Al-Fatah (the reverse acronym of the Arabic for Palestine Liberation Movement, and meaning Conquest) was established in 1959 and is the core component of the PLO. It has always been primarily nationalist in orientation. *Fatah* leader Yassir Arafat was elected PLO chairman in 1969, and has since remained the dominant political figure on the Palestinian stage. Despite resistance from "rejectionist" PLO factions, he began negotiations with Israel that led, in

1993, to mutual recognition and the beginning of Palestinian self-rule in the occupied territories. On returning to Gaza from exile, *Fatah* initially won back support in this former →*Hamas* stronghold. In the January 1996 elections for a Palestinian Council, *Fatah* candidates won 55 of the 86 seats and "independent *Fatah*" candidates won a further 12, while Arafat was popularly elected to the Council's presidency with 88.1% of the vote. No further elections have been held.

Since 1993, schisms have developed between indigenous *Fatah* activists, mostly veterans of the 1987–91 *intifada*, and *Fatah* leaders who were formerly exiled in Tunis. Likewise, various *Fatah*-affiliated police and paramilitary groups have grown in strength, while Arafat has poured water on attempts to "democratize" the party. The outbreak of the Al Aqsa *intifada* in October 2000 resulted in new status for the grassroots *Fatah* faction called →*Tanzim*. PLC Speaker Ahmed Qurei (Abu Ala) is effectively the Council's *Fatah* faction leader.

AC-Fatah is a consultative member of the Socialist International.

Democratic Front for the Liberation of Palestine (DFLP)

Website. www.alhourriah.org/dflp

Formed in 1969 as a splinter from the →Popular Front for the Liberation of Palestine. It was known for various acts of terrorism within Israel during the 1970s and 1980s, and was active during the first *intifada*. In 1991 the DFLP split after the Madrid peace conference, with the creation of the →Palestinian Democratic Union. After 1993, its main faction under Nayif Hawatmeh has opposed the peace accords with Israel, although others participate in the PNA.

Hamas (Islamic Resistance Movement)

Website. www.palestine-info.com/hamas

A vehemently anti-Israeli, Islamic fundamentalist movement in the occupied territories which rose to prominence in 1988. Opposed to mainstream PLO groups, and particularly popular in Gaza, *Hamas* did not field any official candidates in the 1996 Palestinian Council elections, although five *Hamas*-affiliated members won seats, and one, Imad Faluji, is a PNA cabinet minister. The party's spiritual leader, Sheikh Ahmed Yassin, was released from an Israeli jail in October 1997. External leaders include Moussa Abu Marzouk and Ibrahim Ghawshah, both based in Jordan. *Hamas* social welfare and medical facilities rival those of the PNA. Its military wing, the *Izzat-Din al-Qassem* Brigades, has taken credit for many terror attacks in Israel. Though curbed by the PNA, *Hamas* (which means "zeal") enjoys renewed support as the Al Aqsa *intifada* has radicalised opinions.

Palestine People's Party (PPP)

Website. www.palpeople.org

Formed in 1982 as the Palestine Communist Party, assuming its present name in 1991. It backed the 1993 Israel–PLO peace accord, but only joined the PNA in 1996, and officially withdrew in 1998. The party is well organized in the West Bank, and has links with Israeli Communists, though it has a small membership. It lost its leader, Bashir Barghouti, in September 2000; his successor, Suleiman Najjab, died in August 2001.

Palestine Popular Struggle Front (PPSF)

An offshoot of the →Popular Front for the Liberation of Palestine. Its mainstream faction endorsed the 1993 Israel–PLO peace accord.

Palestinian Democratic Union (PDU)

Also known as *Fida* (sacrifice), created in 1991 by members of the →Democratic Front for the Liberation of Palestine. It supports the Israel–PLO peace process, and its leader Yasser Abed-Rabbo serves as a key ministerial ally of Arafat's. FIDA won a single PLC seat in 1996.

Popular Front for the Liberation of Palestine (PFLP)

Website. www.pflp-pal.org

Established in 1967 by members of the Arab National Movement (founded in 1951) and other factions. Its ideology combines Marxism with pan-Arabism, and it endorsed hijackings and terrorism in the early 1970s. Led by the charismatic Georges Habash, the PFLP grew into the second largest PLO faction after →*Fatah*, despite suffering numerous defections. Its hitherto dormant West Bank branch acquired new status during the 1987–91 *intifada*.

The PFLP returned to the PLO fold and endorsed the "two-state solution" of the Palestine National Council's Algiers Declaration in 1988. However, it subsequently led a ten-member Damascus-based "Rejection Front" that condemned the peace accord of September 1993 and officially boycotted the Palestine Authority's first indigenous elections, in January 1996, despite qualms from local leader, Riyad Malki and the election of PFLP-affiliated independents.

In 1999 some PFLP leaders were allowed to return to the West Bank, including PFLP deputy leader, Abu Ali Mustafa (born Mustafa Zibri). In 2000 he was elected as Habash's successor. Israeli forces assassinated Mustafa in August 2001, following several car bombings attributed to the PFLP in Jerusalem. The PFLP retaliated in October 2001, by shooting dead an Israeli minister, Rehavam Ze'evi, after which the PNA arrested several PFLP figures. Overall, the PFLP has lost support amongst radicals to the Islamic movement, →*Hamas*. The PFLP's new secretary-general is Ahmad Saadat.

Other Groups

Arab Liberation Front (ALF), an Iraqi-backed group that in 1995 split between "rejectionists" and those favouring the peace process.

Islamic Holy War (*Al-Jihad al-Islami*), militant fundamentalist and anti-Israeli group, responsible for suicide bombing attacks on Israeli military and civilian targets in the 1990s, opposed to the Israel–PLO peace process. Founded in the late 1970s by the Hebronite sheikh, Asad al-Tamimi, the group enjoys less mass support than fellow Islamic radicals, →*Hamas*. Its secretary-general, Fathi Shqaqi, was shot dead in Malta in October 1995 by Israeli agents. His successor is the Damascus-based Ramadan Abdallah Shalah.

Palestine Liberation Front (PLF), originally Iraqi-backed, it later split into various factions (some affiliated to →*Fatah*). The PLF was associated with terrorist attacks, notably the *Achille Lauro* hijacking in 1985; reported to be more united in the early 1990s.

Popular Front for the Liberation of Palestine – General Command, a militant offshoot of the main PFLP led by Ahmed Jibril. It maintains support in Lebanon, but less so in PNA-ruled areas.

Revolutionary Council of Fatah (also known as the Abu Nidal Group), an anti-Arafat guerrilla organization responsible for numerous terrorist incidents around the world over the last 20 years.

Revolutionary Palestinian Communist Party (RPCP), led by Abdullah Awwad, founded in the late 1980s by a faction of what became the →Palestine People's Party. The RPCP supported the first *intifada* and later criticized the Israel-PLO peace process.

Tanzim, meaning "organization", represents many grassroots →*Fatah* supporters in the West Bank; under Marwan Barghouti it has played a prominent part in fomenting the Al Aqsa *intifada*.

Panama

Capital: Panama City   **Population**: 2,808,268 (2000E)

The Republic of Panama seceded from Colombia in 1903 and immediately ceded in perpetuity to the United States the right to construct an inter-oceanic canal. Until 1979 the Canal Zone was US sovereign territory and the rest of the country essentially a protectorate of the United States. Internal politics, punctuated by military intervention, were turbulent and elected governments were overthrown in 1941, 1949, 1951 and 1968, usually after disputed elections. There were serious constitutional crises in 1918, 1948 and 1955. In 1968 a reforming military government seized power, led by Omar Torrijos Herrera. In the 1972 and 1978 elections to the then National Assembly of Community Representatives, no candidate was allowed to represent a political party. Meanwhile the Torrijos government negotiated the Panama Canal Treaties of 1977 by which the USA relinquished its claims (with control of the Canal passing to Panama on Dec. 31, 1999).

Constitutional reforms adopted in April 1983 established a unicameral Legislative Assembly consisting of 67 members. Executive power rests with the President, assisted by two Vice Presidents, elected for a term of five years. The President appoints a Cabinet and numerous other officials including the president of the Panama Canal Commission.

A tentative return to democratic government in the early 1980s was overshadowed by the presence of the National Guard, whose commander, Gen. Manuel Antonio Noriega Moreno, effectively ruled the country. Nicolás Ardito Barletta of the Democratic Revolutionary Party (PRD), the winner of the May 1984 presidential election, was initially favoured by the military and his election campaign was supported by a centre-right coalition of six parties led by the now defunct National Democratic Union (UNADE). He was forced to resign by the military in September 1985 when he announced that he would investigate charges that Noriega had ordered the killing of a political opponent, Hugo Spadafora. Barletta's successor, Eric Arturo Delvalle, was in turn forced to flee the country after an abortive attempt to dismiss Noriega but still claimed to be president from exile. An interim President, Manuel Solís Palma, was then appointed by the military. Domestic and international pressure, especially from the USA, for the removal of Noriega, who had also been implicated in drug smuggling, continued to mount. His attempt to deny the Civic Opposition Democratic Alliance (ADOC) victory in the May 1989 presidential and legislative elections, by annulling the result, led to rapidly deteriorating relations with the United States culminating in a US military invasion in December.

The results of the May 1989 elections, which had been held in safe keeping by the Roman Catholic Church, were then declared valid on Dec. 27 though they were incomplete and covered only 64% of voters. Guillermo Endara Galimany was duly sworn in as "constitutional President" to head a democratic government of reconstruction and national reconciliation, which, however, was not a success. Endara's austerity policies were highly unpopular and not only did Panama receive negligible compensation from the USA for the damage done by the invasion but it also suffered from the effect of the US anti-narcotics campaign.

Ernesto Pérez Balladares of the PRD won the presidential elections held on May 8, 1994, with 33.3% of the vote. In simultaneous legislative elections, the PRD emerged as the largest single party, with 21 out of 72 seats. Pérez Balladares took office on Sept. 1, including in his Cabinet independents and members of the Arnulfista Party (PA) and Christian Democratic Party (PDC).

Panama has historically had a highly fragmented party system, characterised by the importance of personalities and family ties. One person, Arnulfo Arias Madrid, dominated Panamanian politics from his first election as president in 1940 until his death in 1988, balancing, not always successfully, opposition to US hegemony with political realism. De-registration of parties in Panamanian politics occurs at the comparatively high cut-off point of 5% of the vote. Those parties that fail to gain this minimum level of support in an election providing legislative representation are subsequently banned from the electoral process. The number of parties represented fell from 13 in the 1994 elections to 9 in 1999. All adult citizens over the age of 18 can vote and voting is compulsory.

In elections held in May 1999 parties competed in three groupings. The New Nation (*Nueva Nación*, NN) group won the most seats (42), these being taken by the Democratic Revolutionary Party (PRD) 34, the Solidarity Party (PS) 4 and the National Liberal Party (PLN) 4. In second place, the Union for Panama (*Unión por Panamá*, UPP) won 24 seats, shared by the *Arnulfista* Party (PA) 18, the Nationalist Republican Liberal Movement (MOLIRENA) 3, Democratic Change (CD) 2 and the National Renewal Movement (Morena) 1. The Opposition Action alliance (*Acción Opositora*, AO) took 6 seats, won by the Christian Democratic Party (PDC) 5 and the Civic Renewal Party (PRC) 1. Simultaneous presidential elections were won by the candidate of the Union for Panama, *Arnulfista* Party leader Mireya Elisa Moscoso Rodríguez de Gruber, who took 44.9% of the votes. The defeated candidates were Martín Torrijos Espino of the PRD, with 37.6% of the vote, and Alberto Vallarino Clement of the PDC, with 17.5%. The government is formed by the parties of the Union for Panama led by the PA.

Arnulfista Party
Partido Arnulfista (PA)
Address. Avda. Perú y Calle 37 N° 37–41, Apartado 9610, Zona 4, Panamá

Telephone. (+507) 227–1744
Fax. (+507) 217–2645
Leadership. Mireya Elisa Moscoso Rodríguez de Gruber (president); Víctor M. Juliao (secretary-general)

Founded in 1990 and with a registered membership in January 2001 of 150,100, the PA is now the main right-wing party in Panama. It was established by a faction of the now defunct Authentic *Panameñista* Party *(Partido Panameñista Auténtico,* PPA) led by the late veteran politician Arnulfo Arias Madrid. Arias was President of Panama in 1940–41, 1949–51 and for an eleven-day period in 1968 as the successful candidate of the five-party Opposition National Union (UNO) before being deposed in a coup d'état. The PPA itself had been launched in 1984 as the "authentic" *Panameñista* party, as distinct from a rival *Panameñista* Party (PP) set up against Arias' wishes by Alonso Pinzón and Luis Suarez to contest the 1980 legislative elections.

The PPA, along with the →Nationalist Republican Liberal Movement (MOLIRENA) and the →Christian Democratic Party (PDC), joined the Civic Opposition Democratic Alliance (ADOC) to back Arias's fifth presidential campaign in 1984 against the military's choice, Nicolas Ardito Barletta of the National Democratic Union (UNADE), whose victory the ADOC later claimed was fraudulent. The opposition also refused to accept the official results giving ADOC only 27 of the 67 seats in the Legislative Assembly.

The PPA, which gradually lost the leadership of the ADOC to the PDC, itself split in August 1988 following Arias's death. One faction, again taking the party's original name (PP) and willing to collaborate with the military-backed regime, nominated Hildebrando Nicosia as their candidate in the May 1989 presidential elections. The other faction, however, received ADOC's endorsement of its presidential candidate, Guillermo Endara Gallimany. Endara was judged to have won the election, despite the result being annulled by the military, and was sworn in as president on a US marine base immediately before the US invasion of December 1989. To confirm a break with the past, Endara's supporters then established the PA, which was legalized in May 1990.

The ruling ADOC coalition government weathered massive public opposition to its October 1990 austerity policies only to face sustained protests by the trade unions, especially public sector workers, in the new year. Internal divisions and evidence of official corruption and drug-related scandals, some involving Endara's own law firm, severely damaged Endara's reputation. In April 1991, he dismissed five PDC cabinet ministers whom he accused of "disloyalty and arrogance", leaving the *Arnulfistas* without an assured majority in the Legislative Assembly. The PDC had 28 seats to the 16, seven and four respectively of the remaining ADOC members, MOLIRENA, the AP and the PLA.

Endara was also increasingly accused of sacrificing national sovereignty by being subservient to the US government, especially in his harsh public criticism of Cuba and most controversially in agreeing to the radical reform of the country's banking secrecy laws in July 1991, which critics said would do little to stop drug trafficking and money laundering but would drain the country of foreign exchange. Critics, led by the PDC, also accused the government of fomenting military coup scares in order to keep the country in a perpetual state of emergency. This, they alleged, allowed state security forces more effectively to quell opposition protest. Endara was also blamed for not pressing the US government for adequate compensation for the civilian victims of the December 1989 military invasion, and for not placing imprisoned military associates of Noriega on trial. In September 1991 Endara's choice for Legislative Assembly president was defeated when Marco Ameglio, a PLA member, aligned himself with the opposition.

The widow of former President Arias Madrid, Mireya Elisa Moscoso Rodríguez de Gruber, stood as the party's presidential candidate in the 1994 elections, which she lost to the →Democratic Revolutionary Party (PRD) candidate, Ernesto Pérez Balladares. In May 1999, however, as candidate of the Union for Panama, she gained 44.9% of the votes

cast in a three-way contest. It fell to her therefore to be the President who formally received the Canal from former President Jimmy Carter of the United States who said: "Take it, it's yours".

Christian Democratic Party
Partido Demócrata Cristiano (PDC)

Address. Avda. Perú (frente Plaza Porras), Edf. María No. 55, Apdo. 6322, Zona 5, Panamá
Telephone. (+507) 227–3204
Fax. (+507) 225–8298
Email. pdcpanama@cwpanama.net
Leadership. Rubén Arosemena Valdés (president); José Domingo Torres (secretary-general)

Founded in 1960, the centre-right PDC had its origins in the student National Civic Union (1957–1960), where the tradition of European Christian democratic parties was assimilated. Middle-class professionals, intellectuals and students swelled its ranks but the Federation of Christian Workers (FTC) was also an early affiliate. The PDC contested the 1964 and 1968 presidential elections without much success. During the period when party politics were effectively banned by the Torrijos government (1968–1978), the party reorganized itself, winning 20% of the vote in the 1980 legislative elections and taking 19 of the 56 seats in the newly formed National Legislative Council (the other 37 being filled by nominees of a non-party National Assembly of Community Representatives established in 1972). In 1984, the PDC was part of the Civic Opposition Democratic Alliance (ADOC) which lost the presidential and legislative elections following suspected widespread fraud by the military.

During 1987, the PDC became increasingly involved in confrontations with the government, openly campaigning through strikes (supported mainly by businesses rather than trade unions) and street demonstrations (which were violently suppressed) for the resignation and removal of Gen. Manuel Noriega, who was accused of drug trafficking, electoral fraud, corruption and murder. The PDC was again part of the ADOC electoral alliance in May 1989 which supported the presidential candidacy of Guillermo Endara of the →Arnulfista Party, PA) and, after the official ratification of the results following the US military invasion in December. Ricardo Arias Calderón became First Vice-President and the PDC the largest party in the Legislative Assembly with 28 of the 67 seats. Its subsequent withdrawal from the ADOC coalition government in April 1991, when Endara dismissed five PDC cabinet ministers, caused a political crisis. This had followed months of in-fighting during which Arias Calderón had publicly described Endara's economic programme, which advocated severe austerity measures and the privatization of state enterprises, as "senseless". Although Arias Calderón was stripped of his Interior and Justice Ministry post he won the May 1989 presidential election annulled by Noriega.

In succeeding months, the PDC became the leader of the opposition, to such an extent that it was exerting strong influence within such organizations as the Civic Crusade, an organization from which Endara had drawn his strongest support and which in June called for a plebiscite to decide on the desirability of Endara remaining in office. In September 1991, the PDC was judged firmly to have secured its political influence on parliamentary committees as a direct result of facilitating the victory of a dissident PLA candidate in the election of a new president of the Legislative Assembly.

Arias Calderón resigned the Vice Presidency in December 1992 in a move designed to distance himself from President Endara in the run-up to the May 1994 presidential election. However, the party managed to gain only one seat in the legislative elections. In the 1999 presidential election its candidate, Alberto Vallarino Clement, ran a distant third with 17.5% of the poll but as part of Opposition Action the PDC won 5 legislative seats.

With a registered membership in January 2001 of 51,627 the PDC is a full member of the Christian Democrat International.

Civic Renewal Party
Partido Renovación Civilista (PRC)
Address. 1a/Of.4 Edif. Casa Oceánica, Avda. Aquilino de la Guardia, Panamá
Telephone. (+507) 263–8971
Fax. (+507) 263–8975
Leadership. Serguei de la Rosa; Tomás Herrera (president): Carlos Harris (secretary-general)
Registered in 1992 shortly after the 1991 elections, the PRC is an anti-military grouping which succeeded in winning three legislative seats in the 1994 elections. In the 1999 legislative elections it ran as part of Opposition Action (AO) with the →Christian Democratic Party, and secured one seat, but lost its registration.

Democratic Change
Partido Cambio Democrático (CD)
Address. Parque Lefevre, Plaza Carolina, arriba de la Juguetería del Super 99, Panamá
Telephone. (+507) 217–2643
Fax. (+507) 217–2645
Leadership. Ricardo Martinelli (president); Jaime E. Arosemena (secretary-general)
Alternatively called the Democratic Party (PD), the CD campaigned in 1999 as part of the UPP coalition and gained two seats in the Legislative Assembly. Its registered membership in January 2001 was 47,671.

Democratic Revolutionary Party
Partido Revolucionario Democrático (PRD)
Address. Calle 42 Bella Vista, entre Ave. Perú y Ave. Cuba, bajando por el teatro Bella Vista
Telephone. (+507) 225–1050, 225–5525
Fax. (+507) 225–1802
Email. secreprd@sinfo.net
Leadership. Balbín Herrera (president); Martín Torrijos Espino (secretary-general); Ernesto Pérez Balladares (former President)
The PRD was originally dedicated to the nationalist revolutionary beliefs of Gen. Omar Torrijos Herrera, Commander-in-Chief of the National Guard, who had led a coup in October 1968. Torrijos campaigned against imperialism and the oligarchy and in favour of national independence. The Torrijos years (1968–79) included land re-distribution, the creation of a non-party National Assembly of Community Representatives in 1972 to replace a dissolved National Assembly, and the signing, in 1977, of the Panama Canal Treaties. The party subsequently in the 1980s became a vehicle for Gen. Manuel Noriega and after his fall was characterized by its critics as the mainstay of the right-wing Noriega tradition.

Formally created in 1979 by Torrijos supporters, who included businessmen, Christian Democrats and Marxists, the party retained its progressive-populist image until the death of Torrijos in an air crash in July 1981. The military continued the tradition of Torrijos, albeit manipulating political power from the right of the political spectrum. By the time of the May 1984 presidential and legislative elections, the PRD-led National Democratic Union (UNADE) coalition was a tool of the military and was duly declared the clear winner despite evidence of widespread fraud. The lack of PRD political autonomy was amply demonstrated when the UNADE President Nicolas Ardito Barletta was forced to stand down by the military in 1985 after indicating his intention of investigating allegations that Noriega was implicated in the murder of an opposition candidate Hugo Spadafora. Well-publicized allegations in 1985–88 of Noriega's involvement in murders, drug-dealing, money-laundering, gun-running and espionage for and against the United States did not deflect PRD support for the military.

The party was a member of the Coalition of National Liberation (COLINA) alliance in the May 1989 presidential and legislative alliance and served as apologists for Noriega's annulment of the result until the US military invasion in December. Subsequently, in pursuit of a popular grass-roots base, it allied itself with domestic groups demonstrating for adequate compensation from the US government for civilians killed and property destroyed during the invasion. It backed popular protests against corruption in the government and against its austerity policies. In July it opposed government moves to abolish the army, stating that it was needed to guarantee the security of the Panama Canal, and also spearheaded opposition to US demands that Panama's banking secrecy laws be repealed to assist in the detection of drug traffickers and money launderers.

In early 1990 a new group of PRD leaders emerged, distancing themselves from General Noriega and declaring themselves for democracy. In the elections of 1994 the PRD finally took power with a plurality of 31 seats in the legislature and victory for Ernesto Pérez Balladares in the presidential contest. In 1999 as part of the New Nation coalition its presidential candidate, Martín Torrijos Espino, obtained 37.6% of the vote but was defeated by Mireya Moscoso de Gruber of the →Arnulfista Party. However the coalition gained 57.7% of the vote in the legislative elections and the PRD increased its legislative representation to 34, making it the largest party. With a registered membership of 326,705 the PRD is an observer member of the Socialist International.

National Liberal Party
Partido Liberal Nacional (PLN)
Address. Vía Fernández de Córdoba, Vista Hermosa, Plaza Córdoba, antigua Ersa, Local 6–7, Panamá
Telephone. (+507) 229–7523
Fax. (+507) 229–7524
Email. pln@sinfo.net
Leadership. Dr Roberto Alemán Zubieta; Raúl Urango Gasteazoro (president); Juan José Vallarino Amado (secretary-general)
The PLN was founded in 1979 and is broadly liberal. It campaigned as part of the New Nation coalition at the 1999 elections and won 4 seats in the Legislative Assembly. The PLN's registered membership was 64,896 in January 2001 and it is an observe member of the Liberal International.

National Renewal Movement
Movimiento de Renovación Nacional (MORENA)
Leadership. Joaquín José Vallarino Cox (president); Demetrio Decerega (secretary-general)
Founded and registered in 1993, MORENA gained one legislative seat in the 1994 elections. In the 1999 elections it campaigned as part of the successful Union for Panama coalition for the presidency and retained its one seat in the Legislative Assembly, but lost its registration.

Nationalist Republican Liberal Movement
Movimiento Liberal Republicano Nacionalista (MOLIRENA)
Address. Calle Venezuela, Bella Vista, Casa N° 5, entre Calle 50 y Vía España (Antiguo Restaurante La Casona), Apartado 7468, Panamá 5
Telephone. (+507) 213–5928/9
Fax. (+507) 265–6004
Email. molirena@hotmail.com
Leadership. Jesús L. Rojas (president); Arturo Vallarino (secretary-general)
Founded in October 1981, MOLIRENA is a right-wing libertarian party that preaches the principles of a free market. The party was established by breakaway groups of the now defunct Third Nationalist Party (TPN), Republican Party (PR) and the Liberal Party (PL). Opposed to the military's hold on the country, it joined the Opposition Democratic

Alliance (ADO) to contest the 1984 presidential and legislative elections and thereafter supported the campaign of the National Civic Crusade for the removal of the Commander of the Defence forces, Gen. Manuel Noriega. The party was a member of the Opposition Civic Democratic Alliance (ADOC) denied power by Noriega following the presidential and legislative elections of May 1989. Once the ADOC was installed in power following the US military invasion in December, the party received 15 seats in the Legislative Assembly. The party backed the government's IMF-approved economic austerity programme and proposals for the wholesale privatization of the state sector, including, most controversially, social welfare agencies.

The party suffered as a result of the unpopularity of these policies, its representation falling from 15 to 5 seats in 1994. In 1999 the party campaigned as part of the successful Union for Panama coalition. Its candidate, Arturo Ulises Vallarino Bartuano was elected First Vice President but the party won only 3 seats in the Legislative Assembly. It had a registered membership of 57,890 in January 2001.

Solidarity Party
Partido Solidaridad (PS)
Address. Calle 39, Avda. Justo Arosemena, casa N°17, Panamá
Telephone. (+507) 263–4097
Fax. (+507) 212–1060
Leadership. Carlos Antonio Clement Icaza (president); Enrique Lau Cortez (secretary-general)
Founded and registered in 1993 the PS won two Assembly seats in the May 1994 polls. In 1999 it ran as part of the New Nation coalition and increased its representation in the Assembly to 4. Its registered membership was 33,458 in January 2001.

Other Parties

Authentic Liberal Party (*Partido Liberal Auténtico, PLA*), originated as a breakaway from the →National Liberal Party

in 1987; it held two seats as a result of the 1994 legislative elections but lost both of them and its registration in 1999. *Leadership.* Arnulfo Escalona Riós (president)

Independent Democratic Union (*Union Democrática Independiente, UDI*), won one seat in the 1994 legislative elections but lost both its representation and its registration in 1999.
Leadership. Jacinto Cárdenas

Labour Party (*Partido Laborista, PALA*), founded in September 1982 by Azael Vargas to establish a strong party on the extreme right; won one seat in the 1994 legislative elections but is currently unrepresented.

Liberal Party (*Partido Liberal*), won one seat in the 1994 legislative elections but is currently unrepresented and unregistered.

Motherland Movement (*Movimiento Papa Egoro/Tierra Madre*), an unusual party that rapidly grew from inauspicious beginnings in November 1991 to being the third placed grouping in the 1994 presidential elections. The party's founder was the film star, singer and sometime lawyer, Rubén Blades, who in both 1992 and 1993 was quoted in opinion polls as being the favourite for the presidency in 1994. Blades, however, found it hard to shake off the rumours that his nomination in 1993 was no more than a stunt to advance his career, especially in the United States.

After the May 1994 elections, in which his party won 6 seats in the Legislative Assembly, Blades returned to California to resume his show business career, leaving the party to its current leader Fernando Manfredo. It lost all its seats and its registration in 1999.

Republican Liberal Party (*Partido Liberal Republicano, Libre,* PLR)
Libre won two seats in the 1994 legislative elections, but lost both seats and its registration in 1999.

Papua New Guinea

Capital: Port Moresby   **Population:** 5,130,000 (2000 census)

Papua New Guinea achieved full independence from Australia in 1975. The head of state is the British sovereign (represented by a locally nominated Governor-General). The head of government is the Prime Minister, who is elected by the legislature and appoints the National Executive Council (Cabinet). There is a unicameral National Parliament of 109 members. All are elected under the first-past-the-post voting system from single-member constituencies, but twenty seats are allotted to the nineteen provinces and National Capital District, so that each voter elects two members, one constituency and one provincial. Members are elected for a five-year term.

Every government since independence in 1975 has been a coalition. Coalitions tend to emerge only after elections have been completed, and have proved fluid. Constitutional provision is made for votes of no confidence in the government, eighteen months after an election and up to twelve months before a new election, and every parliament has seen a mid-term change of government.

Parties mostly revolve around personalities, and lack both clear ideological differentiation and mass bases. New parties are continuously being created – especially on the eve of elections – and often prove short-lived. Since the 1970s almost every major political party has at some stage been in coalition with every other. Also, since the pre-independence election of 1972 the number of candidates contesting elections has increased steadily, notwithstanding a substantial increase in candidate fees, to an average of 22 per constituency in 1997. The proportion of candidates standing as independents has also increased. In an attempt to strengthen the party system, in late 2000 the Papua New Guinea parliament passed an Organic Law on the Integrity of Political Parties and Candidates (OLIPPC). This provides for the registration and public funding of parties (on the basis of the number of MPs), and sanctions (including loss of seat) against MPs who change party affiliation during the life of the parliament. This legislation was being implemented in 2001 with elections due in 2002. Additional legislation seeks to change the system of voting from first-past-the-post to preferential by 2007, and to abolish the provincial electorates.

369

In the elections of June 14 and 28, 1997, twenty parties were registered with the Electoral Commission though several others were listed against the names of the 2,371 candidates. In the event, however, a third of the winning candidates had stood as independents. Of those claiming party endorsement, 16 were aligned with the People's Progress Party (PPP), 15 with *Pangu Pati*, 8 each with the National Alliance (NA) and People's Democratic Movement (PDM), and 6 with the People's National Congress (PNC). Nine other parties gained between one and 5 MPs. In the post-election scramble for numbers, PNC leader Bill Skate emerged as the head of the winning coalition. However in July 1999, following several shifts in party allegiance, Skate lost office and Sir Mekere Morauta was voted in as Prime Minister. Morauta had stood as an independent in 1997 but had become parliamentary leader of the PDM. He headed a coalition of PDM, *Pangu*, and National Alliance. Under Morauta's leadership, and following the passage of the OLIPPC, the PDM attracted members across the floor of the house and became the first party in Papua New Guinea's political history to hold an absolute majority in the National Parliament.

Melanesian Alliance (MA)

Leadership. John Momis (leader)

The Melanesian Alliance had its origins in a group established within the Constitutional Planning Committee (CPC) by CPC deputy chairman John Momis and member John Kaputin, together with Bernard Narokobi, who in 1997 became speaker of the National Parliament. The MA is a progressive party with a strong base in the New Guinea Islands Region and links to the Catholic Church. In 1997 it joined the →National Alliance.

National Alliance (NA)

Leadership. Sir Michael Somare (leader)

Formed by Sir Michael Somare before the 1997 elections, the NA comprised the →Melanesian Alliance (MA), Stephen Pokawin of the →Movement for Greater Autonomy, and some →*Pangu* supporters and progressive independents. On the basis of party identification shown in the Electoral Commission's pre-poll list of candidates, the NA (including the MA) gained eleven seats in 1997 and in the immediate post-election period looked likely to form a government. But the NA failed to get the numbers when Bill Skate, who had promised support, reneged and took his →People's National Congress into a rival grouping and became Prime Minister. Following Skate's ouster in 1999, the NA joined the new governing coalition. In 2001 Somare was dropped from the Morauta government's cabinet and moved to the opposition, but other NA members remained with the government.

Pangu Pati

Leadership. Chris Haiveta (leader)

Pangu is one of Papua New Guinea's first significant parties, forming a coalition government after the elections of 1972 and leading the country to independence in 1975. Its former parliamentary leader, Sir Michael Somare, was Papua New Guinea's first Prime Minister. The party subsequently suffered three major splits. In 1985 Paias Wingti left to form the →People's Democratic Movement (PDM), and in 1986 Anthony Siaguru broke away to form the →League for National Advancement. Ten years later, Somare, then a member of a coalition government headed by Sir Julius Chan (→People's Progress Party), opposed legislation which fundamentally changed the country's provincial government system and was dropped from cabinet. He subsequently founded the →National Alliance. From about this time, *Pangu* was weakened by internal differences. Following the 1997 elections *Pangu*, under the leadership of Chris Haiveta, joined Prime Minister Bill Skate's coalition, and Haiveta was for a while deputy Prime Minister. But Skate and Haiveta later had differences and when in 1999 Skate dropped Haiveta from the cabinet *Pangu* withdrew from the coalition, subsequently backing the PDM in its ouster of Skate and participating in the new PDM-led coalition government. Also in 2000 Somare's membership of *Pangu* was terminated, further deepening the rifts within the party.

Papua New Guinea National Party (NP)

Leadership. Paul Pora (leader); John Munnul (president)

The Papua New Guinea National Party (originally the New Guinea National Party) was formed in 1971 in the New Guinea highlands, largely as a reaction to the conservative political orientation of the →United Party. It was once described as "the highlands equivalent of →*Pangu*". The NP was a member of the governing coalition in the 1972–77 parliament, but after its leader and deputy leader were dropped from cabinet in 1976 the party split and virtually collapsed. Two years later the party was revived under colourful NP politician Iambakey Okuk, who became leader of the parliamentary opposition, and in 1980 deputy Prime Minister. The party split again in 1985 and in 1987 following the death of Okuk. It was revived in the 1990s under the leadership of another highlands politician, Paul Pora, but in the 1997 elections secured only one seat. In May 2001 it was re-launched in the highlands with a view to contesting the 2002 elections.

People's Action Party (PAP)

Leadership. Ted Diro (leader)

In 1981 a Papua Action Party was formed as a regional party, drawing on Papuan separatist sentiments. It was aligned with the →Papua New Guinea National Party. Around the same time, former Papua New Guinea Defence Force commander, Ted Diro, a Papuan, stood successfully in the 1982 elections, in association with several candidates, mostly Papuans, who formed an "Independent Group". In 1982 Diro became opposition leader before stepping down in favour of National Party leader Okuk. The People's Action Party was founded shortly before the 1987 elections, with Diro as leader and strong support from Papua (including members of the Papua Action Party and the Independent Group). It gained six seats in 1987 and double that number in 1992, becoming the third largest parliamentary party. In 1997 it secured five seats.

People's Democratic Movement (PDM)

Leadership. Sir Mekere Morauta (party leader); Thomas Negints (acting convenor); Agonia Tamarua (acting secretary)

Address. PO Box 37, Jacksons Airport, NCD

Telephone. (+675) 323 3744

The PDM was formed by a breakaway from *Pangu Pati* in 1985, led by prominent highlander member Paias Wingti. Wingti subsequently became Prime Minister, following a vote of no confidence. The Wingti-led coalition was returned to office in the election of 1987 but was itself removed in mid-term in 1988. After the 1992 election Wingti again became Prime Minister in a coalition government. However, in 1994 he was removed as Prime Minister by a Supreme Court ruling, and in 1997 lost his seat. Following the 1997 elections, the PDM was initially in opposition, but led a successful challenge to Prime Minister Skate and in 1999 became the major partner in a coalition headed by Sir Mekere Morauta, who became parliamentary leader of the PDM in 1998. Following the passage of the OLIPPC (see above), in 2001 a number of members switched allegiance to the PDM, giving it an absolute majority in parliament.

People's National Congress (PNC)
Leadership. Bill Skate (leader)
Formed prior to the 1997 elections, principally as the electoral vehicle for National Capital member Bill Skate, the PNC gained six seats in 1997 (all in Papuan electorates) and Skate emerged as Prime Minister in a coalition government. He lost office in 1999.

People's Progress Party (PPP)
Leadership. Sir Julius Chan (party leader); Michael Nali (parliamentary party leader)
PPP is one of the country's oldest and most successful parties, and remains a major player. It is generally regarded as having a pro-business orientation. Its leader, Sir Julius Chan, was deputy Prime Minister in the first post-independence government and has twice been Prime Minister, but lost his seat in 1997 after his government attempted to employ mercenaries to end a rebellion on the island of Bougainville. In 2001 the PPP had five MPs.

United Party (UP)
Leadership. Gabia Gagarimabu (party leader)
The UP was founded, initially as the Combined Political Associations (Compass), in 1970. Its political base was in the highlands, and its principal platform was opposition to a rapid movement to independence. In the pre-independence elections of 1972 it gained more seats than any other party but was out-manœuvred in the formation of coalitions and became the leading opposition party. Subsequently it lost support and in 1978 split, with a number of its members joining the →Papua New Guinea National Party. It remains as a minor party (having gained three seats in the 1997 elections), still predominantly highlands-based, and has been a junior partner in several governing coalitions.

Other parties

Advance Papua New Guinea Party (APP), emerged on the eve of the 1997 elections, and its parliamentary party leader, John Pundari, subsequently played a crucial role in the moves which brought down the Skate government and installed Sir Mekere Morauta as prime minister. In May 2001 Pundari announced that the predominantly highlander APP was merging its name and identity with the governing →People's Democratic Movement. Soon after, however, Bonny Igime, who had been secretary-general of the APP, proclaimed himself "caretaker" of the party, which, he said, would contest the 2002 elections.

Christian Country Party, formed on the eve of the 1997 elections by a highlander MP, who failed to gain re-election, it was not among the parties registered under the new legislation in 2001.
Leadership. Avusi Tanao

Christian Democratic Party (CDP), launched in 1995 'with the vision to provide Christian leadership in all levels of government'; gained one seat in the elections of 1997.

Leadership. Dilu Goma (chairman); Muki Taranupi (parliamentary leader)

League for National Advancement (LNA), initially known as the *Pangu* Independent Group and formed as a breakaway from the →*Pangu Pati* in 1986. It enjoyed modest electoral success, and was a member of governing coalitions, until 1997, when it faded out.

Liberal Party, gained one seat in 1992, but failed to win a seat in 1997.
Leadership. Thomas Pupun (leader)

Movement for Greater Autonomy (MGA), formed prior to the 1997 elections by former Manus Province governor, Stephen Pokawin, who had been an outspoken opponent of changes to the provincial government system in 1995, the MGA drew support from the New Guinea Islands Region. Pokawin was elected in 1997, when he and the MGA joined the →National Alliance.
Leadership. Stephen Pokawin (leader)

National Vision for Humanity Party, a new party registered in August 2001.

Papua New Guinea Country Party, established prior to the 1992 elections, with predominantly highlander backing, it failed to win a seat in 1997.

Papua New Guinea First Party, led by John Gundu.

Papua New Guinea Labour Party (PNGLP), launched in August 2001 by the PNG Trade Union Congress, as the latest of a series of union-linked parties, none of which has had significant electoral success.
Leadership. Dr Bob Danaya (president)

People's Freedom Party (PFP), formed in mid-2001 by three lawyers with no links to parliamentary members, the PFP 'aims to provide leadership based on honesty, purity and love'.

People's Labour Party (PLP), launched in the highlands in July 2001 by Madang businessman and politician, Peter Yama, with a view to contesting the 2002 elections.

People's Resource Awareness Party (PRAP), launched prior to the 1997 elections, with a platform calling for sustainability in resource exploitation, the PRAP gained two seats in 1997, but was not listed as a registered party in September 2001.

People's Solidarity Party (PSP), whose leader Kala Swokin gained a seat in 1997 but in 2000 was reported to have joined the →United Party.

United Resources Party (URP), created amongst mostly highlander MPs during the 1997–2002 parliament, but by 2001 had been weakened by defections to the →People's Democratic Movement.

Paraguay

Capital: Asunción

Population: 5,585,828 (2000E)

Paraguay was in 1811 the first Latin American country to achieve independence from Spain. Its first constitution was introduced in 1844 in order to legitimize the power of Carlos Antonio López, one of the three consecutive dictators to rule Paraguay up to the end of the War of the Triple Alliance or National Epic (*Epopeya Nacional*) in 1870, in which Paraguay's population was halved. Political forces subsequently developed into the *Colorado* and Liberal parties, which have dominated Paraguayan politics since 1876. A three-year period of military rule, albeit by reformist officers, followed the 1932–37 Chaco War with Bolivia. A new constitution introduced in 1940 failed to bring about needed changes and, after a succession of unstable governments, Gen. Alfredo Stroessner took power in a military coup in 1954.

During Stroessner's 35-year rule Paraguay was under a permanent state of siege and all constitutional rights and civil liberties were suspended. The country's economic and political structure was nonetheless stabilized and its infrastructure greatly modernized. Stroessner was declared the winner of all eight elections, which were held at five-year intervals. He was overthrown on Feb. 3, 1989, in a "palace coup" led by his son-in-law Gen. Andrés Rodríguez, who was sworn in immediately as interim President. The subsequent presidential and congressional elections on May 1, 1989, in which Rodríguez and the *Colorado* Party won a sweeping victory, were considered to have been relatively free and open by international observers. Election to membership of the Group of Rio in October 1990 and entry in March 1991 into the Southern Common Market (MERCOSUR), with Argentina, Brazil and Uruguay, did much to restore the country's international credibility. The *Colorado* Party (ANR-PC) has remained the leading party since the restoration of democratic institutions with the Authentic Radical Liberal Party (PLRA) the principal party of opposition.

Under the 1992 constitution, which curtailed his previously extensive powers, executive power is vested in the President, who is directly elected by simple plurality for a non-renewable five-year term and who governs with the assistance of the Council of Ministers, which he appoints. Legislative authority is vested in the bicameral National Congress, consisting of a 45-member Senate and 80-member Chamber of Deputies, directly elected by proportional representation for five-year terms. Voting is compulsory for all men and women of 18 years of age and older. Women have been allowed to vote since 1958.

Presidential and legislative elections were held in May 1998, with the PLRA and National Encounter (EN) allying in the Democratic Alliance (AD). The contest for the Chamber of Deputies resulted in the ANR–PC taking 45 seats, the PLRA 27 and EN 8. In the Senate contest the ANR–PC took 24 seats, the PLRA 13, the EN 7 and the White Party 1. In the concurrent presidential elections Raúl Alberto Cubas Grau (ANR–PC), with 55.4% of the votes cast, defeated Domingo Laíno (PLRA–EN) with 43.9%. Following the assassination of his Vice President, Luís María Argaña, however, in which he was widely seen as implicated, Cubas fled the country in March 1999. He was succeeded as President by the President of the Senate, Luís González Macchi and a special election held on Aug. 13, 2000, to choose a new Vice President.

Authentic Radical Liberal Party
Partido Liberal Radical Auténtico (PLRA)
Address. Mariscal López 435, 1750 Asunción
Telephone. (+595–21) 24–4867
Fax. (+595–21) 20–4867
Leadership. Julio César Franco (Vice President of the Republic and president); Domingo Isabelino Laíno Figueredo (founder and 1998 presidential candidate)
This centrist party is a descendant of the →Liberal Party (PL) which dominated Paraguayan politics from 1904 to 1936. It was founded in 1978 by Domingo Laíno, and has been the second party in Paraguayan politics since that time. The party was a founder member of the National Agreement (*Acuerdo Nacional*, AN), a coalition of four opposition parties with the aim of pressing for democratization and respect for human rights under the Stroessner regime. The PLRA was denied legal status and boycotted all elections and organized anti-government rallies.

The PLRA was legalized on March 8, 1989, a month after the military coup that overthrew Stroessner. In the May 1989 elections Laíno stood as the PLRA presidential candidate and the party came second in both the presidential and the congressional contests, although its share of the vote was far smaller than that of the ruling →National Republican Association–*Colorado* Party. This pattern was repeated in the 1991 Constituent Assembly elections and the 1993 and 1998 elections. In 1998, the party (running in alliance with →National Encounter (EN)) won 27 seats in the Chamber of Deputies and 13 in the Senate, while Laíno came second, with 43.9% of the vote, in the presidential contest. In the 2000 special vice presidential election the PLRA candidate, Julio César Franco, won a narrow victory, taking 49.64% of the votes cast to 48.82% for the ANR–PC candidate, Félix Argaña, brother of the assassinated vice president.

The PLRA is a member party of the Liberal International.

National Encounter
Encuentro Nacional (EN or PEN)
Address. Senador Long 370, esq. Del Maestro, Asunción
Telephone. (+595–21) 61–0699, 61–0701
Fax. (+595–21) 61–0699
Leadership. Guillermo Caballero Vargas (leader)
EN was founded in 1992 as an electoral vehicle for Guillermo Caballero Vargas, who took 23.14% of the votes in the 1993 presidential contest while his party won eight seats in each house and entered into opposition with the →Authentic Radical Liberal Party (PLRA). As the Democratic Alliance (*Alianza Democrática*, AD), the EN and PLRA jointly contested the 1998 election, when the EN won 7 seats in the Senate and 8 in the Chamber of Deputies.

National Republican Association–Colorado Party
Asociación Nacional Republicana–Partido Colorado (ANR-PC)
Address. 25 de Mayo 842, calle Tacuary, Asunción
Telephone. (+595–21) 44–4137, 49–8669
Fax. (+595–21) 44–4210
Email. anr@uninet.com.py
Leadership. Luís González Macchi (President of the Republic); Bader Rachid Lichi (acting party president)
The right-wing *Colorado* ("Red") Party was founded in 1887 and has been a major force in Paraguayan politics ever since. It originated in a conservative faction created by Gen. Bernardino Caballero (President of Paraguay 1882–91) and it took its name from the faction's red banners.

The *Colorado*s were in power from 1887 until 1904 when the Liberals took power in a popular uprising. They remained in opposition to Liberal governments until the brief *Febrerista* interlude in 1936–37 and the sudden death in an accident of the war hero Marshal José Félix Estigarribian in 1940. They opposed the pro-Axis regime of Higinio Moríngo, until a *Colorado*/→*Febrerista* Revolutionary Party (PRF) coalition government was installed in 1946 after the USA put pressure on the regime to oust fascist sympathizers. A series of coups and fraudulent elections followed, the PRF were edged out and the *Colorado*s were the only legal party between 1947 and 1963.

The military coup of May 5, 1954, marked the beginning of Gen. Alfredo Stroessner's 35-year dictatorship. Then an army commander, he was officially elected President in July 1954. In 1956 Stroessner re-organized the party after exiling his main *Colorado* rival, Epifanio Méndez Fleitas. The 1958 elections were, like all six later elections held under his rule, completely stage-managed. To give a semblance of democracy, after 1963 selected opposition parties or acceptable fractions of parties were permitted to take part (and even win some seats in Congress from 1968 onwards). The manipulated results invariably showed overwhelming support for Stroessner, despite the reality of exile, arrests, long prison sentences and torture being meted out to his political opponents. However after 1979 an extra-parliamentary opposition, the National Agreement (*Acuerdo Nacional*) emerged, made up of the →Authentic Radical Liberal Party (PLRA), the →*Febrerista* Revolutionary Party (PRF), →Christian Democratic Party (PDC) and the Popular *Colorado* Movement (*Movimiento Popular Colorado*, MOPOCO), an anti-Stroessner faction of the *Colorado*s.

The violent coup of Feb. 3, 1989 which toppled Stroessner took place shortly before his former close ally and son-in-law, Andrés Rodríguez, was due to be transferred from his top army position of First Army Commander to the passive role of Defence Minister. Rodríguez, as interim President, legalized most opposition parties and called a general election for May 1, 1989. As the *Colorado*'s presidential candidate, Rodríguez won 78.18% of the valid vote and the party polled 72.8% of the vote in the congressional elections. Under the then Constitution, however, the winning party automatically gained two-thirds of the seats in Congress. Promising that he would hold elections in 1993 and not stand for a second term, Rodríguez was sworn in on May 15, 1989, and retained his interim Cabinet.

The ensuing power struggle between the "traditionalists" and the newly formed "democratic" wing led, however to a severe rift in the party. A *Colorado* Party convention, dominated by "traditionalists", went ahead in early December 1989 despite a court injunction brought by the "democratic" faction, led by Blas Riquelme, and said to be supported by Rodríguez. This was followed on Dec. 11, 1989, by the resignation of the whole Cabinet. The leader of the "traditionalists", the Foreign Minister Dr José María Argaña, was dismissed in mid-August 1990 after making a defiant public statement that the *Colorado*s would never give up power.

At an extraordinary *Colorado* convention in February 1993 the military-backed Juan Carlos Wasmosy defeated Argaña for the party's presidential nomination. Following this rejection, Argaña campaigned against Wasmosy in the May 1993 general elections. Following the elections (won by Wasmosy), Argaña set up a new break-away party called the National Reconciliation Movement (*Movimiento Reconciliación Nacional*, MRN), which formed a rival legislative block with the PLRA and EN. In late 1994 three generals accused Wasmosy of vote-rigging and officially called for his impeachment. This clash between the *Colorado* Party and the military continued into 1995 with General Lino César Oviedo Silva emerging as the leader of the fight against Wasmosy. A new party faction was launched, fuelled by Oviedo, which began making overtures to the exiled Albert Stroessner, son of the former dictator, thus prompting the possibility of a new *stronista* faction within the *Colorado* party. In April 1996, however, Oviedo and his supporters attempted to launch a coup, which was defeated after the Organization of American States (OAS) had made it clear it would not be recognized.

Although imprisoned, Oviedo was chosen as the *Colorado* candidate for the presidency in 1998. Legally barred from running, he was then replaced by his proposed running mate, Raúl Cubas Grau, who was elected in May 1998 in an election generally regarded as free and fair. On taking office, Cubas commuted Oviedo's sentence and ordered his release. In March 1999 Vice President Luís María Argaña was assassinated and it was widely believed that this was the result of a conspiracy between Cubas and Oviedo. After several days of mounting crisis, with widespread strikes and demonstrations and impeachment pending in Congress, Cubas fled to Brazil, where he was given political asylum. He was succeeded as President by the President of the Senate, Luís González Macchi, who formed a government of national unity. In a special election held on Aug. 13, 2000 to choose a new Vice President the Colorado candidate, Félix Argaña, the brother of the assassinated vice president, was narrowly defeated by the PLRA candidate.

Other Parties

Christian Democratic Party (*Partido Demócrata Cristiano, PDC*), founded in 1960 but was illegal until following the February 1989 coup which toppled Stroessner; won one seat in the Chamber in the 1989 and 1991 elections but has been unrepresented since 1993; affiliated to the Christian Democrat International.
Leadership. Jorge Darío Cristaldo (president)
Address. Francisco Dupuys 962, Casi Colón, Asunción
Telephone. (+595–21) 42–0434
Fax. (+595–21) 423 539
Email. idcm@infonet.com.py

Constitution for All (*Constitución Para Todos, CPT*), founded in 1991 with support from within the Church and the CUT and CNT trade union confederations; grew out of Asunción for All (*Asunción para Todos,* APTO), a progressive movement led by Carlos Filizzola, a former president of the Association of Physicians, which won the May 1991 municipal elections in the capital; took 16 seats in the 1991 Constituent Assembly elections, but failed to win a seat in the 1993 or 1998 elections. In 1998 Filizzola ran as vice presidential candidate on the Democratic Alliance ticket with Domingo Laíno of the →Authentic Radical Liberal Party.
Leadership. Carlos Alberto Filizzola Pallares

Febrerista Revolutionary Party (*Partido Revolucionario Febrerista, PRF*), originated among the junior ranks of the armed forces, who carried out a radical nationalist coup of Feb. 17, 1936, which inspired the party's name; called anti-government protests in the mid-1980s; failed to win a seat in the 1993 and 1998 legislative elections. It is a member party of the Socialist International.
Address. Casa del Pueblo, Manduvira 552, Asunción
Telephone. (+595–21) 49–4041
Fax. (+595–21) 49–3995
Email. partyce@mixmail.com
Leadership. Carlos María Liubetic (president); Ricardo Estigarribia Velásquez (secretary-general)

Humanist Party (*Partido Humanista, PH*), party candidate Ricardo Buman, polled 1.54% of the vote in the vice presidential elections of Aug. 13, 2000.
Address. Rca. de Colombia 1260, esq. Rojas Silva y Cptán. Fayol, Asunción
Telephone. (+595–21) 21–3211
Fax. (+595–21) 21–3211
Email. ph@humanista,org.py

Liberal Party (*Partido Liberal, PL*), founded in 1887 in opposition to the *Colorado*s, and dominated Paraguayan politics between 1904 and 1936. The two remaining factions merged with the →Authentic Radical Liberal Party (PRLA) in 1990 but a candidate, Abraham Zapag Bazas, contested the 1993 presidential elections, winning only 0.17% of the votes cast.

White Party (*Partido Blanco, PB*), presidential candidate Gustavo Bader won 0.25% of the votes cast in the 1998 presidential election; PB candidates obtained 2.3% of the votes cast and won one Senate seat in the 1998 legislative elections but failed to win a seat in the Chamber of Deputies.

Peru

Capital: Lima   **Population**: 27,000,000 (2000E)

The Republic of Peru achieved independence from Spain in 1826, since when there have been periods of civilian government alternating with military rule. Under the 1993 constitution executive power is vested in a President, who is directly elected for a five-year term and is eligible for re-election. The President governs with the assistance of a Prime Minister and an appointed Council of Ministers. Legislative authority is vested in a unicameral 120 member National Congress elected for a five-year term from a single national list. Voting is compulsory from the ages of 18 to 70.

Alberto Keinya Fujimori, of Change 90 (*Cambio* 90), was elected as President in June 1990. Fujimori staged a presidential coup (*autogolpe*), with the support of the military, in April 1992, when he dissolved the legislature and suspended the constitution. He survived an abortive counter-coup put down by loyal forces in November 1992 and a new constitution was approved by referendum in October 1993. Fujimori was a comfortable victor in presidential elections held in April 1995, becoming the first incumbent in the country's history to be re-elected for a consecutive term. His ruling New Majority–Change 90 (NM–C90) alliance also secured a majority in Congress by winning the simultaneous legislative elections. In December 1999 Fujimori announced that he would run as the presidential candidate of the Peru 2000 alliance in the forthcoming elections. The opposition launched a legal challenge to Fujimori's candidacy on the grounds that the constitution barred a third term. However, the national election board declared that because the constitution was last amended in 1993, Fujimori had in fact stood for election only once under the current constitution and, therefore, was eligible for a further term. In May 2000 Fujimori won a comfortable victory, his opponent, Alejandro Toledo, having decided to boycott a run-off poll because of the widespread view that it would not be conducted fairly. In simultaneous elections to the Congress, Fujimori's Peru 2000 alliance lost its absolute majority. In July 2000 Fujimori was sworn in for a third presidential term amid threats of international isolation and uproar on the streets of the capital, Lima. However, in a dramatic development, Fujimori made a televised announcement in September 2000 in which he stated that he intended to step down and call an election in which he would not be a candidate. Two months later, in a development that stunned the country, Fujimori (the son of Japanese immigrants) fled to Japan and announced his resignation as President.

In fresh presidential elections held in April and June 2001, Toledo, backed by his centrist Peru Possible (PP) party, took 53.1% of the vote in a run-off victory over Alan García of the populist left-of-centre Peruvian *Aprista* Party (APRA). In legislative elections held in April 2001, Toledo's PP emerged as the largest single party, with 45 seats (from 26.3% of the vote), while APRA took 26 seats and nine other parties shared the remaining seats.

Independent Moralizing Front
Frente Independiente Moralizador (FIM)
Address. C/o Congreso de la República, Plaza Bolivar S/N, Lima 1
Leadership. Luis Fernando Olivera Vega
The FIM was launched in 1990 by Fernando Olivera, a former investigator for the State Prosecutor's Office who had pursued former President Alan García of the →Peruvian *Aprista* Party on corruption charges. The party has adopted a consistent anti-corruption stance and support for it and its leader has grown over the years. In the 2001 presidential election, Olivera finished fourth, gaining just under 10% of the vote. The party won 12 seats in the accompanying legislative elections, making it one of only four parties to achieve double figures.

National Unity
Unidad Nacional (UN)
Address. C/o Congreso de la República, Plaza Bolivar S/N, Lima 1
Leadership. Lourdes Celmira Rosario Flores Nano (2001 presidential candidate)
The centre-right National Unity electoral alliance was created as a vehicle for the presidential ambitions of Lourdes Flores Nano, who had led the Popular Christian Party (*Partido Popular Cristiano*, PPC) for a number of years. In the first round of the 2001 presidential election (held in April), Flores finished in third place having secured 24.3% of the vote, narrowly missing the run off. In the legislative elections (also in April), the UN emerged as the third strongest party, winning almost 14% of the vote and 17 seats in the 120-member Congress.

Peru 2000
A four-party coalition formed in 1999 to support President Alberto Keinya Fujimori in his bid to win a third presidential term. It included Change 90 (*Cambio 90*), the grouping originally founded in 1989 to help Fujimori's presidential aspirations, and the New Majority (*Nueva Mayoría*), formed by Fujimori in the early 1990s. Following the creation of Peru 2000, the main opposition parties mounted an unsuccessful legal challenge to Fujimori's candidacy on the ground that he was running for a third term, barred by the constitution. In the May 2000 elections the Peru 2000 parties took 51 seats and Fujimori was re-elected, but he subsequently resigned and fled the country amid widespread discontent. With the departure of Fujimori, the Peru 2000 alliance collapsed. Two of the member parties – Change 90 and New Majority – contested the 2001 legislative election on a joint ticket, but were soundly defeated, winning only four seats in the Congress.

Peru Possible
Perú Posible (PP)

Address. Bajada Balta 131 Oficina 11, Miraflores, Lima
Telephone. (+51–1) 447–4413
Website. www.peruposible.org.pe
Leadership. Alejandro Toledo Manrique

Peru Possible was formed in 1994 by Alejandro Toledo, an American Indian who had risen from poverty to become a business-school professor and World Bank official. Toledo contested the presidency in 1995 as the candidate of the (now defunct) Democratic Co-ordinating Movement–Peru Viable Nation (Code), winning just over 3% of the vote and finishing well behind President Fujimori and three other candidates. However, by the time of the 2000 elections, Toledo and the PP posed the main challenge to Fujimori. In a highly charged atmosphere, Fujimori and Toledo went through to a second round of voting in the presidential election, but the latter boycotted the poll after accusing the incumbent President of electoral malpractice and Fujimori won a third consecutive term. In the legislative elections held in April 2000, Fujimori's Peru 2000 party lost its absolute majority in Congress with the PP becoming the largest opposition force, with 28 seats in the 120-member Congress.

In Nov. 2000 Fujimori resigned the presidency and fled the country, forcing a new round of elections in 2001. In the first round of the presidential election in April Toledo secured over 36% of the vote in the first round (against 26% for Alan García of the →Peruvian *Aprista* Party (APRA)). In the second round of voting held in June, Toledo defeated García, taking 53.1% of the vote. In the April 2001 legislative poll, the PP had emerged as the strongest party, winning 45 seats, against 26 for APRA and 17 for the →National Unity Party.

Peruvian Aprista Party
Partido Aprista Peruano (APRA) (also known as Alianza Popular Revolucionaria Americana)

Address. Avenida Alfonso Ugarte 1012, Lima
Telephone. (+51–1) 440–6886
Fax. (+51–1) 445–2986
Leadership. Jorge del Castillo (secretary-general); Alan Gabriel Ludwig García Pérez (2001 presidential candidate)

APRA has historically been the leading centre-left force in Peruvian politics. APRA started as a continent-wide anti-imperialist movement formed in the 1920s by Victor Raúl Haya de la Torre, a Peruvian Marxist in exile in Mexico. Its original purpose was to unite Latin America politically, obtain joint control of the Panama Canal and gain social control of land and industry. The Peruvian branch of APRA, the Peruvian *Aprista* Party (PAP), was founded in 1930 when Haya returned to Peru. As it became the sole surviving *Aprista* party, the PAP was increasingly referred to as APRA.

Alan García took over as secretary general in 1982 and led the party to victory in the April 1985 elections, thereby becoming the first *Aprista* to be elected President, and the youngest Peruvian ever to hold the office. García's principal election promise was to halt the country's economic decline by devoting no more than 10% of export earnings to service the huge foreign debt. In an attempt to address widespread and escalating guerrilla activity, he set up a Peace Commission. In June 1986, however, García ordered the quelling of mutinies in three different prisons, staged mainly by Shining Path guerrillas, as a result of which an estimated 254 guerrillas were killed by the security forces. All the members of the Peace Commission resigned in protest. In addition, accusations that the government was using the right-wing Commando Rodrigo Franco death squads to intimidate left-wing opponents dented APRA's liberal image.

In the 1990 elections, APRA won only 16 senatorial seats and 49 seats in the Chamber of Deputies. Its presidential candidate and secretary general Luís Alvaro Castro, was beaten into third place in the presidential contest and the party backed Alberto Keinya Fujimori of Change 90, the victor, in the run-off.

In the aftermath of Fujimori's April 1992 presidential coup, García went into hiding from where he called for popular resistance to restore democratic rule. In early 1993, an extradition request made to Colombia to hand over the exiled García was rejected. Following attempts by García to obtain Colombian citizenship, he was stripped of the position of secretary general of APRA and a new leadership was installed. The internal strife and unpopularity of the party led to its candidate, Mercedes Cabanillas, achieving a dismal 5% of the presidential vote in April 1995 while in 1996 García was convicted in absentia on corruption charges.

In the 2000 elections the party again performed badly. APRA's candidate in the presidential poll, Abel Salinas Eyzaguirre, was eliminated in the first round of voting after gaining just over 1% of the vote and in the legislative elections the party gained only just over 5% of the total vote, having failed to compete effectively with either →Peru 2000 or →Peru Possible (PP).

The catalyst for the party's revival occurred in early 2001 when García returned to Peru from Colombia and announced his intention to contest the April presidential election. After his return, the Supreme Court lifted all arrest warrants against him, following an earlier ruling of the Inter-American Court on Human Rights that his 1996 conviction was spent under a statute of limitations. The subsequent performance of García was impressive, but he still failed to defeat the PP candidate, Alejandro Toledo, who won by a margin of 53% to 47% in a second round of voting held in June. In the legislative elections, APRA also did well but again the party failed to overtake the PP, winning 20% cent of the popular vote and 26 seats.

APRA is a full member party of the Socialist International.

Popular Action
Acción Popular (AP)

Address. Paseo Colon 218, Lima
Telephone. (+51–1) 423–4177
Website. www.geocities.com/accionpopular_2000
Leadership. Victor Andres Garcia Belaunde (presidential candidate); Javier Diaz Orihuela (secretary general)

The right-wing AP was founded by Fernando Belaunde Terry in 1956 and is a strong proponent of free-market policies. Belaunde Terry was among prominent politicians opposed to Fujimori's April 1992 army-backed presidential coup. The party has made little headway in recent years. In the April 2001 elections it won three seats.

Union for Peru
Unión por el Perú (UPP)

Address. C/o Congreso de la República, Plaza Bolivar S/N, Lima 1
Website. www.unionporelperu.org
Leadership. Javier Pérez de Cuellar (honorary president)

The independent social democratic UPP was founded in 1994 by the former UN Secretary-General, Javier Pérez de Cuellar. In the 1995 presidential election, incumbent President Alberto Fujimori easily defeated Pérez de Cuellar, who finished second but only managed to win some 22% of the vote. The UPP emerged as the main opposition party to the pro-Fujimori alliance in the legislature, but only with 17 seats. In the 2000 presidential election, the party's candidate, Maximo San Roman, won less than 0.4% of the vote. The party did not field a candidate in the 2001 presidential poll, but won six seats in the legislature.

We Are Peru
Somos Perú (SP)

Address. Ate Vitarte, Mz E Lote 21 Asoc Los Angeles, Lima
Telephone. (+51–1) 995–8528

Website. www.somosperu.org.pe
Leadership. Alberto Andrade Carmona (leader)
This party was formed in 1998 by Alberto Andrade, the populist mayor of Lima, who converted his *Somos Lima* (We Are Lima) Movement into *Somos Perú* (We Are Peru). The party competed in the municipal elections of 1998 and won control of Lima and various other provinces and districts. In the 2000 presidential election, however, Andrade failed to make an impact, finishing a distant third behind incumbent President Fujimori and Alejandro Toledo of the →Peru Possible party. Andrade did not compete in the 2001 presidential poll, but in the legislative elections the SP won four seats.

Other Parties

Agrarian People's Front of Peru (*Frente Popular Agrícola del Perú, FREPAP*), formed in 1989 by members of the religious sect, the Israelites of the New Universal Pact. In the April 2001 congressional election it won 1.7% of the vote but no seats.

All For Victory (*Todos por la Victoria, TV*), won one seat in the April 2001 elections.

Andean Renaissance (*Renacimiento Andino, RA*), won one seat in the April 2001 elections.

Christian Democrat Union (*Union Demócrata Cristiano, UDC*), is a member party of the Christian Democrat International.
Address. Avenida España 321, Lima
Email. sluti@lullitec.com.pe
Leadership. Julio Luque Tijero (president)

Christian People's Party (*Partido Popular Cristiano, PPC*), is a member party of the Christian Democrat International.
Address. Avenida Alfonso Ugarte 1484, Lima
Email. aflores@congreso.go.be
Leadership. Antero Flores-Araoz (president)

People's Solution (*Solución Popular, SP*), won one seat in the April 2001 congressional elections.

Project Country (*Proyecto Pais, PrP*), took 1.6% of the vote but no seats in the April 2001 elections.

Philippines

Capital: Manila

Population: 81,000,000 (2000E)

The Republic of the Philippines became an independent state in 1946. From its previous colonial ruler, the USA, it inherited a democratic system with two dominant parties, the *Nacionalista* Party and the Liberal Party. In 1972 the then president, Ferdinand Marcos, suspended the constitution and declared martial law. Political parties were for a time illegal; subsequently politics were dominated by President Marcos's *Kilusang Bagong Lipunan* (New Society Movement, KBL). In 1986, facing mounting opposition, Marcos called a "snap election" which precipitated the "People Power revolution", and Corazon Aquino, widow of assassinated opposition leader Benigno Aquino, was installed as president. A new constitution was passed by plebiscite in 1987 and elections were held in that year for the bicameral legislature, and for provincial and local offices.

The constitution provides for a House of Representatives (in 2001 comprising 262 members). Of these 20% are elected from a party-list of organizations, approved by the Commission on Elections, representing marginalized and under-represented sectors (the introduction of the party-list system being intended to help prevent a return to the pattern of pre-Marcos "traditional politics"). Other members of the lower house are elected from single-member constituencies for a three year term, with a limit of three terms. The party-list system was not fully implemented until 1998 (prior to this sectoral representatives were nominated by groups and appointed by the president). The 24 members of the Senate are elected directly for a six-year term (with a limit of two terms), half of them being elected every three years. Executive authority rests with the president, directly elected for a single six-year term, and a vice president, elected separately.

Expectations in some circles of a return to a dominant two party system after 1986 were not borne out. The Liberal and *Nacionalista* parties re-emerged, but have become minor parties. Marcos's KBL suffered a massive decline. For the most part, parties revolve around key personalities and allegiance is fluid. New groupings appear before each election and have frequently disappeared before the next. In 2001, 162 parties and organizations applied for party-list registration. Virtually all political leaders since 1986 have been associated with two or more parties or coalitions.

President Aquino did not identify with a political party although in 1987 Congress was dominated by successful candidates who identified with Aquino. In 1988 her supporters formed a coalition, *Laban ng Demokratikong Pilipino* (LDP), to support the candidature of pro-Aquino candidates. In elections in 1992, LDP emerged as the most successful group, though its presidential candidate failed after President Aquino had endorsed former Philippines National Police chief, Fidel Ramos. Ramos, who had been a member of the LDP, formed a new party, *Partido Lakas-Tao* (*Lakas*) and, campaigning in alliance with the National Union of Christian Democrats (NUCD) and United Muslim Democrats of the Philippines (UMDP), was elected president. In 1992 *Lakas*–NUCD-UMDP gained less than 24% of the presidential vote, only two Senate seats, and about a fifth of the seats in the lower house. By 1994, however, *Lakas*–NUCD-UMDP had gained through defections from other parties (especially the LDP) and in 1995, in alliance with LDP, won a substantial majority in the lower house and nine of the twelve Senate seats being contested.

In the presidential elections of 1998, however, *Lakas*–NUCD-UMDP's candidate lost to Joseph Estrada, whose party, the *Partido ng Masang Pilipino* formed a coalition with LDP and the Nationalist People's Coalition (NPC) known as *Laban ng Makabayan Masang Pilipino* (LAMMP). Three years later, Estrada was accused of corruption and as a result of impeachment proceedings and popular pressure he vacated the presidency in January 2001 and was replaced by Vice President Gloria Macapagal-Arroyo, who had stood in 1998 as the *Lakas*–NUCD–UMDP's vice presidential candidate. Mid-term elections in May 2001 were seen by many as a test of strength between the supporters, respectively, of Macapagal-Arroyo and Estrada. The pro-Macapagal-Arroyo People Power Coalition (PPC) included *Lakas*–NUCD, the Liberal Party, *Partido Demokratikong Pilipino*, *Aksyon Demokratiko*, *Partido ng Demokratikong Reporma-Lapiang Manggagawa*, and *Promdi*. The pro-Estrada coalition, *Puwersa ng Masa* (Power of the Masses), comprised the three elements of LAMMP plus the People's Reform Party. The outcome was a victory for the PPC, consolidating the position of *Lakas*–NUCD–UMDP. The party-list vote also saw the emergence of significant support for the left, with the Communist Party of the Philippines (CPP)-aligned *Bayan Muna* topping the party-list vote and another leftist group, *Akbayan*! also polling well.

Kilusang Bagong Lipunan (New Society Movement, KBL)

The KBL was founded by President Marcos in 1978, initially as an umbrella organization which recruited Marcos supporters from both the →*Nacionalista* Party and the →Liberal Party. It went into decline following the demise of Marcos in 1986, but survives, principally as a political vehicle for the political careers of the Marcos family, notably former first lady Imelda Marcos, who was a presidential candidate in 1992, and nominated again (but withdrew) in 1998.

Laban ng Demokratikong Pilipino (Fight of Democratic Filipinos, LDP)

Leadership. Edgardo Angara (president)
Established in 1988 by President Aquino's brother Jose Cojuangco, through a merger of the *Laban* wing of →PDP–*Laban* and *Lakas ng Bansa* (People Power), a party formed in 1987 as an electoral vehicle for pro-Aquino politicians. From 1988 to 1992 the LDP was in effect the government party, though President Aquino declined to be a member of a party. The LDP did well in the congressional and local elections in 1992 but its presidential candidate, Ramon Mitra, lost out to Fidel Ramos and the party was subsequently weakened by defections. In the 1995 elections it campaigned in alliance with →*Lakas*–NUCD–UMDP, and polled well. However it split in August 1995. In 1998 the LDP was part of →*Laban ng Makabayan Masang Pilipino* (LAMMP) and in 2001 elections it joined the →*Puwersa ng Masa* coalition which lost out to the pro-Macapagal–Arroyo →People Power Coalition.

Laban ng Makabayan Masang Pilipino (Fight of the Patriotic Filipino Masses, LAMMP)

Leadership. Joseph Estrada (leader); Edgardo Angara (president)
Coalition formed prior to the 1998 elections, comprising Joseph Estrada's →*Partido ng Masang Pilipino* (PMP), the →Nationalist People's Coalition (NPC) and →*Laban ng Demokratikong Pilipino*.

Lakas–NUCD–UMDP

Leadership. Teofisto Guingona (president); Raul Manglapus (chairman)
Partido Lakas-Tao (People Power Party) was formed by Fidel Ramos in 1992 after he failed to gain the →*Laban ng Demokratikong Pilipino* (LDP) presidential nomination. In the 1992 elections *Lakas* entered into alliance with the National Union of Christian Democrats (NUCD), headed by Raul Manglapus, and the United Muslim Democrats of the Philippines (a Mindanao–Sulu based party). After Ramos became president in 1992 *Lakas* gained by defections from other parties (principally the LDP) and in 1995 emerged as the dominant group in Congress. In 1998 the *Lakas*–NUCD–UMDP presidential candidate lost out to Joseph Estrada, but the coalition's vice presidential candidate, Gloria Macapagal-Arroyo was successful. *Lakas* also polled well in congressional and local elections, but in the months following the elections support drifted across to

Estrada's →*Laban ng Makabayan Masang Pilipino* (LAMMP). When impeachment proceedings against Estrada began in 2000, much of this support began flowing back to *Lakas*–NUCD, and in the elections of May 2001 *Lakas*–NUCD gained a clear congressional majority.

Liberal Party (LP)

Leadership. Raul Daza (party president); Jovito Salonga (chairman); Florencio Abad (secretary-general)
A remnant of pre-Marcos politics, having been formed as a breakaway from the →*Nacionalista* Party in 1945. Revived in the 1980s as part of the traditional political opposition to Ferdinand Marcos, the LP polled well in 1987, under the leadership of Jovito Salonga, who became Senate president; however it has suffered from internal factionalism. In 2001 the LP was a minor player in the →People Power Coalition (PPC). It is a member of the Liberal International.

Nacionalista Party (NP)

The older of the two dominant pre-martial-law parties, the NP was established in 1907. Ferdinand Marcos was elected as the *Nacionalista* Party candidate in 1965. In the "snap election" of 1986 NP leader Salvador Laurel stood with Corazon Aquino, but in 1992 the party split over the nomination of its presidential candidate, with major factions led by Laurel, Juan Ponce Enrile and Eduardo Cojuangco (the latter forming the →Nationalist People's Coalition (NPC). It survives as a minor party.

Nationalist People's Coalition (NPC)

Leadership. Eduardo Cojuangco (chairman)
Formed in 1992 by former Marcos crony Eduardo Cojuangco, as a centre-right coalition. It derives much of its support from politicians who split from the →*Nacionalista* Party and the →*Kilusang Bagong Lipunan* (KBL). In the 1992 presidential contest Cojuangco received 18% of the vote (compared with Ramos's 24%) and the NPC polled strongly in the congressional elections. It subsequently became part of a "rainbow coalition" with →*Lakas*–NUCD–UMDP, and in 2001 was part of the pro-Estrada →*Puwersa ng Masa* coalition.

Partido ng Masang Pilipino (Party of the Filipino Masses, PMP)

Leadership. Joseph Estrada (leader)
Formed in 1997 as the political vehicle for then Vice President Joseph Estrada's bid for the presidency, it was initially aligned with the Nationalist People's Coalition (NPC) and the →*Laban ng Demokratikong Pilipino* (LDP) in the →*Laban ng Makabayan Masang Pilipino* (LAMMP) coalition, and was part of the →*Puwersa ng Masa* coalition in 2001.

PDP-Laban

Email. mail@pdp-laban.com
Website. www.pdp-laban.com
The PDP–Laban was formed in 1982 as a merger of the *Partido Demokratikong Pilipino* (PDP), a broadly social democrat/Christian democrat grouping formed during the

martial law years with strong support in Mindanao, and the *Lakas ng Bayan* (National Struggle) (*Laban*) party founded by opposition leader and former →Liberal Party (LP) candidate Benigno Aquino. In 1988 President Aquino's brother, Jose Cojuangco, led a merger of PDP–Laban with *Lakas ng Bansa,* together with some members of the →*Kilusang Bagong Lipunan* (KBL), to form the →*Laban ng Demokratikong Pilipino* as a vehicle for Aquino supporters. However, a faction of PDP–Laban, led by Aquilino Pimentel and regarded as more progressive than the faction led by Cojuangco, opposed the merger and has continued to operate as a separate political group. In 1992 Pimentel stood as vice presidential candidate with the LP's Salonga, but in 1998 stood for the Senate on the →*Laban ng Makabayan Masang Pilipino* (LAMMP) list.

People Power Coalition (PPC)

Alliance formed by supporters of President Macapagal-Arroyo in the May 2001 elections. It included →*Lakas*–NUCD, the →*Liberal Party, Partido Demokratikong Pilipino,* →*Aksyon Demokratiko,* →*Partido ng Demokratikong Reporma–Lapiang Manggagawa,* and →*Probinsya Muna* Development Initiative (*Promdi*). The outcome was a victory for the PPC, consolidating the position of *Lakas*–NUCD–UMDP as the leading political force.

Puwersa ng Masa (Power of the Masses)

Alliance formed by supporters of former President Estrada in the May 2001 elections. It comprised the three elements of →*Laban ng Makabayan Masang Pilipino* (LAMMP) plus the →People's Reform Party.

Other Parties

Akbyan! (*Citizens' Action Party*), formed in 1998 as a coalition of progressive groups and polled well in the party-list vote in 2001.
Address. 14 Mapagkumbaba St., Sikatuna Village, Quezon City
Telephone. (+63–2) 433–6933/6831
Fax. (+63–2) 925–2936
Email. secretariat@surfshop.net
Website. www.akbayan.org

Aksyon Demokratiko (*Democratic Action*), formed in 1997 by Senator Raul Roco after he failed to secure the →*Laban* nomination for the presidential contest; in 2001 Aksyon was part of the →People Power Coalition.
Address. 16th Floor Strata 2000 Building, Emerald Ave., Ortigas Centre, Pasig City 1600.
Telephone. (+63–2) 638–5381
Fax. (+63–2) 634–3073
Email. rroco@starnet.net.ph
Website. www.raulroco.com/Aksyon

Alayon, a Visayan regional party founded in Cebu in 2000 by Senator John Osmeña and drawing membership primarily from former Estrada supporters, including twelve Congressmen who resigned from →*Laban ng Makabayan Masang Pilipino* (LAMMP).
Leadership. John Osmeña (president)

Bagong Lakas ng Nueva Ecija (Balane), a regional party, dominated by the Joson clan of the province of Nueva Ecija.

Bayan Muna (*Nation First*), emerged on the left prior to the 2001 elections to contest the party-list vote. It topped the poll and secured the maximum possible three party-list members.
Leadership. Satur Ocampo (chairman)

Bileg Party, a regional party of Ilocos Sur, backed by Governor Luis Singson.

Communist Party of the Philippines (CPP), founded in 1968 as the Communist Party of the Philippines – Marxist-Leninist-Mao Tse Tung Thought, as a breakaway from the *Partido Komunista ng Pilipinas* (PKP). (The PKP, founded in 1930 was for most of its existence an illegal organization. It followed a pro-Soviet orientation and by the 1970s was a largely spent force.) Under the leadership of Jose Maria Sison, the CPP formed a National Democratic Front (NDF) and from 1969 carried on an armed insurgency through its military wing, the New People's Army. In 2001 the CPP-aligned →*Bayan Muna* topped the party-list poll.

Partido ng Demokratikong Reporma (*Democratic Reform Party, Reporma*), formed by former Defence Secretary Renato de Villa before the 1998 elections, after he lost the →*Lakas* Party's presidential nomination to Jose de Venecia. In 2001 *Reporma* was part of the →People Power Coalition.

People's Reform Party (PRP), formed in 1991 as a vehicle for the presidential bid of Miriam Defensor-Santiago. Santiago finished second in the 1992 presidential race, with 20 per cent of the vote, behind Fidel Ramos (24 per cent). In 1995 she was elected to the Senate, but failed in a re-election bid in 2001, in which she was aligned with the →*Puwersa ng Masa.*

Philippines Democratic Socialist Party (*Partido Demokratiko-Sosyalista ng Pilipinas, PDSP*), founded in 1973, is a consultative member of the Socialist International.
Address. #7 Big Horseshoe Drive, Horseshoe Village, Quezon City
Telephone. (+63–2) 726–6991
Fax. (+63–2) 726–8072

Probinsya Muna Development Initiatives (Promdi), formed in 1997 by Cebu Governor and Ramos advisor Emilio Osmeña, as a vehicle for his presidential bid in 1998; draws on regional resentment in the Visayas and Mindanao towards the political dominance of Manila (*promdi* is a slang term for someone "from the provinces"). In 2001 Promdi was part of the →People Power Coalition.

United Negros Alliance (UNA), a regional party of Negros province supporting the interests of Eduardo Cojuangco, and aligned in 2001 with the →People Power Coalition.

Poland

Capital: Warsaw **Population:** 38,600,000 (2000E)

The communist-ruled People's Republic of Poland established in 1947 gave way in 1989 to the pluralist Polish Republic. Under a new constitution approved by referendum in 1997, the President (head of state) is popularly elected in two voting rounds (if required) for a five-year term and appoints the Prime Minister subject to parliamentary approval. Legislative authority is vested in a bicameral National Assembly (*Zgromadzente Narodowe*) elected by universal adult suffrage for a four-year term, consisting of (i) a directly-elected Senate (*Senat*) of 100 members, of whom 94 are returned from 47 two-member provinces and three each from Warsaw and Krakow provinces; and (ii) a National Assembly (*Sejm*) of 460 members, who are elected by a system of proportional representation that requires party lists (except those representing ethnic minority communities) to obtain at least 7% of the vote. The threshold rule was introduced (initially at 5%) because the parliamentary elections of October 1991 had produced a highly fragmented *Sejm* in which 29 parties or groups had obtained representation.

The first round of presidential elections on Oct. 8, 2000, resulted in outright victory for the incumbent Democratic Left Alliance (SLD) candidate, Aleksander Kwaśniewski, with 53.9% of the vote against 11 other candidates. Elections to the *Sejm* on Sept. 23, 2001, resulted in a coalition of the Democratic Left Alliance (SLD) and the Union of Labour (UP) winning 219 seats (with 41.3% of the vote), the Citizens' Platform (PO) 63 (12.7%), Self-Defence (*Samoobrona*) 53 (10.0%), Law and Justice (PiS) 47 (9.8%), the Polish Peasant Party (PSL) 42 (8.8%) and the League of Polish Families (LPR) 34 (7.7%), with one seat going to a representative of the ethnic German minority. The previous government party, Solidarity Electoral Action (AWS), failed to surmount the 7% barrier to representation. In simultaneous Senate elections, the SLD–UP coalition won 68 of the 100 seats.

The post-communist fluidity of the Polish party structure intensified in the run-up to the September 2001 elections (by which time well over 300 parties were registered) and was expected to continue in the wake of the defeat of the disparate forces of the centre-right. Covered below are those parties which emerged from the elections with representation in the *Sejm* and/or the Senate.

Citizens' Platform
Platforma Obywatelska (PO)
Address. c/o Sejm, Warsaw 00902
Leadership. Maciej Plazynski (chairman)
The centrist strongly pro-EU PO was launched in January 2001 by Maciej Plazynski, Speaker of the *Sejm* and hitherto a member of the then ruling →Solidarity Electoral Action (AWS), supported by such luminaries as Donald Tusk, Deputy Speaker of the Senate and hitherto a member of the →Freedom Union (UW), and independent politician Andrzej Olechowski, who had come second in the 2000 presidential election with 17.3% of the vote. Declaring its basic aim as being to prevent the →Democratic Left Alliance (SLD) from regaining power in the forthcoming parliamentary elections, the new formation quickly attracted substantial support from within both the UW and the AWS.

In the September 2001 parliamentary elections the PO failed to prevent an SLD victory, but came a creditable second with 63 of the 460 lower house seats. In the simultaneous upper house elections the PO formed part of the five-party Senate 2001 Bloc, which won 16 seats.

Democratic Left Alliance
Sojusz Lewicy Demokratycznej (SLD)
Address. 44A ul. Rozbrat, Warsaw 00419
Telephone. (+48–22) 621–0341
Fax. (+48–22) 621–6657
Website. www.sld.org.pl
Leadership. Leszek Miller (chairman); Marek Borowski, Andrzej Celiński & Jerzy Szmajdziński (deputy chairmen); Krzysztof Janik (secretary-general)
The SLD was created prior to the 1991 elections as an alliance of Social Democracy of the Polish Republic (SRP) and the All-Poland Trade Unions' Federation (OPZZ). The SRP had been founded in January 1990 upon the dissolution of the former ruling (Communist) Polish United Workers' Party (PZPR), of which it was the organizational successor, although with democratic socialism replacing its previous Marxism–Leninism. The OPZZ derived from the official trade union federation of the communist era.

The PZPR had been created in 1948 as an enforced merger of the Polish Workers' Party (successor to the Polish Communist Party established in 1918) and the Polish Socialist Party. It had then been in power through four decades of Soviet-decreed one-party rule, featuring a renunciation of Stalinism and some liberalization under Wladyslaw Gomulka (1956–70) and further reforms under Edward Gierek (1970–80), although the regime had

remained essentially authoritarian and loyal to Moscow. PZPR rule had therefore come under severe challenge in the 1980s from the Solidarity free trade union movement led by Lech Walesa, which in June 1989 had made a virtual clean sweep of unreserved seats in partially democratic elections. Constitutional amendments in December 1989 had deleted reference to the PZDR's "leading role" and the goal of socialism, following which the PZDR had transformed itself into the SRP.

The SRP's communist-era organizational strength enabled the SLD alliance to win 60 lower house seats in the October 1991 elections on a 12% vote share. Its deputies faced considerable hostility in the new legislature, but the SDL's image improved rapidly as transition to a market economy took a social toll and the ruling centre-right parties became increasingly fragmented. In the September 1993 parliamentary elections the SLD became the largest formation in the *Sejm*, winning 171 seats with 20.4% of the vote. Despite its seniority, the SRP opted to accept participation in a coalition headed by the →Polish Peasant Party (PSL), being conscious of its need to prove its democratic credentials. The PSL held the premiership until February 1995, when Józef Oleksy of the SDL/SRP took the post, amid chronic strains between the government and President Walesa, who used his power of veto on a series of measures adopted by parliament.

The SLD candidate in the November 1995 presidential elections was the then SRP leader, Aleksander Kwaśniewski, who headed the first-round polling with 35.1% of the vote and defeated Walesa in the second with 51.7%, supported by over 30 other groupings. In February 1996 Oleksy was replaced as Prime Minister by Wlodzimierz Cimoszewicz, an adherent of the SLD but not of any of its constituent parts. In the September 1997 parliamentary elections the SLD increased its share of the vote to 27.1%, but its lower house representation fell to 164 seats, well below the total achieved by the new centre-right →Solidarity Electoral Action (AWS). The SLD therefore went in opposition, taking some consolation from a strong performance in local elections in October 1998.

Having supported Poland's accession to the North Atlantic Treaty Organization (NATO) in March 1999, the SLD formally established itself as a unitary party two months later. At the first congress of the new SLD in December 1999, former Interior Minister Leszek Miller was elected chairman and the party undertook to support pro-market reforms but in a way that would soften their impact. The party also reiterated its strong support for Polish accession to the European Union. Benefiting from the unpopularity of the AWS-led government, the SLD secured the re-election of Kwaśniewski in presidential elections in October 2000 in which he won 53.9% in the first round.

The SLD contested the September 2001 parliamentary elections in alliance with the →Union of Labour (UP), their joint list achieving a relative lower house majority of 219 of the 460 seats and an overall Senate majority of 68 out of 100 seats. Miller therefore entered into talks with other parties on the formation of a majority government.

The SLD is a full member of the Socialist International.

Freedom Union
Unia Wolnośći (UW)
Address. 77–79 ul. Marszalkowska, Warsaw 00024
Telephone. (+48–22) 827–5047
Fax. (+48–22) 827–7851
Email. uw@uw.org.pl
Website. www.uw.org.pl
Leadership. Wladyslaw Frasyniuk (chairman)
The UW was founded in April 1994 as a merger of the Democratic Union (UD) and the smaller Liberal Democratic Congress (KLD). The new formation declared itself to be strongly of the democratic social centre, favouring market-oriented reforms but urging sensitivity to resultant social problems.

Of the UW components, the pro-privatization KLD had been founded in 1990 under the leadership of journalist Donald Tusk and had won 37 seats in 1991, but had failed to reach the 5% threshold for representation in the 1993 elections. The UD had been created in 1990 to support the presidential candidacy of then Prime Minister Tadeusz Mazowiecki (unsuccessfully) and had been identified with the "shock therapy" economic programme of then Finance Minister Leszek Balcerowicz, although it had called for more consideration to be given to its social consequences. In the October 1991 parliamentary elections the UD had won 62 seats on a 12.3% vote share, gaining the dubious distinction of having more seats than any of the other 28 parties with representation. Its then leader, Bronislaw Geremek, had tried and failed to form a government, so that the UD had become the main opposition to the 1991–92 government headed by the →Democratic Left Alliance (SLD). Upon its fall in June 1992, Hanna Suchocka of the UD had formed a seven-party coalition, becoming Poland's first female Prime Minister; but her government had fallen in May 1993. In the September 1993 parliamentary elections the UD had improved its representation to 74 seats under the new leadership of Balcerowicz, but had slipped to 10.6% of the vote and third place in the parliamentary order, becoming the principal opposition to an SLD-dominated government.

The candidate of the merged UW in the 1995 presidential elections was Jacek Kurón, who achieved third place in the first round with 9.2% of the vote. In the September 1997 parliamentary elections the UW won 13.4% and 60 seats and decided, somewhat reluctantly, to join a centre-right coalition headed by →Solidarity Electoral Action (AWS) in which Balcerowicz returned to the Finance Ministry and Geremek became Foreign Minister. Both ministers won international praise, Geremek for supervising Poland's admission to NATO in 1999 and both for advancing Poland's aspiration to join the European Union. However, opposition to Balcerowicz's further economic reform plans on the populist wing of the AWS resulted in the UW leaving the government in June 2000. The UW did not present a candidate in the October 2000 presidential election.

Following Balcerowicz's appointment as president of the Polish central bank in December 2000, Geremek resumed the UW chairmanship. In January 2001 the UW was weakened when Tusk and other prominent centrist politicians formed the →Citizens' Platform (PO), which was joined by a substantial number of UW members. The rump UW accordingly failed to retain any seats in the September 2001 lower house elections, winning only 3.1% of the vote,

although in simultaneous upper house elections it retained representation within the five-party Senate 2001 Bloc, which won 16 seats. Soon after the elections Geremek resigned as UW chairman and was replaced by Wladyslaw Frasyniuk.

The UW is a member of the European Democrat Union and an associate member of the European People's Party.

Law and Justice
Prawo i Sprawieliwosc (PiS)
Address. 47 ul. Zawojska, Warsaw 02927
Telephone. (+44–22) 642–8289
Fax. (+44–22) 642–6987
Leadership. Lech Kaczyński (chairman)
This centre-right formation was launched in April 2001 by Lech Kaczyński (a former Justice Minister) and his twin brother Jaroslaw Kaczyński, who had been close associates of Lech Walesa before and during the latter's presidency (1990–95). Declaring its opposition to the incumbent →Solidarity Electoral Action (AWS) government, the PiS effectively succeeded the Centre Alliance (*Porozumienie Centrum*, PC), which had been allied with the AWS in the 1997 parliamentary elections.

The PC had been founded in 1990 as an attempt to create a Polish version of the German →Christian Democratic Union, i.e. a broad-based Christian-oriented party of the centre-right. It had backed the presidential candidacy of Walesa and had subsequently became the core component of the Centre Citizens' Alliance (POC), which had won 44 *Sejm* seats (with 8.7% of the vote) in the October 1991 parliamentary elections, becoming the fourth largest grouping and providing the Prime Minister (Jan Olszewski) of the subsequent centre-right government. Following the collapse of the latter in June 1992, a PC congress had voted to expel Olszewski and other elements (later regrouped in the →Movement for the Reconstruction of Poland). After agreeing to join the seven-party government formed in July 1992 by Hanna Suchocka of the Democratic Union (later the →Freedom Union), the PC had unexpectedly withdrawn its support later in the year to become part of the "soft" opposition. Having narrowly failed to retain representation in the September 1993 elections (winning only 4.4% of the vote), the PC had supported Walesa's unsuccessful re-election bid in November 1995 before becoming part of the victorious AWS bloc in the 1997 elections.

Drawing support previously given to the AWS, the new PiS polled strongly in the September 2001 parliamentary elections on an anti-corruption platform, winning 47 lower house seats with 9.8% of the vote. In the simultaneous upper house elections the PiS was part of the five-party Senate 2001 Bloc, which won 16 seats.

The PC was an affiliate of the Christian Democrat International and of the International Democrat Union.

League of Polish Families
Liga Polskich Rodzin (LPR)
Address. c/o Zgromadzente Narodowe, Warsaw 00902
Leadership. Antoni Macierowicz
The radical Catholic LPR was formed in advance of the September 2001 parliamentary elections, on a platform of opposition to Polish membership of the European Union because of its liberal abortion laws. It also advocated close alliance with the USA to protect Poland from domination by either Germany or Russia. Attracting rural voters who had previously supported →Solidarity Electoral Action (AWS), the LPR entered the *Sejm* at its first attempt, winning 34 seats with 7.7% of the vote, and also securing two Senate seats.

Movement for the Reconstruction of Poland
Ruch Odrodzenia Polski (ROP)
Address. c/o Zgromadzente Narodowe, Warsaw 00902
Email. kprop@sejm.gov.pl
Website. www.rop-jo.com

Leadership. Jan Olszewski (chairman)

The ROP was launched by former Prime Minister Jan Olszewski on a strongly pro-market platform following his respectable fourth place (with 6.9% of the vote) in the first round of the November 1995 presidential elections. Then identified with the Centre Alliance (PC), Olszewski had become Prime Minister in the wake of the 1991 parliamentary elections, heading a centre-right coalition which had eventually fallen in June 1992 in acrimonious circumstances related to the government's proposal to publish lists of communist-era collaborators. Expelled from the PC, Olszewski had become leader of the more right-wing Movement for the Republic (RdR) but had been replaced in December 1993 following the general defeat of pro-market formations in the September 1993 parliamentary elections, although in April 1994 he had become honorary chairman of a deeply divided RdR.

The ROP won only six lower house seats (from 5.6% of the vote) and five Senate seats in the September 1997 parliamentary elections, thereafter becoming part of the ruling →Solidarity Electoral Action (AWS) bloc. In the September 2001 elections much of AWS/ROP support switched to new centre-right formations such as →Law and Justice (successor to the PC), so that the ROP shared in the AWS failure to retain any lower house seats. In the simultaneous upper house elections, however, the ROP retained representation within the five-party Senate 2001 Bloc, which won 16 seats.

Polish Peasant Party
Polskie Stronnictwo Ludowe (PSL)

Address. 4 ul. Grzybowska, Warsaw 00131
Telephone. (+48–22) 206020
Website. www.psl.org.pl
Leadership. Jaroslaw Kalinowski (chairman)

The PSL was founded in 1945 by Stanislaw Mikolajczyk after the leadership of the historic Peasant Party (founded in Galicia in 1895) had opted for close co-operation with the Communists. In November 1949, after Mikolajczyk had been ousted by leftist PSL members, the two groups merged as the United Peasant Party (ZSL), which became part of the Communist-dominated National Unity Front. The ZSL was thus committed to the goal of transforming Poland into a socialist society, although private peasant ownership of land was guaranteed by the Communist regime from 1956 and by constitutional guarantee from 1983. ZSL members were consistently included in the government and other state bodies under Communist rule. In 1987 the party backed a government programme for the democratization of political life and introduction of market mechanisms, while supporting the maintenance of the existing power structure.

In August 1989 a group of rural activists revived the PSL on the basis of its 1946 programme, becoming known as the Polish Peasant Party–Wilnanóv (PSL–W). The following month the ZSL was included in the new Solidarity-led coalition government and in November relaunched itself as the Reborn Polish Peasant Party (PSL–O). Six months later, in May 1990, the PSL–O, PSL–W and some members of Rural Solidarity held a unification congress to constitute the present PSL, which aimed to establish itself as the "third force" in Polish politics. In September 1990 the PSL withdrew its support from the Solidarity-led government. The then PSL leader, Roman Bartoszcze, received 7.2% of the vote in the first round of presidential elections in November 1990.

In June 1991 Bartoszcze was replaced as PSL leader by Waldemar Pawlak, who restored unity to the party and led it to a creditable 8.7% of the vote and 48 seats in the October 1991 *Sejm* elections, in which it headed a Programmatic Alliance list. Although it broadly supported the subsequent centre-right government, the PSL opposed its proposal to release secret police files to expose informers of the communist era. This issue brought down the government in June 1992, whereupon Pawlak was endorsed by the *Sejm* as the new Prime Minister, but was unable to form a government.

Benefiting from rural disenchantment with economic "shock therapy", the PSL polled strongly in the September 1993 parliamentary elections, becoming the second largest party with 132 seats in the *Sejm* on an overall vote share of 15.4% (and a historically high 46% of the peasant vote). It then opted to join a coalition government with →Democratic Left Alliance (SLD), which agreed that Pawlak should be Prime Minister in light of doubts about the SLD's political ancestry in the previous regime. The new coalition displayed tensions almost from the start, notably over government appointments, and in November 1994 the PSL deputy president was dismissed as chairman of the *Sejm*'s privatization committee on the grounds that he had tried to block or slow down the sell-off of state enterprises. It also came into protracted conflict with President Walesa and the latter's concepts of presidential government, the eventual result being Pawlak's resignation in February 1995 and the appointment of an SRP Prime Minister, although the SRP/SLD coalition was maintained. In the November 1995 presidential elections Pawlak received a modest 4.3% of the first-round vote.

The PSL's government participation came to an end at the September 1997 parliamentary elections, in which its vote share slumped to 7.3% and its *Sejm* representation to 27 seats. The following month Pawlak was replaced as party chairman by former Agriculture Minister Jaroslaw Kalinowski, a representative of the PSL's conservative Christian democratic wing which favoured tariff protection for Polish farmers. Over the next two years the PSL was weakened by the formation of at least two breakaway peasant parties, although in the October 2000 presidential election Kalinowski did better than his predecessor, winning 6% of the first-round vote.

The PSL further improved its position in the September 2001 parliamentary elections, winning 42 lower house seats on an 8.8% vote share, and also electing seven candidates to the Senate.

Self-Defence
Samoobrona

Address. c/o Zgromadzente Narodowe, Warsaw 00902
Leadership. Andrzej Lepper

The rural populist *Samoobrona* movement was launched in mid-2001 in opposition to Polish accession to the European Union, claiming that Poland's attempts to prepare for membership were already impoverishing Polish farmers. Its leader, Andrzej Lepper, had once been a farm labourer and had risen to public prominence by mounting a series of French-style road blockade protests which had resulted in violent clashes between farmers and police. Standing in the October 2000 presidential elections, Lepper had come fifth with 3.1% of the vote. In the September 2001 parliamentary elections the *Samoobrona* list achieved a remarkable 10% vote share, which made it the third strongest group in the *Sejm* with 53 seats. For good measure, it also won three Senate seats.

Solidarity Electoral Action
Akcja Wyborcza Solidarność (AWS)

Address. c/o Zgromadzente Narodowe, Warsaw 00902
Telephone. (+48–22) 694–1934
Fax. (+48–22) 694–1943
Website. www.aws.org.pl
Leadership. Jerzy Buzek (chairman)

The centre-right multi-party AWS is descended indirectly from the Solidarity independent trade union movement responsible for accelerating the demise of European communism in the 1980s under the leadership of Lech Walesa. Having been disowned by Walesa after his election as President in 1990, the Solidarity political wing had played a minor role in the early 1990s, failing to win *Sejm* representation in 1993. Following Walesa's narrow failure to secure re-election in 1995, a Solidarity congress in June 1996 resolved to form the AWS as a broad alliance to challenge the incumbent government dominated by the →Democratic Left Alliance (SLD). Chaired by Solidarity leader Marian Krzaklewski, the new grouping attracted some 35 existing formations to its banner, notably the Christian National Union (ZChN), the Centre Alliance (PC), the Conservative Peasant Party (SKL), the Christian Democratic Labour Party (ChDSP) and the Christian Democratic Party (PChD).

Attracting substantial rural support, the AWS led the polling in the September 1997 parliamentary elections, winning 201 of the 460 lower house seats with 33.8% of the vote, well ahead of the SLD. It therefore formed a coalition government with the liberal →Freedom Union (UW) under the premiership of Jerzy Buzek, while Krzaklewski became chairman of the AWS parliamentary group. At the end of 1997 about half of the AWS deputies formed the AWS Social Movement (AWS–RS), also under Krzaklewski's chairmanship, in a move to create a unitary party; the other half, however, preferred to remain affiliated to AWS component parties. In September 1998 Krzaklewski was re-elected leader of the Solidarity trade union at a congress which resolved that senior union and party posts could not be held by the same person. Accordingly, Krzaklewski was succeeded by Buzek as AWS–RS chairman in January 1999, although he remained chairman of the AWS parliamentary group.

Growing tensions in the coalition government culminated in the withdrawal of the UW in June 2000, leaving Buzek as head of a minority AWS government with eroding parliamentary and popular support. In the October 2000 presidential elections Krzaklewski came a poor third with only 15.6% of the vote, the SLD candidate being elected outright in the first round. In a bid to revive centre-right fortunes in advance of the forthcoming parliamentary elections, Buzek in January 2001, as chairman of the AWS–RS, took over the leadership of the overall AWS from Krzaklewski, who had been under further attack since his presidential election defeat. However, Buzek's efforts to create a more cohesive AWS bloc were rebuffed by the SKL (which in March 2001 withdrew from the AWS and aligned itself with the new →Citizens' Platform), while the PC component mostly joined the new →Law and Justice grouping. In May 2001, moreover, the Solidarity trade union federation formally withdrew from the AWS bloc.

In considerable disarray, what remained of the AWS

adopted the suffix "of the Right" for the September 2001 parliamentary elections, only to experience widely forecast decimation. The grouping obtained only 5.6% of the vote and so failed to win any lower house seats, while in the simultaneous upper house elections it retained slender representation only by forming part of the five-party Senate 2001 Bloc, which won 16 seats.

The AWS is an associate member of the European People's Party.

Union of Labour
Unia Pracy (UP)
Address. 4 ul. Nowogrodzka, Warsaw 00513
Telephone. (+48–22) 625–6776
Fax. (+48–22) 625–6776
Website. www.uniapracy.org.pl
Leadership. Marek Pol (chairman)
The social democratic UP was founded in June 1992 as a merger of two small parliamentary groupings of Solidarity provenance, namely Labour Solidarity (SP) and the Democratic Social Movement (RDS), plus elements of the divided Polish Socialist Party (PPS) and the Great Poland Social Democratic Union. Its first leader was Prof. Ryszard Bugaj, a former underground Solidarity leader who had previously been prominent in the Democratic Action Civil Movement (ROAD) – later part of the Democratic Union, which became the →Freedom Union – and had been an articulate critic of the economic "shock therapy" policies of the immediate post-communist period.

Despite the paucity of its resources, the UP achieved an impressive 7.3% of the vote in the September 1993 parliamentary elections, winning 41 *Sejm* seats and becoming the main left-wing opposition to the new government dominated by the →Democratic Left Alliance (SDL). It nevertheless suffered from a general swing to the right in the September 1997 parliamentary elections, slipping below the then applicable 5% barrier, and in 1998 lost several prominent members to the →Freedom Union and other parties. Under the new leadership of Marek Pol, the rump UP responded by opting for a left-wing course, presenting a joint list with the SDL in the September 2001 parliamentary elections and sharing in the list's success.

The UP is a full member of the Socialist International.

Portugal

Capital: Lisbon   **Population:** 10,200,000 (2000E)

Under Portugal's 1976 constitution as amended, legislative authority is vested in the unicameral Assembly of the Republic (*Assembléia da República*), currently consisting of 230 members elected for a four-year term (subject to dissolution) by universal adult suffrage of those aged 18 and over according to a system of proportional representation in multi-member constituencies. The head of state is the President, who is popularly elected for a five-year term (once renewable) by absolute majority, a failure to achieve which in a first round of voting requires the two leading candidates to contest a second round. The President appoints the Prime Minister, who selects his or her ministerial team, all subject to approval by the Assembly. There is also a Supreme Council of National Defence, a 13-member Constitutional Tribunal and an advisory Council of State chaired by the President. Portugal joined what became the European Union on Jan. 1, 1986, and elects 25 members of the European Parliament.

Portuguese political parties and parliamentary groups are eligible for annual subsidies from public funds, on the following basis: (i) a sum equivalent to 1/225th of the minimum national salary is payable on each vote obtained at the most recent Assembly elections; (ii) a sum equivalent to four times the minimum salary, plus one-third of the minimum national salary multiplied by the number of deputies in an Assembly group, is payable to defray deputies' secretarial costs.

Elections to the Assembly on Oct. 10, 1999, resulted as follows: Socialist Party (PS) 115 seats (with 44.1% of the vote), Social Democratic Party (PSD) 81 (32.3%), United Democratic Coalition (CDU) 17 (9.0%), Popular Party (PP) 15 (8.3%), Left Bloc (BE) 2 (2.4%). In a presidential election on Jan. 14, 2001, Jorge Sampaio (PS) was re-elected for a second five-year term with 55.8% of the vote.

Ecologist Party The Greens
Partido Ecologista Os Verdes (PEV)
Address. Calçada Salvador Correia de Sá 4–0° Dt, 1200 Lisbon
Telephone. (+351–21) 343–2763
Fax. (+351–21) 343–2764
Email. osverdes@mail.telepac.pt
Leadership. Maria Santos & Isabel Castro (spokespersons)
The left-leaning PEV joined the Communist-dominated →United Democratic Coalition (CDU) prior to the 1987 Assembly elections, obtaining representation in that and subsequent contests. In the October 1999 elections the PEV took two of the 17 Assembly seats won by the CDU. The party is affiliated to the European Federation of Green Parties.

Left Bloc
Bloco do Esquerda (BE)
Address. Rua de S. Bento 698–1°, 1250–223 Lisbon
Telephone. (+351–21) 388–5034
Fax. (+351–21) 388–5035
Email. udp@esoterica.pt
Website. www.bloco-do-esquerda.pt
Leadership. Luís Fazenda (president)
The BE was formed for the 1999 elections by three far-left parties, namely the Marxist–Leninist Popular Democratic Union (*União Democrática Popular*, UDP), the Trotskyist Revolutionary Socialist Party (*Partido Socialista Revolucionario*, PSR) and Politics XXI (*Politica XXI*). In the June 1999 European Parliament elections the alliance took 1.8% of the vote and no seats. Standing on a platform of opposition to the "anti-working class" policies of the incumbent →Socialist Party government, the alliance won 2.4% of the vote and two Assembly seats in the October 1999 national elections. In the January 2001 presidential election Fernando Rosas of the BE took 3% of the vote.

Popular Party
Partido Popular (PP)
Address. Largo Adelino Amaro da Costa 5, 1196 Lisbon
Telephone. (+351–21) 886–9730
Fax. (+351–21) 886–0454
Email. cds-pp@esoterica.pt
Website. www.partido-popular.pt
Leadership. Paulo Portas (president)
Advocating a social market economy, the conservative Christian democratic PP was established in 1974 as the Democratic Social Centre (*Centro Democrático Social*, CDS). It quickly began using the suffix "Popular Party" to distinguish itself from the main →Social Democratic Party (PSD), being formally known as the CDS–PP until opting for the shorter PP title in the 1990s.

The CDS was founded on the basis of an earlier Manifesto Association, (*Associação Programa*) by Prof. Diogo Freitas do Amaral, who had been a member of the Council of State under the quasi-fascist Salazarist regime overthrown in 1974. The CDS was attacked by left-wing groups in 1974–75. In the April 1975 constituent elections, in which it allied with the Christian Democrats, it won 16 of the 250 seats. In 1976 it became the largest party in the new Assembly, with 15.9% of the vote and 42 of the 263 seats. The CDS joined a government headed by the →Socialist Party (PS) in January–July 1978, but fought the 1979 and 1980 elections as part of the victorious Democratic Alliance, led by the PSD; Freitas do Amaral became Deputy Prime Minister in the ensuing coalition government.

The coalition ended in April 1983, and the CDS, standing alone, won only 12.4% and 30 seats in that month's Assembly elections; it then elected a new leader, Dr Francisco Antonio Lucas Pires. In 1985 the CDS declined further, to 9.8% and 22 seats. The leadership of the CDS passed in 1985 to a former Salazarist minister, Prof. Adriano Alves Moreira. Freitas do Amaral, endorsed by the CDS and PSD, narrowly lost the second round of the 1986 presiden-

tial elections to Mário Soares of the PS. The CDS continued to decline, securing only 4.4% and four seats in the 1987 Assembly elections, and Freitas do Amaral was re-elected leader at a congress in January 1988.

What was now known as the PP won only five Assembly seats in the 1991 elections (again with a 4.4% vote share), after which Freitas do Amaral finally resigned the party leadership and was succeeded by Manuel Monteiro. In the European Parliament elections of June 1994, the party regained support, winning three of Portugal's 25 seats on a 12.5% vote share. This European success did not moderate the party's deep reservations about Portuguese membership of the European Union, which struck something of a chord with voters in the October 1995 Assembly elections, when the PP advanced to 9.1% of the vote and 15 seats.

Internal divisions in the PP from September 1996 eventually resulted in Monteiro being succeeded as leader by Paulo Portas. After an attempted alliance with the PSD had collapsed in March 1999, the PP contested the June 1999 European elections on its own, slipping to 8.2% of the vote and two seats. The party also lost ground in the October 1999 Assembly elections, winning a vote share of 8.3% and 15 seats.

The PP is an affiliate of the International Democrat Union. Its two European Parliament members sit in the Europe of Nations group.

Portuguese Communist Party
Partido Comunista Português (PCP)
Address. Rua Soeiro Pereira Gomes 3, 1600 Lisbon
Telephone. (+351–21) 781–3800
Fax. (+351–21) 796–9126
Email. pcp.dep@mail.telepac.pt
Website. www.pcp.pt
Leadership. Carlos Carvalhas (secretary-general); Octávio Teixeira (parliamentary leader)
The PCP was founded in March 1921 by the pro-Bolshevik wing of the →Socialist Party (PS) and was banned from May 1926 until April 1974. Its leader from the 1940s was Alvaro Barreirinhas Cunhal, a charismatic Stalinist who was imprisoned throughout the 1950s and was then in exile until 1974. The PCP took part in interim governments between May 1974 and July 1976. In April 1975 it won 30 seats (out of 250) in constituent elections, with 12.5% of the vote; in April 1976 it won 40 seats in the Assembly, with 14.6%, but in June its presidential candidate took only 7.6%. From 1979 to 1986 the PCP was in an electoral front – the Popular Unity Alliance (APU) – with the small Portuguese Democratic Movement (MDP/CDE). The PCP itself won 44 seats in the Assembly in 1979, 39 in 1980 and 44 in 1983. In 1985 the APU won 15.4% and 38 seats, almost all for the PCP. In the 1986 presidential elections the PCP at first backed Dr Francisco Salgado Zenha, but in the second round it reluctantly endorsed Mário Soares of the PS.

In the 1987 elections the PCP formed a new front, the →United Democratic Coalition (CDU), along with a minority section of the MDP known as the Democratic Intervention (ID), some independent left-wingers and the →Ecologist Party The Greens (PEV). The CDU secured 31 seats with 12.1% of the vote, but the PCP-led parliamentary bloc rose from fourth to third place as a result of the eclipse of the Democratic Renewal Party (PRD); it also retained its three seats in Portugal's first direct elections to the European Parliament held simultaneously. In early 1988 the PCP experienced internal divisions as it prepared for a congress, some members calling for "democratization" and the Cunhal leadership insisting on maintaining rigid pro-Soviet orthodoxy.

In the event, the 12th PCP congress in December 1988 showed some awareness of developments in the Soviet Union by making a formal commitment to freedom of the press and multi-party politics, the CDU) being rewarded in the June 1989 European Parliament elections with four seats and 14.4% of the vote. Yet even as communism was collapsing all over Eastern Europe in 1989–90, the PCP majority maintained a hardline view of events, showing no sympathy with the popular aspirations to multi-party democracy. The electoral consequence was that the PCP-dominated CDU fell back to 17 seats (8.8% of the vote) in the 1991 elections and to 15 seats (8.6%) in October 1995. In between, the CDU slipped to three seats and an 11.2% vote share in the June 1994 European elections.

The June 1999 European elections brought a further reverse for the CDU, to 10.3% of the vote and two seats. In the October 1999 Assembly elections, however, the CDU reversed its long decline, winning 9.0% of the vote and 17 seats, of which the PCP took 15 and the PEV two. The PCP candidate in the January 2001 presidential election was António Simões de Abreu, who took 5.1% of the vote.

Social Democratic Party
Partido Social Democrata (PSD)

Address. Rua de São Caetano 9, 1296 Lisbon
Telephone. (+351–21) 395–2140
Fax. (+351–21) 397–6967
Email. psd@mail.telepac.pt
Website. www.psd.pt
Leadership. José Manuel Durão Barroso (leader); Artur Torres Pereira (secretary-general)

Centre-right rather than social democratic in orientation, the PSD was founded in May 1974 as the Popular Democratic Party (*Partido Popular Democrático*, PPD) and adopted the PSD label in 1976, when the Portuguese political scene created by the 1974 revolution was heavily tilted to the left. The party took part in five of the first six provisional governments established after the April 1974 revolution. It was in opposition in June-September 1975 and in 1976–79; it supported the election of Gen. Antonio Ramalho Eanes as President in 1976. It was the second largest party in the April 1975 constituent elections, with 27% of the vote, and in the April 1976 legislative elections, in which it took 24%.

Having supported the non-party government of November 1978-June 1979, the PSD fought the 1979 elections along with the Democratic Social Centre (CDS, later the →Popular Party, PP) as the Democratic Alliance, winning 79 seats for itself. The then PSD leader (and party co-founder), Dr Francisco Sa Carneiro, became Prime Minister and continued in office after fresh elections in October 1980, in which PSD representation increased to 82 seats. Sa Carneiro died in December 1980 at the age of 46 and was succeeded by Dr Francisco Pinto Balsemão, also a co-founder of the PSD, who brought the Popular Monarchist Party (PPM) into the coalition in September 1981. The PSD held 75 seats in the April 1983 elections, which it fought alone, and in June it joined the →Socialist Party (PS) in a new coalition government, with a new PSD leader, former Prime Minister (1978-79) Carlos Mota Pinto, as Deputy Prime Minister.

In October 1985 the PSD increased its vote share to 29.9% and won 88 seats – the largest bloc – in the Assembly, allowing it to form a minority government under Aníbal Cavaco Silva, who had been elected party leader in May 1985. He subsequently strengthened his control over the party and after the presidential elections of 1986, in which the PSD endorsed the losing CDS candidate, he opposed all suggestions of alliance with other parties. On April 3, 1987, his government lost a vote of confidence concerning the integration of Portugal into what became the European Union. In early elections in July 1987 the PSD greatly increased its vote, to 50.2% and 148 seats, giving it an absolute majority (the first in the Assembly since 1974). In simultaneous elections to the European Parliament, the nine PSD members appointed in January 1986 were replaced by 10 popularly-elected PSD members (from the total of 24 Portuguese representatives). In August 1987 Cavaco Silva was reappointed Prime Minister of an almost wholly PSD government.

The PSD retained governmental office in the October 1991 parliamentary elections, although with a slightly reduced majority of 135 of 230 seats on a 50.4% vote share. In the June 1994 European Parliament elections the party fell to 34.4%, taking only nine of the 25 Portuguese seats. This result and the PSD's negative opinion poll ratings impelled Cavaco Silva to resign from the party leadership in January 1995, although he remained Prime Minister until the October elections to prepare for a presidential challenge. Under the new leadership of Joaquim Fernando Nogueira, the PSD lost the October contest, although its retention of 88 seats on a 34% vote share was a better performance than many had predicted. Cavaco Silva's presidential ambitions were also thwarted by the swing of the political pendulum to the left. Standing as the PSD candidate in January 1996, he was defeated by the Socialist candidate in the first voting round, winning only 46.2% of the vote. The PSD's somewhat drastic response to these twin setbacks was to elect a new leader, namely Marcelo Rebelo de Sousa, a popular media pundit who had never held ministerial office.

Rebelo de Sousa lasted as PSD leader until March 1999, when the acrimonious collapse of plans for an alliance with the PP precipitated his resignation. He was succeeded by José Manuel Durão Barroso, under whom the PSD retained nine European Parliament seats in June 1999 (on a reduced vote share of 31.1%). In the October 1999 national elections the PSD slipped to 81 Assembly seats on a vote share of 32.3%. The PSD candidate in the January 2001 presidential election, Joaquim Martíns Ferreira do Amaral, was defeated by the Socialist incumbent with 34.5% of the vote.

The PSD is affiliated to the International Democrat Union and the Christian Democrat International. Its nine European Parliament representatives belong to the European People's Party/European Democrats group.

Socialist Party
Partido Socialista (PS)

Address. Largo do Rato 2, 1269–143 Lisbon
Telephone. (+351–21) 382–2021
Fax. (+351–21) 382–2023
Email. info@ps.pt
Website. www.ps.pt
Leadership. António Guterres (general secretary); Jorge Coelho (deputy general secretary); António Almeida Santos (president); Francisco Assis (parliamentary group chairman)

Originally founded in 1875, the early Portuguese Socialist Party was a member of the Second International and played a minor role in the first period of democratic government in Portugal (1910–26). Forced underground during the period of the fascistic "New State" (1928–74), Socialists were active in various democratic movements. In 1964 Dr Mario Alberto Nobre Lopes Soares and others formed Portuguese Socialist Action (*Accão Socialista Portuguesa*, ASP), which led to the revival of the Socialist Party (PS) among exiles in West Germany in April 1973.

Soares was repeatedly arrested and banished from Portugal, but the April 1974 revolution permitted his return and the PS took part in the coalition government formed in May 1974. In April 1975 the party won 116 of the 250 seats in a Constituent Assembly which drew up a constitution aspiring to a "transition to socialism", although in July-September the PS was excluded from the government, along with other parties except the →Portuguese Communist Party (PCP). In April 1976 the PS won 35% of the vote and 107 of the 263 seats in the new Assembly. In June it supported the successful presidential candidate, Gen. Antonio Ramalho Eanes, who in July appointed Soares as Prime Minister of a minority PS government including independents and military men. That was followed in January-July 1978 by a coalition, also led by Soares, of the PS and the Democratic Social Centre (CDS, later the Popular Party, PP). The PS subsequently supported a government of independents formed in October 1978.

The PS later suffered numerous defections, was decisively defeated in the 1979 Assembly elections, and went into opposition. In June 1980 it formed the Republican and Socialist Front *(Frente Republicana e Socialista,* FRS) electoral coalition with the (now defunct) Independent Social Democratic Action party (ASDI) and the Left Union for a Socialist Democracy (UEDS, formed in 1978 by Antonio Lopes Cardoso, a former PS Agriculture Minister). The FRS won 74 seats in the October 1980 Assembly elections. Reforms in 1981 (since reversed) increased the power of the PS general secretary, leading to dissent within the party. In the April 1983 elections the PS obtained 36.2% of the valid vote and 101 (out of 250) seats; it then formed a coalition government with the →Social Democratic Party (PSD). In 1985 that government lost a vote of confidence and in the ensuing elections the PS fell to 20.7% and 57 seats, being excluded from the minority government formed by the PSD. In February 1986, however, Soares was elected as the country's first civilian President in over 50 years, whereupon he resigned his PS posts. His 1986 opponents included two former PS ministers – Maria de Lourdes Pintasilgo, backed by the Popular Democratic Union (UDP) and Dr Francisco Salgado Zenha, backed by the PCP.

The sixth PS congress in June 1986 elected Manuel Vitor Ribeiro Constâncio (a former Finance Minister and central bank governor, regarded as a pragmatic left-winger) as party leader. It also significantly moderated the party's programme and altered its structure. A minority faction developed around Dr Jaime Gama, a former Foreign Minister close to Soares, but he was later reconciled with the leadership, whereafter the *Soaristas* (who wanted more active opposition to the PSD, including co-operation with the Communists) were led by the President's son, João Soares. Elections in July 1987 gave the PS 22.3% of the vote and 60 seats, so that it remained the leading opposition party; it also held its six European Parliament seats, which were subject to direct election for the first time. The October 1991 parliamentary elections resulted in the PS advancing to 72 seats (on a 30% vote share), but the party remained in opposition, with its leadership passing in February 1992 from Jorge Sampaio to António Gutteres, a young technocrat with a non-ideological approach to politics. The party achieved an all-time high national vote in the December 1993 local elections and again outpolled the ruling PSD in the June 1994 European Parliament elections, in which its vote share was 34.9% and its seat tally 10 of the 25 allocated to Portugal.

In the October 1995 Assembly elections Gutteres led the PS back to governmental office, albeit in a narrow minority position in terms of strict parliamentary arithmetic, its seat tally being 112 out of 230 (on a 43.9% vote share). The new minority PS government, which was expected to obtain the external support of the →United Democratic Coalition on most key issues, announced a programme of accelerated privatization of state enterprises, combined with introduction of a guaranteed minimum wage, social and educational improvements and regional devolution for mainland Portugal. In January 1996 Socialist political authority was consolidated when PS presidential candidate Sampaio (who had become mayor of Lisbon) was elected to the top state post with a commanding 53.8% of the first-round vote.

The PS polled strongly in local elections in December 1997 and also in the June 1999 European Parliament elections, in which it advanced to 43.1% of the national vote and 12 seats. In the October 1999 national elections the PS retained power, winning exactly half of the 230 Assembly seats with a 44.1% vote share. In January 2001 Sampaio was re-elected for a second presidential term with 55.8% of the vote.

The PS is a member of the Socialist International, of which Guterres became president in 1999. Its representatives in the European Parliament sit in the Party of European Socialists group. The party has a membership of 126,000.

United Democratic Coalition
Coligação Democrático Unitária (CDU)
Address. Rua Soeiro Pereira Gomes 3, 1600–196 Lisbon
Telephone. (+351–21) 793–6272
Fax. (+351–21) 796–9126
Leadership. Vested in the leaderships of component parties

The CDU is the electoral front organization of the →Portuguese Communist Party (PCP), effectively dating from prior to the 1979 Assembly elections, in which the PCP presented a joint list with the Portuguese Democratic Movement (MDP) called the United People's Alliance (APU). The APU won 47 seats in 1979, before falling to 41 in 1980 and to 38 in 1985, its constituent formations having campaigned separately in 1983. In the 1986 presidential election the APU backed the independent candidacy of former Prime Minister Maria de Lourdes Pintasilgo in the first round, switching with reluctance in the second to Mario Soares of the →Socialist Party (PS). Following the MDP's withdrawal in November 1986, the pro-Soviet PCP converted the APU into the CDU, which also included a group of MDP dissidents, the →Ecologist Party The Greens (PEV) and a number of independent leftists.

The new CDU won 31 Assembly seats in 1987, seven less than the APU in 1985. In the October 1991 elections, with the Soviet Union in its death throes, CDU representation was further reduced to 17 seats (from 8.8% of the vote). In the June 1994 European Parliament elections the CDU list (in which the PEV was prominent) improved to 11.2% and won three of Portugal's 25 seats. In the October 1995 Assembly elections the CDU slipped further to 15 seats (from 8.6% of the vote), thereafter offering qualified parliamentary backing to the new PS minority government. Having lost one of its three seats in the June 1999 European elections (with a vote share of 10.3%), the CDU improved to 9.0% in the October 1999 Assembly elections, winning 17 seats (15 for the PCP and two for the PEV).

The two CDU representatives in the European Parliament sit in the European United Left/Nordic Green Left group.

Other Parties

Communist Party of Portuguese Workers (*Partido Comunista dos Trabalhadores Portugueses, PCTP*), a Maoist faction which won 0.9% vote share in the June 1999 European Parliament elections. Its leader obtained 1.6% in the January 2001 presidential election, standing as the candidate of the PCTB and the Portuguese Proletarian Revolutionary Movement (MRPP).
Leadership. António Garcia Pereira

National Solidarity Party (*Partido Solidariedade Nacional, PSN*), pensioners' party founded in 1990, won one Assembly seat on 1991, but none in 1995 or 1999; obtained 0.3% in the June 1999 European Parliament elections.
Leadership. Manuel Sergio

Popular Monarchist Party (*Partido Popular Monárquico, PPM*), pro-market monarchist formation, won six Assembly seats in 1980, but none in subsequent elections; took 0.5% in the June 1999 European Parliament elections.
Leadership. Gonçalo Ribeiro Telles & Augusto Ferreira do Amaral

Workers' Party of Socialist Unity (*Partido Operário de Unidade Socialista, POUS*), Trotskyist cell formed in 1979 by →Socialist Party dissidents; won 0.2% in June 1999 European Parliament elections.

Qatar

Capital: Doha   **Population**: 745,000 (2000E)

The state of Qatar has a Council of Ministers appointed and presided over by the head of state (the Amir) and assisted by an appointed 35-member Advisory Council. There is no parliament and there are no political parties. A committee was appointed in June 1999 by the Amir to draw up a new constitution with provision for a national elected legislature.

Romania

Capital: Bucharest   **Population:** 23,000,000 (2000E)

The communist-ruled People's Socialist Republic of Romania became simply Romania in December 1989 on the violent overthrow of the Ceauşescu regime. A new constitution approved by referendum in December 1991 provided for a strong presidency, political pluralism, human rights guarantees and a commitment to the market economy. Under a law passed in early 1990 Romania opted for the French system of executive-legislative separation by barring members of parliament from holding ministerial posts and by according substantial powers to the President, who is directly elected for a four-year term in two rounds of voting (if required) and who appoints the Prime Minister and other ministers subject to approval by the legislature. The latter is bicameral, consisting of the 140-member Senate (*Senat*) and the 346-member Chamber of Deputies (*Cameră Deputatilor*), both elected for a four-year term by proportional representation on the basis of party lists, subject to a minimum of 5% of the national vote being obtained by individual parties, 8% by two-party alliances, 9% by those of three parties and 10% by those of four or more. The threshold requirement presents no barrier to parties representing Romania's ethnic Hungarians winning national representation, since they are the largest national minority in any European country (making up about 9% of the population). For other minorities, 19 Chamber seats were allocated in the 2000 elections.

Under the 1996 Political Parties Law, state subsidies are available to parties to a maximum amount of 0.04% of budgeted government revenue. A third of the total sum is distributed as an equal basic subvention to each party group in the Chamber and Senate, the remaining two-thirds being distributed as an additional subvention to all represented parties in proportion to seats held, up to a maximum of five times the basic subvention. Unrepresented parties which obtained at least 2% of the total vote in the most recent elections also receive subsidies, which are calculated by dividing equally between them the unused part of the additional subvention to parliamentary parties up to a maximum of one basic subvention for each unrepresented party. Under the 2001 budget, the total sum available in subsidies to parties was 58 billion lei (about US$2 million).

Electoral contests since 1992 have produced successive major swings of the political pendulum. A government of the post-communist left was replaced in November 1996 by one of the centre-right headed by the Christian Democratic National Peasants' Party (PNTCD), which was in turn heavily defeated by the left in parliamentary and presidential elections in late 2000. Elections to the Chamber of Deputies on Nov. 26, 2000, resulted in the Social Democratic Pole – an alliance of the Social Democracy Party of Romania (PDSR), the Romanian Social Democratic Party (PSDR) and the Humanist Party of Romania (PUR) – winning 155 seats (with 36.6% of the vote), the Greater Romania Party (PRM) 84 (19.5%), the Democratic Party (PD) 31 (7.0%), the National Liberal Party (PLN) 30 (6.9%) and the Hungarian Democratic Union of Romania (UDMR) 27 (6.8%), with the remaining 19 seats being allocated to 19 ethnic minority parties. In simultaneous Senate elections the Pole parties won 65 seats, the PRM 37, the PD 13, the PLN 13 and the UDMR 12.

In presidential elections on Nov. 26 and Dec. 10, 2000, Ion Iliescu of the PDSR (who had previously been President in 1990-96) won in the second round with 66.8% of the vote, defeating Corneliu Vadim Tudor of the populist PRM. In June 2001 the PDSR formally merged with the PSDR under the title Social Democratic Party (PSD).

Christian Democratic National Peasants' Party
Partidul National Tărănesc Cretin Democrat (PNTCD)
Address. 34 bd. Carol I, sector 2, Bucharest 70334
Telephone. (+40–1) 312–0603
Fax. (+40–1) 312–3436
Email. contact@pntcd.ro
Website. www.pntcd.ro
Leadership. Victor Ciorbea (chairman); Ion Diaconescu

(honorary chairman); Constantin Dudu Ionescu (secretary-general)
The PNTCD is descended from the National Peasants' Party (PNT) founded in 1869, which was of political importance in the inter-war period and was banned by the Communists in 1947. Revived in December 1989 under veteran leader Ion Puiu, the party refused to co-operate with the post-communist National Salvation Front (FSN) because of the large

number of former Communists within FSN ranks. Prior to the May 1990 elections the bulk of the "historic" PNT opted to merge with a younger group of Christian democratic orientation under the chairmanship of Corneliu Coposu, another veteran peasant leader who had served 17 years in prison under the Communist regime before becoming Prime Minister in its final phase. The result of the merger was the present PNTCD, which favours a market economy and the recovery of Romanian-populated territories lost during World War II.

Having won 12 Chamber seats in 1990, the PNTCD, as a leading component of the centre-right Democratic Convention of Romania (CDR), advanced to 42 seats in September 1992, when it also won 21 Senate seats. Coposu died in November 1995 and was succeeded by Ion Diaconescu, who led the PNTCD and the CDR to a relative majority in the November 1996 elections, in which the CDR candidate, Emil Constantinescu, was elected President with 54.4% of the second-round vote and the PNTCD won 88 of the CDR's 122 Chamber seats. Victor Ciorbea of the PNTCD became Prime Minister of a centre-right coalition, which included the →Democratic Party (PD), the →National Liberal Party (PNL) and the →Hungarian Democratic Union of Romania (UDMR), but inter-party feuding resulted in his replacement by Radu Vasile of the PNTCD in March 1998.

Ciorbea reacted to losing the premiership by founding the breakaway Christian Democratic National Alliance (ANCD) in April 1999, as the PNTCD-led government descended into disarray amidst accelerating economic and social deterioration. In August 2000 the PNTCD and four other parties re-launched the CDR, but in the November elections the so-called "CDR 2000" and its allies failed to surmount the threshold for representation. The PNTCD's presidential candidate, Constantin Mugur Isărescu, came a poor fourth with only 9.5% of the first-round vote.

In January 2001 Diaconescu was replaced as PNTCD chairman by former Education Minister Andrei Marga, who quickly succeeded in bringing Ciorbea's ANCD (also now without parliamentary representation) back into the party. However, the election of Ciorbea as chairman of the PNTCD national committee in June 2001 prompted Marga to resign as party chairman the following month, complaining that he had been thwarted in his attempts to bring corrupt former PNTCD ministers to book. In August 2001 Ciorbea was elected PNTCD chairman by an extraordinary party congress, whereupon a dissident faction of supporters of Marga and former deputy chairman Vasile Lupu held a rival congress which elected Lupu as chairman and decided that a new Party of Christian Democracy would be established before the end of 2001.

The PNTCD is a member of the Christian Democrat International and an associate member of the European People's Party, as well as an affiliate of the European Democrat Union.

Democratic Party
Partidul Democrat (PD)
Address. 1 allea Modrogan, sector 1, 71274 Bucharest
Telephone. (+40–1) 230–1332
Fax. (+40–1) 230–1332
Email. office@pd.ro
Website. www.pd.ro
Leadership. Traian Basescu (chairman); Alexandru Sassu (Chamber group leader); Marian Viorel Pana (Senate group leader); Mihai Stanisoara (executive secretary)
The PD derives from the National Salvation Front (FSN) which took power on the overthrow of the Ceauşescu regime in December 1989, most of its leaders having previously been members of the *nomenklatura*. Having taken on a party identity in February 1990, the FSN had a landslide victory in the May elections, winning 66.3% of the vote and 263 Chamber seats, while FSN leader Ion Iliescu was elected President with 85.1% of the vote. Iliescu there-

upon vacated the FSN leadership (in compliance with a law barring the head of state from serving as the leader of a political party) and the Front became divided between those favouring rapid economic reform to create a market economy and those supporting the President's more cautious approach. In March 1991 the first FSN national conference, against the advice of the Iliescu faction, approved a radical free-market reform programme presented by then Prime Minister Petre Roman. The latter vacated the premiership in October 1991 and was re-elected FSN leader in March 1992, whereupon the Iliescu faction broke away to form the Democratic National Salvation Front (which later became the Social Democracy Party of Romania, which in turn became the →Social Democratic Party).

The FSN candidate, Caius Dragomir, came a poor fourth in the autumn 1992 presidential election, winning only 4.8% of the first-round vote. The party fared better in the concurrent parliamentary elections, winning 43 Chamber and 18 Senate seats on a vote share of over 10%. The following year it adopted the prefix "Democratic Party", and eventually dropped the FSN suffix. The PD contested the November 1996 elections within the Social Democratic Union (USD) alliance with the Romanian Social Democratic Party (PSDR), Roman coming third in the presidential poll with 20.5% of the vote and the PD again winning 43 Chamber seats its own right. The PD joined the subsequent coalition government headed by the centre-right →Christian Democratic National Peasants' Party (PNTCD), left it in February 1998 and rejoined it two month later when a new Prime Minister was appointed. But it continued to have strained relations with the other coalition parties during the remainder of the government's term.

Having lost its previous alliance with the Social Democrats, the PD contested the November-December 2000 elections on its own and was damaged by its membership of a deeply unpopular outgoing government. Roman sank to sixth place and less than 3% of the vote in the first round of the presidential contest, whereupon the PD backed Iliescu in his second-round victory over the leader of the far-right →Greater Romania Party. In the parliamentary elections the PD was reduced to 31 Chamber seats and 7% of the vote and to 13 Senate seats. It thereafter gave qualified external support to a minority government headed by what became the →Social Democratic Party.

A post-election internal power struggle culminated in Roman being ousted from the PD chairmanship by an extraordinary party convention in May 2001 and replaced by the popular mayor of Bucharest, Traian Basescu, who declared his intention to restore the party's social democratic image. A declaration adopted by the convention stated that the party favoured "a market economy but not a market society". Roman showed his displeasure by resigning as PD leader in the Senate, while some of his supporters left the PD parliamentary caucus. The PD leadership responded by negotiating the absorption of the small National Alliance Party led by Virgil Măgureanu, following the latter's separation from the →Romanian National Unity Party (PUNR). Magureanu expressed confidence that the PD would assimilate the PD's nationalist doctrines.

The PD was admitted to membership of the Socialist International in November 1999.

Greater Romania Party
Partidul România Mare (PRM)
Address. 39A calea Victoriei, 70101 Bucharest
Telephone. (+40–1) 613–9796
Fax. (+40–1) 615–0229
Email. prm@romare.ro
Website. www.romare.ro
Leadership. Corneliu Vadim Tudor (chairman); Augustin Lucian Bolcas (Chamber group leader); Gheorghe Funar (executive secretary)
Registered in June 1991, the PRM is the political wing of the extreme nationalist Greater Romania movement, which

advocates strong government in pursuit of Romanian nationalist interests, the recovery of Romanian-populated territories lost during World War II and recognition of wartime pro-fascist dictator Marshal Ion Antonescu as a great leader. Often accused of antisemitism, the party also sees merit in the "patriotic achievements" of the Ceauşescu regime.

The PRM won 16 Chamber and six Senate seats in the 1992 elections (on a vote share of 3.9%) and became one of the so-called "Pentagon" parties giving external support to the government of the Social Democracy Party of Romania (PDSR). In 1995 party leader Corneliu Vadim Tudor repeatedly urged the government to ban the →Hungarian Democratic Union of Romania (UDMR), which he accused of planning a Yugoslavia-style dismemberment of Romania. This and other differences resulted in the PRM withdrawing its support from the government in October 1995, with a political eye to the elections due a year later.

Tudor encountered problems in April 1996 when the Senate voted to withdraw his parliamentary immunity, thus exposing him to a range of legal actions, including some related to his extremist political views. Also in April 1996, a PRM congress endorsed a programme of action for the party in government, its proposed measures including the banning of the UDMR and restrictions on foreign investment in Romania. In September 1996 the PRM absorbed the small Romanian Party for a New Society (PRNS) led by Gen. Victor Voichita. In the November 1996 elections Tudor came fifth in the presidential polling with 4.7% of the vote and the party won 19 Chamber seats with 4.5%. In late 1998 the PRM was strengthened when it was joined by Gheorghe Funar, former leader of the →Romanian National Unity Party (PUNR), while in mid-1999 it absorbed the Democratic Forces Party (PFD) led by Dorin Lazar Maior.

In the November–December 2000 elections the PRM drew substantial benefit from the deep unpopularity of the centre-right government headed by the →Christian Democratic National Peasants' Party (PNTCD). Tudor came second in the first round of the presidential contest with 28.3% of the vote and therefore went forward to second round, in which he obtained 33.2% against the victorious Ion Iliescu of what became the →Social Democratic Party (PSD). In the parliamentary contest the PRM became the second largest party with 84 of the 346 Chamber seats on a vote share of 19.5%.

In 2001 the PRM mounted vigorous opposition to a bill granting certain language rights to ethnic Hungarians and other minorities and renewed its campaign to get the UDMR outlawed because of its alleged treachery. It also accused the PSD government of not properly opposing new Hungarian legislation according special status to Hungarian minorities in neighbouring countries such as Romania. In May 2001 the PRM was boosted by the release by the authorities in the breakaway republic of Transdnestria (Moldova) of Ilie Ilascu, a "greater Romania" activist who had been elected to the Senate on the PRM ticket while still in prison in Tiraspol.

Humanist Party of Romania
Partidul Umanist din România (PUR)
Address. 118 calea Victoriei, etaj 5, Bucharest
Telephone. (+40–1) 212–5302
Fax. (+40–1) 212–5301
Email. pur@itcnet.ro
Website. www.pur.ro
Leadership. Dan Voiculescu (chairman); Ioan Pop de Popa (first vice-president); Dorel Bahrin (secretary-general)
The PUR was founded in December 1991 as a social liberal formation aiming to build post-communist democracy and civil society. It obtained strong local representation in municipal elections in June 1996 but failed to win seats in the national parliamentary elections in November 1996. For the November 2000 elections the PUR joined the left-wing Social Democratic Pole, mainly consisting of what later

become the →Social Democratic Party, and participated in the Pole's victory by winning six Chamber seats and four in the Senate. The party therefore became a component of the resultant minority government.

Hungarian Democratic Union of Romania
Uniunea Democrată Maghiară din România (UDMR)
Romániai Magyar Demokraták Szövetsége (RMDSz)
Address. 8 str. Avram Iancu, sector 2, Bucharest
Telephone. (+40–1) 314–6849
Fax. (+40–1) 314–4356
Email. elhivbuk@rmdsz.rdsnet.ro
Website. www.rmdsz.ro
Leadership. Béla Markó (chairman); Csaba Takács (executive chairman); Bishop László Tökes (honorary chairman); Atilla Kelemen (Chamber group leader); Károly Szabó (Senate group leader)
The principal political vehicle of Romania's ethnic Hungarian minority, the UDMR was registered in January 1990 with the aim of furthering ethnic Hungarian rights within the framework of a democratic Romania. It took 7.2% of the vote in the May 1990 parliamentary elections, winning 29 Chamber and 12 Senate seats, so that it became the largest single opposition formation. Despite being affiliated to the centre-right Democratic Convention of Romania (CDR), the UDMR contested the September 1992 elections separately, winning 7.5% of the vote and 27 Chamber seats, while again returning 12 senators.

Following the resignation of Géza Domokos as UDMR chairman, the moderate Béla Markó was elected as his successor at a party congress in January 1993, after the more radical Bishop László Tökes (hero of anti-Ceauşescu protest actions in Timisoara, Northern Transylvania, in the late 1980s) had withdrawn his candidacy and accepted appointment as honorary chairman. The same congress called on the government to assist with the preservation of Hungarian language and culture, while calling for self-administration of majority Hungarian districts rather than full autonomy (as urged by some radicals). In mid-1995 the UDMR was rebuffed in its efforts to re-establish political co-operation with the CDR parties, whose spokesmen contended that the UDMR had become a party of extreme nationalism.

In 1996 the UDMR came under increasingly fierce attack from the extreme nationalist →Greater Romania Party (PRM), which called openly for the UDMR to be banned. For the November 1996 presidential election the UDMR candidate was Senator György Frunda, who came fourth with 6% of the first-round vote, while in the simultaneous Chamber elections the UDMR slipped to 25 seats with 6.6% of the vote. It then opted to join a coalition government headed by the CDR.

Despite frequent strains with CDR parties over Hungarian language rights, the UDMR's government participation survived until the November–December 2000 elections, in which Frunda came fifth in the presidential contest with 6.2% of the vote, while in the parliamentary contest the UDMR improved slightly to 27 seats, again with 6.8%. It thereafter gave qualified external support to a minority government of what became the →Social Democratic Party (PSD) on the understanding that legislation would be enacted granting more language rights to ethnic Hungarians. In 2001 the UDMR came under renewed attack from the PRM, this time for supporting Hungary's new legislation giving special status to ethnic Hungarians abroad, while also experiencing internal dissent over its backing for the PSD government.

The UDMR is a member of the European Democrat Union and the Christian Democrat International and an associate member of the European People's Party.

National Liberal Party
Partidul National Liberal (PNL)
Address. 86 bd. Aviatorilor, sector 1, 71299 Bucharest
Telephone. (+40–1) 231–0795

Fax. (+40–1) 231–0796
Email. compas@pro.ro
Website. www.pnl.ro
Leadership. Valeriu Stoica (chairman); Mihai Voicu (secretary-general)

Dating from 1848 and founded as a party in 1875, the centre-right PNL suspended operations in 1947, so as not to expose members to Communist persecution, and was revived in January 1990. The party took third place in the May 1990 elections, winning 29 Chamber seats on a 6.4% vote share and 10 Senate seats, but was weakened by internal divisions that produced the breakaway Liberal Union. The PNL was a founding member of the Democratic Convention of Romania (CDR) but withdrew in April 1992 because of policy differences, although two PNL splinter groups refused to endorse the action and remained within the CDR.

A PNL congress in February 1993 approved a merger with the New Liberal Party and elected Mircea Ionescu-Quintus as chairman. The latter decision was contested by the previous leader, Radu Câmpeanu, who had been the PNL candidate in the 1990 presidential elections. Câmpeanu was reinstated by a Bucharest court in early 1994, but Ionescu-Quintus showed that he had majority support among party members. Merger with the New Liberals was finalized in May 1995, when the PNL also absorbed a faction of the Civic Alliance Party. It thus regained parliamentary representation of about a dozen deputies, who were technically classified as independents.

A feature of the PNL programme is its call for the restoration to the Romanian throne of the exiled King Michael, who had been deposed by the Communists in 1947. In 1992 the former monarch declined nomination as the PNL presidential candidate, having briefly visited Romania in April that year (but later being twice barred from entry). Complications ensued for Michael's claim to the throne when a Romanian court ruled in October 1995 that the first son of his father, the pre-war Carol II, was the rightful heir despite having been the product of a morganatic marriage.

The PNL rejoined the CDR for the November 1996 elections, backing the successful presidential candidacy of Emil Constantinescu (CDR) and winning 25 Chamber seats under the CDR banner. The party became a component of the resultant CDR-led coalition government and was strengthened in February 1998 by absorbing the Civic Alliance Party (PAC). Nevertheless, frequent strains between the PNL and other CDR components were accompanied by internal divisions and defections, notably over the choice of a presidential candidate for 2000. In the event, the PNL contested the November–December 2000 elections outside the CDR and therefore escaped the obliteration suffered by the latter. The party's presidential candidate, Theodor Dumitru Stolojan, came third in the first round with 11.8% of the vote, while in the parliamentary elections the PNL advanced to 30 Chamber seats on a vote share of 6.9% and also won 13 Senate seats. A breakaway PNL list headed by former leader Radu Câmpeanu took only 1.4% of the vote.

In December 2000 the PNL agreed to give qualified external support to a minority government of what became the →Social Democratic Party (PSD). Opposition to this arrangement was strongly expressed at a PNL congress in February 2001, which elected former Deputy Premier and Justice Minister Valeriu Stoica as party chairman in succession to Ionescu-Quintus. In May 2001 Stoica announced the abrogation of the agreement with the PSD, claiming that the government had failed to bring forward economic and political reforms. In September 2001 the PNL announced that in mid-2002 it would merge with the →Alliance for Romania (ApR) under a title yet to be decided.

The PLN is a member of the Liberal International.

Romanian National Unity Party
Partidul Unitaii Nationale Române (PUNR)

Address. 1/B Str. Negustori, 70481 Bucharest
Telephone. (+40–1) 613–5375

Fax. (+40–1) 311–2428
Leadership. Valeriu Tabără (chairman)

The right-wing PUNR was founded in March 1990 as the political arm of the nationalist Romanian Hearth (*Vátra Româneasca*) movement, which aspires to the recovery of the "greater Romania" borders of the inter-war period and is strongly opposed to any special recognition of the rights of Romania's ethnic Hungarian minority. The party was fifth-placed in the September 1992 parliamentary elections, winning 30 Chamber and 14 Senate seats on a vote share of some 8%. In August 1994 it opted to join the government coalition headed by the Social Democracy Party of Romania (PDSR). In mid-1995 serious coalition tensions arose when the PUNR demanded the foreign affairs portfolio and asserted that too many concessions were being made by Romania in its quest for better relations with Hungary. However, after the PDSR had threatened either to continue as a minority government or to bring about an early election, the PUNR moderated its position and remained in the ruling coalition.

Underlying differences remained, however, and were sharpened in October 1995 by the decisions of the Socialist Party of Labour and the →Greater Romania Party (PRM) to withdraw external support from the government. The dismissal of the PUNR Communications Minister in January 1996 caused a new crisis, in which the PUNR in March announced that it was definitely leaving the government. It was again persuaded to change its mind, although by then it had become an opposition party in all but ministerial status. An important factor at play was the party's desire to establish an independent image for the elections scheduled for November 1996 and in particular not to be outflanked on the nationalist right by the PRM.

In the latter context, the PUNR's then leader and presidential candidate, Gheorghe Funar, became a vocal critic of a draft treaty with Hungary tabled by the government in mid-1996, contending that its provisions on the rights of Romania's Hungarian minority amounted to a "national betrayal". One such outburst in early September 1996, in which he made a fierce personal attack on the President, finally brought matters to a head, the PUNR being ejected from the government by the Prime Minister (although one of the four PUNR ministers preferred to leave the party rather than give up his ministerial office). The party derived no benefit in the November 1996 elections, being out-polled by the PRM in both the presidential contest, in which Funar came sixth with only 3.2%, and in the parliamentary polls, in which the PUNR slumped to 18 Chamber and seven Senate seats.

A period of intense internal feuding ensued, in which Funar was ousted as chairman in February 1997 (and later expelled from the party) and replaced by Valeriu Tabără. In early 1998 Funar's supporters mustered a majority in the party's national council and restored him to the leadership, but the courts ruled that Tabără remained chairman. Funar then attempted to launch his own party, but failed to secure official registration, whereupon he threw in his lot with the PRM.

For the November 2000 parliamentary elections the rump PUNR joined with the Romanian National Party (PNR) to form the National Alliance Party (PAN), but the PAN list secured only 1.4% of the vote and no seats. This failure provoked further feuding which culminated in the PUNR re-establishing itself as an independent party in June 2001 and the rump PAN opting for an unlikely merger with the centre-left →Democratic Party.

Social Democratic Party
Partidul Social Democrat (PSD)

Address. 10 str. Kiseleff, 71271 Bucharest
Telephone. (+40–1) 222–2952
Fax. (+40–1) 222–2879
Email. psd@psd.ro
Website. www.psd.ro

Leadership. Adrian Nastase (chairman); Alexandru Athanasiu (chairman of national council)

The PSD was created in June 2001 as a merger of the Social Democracy Party of Romania (PDSR) and the smaller Romanian Social Democratic Party (PSDR), which had won a relative majority in the 2000 elections in the Social Democratic Pole alliance and taken office as a minority government.

The PDSR had been launched in 1993 as a merger of the Democratic National Salvation Front (FSND), the Romanian Socialist Democratic Party and the Republican Party, to provide a political base for President Ion Iliescu, a former senior communist-era apparatchik. The FSND had come into being in March 1992, when a group of pro-Iliescu deputies of the National Salvation Front (FSN) opposed to rapid economic reform had withdrawn from the parent party. The FSND had then won a relative majority of seats in both houses of parliament in the September 1992 elections and had backed Iliescu's successful re-election bid in the concurrent presidential contest. The new PDSR had defined itself as a social democratic, popular and national party supporting transition to a market economy on the basis of social responsibility.

The PSDR was descended from the historic party of that name founded in 1893, which had been forced to merge with the Communist Party in 1948 and had thereafter been maintained in exile. Revived in Romania after the overthrow of the Ceauşescu regime, the party had won only one Chamber seat in the May 1990 elections, improving to 10 in 1992 as a component of the mainly centre-right Democratic Convention of Romania (CDR).

Having formed a minority government as a result of the 1992 elections, the PDSR had in August 1994 entered into a coalition with the right-wing Romanian National Unity Party (PUNR), with external support from the even more nationalist →Greater Romania Party (PRM) and from the neo-communist Socialist Party of Labour (PSM). By mid-1995, however, serious differences had developed between the government parties, with the result that the PRM and the PSM had withdrawn their support in late 1995, while the PUNR had been ejected from the government in September 1996. Meanwhile, the PSDR had left the CDR in January 1996, instead joining an alliance with the →Democratic Party (PD), itself deriving from the anti-Iliescu rump of the original FSN. In the November 1996 elections Iliescu had failed to secure re-election as President, being defeated in the second round by 54.4% to 45.9% by CDR candidate Emil Constantinescu, while in the parliamentary contest the PDSR had won only 91 Chamber seats with 21.5% of the vote. It had therefore done into opposition to a CDR-led coalition that included the PSDR, whose Chamber representation had remained at 10 seats.

The PSDR withdrew from the government in September 2000, abandoning its alliance with the PD to form the Social Democratic Pole with the PDSR and the →Humanist Party of Romania (PUR). In the November-December 2000 elections, Iliescu regained the presidency as the Pole candidate, winning 66.8% of the second-round vote against a challenge by the PRM leader, while in the parliamentary contest the Pole parties won a total of 155 of the 346 Chamber seats (and 36.6% of the vote), of which the PDSR obtained 142, the PSDR a disappointing seven and the PUR four. The Pole parties therefore formed a minority government under the premiership of Adrian Nastase, which obtained qualified pledges of support from the PD, the →National Liberal Party (PLN) and the →Hungarian Democratic Union of Romania.

In January 2001 Nastase was elected chairman of the PDSR in succession to Iliescu (who was disqualified from party affiliation during his presidential term). The party then embarked upon negotiations for a formal merger with the PSDR, which came to fruition in June 2001, with Nastase being elected chairman of the unified PSD and former PSDR leader Alexandru Athanasiu becoming chairman of the PSD national council. Meanwhile, the PLN had withdrawn its support for the minority government.

The unified PSD did not automatically inherit the PSDR's membership of the Socialist International (SI), which had refused to admit the PDSR because of doubts about its democratic credentials. Instead, the SI gave the PSD the status of "permanent guest" pending further evaluation of its suitability for membership.

Ethnic Minority Parties

The 19 formations listed below were each allocated one Chamber seat in the November 2000 parliamentary elections.

Albanian League of Romania (*Liga Albanezilor din România, LAR*)
Leadership. Oana Manolescu

Armenian Union of Romania (*Uniunea Armenilor din România, UAR*)
Leadership. Varujan Pambuccian

Bulgarian Union of the Banat–Romania (*Uniunea Bulgara din Banat-România, UBBR*)
Leadership. Petru Mirciov

Croatian Union of Romania (*Uniunea Croatilor din România, UCR*)
Leadership. Mihai Radan

Cultural Union of Ruthenians of Romania (*Uniunea Culturala a Rutenilor din România*, UCRR)
Leadership. Gheorghe Firczak

Democratic Union of Tatar Turkish-Muslims of Romania (*Uniunea Democrata a Tatarilor Turco-Musulmani din România*, UDTTMR)
Leadership. Negiat Sali

Democratic Union of Slovaks and Czechs of Romania (*Uniunea Democratica a Slovacilor si Cehilor din România*, UDSCR)
Leadership. Ana Florea

German Democratic Forum of Romania (*Forumul Democrat al Germanilor din Romania*, FDGR)
Leadership. Eberhard-Wolfgang Wittstock

Greek Union of Romania (*Uniunea Elena din Romania*, UER)
Leadership. Sotiris Fotopolos

Italian Community of Romania (*Comunitatea Italiana din Romania*, CIR)
Leadership. Ileana Stana-Ionescu

Jewish Community Federation of Romania (*Federatia Comunitatilor Evreiesti din România, FCER*)
Leadership. Dorel Dorian

Lipova Russian Community of Romania (*Comunitatea Rusilor Lipoveni din România, CRLR*)
Leadership. Miron Ignat

Polish Union of Romania (*Uniunea Polonezilor din România, UPR*)
Leadership. Iohan-Peter Babias

Roma Party (*Partida Romilor, PR*)
Leadership. Nicolae Păun

Serbian Union of Romania (*Uniunea Sarbilor din România, USR*)
Leadership. Slavomir Gvozdenovici

Slav Macedonian Association of Romania (*Asociatia Macedonenilor Slavi din România, AMSR*)
Leadership. Vasile Ioan Savu

Turkish Democratic Union of Romania (*Uniunea Democrata Turca din România, UDTR*)
Leadership. Metin Cerchez

Ukrainian Union of Romania (*Uniunea Ucrainienilor din România, UUR*)
Leadership. Stefan Tcaciuc

General Union of Ethnic Associations of Romania (*Uniunea Generala a Asociatiilor Etniei Hutule din România, UGAEHR*)

Other Parties

Among well over 100 other registered parties in Romania, those listed below featured unsuccessfully in the 2000 elections.

Alliance for Romania (*Alianta pentru România, ApR*), formed in mid-1997 by dissidents of the Social Democracy Party of Romania (later the →Social Democratic Party), being backed by about a dozen deputies and two senators.

None were re-elected on the ApR ticket in the November 2000 elections, the party winning only 4.1% of the vote. In September 2001 the ApR agreed to merge with the →National Liberal Party in mid-2002.
Leadership. Teodor Meleşcanu (chairman)

Christian Democratic National Alliance (*Alianta Nationala Crestin Democrata, ANCD*), a coalition of groupings of Christian orientation which formed part of the defeated Democratic Convention of Romania 2000 alliance in the November 2000 parliamentary elections, including the Hungarian Christian Party of Romania (RMKDM) led by Kálmán Kelemen.

Ecologist Federation of Romania (*Federatia Ecologista din România, FER*), the latest of various manifestations of the Green movement in Romania, which obtained five Chamber seats in the 1996 elections. In 2000 the FER was part of the defeated Democratic Convention of Romania 2000 alliance.

Union of Right-Wing Forces (*Uniunea Fort,elor de Dreapta, UFD*), an amalgam of various groups which formed part of the defeated Democratic Convention of Romania 2000 alliance in the 2000 elections.
Website. www.ufd.ro

Russia

Capital: Moscow   **Population:** 146,500,000 (2000E)

The Russian Federation was formerly the Russian Soviet Federative Socialist Republic, the largest constituent republic of the USSR, and became a sovereign member of the Commonwealth of Independent States on Dec. 21, 1991. Approved by referendum in December 1993, its present constitution defines Russia as a democratic, pluralist federation headed by an executive President, directly elected for a four-year term (once renewable consecutively), who guides the domestic and foreign policy of the state, serves as commander-in-chief of the armed forces and nominates the Prime Minister and other ministers, subject to approval by the legislature. The latter body is the bicameral Federal Assembly (*Federalnoe Sobranie*), consisting of (i) the upper Federation Council (*Sovet Federatsii*) of 178 members, to which each of the Federation's 89 territorial entities sends two representatives; and (ii) the lower State Duma (*Gosudarstvennaya Duma*) of 450 members elected for a four-year term, half of whom are returned by proportional representation from party lists obtaining at least 5% of the vote and the other half from single-member constituencies on the basis of majority voting. The President may reject a first vote of no confidence by the legislature, but upon the re-adoption of such a measure within three months must either resign or dissolve the legislature and call new elections. A presidential veto on legislation may only be overridden by a two-thirds majority of the whole membership of the Federal Assembly. The President has considerable scope under the constitution to govern by decree.

Elections to the State Duma on Dec. 19, 1999, and further polling on March 19, 2000, in eight constituencies where majorities had been cast against all candidates, produced the following results: Communist Party of the Russian Federation (KPRF) 113 seats (with 24.3% of the proportional vote), Unity Inter-Regional Movement (*Medved*) 72 (23.3%), Fatherland–All Russia 67 (13.3%), Union of Rightist Forces 29 (8.5%), Yabloko 21 (5.9%), Liberal Democratic Party of Russia 17 (6.0%), Our Home is Russia (NDR) 7 (1.2%), All-Russian Political Movement in Support of the Army 2 (0.6%), Russian All-People's Union 2 (0.4%), five other lists 5, independents 114. Postponed polling for the Chechnya seat took place in August 2000. In February 2001 the NDR was absorbed by *Medved*.

In the first round of presidential elections on March 26, 2000, Vladimir Putin, standing without party affiliation but supported by most centre-right formations, was elected outright with 52.9% of the vote against 10 other candidates. Putin had been appointed Prime Minister in August 1999 and had become acting President on the resignation of Boris Yeltsin on Dec. 31, 1999.

A new Parties Law enacted in July 2001 was intended to reduce the proliferation of registered political parties in Russia, currently numbering some 200, by introducing stricter registration requirements and obliging existing parties to re-register within two years. Parties were required to have at least 10,000 members and at least 100 in at least half of Russia's territorial entities, multiple party membership was banned, and only registered parties would be able to present candidates in elections. Limits were placed on individual and corporate financial contributions to parties, which would be eligible for state financial assistance in proportion to their electoral support if they obtained at least 3% of the vote.

391

Agrarian Party of Russia
Agrarnaya Partiya Rossii (APR)

Address. 15 ul. Malaya Kaluzhskaya, 121019 Moscow
Telephone. (+7–095) 292–9669
Leadership. Mikhail Lapshin (chairman)

The APR was founded in February 1992 to provide political representation for collective and state farmers, as well as for agro-industrial workers and managers, initially on a platform opposed to the introduction of a free market in land. Its predominantly conservative constituent organizations included the Agrarian Union of Russia (*Agrarnyi Soyuz Rossii*, ASR) led by Vasily Starodubtsev, which had held its inaugural congress in June 1990. APR spokesmen made a point of stressing that the APR was not the agrarian branch of the →Communist Party of the Russian Federation (KPRF). But in policy terms the two parties shared much common ground, notably a conviction that the free-market programme of the Yeltsin administration was damaging Russia.

The APR took fourth place in the December 1993 State Duma elections, winning 7.9% of the popular vote and 47 seats (later increased by the adhesion of deputies elected as independents). The party subsequently aligned itself with the KPRF/nationalist opposition in the new parliament, even though the Agriculture Minister in a more conservative Yeltsin administration was identified with the APR. In the December 1995 parliamentary elections, the APR received only 3.8% of the party list vote, so that it did not qualify for proportional seats; but it won 20 seats in the constituency section and had the unofficial support of some of the 77 deputies returned as independents.

The APR backed the unsuccessful candidacy of the KPRF leader in the mid-1996 presidential elections and subsequently, without great enthusiasm, joined the new KPRF-inspired Popular-Patriotic Union of Russia. An APR congress in April 1997 adopted a new policy platform accepting the privatization of state-owned land in some circumstances and generally moving to a more centrist stance.

The APR again secured representation in the December 1999 State Duma elections, returning some candidates on the KPRF list and others as "independents", one of its deputies again being party chairman Mikhail Lapshin. In January 2001 Lapshin reverted to the APR's original line by calling for a moratorium on the buying and selling of land that had been owned by the state. In September 2001 the party initiated the procedure for the collecting the 2 million signatures required to trigger a referendum, in which it would seek approval for a moratorium on the buying and selling of land.

All-Russian Political Movement in Support of the Army
Obsherossiskoe Politcheskoye Dvizhenie v Podderzhku Armii (OPDPA)

Address. c/o Gosudarstvennaya Duma, Okhotniy ryad 1, Moscow 103265
Leadership. Viktor Ilyukhin (chairman)

The OPDPA was launched in September 1997, describing itself as "an opposition movement of the left" aiming to reverse the rapid post-Soviet deterioration in Russia's military capability and service conditions. Its first leader was Gen. (retd.) Lev Rokhlin, a popular hero of the first Chechnya war who had been elected to the State Duma in 1995 for Our Home is Russia (→Unity Inter-Regional Movement). As chairman of the State Duma's defence committee, he was a vociferous critic of the Yeltsin administration until being shot dead at his country dacha in July 1998 in what his family claimed was a political murder. Over 10,000 mourners at his funeral included several opposition leaders.

Rokhlin's successor as OPDPA leader was Viktor Ilyukhin, chairman of the State Duma's security committee and a member of the →Communist Party of the Russian Federation. Presenting candidates in its own right in the December 1999 parliamentary elections, the OPDPA won two constituency seats and 0.6% of the proportional vote.

Communist Party of the Russian Federation
Kommunisticheskaya Partiya Rossiiskoi Federatisii (KPRF)

Address. 3 M. Sukharevskii per., 101007 Moscow
Telephone. (+7–95) 207–0791
Fax. (+7–95) 292–9050
Website. www.kprf.ru
Leadership. Gennady Zyuganov (chairman)

The KPRF was registered in March 1993 after a Communist "revival/unification" congress had been held at Klyazm (near Moscow) the previous month, following a Constitutional Court ruling in December 1992 that the banning in November 1991 of the Communist Party of the Soviet Union (KPSS) had been unconstitutional. The KPRF is therefore the self-proclaimed successor to the Russian branch of the KPSS (not least to its financial assets), albeit without those parts of the latter's Marxist–Leninist ideology which had underpinned 70 years of authoritarian, one-party rule.

The KPSS was directly descended from Vladimir Ilyich Ulyanov Lenin's majority (Bolshevik) wing of the Russian Social Democratic Labour Party (itself established in 1898), which at the party's second congress held in London in 1903 out-voted the minority (Menshevik) wing on Lenin's proposal that in existing Russian conditions the party must become a tightly-disciplined vanguard of professional revolutionaries. In 1912 the Bolshevik wing established itself as a separate formation, which became a legal party in Russia following the overthrow of the Tsar in February 1917 and which in October 1917 seized power from the Mensheviks. The party changed its name to Russian Communist Party (Bolsheviks) in 1918, to All-Union Communist Party (Bolsheviks) in 1925 and to the KPSS designation in 1952.

Following Lenin's death in January 1924, Joseph Stalin (who had become general secretary of the central committee in April 1922) took full control over the party and government. He proceeded to eliminate all actual and potential rivals on the right and left of the party, notably Leon Trotsky (the architect of the Communist victory in the post-revolution civil war), who was expelled from the party in November 1927, exiled in January 1929 and finally murdered by Stalin's agent in his Mexican home in August 1940.

From October 1925 Stalin adopted the programme of the eliminated leftist opposition by launching the first five-year plan of rapid industrialization and forcible collectivization of agriculture (the latter involving the virtual elimination of the land-owning peasants, or *kulaks,* as a class). Between 1928 and 1938 total industrial output almost quadrupled, although agricultural output declined. The assassination of politburo member Sergei Kirov in December 1934 led to the great purges of the late 1930s, in which almost the entire generation of party activists formerly associated with Lenin disappeared. In December 1936 a new constitution was promulgated under which the Communist Party was enshrined as the leading force in the state.

After the interval provided by the August 1939 Nazi–Soviet Pact, the German invasion of the Soviet Union in June 1941 coincided with Stalin's assumption for the first time of formal government responsibilities as Prime Minister and supreme commander of the Soviet armed forces. The eventual victory of the Red Army and its penetration into Eastern Europe led to the establishment of Soviet-aligned Communist regimes in a number of states, causing post-war tensions in relations with the Western powers which eventually deteriorated into the Cold War. During the post-war period Stalin remained in absolute control of the party and state apparatus and mounted further purges of suspected opponents.

Immediately after Stalin's death in March 1953 moves were initiated to reverse the Stalinist system and the cult of his personality. Stalin's secret police chief, Lavrenti Beria, was executed and Stalin's designated successor, Georgy Malenkov, was immediately ousted from the party leadership by Nikita Khrushchev and replaced as Prime Minister by Nikolai Bulganin in February 1955. Under Khrushchev's leadership, the KPSS in 1955 re-established relations with the Yugoslav Communists (hitherto regarded as right-wing deviationists) and in his celebrated "secret" speech to the 20th party congress in February 1956 Khrushchev denounced the Stalinist terror and cult of personality.

Khrushchev's denunciation of Stalin triggered serious challenges to the Communist regimes in Poland and also in Hungary, where orthodox Communist rule was re-established by Soviet military intervention in November 1956. In March 1958 Khrushchev added the premiership to his party leadership, but growing doubts within the KPSS hierarchy about his policies and leadership style culminated in his removal from the party and government leadership in October 1964, in which posts he was succeeded by Leonid Brezhnev and Alexei Kosygin respectively.

Under Brezhnev's leadership the cautious liberalization policy of the Khrushchev era was largely halted or reversed. Although the Soviet government pursued a policy of detente with the West, its refusal to countenance deviation from Communist orthodoxy was demonstrated by the Soviet-led intervention in Czechoslovakia in 1968, following which Brezhnev enunciated his doctrine that Communist countries were entitled to intervene in other Communist countries if the preservation of socialism was deemed to be threatened. Having established a position of complete authority as party leader, Brezhnev was elected USSR head of state in June 1977.

The Brezhnev era was essentially a period of conservatism and stagnation, this being acknowledged by the party itself after his death in November 1982. He was succeeded as party leader by former KGB chief Yury Andropov, who died in February 1984. His successor, Konstantin Chernenko, also lasted only a year before he too died in office. The party then opted for the relatively young Mikhail Gorbachev (54), who embarked upon a reform programme that was ultimately to lead to the demise of the Soviet Union.

At the April 1985 plenary meeting of the KPSS central committee and the 27th party congress in March 1986, Gorbachev advanced the concept of a "restructuring" (*perestroika*) of social relations based on "resolute efforts to overcome elements of stagnation and negative phenomena to accelerate the country's socio-economic development". At the same time, the party became committed to a new "openness" (*glasnost*) in public and media discussion of present and past conditions in the Soviet Union. Perhaps most controversially of all, Gorbachev proposed electoral reform, including the multiple choice of candidates and the introduction of secret ballots in the election of party secretaries; however, this proposal was not specifically endorsed in the central committee's resolution giving general formal backing to Gorbachev's plans.

In order to encourage the policy of *glasnost,* Gorbachev declared that the activities of state and public organizations should be more open to public scrutiny through the official media, and be more receptive to criticism. He also announced the preparation of a law on the procedure for filing a complaint against a party official who had infringed the rights of a citizen. Such a law was passed by the Supreme Soviet on June 30, 1987, and came into effect on Jan. 1, 1988.

Differences within the KPSS leadership over the desirable pace of reform were demonstrated by the dismissal of Boris Yeltsin as first secretary of the Moscow party committee in November 1987, as a direct consequence of a speech by him to the KPSS central committee the previous month in which he had accused other senior leaders of frustrating the *perestroika* process and had also criticized aspects of the present leadership style, including the high profile accorded to Gorbachev's wife, Raisa Gorbachev. Formerly a close associate of the party leader, Yeltsin was in February 1988 dropped from alternate membership of the

KPSS political bureau. He thereafter effectively ceased to be a KPSS member, becoming the leading advocate of democratization and economic liberalization in the Russian Federation, of which he was elected President in May 1990 (by a legislature itself elected competitively two months earlier).

Meanwhile, Gorbachev had succeeded Andrei Gromyko as USSR head of state in October 1988, subsequently introducing historic constitutional changes to allow for a multiparty system and private economic enterprise, although he himself remained a Communist, convinced that the KPSS would retain its dominance in genuinely competitive elections. Others in the KPSS hierarchy did not share his confidence, nor his belief that the Soviet Union could be preserved as a voluntary association. Gorbachev's proposed new Union Treaty, envisaging an association of "sovereign" republics with extensive powers of self-government, was the final straw for his hardline conservative opponents, who in August 1991 attempted to assume power in Moscow while Gorbachev was on holiday. The coup attempt quickly crumbled, not least because of the courageous opposition displayed by Yeltsin; but it served to accelerate the unravelling of the Soviet system, in that most of the republican Communist parties withdrew from the KPSS while it was in progress, and were subsequently banned or suspended as the republics moved to independence. In the Russian Federation both the KPSS and the KPRF were banned under a presidential decree issued on Nov. 6, 1991, their assets being declared state property.

The leadership of the revived KPRF elected at the February 1993 Klyazm congress was headed by Gennady Zyuganov, a former Soviet apparatchik who had been co-chair of the National Salvation Front formed in October 1992 by Communists and Russian nationalists who deplored the passing of the supposed glories of the Soviet era. The KPRF was thus placed in uneasy spiritual alliance with the non-Communist nationalist right in opposition to the reformist forces of the centre in governmental power in Moscow, in particular to the Yeltsin presidency. The manifest negative effects of economic transition, including rampant crime and spiralling unemployment and inflation, provided the KPRF with powerful ammunition in its unaccustomed role as a party seeking electoral support in a multi-party system. In the State Duma elections of December 1993 it took third place with 65 seats and 12.4% of the proportional vote, thereafter becoming the principal focus of opposition to the Yeltsin administration. The appointment in January 1995 of an acknowledged Communist as Justice Minister did not mean that the KPRF had become a government party. Using the slogan "For our Soviet motherland", it contested the December 1995 State Duma elections on a platform promising the restoration of "social justice", its reward being to become the largest party with 157 seats, of which 99 came from a 22.3% share of the vote in the proportional half of the contest.

Remaining in opposition (although welcoming a more conservative government orientation), the KPRF presented Zyuganov as its candidate for the mid-1996 presidential election, on a platform condemning the devastation of Russia's industrial base by IMF-dictated policies and promising to restore economic sovereignty. He came a close second to Yeltsin in the first round of voting on June 16, winning 32.04%, but lost to the incumbent in the second round, when he won 40.4%. The KPRF thereupon initiated the launching in August 1996 of the Popular–Patriotic Union of Russia (*Narodno-Patrioticheskii Soyuz Rossii*, NPSR), which was designed to rally all anti-Yeltsin forces, although Zyuganov insisted, shortly before being elected as its leader, that it was not a Communist front organization.

In the late 1990s the KPRF sought to distance itself from the nationalist right, while continuing to espouse a form of Russian nationalism harking back to the Soviet era. The party urged a return to centralized government and the transfer of presidential powers to the government and the legislature, as well as the creation of a "Slavic union" of Russia, Ukraine and Belarus, arguing that only a KPRF government could resurrect Russia's status as a great power. However, the KPRF's opposition to the war in Chechnya cost it some popular support, so that the party fell back to 113 seats in the December 1999 State Duma elections, although its share of the proportional vote increased to 24.3% and it remained the largest single party.

President Yeltsin's unexpected resignation at the end of 1999 presented a particular challenge to the KPRF, because his designated successor, Vladimir Putin, was popularly perceived as having strong nationalist and pro-authority credentials. In presidential elections in March 2000, Zyuganov was again the KPRF candidate but was heavily defeated by Putin in the first round, receiving only 29.2% of the vote. The KPRF subsequently declared its readiness to provide "constructive opposition" to the new government, although following the re-election of Zyuganov as chairman at the 7th party congress in December 2000 the KPRF embarked upon "active opposition" to what it described as the elitist and "anti-people" Putin administration.

In January 2001 Zyuganov was elected chairman of the Council of Communist Parties in the Former Soviet Republics. Within the Russian Federation, the party in September 2001 launched the "Russian Patriots" movement, intended as a broad front of left-wing parties opposed to the Putin administration's policies. The founding congress of the movement censured Putin for joining the US-led coalition against terrorism launched in the wake of the attacks on the USA on Sept. 11.

Congress of Russian Communities
Kongress Russkikh Obshchin (KRO)

Address. c/o Federalnoe Sobranie, Moscow
Leadership. Dmitry Rogozin (chairman)
Founded in May 1993, the nationalist KRO stresses the need to preserve the unity of the Russian nation and to protect the rights of Russian communities in neighbouring republics. The grouping was boosted when the controversial but popular former commander of Russia's 14th Army in Moldova's Russian-populated Transdnestria region, Gen. Aleksandr Lebed, agreed to take a prominent place on the KRO's list of candidates for the December 1995 elections, following his resignation from the armed forces in May 1995. However, favourable early opinion poll ratings for the KRO were not sustained in the actual voting, which gave it only 4.3% of the national vote (and therefore no proportional seats), its tally of five State Duma seats coming from the constituency contests.

Disappointed with the election outcome, delegates at a special KRO congress in late May 1996 ousted Yury Skokov from the leadership and replaced him with the more nationalistic Dmitry Rogozin. There was an immediate dividend for Lebed in the following month's presidential elections, when he came third in the first round with 14.5% of the national vote and therefore became a very marketable political commodity. President Yeltsin speedily made him his National Security Adviser, thus securing his backing in his successful second-round contest with the candidate of the →Communist Party of the Russian Federation.

Lebed was dismissed by Yeltsin in October 1996 and quickly left the KRO to launch another party (which made little impact). The rump KRO subsequently flirted with the idea of joining the new →Fatherland–All Russia (OVR) bloc launched in November 1998, but in the event could not accept the OVR's pro-decentralization stance. Contesting the December 1999 State Duma elections jointly with the Yury Boldurev Movement, the KOR won only one constituency seat and only 0.6% of the proportional vote. In March 2000 it backed the successful presidential candidacy of Vladimir Putin.

Fatherland–All Russia
Otechestvo–Vsya Rossiya (OVR)

Address. c/o Gosudarstvennaya Duma, Okhotniy ryad 1, Moscow 103265
Email. info@otech.ru
Website. www.luzhkov-otechestvo.ru
Leadership. Yury Luzhkov (chairman); Vyacheslav Volodin (leader in State Duma)
The moderate conservative OVR bloc was formed in April 1999 to rally opposition to the increasingly troubled presidency of Boris Yeltsin. Fatherland had been launched in November 1998 by Yury Luzhkov, the popular mayor of Moscow, attracting considerable support from regional governors and business leaders for its call for a better balance between the free market and state economic control. The more recent All Russia movement had a strong regional orientation and aimed to transform what it regarded as the corrupt and discredited politics in Moscow.

Initially seen as the likely successor to the Yeltsin administration, the OVR from September 1999 faced strong competition on the right from the new →Unity Inter-Regional Movement (*Medved*), which backed then Prime Minister Vladimir Putin for the presidential succession. In the December 1999 State Duma elections the OVR was outpolled by *Medved* and took a disappointing third place, winning 66 seats with a proportional vote share of 13.3%. Yeltsin's surprise resignation after the elections and the elevation of Putin as his designated successor resulted in Luzhkov, in recognition of Putin's popular appeal and the similarity of his programme to that of the OVR, abandoning his own presidential ambitions and backing Putin in his successful candidacy in the March 2000 presidential elections.

The OVR group subsequently formed part of the pro-government parliamentary majority and entered into negotiations for a merger with *Medved*. Luzhkov became chairman of an OVR–Medved co-ordinating council in April 2001, with a full merger being set for December 2001. In September 2001 former Prime Minister Yevgeniy Primakov resigned as leader of the OVR group in the State Duma and was replaced by Vyacheslav Volodin.

Liberal Democratic Party of Russia
Liberalno–Demokraticheskaya Partiya Rossii (LDPR)

Address. Lukov per. 9, Moscow 103045
Telephone. (+7–95) 261–0033
Fax. (+7–95) 928–2444
Leadership. Vladimir Zhirinovsky (chairman)
The right-wing ultra-nationalist LDPR was founded in March 1990 in the era of the Soviet Union, the borders of which it wishes to restore to Russian hegemony, although it does not favour the Communist economic system. Its leader, the controversial Vladimir Zhirinovsky, attracted 6,211,007 votes (7.8%) in the 1991 presidential poll on an openly xenophobic platform with racist and antisemitic overtones. Among his more extravagant proposals was one for a Russian re-conquest of Finland (which had been part of the Tsarist empire until World War I). The party was technically banned in August 1992 on the grounds that it had falsified its membership records. However, it was allowed to contest the December 1993 parliamentary elections, in which it became the second strongest State Duma party with 64 seats and actually headed the proportional voting with 22.8% of the national poll.

Although forming the main parliamentary opposition to the Yeltsin administration, the LDPR lost momentum in 1994–95, as its leader made increasingly bizarre utterances and was shunned by other politicians close to him in the ideological spectrum. Zhirinovsky's decision to sign the April 1994 "treaty on civil accord" between Yeltsin and over 200 political and social groups failed to improve his standing in the political class and served to alienate some of his natural supporters. In the December 1995 State Duma elections the LDPR again took second place with 51 seats, but slumped to 11.4% of the proportional vote. In the 1996 presidential elections, moreover, Zhirinovsky came a poor fifth in the first round, with only 5.7% of the vote.

Because of irregularities in its paperwork, the LDPR was denied registration for the December 1999 State Duma elections, which it therefore contested as the "Zhirinovsky Bloc". In a further major setback, the formation slumped to 17 seats and 6% of the proportional vote. Worse followed in the March 2000 presidential elections, in which the LDPR leader came a distant fifth with only 2.7% of the vote. Undeterred, the 12th LDPR congress in May 2001 called for an alliance of ex-Soviet republics as a counterweight to NATO, the adoption of Tsarist territorial divisions in Russia, greater state control of the economy and the reactivation of the death penalty.

Notorious for his outbursts on alleged Jewish domination of business and the media, Zhirinovsky in July 2001 acknowledged for the first time that his father was Jewish. In September 2001 he urged President Putin to take advantage of the terrorist attacks on the USA to secure US support for Russian regional aims as the price for joining an international coalition against terrorism.

Union of Rightist Forces
Soyuz Pravikh Sil (SPS)
Address. c/o Gosudarstvennaya Duma, Okhotniy ryad 1, Moscow 103265
Leadership. Boris Nemtsov (chairman); Eldar Yanbukhtin (executive committee chairman)

The pro-market SPS was launched prior to the December 1999 State Duma elections as an alliance of parties and groups broadly descended, through many complex changes of name and alignment, from those which had supported the "shock therapy" economic policies of the early 1990s, notably Yegor Gaidar's Russia's Democratic Choice (DVR). These formations had lost influence in the more conservative later years of the presidency of Boris Yeltsin, with whom Gaidar had broken irrevocably in 1996, and had been widely blamed for the deterioration and corruption engendered by the early rush to a market economy.

The DVR had originally been founded in November 1993 as Russia's Choice (VR), deriving from the Bloc of Reformist Forces–Russia's Choice (BRVR) created five months earlier by a group of radical pro-market reformers which had included Gaidar. The BRVR had itself derived from the pro-Yeltsin Democratic Choice (DV) bloc created by a large number of centre-right groups in July 1992. The new VR grouping had been part of an attempt to provide a stable political framework for centre-right reformist forces hitherto operating under a host of different and constantly changing party or alliance labels. It had become the largest parliamentary grouping in the December 1993 State Duma elections, winning 76 seats and 15.4% of the national vote. But strong advances by anti-reform parties had resulted in Gaidar and most other radical reformers being dropped from the government in January 1994. In April 1994, in securing Gaidar's signature of his "treaty on civil accord", President Yeltsin had expressed a desire for close co-operation with the VR bloc, while explaining that he could not, as head of state, become an actual member.

In June 1994 the VR had formally established itself as a political party, adding "Democratic" to its title, to become the DVR. Thereafter, DVR criticism of the slow pace of economic reform under the government of Viktor Chernomyrdin had continued despite the promotion of Anatoly Chubais (then of the DVR) to the rank of First Deputy Prime Minister in November 1994. In March 1995 the DVR had withdrawn support from President Yeltsin in protest against the Russian military action in Chechnya. Two months later Chubais had announced that he was suspending his DVR membership and giving his support to Chernomyrdin's new Our Home is Russia formation (→Unity Inter-Regional Movement). The centre-right's incorrigible addiction to new nomenclature had then been displayed in June 1995 when the DVR had launched the

United Democrats (OD) as its electoral bloc, including over 20 ethnic minority groups. The December 1995 elections had proved dismal for the DVR/OD, which had slumped to 3.9% of the national vote and no proportional seats, although it had won nine constituency seats. The Yeltsin administration's shift to an even more conservative posture as a result of the electoral verdict had caused Yegor Gaidar to resign from the Presidential Advisory Council in January 1996 in what he had described as a "final and irrevocable" breach with Yeltsin. In the same month Chubais had been dismissed from the government for disregarding presidential instructions. In June-July 1996 most DVR elements had nevertheless backed President Yeltsin's successful re-election bid, although some had preferred the candidacy of Grigory Yavlinsky of →Yabloko.

Gaidar and the DVR had then embarked upon yet another attempt to create a centre-right bloc, launching in late 1998 the Just Cause (*Pravoye Delo*, PD) alliance, partly in response to the murder in St Petersburg of Galina Starovoitova, a DVR State Duma deputy and prominent human rights campaigner. However, the unwillingness of the other major centre-right formations to join the PD initiative had eventually persuaded the DVR to become part of the SPS on its creation in 1999.

The SPS won 29 State Duma seats in the December 1999 elections, with 8.5% of the proportional vote. It subsequently gave broad support to the new presidency of Vladimir Putin, while maintaining its distance from the main pro-Putin →Unity Inter-Regional Movement (*Medved*). In May 2000 the SPS alliance formally constituted itself as a national organization and in May 2001 held a constituent congress in Moscow at which former Prime Minister Boris Nemtsov was elected chairman and Gaidar one of five co-chairmen. In June 2001 it was confirmed that a suggested merger between the SPS and Yabloko would not come to pass, although the two parties pledged continued co-operation in areas where they had the same policies.

The SPS was accepted as a member of the International Democrat Union in succession to the DVR.

Unity Inter-Regional Movement
Mezhregional'noye Dvizhenie Edinstvo (Medved)
Address. 12 pr. Akad. Sakharova, Moscow
Telephone. (+7–095) 921–8815
Fax. (+7–095) 923–0746
Email. shoigu.sergey@partia.edin.ru
Website. www.edin.ru
Leadership: Sergey Shoigu (chairman); Boris Gryzlov (State Duma group leader)

Its acronym meaning "bear" in Russian, the moderate nationalist *Medved* was founded in September 1999 by strategists associated with the then President, Boris Yeltsin, with the aim of countering the growing strength of the →Fatherland–All Russia (OVR) bloc. It subsequently became the principal political vehicle of the Vladimir Putin, although he did not formally join the party. *Medved* outpolled the OVR in the December 1999 State Duma elections, taking second place by winning 72 seats with 23.3% of the proportional vote. In the new legislature it attracted a number of independents to its parliamentary group, which became of similar size to that of the →Communist Party of the Russian Federation (KPRF).

Medved provided the core support for Putin in the March 2000 presidential elections, his outright first-round victory with 52.9% of the vote being achieved with broad backing from moderate nationalist and pro-market formations. In May 2000 *Medved* held its first congress in the Kremlin, declaring its aim of becoming Russia's governing party and re-electing Sergey Shoigu (the Minister for Emergency Situations) as party chairman.

In February 2001 *Medved* absorbed the Our Home is Russia (NDR) grouping, which had been launched in May 1995 mainly to provide a party political base for the cautious pro-market reform programme of the then Prime Minister, Viktor Chernomyrdin, and by extension for President Yeltsin, although the latter had not publicly endorsed the new formation. Supported by most government ministers, the NDR had quickly been branded by the more radical pro-market elements (and by the ultra-nationalist opposition) as being funded by Gazprom, which Chernomyrdin (a former USSR Gas Minister) had run before joining the Russian government. In the December 1995 State Duma elections it had taken 10.1% of the national vote and 55 seats, and its organizational resources had made a significant contribution to Yeltsin's second-round presidential victory in July 1996, after which Chernomyrdin had been Prime Minister again, until March 1998. In the December 1999 State Duma elections, however, the NDR had slumped to only seven seats.

Enlarged by the NDR's accession, *Medved* entered into negotiations for a merger with the OVR bloc, for which a co-ordinating council was set up in April 2001, followed three months later by the creation of the joint All-Russia Union bloc in the State Duma. A full merger was set for December 2001.

Yabloko

Address. 36 Novyi Arbat, Moscow
Telephone. (+7–95) 292–8942
Website. www.eng.yabloko.ru
Leadership. Grigoriy Yavlinsky (chairman)

Yabloko (meaning "apple" in Russian) was launched in October 1993 as the Yavlinsky–Boldyrev–Lukin Bloc by Grigoriy Yavlinsky, Yuri Boldyrev and Vladimir Lukin, who supported transition to a market economy but strongly opposed the "shock therapy" then being administered by the Yeltsin administration. Yavlinksy was a well-known economist, Boldyrev a scientist and Lukin a former ambassador to the United States. Having won 33 seats and 7.8% of the proportional vote in the December 1993 elections, Yabloko was one of the few State Duma groups which declined to sign the April 1994 "civic accord treaty" between the government and most political groupings, on the grounds that the initiative contravened constitutional provisions. Yabloko also condemned the Russian military operation in Chechnya launched in December 1994.

In the December 1995 State Duma elections, Yabloko took a creditable fourth place, winning 45 seats on a proportional vote share of 6.9%. Its candidate in the 1996 presidential election was Yavlinsky, who came fourth in the first round with 7.3% and gave qualified support to incumbent Boris Yeltsin in the second. The party nevertheless opposed many aspects of the new government's economic policy, drawing particular support from older professionals. In the December 1999 State Duma elections, Yabloko fell back to 21 seats with 5.9% of the proportional vote, while Yavlinsky came third (with 5.8%) in the March 2000 presidential elections won by Vladimir Putin. Yabkloko thereafter adopted a stance of "constructive opposition" to the Putin administration.

Plans were announced in June 2000 for an alliance between Yabloko and the →Union of Right Forces (SPS), providing initially for the presentation of joint candidates in forthcoming elections and possibly leading to a full merger. However, although the two formations had similar pro-market economic and social programmes, doubts about the viability of the alliance centred on whether it would follow Yabloko's line of opposing the Putin administration or the SPS line of giving it qualified support.

Yabloko is an observer member of the Liberal International.

Other Parties

The following selection from the large number of minor parties and groupings in existence in Russia focuses on those which featured in the December 1999 elections to the State Duma. Numerous new parties have been launched since those elections, but in most cases it is uncertain that they will meet the requirements for official registration contained in the 2001 Parties Law (see introduction).

Christian Democratic Union–Christians of Russia, member party of the Christian Democrat International.
Leadership. Vladimir Bauer (chairman)

Eurasian Party of Russia, launched in June 2001 by several formations representing Muslim, Buddhist and other non-European communities to promote the unity of "Russian Orthodoxy, Islam and devotion to the fatherland". Officially registered in August 2001, the party advanced proposals for the territorial re-division of Russia to take more account of ethnic population distribution.
Leadership. Abdul-Vakhed Niyazov (chairman)

Inter-regional Green Party, affiliated to the European Federation of Green Parties.
Leadership. Oleg Kouznetsov

Islamic Party of Russia, umbrella formation of many Muslim groupings. Its September 2001 congress expressed condolences for the victims of the terrorist attacks on the USA, whilst also calling for the creation of a "Council of Islam" within the Russian presidential administration.

Pensioners' Party (*Partiya Pensionerov, PP*), founded in late 1997 to promote the interests of the 25% of the population who are pensioners; won one State Duma seat in 1999 and 2% of the proportional vote.
Leadership. Yakov Ryabov (chairman)

Russian All-People's Union (*Rossiskoi Obshenarodny Soyuz, ROS*), left-wing formation which won two State Duma seats in 1999 and 0.4% of the proportional vote.
Leadership. Sergey Baburin (chairman)

Russian Socialist Party (*Russkaya Sotsialisticheskaya Partiya, RSP*), launched in April 1996 by millionaire presidential candidate Vladimir Bryntsalov, whose advocacy of "a truly Russian model of socialism" brought him last place out of 10 candidates in the June polling with 0.2% of the vote. The RSP won one State Duma seat in 1999 and 0.2% of the proportional vote.
Leadership. Vladimir Bryntsalov (chairman)

Socialist Party of Russia (*Sotsialisticheskaya Partiya Rossii, SPR*), launched in April 1996 by Ivan Rybkin, then chairman of the State Duma and hitherto a member of the →Agrarian Party of Russia, in what at first appeared to be a promising unification of various non-Communist left-wing groups reported to be financed by business magnate Boris Berezovsky. In the December 1999 elections, however, the SPR won only 0.1% of the vote and no seats.
Leadership. Ivan Rybkin (chairman)

Spiritual Heritage (*Dukhovnoe Nasledie, DN*), left-wing list which won one State Duma seat in 1999 and 0.1% of the proportional vote.
Leadership. Aleksei Podberezkin (chairman)

Union of People's Power and Labour (*Soyuz Narodovlastiya i Truda, SNT*), founded in mid-1998 by Gen. (retd) Andrei Nikolayev on a moderate left platform favouring a social market economy. Having failed to build a larger centre-left alliance for the 1999 State Duma elections, Nikolayev stood on a joint personalized list with veteran political activist Academician Svyatoslav Fyodorov, their return being one constituency seat and 0.6% of the proportional vote.
Leadership. Gen. (retd) Andrei Nikolayev (chairman)

United Social Democratic Party (*Obyedinyonnaya Sotsial-Demokraticheskaya Partiya, OSDP*), one of many attempts to create a European-style social democratic party in post-Soviet Russia, assisted internationally by the reputation of its leader as the terminator of the Soviet Union but with little domestic support. Having won only 0.1% in the 1999 elections, the party backed Vladimir Putin in the 2000 presidential elections. In April 2001 it agreed to a merger with the Russian Party of Social Democracy led by Konstantin Titov.
Leadership. Mikhail Gorbachev (chairman)

Women of Russia (*Zhenshchiny Rossii, ZR*), centre-left formation aspiring to bring about the equality of women. Having won 25 seats in the 1993 State Duma elections (with 8.1% of the vote), the ZR was reduced to three constituency seats in 1995, having narrowly failed to surmount the 5% barrier in the proportional section. Having endorsed President Yeltsin in his successful re-election bid in mid-1996, the ZR failed to gain representation in 1999, taking only 2.1% of the national vote.
Leadership. Alevtina Fedulova (chairperson)

Rwanda

Capital: Kigali

Population: 7,300,000 (2000E)

The Republic of Rwanda achieved independence from Belgium in 1962. Following a military coup led by Gen. Juvénal Habyarimana in 1973, the Hutu-dominated regime created the National Republican Movement for Democracy and Development (MRNDD), which remained the sole legal political party until the adoption of a multi-party constitution in 1991. By then a rebellion had been launched by the predominantly Tutsi Rwandan Patriotic Front (FPR), with which the government signed the Arusha Accord of August 1993 providing for the establishment of interim institutions in a transition period leading to multi-party elections. However, delays in the deployment of a UN observer force and divisions within various political parties led to the repeated postponement of the start of the transition period.

The fragile peace process ended abruptly in April 1994 when President Habyarimana was killed in a plane crash and mass violence of genocidal proportions ensued. Although generally presented as an ethnic conflict between the majority Hutu and minority Tutsi, the violence was also politically-motivated, in that supporters of the Habyarimana regime sought to eliminate all opposition, Tutsi and Hutu. The violence prompted the resumption of the rebellion by the FPR which, by July 1994, claimed military victory. In the same month Pasteur Bizimungu, a senior FPR figure, was inaugurated as President for a five-year term and the composition of a new government of national unity was announced. Posts in the Council of Ministers were assigned to the FPR, the Republican Democratic Movement, the Liberal Party, the Social Democratic Party and the Christian Democratic Party. The new administration declared its intention to honour the terms of the 1993 Arusha Accord within the context of an extended period of transition (to June 1999). However, the MRNDD and the Coalition for the Defence of the Republic (CDR) were excluded from participation in the government.

A 70-member Transitional National Assembly was inaugurated in December 1994 (without benefit of election). Seats in the Assembly were awarded to the FPR, the Republican Democratic Movement, the Liberal Party, the Social Democratic Party, the Christian Democratic Party, the Islamic Democratic Party, the Rwandan People's Democratic Union and the Rwandan Socialist Party. In May 1995 the Assembly adopted a new constitution which brought together elements of the 1991 constitution, the 1993 Arusha Accord, the FPR's victory declaration of July 1994 and a protocol of understanding signed in November 1994 by political parties not implicated in the earlier massacres.

In June 1999 the Transitional National Assembly was extended for a further four years. President Bizimungu resigned in March 2000; he was succeeded in April by Maj.-Gen. Paul Kagame who was elected in a special parliamentary vote. Kagame, the FPR military chief, had formerly been Vice-President and Minister of National Defence. Presidential and legislative elections were last held (on a single-party basis) in December 1988.

Christian Democratic Party
Parti Démocratique Chrétien (PDC)
The PDC, established in 1990, was included in the →Rwandan Patriotic Front-led administration that came to power in July 1994.

Coalition for the Defence of the Republic
Coalition pour la Défense de la République (CDR)
The CDR was formed in 1992, drawing support from uncompromising Hutu groups. In the mass violence between April and June 1994, its unofficial militia (*Impuza Mugambi,* or "Single-Minded Ones") was reported to have taken a leading role in the slaughter of Tutsis and moderate Hutus. CDR participation in the transitional government and legislature was subsequently proscribed by the new administration led by the →Rwandan Patriotic Front.

Liberal Party
Parti Libéral (PL)
The PL was formed in 1991 but split into two factions during late 1993 and early 1994, one faction joining the coalition government installed by the →Rwandan Patriotic Front following its military victory in July 1994.

National Republican Movement for Democracy and Development
Mouvement Républicain National pour la Démocratie et le Développement (MRNDD)
The MRNDD (known as the National Revolutionary Movement for Democracy until 1991) was founded in 1975 by Gen. Juvénal Habyarimana as a single national party embracing both military and civilian elements. Of Catholic orientation, it remained the sole legal party until the promulgation of legislation authorizing the formation of political parties in June 1991. The party retained a strong presence in subsequent coalition governments, ensuring President

Habyarimana's continuing powerful influence. In the carnage that followed the President's death in April 1994, the MRNDD's large unofficial militia (*Interahamwe,* or "Those Who Stand Together") was reported to be extensively involved in Hutu atrocities. The party was consequently excluded from the transitional government formed in July 1994 following the defeat of government forces by the →Rwandan Patriotic Front. The *Interahamwe* remain active militarily in the volatile eastern region of the Democratic Republic of the Congo.

Republican Democratic Movement
Mouvement Démocratique Républicain (MDR)
Leadership. Pierre-Celestin Rwigyema (chairman)
The current MDR, legalized in July 1991, stems from the *Parmehutu*-MDR which was the dominant party until 1973 when it was banned by the Habyarimana regime. The MDR led the campaign in late 1991 for the creation of a provisional government of all parties to manage the transition to pluralism and, from April 1992, headed successive coalition governments. The party was a signatory of the August 1993 Arusha Accord with the then rebel →Rwandan Patriotic Front (FPR), and Faustin Twagiramungu (on the anti-Habyarimana wing of the party) became the agreed nominee of the pro-democracy parties for the premiership in the envisaged transitional government. Many MDR members were subsequently victims of Hutu extremism in the atrocities perpetrated from April 1994. Twagiramungu was appointed Prime Minister in the FPR-dominated administration formed in July 1994. However, in August 1995, he was dismissed by President Bizimungu and replaced by Pierre-Celestin Rwigyema. Rwigyema served as Prime Minister until his resignation in February 2000, and was replaced by Bernard Makuza, also of the MDR, the following month.

Rwandan Patriotic Front
Front Patriotique Rwandais (FPR)
Leadership. Maj.-Gen. Paul Kagame (chairman); Charles Muligande (secretary-general)
The largely Tutsi FPR launched an insurgency from Uganda against the Habyarimana regime in October 1990. By 1992, in the light of extensive territorial gains by the FPR in northern Rwanda, the government was obliged to enter into negotiations which, a year later in August 1993, culminated in the signing of the Arusha Accord. The peace process was shattered in April 1994 by the massacres of Tutsis and moderate Hutus which followed the death of President Habyarimana, as a consequence of which the FPR, under the command of Kagame, renewed the military offensive that brought it to power three months later. Pasteur Bizimungu, who had become national President in July 1994, resigned in March 2000. He was replaced the following month by Kagame, who had previously served as Vice-President and Minister of National Defence. Kagame was the first Tutsi President since Rwanda gained independence in 1962.

Social Democratic Party
Parti Social–Démocrate (PSD)
Leadership. Charles Niakirutinka
The PSD was one of the first three opposition parties to be recognized under the 1991 constitution, and participated in government coalitions from April 1992. The party's president and vice-president were both killed in the mass violence from April 1994, their bodies being discovered and identified in February 1995. The PSD is represented in the coalition government dominated by the →Rwandan Patriotic Front.

AC-Fatah   365
Al-Jihad al-Islami   365
Aliança Popular, AP   404

St. Christopher and Nevis

Capital: Basseterre (St. Kitts)   **Population:** 39,000 (2000E)

The former British dependency of Saint Christopher (St. Kitts) and Nevis has been an independent member of the Commonwealth since 1983. The head of state is the British sovereign, represented by a Governor-General, who is appointed on the recommendation of the Prime Minister, the head of government. The unicameral federal Parliament or National Assembly, which has a five-year mandate, consists of 11 elected members together with three appointed senators (nominated by the Governor-General on the advice of the government and the opposition). It also includes the Speaker (elected by the members) and the Attorney General, either of whom may or may not be elected members.

The strength of separatist sentiment in the island of Nevis (which has a population of less than 9,000) was acknowledged in the independence constitution under which Nevis was granted considerable local autonomy, including its own Assembly, executive and Premier (parallel structures do not exist in St. Kitts). The constitution also granted Nevis the right to secede subject to various conditions. In August 1998 a referendum resulted in 62% of Nevisians voting for independence, but this fell short of the 2/3 majority required under the constitution.

In St. Kitts there are two political parties, the St. Kitts–Nevis Labour Party (SKNLP) and the People's Action Movement (PAM), while the two parties in Nevis are the Concerned Citizens' Movement (CCM) and the Nevis Reformation Party (NRP). In federal elections on March 6, 2000, Labour (in office since 1995) won a further five-year term, taking all eight elected seats on St. Kitts. The CCM took two of the three seats in Nevis and the NRP the third. The CCM forms the local administration in Nevis, where elections were last held in 1997. The perceived influence of organized crime on politics in St. Kitts and Nevis has attracted increasing concern.

Concerned Citizens' Movement (CCM)
Address. c/o Assembly, Charlestown, Nevis
Leadership. Vance Amory (leader)
The Nevis-based CCM has held a majority in the local Nevis Assembly since 1992. In federal elections it won two of the three Nevis seats in each of the elections of 1993, 1995 and 2000. The CCM urged a vote for secession from St. Kitts at a referendum in August 1998 but this proposal narrowly failed to win the required 2/3 majority. The CCM believes that the many thousands of offshore businesses operating from Nevis provide a basis for economic independence from St. Kitts, while opponents of secession maintain that it would effectively hand over control of the island to money launderers and drug cartels.

Nevis Reformation Party (NRP)

Address. Government Road, Charlestown, Nevis
Telephone. (+1–869) 469–0630
Leadership. Joseph Parry (leader)

The NRP was formed in 1970, advocating the separation of Nevis from St. Kitts. In 1980, having retained two National Assembly seats, the party formed a coalition government with the →People's Action Movement, which in 1983 oversaw the independence of St. Kitts and Nevis as a federation with considerable local autonomy for Nevis. In the 1990s the NRP has been displaced as the major party on Nevis by the →Concerned Citizens' Movement, retaining only one National Assembly seat in each of the 1993, 1995 and 2000 elections. In the 1998 referendum on independence for Nevis the NRP opposed secession, party leader Joseph Parry warning that Nevis lacked the human and economic resources to sustain itself as an independent nation.

The NRP is a member of the Caribbean Democrat Union, a regional organization of the International Democrat Union.

People's Action Movement (PAM)

Address. Lockhart Street, Basseterre
Telephone. (+1–869) 465–9335
Email. exec@pamskb.com
Leadership. Kennedy A. Simmonds (leader)

The centre-right PAM was formed in 1965. In 1979 Dr. Kennedy Simmonds became (in a by-election) the first person ever elected on the island of St. Kitts who was not from the Labour Party. Campaigning in the 1980 elections on a platform of early independence, the party won three of the (then) nine elective seats, which with the two seats won by the →Nevis Reformation Party (NRP) allowed it to form a coalition government. The coalition led St. Kitts–Nevis to independence in 1983, and Simmonds became the first Prime Minister. The PAM remained in government through the 1984 and 1989 elections. In the 1993 elections, although finishing second in the popular vote and returning only four of the 11 National Assembly members, the PAM retained office as a minority government with the support of the NRP. As a result of political instability and civil disorder, together with allegations of government corruption and links with organized crime, an early election was called for July 1995, in which the party lost all but one seat and was forced into opposition. In the 2000 elections the PAM campaigned on a platform that argued the ruling Labour Party had failed to revive the sugar industry or tackle the country's external debt, and had allowed organized crime and drug racketeering to flourish, but it won no seats. The PAM alleged that the result was flawed because of electoral fraud arising from improper voter registration and bribery, and criticized the government for failing to invite a Commonwealth observer group to monitor the election.

The PAM is a member of the Caribbean Democrat Union, a regional organization of the International Democrat Union.

St. Kitts–Nevis Labour Party (SKNLP)

Address. Box 1577, Church Street, Basseterre
Telephone. (+1–869) 465–5347
Fax. (+1–869) 465–8328
Email. labourleads@caribsurf.com
Website. www.sknlabourparty.org
Leadership. Denzil L. Douglas (political leader)

Originating in 1932 as the St. Kitts Workers' League, the Labour Party had a majority in the legislature in every election from the introduction of adult suffrage in 1952 until 1980. Having lost power in the 1980 elections to a coalition of the →People's Action Movement (PAM) and the →Nevis Reformation Party (NRP), Labour opposed what it regarded as the disproportionate amount of power given to Nevis by the independence constitution of 1983. Denzil Douglas became party leader in 1989. Elections in November 1993 resulted in both the PAM and the Labour Party winning four seats (although Labour won 54.5% of the vote in St. Kitts compared with the 41.7% won by the PAM), with PAM continuing in office with the support of the NRP. Labour and its supporters then agitated for early fresh elections with political instability and violence resulting; a state of emergency was declared for ten days in December 1993 because of disturbances and in 1994 there was further unrest with Labour boycotting the Assembly. In November 1994 the political parties and civic groups reached agreement to hold early general elections. When these took place in July 1995 Labour won seven of the eight seats in St. Kitts and returned to power. In 1998 US magazine *Newsweek* charged that the 1995 Labour campaign had been in part financed by Charles "Little Nut" Miller, wanted in the United States on drug trafficking charges. Efforts by the US authorities to extradite Miller, who had substantial business interests in St. Kitts and was widely seen as above the law, failed until the eve of the March 2000 election when (after a Cabinet decision) he was arrested and handed over to US law enforcement officials. The action, described by Douglas as being taken to eradicate the threat to foreign investment posed by intimidation and blackmail, was seen as bolstering the government's popularity. Labour went on to retain power, taking all eight seats in St. Kitts. Labour's 2000 election programme pledged an inclusive society and poverty eradication as priorities, "zero tolerance" for crime, full employment and never to re-introduce personal income tax.

The Labour Party is a consultative member of the Socialist International.

St. Lucia

Capital: Castries   **Population**: 156,000 (2000E)

Saint Lucia gained independence from the United Kingdom in 1979, remaining within the Commonwealth. The head of state is the British sovereign, represented by a Governor-General. The head of government is the Prime Minister. There is a bicameral parliament consisting of an appointed 11-member Senate and a 17-member House of Assembly. Assembly members are elected on the Westminster model for five-year terms on the basis of first past the post in single-seat constituencies. Senators are appointed by the Governor-General, six on the advice of the Prime Minister, three on the advice of the Leader of the Opposition and two at the discretion of the Governor-General after consulting religious, economic and social bodies.

The St. Lucia Labour Party (SLP) returned to power after 15 years when, in elections on May 23, 1997, it won 16 of the 17 Assembly seats, taking 61.3% of the vote. One seat was won by the previously governing United Workers' Party, which gained 36.6% of the vote.

St. Lucia Labour Party (SLP)

Address. Tom Walcott Building, PO Box 427, Jeremie Street, Castries
Telephone. (+1–758) 451–8446
Fax. (+1–758) 451–9389
Email. slp@candw.lc
Website. www.geocities.com/capitolhill/6166
Leadership. Kenny D. Anthony (political leader)

The centre-left SLP originated in the late 1940s as the political arm of the St. Lucia Workers' Cooperative Union, a trade union. It won the first elections held under universal adult suffrage in 1951 and formed the administration in the then colony until 1964. Other than in the period 1979–82 it was thereafter continuously in opposition to the governing →United Workers' Party (UWP) until the elections of May 1997 when, led by former law lecturer Kenny Anthony, it took 16 of the 17 Assembly seats. It came to office on a platform promising "people centred" government, economic development and improved health care and education, while capitalizing on allegations of corruption and scandal surrounding the outgoing UWP government.

The SLP is a consultative member of the Socialist International.

United Workers' Party (UWP)

Address. 1 Riverside Road, Castries
Telephone. (+1–809) 452–3438
Email. uwp@iname.com
Website. www.geocities.com/capitolhill/8393
Leadership. Morella Joseph (political leader)

The conservative UWP was formed in 1964 and, under the leadership of John Compton, ruled from 1964 until 1979, when it was decisively beaten in the first post-independence election. It returned to power in May 1982 and then remained in government until 1997. In April 1996 Compton was succeeded as party leader and Prime Minister by Vaughan Lewis, under whom the UWP slumped to defeat in the May 1997 elections, taking only one seat. Morella Joseph was elected party leader in October 2000 following Lewis's resignation, becoming the first woman party leader in St. Lucia. In May 2001 she also became the vice-president of the anti-SLP →National Alliance.

The UWP is a member of the Caribbean Democrat Union, a regional organization of the International Democrat Union.

Other Parties

National Alliance, emerged in Spring 2001 as an umbrella for opponents of the →St. Lucia Labour Party (SLP) government in preparation for the general election due by May 2002, promising to establish a "national unity government". Its three co-leaders were George Odlum, dismissed as the SLP government's Foreign Affairs Minister on March 29, 2001, because of reports of his involvement in the formation of the Alliance, Sir John Compton, former UWP leader and Prime Minister, and current UWP leader Morella Joseph. In May 2001 Odlum was named NA political leader, with Compton and Joseph as president and vice-president respectively.

St. Vincent and the Grenadines

Capital: Kingstown

Population: 115,000 (2000E)

A former British dependency, Saint Vincent and the Grenadines became fully independent within the Commonwealth in 1979. The head of state is the British sovereign, represented by a Governor-General. The head of government is the Prime Minister. The unicameral House of Assembly, which serves a term of office of up to five years, comprises six appointed Senators (four nominated by the government and two by the opposition) and 15 representatives elected on the first past the post system in single member constituencies.

The conservative New Democratic Party (NDP) of Sir James F. Mitchell won four successive elections in 1984, 1989, 1994 and 1998. In the June 1998 election, however, the opposition social democratic Unity Labour Party (ULP), although winning only seven seats to the NDP's eight, took 55% of the vote to the NDP's 45%. The ULP demanded fresh elections and a period of unrest culminated in Prime Minister Mitchell, in the Grand Beach Accord of May 2000, agreeing to hold a further general election by end March 2001. In the run-up to the elections, which were held on March 28, 2001, the three contesting party leaders signed a code of conduct agreeing equal access to the media and not to incite or encourage violence. The elections, which were monitored by Commonwealth observers at the government's request, resulted in victory for the ULP. The ULP won 12 of the 15 elected seats, with 56.7% of the vote, while the NDP took the remaining three seats with 40.7% of the vote.

New Democratic Party (NDP)

Address. Democrat House, PO Box 1300, Kingstown
Telephone. (1–784) 456–2114
Fax. (+1–784) 456–2114
Email. ndp@caribsurf.com
Leadership. Arnhim Eustace (leader)

The conservative NDP was founded by James Mitchell (later Sir James) in 1975, advocating political unity in the East Caribbean, social development and free enterprise. In 1984 the NDP formed the government for the first time, with Prime Minister Mitchell then winning three further successive elections (in 1989, 1994 and 1998). In the 1998 election, however, although the NDP took eight seats to the →Unity Labour Party's seven, it won fewer votes. The ULP demanded fresh elections and tensions climaxed in April-

May 2000 in work stoppages, road blockades and demonstrations against plans to provide improved benefits for parliamentarians. Mitchell refused to resign, warning of the damage being done to the country's reputation by the instability, but in the Grand Beach Accord, brokered by heads of other Caribbean states in May 2000, he agreed to hold elections two years ahead of schedule. In October 2000 Mitchell stood down as Prime Minister and was replaced by his Finance Minister, economist Arnhim Eustace. In the run-up to the March 2001 elections Eustace warned that failing to re-elect the NDP with an increased majority would jeopardize foreign investment and he promised to accelerate restructuring of the economy, which had been damaged by the decline of exports of bananas, the principal commodity. However, the NDP lost office, retaining only three seats. In

June 2001 Eustace said that some 569 people had been dismissed since the election "for no other reason than they supported the New Democratic Party".

The NDP is an associate member of the International Democrat Union (IDU) and a member of the IDU's regional organizations, the Americas Democrat Union and the Caribbean Democrat Union.

Unity Labour Party (ULP)
Address. Beachmount, Kingstown
Telephone. (+1–784) 457–2761
Fax. (+1–784) 456–2811
Email. headquarters@ulpsvg.com
Website. www.ulpsvg.com
Leadership. Ralph E. Gonsalves (political leader)
The centre-left ULP was established in September 1994 by the merger of the moderate social democratic St. Vincent Labour Party (SVLP) and the more left-wing Movement for National Unity (MNU), founded in 1982 by lawyer Ralph Gonsalves. The SVLP was in power from 1967–84 and led the country to independence in 1979. The conservative →New Democratic Party then won a string of election victories in 1984, 1989, 1994 and 1998. The ULP's first leader, Vincent Beache, was succeeded by Gonsalves in December 1998. The ULP disputed the result of the 1998 elections (which the NDP won by one seat) and was behind subsequent anti-government demonstrations that forced the government to accept early elections. Gonsalves then led the ULP to victory in the March 2001 election, when it won 12 seats with 56.7% of the vote. The ULP election programme emphasized "good governance", including job creation and sustainable development, a tough approach on crime and the causes of crime, and action to root out corruption in government. It also promised constitutional reform to strengthen the country's democracy and individual liberties, including the establishment of an Electoral and Boundaries Commission. On taking office Gonsalves pledged to clean up St. Vincent's offshore financial sector, which had attracted criticism from the OECD's Financial Action Task Force.

The ULP is a consultative member of the Socialist International.

Other Parties

People's Progressive Movement (PPM), founded by Ormiston (Ken) Boyea, a former leading figure in the →Unity Labour Party, in 2000. It won only 2.6% of the vote and no seats in the March 2001 election.

Samoa

Capital: Apia

Population: 168,000 (2000E)

Administered by New Zealand after World War I (in later years with self-government), Western Samoa achieved full independence in 1962 and opted for the shortened name Samoa in 1997. The head of state acts as a constitutional monarch with the power to dissolve the unicameral 49-member legislative assembly (the *Fono)* and to appoint a Prime Minister upon its recommendation. The *Fono* is elected by universal adult suffrage for up to five years, although the right to stand for election remains confined to members of the *Matai* (elected clan leaders).

In general elections on March 2, 2001, the ruling Human Rights Protection Party (HRPP) won 23 seats against 13 for the Samoan National Development Party, while 13 independents were elected. On March 16 the leader of the HRPP and incumbent Premier, Tuilaepa Sailele Malielegaoi, was re-elected by members of the *Fono*.

Human Rights Protection Party (HRPP)
Address. POB 3898, Apia
Leadership. Tuilaepa Sailele Malielegaoi (leader)
The HRPP was founded in 1979 as Western Samoa's first formal political party. Having won 22 parliamentary seats in the 1982 general elections, the party won an overall majority in 1985. However, subsequent defections brought down the government headed by Tofilau Eti Alesana at the end of that year. Tofilau Eti formed a new HRPP administration following the 1988 election, and the party's majority was enhanced in polling in 1991. In the 1996 elections, the HRPP won 24 of the 49 seats but quickly drew in enough independent deputies to retain a comfortable overall majority.

Tofilau Eti resigned for health reasons in November 1998 and was succeeded by his deputy, Tuilaepa Sailele Malielegaoi. Campaigning for elections to the *Fono* in March 2001 featured opposition allegations of corruption against the government and a demand, rejected by the Prime Minister, that the franchise and the right to stand in elections should be extended to Samoans resident abroad. In the event, the HRPP lost ground slightly, winning 23 seats, but again used its control of the levers of government to attract sufficient independents to ensure a continued majority.

In the wake of the elections the HRPP moved to appease its critics by setting up an electoral commission, but failed to convince the opposition that it would be independent. In August 2001 three HRPP ministers appeared in court on charges of bribery in the recent elections.

Samoan National Development Party (SNDP)
Address c/o Fono, Apia
Leadership. Tupua Tamasese Efi (leader)
The SNDP was created following the 1988 elections as an alliance of independents and Christian Democratic Party (CDP) members. The CDP had been formed by Tupua Tamasese Efi prior to the February 1985 general election and, in January 1986, had entered into a coalition government with a dissident faction of the →Human Rights Protection Party (HRPP). The coalition had been defeated in SNDP was constituted following the 1988 elections, which saw the return to power of the HRPP.

The SNDP remained the principal opposition party through the 1990s. In the campaign for the March 2001 elections the party accused the HRPP government of corruption, notably by selling Samoan passports to Chinese and Taiwanese nationals and in its management of Polynesian Airlines, the national carrier. However, the SNDP made only limited progress at the polls, returning 13 members of the *Fono*, and remained in opposition.

Other Parties

Samoa Democratic Party (SDP), formed in 1993 by a previously independent deputy in the *Fono* who objected to the extension of the legislature's term from three to five years without popular endorsement in a referendum.
Leadership. Le Tagaloa Pita

Samoa Labour Party (SLP), launched in 1994 by Toleapaialii Toesulusulu Siueva, a hotel owner who accused the ruling →Human Rights Protection Party of corruption. He won a seat in the 1996 elections but resigned after being accused of bribery.
Leadership. Toleapaialii Toesulusulu Siueva

Samoa Liberal Party (SLP), established in early 1994 mainly by dissidents of the ruling →Human Rights Protection Party opposed to the introduction of value-added tax.
Leadership. Nonumalo Leulumoega Sofara

Samoa National Party (SNP), established in January 2001, but unsuccessful in the March elections.

Samoans For Tomorrow (SFT), founded in 1998 and subsequently prominent in popular opposition to the ruling →Human Rights Protection Party.
Leadership. Tuifa'asisina Meaole Keil

San Marino

Capital: San Marino

Population: 25,000 (2000E)

The Most Serene Republic of San Marino, which traces its independent history back to 301 AD and its constitution to 1600, is a parliamentary democracy with a flourishing multi-party system. Legislative power is vested in the 60-member Grand and General Council (*Consiglio Grande e Generale*), which is directly elected by a system of proportional representation by citizens aged 18 and over, serving a five-year term subject to dissolution. A 10-member Congress of State (*Congresso di Stato*), or government, is elected by the Council for the duration of its term. Two members of the Council are designated for six-month terms as executive Captains Regent (*Capitani Reggenti*), one representing the city of San Marino and the other the countryside. An interval of three months must elapse before a councillor can be re-elected as a Captain Regent.

Early elections to the Grand and General Council on June 10, 2001, resulted as follows: Christian Democratic Party of San Marino 25 seats (with 41.4% of the vote), Socialist Party of San Marino 15 (24.2%), Party of Democrats 12 (20.8%), Popular Alliance of San Marino Democrats for the Republic 5 (8.2%), Communist Refoundation 2 (3.4%), San Marino National Alliance 1 (1.9%).

Christian Democratic Party of San Marino
Partito Democratico Cristiano Sammarinese (PDCS)
Address. 6 via delle Scalette, 47890 San Marino
Telephone. (+39–549) 991193
Fax. (+39–549) 992694
Email. pdcs@omniway.sm
Website. www.pdcs.sm
Leadership. Pier Marino Menicucci (political secretary); Pier Marino Mularoni (Council group leader); Ernesto Benedettini (president)
Founded in 1948, the PDCS was in opposition to a left-wing coalition until 1957, following which it headed centre-left coalitions until reverting to opposition in 1978. The party achieved narrow pluralities in successive Council elections, winning 25 seats in 1974, 26 in both 1978 and 1983 and 27 in 1988. The PDCS returned to power in July 1986, when the left-wing government collapsed and was replaced by San Marino's (and Europe's) first-ever coalition between Christian Democrats and Communists. This lasted until February 1992, when the PDCS opted to form a coalition with the →Socialist Party of San Marino (PSS).

The Christian Democrats retained their Council dominance in the 1993 and 1998 elections, albeit with slightly reduced representation of 26 and 25 seats respectively, and continued to govern in coalition with the PSS. In early elections in June 2001 the party again won 25 seats, opting this time to broaden the ruling coalition to include both the PSS and the →Party of Democrats.

The PDCS is affiliated to the Christian Democrat International. Party of Democrats

Party of Democrats
Partito dei Democratici (PdD)
Address. 1 via Sentier Rosso, San Marino
Telephone. (+39–541) 991199

Email. info@democratici.sm
Website. www.democratici.sm
Leadership. Claudio Felici (secretary-general); Emma Rossi (president)
The PdD was founded in April 1990 as the Progressive Democratic Party (PDP), which was the successor to the San Marino Communist Party (PCS) in line with similar conversions to democratic socialism on the part of communist parties elsewhere in Europe. Founded in 1941, the PCS had been an orthodox pro-Soviet party after World War II and had been in government with the →San Marino Socialist Party (PSS) until 1957 and again from 1978 until 1986, when the coalition had collapsed in 1986 amid differences over foreign and domestic issues. It had been replaced by the first-ever coalition of the PCS and the →San Marino Christian Democratic Party (PDCS). PCS representation in the Council had risen to 18 at the May 1988 elections, although its conversion into the PDP in 1990 resulted in two of its councillors joining the breakaway →Communist Refoundation.

The new PDP was forced into opposition in February 1992, when the PDCS decided that the PSS was a more suitable partner, and won only 11 seats in both the 1993 and the 1998 elections, remaining in opposition to a PDCS–PSS coalition. Having changed its name to the PdD, the party improved to 12 seats in the June 2001 elections and agreed to join a three-party "grand coalition" with the PDCS and PSS.

Popular Alliance of San Marino Democrats for the Republic
Alleanza Popolare dei Democratici Sammarinesi per la Repubblica (APDSR)
Address. 26 via Ca' Bartoletto, Cailungo, 47890 San Marino
Telephone. (+39–549) 907080
Fax. (+39–549) 907082

Email. apds@omniway.sm
Website. www.infotel.it/apds
Leadership. Mario Venturini

The centrist APDSR was founded before the May 1993 Council elections, in which it took fourth place behind the three main parties, winning four seats on a platform advocating constitutional and institutional reform. It improved to six seats in 1998 but fell back to five in 2001.

Socialist Party of San Marino
Partito Socialista Sammarinese (PSS)
Address. 46 via G. Ordelaffi, Borgo Maggiore, 47031 San Marino
Telephone. (+39–549) 902016
Fax. (+39–549) 906438
Website. pss.smn.sm
Leadership. Augusto Casali (secretary-general); Alberto Cecchetti (president)

The PSS was in coalition government with the Communists from 1945 until 1957 and then in opposition until 1973, when it entered a coalition with the →Christian Democratic Party of San Marino (PDCS). Through this period the Socialists were a distant second to the PDCS in successive Council elections, winning eight seats in 1974 against 25 for the PDCS. The PDCS-PSS coalition continued until November 1977, when the Socialists withdrew because of economic policy differences. The party retained eight Council seats in the 1978 elections, thereafter entering a left-wing coalition with the Communists and the Unitarian Socialists (PSU) which continued after the 1983 elections, in which the PSS advanced to nine seats. The left-wing coalition collapsed in mid-1986, when the PSS went into formal opposition for the first time since World War II. In 1990 the PSU (which had been formed in 1975 by a left-wing faction of the Independent Social Democrats, themselves originally a right-wing splinter of the PSS) merged with the PSS.

The PSS revived its coalition with the PDCS in February 1992, continuing it after the May 1993 elections, when it advanced to 14 seats, and after those of May 1998, in which it retained 14 seats. In the early elections of June 2001 the party advanced to 15 seats, thereafter becoming part of a three-party coalition led by the PDCS and including the →Party of Democrats.

The PSS is affiliated to the Socialist International.

Other Parties

Communist Refoundation (*Rifondazione Comunista, RC*), founded in 1990 by a minority Marxist-Leninist faction of the San Marino Communist Party which declined to accept the conversion of the latter into the democratic socialist Progressive Democratic Party in April 1990 (→Party of Democrats). The RC won two Council seats in May 1993, retaining them in October 1998 and June 2001.
Leadership. Ivan Foschi

San Marino National Alliance (*Alleanza Nazionale Sammarinese, ANS*), new formation which won a single seat in the June 2001 Council elections.
Leadership. Glauco Sansovini

São Tomé and Príncipe

Capital: São Tomé

Population: 160,000 (2000E)

The Democratic Republic of São Tomé and Príncipe achieved full independence from Portugal in 1975. There was only one legal political party — the Movement for the Liberation of São Tomé and Príncipe–Social Democratic Party (MLSTP-PSD) — until August 1990, when a new constitution providing for a multi-party democratic system was approved by referendum. Under the constitution, executive power is vested in a directly-elected President who may serve for a maximum of two consecutive five-year terms. Legislative power is vested in a 55-member National Assembly (*Assembléia Nacional*) with a maximum four-year term. A regional government looks after the affairs of the island of Príncipe, which assumed autonomous status in April 1995.

Presidential elections in March 1991 were won by independent candidate Miguel Trovoada, who was supported by the Democratic Convergence Party–Reflection Group (PCD–GR), which had defeated the ruling party in the first multi-party legislative elections two months earlier. Further legislative elections in October 1994 resulted in the MLSTP–PSD winning a plurality of 27 seats and regaining governmental power. In August 1995 a group of young army officers temporarily seized power in a bloodless coup. However, following mediation by Angolan representatives, the President and civilian government were restored to office.

In further presidential elections on June 30 and July 21, 1996, incumbent Miguel Trovoada (Independent Democratic Action, ADI) was re-elected in the second round with 52.7% of the vote. Another brief military takeover by young army officers followed in August, but President Trovoada was restored to power on Aug. 22. Eight political parties contested the National Assembly elections held on Nov. 8, 1998, which returned the MLSTP–PSD to power with 31 seats and an outright majority. The ADI and PCD–GR won 16 and 8 seats respectively, and were the only opposition parties to secure representation.

In a presidential election held on July 29, 2001, ADI candidate Fradique de Menezes won in the first round by polling 56.3% of the vote; his closest rival, former President Manuel Pinto da Costa of the MLSTP–PSD, gained 38.7%.

Democratic Convergence Party–Reflection Group
Partido de Convergencia Democrática–Grupo de Reflexão (PCD-GR)
Address. c/o Assembléia Nacional, São Tomé
Leadership. Alda Bandeira (president)

Initially an underground opposition movement, the PCD–GR formally came into existence following the constitutional changes in 1990. In the January 1991 legislative elections the party won a majority with just over 54% of the votes cast, and in March it supported the successful presidential candidacy of Miguel Trovoada. Relations between the PCD-GR and the President subsequently deteriorated, as did the party's popularity, culminating in defeat in the legislative elections in October 1994, in which its representation in the National Assembly fell from 33 to 14.

Having supported a no-confidence motion against the government and signed an agreement which provided for the formation of a nine-member coalition with the →Movement for the Liberation of São Tomé and Príncipe-Social Democratic Party (MLSTP–PSD), three members of the PCD–GR were appointed to the new administration formed in October 1996. However, the party came third in the 1998 legislative elections, declining to 8 seats (with just 16% of the vote).

Independent Democratic Action
Ação Democrática Independente (ADI)
Address. c/o Assembléia Nacional, São Tomé
Leadership. Carlos Agostinho das Neves
Founded in 1992 under the leadership of an adviser to President Trovoada, the centrist ADI won 14 of the 55 seats in the National Assembly in the 1994 elections, making it the joint runner-up with the →Democratic Convergence Party-Reflection Group. In January 1996 the ADI accepted representation in a government of national unity headed by the →Movement for the Liberation of São Tomé and Príncipe–Social Democratic Party (MLSTP-PSD). Trovoada was re-elected President in the second round of voting in July, having come a poor second in the first round with only 25% of the vote. The party refused to participate in the next MLSTP-PSD coalition government formed in October 1996 with the →Democratic Convergence Party-Reflection Group (PCD-GR). In the 1998 legislative elections, the ADI came second (increasing its representation by two seats), although it complained of irregularities in the elections.

President Trovoada stepped down after the two five-year terms permitted under the constitution, and in the presidential elections in July 2001 ADI candidate Fradique de Menezes, a businessman, was elected in the first round with 56.3% of the vote.

Movement for the Liberation of São Tomé and Príncipe–Social Democratic Party (MLSTP–PSD)
Movimento de Libertação de São Tomé e Príncipe–Partido Social Democrata (MLSTP–PSD)
Address. c/o Assembléia Nacional, São Tomé
Leadership. Manuel Pinto da Costa (president); Carlos Alberto da Graça (secretary-general)
The leftist MLSTP was formed in the early 1970s and became the driving force in the campaign against Portuguese rule. After independence it maintained its position as the sole legal political organization until the adoption of multi-partyism in 1990, at which point the Social Democratic Party designation was added to its title and the longstanding leader and former President, Manuel Pinto da Costa, stood down. The party was defeated by the →Democratic Convergence Party–Reflection Group (PCD-GR) in the January 1991 legislative elections and did not endorse any candidates in the presidential poll the following March. However, in the October 1994 legislative elections, the MLSTP-PSD was returned to power winning 27 of the seats in the 55-member National Assembly. The party's secretary-general, Carlos Alberto da Graça, was appointed Prime Minister of a Cabinet largely composed of MLSTP-PSD members. In December 1995, however, he was replaced by his party deputy, Armindo Vaz de Almeida, who formed a national unity government also including the →Independent Democratic Alliance (ADI) and the extra-parliamentary →Opposition Democratic Coalition. The MLSTP-PSD candidate in the mid-1996 presidential elections was da Costa, who headed the field in the first round with 40% of the vote but lost to the incumbent in the second round, when he received 47.3%.

The De Almeida government was dissolved after its defeat in a confidence motion in September 1996. President Trovoada refused to appoint the party's first choice of Prime Minister and Raúl Wagner da Conceição Bragança Neto was appointed to form a nine-member coalition government with the PCD-GR and one independent in October 1996. (De Almeida was expelled from the party in December, accused of corruption).

Following an extraordinary party congress in May 1998, the party approved new statutes providing for: the creation of the position of party president, to which Pinto da Costa was elected; three vice-presidential appointments; and the enlargement of the national council from 95 to 120 members. The party held power securing a further four parliamentary seats (with over 50% of the vote) in the 1998 elections. Guilherme Posser da Costa was appointed Prime Minister, but his first nominations for the Council of Ministers were rejected by the President.

The power struggle between government and President has blocked decisions on important political and economic issues. In the July 2001 presidential elections, Pinto da Costa stood for the MLSTP but was beaten in the first round of voting by the ADI candidate backed by the outgoing President.

Other Parties

Christian Democratic Front (*Frente Democrata Cristão, FDC*), launched in late 1990 but failed to secure legislative representation in the 1991, 1994 or 1998 elections.
Leadership. Sabino Dos Santos (president)

Opposition Democratic Coalition (*Coligação Democrática da Oposição, CODO*), originated in the mid-1980s as an alliance of Portugal-based exile groups in opposition to the then single-party regime; won one seat in 1991 but unrepresented in the legislature since the 1994 elections.

Popular Alliance (*Aliança Popular, AP*), a small Portugal-based expatriate party, recognized in 1993.

Saudi Arabia

Capital: Riyadh

Population: 22,023,000 (2000E)

The Kingdom of Saudi Arabia is under the direct rule of the King, who is also the Prime Minister and who presides over a Council of Ministers. There is no parliament nor are there any legal political parties. A royal decree in March 1992 provided for the establishment of a Consultative Council, composed initially of 60 members and a chairman and appointed every four years in accordance with the Islamic principle of "consultation". The Consultative Council, which has only an advisory role, was inaugurated in December 1993. The King expanded the membership of the Council to 90 in July 1997 and then to 120 in May 2001. Extra-legal opposition to the regime has been fuelled by resentment of Islamic militants towards the presence of Western (mainly US) military forces in the country.

Senegal

Capital: Dakar

Population: 9,987,000 (2000E)

Senegal was under French rule until it achieved independence in federation with Mali in June 1960. The federation was dissolved in August 1960 when Senegal withdrew. The following month the Republic of Senegal was proclaimed. Under the constitution (most recently amended in 2001), executive power is vested in the President, who is directly elected by universal suffrage for a five-year term. The President, as head of state and head of government, appoints the Prime Minister, who appoints the Council of Ministers in consultation with the President. Legislative power is vested in the 120-member National Assembly (*Asssemblée Nationale*), which is also directly elected for a five-year term.

In presidential elections on Feb. 21, 1993, President Abdou Diouf of the Senegal Socialist Party (PSS) won his third term of office (extended from five to seven years following a constitutional amendment in 1991), with 58.4% of the votes cast. In Assembly elections on May 9, 1993, the PSS obtained 84 seats, the Senegalese Democratic Party (PDS) 27 and four minor parties or alliances the other nine seats. In March 1998 the National Assembly voted to increase the number of its deputies from 120 to 140. At the following elections held on May 24, 1998, the PSS won 93 of the 140 seats, with the PDS again in second place with 23.

In January 1999 elections were held for the newly-established Senate; 45 of the 60 senators were elected by the National Assembly and local, municipal and regional councillors (and all were returned for the PSS), with 12 appointed by the President and three elected by Senegalese living abroad. Eight candidates stood in the presidential elections held on Feb. 27, 2000. After a second round on March 19, Abdoulaye Wade of the PDS with 58.5% of the vote beat the PSS incumbent Diouf (who took 41.5% of the vote). Diouf had led after the first round but lost after five of the six candidates who dropped out after the first round gave their support to Wade, so ending 40 years of uninterrupted socialist rule.

In a referendum on Jan. 7, 2001, an amended constitution was approved by over 90% of voters. It provided for the dissolution of the Senate, the reduction of the number of deputies in the National Assembly from 140 to 120 members, and the limiting of the presidential term from seven to five years. It also gave the President power to dissolve the Assembly without the agreement of a two-thirds majority. Early legislative elections were held on April 29, 2001, in which the *Sopi* ("Change") coalition, led by President Wade's PDS, won a landslide victory over the former ruling party, taking 89 of the 120 seats. Mame Madior Boyle, who had been appointed as Senegal's first woman Prime Minister in March 2001, was re-appointed in May.

African Party for Democracy and Socialism/And Jëf
Parti Africain pour la Démocratie et le Socialisme/And Jëf (PADS/AJ)

Address. BP 12136, Dakar
Telephone. (+221) 825–7267
Fax. (+221) 823–5860
Website. www.ajpads.org
Leadership. Landing Savané (secretary-general)

The progressive and pan-Africanist PADS/AJ was formed in 1991 by a merger of the And-Jëf-Revolutionary Movement for the New Democracy with three other left-wing groups. The party's leader, Landing Savané, took third place in the February 1993 presidential election but gained less than 3% of the votes cast. In May 1993 the party contested the legislative elections in an alliance with the →National Democratic Rally and the →Convention of Democrats and Patriots, which was called *Jappoo Liggeeyal* (Let Us Unite) and which won three National Assembly seats (and 4.9% of the vote). In February 1994 Savané and the leader of the →Senegalese Democratic Party (PDS) were arrested and charged with provoking anti-government riots. The charges against them were dropped later in the year. The party won four seats in the 1998 National Assembly polling, and contested the Senate elections the following year in a coalition which included the →Independence and Labour Party (PIT), although it failed to gain representation. Savané backed the successful candidature of Abdoulaye Wade for the presidential election in 2000 and was appointed minister for industry and mines in the new government. The PADS/AJ retained two of its seats in the 2001 Assembly elections with 4% of the vote.

Alliance of Progressive Forces
Alliance des Forces de Progrès (AFP)

Address. BP 5825, Dakar Fann
Telephone. (+221) 825–1488
Fax. (+221) 825–7770
Email. Admin@afp-senegal.org
Website. www.afp-senegal.org
Leadership. Moustapha Niasse (secretary-general)

The AFP was formed in June 1999 by a dissident faction of the →Senegal Socialist Party (PSS) led by Moustapha Niasse, a former minister of foreign affairs. Niasse stood in the first round of the presidential election in 2000, coming third with 16.8% of the vote, and then transferred his support to Abdoulaye Wade in the run-off. Appointed Prime Minister in the subsequent new government, he was dismissed in March 2001 following his decision to contest the legislative elections the following month as leader of the AFP. The party came second in the polling, winning 11 seats.

Democratic League–Labour Party Movement
Ligue Démocratique-Mouvement pour le Parti du Travail (LD–MPT)

Address. BP 10172, Dakar Liberté
Leadership. Abdoulaye Bathily (secretary-general)

The LD–MPT originated as a Marxist party in 1981. Increasingly critical of the Diouf administration, party leader Bathily launched a campaign in 1990 for a "non-Diouf unity government". His unsuccessful presidential candidacy in February 1993 attracted only 2.4% of the votes cast, although the party secured three seats in the National Assembly elections the following May. The LD–MPT retained its Assembly seats in the 1998 elections with nearly 4% of the vote. In March 1999 it joined a left-wing coalition to back the →Senegalese Democratic Party (PDS) candidate in the presidential election and Bathily was appointed minister for energy and water in the subsequent new government. In the 2001 Assembly elections the party joined the PDS-led *Sopi* Coalition (Coalition for Change), which won a landslide victory with 89 seats.

Independence and Labour Party
Parti de l'Indépendance et du Travail (PIT)

Address. BP 5612, Dakar Fann
Website. www.pit-senegal.com
Leadership. Amath Dansokho (secretary-general)

The left-wing PIT was registered in 1981. Party leader Dansokho served in the Diouf government from 1991–95. It allied with the →Senegalese Democratic Party (PDS) to back the victorious PDS candidate in the 2000 presidential election and Dansokho was appointed minister for urban planning in the new government. The party retained its single seat in the 2001 legislative polling.

Senegal Socialist Party
Parti Socialiste Sénégalais (PSS)

Address. BP 12010, Dakar
Telephone. (+221) 252232
Fax. (+221) 258054
Leadership. Abdou Diouf (chairman); Ousmane Tanor Dieng (executive secretary)

Founded in 1958 but descended from pre-war socialist movements in French West Africa, the democratic socialist PSS has been the ruling party in Senegal since independence in 1960, adopting its present name at the end of 1976, before which change it had been called the Senegalese Progressive Union (UPS). Although it was in effect the country's only legal party between 1964 and 1974 under the presidency of its founder, Léopold Sédar Senghor, the constitution continued to guarantee a plurality of political parties and in 1974 the →Senegalese Democratic Party (PDS) was officially recognized as an opposition party. A three-party system, introduced in 1976, was later extended to allow a multiplicity of parties. Abdou Diouf assumed the leadership of the PSS in 1981, after which new agricultural and industrial policies, intended to give a greater role to the private sector, were adopted.

The PSS dominated all Senegalese elections until 2000. Having retained the Presidency of the Republic in 1993, Diouf was elected to the new post of party chairman in 1996 and a new position of executive secretary was also created. During 1997 there were rumours of serious divisions within the PSS and a dissident group which had begun a campaign for party reform broke away in 1998 prior to the legislative elections that year. However, the PSS secured 93 of the 140 seats in the National Assembly and all the elected seats to the newly created Senate in 1999.

Diouf narrowly won the first round of the presidential elections in 2000 (with 41% of the vote) but lost the second round to the PDS candidate, Abdoulaye Wade, who was backed by the major opposition parties. Weakened by further defections from the party, the PSS lost out badly in the 2001 legislative elections, winning only ten seats with 17% of the vote.

The party is a member of the Socialist International

Senegalese Democratic Party
Parti Démocratique Sénégalais (PDS)

Address. ave Gen. de Gaulle, Dakar
Leadership. Abdoulaye Wade (secretary-general)

Founded in 1974, the liberal democratic PDS was required by a constitutional amendment of March 1976 to adopt a formal political position to the right of the government party (in a three-party system which was later expanded to cover further parties). In successive legislative elections from 1970 until 2001, it was runner-up to, but some distance behind, the →Senegal Socialist Party (PSS). In presidential elections until 2000, party leader Wade was similarly placed.

Although the PDS was the major element in the growing opposition movement at the end of the 1980s, the party was persuaded by early 1991 (like the →Independence and Labour Party, PIT) to accept the government's offer of participation in a coalition administration. This continued until October 1992, when Wade and the other PDS members in the government resigned their posts. In May 1994 charges against Wade for his alleged role in the assassination of a member of the Constitutional Court in May 1993 were dismissed. Other charges, linked to anti-government rioting in February 1994, were similarly dropped later in the year. In March 1995 the PDS resumed its participation in the PSS-dominated coalition government, being assigned five portfolios.

In February 1998 Wade lodged an appeal to overturn legislation to enlarge the National Assembly and withdrew the party from government in March to prepare for the legislative elections scheduled for May. At the elections, however, the PDS secured only 23 seats with less than 20% of the vote.

Returning from a year in exile, Wade formed an alliance with the →African Party for Democracy and Socialism (AJPADS), the PIT and the →Democratic League–Labour Party Movement (LD–MPT) in 1999 and he was nominated as their joint candidate for the presidential elections in 2000. Wade won a substantial victory over Diouf with 58.5% of the vote in the second round and negotiated the new constitution by referendum which enabled him to dissolve the PSS-dominated parliament. Under the name of *Sopi* ("Change"), a PDS-led coalition won 89 seats, giving it a commanding majority, in the new National Assembly.

The PDS is a member of the Liberal International.

Union for Democratic Renewal
Union pour le Renouveau Démocratique (URD)

Address. c/o Assemblée Nationale, Dakar
Leadership. Djibo Leyti Kâ (leader)

Founded by former minister Kâ in April 1998. Kâ came fourth in the first round (with 7% of the vote) of the presidential elections in 2000 and was the only opposition member to support incumbent President Diouf in the run-off. In the 2001 Assembly elections the URD won three seats with just under 4% of the vote.

Other Parties

Alliance Jëf Jël, formerly the centrist Alliance for Progress and Justice (*Alliance pour le Progrès et la Justice*), its name was changed to its present style in 2000. In the 2001 National Assembly elections, the party won a single seat.

Convention of Democrats and Patriots (*Convention des Démocrates et des Patriotes*, CDP), founded in 1992 by former minister Iba Der Thiam; he took 1.2% of the vote in the first round of the 2000 presidential poll; the party has no seats in the legislature.

National Democratic Rally, (*Rassemblement National Démocratique, RND*), leftist party originating in 1976; won one seat in the 2001 Assembly elections.

Party for Progress and Citizenship (*Parti pour le Progrès et la Citoyenneté, PPC*), won a single seat in the 2001 elections with less than 1% of the vote.

Senegalese Liberal Party (*Parti Libéral Sénégalais, PLS*), led by Ousmane Ngom; formed in 1998 by a breakaway faction of the →Senegalese Democratic Party; unsuccessfully contested the Senate elections in 1999 but gained one seat in the 2001 National Assembly polling.

Seychelles

Capital: Victoria

Population: 79,300 (2000E)

The Republic of Seychelles achieved independence from Britain in June 1976. President James Mancham, who at that time led the Seychelles Democratic Party, was ousted in a coup in 1977 by France-Albert René. René established a one-party state with the Seychelles People's Progressive Front (SPPF) as the sole legal party. Pressure for democratic reform was resisted until December 1991, when the SPPF endorsed a return to political pluralism. A new constitution, drafted by an elected constitutional commission, was approved in a popular referendum in June 1993. It provided for the simultaneous direct election for five-year terms of the President and unicameral National Assembly (with 11 of the Assembly's 33 seats allocated on a proportional basis to parties obtaining at least 9% of the total votes cast). The President may hold office for a maximum of three consecutive terms.

Multi-party Assembly elections on July 23, 1993, resulted in the SPPF obtaining 28 seats, the Democratic Party 4 and the United Opposition one. In a simultaneous presidential contest, President René was re-elected with 59.5% of the vote. In 1996 the constitution was amended to redefine the composition of the National Assembly as 25 directly elective seats and a maximum of 10 proportionally allocated seats. At the next elections, held on March 22, 1998, for an Assembly of 34 seats (including 9 proportionally allocated), the SPPF won a total of 30 seats with 61.7% of the vote, the United Opposition (subsequently renamed Seychelles National Party, SNP) three (26.1%) and the Democratic Party one (12.1%). President René won the simultaneous presidential election with 66.7% of the vote. A further presidential election, called two years early on Aug. 31–Sept. 2, 2001 and without there being simultaneous legislative elections, resulted in René being re-elected on a 54.2% vote share, with Wavel Ramkalawan of the SNP taking 44.9% of the vote.

Democratic Party (DP)

Address. POB 169, Mont Fleuri
Telephone. (+248) 224916
Fax. (+248) 224302
Leadership. Sir James Mancham (leader); Daniel Belle (secretary-general)

The DP was registered in March 1992 as a revival of the former Social Democratic Party, which had been effectively dissolved following the declaration of a one-party state in the late 1970s. Party leader and former President of the Republic, Sir James Mancham, returned from exile in April 1992. In July 1992 the DP won eight of the 22 seats on the constitutional commission elected to draft a new constitution. In multi-party presidential elections held the following July, Mancham was runner-up to incumbent President René of the →Seychelles People's Progressive Front (SPPF), taking 36.7% of the vote. At the same time, in elections to the National Assembly, the DP obtained four seats allocated on a proportional basis. The DP adopted a policy of "reconciliation" with the SPPF in the aftermath of the 1993 elections, and in late 1997 rejected an invitation from the United Opposition (as the →Seychelles National Party was then known) to form an alliance at the 1998 elections. In these elections Mancham (with 13.8% of the vote) took third place in the presidential election and lost his seat in the National Assembly (where the DP won only one seat). The party did not contest the 2001 presidential election.

The DP is associated with the International Democrat Union through the Democrat Union of Africa.

Seychelles National Party (SNP)

Address. PO Box 81, Victoria
Telephone. (+248) 224124
Fax. (+248) 224124
Leadership. Wavel Ramkalawan (leader); Roger Mancienne (secretary)

Seychelles National Party is the name adopted in July 1998 by the United Opposition. This had been formed in 1995 through the merger of three parties (Seychelles Party, National Alliance Party and Seychelles National Movement) which had contested the 1993 elections as a coalition, winning one proportionally allocated Assembly seat and receiving less than 4% of the vote in the presidential election. In the March 1998 legislative elections the party won three Assembly seats with 26.1% of the vote, while its leader was runner-up in the simultaneous presidential election, winning 19.5% of the vote. In an early presidential election held on Aug. 31–Sept. 2, 2001, Ramkalawan made a substantial advance, taking 44.9% of the vote, but was again defeated by incumbent President René. Ramkalawan's subsequent complaints that there had been vote rigging, including intimidation, bribery and under-age voting, were rejected by the Elections Commissioner.

The SNP is an observer member of the Liberal International.

Seychelles People's Progressive Front (SPPF)
Front Populaire Progressiste des Seychelles (FPPS)

Address. PO Box 91, Victoria
Telephone. (+248) 224455
Fax. (+248) 225351
Leadership. France-Albert René (president); James Michel (secretary-general)

Founded in 1964 as the left-of-centre Seychelles People's United Party, the SPPF adopted its present name in 1978, a successful coup having been staged the previous year by party leader René, who was then Prime Minister. René assumed the presidency of the Republic and the SPPF became the sole legal party until December 1991, when the ban on political activity by other parties was suspended. In elections to the constitutional commission in July 1992, the SPPF won the majority of the votes cast and was awarded 14 of the 22 seats on the commission. In the presidential and legislative elections in July 1993, René and the SPPF won an emphatic victory. René retained the presidency with almost 59.5% of the vote, while the party won 28 seats (22 of them directly elected) in the National Assembly. In March 1998 President René was re-elected with 66.7% of the vote, while the SPPF won 30 seats in the National Assembly.

René called further presidential elections two years ahead of time, on Aug. 31–Sept. 2, 2001, citing the need to demonstrate political stability to investors concerned about the country's economic difficulties. He was re-elected, but with a significantly reduced share of the vote (54.2%) compared with 1998.

Sierra Leone

Capital: Freetown

Population: 5,232,500 (2000E)

The Republic of Sierra Leone achieved independence from the United Kingdom in 1961, originally as a constitutional monarchy. In 1971 a republican constitution was adopted and Siaka Stevens, leader of the All People's Congress (APC), became President. The APC was declared the sole legal party in 1978, and the country remained a one-party state until a referendum in 1991 endorsed the introduction of multi-party politics. General elections were arranged for the following year, but the process was curtailed in April 1992 by a military coup led by Capt. Valentine Strasser. Under the Strasser regime a National Provisional Ruling Council (NPRC) was set up in May 1992, the legislature was dissolved and all political activity suspended. In July 1992 the NPRC was designated the Supreme Council of State, and the Cabinet was reconstituted as the Council of State Secretaries, including civilian and military figures.

In 1993 the regime announced the adoption of a transitional programme envisaging a return to civilian government in early 1996 following multi-party elections. In April 1995 Strasser lifted the ban on political activity, stating that parties wishing to participate in elections should register with an Interim National Electoral Commission. These developments took place against a background of intensifying rebel activity by the Revolutionary United Front (RUF). In January 1996 Strasser was deposed by Brig. Julius Maada Bio, who became the new chairman of the NPRC and head of state. Nevertheless, elections went ahead as planned on Feb. 26–27 under the provisions of the 1991 constitution (which had been suspended since April 1992). This provided for a unicameral legislature with 12 indirectly elected members (Paramount Chiefs drawn from the different provincial districts of Sierra Leone) and 68 members directly elected for a 5-year term by universal adult suffrage under a system of proportional representation. Executive power was vested in a directly elected President, who could serve for no more than two 5-year terms. The minimum voting age was 21 years.

The February 1996 parliamentary election was contested by 13 parties, of which six won seats as follows: Sierra Leone People's Party (SLPP) 27, United National People's Party (UNPP) 17, People's Democratic Party (PDP) 12, APC 5, National Unity Party 4, Democratic Centre Party (DCP) 3. All 13 parties fielded candidates in simultaneous voting for the presidency, but no candidate won an absolute majority in the first round of voting. In a run-off ballot on March 15, 1996, Ahmed Tejan Kabbah, the SLPP candidate, was elected with 59.5% of the vote, as against 40.5% for the UNPP candidate, John Karefa-Smart. President Kabbah was inaugurated on March 29, 1996. On May 25, 1997, he was deposed in a military coup led by Maj. Johnny Paul Koroma, who formed an Armed Forces Revolutionary Council (AFRC), suspended the existing constitution and banned political activity. Members of the suspended legislature nevertheless met to debate proposals for a peace settlement, the latest coup being widely opposed by civilians in Sierra Leone and universally condemned by the international community. Although the coup leaders were dissident members of the Sierra Leone armed forces (and had links with the former NRPC), some leaders of the RUF were appointed to the AFRC. Other elements of the Sierra Leone armed forces remained loyal to the exiled President Kabbah, whose restoration was also an objective of ECOMOG, the regional peacekeeping force operating in Sierra Leone. Key concentrations of AFRC troops were defeated in February 1998 by ECOMOG forces, which also clashed with RUF rebels.

On March 10, 1998, President Kabbah was restored to office and the civilian government institutions were formally reinstated. A further round of armed conflict, in which RUF forces were backed by former AFRC elements, led to a ceasefire agreement between the RUF and the Kabbah Government in May 1999. An accord was signed in July 1999 under which the RUF pledged to disarm and to reconstitute itself as a political organization, with an entitlement to representation in a proposed government of national unity. The RUF was duly registered as a political party in November 1999, but it failed to fulfil its disarmament pledges and in early 2000 objected to the replacement of ECOMOG by a larger UN peacekeeping force (UNAMSIL). The peace process broke down and there was a fresh cycle of armed conflict before the RUF signed another ceasefire agreement with the Kabbah Government in November 2000. In October 2001 the RUF said it would hand over weapons by the end of the month under the terms of a UN-brokered agreement.

Six of Sierra Leone's political parties (the APC, PDP, UNPP, People's Democratic Alliance, People's National Convention and People's Progressive Party) announced in August 2000 that they had agreed in principle to merge into a single party and had established a "Grand Alliance" as a first step towards this objective. In January 2001 the chairman of the National Electoral Commission advised President Kabbah that it would be unrealistic to hold national elections in the following month (the normal expiry date for the five-year mandates won in 1996). In February 2001 Parliament unanimously voted for a (renewable) six-month postponement of the parliamentary and presidential elections on the grounds that two-thirds of the country was currently under the control of RUF rebels.

All People's Congress (APC)

Address. c/o Sierra Leone Parliament, Freetown
Leadership. Edward Mohammed Turay (leader)
Established in 1960 by Siaka Stevens (who died in 1988),

the leftist APC was the dominant party from 1968 and the sole authorized political formation between 1978 and 1991. In the 1996 legislative elections the party came in fourth place with less than 6% of the vote and only five seats. In the presidential poll the APC candidate finished fifth.

Democratic Centre Party (DCP)
Address. c/o Sierra Leone Parliament, Freetown
Leadership. Adu Aiah Koroma (leader)
Following the February 1996 elections the DCP was awarded three parliamentary seats, having secured 4.8% of the vote. In the presidential poll the party's candidate took sixth place.

National Unity Party (NUP)
Address. c/o Sierra Leone Parliament, Freetown
Website. www.nupsl.org
Leadership. John Oponjo Benjamin (interim leader)
With 5.3% of the vote in both the legislative and presidential elections in February 1996, the NUP secured four seats in the 68-member Parliament.

People's Democratic Party (PDP)
Address. c/o Sierra Leone Parliament, Freetown
Leadership. Osman Kamara (leader)
The PDP was first registered in 1991. In the February 1996 polling it took third place, securing 15.3% of the vote and 12 seats in the legislative election and 16.1% of the vote in the presidential election.

Sierra Leone People's Party (SLPP)
Address. 29 Rawdon Street, Freetown
Telephone. (+232–22) 228222
Website. www.slpp.ws
Leadership. Ahmad Tejan Kabbah (leader); Maigore Kallon (chairman); Prince A. Harding (secretary general)
The SLPP was the dominant party at independence and the party of government until 1967. It was then banned in 1978 but resurfaced in 1991 under the leadership of Salia Jusu-Sheriff. In the February 1996 elections the party won the largest share of the votes in both the legislative and presidential polls (36.1% and 35.8% respectively), securing 27 seats in Parliament. The SLPP's presidential candidate, Ahmad Tejan Kabbah, won the second round run-off in March against his nearest rival from the →United National People's Party (UNPP), taking 59.5% of the vote.

United National People's Party (UNPP)
Address. Sierra Leone Parliament, Freetown
Leadership. John Karefa-Smart (leader); Joe Conteh (secretary general)
The UNPP was runner-up to the SLPP in the 1996 elections, winning 21.6% of the vote and 17 seats in the legislative poll and 40.5% of the vote in the final round of the presidential contest. In January 1997 the party leadership expelled 14 UNPP members of Parliament from the party but failed to persuade the Speaker to declare their seats vacant. John Karefa-Smart, who had lived in self-imposed exile in the USA since 1997, returned to Freetown in April 2001 to make a personal application for a High Court judgement on the status of the 14 dissident MPs.

Other Political Organizations

National Alliance Democratic Party (NADP), won 0.6% of the vote in the 1996 legislative elections.

National Democratic Alliance (NDA), won 2.7% of the vote in the 1996 legislative elections.

National People's Party (NPP), won 0.5% of the vote in the 1996 legislative elections.

National Unity Movement (NUM), won 1.2% of the vote in the 1996 legislative elections.

People's Democratic Alliance (PDA), registered in March 2000 by former members of the →People's Democratic Party (PDP), who were subsequently reported to have held discussions with former members of the Armed Forces Revolutionary Council seeking a route into civilian politics.
Leadership. Abdul Rahman Kamara (leader)

People's National Convention (PNC), won 2.5% of the vote in the 1996 legislative elections.

People's Progressive Party (PPP), won 2.9% of the vote in the 1996 legislative elections.

Revolutionary United Front (RUF), engaged in armed conflict with the government since 1991 and linked to the National Patriotic Front of Liberia (which subsequently evolved into Liberia's ruling →→National Patriotic Party). Some RUF leaders were appointed to the Armed Forces Revolutionary Council which held power in Sierra Leone from May 1997 to February 1998. In July 1999 the RUF signed an agreement with the restored civilian government of President Kabbah to disarm and reform itself into a political organization. Despite registering the name Revolutionary United Front Party (RUFP, to be led by the then RUF leader, Foday Sanko) in late 1999, the RUF continued to engage in armed conflict, leading to another cease-fire agreement in November 2000. In early 2001 the Sierra Leone Parliament estimated that two-thirds of the country was controlled by the RUF. The RUF Military High Command in March 2001 approved the formation of a Political and Peace Council to conduct a "formal dialogue with the government and the international community" on "efforts to seek a peaceful conclusion to this unfortunate episode". In October 2001 the RUF said it would disarm under the terms of a UN-brokered agreement.
Leadership. Gen. Issa Sesay (interim leader of Military High Command); Omrie Golley (chairman of Political and Peace Council)

Social Democratic Party (SDP), won 0.8% of the vote in the 1996 legislative elections.

Singapore

Capital: Singapore City

Population: 4,000,000 (2000E)

Singapore achieved internal self-rule from the United Kingdom in 1959, and four years later joined the Federation of Malaysia. On leaving the federation in 1965, Singapore became an independent sovereign state.

Singapore is a republic with a parliamentary system based on the Westminster model in which the Prime Minister is head of government. The constitution provides for a President who is the head of state. Prior to 1991, the President was appointed by Parliament and held a largely ceremonial role. Following constitutional amendments that year, an elected presidency was created, with wider powers of veto and oversight of government activities. Presidential candidates are first vetted by a Presidential Elections Committee, and in the first elections on Aug. 28, 1993, Ong Teng Cheong of the People's Action Party (PAP) became Singapore's first directly elected President. The current President, Sellapa Rama Nathan, was declared President-elect on Nomination Day when he was the sole candidate approved by the Committee. He was sworn in on Sept. 1, 1999.

Parliament is a unicameral chamber currently comprising 84 Members of Parliament (MPs) elected by universal adult suffrage for five years and six appointed members. In an early general election, held on Nov.4, 2001, the PAP (which has held a majority continuously since 1959) won 82 of the 84 elective seats taking 75.3% of the vote in the 29 contested seats. The PAP was unopposed for 55 seats, with the Singapore People's Party (SPP) and the Workers' Party (WP) taking one seat each. Most MPs were elected from 14 wards, each with five or six seats, the party winning the ward taking all the seats, a system seen as favouring the PAP. Only nine MPs were elected from single-seat wards.

People's Action Party (PAP)

Address. Blk 57B, New Upper Changi Road, #01–1402, PCF Building, Singapore 463057
Telephone. (+65) 244–4600
Fax. (+65) 243–0114
Email. paphq@pap.org.sg
Website. www.pap.org.sg
Leadership. Goh Chok Tong (secretary-general)
The PAP, founded as a radical socialist party in 1954, has been Singapore's ruling party since 1959. After the defection of its more militant members to form the Socialist Front (*Barisan Sosialis*) in 1961, the PAP leadership effectively transformed the party into a moderate, anti-communist organization, supporting a pragmatic socialist programme emphasizing economic development and social welfare. Despite its overwhelming legislative dominance, the PAP's share of the total vote fell steadily from 1980 (down to 61% in 1991). However, the January 1997 election results showed the party raising its share of the total vote to 65% and recapturing two of the four seats previously lost to the opposition. In the November 2001 elections it further improved its vote share to over 75%. The party had emphasized the need to retain continuity in government in the face of Singapore's worst recession since the 1960s.

Until the end of 1992, the party's secretary-general (i.e. leader) was Lee Kuan Yew, who was also Prime Minister from 1959 to 1990. He remains a senior figure in the party and in the current government led by his successor, Goh Chok Tong.

Singapore People's Party (SPP)

Address. 1 North Bridge Road, #17–08, High Street Centre, Singapore 179094
Telephone. (+65) 3380378
Leadership. Chiam See Tong (secretary-general)
Formed largely by defecting →Singapore Democratic Party (SDP) members in 1993, the SPP is similarly liberal and centrist in its tendencies. It has, however, adopted a less confrontational approach to the ruling →People's Action Party, thereby cultivating an image of a more moderate and responsible opposition. In its first electoral effort in the 1997 elections, it fielded three candidates, including Chiam See Tong, who had earlier defected from the SDP. Chiam was the only successful candidate, delivering the SPP a single seat in parliament.

In June 2001, the SPP formed the Singapore Democratic Alliance with four other smaller opposition parties (the →Singapore Justice Party, →Singapore National Front, →National Solidarity Party and →Singapore Malays National Organization) to contest the next general elections. In the November 2001 elections Chiam See Tong retained his seat for the SPP, but the alliance had no other successes.

Workers' Party (WP)

Address. 411B Jalan Besar, Singapore 209014
Telephone. (+65) 337–2371
Fax. (+65) 337–2035
Email. wp@wp.org.sg
Website. www.wp.org.sg
Leadership. Low Thia Khiang (secretary-general)
The WP, originally founded in 1957, was revived by its previous secretary-general, J. B. Jeyaretnam, in 1971. The party advocates the establishment of a democratic socialist government, with a constitution guaranteeing fundamental citizens' rights. In a by-election in 1981, Jeyaretnam became the first opposition member of Parliament since 1968, although he forfeited the seat in 1986 following a controversial conviction. In 1988, the WP merged with the left-wing Socialist Front (*Barisan Sosialis*), which had been established by →People's Action Party dissidents in 1961, and with the Singapore United Front (dating from 1973). Although the party won no seats in the 1988 legislative elections, it attracted nearly 17% of the total votes cast. In the 1991 poll, the WP contested 13 seats, won one and gained over 14% of the total vote. This performance was repeated in the 1997 elections, when it won one of 14 seats contested and again received more than 14% of total votes. It retained its single seat in the November 2001 elections.

Other Parties

According to the Registrar of Societies, there are 21 other registered political parties in Singapore. A number of these exist in name only: party activities are minimal and they have not contested general elections for some time. Some others lie dormant in the intervals between elections, springing to life once these are called and fielding a token number of candidates. Only a few parties have an active and ongoing political programme. The listing below only includes parties that have contested recent elections and/or have an active programme of political activity.

Democratic Progressive Party (DPP), a small and somewhat obscure party founded in 1973 which is unrepresented in parliament. In the 1999 presidential election, leader Tan Soo Phuan was one of two candidates that sought, and was denied, a Certificate of Eligibility to run for President by the Presidential Elections Committee. In the absence of any other contenders, Sellapa Rama Nathan was subsequently declared President-elect.
Leadership. Tan Soo Phuan

National Solidarity Party (NSP), centrist party formed in 1987 by mainly young professionals. The party seeks to broaden popular political participation in Singapore, while functioning as a credible opposition providing checks and balances against the ruling →People's Action Party. It contested three constituencies in the 1997 elections and, although failing to win a parliamentary seat, attracted over 6% of total votes cast. The NSP is one of five opposition parties that are members of the Singapore Democratic Alliance launched in June 2001.

Address. Hong Lim Complex, Blk 531 Upper Cross Street, #03–30, Singapore 050531
Telephone. (+65) 536–6388
Fax. (+65) 536–6388
Email. nsp@nsp-singapore.org
Website. www.nsp.org.sg
Leadership. Yip Yew Weng (president); Steve Chia (secretary-general)

Singapore Democratic Party (SDP), a liberal and centrist party founded in 1980 by Chiam See Tong in an attempt to create a credible opposition to the ruling →People's Action Party (PAP). In the 1991 elections, the SDP was the most successful of the opposition parties, winning three of the nine parliamentary seats it contested (Chiam See Tong retaining the seat he had held since 1984). In June 1993, Chiam resigned as secretary-general of the party, apparently as the result of an internal power struggle, and later joined the →Singapore People's Party just prior to the 1997 elections. Under the leadership of his successor, Chee Soon Juan, the SDP adopted a more aggressive and vocal stance against the PAP. In the 1997 elections, the SDP contested 12 seats. It lost in all, but received more than 10% of total votes. It again failed to win a seat in the 2001 elections.
Address. 1357A Serangoon Road, Singapore 328240
Telephone. (+65) 352–8925
Leadership. Chee Soon Juan (secretary-general)

Singapore Justice Party (SJP), established in 1972 but has yet to win any parliamentary representation. The party joined the Singapore Democratic Alliance formed in June 2001 to contest the next general election.
Leadership. Muthusamy Ramasamy (secretary-general)

Singapore Malays National Organization (*Pertubuhan Kebangsaan Melayu Singapura, PKMS*), founded as an affiliate of the →→United Malays National Organization in Malaysia in the early 1950s, assuming its present title in 1967. It seeks to advance the rights of Malays in Singapore, to safeguard and promote Islam, and to encourage racial harmony. It has so far failed to gain parliamentary representation. Together with four other parties, it joined the Singapore Democratic Alliance to contest the 2002 general election.
Leadership. Mohammed Aziz Ibrahim (secretary-general)
Address. 218F Changi Rd, PKM Bldg, Fourth Floor, Singapore 419737
Telephone. (+65) 345–5275
Fax. (+65) 345–8724

Singapore National Front (SNF), a small and little-known party formed in 1991 that has not contested general elections and has no parliamentary representation. With four other opposition parties, the SNF is a member of the Singapore Democratic Alliance launched in June 2001.
Address. Katong Mall, 112 East Coast Road, Singapore 428802.
Telephone. (+65) 346–6856

Slovakia

Capital: Bratislava

Population: 5,400,000 (2000E)

The independent Slovak Republic came into being on Jan. 1, 1993, upon the dissolution of the Czech and Slovak Federative Republic, which had been proclaimed in April 1990 as successor to the (Communist-ruled) Czechoslovak Socialist Republic declared in 1960, itself successor to the People's Republic of Czechoslovakia established in 1948. Adopted in September 1992, its constitution vests supreme legislative authority in the unicameral National Council (*Národná Rada*) of 150 members, who are elected for a four-year term by citizens aged 18 and over. Elections are by a system of proportional representation under which single parties must obtain at least 5% of the national vote to be allocated seats whether or not they run in alliances. The head of state is the President, who under a 1999 constitutional amendment is directly elected for a five-year term (renewable once) and who appoints the Prime Minister subject to approval by the National Council.

Under legislation dating from 1990, Slovakian parties are eligible for direct and indirect subsidies from the state to cover election campaign costs and to fund their political work inside and outside parliament. Direct funding consists of (i) reimbursement of election expenses to parties obtaining at least 3% of the vote at a rate of SK60 per vote; and (ii) annual general grants to the same parties at the same rate plus (from 2001) an additional annual subsidy of SK500,000 per elected deputy. In the parliamentary election year 1998 a total of SK189,894,720 was received by parties as reimbursement of election expenses, while in 2001 the totals allocated in general and parliamentary mandate grants were SK47,473,680 and SK74,500,000 respectively. Of the 2001 grants, the Movement for a Democratic Slovakia, for example, received a total of SK35,106,545 (about US$740,000). Indirect state financial support for parties, covering such items as office rentals and the services of political assistants, totalled SK98,300,000 in 2001.

The Constitutional Court ruled in September 2001 that it was permissible to be a member of more than one party, thus striking down a recently enacted ban on dual membership. The ruling meant that members of a party participating in an alliance which had constituted itself into a single party (so that it would only have to achieve the 5% threshold to obtain parliamentary representation) could be members of both their first party and the alliance party.

National Council elections on Sept. 25–26, 1998, resulted as follows: Movement for a Democratic Slovakia (HZDS) 43 seats (with 27.0% of the vote), Slovak Democratic Coalition (consisting of the Christian Democratic Movement, the Democratic Union of Slovakia, the Social Democratic Party of Slovakia, the Green Party in Slovakia and the Democratic Party) 42 (26.3%), Party of the Democratic Left 23 (14.7%), Hungarian Coalition Party 15 (9.1%), Slovak National Party 14 (9.1%), Party of Civic Understanding (SOP) 13 (8.0%).

In presidential elections on May 15 and 29, 1999, Rudolf Schuster of the SOP was elected with 57.2% of the second-round vote, defeating Vladimír Mečiar of the HZDS.

411

Christian Democratic Movement
Krest'ansko–demokratické Hnutie (KDH)
Address. 2 Žabotova, 81104 Bratislava
Telephone. (+421–2) 5249–2541
Fax. (+421–2) 5249–6313
Email. kdhba@isternet.sk
Website. www.kdh.sk
Leadership. Pavol Hrušovský (chairman); František Mikloško (parliamentary group leader); Martin Šrank (secretary-general)

Founded in February 1990 under the leadership of communist-era Catholic dissident Ján Carnogurský, the centrist strongly pro-European KDH began as the Slovak wing of the Czechoslovak Christian Democrats but presented its own list in Slovakia for the 1990 National Council elections, coming in second place with 31 seats and 19.2% of the vote. Carnogurský became Prime Minister of Slovakia following the dismissal of Vladimír Mečiar of the →Movement for a Democratic Slovakia (HZDS) in April 1991.

The party went into opposition after the June 1992 elections, in which it fell back to 18 seats with 8.9% of the vote. The KDH returned to government in March 1994 in the centre-left coalition headed by what became the →Democratic Union of Slovakia, but went into opposition again after the autumn 1994 parliamentary elections. In that contest it was allied with the non-party Standing Conference of the Civic Institute, the combined list taking a creditable 10.1% vote share and 17 seats. The KDH subsequently rebuffed suggestions that it should join a government coalition with the HZDS.

For the September 1998 parliamentary elections the KDH took the lead in creating the five-party →Slovak Democratic Coalition (SDK), which narrowly failed to outpoll the HZDS, winning 42 seats from 26.3% of the vote. It was nevertheless able to form a centre-left coalition government with the →Party of the Democratic Left (SDL'), the →Party of Civic Understanding (SOP) and the →Hungarian Coalition Party (SMK), under the premiership of Mikuláš Dzurinda (a former KDH minister).

The KDH was part of the coalition which secured the election of Rudolf Schuster (SOP) as President in May 1999. But the party subsequently resisted Dzurinda's moves to convert the SDK into a fully integrated single party, arguing that this would effectively weaken centrist forces. In October 2000 Carnogurský was succeeded as party chairman by Pavol Hrušovský. The following month the KDH deputies signalled the party's intention to maintain itself in being by withdrawing from the SDK parliamentary caucus and forming a separate group.

The KDH is affiliated to both the Christian Democrat International and the International Democrat Union.

Democratic Party
Demokratická Strana (DS)
Address. 70 Šancová, 81347 Bratislava
Telephone. (+421–2) 5249–6885
Fax. (+421–2) 5249–5893
Email. sekret@demstrana.sk
Website. www.demstrana.sk
Leadership. L'udovit Kanik (chairman)

The conservative DS is descended from a party of the same name founded in 1944 but suspended in 1948 when the Communists came to power. Revived in 1989, the DS joined the Slovak government in 1990 but failed to win representation in the 1992 elections. Although the party absorbed several small centre-right groupings in 1994, a joint list of the DS and the Party of Entrepreneurs and Tradesmen won only 3.4% and no seats in the autumn 1994 parliamentary elections.

For the September 1998 parliamentary elections the DS joined the →Slovak Democratic Coalition (SDK), obtaining six deputies on the SDK list. It therefore formed part of the resultant ruling coalition headed by the SDK, although the party was one of the SDK components which resisted moves to convert the SDK into a unitary party. In December 2000 the six DS deputies withdrew from the SDK parliamentary caucus, though they were too few to form their own group. This step provoked the resignation from the party of Deputy Prime Minister Iván Miklós (who remained in the government), while in January 2001 Ján Langós announced his departure from the SD chairmanship. The following month an SD congress first elected deputy chairman František Sebej, a right-winger, as chairman and L'udovit Kanik, a reformist, as a deputy chairman. When Sebej immediately handed back the post on the grounds that he could not work with Kanik, the congress elected Kanik as chairman.

Democratic Union of Slovakia
Demokratická Unia Slovenska (DÚS)
Address. 10 Medená, 81102 Bratislava
Telephone. (+421–7) 392564
Fax. (+421–7) 397877
Leadership. Eduard Kukan (chairman); Eva María Harvannová (secretary-general)

The centrist DÚS was founded in April 1994 as a merger of two elements of the coalition government which had come to power the previous month, namely: (i) the Democratic Union of Slovakia, led by then Prime Minister Jozef Moravčik, which had originated in February 1994 as the "Realistic Political Alternative" breakaway group of the then ruling →Movement for a Democratic Slovakia (HZDS); and (ii) the Alliance of Democrats of the Slovak Republic (ADSR), another HZDS splinter group created in June 1993 by Milan Kňažko, who had been dismissed as Foreign Minister three months earlier.

Commanding the support of 18 members of the National Council at the time of the merger, the DÚS subsequently failed in its aim of constructing a broad centrist alliance. The only significant grouping to come under its banner was a moderate splinter group of the right-wing →Slovak National Party called the National Democratic Party-New Alternative (NDS–NA), led by L'udovit Černák. In the autumn 1994 elections the DÚS list came in fifth place with 8.6% of the vote and only 15 seats. For the 1998 elections the DÚS joined the →Slovak Democratic Coalition and therefore became part of the resultant centre-left coalition government.

The DÚS is affiliated to the Liberal International.

Hungarian Coalition Party
Strana Mad'arskej Koalície (SMK)
Magyar Koalíció Pártja (MKP)
Address. 2 Žabotova, 81104 Bratislava
Telephone. (+421–2) 5249–5164
Fax. (+421–2) 5249–5264
Email. agardi@smk.sk
Website. www.mkp.sk
Leadership. Béla Bugár (chairman); Gyula Bárdos (parliamentary group leader)

Based in Slovakia's 650,000-strong ethnic Hungarian community, the SMK is committed to defending the rights of all minorities in Slovakia, including Poles, Ruthenians and Ukrainians. It was launched in January 1998 as an alliance of three ethnic Hungarian parties, namely the Coexistence Political Movement (ESWS), the Hungarian Christian Democratic Movement (MKdH/MKdM) and the Hungarian Civic Party (MOS). In July 1998 the SMK registered as a single party, in light of new electoral rules specifying that each component of an alliance must surmount the 5% threshold to obtain representation. Its component parties nevertheless remained in existence.

The liberal democratic Coexistence (*Egytélés-Spolužitie-Wspoinota-Suzitie*, ESWS) had been founded in March 1990 and had been allied in the 1990 and 1992 Council elections with the Hungarian Christian Democratic Movement (*Mad'arská Krest'ansko-demokratické Hnutie*, MKdH/*Magyar Keresztény-demokrata Mozgalom*, MKdM), their list winning 14 seats on the latter occasion. The

MKdH/MKdM had also been founded in March 1990, on a Christian-oriented, pro-market platform. In the autumn 1994 elections the ESWS and MKdH/MKdM had been part of the broader Hungarian Coalition (MK), including the Hungarian Civic Party (*Mad'arská Obianská Strana*, MOS/*Magyár Polgári Párt*, MPP), which had been founded in February 1990 as the Hungarian Independent Initiative and had secured representation in 1990 on the pro-democracy Public Against Violence list. In the 1994 contest the MK list had won 17 seats and had subsequently come into increasing conflict with the populist policies of the government of the Movement for a Democratic Slovakia (HZDS), seeing them as intended to impose an exclusively Slovak concept of national identity.

In the September 1998 parliamentary elections, the SMK lost ground slightly compared with the aggregate results in 1994, returning 15 deputies on a vote share of 9.1%. It opted to join a centre-left coalition government headed by the →Slovak Democratic Coalition (SDK), receiving three ministerial portfolios and a promise that more ethnic Hungarian rights would be enacted. Inevitably disappointed by the slow progress on that front, the SMK on several occasions threatened to leave the coalition, notably in August 2001, when the SMK executive committee voted unanimously for withdrawal. As in previous crises, however, the party was persuaded to remain in the government by new promises from the other coalition parties.

The overall SMK is a full member of the European Democrat Union and an associate member of the European People's Party as well as an observer member of the Christian Democrat International. Of the component parties, the ESWS is a member of the Liberal International.

Movement for a Democratic Slovakia
Hnutie za Demokratické Slovensko (HZDS)

Address. 32A Tomášikova, PO Box 49, 83000 Bratislava
Telephone. (+421–7) 4329–3800
Fax. (+421–7) 4341–0225
Email. webmaster@hzds.sk
Website. www.hzds.sk
Leadership. Vladimír Mečiar (chairman); Tibor Cabaj (parliamentary group leader)
The populist HZDS was registered in May 1991 a month after Vladimír Mečiar (a former Communist) had been ousted from the premiership of Slovakia (then still part of Czechoslovakia) after coming into conflict with the mainstream leadership of the pro-democracy Public Against Violence (VPN) movement. In an explicitly nationalist appeal called "For a Democratic Slovakia" and issued in April 1991, Mečiar had argued in favour of a diluted form of federalism providing greater protection for Slovak economic and political interests than was contemplated in Prague. The HZDS quickly confirmed that it was Slovakia's leading political formation, winning 74 of the 150 Slovak Council seats in the June 1992 elections. Restored to the premiership, Mečiar at first resisted Czech insistence that either the federation should have real authority at government level or the two parts should separate. By late 1992, however, he had embraced the latter option, leading Slovakia to sovereignty on Jan. 1, 1993, and forming a governmental coalition with the radical right-wing →Slovak National Party (SNS).

The Mečiar government of independent Slovakia quickly came under attack for its perceived authoritarian tendencies and acceptance of the entrenched position of former Communists in the state bureaucracy. Policy and personal clashes precipitated a series of defections from the HZDS in 1993–94, while Mečiar's appointment of a former Communist as Defence Minister in March 1993 caused the SNS to leave the government, which was thus reduced to minority status. Having failed to persuade the (ex-communist) →Party of the Democratic Left (SDL') to accept ministerial office, Mečiar restored the coalition with the SNS in October 1993; but chronic divisions within the HZDS led to the Prime Minister's defeat on a no-confidence motion and

reluctant resignation in March 1994. In opposition to a centrist coalition headed by what became the →Democratic Union of Slovakia, the HZDS remained the country's strongest formation, with a large following for its combination of economic conservatism and fiery nationalism.

Allied in the autumn 1994 elections with the small →Agrarian Party of Slovakia, the HZDS won a decisive plurality of 61 seats (on a 34.9% vote share) and became the lead partner in a "red-brown" government coalition with the SNS and the left-wing →Slovak Workers' Front. Promises notwithstanding, the return of the HZDS to power meant a slow-down in transition to a market economy. It also revived earlier conflict between Mečiar and President Michal Kováč, who had been elected by the legislature in February 1993 as candidate of the HZDS but who had subsequently distanced himself from the movement as he became embattled with the Prime Minister on a series of issues. The tension flared in March 1995 when the President refused at first to sign a bill transferring overall control of the security services from the head of state to the government. Although he signed the measure the following month when the National Council had readopted it, HZDS deputies engineered the passage of a vote of censure on the President (although with well short of the two-thirds majority needed to remove him), while the HZDS executive called for his resignation and expulsion from the party.

The confrontation between Mečiar and President Kováč remained unresolved in 1996–97, with the HZDS government blocking opposition moves for a referendum on a proposal that the President should be directly elected. As Kováč's five-year term came to an end, the legislature failed in several votes to produce the required two-thirds majority for a successor, so that in March 1998 Mečiar, as Prime Minister, assumed important presidential functions. HZDS deputies thereafter blocked further attempts to elect a President, with damaging effects on the party's public standing. In National Council elections in September 1998 the HZDS narrowly remained the largest party, but slumped to 43 seats on a 27% vote share and went into opposition to a centre-left coalition led by the →Slovak Democratic Coalition (SDK).

After the new National Cocucil had in January 1999 adopted a constitutional amendment providing for direct presidential elections, Mečiar emerged from post-election seclusion to run as the HZDS candidate. However, in the elections in May 1999 he was defeated in the second round by the centre-left nominee on a 57.2% to 42.8% split. In March 2000 Mečiar was re-elected HZDS chairman by a party congress which also approved the conversion of the HZDS into a formal political party with the suffix "People's Party", signifying a shift to a less nationalistic stance, while the party declared its full support for membership of the European Union and NATO.

In April 2000 Mečiar was arrested and fined for refusing to testify on the murky affair of the kidnapping of President Kováč's son in 1995 at the height of the HZDS leader's dispute with the President. The HZDS then succeeded in collecting sufficient signatures to force a referendum on its proposal that early parliamentary elections should be held. However, only 20% of the electorate voted when the consultation was held in November 2000, so that the result had no validity. Undeterred, Mečiar continued to castigate the ruling coalition in 2001, contending that after the 2002 elections a stable government which did not include the HZDS was "unthinkable".

Party of Civic Understanding
Strana Občianského Porozumenia (SOP)

Address. 6 Ružová dolina, 82108 Bratislava
Telephone. (+421–7) 5022–1161
Fax. (+421–7) 5022–1121
Email. rk@sop.sk
Website. www.sop.sk
Leadership: Pavol Hamžik (chairman); Igor Presperin (first vice-chairman)

The centre-left SOP was launched in April 1988 under the leadership of Rudolf Schuster, the ethnic German mayor of Košice, and included among its prominent members Pavol Hamžik, who had served as non-party Foreign Minister in 1996-97 in the government headed by the →Movement for a Democratic Slovakia (HZDS). In its first parliamentary elections in September 1998, the SOP won 13 seats on a vote share of 8% and opted to join a centre-left coalition headed by the →Slovak Democratic Coalition (SDK), in which Hamžik became Deputy Prime Minister responsible for relations with the European Union. After the new government had enacted a constitutional amendment providing for direct presidential elections, Schuster was chosen as the candidate of the ruling parties. In the polling in May 1999, Schuster was the comfortable victor, heading the first-round vote with 47.4% and defeating HZDS leader Vladimír Mečiar in the second by 57.2% to 42.8%.

After being installed as President, Schuster was succeeded as SOP chairman by Hamžik. In May 2001 Hamžik was dismissed from the government over allegations of improper use of EU funds and replaced by another SOP member, Maria Kadlecikova. He was nevertheless re-elected as SOP chairman the following month. An SOP congress in September 2001 decided that the party should seek political allies on the left and "stop toying with liberal orientations", although a significant minority faction rejected this strategy.

Party of the Democratic Left
Strana Demokratickej L'avice (SDL')
Address. 12 Gunduličova, 81105 Bratislava
Telephone. (+421–2) 5443–3617
Fax. (+421–2) 5443–5574
Email. hovorca@sdl.sk
Website. www.sdl.sk
Leadership. Pavol Konkos (chairman); Anton Hoffmann (parliamentary group leader)
The collapse of communist rule in Czechoslovakia in late 1989 inspired the Slovak Communists, somewhat paradoxically, to re-establish a separate →Communist Party of Slovakia (KSS), in indirect succession to the KSS originally founded in 1939 but later absorbed into the Communist Party of Czechoslovakia (KSČ). In October 1990 the KSS majority wing adopted the new name Communist Party of Slovakia–Party of the Democratic Left, which became simply Party of the Democratic Left (SDL') later in the year, while a dissident minority maintained the KSS in being.

Having embraced democratic socialism, the SDL' emerged from the June 1992 general elections as the second largest party in the Slovak National Council, winning 29 seats on a 14.7% vote share. After the government of the right-wing →Movement for a Democratic Slovakia (HZDS) had been reduced to minority status in March 1993, the SDL' rejected HZDS offers of ministerial status and instead became the leading party in a centre-left opposition alliance called Common Choice (SV). In the autumn 1994 general elections, however, the SDL' failed to emulate the recent electoral successes of other East European ex-communist formations, falling back to 13 seats. Many commentators attributed this relative failure to voters' perception of the HZDS as being the real "party of continuity" with the communist era.

In 1995–96 the SDL' became increasingly divided over whether to accept persistent HZDS offers of coalition status, the election of the relatively unknown Józef Migas as party chairman in April 1996 being a compromise between the contending factions. During a major coalition crisis in June 1996 the decision of the SDL' to give qualified external support to the government attracted much criticism from other opposition parties.

Standing on its own in the September 1998 National Council elections, the SDL' advanced to 23 seats on a 14.7% vote share. It then joined a centre-left coalition government headed by the centrist →Slovak Democratic Coalition (SDK) and also including the →Party of Civic Understanding (SOP) and the →Hungarian Coalition Party (SMK). The SDL' obtained six portfolios in the new government, which was committed to accession to both the European Union and NATO, and Migas became Speaker of the National Council. In the May 1999 direct presidential elections, the SDL' backed the successful candidacy of Rudolf Schuster of the SOP.

In June 2001 Migas confirmed that he would not be the SDL' candidate for the premiership in the 2002 parliamentary elections, and in November 2001 he was succeeded as party chairman by Pavol Konkos.

The SDL' is a member party of the Socialist International.

Slovak Democratic Coalition
Slovenská Demokratická Koalícia (SDK)
Address. 1 Nábrežie Ludvíka Svobodu, 81101 Bratislava
Telephone. (+421–7) 5441–6207
Fax. (+421–7) 4341–4114
Email. sdk@sdk.sk
Website. www.sdk.sk
Leadership. Mikuláš Dzurinda (chairman); Ján Rusnák (parliamentary group leader)
The SDK was founded in April 1998 as an electoral alliance of five centre-left parties then in opposition, namely the →Christian Democratic Movement (KDH), the →Democratic Party (DS), the →Democratic Union of Slovakia (DÚS), the →Social Democratic Party of Slovakia (SDSS) and the →Green Party in Slovakia (SZS). Under the leadership of Mikuláš Dzurinda (a former KDH minister), the SDK in July 1998 registered as a single party, in light of new electoral rules specifying that each component of an alliance must surmount the 5% threshold to obtain representation. The component parties nevertheless remained in being, with members of these having dual membership (a practice which was later authorized by the Constitutional Court).

In the September 1998 parliamentary elections, the SDK narrowly failed to overtake the then ruling →Movement for a Democratic Slovakia (HZDS), winning 42 of the 150 seats with 26.3% of the vote. Nevertheless, on the basis of a pre-election agreement, Dzurinda was able to form a majority coalition government which included the SDL', the →Party of Civic Understanding (SOP) and the →Hungarian Coalition Party (SMK), on a programme of accelerated pro-market reform and accession to the European Union and NATO. In direct presidential elections in May 1999, the SDK officially backed the successful candidacy of Rudolf Schuster of the SOP.

Strains then developed between the SDK leadership's aspiration to create a unitary party and the unwillingness of some constituent parties to abandon their separate identities. In January 2000 Prime Minister Dzurinda announced the creation of the Slovak Democratic and Christian Union (SDKU) as the effective successor of the SDK, being elected SDKU chairman at its founding conference in November. However, in order not to provoke defections by SDK components, activation of the SDKU was deferred until the 2002 elections, pending which the SDK would remain in being under Dzurinda's chairmanship. Nevertheless, the nine KDH deputies in the SDK caucus opted to set up a separate parliamentary group, while in December 2000 the six DS deputies also left the SDK caucus. At the same time, other SDK deputies led by Ján Budaj launched the Liberal Democratic Union to further liberal values, while the SDSS component of the SDK entered into "parallel" talks for a possible merger with either the SDL' or the SOP. Although all the SDK components said that they would continue to support the government, Prime Minister Dzurinda expressed disappointment at the response to his SDKU concept.

Slovak National Party
Slovenská Národná Strana (SNS)

Address. Šafárikovo nám. 3, 81499 Bratislava
Telephone. (+421–7) 5292–4260
Fax. (+421–7) 5296–6188
Email. sns@isnet.sk
Website. www.sns.sk
Leadership. Anna Malíková (chairperson)

Descended from a party founded in 1871, the nationalistic and anti-Hungarian SNS was launched in December 1989 and registered in March 1990, its programme calling for the assertion of Slovak rights and the revival of national pride and patriotism. It advocates the establishment of Slovak-language schools in every district (including those with ethnic Hungarian majorities) and exclusive use of Slovak at all official levels. It obtained 13.9% of the vote in the 1990 Slovak National Council elections, but only 7.9% (and nine seats) in the June 1992 contest, after which it joined a coalition with the dominant →Movement for a Democratic Slovakia (HZDS). It continued to support the government after the resignation of its sole minister in March 1993, and in October resumed formal coalition status, obtaining several key ministries.

In February 1994 the SNS was weakened by a split involving the defection of the party's "moderate" wing led by the then chairman, L'udovit Černák, this faction later joining the →Democratic Union of Slovakia. The following month, on the fall of the HZDS government, the rump SNS went into opposition, whereupon the SNS central council decided in May that only ethnic Slovaks were eligible to be members of the party. In the autumn 1994 elections the SNS took only 5.4% of the vote (and nine seats), being nevertheless awarded two portfolios in a new HZDS-led coalition. Thereafter the party resolutely opposed the granting of any form of autonomy to ethnic Hungarian areas of Slovakia under the March 1995 Slovak–Hungarian friendship treaty, tabling proposed constitutional amendments in July 1996 whereby minorities would have not only the right but also the duty to master the state language, Slovak. It also promised to block Slovakia's entry into NATO (if such became a possibility), despite the goal of accession being official government policy.

In the September 1998 parliamentary elections, the SNS advanced to 14 seats with 9.1% of the vote but went into opposition to a centre-left coalition headed by the →Slovak Democratic Coalition (SDK). In the May 1999 presidential elections, then SNS leader Ján Slota took a distant fifth place with only 2.5% of the first-round vote, having attracted criticism for his anti-Hungarian outbursts during the campaign. In September 1999 Slota was ousted as SNS chairman by a party congress, being succeeded the following month by Anna Malíková, hitherto deputy chairperson.

Malíková reiterated her party's opposition to NATO membership in October 2000, principally on grounds of cost, and its advocacy of an independent European security system. In January 2001 the SNS set out a controversial plan for "reservations" in which "unadaptable" Roma (Gypsies) would be educated to become good citizens. In June 2001 she strongly rejected press reports that in a recent meeting with President Schuster she had moderated SNS opposition to NATO membership, telling a Bratislava rally marking the 130th anniversary of the party's foundation that the idea that joining NATO would solve all of Slovakia's problems was "shameful". She also asserted that Slovaks would never forget "the death and suffering of our Slav and Christian brothers" in Yugoslavia as a result of the NATO bombardment during the Kosovo crisis.

Growing opposition to Malíková's leadership from July 2001 was attributed in part to her recent marriage to a Russian businessman. On her proposal, no less than eight of the SNS parliamentary deputies were suspended for "destabilizing" the party and five were expelled in September 2001, including former leader Ján Slota. Meanwhile, Malíková's new Russian husband had sued dissident SNS deputy Ratislav Septak for allegedly blackening his name. The response of Slota was to launch the "Real Slovak National Party", which declared its opposition to NATO membership and "the sellout of the national economy".

Social Democratic Party of Slovakia
Sociálnodemokratická Strana na Slovensku (SDSS)

Address. 2 Žabotova, 81104 Bratislava
Telephone. (+421–2) 5262–1401
Fax. (+421–2) 5249–4621
Email. sdss@ba.psg.sk
Website. www.sdss.sk
Leadership. L'udomir Šlahor (chairman); Peter Škriečka (secretary)

The SDSS derives from the historic Czechoslovak Social Democratic Party, which was a leading formation in the inter-war period but was forcibly merged with the Communist Party in 1948, after which the authentic party was maintained by exiled groups in Britain and elsewhere. When the party was re-launched in post-communist Czechoslovakia in February 1990, the Slovak branch quickly asserted its separate identity. The SDSS list in the June 1992 general elections was headed by the 1968 "Prague Spring" Communist leader, Alexander Dubček. It failed to win representation in either the federal or the Slovak lower chambers, but did obtain five seats in the federal upper chamber on a 6.1% share of the vote. Dubček died in November 1992 as the result of a road accident that many regarded as suspicious.

The SDSS regained national representation in the autumn 1994 elections, winning two seats as a component of a centre-left opposition alliance called Common Choice (SV), which also included the (ex-communist) →Party of the Democratic Left (SDL'), the →Green Party in Slovakia and the →Farmers' Movement of Slovakia. The party's participation in the SV was opposed by a minority faction styling itself "Revival of Social Democracy", under the leadership of Boris Zala.

For the 1998 parliamentary elections the SDSS formed part of the →Slovak Democratic Coalition (SDK) and therefore became part of the resultant centre-left ruling coalition, although without parliamentary representation in its own right. It displayed its independence by running its own candidate, Boris Zala, in the May 1999 presidential elections, but he managed only 2.5% of the vote. By late 2000 divisions within the SDK had impelled the SDSS into "parallel" negotiations on a possible union with either the SDL' on the left or the more centrist →Party of Civic Understanding (SOP). The replacement of Jaroslav Volf as SDSS chairman by Eximbanka governor L'udomir Šlahor in May 2001 appeared to slow down such negotiations. In September 2001 an SDSS conference resolved that the party would continue to support the ruling centre-left coalition.

The SDSS is a member party of the Socialist International.

Other Parties

Agrarian Party of Slovakia (*Rol'nícka Strana Slovenska, RSS*), founded in October 1990 to protect communist-era agricultural interests, the conservative RSS was at first allied with the →Farmers' Movement of Slovakia in the 1990 local elections but later opted to ally itself with the →Movement for a Democratic Slovakia.
Leadership. Pavol Delinga (chairman)

Communist Party of Slovakia (*Komunistická Strana Slovenska, KSS*), descended from the original Slovak Communist Party founded in 1939, now consisting of the Marxist-Leninist minority which rejected conversion into the democratic socialist →Party of the Democratic Left in 1990; obtained 2.7% in the 1994 elections and 2.8% in 1998.
Leadership. Vladimír Dado

Direction (*Smer*), populist formation launched in 2000, favouring the abolition of proportional representation to reduce party fragmention and back-room deals, also a tougher approach to Roma (Gypsies), including the restriction of welfare benefits to the first three children per family; supports NATO and EU membership. By mid-2001 *Smer* was obtaining around 20% in polls of voting intentions in the 2002 elections.
Website. www.strana-smer.sk
Leadership. Robert Fico (chairman)

Farmers' Movement of Slovakia (*Hnutie Pol'nohospodárov Slovenska, HPS*), left-leaning formation which in 1994 won one seat as part of the Common Choice (SV) alliance headed by the →Party of the Democratic Left.
Leadership. Józef Klein (chairman)

Green Party in Slovakia (*Strana Zelench na Slovenska, SZS*), founded as a party in late 1989, arguing that the creation of a market economy was not an end in itself but rather the means of improving the quality of life. It won six Slovak seats in 1990, lost them all in 1992 and regained two in 1994, when it was part of the centre-left Common Choice (SV), alliance headed by the →Party of the Democratic Left. In 1998 it was part of the →Slovak Democratic Coalition, which thereafter headed the government. The SZS is affiliated to the European Federation of Green Parties.
Leadership. Zdenka Tothová

Slovak People's Party (*Slovenská L'udová Strana, SL'S*), presented 56 candidates in the 1998 parliamentary elections, but won only 0.3% of the vote.
Leadership. Andrej Trnovec (chairman)

Slovak Workers' Front (*Zdruzenie Robotníkov Slovenska, ZRS*), established as an independent party in April 1994, having previously been a trade union component of the →Party of the Democratic Left. Standing on a left-wing platform urging protection of workers' rights and neutrality, it obtained 7.3% and 13 seats in the 1994 elections, opting to join a coalition government headed by the →Movement for a Democratic Slovakia. Internal division contributed to the party's failure to win any seats in 1998, when its vote slumped to 1.3%.
Leadership. Ján L'upták (chairman)

Union of Romany Political Parties of Slovakia, founded in 1995 in an attempt to unite the many parties aiming to represent Slovakia's Roma (Gypsy) minority, including the League of Romany Unity, the Party of Integration of Romanies in Slovakia, the Party of the Democratic Union of Romanies in Slovakia, the Romany Civic Initiative, the Romany National Congress and the Social Democratic Party of Romanies in Slovakia.
Leadership. Mikuláš Horváth (chairman)

Slovenia

Capital: Ljubljana

Population: 1,930,000 (2000E)

Having been a constituent republic of the Communist-ruled Socialist Federal Republic of Yugoslavia since World War II, Slovenia declared independence in June 1991 on the basis of a referendum held in December 1990. Its constitution adopted in December 1991 provides for a multi-party democracy, in which the largely ceremonial President is directly elected for a five-year term (once renewable) and the head of government is the Prime Minister, who is designated by (and may be removed by) the legislature. The latter is a bicameral body, consisting of the (i) the upper National Council (*Državni Svet*), whose 40 members serve five-year terms, 22 being directly elected and 18 indirectly elected by socio-economic interest groups; and (ii) the lower National Assembly (*Državni Zbor*), whose 90 members are elected for a four-year term, 40 by constituency-based majority voting and 50 by proportional representation from party lists which obtain at least 3% of the vote. One seat each is reserved for Slovenia's Hungarian and Italian ethnic minorities.

In presidential elections on Nov. 23, 1997, Milan Kučan, standing without party attribution, was re-elected for a second five-year term with 55.6% of the vote. Elections to the National Assembly on Oct. 15, 2000, resulted as follows: Liberal Democracy of Slovenia 34 seats (with 36.3% of the vote), the Social Democratic Party of Slovenia 14 (15.8%), the United List of Social Democrats 11 (12.1%), the Slovenian People's Party 9 (9.6%), the New Slovenia–Christian People's Party 8 (8.6%), the Democratic Party of Slovenian Pensioners 4 (5.2%), the Slovenian National Party 4 (4.8%), the Party of Slovenian Youth 4 (4.3%). The ethnic Hungarian and Italian minorities each returned one Assembly member.

Democratic Party of Slovenian Pensioners
Demokratska Stranka Upokojencev Slovenije (DeSUS)
Address. Kopališka 6, Ljubljana
Telephone. (+386–1) 439–7350
Fax. (+386–1) 431–4113
Email. janez.cemazar@siol.net
Website. www.desus.si
Leadership. Janko Kušar (chairman); Ivan Kebrič (Assembly group leader); Janez Čemažar (general secretary)
Also known as the Grey Panthers, the DeSUS seeks to defend the rights of the elderly generally and of pensioners in particular. It was part of the (ex-communist) →United List of Social Democrats (ZLSD) in the 1992 parliamentary elections, but contested those of 1996 independently, winning five seats with 4.3% of the vote. It then joined a coalition government headed by the →Liberal Democracy of Slovenia (LDS), successfully opposing proposals for the privatization of the pensions system. In the October 2000 parliamentary elections, the party slipped to four seats (while improving to 5.2% of the vote), but was included in a new ruling coalition headed by the LDS and also including the ZLSD and the →Slovenian People's Party (SLS+SKD).

Liberal Democracy of Slovenia
Liberalna Demokracija Slovenije (LDS)
Address. Trg Republike 3, 1001 Ljubljana
Telephone. (+386–1) 231–2659
Fax. (+386–1) 425–6150
Email. lds@lds.si

Website. www.2000.lds.si

Leadership. Janez Drnovšek (chairman); Anton Anderlič (Assembly group leader); Gregor Golobič (general secretary)

The centre-left and staunchly secular LDS was founded in March 1994 as a merger of the ruling Liberal Democratic Party (LDS), itself derived from the communist-era Federation of Socialist Youth of Slovenia (ZSMS), and three small formations, namely (i) a moderate faction of the →Democratic Party of Slovenia, including half of its Assembly contingent of six deputies; (ii) all five deputies of the Greens of Slovenia (→United Greens); and (iii) the Socialist Party of Slovenia (SSS), which was derived from the communist-era front organization (and had no Assembly representation). A third of the deputies in the 90-member Assembly accepted the authority of the new formation, which espoused classical liberal principles regarding individual rights and liberties, also advocating decentralization of power, rapid transition to a market economy and accession to the European Union and NATO.

The former LDS had come down the list of parties winning seats in the April 1990 Slovenian elections, which were the first multi-party contest in over half a century in what was then still Yugoslavia. Following the achievement of independence in 1991, however, LDS leader Janez Drnovšek had become Prime Minister in April 1992, heading a centre-left coalition government committed to privatization of the economy. In the first post-independence elections in December 1992, the LDS had become the strongest Assembly party, winning 22 seats on a 21.4% vote share. Drnovšek had accordingly formed a new centre-left government that included the Slovenian Christian Democrats (SKD, later the →Slovenian People's Party, SLS+SKD), the →United List of Social Democrats (ZLSD) and the →Social Democratic Party of Slovenia (SDS).

The launching of the new LDS in March 1994 coincided with the exit of the SDS from the ruling coalition in acrimonious circumstances, followed in January 1996 by the ZLSD. The LDS nevertheless retained power until the November 1996 Assembly elections, in which it remained the largest single party but with only 25 seats on a 27% vote share. The following month Drnovšek narrowly secured re-election as Prime Minister on the basis of a disparate coalition that included the ZLSD on the left and the far-right →Slovenian National Party (SNS). In February 1997, however, he succeeded in forming a more stable coalition which included the SLS and the →Democratic Party of Slovenian Pensioners (DeSUS).

In presidential elections in November 1997 the LDS candidate, Bogomir Kovač, came a distant seventh with only 2.7% of the vote. Mounting strains in the coalition culminated in the withdrawal of the SLS in April 2000 and Drnovšek's resignation after he had lost a confidence vote, whereupon an SLS-led coalition took office in June. Drnovšek obtained revenge in parliamentary elections in October 2000, when the LDS advanced to 34 of the 90 seats on a vote share of 36.3%. He proceeded to form a broad-based centre-left coalition which included what had become the SLS+SKD, the ZLSD and DeSUS.

The LDS is a member of the Liberal International.

New Slovenia–Christian People's Party
Nova Slovenija–Kršćanska Ljudska Stranka (NSi)

Address. Cankarjeva cesta 11, 1000 Ljubljana

Telephone. (+386–1) 241–6650

Fax. (+386–1) 241–6670

Email. tajnistvo@nsi.si

Website. www.nsi.si

Leadership. Andrej Bajuk (chairman); Anton Kokalj (general secretary)

The centrist NSi was launched prior to the October 2000 Assembly elections by then Prime Minister Andrej Bajuk, who hoped that the new party would help to maintain him in office. Then deputy chairman of the →Slovenian People's Party (SLS+SKD), Bajuk had come to the premiership in June 2000 following the fall of the government headed by →Liberal Democracy of Slovenia (LDS). The following month he responded to the Assembly's rejection of his proposal for the abandonment of proportional representation by leaving the SLS+SKD (which had voted against any change) and announcing the creation of the NSi (the preferred abbreviation despite the party's longer official title).

The NSi formation attracted support from some prominent centrists, especially members of the Slovenian Christian Democrats (SKD) opposed to the SKD's merger with the SLS. However, in the October 2000 parliamentary elections it obtained only eight seats and 8.6% of the vote. Bajuk accordingly resigned as Prime Minister and took his new party into opposition to a new government led by the LDS, having headed the shortest-lived administration since independence.

Having a membership of 7,300, the NSi is an associate member of the European People's Party.

Party of Slovenian Youth
Stranka Mladih Slovenije (SMS)

Address. Tržaška 2, 1000 Ljubljana

Telephone. (+386–1) 425–4014

Fax. (+386–1) 425–2821

Email. info@sms.si

Leadership. Dominik Černjak (chairman); Tadej Slapnik (deputy chairman); Peter Levič (Assembly group leader); Jože Vozelj (secretary-general)

The SMS was launched in 1999 as an ecologically oriented formation believing that the established parties did not properly represent young people. In its first Assembly elections in October 2000, the SMS unexpectedly surmounted the 3% barrier to representation, winning 4.3% of the vote and being allocated four seats.

Slovenian National Party
Slovenska Narodna Stranka (SNS)

Address. Tivolska 13, 1000 Ljubljana

Telephone. (+386–1) 421–3250

Fax. (+386–1) 422–4241

Email. s.n.s.@siol.net

Website. www.sns.si

Leadership. Zmago Jelinčič (chairman)

Founded in 1991, the SNS is an extreme right-wing formation advocating a militarily strong Slovenia, revival of the Slovenes' cultural heritage and protection of the family as the basic unit of society. It is also strongly opposed to any consideration being given to Italian and Croatian irredentist claims on Slovenian territory or property. The party won 9.9% of the vote and 12 lower house seats in December 1992 but became deeply divided in 1993 after party leader Zmago Jelinčič was named as a federal Yugoslav agent. Also problematical for the party were reports that leading members were listed in security service files as having been informers in the communist era. As a result of these and other embarrassments, five SNS deputies formed an independent Assembly group that became the core of the breakaway Slovenian National Right.

The rump SNS slumped to only four lower house seats and 3.2% of the vote in the November 1996 parliamentary elections. It was then brought into a mixed coalition government headed by →Liberal Democracy of Slovenia (LDS), but reverted to opposition status when the LDS found a larger partner in February 1997. In the October 2000 parliamentary elections, the SNS improved slightly to 4.4% of the vote but again won only four lower house seats.

Slovenian People's Party
Slovenska Ljudska Stranka (SLS+SKD)

Address. Beethovnova 4, 1000 Ljubljana

Telephone. (+386–1) 426–2179 *Fax*. (+386–1) 426–3314

Email. janez.vertacrik@sls-skd.si

Website. www.sls-skd.si
Leadership. Janez Podobnik (chairman)

The centre-right SLS+SKD was launched in mid-2000 as a merger of the Slovenian People's Party (SLS) and the Slovenian Christian Democrats (SKD), the name of the first becoming the name of the new party, although the abbreviations of both were retained.

Identifying its antecedents in a pre-war Catholic/populist party of the same name, the SLS had been founded in May 1988 as the non-political Slovene Peasant League (SKZ), which had registered as a party in January 1990. The party had won 11 Assembly seats in 1990 as a member of the victorious Democratic United Opposition (DEMOS) alliance and had adopted the SLS label in 1991. In the December 1992 elections it had won 11 Assembly seats on the strength of 8.96% of the national vote.

Also claiming descent from a pre-war Christian democratic party, the SKD had been founded in March 1990 by a group of "non-clerical Catholic intellectuals" advocating the full sovereignty of Slovenia, gradual transition to a market economy and integration into European organizations, especially the European Union. For the April 1990 elections it had been the largest component of the DEMOS alliance, winning 11 Assembly seats in its own right, so that SKD leader Lojze Peterle had become Prime Minister and led Slovenia to the achievement of full independence in 1991. He had remained Prime Minister despite the break-up of DEMOS at the end of 1991 but been forced to resign in April 1992 by a successful no-confidence motion criticizing the slow pace of economic reform. In the December 1992 Assembly elections the SKD had advanced to 15 seats (on a 13.9% vote share), thereafter joining a new centre-left coalition headed by what became →Liberal Democracy of Slovenia (LDS). Strains in the SKD's relations with the LDS had sharpened in 1994, leading to Peterle's resignation in September in protest against the induction of an LDS president of the National Assembly. The SKD had remained a government party, but renewed coalition tensions in 1996 had been highlighted by the support which SKD deputies gave to a motion of no confidence in the LDS Foreign Minister in May.

The SLS and the SKD had contested the November 1996 parliamentary elections within the Slovenian Spring (SP) alliance, the former party advancing to 19 seats on 19.4% vote share, whereas the latter fell back to 10 seats and 9.6%. The SLS had then deserted the SP and joined a coalition government headed by the LDS, whereas the SKD had gone into opposition. In the November 1997 presidential elections, Janez Podobnik of the SLS had come a poor second to the incumbent, Milan Kučan (non-party), winning only 18.4% of the vote, while the joint nominee of the SKD and the →Social Democratic Party of Slovenia had come third with 9.4%.

Strains in the SLS's relations with the LDS had culminated in April 2000 in the party's withdrawal from the government, which fell and was replaced in June by an SLS-led coalition under the premiership of Andrej Bajuk. The new Prime Minister promptly left the SLS to launch →New Slovenia–Christian People's Party, while the rump SLS joined forces with the SKD to contest the October 2000 parliamentary elections as the SLS+SKD. The merged party obtained a disappointing nine seats with 9.6% of the vote, but was included in the new government coalition headed by the LDS and also including the →United List of Social Democrats (ZLSD) and the →Democratic Party of Slovenian Pensioners (DeSUS).

The SLS+SKD inherited the SKD's affiliation to the Christian Democrat International and associate membership of the European People's Party, as well as its membership of the European Democrat Union.

Social Democratic Party of Slovenia
Socialdemokratska Stranka Slovenije (SDS)
Address. Komenskega 11, 1000 Ljubljana

Telephone. (+386–1) 231–4086
Fax. (+386–1) 230–1143
Email. tajnistvo@sds.si
Website. www.sds.si
Leadership. Janez Janša (chairman); Miha Brejca (vice-chairman); Andrej Vizjak (Assembly group leader); Du_an Strnad (secretary-general)

Founded in February 1989, the SDS seeks to be the authentic Slovenian party of European social democracy but has been obliged to compete for the left-wing vote with the organizationally powerful →United List of Social Democrats (ZLSD). The party was a component of the victorious Democratic United Opposition (DEMOS) alliance in the 1990 elections. In December 1992 its presidential candidate took only 0.6% of the first-round vote, but the party won 3.1% and four seats in the simultaneous legislative elections, subsequently participating in the centre-left coalition government headed by →Liberal Democracy of Slovenia (LDS). In 1993 the SDS Defence Minister and party leader, Janez Janša, became enmeshed in an arms-trading scandal, which led indirectly to his dismissal in March 1994, whereupon the SDS joined the parliamentary opposition.

The SDS contested the November 1996 parliamentary elections as part of the Slovenian Spring (SP) alliance with the →Slovenian People's Party (SLS) and the Slovenian Christian Democrats (SKD), making a breakthrough by winning 16 seats on a 16.1% vote share. It continued in opposition, making little impact in the November 1997 presidential elections but contributing to the fall of the LDS-led coalition in April 2000 and becoming part of the SLS-led coalition formed in June 2000. In the October 2000 parliamentary elections the SDS fell back to 14 seats and was not included in the new LDS-led coalition.

The SDS was an observer member of the Socialist International until 1996, when it was replaced as the SI's Slovenian affiliate by the ZLSD. Instead, the party became an observer member of the European People's Party.

United List of Social Democrats
Združena Lista Socialnih Demokratov (ZLSD)
Address. Levstikova 15, 1000 Ljubljana
Telephone. (+386–1) 425–4222
Fax. (+386–1) 25158
Email. office@zlsd.si
Website. www.zlsd.si
Leadership. Borut Pahor (chairman); Miran Potrč (Assembly group leader); Dušan Kumer (secretary-general)

The ZLSD was created prior to the December 1992 elections as an alliance of formations deriving from the former ruling League of Communists and its front organization, including the →Democratic Party of Slovenian Pensioners (DeSUS), the Social Democratic Union (SDU), the Workers' Party of Slovenia (DSS) and the →Party of Democratic Reform (SDR). The 1992 electoral outcome was third place in the new Assembly, with 14 seats and 12.1% of the vote, on the strength of which the ZLSD joined a centre-left coalition government headed by what became →Liberal Democracy of Slovenia (LDS). Of the four constituent groupings, the DeSUS, SDU and DSS formally merged in April 1993 to become the ZLSD, whereas the SDR preferred to maintain a separate identity.

The ZLSD lasted as a coalition partner until January 1996, when the LDS Prime Minister's move to dismiss one of its four ministers caused the party to withdraw from the government. Later in 1996 the ZLSD was admitted to membership of the Socialist International, replacing the conservative-leaning →Social Democratic Party of Slovenia (SDS). But the decision of the DeSUS to re-establish itself as an autonomous party weakened the ZLSD in the November 1996 parliamentary elections, the party representation falling to nine seats from 9% of the vote. Having continued in opposition, the ZLSD advanced to 11 seats and

12.1% in the October 2000 elections, opting thereafter to join a coalition government headed by the LDS and also including the →Slovenian People's Party (SLS+SKD) and the DeSUS.

The ZLSD is a full member of the Socialist International.

Other Parties

Democratic Party of Slovenia (*Demokratska Stranka Slovenije, DSS*), descended from the Slovene Democratic League (SDZ), which registered as a party in March 1990. A leading proponent of secession from Yugoslavia, the SDZ contested the 1990 elections within the victorious Democratic United Opposition (DEMOS). It stood on its own in 1992, winning six lower house seats with 3.1% of the vote, following which it absorbed a small social democratic faction to become the DSS. In March 1994 three of the DSS deputies joined the restructured →Liberal Democracy of Slovenia, while one became an independent and two opted to retain the DSS label. The DSS failed to surmount the 3% threshold in the 1996 and 2000 parliamentary elections, declining from 2.7% to 0.6%, although then leader Anton Peršak scored 3.1% in the 1997 presidential contest.
Address. Linhartova 13, 1000 Ljubljana

Telephone/Fax. (+386–1) 431–4392
Email. dss@netsi.net
Leadership. Mihael Jurak (chairman)

Party of Albanian Democratic Union (*Partia Bashkimi Demokratike Shqiptare, PBDSh*), launched in January 2000 as an independent formation seeking to represent Slovenia's small ethnic Albanian population.
Leadership. Besnik Tallaj (chairman)

United Greens (*Združeni Zeleni, ZZ*), embracing the Greens of Slovenia (Zeleni Slovenije, ZS) and the Green Alternative (Zelena Alternativa, ZA). Founded as a party in June 1989, the ZS had elected five deputies in 1992, all of whom had joined the restructured →Liberal Democracy of Slovenia in 1994, leaving the parent group without representation, which it failed to recover in 1996. In 2000 the broader ZZ won 0.9% of the vote.
Address. Komenskega 11, 1000 Ljubljana
Telephone. (+386–1) 231–2368
Fax. (+386–1) 231–1629
Email. zeleni@email.si
Website. www.zeleni.si
Leadership. Stefan Han (chairman)

Solomon Islands

Capital: Honiara (Guadalcanal)　　　　　　　　　　　　　　　　　　　　　　　　**Population:** 418,000 (2000E)

The Solomon Islands achieved internal self-government in 1976 and became independent in July 1978. The head of state is the British sovereign represented by a Governor-General. Legislative authority is vested in a unicameral National Parliament, the 50 members of which are popularly elected from single-member constituencies for up to four years. The Prime Minister (who is elected by members of Parliament from among their number) and an appointed Cabinet exercise executive power and are responsible to Parliament.

Government composition since independence has been determined by an extremely fluid party structure and constantly shifting coalitions. Parliamentary elections on Aug. 6, 1997, resulted in the Group for National Unity and Reconciliation (GNUR) led by incumbent Prime Minister Solomon Mamaloni winning command of 24 seats but losing power to the multi-party Solomon Islands Alliance for Change (SIAC), which mustered 26 seats and installed Bartholomew Ulufa'alu as Prime Minister. From mid-1999 inter-ethnic conflict between the indigenous inhabitants of Guadalcanal (Isatabu) and settlers from the neighbouring island of Malaita escalated into virtual civil war, fought between the paramilitary Isatabu Freedom Movement (IFM) and the Malaita Eagles Force (MEF). In June 2000 Ulufa'alu was briefly taken prisoner by the MEF and resigned shortly after his release, whereupon a government of "national unity, reconciliation and peace" was installed. The new Prime Minister was Manasseh Sogavare, who had become leader of the opposition People's Progressive Party (successor to the GNUR) following Mamaloni's death in January 2000.

People's Progressive Party (PPP)
Address. c/o National Parliament, Honiara
Leadership. Manasseh Sogavare

The PPP was originally founded under British rule by Solomon Mamaloni, who served as Chief Minister in 1974–76 and as Prime Minister in 1981–84, 1989–93 and 1994–97, during which his party went through numerous name and composition changes. The PPP title was revived on Mamaloni's death in January 2000 as a tribute to him.

Following independence, Mamaloni in 1979 merged the PPP with the Rural Alliance Party to form the People's Alliance Party (PAP), which provided his power-base in the 1980s. Having regained the premiership in 1989, Mamaloni in October 1990 resigned as PAP leader to lead a broader-based government, the components of which were organized as the Group for National Unity and Reconstruction (GNUR) in the May 1993 elections. Under Mamaloni's leadership the GNUR secured the most seats, winning 21, but an alliance of anti-Mamaloni parties and independents

formed a new administration, which remained in power until losing its slim majority in October 1994. The following month Mamaloni resumed the post of Prime Minister.

Mamaloni's fourth and last premiership proved to be the most controversial, as his government repealed or relaxed many of the regulations introduced by the previous government to conserve forestry resources. It also attracted opposition charges of general economic incompetence and political corruption. In the August 1997 elections for a Parliament enlarged from 47 to 50 members, the GNUR grouping (which was also known as the National Unity and Reconciliation Progressive Party) again won a plurality of 21 seats, and was backed by three independents. But the anti-Mamaloni →Solomon Islands Alliance for Change (SIAC) mustered 26 seats and was able to form a government.

In opposition, Mamaloni adopted the designation Coalition for National Advancement (CNA) for his followers. His successor when he died in January 2000 was former

419

Finance Minister Manasseh Sogavare, whose adoption of the historic PPP rubric coincided with rising inter-ethnic conflict on Guadalcanal. Sogavare denied government claims that the PPP was involved in fomenting the indigenous unrest, which led directly to the government's resignation in June 2000. Sogavare was the political beneficiary, being installed as Prime Minister of a national unity government committed to national reconciliation and including some SIAC representatives.

Solomon Islands Alliance for Change (SIAC)
Address. c/o National Parliament, Honiara
Leadership. Bartholomew Ulufa'alu

The SIAC was formed prior to the 1997 elections by the disparate forces opposed to the government headed by Solomon Mamaloni, then leader of the Group for National Unity and Reconciliation (GNUR), which later became the →People's Progressive Party (PPP). The alliance was effectively the successor to the National Coalition Partners (NCP) combination which had ousted Mamaloni after the 1993 elections and installed a government led by Francis Billy Hilly, who had survived until October 1994, when Mamaloni had returned to power.

The SIAC formations included (i) the Solomon Islands Liberal Party led by Bartholomew Ulufa'alu, which had been founded in 1976 as the National Democratic Party and had participated in the 1981–84 Mamaloni government; (ii) the National Action Party of the Solomon Islands led by Francis Saemala; (iii) the People's Alliance Party led by Sir David Kausimae, originally established in 1979 under the leadership of Mamaloni, who had deserted the party in 1990; (iv) the Solomon Islands United Party led by Ezekiel Alebua, which had been founded by Sir Peter Kenilorea (the first post-independence Prime Minister) and had been the senior partner in the 1984–89 coalition government; and (v) the Solomon Islands Labour Party led by Joses Tuhanuku, which dated from 1988.

Castigating the Mamaloni government for its alleged corruption and subservience to foreign logging companies, the SIAC parties emerged from the 1997 elections commanding 26 of the 50 Assembly seats and so were able to install Ulufa'alu as Prime Minister. From mid-1999, however, his government was powerless to prevent a descent into virtual civil war between the indigenous population of Guadalcanal and immigrants from Malaita. Though himself a Malaitese, Ulufa'alu was in June 2000 abducted and held captive by Malaitese guerrillas for five days, in what proved to be tantamount to an armed coup. Emerging from captivity, Ulufa'alu tendered his resignation as demanded and was replaced by Manasseh Sogavare of the PPP, with some SIAC figures joining the new government. In June 2001 Ulufa'alu filed a somewhat belated suit challenging the legality of the Sogavare government.

Somalia

Capital: Mogadishu

Population: 7,253,000 (2000E)

The Republic of Somalia was formed by the unification of the British Somaliland Protectorate and the UN Trust Territory of Somalia at independence in 1960. In 1969 President Mohammed Siyad Barre seized power, and under his regime the Somali Revolutionary Socialist Party (SRSP) became the sole legal party. Siyad Barre was overthrown in a rebellion led by United Somali Congress (USC) guerrillas in January 1991. Ali Mahdi Mohamed was installed as interim President and free elections were promised. In July 1991 the USC and five other groups agreed on the re-adoption of the constitution which had been in force from 1961 until Siyad Barre's coup. A Cabinet appointed in October 1991 represented an attempt to unite various groups behind the USC, but after fighting between opposing USC factions—one led by Ali Mahdi Mohamed and the other by Gen. Mohamed Farah Aidid—had broken out in Mogadishu in November 1991, the attempt to establish a national government was suspended. Other leading political groups subsequently split into pro-Aidid and pro-Mahdi factions.

In May 1991 the area which had formerly constituted the British Somaliland Protectorate, in the north-west, was proclaimed independent by the Somali National Movement (SNM), as the Republic of Somaliland, with its capital at Hargeisa, but received no international recognition. In February 1997 representatives of the self-proclaimed republic announced the promulgation of an interim constitution. In May 2001 the "Somaliland" authorities were finalizing preparations to hold a referendum on an independence constitution. This move was condemned both by the current transitional national government in Mogadishu (for which see below) and by the government of neighbouring "Puntland" (the name assumed by an area of north-eastern Somalia when an autonomous regional administration was established in 1998 under the presidency of Col. Abdullahi Yusuf Ahmed, a former leader of the Somali Salvation Democratic Front). The "Puntland" government, currently organized on a non-party basis, supported a federal solution to Somalia's political problems and stated that it would be "unwise and provocative" for "Somaliland" to conduct its referendum in several districts whose historic clan affiliations were with "Puntland".

A United Nations peace-keeping presence in Somalia between 1992 and March 1995, aiming to disarm warring factions and protect relief operations, was unable to restore order, and essentially anarchic conditions persisted in the country. In mid-June 1995 factions allied with Gen. Aidid elected him President of the country, and the appointment of a Cabinet was subsequently announced. On Gen. Aidid's death shortly thereafter, his supporters elected his son, Hussein Aidid, to succeed him as "interim President". In January 1997 representatives of 26 anti-Aidid factions established a 41-member National Salvation Council pending the holding of a national reconciliation conference. In May 2000 a reconciliation conference, attended by 400 delegates (but rejected by three of the five main faction leaders, including Hussein Aidid), opened in Djibouti. In July the conference (now attended by an estimated 900 delegates) drew up proposals for Somalia to make a three-year transition to a federal government structure with 18 regional administrations. On Aug. 13, 2000, a 245-member transitional national assembly, in which seats were apportioned after detailed negotiations between representatives of different Somali clans, was inaugurated and went on to elect Abdulkasim Salat Hassan (a former minister under Siyad

Barre) as President of Somalia. His transitional national government (TNG) established a presence in Mogadishu from mid-October 2000 but remained highly vulnerable to continuing outbreaks of faction fighting (an Aidid faction being involved in a major battle in the port area on May 11–12, 2001).

Representatives of 17 factions opposed to the TNG agreed in March 2001 to set up their own Somali Reconciliation and Reconstruction Council (SRRC) in the town of Baidoa to organize a new reconciliation conference in Somalia. The SRRC, whose formation was endorsed by the government of "Puntland", was co-chaired by Hussein Aidid, who said that he had formed a 23-member Cabinet to undertake state functions.

Allegiances within Somalia are primarily clan-based, with fluctuating alliances, and there is no functioning political party system.

South Africa

Capital: Pretoria (administrative), Cape Town (legislative), Bloemfontein (judicial)

Population: 43,421,000 (2000E)

The Republic of South Africa was established in 1961, evolving from the Union of South Africa which had been formed in 1910 and achieved independence from the United Kingdom in 1931. The National Party (NP), which was the ruling party from 1948 until May 1994, pioneered the system of apartheid under which the population was divided into four different racial categories (Whites, Coloureds, Indians and Africans), each entitled to varying degrees of political, social and economic rights. In practice, the system maintained the supremacy of the minority white (particularly Afrikaner) population. In the face of domestic and international pressure, the NP government in 1989 indicated a preparedness to negotiate an end to apartheid, the following year lifting restrictive measures against the African National Congress (ANC) and other proscribed organizations. Multi-party negotiations began in December 1991 and resulted in the adoption in November 1993 of an interim constitution, under which South Africa's first non-racial, multi-party legislative elections took place on April 26–29, 1994. These resulted in a decisive victory for the ANC, which had been in the forefront of the struggle against the apartheid regime. In May 1994 the ANC leader, Nelson Mandela, was elected President of the Republic by the National Assembly (lower house of parliament), and a transitional government of national unity assumed office. The two houses of parliament sat jointly as a Constituent Assembly to draft a permanent constitution, which entered into force in February 1997.

The 1997 constitution provides for a bicameral parliament comprising a National Assembly of 400 members, popularly elected by universal adult suffrage (200 from national party lists and 200 from regional party lists) under a system of proportional representation, and a 90-seat National Council of Provinces, appointed by the members of the elected legislatures of the nine South African provinces. Any vacancy occurring in the National Assembly in the period between general elections is filled by the "next-in-line" candidate on the same party list. The President, who is head of state and head of the executive, is elected by the National Assembly from among its members. No person may serve more than two presidential terms.

A general election held on June 2, 1999, produced an increased ANC majority in the National Assembly, where the distribution of seats among the larger parties was ANC 266, Democratic Party 38, *Inkatha* Freedom Party 34, New National Party (successor to the NP) 28 and United Democratic Movement 14. Nine small parties accounted for the remaining 20 seats. The Democratic Party formed the official opposition in the new Assembly, while the *Inkatha* Freedom Party concluded a coalition agreement with the ANC. Thabo Mbeki (who had succeeded Nelson Mandela as ANC party president at the end of 1997) was elected President of South Africa by the new Assembly and was formally inaugurated in office on June 16, 1999.

African Christian Democratic Party (ACDP)
Address. PO Box 2417, Durbanville 7551
Telephone. (+27–21) 461–2048
Fax. (+27–21) 462–5394
Website. www.acdp.org.za
Leadership. Kenneth Meshoe (president); Louis Green (deputy president)
The ACDP won two National Assembly seats in the April 1994 elections, having campaigned for the social and economic transformation of the country based on a "moral, judicial and ethical system, open market economics and direct democracy". It won 6 seats in the 1999 National Assembly elections.

African National Congress (ANC)
Address. 54 Sauer Street, Johannesburg 2001; POB 61884, Marshalltown 2107
Telephone. (+27–11) 376–1000
Fax. (+27–11) 376–1134

Email. anchq@anc.org.za
Website. www.anc.org.za
Leadership. Thabo Mbeki (president); Jacob Zuma (vice-president); Kgalema Motlanthe (secretary-general); Patrick Lekota (national chairman)
Founded in 1912, the ANC became the leading black formation in South Africa. It was banned by the apartheid regime from 1960 to 1990, its most prominent figures being imprisoned (in particular, Nelson Mandela and Walter Sisulu) or exiled. From the late 1970s, as ANC guerrilla attacks within the country escalated, the South African armed forces increased counter-insurgency operations against the liberation movement's camps in neighbouring states.

While emphasizing that it was prepared for an armed seizure of power in order to establish a non-racial political system, the ANC indicated that this position did not preclude a negotiated transition to democracy. ANC proposals, set out in 1989, argued that negotiations would only be possible in a free political climate. Having released Walter Sisulu from detention in October of that year, the National Party (NP) government then released Mandela in February 1990 and legalized all previously banned organizations. The ANC began the transformation from liberation movement to political party, suspending its armed struggle and engaging in constitutional talks with the government.

Substantive multi-party negotiations on a future constitution took place from 1991 to 1993, although the process was frequently threatened by escalating political violence, for which the ANC blamed the →Inkatha Freedom Party (IFP) and members of the state security forces.

Although the ANC had replaced its commitment to comprehensive nationalization with an emphasis on a mixed economy, the organization announced a radical plan in January 1994 to end the economic and social inequities of the apartheid era. This Reconstruction and Development Programme gave priority to housing, education, health improvement and economic growth.

The non-racial, multi-party legislative elections in April 1994 resulted in an overwhelming victory for the ANC, which secured 252 National Assembly seats with 62.6% of the vote and took control of seven of the nine provincial assemblies. The following month Nelson Mandela became President of the Republic. The new Cabinet was dominated by the ANC, but also included members of the NP and the IFP. (The NP, later renamed the →New National Party, withdrew from the government in 1996.)

Thabo Mbeki succeeded Walter Sisulu as ANC vice-president in December 1994, subsequently becoming president of the ANC in succession to Nelson Mandela in December 1997. With the support of the →South African Communist Party (SACP) and the Congress of South African Trade Unions (COSATU), Mbeki led the ANC to victory in the June 1999 general election, when it won 66.4% of the vote and 266 seats in the National Assembly. Having been elected President of South Africa by the National Assembly, he appointed a Cabinet which included three members of the IFP. President Mbeki's government came under strong pressure from its SACP and trade union allies for its perceived conservatism on economic policy issues, while Mbeki himself attracted much national and international criticism for his controversial views on South Africa's HIV/AIDS crisis. In nationwide municipal elections in December 2000 the ANC's share of the total vote was about 59%, a fall of over 7% compared with the 1999 general election.

Afrikaner Unity Movement
Afrikaner Eenheidsbeweging (AEB)
Address. PO Box 5460, Pretoria
Telephone. (+27–12) 329–1220
Fax. (+27–12) 329–1229
Website. www.aeb.org.za
The AEB, a right-wing Afrikaner movement, won one National Assembly seat in the June 1999 general election.

Azanian People's Organization (AZAPO)
Address. PO Box 4230, Johannesburg 2000
Telephone. (+27–11) 336–3556
Fax. (+27–11) 333–6681
Website. www.azapo.org.za
Leadership. Mosibudi Mangena (president)
The AZAPO is a black consciousness movement that was launched in 1978. Its leader, Mosibudi Mangena, had been imprisoned on Robben Island for five years from 1973. AZAPO rejected constitutional negotiations with the white minority government and declared its opposition to the April 1994 elections. It excludes white members. The AZAPO registered to contest the June 1999 general election, in which Mangena won the party's sole seat in the National Assembly. In January 2001 Mangena became Deputy Minister of Education.

Democratic Alliance (DA)
Address. PO Box 1698, Cape Town 8000
Telephone. (+27–21) 461–5833
Fax. (+27–21) 461–5329
Email. info@da.org.za
Website. www.da.org.za
Leadership. Tony Leon (leader); Marthinus van Schalkwyk (deputy leader); Joe Seremane (chairman); Daryl Swanepoel (national executive secretary)
The DA was formed in June 2000 through the merger of the →Democratic Party (DP, which won 38 seats in the National Assembly in 1999) and the →New National Party (NNP, which won 28 seats in the 1999 National Assembly elections). The aim of the new party was "to consolidate the support of opposition voters in South Africa based on common values for a better South Africa for all its citizens". The values in question were broadly liberal ones, long held by the DP (the senior partner in the merged party) but rather more recently adopted by the NNP (formerly the National Party). The DA's primary electoral challenge was to attract black votes away from the ruling →African National Congress (which sought to portray the DA as the party of the white opposition in South Africa). In December 2000 the DA stood as a merged party in nationwide municipal elections, fielding candidates of all races (over half of them black) and receiving 23% of the total vote, compared with the 16.4% combined share of the DP and the NNP at the June 1999 general election. The new party won control of the Cape Town "megacity" administration.

South African electoral law made it impractical for the Democratic Alliance to register as a merged party in the current National Assembly, where the DP and the NNP continued to be represented as separate parties. Unless there was an early change in the law to facilitate mergers of sitting parties, the DP and the NNP did not intend to disband until the end of the Assembly's term in 2004, at which point the DA would be registered in their place to contest the next general election. In the meantime, a merged party structure was put in place at national and provincial levels, the composition of each DA committee being determined on the basis of votes received by the DP and NNP at the June 1999 elections. The DP accordingly became the dominant component of the DA at national level and in seven of South Africa's nine provinces.

Democratic Party (DP)
Address. PO Box 1475, Cape Town 8000
Telephone. (+27–21) 465–1431
Fax. (+27–21) 461–5276
Email. headoffice@dp.org.za
Website. www.dp.org.za
Leadership. Tony Leon (leader); Joe Seremane (federal chairman)
The moderate, predominantly white DP was formed in 1989 (by the merger of the Progressive Federal Party, the Independent Party and the National Democratic Movement), advocating the establishment of a democratic, non-racial society by peaceful means. It traced its own origins back to the formation in 1959 of the Progressive Party, whose MP Helen Suzman was for 13 years the sole anti-apartheid campaigner in the South African parliament. In the April 1994 elections the DP took fifth place, winning seven National Assembly seats with just over 1.7% of the votes cast. In the June 1999 general election the DP was placed second, with 9.5% of the vote and 38 seats in the National Assembly, and its leader became the leader of the official opposition in the Assembly. The June 1999 provincial election in Western Cape resulted in the formation of a provincial coalition government between the DP and the →New National Party (NNP) (respectively the third and second largest parties in the provincial legislature), with the →African National Congress (the largest party) forming the provincial opposition. In June 2000 the DP merged with the NNP to form the →Democratic Alliance, although neither of the constituent parties was disbanded at this stage.

The DP is a member of the Liberal International.

Federal Alliance (FA)

Address. PO Box 767, Saxonwold 2132
Telephone. (+27–11) 402–9551
Fax. (+27–11) 402–7282
Email. media@federalalliance.org.za
Website. www.federalalliance.org.za
Leadership. Louis Luyt (leader)

The Federal Alliance, established in September 1998 by Louis Luyt, a wealthy businessman and former president of South Africa's Rugby Football Union, won two seats in the National Assembly at the June 1999 general election. It subsequently concluded a parliamentary co-operation agreement with the →United Democratic Movement (UDM) whereby FA members may attend UDM caucus meetings. In June 2000, prior to the merger between the →Democratic Party (DP) and the →New National Party, the FA reached an electoral pact with the DP to field joint candidates in the 2000 municipal elections. (The DP subsequently contested these elections through the →Democratic Alliance, which retained the FA's support under the electoral pact.)

Freedom Front
Vryheidsfront (VF)

Address. POB 74693, Lynnwood Ridge 0040, Pretoria
Telephone. (+27–12) 322–7141
Fax. (+27–12) 322–7144
Website. www.vryheidsfront.co.za
Leadership. Gen. Constand Viljoen (leader)

The VF was launched by its leader in March 1994 following a rift in the right-wing Afrikaner People's Front (linking groups opposed to black majority rule) over the issue of participation in the forthcoming April elections. Viljoen opted to register the new party in order to promote the objective of a confederal South Africa based on the right of self-determination for Afrikaners and all other groups. The VF was the only white far-right party to contest the elections, in which it secured nine National Assembly seats with almost 2.2% of the vote. In the 1999 general election the VF won three seats with 0.8% of the vote.

Inkatha Freedom Party (IFP)

Address. POB 4432, Durban 4000
Telephone. (+27–31) 307–4962
Fax. (+27–31) 307–4964
Website. www.ifp.org.za
Leadership. Chief Mangosuthu Buthelezi (leader); Zakhele Khumalo (secretary-general)

The IFP, formed originally as a liberation movement, was re-launched in 1990 as a multi-racial political party, although it remains a predominantly Zulu organization with its power base in KwaZulu/Natal. Hostility between the IFP and the →Afican National Congress (which accused the IFP of being an ally of the white minority regime) engendered serious political violence, particularly in the early 1990s, and major differences over constitutional and other issues continued to cause friction for some years. Having belatedly agreed to participate in the April 1994 elections, the IFP took third place with 43 National Assembly seats and about 10.5% of the votes cast. It also won a majority of seats in the KwaZulu/Natal provincial assembly. The party was awarded three portfolios in the ensuing ANC-dominated Cabinet. However, the disaffection of the IFP and its Zulu supporters continued, centring on the demand for separate status for KwaZulu/Natal. In April 1995 IFP members withdrew from the Constituent Assembly charged with the drafting a permanent constitution. During the latter part of the Mandela presidency relations between the IFP and the ANC improved considerably, thanks largely to the efforts of the new ANC leader, Thabo Mbeki. In the 1999 general election the IFP won 34 National Assembly seats with 8.6% of the vote and entered into a new coalition agreement with the ANC. Chief Buthelezi (one of three IFP cabinet ministers) continued to hold the home affairs portfolio.

Minority Front

Address. 76 Trisula Avenue, Arena Park 4037
Telephone. (+27–31) 404–1993
Fax. (+27–31) 404–9059
Leadership. Amichand Rajbansi (leader)

The Minority Front, based in Durban and supported mainly by the Indian community, won no seats in the 1994 national elections and one National Assembly seat in the June 1999 general election. It formed a political alliance with the →African National Congress in June 1999.

New National Party (NNP)

Address. PO Box 1698, Cape Town
Telephone. (+27–21) 461–5833
Fax. (+27–21) 461–5329
Email. info@natweb.co.za
Website. www.natweb.co.za
Leadership. Marthinus van Schalwyk (national leader)

The name New National Party was adopted by the former National Party (NP) prior to the 1999 general election. The conservative NP had come to power in 1948, and was the instigator of the system of apartheid in South Africa which was maintained repressively until the end of the 1980s. At that point the party, under the new leadership of F.W. de Klerk, abandoned its defence of apartheid in favour of reform of the political system, although it continued to advocate the constitutional protection of minority rights.

Following his inauguration as State President in 1989, de Klerk implemented a number of dramatic measures, including the release of political prisoners and the legalization of banned organizations, as a prelude to substantive constitutional negotiations with anti-apartheid groups. South Africa's white population voted in support of continuing the reform process in a referendum in March 1992, after which de Klerk declared "today we have closed the book on apartheid".

In the multi-party elections in April 1994 the NP was runner-up to the ANC, winning 82 National Assembly seats with just over 20% of the votes cast. The party also won a majority of seats in the Western Cape regional assembly. De Klerk was subsequently named as one of two Executive Deputy Presidents in the new Mandela administration, which also included several other NP ministers. Following the advent of majority rule, the NP suffered a number of defections to the ANC. In February 1996 Roelf Meyer took up the new post of NP secretary-general, charged with charting a new future for the party, which withdrew from the government at the end of June 1996. Meyer's proposals for radical restructuring were rejected by the party, prompting his resignation from the NP; he later co-founded the →United Democratic Movement.

Meyer's successor as NP secretary-general, Marthinus van Schalkwyk, became party leader after de Klerk's resignation in August 1997. Renamed the NNP, the party won only 6.9% of the vote and 28 National Assembly seats in the June 1999 general election, after which it was superseded as the official national opposition party by the →Democratic Party (DP). In Western Cape province, the NNP and the DP formed a coalition government after the June 1999 provincial election. In June 2000 the NNP responded to pressure from the leadership of the DP (which had been attracting increasing numbers of former NNP members) to negotiate a merger agreement. Van Schalkwyk agreed to become deputy leader of a new →Democratic Alliance led by the DP's Tony Leon, although the NNP and the DP did not immediately disband their separate party organizations.

The NNP is an associate member of the International Democrat Union and a member party of its regional organization, the Democrat Union of Africa.

Pan-Africanist Congress of Azania (PAC)

Address. Box 13412, The Tramshed 0126
Telephone. (+27–12) 320–6243
Fax. (+27–12) 320–1509

Email. azania@icon.co.za
Website. www.paca.org.za
Leadership. Mmutlanyane Mogoba (president); Michael Muendane (secretary-general)

The PAC was formed in 1959 by a breakaway faction of the ANC and advocated the establishment of a democratic society through African, and not multi-racial, organizations. It rejected multi-racial co-operation on the grounds that it was a means of safeguarding white interests. Like the ANC, the PAC was banned by the apartheid regime between 1960 and 1990. Having announced in January 1994 that it was abandoning armed struggle, and claiming to be the authentic voice of the black population, the PAC registered for the April elections, in which it secured 1.25% of the vote and five National Assembly seats. In the June 1999 general election it won 0.7% of the vote and three National Assembly seats.

South African Communist Party (SACP)

Address. PO Box 1027, Johannesburg 2000
Telephone. (+27–11) 339–3633
Fax. (+27–11) 339–4244
Email. sacp@wn.apc.org
Website. www.sapc.org.za
Leadership. Charles Nqakula (national chairman); Blade Nzimande (secretary-general)

The Communist Party of South Africa was formed in 1921 and re-founded as the SACP in 1953. Banned until 1990, it has long co-operated closely with the →African National Congress (ANC), some senior appointments within which have been held by SACP members. SACP candidates were included on the ANC list for the April 1994 elections after which the then party chairman, Joe Slovo (who died in January 1995), was appointed to President Mandela's new administration. In the 1999 general election the SACP called on its members to vote for the ANC (as did the Congress of South African Trade Unions, the third component of the "tripartite alliance").

United Christian Democratic Party (UCDP)

Address. PO Box 3010, Mafikeng
Telephone. (+27–18) 381–5691
Fax. (+27–18) 381–5603
Leadership. Lucas Mangope (leader)

The UCDP was registered to contest the June 1999 elections by Lucas Mangope, the former president of the "independent homeland" of Bophuthatswana (whose government had been overthrown by an uprising in March 1994). Drawing many of its officials from the leadership of Mangope's former Bophuthatswana Democratic Party, the UCDP won three seats in the National Assembly in 1999, while at provincial level it became the official opposition party in the legislature of the North West province (largely corresponding to the former Bophuthatswana). In January 2000 the UCDP concluded a co-operation agreement with the →Democratic Party.

United Democratic Movement (UDM)

Address. PO Box 26290, Arcadia 0007
Telephone. (+27–12) 321–0010
Fax. (+27–12) 321–0014
Email. info@udm.org.za
Website. www.udm.org.za
Leadership. Bantu Holomisa (president); Masilo Mabeta (national chairman); Malizole Diko (national secretary)

The UDM, which claimed to have a membership "directly corresponding to the demographic composition of South Africa", was co-founded in September 1997 by Bantu Holomisa and Roelf Meyer. Holomisa, a former head of government (1987-94) in the "independent homeland" of Transkei, had been dismissed as a deputy minister in Nelson Mandela's government of national unity and expelled from the →African National Congress after making corruption allegations against another ANC minister in testimony to South Africa's truth and reconciliation commission. Meyer, a former secretary-general of the National Party, had been obliged to resign from the NP after the party's rejection of his call for it to disband and/or undergo radical restructuring following its withdrawal from the government of national unity in 1996. In 1998 Holomisa became president, and Meyer deputy president, of the UDM, which won 14 National Assembly seats in the June 1999 general election. The UDM subsequently concluded a parliamentary co-operation agreement with the →Federal Alliance. In January 2000 Roelf Meyer resigned from his parliamentary seat and his UDM position, stating that he was retiring from politics. The position of UDM deputy president was left vacant, reflecting a lack of agreement between different sections of the party over the selection of a successor.

Other Parties

Christian Democratic Party, Afrikaner-led group calling for a government based on Christian values.
Website. www.christiandemocraticparty.org.za
Leadership. Revd. Theunis Botha & Revd. Rudi du Plooy

Conservative Party of South Africa (*Konsertwatiewe Party van Suid-Afrika*), launched in 1982 by former National Party members who rejected any constitutional moves towards power-sharing with the non-white population. The party was runner-up to the National Party at the elections in 1987 and 1989. It unsuccessfully urged white voters to reject the reform process in the March 1992 referendum, thereafter insisting on the right to self-determination including the possibility of a white homeland. The party did not register to contest elections held in the 1990s.
Address. Private Bag X847, Pretoria 0001
Telephone. (+27–12) 329–1220
Fax. (+27–12) 329–1229
Email. kp@kp.co.za
Website. www.kp.co.za
Leadership. Dr Ferdi Hartzenberg (leader)

Green Party of South Africa, formerly known as the Government by the People Green Party, contested the 1999 general election but won no seats in the National Assembly.
Email. info@greenparty.org.za
Website. www.greenparty.org.za
Leadership. Judy Sole (founder)

Reconstituted National Party (*Herstigte Nasionale Party, HNP*), founded in 1969 by extreme right-wing former members of the National Party. The HNP, advocating "Christian nationalism" and strict apartheid, briefly held one parliamentary seat (following a by-election) between 1985 and 1987. It opposed the constitutional reform process and did not register to contest elections held in the 1990s.
Address. PO Box 1888, Pretoria 0001
Telephone. (+27–12) 342–3410
Fax. (+27–12) 342–3417
Email. info@hnp.org.za
Website. www.hnp.org.za

Socialist Party of Azania (SOPA), contested the 1999 general election but won no seats in the National Assembly.

Spain

Capital: Madrid

Population: 40,000,000 (2000E)

The Kingdom of Spain's 1978 constitution rescinded the "fundamental principles" and organic legislation under which General Franco had ruled as Chief of State until his death in 1975 and inaugurated an hereditary constitutional monarchy. Executive power is exercised by the Prime Minister and the Council of Ministers nominally appointed by the King but collectively responsible to the legislature, in which they must command majority support. Legislative authority is vested in the bicameral *Cortes Generales*, both houses of which are elected for four-year terms (subject to dissolution) by universal adult suffrage of those aged 18 and over. The upper Senate (*Senado*) has had 259 members since the 2000 elections, of whom 208 were directly elected and 51 designated by 17 autonomous regional legislatures. The lower Congress of Deputies (*Congreso de los Diputados*) consists of 350 deputies elected from party lists by province-based proportional representation, with each of the 50 provinces being entitled to a minimum of three deputies. Spain joined what became the European Union on Jan. 1, 1986, and elects 64 members of the European Parliament.

Pursuant to the constitutional description of political parties as the expression of pluralism and an essential instrument of political participation, subsidies are available from state funds for parties represented in the Congress of Deputies, in proportion to number of seats and votes obtained at the most recent general elections. Parties are also eligible for state subsidies to defray election campaign expenses, again in proportion to representation obtained, and to certain benefits during campaigns, such as free advertising space in the media. A separate channel of public subsidy is the entitlement of parliamentary groups in the national and regional legislatures to financial assistance according to their number of members.

Elections to the Congress of Deputies on March 12, 2000, resulted as follows: Popular Party 183 seats (with 44.6% of the vote), Spanish Socialist Workers' Party 125 (34.1%), Convergence and Union 15 (4.2%), United Left (led by the Communist Party of Spain) 8 (5.5%), Basque Nationalist Party 7 (1.5%), Canarian Coalition 4 (1.1%), Galician Nationalist Bloc 3 (1.3%), Andalusian Party 1 (0.9%), Republican Left of Catalonia 1 (0.8%), Initiative for Catalonia–Greens 1 (0.5%), Basque Solidarity 1 (0.4%), Aragonese Union 1 (0.3%).

Communist Party of Spain
Partido Comunista de España (PCE)

Address. Calle Toronga 27, 28043 Madrid
Telephone. (+34–91) 300–4969
Fax. (+34–91) 300–4744
Email. internacional@pce.es
Website. www.pce.es
Leadership. Francisco Frutos (secretary-general)

The PCE was founded in April 1920 by dissident members of the youth wing of the →Spanish Socialist Workers' Party (PSOE) who wished to join the Third (Communist) International and who united in November 1921 with the *Partido Comunista Obrero Español* (PCOE), formed by further defections from the PSOE. The PCE held its first congress in 1922 but was forced underground by the Primo de Rivera dictatorship and had only 800 members by 1929. The party formed part of the republican Popular Front from January 1936, winning 17 seats in the Congress in that year. During the Francoist uprising the PCE policy was "victory first, then revolution", in contrast to the Trotskyists and anarcho-syndicalists. Under the subsequent Franco regime, the PCE was active in the clandestine resistance, its general secretaries (in exile) being Dolores Ibárruri Gómez ("*La Pasionaria*") in 1942–60 and Santiago Carrillo Solares from 1960 (when Ibárruri was appointed honorary president of the party). Undergoing various splits during the 1960s, the PCE developed links with the Italian Communist Party (PCI), sharing the latter's opposition to Moscow's leadership and the 1968 Czechoslovakia intervention, and its support for co-operation with other democratic parties.

In July 1974 the exiled PCE leadership joined other anti-Franco parties in the *Junta Democrática*, which in March 1976 joined the Socialist-led Democratic Platform to form the Democratic Co-ordination. Legalized in April 1977, when it had some 200,000 members, the PCE supported the restoration of a constitutional monarchy and won 20 seats in the Congress of Deputies elected in June 1977 (and three in the Senate). The ninth (1978) PCE congress was the first to be held in Spain for 46 years. The party's congressional strength increased to 23 in the elections of March 1979, but it became internally divided between two large and broadly Euro-communist factions and two smaller and broadly pro-Soviet factions. The weakened party was reduced to 4.1% of the vote and four deputies in the October 1982 elections, whereupon Carrillo resigned and was succeeded as PCE secretary-general (in November) by a more committed Euro-communist, Gerardo Iglesias Argüelles.

In local elections in May 1983 the PCE vote recovered to 7.9%, but in the following months it suffered a series of splits, mainly between "*gerardistas*" favouring a broad left alliance and "*carrillistas*" opposed to such a strategy. In March 1985 Carrillo was forced out of the PCE leadership, his supporters being purged from the central committee. In April 1986 the PCE was a founder-member of the →United Left (IU), which secured 4.6% of the vote and seven lower house seats in the June general elections. The then deputy general secretary, Enrique Curiel, resigned in December 1987, and Iglesias himself resigned in February 1988 after losing the support of the large Madrid, Catalan and Andalusian sections. Later that month the 12th PCE congress elected Julio Anguita (a former mayor of Córdoba) as his successor. Meanwhile, the PCE had become involved in sporadic efforts to reunify the Spanish communist movement following the establishment by Ignacio Gallego of the People's Communist Party of Spain (PCPE) and by Carrillo of what became the Workers' Party of Spain (PTE).

PCE president Dolores Ibárruri died in November 1989, whereafter the PCE continued its "broad left" strategy in the 1993, 1996 and 2000 elections, deriving some benefit in 1996 from the troubles of the then ruling PSOE and the broadly conservative policies of the González government, but falling back sharply in 2000. At the 15th PCE congress in December 1998, Anguita was succeeded as secretary-general by Francisco Frutos.

Popular Party
Partido Popular (PP)

Address. Génova 13, 28004 Madrid
Telephone. (+34–91) 557–7300
Fax. (+34–91) 308–4618
Email. oipp@pp.es
Website. www.pp.es
Leadership. José María Aznar López (president); Luis de Grandes Pascual (Congress spokesman); Esteban González Pons (Senate spokesman); Javier Arenas Bocanegra (secretary-general)

The moderate conservative PP was established in its present form in January 1989 as successor to the Popular Alliance (*Alianza Popular*, AP), which been created in October 1976 as a distinctly right-wing grouping embracing the dominant political forces of the Franco era. The AP had been formed as a coalition of seven right-wing and centre-right parties: *Reforma Democrática* (RD), led by a former Francoist minister Manuel Fraga Iribarne; *Acción Regional* (AR), led by Laureano López Rodó; *Acción Democrática Española* (ADE), formed in 1976 and led by Federico Silva Muñoz; *Democracia Social* (DS), led by Licinio de la Fuente; *Unión del Pueblo Español* (UDPE), led by Cruz Martínez Esteruelas; *Unión Nacional Española* (UNE), led by Gonzalo Fernández de la Mora, and *Unión Social Popular* (USP), led by Enrique Thomas de Carranza. In March 1977 five of these parties merged as a single organization named the *Partido Unido de Alianza Popular* (PUAP) led by Fraga Iribarne as secretary-general. The two non-participating parties were the ADE and the UNE, both led by former Francoist ministers, but they remained in alliance with the PUAP until late 1979.

In the June 1977 general elections the AP, then widely regarded as a Francoist grouping, won 8.2% of the vote, giving it 16 seats in the Congress of Deputies and two in the Senate. Divided over whether to endorse the 1978 constitution (which Fraga Iribarne in the event supported), the AP lost support. In the March 1979 general elections the Democratic Coalition which it had formed with other right-wing groups, including *Acción Ciudadana Liberal*, the *Partido Popular de Cataluña*, *Renovación Española* (RE) and the Popular Democratic Party (PDP), won only 6% of the vote, giving it nine seats in the Congress and three in the Senate. At the 1979 and 1980 party congresses, the AP leadership moved the party, with some difficulty, towards a mainstream conservative orientation, a leading advocate of which was Fraga Iribarne, who was elected AP president in 1979. In mid-1980 the AP merged with the PDP and RE; the combined party, projecting a moderate image (and denouncing the 1981 coup attempt), doubled its membership in 1981–82.

The Galician elections of October 1981 enabled the AP to form a minority government in that region, where it secured a majority in 1983 by recruiting members of the by then dissolved Union of the Democratic Centre (UCD). Meanwhile, in the national parliamentary elections of October 1982 the AP-led bloc won 26.6% of the vote and 106 seats in the lower chamber (and 54 in the upper), so eclipsing the UCD and becoming the main opposition formation. From 1983 the AP led a regional and national electoral alliance, the Popular Coalition (*Coalición Popular*, CP), including the PDP, the Liberal Union (UL) and regional formations such as the →Union of the Navarrese People (UPN), the →Aragonese Party and the →Valencian Union. The CP came under severe strain following the June 1986 general elections, in which it secured 26% of the vote and 105 seats in the lower house (and 63 in the Senate). In July 1986 the PDP broke away. In December, after an electoral rout in the Basque Country, Fraga resigned as AP president. In January 1987 the national AP broke with the Liberal Party (PL, as the UL had become) although the AP-PL alliance remained in existence in some regions. The 8th AP congress, in February 1987, installed a new youthful party leadership headed by Antonio Hernández Mancha, who had been AP leader in Andalusía. During 1987 the AP contested elections at various levels, securing 231 seats in autonomous parliaments, over 13,000 local council seats and 17 seats in the European Parliament (for which its list was led by Fraga Iribarne). However, by late 1987 defections resulting from chronic internal infighting had reduced the party's strength in the national Congress of Deputies to 67.

The conversion of the AP into the PP at a party congress in January 1989 reflected the wish of most AP currents to present a moderate conservative alternative to the ruling →Spanish Socialist Workers' Party (PSOE) and to eschew any remaining identification with the Franco era. The congress was preceded by a power struggle between Hernández and Fraga Iribarne, the latter having been persuaded by supporters that he should try to regain the leadership. In the event, Hernández opted out of the contest shortly before the congress, so that Fraga Iribarne resumed the leadership of a more united party, which subsequently made particular efforts to build alliances with regional conservative parties. In the October 1989 general elections it advanced marginally to 106 seats and 30.3% of the vote, but remained far behind the PSOE. In December 1989 the PP won an absolute majority in the Galician assembly, whereupon Fraga Iribarne became regional president, being succeeded as PP leader by José María Aznar López.

In the early 1990s the PP was not immune from scandals concerning irregular party financing, of the type affecting most of Latin Europe; but it remained relatively untarnished compared with the ruling PSOE. In general elections in June 1993 the party increased its Chamber representation to 141 seats and its vote share to 34.8%, less than four points behind the PSOE. Continuing in opposition, the PP registered major victories in the October 1993 Galician regional election and in the June 1994 European Parliament elections, on the latter occasion overtaking the PSOE by winning 40.6% of the vote and 28 of the 64 seats. Further advances followed in regional and local elections in May 1995, although in actual voting the PP failed to match its large opinion poll lead over the PSOE. Aznar's public standing was boosted by a car-bomb assassination attempt against him in Madrid in April 1995.

In early general elections in March 1996 the PP at last overtook the PSOE as the largest Chamber party, but its 156 seats (from 38.9% of the vote) left it well short of an overall majority. Aznar was accordingly obliged to form a minority government, which received qualified pledges of external support from the Catalan →Convergence and Union (CiU), the →Basque Nationalist Party (PNV) and the →Canarian Coalition (CC) in return for concessions to their regional agendas. His government programme promised urgent economic austerity measures to achieve the "national objective" of meeting the Maastricht treaty criteria for participation in a single European currency. The PNV withdrew its support from the PP government in September 1997, without affecting its ability to survive. The PNV withdrawal was confirmed in June 1999 following municipal and regional elections in which the PP maintained its status as the leading political formation, retaining control in nine of the 13 autonomous regions where elections were held. In simultaneous European Parliament elections the PP slipped to 39.8% of the national vote and 27 seats.

Economic progress related to the discipline required for joining the euro boosted the PP's popularity in the run-up to the March 2000 parliamentary elections, the party also being assisted by a public desire for continuity following the ending of the Basque separatist ETA's ceasefire in December 1999. The results showed that the party had secured an historic overall majority of 183 lower house seats on a 44.6% vote share as well as an overall majority of 150 seats in the Senate. The new Aznar government therefore had the unfettered authority to enact long-discussed legislation, including a tough new immigration bill and the standardization of the teaching of humanities throughout Spain's regions. Although it no longer needed their votes, the PP again negotiated external support agreements with the CiU and the CC, but made no attempt to establish a new accord with the PNV.

The PP is affiliated to the Christian Democrat International and the International Democrat Union. Its representatives in the European Parliament sit in the European People's Party/European Democrats group.

Spanish Socialist Workers' Party
Partido Socialista Obrero Español (PSOE)

Address. Ferraz 68–70, Madrid 28008
Telephone. (+34–91) 582–0444
Fax. (+34–91) 582–0525
Email. internacional@psoe.es
Website. www.psoe.es
Leadership. José Luis Rodríguez Zapatero (secretary-general); Jesús Caldera Sánchez-Capitán (Congress spokesman); Juan José Laborda Martín (Senate spokesman) Of social democratic orientation, the PSOE seeks a fairer and more united society based on social, economic and political democracy. It supports Spanish membership of the European Union (EU) and of the Atlantic Alliance, having opposed the latter until 1986. It defined itself as Marxist in 1976, but since 1979 has regarded Marxism as merely an analytical tool. It defends divorce and the decriminalization of abortion in certain circumstances.

Originally founded in 1879 from socialist groups in Madrid and Guadalajara, the PSOE held its first congress in 1888 and became a leading party of the Second International. It was allied with the Republicans from 1909, as a result of which its founder, Pablo Iglesias, was elected to the Congress of Deputies in 1910. The party had some 40,000 members when its left wing broke away in 1920–21 to form the →Communist Party of Spain (PCE). The PSOE doubled its membership during the 1920s and returned about one third of the deputies in the Congress in 1931. It played an important role in the history of the Spanish Republic until the end of the Civil War in 1939, when it was banned by the Franco regime. The exiled leadership, based in Toulouse (France), refused to ally with other anti-Franco forces, but a more radical internally-based *"renovador"* faction began to organize in the late 1960s. The internal section gained control at a congress in Paris in 1972, and in 1974 it elected Felipe González as first secretary (although a rival *"historico"* faction survived in France and evolved into the →Socialist Action Party). Both the PSOE and various regional socialist parties experienced rapid growth in Spain at about this time, partly due to the death of Franco.

In June 1975 the PSOE joined other non-Communist opposition parties in the *Plataforma Democrática* alliance, which in March 1976 merged with the PCE-led *Junta Democrática*. The latter had been created in 1974 and included the Popular Socialist Party (*Partido Socialista Popular*, PSP), which had been formed in 1967 as the *Partido Socialista del Interior* (PSI). The PSOE was also a component of the even broader *Coordinación Democrática*, which negotiated with the post-Franco government for the restoration of civil and political rights, regional autonomy and popular consultation on the future form of government. During 1976 the PSOE formed the *Federación de Partidos Socialistas* along with groups such as the →Party of Socialists of Catalonia (PSC), *Convergencia Socialista Madrileña*, the *Partit Socialiste des Illes*, the *Partido Socialista Bilzarrea* and the Aragonese and Galician Socialist parties.

In December 1976 the PSOE, the largest socialist group with about 75,000 members, held its first congress inside Spain for 44 years, the venue being in Madrid. It was formally legalized on Feb. 17, 1977, along with a number of other parties. The PSOE participated in the June 1977 general elections together with the PSC and the Basque Socialist Party (PSE–PSOE), winning a total of 118 seats in the Congress of Deputies and 47 in the Senate. In February 1978 the PSC formally affiliated to the national party, as the PSC–PSOE, and in April the PSOE absorbed the PSP, which had six deputies and four senators. The Aragonese and Galician parties were similarly absorbed in May and July 1978. In the March 1979 general elections the PSOE, with its Basque and Catalan affiliates, won 121 seats in the Congress and 68 in the Senate, therefore remaining in opposition. At a centennial congress in May 1979 González unexpectedly stepped down as party leader after a majority of delegates refused to abandon a doctrinal commitment to Marxism. His control was re-established during a special congress in late September 1979, the hard-liners being defeated by a 10 to 1 majority.

The PSOE made further gains in the October 1982 general elections, in which it won 48.7% of the vote (passing the 10 million mark for the first time) and gained an absolute majority in both chambers (with 202 of the 350 deputies and 134 of the 208 senators). A PSOE government was formed on Dec. 1, with González as Prime Minister; it subsequently negotiated Spain's entry into what became the European Union (EU) with effect from Jan. 1, 1986. In January 1983 the PSOE absorbed the Democratic Action Party (*Partido de Acción Democráta*, PAD), which had been formed in March 1982 by centre-left defectors from the then ruling Union of the Democratic Centre (UCD). In 1985 the PSOE experienced serious internal divisions over the government's pro-NATO policy, which ran counter to the party's longstanding rejection of participation in any military alliance. The issue was resolved by a referendum of March 1986 which delivered a majority in favour of NATO membership on certain conditions, including reduction of the US military presence in Spain.

The PSOE retained power in the June 1986 general elections with a reduced vote share of 43.4% but a renewed majority of 184 lower house seats and 124 in the Senate. It thereafter pursued what were generally seen as moderate and somewhat conservative policies, particularly in the economic sphere. The PSOE's narrow loss of an overall majority in the October 1989 general elections (in which it slipped to 175 seats in the lower house on a 39.6% vote share) was attributed in part to internal divisions, highlighted by the prior emergence of the dissident →Socialist Democracy splinter group and by the defection of a substantial PSOE group to the →United Left (IU). In the early 1990s the PSOE's standing was damaged further by a series of financial scandals involving prominent party figures, combined with familiar left/right tensions. At the 32nd PSOE congress in November 1990 the left-leaning Deputy Prime Minister and deputy party leader, Alfonso Guerra, was able to block a move by the party's right to strengthen its base in leadership bodies. However, a corruption scandal involving his brother compelled Guerra to resign from the government in January 1991; although he remained deputy léader of the party, the PSOE right became increasingly dominant thereafter.

In early general elections in June 1993 the party retained a narrow relative majority of 159 Chamber seats (on a 38.7% vote share), sufficient for González to form a minority government with regional party support. Held amid further disclosures about irregular party financing, the 33rd PSOE congress in March 1994 resulted in the transfer of the party's controversial organization secretary, José María ("Txiki") Benegas, to another post. In the June 1994 European Parliament elections PSOE support slumped to 31.1%, so that the party took only 22 of the 64 Spanish seats, while in simultaneous regional elections the PSOE lost overall control of its stronghold of Andalusia. Further setbacks followed in Basque Country elections in October 1994 and in regional/municipal polling in May 1995, although the PSOE retained control of Madrid and Barcelona.

The tide of corruption and security scandals rose inexorably through 1995, with the CESID phone-tapping disclosures in June, causing the small Catalan →Convergence and Union party to withdraw its external support from the PSOE government the following month. The eventual upshot was another early general election in March 1996 in which the PSOE finally lost power, although the margin of its defeat was less wide than many had predicted: it retained 141 seats with 37.5% of the vote, only slightly down on its 1993 showing and only 1.5% behind the →Popular Party, which was therefore obliged to form a minority government.

González finally vacated the PSOE leadership at the 34th party congress in Madrid in June 1997, being succeeded by Joaquín Almunia Amann, an uncharismatic Basque politician. On Almunia's proposal the first-ever "primary" elections were held in April 1998 to choose the party's prime ministerial candidate, the unexpected victor being not Almunia but articulate former minister Josep Borrell Fontelles. An uneasy dual leadership ensued, until Borrell resigned as Prime Minister-candidate in May 1999 over a controversial financial investment by his now-estranged wife in the 1980s. In the June 1999 European Parliament elections the PSOE presented a joint list with the →Democratic Party of the New Left (PDNI), advancing to 35.3% of the vote and 24 of the 64 Spanish seats. The following month Almunia was elected unopposed as the PSOE candidate for Prime Minister.

In the run-up to the March 20000 parliamentary elections the PSOE entered into a ground-breaking agreement to co-operate with the Communist-led IU in the contest, although at IU insistence the pact to present joint lists extended only to the Senate elections. In the event, both parties fared badly, with the PSOE falling to 125 lower house seats and 34.1% of the vote, while the combined efforts of the parties yielded only 69 Senate seats. Almunia immediately resigned as PSOE leader and was replaced in July 2000 by 39-year-old José Luis Rodríguez Zapatero, a Castilean lawyer, who embarked upon a rejuvenation of the party's leadership bodies.

The PSOE is a member party of the Socialist International and its European Parliament representatives sit in the Party of European Socialists group.

United Left
Izquierda Unida (IU)
Address. Olimpo 35, 28043 Madrid
Telephone. (+34–91) 300–3233
Fax. (+34–91) 388–0405
Email. org.federal@izquierda-unida.es
Website. www.izquierda-unida.es
Leadership. Gaspar Llamazares (secretary)
The radical left-wing (mainly Marxist) IU was founded in April 1986 as an electoral alliance, its first president being the then PCE leader, Gerardo Iglesias. The IU originally consisted of the →Communist Party of Spain (PCE), the →Socialist Action Party (PASOC), the Peoples' Communist Party of Spain (PCPE), the Progressive Federation (FP) and the Communist Union of Spain (UCE). It was expanded in 1988–89 to include the →Republican Left (IR) and the Unitarian Candidature of Workers (*Candidatura Unitaria de Trabajadores*, CUT), led by Juan Manuel Sánchez Gordillo. Later temporary participants included the →Carlist Party, the →Humanist Party (PH) and the →Unity of the Valencian People (UPV).

In the June 1986 general elections the IU won seven seats in the Congress of Deputies and none in the Senate. The FP left the IU in late 1987, partly as a result of the unilateral decision of the PCE to sign a parliamentary accord against political violence without consulting the other IU parties. In December 1987 the IU leadership adopted a strategy seeking to make the IU a permanent rather than *ad hoc* alliance, and to broaden its base during 1988 beyond the member parties to incorporate independent left-wingers and pressure groups. In the October 1989 general elections the IU increased its lower house representation to 18 seats (on a 9.1% vote share) and also won one Senate seat.

Proposals for a formal merger between the IU parties caused dissension in 1991–92, the outcome being that com-

ponent formations retained their autonomous identity. In the June 1993 general elections the IU made only marginal headway, again winning 18 lower house seats but with 9.6% of the vote. It fared substantially better in the June 1994 European Parliament elections, obtaining nine of the 64 Spanish seats on a 13.5% vote share. In simultaneous regional elections in Andalusia, it won 19.2% of the vote. In the March 1996 general elections the IU derived some benefit from the defeat of the →Spanish Socialist Workers' Party (PSOE), winning 10.6% of the national vote and 21 lower house seats (although none in the Senate). However, the June 1999 European elections brought a sharp reverse for the IU, to only 5.8% of the vote and four seats.

In February 2000 the IU concluded its first-ever electoral pact with the PSOE, but covering only the forthcoming Senate elections and not those to the Congress of Deputies. The results of the polling the following month showed a slump in IU support, to 5.5% of the vote, which yielded only eight seats. Veteran IU secretary Julio Anguita González immediately resigned and was succeeded by Gaspar Llamazares.

The IU representatives in the European Parliament sit in the European United Left/Nordic Green Left group. The IU has an official membership of 68,000.

Other National Parties

Alliance for National Union (*Alianza por l'Unión Nacional, AUN*), radical far-right formation seeking the preservation of the unity of the Spanish state and a halt to immigration.
Leadership. Ricardo Saenz de Ynestrillas

Carlist Party (*Partido Carlista, PC*), formed in 1934, a left-wing group which arose from a 19th-century Catholic monarchist movement; strongest in the north of Spain, the Carlists turned against the Franco regime after 1939 and many of its leaders were exiled; in the post-Franco era it became a component of the →United Left alliance.

Centrist Union (*Unión Centrista, UC*), launched in early 1995 by elements that included former members of the Democratic and Social Centre (*Centro Democrático y Social*, CDS), which had been founded prior to the 1982 elections by Adolfo Suárez González, who had vacated the leadership of the Union of the Democratic Centre (*Unión de Centro Democrático*, UCD) on resigning as Prime Minister in January 1981 and had been rebuffed when he tried to regain the party leadership in July 1982; allied regionally and locally with the →Popular Party (PP) and an affiliate of the Liberal International, the CDS had won 14 lower house seats and five European Parliament seats in 1989, although the resignation of Suárez González in September 1991 had heralded virtual extinction in the 1993 national and 1994 European elections; the new UC fared little better in the 1996 general elections.
Address. Jorge Juan 30, 28001 Madrid
Leadership. Fernando García Fructuoso

Feminist Party of Spain (*Partido Feminista de España, PFE*), founded in 1979, aiming to spread the gospel of women's liberation at the political and social levels, but not making much headway in Catholic and socially conservative Spain.
Address. Magdalena 29/1A, 28012 Madrid
Leadership. Lidia Falcón O'Neill

The Greens (*Los Verdes*), confederation resulting from ecologist conferences in Tenerife in May 1983 and in Malaga in June 1984, legally registered in November 1984, inaugurated at a congress in Barcelona in February 1985; the resultant Green Alternative (*Alternativa Verde*) electoral alliance won less than 1% of the vote in the 1986 general

elections, and subsequent assorted electoral variants (sometimes simultaneous and competing) have made no further progress, although the movement has gained some representation at local level and won 1.4% in the June 1999 European Parliament elections.
Address. Calle Navellos 9/2°, 46003 Valencia
Telephone/Fax. (+34–96) 392–1314
Email. verdspv@xarxaneta.org
Website. www.xarxaneta.org/losverdes

Humanist Party of Spain (*Partido Humanista de España, PHE*), formed in 1984, a member of the →United Left electoral coalition (IU) in the 1986 general elections, subsequently independent.
Website. www.mdnh.org
Leadership. Rafael de la Rubia

Liberal Party (*Partido Liberal, PL*), founded in 1977, absorbed the small Liberal Union (*Unión Liberal*, UL) in 1985, closely allied with the →Popular Party from 1989, although retaining independent party status.
Address. Plaza de las Cortes 4, 28014 Madrid
Website. www.website.es/liberal
Leadership. José Antonio Segurado

National Democracy (*Democracia Nacional, DN*), right-wing formation founded in 1995.
Email. demnac@arrakis.es
Website. www.ecomix.es/~demnac
Leadership. Francisco Pérez Corrales

National Front (*Frente Nacional, FN*), far-right party founded in October 1986 aiming to rally Francoist forces against the then ruling →Spanish Socialist Workers' Party.
Leadership. Blas Piñar López

Republican Left (*Izquierda Republicana, IR*), left-wing formation dating from 1934, became a component of the →United Left (IU) in 1988.
Address. Calle Príncipe de Vergana 55/4°/A, 28006 Madrid
Telephone. (+34–91) 564–8719
Fax. (+34–91) 564–8655

Email. ir@bitmailer.net
Website. www.izqrepublicana.es
Leadership. Albert Vela Antón (president); Isabelo Herreros Martín-Maestro (secretary-general)

Socialist Action Party (*Partido de Acción Socialista, PASOC*), founded in January 1983 by left-wing socialists who regarded the then ruling →Spanish Socialist Workers' Party (PSOE) as having betrayed the working class; succeeded the PSOE *Histórico*, which arose from the 1974 split between the *renovadores* ("renewal") group based inside Spain (led by Felipe González) and the *historicos* loyal to the exiled leadership of Rodolfo Llopis; having absorbed some even smaller socialist formations, PASOC was a founder member of the →United Left alliance in 1986, through which it gained representation at national, regional and European levels.
Address. Espoz y Mina 5, 28012 Madrid
Leadership. Pablo Castellano & Alonso Puerta

Socialist Democracy (*Democracia Socialista, DS*), founded in 1990 by a left-wing dissident faction of the then ruling →Spanish Socialist Workers' Party.
Leadership. Ricardo García Damborenea

Spanish Falange (*Falange Española*), residual survival of the ruling formation of the Franco era, won one lower house seat in 1979 in a National Union (*Unión Nacional*) with other neo-fascist groups; other far-right formations appeared to supersede the Falange in the 1980s, notably the →National Front; in the 1990s it has sought to articulate right-wing sentiment among those damaged by free-market government policies.
Address. Calle Silva 2, 4–3, 28015 Madrid
Telephone. (+34–91) 541–9699
Fax. (+34–91) 559–9210
Website. www.falange.es
Leadership. Carmen Franco & Diego Marquez Jorrillo

Revolutionary Workers' Party (*Partido Obrero Revolucionario, POR*), Trotskyist formation founded in 1974.
Email. por@pangea.org
Website. www.pangea.org/por

Regional Parties

As the leading national formations, the →Popular Party (PP), →Spanish Socialist Workers' Party (PSOE) and →United Left (IU) are organized in most of Spain's autonomous regions, either under their own name or in alliance with autonomous regional parties. There are also many regional parties without national affiliation.

ANDALUSIA

Regional assembly elections on March 3, 1996, resulted as follows: PSOE 52 seats, PP 20, a joint list of the IU, Greens and local progressives (the *Convocatoria por Andalucía*) 13, Andalusian Party 4.

Andalusian Party
Partido Andalucista (PA)
Address. Av. San Francisco Javier 24, Edificio Seville 1/9A-2, 41005 Seville
Telephone. (+34–95) 422–6855
Fax. (+34–95) 421–0446
Email. pa-secretaria@p-andalucista.org
Website. www.p-andalucista.org
Leadership. Alejandro Rojas-Marcos de la Viesca (president); Antonio Ortega García (secretary-general)
The PA was founded in 1976 (as the Socialist Party of Andalusia) on a progressive nationalist platform, seeking self-determination for Andalusia on terms more concessionary than those of the 1981 autonomy statute. Legalized in 1977, the party fought the 1979 general elections on a moderate regionalist manifesto, securing five seats in the Congress of Deputies (which it failed to hold in 1982). It won two seats in the Catalan assembly in March 1980 and three seats in the Andalusian assembly in May 1982 (with 5.4% of the vote). The party adopted its present name at its fifth congress in February 1984. In the 1986 Andalusian elections it was reduced to two seats, but it slightly raised its vote in the 1987 local elections.

The PA regained national representation in 1989, winning two lower house seats, and advanced strongly to 10 seats in the Andalusian regional assembly in 1990. However, it lost its national seats in 1993 and fell back to three regional seats in 1994. In the 1996 contests the PA again failed at national level, while improving to four seats in the Andalusian assembly. It contested the June 1999 European elections as part of the European Coalition (*Coalición Europea*, CE) of regional parties, winning one of the CE's two seats. In March 2000 the party regained national representation, winning one lower house seat with 0.9% of the vote.

The PA's representative in the European Parliament sits in the Greens/European Free Alliance group.

ARAGON

Regional assembly elections on June 13, 1999, resulted as follows: PP 28 seats, PSOE 23, Aragonese Party 10, Aragonese Union 5, IU 1.

Aragonese Party
Partido Aragonés (PAR)
Address. Coso 87, 50001 Zaragoza, Aragon
Telephone. (+34–976) 200–616
Fax. (+34–976) 200–987
Leadership. José María Mur Bernad (president); Emilio Eiroa García (secretary-general)
Officially called the Aragonese Regionalist Party (*Partido Aragonés Regionalista*) until 1990, the PAR was founded in January 1978 to campaign for greatly increased internal autonomy for the provinces of Aragon within the Spanish state. Having its main strength in Zaragoza, it secured one of the region's 13 seats in the national lower house in 1977, retaining it in 1979. In the 1982 general elections the PAR was allied with the conservative Popular Alliance (later the →Popular Party) and lost its seat. It became the third-largest bloc in the regional assembly in the May 1983 elections, which gave it 13 seats. Standing alone in the 1986 national elections, it regained a lower house seat. After the 1987 regional elections, which produced no overall majority, the then PAR president, Hipólito Gómez de las Roces, was elected regional premier. The party retained its one national seat in 1989 and 1993, but lost it in 1996 (despite being allied with the PP). In the interim, it won 14 seats in the regional assembly in March 1995. It contested the June 1999 European elections as part of the European Coalition (*Coalición Europea*, CE) of regional parties, failing to win representation.

Other Party

Aragonese Union (*Chunta Aragonesista, ChA*), of socialist and ecological orientation, advanced from two to five seats in June 1999 regional elections in Aragon and won one national lower house seat in March 2000; claims 2,000 members.
Address. c/ Conde de Aranda 14/16/1°, 50003 Zaragoza
Telephone. (+34–97) 628–4242
Fax. (+34–97) 628–1311
Email. sedenacional@chunta.com
Website. www.chunta.com
Leadership. Bizén Fuster Santaliestra (chairman); José Antonio Acero (secretary-general)

ASTURIAS

Regional assembly elections on June 13, 1999, resulted as follows: PSOE 24 seats, PP 15, IU 3, Asturian Renewal Union 3.

Asturian Renewal Union (*Unión Renovadora Asturiana, URAS*), led by Sergio Marqués Fernández, founded in 1998 by dissident faction of regional Popular Party (PP), won three seats in June 1999 regional elections.

BALEARIC ISLANDS

Regional assembly elections on June 13, 1999, resulted as follows: PP 28 seats, PSOE 13, Socialist Party of Majorca–Nationalists of Majorca 5, IU 3, Majorcan Union 3, others 7.

Majorcan Union
Unió Mallorquina (UM)
Address. Av. de Joan March 1/3/3, 07004 Palma de Mallorca
Telephone. (+34–971) 726–336
Fax. (+34–971) 728–116
Email. um@ctv.es
Website. www.unio-mallorquina.es
Leadership. Bartomeu Vicens (secretary-general)
The regionalist UM has a centrist political orientation. It won six of the 52 regional assembly seats in 1983, so that it held the balance of power between the PP and the PSOE. By 1995 it had slipped to only two seats, recovering to three in June 1999. On the latter occasion it contested the European elections as part of the Nationalist Coalition/Europe of the Peoples (*Coalición Nacionalista/Europa de los Pueblos* alliance, without winning representation.

The UM became an observer member of the Liberal International in 2000.

Socialist Party of Majorca–Nationalists of Majorca
(*Partit Socialista de Mallorca–Nacionalistes de Mallorca, PSM-NM*), left-oriented nationalist formation, won six out of 59 regional assembly seats in 1995, falling to five in 1999.

BASQUE COUNTRY (EUSKADI)

Regional assembly elections on May 13, 2001 resulted as follows: Basque Nationalist Party/Basque Solidarity alliance 33 seats, PP 19, Basque Socialist Party-Basque Left 13, We Basques 7, IU 3.

Basque Nationalist Party
Partido Nacionalista Vasco (PNV)
Euzko Alderdi Jeltzalea (EAJ)
Address. Ibáñez de Bilbao 16, 48001 Bilbao, Euzkadi
Telephone. (+34–94) 435–9400
Fax. (+34–94) 435–9415
Email. ebb@eaj-pnv.com
Website. www.eaj-pnv.com
Leadership. Juan José Ibarretxe Markuartu (*lendakari* of Basque government); Xabier Arzallus Antía (president); Ricardo Ansotegui (secretary)
Dating from 1895, the Christian democratic PNV stands for an internally autonomous Basque region (including Navarra) within Spain and is opposed to the terrorist campaign for independence being waged by the Basque Homeland and Liberty (*Euzkadi ta Azkatasuna*, ETA), although it favours dialogue with the ETA political wing. It opposes unrestrained capitalism and supports a mixed economy.

The PNV developed from the Basque Catholic traditionalist movement led by its founder, Sabino Arana y Goiri. It returned seven deputies to the Spanish *Cortes* in 1918, 12 in 1933 and nine in 1936, succeeding in the latter year in establishing an autonomous Basque government under José Antonio Aguirre. Allied with the republican regime in the Spanish civil war, its leadership was forced into exile by Gen. Franco's victory, and the party was suppressed throughout the Franco era. Aguirre died in 1960 and the Basque "government in exile" nominated Jesus María de Leizaola to succeed him as *lendakari* (president of the Basque government).

In the 1977 Spanish general elections the PNV won seven seats in the Congress of Deputies and eight in the Senate; its representatives abstained in the parliamentary vote on the 1978 constitution, and its supporters were among the 56% of voters in Guipúzcoa and Vizcaya (the two largest Basque provinces) who abstained in the ensuing referendum. It lost one of its seats in Congress in 1979, but in that year's elections to the Basque general junta the PNV won 73 of the 171 seats in the two main provinces, whereupon de Leizaola returned from France, ending the 43-year-old "government in exile". In the March 1980 elections to the new Basque parliament it won 37.6% of the vote and 25 of the 60 seats. The then PNV leader, Carlos Garaikoetxea, became *lendakari* of the autonomous Basque government in April 1980.

In 1982 the PNV secured eight seats in the Spanish Congress and nine in the Senate. In the February 1984

Basque elections it won 42% of the vote and 32 of the 75 seats. Garaikoetxea was forced to resign due to intra-party disputes in December 1984, and in February 1985 was succeeded as party leader by Xabier Arzallus and as *lendakari* by José Antonio Ardanza Garro, a PNV member, who agreed a "pact of government" with the Basque Socialist Party (later the →Basque Socialist Party–Basque Left, PSE–EE). In June 1986 the PNV's representation in the *Cortes* fell to six seats in the lower chamber and seven in the upper. The party split in September, with supporters of Garaikoetxea leaving to form →Basque Solidarity (EA). In the Basque elections of November 1986 the PNV held only 17 of its seats and was again obliged to govern in coalition with the PSE (which won fewer votes but more seats than the PNV).

In January and March 1989 the PNV organized huge demonstrations in Bilbao calling upon separatist militants to end their armed struggle. However, subsequent efforts to form an electoral alliance with the EA and the →Basque Left (EE) failed, with the result that in October 1989 the PNV's national representation fell to five Congress and four Senate seats, although it was confirmed as the largest party in the 1990 Basque parliament elections, with 22 seats. The PNV again won five lower house seats in the 1993 general elections, after which the PNV usually gave external support to the PSOE minority government. In the June 1994 European Parliament election the PNV headed a regional list which won 2.8% of the vote and two seats, one of which was taken by a PNV candidate. In regional elections in October 1994, the PNV won 22 of the 75 Basque parliament seats and formed a coalition with the Basque Socialist Party–Basque Left (PSE–EE).

In the March 1996 national elections the PNV retained five lower house seats and improved from three to four in the Senate. The following month it joined with the Catalan →Convergence and Union and the →Canarian Coalition in undertaking to give external parliamentary support to a minority →Popular Party (PP) government, in exchange for certain concessions to its regionalist agenda. Having withdrawn its backing for the PP national government in September 1997, the PNV fell out with the PSE-EE in the regional government in June 1998. In the October 1998 Basque regional elections, held a month after ETA had declared a ceasefire, the PNV slipped to 21 seats under the new leadership of Juan José Ibarretxe Markuartu. It nevertheless became the leading party in the region's first-ever wholly nationalist coalition, including the EA and, controversially, ETA's political wing, →We Basques (EH). In the June 1999 European elections the PNV was part of the Nationalist Coalition/Europe of the Peoples (*Coalición Nacionalista/Europa de los Pueblos*) regional alliance, winning one seat.

ETA's return to violence in December 1999 appeared to strengthen the appeal of the PNV, which advanced to seven lower house seats and six in the Senate in the March 2000 national elections. In early regional elections in May 2001, moreover, a joint PNV–EA list won a commanding 33 seats (out of 75) and 43% of the vote in a high turnout, with the PNV taking 25 seats. It therefore claimed that the public supported its policy of dialogue with ETA and that the PP government in Madrid had failed in its efforts to tarnish the party with association with terrorism. Ruling out any further co-operation with the EH while ETA violence continued, Ibarretxe formed a minority coalition with the EA and the Basque →United Left (which had won three seats).

The PNV's European Parliament representative sits in the Greens/European Free Alliance group. The party was for many years a member of the Christian Democrat International, but in 2000 it was expelled on the proposal of the PP because of its advocacy of dialogue with ETA.

Basque Socialist Party–Basque Left
Partido Socialista de Euskadi–Euskadiko Ezkerra (PSE-EE)
Address. Plaza de San José 3, Bilbao 9, Euzkadi
Telephone. (+34–94) 424–1606

Leadership. José María (Txiki) Benegas (president); Nicolás Redondo Terreros (secretary-general)

The PSE–EE was created in March 1993 when the PSE (the autonomous Basque federation of the →Spanish Socialist Workers' Party, PSOE) merged with the smaller and more radical EE. The merged party continued with the PSE's pro-autonomy line, whereas the Marxist EE had previously been committed to independence for the Basque provinces. That the latter was able to accept the PSE's stance for the merged party was in part because its militant pro-independence wing rejected the merger and broke away to maintain the →Basque Left (EuE) in being as an independent formation.

Founded in 1977, the PSE won seven seats in the Congress of Deputies in 1977, and five in 1979. It was in an autonomist pact until late 1979, when it parted company with the →Basque Nationalist Party (PNV) over the latter's insistence on the necessity of including Navarra in the Basque autonomy statute. However, having won eight lower house seats in the 1982 national elections, the PSE from early 1985 agreed to support a PNV administration. In June 1986, for the first time, the PSE–PSOE won more seats in the Congress than any other party in the region, with seven deputies to the PNV's six, although the Socialist vote in the three provinces of the Basque autonomous region was the lowest anywhere in Spain, at around 25%. In November 1986, after a split in the PNV, the PSE was confirmed as the largest single party, winning 19 of the 75 seats in elections to the Basque parliament. Early in 1987 the PSE joined a coalition administration with the PNV, with a PSE member Jesus Eguiguren, being elected president of the parliament. In the 1990 Basque elections the PSE slipped to 16 seats.

The EE had been launched in 1976 as a pro-independence electoral alliance which had as its main component the Basque Revolutionary Party (*Euskal Iraultzarako Alderdia*, EIA), which had been formed by supporters of Mario Onaindía Machiondo, then a political prisoner, as a non-violent Marxist offshoot of the *Politico-Militar* faction of the terrorist group, Basque Nation and Liberty (ETA). Onaindía was secretary-general of the EE for some ten years after its foundation. In June 1977 the EE secured one seat in each chamber of the Spanish parliament, both EE representatives subsequently voting against the 1978 constitution because of its limited provisions for Basque autonomy. The party lost its Senate seat in 1979, but in the 1980 elections to the Basque parliament the EE won 9.7% of the vote and six seats (out of 60). The EIA dissolved itself in mid-1981, and the EE was reorganized shortly afterwards, incorporating Roberto Lertxundi Baraffano's faction of the Basque Communist Party (EPK). It was relaunched in March 1982, as the Basque Left–Left for Socialism alliance (EE–IS), and retained its Congress seat in October. A radical nationalist faction, the New Left (*Nueva Izquierda*), led by José Ignacio Múgica Arregui, broke away from the EE later in 1982; *Ezkerra Marxista*, a similar tendency formed in October 1983, sought to remain within the EE, but the leadership declared its intention to purge any dissident groups. The EE held its six Basque parliament seats in 1984, following which Onaindía resigned as general secretary in January 1985. In 1986 the EE won a second seat in the Congress, and nine in the Basque parliament. In the 1990 Basque elections the EE tally was again six seats.

The merged PSE–EE did not aggregate the two parties' previous electoral support, winning only 12 seats in the 1994 Basque parliament elections, although it joined a regional coalition headed by the PNV. In the October 1998 Basque elections the PSE–EE advanced to 14 seats, thereafter becoming part of the regional opposition. It fell back to 13 seats in May 2001, continuing in opposition after talks on joining a coalition with the PNV had come to nothing.

Basque Solidarity
Eusko Alkartasuna (EA)
Address. Camino de Portuetxe 23/1°, 20009 Donostia-San Sebastián
Telephone. (+34–943) 020–130
Fax. (+34–943) 020–132
Email. prentsa@euskoalkartasuna.org

Website. www.euskoalkartasuna.org
Leadership. Begoña Errazti Esnal (president); Gorka Knörr Borras (secretary-general)

The EA is a radical nationalist (pro-independence), pacifist and social democratic movement, which rejects revolutionary nationalism. Its ideological determinants have included the anti-communist *Bultzagilleak* group from Guipúzcoa, the traditional nationalists known as *sabinianos* after early nationalist leader Sabino Arana and the *abertzales* or patriots. The party was founded in September 1986 as the Basque Patriots (*Eusko Abertzaleak*) by a breakaway faction of the →Basque Nationalist Party (PNV) led by Carlos Garaikoetxea, who as then PNV leader had been *lendakari* (president of the Basque government) in 1980-84. The split precipitated early elections to the Basque parliament in November, when the EA won 14 seats against 17 for the parent party. Its first congress in April 1987 showed that it then had the support of several hundred mayors and local councillors.

In January 1987 the EA agreed a joint programme for government with the →Basque Left (EE/EuE), this document later applying to the EA's relations with the radical EuE following the main EE's decision to create the →Basque Socialist Party–Basque Left. In June 1987 the EA contested European Parliament elections as part of the autonomist Europe of the People's Coalition (EPC), with Garaikoetxea winning a seat. In November the EA declined to sign an inter-party Basque accord against terrorism paralleling that signed by parties in the Spanish parliament; the EA stated that the accord did not address the fundamental issues of self-determination and national reintegration. It slipped to nine seats in the 1990 Basque parliament elections and to eight in 1994, but retained its single national lower house seat in the March 1996 elections on a joint list with the EuE.

The EA won only six seats in the October 1998 Basque regional elections but joined a minority coalition with the PNV and →We Basques, the first to be formed entirely by nationalist parties. In the June 1999 European elections it was part of the Nationalist Coalition/Europe of the Peoples (*Coalición Nacionalista/Europa de los Pueblos*) alliance, winning one seat, whose holder joined Greens/European Free Alliance group. Under the new leadership of Begoña Errazti Esnal, the EA retained its single national seat in March 2000 and recovered to eight seats in Basque regional elections in May 2001, standing on a joint list with the PNV. It was allocated three portfolios in the resultant PNV-led government.

The EA is a member of the Democratic Party of the Peoples of Europe–European Free Alliance.

We Basques
Euskal Herritarrok (EH)

Address. Astarioa 8/3°, 48001 Bilbao, Euzkadi
Telephone. (+34–943) 424–0799
Fax. (+34–943) 423–5932
Leadership. Arnaldo Otegi

The EH was launched in 1998 as successor to United People (*Herri Batasuna*, HB) following action against the latter by the Spanish authorities. A Marxist-oriented Basque nationalist formation, HB/EH has called for the withdrawal of "occupation forces", i.e. the Spanish military and police, and negotiations leading to the complete independence of Euzkadi. It is regarded as the closest of the main parties to the illegal terrorist group Basque Nation and Liberty (*Euzkadi ta Askatasuna*, ETA).

HB was founded in 1978 as an alliance of two legal Basque nationalist groups, the social democratic Basque Nationalist Action (*Accion Nacionalista Vasca*, ANV), formed in 1930, and the Basque Socialist Party (*Euskal Socialista Biltzarrea*, ESB), formed in 1976, with two illegal groups, the People's Revolutionary Socialist Party (HASI) and the Patriotic Workers' Revolutionary Party (LAIA). HASI and LAIA had formed the *Koordinadora Abertzale Sozialista* (KAS), which functioned in effect as the political wing of the main ETA faction, ETA *Militar*, and the KAS manifesto was adopted more or less in full by HB.

HB contested Basque and Spanish elections from 1979, when it won three seats (which it refused to occupy) in the Spanish Congress of Deputies, one in the Senate and a total of 48 seats (out of 248) in the provincial assemblies of Guipúzcoa, Vizcaya and Navarra. In October 1979 HB called for abstention in the referendum on the creation of an autonomous Basque region excluding Navarra; in a 59% turnout the draft statute was supported by some 90.3% of voters. In March 1980 HB won 16.3% of the vote and 11 of the 60 seats in elections to the new Basque parliament, although it refused to take up its seats in assemblies above the level of *ayuntamientos* (local councils). Although it lost one of its Congress seats in the elections of October 1982, albeit with an increased vote, it won 12 seats (out of 75) in the Basque parliamentary elections of February 1984. Also in 1984 it won a High Court ruling obliging the Interior Ministry to recognize it as a party despite its alleged links with ETA.

In 1986 HB secured five seats in the Spanish Congress, one in the Senate and 13 in the Basque parliament. In February 1987 HB (unsuccessfully) nominated one of its leaders, Juan Carlos Yoldi (then in prison charged with ETA activities), as its candidate for *lendakari* (Basque premier). Also in early 1987 HB called for the formulation of a joint nationalist strategy with the →Basque Nationalist Party (PNV) and →Basque Solidarity (EA). In June 1987 an HB candidate was elected to the European Parliament (with 1.7% of the national vote). In January 1988 HB was the only one of the seven parties represented in the Basque parliament which was not invited to sign a pact against terrorism.

In the 1989 national elections HB lost one lower house seat and surprised observers by announcing that it would occupy its four remaining seats, ending a decade-long boycott of representation at that level. However, on the eve of the opening of parliament, HB deputy-elect Josh Muguruza was killed and HB leader Iñaki Esnaola wounded in an attack apparently carried out by right-wing terrorists. Later, the remaining HB deputies were expelled for refusing to pledge allegiance to the constitution. HB won two Congress seats and one in the Senate in the 1993 national elections, while the October 1994 Basque parliament balloting yielded 11 seats (two less than in 1990). Meanwhile, HB had lost its European Parliament seat in June 1994, its share of the national vote falling to 0.97%. In the 1996 national elections the HB again won two lower house seats.

In December 1997 the entire 23-member HB leadership received seven-year prison terms for "collaborating with an armed band" (i.e. ETA). A new leadership was elected in February 1998, following which the party opted to change its name to *Euskal Herritarrok* (EH) and to take its seats in the regional parliament. In the October 1998 Basque elections EH improved to 14 seats, whereupon the party took the historic step of joining a minority regional government headed by the PNV and including the EA. In the June 1999 European Parliament elections the EH regained a seat with a 1.5% national vote share, its representative becoming one of the non-attached members. The following month the old HB leadership was released from prison.

ETA's decision to call off a 14-month truce in December 1999 damaged the EH in terms of electoral support. Having failed to win any seats in the March 2000 national elections, it slumped to only seven seats (with 10% of the vote) in the Basque regional elections in May 2001, following which it went into opposition to a PNV-led coalition.

Other Parties

Alavan Unity (*Unidad Alavesa, UA*), a →Popular Party splinter group founded in 1989, campaigning for recognition of the rights of the province of Alava within the Basque Country. It won three seats in the 1990 Basque parliament elections, five in 1994 and two in 1998.
Leadership. José Luis Añúa (president)

Basque Left (*Euskal Ezkerra, EuE*), formed by militant pro-independence elements of the previous Basque Left grouping who rejected the 1993 merger with the Basque federation of the →Spanish Socialist Workers' Party to create the →Basque Socialist Party–Basque Left. In the March 1996 national elections the EuE presented a joint list with →Basque Solidarity, returning one deputy to the lower house, but the alliance was not sustained in subsequent national and regional elections.

Address. Jardines 5/1°, 48005 Bilbao, Euzkadi
Leadership. Xabier Gurrutxaga (secretary-general)

CANARY ISLANDS

Regional assembly elections on June 13, 1999, resulted as follows: Canarian Coalition 25 seats, PSOE 19, PP 14, Hierro Independent Grouping 2.

Canarian Coalition
Coalición Canaria (CC)
Address. Galcerán 7–9, 38004 Santa Cruz de Tenerife
Leadership. Román Rodríquez (president); Victoriano Ríos Pérez (Senate spokesman)

The broadly centrist CC was created prior to the 1993 general elections by the following parties: (i) the Canarian Independent Groupings (*Agrupaciones Independientes de Canarias*, AIC) led by Manuel Hermoso Rojas and Paulino Rivero; (ii) the Canarian Independent Centre (*Centro Canario Independiente*, CCI) led by Lorenzo Olarte Cullén; (iii) the Canarian Initiative/Left (*Iniciativa/Izquierda Canaria*, ICAN) led by José Mendoza Cabrero and José Carlos Mauricio Rodríguez; and (iv) the Majorca Assembly (*Asamblea Majorera*, AM) led by José Miguel Barragan Cabrera.

Of these components, the AIC was formed in 1985 as an alliance of Hermoso's *Agrupación Tinerfeña Independiente* (ATI) of Santa Cruz de Tenerife with the *Agrupación Palmera Independiente* (API) of Las Palmas and the *Agrupación Gomera Independiente* (AGI) of Tenerife. In the June 1986 general elections the AIC won about 60,000 votes, securing one seat in the Congress of Deputies and two in the Senate. The AIC retained one lower house seat in the 1989 general elections and was subsequently the only party to support Prime Minister González's re-election apart from his own →Spanish Socialist Workers' Party (PSOE). In the 1991 Canaries regional elections the AIC, with 16 seats, took second place behind the PSOE and the AIC candidate, Manuel Hermoso Rojas, was elected to the island presidency with support from the ICAN (five seats), the AM (two) and other parties.

In the 1993 national elections the CC returned four deputies and six senators, who subsequently gave qualified support to the minority PSOE government. In June 1994 the CC captured one seat in elections to the European Parliament. In September 1994 the CC-led regional government lost its narrow majority when the →Canarian Nationalist Party (PNC) left the alliance. In the May 1995 regional elections the CC obtained a plurality of 21 assembly seats out of 60 and continued to lead the islands' government. In the March 1996 national elections the CC retained four lower house seats but won only two of the directly elected Senate seats. It thereupon pledged qualified external support for a minority government of the centre-right →Popular Party (PP).

The CC increased its regional representation to 25 seats in June 1999, thus retaining leadership of the islands' government. In simultaneous European elections the CC was part of the European Coalition (*Coalición Europea*) of moderate regional parties, winning one seat. In the March 2000 national elections the CC again won four lower house seats and increased its representation in the Senate to five seats. Although the PP now had an absolute majority, it again concluded an external support agreement with the CC.

The CC's representative in the European Parliament sits in the European Liberal, Democratic and Reformist group.

Other Parties

Canarian Nationalist Party (*Partido Nacionalista Canario, PNC*), was original component of →Canarian Coalition, but withdrew in 1994, won four seats in 1995 Canaries regional elections.
Address. Sagasta 92, 35008 Las Palmas de Gran Canaria
Telephone/Fax. (+34–928) 221–736
Leadership. Pablo Betancor Betancor & José Luis Alamo Suárez

Hierro Independent Grouping (*Agrupación Herreña Independiente, AHI*), won one regional assembly seat in 1995 and two in 1999.
Address. La Constitución 4, 38900 Valverde, El Hierro, Santa Cruz de Tenerife
Telephone. (+34–922) 551–134
Fax. (+34–922) 551–224
Leadership. Tomás Padrón Hernández

Lanzarote Independents' Party (*Partido de Independientes de Lazarote, PIL*), returned one candidate to the Senate in the March 2000 national elections.
Leadership. Juan Pedro Hernández Rodríguez

National Congress of the Canaries (*Congreso Nacional de Canarias, CNC*), pro-independence group founded in 1986, favours leaving the EU and joining the OAU.
Address. Avda 3 de Mayo 81, 1° y 2°, Santa Cruz de Tenerife
Telephone/Fax. (+34–922) 283–353
Leadership. Antoni Cubillo Ferreira

CANTABRIA

Regional assembly elections on June 13, 1999, resulted as follows: PP 19 seats, PSOE 14, Regionalist Party of Cantabria 6.

Regionalist Party of Cantabria (*Partido Regionalista Cántabro, PRC*), centre-right formation which obtained two of the 35 seats in the May 1983 elections to the regional parliament; by the June 1999 elections it had improved to six seats out of 39.
Leadership. Migel Angel Revilla

Union for the Progress of Cantabria (*Unión para el Progreso de Cantabria, UPCA*), conservative formation, contested the 1991 regional elections on the →Popular Party (PP) list, winning 15 of that list's 21 seats (out of 39). In June 1993, however, the UPCA president of the regional government, Juan Hormaechea Cázon, broke with the PP, with the result that his party was reduced to seven seats in the May 1995 regional elections and lost the government presidency.
Leadership. Juan Hormaechea Cazón

CASTILLA Y LEON

Regional assembly elections on June 13, 1999, resulted as follows: PP 48 seats, PSOE 30, Union of the León People 3, IU 1, others 1.

Union of the León People (*Unión del Pueblo Leonés, UPL*), separatist formation that won two seats (out of 84) in the 1995 regional elections, rising to three in 1999.

CASTILLA–LA MANCHA

Regional assembly elections on June 13, 1999, resulted as follows: PSOE 26 seats, PP 21.

CATALONIA

Regional assembly elections on Oct. 17, 1999, resulted as follows: Convergence and Union 56 seats, Party of Socialists of Catalonia 52, PP 12, Republican Left of Catalonia 12, Initiative for Catalonia/Greens 3.

Convergence and Union
Convergència i Unió (CiU)

Address. Valencia 231, 08007 Barcelona, Catalunya
Telephone. (+34–93) 487–0111
Fax. (+34–93) 215–8428
Email. gpc.ciu@convergencia.org
Website. www.convergencia-i-unio.org
Leadership. Jordí Pujol i Soley (secretary-general); Francesc Xavier Marimon i Sabaté (Senate spokesman)

The pro-autonomy CiU was founded in 1979 as an alliance of the Democratic Convergence of Catalonia (Convergència Democrática de Catalunya, CDC) and the Democratic Union of Catalonia (Unió Democrática de Catalunya, UDC), and later absorbed the small Catalan Democratic Left Party (*Esquerra Democrática de Catalunya*, EDC). The CDC and UDC had contested the 1977 general elections as part of a Democratic Pact (*Pacte Democràtic*), which obtained 11 seats in the Congress of Deputies (and voted for the 1978 constitution). In the 1979 elections the CiU won eight seats in the Congress and one in the Senate. In elections to the new Catalan parliament in March 1980 the CiU displaced the →Party of Socialists of Catalonia (PSC) as the region's main political force, winning 28% of the vote and 43 of the 135 seats. Pujol was elected premier of the *Generalitat* (the Catalan administration) and formed a coalition with the local affiliate of the Union of the Democratic Centre, then the ruling party in Madrid, and a number of independents. In the October 1982 general elections the CiU increased its representation in the Spanish Congress to 12 members (and nine in the Senate). In the April 1984 Catalan elections the CiU won 46.8% of the vote and 72 seats, enabling it to form a majority administration.

In the 1986 national elections the CiU returned 18 deputies and eight senators, thus becoming the fourth-largest party in the Spanish parliament. It was allied with the new liberal Democratic Reformist Party (PRD), which failed to win any seats, their joint candidate for Prime Minister having been Miquel Roca Junyent, the CiU parliamentary leader who had formed the PRD and was regarded as the national leader of the reformist–liberal bloc. The CiU obtained three seats in the 1987 European Parliament elections. In March 1992 the CiU confirmed its regional dominance by winning 71 of the 135 seats in the Catalan assembly, while national elections in June 1993 yielded 17 Catalan lower house and 14 Senate seats, on a vote share of nearly 5%. The party thereafter gave qualified parliamentary support to the minority government of the →Spanish Socialist Workers' Party (PSOE). In June 1994 the CiU retained three seats in the European Parliament elections with 4.7% of the vote.

The travails of the PSOE government in 1994–95 encouraged the CiU to attach more autonomist conditions to its continued support, beyond the original demand for greater transfer of tax receipts to the Catalan government. After much confusion, the CESID phone-tapping scandal of mid-1995 finally impelled the CiU into formal opposition and support for new general elections. This switch enabled the party to maintain its ascendancy in regional elections in Catalonia in November 1995, although it fell back to 60 seats (out of 135). Held in March 1996, early national elections resulted in the CiU slipping to 16 lower house and

eight Senate seats, with 4.6% of the overall vote. After protracted negotiations, the CiU agreed to give external support to a minority government of the anti-regionalization →Popular Party (PP), which in return was obliged to swallow a dose of further devolution and to express admiration for Catalan culture. Featuring a doubling (to 30%) of tax receipt transfers from Madrid to Barcelona (and to the other autonomous regions), the deal with the PP was approved by the CiU executive in late April 1996 by 188 votes to 20 with 21 abstentions.

The CiU retained three seats in the June 1999 European elections (two for the CDC and one for the UDC), with 4.4% of the vote. In regional elections in October 1999 the CiU's long dominance came under serious challenge from the PSC, but the party just managed to remain the largest party with 56 seats (though with only 37.7% of the vote against 37.9% for the PSC). Pujol was therefore able to form a further minority administration. In the March 2000 national elections the CiU declined further to 15 lower house seats (with 4.2% of the vote), while retaining eight Senate seats. Although the PP now had an absolute majority, it again concluded an external support agreement with the CiU.

Of the CiU components, the UDC is affiliated to the Christian Democrat International and its representative in the European Parliament sits in the European People's Party/European Democrats group. The two CDC representatives sit in the European Liberal, Democratic and Reformist group.

Initiative for Catalonia
Iniciativa per Catalunya (IC)

Address. Ciutat 7, 08002 Barcelona, Catalunya
Telephone. (+34–93) 301–0612
Fax. (+34–93) 412–4252
Leadership. Rafael Ribó Massó (president)

The IC was launched in 1986 as an alliance of Communist and other left-wing formations in Catalonia, headed by the Unified Socialist Party of Catalonia (*Partit Socialista Unificat de Catalunya*, PSUC) led by Ribó Massó and also including the Party of Communists of Catalonia (*Partit dels Comunistes de Catalunya*, PCC) and the Union of Left Nationalists (*Entesa des Nacionalistas d'Esquerra*, ENE).

Founded in 1936 by the merger of four left-wing groups, the PSUC took part in the government of Catalonia until 1939, when it was forced underground by the Francoist victory. Legalized again in 1976, it became a member of the provisional government of Catalonia. In the 1980 elections to the new Catalan parliament the PSUC obtained 19% of the vote and 25 of the 135 seats; but in the 1984 elections it was reduced to six seats and 5.8% of the vote. In the June 1986 national elections the PSUC retained the single seat in the Congress of Deputies which it had won in 1982 (as against eight won in 1979 and 1977).

Contesting the 1992 regional and 1993 national elections as effectively the Catalan version of the national →United Left, the IC made little impact. For the November 1995 regional elections it formed an alliance with the Catalan →Greens (*Els Verds*), their joint list obtaining 11 of the 135 seats. It maintained the alliance in the October 1999 regional elections but also gave tactical support to the →Party of Socialists of Catalonia and confined its own effort to Barcelona, with the result that its representation fell to three seats. In the March 2000 national elections a joint IC–Green list won a single lower house seat.

Party of Socialists of Catalonia
Partit dels Socialistes de Catalunya (PSC)

Address. Calle Nicaragua 75–77, 08029 Barcelona, Catalunya
Telephone. (+34–93) 495–5400
Fax. (+34–3) 495–5435
Email. psc@psc.es
Website. www.psc.es
Leadership. Pasqual Maragall (president); Narcís Serra (first secretary)

The PSC is affiliated to, but not formally part of, the →Spanish Socialist Workers' Party (PSOE), pursuing similar economic and social policies but seeking the transformation of the current autonomist constitution into a federal one. The present party was founded in July 1978 as a merger of three pre-existing socialist formations, including the Catalan branch of the PSOE. After winning 15 lower house seats in the 1977 national elections, the following year the PSC affiliated to the PSOE, contesting subsequent national elections as a federation of the Spanish party.

In the 1979 general elections the PSC returned 17 lower house deputies, but was defeated by the centrist →Convergence and Union (CiU) alliance in the 1980 elections to the Catalan parliament, obtaining 33 of the 135 seats. In the 1982 national elections the PSC won an absolute majority (25) of the Catalan seats in the lower house. In the 1984 Catalan elections it obtained 30% of the vote and 41 seats, while in the 1986 national elections it fell back to 21 seats but remained ahead of other Catalan parties. The same pattern of ascendancy in national contests and inferiority at regional level was apparent in subsequent elections. In the November 1995 Catalan elections the PSC won 34 seats (against 39 in 1992), again coming a distant second to the CiU.

In June 1999 three PSC members were elected to the European Parliament on the PSOE list. In the October 1999 regional elections the PSC mounted a strong challenge against the CiU, on a platform of less strident Catalan nationalism and greater accommodation with the rest of Spain. It outpolled the CiU in popular vote terms (37.9% to 37.7%) and increased its representation to 52 seats, but narrowly failed to become the leading party and so remained in opposition.

Republican Left of Catalonia
Esquerra Republicana de Catalunya (ERC)
Address. c/ Villarroel 45 ent., 08011 Barcelona, Catalonia
Telephone. (+34–93) 453–6005
Fax. (+34–93) 323–7122
Email. internacional@esquerra.org
Website. www.esquerra.org
Leadership. Josep Lluís Carod-Rovira (secretary-general and parliamentary leader); Jordí Carbonell (president)
Dating from 1931, the ERC was the majority party in the Catalan parliament of 1932 but was forced underground during the Franco era. Re-legalized in 1977, it adopted a moderate left-wing economic programme, also advocating Catalan self-determination and defining languages other than Catalan as foreign. It contested the June 1977 national elections along with the *Partido del Trabajo de España*, other groups and independent candidates in an alliance, the *Esquerra de Catalunya–Front Electoral Democràtic*, and elected one deputy. In 1979 the ERC allied with the *Front Nacional de Catalunya*, and won one seat each in the Spanish Congress of Deputies and the Senate. In elections for the new Catalan parliament in March 1980 the ERC gained 9% of the vote and 14 of the 135 seats. In the October 1982 Spanish elections it held its single seat in the Congress, and in the Catalan elections in April 1984 it won 4.4% and its strength was reduced to five members.

The ERC divided during the 1980s between a liberal wing, which favoured participation in the Catalan *Generalitat* (government), and the left, which favoured an independent line. The 15th (1985) ERC congress elected the liberal Joan Hortalà i Arau (the Catalan industry minister) as the party's leader, succeeding the more nationalistic Heribert Barrera i Costa. The 1986 elections deprived the ERC of its representation in the Madrid parliament, but in 1987 the party was part of the Europe of the Peoples Coalition (CEP) that secured a seat in the European Parliament (this being retained in 1989 but lost in 1994).

In 1991 the ERC absorbed the radical separatist Free Land (*Terre Lliure*) movement, the consequences being a switch from a pro-federalism line to advocacy of outright independence for Catalonia. The ERC retained its single seat in the national lower house in the 1993, 1996 and 2000 elections. In Catalonia it won 11 of 135 regional parliament

seats in 1992, rising to 13 in November 1995. The ERC was part of the Nationalist Coalition/Europe of the Peoples (*Coalición Nacionalista/Europa de los Pueblos*) of regional parties in the June 1999 European elections, though it failed to win one of the Coalition's two seats. In the October 1999 regional elections the ERC slipped to 12 seats on a vote share of 8.7%.

Having some 5,000 members, the ERC is a member of the Democratic Party of the Peoples of Europe–European Free Alliance.

Other Party

Liberty and Democracy (*Libertat i Democracia, LiD*), the small centrist LiD has made little electoral impact, although it has been a member of the Liberal International since 1975.
Address. Corsega 331–33/1r, 08037 Barcelona
Telephone. (+34–93) 488–1580
Fax. (+34–93) 236–3115
Email. josepsoler@bcn.servicom.es
Leadership. Josep Soler (secretary-general)

EXTREMADURA

Regional elections on June 13, 1999, resulted as follows: PSOE 34 seats, PP 28, IU 3.

GALICIA

Regional elections on Oct. 21, 2001, resulted as follows: PP 41, Galician Nationalist Bloc 17, Party of Galician Socialists 17.

Galician Nationalist Bloc
Bloque Nacionalista Galego (BNG)
Address. Avda Rodríguez de Viguri, Bloque 3 Baixo, 15703 Santiago de Compostela, Galicia
Telephone. (+34–981) 555–850
Fax. (+34–981) 555–851
Email. beiras@bng-galiza.org
Website. www.bng-galiza.org
Leadership. Xosé Manuel Beiras (secretary-general)
Founded in 1983, the BNG advocates greater autonomy for Galicia and moderate left-wing economic policies. In 1991 it absorbed the more centrist Galician National Party (*Partido Nacionalista Galego*, PNG) led by Pablo González Mariñas, which had been formed in 1986 by a progressive faction of the Galician Coalition. The BNG's regional electoral support rose steadily, from five seats in 1989, 13 in 1993 and 18 in October 1997. Meanwhile, it had won two lower house seats in the 1996 national elections. Having taken one seat in the June 1999 European elections (with 1.7% of the national vote), the BNG improved its national lower house representation to three seats in March 2000 but lost one of its regional seats in October 2001.

The BNG's representative in the European Parliament sits in the Greens/European Free Alliance group.

Party of Galician Socialists
Partido dos Socialistas de Galicia (PSdG)
Address. Pino 1–9, 15704 Santiago de Compostela
Telephone. (+34–981) 589–622
Leadership. Emilio Pérez Touriño (secretary-general)
The PSdG is the autonomous regional federation of the →Spanish Socialist Workers' Party (PSOE). Although it increased its representation in the Galician parliament from 17 seats to 22 in 1985, control of the Xunta passed to what became the →Popular Party (PP). The PSdG re-established control in 1987, but went into opposition to the PP after the 1989 regional elections, despite advancing to 28 seats. It slumped to 19 seats in the 1993 regional elections and continued in opposition, falling further to 15 seats in October

1997, when it was allied with the regional United Left–Galiciian Left (*Esquerda Unida–Esquerda Galega*, EU-EG) and the →Greens. In the October 2001 regional elections the PSdG recovered to 17 seats.

MADRID

Regional elections on June 13, 1999, resulted as follows: PP 55 seats, PSOE 39, IU 8.

MURCIA

Regional elections on June 13, 1999, resulted as follows: PP 27 seats, PSOE 17, IU 1.

NAVARRE

Regional elections on June 13, 1999, resulted as follows: Union of the Navarrese People 22 seats, Socialist Party of Navarra 11, We Basques (EH) 8, Basque Solidarity (EA) 3, Convergence of Navarran Democrats 3, IU 3. (The EH and EA are covered under Basque Country, above.)

Socialist Party of Navarra
Partido Socialista de Navarra (PSN)
Address. c/o Regional Assembly, Pamplona, Navarra
Leadership. Víctor Manuel Arbeloa (president); Juan José Lizarbe (secretary-general)
The PSN is the regional federation of the →Spanish Socialist Workers' Party (PSOE). Formed in 1975 as the *Federación Socialista de Navarra*, it was integrated into the PSOE in 1982, although it retained its own identity and structure. Having won 19 of the 50 regional seats in 1991, the PSN was in opposition to the →Union of the Navarrese People until the 1995 elections, in which it fell back to 11 seats but nevertheless secured the election of Javier Otano as regional premier by virtue of support from other parties. It again won 11 seats in the June 1999 regional elections.

Union of the Navarrese People
Union del Pueblo Navarro (UPN)
Address. Plaza Príncipe de Viana 1/4°, 31002 Pamplona, Navarra
Telephone. (+34–948) 227–211
Fax. (+34–948) 210–810
Leadership. Miguel Sanz Sesma (president); Rafael Gurrea Induraín (secretary)
Founded in 1979, the conservative and Christian democratic UPN won a single seat in the Congress of Deputies in 1979 but lost it in 1982. In the 1982 and 1986 national elections the UPN allied with the right-wing Popular Alliance, precursor of the →Popular Party (PP); it also co-operated with the Popular Democratic Party (PDP) and the Liberal Union (UL), now the →Liberal Party. In the 1983 Navarra regional elections the UPN (then led by Javier Gomara) won 13 of the 50 seats, increasing to 14 in 1987 and to a plurality of 20 in 1991, when its candidate Juan Cruz Alli Aranguren was elected president of the regional government. It slipped to 17 seats in 1995 and went into opposition to a coalition headed by the →Socialist Party of Navarra but won 22 seats in 1999.

LA RIOJA

Regional assembly elections on June 13, 1999, resulted as follows: PP 18 seats, PSOE 13, Rioja Party 2.

Rioja Party
Partido Riojano (PR)
Address. Portales 17/1°, 26001 Logroño, La Rioja
Telephone. (+34–941) 238–199

Fax. (+34–941) 254–396
Leadership. Miguel González de Legarra (president); Jesús María Resa Fernández de Manzanos (secretary-general)
This small regionalist grouping has attempted, with little success, to challenge the dominance in the Rioja region of the national parties (mainly the PP and the PSOE, the latter organized locally as the *Partido Socialista de La Rioja*). It has usually returned two candidates in regional elections, most recently in June 1999.

VALENCIA

Regional elections on June 13, 1999, resulted as follows: PP 49 seats, Socialist Party of Valencia 35, Unity of the Valencian People 5.

Socialist Party of Valencia
Partido Socialista del País Valenciano (PSPV)
Address. Almirante 3, 46003 Valencia
Leadership. Antonio García Miralles (president); Antoni Asunción (secretary-general)
The PSPV is the autonomous Valancian wing of the →Spanish Socialist Workers' Party (PSOE) and was the dominant Valencian party in regional and national elections of the 1980s and early 1990s. In both the May 1995 and June 1999 regional elections, however, it came a poor second to the →Popular Party, winning only 32 and 35 of the 89 seats respectively.

Unity of the Valencian People
Unitat del Poble Valencià (UPV)
Leadership. Pere Mayor Penadés (chairman)
The UPV was founded in 1982 by two regionalist parties as a "democratic, left nationalist, egalitarian, ecologist and pacifist" formation; in alliance with the →United Left, it won two regional seats in 1987, failed to win representation in 1995 and advanced to five seats in June 1999.

Valencian Union
Unió Valenciana (UV)
Address. Avda de César Giorgeta 16/1°, 46007 Valencia
Telephone. (+34–96) 380–6267
Fax. (+34–96) 380–2308
Leadership. Héctor Villalba Chirivella (president)
The centre-right regionalist UV was founded in 1982, describing itself as "progressive and independent, inter-classist and democratic". At first allied with national conservative parties, it stood on its own in the 1986 national elections and won one lower house seat, which it has retained in subsequent elections. At regional level it maintained a small but significant presence, winning five seats in May 1995 and securing the election of its leader as president of the regional parliament. It failed to win representation in June 1999.

Other Party

Valencian Nationalist Party (*Partido Valenciano Nacionalista/Partit Valencià Nacionalista, PVN*), seeking the restoration of the ancient Valencian kingdom.
Address. Passeig de Russafa 10/3r/4, 46002 Ciutat de Valencia
Telephone/Fax. (+34–96) 394–2615
Email. pvn@arrakis.es

CEUTA AND MELILLA

Under legislation approved in September 1994, the North African enclaves of Ceuta and Melilla acquired full autonomous status as regions of Spain. Political life in both possessions was dominated until recently by local branches of metropolitan formations, notably the →Popular Party (PP) and the →Spanish Socialist Workers' Party (PSOE). However, elections on June 13, 1999, in Ceuta resulted in the newly-founded Independent Liberal Group (GIL) winning 12 seats, against eight for the PP, two for the PSOE and three for others, while in Melilla the GIL won seven seats, the Coalition for Melilla five, the PP five, the PSOE two and others six.

Independent Liberal Group (*Grupo Independiente Liberal, GIL*), led by the mayor of the mainland city of Marbella, won pluralities in both Ceuta and Melilla in June 1999, on a platform of closer integration of the enclaves with mainland Spain.
Leadership. Jesús Gil

Initiative for Ceuta (*Iniciativa por Ceuta, IC*), leftist grouping formed in December 1990, based in the Muslim community and named after the →Initiative for Catalonia.
Leadership. Ahmed Subair

Progress and Future of Ceuta (*Progreso y Futuro de Ceuta, PFC*), supports continued Spanish status, won six Ceuta assembly seats in 1995, its leader being elected government president with support from other parties.
Leadership. Francisco Fraiz Armada

Coalition for Melilla (*Coalición por Melilla, CpM*), won five seats in June 1999 elections.
Leadership. Mustafa Aberchan Hamed

Union of the Melilla People (*Unión del Pueblo Melillense, UPM*), right-wing formation founded in 1985.
Leadership. Juan José Imbroda Ortíz

Sri Lanka

Capital: Colombo

Population: 18,500,000 (2001E)

Ceylon gained its independence from the United Kingdom in 1948, and in 1972 was redesignated the Republic of Sri Lanka. Under the present constitution, promulgated in 1978, its name was changed again to the Democratic Socialist Republic of Sri Lanka, and a presidential form of government was adopted. The President, who is directly elected by universal suffrage for a six-year term, has the power to appoint or dismiss members of the Cabinet, including the Prime Minister, and to dissolve Parliament. The unicameral Parliament has 225 members, directly elected for a period of six years under a system of proportional representation first introduced in 1989.

In a general election held on Aug. 16, 1994, the United National Party (UNP), in power since 1977, was defeated by a left-wing coalition, the People's Alliance, which emerged as the largest grouping. Chandrika Bandaranaike Kumaratunga was sworn in as Prime Minister of a coalition government dominated by her Sri Lanka Freedom Party (SLFP), and including the Lanka Equal Society Party (LSSP), the Democratic United National Front (DUNF), the Sri Lanka Muslim Congress (SLMC), the Communist Party of Sri Lanka (CPSL) and later, the Ceylon Workers' Congress (CWC).

On Nov. 12, 1994, Kumaratunga was elected President with 62.3% of the popular vote, being succeeded as Prime Minister by her mother, Sirimavo Bandaranaike. Kumaratunga's first term in office was dominated by the civil war against the Liberation Tigers of Tamil Ealam and, after her peace strategy based on constitutional reform was blocked in parliament, she called an early presidential election in December 1999. This confirmed her in office but with a proportion (51%) of the vote sufficiently reduced for her not to consider calling early parliamentary elections as well. When parliament completed its six-year term, a general election was held on Oct. 11, 2000. Kumaratunga's People's Alliance was returned again as the largest grouping with 107 seats in the 225-member House. To secure a majority for her government, Kumaratunga had to include new elements in her ruling coalition - specifically, the National Unity Alliance (which was part of the SLMC) and the Eelam People's Democratic Party (EPDP) – and expand her cabinet to 44 members (or almost a sixth of the total House). But bitter faction fighting soon broke out within the new government and, in June 2001, the SLMC withdrew its support. Faced with a no-confidence motion, Kumaratunga utilised presidential prerogative to suspend parliament for up to 60 days. When the House re-convened on September 3, Kumaratunga revealed that she had obtained back-bench support from the far-left People's Liberation Front (JVP) to sustain the government. However, further defections from the ruling coalition followed and, on Oct. 11, 2001, she dissolved parliament and called a new general election for December.

Ceylon Workers' Congress (CWC)
Address. PO Box 1294, Colombo 3
Leadership. Arumugam Thondaman (president)
The CWC is both a trade union (with its main strength being among Tamil workers of Indian origin on tea plantations) and a political party, seen as representing the community of Indian descent. It has held the rural development portfolio in the government since 1978 through changes of administration. It has long been split into two factions. The dominant faction contested the general elections of 1994 and 2000 as part of the →People's Alliance and was represented in government. But a dissident faction stood, on both occasions, under the →United National Party banner.

Communist Party of Sri Lanka (CPSL)
Address. c/o Parliament, Colombo

Leadership. Pieter Keuneman (chair)
Formerly a Soviet-oriented party. Following the victory of the left-wing →People's Alliance in the 1994 elections, the party secured one portfolio in the government led by the →Sri Lanka Freedom Party and retained it after the 2000 election.

Democratic People's Liberation Front (DPLF)
Address. c/o Parliament, Colombo
Leadership. Dharmalingam Sithadthan (leader)
The DPLF is the political wing of the Tamil separatist People's Liberation Organization of Tamil Eelam (PLOTE), and has operated as a national political party since 1988. In the 1994 legislative elections it secured three parliamentary seats but lost them in the 2000 election.

Democratic United National Front (DUNF)

Address. c/o Parliament, Colombo

Leadership. G.M. Premachandra (general secretary)

The DUNF was formed in 1992 by a dissident group of →United National Party (UNP) politicians. Following the electoral victory of the →People's Alliance in the 1994 legislative polling, the party joined the coalition administration headed by the →Sri Lanka Freedom Party and continued to support it at the 2000 election.

Eelam People's Democratic Party (EPDP)

Address. c/o Parliament, Colombo

Leadership. Douglas Devananda (general secretary)

The EPDP is a Tamil regionalist party, nine members of which secured parliamentary seats as independents from Jaffna in the 1994 legislative elections. At the 2000 election, it won four seats and joined the coalition government headed by the →Sri Lanka Freedom Party.

Lanka Equal Society Party
Lanka Sama Samaja Party (LSSP)

Address. 457 Union Place, Colombo 2

Leadership. Bernard Soysa (leader)

The LSSP originated in the 1930s and has been a rare example worldwide of a Trotskyist party with significant political influence, participating in left-wing governments from 1964. Upon the defeat of the →United National Party by the →People's Alliance in the August 1994 parliamentary elections, the LSSP leader joined the new coalition government headed by the →Sri Lanka Freedom Party and continued to support it at the 2000 election.

People's Alliance

Address. c/o Parliament, Colombo

Leadership. Chandrika Bandaranaike Kumaratunga (leader)

The People's Alliance was formed in 1993 as a coalition of left-wing groups dominated by the →Sri Lanka Freedom Party (SLFP). In the 1994 legislative elections it secured 105 of the 225 seats, subsequently forming a new administration with the parliamentary support of moderate Tamil parties and the →Sri Lanka Muslim Congress. In November 1994 Kumaratunga won the presidential election as the People's Alliance candidate, with 62.3% of the popular vote. She retained the presidency in December 1999 with 51% of the vote and led the Alliance to victory in the October 2000 general election where it secured 107 parliamentary seats.

People's Liberation Front
Janatha Vimukthi Peramuna (JVP)

Address. 198/19, Panchikawattha Road, Colombo 10

Telephone. (+94–1) 822379

Fax. (+94–1) 819775

Email. contact@jvpsrilanka.com

Website. www.jvpsrilanka.com

Leadership. Somawansa Amarasinghe (leader); Tilvin Silva (general secretary)

A Sinhalese-based Marxist party with a continuing pro-Chinese orientation, the People's Liberation Front (JVP) was founded in 1965 in opposition to the participation of other left-wing parties in the Bandaranaike government. In 1971, it attempted to overthrow the government and again, in the late 1980s, sought to raise insurrection, after which it was severely repressed (with many supporters killed) and legally proscribed. However, it was rehabilitated after the victory of the →People's Alliance in 1994 and, adopting a constitutionalist strategy, stood at the October 2000 general election, winning 10 seats in parliament. In September 2001, it briefly offered back-bench support to the coalition government led by the →Sri Lanka Freedom Party, keeping it in office for an additional month, citing efforts to destabilize the country by the "murderous" →United National Party (which it blamed for past massacres of JVP supporters), imperialists, and Tamil separatist forces.

Sri Lanka Freedom Party (SLFP)

Address. 301 T.B. Jayah Mawatha, Colombo 10

Telephone. (+94–1) 696289

Website. www.slfp.lk

Leadership. Chandrika Bandaranaike Kumaratunga (leader)

Founded in 1951, the SLFP campaigned for the attainment of republican status for Sri Lanka prior to adoption of the 1972 constitution. With a democratic socialist orientation, the party advocated a non-aligned foreign policy, industrial development in both the state and private sectors, and safeguards for national minorities. One family has led the party throughout its history. S.W.R.D. Bandaranaike (originally a leading figure in the →United National Party (UNP), historically the country's other major party) was the party's founder and first Prime Minister from 1956 until his assassination in September 1959. His widow, Sirimavo Bandaranaike, in 1960 became the world's first woman Prime Minister (when the Prime Minister was head of government), holding this post until 1965 and again from 1970-77. Following the party's return to power after 17 years in the August 1994 elections, she was again Prime Minister (the post by now being largely ceremonial) from November 1994 until her death in October 2000. Chandrika Bandaranaike Kumaratunga, the daughter of S.W.R.D. and Sirimavo, was Prime Minister from August-November 1994, becoming the elected President (the head of government) in November 1994.

The party slumped to defeat in the 1977 elections, when it won only eight seats. During the 1980s it faced periodic harassment from the ruling UNP including Sirimavo's expulsion from parliament and detention. In August 1994, however, the SLFP returned to power heading the →People's Alliance coalition, which emerged as the largest parliamentary grouping in the legislative elections with 49% of the vote. The party formed a new government under the premiership of Chandrika Kumaratunga, who was subsequently elected President of the Republic in direct balloting in November. As President she sought reconciliation with Tamil separatists in the face of entrenched opposition and violence from hardliners in both the Tamil and majority Sinhalese communities. Kumaratunga retained the presidency at the December 1999 election and led the People's Alliance to another victory in the October 2000 general election, where it won 48% of the vote and formed another coalition government. However, in October 2001, following defections from the People's Alliance coalition, Kumaratunga called new elections for December 2001.

Sri Lanka Muslim Congress (SLMC)

Address. c/o Parliament, Colombo

Website. www.slmc.org

Leadership. Rauf Hakeem (leader of majority section)

The SLMC was formed under the leadership of M.H.M. Ashraff in 1981 to represent the Tamil-speaking Muslim population of the Eastern province and was organized as an all-island party in 1986. In the August 1994 elections the party won six parliamentary seats in its own right and three on the →People's Alliance national list, with Ashraff securing a post in the new coalition Cabinet headed by the →Sri Lanka Freedom Party (SLFP). Immediately before his death in a helicopter crash in September 2000 SLMC leader Ashraff said that he intended the associated National Unity Alliance (NUA), of which he was convenor, to be a separate political party. In 2001 the SLMC/NUA (which in practice were indivisible) split into a majority faction backing Rauf Hakeem while three of the 11 SLMC/NUA MPs elected in October 2000 backed Ashraff's widow, Ferial Ashraff, who in February 2001 joined the government as Minister of Eastern Rehabilitation and Reconstruction. In June 2001 President Kumaratunga dismissed Hakeem from the government, precipitating a withdrawal of support for the government by his supporters and, after internal party pressure, those of Ashraff. Ashraff resigned her Cabinet post but said she would continue to support the President.

Tamil United Liberation Front (TULF)

Address. 238 Main Street, Jaffna

Leadership. Murugesu Sivasithamraram (president)

The moderate TULF was formed in 1976 by a number of Tamil groups. It aims to establish a Tamil homeland (Tamil Eelam) in north-eastern Sri Lanka with the right of self-determination. In the August 1994 elections, its parliamentary representation fell from 10 to five seats, which it retained in the 2000 general election.

United National Party (UNP)

Address. Sirikotha, 400 Kotte Road, Sri Jayawardenepura

Telephone. (+94–1) 8653758

Fax. (+94–1) 865380

Email. unp@unp.itmin.com

Website. www.unplanka.org/unp

Leadership. Ranil Wickremasinghe (leader)

The conservative UNP, with the →Sri Lanka Freedom Party historically one of the country's two leading parties, was founded in 1947. It advocates the development of the country though free markets and inter-communal co-operation. It formed the government from 1947–1956 and again from 1965–70. In 1977 it secured a landslide victory under J. R. Jayawardene (who became the country's first executive President under the Constitution adopted in 1978) and then held office for 17 years. In 1989 Jayawardene was succeeded as President by Ranasinghe Premadasa, but he was assassinated on May 1, 1993. The party lost power in August 1994 when it secured only 94 of the 225 seats in Parliament. In the presidential election of November 1994 the replacement UNP contender, Srima Dissanayake (whose husband Gamini Dissanayake had been the party's candidate prior to his assassination in October), came second with 35.9% of the vote. In the presidential election of December 1999, Ranil Wickremasinghe, who became party leader in November 1994, stood in his own right and was defeated, taking 42% of the vote. At the general election in October 2000, the UNP won 89 seats and remained in opposition.

The UNP claims 1.4 million members and is a member party of the International Democrat Union.

Other Parties

Liberal Party, closely aligned with →Sri Lanka Freedom Party and a member of the Liberal International.

Address. 88/1 Rosmead Place, Colombo 7

Telephone. (+94–1) 691589

Leadership. Rajiva Wijesinha (president)

Sihala Urumaya (SU), a Sinhalese nationalist organisation, initially led by S.L. Gunasekere, which won one seat in parliament at the 2000 general election. However, the seat then fell vacant when Gunasekere, a Christian, was forced to resign from the SU by its Buddhist majority.

Website. www.sihalaurumaya.org

Leadership. Thilak Karunaratne (general secretary)

Sinhalese Freedom Front (*Singhalaye Nithahas Peramuna, SNP*), led by Arya Sena Tera, a Buddhist-centred nationalist group launched in 1994.

Tamil Eelam Liberation Organization (TELO), stood in the 2000 general election in Northern province and won three seats in parliament.

Separatist Organization

Liberation Tigers of Tamil Eelam (LTTE), the largest and most hardline of the militant Tamil separatist groups, has been fighting Sri Lankan forces for control of the Tamil majority areas in the north and east of the country since 1983; a major government offensive at the end of 1995 succeeded in capturing the main LTTE stronghold of Jaffna city but broke down in the northern mainland; in 1999, 'the Tigers' struck back re-capturing much of the lost ground – although not Jaffna city – and restoring a military stalemate with the government. Since 1999, several attempts to broker peace negotiations under Norwegian auspices have taken place, but without success.

Website. www.eelam.com

Sudan

Capital: Khartoum

Population: 29,490,000 (2000E)

The Republic of Sudan has, since its establishment in 1956, experienced political instability, north-south division and civil war. At the end of the 1990s the population included up to 4,000,000 displaced people, of whom an estimated 2,600,000 were in government-controlled areas of the country. A period of transitional military rule followed the coup of 1985 in which the army seized power from President Jaafar al-Nemery, who had himself come to power in a coup in 1969 and established a one-party state. Power was transferred to a civilian regime in May 1986, and for three years a series of coalition governments held office, with Sadiq al-Mahdi as the most prominent political figure (as he had been in civilian administrations prior to the Nemery coup). In June 1989, another military coup installed a Revolutionary Command Council (RCC) led by Lt.-Gen. Omar Hassan Ahmad al-Bashir. In October 1993 the RCC dissolved itself and named Bashir as President of a new civilian government which included most ministers from the outgoing administration. Elections were held on a non-party basis in March 1996 for 265 of the 275 elective seats in a 400-seat National Assembly (unicameral legislature) with a term of four years. Hassan al-Turabi, secretary-general of the National Islamic Front (NIF, a fundamentalist party with close links to successive Bashir governments) was unanimously elected president of the new legislature. Omar al-Bashir was elected to a five-year term as President of Sudan in March 1996, winning 75.5% of the vote in a contest with 40 other candidates.

A new constitution, approved by the National Assembly and endorsed by a referendum, came into force in July 1998. Organized political activity, banned since the 1989 coup, resumed in November 1998, the first approvals of party registration applications being announced in early 1999 (although the most important opposition parties remained in exile). The NIF evolved into the National Congress (NC) party, with President Bashir as its president and Hassan al-Turabi as its secretary-general. Relations between the two men deteriorated progressively during the second half of 1999, which also brought a reopening of contacts between Bashir and Sadiq al-Mahdi, the exiled leader of the *Umma* Party (one of the two major parties which, together with the NIF, had dominated

Sudanese politics before the 1989 coup). In December 1999 President Bashir suspended the National Assembly before it could vote on a bill (supported by Turabi) to reduce the powers of the President. The Assembly was dissolved in February 2000, and in June 2000 Turabi (who had been suspended as secretary-general of the NC) set up a Popular National Congress (PNC) party in opposition to Bashir. Sudan's 1998 law on political associations (widely criticized for imposing restrictive registration requirements) was replaced in March 2000 by a more liberal political organizations act which the government said was designed "to open doors for national dialogue that could provide peaceful solutions to the country's problems". Presidential and legislative elections held from Dec. 13 to 23, 2000, were boycotted by the PNC and other principal opposition parties (including the *Umma* Party, whose leadership had returned from exile between April and November 2000). In a five-way presidential contest President Bashir was re-elected with 86.5% of the vote; the runner-up, with 9.6% of the vote, was former President Nemery, who had returned to Khartoum under an amnesty granted in May 2000. The National Assembly elected in December 2000 had 360 members, of whom 270 were directly elected by universal adult suffrage (with a voting age of 17 years) and 90 were indirectly elected to represent women, university graduates and trade unions. Voting did not take place in three southern states currently under rebel control. The NC won a total of 355 Assembly seats (112 of them unopposed) with the 5 remaining seats going to independent candidates.

Democratic Unionist Party (DUP)

Leadership. Mohammed Osman al-Mirghani (leader)

The DUP, formed in 1968 through the merger of two long-established parties, is a largely secularist Islamic centre party, supported primarily by the *Khatmiya* sect. In November 1988 (while participating in a government of national unity led by the →*Umma* Party) the DUP played a leading role in opening peace talks with the rebel →Sudan People's Liberation Movement. After the 1989 military coup the DUP leader, Osman al-Mirghani, went into exile and aligned the party with the →National Democratic Alliance (NDA), of which he became chairman in 1995. It was in his capacity as NDA chairman that Mirghani held talks with President Bashir in Eritrea in September 2000 (this being their first meeting since the 1989 coup). A statement issued after the meeting recorded the two sides' "determination to bring about a quick end" to Sudan's civil war and to strive to create "suitable conditions for voluntary unity between the north and the south". However, Mirghani did not announce any plans to return to Sudan or to end the DUP's participation in the NDA (whereas the *Umma* Party leader, who had broken with the NDA in March 2000, was about to return to Sudan). Mirghani advised his followers to boycott the presidential and legislative elections held in December 2000, and in February 2001 a DUP spokesman praised the *Umma* Party for refusing an offer to participate in the Bashir Cabinet. Not all DUP members supported Mirghani's insistence that the DUP should maintain its stance as a party in exile. Siddiq al-Hindi, a former deputy prime minister of Sudan, returned to the country in 1997 to establish an internal faction of the DUP (sometimes known as the "DUP General Secretariat") with himself as chairman. In February 2001 Hindi and two other members of his internal DUP faction accepted ministerial portfolios in the Bashir Cabinet.

Muslim Brotherhood

Leadership. Habir Nur al-Din

The Muslim Brotherhood was a main focus of Islamic fundamentalism in Sudan until the mid-1980s, when its dominant faction leader, Hassan al-Turabi, set up a separate National Islamic Front which later evolved into the →National Congress (NC). After Turabi's departure the Brotherhood took little active part in Sudanese politics. In February 2001 a member of the Brotherhood, Isam Ahmed al-Bashir (described as a moderate Muslim scholar and staunch advocate of national reconciliation), joined the government as minister for religious guidance and endowments.

National Congress (NC)

Address. c/o National Assembly, Omdurman

Leadership. Lt.-Gen. Omar Hassan Ahmad al-Bashir (president); Ibrahim Ahmed Omar (secretary-general)

The NC was founded in 1999, having evolved out of the National Islamic Front (NIF), an Islamic fundamentalist party established in the mid-1980s which had become a de facto government party under the Bashir regime. The secretary-general of the NIF, Hassan al-Turabi, became the first secretary-general of the NC but was suspended from that office in May 2000 (together with the other members of the party's national secretariat and its regional leaders) after he had called on party members to ignore Lt.-Gen. Bashir's announcement of a meeting to launch his presidential re-election campaign. Turabi subsequently left the NC to found the →Popular National Congress, which participated in an opposition boycott of the presidential and legislative elections held in December 2000. In these elections President Bashir was re-elected with 86.5% of the vote, while the NC won 355 of the 360 seats in the National Assembly (112 of them unopposed).

National Democratic Alliance (NDA)

Leadership. Mohammed Osman al-Mirghani (chairman); Joseph Okelo (secretary-general)

The NDA was formed after the 1989 military coup as an umbrella organization linking a disparate group of opponents of the Bashir regime, including Sudan's two main centrist parties, the →Democratic Unionist Party (DUP) and the →*Umma* Party (UP); several smaller parties with more radical ideologies (including the Sudan Communist Party and the Arab Ba'ath Party); trade union organizations (whose activities were included in the post-coup ban on political activities); and political representatives of various armed rebel groups operating in southern Sudan (including the →Sudan People's Liberation Movement/Army). From 1995 the NDA was chaired by Osman al-Mirghani, the exiled leader of the DUP. Mubarak al-Mahdi, a senior member of the UP (and cousin of its leader), was suspended as secretary-general of the NDA in November 1999 after the UP leader met President Bashir without first consulting other NDA members. Mubarak al-Mahdi resigned as NDA secretary-general in March 2000 when the UP suspended its contacts with the NDA's external leadership, and in April 2000 he was one of the first group of UP leaders to return to Khartoum. At an "exploratory" meeting with President Bashir in Eritrea in September 2000, Mirghani spoke on behalf of all the current members of the NDA, including rebel military forces (who were represented by a field commander). In December 2000 the authorities in Khartoum arrested the NDA's current secretary-general, Joseph Okelo, and six other members of the NDA's Khartoum secretariat on charges including espionage and plotting armed opposition to the government. A US diplomat who had held a meeting with the NDA officials was expelled from Sudan.

Popular National Congress (PNC)

Leadership. Hassan Abdallah al-Turabi

The National Islamic Front, formed by Hassan al-Turabi (a leading Islamic theoretician and former member of the →Muslim Brotherhood) to contest the April 1986 general election, was reconstituted in 1999 as the →National Congress (NC) under the leadership of President Bashir, setting the scene for a power struggle which culminated in Turabi's departure from the NC in June 2000 to set up the PNC. The new party was formally registered in September 2000 but boycotted the December 2000 elections, in which the NC was the only party to win seats in the National Assembly, while President Bashir was re-elected to office by a massive margin. In February 2001 the PNC signed a "memorandum of understanding" with the →Sudan People's Liberation Movement (SPLM), reportedly calling for "an escalation of popular and peaceful resistance against the government". According to the authorities, the PNC had claimed that it had a "sacred duty to overthrow the government", and its contacts with the SPLM (whose military wing had been engaged in armed rebellion in southern Sudan since 1983) represented a conspiracy to overthrow the government. Turabi and three other PNC officials were detained on conspiracy charges on Feb. 21, 2001. A PNC spokesman said in April 2001 that the party had no intention of rescinding its accord with the SPLM. President Bashir was quoted as saying in May 2001 that the government would "never allow" Turabi to return to politics.

Sudan People's Liberation Movement/Army (SPLM/A)
Leadership. Col. John Garang (chairman and commander-in-chief); James Wani Igga (secretary-general)
The SPLM is the political wing of the Sudan People's Liberation Army (SPLA, formed in 1983), the principal armed rebel force in southern Sudan. The SPLM/A was one of the founder members of the →National Democratic Alliance (NDA) set up after the military coup of 1989 to provide a joint forum for a wide range of opponents of the Bashir regime (including mainstream political parties). The broad political objective of the SPLM/A has been represented as a form of self-determination for the south within the framework of a secular Sudanese state, and its leaders have denied accusations that it has a "hidden agenda" involving the secession of the south to form a separate state. After the December 2000 elections there was an intensification of national and international efforts to negotiate a peaceful solution to the conflict in Sudan. In addition to maintaining close links with its partners in the NDA, the SPLM concluded a controversial accord with the →Popular National Congress in February 2001, while in May 2001 Col. Garang held talks with the leader of the →*Umma* Party (which had withdrawn from the NDA in March 2000), who urged him to declare a ceasefire to prepare the way for talks between the Government and all the opposition groups in Sudan.

Umma Party (UP)
Leadership. Sadiq al-Mahdi (leader); Omar Nur al-Dayem (secretary-general)

The UP is a largely secularist Islamic centre party, supported primarily by the Ansar sect. Led by Sadiq al-Madhi (Prime Minister of Sudan in 1966–67 and 1986–89), the UP operated from exile in Eritrea in the latter part of the 1990s, allying itself with other exiled political organizations (and with armed opponents of the Bashir regime) through its membership of the →National Democratic Alliance (NDA). In late November 1999 Mahdi held talks with President Bashir in Djibouti, resulting in the signature of a declaration (envisaging the holding of a referendum on key issues within four years) which was rejected by other NDA members. The UP suspended contacts with the NDA's external leadership in March 2000, whereupon the Bashir government released the UP's Khartoum premises (confiscated in 1989) in preparation for the return to Sudan of 30 leading UP officials in the following month. Sadiq al-Mahdi himself returned to Khartoum in November 2000. The UP did not contest the December 2000 elections (joining an opposition boycott to protest at the holding of elections while a state of emergency remained in force), nor did it accept an offer of ministerial representation in the Cabinet appointed in February 2001. However, Mahdi did play an active role in the first half of 2001 in the search for a peaceful solution to the conflict in Sudan, travelling abroad to attend meetings organized by various mediators between rival Sudanese factions.

United Democratic Salvation Front (UDSF)
Leadership. Maj.-Gen. Elijah Hon Top (chairman)
The UDSF was registered in January 1999 to represent various former southern Sudanese rebel factions which had concluded a peace agreement with the Government in 1997 (and had participated in government since 1998).

Other Parties

Alliance of the People's Working Forces, formed as a platform for a future presidential election bid by Jaafar al-Nemery (president of Sudan from 1969 to 1985) on his return from exile in May 1999 after being granted an amnesty by the Bashir Government. When the presidential election took place in December 2000, Nemery received only 9.6% of the vote, compared with 86.5% for the incumbent, President Bashir. (The remaining 3.9% of the vote went to three previously unknown independent candidates.)
Leadership. Jaafar al-Nemery

Arab Ba'ath Party, one of the constituent parties of the →National Democratic Alliance.

Sudan Communist Party (SCP), one of the constituent parties of the →National Democratic Alliance.

Suriname

Capital: Paramaribo   **Population**: 430,000 (2000E)

Formerly Dutch Guiana, the Republic of Suriname achieved complete independence from the Netherlands in 1975. In 1980 the constitution was suspended and the legislature dissolved following the overthrow of the elected government and the formation of a military junta, the National Military Council (NMR). Behind a democratic façade real power remained with Lt-Col Désiré "Desi" Bouterse, commander-in-chief of the army until his resignation in 1992.

Under a new constitution approved in a national referendum in 1987, ultimate authority rests with a 51-member National Assembly, elected for a five-year term, while executive authority rests with the President (elected by the National Assembly) as head of state, head of government, head of the armed forces, chair of the Council of State and of the Security Council which, in the event of "war, state of siege or exceptional circumstances to be determined by law", assumes all government functions. The President is assisted by a

Vice-President, who is also elected by the National Assembly, and a Cabinet appointed by the President and responsible to the Assembly. Constitutional amendments, unanimously approved by the National Assembly in 1992, restricted the role of the army to national defence and combating "organized subversion". Serving members of the armed forces were restricted from holding representative political office but not denied personal involvement in political activity.

Former President Ronald Venetiaan's opposition four-party coalition, the New Front for Democracy (NF), won elections to the National Assembly held in May 2000, taking 32 of the 51 seats. The NF easily defeated its closest rival, the Millennium Combination, an alliance of the National Democratic Party (NDP), led by Bouterse, and two smaller parties, which took 10 seats. The Democratic National Platform 2000 (DNP 2000), headed by outgoing President Jules Wijdenbosch, came third, suffering a resounding defeat in taking only 3 seats. President Wijdenbosch had called the general election a year earlier to quell street demonstrations demanding his resignation after the economy collapsed and a series of resignations from his Cabinet had left him with a minority in the National Assembly.

In August 2000, Ronald Venetiaan was sworn in as the new President of the country, after being elected by a two-thirds majority of National Assembly members.

Democratic Alternative
Democratisch Alternatief

Address. c/o National Assembly, Paramaribo
This offshoot of the →Democratic Alternative '91 contested the May 2000 general election as a member of the →Millennium Combination coalition.

Democratic Alternative '91
Democratisch Alternatief '91 (DA '91)

Address. c/o National Assembly, Paramaribo
Email. info@da91.sr
Website. www.da91.sr
Leadership. Winston Jessurun (president)
Formed in 1991 as an anti-military, centre-left grouping of parties, DA '91 has campaigned for the constitutional exclusion of the military from involvement in the political process. The party contested the May 2000 general election, gaining over 6% of the vote and two seats in the legislature.

Democratic National Platform 2000
Democratisch Nationaal Platform 2000 (DNP 2000)

Following calls for his resignation after the virtual collapse of the economy, President Jules Wijdenbosch called an early general election in May 2000 and formed the DNP 2000 to contest the poll. Wijdenbosch had hitherto been a member of the →National Democratic Party. The DNP 2000 performed poorly in the elections, winning only 10% of the vote and three seats in the legislature. Wijdenbosch was subsequently replaced as President by Ronald Venetiaan, leader of the →New Front for Democracy coalition.

Millennium Combination
Millennium Combinatie (MC)

The MC was created to contest the May 2000 general election. Dominated by the →National Democratic Party of former military strongman Désiré Bouterse, the MC also includes the →Democratic Alternative and the →Party of Unity and Harmony. In the May election the MC won only 10 seats, being easily defeated by the →New Front for Democracy alliance.

National Democratic Party
Nationale Democratische Partij (NDP)

Address. c/o National Assembly, Paramaribo
Telephone. (+597) 499–183
Fax. (+597) 432–174
Email. ndp@cq-link.sr
Website. www.cq-link.sr/ndp
Leadership. Lt.-Col. Désiré Bouterse (leader)
Founded in 1987, the NDP is a right-wing party, which is backed by the Suriname military. The NDP was formed by *Standvaste*, the 25 February Movement, under Lt.-Col. Désiré Bouterse, and has played a major role in the country's political life, vying for power with the multi-ethnic, centre-left →New Front for Democracy (NF). Prior

to the May 2000 general election the NDP aligned itself with two smaller parties to form the →Millennium Combination but this took only 10 seats in the election.

New Front for Democracy
Nieuwe Front voor Democratie (NF)

Address. c/o National Assembly, Paramaribo
Leadership. Ronald Venetiaan (leader)
Founded in 1987 as a coalition of Indian, Javanese and mixed-race ethnic groups, the NF alliance won a decisive victory in the May 2000 general election. The NF leader, Ronald Venetiaan, was elected as President shortly thereafter. The four components of the NF are Venetiaan's →National Party of Suriname (NPS), the →Progressive Reform Party (VHP), the →*Pertjajah Luhur* (PL) and the →Suriname Labour Party (SPA).

The NF had its origins in the Front for Democracy and Development (*Front voor Demokratie en Onnvikkeling*, FDO) led by former President Henck Arron (toppled by the Bouterse-led army in 1980). In November 1987 the FDO won the election with an overwhelming 85% of the vote. Following the December 1990 military coup, dissident groups, critical of the NF's failure to curb military influence, left in March 1991 to form the →Democratic Alternative 1991 (DA' 91). The NF had its ranks swelled by the →Suriname Labour Party (SLA), who joined shortly before the May 1991 general election which it convincingly won, taking 30 seats and over 54% of the vote. The NF won 24 out of the 51 National Assembly seats in the 1996 general election It subsequently disintegrated, to the benefit of the →National Democratic Party, but managed to put a halt to divisive infighting ahead of the 2000 elections.

National Party of Suriname
Nationale Partij Suriname (NPS)

Address. Wanicastraat 77, Paramaribo
Telephone. (+597) 477–302
Fax. (+597) 475–796
Email. nps@sr.net
Website. www.nps.sr
Leadership. Ronald Venetiaan (leader)
Founded in 1946, the Creole-based NPS is a mainstay of the ruling coalition, the →New Front for Democracy (NF). Led by Ronald Venetiaan, the party won 14 of the 32 seats taken by the NF in the May 2000 general election, thereby becoming the largest single party in the National Assembly and Venetiian subsequently becoming President.

Party of Unity and Harmony
Kerukanan Tulodo Pranatan Ingil (KTPI)

Address. Weidestraat, Paramaribo
Founded in 1947, the party has been the traditional protector and promoter of the interests of the ethnic Indonesian community and has switched its political allegiances to further this end. The party was a founder member of the →New

Front for Democracy (NF) in the late 1980s, but, prior to the May 2000 general election it joined forces with former military leader Désiré Bouterse in his →Millennium Combination. The coalition performed poorly, winning only 10 seats in the legislature.

Pertjajah Luhur (PL)
Address. c/o National Assembly, Paramaribo
The PL is the Javan-based member of the ruling coalition, the →New Front for Democracy (NF). The party won seven National Assembly seats in elections held in May 2000.

Political Wing of the FAL
Politieke Vlevgel Van de FAL (PVF)
Address. c/o National Assembly, Paramaribo
The PVF won 4.1 % of the vote and two legislative seats in the May 2000 general election.

Progressive Reform Party
Vooruuitstrevende Hervormings Partij (VHP)
Address. c/o National Assembly, Paramaribo
Website. www.parbo.com/vhp
Leadership. Jagernath Lachmon (chairman)
Founded in 1949 (with several changes of name thereafter and also styled the *Verenigde Hervormings Partij*), the VHP is the leading left-wing party, a Hindustani-based grouping that stresses Suriname's cultural diversity and need for co-existence. It has alternated in opposition and as part of governing coalitions. In the 1996 elections it won nine seats but subsequently suffered five defections and joined the opposition. A founder member of the →New Front for Democracy (NF), the party won nine National Assembly seats in elections held in May 2000 that resulted in victory for the NF coalition.

Progressive Workers' and Farm Labourers' Union
Progressieve Arbeiders en Landbouwers Unie (PALU)
Address. c/o National Assembly, Paramaribo
Founded in the late 1970s, the PALO is a nominal socialist party that supported the Bouterse regime (1980–87) and in the May 2000 general election won only one seat.

Suriname Labour Party
Suriname Partij voor Arbeid (SPA)
Address. c/o National Assembly, Paramaribo
The SPA, whose membership is predominantly Creole, is a member of the ruling coalition, the →New Front for Democracy (NF). The party won two National Assembly seats in elections held in May 2000. The party has links with the C-47 trade union.

Other Parties

Basic Party for Renewal and Democracy (*Basispartij voor Vernieuwing en Democratie, BVD*), predominantly Hindustani-based membership; gained 3.2% of the vote in the May 2000 general election, but no seats.

Democrats of the 21st Century (*Democraten van de 21ste Eeue, D21*), gained 1.3% of the vote but no seats in the May 2000 general election.

General Liberation and Development Party (*Algemene Bevrijdings – en Ontwikkelingsparkj, ABOP*), gained 1.7% of the vote but no seats in the May 2000 general election.

National Party for Leadership and Development (*Nationale Partij voor Leiderschap en Ontwikkeling, NPLO*), gained 1% of the vote but no seats in the May 2000 general election.

Naya Kadan, took 2.4% of the vote in the May 2000 general election, but failed to win a seat.

Party for Democracy and Development Through Unity (*Partij voor Democratie en Ontwikkeling door Eenheid, DOE*), won 2.5% of the vote, but no seats, in the May 2000 general election.

Pendawa Lima, Javanese-based party which won 1% of the vote but no seats in the May 2000 general election.

Progressive People's Party of Suriname (*Progressieve Surinaamse Volkspartij, PSV*), a member of the Christian Democrat International and of the Christian Democrat Organization of America.
Address. Keizerstraat 122, PO Box 195, Paramaribo
Telephone. (+597) 472–979
Fax. (+597) 410–555
Leadership. Eugene Wong Loi Sing (president); S. E. Van Dal (secretary general)

Renewed Progressive Party (*Hernieuwde Progressieve Partij, HPP*), founded in the 1970s and social democratic in orientation, the HPP won 2.5% of the vote in the May 2000 general election, but failed to win representation in the legislature.
Email. hpp@cq-link.sr
Website. www.cq-link.sr/hpp
Leadership. Harry Kisoensingh (persident)

Swaziland

Capital: Mbabane (administrative); Lobamba (legislative)   **Population**: 1,083,300 (2000E)

The Kingdom of Swaziland achieved full independence from the United Kingdom in 1968. The country is ruled by a King (*Ngwenyama* or Paramount Chief) whose succession is governed by Swazi law and custom. The present King, Mswati III, acceded to the throne in 1986. Under the 1978 constitution considerable executive power is vested in the King and is exercised by a Cabinet appointed by him. The bicameral Parliament consists of a Senate and a House of Assembly, with limited powers. The House of Assembly has 65 members, 55 of whom were directly elected for the first time in September–October 1993 (on a non-party basis), with voters electing one representative from each of the *Tinkhundla* (tribal assemblies). A further 10 members are appointed by the King. There are 30 members of the Senate, 20 of whom are nominated by the King and 10 elected by the House of Assembly. Party political activity, banned in 1973, was formally prohibited under the 1978 constitution. However, following indications that the constitution might be revised, a number of political associations re-emerged during the 1990s. The Swaziland Federation of Trade Unions called a two-day general strike in November 2000 in support of a petition (backed by several political pressure groups) calling for revocation of restrictive labour laws and for the lifting of the ban on party politics. A constitutional review commission appointed in 1996 had presented its report to the King in October 2000. Non-party National Assembly elections were held in October 1998.

Confederation for Full Democracy in Swaziland, formed in 1992 as an alliance of organizations advocating democratic reform, including the →People's United Democratic Movement and the →Swaziland Youth Congress.

Imbokodvo National Movement (INM), founded in 1964, a traditionalist and royalist organization, but also advocates policies of development and the elimination of illiteracy.

Ngwane National Liberatory Congress (NNLC), founded in 1962 as a result of a split in the →Swaziland Progressive Party; seeks an extension of democratic freedoms and universal suffrage.
Leadership. Obed Dlamini (president)

People's United Democratic Movement (PUDEMO), emerged in the 1980s, circulating pamphlets critical of the King, thus attracting official hostility and suppression; campaigns for electoral reform, multi-party democracy and limits on the power of the monarchy.
Leadership. Mario Masuku (president)

Swaziland National Front (SWANAFRO)
Leadership. Elmond Shongwe (president)

Swaziland Progressive Party (SPP), founded in 1929 as the Swazi Progressive Association, adopted present title in 1960, after which it suffered from factional divisions and defections.
Leadership. J.J. Nquku (president)

Swaziland United Front (SUF), founded in 1962 following a split within the →Swaziland Progressive Party.
Leadership. Matsapa Shongwe

Swaziland Youth Congress (SWAYOCO), a constituent of the →Confederation for Full Democracy in Swaziland.
Leadership. Bongani Masuku (president)

Sweden

Capital: Stockholm

Population: 8,900,000 (2000E)

The Kingdom of Sweden is a parliamentary democracy in which the monarch has purely ceremonial functions as head of state. There is a Cabinet headed by a Prime Minister and responsible to a unicameral Parliament (*Riksdag*) of 349 members elected for a four-year term by universal adult suffrage of citizens above the age of 18 years under a system of proportional representation, with 310 seats being filled in 28 multi-member constituencies and the remaining 39 allocated to parties according to a complex formula. A party must obtain 4% of the national vote to qualify for a seat. Sweden joined what became the European Union on Jan. 1, 1995, and elects 22 members of the European Parliament.

Since 1966 state subsidies have been paid to political parties which have at least one representative in the *Riksdag* or have obtained at least 2.5% of the national vote in either of the two most recent elections, with an additional "secretariat subsidy" being available for parties achieving 4% or more of the vote. The amount of the subsidies is related to party representation or voting strength, but "secretariat subsidies" are higher for opposition parties than for those in the government. Similar arrangements apply at the level of regional and local government. In 1999 the total amount allocated for party subsidies in the state budget was Skr221.2 million (about US$26 million), of which the Social Democratic Labour Party, for example, was eligible for Skr74 million (about $8.7 million).

Parliamentary elections on Sept. 22, 1998, resulted as follows: Swedish Social Democratic Labour Party 131 seats (with 36.4% of the vote), Moderate Party 82 (22.9%), Left Party 43 (11.9%), Christian Democratic Community Party 42 (11.8%), Centre Party 18 (5.1%), Liberal People's Party 17 (4.7%), Green Ecology Party 16 (4.5%).

Centre Party
Centerpartiet (CP)
Address. Bergsgatan 7B, PO Box 22107, 104 22 Stockholm
Telephone. (+46–8) 617–3800
Fax. (+46–8) 652–6440
Email. centerpartiet@centerpartiet.se
Website. www.centerpartiet.se
Leadership. Lennart Daléus (chairman); Agne Hansson (parliamentary group leader); Ola Alterå (secretary-general)
The Centre Party works for a decentralized society with a social market economy, with all parts of the country having an equal chance to develop; for the protection of the environment; and for the use of technology not only for man's material welfare but also for his mental well-being. The party is strongly opposed to the development of nuclear energy.

The party was founded in 1910 as the Farmers' Union Party to represent the population in rural areas but now has both rural and urban support. It first gained parliamentary representation in 1917 and formed its first government in

June 1936. From October 1936 it co-operated in government with the →Swedish Social Democratic Labour Party (SAP), and in 1939–45 in a national coalition government. In 1951–57 the party was again a partner with the SAP in a coalition government, at the end of which it changed its name to Centre Party–Farmers' Union Party (1957), shortening this to Centre Party a year later.

In 1976–78 the CP headed a three-party non-socialist government including also the →Liberal People's (FP) and →Moderate (MSP) parties, this coalition, led by Thorbjörn Fälldin, being re-established after the September 1979 elections. In elections to the *Riksdag* in September 1982 the CP obtained 15.5% of the valid votes and 56 (out of 349) seats and went into opposition. In the September 1985 elections, which it contested jointly with the →Christian Democratic Community Party (KdS), the CP slipped to 12.4% and 44 seats (including one Christian Democrat) and continued in opposition. In view of this setback Fälldin resigned the party leadership in December 1985, having come under sharp criticism for his opposition to a rapprochement with the SAP, the party's traditional allies. He was replaced by Karin Söder (who became Sweden's first female party leader), but she resigned in January 1987 for health reasons and was succeeded by Olof Johansson.

The CP's decline continued in the 1988 and 1991 elections, to 42 and 31 seats respectively, but after the latter contest the party entered a centre-right coalition headed by the MSP. In June 1994 its participation was shaken by the resignation of party chairman Johansson as Environment Minister, in opposition to the controversial Öresund Sound bridge project. In the September 1994 parliamentary elections the CP was further reduced to 27 seats (on a vote share of 7.7%) and again went into opposition. The CP supported Swedish accession to the European Union (EU), while advocating non-participation in a single European currency or in any EU defence co-operation. In Sweden's first direct elections to the European Parliament in September 1995, the CP won two of the 22 seats on a 7.2% vote share.

In April 1998 Olof Johansson was succeeded as CP leader by Lennart Daléus, who led the party to a further defeat in the September 1998 general elections, when its vote fell to 5.1% and its representation to only 18 seats. In the June 1999 European elections the CP vote slipped to 6.0%, giving the party only one seat.

The CP's representative in the European Parliament sits in the European Liberal, Democratic and Reformist group.

Christian Democratic Community Party
Kristdemokratiska Samhällspartiet (KdS)
Address. Malargatan 7, PO Box 451, 101 26 Stockholm
Telephone. (+46–8) 723–2550
Fax. (+46–8) 723–2510
Email. brev.till@kristdemokrat.se
Website. www.kristdemokrat.se
Leadership. Alf Svensson (chairman); Göran Hägglund (parliamentary group chairman); Sven Gunnar Persson (secretary-general)

The KdS has described itself as "the third alternative in Sweden, where all [other] parties are socialistic or non-socialistic". It propagates "a new way of life" and concentrates on social problems, calling for a review of the abortion law among other things. It also opposes the development of nuclear energy. The party was founded in 1964 and obtained some 78,000 votes in its first general election in 1964. By 1982 this total had increased to 103,820 (1.9%). Having thus failed to pass the 4% barrier to representation in the *Riksdag*, in September 1985 it entered into an electoral pact with the →Centre Party, winning some 2.6% of the vote in its own right and being allocated one of the Centre Party's 44 seats (Alf Svensson becoming the party's first representative in the *Riksdag*). Meanwhile, the party had established a significant local government presence, with almost 300 elected councillors by the mid-1980s.

Originally called the Christian Democratic Assembly (*Kristen Demokratisk Samling*), the party assumed its present name in 1987, when it also adopted a new programme. The KdS failed to secure representation in the 1988 parliamentary elections, but again came back strongly three years later, winning 26 *Riksdag* seats in 1991 (with 7.1% of the vote) and becoming a member of a centre-right coalition government. It slipped back in the 1994 contest, only just clearing the 4% barrier and winning 15 seats. It thereupon went into opposition to a minority government of the →Swedish Social Democratic Labour Party. The KdS was strongly in favour of Swedish accession to the EU in 1995.

Campaigning on a platform of family values and opposition to sleaze, the KdS registered a record advance in the September 1998 general elections, winning 42 seats on a vote share of 11.8%. It remained in opposition and lost impetus by the time of the June 1999 European elections, in which it won two seats and 7.6% of the vote.

The KdS is affiliated to the Christian Democrat International. Its representatives in the European Parliament sit in the European People's Party/European Democrats group.

Green Ecology Party
Miljöpartiet de Gröna
Address. PO Box 12660, 112 93, Stockholm
Telephone. (+46–8) 208–050
Fax. (+46–8) 201–577
Email. ursula@mp.se
Website. www.mp.se
Leadership. Lotta Nilsson Hedström & Birger Schlaug (spokespersons); Gunnar Goude & Marianne Samuelsson (parliamentary group leaders); Håkan Wåhlstedt (secretary)

Founded in September 1981, the party has developed a mainstream environmentalist programme based on "fourfold solidarity" with (i) animals, nature and the eco-system, (ii) future generations, (iii) the people of the world and (iv) the people of Sweden. It advocates enhanced international co-operation on environmental issues, human rights, cultural development, disarmament and peace, and favours the establishment of an international court on environmental matters. It also demands a halt to all exports of weapons from Sweden and the subordination of free trade to environmental requirements and labour conditions, "so that the environment, poor people and individuals are not exploited by the wealthy". Unlike most other EU Green parties, it is opposed to EU membership on the grounds that it is damaging for Sweden, and has called for a referendum to be held on withdrawal.

In the 1982 and 1985 general elections the party fell well short of the 4% vote minimum required for representation in the *Riksdag*, not least because the major parties, particularly the →Swedish Social Democratic Labour Party (SAP) and the →Centre Party, have incorporated a strong environmentalist strand in their platforms. On the other hand, it succeeded in obtaining representation in over 30% of local councils by 1988, in which year it became the first new party to enter the *Riksdag* for 70 years, winning 20 seats on a 5.5% vote share. It slumped to 3.4% in 1991 and so failed to gain representation; but in 1994 it recovered strongly to 5.0% and 18 *Riksdag* seats, thereafter giving qualified external support to the minority government of the SAP.

Opposed to Sweden's accession to the EU, the Greens were prominent in the "no" campaign for the November 1994 referendum on EU membership, finishing on the losing side. The party nevertheless polled strongly in Sweden's first direct elections to the European Parliament in September 1995 winning four seats on a vote share of 17.2%. In the September 1998 general elections, however, the party slipped to 4.5% and 16 seats, thereafter giving external support to a further minority SAP government. In the June 1999 European elections the Greens were reduced to two seats, with a 9.5% vote share.

The Greens are affiliated to the European Federation of Green Parties. The party's representatives in the European Parliament are members of the Greens/European Free Alliance group.

Left Party
Vänsterpartiet (VP)
Address. Kungsgatan 84, PO Box 12660, 112 93 Stockholm
Telephone. (+46–8) 654–0820
Fax. (+46–8) 653–2385
Email. orjan.svedberg@vansterpartiet.se
Website. www.vansterpartiet.se
Leadership. Gudrun Schyman (chairman); Lars Bäckström (parliamentary group leader); Pernilla Zethraeus (secretary-general)

The VP is the latter-day successor to the historic Swedish Communist Party, which was founded as early as May 1917 under the name Left Social Democratic Party by the revolutionary wing of the →Swedish Social Democratic Labour Party (SAP). It changed its name to Communist Party in 1921, having joined the Communist International (Comintern), to which it belonged until that organization's dissolution in 1943. In the post-1945 era, the party at first displayed pro-Soviet orthodoxy but in the 1960s embarked upon a revisionist course in line with "Euro-communist" prescriptions. To signify the party's aim of becoming "a forum for the whole socialist left", the new designation Left Party–Communists (*Vänsterpartiet–Kommunisterna*, VPK) was adopted in 1967. This decision, combined with attendant policy evolution, generated much dissension within the party prior to the withdrawal of an orthodox faction in early 1977 to form the Communist Workers' Party. The suffix "Communists" was dropped from the party's title by a congress decision of May 1990.

The party has been represented in the *Riksdag* since its foundation, and for long periods minority SAP governments have relied on its support. In both the 1979 and 1982 general elections what was then the VPK obtained 20 seats and 5.6% of the valid votes, while in September 1985 it slipped to 5.4% and 19 seats (out of 349); but a concurrent SAP decline meant that VPK voting strength became crucial to the SAP government's survival in the late 1980s. The renamed VP won 16 seats in the 1991 general elections (on a vote share of 4.5%), thereafter going into full opposition to a centre-right coalition government. In a general swing to the left in September 1994, the VP achieved the party's best result since 1948, winning 6.2% of the vote and 22 seats.

The VP campaigned vigorously against Sweden's accession to the European Union (the only parliamentary party to do so), but was on the losing side in the November 1994 referendum. In Sweden's first direct elections to the European Parliament in September 1995 the VP won three seats on a 12.9% vote share. In September 1997 party leader Gudrun Schyman announced that she was taking leave of absence for the latest round in her long public struggle against alcoholism. She returned to lead the party to a record result in the September 1998 general elections, in which the VP vote, boosted by disaffected SAP supporters, climbed to 11.9% and its representation to 43 seats. It thereafter gave external support to a further SAP minority government and maintained its forward impetus in the June 1999 European elections, in which it again won three seats with an increased vote share of 15.8%.

In September 2000 the VP warmly welcomed Denmark's referendum decision not to join the single European currency, contending that it strengthened the case for Sweden remaining a non-participant.

The party's representatives in the European Parliament sit in the European United Left/Nordic Green Left group.

Liberal People's Party
Folkpartiet Liberalerna (FPL)
Address. Drottninggatan 97/1tr, PO Box 6508, 113 83 Stockholm
Telephone. (+46–8) 5091–1600
Fax. (+46–8) 5091–1660
Email. info@liberal.se
Website. www.folkpartiet.se
Leadership. Lars Leijonborg (chairman); Bo Könberg (parliamentary group leader); Johan Pehrson (secretary-general)
Although the present party dates from 1934, organized liberalism began in Sweden at the end of the 19th century with the objectives of social justice, universal suffrage and equality. After World War I a coalition government with the →Swedish Social Democratic Labour Party (SAP), led by a Liberal Prime Minister, completed the process of democratization. At the same time, the introduction of universal suffrage reduced the party's influence, while between 1923 and 1934 the party was split over the issue of alcohol prohibition. Nevertheless, it formed governments in 1926–28 and 1930–32 and it took part in the national government during World War II.

In 1948 the party became the second strongest in the then lower chamber of the *Riksdag*, with 57 seats, but by 1968 its representation had declined to 34. In the unicameral *Riksdag* established in January 1971 the party won 58 seats in 1970, but only 34 in 1973 and 39 in 1976. It then took part in the first non-socialist government to be formed in Sweden for 44 years in coalition with the →Centre and →Moderate

(Conservative) parties. The collapse of this coalition in October 1978 over the nuclear issue was followed by a year of minority Liberal rule under Ola Ullsten; but as a result of the September 1979 elections the three-party non-socialist coalition was re-established. However, the Conservatives left this government in 1981 after disagreements on taxation, and the Liberal and Centre parties formed a minority government until the September 1982 elections brought the Social Democrats back to power. In those elections the Liberal vote dropped to 5.9% and its representation to 21 seats.

The FPL staged a significant recovery in the September 1985 elections, winning 14.2% of the vote and 51 seats, but remaining in opposition. It fell back to 44 seats to 1988 (12.2%) and to 33 in 1991 (9.1%), when it joined a four-party centre-right coalition. Another setback followed in the September 1994 elections, which yielded only 7.2% and 26 seats, after which the party reverted to opposition status and party leader Bengt Westerberg gave way to Maria Leissner. The FPL was strongly in favour of Swedish accession to the EU in January 1995, but in Sweden's first direct elections to the European Parliament in September 1995 it managed only 4.8% of the vote and one seat.

Elected party leader in March 1997, Lars Leijonborg led the FPL to a further defeat in the September 1998 general elections, in which the party fell back to 4.7% of the vote and 17 seats. In the June 1999 European elections, however, the FPL recovered strongly to 13.9% of the vote, which gave it three seats.

With an official membership of 19,600, the FPL is a member of the Liberal International. Its representatives in the European Parliament sit in the European Liberal, Democratic and Reformist group.

Moderate Party
Moderata Samlingspartiet (MSP)
Address. PO Box 1243, SE–111 82 Stockholm
Telephone. (+46–8) 676–8000
Fax. (+46–8) 216–123
Email. info@moderat.se
Website. www.moderat.se
Leadership. Bo Lundgren (chairman); Chris Heister (first vice-chairman); Gunilla Carlsson (second vice-chairperson); Per Unckel (parliamentary group leader); Johnny Magnusson (secretary-general)
The MSP combines a conservative heritage with liberal ideas to advocate a moderate, anti-socialist policy in favour of a free-market economy and individual freedom of choice. The party was originally founded in 1904 as the political expression of better-off peasants and the emerging industrial bourgeoisie. It participated in coalitions or formed minority governments several times before 1932, after which the →Swedish Social Democratic Labour Party (SAP) was in almost uninterrupted power for 44 years (though during World War II all democratic parties took part in the government). The party increased its support during the 1950s, winning more than 20% of the vote in the 1958 general elections. It declined in subsequent contests, obtaining only 11.6% in the 1970 elections, prior to which it changed its name from Conservative to Moderate Party (its preferred English translation, although the Swedish means something like "Moderate Alliance Party").

Later the party advanced again, gaining 15.6% of the vote in the 1976 elections whereupon it entered the first non-socialist coalition for 40 years (with the →Centre and →Liberal parties). This was dissolved in October 1978 but re-established after the September 1979 elections, in which the party made a significant advance, to 20.3% and 73 seats. It withdrew from the coalition in May 1981 amid disagreements over fiscal policy, although it generally gave external support to the government thereafter. In the elections of September 1982 the party gained further support (23.6% of the vote and 86 seats) and thus became the dominant non-socialist party in Sweden, although the Social Democrats were returned to power as a minority government. In the September 1985 elections the MSP slipped to 21.3% and 76 seats (out of 349) and continued in opposition. In light of this setback, Ulf Adelsohn resigned as party chairman in June 1986 and was succeeded by Carl Bildt (son-in-law of Adelsohn's immediate predecessor, Gösta Bohman).

A further decline in 1988 (to 18.3% and 66 seats) was followed by recovery in 1991 to 21.9% and 80 seats, enabling Bildt to form a four-party centre-right coalition with the Centre, →Christian Democratic Community and Liberal People's parties. In the September 1994 elections the MSP again won 80 seats (and a slightly higher 22.4% vote share), but a general swing to the left resulted in a minority SAP government. Two months later the MSP warmly welcomed the referendum decision in favour of EU membership. Released of the burdens of government, Bildt accepted appointment as the EU's chief mediator in former Yugoslavia, while retaining the less taxing post of MSP chairman. In Sweden's first direct elections to the European Parliament in September 1995 the MSP took five of the 22 seats with a vote share of 23.2%.

Despite the unpopularity of the SAP government, the MSP failed to make major inroads in the September 1998 general elections, winning 82 seats on a slightly higher vote of 22.9%. Remaining in opposition, the party also registered a lacklustre performance in the June 1999 European elections, retaining five seats but on a reduced vote share of 20.7%. In August 1999 Bildt was succeeded as party leader by Bo Lundgren, a former MSP Finance Minister.

With an official membership of 77,000, the MSP is affiliated to the Christian Democrat International, the International Democrat Union and the European Democrat Union. Its members of the European Parliament sit in the European People's Party/European Democrats group.

Swedish Social Democratic Labour Party
Sveriges Socialdemokratiska Arbetareparti (SAP)

Address. Socialdemokraterna, Sveavägen 68, 105 60 Stockholm
Telephone. (+46–8) 700–2600
Fax. (+46–8) 219–331
Email. sap.international@sap.se
Website. www.sap.se
Leadership. Göran Persson (chairman); Sven Hulterström (parliamentary group leader); Lars Stjernkvist (general secretary)

The SAP seeks "to transform society in such a way that the right of decision over production and its distribution is placed in the hands of the entire nation"; to replace "a social order based on classes" by "a community of people in partnership on a basis of liberty and equality"; to maintain "Sweden's non-alignment and neutrality in war"; and to work for "world peace on the basis of self-determination for every nation, of social and economic justice, of détente and disarmament and of international co-operation". The party has shown majority support for Sweden's participation in the European Union (EU), though a significant SAP minority is opposed to further EU integration.

Founded in April 1889, the party sent its first member to the *Riksdag* in 1896, namely Hjalmar Branting, who, after serving as Minister of Finance in 1917–18, became Prime Minister in Sweden's first Social Democratic government in 1920; he was Prime Minister again in 1921–23 and in 1924–25. The share of national vote gained by the party in elections rose from 28.5% in 1911 to 53.8% in 1940, whereafter it declined to 46.7% in 1944 and remained more or less stable until 1968, when it rose to 50.1%. In the four succeeding elections the SAP share fell to 42.9% in 1976, rose slightly to 43.3% in 1979 and to 45.6% in 1982, but slipped to 45.1% in September 1985, when it won 159 seats in the *Riksdag* (out of 349).

Except for a short interval in 1936, the party was in office from 1932 to 1976, in coalition with the →Centre Party between 1936 and 1939 and between 1951 and 1957, in a four-party coalition during World War II, and at other times as a minority party requiring the support of one or more other parties on important issues. The party's 44 years of virtually uninterrupted power established the record for continuous governmental power by a social democratic party, and also resulted in Sweden becoming what was widely regarded as a model social democracy. In over 100 years of existence, the SAP has had only six leaders, namely Hjalmar Branting, Per-Albin Hansson, Tage Erlander, Olof Palme, Ingvar Carlsson and Göran Persson (since March 1996). Carlsson succeeded to the party leadership and premiership following the (still unexplained) assassination of Palme on a Stockholm street on Feb. 28, 1986.

Having formed a minority government since 1982, the SAP went into opposition after the September 1991 elections, when its share of the vote fell from 43.2% in 1988 to 37.6% and its representation from 156 seats to 138. It recovered in a general swing to the left in the September 1994 elections, bringing it 45.3% of the vote and 161 seats and enabling it to form another minority government under Carlsson. For the November 1994 referendum on EU membership, the official government and party line was to favour a "yes" vote but the extent of anti-EU opinion within SAP ranks compelled the leadership to allow the contrary case to be made within the party. In both the 1994 general elections and the September 1995 European Parliament polling anti-EU candidates were included on the SAP lists. The result on the latter occasion was that three of the seven Social Democrats elected (on a vote share of only 28%) were "Eurosceptic" to a greater or lesser extent.

Meanwhile, Carlsson had surprised the political world by announcing in August 1995 that he intended to stand down as party leader and Prime Minister the following March, marking the 10th anniversary of his elevation. The initial favourite to succeed him was Deputy Prime Minister Mona Sahlin but disclosures about irregularities in her financial affairs forced her not only to withdraw from the leadership race but also to resign from the government. Instead, the succession went to the Finance Minister, Göran Persson, who was elected SAP chairman unopposed at a special party congress on March 15, 1996, and appointed Prime Minister two days later.

The Persson government came under pressure in 1997–98 for sticking to unpopular economic retrenchment policies. In the September 1998 general elections the SAP recorded its worst result for 70 years, winning only 36.4% of the vote and 131 seats. It nevertheless continued as a minority government, with the external support of the →Left Party and the →Green Ecology Party. In the June 1999 European elections the SAP slipped to 26.0% of the vote, winning only six seats.

An SAP congress in March 2000 voted by 234 to 133 to make participation in the single European currency official party policy, coupled with a stipulation that approval in a referendum would be required before Sweden adopted the euro. However, although strongly supported by Persson, euro membership was opposed by several ministers and by a substantial section of the SAP rank-and-file. When Denmark voted against euro membership in September 2000, Persson contended that it had been "purely a Danish decision" but SAP opponents of the euro saw it as strengthening their case. Also in September 2000, the SAP government suffered some embarrassment when long-serving Justice Minister Laila Freivalds was forced to resign over disclosures that she had bought her council-owned apartment in central Stockholm in contravention of SAP policy in the capital (where the party was in opposition).

In November 2000 Persson opened another debate within the SAP by proposing that Sweden should abandon its 100-year-old policy of neutrality, arguing that the end of the Cold War had rendered it irrelevant. Although he said that Sweden should remain non-aligned and should not join NATO, his proposal sparked immediate contention within the party, which would be required to revise its commitment to neutrality before an SAP government could act on the proposal. As that debate continued, Persson disclosed in August 2001 that after the 2002 elections an SAP government would begin evaluating whether to recommend euro membership in a referendum. He expressed confidence that, provided the January 2002 change-over to the euro in other EU states went well, Sweden would approve participation and would join in 2005.

Having an official membership of 177,300, the SAP is a member party of the Socialist International. Its European Parliament representatives are members of the Party of European Socialists group.

Other Parties

Alliance Party (*Allianspartiet, AP*), centrist formation; won 175 votes in 1998 general election.
Address. Wemmenhögsgatan 23, 231 45 Trelleborg
Telephone/Fax. (+46–410) 40904
Email. jlm-trbg@algonet.se
Website. www.alli9anspartiet.se
Leadership. Jerry Larsson (chairman)

Centre Democrats (*Centrum-Demokraterna, CD*), right-wing party advocating traditional values; won 377 votes in 1998 general election.
Address. Mariceholmsvägen 10, 260 24 Röstånga
Telephone. (+46-435) 91054
Fax. (+46-435) 91092
Leadership. Harry Franzén (chairman)

Communist Party of Marxist–Leninists (Revolutionaries) (*Kommunistiska Partiet Marxist-Leninisterna (Revolutionärerna), KPML(r))*, founded in 1970 as a pro-Albanian party originally; has contested elections with minimal national support, although it elected about a dozen local councilllors in 1998.
Address. PO Box 31187, 400 32 Göteborg
Telephone. (+46–31) 122–631
Fax. (+46–31) 244–464
Email. kpmlr@proletaren.se
Website. www.proletaren.se/kpmlr
Leadership. Anders Carlsson (chairman)

Conservative Party (*Konservativa Partiet, KP*), standing for traditional Swedish family values, critical of the main →Moderate Party.
Address. PO Box 1700, 114 79 Stockholm
Telephone. (+46–8) 600–3345
Email. kp@altmedia.se
Website. www.flashback.net/~grinden

European Labour Party (*Europeiska Arbertarpartiet, EAP*), won 117 votes in 1998 general election.
Address. PO Box 11918, 161 11 Bromma
Leadership. Tore Fredin (chairman)

Freedom Front (*Frihetsfronten*), radical free market formation.
Address. PO Pox 620, 114 79 Stockholm
Telephone. (+46–8) 345–647
Fax. (+46–8) 328–664
Email. frihetsfronten@bahnhof.se
Website. www.frihetsfronten.pp.se
Leadership. Henrik Bejke

New Democracy (*NyDemokrati, NyD*), founded in February 1990 on a populist platform of massive tax cuts, abolition of the welfare state, stringent curbs on immigration, opposition to EU membership and cheaper alcohol. It caused a sensation in the 1991 general elections, winning 24 *Riksdag* seats with a vote share of 6.7%. For most of the subsequent parliamentary term it gave often vital external voting support to the centre-right minority government. In March 1994, however, the resignation of its controversial leader, Count Ian Wachmeister (sometimes labelled "the crazy count"), assisted a reorientation which resulted in the party joining the opposition. Having lost its early momentum, New Democracy fell well short of the 4% barrier to representation in the 1994 elections, taking only 1.2% of the vote; it failed again in 1998, winning only 8,297 votes.
Address. PO Box 1255, 111 82 Stockholm
Telephone/Fax. (+46–31) 262–543
Email. info@nydemokrati.org
Website. www.nydemokrati.org
Leadership. Ulf Eriksson (chairman)

New Progress (*Ny Framtid*), won 9,171 votes in 1998 general election.
Address. PO Box 84, 565 22 Mullsjö
Telephone. (+46–392) 31500
Fax. (+46–392) 12610
Email. feedback@nyframtid.com
Leadership. Sune Lyxell

Socialist Justice Party (*Rättvisepartiet Socialisterna, RS*), Trotskyist formation founded in 1997, claims to be biggest Trotskyist party in Scandinavia, affiliated to Committee for a Workers' International; won 3,044 votes in 1998 general election.
Website. www.socialisterna.org/rs

Socialist Party (*Socialistiska Partiet, SP*), a Trotskyist grouping founded in 1953 as the Communist Workers' League by dissidents of the main Communist Party (later the →Left Party); took its present name in 1982; has contested elections but with minimal support (winning only 1,466 votes in 1998).
Address. PO Box 6087, 102 32 Stockholm
Telephone. (+46–8) 310–850
Fax. (+46–8) 441–4576
Email. intis@internationalen.se
Website. www.internationalen.se/sp

Stockholm Party (*Stockholmspartiet*), aiming to promote the interests of Sweden's capital city.
Address. Kungsgatan 37/2tr, 111 56 Stockholm.
Telephone. (+46–8) 219–959
Fax. (+46–8) 219–279
Email. kontakt@stockholmspartiet.se
Website. www.stockholmspartiet.se

Swedish Communist Party (*Sveriges Kommunistiska Parti, SKP*), founded in 1977 as the Communist Workers' Party by a pro-Soviet faction of what later became the →Left Party, renamed in 1979; unrepresented nationally since 1979, it contested the 1998 elections as simply "Communists".
Address. PO Box 1566, 171 29 Solna
Telephone. (+46–8) 735–8640
Fax. (+46–8) 735–7902
Email. skp@skp.se
Website. www.skp.se
Leadership. Roland Pettersson (chairman); Jan-Olof Norell (secretary)

Swedish Democrats (*Sverigedemokraterna, SD*), radical right-wing formation opposed to immigration and multiculturalism; claiming 5,000 members, it received 19,624 votes in 1998 general election.
Address. PO Box 20085, 104 60 Stockholm
Telephone. (+46–8) 641–2011
Fax. (+46–8) 643–9260
Email. kansli@sverigedemokraterna.se
Website. www.sverigedemokraterna.se
Leadership. Mikael Jansson (chairman)

Swedish Pensioners' Interests Party (*Sveriges Pensionärers Intresseparti, SPI*), won 52,869 votes in 1998 general election.
Address. PO Box 5187, 200 72 Malmö
Leadership. Nils-Olof Persson (chairman)

Viking Party (*Vikingapartiet, VP*), advocating principles and policies drawn from a former age; won a total of 28 votes in 1998 general election.

Address. PO Box 4403, 203 15 Malmö
Telephone. (+46–40) 943–031
Email. m-2829@mailbox.swipnet.se
Leadership. Bosse Persson (chairman)

Switzerland

Capital: Bern

Population: 7,200,000 (2000E)

The Swiss Confederation, dating its independence from 1291, is a republic in which power is held by the electorate (consisting of all citizens above the age of 20 years). The latter not only elects members of the Federal Assembly (*Bundesversammlung* or *Assemblée Fédérale*) and of cantonal and local councils but also has powers to vote on constitutional amendments or on other matters. Constitutional amendments may be enacted as a result of an initiative supported by at least 100,000 voters and either containing a draft amendment or proposing the substance of an amendment and leaving the drafting to Parliament. A referendum may be held on a matter already approved by Parliament. Constitutional amendments and the most important international treaties are subject to approval by popular vote and by the cantons in a "compulsory referendum". A national "faciltative referendum" may be held on other matters of general validity (but not on the budget) already approved by Parliament if, within 90 days of parliamentary adoption, 50,000 voters or eight cantons request a vote on the specific act or decree.

The bicameral Federal Assembly comprises (i) a Council of States (*Standerat* or *Conseil des États*) consisting of two members for each of 20 cantons and one for each of six half-cantons, the electoral process being left to the decision of each of the cantons or half-cantons, and (ii) a 200-member National Council (*Nationalrat* or *Conseil National*) elected for a four-year term in proportion to the population of the cantons (each of the 20 cantons and six half-cantons being represented by at least one member). In all cantons and half-cantons the elections to the National Council are conducted under a list system with proportional representation, with voters being able to cast preferential votes; in all but one canton and one half-canton a simple majority system applies for elections to the Council of States. The President of the Confederation, who is also President of the *Bundesrat* or *Conseil Fédéral* (seven-member government), is elected, together with a Vice-President, for a one-year term by the two Houses of Parliament, which also elect the members of the government for a four-year term.

While there is no state financial support for party organizations, parliamentary groups receive a basic payment of SwF90,000 per annum plus SwF16,500 per member. Thus in 2001, for example, the Social Democratic Party of Switzerland group, numbering 58 in the two chambers, received SwF1,047,000 (about US$640,000).

Elections to the National Council on Oct. 24, 1999, resulted as follows: Social Democratic Party of Switzerland 51 seats (with 22.5% of the vote), Swiss People's Party 44 (22.5%), Radical Democratic Party of Switzerland 43 (19.9%), Christian Democratic People's Party of Switzerland 35 (15.8%), Green Party 9 (5.0%), Liberal Party of Switzerland 6 (2.2%), Evangelical People's Party 3 (1.8%), Swiss Party of Labour 2 (1.0%), Ticino League 2 (0.9%), Swiss Democrats 1 (1.8%), Federal Democratic Union 1 (1.2%), Independents' Alliance 1 (0.7%), Left Alliance 1 (0.5%), Christian Social Party 1 (0.4%). The outcome was a continuation of the existing government coalition of the four largest parties (first established in 1959).

Note. The non-English party titles given below begin with the one to which the party itself accords senior status, the official abbreviation of that version being used thereafter in entries. It will be noted that not all parties have a version of their title in all four official languages (German, French, Italian and Romansch).

Christian Democratic People's Party of Switzerland
Christlichdemokratische Volkspartei der Schweiz (CVP)
Parti Démocrate–Chrétien Suisse (PDC)
Partito Popolare Democratico Svizzero (PPD)
Partida Cristiandemocratica dalla Svizra (PCD)
Address. Klaraweg 6, Postfach 5835, 3001 Bern
Telephone. (+41–31) 352–2364
Fax. (+41–31) 352–2430
Email. info@cvp.ch
Website. www.cvp.ch

Leadership. Philipp Stähelin (chairman); Jean-Philippe Maître (parliamentary leader); Reto Nause (general secretary)

The CVP is a mainstream Christian democratic party, advocating the encouragement of family life, a social market economy, peace in independence and freedom (i.e. maintenance of the country's armed forces) and solidarity with the Third World poor. The party was founded in 1912 as the Swiss Conservative Party (*Parti Conservateur Suisse*), following the establishment of national (i.e. not cantonal) parties by the Social Democrats in 1882 and the Radicals in

1894 and a call for the creation of a Swiss Catholic party. By adopting the name Conservative Party, the founders emphasized the political rather than the denominational character of the new party, which was joined by representatives of Christian trade union groups in denominationally-mixed cantons. Having in 1957 become the *Parti Conservateur Chrétien–Social Suisse*, the party took its present name in 1970, becoming a party organized at federal level and no longer a union of cantonal parties.

The party has had two representatives in the seven-member federal government since 1959, although its share of the national vote has declined in recent elections. It was the strongest party in the *Nationalrat* between 1975 and 1983, falling to third place in the latter year but recovering to second place in 1987, with 42 seats and 20% of the vote. It fell back to third place in 1991, with 36 seats and 18.3% of the vote, and slipped further in 1995 to 34 seats and 17.0%. The party then sought to develop new policies for the 21st century, based on its view that Switzerland's destiny was to join the European Union. However, in the October 1999 parliamentary elections the party became the smallest of the four coalition parties with 15.8% of the vote, even though it made a one-seat gain to 35.

The CVS is a member party of the Christian Democrat International, an associate member of the European People's Party and a member of the European Democrat Union.

Christian Social Party
Christlichsoziale Partei (CSP)
Parti Chrétien–Social (PCS)
Partito Cristiano–Sociale (PCS)

Address. Bruneggweg 4, 8002 Zurich
Telephone. (+41–1) 201–1941
Fax. (+41–1) 201–2114
Email. bloch.suess@bluewin.ch
Leadership. Monika Bloch Süss (chairperson); Marlies Schafer-Jungo (secretary)

The small CSP stands on the progressive wing of Christian democracy, advocating that governments have important social responsibilities to which resources must be allocated. The party won one *Nationalrat* seat in the October 1995 general elections and retained it four years later, its elected member joining the →Green Party parliamentary group.

Evangelical People's Party
Evangelische Volkspartei (EVP)
Parti Évangelique (PEV)
Partito Evangelico (PEV)

Address. Josefstrasse 32, 8005 Zurich
Telephone. (+41–1) 272–7100
Fax. (+41–1) 272–1437
Email. info@evp-pev.ch
Website. www.evp-pev.ch
Leadership. Ruedi Äschbacher (chairman); Roland Wiederkehr (parliamentary leader); Daniel Reuter (general secretary)

Founded in 1919, the EVP is a centrist party based on Protestant precepts, advocating a social market economy, avoidance of damage to the environment, a restructuring of agriculture, land reform, strict control of traffic, civilian service for conscientious objectors and a halt to the construction of nuclear power stations. First represented in the *Nationalrat* in 1919, the party has maintained a small but consistent presence in the post-war era, winning three seats in 1991 (with 1.9% of the vote), slipping to two seats in 1995 (with 1.8%) but recovering to three seats (again with 1.8%) in 1999. In the *Nationalrat* the EVP has been closely aligned with the →Independents' Alliance.

The EVP is affiliated to the Christian Democrat International.

Federal Democratic Union
Eidgenössisch–Demokratische Union (EDU)
Union Démocratique Fédérale (UDF)
Unione Democratica Federale (UDF)

Address. Frutigerstrasse 16, 3607 Thun
Telephone. (+41–33) 222–3637
Fax. (+41–33) 222–3744
Email. info@edu-udf.ch
Website. www.edu-udf.ch
Leadership. Hans Moser (chairman)

The EDU was founded in 1975 on a policy platform deriving from a conservative and fundamentalist Protestant interpretation of the Bible. The party was established by Max Wahl and other members of the (now defunct) Swiss Republican Movement, which had itself been created in 1971 by James Schwarzenbach, who had previously founded what later became the →Swiss Democrats. Advocating restrictions on the permanent settlement of foreigners in Switzerland, the EDU won four *Nationalrat* seats in 1975 and one in 1983. It failed to win representation in the 1987 general elections, but obtained one seat in 1991, which it retained in 1995 and increased to three in 1999.

Green Party–Greens
Grüne Partei–Grüne
Parti Écologiste–Les Verts
Partida Ecologista–I Verdi

Address. Waisenhausplatz 21, 3011 Bern
Telephone. (+41–31) 312–6660
Fax. (+41–31) 312–666
Email. gruene@gruene.ch
Website. www.gruene.ch
Leadership. Ruedli Baumann (chairman); Cécile Bühlmann (parliamentary leader); Hubert Zurkinden (general secretary)

The mainstream environmentalist GPS was founded in May 1983 as the Federation of Green Parties of Switzerland, embracing nine groupings, among them the *Groupement pour l'Environnement* in the canton of Vaud (which had gained one seat in the *Nationalrat* in 1979), the *Parti Écologique* of Geneva, the *Mouvement pour l'Environnement* of Neuchâtel, the Green Party of Zurich and the Green Party of North-West Switzerland. In the 1983 general elections the federated party obtained 2.9% of the vote and three seats in the *Nationalrat*. After it had been joined by further groups, it changed its name to Green Party in 1985. Thereafter the Greens operated both as a federal party and as a collection of cantonal groups, which were free to make their own electoral alliances.

In the October 1987 federal elections the GPS obtained nine seats in the *Nationalrat* (and 4.8% of the vote), rather less than had been expected in view of public alarm over recent chemical pollution of the Rhine and also over the Chernobyl nuclear disaster in the then Soviet Union. Part of the reason was that some pro-ecology voting support went to the Progressive Organizations of Switzerland, which included left-oriented Greens (but later became inactive). The mainstream GPS made a substantial advance in the 1991 elections, to 14 seats and 6.1% of the vote.

The tide of environmental concern had receded by the time of the October 1995 federal elections, in which the Greens fell back to nine seats on a 5% vote share. Four years later the party achieved precisely the same result, despite campaigning jointly with the left-leaning →Green Alliance, although its parliamentary group was increased to 10 by the adhesion of the →Christian Social Party representative. Thereafter the Greens were active with the →Social Democratic Party of Switzerland in demanding that Swiss defence expenditure should be reduced by a third over 10 years (a proposal to that effect being decisively defeated in a referendum in November 2000)).

The Swiss Greens are members of the European Federation of Green Parties.

450

Independents' Alliance
Landesring der Unabhängigen (LdU)
Alliance des Indépendants (AdI)

Address. Gutenbergstrasse 9, Postfach 7075, 3001 Bern
Telephone. (+41–31) 382–1636
Fax. (+41–31) 382–3695
Leadership. Monica Weber (chairperson); Rudolf Hofer (secretary)

The LdU was founded in 1936 to represent the interests of socially responsible citizens and consumers outside the conventional party framework. In the post-war era, operating very much like a conventional party, the formation achieved significant *Nationalrat* representation, of 10 seats between 1951 and 1967, when its tally rose to 16. Since then it has been in steady decline, in part because of the emergence of the →Green Party of Switzerland and other formations representing particular interests. Having won five seats from 2.8% of the vote in 1991, the LdU fell to three seats (1.8%) in 1995 and to one seat (0.7%) in October 1999.

Liberal Party of Switzerland
Liberale Partei der Schweiz (LPS)
Parti Libéral Suisse (PLS)
Partito Liberale Svizzero (PLS)

Address. Spitalgasse 32, Postfach 7107, 3001 Bern
Telephone. (+41–31) 311–6404
Fax. (+41–31) 312–5474
Email. info@liberal.ch
Website. www.liberal.ch
Leadership. Jacques-Simon Eggly (chairman); Rémy Scheurer (parliamentary leader); Nelly Sellenet (secretary)

The LPS stands for "the maintenance of federalism and of the market economy and the guaranteeing of individual freedom and responsibility, without ignoring the need for solidarity and the necessity of the functions of the state". It also calls for protection of the individual, the maintenance of an efficient defence force and of "armed neutrality", cooperation with the Third World, improvement of the quality of life, the use of natural gas and nuclear power as an alternative to oil, and freedom of information (but with state control over radio and television frequencies).

Descended from the liberal movement of the late 19th century, the LPS is based in the four mainly Protestant cantons of Geneva, Vaud, Neuchâtel and Basel-Stadt, where the party maintained an independent identity as liberals in other cantons were absorbed into the →Radical Democratic and →Christian Democratic People's parties. The party took its present name in 1977, having previously been the Liberal Democratic Union of Switzerland.

In the 1983 general elections the LPS retained eight *Nationalrat* seats on the basis of 2.8% of the vote, advancing in 1987 to nine seats (although with 2.7% of the vote). A further advance in 1991 to 10 seats and 3.0% was followed by a decline to seven seats and 2.7% of the vote in October 1995 and to six seats (2.2%) in October 1999.

The LPS is a member of the Liberal International.

Radical Democratic Party of Switzerland
Freisinnig–Demokratische Partei der Schweiz (FDP)
Parti Radical–Démocratique Suisse (PRD)
Partito Liberale–Radicale Svizzero (PLR)

Address. Postfach 6136, 3001 Bern
Telephone. (+41–31) 320–3535
Fax. (+41–31) 320–3500
Email. gs@fdp-prd.ch
Website. www.fdp.ch
Leadership. Gerold Bührer (chairman); Christine Beerli (parliamentary leader); Guido Schommer (secretary-general)

The FDP claims to be "the founder of modern Switzerland" in that "after a confrontation with conservative forces in 1848 it laid the foundations for the Swiss federal state as it exists today". A Radical Democratic group was first established in the Federal Assembly in 1878, 16 years before the establishment of the party as such in 1894. The introduction of proportional representation in 1919 diminished the party's influence in the *Nationalrat*, but it held a dominant position in the federal government until 1959. In that year it formed a coalition with the →Social Democratic Party, the →Christian Democratic People's Party and the Agrarians (later the →Swiss People's Party), which has been maintained ever since.

The 1983 general elections resulted in the FDP becoming the country's strongest party, with 23.4% of the vote and 54 of the 200 *Nationalrat* seats. It remained so in 1987, with 51 seats and 22.9% of the vote, and in 1991, despite slipping to 44 seats and 21.0%. In the October 1995 elections, however, it yielded first place to the Social Democrats, despite improving marginally to 45 seats on a lower vote share of 20.2%. In October 1999 it slipped to third place, with 43 seats and 19.9% of the vote.

The FDP is a member of the Liberal International.

Social Democratic Party of Switzerland
Sozialdemokratische Partei der Schweiz (SPS)
Parti Socialiste Suisse (PSS)
Partito Socialista Svizzero (PSS)

Address. Spitalgasse 34, Postfach 7876, 3001 Bern
Telephone. (+41–31) 329–6969
Fax. (+41–31) 329–6970
Email. sekretariat@sp-ps.ch
Website. www.sp-ps.ch
Leadership. Christiane Brunner (chairperson); Franco Cavalli (parliamentary leader); Reto Gamma (general secretary)

Founded as a federal party in 1888, the SPS quickly became a powerful political force in the country, particularly after the introduction of proportional representation in 1919. In the post-1945 period it has regularly obtained about 25% of the total vote and since 1959 has held two of the seven seats in a four-party coalition government also including the →Radical Democratic (FDP), →Christian Democratic People's (CVP) and →Swiss People's (SVP) parties. During the 1970s "new left" elements were in the ascendancy within the party, which accordingly adopted more radical policies (although with little effect on governmental action). However, at a congress held in Lugano in November 1982 a new programme of basic principles was adopted by a large majority, confirming the reformist, social democratic character of the party and thus representing a defeat for the left wing, which had argued for a socialist programme based on the concept of self-management.

In the 1983 general elections the SPS was outpolled by the FDP for the first time for 58 years, being reduced to 22.8% of the vote and 47 of the 200 *Nationalrat* seats as against 24.4% and 51 seats in 1979. Thereafter opposition within the SPS to continued participation in the federal coalition government came to a head when the party's nomination of female left-winger Lillian Uchtenhagen for a ministerial post failed to secure the support of the other coalition parties. However, a recommendation from the executive in favour of withdrawal from the government was effectively rejected by an emergency party congress in Bern in February 1984 by 773 votes to 511.

The SPS contested the 1987 general elections on a platform including ecological objectives; it lost six lower house seats, polling only 18.4% of the vote and obtaining the party's lowest representation (41 seats) since 1919. In the canton of St Gallen the SPS held its two seats in alliance with a Green List for People, Animals and the Environment (*Grüne Liste für Mensch, Tier und Umwelt*). The 1991 federal elections were also bad for the SPS, which languished on 18.5% of the vote, although the canton-based voting system gave it three additional seats, for a total of 44.

Demonstrating its commitment to women's equality by having a rule that at least one-third of its election candidates must be women, in 1993 the SPS again became exercised by the resistance of its coalition partners to female ministerial participation when its nomination of Christiane Brunner was rejected, apparently because of her unorthodox life style and outspoken feminism. The SPS promptly nominated another woman, Ruth Dreifuss, and warned that it would leave the coalition if she too were blackballed. The result was that Dreifuss was elected to the government, becoming Interior Minister.

Benefiting from a swing to the left in the October 1995 general elections, the SPS recovered its position as the premier party, advancing to 54 seats in the *Nationalrat* on a vote share of 21.8%. It retained the leading position in the October 1999 elections with 51 seats and 22.5%, although it was narrowly outpolled in terms of the popular vote by the SVP. In the new *Nationalrat*, the SPS group was joined by the single representative of the →Left Alliance. In the subsequent government formation, the SPS successfully resisted SVP demands for an additional seat on the seven-member Federal Council, but failed in its attempt to have the SVP ejected from the ruling coalition.

Internal dissension contributed to the resignation of Ursula Koch from the SPS chairmanship in April 2000. She was succeeded in October 2000 by Brunner, in a victory for the party's radical wing. The following month the SPS, alone among the four coalition parties, supported a referendum proposal that Swiss defence expenditure should be reduced by a third over 10 years, expressing disappointment at the decisive rejection given by the voters.

The SPS is a member of the Socialist International.

Swiss Democrats
Schweizer Demokraten (SD)
Démocrates Suisses (SD)
Democratici Svizzeri (DS)
Address. Postfach 8116, 3001 Bern
Telephone. (+41–31) 974–2010
Fax. (+41–31) 974–2011
Email. sd-ds@bluewin.ch
Website. www.schweizer-demokraten.ch
Leadership. Rudolf Keller (chairman); Bernhard Hess (secretary)

The party was founded in 1961 as the National Action Against Foreign Infiltration of People and Homeland (*Nationale Aktion Gegen Überfremdung von Volk und Heimat*), which was later shortened to National Action for People and Homeland (*Nationale Aktion für Volk und Heimat*) and abbreviated to National Action (NA). It called for strict curbs on immigration, an end to the "misuse" of the right to asylum and measures to limit the sale of property to foreigners. It also advocated "the protection of the natural environment, full employment of the Swiss population, political independence, and security, law and order in liberty".

In 1968 the NA launched a campaign for setting a ceiling on the proportion of foreigners resident in Switzerland and initiated a national referendum to that end, which was defeated by a slight majority in June 1970. Although the government subsequently issued certain restrictive regulations on foreign residents the NA continued its campaign and launched another initiative, which was also rejected by a majority of citizens in 1974. Following an increase in the number of naturalizations, the NA undertook a further initiative together with one demanding the submission of all future treaties with foreign countries to a referendum. The Federal Council thereupon drafted a counter-proposal which was approved in a referendum in March 1977. In 1981 the NA asked for a referendum on a proposed bill relaxing some of the existing restrictions on foreign workers, and in a referendum in June 1982 this bill was rejected by a large majority.

In the 1967 elections to the *Nationalrat* the NA won one seat for its founder, James Schwarzenbach, who left the NA in 1970 and later founded the (now defunct) Swiss Republican Movement. In the 1971 *Nationalrat* elections the NA won four seats (while the Swiss Republican

Movement obtained seven). By October 1979 the NA's representation had fallen to two but in the 1983 elections it rose again to four seats, after the party had contested the elections on a joint list with the Swiss Republican Movement which obtained 3.5% of the vote. In August 1985 Hans Zwicky (who was then president of the NA) asserted that there was no connection between the NA and the newly formed →National Socialist Party.

Despite scoring some local election successes in the mid-1980s, in the general elections of October 1987 the NA lost one of its four seats in the *Nationalrat* and obtained only 2.9% of the vote. The new SD title was adopted prior to the 1991 federal elections, in which the party rose to five seats, having presented a joint list with the →Ticino League which took 3.4% of the vote. Standing alone, it dropped back to three seats and 3.1% in the October 1995 elections and to only one seat and 1.8% in October 1999. The SD was subsequently prominent in the campaign for a constitutional limit of 18% on the proportion of foreigners in the Swiss population, which was heavily defeated in a national referendum in September 2000.

Swiss Party of Labour
Parti Suisse du Travail (PST)
Partei der Arbeit der Schweiz (PAS)
Partito Svizzero del Lavoro (PSL)
Address. Rue du Vieux-Billard 25, CP 232, 1211 Geneva 8
Telephone. (+41–22) 322–2299
Fax. (+41–22) 322–2295
Email. pst-pda@bluemail.ch
Website. www.pst.ch
Leadership. Christiane Jaquet-Berger (chairperson)

The PST was founded in October 1944 by members of the pre-war Communist Party (formed in 1921 but banned in 1939) and left-wing socialists who had been expelled or had resigned from the →Social Democratic Party of Switzerland. The party is organized in a dozen cantons, in particular in Geneva, Vaud, Neuchâtel and Basel (all predominantly French-speaking) and in Italian-speaking Ticino. Formerly an orthodox pro-Soviet party, the PST converted to democratic socialism on the demise of the USSR in 1991. Its reward in the 1991 elections was a tripling of its *Nationalrat* representation from one to three seats, which it retained in 1995 with 1.2% of the vote. In October 1999, however, it fell back to two seats and 1%.

Swiss People's Party
Schweizerische Volkspartei (SVP)
Union Démocratique du Centre (UDC)
Unione Democratica di Centro (UDC)
Uniun Democratica dal Center (UDC)
Address. Brückfeldstrasse 18, 3000 Bern 26
Telephone. (+41–31) 302–5858
Fax. (+41–31) 301–7585
Email. gs@svp.ch
Website. www.svp.ch
Leadership. Christoph Blocher (leader); Ueli Maurer (chairman); Walter Frey (parliamentary leader); Gregor Rutz (general secretary)

The right-wing populist SVP was founded in its present form in 1971 as successor to (i) the Farmers', Traders' and Citizens' (i.e. Agrarian) Party, which had been formed in Zurich in 1917 and in Bern in 1918, and which was joined by the artisans and former Conservative Liberals of the canton of Bern in 1921, becoming a government party in 1929; and (ii) the former Swiss Democratic Party (founded in 1942), which had its origins in the Democratic Party established in the canton of Zurich in 1867, the Democratic and Workers' Party set up in the canton of Glarus in 1890 and the Democratic Party founded in Grisons in 1942. Since the 1971 union, the SVP has continued to hold the one seat in the federal government which the Agrarian Party had held since 1959 in coalition with the →Radical Democratic, →Social Democratic and →Christian Democratic People's parties.

In the 1983 general elections the SVP retained 23 seats in the *Nationalrat* on the basis of 11.1% of the vote. In the 1987 contest the party obtained 25 seats on a slightly reduced vote share, which it increased to 11.9% in 1991 while still winning 25 seats. The October 1995 elections brought something of a breakthrough by Swiss standards, to 14.9% of the vote and 29 seats, only five less than the Christian Democrats (which held two government posts). The SVP's success in 1995 was attributed in particular to its participation, alone among the coalition parties, in the successful campaign against Swiss membership of the European Economic Area and its consistent opposition to accession to the European Union. Also important was the party's articulation of growing public concern about immigration and the number of foreign workers in Switzerland.

Building on this populist platform, the SVP scored a major victory in the October 1999 parliamentary elections, winning more votes than any other party, although the peculiarities of the electoral system gave it second representative place with 44 seats. Despite now being stronger than two of the other three coalition parties, the SVP's demand for equal representation in the government was successfully resisted, especially by the Social Democrats. The SVP was subsequently prominent in the campaign that resulted in March 2001 in a decisive referendum decision against opening negotiations on EU membership.

Ticino League
Lega dei Ticinesi (LdT)
Address. Via Monte Boglia 7, CP 2311, 6901 Lugano
Telephone. (+41–91) 971–3033
Fax. (+41–91) 972–7492
Website. www.legaticinesi.com
Leadership. Giuliano Bignasca (chairman); Mauro Malandra & Guido Quadri (secretaries)
Based exclusively in the Italian-speaking canton of Ticino, the LdT combines right-wing economic and social policy prescriptions with advocacy of greater autonomy for Ticino within the confederation. It won two *Nationalrat* seats in 1991 on a joint list with the equally right-ring →Swiss Democrats. Standing on its own, it retained only one seat in the October 1995 contest, improving to two in October 1999 with 0.9% of the vote.

Other Parties

Freedom Party of Switzerland (*Freiheits Partei der Schweiz, FPS*), better known as the Automobile or Car Party, the name under which it was launched in March 1985 to represent motorists' "rights", to support the construction of motorways and the provision of parking facilities in towns, and to oppose increases in car tax or a levy on vehicles using motorways. More broadly, the party espouses free enterprise and anti-state precepts, akin to those of the conservative wing of the →Radical Democratic Party (of which its first leader, Michael Dreher, had been a member). The FPS title was adopted in 1994, by which time the party was combining concern for the interests of motorists with a demand for curbs on immigration. Having won two *Nationalrat* seats at its first election in 1987 (with 2.6% of the vote), the party advanced strongly to eight seats on a 5.1% vote share in 1991, but fell back to seven seats and 4.0% in 1995. In October 1999 it failed to gain representation, taking only 0.9% of the vote.
Leadership. Roland F. Borer (president)

Green Alliance (*Grünes Bundnis, GB/Alliance Verte et Sociale, AVeS/Alleanza Verde e Sociale, AVeS*), left-wing ecologist grouping which urges the eventual abolition of the Swiss Army. It established a presence in the Lucerne cantonal parliament, before contesting the 1987 general elections on a joint list with the (now inactive) Progressive Organizations of Switzerland (POCH), winning four seats and 3.5% of the vote. Having failed to gain representation in 1991 and 1995, it overcame its original hostility to the mainstream →Green Party by presenting joint lists with the latter in 1999, winning one of the Greens' nine seats. The GB is a member of the European Federation of Green Parties.
Address. Neubrückstrasse 17, 3001 Bern
Telephone. (+41–31) 301–8209
Fax. (+41–31) 302–8878
Email. gbbern@infodelta.ch
Website. www.gbbern.ch
Leadership. Franziska Teuscher (*Nationalrat* member); Isabel Jordi-Ertler (secretary)

Left Alliance (*Alliance de Gauche*), left-wing alternative movement advocating a "new citizenship" and rights for foreign workers, opposing gender discrimination and social exclusion; standing as Solidarités, it won one *Nationalrat* seat in Geneva in October 1999, its member joining the group of the →Social Democratic Party of Switzerland.
Address. CP 2089, 1211 Geneva
Telephone. (+41–22) 740–0740
Fax. (+41–22) 740–0887
Email. info@solidarites.ch
Website. www.solidarites.ch
Leadership. Christian Grobet (*Nationalrat* member)

National Socialist Party (*Nationalsozialistische Partei, NSP*), radical right-wing party founded in 1985 by a faction of what became the →Swiss Democrats "to improve the image of national socialism" and to combat "over-population by foreigners".
Leadership. Ernst Meister

Ticino Socialist Party (*Partito Socialista, Sezione Ticinese*), left-wing socialist grouping based in Italian-speaking Switzerland, founded in 1988 as the Unitarian Socialist Party (PSU), which was a merger of the Autonomous Socialist Party with a section of the smaller Community of Ticinese Socialists (CST). Since 1992 the party has operated as an autonomous section of the →Social Democratic Party of Switzerland.
Leadership Anna Biscossa

Women Do Politics! (*Frauen Macht Politik!, FraP!*), seeking to change what it regards as ingrained resistance to female participation within established Swiss parties by persuading more women to become involved in politics. It established a bridgehead in the October 1995 elections, winning one *Nationalrat* seat, but lost it in 1999.
Address. Postfach 9353, 8036 Zurich
Telephone. (+41–1) 242–4418
Fax. (+41–1) 242–4418
Leadership. Barbara Huber & Claudia Schätti (joint secretaries)

Syria

Capital: Damascus   **Population**: 16,304,000 (2001E)

The Syrian Arab Republic is, under its 1973 constitution, a "socialist popular democracy". It has an executive President, who is secretary-general of the *Baath* Arab Socialist Party and also chairman of the National Progressive Front (NPF), embracing the country's legal parties. These are the *Baath*, the Socialist Unionist Movement, the Arab Socialist Union (ASU), the Arab Socialist Party (ASP), the Syrian Communist Party (SCP) and (since 1990) the Socialist Unionist Democratic Party. Legislative authority rests with the People's Assembly (*Majlis al-Sha'ab*), which is elected for a four-year term by universal adult suffrage of citizens over the age of 18 years and under a simple-majority system in multi-member constituencies. In elections held in August 1994, the *Baath* Party and its allies within the NPF won a guaranteed 167 of the 250 Assembly seats, with the remaining 83 going to independents. The same returns were recorded in the next elections held Nov. 30 and Dec. 1, 1998.

The President is elected every seven years in a nation-wide referendum after nomination as sole candidate by the People's Assembly on the recommendation of the ruling *Baath* Party. In a referendum held on July 10, 2000, Bashar al-Assad was confirmed as President following the death the previous month of his father, Hafez al-Assad, who had been President since 1971. The President appoints the Vice-Presidents and the Council of Ministers.

A tentative liberalization of political dialogue (including the release of 600 political prisoners) following the appointment of President Bashar al-Assad was termed the "Damascus Spring" but in August–September 2001 one member of the Assembly was jailed after issuing a manifesto and another detained for leading a "national dialogue" discussion group.

Arab Socialist Party (ASP)
Hizb al-Ishtiraki al-Arabi
Address. c/o Majlis al-Sha'ab, Damascus
Leadership. Abd al-Ghani Kannut
The party has taken part in government since 1970, normally being allocated one ministerial post. It has been represented in the People's Assembly since 1973, as part of the NPF structure, obtaining six seats in the 1994 and 1998 legislative elections. It is anti-Egyptian and seeks a revival of free competition among political parties.

Arab Socialist Union (ASU)
Ittihad al-Ishtiraki al-Arabi
Address. c/o Majlis al-Sha'ab, Damascus
The party has long been a "Nasserite" group (subscribing to the socialist ideals of the former Egyptian President, Abdel Gamal Nasser). It has been represented in every People's Assembly, as part of the NPF, and took seven seats in both the 1994 and 1998 elections.

Baath Arab Socialist Party
Hizb al-Baath al-Arabi al-Ishtiraki
Address. BP 9389, Damascus
Leadership. Bashar al-Assad (secretary-general, chairman of the National Progressive Front); Abdallah al-Ahmar (assistant secretary-general)
Website. www.albaath.com
The *Baath* (Renaissance) stands for secular pan-Arabism, socialism, anti-imperialism and anti-Zionism. It is historically (but now only theoretically) a regional party of which the Syrian party is one "regional command", others being in Iraq and Lebanon. Founded originally by Michel Aflaq in Syria in the latter part of the 1940s, the *Baath* absorbed the Syrian Arab Socialist Party in December 1953 and assumed its current name. The party was behind the March 1963 coup (the month after its involvement in a coup in Iraq) and it has held office in Syria ever since, although following a crisis in its ranks in 1966 the party expelled its rightist wing in which Aflaq was prominent. The Iraqi *Baath* returned to power in 1968, having been ousted at the end of 1963, but the theoretical unity of the party was not restored. The Syrian and Iraqi wings became fierce enemies, the former regularly denouncing the latter as a "rightist clique", and both sides have sponsored violent action against the other.

Hafez al-Assad's group within the *Baath* seized power in late 1970 and he maintained his dominance of the Syrian political scene until his death in 2000. The *Baath* has, in turn, consistently dominated the National Progressive Front which it formed as a broad umbrella group in 1972, providing the framework for putting forward approved lists of candidates for legislative elections. In both the 1994 and 1998 elections, 135 *Baath* candidates were returned. After the death of his father, Bashar al-Assad took over as *Baath* secretary-general and NPF chairman.

Socialist Unionist Democratic Party
Hizb al-Dimuqrati al-Tawdhidi al-Ishtiraki
Address. c/o Majlis al-Sha'ab, Damascus
The party first appeared as one of the constituent parts of the National Progressive Front at the legislative elections held in May 1990. In the 1994 and 1998 elections to the People's Assembly it took four seats.

Socialist Unionist Movement
Haraka at-Tawhidiyah al-Ishtiraki-yah
Address. c/o Majlis al-Sha'ab, Damascus
The party proclaims "Nasserite" socialist ideals. It has been represented in government since 1967, and is also represented in the People's Assembly through its membership of the NPF, obtaining seven seats in the 1994 and 1998 legislative elections.

Syrian Communist Party (SCP)
Hizb al-Shuyui al-Suri
Address. c/o Majlis al-Sha'ab, Damascus
Leadership. Yusuf Faysal (secretary-general)
Founded in 1925 (as part of a joint Communist Party of Syria and Lebanon until 1958), the SCP is generally regarded as the largest Communist Party in the Arab world, and was pro-Soviet in orientation until the collapse of the Soviet bloc. It is technically illegal, but is permitted to operate openly and has been represented in the Cabinet since 1966. The SCP is a part of the NPF framework, taking eight seats in the 1994 and 1998 elections to the People's Assembly.

Taiwan

Capital: Taipei   **Population**: 22,191,087 (2000E)

The government of Taiwan (Formosa) is derived from that which ruled the Chinese mainland prior to the 1949 communist revolution and the establishment of the People's Republic of China (PRC). The Taiwan government continues to be called the Republic of China, though it abandoned claims to the mainland in 1991. Martial law, imposed in 1949, was lifted in 1987, this decision opening the way for the legalization of opposition parties. Since a constitutional revision in 2000 the National Assembly (*Kuomin Tahui*) confines itself largely to constitutional matters, whilst other legislation is the preserve of the elective Legislative *Yuan* (*Lifa Yuan*, LY).

Elections in December 1991 for 325 seats in the new National Assembly resulted in the Nationalist Party (*Kuomintang* or KMT) winning 254, the Democratic Progressive Party (DPP) 66, the National Democratic Independent Political Alliance 3 and independents 2. In elections to the 164-member LY in 1995, however, the KMT achieved only a narrow majority, winning 85 seats, against 54 for the DPP, 21 for the New Party and 4 for independents. For the December 1998 LY election the number of seats was increased to 225, with 41 elected from national lists including 8 for Overseas Chinese. The KMT confirmed their supremacy, winning 123, whilst the DPP won only 70, and the New Party 11. By April 2000 91 parties had registered with the government, but only four have representatives in the LY.

Constitutional reforms approved in July 1994 provided for the direct election of the executive President (previously elected by the National Assembly). In March 1996 the incumbent, President Lee Teng-hui of the KMT, was re-elected with 54% of the votes cast despite strident military threats from the PRC. In 2000, however, rivalry between two potential candidates from the KMT, Lien Chan and James Soong, led to the latter standing at the head of his own People First Party (PFP). This, combined with increasing public exasperation over corruption scandals, let in Chen Shui-bian as the first President from the DPP, with Soong second and Lien an embarrassing third.

Democratic Progressive Party (DPP)
Minchu Chinpu Tang
Address. 10th Fl, 30 Peiping E. Road, Taipei 100
Telephone. (+886–2) 2392–9989
Fax. (+886–2) 2393–0342
Email. dpp@dpp.org.tw
Website. www.dpp.org.tw
Leadership. Lin Yi-hsiung (chair)

The DPP was formed in 1986 (although the restrictions of martial law still applied at that time) by a dissident movement (*Tangwai*, meaning "outside the party"), which had been set up to promote multi-party democracy. Its base support comes from the "Taiwanese", i.e. those born on the island, and they are more concentrated in the south. Accorded legal status in 1989, the party supports an independent sovereign Taiwan, although it has accepted that a referendum would be required if Taiwan were to declare itself independent. During the 1990s it gradually increased its share of seats in the Legislative *Yuan*, from 21 in 1989 to 70 in 1998, but it never seemed likely to overtake the ruling →Nationalist Party (KMT). It seemed trapped in a strategy of appealing for Taiwanese independence that was not enough to win majority support. In the March 1996 presidential election the party's candidate, Peng Ming-min, came second with 21% of the vote. In 2000, however, a split within the KMT ranks allowed Chen Shui-bian to win with 39%, though he has had to cohabit with a KMT-dominated Legislative *Yuan*. Currently the DPP claims around 200,000 members. They choose their presidential candidate. The DPP has always consisted of a number of factions that coexist uneasily, central discipline is weak and Chen is not the party leader.

The DPP has observer status in the Liberal International.

Nationalist Party
Kuomintang
Address. 9th Floor, 11 Chung Shan South Road, Taipei
Telephone. (+886–2) 2343–4847
Fax. (+886–2) 2343–4850

Website. www.kmt.org.tw
Leadership. Lien Chan (chair)

Dating from 1894, the *Kuomintang*, or KMT, was dominant at all levels of government from the proclamation of the Republic of China in 1949 until the 2000 presidential election. Its platform is still based on the "three principles of the people" (nationalism, democracy and social well-being) originally enunciated by Sun Yat-sen, the party's founder. Organizationally it was modelled on Leninist Bolshevism until recently. The loser in the Chinese civil war, until the 1990s it still aspired to return to the mainland, but now it has effectively reconciled itself to a future on Taiwan. Over the decades people born on the island came to displace those born on the mainland within the leading ranks of the party. This was symbolized by Lee Teng-hui, who succeeded Chiang Ching-kuo as President of Taiwan and leader of the party in 1988. Later, in 1998, he launched the concept of the "New Taiwanese" as a call for national unity.

Once competitive party elections were allowed, the KMT's supremacy gradually declined. It was hit from without by increasing allegations of corruption and from within by suspicions that Lee Teng-hui was moving towards a position favouring Taiwanese independence. In 1993 members of a younger and more reform-minded New KMT Alliance faction within the party defected to form the →New Party (NP). In 1995 two conservative KMT vice-chairs who favoured closer ties with China were expelled for aligning themselves with the NP.

Nevertheless Lee Teng-hui won Taiwan's first direct presidential election in March 1996, drawing 54% of the total vote. The KMT also remained the leading party in the Legislative *Yuan* as a result of the December 1998 elections, when it took 123 seats. For the March 2000 presidential election, however, the Vice-President, Lien Chan, and a former secretary general of the KMT, James Soong, both sought the party nomination, Lee being constitutionally barred. Lien won the nomination but Soong refused to withdraw, forming the →People First Party (PFP). In the election the candidate of the opposition →Democratic

Progressive Party (DPP) came first, while Soong pushed Lien into third place, taking 37% of the vote to Lien's 23%. In the recriminations that followed, Lee was forced to step down early as KMT chair, being replaced by Lien.

Since the victory of the DPP in March 2000, a re-registration of KMT party members has shown 2.5 million instead of 3.5 million. In future the party leader will be chosen by all the members. Politicians with a mainland background have made a come-back in the KMT under Lien and the party has expanded its contacts with the People's Republic of China (PRC) and the Communist Party of China (CPC). Where Lee advocated that cross-Straits relations be handled on the basis of full equality, Lien has floated the concept of a confederation with the PRC. Partly in protest against these moves, Lee set up the Taiwan Solidarity Alliance in August 2001 and expressed support for President Chen Shui-bian.

The KMT is an affiliate of the International Democrat Union.

New Party (NP)
Hsin Tang
Address. 4th Floor, 65 Kuangfu Nanlu, Taipei 105
Telephone. (+886–2) 2756–2222
Fax. (+886–2) 2756–5555
Website. www.np.org.tw
Leadership. Chou Yang-sun (chair)
The New Party was set up in mid-1993 by dissident →Nationalist Party (KMT) members in the Legislative *Yuan*

and merged later that year with the China Social Democratic Party (which had broken away from the →Democratic Progressive Party (DPP) in 1991). The party advocates a "one China" policy while supporting the concept of direct talks with the mainland communist government. In the December 1995 elections the NP's representation in the Legislative *Yuan* rose to 21, making it the third largest formation. In the March 1996 presidential election the NP-backed candidate was former KMT vice-chair Lin Yang-kang, who came third with 15% of the popular vote. In 1998, however, its representation in the Legislative *Yuan* fell to 11 seats and its candidate in the 2000 presidential election only polled 0.13% of the votes after urging voters to support James Soong. Currently it claims nearly 68,000 members. Its chief office-holders, not rank-and-file members, choose the leader.

People First Party
Ch'in Min Tang
Email. webservice@pfp.org.tw
Website. www.pfp.org.tw
Leadership. James Soong (chairman); Jong-chi Chung (secretary general)
Initially formed as a vehicle to support the 2000 presidential campaign of James Soong, a former secretary general of the →Nationalist Party (KMT). His success in coming came second with 37% of the vote encouraged him to turn it into a regular party, attracting a number of defections by KMT legislators.

Tajikistan

Capital: Dushanbe

Population: 6,500,000 (2001E)

The Soviet Socialist Republic of Tajikistan declared independence from the USSR in September 1991 as the Republic of Tajikistan, which became a sovereign member of the Commonwealth of Independent States (CIS) in December 1991. The post-Soviet constitution adopted by referendum in November 1994 established an executive presidency, with the President as head of state, chief executive and commander-in-chief, being popularly elected for a five-year term (once renewable consecutively) and having the authority to appoint and dismiss the Prime Minister and other ministers, subject to approval by the legislature.

The Soviet-era Communist establishment remained in power in independent Tajikistan until civil war erupted in mid-1992, when allied pro-democracy and Islamic parties briefly took control, before being driven into opposition and armed insurgency by the resurgent Communists. Five years of bitter internal conflict followed, until on June 27, 1997, a peace agreement was concluded in Moscow between the Tajikistan government and the United Tajik Opposition (UTO) providing for UTO participation in government and the legalization of opposition parties. Implementation of the agreement proved slow and difficult, however, as disaffected Islamic groups and others continued their armed struggle.

As provided for under the Moscow agreement, important changes to the constitution were adopted by referendum in September 1999. These included the extension of the presidential term of office to seven years and the reform of the Supreme Assembly, introducing a bicameral system in place of the unicameral Soviet-era body. The highest legislative body remains the Supreme Assembly (*Majlisi Oli*). The lower Chamber of Representatives (*Majlisi Namoyandagon*) has 63 members, elected by universal adult suffrage on the basis of a mixed voting system of constituency seats (41) and proportional representation of parties (22 seats) subject to a threshold of 5% of the national vote. The upper National Chamber (*Majlisi Milli*) has 33 members, 25 elected by members of the provincial governments and eight appointed by the President. Both houses hold office for five-year terms.

Having been returned to office in November 1994 as interim incumbent, President Imomali Rakhmonov of the People's Democratic Party of Tajikistan (HDKT) was re-elected with a landslide 96.97% of the vote in presidential elections on Nov. 6, 1999. For elections to the newly-established Chamber of Representatives on Feb. 27 and March 12, 2000, six parties satisfied the requirements for registration and hence were allowed to nominate candidates. According to results published in May 2000 by the OSCE's Office for Democratic Institutions and Human Rights (ODIHR), the HDKT won 36 seats (with 63.4% of the proportional vote), the Communist Party of Tajikistan 13 (20.4%) and the Islamic Renaissance Party 2 (6.8%), the remaining 12 seats being won by independents or not decided.

Communist Party of Tajikistan (CPT)

Address. c/o Supreme Assembly, Dushanbe
Leadership. Shodi Shabdollov (first secretary)

Having been the ruling (and only legal) party since 1924 as the republican branch of the Communist Party of the Soviet Union, the CPT entered the era of independence still very much in charge in conservative Tajikistan, with a substantial genuine membership concentrated in areas of high ethnic Uzbek or Russian population such as the northern industrial region of Khodjent (formerly Leninabad). Twelve days after Tajikistan's declaration of independence, a CPT congress voted on Sept. 21, 1991, to convert the party into the Tajik Socialist Party, with a democratic socialist orientation. In response to immediate mass protests, a presidential decree of Sept. 22 banned the party and nationalized its assets. One day after that, the Communist-dominated Supreme Soviet voted to rescind the prohibition, triggering further popular protests which resulted in the ban being confirmed on Oct. 2. However, the direct election of Communist Rakhman Nabiyev to the presidency in November 1991 with 58% of the popular vote resulted in the ban being officially lifted in January 1992; thereafter the party resumed activities under the CPT title, while maintaining its new commitment to democratic socialist principles.

The onset of civil conflict in 1992 ranged the Communist-era establishment against the allied forces of the Islamic and pro-democracy opposition, with the establishment emerging victorious, as indicated by the accession of Imomali Rakhmonov to the presidency in November 1992. The Supreme Court's decision in June 1993 to ban the four leading opposition parties served to confirm the CPT in its resumed role as effectively the ruling formation. Several new parties were launched in 1993–94, the most significant of which was the pro-presidential →People's Democratic Party of Tajikistan (HDKT). Some observers initially regarded the HDKT as part of the CPT network, but the two parties soon diverged. When Rakhmonov formally opted for the HDKT in March 1998, the CPT effectively became part of the secular opposition.

The continuing strength of the CPT's countrywide organization was apparent in the February–March 2000 parliamentary elections, in which the party won over 20% of the national vote and 13 lower house seats, as well as four seats in the indirectly-elected upper house. In March 2001 the CPT announced that 1,200 people had applied to join the party in 2000, bringing its membership to 65,000.

Democratic Party of Tajikistan (DPT)

Address. c/o Supreme Assembly, Dushanbe
Leadership. Mahmadruzi Iskandarov (chairman)

The strongly anti-Communist DPT was launched in 1990 on a platform advocating Tajik sovereignty, the introduction of a market economy and a cultural revival. Its candidate in the October 1991 presidential election was Davlat Khudonazarov, who came a creditable second on the strength of an alliance with the →Islamic Renaissance Party (IRP) against the ruling establishment of the →Communist Party of Tajikistan. The DPT was prominent in the "government of national reconciliation" of May–November 1992, but the reassertion of Communist authority in late 1992 forced it into armed resistance. It was one of four opposition parties banned by the Supreme Court in June 1993, amid escalating internal conflict ranging pro-democracy and Islamic forces against the government. Peace talks resulting in a notional cease-fire agreement in September 1994 failed to bring the DPT and other opposition parties into the elections of late 1994 and early 1995.

Divisions between the moderate and hard-line wings of the DPT led to an open split in June 1995, when Shodmon Yusuf was deposed from the leadership but refused to recognize the election of Jumaboy Niyazov as his successor. Claiming to be the authentic DPT leader, Yusuf came to an agreement with the government under which his faction of the party, the DPT–Tehran, was re-legalized in July, whereas the Niyazov faction, the DPT–Almaty, entered into a formal opposition alliance with the IRP. Yusuf later fell out with the government and sought political asylum in Austria.

The DPT–Almaty was re-registered in August 1999, whereas in November that year the DPT–Tehran was denied registration because it had essentially the same name as a registered party. In the run-up to the February-March 2000 parliamentary elections the DPT–Almaty itself became seriously divided between supporters of new chairman Mahmadruzi Iskandarov (a former Emergency Situations Minister) and Niyazov's faction, which criticized Iskandarov for being too accommodating to the government. In the elections the DPT–Almaty obtained only 3.5% of the vote, thus failing to qualify for proportional representation seats. In February 2001 Niyazov initiated moves for a reconciliation of the DPT–Almaty factions, whereas the former DPT–Tehran in May 2001 re-launched itself as the →Development Party.

Islamic Renaissance Party (IRP)
Nahzati Islomi Tojikistan

Address. c/o Supreme Assembly, Dushanbe
Leadership. Sayed Abdullo Nuri (leader); Mohieddin Kabiri (deputy leader); Muhammad Sharif Himatzada (chairman)

The IRP was founded in June 1990 as the Tajik branch of a network of Islamic parties that emerged in the last phase of the USSR. Based in the rural population, the IRP has declared its long-term objective to be the conversion of Tajikistan into an Islamic republic, although it rejects the label "Islamic fundamentalist". The party was refused permission to hold its founding congress in Dushanbe in October 1990 and was subsequently proscribed by the presidium of the then Tajikistan Supreme Soviet. It nevertheless took an active part in organizing the mass protests that followed the Dushanbe government's support for the attempted coup by hard-liners in Moscow in August 1991. Legalized in October 1991, the IRP supported the unsuccessful presidential candidacy of Davlat Khudonazarov of the →Democratic Party of Tajikistan in October 1991.

The IRP was again banned in June 1993, along with three other opposition parties, and became a leading component of the insurgent Islamic Revival Movement, which in 1996 was renamed the United Tajik Opposition (UTO). The IRP's then deputy leader, Ali Akbar Turadzhonzoda, had been Tajikistan's chief *kazi* (senior Muslim cleric) until February 1993; thereafter he acted as an opposition spokesman in peace negotiations with the government. Their failure to produce political agreement resulted in an IRP boycott of the presidential and legislative elections of late 1994 and early 1995. The IRP leader, as chairman of the UTO, then entered into "inter-Tajik" peace talks under the auspices of Iran, Russia and the UN, with support from the OSCE, the USA and neighbouring states such as Uzbekistan and Pakistan. Armed conflict between government troops and UTO forces continued intermittently in 1995–96, but on June 27, 1997, after eight rounds of negotiations, a "general agreement on the establishment of peace and national accord" was signed by President Rakhmonov and Nuri in Moscow, in the presence of President Yeltsin of Russia and senior representatives of the UN and other supporters of the peace process. Under the agreement, UTO representatives were subsequently appointed to the government, although full reconciliation proved to be a slow process.

The IRP was officially re-registered in August 1999 and put forward government minister Davlat Usmon as its candidate for the presidential elections in October. Although he withdrew at the last moment, his name remained on ballot papers and attracted 2% of the vote, as incumbent President Rakhmonov was re-elected with a massive majority that was dismissed as fraudulent by the IRP. The IRP was allowed to contest the February–March 2000 parliamentary elections, winning two seats in the lower house with 6.8% of the proportional vote. At an IRP congress in December 1999, Nuri affirmed that the party would observe the constraint of

Tajikistan's constitution in its efforts to create an Islamic state. People's Democratic Party of Tajikistan

People's Democratic Party of Tajikistan
Hizbi Demokrati Khalkii Tojikston (HDKT)
Address. c/o Supreme Assembly, Dushanbe
Leadership. Imomali Rakhmonov (chairman)
Initially launched in August 1993 in the wake of the banning of the main opposition parties two months previously, the People's Party of Tajikistan (PPT) – renamed the People's Democratic Party of Tajikistan (HDKT) in June 1997 – was formally constituted in April 1994, apparently as a product of the ruling establishment's wish to demonstrate the multi-party character of the new Tajikistan. Reports that the new party was intended as a successor to the →Communist Party of Tajikistan (CPT) proved to be premature, as the CPT remained in being on its own account. In the 1995 parliamentary elections the PPT was credited with winning five seats in the 181-member Supreme Assembly.

Having become the HDKT, the party rapidly became the dominant formation in Tajikistan, with a membership of some 20,000 by 1998. President Rakhmonov formally joined the party in March 1998 and was elected as its chairman the following month. He was therefore the HDKT candidate in the November 1999 presidential elections, his 97% vote in which was regarded as highly suspect by the opposition. The HDKT also dominated the February–March 2000 parliamentary elections, winning 36 of the 63 lower house seats with 63.4% of the proportional vote. The party also won a majority of the seats in the March 2000 indirect elections to the upper house.

Other Parties

Agrarian Party of Tajikistan, founded in 1998, but banned in September 1999 and so did not contest the 2000 parliamentary elections.
Leadership. Hikmatullo Nasriddinov (chairman)

Badakhshan Ruby Movement (*Lali Badakhshan*), founded in the late 1980s to represent the distinctive Pamiri (Ismaili Muslim) people of Gorny-Badakhshan; it originally demanded full autonomy, to which end it joined the opposition alliance headed by the →Democratic and →Islamic Renaissance parties in armed struggle against the Dushanbe government and was banned in June 1993. The ban was lifted in August 1999, but the party was unsuccessful in the 2000 parliamentary elections.
Leadership. Atobek Amirbek (chairman)

Civil Patriotic Party of Tajikistan Unity (*Soyuz*), founded in 1994; banned in April 1999 and so did not contest the 2000 parliamentary elections.
Leadership. Bobohan Mahmadov (chairman)

Development Party (*Taraqqiyot*), founded as a "constructive opposition" formation in May 2001 by the former "Tehran faction" of the →Democratic Party of Tajikistan (DPT), aspiring to reunite the various currents of the DPT.
Leadership. Sulton Quvvatov (chairman).

Justice and Development Party, founded in 1998 and registered in February 1999; did not contest 2000 parliamentary elections.
Leadership. Rahmatullo Zoirov (chairman)

Justice Party (*Adolatho*), founded in 1995; contested the 2000 parliamentary elections, winning only 1.4% of the vote and no seats; suspended for six months in January 2001 for contravening the electoral law and banned outright in August.
Leadership. Abdurahmon Karimov (secretary-general)

National Movement (*Jumbish*), founded in February, favouring integration with CIS, denied registration in April 1999, and so did not contest 2000 parliamentary elections.
Leadership. Hakim Muhabbatov (chairman)

Rebirth Movement (*Rastokhez*), founded in 1990 as a nationalist/religious movement advocating the revival of Tajik culture and traditions; participated in the anti-communist, pro-independence agitation of 1990–91 and in the "government of national reconciliation" of May–November 1992, prior to being banned in June 1993. The ban was lifted in August 1999 but the party did not contest the 2000 parliamentary elections.

Socialist Party of Tajikistan, founded in 1996 and based in the Leninobod region; its first leader, Safarali Kenjayev, was murdered in April 1999 and succeeded by his son; contested the 2000 parliamentary elections but took only 1.2% of the vote.
Leadership. Sherali Kenjayev (chairman)

Tajikistan Party of Political and Economic Renewal, founded in 1993 as a pro-market formation, credited with winning one seat in the 1995 elections. Then leader Mukhtor Boboyev was murdered in northern Tajikistan by unknown gunmen; the party was suspended in April 1999 owing to administrative irregularities and did not contest the 2000 elections.
Leadership. Vali Babayev (chairman)

Tanzania

Capital: Dodoma   **Population**: 35,300,000 (2000E)

The United Republic of Tanzania was established in 1964, when the newly independent states of Tanganyika and Zanzibar merged. Under the constitution, executive power is vested in the President of the United Republic, who is elected by direct popular vote for a five-year term, renewable once only. Legislative power is exercised by the National Assembly, which serves a five-year term. It comprises 232 members directly elected from single seat constituencies, 37 women nominated by the President, and five seats reserved for members of the Zanzibar House of Representatives. Zanzibar's internal administration provides for a popularly elected President and House of Representatives. In December 1994 a constitutional amendment was introduced ending the convention that the President of Zanzibar would automatically serve as a Vice-President of the United Republic.

The ruling Revolutionary Party of Tanzania (*Chama Cha Mapinduzi*, CCM) was the sole legal political party until 1992.

Multi-party presidential and legislative elections were held throughout Tanzania in October-November 1995 resulting in victory in the presidential election to the CCM candidate, Benjamin Mkapa, with 61.8% of the vote, while the CCM also gained an overwhelming majority in the legislature. Zanzibar also held elections for its own president and legislature in October 1995. The CCM's incumbent presidential candidate, Salmin Amour, was narrowly re-elected with 50.2% of the votes cast, while in the House of Representatives the party secured 26 of the 50 elective seats, the other 24 going to the Zanzibar-based Civic United Front (CUF).

In 2000 Zanzibar held its internal elections at the same time as the Tanzanian national presidential and legislative elections. Polling took place throughout Tanzania on Oct. 29, 2000, with re-runs in 16 of the 50 Zanzibar constituencies on Nov. 5. The conduct of the October elections throughout Zanzibar was strongly criticized by international observers, and the 16 re-runs (in constituencies containing 42% of Zanzibar's electorate) were boycotted by opposition parties, which called for fresh elections in all 50 Zanzibar constituencies. Benjamin Mpaka was re-elected President of Tanzania, having received 71.7% of the national vote in a four-way contest, while the CCM's candidate for the presidency of Zanzibar, Amani Abeid Karume, was elected with 67% of the local vote in a two-way contest with Seif Shariff Hamad of the CUF. The elections to the Tanzanian legislature (including nominated women members) resulted in the CCM holding 244 seats, the CUF 15, the Party for Democracy and Progress (CHADEMA) 4, the Tanzania Labour Party (TLP) 3, and the United Democratic Party (UDP) 2.

In the Zanzibar House of Representatives, the CCM won 33 of the elective seats, the remaining 17 seats going to the CUF. In April 2001 CUF members of the National Assembly and the Zanzibar House of Representatives, who had boycotted their respective legislatures in protest at the conduct of the 2000 elections in Zanzibar, were declared to have forfeited their seats because they had committed technical breaches of parliamentary standing orders. This action followed the introduction of legislation to extend from 90 days to two years the maximum period for holding by-elections to fill vacant seats in the National Assembly and the Zanzibar House of Representatives.

Civic United Front (CUF)
Chama Cha Wananchi
Address. Mtendeni Street, PO Box 3637, Zanzibar
Telephone. (+255–54) 237446
Fax. (+255–54) 237445
Leadership. Ibrahim Haruna Lipumba (chairman); Shaaban Khamis Mloo (vice-chairman); Seif Shariff Hamad (secretary-general)
The mainly Zanzibar-based CUF was formed in 1992 through the merger of *Kamahuru* (a Zanzibar-based pro-democracy pressure group) and the Civic Movement (a mainland-based human-rights organization). In the 1995 Tanzanian presidential election the CUF candidate, Ibrahim Lipumba, took third place with 6.4% of the votes cast, while in the National Assembly elections the party won 24 of the directly-elected seats and was allocated three of the nominated women's seats. In the Zanzibar presidential poll, the CUF's Seif Shariff Hamad was narrowly beaten into second place, having secured 49.8% of the vote, while the CUF won 24 of the 52 elective seats in the Zanzibar House of Representatives. The authorities in Zanzibar arrested 18 members of the CUF (including members of the House of Representatives) in late 1997 and early 1998 on charges of "plotting to destabilize Zanzibar". They were held in detention for the remainder of the President Amour's term of office but were released as part of an amnesty to mark his successor's inauguration in November 2000.

The 2000 elections, which were described by Commonwealth observers as "falling far short of minimum standards", resulted in the CUF holding 15 seats in the National Assembly and 17 in the Zanzibar House of Representatives. Ibrahim Lipumba was runner-up in the national presidential election, with 16.3% of the vote, while Said Shariff Said came second with 33% of the vote in the Zanzibar presidential election. Having called for re-runs of the 2000 elections in all 50 Zanzibar constituencies, the CUF boycotted the re-runs that were held in 16 of the constituencies. CUF MPs subsequently boycotted the proceedings of the national and Zanzibar legislatures, their seats in which were formally declared vacant in early April 2001, when it was ruled that such a boycott was in breach of correct procedure. Not all members of the CUF supported the recent policy trends, and it was reported in April 2001 that a splinter group had applied to register itself as a separate party under the name Forum for the Restoration of Democracy (FORD).

The CUF has had observer status with the Liberal International since 1997.

Party for Democracy and Development
Chama Cha Demokrasia na Maendeleo (CHADEMA)
Address. PO Box 31191, Dar es Salaam
Telephone. (+255–22) 2668866
Website. www.democratafrica.org/tanzania/chadema
Leadership. Bob N. Makani (chairman); Willibrod Slaa (vice-chairman); Aman Walid Kabourou (secretary-general)
CHADEMA was registered in 1993, advocating democracy and social development. It has a broadly right-of-centre pro-business orientation. It took four seats in the 2000 National Assembly elections.

The party is associated with the International Democrat Union through the Democrat Union of Africa.

Revolutionary Party of Tanzania
Chama Cha Mapinduzi (CCM)
Address. PO Box 50, Dodoma
Telephone. (+255–61) 2282
Website. www.ccm.or.tz
Leadership. Benjamin Mkapa (leader); Philip J. Mangula (secretary-general)
The CCM was formally launched in 1977 upon the merger of the Tanganyika African National Union (TANU) with the Afro-*Shirazi* Party (ASP) of Zanzibar. Since the adoption of a one-party constitution in 1965, TANU had been the sole party of mainland Tanzania and the ASP the sole party of Zanzibar. Under President Julius Nyerere, the party had pursued a policy of socialism and self-reliance. However, Ali Hassan Mwinyi, who succeeded Nyerere as President of Tanzania in 1985 and as CCM chairman in 1990, implemented free-market reforms and economic liberalization. In February 1992 an extraordinary national conference of the CCM unanimously endorsed the introduction of a multi-party system, reflecting developments in much of Africa at that time.

In July 1995 Benjamin Mkapa was selected in succession to Mwinyi as presidential candidate for the CCM. The party reasserted its political dominance in the multi-party elections in October–November 1995, retaining the presidency and achieving an overwhelming majority in the National Assembly, although its victories in the Zanzibar polls were much narrower. The 2000 elections further increased the CCM's dominance, Mpaka being re-elected Tanzanian President with 71.7% of the vote and Amani Abeid Karume winning the Zanzibar presidency with 67% of the vote. The CCM held 244 seats in the National Assembly and 33 of the 50 elective seats in the Zanzibar House of Representatives.

Tanzania Labour Party (TLP)
Address. c/o National Assembly, PO Box 941, Dodoma
Leadership. Augustine Mrema (chairman)
The TLP, founded by Leo Herman Lwekamwa, gained representation in the National Assembly in April 1999 through the defection to it of a faction of the →National Convention for Construction and Reform-*Mageuzi* led by Augustine Mrema. In the 2000 elections Mrema came third (with 7.8% of the vote) in the contest for the Tanzanian presidency, while the TLP won 3 seats in the National Assembly. In April 2001 Leo Herman Lwekamwa (a vice-chairman of the TLP) and 29 other TLP members claimed to have removed Mrema from the party chairmanship. In the following month Mrema contested this claim, stating that his opponents had "abdicated their membership of the party".

United Democratic Party (UDP)
Address. PO Box 5918, Dar-es-Salaam
Telephone. (+255–22) 2628131
Leadership. Richard Kasella-Bantu (secretary-general)
In the 2000 elections the UDP presidential candidate, John Cheyo, took fourth place in the Tanzanian presidential election with 4.2% of the vote, while the UDP won two seats in the National Assembly. The party has had observer status with the Liberal International since 1996.

Other Parties

National Convention for Construction and Reform–Mageuzi (NCCR-M), launched in 1992; in the 1995 elections its presidential candidate Augustine Mrema (who had resigned from the ruling →Revolutionary Party of Tanzania in March 1995) took second place with almost 28% of the vote and the party gained 19 seats; the party subsequently split with a majority faction led by Mrema defecting to the →Tanzania Labour Party. Having been seriously undermined by this development, the NCCR-M did not win any seats in the 2000 elections.
Address. PO Box 5316, Dar es Salaam
Leadership. Kassim Magutu (chairman); Mabene Marando (secretary-general)

National League for Democracy (NLD), registered in 1993. In June 1999 the NLD chairman became chairman of an umbrella organization linking six opposition parties with no representation in the National Assembly.
Address. PO Box 352, Dar es Salaam
Leadership. Emmanuel Makaidi (chairman)

Thailand

Capital: Bangkok

Population: 60,606,947 (2000)

The Kingdom of Thailand is the only south-east Asian country not to have been colonized by a European power. Modern Thailand came into being in 1932 when a civilian-military group carried out a coup replacing the country's absolute monarchy with a system modelled on European constitutional monarchies. From 1938 to 1979 military rule prevailed, interspersed with short periods of democratic government. Since 1979 an elected parliament has prevailed, interrupted only by a coup in February 1991 and a period of military rule before democratic procedures were restored after mass street demonstrations in May 1992.

In reaction to this most recent military intervention, a popular movement demanded a new constitution, which was finally approved by parliament in August 1997. It confirmed Thailand as a parliamentary democracy in which the Prime Minister and the Cabinet appointed by the Prime Minister must have the confidence of the elected legislature. The National Assembly (*Ratha Sapha*) consists of a House of Representatives (*Sapha Phu Thaen Ratsadorn*) and Senate (*Wuthi Sapha*), both elected by universal adult suffrage at 18 years and above. The 200 senators, who must not be members of political parties, are returned by territorial constituencies. The 500-member lower house has 400 MPs elected by single-member territorial constituencies and 100 returned from party lists which secure at least 5% of valid votes. All MPs must be members of a registered political party. The Cabinet is restricted to 25 persons. MPs chosen as ministers must resign their seats.

The first elections under the new constitution, supervised by an independent Election Commission, were held for the Senate in March–June 2000 and for the House of Representatives on Jan. 6, 2001. The results of the polling for the House (after re-runs in several constituencies where malpractice was found by the Election Commission) were as follows: Thais Love Thais (*Thai Rak Thai*) 248 seats, Democrat Party 128, Thai Nation Party (*Chart Thai*) 41, New Aspiration Party 36, National Development Party (*Chart Pattana*) 29, Liberal Democratic Party (*Seri Tham*) 14, Citizens' Party (*Ratsadorn*) 2, Social Action Party 1, Thai Motherland Party 1. In February 2001 *Seri Tham* merged into the *Thai Rak Thai*.

Citizens' Party
Phak Ratsadorn
Address. c/o Sapha Phu Thaen Ratsadorn, Bangkok 10300
Leadership. Somboon Rahong (chairman)
Originally formed in 1986 by elements with military links, *Ratsardorn* became moribund in the mid-1990s but was revived in 1999 as a vehicle for a small group of old politicians found unacceptable by other parties. The party won only two seats in the 2001 elections, so that its future again came into question.

Democrat Party (DP)
Phak Prachathiphat
Address. 67 Setsiri Road, Samsen Nai, Phaythai, Bangkok 10400
Telephone. (+66–2) 270–1683
Fax. (+66–2) 279–6086
Email. admin@democrat.or.th
Website. www.democrat.or.th
Leadership. Chuan Leekpai (leader)
Established in 1946, the liberal DP is Thailand's oldest political party. Having won by far the largest number of

legislative seats in 1986, the party split in 1988, in which year it experienced a dramatic fall in electoral support, becoming a party of the southern region. However, Chuan Leekpai subsequently re-established a Bangkok following by recruiting several technocrats and new young politicians. On this base, the DP became the "party of government" through the 1990s, heading the ruling coalition from September 1992 until May 1995. Having increased its representation to 86 seats (out of 391) in July 1995, it returned to power in November 1997 without a new election, after the →New Aspiration-led government had collapsed in the face of urban demonstrations.

The post-1997 DP-led government headed by Chuan Leekpai lost popularity through its association with the IMF programme to manage Thailand's 1997–98 financial crisis. It was again reduced to a southern regional party at the January 2001 elections, in which it won 128 seats (out of 500), becoming the leading opposition party.

National Development Party
Phak Chart Patthana (CP)
Address. 10 Soi Phaholyothin 3, Phyathai, Bangkok 10400
Telephone. (+66–2) 279–3104
Fax. (+66–2) 279–4284
Website. www.chartpattana.or.th
Leadership. Korn Dabbaransi (leader)
Launched in mid-1992 by Chatichai Choonhavan following his defection from the →Thai Nation Party (*Chart Thai*), the CP won 50–60 seats in the elections of 1992, 1995 and 1996, serving as a junior partner in all the subsequent coalition governments, including that led by the →Democrat Party from late 1997. After Chatichai's death in 1998, the party leadership passed to his nephew. At the January 2001 polls, the party won only 28 seats and was excluded from the subsequent governing coalition.

New Aspiration Party (NAP)
Phak Khwam Wang Mai
Address. 310 Soi Ruamchit, Nakhornchaisri Road, Dusit, Bangkok 10300
Telephone. (+66–2) 243–5000
Fax. (+66–2) 241–2280
Website. www.nap.or.th
Leadership. Gen. Chavalit Yongchaiyut (leader)
The NAP was set up in 1990 as a vehicle for the political ambitions of its leader, a former army commander and self-styled "soldier for democracy". Despite his background, Chavalit was strongly critical of the military's intervention in national politics in 1991–92. The NAP won 51 seats at the September 1992 elections, and joined the ruling coalition until December 1994, when it withdrew. In July 1995 the party won 57 seats and joined the government led by the →Thai Nation Party (*Chart Thai*). After the opposition mounted two no-confidence debates against this coalition, Chavalit pressured the *Chart Thai* Prime Minister into resigning in September 1996. Attracting many *Chart Thai* defectors, the NAP emerged as the largest party with 125 seats (out of 391) at the November 1996 polls, whereupon Chavalit formed a coalition government.

The Chavalit government failed to manage the onset of Thailand's financial crisis in mid-1997 and was driven from power by pressure from the IMF, army and business leaders and by white-collar street demonstrations. In 1998 the small Mass Party (*Phak Muan Chon*) merged into the NAP, but the party was weakened when a major faction defected to the new →Thais Love Thais Party (*Thai Rak Thai*). The rump NAP won only 36 seats (out of 500) at the January 2001 elections, but became a junior partner in the resultant governing coalition.

Social Action Party (SAP)
Phak Kit Sangkhom
Address. 126 Soi Ongkarak, Nakhon Chaisi Road, Dusit, Bangkok 10300
Telephone. (+66–2) 243–0100
Fax. (+66–2) 243–3224
Website. www.sap.or.th
Leadership. Bunphan Khaewattana (leader)
The SAP was formed in 1974 by a conservative faction of the →Democrat Party (DP) led by Kukrit Pramoj. It became the largest parliamentary party in 1979 and again in 1983. In 1991 the leadership passed to Montri Pongpanich, following which the SAP joined coalition governments in 1992 (briefly), 1995 and 1996. The party split in November 1997, some members joining the DP-led coalition. It declined further after Montri's death in 1998. At the January 2001 polls it won only one seat.

Thai Motherland Party
Phak Thin Thai
Address. 577 Pracha Uthit Road, Samsen, Bangkok 10320
Telephone. (+66–2) 691–1571–4
Email. info@tmp.or.th
Website. www.tmp.or.th
Leadership. Bhichai Rattakul (leader)
This party was formed in 2000 by the outgoing Bangkok mayor, Bhichai Rattakul. It campaigned on an environmental platform in the January 2001 parliamentary elections, but won only a single seat.

Thai Nation Party
Phak Chart Thai
Address. 325/74–76 Lukluang Road, Dusit, Bangkok 10300
Telephone. (+66–2) 280–7054
Fax. (+66–2) 282–4003
Website. www.chartthai.or.th
Leadership. Banharn Silpa-Archa (leader)
Established in the mid-1970s by a right-wing, pro-business group of retired military officers, *Chart Thai* rose in the late 1980s by attracting the new generation of "godfather" provincial politicians. It won the most seats in the 1988 elections, and headed the coalition later thrown out by a military coup in February 1991. In 1992 party leader Chatichai Choonhavan defected to form the →National Development Party (*Chart Pattana*), and the original ex-military group was supplanted by provincial notables such as the new leader, Banharn Silpa-Archa.

In the July 1995 elections *Chart Thai* emerged as the largest legislative party, increasing its representation from 77 to 92 seats and forming a new seven-party coalition administration. The coalition collapsed in September 1996 after two no-confidence debates had detailed charges of corruption and maladministration against Banharn and several other ministers. Many members defected. At the polls in November 1996, the party was reduced to 39 seats (out of 393), although it participated in subsequent ruling coalitions.

For the 2001 election, *Chart Thai* brought in some new faces and proclaimed a programme of rural reform, but won only 41 seats (out of 500), mostly in a few isolated areas of the central and north-eastern regions, and only narrowly surmounted the 5% threshold for party-list seats. Nevertheless, the party was invited to join the subsequent coalition headed by the →Thais Love Thais Party.

Thais Love Thais Party
Phak Thai Rak Thai (TRT)
Address. 237/2 Ratchawithi Road, Chitlada, Dusit, Bangkok 10300
Telephone. (+66–2) 668–2000
Fax. (+66–2) 668–6000
Email. public@thairakthai.or.th
Website. www.thairakthai.or.th
Leadership. Thaksin Shinawatra (leader)
Launched in July 1998 by Thaksin Shinawatra, who became one of Thailand's richest entrepreneurs in the early 1990s from telecommunications concessions. In the early 1990s, Thaksin joined the →Moral Force Party (*Palang Dharma*)

and briefly served as Foreign Minister and Deputy Prime Minister. The TRT was launched to capture the soft nationalism generated in reaction to the IMF's perceived botched management of the 1997–98 financial crisis. With an initial slogan of "think new, act new", Thaksin attracted many old activists as well as intellectuals and new political aspirants. He also welcomed the defection of a large faction of old-style politicians from the crumbling →New Aspiration Party (NAP).

To contest the 2001 polls, Thaksin announced a programme of financial reforms and rural uplift, investing part of his considerable fortune in grassroots political organization and American-style campaign techniques—all innovations in Thai political life. The party swept to an overall majority of 248 seats and Thaksin became Prime Minister of a coalition government which included the NAP and the →Thai Nation Party (*Chart Thai*). Immediately after the elections the TRT absorbed the small Liberal Democratic Party (*Seri Tham*, ST), which had won 14 seats in northeastern Thailand.

In June 2001 Thaksin appeared before the Constitutional Court on charges (filed by the anti-corruption commission shortly before the January elections) that he had made false asset declarations while in government in the 1990s.

Other Parties

Moral Force Party (*Palang Dharma*), formed in 1988 by the then governor of Bangkok, Chamlong Sirimaung, as a vehicle to enter national politics; declined after 1992 when Chamlong withdrew into community work. The party failed to win any seats at the 2001 national elections, but remained active in Bangkok municipal politics.
Address. 445/15 Soi Ramkhaeng 39, Wangthonglang, Bangkapi, Bangkok 10310
Telephone. (+66–2) 718–5626
Leadership. Chaiwat Sinsuwong (leader)

Solidarity Party (*Phak Ekkaphap*), formed in 1989 from the merger of four opposition parties (*Ruam Thai*, Community Action, Progressive Party and *Prachachon*), briefly acceded to the governing coalition prior to the 1991 military coup. In the 1992, 1995 and 1996 general elections the party won eight seats, but failed to win any in 2001.

Thai Citizens' Party *Prachakorn Thai, PT*, formed in 1979 a vehicle for the right-wing populist, Samak Sundaravej. The party split in 1997, while Samak resigned from parliament and was elected mayor of Bangkok in 2000. The party failed to win representation in the January 2001 legislative elections.
Address. 9/250 Soi Ladprao 55, Lardrap Road, Bangkapi, Bangkok 10310
Telephone. (+66–2) 559–0008
Leadership. Samak Sundaravej (leader)

Togo

Capital: Lomé

Population: 5,020,000 (2000E)

The Republic of Togo gained full independence in 1960, having previously been administered by France as a United Nations Trust Territory. In 1967 the present head of state, Gen. Gnassingbé Eyadéma, seized power in a bloodless coup and assumed the title of President. Existing political parties were banned, and in 1969 the Rally of the Togolese People (RPT) was established as the ruling and sole legal party. By early 1991 Eyadéma was facing increasing opposition pressure for the introduction of multi-party democracy, and he agreed to the holding of a National Conference, in July and August of that year, to determine the political future. The Conference set up a transitional High Council of the Republic which subsequently engaged in a power struggle with President Eyadéma. Amid the continuing political tension, a multi-party constitution was given approval in a referendum in September 1992. This vested executive power in the President and legislative power in an 81-member National Assembly (*Assemblée Nationale*), both directly elected for five-year terms of office.

Togo's first multi-party presidential elections in August 1993 resulted in victory for the incumbent Eyadéma, although the contest was marked by the absence of any serious challengers and accusations of electoral malpractice. In legislative elections in February 1994, the opposition Action Committee for Renewal (CAR) and Togolese Union for Democracy (UTD) won 36 and 7 Assembly seats respectively (although the results in three constituencies were subsequently declared invalid by the Supreme Court), while the ruling RPT took 35 seats.

In further presidential elections held on June 21, 1998, Eyadéma was re-elected with 52% of the vote. Opposition groups claimed irregularities and international observers expressed doubts about the credibility of the results. The legislative elections held on March 21, 1999, which returned the RPT to power, were boycotted by the major opposition parties, which claimed that their concerns over the earlier disputed presidential polling had not been resolved. In July 1999, the European Union brokered the Lomé Framework Agreement, by which the opposition parties entered into negotiations with the President to establish an independent electoral commission and prepare for a new round of legislative elections.

Action Committee for Renewal
Comité d'Action pour la Renouveau (CAR)

Leadership. Yao Agboyibo (leader)
Part of an opposition coalition with the →Togolese Union for Democracy (UTD), the CAR boycotted the presidential election in August 1993 but participated in the legislative balloting in February 1994. Initially the party gained the highest number of seats, with 36, although this was subsequently reduced to 34 by a controversial Supreme Court decision that prompted a CAR boycott of the new National Assembly. In the light of the election results, the CAR/UTD coalition declared in March 1994 that CAR leader Agboyibo had been selected for appointment as the new Prime Minister. However, President Eyadéma refused to endorse this, and in April he appointed the UDT leader, Edem Kodjo, as Prime Minister in a move which fractured the

unity of the CAR/UTD coalition. The CAR rejected the appointment, continuing to assert that the new Prime Minister should come from within its own ranks, and boycotted the Assembly for a period.

As the party's presidential candidate in the June 1998 election, Agboyibo came third with 9.6% of the vote. Following further claims of irregularities in that election the CAR boycotted the National Assembly elections held in 1999 and refused to serve in the new administration.

Co-ordination of New Forces
Co-ordination des Forces Nouvelles (CFN)
Leadership. Joseph Kokou Koffigoh (president)
The CFN was formed in 1993, comprising six political organizations and led by the (then) Prime Minister, Koffigoh. He resigned as premier in March 1994, following the legislative elections the previous month in which the CFN won one seat. The party stood in the March 1999 legislative elections but failed to secure representation.

Patriotic Pan-African Convergence
Convergence Patriotique Panafricaine (CPP)
Leadership. Edem Kodjo (president)
Launched in 1999, the party was a merger of the →Togolese Union for Democracy (UTD), the Party of Action for Democracy (*Parti d'Action pour la Démocratie*, PAD) led by Francis Ekoh, the Party of Democrats for Unity (*Parti des Démocrates pour l'Unité*, PDU) and the Union for Democracy and Solidarity (*Union pour la Démocratie et la Solidarité*, UDS) headed by Antoine Foly.

Rally of the Togolese People
Rassemblement du Peuple Togolais (RPT)
Address. Place de l'Indépendance, BP 1208, Lomé
Telephone. (+228) 212018
Leadership. Gen. Gnassingbé Eyadéma (president)
The RPT was established in 1969 under the sponsorship of President Eyadéma, and ruled on a single-party basis until its constitutional mandate was abrogated in 1991 by the National Conference. The Conference, convened in response to increasing opposition to the regime, set up a transitional High Council of the Republic and a serious power struggle subsequently developed between this body and Eyadéma.

In presidential elections held in August 1993, which were boycotted by the main opposition parties, Eyadéma was confirmed in office with about 96.5% of the votes cast, although voter turnout was extremely low. In January 1994 an attempt was made on the President's life; the government alleged that the →Union of Forces for Change (UFC), with Ghanaian support, was responsible. In legislative elections in February 1994, the RPT took only 35 National Assembly seats, leaving it without a majority. President Eyadéma subsequently split the opposition ranks by appointing the leader of the →Togolese Union for Democracy (UTD) as the new Prime Minister and RPT members secured key portfolios in a coalition Cabinet. The RPT gained a parliamentary majority by winning three by-elections held in August 1996; following this, Kwassi Klutse, the former Minister of Planning, was appointed Prime Minister of a new government of mainly Eyadéma supporters, since the main opposition parties refused to serve.

Early returns suggested that Eyadéma might lose the presidential elections in June 1998. Voting was suspended and, once the head of Togo's electoral commission resigned, the Minister of the Interior declared Eyadéma the winner without resuming the count. The government survived a vote of no confidence in September 1998 and went on to win the legislative elections in March 1999 without the outcome of the presidential elections being resolved. Condemned by the opposition, the RPT stood virtually unopposed, winning 79 seats in the new National Assembly (the remaining two seats going to independent candidates). Koffi Eugene Adoboli, a former United Nations official, was appointed as the new Prime Minister in May 1999. Following a Constitutional Court ruling that the Minister of the Interior had violated the electoral code and EU mediation with the opposition, Eyadéma pledged to stand down at the next presidential election due in 2003. In August 2000, Kodjo Agbéyomè, the president of the National Assembly, was appointed Prime Minister.

Togolese Union for Democracy
Union Togolaise pour la Démocratie (UTD)
In alliance with the →Action Committee for Renewal (CAR), the UTD boycotted the presidential polls in 1993 but participated in the National Assembly elections in February 1994. The party secured seven seats initially, although the election of one UTD member was subsequently invalidated. Having refused to appoint the CAR leader as the new Prime Minister, President Eyadéma chose UTD leader Edem Kodjo in April 1994 to head a new government drawn heavily from the President's →Rally of the Togolese People. Kodjo's acceptance caused a breach in relations between the UTD and the CAR. The UTD left the government in 1996. In 1999 it boycotted the National Assembly elections and merged with the newly formed →Patriotic Pan-African Convergence (CPP).

Union of Forces for Change
Union des Forces du Changement (UFC)
Email. contact@ufc-togo.com
Website. www.ufc-togo.com
Leadership. Gilchrist Olympio; Jean-Pierre Fabre (secretary-general).
Initially a coalition of anti-Eyadéma organizations under Olympio, the UFC was launched as a social democratic party in 1993. Having been exiled in Ghana with other Togolese dissidents, Olympio's candidature for the 1993 presidential election was disallowed on a legal technicality. Following government allegations that he was involved in an attack on the President in 1994 (which he denied), the UFC boycotted the legislative elections that year.

Olympio returned from exile to stand as the party presidential candidate in 1998. Although early voting figures suggested that he was ahead of President Eyadéma, once voting was suspended Olympio was declared to have come second with 34% of the vote. The UFC staged demonstrations, claiming that that the results were fraudulent, and boycotted the National Assembly elections in 1999.

Other Parties

Democratic Convention of African Peoples (*Convention Démocratique des Peuples Africains, CDPA*), one of the earliest identifiable opposition movements to emerge under the Eyadéma regime at the end of the 1980s. Party leader Gnininvi took fifth place in the presidential elections held in 1998 with less than 1% of the vote. The CDPA has consultative status with the Socialist International.
Leadership. Leopold Mensan Gnininvi

Party for Democracy and Renewal (*Parti pour la Démocratie et le Renouveau, PDR*), launched in 1991. Party leader Ayewa came fourth in the presidential election in 1998 with only 3% of the vote.
Leadership. Zarifou Ayewa

Union of Independent Liberals (*Union des Libéraux Indépendants, ULI*), launched by Jacques Amouzou, who contested the 1993 presidential election but came a very distant second to Gen. Eyadéma with 1.87% of the vote. Amouzou took sixth place in the presidential elections in 1998 with less than 1% of the vote.
Leadership. Jacques Amouzou

Tonga

Capital: Nuku'alofa (Tongapatu) **Population:** 100,000 (2000E)

The Kingdom of Tonga, an independent constitutional monarchy within the Commonwealth, was a British Protected State for 70 years prior to achieving full independence in 1970. The Tongan sovereign is head of state and exercises executive power in conjunction with an appointed 11-member Privy Council which functions as a Cabinet. The 30-member unicameral Legislative Assembly consists of the King, Privy Council, nine nobles elected by the country's 33 hereditary peers, and nine popularly elected representatives. In recent years this system has faced an increasingly determined challenge from a pro-democracy movement, members of which in 1994 founded a formal organization, initially called the People's Party and later the Human Rights and Democracy Movement (HRDM). In the most recent general election, which was held on March 12, 1999, candidates associated with the HRDM won five of the nine seats open to popular vote.

Trinidad and Tobago

Capital: Port of Spain **Population:** 1,180,000 (2000E)

Trinidad and Tobago gained independence from the United Kingdom in 1962 and became a republic in 1976. Under the 1976 constitution the head of state is the President, who is elected for a five-year term by a parliamentary electoral college. The head of government is the Prime Minister. There is a bicameral parliament. The House of Representatives has 36 members (34 from Trinidad, two from Tobago), elected for five-year terms in single seat constituencies. The Senate has 31 members appointed by the President: of these, 16 are appointed on the advice of the Prime Minister, six on that of the Leader of the Opposition, and nine at the President's own discretion to represent economic, social and community organizations. Tobago, the smaller of the country's two main constituent islands with a population of only 50,000, enjoys a measure of internal self-government. Its House of Assembly, established in 1980 and given extended powers in 1996, has 15 members (12 directly elected and three chosen by the majority party), who serve four-year terms.

In a general election on Dec. 11, 2000, the United National Congress (UNC), which had headed a coalition government since 1995, won 19 of the House seats, with 16 going to the opposition People's National Movement (PNM) and one to the National Alliance for Reconstruction (NAR). A Commonwealth Observer Group monitored the election and said it had been fairly conducted. However, the PNM charged that there had been widespread vote-rigging in marginal constituencies.

Elections to the local Tobago House of Assembly were held most recently on Jan. 29, 2001, and resulted in the PNM winning 8 of the 12 elected seats with the NAR, previously the dominant party in Tobago, taking four.

There is a distinct racial element to support for the two main parties, which intensifies at election time. The PNM is backed mainly by the African-descended population whereas the UNC's main strength is among people of East Indian descent, the two communities each constituting about 40% of the population with the balance being mainly of mixed race.

National Alliance for Reconstruction (NAR)
Address. 71 Dundonald Street, Port of Spain/Robinson and Main Streets, Scarborough, Tobago
Telephone. (+1–868) 627–6163 (Port of Spain)/(+1–868) 639–4431 (Tobago)
Leadership. Hochoy Charles (leader in Tobago)
The NAR was formed in February 1986 as a "rainbow coalition" of opposition parties aiming to unite support among both the African and Indian communities and adopting the slogan "One Love". Although the NAR, under the leadership of Arthur N.R. Robinson, won a landslide victory in the 1986 general election, taking 33 of the 36 seats, it subsequently broke apart against a background of worsening economic conditions, with dissidents forming the →United National Congress (UNC) in 1989. Since 1991 the NAR has held seats only in Tobago (Robinson's home island), although following the 1995 election it held the balance of power and supported the formation of a UNC-led government in exchange for a Cabinet seat for Robinson and

increased autonomy for Tobago. There have also been tensions between party supporters in the two islands of Trinidad and Tobago. In the most recent general election in December 2000 (when it put up candidates only in Tobago), it lost one of its two seats. In January 2001 elections the NAR, which had dominated the Tobago House of Assembly since its creation in 1980, lost control of the Assembly to the PNM, which took 8 of the 12 elected seats to four for the NAR. Former NAR Prime Minister Arthur Robinson has been national President (head of state) since 1997.

People's National Movement (PNM)
Address. Balisier House, Tranquility Street, Port of Spain
Telephone. (+1–868) 625-1533
Email. pnm@carib-link.net
Website. www.pnm.org.tt
Leadership. Patrick Manning (political leader); Martin R. Joseph (general secretary)
The centre-right PNM has traditionally derived its main sup-

port from Trinidadians of African descent. It won every election in Trinidad and Tobago from its formation in 1956 until 1986. The party's founder, Eric Williams, Chief Minister under colonial rule from 1956, became the first Prime Minister on independence in 1962 and died in office on March 29, 1981. In December 1986 the party lost a general election for the first time, being heavily defeated by the newly formed →National Alliance for Reconstruction (NAR). George Chambers, who had assumed the leadership on the death in 1981 of the party's founder, lost his seat in the election and resigned as party leader, being replaced by Patrick Manning. The PNM returned to office at the 1991 general election, winning 21 seats, but went into opposition again after the November 1995 election when it and the →United National Congress (UNC) each won 17 seats and the UNC went on to form a government with NAR support. The PNM remained in opposition after the December 2000 election, when it won 16 of the 36 seats. However, the party alleged widespread voting irregularities by the UNC and filed legal challenges against two successful UNC candidates. In January 2001 the PNM gained control of the Tobago House of Assembly for the first time, winning eight of the 12 seats.

United National Congress (UNC)

Address. Rienzi Complex, 78-81 Southern Main Road, Couva
Telephone. (+1–868) 636 8145
Email. unc@tstt.net.tt
Website. www.unc.org.tt
Leadership. Basdeo Panday (leader); Fazal Karim (general secretary)

The UNC, in government since 1995, has its base in the East Indian-descended 40% of the population and its leader, Basdeo Panday, is the first Prime Minister of Indian extraction. In 1975, Panday, then (and until 1995) president of the All Trinidad Sugar and General Workers' Trade Union (ATS/GWTU), formed the United Labour Front (ULF). In the 1976 elections the ULF won 10 of the 36 House seats on a platform that included worker participation, nationalization of key enterprises and land reform. The ULF subsequently participated in the →National Alliance for Reconstruction (NAR), which won the 1986 general election. Panday was expelled from the NAR in 1988 and in 1989 with other former ULF members formed the UNC.

The UNC won 13 seats in the 1991 elections and then in 1995 won 17, enabling it to form the government with the support of the weakened NAR.

In office from 1995 the UNC pursued similar policies of economic restructuring and encouragement of foreign investment as had the preceding →People's National Movement (PNM) government. It also benefited from the rise in the world price of oil, hydrocarbons being the bulwark of the economy. In the December 2000 election the UNC retained power, winning 19 seats. The government ran on its record in creating jobs and tackling the country's problems of violent crime and drug trafficking. However, the campaign was dominated by racial tension and PNM claims that the UNC was engaged in systematic electoral fraud, targeted particularly on five marginal seats (all of which the UNC won). In response to charges by PNM leader Patrick Manning that the election would be "stolen", Panday invited a Commonwealth Observer Group to monitor the polling, but the conclusion of its small team of observers that the elections were fair had little impact on the domestic controversy. With PNM accusations of electoral fraud continuing post-election, and Manning threatening to call anti-government demonstrations, Panday on Jan. 24, 2001, warned Parliament that "certain groups" were amassing arms "for what is believed to be a violent attempt to take control of the country".

In January 2001 the UNC contested the local elections to the House of Assembly in Tobago (which has only a small Asian community) for the first time, but failed to win a seat.

The UNC is an affiliate of the Christian Democrat International.

Other Parties

People's Empowerment Party (PEP), based in Tobago and led by lawyer Deborah Moore-Miggins, a former NAR member, was founded in December 1999. It put forward candidates without success in the two Tobago constituencies in the December 2000 national elections and in the January 2001 Tobago House of Assembly elections.
Address. Miggins Chamber, Young Street, Scarborough, Tobago
Telephone. (+1–868) 649–3175

Tunisia

Capital: Tunis   **Population:** 9,593,000 (2000E)

The Republic of Tunisia was declared in 1957, a year after the country achieved independence from France. Under the 1959 constitution executive power is held by the President, elected every five years, who appoints the Prime Minister and the Council of Ministers. The unicameral Chamber of Deputies (*Majlis al-Nuwab/Chambre des Députés*) is also elected for a five-year term by universal suffrage (with a minimum voting age of 20). Following the deposition in November 1987 of "President-for-Life" Habib Bourguiba and his replacement by Gen. Zine El Abidine Ben Ali, the Chamber voted to limit the President to a maximum of three five-year terms.

In presidential elections on March 20, 1994, Ben Ali was the sole candidate (standing for the ruling Democratic Constitutional Rally, RCD) and was officially stated to have been re-elected with over 99% of the votes cast. In simultaneous elections for the Chamber of Deputies, the RCD won all 144 seats contested in the traditional first-past-the-post district list system. Four of the six legal opposition parties shared the remaining 19 seats, reserved under a newly instituted system for parties which did not secure a majority in the constituencies. In November 1998 a further electoral reform increased the total number of seats in the Chamber of Deputies from 163 to 182, out of which opposition candidates were to be guaranteed at least 34 seats (allocated according to the proportion of votes received nationally by each party). For the first time in the country's history, two candidates stood against the incumbent President in the presidential elections held on Oct. 24, 1999 but Ben Ali was re-elected with a declared 99.4% of the vote for a third term of office. In the simultaneous legislative elections, the RCD won 148 seats while five parties shared the 34 seats reserved for the opposition.

Despite introducing electoral and some press reform, the governing party has been criticized by human rights groups for its treatment of its opponents. It was reported in August 2001 that a proposed constitutional amendment to allow Ben Ali to compete in the next presidential election for a fourth term of office is expected to produce political controversy.

Democratic Constitutional Rally
Rassemblement Constitutionnel Démocratique (RCD)
Address. blvd 9 Avril 1938, Tunis
Telephone. (+216–1) 560393
Fax. (+216–1) 569143
Email. info@rcd.tn
Website. www.rcd.tn
Leadership. Zine El Abidine Ben Ali (chairman); Hamed Karoui (deputy chairman); Abderrahim Zouari (secretary-general)
Founded in 1934 as the Neo-Destour Party – a breakaway group from the old Destour (Constitution) Party – the organization led the movement for independence and for a republic, adopting in effect a single party framework between 1963 and the early 1980s. The party used the name Destourian Socialist Party from 1964 to 1988. The change to its present name at the end of that period was intended to reflect a greater political openness under President Ben Ali.

The RCD has a moderate left-wing republican orientation. At a congress held in July 1993 it confirmed its commitment to free-market economic policies and its opposition to Islamic fundamentalist militancy. Despite the controlled and limited multi-partyism implemented since 1991, the RCD has retained its monopoly of power. It won 144 of the 163 seats in the Chamber of Deputies in the 1994 elections against nominal opposition from six parties, and took 148 seats (all the seats other than those reserved for opposition parties) with 91.6% of the vote in the 1999 polling. In the 1999 presidential elections Ben Ali won 99.4% of the vote standing against two opposition candidates.

The RCD is a member party of the Socialist International.

Democratic Socialist Movement
Mouvement des Démocrates Socialistes (MDS)
Address. c/o Chambre des Députés, Tunis
Leadership. Ismail Boulahya (secretary-general)
Legally registered in 1983, the MDS was originally organized in 1977 by a number of former cabinet members from the ruling party who sought greater political liberalization in Tunisia. The MDS boycotted legislative elections in 1986, following the arrest and disqualification of its leader Ahmed Mestiri from running for legislative office, and failed to secure representation in the 1989 poll, after which Mestiri resigned as secretary-general. The party also boycotted municipal elections in June 1990 in protest against the failure of democratization efforts in the country.

In March 1994 the MDS supported Zine El Abidine Ben Ali for re-election as President but challenged the ruling →Democratic Constitutional Rally in the national legislative balloting. Although no MDS candidates were successful on their own, 10 subsequently entered the Chamber of Deputies under the new electoral arrangement guaranteeing the opposition a minimal number of seats. The MDS gained 13 seats in the 1999 elections under electoral reforms which increased the number of seats guaranteed to opposition parties.

Liberal Social Party
Parti Social Liberal (PSL)
Address. c/o Mondher Thabet, 31 Rue des Lys Bellevue, 1001 Tunis
Telephone. (+216–1) 493118
Fax. (+216–1) 336697
Leadership. Mounir Beji (president); Hosni Lahmar (vice-president)
Advocating liberal social and political policies and economic reforms, the PSL was officially recognized as a legal party in September 1988 under the name of the Social Party for Progress (*Parti Social pour le Progrès*, PSP). The party assumed its present name in October 1994. The party was allotted two seats in the Chamber of Deputies following the 1999 legislative elections. It has been an observer member of the Liberal International since 1997.

Popular Union Party
Parti de l'Unité Populaire (PUP)
Address. 7 rue d'Autriche, 1002 Tunis
Telephone. (+216–1) 289678
Fax. (+216–1) 796031
Leadership. Muhammad Bouchire (leader)
The PUP evolved out of a factional conflict within the →Popular Unity Movement over the issue of participation in the 1981 legislative elections. It was officially recognized in 1983 as a legal organization. The party failed to win legislative representation in the elections in 1989, but secured two of the 19 seats proportionally allocated in the Chamber of Deputies to opposition parties in March 1994. In October 1999 Muhammad Belhadj Amor stood as the party candidate in the presidential elections, coming second but with only 0.3% of the vote. The party was allocated seven seats in the Chamber of Deputies following the legislative elections held at the same time.

Renewal Movement
Mouvement de la Rénovation (MR)
Address. 6 Rue Metouia, 1000 Tunis
Leadership. Mohamed Harmel (secretary-general); Mohamed Ali el Halouani (chairman)
Formerly the Tunisian Communist Party (PCT), the MR adopted its new name at an April 1993 congress when it was announced that Marxism had been abandoned as official party doctrine. The PCT had been banned in 1963, regaining legality in 1981. In 1986 it boycotted the legislative elections because it was debarred from presenting a "Democratic Alliance" list with the then illegal Progressive Socialist Rally. The party was critical of the government's emphasis on free-market economic policies but initially welcomed President Ben Ali's political liberalization measures in the late 1980s. However, it subsequently became disillusioned over the lack of progress on full democratization, boycotting the June 1990 municipal elections, having earlier failed to win any seats in the 1989 national legislative poll. No MR candidates were successful in the 1994 elections, although four party members were subsequently seated in the Chamber of Deputies under the new electoral arrangement established for opposition parties. Following the 1999 polling, the party was allotted five legislative seats.

Unionist Democratic Union
Union Démocratique Unioniste (UDU)
Address. c/o Chambre des Députés, Tunis
Leadership. Abderrahmane Tlili (secretary-general)
Legalized in November 1988, the UDU is led by a former member of the →Democratic Constitutional Rally who resigned from the ruling party to promote the unification of various Arab nationalist tendencies in Tunisia. Under the proportional arrangement for opposition parties, three UDU members were seated in the Chamber of Deputies following the March 1994 elections. Tlili stood as the party candidate in the 1999 presidential elections, taking third place with 0.2% of the vote. Seven party members were allocated seats in the Chamber following the legislative polling.

Illegal Groups

Communist Workers' Party (*Parti des Travailleurs Communistes, PTC*), an unrecognized splinter group of the former Tunisian Communist Party.
Leadership. Hamma Hammani

National Arab Rally (*Rassemblement National Arabe, RNA*), banned following its launch in 1981; the organization advocates unity among Arab countries.
Leadership. Bashir Assad

Popular Unity Movement (*Mouvement de l'Unité Populaire, MUP*), formed in 1973 by Ahmed Ben Salah, a former minister who fell out of favour with President Habib Bourguiba and who directed the party from exile. The movement reorganized itself as a political party in 1978 but was unable to gain legal recognition. In 1981 Ben Salah was excluded from a government amnesty and he urged the party not to participate in national elections in that year. This caused a split between his supporters and the faction which broke away to form the →Popular Union Party. Although

Ben Salah returned to Tunisia in 1988, the government refused to restore his civil rights, thereby preventing his participation in national elections. The MUP is a consultative member of the Socialist International.

Renaissance Party (*Hizb al-Nahda/Parti de la Renaissance*), formed in 1981 as the Islamic Tendency Movement (*Mouvement de la Tendance Islamique*, MTI) by fundamentalists inspired by the 1979 Iranian revolution, and renamed in 1989. MTI adherents were harassed under the Bourguiba regime, and although President Ben Ali initially adopted a more conciliatory approach, the movement was denied legal status on the grounds that it remained religion-based. Despite the party's denials of any complicity in violent or revolutionary activity, the government labelled it a terrorist organization in the early 1990s and took repressive action against it, including sentencing its leader in exile to life imprisonment.
Email. nahdha@ezzeitouna.org
Website. www.ezzeitouna.org/annahdha
Leadership. Rachid Ghanouchi (leader); Abd al-Fatha Mourou (secretary-general)

Turkey

Capital: Ankara   **Population:** 67,700,000 (2001E)

Under a new constitution approved by referendum in November 1982, Turkey is a democratic secular state in which legislative authority is vested in a unicameral Grand National Assembly (*Türkiye Büyük Millet Meclisi*) currently of 550 members, who are elected by compulsory universal adult suffrage for a maximum five-year term by a system of proportional representation in 79 multi-member constituencies corresponding to the country's regions. Executive power is exercised by a President and a Council of Ministers headed by a Prime Minister appointed by the President subject to parliamentary approval. The new constitutional arrangements were introduced by the National Security Council (NSC), in power since the military coup of September 1980; in accordance with its provisions, the chairman of the NSC, Gen. Kenan Evren, continued as head of state until 1989, when a new President was elected by the Grand National Assembly for a seven-year term. The 1982 constitution bars the formation of political parties on an ethnic, class or trade union basis, as well as those professing communism, fascism or religious fundamentalism. It also specifies, in Article 96, that Assembly deputies are debarred from changing party allegiance once elected (although this provision has been circumvented by the stratagem of founding new parties and then dissolving them prior to mergers with other parties).

Following a partial lifting of the ban on political activity in April 1983, elections to the Grand National Assembly were held in November 1983 under close supervision by the NSC. By March 1987 martial law had been lifted in all provinces except the four with Kurdish-speaking majorities. Further elections to the Assembly, enlarged from 400 to 450 members, were held in November 1987 under freer conditions, although a stipulation that at least 10% of the valid votes was required for representation restricted the number of parties obtaining seats to three. Prior to those elections, a referendum in September 1987 had produced a narrow majority (50.2%) in favour of lifting the current 10-year ban (until 1992) on over 100 political figures who had been prominent before the 1980 military coup. This decision did not affect the continuing ban on Marxist parties such as the United Communist Party of Turkey (TBLP) or that on militant Kurdish groupings such as the Kurdistan Workers' Party (PKK).

The size of the Assembly was further increased to 550 members in the December 1995 elections. The most recent elections were held on April 18, 1999, and resulted as follows: Democratic Left Party 136 seats (with 22.3% of the vote), Nationalist Action Party 129 (18.1%), Virtue Party 111 seats (15.5%), Motherland Party 86 (13.3%), True Path Party 85 (12.1%), independents 3. The Virtue Party was banned in June 2001, whereupon the Felicity Party and the Justice and Development Party were launched as successor Islamist formations.

Democratic Left Party
Demokratik Sol Partisi (DSP)
Address. Maresal Fevzi Cakmak cad. 17, Besevler, Ankara
Telephone. (+90–312) 212–4950
Fax. (+90–312) 221–3474
Email. info@dsp.org.tr
Website. www.dsp.org.tr
Leadership. Bülent Ecevit (chairman); Hasan Gülay (secretary-general)

The DSP has a social democratic orientation, following the secular and republican principles enunciated by Kemal Atatürk, founder of modern Turkey and of the historic →Republican People's Party (CHP). The DSP was founded in July 1984 mainly by former members of the CHP, which until it was banned following the October 1980 military coup had been led by Bülent Ecevit, who had served two terms as Prime Minister in the 1970s. On the creation in November 1985 of the rival Social Democratic Popular

Party (SHP), the DSP was formally established as a party under the chairmanship of Rahsan Ecevit, wife of the former Prime Minister, who himself remained subject to a 10-year political ban under transitional provisions of the 1982 constitution.

Having accused the SHP of falsely claiming to represent Turkey's social democrats, Rahsan Ecevit in January 1986 concluded an agreement with the conservative →True Path Party (DYP) on the need for a "constitution of national reconciliation". In December 1986 the DSP was joined by 20 SHP Assembly deputies (by way of a short-lived People's Party) and thus was able to form an official parliamentary group (then numbering 23 members). Over this period Bülent Ecevit was prosecuted several times for allegedly contravening the political ban to which he was still subject. However, following a September 1987 referendum decision in favour of lifting the ban, he was elected chairman of the DSP, with his wife becoming his deputy. In the November 1987 Assembly elections the DSP failed to achieve the 10% minimum of the valid votes required for representation, although it headed the list of unsuccessful parties with 8.5% of the vote. After the elections Ecevit announced his intention to resign as DSP chair, this being formally accomplished at a party congress in March 1988, when Necdet Karababa was elected as his successor. In January 1989, however, Ecevit made a comeback, being once again elected DSP leader.

The DSP achieved Assembly representation in the October 1991 elections, although it was allocated only seven seats, whereas the SHP and its allies won 88. The lifting in July 1992 of the ban on organization of the CHP gave rise to a fierce struggle between the DSP and the SHP to acquire the mantle of the historic party, this being "won" by the SHP to the extent that the SHP eventually dissolved itself into the revived CHP. The DSP took its revenge in the December 1995 Assembly elections, decisively out-polling the CHP and advancing strongly to 76 seats on a 14.6% vote share. It then participated in talks between the secular parties on forming a coalition government, but these became deadlocked over who should be the Prime Minister, to which post Ecevit laid claim on the strength of his party's gains. The consequence was that the DSP continued in opposition, initially to a government of the secular centre-right parties and from June 1996 to a coalition of the Islamist Welfare Party (RP) and the secular DYP.

The collapse of the RP–DYP government in June 1997 brought the DSP back to office as junior coalition partner to the →Motherland Party (ANAP). The collapse of this government in November 1998 resulted, after a prolonged political crisis, in Ecevit forming a minority DSP administration in January 1999 pending early general elections, just in time to be able to take the credit for the capture in Kenya of Abdullah Öcalan, leader of the banned Kurdistan Workers' Party (PKK). Held in April 1999, the elections produced a major advance for the DSP, which became the largest party with 136 seats from 22.3% of the vote. Ecevit was therefore able to form a majority coalition with the ANAP and the right-wing Nationalist Action Party (MHP), committed to undertaking long-delayed privatization of the large state-owned sector and to furthering Turkey's candidacy for admission to the European Union.

Two massive earthquakes in north-western Turkey in August and November 1999 threw the Ecevit government's economic policy off course, which was only partially disguised in December by the EU's acceptance of Turkey as an official candidate for membership. In March 2000, moreover, the DSP and the other government parties failed to secure parliamentary approval for constitutional amendments which would have allowed incumbent President Süleyman Demirel to seek a second term. The DSP accordingly joined the other coalition partners in securing the election in May 2000 of Ahmet Necdet Sezer, hitherto president of the Constitutional Court, as Turkey's 10th President.

Political conflict between Ecevit and Sezer quickly developed, culminating in February 2001 in a public clash over the Prime Minister's apparent reluctance to root out corruption in ministerial ranks. The confrontation precipitated Turkey's most serious financial crisis for decades, forcing the devaluation of the currency by more than a third, which in turn provoked widespread anti-government demonstrations as consumer prices rose sharply. Ecevit rejected calls for his resignation, arguing that there was no viable alternative to his government, which embarked upon a more serious attempt to implement economic reforms long demanded by the IMF. It also tabled extensive amendments to the 1982 constitution designed to bring Turkey's judicial and other procedures into line with European norms, in the hope that such reform would expedite accession to the EU.

Felicity Party
Saadet Partisi (SP)

Address. Çetin Emeç Bul. Hürriyet cad. 1/13, Dikmen, Ankara

Leadership. Recai Kutan (chairman)

The Islamist SP (also rendered in English as "Happiness" or "Prosperity" Party) was launched in July 2001 as a successor to the Virtue Party (*Fazilet Partisi*, FP), which in June had become the fourth mainstream Islamist party to be banned since 1971 on the grounds that its activities were in contravention of Turkey's secular constitution. The new conservative-oriented party attracted just under half of the former FP Assembly representatives, the reformist members preferring to join the new →Justice and Development Party (AK).

The sequence of proscribed Islamist parties began with the National Order Party (banned after the 1971 military coup) and continued with the National Salvation Party (banned after the 1980 military coup). Both had been led by Necmettin Erbakan, who in 1983 launched the successor Welfare Party (*Refah Partisi*, RP), which won only 7% of the vote in the 1987 Assembly elections, thus failing to surmount the 10% barrier to representation. Determined to overcome the 10% hurdle in the 1991 elections, the RP headed a joint list with what later became the →Nationalist Action Party (MHP) and the small →Nation Party, the combined slate winning 62 Assembly seats with 17% of the vote. Local elections in March 1994 yielded a doubling of the RP share of the previous such vote in 1989, to 18.3% (and third place in the party order), with its victories including the mayoralties of both Istanbul and Ankara. In Istanbul the new RP mayor was Reçep Yayyıp Erdogan, who quickly achieved wide popularity for his dynamic approach.

The problems of the post-1991 centre-left coalition government of the →True Path Party (DYP) and what became the →Republican People's Party (CHP) assisted the RP cause in the December 1995 Assembly elections. The party startled foreign observers by achieving a clear plurality of 158 seats (out of 550) with a vote share of 21.4%, thus establishing its right to take national government responsibility. The response of the DYP was to conclude a coalition agreement with the →Motherland Party (ANAP), as the other major conservative secular party. But this arrangement broke down by May 1996, with the result that the RP was able to reach a coalition agreement with the DYP under which Erbakan became Turkey's first Islamist government leader since the demise of the Ottoman Empire.

On taking office in June 1996, Erbakan sought to allay fears about the RP's intentions by stressing that "the Turkish Republic is a democratic, secular and social state based on law and the principles of Atatürk". At the same time, he indicated that Turkey's long-standing pro-Western orientation would now have the admixture of closer co-operation with Islamic countries, particularly those of central Asia and the Balkans. Such assurances did not satisfy the powerful and intensely secular military leadership, which eventually engineered Erbakan's resignation in June 1997, following which the party went into opposition facing an official challenge to its constitutional legality.

The outcome was a decision by the Constitutional Court in January 1998 to ban the RP, on grounds of the party's "hidden" Islamic fundamentalist agenda and its "conspiracies" against the secular order. Erbakan and six other RP leaders were barred from holding any political office for five years. The following month some former 100 RP deputies declared their allegiance to the recently formed Virtue Party (FP), which thus became the largest single party in the Assembly. In early parliamentary elections in April 1999, however, the FP slipped to third place with 111 seats and 15.5% of the vote, some of the party's support switching to the →Nationalist Action Party (MHP). As the FP began a further period of opposition, the Chief Prosecutor launched banning proceedings against the party, the final straw having apparently been the wearing of the Islamic headscarf by a female FP deputy when she arrived for her investiture.

The FP then experienced bitter internal feuding, with Erbakan continuing to hold sway over the party and backing conservative chairman Recai Kutan in successfully resisting a leadership challenge by FP reformists. Erbakan himself was sentenced to a year's imprisonment in March 2000 for making an inflammatory speech in 1994, later becoming the subject of an arrest warrant when he ignored an appeal court ruling upholding the sentence. There was little surprise, therefore, when the Constitutional Court in June 2001 banned the FP, although without accepting the prosecution's demand that all FP deputies should lose their Assembly seats. Instead, the Court expelled only the 1999 headscarf wearer and her sponsor, ruling that the other FP deputies should cease to have FP affiliation. Kutan described the banning as "a blow to Turkey's search for democracy and law", while Prime Minister Bülent Ecevit of the →Democratic Left Party (DSP) regretted the decision because of its potential for destabilization at a time of grave economic difficulty.

Following precedent, Kutan responded by launching the new Felicity Party (SP) in July 2001, receiving the backing of Erbakan (who remained unarrested) for an Islamist party with a conservative orientation. Kutan said that the SP would not challenge the principles of the secular state but would seek to further religious rights, including legalization of the wearing of Islamic headscarves in schools and public offices. By late September 2001 the SP had been joined by 48 former FP deputies, whereas 52 had opted for the reformist AK.

Justice and Development Party
Adalet ve Kalkinma Partisi (AK)
Address. Ceyhun Atif cad. 202, Balgat, Ankara
Leadership. Reçep Yayyıp Erdogan (chairman)
The Islamist AK (also rendered in English as "Justice and Progress Party") was launched in August 2001 as a reformist successor to the Virtue Party (*Fazilet Partisi*, FP), which in June had become the fourth mainstream Islamist party to be banned since 1971 on the grounds that it contravened Turkey's secular constitution. The new party's AK abbreviation means "white" or "clean" in Turkish. Led by the popular former FP mayor of Istanbul, Reçep Yayyıp Erdogan, the AK had by late September 2001 been joined by 52 former FP Assembly deputies, whereas 48 had opted for the more conservative →Felicity Party, which claimed to be the real successor to the FP.

Elected mayor of Istanbul in 1994, Erdogan had been banned from politics in 1998 for inciting religious hatred (by reciting a poem with an Islamic message) and had served four months in prison in 1999 before benefiting from a 2000 amnesty law allowing him to resume political activity. On launching the AK, Erdogan distanced the new party from the previous FP and declared that it would be truly democratic and financially transparent and would seek a reconciliation between Turkey's Islamic traditions and Western democratic values. He also declared the party's support for Turkish membership of the European Union.

Motherland Party
Anavatan Partisi (ANAP)
Address. Karsisi 13 cad. 3, Balgat, Ankara
Telephone. (+90–312) 286–5000
Fax. (+90–312) 286–5019
Email. anavatan@anap.org.tr
Website. www.anap.org.tr
Leadership. Mesut Yılmaz (chairman); Yaşar Okuyan (secretary-general)
Founded in May 1983 by former senior minister Turgut Özal, the conservative and nationalist ANAP aspires to occupy the political ground held by the pre-1980 Justice Party. It supports a free market economy and closer relations with other Islamic countries, while favouring Turkish accession to the European Union. Launched in the wake of the partial restoration of open political activity in March 1983, the ANAP had some initial skirmishes with the military but was allowed to contest the November 1983 Assembly elections. It won an absolute majority (212 of the 400 seats) against two other parties, whereupon Özal became Prime Minister.

By now favoured by the military as a guarantor of political stability, the ANAP subsequently experienced internal dissension between its moderate and Islamist factions; but the party was strengthened by the adherence of 22 independent Assembly deputies in May 1986, following the dissolution of the Nationalist Democracy Party (MDP). In December 1986, moreover, the small Free Democratic Party, founded in May 1986 by other independent deputies who had in many cases previously been members of the MDP, decided to merge with the ANAP, although about a quarter of the FDP Assembly contingent of some 20 deputies decided instead to join the →True Path Party (DYP).

In the November 1987 Assembly elections, the ANAP retained its overall majority, winning 292 of the 450 seats on the strength of 36.3% of the vote. The following month Özal formed a new government notable for the inclusion of two prominent liberals (one of them his own younger brother, Yusuf Özal) and for the exclusion (apparently at the insistence of President Evren) of the then ANAP deputy chairman, Mehmet Kececiler, a prominent Islamic fundamentalist. Prime Minister Özal in 1988 proposed a merger between the ANAP and the DYP, with the aim of creating a parliamentary majority large enough to pass constitutional amendments without need to obtain referendum endorsement. He was rebuffed by the DYP, however, whose then leader, Süleyman Demirel, described Özal as "a calamity for the nation".

On Özal's elevation to the presidency in November 1989, he effectively conferred the succession to the ANAP leadership and premiership on the Assembly's Speaker, Yıldırım Akbulut. Amid deteriorating economic conditions, Akbulut presided over a catastrophic slump in the ANAP's popular standing, not least because of a furore surrounding the installation of the President's wife, Semra Özal, as chairperson of the ANAP's powerful Istanbul section in April 1991. Although supposedly now above party politics, President Özal continued to pull the ANAP strings through his wife and others, as evidenced in June 1991 when Akbulut was defeated in an ANAP leadership contest by Mesut Yılmaz (a former Foreign Minister), who thus became Prime Minister. Persuaded to call early general elections in October 1991, Yılmaz led the ANAP to comprehensive defeat, its Assembly representation slumping from 275 to 115 seats (out of 450), on a vote share of 24%.

In opposition to a centre-left coalition headed by the DYP, the ANAP experienced much factionalism and lost its founder and supreme leader when President Özal died of a heart attack in April 1993. Despite the travails of the resultant Çiller government, the ANAP came under increasing challenge on the conservative/Islamist right from the Welfare Party (RP), to which it lost heavily in local elections in March 1994. When the Çiller government collapsed in September 1995, personal antipathy between Yılmaz and Turkey's first female leader at that stage precluded the obvious solution of an ANAP/DYP coalition. General elections in December 1995 served to chasten both secular centre-right parties but the ANAP at least gained seats on the strength of the expansion of the Assembly complement from 450 to 550 members, returning 132 on a reduced vote of 19.7%.

In protracted post-election negotiations, the ANAP found no basis for co-operation with the RP; instead, Yılmaz and Çiller were sufficiently reconciled to enable the formation of an ANAP/DYP coalition in March 1996, with the ANAP leader taking first turn as Prime Minister. He had only three months in the top political job, however, being forced to resign in early June after the DYP had withdrawn from the coalition in late May when Yılmaz declined to back Çiller against allegations of corruption under her recent premiership. The upshot was that the ANAP again found itself in opposition, this time to a coalition of the RP and the DYP. In local elections in June 1996 the ANAP improved marginally on its general election performance, to 21% of the vote, but was again out-polled by the RP.

The collapse of the RP/DYP government in June 1997 brought Yılmaz back to the premiership, heading a coalition with the →Democratic Left Party (DSP) and the small →Democratic Turkey Party. This government collapsed in November 1998 on losing a vote of confidence arising from corruption allegations against some ministers. The ANAP then agreed to give external support to a caretaker DSP administration pending early general elections in April 1999. These produced a further setback for the ANAP, which fell back to 86 seats and 13.3% of the vote. It therefore accepted the status of junior partner in a three-party coalition headed by the DSP and also including the ultra-nationalist →Nationalist Action Party.

Parliamentary investigation of the conduct of the recent Yılmaz governments resulted in a recommendation in June 2000 that the ANAP leader should be arraigned before the supreme court on corruption and abuse of power charges. However, the full Assembly voted to reject the recommendation, the other coalition parties rallying to Yılmaz's defence in the interests of preserving the coalition. In July 2000 Yılmaz was appointed Deputy Prime Minister with responsibility for EU affairs.

The ANAP is a member of the European Democrat Union.

Nationalist Action Party
Milliyetçi Hareket Partisi (MHP)
Address. Strazburg cad. 36, Sihhiye, Ankara
Telephone. (+90–312) 231–8700
Fax. (+90–312) 231–1424
Website. www.mhp.org.tr
Leadership. Devlet Bahçeli (chairman); Koray Aydin (secretary-general)

The ultra-nationalist and mainly secular MHP dates from 1948 and was known until 1969 as the Republican Peasant Nation Party. Under the leadership of Alpaslan Türkes, the MHP was linked in the 1970s with the radical "Hearths of the Ideal" movement, whose militants were known as the Grey Wolves and were heavily involved in murders of leftists and Kurdish activists. Banned in 1980, the party was revived by its adherents in 1985 as the Nationalist Labour Party (MÇP), which reverted to the MHP title in 1992. The MHP failed to surmount the 10% barrier in the 1995 Assembly elections, winning 8.2% of the vote.

The death of Türkes in April 1997 (at the age of 80) and the election of Devlet Bahçeli as chairman brought a new generation to the MHP leadership. Benefiting from nationalist euphoria generated by the capture of Kurdish separatist leader Abdullah Öcalan, the MHP achieved a major breakthrough in the April 1999 Assembly elections, winning 129 seats from an 18.1% vote share and becoming the second largest parliamentary party. Its reward was inclusion in a

majority three-party government headed by the →Democratic Left Party (DSP) and also including the →Motherland Party (ANAP), with Bahçeli becoming a Deputy Prime Minister.

Coalition relations became increasingly strained in 2000 over corruption allegations against certain ministers, including Public Works and Housing Minister Koray Aydin of the MHP. Aydin and the others survived in their posts, mainly because of Prime Minister Ecevit's desire to preserve the coalition. But the price paid by Turkey was the massive financial crisis and devaluation of February 2001. In the wake of the crisis, MHP ministers and deputies were prominent in the resistance to IMF-decreed economic restructuring, notably to the privatization of the telecommunications sector, over which the MHP Minister of Transport and Communications, Enis Öksüz, resigned in July 2001.

Republican People's Party
Cumhuriyet Halk Partisi (CHP)
Address. Çevre Sok. 38, Cankaya, Ankara
Telephone. (+90–312) 468–5969
Fax. (+90–312) 468–5969
Email. info@chp.org.tr
Website. www.chp.org.tr
Leadership. Altan Öymen (chairman); Tarhan Erdem (general secretary)

The original CHP was established in 1923 by Kemal Atatürk, the founder of modern Turkey, and became the country's main force for modernization and secularization. It was the only political party until 1946, thereafter becoming a mainstream moderate left-wing formation which was in power in the 1970s under the premiership of Bülent Ecevit but was proscribed following the 1980 military coup. Successor parties included the Social Democratic Popular Party (SHP), the forerunner of the CHP, as well as the →Democratic Left Party (DSP) led by Ecevit.

Founded in November 1985, the SHP was a merger of the Popular Party (PP) and the Social Democratic Party (SODEP) led by Prof. Erdal Inönü (son of former President Ismet Inönü, a pre-1980 leader of the CHP). Of these, the PP had been formed in May 1983 under the leadership of Necdet Calp and became the main parliamentary opposition party in the November 1983 elections, winning 117 of the 400 Assembly seats and about 30% of the vote, in part because other left-wing parties had been excluded from participation. Thereafter the PP had become divided as to its future strategy, and Calp was replaced in June 1985 by Prof. Aydin Guven Gurkan, who at first explored the possibility of a merger with the DSP but in July 1985 signed a unity protocol with SODEP under which the latter would be absorbed into the PP's legal structure. Meanwhile, a proposal that SODEP should itself unite with the DSP had also proved abortive. On the formal accomplishment of the PP-SODEP merger (in November 1985), a number of PP Assembly deputies resigned from the party in protest; nevertheless, the new formation was the largest opposition group in the Assembly at that point.

Prof. Inönü replaced Prof. Guven Gurken as leader of the new SHP at its first congress in June 1986 and in September 1986 was elected to the Grand National Assembly in one of a series of by-elections in which the SHP polled 22.7% of the vote. In December 1986 the SHP was weakened by the defection of 20 of its Assembly deputies to the DSP (via a short-lived People's Party). Nevertheless, in the November 1987 Assembly elections the SHP emerged as substantially the strongest left-wing party (and still the main parliamentary opposition), winning 99 of the 450 seats and 24.8% of the vote. It was further weakened in late 1989 when 10 Kurdish SHP deputies left the party in protest against the earlier expulsion of seven Kurdish deputies who had participated in a Kurdish conference in Paris in defiance of party policy. However, the People's Labour Party (*Halkim Emek Partisi*, HEP) formed by these dissidents in June 1990 contested the October 1991 Assembly elections on a joint list with the SHP, their respective seat tallies being 22 and 66. The outcome was that the SHP became the junior partner in a coalition with the →True Path Party (DYP) committed to an ambitious programme of economic and social reform.

The SHP's role as guarantor of a parliamentary majority for the DYP became increasingly difficult in 1992–93. First, most of the HEP contingent opted for independence, forming the Democracy Party (*Demokrasi Partisi*, DP) when the HEP was banned in June 1993 and the →People's Democracy Party (HADEP) when the DP was banned in June 1994. Second, the lifting of the official ban on the CHP in July 1992 divided the SHP between those who wished to return to the banner of the historic party and those preferring to maintain the SHP as the authentic successor to the CHP. The formal re-launching of the CHP in September 1992, under the leadership of Demiz Baykal and with 21 SHP deputies declaring support, added to the flux. By June 1993 Inönü was ready to announce his retirement, being succeeded in September by Murat Karayalcins both as party leader and as Deputy Prime Minister. More infighting ensued, until in February 1995 the SHP was formally merged into the CHP under the chairmanship of Hikmet Çetin, a former SHP Foreign Minister and an ethnic Kurd. After some initial uncertainty, the CHP became the DYP's junior coalition partner, with changes in its ministerial team that included the return of Inönü as Foreign Minister.

Participation in an unpopular government became increasingly unpopular in the CHP, which in September 1995 restored Baykal to the leadership on a pledge, carried out immediately, to take the party out of the ruling coalition. In the resultant general elections in December 1995, the CHP was punished by the electorate, winning only 10.7% of the vote and 49 seats, well behind the DSP. Discussions on a broad-based coalition of secular parties (including the CHP and the DSP) came to nothing, so the CHP went into opposition, first to a coalition of the →Motherland Party (ANAP) and the DYP and from June 1996 to one of the Islamist Welfare Party (RP) and the DYP.

From July 1997 the CHP gave external support to a new minority coalition government headed by the ANAP and including the DSP. In November 1998, however, the CHP was instrumental in moving the no confidence motion which brought down the government on grounds of ministerial corruption. This action yielded no reward for the CHP in early Assembly elections in April 1999, in which it fell below the 10% threshold with 8.9% of the vote and so became an extra-parliamentary party for the first time since its foundation by Atatürk. Baykal took responsibility for the defeat by resigning as CHP chairman, being succeeded by Altan Öymen, a prominent journalist and former Tourism Minister.

The CHP is a member party of the Socialist International.

True Path Party
Doğru Yol Partisi (DYP)

Address. Selanik cad. 40, Kizilay, Ankara
Telephone. (+90–312) 417–2241
Fax. (+90–312) 418–5657
Email. info@dyp.org.tr
Website. www.dyp.org.tr
Leadership. Tansu Çiller (chairperson); Nurhan Tekinel (secretary-general)

The moderate conservative DYP was founded in May 1983 with the aim of occupying the same political ground as the pre-1980 Justice Party, which had been in government at the time of the October 1980 military coup under the premiership of Süleyman Demirel. The latter was regarded as the principal influence behind the new party (of which Yıldırım Avçi became the first leader), although at that stage he was barred from political activity by a 10-year ban applied to prominent pre-1980 politicians under transitional provisions of the 1982 constitution. After being excluded from the 1983 Assembly elections, the DYP took part in local

elections in March 1984, coming in third place with some 13.5% of the vote. The following month the state prosecutor applied to the Constitutional Court for a ruling that the DYP should be closed down on the grounds that it was in fact a continuation of a banned party; but this application was rejected by the court in September 1984.

In January 1986 the then DYP leader, Husamettin Çindoruk (who had succeeded Avçi in May 1985), signed an agreement with the then leader of the →Democratic Left Party (DSP), Rahsan Ecevit, on the need for a "constitution of reconciliation". In May 1986 the DYP was strengthened by the adherence of about 20 independent Assembly deputies, most of whom had previously been members of the Nationalist Democracy Party prior to its dissolution earlier that month. Moreover, in December 1986 not only did a majority faction of the small Citizens' Party formed in March 1986 as a breakaway from the then ruling →Motherland Party (ANAP) decide to merge with the DYP but also five Assembly members of the Free Democratic Party disregarded a majority decision to merge with the ANAP and instead joined the DYP.

Süleyman Demirel assumed the leadership of the DYP in September 1987, following a referendum decision that month in favour of lifting the existing ban on him and other pre-1980 political leaders. In the Assembly elections of November 1987 the DYP came in third place (of only three parties which secured representation), with 59 of the 450 seats and 19.3% of the vote. It therefore remained in opposition to another government of the ANAP, which became increasingly erratic after Prime Minister Özal's elevation to the presidency in November 1989. In the October 1991 Assembly elections the DYP became the leading party, winning 178 of the 450 seats and thereafter forming a coalition with the Social Democratic Popular Party (which later merged into the revived →Republican People's Party, CHP), under the premiership of Demirel.

Demirel was elected President in May 1993 following Özal's death in office the previous month, being succeeded as DYP leader and Prime Minister by Tansu Çiller, a youngish American-educated economics professor, who defeated two other candidates to become Turkey's first woman leader. She brought in a new generation of DYP ministers, but economic woes, never-ending Kurdish insurgency in the south-east and an unstable junior coalition partner were only some of the problems with which she had to contend. The CHP's abrupt exit from the government in September 1995 precipitated general elections in December, when the DYP slumped to 135 seats (in an Assembly enlarged by 100 seats) and a vote share of 19.2%, being overtaken as the largest party by the Islamist Welfare Party (RP).

Faced with the RP challenge, Çiller briefly overcame her personal differences with ANAP leader Mesut Yılmaz and in March 1996 took the DYP into a coalition with the other conservative secular party, with Yılmaz being accorded first occupancy of the premiership under an agreement that it would revert to the DYP later on. This part of the coalition agreement was not tested, however, because Çiller and Yılmaz quickly rediscovered their personal antipathy. When the latter declined to back Çiller over corruption allegations against her, the DYP withdrew from the coalition in May 1996 on a technical constitutional issue, forcing Yılmaz to resign. Çiller then sank her previous distaste for the policies of the Islamist RP, agreeing that the DYP should be the junior coalition partner in the first Islamist-led government of modern Turkey.

Much opposed by some DYP factions, the RP-DYP coalition collapsed in June 1997, after which the DYP went into opposition. The party gave external support to a DSP minority government formed in advance of early Assembly elections in April 1999, in which the DSP declined to 85 seats and 12.1% of the vote. The party thereafter formed part of the parliamentary opposition to a new government headed by the DSP.

The DYP is a member of the European Democrat Union.

Other Parties

The listing below focuses on parties that contested the April 1999 parliamentary elections without winning representation.

Changing Turkey Party (*Değişen Türkiye Partisi, DEPAR*), founded in February 1998, won 0.1% in 1999 elections.
Address. Cad. 6/78, Sok. 15/2, Öveçler, Ankara
Telephone. (+90–312) 478–4566

Democracy and Peace Party (*Demokrasi ve Barış Partisi, DBP*), founded in March 1996 to advocate Kurdish autonomy, won only 0.1% of the vote in 1999.
Address. Menekşe sok. 10A/7, Kızılay, Ankara
Leadership. Yılmaz Çamlıbel (chairman)

Democratic Party (*Demokrat Partisi, DP*), founded in November 1992, won 0.3% in 1999 elections.
Address. Ziyabey cad. 3, Sok. 26/456, Balgat, Ankara
Telephone. (+90–312) 285–9515
Leadership. Yalçın Koçak (chairman)

Democratic Turkey Party (*Demokrat Türkiye Partisi, DTP*), founded in January 1997, won 0.6% in 1999 elections.
Address. Mesnevi Sok. 27, Ankara
Telephone. (+90–312) 442–0151
Leadership. Ismet Sezgin (chairman)

Freedom and Solidarity Party (*Özgürlük ve Dayanışma Partisi, ÖDP*), environmentalist formation founded in 1996, won 0.8% in 1999.
Address. Necatibey cad. 23/11, Sıhhıye, Ankara
Telephone. (+90–312) 229–9706
Leadership. Mohammed Ufuk Uras (chairman)

Grand Union Party (*Buyuk Birlik Partisi, BBP*), formed in 1993, won a creditable 1.5% of the vote 1999.
Address. Tuna cad. 28, Yenişehir, Ankara
Telephone. (+90–312) 434–0920
Leadership. Muhsin Yazıcıoğlu (chairman)

Labour Party (*Emeğin Partisi, IP*), left-wing formation founded in November 1996, won 0.2% in 1999.
Address. Karanfil sok. 11/12, Kızılay, Ankara
Leadership. Abdullah Levent Tüzel (chairman)

Liberal Democratic Party (*Liberal Demokrat Partisi, LDP*), founded in July 1994, won 0.4% in 1999 elections; observer member of Liberal International.
Address. G.M.K. Bulvari 198/18, Maltepe, Ankara
Telephone. (+90–312) 232–3374
Leadership. Besim Tibuk (chairman)

Nation Party (*Millet Partisi, MP*), founded in 1992 as successor to the centre-right Reformist Democracy Party (IDP), itself descended from the original MP; obtained 0.5% of the national vote in 1995 and 0.3% in 1999.
Address. Rüzgarli Mah. Gayret sok 2, Ulus, Ankara
Leadership. Aykut Edibali (chairman)

People's Democracy Party (*Halkin Demokrasi Partisi, HADEP*), moderate Kurdish formation created in 1995 as successor to the Democratic Party (banned in June 1994), which was itself successor to the People's Labour Party (banned in July 1993), which had contested the 1991 elections on a joint list with the Social Democratic Popular Party (later merged into the →Republican People's Party). HADEP obtained 4.2% (and no seats) in the 1995 elections, thereafter coming under official pressure in 1996, being accused of "leadership of an armed gang". The party won 4.7% of the vote and no seats in 1999. In February 2000 then leader Ahmet Turan Demir and 17 other HADEP activists received four-year prison sentences for aiding and abetting the banned Kurdistan Workers' Party (KPP).
Address. 2 Cad. 32 Sok. 37, Balgat, Ankara
Telephone. (+90–312) 285–2200
Leadership. Murat Bozlak (chairman)

Renaissance Party (*Yeniden Doğuş Partisi, YDP*), obtained 0.3% of the national vote in 1995 and 0.1% in 1999.
Address. Ziyabey cad. 52/3, Balgat, Ankara
Telephone. (+90–312) 285–2002
Leadership. Ahmet Rü_tü Çelebi (chairman)

Socialist Rule Party (*Sosyalist Iktidar Partisi, SIP*), founded in November 1992, won 0.1% in 1999 elections.
Address. G.M.K. Bulvarı 42/7, Maltepe, Ankara
Telephone. (+90–312) 231–4238
Leadership. Aydemir Güler (chairman)

Workers' Party (*Işçi Partisi, IP*), founded in March 1992, won 0.2% in 1999 elections.
Address. Mithatpaşa cad. 10/8, Sıhhiye, Ankara
Telephone. (+90–312) 430–4123
Leadership. Doğu Perinçek (chairman)

Turkmenistan

Capital: Ashkhabad

Population: 5,100,000 (2001E)

The Turkmen Soviet Socialist Republic declared independence from the USSR in October 1991 as the Republic of Turkmenistan. It became a sovereign member of the Commonwealth of Independent States (CIS) in December 1991. A new constitution was adopted in May 1992, providing for an executive President as head of state and government. Legislative authority is vested in the 50-member Assembly (*Majlis*), elected by popular vote for a five-year term. A non-legislative People's Council (*Khalk Maslakhaty*) is the supreme representative and supervisory body, consisting of 50 directly elected members as well as the 50 *Majlis* deputies, the members of the Council of Ministers, 10 appointed regional representatives and other senior executive and judicial officials. The Communist Party of Turkmenistan was transformed into the Democratic Party of Turkmenistan (DPT) on the eve of the demise of the USSR.

A presidential election on June 21, 1992, resulted in incumbent head of state Saparmurad Niyazov (former First Secretary of the Communist Party of Turkmenistan) being elected unopposed. In a referendum on Jan. 15, 1994, almost unanimous approval was given to a proposal that Niyazov's term of office be extended until January 1999, so that he was not required to seek re-election in 1997. On Dec. 28, 1999, moreover, the *Majlis* voted unanimously in favour of a recommendation by the People's Council that there should be no limit to Niyazov's term of office.

Although the 1992 constitution allows for multi-partyism, the DPT remains the only party with legal status, attempts to create opposition formations having quickly withered. Elections to the *Majlis* on Dec. 11, 1994, and Dec. 12, 1999, accordingly endorsed the DPT as the sole legislative party, although on the latter occasion the 50 seats were contested by 102 DPT candidates. After the December 1999 elections, President Niyazov ruled out the legalization of other parties for at least a decade.

Democratic Party of Turkmenistan (DPT)
Address. 28 Gogolya Street, 744014 Ashkhabad 14
Telephone. (+7–3632) 251212
Leadership. Saparmurad Niyazov (chairman)
The DPT was founded in November 1991 as in effect the successor to the former ruling Communist Party (CP) of the Turkmen SSR, which had been suspended immediately after the attempted coup by hardliners in Moscow in August 1991 and was officially dissolved by decision of its 25th congress on Dec 16, 1991. At its inauguration, the DPT distanced itself from its predecessor's "mistakes" but declared itself to be the country's "mother party", dominating all political activity but seeking to engender a "loyal" political opposition. In succeeding years very little of the latter made its presence felt, as the DPT maintained a grip on power every bit as firm as that exercised by its predecessor.

In February 1992 President Niyazov gave an outline of his version of a multi-party system in Turkmenistan, suggesting that former CP officials and supporters in rural areas should set up a peasant party, and that everyone else should join the DPT. In a further pronouncement in December 1993, the President said that a peasants' party would be granted official registration as the first step towards a multi-party system. In the event, however, registration was not granted.

As the only legal party, the DPT retained its legislative monopoly in elections to the *Majlis* in December 1994 and December 1999. Amidst a burgeoning cult of personality surrounding the former general turned politician, Niyazov was in December 1999 effectively confirmed as having life tenure of the presidency, without need of re-election. In February 2001 Niyazov said that the next presidential elections would be held in 2010 and confirmed that no other parties would be legalized until then.

Tuvalu

Capital: Fongafale (Funafuti atoll) **Population:** 10,000 (2000E)

Tuvalu, formerly the Ellice Islands, became a fully independent country in 1978. The head of state is the British sovereign, represented by a Governor-General. Legislative authority is vested in a unicameral Parliament (*Parlamene o Tuvalu*) of 13 members, 12 of whom are popularly elected for up to four years. Executive power is exercised by a Cabinet drawn from, and answerable to, Parliament, and headed by a Prime Minister elected by Parliament. There are no political parties in Tuvalu, where members of Parliament tend to be aligned with the leading political personalities. The most recent elections, held on March 26, 1998, featured much trading of allegations of sexual and financial misconduct between prominent candidates.

Uganda

Capital: Kampala **Population:** 23,317,500 (2000E)

Uganda became an independent state in 1962 after some 70 years of British rule, a republic being instituted in 1967. In 1971 President Milton Obote and his Uganda People's Congress (UPC) regime were deposed by Idi Amin Dada, whose military government was in turn overthrown in 1979 following internal rebellion and military intervention by Tanzania. General elections were held the following year in which Obote and the UPC were returned to power. The current President, Yoweri Museveni, assumed power in January 1986 as leader of the National Resistance Movement (NRM). The NRM had waged a guerrilla war since 1981, firstly against the Obote government and subsequently against the military regime which deposed Obote in July 1985.

Although political activity is banned, political parties are permitted to exist and the main traditional groupings, the UPC and the Democratic Party, have been represented in the NRM-dominated government. In 1993 the Government published a draft constitution. The following year a Constituent Assembly was elected, on a non-party basis, to debate, amend and enact the new constitution. Having extended the NRM's term of office in November 1994, the Assembly voted in June 1995 to retain the current system of non-party government. The constitution came into effect in October 1995, after which the Constituent Assembly was disbanded.

In non-party presidential and legislative elections on May 9 and June 27, 1996, respectively, President Museveni was victorious in the former with 74.2% of the vote, while the latter resulted in presidential supporters winning a majority in the new 276-seat unicameral Parliament. On June 29, 2000, the continuation of the existing non-party political system (known officially as the Movement system) was approved by 90.7% of the vote in a national referendum, with only 9.3% of voters favouring a return to a multi-party system. However, opposition forces boycotted the referendum and there was a turnout of only 47.2%. President Museveni was re-elected with 69.3% of the vote in a presidential election held on March 12, 2001. Kizza Besigye, the runner-up (with 27.8% of the vote), claimed that the conduct of the election had been "massively fraudulent". There were four other candidates in the election. Besigye, a former NRM colleague of Museveni, had accused the incumbent President of heading a corrupt and nepotistic administration.

Democratic Party (DP)
Address. PO Box 458, Kampala
Telephone. (+256–41) 344155
Email. ssemo2@swiftuganda.com
Website. www.framework.co.za/dua/uganda/dp
Leadership. Paul Ssemogerere (president general); Byanyima Boniface (chairman)
The DP was founded in 1954, attracting strong Roman Catholic support in southern Uganda. Having been banned from the late 1960s, it became the main opposition party to the →Uganda People's Congress (UPC) following the parliamentary elections held in December 1980. After the assumption of power by the →National Resistance Movement (NRM) in 1986, the DP was represented in the coalition government under President Museveni. Party leader Ssemogerere, who had continued to campaign against NRM dominance and against the regime's refusal to move more quickly to a multi-party system, resigned his post as Second Deputy Prime Minister and Minister of Public Service in June 1995, announcing that he would contest planned presidential elections as the DP candidate. In the event, under the October 1995 constitution party labels were barred in the May 1996 presidential elections, in which Ssemogerere came a poor second to the incumbent with only 23.7% of the vote. Factors damaging his cause reportedly included his gravitation to an alliance with the unpopular Milton Obote's UPC and his reluctance to make outright condemnation of the militant anti-government Lord's Resistance Army. In the March 2001 presidential election Ssemogerere urged DP members to vote for Kizza Besigye, who was seen as the strongest challenger to Museveni.

The DP is affiliated to the Christian Democrat International and the Democrat Union of Africa.

National Resistance Movement (NRM)
Address. c/o Parliamentary Buildings, PO Box 7178, Kampala
Leadership. Yoweri Museveni (leader); Samson Kisekka (chairman)
The NRM was founded in early 1981 as the political wing of the guerrilla National Resistance Army in opposition to the Obote government. The armed struggle had been launched when the political party formed by Museveni in mid-1980 (the →Uganda Patriotic Movement) was deemed to have won only one seat in the December 1980 legislative elections. The NRM assumed power in early 1986, ousting the short-lived military regime which had deposed Obote, and has since been the dominant force within government.

Uganda Patriotic Movement (UPM)
Leadership. Jaberi Ssali (secretary-general)
Co-founded by Yoweri Museveni in 1980, the UPM controversially won only a single seat in the December 1980 legislative elections, prompting a subsequent guerrilla struggle against the Obote government. Having dissolved upon Museveni's formation of the National Resistance Movement, the UPM re-emerged after the NRM took control in 1986 and several of its members were accorded ministerial positions.

Uganda People's Congress (UPC)
Address. PO Box 1951, Kampala
Website. www.members.home.net/upc
Leadership. Milton Obote (leader in exile); James Rwanyarare (national leader)
The UPC is a mainly Protestant formation, with a socialist-based philosophy, dating from 1960. It led the country to independence in 1962 under Milton Obote and was the ruling party until overthrown in 1971. The UPC returned to power, after the ousting of Idi Amin, with a disputed victory in the December 1980 elections. Obote was again overthrown by the military in 1985, but UPC adherents were included within the broad-based government established by Museveni after the →National Resistance Movement assumed power in early 1986. Friction has persisted between the government and Obote loyalists, and a number of UPC offshoots have reportedly taken up armed resistance to the Museveni government. In May 1999 Museveni announced that Obote would be permitted to return to Uganda, if he so wished, under the terms of a current amnesty for all exiles. Obote chose to remain in exile and to urge his supporters to oppose Museveni. In the non-party presidential election of March 12, 2001, Aggrey Awari, an MP who was a member of the UPC, was placed third with 1.4% of the vote.

Ukraine

Capital: Kyiv (Kiev)   **Population:** 49,500,000 (2000E)

The Ukrainian Soviet Socialist Republic declared independence from the USSR in August 1991 as Ukraine, which became a sovereign member of the Commonwealth of Independent States (CIS) in December 1991. A new constitution adopted in June 1996 defines Ukraine as a democratic pluralist state and recognizes the right to private ownership of property, including land. It vests substantial powers in the executive President, who is directly elected for a five-year term and who nominates the Prime Minister and other members of the government, for approval by the legislature. Legislative authority is vested in a Supreme Council (*Verkhovna Rada*) of 450 members, who are elected for a four-year term by universal adult suffrage. Under an amendment to the Electoral Law adopted in October 1997, half of the Supreme Council deputies are elected by majority vote in single-member constituencies and the other 225 from party lists by proportional representation subject to a threshold of 4% of the national vote.

Elections to the Supreme Council on March 29, 1998, resulted in 445 of the 450 seats being validly filled, as follows: Communist Party of Ukraine (KPU) 121 seats (with 24.7% of the proportional vote), Popular Movement of Ukraine (*Rukh*) 46 (9.4%), a joint list of the Socialist Party of Ukraine and the Peasants' Party of Ukraine 34

(8.6%), Popular Democratic Party 28 (5.0%), *Hromada* All-Ukrainian Association 24 (4.7%), Green Party of Ukraine 19 (5.4%), Social Democratic Party of Ukraine–United 17 (2.9%), Progressive Socialist Party 16 (2.5%), Agrarian Party of Ukraine 9 (3.7%), National Front 5 (2.7%), Party of Reforms and Order 3 (3.1%), Forward Ukraine! 2 (1.7%), Christian Democratic Party of Ukraine 2 (1.3%), Party of Regional Revival 2 (0.9%), six other parties or alliances 6, independents 111. Most of the independents joined parliamentary groups set up by the main parties, with the result that the centre-right factions commanded an overall majority, although the composition and names of the groups changed continually in the post-1998 parliamentary term.

In presidential elections on Oct. 31 and Nov. 14, 1999, incumbent Leonid Kuchma, standing without party affiliation, was re-elected for a second term with 56.3% of the valid second-round vote against 37.8% for the KPU candidate.

In a referendum on April 16, 2000, President Kuchma obtained overwhelming popular approval for proposed constitutional amendments providing for a bicameral parliament, a reduction in the size of the Supreme Council from 450 to 300 members, reduced parliamentary immunity from prosecution and enhanced presidential powers of dissolution. By late 2001, however, none of these proposed changes had secured the necessary parliamentary approval, whilst a new Electoral Law adopted by the Supreme Council in January 2001, under which all seats would be allocated by proportional representation, was vetoed by President Kuchma in March, following which the Council in May 2001 failed to muster the two-thirds majority needed to override the veto.

Agrarian Party of Ukraine
Ahrarna Partiya Ukrainy (APU)
Address. 16 Mechnikova St., Kyiv
Leadership. Mykhaylo Hladiy (chairman)
Favouring the de-collectivization of the agricultural sector, the APU was launched in 1996 as an alternative to the pro-collectivization →Peasants' Party of Ukraine (SelPU). Backed by the presidency of Leonid Kuchma, the party obtained some support in the agriculture bureaucracy. Led by Kateriyna Vashchuk in the 1998 parliamentary elections, the APU failed to achieve the 4% proportional threshold but won nine constituency seats.

Under the new leadership of Mykhaylo Hladiy, the APU in July 2001 joined a "pro-presidential" bloc, later designated "For a United Ukraine", with the →People's Democratic Party, the Labour Party of Ukraine (→Together) and the →Party of Regional Revival of Ukraine, with the aim of creating "a powerful democratic force of centrist orientation". However, the APU resisted moves to weld the bloc into a single political party.

Christian Democratic Party of Ukraine
Khrystiiansko-Demokratychna Partiya Ukrainy (KhDPU)
Address. 5/36 Darvina St., Kyiv
Telephone. (+380–44) 224–2794
Leadership. Vitaly Zhuravskiy (chairman)
The KhDPU was founded in June 1992 by a moderate splinter group of the more nationalistic Ukrainian Christian Democratic Party (UKhDP) (→Forward Ukraine!). Whereas the conservative UKhDP is based in western Ukraine and supported mainly by Uniate Catholics, the KhDPU represents Orthodox Christians in central and eastern Ukraine, a majority of whom are Russian-speakers, and advocates liberal reforms and the creation of a market economy. The KhDPU won two seats in the 1994 parliamentary elections, one in Transcarpathia and the other in Odessa. It retained two constituency seats in 1998, although it won only 1.3% of the proportional vote.

Communist Party of Ukraine
Komunistychna Partiya Ukrainy (KPU)
Address. 1/11 Vynohradnyi St., 252024 Kyiv
Telephone. (+380–44) 226–2297
Fax. (+380–44) 293–3458
Leadership. Petro Symonenko (first secretary)
The Soviet-era KPU was formally banned in August 1991, but a campaign for its revival began as early as the summer of 1992, culminating in two restoration congresses in Donetsk in March and June 1993. The party claims to be the "legal successor" to the Soviet-era KPU, but avoided declaring the June congress to be the "29th" in the party's history and has been unable to claim former KPU property. The

party was officially registered in October 1993, the day after President Yeltsin's troops bombarded the White House in Moscow. Unlike other "successor" parties in Eastern Europe, the KPU remains aggressively anti-capitalist and anti-nationalist. It stands for the restoration of state control over the economy, and for some kind of confederative union between Ukraine and Russia. The KPU's populist nostalgia rapidly gained it support in economically troubled industrial areas of eastern Ukraine, especially in the Donbas, where party leader Petro Symonenko had been second secretary of the Donetsk party under the Soviet regime).

In the mid-1994 presidential elections the KPU gave crucial backing to Leonid Kuchma, then of the Inter-Regional Bloc for Reform (→Social-Liberal Union), in his successful challenge to the incumbent. In the parliamentary elections that began in March 1994, the KPU emerged as substantially the largest single party, with an initial total of 90 seats (nearly all in eastern and southern Ukraine). The party thus became the fulcrum of potential further conflict between the eastern and western regions of Ukraine. In 1995–96 the KPU put up determined resistance to the new "presidential" constitution favoured by President Kuchma, claiming in February 1996 to have collected 2.5 million signatures in support of a referendum on the issues at stake. However, following the final adoption of the new text in June 1996 (without a referendum), the party leadership announced that it would no longer question the constitution's legitimacy, but would instead mount a campaign for early presidential and parliamentary elections, combined with mass industrial action in protest against government economic policy.

The KPU confirmed its position as the largest party in the March 1998 parliamentary elections, advancing to 121 seats on a vote share of 24.7% and subsequently being joined by some independent deputies. Standing for the KPU in the autumn 1999 presidential elections, Symonenko came second to Kuchma in the first round with 22.2% of the vote and lost to the incumbent in the second, receiving 37.8% on the strength of backing from other left-wing parties. The KPU leader complained that the polling had been rigged, as did international observers. In March 2000 the KPU's headquarters in Kyiv were briefly occupied by nationalist militants, who accused the party of promoting the colonization of Ukraine by Russia.

In the major crisis which overtook the Kuchma administration in early 2001 over allegations that he had been involved in the murder of a journalist, the KPU claimed credit for securing the dismissal of "pro-American" Prime Minister Viktor Yushchenko in April and declared itself ready to form a government. At a May Day rally Symonenko asserted that "nationalists and oligarchic capitalists", assisted by the West, were seeking to divide Ukraine into three parts and to detach the country from "fraternal Slavic peoples". Earlier in the year the KPU had signed a co-operation agreement with the →→Communist Party of the Russian Federation and declared its support for Ukrainian membership of the Belarus-Russia Union.

Following the terrorist attacks on the USA in September 2001, the KPU condemned the resultant US-UK military action against Afghanistan as "unleashing a new world war". Calling for Ukraine to declare neutrality and non-alignment, the party castigated the Kuchma administration for granting US military planes the right to use Ukrainian airspace.

Fatherland
Batkivschchyna

Address. c/o Verkhovna Rada, 5 Hrushevskogo, 252019 Kyiv

Leadership. Yuliya Tymoshenko (chairperson)

The moderate conservative Fatherland was launched in March 1999 by a faction of the →*Hromada* All-Ukrainian Association after *Hromada* leader Pavlo Lazarenko had fled to the USA to escape charges of financial corruption when he was Prime Minister in 1996-97. The new party was joined by 23 Supreme Council deputies, 19 of them former *Hromada* members. In January 2000 Fatherland leader Yuliya Tymoshenko was appointed Deputy Prime Minister and given charge of the energy sector. In August 2000 her husband was among several state energy officials arrested on embezzlement charges and was later also accused of paying large bribes to Lazarenko when he was Prime Minister.

Tymoshenko herself was then charged with corruption when she had been a state energy official and was dismissed from the government in January 2001, whereupon Fatherland joined the parliamentary opposition to President Kuchma, who was concurrently under intense pressure to resign over his alleged involvement in the murder of a journalist. The arrest of Tymoshenko in mid-February 2001 was condemned by Fatherland as punishment for her anti-Kuchma stance and her attempts to reform the energy sector. She was released and re-arrested in March, before being re-released by decision of the Supreme Court in April 2001. Under hospital treatment for a stomach ulcer through these machinations, Tymoshenko on her re-release called for Kuchma to be removed by constitutional procedures. She subsequently dismissed as "cheap provocation" the filing of bribery charges against her by military prosecutors in Russia.

In July 2001 Tymoshenko announced the creation of the anti-Kuchma "National Salvation Forum", within which it was envisaged that Fatherland would contest the 2002 elections in an alliance of centre-right parties including the →Christian Democratic Party of Ukraine, the →Social Democratic Party of Ukraine, the Ukrainian Republican Party and the Ukrainian Conservative Republican Party (→National Front). The following month the Forum was joined by the Confederation of Free Trade Unions of Ukraine.

Forward Ukraine!
Vypered Ukrayino!

Address. 3 Khmelnytskoho St., Kyiv

Telephone. (+380–44) 228–7242

Fax. (+380–44) 228–7193

Leadership. Viktor Musiyaka

Adapting the name of a Russian formation of the mid-1990s, Forward Ukraine! was launched for the 1998 elections as an alliance of (i) the Christian Popular Union Party (Partiya Krrystyyansko–Narodny Soyuz, PKNS) led by Volodymyr Stretovych; and (ii) the Ukrainian Christian Democratic Party (Ukrainska Khrystyyansko–Demokratychna Partiya, UKhDP). Plans for a broader electoral front to include the →Party of Reforms and Order came to nothing, with the result that Forward Ukraine! scored only 1.7% of the proportional vote and won only two constituency seats.

Based in the Uniate Catholic population of Galicia, the nationalist UKhDP had been founded in 1990 but had been weakened by a 1992 schism with its more moderate Orthodox wing, which broke away to form the →Christian Democratic Party of Ukraine.

The PKNS is an observer member of the Christian Democrat International.

Green Party of Ukraine
Partiya Zelenykh Ukrainy (PZU)

Address. 38 Shota Rustaveli St., 01021 Kyiv

Telephone. (+388–44) 220–5080

Fax. (+388–44) 220–6694

Email. greenparty@ukrpost.net

Website. greenparty.org.ua

Leadership. Vitaliy Kononov (leader); Oleh Shevchuk (deputy leader and secretary-general)

The PZU was created in 1990 by environmentalist groups which had emerged in the wake of the 1986 Chernobyl nuclear accident, its platform urging government action on the huge environmental problems faced by Ukraine arising from Soviet-era industrialization. It had early links with the →Communist Party of Ukraine (KPU) and generally supported the presidency of Leonid Kravchuk (1991–94), but has been more critical of the successor administration of Leonid Kuchma. Having failed to achieve representation in 1994, the PZU won 19 seats in the 1998 legislative elections on a vote share of 5.4%, becoming part of a fluctuating parliamentary majority defined by its opposition to the KPU-led left. In the 1999 presidential elections, however, PZU leader Vitaliy Kononov obtained only 0.3% of the first-round vote, while by mid-2001 the Green parliamentary group had declined to 17 members.

Hromada All-Ukrainian Association
Vseukrayinske Obyednannya Hromada

Address. 18/7 Kutuzova St., Kyiv

Telephone. (+388–44) 296–3206

Leadership. Pavlo Lazarenko (chairman)

The free-market *Hromada* ("Community") party was re-launched in late 1997 under the leadership of Pavlo Lazarenko, who had been dismissed as Prime Minister by President Leonid Kuchma some months earlier because of corruption allegations against him. Based in Dnipropetrovsk, the party became part of the anti-Kuchma opposition and won 24 seats in the 1998 parliamentary elections (with a vote share of 4.7%), subsequently attracting about 20 independent deputies into its parliamentary group. In February 1999, however, Lazarenko fled to the USA after the Supreme Council had removed his immunity from prosecution, whereupon a substantial section of *Hromada* broke away to form the →Fatherland grouping. By late 2000 Lazarenko was in custody in the USA facing money-laundering charges.

National Front
Natsionalniy Front (NF)

Address. 21/111 Kreshchatyk Street, Kyiv

Telephone. (+388–44) 229–2425

Leadership. Slava Stetsko (KUN chairman); Levko Lukyanenko (URP chairman); Stepan Khmara (UKRP chairman)

The right-wing nationalist NF was created for the March 1998 parliamentary elections as an alliance of (i) the Congress of Ukrainian Nationalists (Kongres Ukrainskykh Natsionalistiv, KUN); (ii) the Ukrainian Republican Party (Ukrainska Respublikanska Partiya, URP); and (iii) the Ukrainian Conservative Republican Party (Ukrainska Konservatyvna Respublikanska Partiya, UKRP). Their joint list fell well below the 4% barrier in the proportional section (obtaining 2.7%), while in the constituency contests its tally of five seats compared unfavourably with the 17 seats won by the three parties in 1994.

The KUN was established in October 1992 by the émigré Organization of Ukrainian Nationalists (OUN) and quickly absorbed other rightist groups. Its programme advocates a strong nation state, independent in all respects from Russia, and withdrawal from the Commonwealth of Independent States (CIS). Economically, the KUN has veered between the strongly pro-capitalist orientation of its émigré members and a recognition of the need for state protection for the enfeebled Ukrainian economy. In the 1994 elections KUN chairman Slava Stetsko was prevented from standing in a Lviv constituency, but the party had considerable support in western Ukraine, where it elected five deputies in its own name and endorsed several successful non-party candidates.

The URP was the first non-communist political party to be openly formed in Ukraine in modern times (in April 1990), as the direct successor of the Ukrainian Helsinki Union (1988–90), itself a revival of the Ukrainian Helsinki Group (1976–80). The party bases its ideology on the conservative Ukrainian philosopher Viacheslav Lypynskiy and supports "the Ukrainian character of national statehood", while advocating a tolerant approach to ethnic minorities. It stands for resolute national defence, immediate withdrawal from the CIS and a strong, unitary, presidential republic. Economically, the party supports the creation of "a society of property owners" but opposes "socially unjust privatization".

The URP became the best organized nationalist party in the early 1990s, but was weakened by the formation in June 1992 of the breakaway UKRP by a radical right-wing faction led by deputy chairman Stepan Khmara. The UKRP adopted a vigorously anti-Russian line and, unlike the URP, strongly opposed any compromise with former Communists such as Leonid Kravchuk (President until July 1994), whom Khmara had accused of being a "traitor" to Ukrainian national interests. Khmara also advocated a nuclear Ukraine and support for ethnic Ukrainians in neighbouring Russian territories. Despite fielding 130 candidates, the URP performed poorly in the 1994 elections, winning only 11 seats. Its then chairman, Mykhailo Horyn, was defeated by Khmara in Lviv, although that was the UKRP's only success.

Party of Reforms and Order
Partiya Reformy i Poryadok (PRiP)
Address. 14/6 Dymiprova St., Lyiv
Leadership. Viktor Pynzenyk (chairman)
The PRiP was launched in advance of the 1998 parliamentary elections by a group of economic reformers led by former Deputy Prime Minister Viktor Pynzenyk, who had resigned from the Kuchma administration in April 1997 in protest against the slow pace of reform. As originally conceived, the "reforms" component of the party's platform was to be represented by Pynzenyk, while Supreme Council committee chairman Hryhoriy Omelchenko was to supply a "law and order" dimension. In the event, Omelchenko opted to join →Forward Ukraine! In the polling the PRiP unexpectedly failed to achieve the 4% minimum in the proportional section (winning 3.1%) and returned only three candidates in the constituency contests.

In political manoeuvring for the 2002 parliamentary elections, the PRiP in July 2001 joined the "Our Ukraine" bloc led by former Prime Minister Viktor Yushchenko and also including both factions of the →Popular Movement of Ukraine (*Rukh*).

Party of Regional Revival of Ukraine
Partiya Rehionalnoho Vidrodzhennya Ukrainy (PRVU)
Address. 7/5 Kotsiubynsky St., Kyiv
Leadership. Volodymyr Rybak (chairman)
The PRVU was founded in November 1997 by Volodymyr Rybak, the mayor of Donetsk, with the declared aim of protecting the socio-economic interests of the regions and promoting regional autonomy. It won only 0.9% of the proportional vote in the March 1998 parliamentary elections, but elected two candidates in constituency contests.

Peasants' Party of Ukraine
Selianska Partiya Ukrainy (SelPU)
Address. 24 Chreshchatyk St., Kyiv
Leadership. Serhiy Dovhan (chairman)
The roots of the SelPU lie in the rural organizations of the former ruling →Communist Party of Ukraine (KPU), which first established the Peasants' Union of Ukraine in September 1990 and then the SelPU in January 1992. While collective farm chairmen and heads of agro-industries usually prefer to remain "non-party" publicly, in practice many support the SelPU, which has been a powerful force maintaining the flow of subsidies to the agricultural sector and obstructing plans for land privatization. In alliance with the KPU and the →Socialist Party of Ukraine (SPU), the SelPU polled strongly in the 1994 parliamentary elections, winning 19 seats in conservative rural areas. In the new Supreme Council, it became the dominant component of the Rural Ukraine faction.

The SelPU contested the 1998 parliamentary elections in an alliance with the SPU called "For the Truth, For the People, For Ukraine", winning about a third of the joint list's 34 seats (with 8.6% of the vote). A prominent SelPU member, Oleksandr Tkachenko, was elected chairman of the new Supreme Council and became a prospective candidate in the 1999 presidential elections, until withdrawing in favour of the KPU leader, Petro Symonenko, and backing his unsuccessful bid. In a lengthy political crisis in early 2000, during which two competing legislatures were sitting at one stage, Tkachenko was ousted from the Council presidency by the centre-right majority.

Popular Democratic Party
Narodne-Demokratychna Partiya (NDP)
Address. 19/6 Liuteranska St., Kyiv
Telephone. (+388–44) 227–7076
Fax. (+388–44) 216–8333
Website. ndp.org.ua
Leadership. Valeriy Pustovoytenko (chairman); Oleksandr Karpov (Council group leader)
The pro-market NDP was formed in mid-1996 as a merger of several small centrist groupings, notably the Democratic Revival Party of Ukraine (PDVU), which had won four parliamentary seats in 1994, and New Wave (NK), which had also won four. From July 1997 to November 1999 the NDP provided the Prime Minister in the person of Valeriy Pustovoytenko. In the March 1998 parliamentary elections the NDP advanced to 28 seats on a proportional vote share of 5% and became part of the centre-right parliamentary majority giving qualified backing to governments appointed by President Kuchma, whom the party supported in his successful re-election bid in 1999.

In September 2000 the NDP parliamentary group chairman, Oleksandr Karpov, was elected head of the centre-right pro-government majority in the Supreme Council. The party subsequently became part of the "For a United Ukraine" centre-left bloc, with the →Agrarian Party of Ukraine, the Labour Party of Ukraine (→Together) and the →Party of Regional Revival of Ukraine.

Popular Movement of Ukraine
Narodniy Rukh Ukrainy
Address. 37/122 T. Shevchenka Blvd., Kyiv
Telephone. (+388–44) 224–9151
Fax. (+388–44) 216–8333
Email. mail@rukhpress-center.kiev.ua
Website. www.rukhpress-center.kiev.ua
Leadership. Yuriy Kostenko, Hennadiy Udovenko (leaders of competing factions)
The first attempt to unite all Ukrainian opposition groups in a "popular front" modelled on similar groups in the Baltic republics was crushed by the authorities in the summer of 1988. The second attempt brought in moderate elements from the →Communist Party of Ukraine (KPU) and the Writers' Union of Ukraine over the winter of 1988–89, and

resulted in the publication of a draft manifesto in February 1989. At that stage, *Rukh* (Ukrainian for "movement") still accepted the leading role of the KPU and refrained from any direct mention of Ukrainian independence. This pattern was largely confirmed by the movement's first congress in September 1989, which elected the writer Ivan Drach as leader. The autumn of 1989 also brought the resignation of the KPU's veteran conservative leader, Volodymyr Shcherbytskiy, and the beginning of the campaign for republican elections, which allowed *Rukh* to expand its influence. *Rukh*'s high-water mark came in March 1990, when the movement's front organization, the Democratic Bloc, won 27% of the seats in the elections to the Ukrainian parliament.

Thereafter, *Rukh* lost its status as the sole opposition group. Other political parties began to appear, and *Rukh* fell increasingly under the control of its nationalist wing. The various elections and referendums of 1991 showed no advance on *Rukh*'s 1990 position, and the movement effectively split at its third congress in February-March 1992, with the more nationalist wing leaving to found the Congress of National Democratic Forces in August 1992. Vyacheslav Chornovil was left in charge of a rump *Rukh*, which formally turned itself into a political party under his leadership at its fourth congress in December 1992.

Under Chornovil's leadership, *Rukh* took a centrist-nationalist line on most questions, supporting market reforms and a liberal democratic state united around territorial rather than ethnic patriotism, but also advocating strong national defence and Ukraine's departure from the Commonwealth of Independent States (CIS). On this platform, it won 20 seats in its own right in the 1994 elections and subsequently attracted half a dozen independent deputies into its parliamentary group. The party subsequently strongly opposed the successful KPU-backed presidential candidacy of Leonid Kuchma, whom Chornovil described as Ukraine's "most dangerous enemy".

Declaring itself to be in favour of Ukrainian membership of the European Union and NATO, *Rukh* sought to rally anti-left forces for the March 1998 parliamentary elections. Benefiting from its substantial following in western Ukraine, *Rukh* emerged as the second largest party (though far behind the KPU), winning 46 seats on a vote share of 9.4%. It then became part of a highly fluid parliamentary majority defined by its opposition to the left and broadly supportive of Kuchma-appointed governments, although critical of Kuchma himself.

Festering divisions within *Rukh* became critical in February 1999 when Chornovil was ousted from the party chairmanship and replaced by Yuriy Kostenko. Chornovil and his supporters thereupon established another version of *Rukh*, of which Hennadiy Udovenko became leader following Chornovil's death in a car crash in March. Both Kostenko and Udovenko were candidates in the autumn 1999 presidential elections, but won only 2.2% and 1.2% of the first-round vote respectively. With hostility between the two factions growing, a third *Rukh* faction was formed in November 2000 under the leadership of Bohdan Boyko with the aim of reuniting the other two. Such efforts resulted in a joint announcement by Kostenko and Udovenko in September 2001 that their factions would reunite under the umbrella of the "Our Ukraine" bloc led by former Prime Minister Viktor Yushchenko.

Progressive Socialist Party
Prohresyvna Sotsialistychna Partiya (PSP)
Address. 27 P. Myrny St., Ap. 51, Kyiv
Leadership. Nataliya Vitrenko (chairperson)
The leftist PSP was launched in 1996 by a dissident faction of the →Socialist Party of Ukraine (SPU). Under the leadership of Nataliya Vitrenko, the party called for a return to "the radiant past" of the Soviet era, opposed privatization of "national security enterprises" and advocated closer links with Russia and Belarus. The PSP just achieved the 4%

threshold in the March 1998 parliamentary elections, winning 16 seats and becoming part of the left-wing parliamentary opposition headed by the →Communist Party of Ukraine (KPU).

Standing for the PSP in the 1999 presidential elections, Vitrenko came a creditable fourth, winning 11% of the first-round vote. In July 2001 she announced that the PSP would contest the 2002 parliamentary elections as "an independent political force".

Social Democratic Party of Ukraine–United
Sotsial-Demokratychna Partiya Ukrainy–Obyednana (SDPU-O)
Address. 22–24 Gegelivska St., Kyiv
Telephone. (+388–44) 290–9116
Fax. (+388–44) 290–9274
Email. sdpu_o@alpha.rada.kiev.ua
Website. sdpu.inter.kiev.ua
Leadership. Viktor Medvedchuk (chairman)
A Ukrainian social democratic movement first emerged in 1988, when various all-USSR groups became active in the republic. In 1989–90 the Ukrainian groups cut their ties with fraternal organizations in the rest of the USSR, organizing a founding congress in May 1990. However, the congress resulted in an immediate split, with the moderates, who supported Ukrainian sovereignty and German-style social democracy, forming the →Social Democratic Party of Ukraine (SDPU) and the more left-wing faction the SDPU–O. After the SDPU won only two seats in the 1994 elections and the SDPU–O none, a reunification attempt was made but broke down in late 1997.

In the 1998 parliamentary elections, most social democratic forces, including former President Leonid Kravchuk and former Prime Minister Yevgeniy Marchuk, swung behind the SDPU–O, but the party won only 17 seats and just over 4% of the proportional vote. In the 1999 presidential elections, SDPU–O candidate Vasyl Onopenko took only 0.5% of the first-round vote, in part because Marchuk, running without party attribution, obtained 8.1%. Thereafter, the SDPU–O parliamentary group became part of a fluid pro-government centre-right majority, of which Kravchuk was the leader until September 2000.

Socialist Party of Ukraine
Sotsialistvchna Partiya Ukrainy (SPU)
Address. 45 Vorovskogo St., Kyiv
Telephone. (+388–44) 291–6063
Leadership. Oleksandr Moroz (chairman)
The SPU was the first would-be successor to the Soviet-era →Communist Party of Ukraine (KPU), being formed only two months after the August 1991 coup attempt in Moscow under the leadership of Oleksandr Moroz, the former KPU chairman of the Ukrainian legislature. Moroz steered the SPU away from open nostalgia for the old system, but in 1992–94 adopted a populist position, attacking the "introduction of capitalism" and the "growth of national-fascism" in Ukraine. He also called for the reintroduction of state direction of the economy, price controls and "socially just privatization". In the sphere of external policy, the party has advocated closer economic and political ties with Russia and the other CIS states (its more radical members supporting a restored USSR). Unlike the revived KPU, however, the SPU is generally reconciled to the fact of Ukrainian independence.

In June 1993 the SPU formed an alliance called "Working Ukraine" with the →Peasants' Party of Ukraine (SelPU) and smaller left-wing groups, in close co-operation of the KPU, although the latter did not join. The SPU claimed the support of 38 deputies in the Ukrainian parliament in 1992–93 while it enjoyed the advantage of being the only organized leftist successor to the KPU. Its pre-eminence on the left disappeared with the rise of the restored KPU in 1993–94, but it nevertheless won 15 seats in the 1994 elections, after which Moroz was elected chairman of the Ukrainian parliament. By mid-1994 the SPU controlled a parliamentary faction of 25 deputies. In early 1996, however, the party was weakened by a split resulting in the formation of the →Progressive Socialist Party (PSP).

The SPU contested the 1998 parliamentary elections in an alliance with the SelPU called "For the Truth, For the People, For Ukraine", their joint list winning 34 seats with 8.6% of the proportional vote. Plans for a joint presidential candidate of the alliance and other left-leaning parties foundered in the run-up to the 1999 contest, with the result that Moroz stood for the SPU and came third with 11.3% of the first-round vote. In the second round the SPU supported KPU leader Petro Symonenko, who was defeated by incumbent Leonid Kuchma. In early 2000 the SPU was prominent in ultimately abortive left-wing attempts to prevent the ousting of Council president Oleksandr Tkachenko (SelPU) by the centre-majority, whose action was described by Moroz as tantamount to a coup d'état.

Moroz and the SPU also took a leading role in the major political crisis which developed from late 2000 over President Kuchma's alleged role in the murder of a journalist. After being sued for slander by Kuchma's chief of staff for revealing apparent presidential involvement in the affair, Moroz described the crisis as "a turning-point" in Ukraine's national history. In May 2001 the SPU initiated moves for a national referendum in which voters would be asked to approve the removal of the President. In May 2001 Moroz announced that the SPU would contest the 2002 parliamentary elections in alliance with at least four other left-wing parties.

Other Parties and Alliances

The following selection from the 100 or more other registered parties in Ukraine focuses on those which contested the March 1998 parliamentary elections, either on their own or within blocs.

All-Ukrainian Party of Women's Initiatives (*Partiya Zhinochi Initiatyvy, PZI*), one of several feminist formations, took 0.6% of the proportional vote in 1998.
Leadership. Valentyna Datsenko (chairperson)

All-Ukrainian Workers' Party (*Vseukrainska Partiya Trudyashchykh*, VPT), founded in 1997 by the head of the official trade union federation, won 0.8% of the proportional vote in 1998.
Leadership. Oleksandr Stoyan (chairman)

Democratic Parties Electoral Bloc (*Vyborchiy Blok Demokratychnykh Partiy, VBDP*), alliance of the **Democratic Party of Ukraine** (*Demokratychna Partiya Ukrainy*, DPU) and the **Party of Economic Rebirth** (*Partiya Ekonomichnoho Vidrodzhennya*, PEV) which in 1998 won 1.2% of the proportional vote and one constituency seat (for the DPU). Founded in 1990, the DPU became the main party of the nationalist intelligentsia in the early 1990s, but representation had collapsed from over 20 seats to a handful in 1994. The Crimea-based and pro-market PEV had won one seat in 1994.
Leadership. Volodymyr Yavorivskiy (DPU chairman); Volodymyr Shevyov (PEV chairman)

European Choice of Ukraine (*Yevropeyskiy Vybir Ukrainy, YVU*), centrist pro-EU alliance of the **Liberal Democratic Party of Ukraine** (*Liberalno-Demokratychna Partiya Ukrainy*, LDPU) and the **Ukrainian Democratic Peasants' Party** (*Ukrainska Selyanska Demokratychna Partiya*, USDP); won 0.1% in 1998.
Leadership. Andriy Koval (LDPU chairman); Viktor Prysyazhnyuk (USDP chairman)

Less Talk (*Menshe Sliv*), far-right alliance of the **Social**

National Party of Ukraine (*Sotsial-Natsionalna Partiya Ukrainy*, SNPU) and **Ukrainian Statehood and Independence** (*Derzhavna Samostiinist Ukrainy*, DSU), claiming to be nationalist and not "neo-fascist", won 0.2% of the proportional vote and one constituency seat (for the SNPU) in 1998.
Leadership. Oleh Tyahnybok (SNPU); Roman Koval (DSU)

Muslim Party of Ukraine (*Partiya Musulman Ukrainy, PMU*), representing the small Muslim population, won 0.2% in 1998.
Leadership. Rashyl Bragin

Party of Defenders of the Fatherland (*Partiya Zakhysnykiv Vitchyzny, PZV*), nationalist formation which won 0.3% in 1998.
Leadership. Volodymyr Kolomyitsev (chairman)

Party of National Economic Development of Ukraine (*Partiya Natsionalno Ekonomichnoho Rozvytku Ukrainy, PNERU*), pro-market formation led by a prominent banker, won 0.9% in 1998.
Leasdership. Volodymyr Malynkovych (chairman)

Party of Spiritual, Economic and Social Progress (*Partiya Dukhovnoho, Ekonomichnoho i Sotsialnoho Prohresu, PDESP*), pro-business, pro-science formation which won 0.2% in 1998.
Leadership. Ivan Burdak (chairman)

Republican Christian Party (*Respublikanska Kkrystyyanska Partiya, RKP*), formed in 1997 mainly by ex-members of the →Popular Movement of Ukraine (*Rukh*), won 0.5% in 1998.
Leadership. Mykola Porovskiy (chairman)

Slavic Unity Party of Ukraine (*Partiya Slovyanskoi Yednosti Ukrainy, PSYU*), advocating unification of the ex-Soviet Slav republics, was not included on ballot papers in the 1998 elections.
Leadership. Oleksandr Bazyliuk (chairman)

Social Democratic Party of Ukraine (*Sotsial-Demokratychna Partiya Ukrainy, SDPU*), one of several small social democratic groupings seeking, without much success, to challenge the →Social Democratic Party of Ukraine–United; won 0.3% in 1998. In July 2001 the SDPU joined the opposition "National Salvation Forum" headed by →Fatherland.
Leadership. Yuriy Buzduhan (chairman)

Social-Liberal Union (*Sotsialno-Liberalne Obyednannya, SLON*), alliance of the **Inter-Regional Bloc for Reform** (*Mizhrehionalnyi Blok Reformiv*, MBR) and the **Constitutional Democratic Party** (*Konstytutsiyno Demokratychna Partiya*, KDP) which in 1998 won 0.9% of the proportional vote and one constituency seat (for the MBR). Formed in 1993, the pro-market MBR had originally included Leonid Kuchma, but his unexpected victory in the mid-1994 presidential elections had marked his break from the party, which had returned some 30 candidates in the 1994 parliamentary elections.
Leadership. Volodymyr Hrynyov (MBR chairman); Volodymyr Zolotaryov (KDP chairman)

Together (*Razom*), alliance of the **Labour Party of Ukraine** (*Partiya Truda Ukrainy*, PTU), founded in 1992, and the **Liberal Party of Ukraine** (*Liberalna Partiia Ukrainy*, LPU), founded in 1993, both strongly based in Donetsk. Whereas the two parties had won some half-a-dozen seats between them in 1994, in 1998 their joint list got only 1.8% of the proportional vote and returned only one constituency candidate (for the LPU, which is an observer member of the Liberal International).

Leadership. Valentyn Landyk (PTU chairman); Volodymyr Shcherban (LPU chairman)

Ukrainian National Assembly (*Ukrainska Natsionalna Asambleya, UNA*), ultra-nationalist formation advocating a Ukrainianized army, won 0.4% in 1998.
Leadership. Oleh Vitovych

Union Party (*Partiya Soyuz*), pro-Russian Crimean party supporting a Ukraine-Russia-Belarus union, won 0.7% in 1998.
Leadership. Svitlana Savchenko (chairperson)

Working Ukraine (*Trudova Ukraina*), electoral bloc of the Donetsk-based **Civil Congress of Ukraine** (*Hromadyanskiy Konhres Ukrainy*, HKU) and the **Ukrainian Justice Party** (*Ukrainska Partiya Spravedlyvosti*, UPS). Founded in 1992 to defend use of the Russian language and to advocate integration with Russia, the HKU won two Council seats in 1994. Containing many ex-servicemen, the joint list won 3.1% of the proportional vote in 1998 and elected one UPS candidate for a constituency seat.
Leadership. Aleksandr Bazeliuk (HKU chairman); Mychaylo Grechka (UPS chairman)

United Arab Emirates

Capital: Abu Dhabi

Population: 2,370,000 (2000E)

The United Arab Emirates (UAE) is a federated state of seven sheikhdoms (Abu Dhabi, Dubai, Sharjah, Ras al-Khaimah, Fujairah, Umm al-Qaiwain and Ajman) without parliament or political parties. The highest federal authority is the Supreme Council of Rulers comprising the seven hereditary rulers of the sheikhdoms. Decisions of the Supreme Council require the approval of at least five members, including the rulers of Abu Dhabi and Dubai. The head of state is the President, who is elected by the Supreme Council from among its members for a five-year renewable term (as is the Vice-President). The Prime Minister and the Council of Ministers are appointed by the President. An appointed consultative Federal National Council, with 40 members drawn proportionately from each sheikhdom, considers legislative proposals submitted by the Council of Ministers.

United Kingdom

Capital: London

Population: (including N. Ireland): 59,500,000 (2000E)

The United Kingdom of Great Britain and Northern Ireland is a hereditary constitutional monarchy in which the monarch, as head of state, has numerous specific responsibilities. The supreme legislative authority is Parliament, consisting of (i) a 659-member House of Commons, with a life of not more than five years, directly elected under a simple-majority system in single-member constituencies, the right to vote being held by British subjects (and citizens of any Commonwealth member country or the Republic of Ireland resident in the United Kingdom) above the age of 18 years, and (ii) a House of Lords. Under a reform enacted in November 1999 the majority hereditary component of the House of Lords was abolished and a 670-member "interim chamber" (of 578 life peers, bishops and law lords plus 92 ex-hereditaries elected by their peers) was set up pending definitive reform of the upper chamber. The government is headed by a Prime Minister who is leader of the party which commands a majority in the House of Commons. Each candidate standing for election to the House of Commons has to pay a deposit of £500, which is forfeited if he or she obtains less than 5% of the valid votes in his constituency. Any vacancies arising are filled through by-elections. The UK joined what became the European Union on Jan. 1, 1973, and elects 87 members of the European Parliament, including three from Northern Ireland.

Opposition parties in the House of Commons receive financial assistance from state funds to assist them in fulfilling their parliamentary duties, the subsidies being known as "Short money", after the minister (Edward Short) who first introduced the arrangement in 1975. To qualify for the subsidies, which are increased annually in line with inflation, a non-government party is required to have at least two MPs, or one MP plus a total of at least 150,000 votes in the most recent general election. For the 2000–01 financial year the assistance available was set at a rate of £11,011.73p per seat and £21.99p per 200 votes won in the most recent election. In addition, £513,000 was made available to defray the running costs of the Leader of the Opposition's Office, while qualifying opposition parties received an additional total of £120,961 to meet travel expenses. Under these headings, the Conservative and Unionist Party received £3,465,132 in subsidies in the 2000–01 financial year, the Liberal Democrats £1,112,906 and other non-government parties lesser sums.

Since 1996 a similar scheme of state financial assistance has operated for non-government parties in the House of Lords, known as "Cranborne money" after the then leader of the upper chamber, Lord Cranborne. Extended to cross-bench peers in 1999, the scheme made £222,480 available to the Conservatives in the 2000-01 financial year, £66,743 to the Liberal Democrats and £20,520 to the convenor of the cross-bench peers.

The 2000 Political Parties, Elections and Referendums Act, implementing most of the recommendations of the Neill Committee report on political funding published in 1998, banned parties from accepting financial donations from foreign sources and laid down disclosure and other rules for donations from domestic sources and for campaign expenditure. It also provided for the creation of an Electoral Commission charged with ensuring compliance with the new rules and with maintaining a register of political parties. On being formally established in February 2001, the new Commission tabled proposals for additional state funding of opposition parties to cover "policy research".

In general elections to the House of Commons in May 1997 the Labour Party ended 18 years of Conservative rule by winning an overwhelming majority. Further elections on June 7, 2001, confirmed Labour in power with a similar majority, the results being as follows: Labour Party 412 seats (with 42.0% of the vote), Conservatives 166 (32.7%), Liberal Democrats 52 (18.8%), Ulster Unionist Party* 6, Democratic Unionist Party* 5, Scottish National Party (SNP) 5, *Plaid Cymru* (in Wales) 4, *Sinn Féin* 4, Social Democratic and Labour Party* 3, Independent Kidderminster Hospital and Health Concern 1, Speaker 1.

Under devolution legislation enacted in 1998, a 129-member Scottish Parliament and a 60-member Welsh Assembly were elected for five-year terms on May 6, 1999, by a combination of single-member constituency voting and proportional representation of party lists. In Scotland the Labour Party won 56 seats, the SNP 35, the Conservatives 18, the Liberal Democrats 17, others 3. In Wales Labour won 28 seats, *Plaid Cymru* 17, the Conservatives 9, the Liberal Democrats 6.

*Northern Ireland party: see separate section below.

Conservative and Unionist Party

Address. Conservative Central Office, 32 Smith Square, London, SWIP 3HH

Telephone. (+44–20) 7222–9000

Fax. (+44–20) 7222–1135

Email. ccoffice@conservative-party.org.uk

Website. www.tory.org

Leadership. Iain Duncan Smith (leader); Michael Ancram (deputy leader); David Davis (chairman)

Founded in the 1830s, the Conservative Party regards freedom of the individual under the rule of law as its guiding principle. It believes that political arrangements should be so designed as to give people "the maximum degree of control over their own lives, whilst restricting the role of government so that the state exists for the benefit of the individual and not vice versa". The party stands for wider ownership of property and wealth and for lower taxes on earnings, and is strongly committed to the free enterprise system. Believing in the maintenance of the United Kingdom, it opposed the devolution of power to Scotland and Wales; it is also opposed to the introduction of proportional representation for House of Commons elections. The party is pledged to the maintenance of strong defence and regards the concept of deterrence as central to the nation's nuclear and conventional defence capability. It favours Britain's continued membership of a European Union of nation states and opposes any further transfer of sovereignty to the EU.

The Conservatives trace their history back to the 17th and 18th century, but the modern party was formed by Sir Robert Peel, who established the first Conservative government in 1834, shortly before which the term "Conservative" was first used as opposed to "Tory" (a term of Irish origins applied to members of the political grouping which from 1679 opposed Whig attempts to exclude the future James II from the succession to the throne). The party assumed its present official name in 1912 when it was formally joined by the Liberal Unionists (former Liberals who opposed home rule for Ireland and had supported the Conservative Party since 1886). During World War I the party took part in a coalition government. It was returned to power in 1922 and remained in government for most of the inter-war years (from 1931 as the dominant party in a National government) and in the World War II all-party coalition (under Winston Churchill from May 1940 to July 1945).

In the post-war era the Conservative Party has been led by Churchill (1940–55), Anthony Eden (1955–57), Harold Macmillan (1957–63), Sir Alec Douglas-Home (1963–65), Edward Heath, the first leader elected by Conservative MPs (1965–75), Margaret Thatcher (1975–90), John Major (1990–97), William Hague (1997–2001) and Iain Duncan Smith, who in 2001 became the first leader to be elected by the party membership as well as by MPs.

After heavily losing the 1945 elections to the →Labour Party, the Conservatives were in opposition until 1951 and thereafter in power until 1964. The next Conservative government, under Heath in 1970–74, successfully negotiated Britain's entry into what later became the European Union (EU). Following his 1974 election defeat, Heath was ousted as leader in 1975 by Margaret Thatcher, who in the May 1979 elections became the UK's first woman Prime Minister. The party was confirmed in power with large majorities in June 1983 (benefiting from the successful British military action in 1982 to recover the Falkland Islands from Argentinian occupation) and again in June 1987, although its percentage share of the vote slipped from 43.9% in 1979 to 42.4% in 1983 and to 42.3% in 1987. Thatcher's 1987 victory, with a Commons majority of 102 seats, made her the first British Prime Minister in modern history to win three consecutive terms in office.

Under the Thatcher premiership the Conservatives pursued radical right-wing social and economic policies, with the party's moderate "one nation" wing being increasingly marginalized (and referred to dismissively by the Thatcherites as "wets"). Major reforms included stringent curbs on the powers of trade unions, the promotion of individual choice and market mechanisms within the welfare state structure, the sale of council houses to their tenants and the privatization of many industries and companies previously under public ownership. Her government also cut income tax rates to pre-war levels (although without appreciably reducing the proportion of GDP spent by the state) and presided over an economic boom in the late 1980s, when for a while there was an actual surplus in government finances. During her third term, however, an attempt to reform the financing of local government so that all residents paid a "community charge" provoked large-scale opposition to what was dubbed a "poll tax". There were also deepening divisions within Conservative ranks over British membership of the EU, which many Conservatives saw as being intent on eroding the national sovereignty of member states.

Thatcher positioned herself on the "Euro-sceptic" wing of the party, delivering a celebrated speech in Bruges (Belgium) in September 1988 in which she categorically rejected schemes for a federal European state. However, a series of by-election defeats in 1989–90 weakened her position, which was fatally undermined by the pro-European Sir Geoffrey Howe, who delivered a blistering critique of her stewardship following his exit from the government in November 1990. The speech precipitated an immediate leadership challenge by the pro-European former Defence Minister, Michael Heseltine, who obtained enough first-round votes to force a second round, whereupon Thatcher resigned in the face of almost certain defeat. Two other contenders then entered the lists, including the Chancellor of the Exchequer, John Major, who was regarded as the Thatcherite candidate and for that reason was elected in the second-round ballot by a comfortable margin.

Becoming at 47 Britain's youngest 20th-century Prime

Minister, Major quickly jettisoned his predecessor's more controversial policies (which he had staunchly supported), including the "poll tax". The Conservatives fought the April 1992 election on a somewhat more centrist platform of further privatization (including British Rail and the coal mines), financial accountability in the National Health Service (NHS) and freedom of choice in the state education sector. In the sphere of economic policy, they contended that the recession into which Britain had descended in the early 1990s would become much worse under a Labour government. Assisted by public doubts as to the prime ministerial calibre of Labour leader Neil Kinnock, the Conservatives won an almost unprecedented fourth term, although by the much narrower margin of 336 seats out of 651 (from an aggregate vote of 14.1 million, representing a 41.9% share).

Also almost unprecedented was the massive post-election slump in the Conservative government's public standing, as evidenced by disastrous local election results in 1993 and 1994 and the more damaging loss of several hitherto safe Conservative parliamentary seats to the →Liberal Democrats. Contributory factors included Britain's humiliating enforced exit from the European exchange rate mechanism in September 1992, representing a traumatic collapse of government economic policy (but not generating any immediate ministerial resignations) and leading to a ramp of additional taxation in direct breach of the party's election pledge to reduce taxes. Also damaging were internal Conservative divisions over Europe, evidenced in protracted resistance to ratification of the 1991 Maastricht Treaty creating the EU (despite the much-trumpeted opt-outs negotiated for Britain by Major), and a never-ending series of "sex and sleaze" scandals featuring prominent Conservatives.

In June 1994 the Conservatives fared badly in elections for the European Parliament, falling from 34 to 18 seats (out of 87) with only 26.8% of the vote and losing several seats in the Conservative heartland of southern England. Further by-election and local election disasters in late 1994 and early 1995, with Labour now the main beneficiary, fuelled increasing Conservative criticism of Major's leadership. In June 1995 the Prime Minister unexpectedly confronted his critics, when he announced his resignation as party leader (although not as Prime Minister) to force a leadership election in which he requested his critics to "put up or shut up". Only one Conservative dared to "put up", namely Welsh Secretary John Redwood, representing the Euro-sceptic right wing of the party. Major was duly re-elected with the support of 218 of the 329 Conservative MPs and therefore continued as Prime Minister, immediately elevating Heseltine to "number two" in the government as reward for his crucial support during the leadership contest.

Major's leadership election victory had no impact on the historically low opinion poll ratings being accorded to the Conservative Party, which kept losing by-elections no matter how "safe" the seat. It also, unusually, suffered defections from the parliamentary party, one to Labour in September 1995, another to the Liberal Democrats at the end of the year and a third who eventually opted for the Liberal Democrats. Yet another by-election defeat in April 1996 reduced the government's overall theoretical majority in the Commons to one and another local election disaster in May all but eliminated the Conservative Party from local government. The following month internal party dissension over Europe intensified when 74 Conservative backbenchers voted in favour of an early referendum on whether Britain should surrender further sovereignty to the EU.

The Conservatives were decimated in the May 1997 general elections, retaining only 165 seats on a vote share of 31.5%, its worst result of the 20th century, which left it without representation in Scotland and Wales. Major immediately resigned as leader and was succeeded by William Hague, who at 36 became the party's youngest leader for over 200 years. Inheritor of the "Thatcherite"

mantle, Hague quickly came into conflict with the party's pro-European wing, as he moved to oppose UK participation in the single European currency (euro). On the eve of the Conservative conference of October 1998 Hague secured 84% endorsement from party members for the proposition that a Conservative government would not join the euro during the lifetime of the next parliament. Nevertheless, infighting on the issue continued, with Heseltine and former Chancellor Kenneth Clarke to the fore in insisting that the party should not rule out participation in the single currency.

The Conservatives showed signs of recovery in the May 1999 local elections, displacing the Liberal Democrats as the second strongest party in local government. The party also secured representation in the new legislatures of Scotland and Wales elected in that month, though they were in opposition in both. In June 1999 the Conservatives were the main victors in European Parliament elections, winning 36 of the 87 UK seats on a vote share of 35.8% despite a powerful performance by the anti-EU →UK Independence Party. However, the party continued to be dogged by internal division and controversy, notably when its candidate for the new post of mayor of London, Lord (Jeffrey) Archer of Weston-super-Mare, was forced to withdraw in November 1999 over allegations that he had suborned a potential witness in a 1987 libel trial. In the same month the return to the Commons of former Defence Secretary Michael Portillo in a London by-election served to increase the pressure on Hague, though Portillo pledged that he would be loyal. In December 1999 Hague suffered another major blow when former front-bench spokesman Shaun Woodward defected to the Labour Party, claiming that the Conservatives had moved too far to the right.

Portillo was rewarded for his loyalty by being appointed shadow Chancellor in February 2000, whereupon he immediately abandoned the Conservatives' opposition to the national minimum wage and the independence of the Bank of England. The following month the Conservatives narrowly gained a directly-elected seat in the Scottish Parliament (from Labour), whilst in May 2000 the party made significant gains in local elections in England and the replacement Conservative candidate for the London mayoralty, Steven Norris, came a creditable second. However, in a simultaneous parliamentary by-election for the "safe" Conservative-held seat of Romsey in Hampshire the party suffered a devastating defeat at the hands of the Liberal Democrats, in part because of anti-Conservative tactical voting by Labour supporters.

In September 2000 the Labour government's disarray in the face of fuel price protests which paralysed the country resulted in the Conservatives taking the lead in opinion polls, but only briefly. Conservative by-election results continued to be poor, causing analysts to note that no opposition party had ever regained power in a general election without winning at least one by-election in the previous parliamentary term. As his party returned to a distant second place behind Labour in the polls, Hague continued to be undermined internally by divisions on Europe and by behinds-the-scenes criticism of his leadership. Also damaging was the preferment of perjury and other charges against Archer (who was later convicted and sent to prison for four years), it being recalled that Hague had publicly endorsed him for the London mayoralty despite warnings about his probity.

In his campaign for the June 2001 parliamentary elections Hague tried to bring the European currency issue to the fore, claiming that it was the last chance to "save the pound" because a further Labour government would join the euro. He also sought to make capital from the failings of the government's political asylum policy, pledging that a Conservative government would introduce detention for all applicants while their cases were assessed and would speedily deport those refused asylum. But such policies seemed to fall on deaf ears. The results showed that the Conservatives had suffered another heavy defeat, making a net gain of only one seat (to 166) and increasing their share of the vote by only 1.2% (to 32.7%).

Hague immediately resigned as party leader, acknowledging that he had failed to attract popular support. Five candidates came forward for a leadership election, which under new rules introduced by Hague involved voting by Conservative MPs to narrow the field to two, who were then submitted for election by the 330,000 individual party members. In the MPs' stage the three candidates eliminated were Portillo (who had begun as the favourite), former party chairman Michael Ancram and former junior minister David Davis. The two who went forward were defence spokesman Iain Duncan Smith from the Eurosceptic right and former Chancellor Kenneth Clarke from the pro-EU wing of the party, who had unsuccessfully sought the leadership in 1997.

The membership stage of the contest in August-September 2001 featured intense personal acrimony and controversy. Hague and Baroness Thatcher endorsed Duncan Smith, whereas Clarke was backed by Major, who launched a fierce attack on Duncan Smith and Thatcher for disloyalty to his 1990–97 government. Other party figures weighed into a level of vituperation seen as unprecedented in the party's history. It then emerged that one of Duncan Smith's campaign team in Wales was the father of the leader of the far-right →British National Party (BNP) and supported the BNP's policies on immigration. He was quickly removed from the Duncan Smith team and expelled from the party (after 53 years of membership), as Clarke depicted himself as the candidate of "one nation" conservatism and assailed Duncan Smith for being a right-wing "hanger and flogger".

Declared in September 2001, the result of the membership ballot was a decisive victory for Duncan Smith with 61% of some 255,000 votes cast. Himself without ministerial experience, the new leader appointed a front-bench team dominated by opponents of euro participation, including Ancram as shadow Foreign Secretary and deputy party leader, Michael Howard (a former Home Secretary) as shadow Chancellor and Oliver Letwin as shadow Home Secretary. The party chairmanship was entrusted to Davis. Seeking to repair damage done during the leadership contest, Hague and Davis decreed that the right-wing Monday Club, which advocated voluntary repatriation of immigrants, was no longer an acceptable pressure-group within the party.

The Conservative Party is a founder member of the International Democrat Union. Its representatives in the European Parliament sit in the European People's Party/European Democrats group (consisting mainly of Christian Democrats).

Green Party of England and Wales (GPEW)

Address. 1A Waterlow Road, Archway, London, N19 5NJ
Telephone. (+44–20) 7272–4474
Fax. (+44–20) 7272–6653
Email. office@greenparty.org.uk
Website. www.greenparty.org.uk
Leadership. Penny Kemp (chairperson); Margaret Wright (female spokesperson); Darren Johnson (male spokesperson)

The Green Party propagates policies which are based on the principle that people must live in harmony with nature within the limitations of the earth's finite supply of resources. Its aims include unilateral disarmament, a ban on all nuclear as well as chemical and biological weapons, an end to Britain's involvement in NATO, an end to nuclear power generation, material security through a Basic National Income scheme, land reform, decentralization, proportional representation and increased aid for third-world countries in the form of grants not loans. The →Scottish Green Party is organizationally separate from the GPEW.

The party was founded in 1973 as the Ecology Party, which nominated 54 candidates for the 1979 general elec-

tions, All of them lost their deposits and gained an average of only 1.2% of the vote in the contested constituencies, the party's best results being 2.8% in two. In the 1983 general elections Ecologists contested 109 seats, the highest vote for any candidate being 2.9%. In September 1985 the party changed its name to Green Party, which in the 1987 general elections fielded 133 candidates, the highest vote obtained by any of them being 3.7%. Meanwhile, the party had elected its first two local councillors in the district elections of May 1986, when its candidates averaged 6% in the wards which it contested.

The Greens seemed to make a breakthrough when they obtained 2.3 million votes (15% of the total) in the June 1989 European Parliament elections in Britain (but no seats). However, internal divisions between the moderates and a radical wing weakened the party in the early 1990s. It was also damaged when well-known television sports commentator David Icke, a party member, announced in 1991 that he was the new messiah sent to save mankind (and also left himself open to charges of anti-semitism in a new book). The party obtained only 171,927 votes (0.5%) in the April 1992 general elections, when all 253 Green candidates lost their deposits. Four months later Sara Parkin resigned as leader, stating that because of perpetual infighting "the Green Party has become a liability to green politics". Britain's other best-known environmentalist, Jonathon Porritt, also distanced himself from the party, becoming an adviser on green issues to the Prince of Wales.

The Greens staged a minor recovery in the June 1994 European Parliament elections, winning 3.1% of the vote (but again no seats). In the May 1997 general elections, however, the Greens' 95 candidates all lost their deposits in amassing an aggregate vote of 63,991 (0.2%). Two years later the Scottish Parliament elections of May 1999 yielded better fortune, with the Scottish Greens winning 3.6% of the vote and returning the first Green candidate ever to be elected in a major UK poll. In the June 1999 European elections, moreover, the Greens won two seats from a national vote share of 6.3%.

In November 1999 the party obtained formal Westminster representation for the first time when Lord Beaumont of Whitley, hitherto a →Liberal Democrat life peer, crossed the floor in the House of Lords. In May 2000, moreover, the Greens won three of the 25 seats on the new Greater London Assembly (with 11.1% of the proportional vote), one of its elected members being given the environment portfolio in the new mayoral administration of Ken Livingstone (formerly of the →Labour Party, now independent). However, the June 2001 general elections produced the familiar universal failure for the Greens' 145 candidates, although their share of a much-reduced national vote rose to 0.6%.

With an official membership of 5,000, the GPEW is affiliated to the European Federation of Green Parties. Its representatives in the European Parliament sit in the Greens/European Free Alliance group.

Labour Party

Address. Millbank Tower, Millbank, London, SW1P 4GT
Telephone. (+44–20) 7802–1000
Fax. (+44–20) 7272–6653
Email. info@new.labour.org.uk
Website. www.labour.org.uk
Leadership. Tony Blair (leader); John Prescott (deputy leader); Charles Clarke (chairman); Margaret Wall (chairperson of national executive committee); David Triesman (general secretary)

The party was founded in 1900 as the Labour Representation Committee at a conference held in London attended by representatives of the trade unions, the Independent Labour Party, the Fabian Society and other socialist societies, having been convened as a result of a decision by the Trades Union Congress (TUC) to seek improved representation of the labour movement in parliament. Later in 1900 two Labour members were elected to parliament. The name of the Committee was changed to Labour Party in 1906, when there were 29 Labour members in the House of Commons. The first (minority) Labour government was in office from January to November 1924 and the second from June 1929 to August 1931, both under the premiership of Ramsay MacDonald, although MacDonald then headed a National government from which the bulk of the Labour Party dissociated itself.

Labour joined an all-party coalition during World War II and won an overwhelming victory in the 1945 general elections under the leadership of Clement Attlee (party leader from 1933 to 1955). His government carried out many social and economic reforms, among them the creation of the National Health Service (NHS), remaining in office until 1951. After 13 years in opposition (for part of which the party was led by Hugh Gaitskell), Labour was narrowly returned to power in 1964 under the leadership of Harold Wilson, who consolidated Labour's majority over the →Conservative Party in further elections in 1966. Wilson's goal of social modernization made little progress and his government became increasingly troubled. Nevertheless, Labour's defeat by the Conservatives in the 1970 elections was unexpected.

In March 1974 Wilson returned to office as head of a minority administration after Labour had become the largest single parliamentary party in elections the previous month. The party subsequently achieved a narrow overall majority in further elections in October 1974. In a referendum in June 1975 the Labour government secured approval for its recommendation that Britain should remain a member of the European Community, despite the party being predominantly anti-European in those days. Wilson unexpectedly vacated the leadership in March 1976 and was succeeded by James Callaghan, who was obliged to enter into a parliamentary pact with the small Liberal Party (later the →Liberal Democrats) after Labour's majority had been eroded by by-election losses. The Callaghan government became increasingly embroiled in disputes with militant public sector unions, culminating in the 1978–79 "winter of discontent", in which civil society seemed to have broken down. In the May 1979 general elections the Labour Party suffered a decisive defeat at the hands of Margaret Thatcher's Conservative Party and was in opposition for the next 18 years.

Labour's 1979 election defeat resulted in the party's left wing gaining the ascendancy. Personifying Labour's "old left", Michael Foot succeeded Callaghan as leader in 1980 and sought to unify the party on the basis of radical policy commitments and opposition to membership of the European Community. The response of leading right-wingers was the formation in March 1981 of the breakaway Social Democratic Party (later mostly subsumed into what became the Liberal Democrats). In the June 1983 elections, Labour went down to a further heavy defeat, its 27.6% vote share being the party's lowest since 1918. Foot quickly resigned and a party conference in October 1983 elected another left-winger, Neil Kinnock (then 41), as the party's youngest-ever leader.

Kinnock failed to mount a credible challenge to the Thatcher government, being shackled by his own left-wing provenance and the influence of the hard left within the party. In June 1987 Labour suffered its third general election defeat in a row, albeit with the consolation of having reversed its electoral decline by increasing its share of the vote to 31.6% and its seat total to 229 (out of 650). Kinnock responded by initiating a major revision of Labour policies in key areas, featuring abandonment of the party's commitment to unilateral nuclear disarmament and of its opposition the UK membership of the European Community, for which the party quickly became a great enthusiast. Labour also moved towards acceptance of the market economy (subject to "regulation" in the general interest), while remaining opposed to privatization. At the same time, Kinnock

launched a major drive to cleanse the Labour Party of hard-left "entryists" of the Militant Tendency.

Nevertheless, Labour was again defeated by the Conservatives in the April 1992 elections, although its seat total of 271 and 11.6 million votes (34.4%) represented a significant improvement. Kinnock resigned immediately after the contest and was succeeded by John Smith, a pro-European Scottish lawyer on Labour's moderate wing. Smith continued with the modernization programme, securing the adoption of "one member one vote" (OMOV) arrangements for the selection of Labour candidates and leadership elections, and led Labour to major advances in the 1993 and 1994 local elections. Smith died of a heart attack in May 1994 and was succeeded in July, under the new voting arrangements, by another "modernizing" and pro-European lawyer, Tony Blair (41). Meanwhile, under the interim leadership of Margaret Beckett, Labour had won a decisive victory in the June 1994 European Parliament elections, taking 62 of the 87 UK seats with 42.7% of the vote and for the first time in recent memory breaking through in hitherto "safe" Conservative areas in southern and central England.

In a symbolic revision of Labour's constitution initiated by Blair, a special party conference in April 1995 approved the abandonment of the party's 77-year-old clause 4 commitment to "the common ownership of the means of production, distribution and exchange". It was replaced by a general statement of democratic socialist aims and values asserting that the party seeks "a dynamic economy, serving the public interest, in which the enterprise of the market and the rigour of competition are joined with the forces of partnership and co-operation to produce the wealth the nation needs and the opportunity for all to work and prosper". In another significant policy shift, the Blair leadership in June 1996 announced that plans for the creation of directly-elected assemblies in Scotland and Wales would be submitted to referendums in each country before the necessary legislation was introduced by a Labour government at Westminster.

Blair led the party to a landslide victory in the May 1997 general elections, achieving a national swing from Conservative to Labour of 10.6%. The party won 418 of the 659 seats (with a vote share of 44.4%), giving it the largest parliamentary majority since 1945. The new Labour cabinet included John Prescott as Deputy Prime Minister and Secretary of State for Environment, Transport and the Regions, as well as Gordon Brown as Chancellor of the Exchequer, Jack Straw as Home Secretary and Robin Cook as Foreign and Commonwealth Secretary. Scottish and Welsh devolution bills were introduced and enacted in 1998, elections to the new legislatures in May 1999 producing Labour pluralities of 56 seats out of 129 in Scotland and 28 out of 60 in Wales. Accordingly, Labour formed a coalition with the Liberal Democrats in Scotland under Donald Dewar as first minister and a minority government in Wales under Alun Michael.

The Blair government was buffeted in 1998 by a series of disclosures involving claims that power and influence under Labour were concentrated in a small group of "Tony's cronies"; it was also accused of "control freakery" and of excessive "spin-doctoring" of the news. In December 1998 close Blair aide Peter Mandelson was forced to resign as Trade and Industry Secretary over a controversial private loan at a preferential rate received from another government minister. In the June 1999 European elections, held for the first time by proportional representation based on regional lists, Labour was out-polled by the Conservatives, winning only 28.0% of the vote and dropping from 62 to 29 seats. Nevertheless, Labour held its own in parliamentary by-elections and remained well ahead of the Conservatives in opinion polls, assisted by a generally buoyant economy and falling unemployment, so that Blair felt able to restore Mandelson to the cabinet in October 1999 as Northern Ireland Secretary. In December 1999, moreover, Labour pulled off a major publicity coup when it persuaded former

Conservative front-bench spokesman Shaun Woodward to defect to the Labour Party.

The resignation in January 2000 of junior minister Peter Kilfoyle on the grounds that Labour was losing touch with its working-class supporters highlighted growing discontent with the Blair leadership in sections of the party. In Wales, Blair appointee Alun Michael was forced to resign as first secretary in February by a revolt of the Labour Assembly members, his successor being the more independent Rhodri Morgan. More damaging was the strong support in London Labour ranks for the candidacy of left-wing Labour MP Ken Livingstone for the post of mayor in a restored administration for the capital. The Blair leadership used every stratagem to block Livingstone, securing the selection of former Cabinet minister Frank Dobson as the official Labour candidate even though 60% of London party members backed Livingstone. The latter responded by running as an independent (and accepting expulsion from the party) and easily winning the election in May 2000, with Dobson trailing a poor third.

A public relations disaster for Blair in June 2000, when he was barracked by a Women's Institute audience, was followed by the leaking in July of memos showing the extent of "control freakery" and "spin-doctoring" in the Prime Minister's Office. In September 2000, moreover, the government was caught entirely unprepared by a fuel price protest which brought the country to a standstill for a time. Overhanging such difficulties was the débâcle of London's Millennium Dome, which the government had insisted on building at huge public expense despite being warned that it would be a financial disaster.

In Scotland, the sudden death of Labour first minister Donald Dewar in October 2000 was a blow to a party under increasing challenge from the →Scottish National Party, the new first minister, Henry McLeish, being much less popular than his predecessor. In Wales, Morgan brought the Liberal Democrats into a majority coalition with Labour in October, partly with the aim of achieving greater leverage with the London government in pursuit of Welsh demands. The second enforced resignation of Mandelson in January 2001, this time over his alleged role in a citizenship application by one of the wealthy Hinduja brothers, caused further embarrassment for the government, although many in the party welcomed Mandelson's downfall because of his reputation as the architect of the Blair "modernization" project.

Notwithstanding such difficulties, and the outbreak of a major epidemic of foot-and-mouth disease in February 2001, Labour continued to ride high in the opinion polls, bolstered by a strong economy and the government's reputation for economic competence. The party's manifesto for the general elections eventually held in June 2001 pledged that the economic success of the post-1997 term would be translated in a second term into a major real increases in spending on the NHS, education and public transport. The outcome was a second overwhelming majority for Labour, which won 412 seats (a net loss of only six) and 42% of the vote (down only 2.4%). However, celebration of an unprecedented full second term for a Labour government was somewhat dampened by a voting turnout of only 59.4%, the lowest since 1918.

Cabinet changes and a government restructuring announced by Blair in the wake of the June 2001 elections were intended to ensure delivery of Labour's core pledge to improve the public services. They included the reallocation of Prescott's departmental responsibilities to other ministers, the demotion of Cook to the leadership of the Commons, the appointment of Straw as Foreign and Commonwealth Secretary and the promotion to the Home Office of David Blunkett, who became the first blind person to hold such a senior office. More controversially, Blair appointed Charles Clarke as chairman of the Labour Party (and Cabinet minister), with the stated objective of ensuring close liaison between government and party. Leaders of Labour-affiliated unions pointed out that the party already

had a chairperson, of its national executive committee, and argued that another was not needed. Following Clarke's appointment, Sheila McDonagh resigned as Labour Party general secretary (after less than three years in the post) and was later succeeded by David Triesman from the Association of University Teachers.

In the new House of Commons Labour backbenchers quickly showed that they would be less subservient than during the first Labour term. In July 2001 they inflicted the first defeat on the government since it came to power in 1997 by rejecting the composition of the new select committees proposed by the Labour Whips' Office because two prominent critics of government policy had been dropped. The two members were quickly reinstated, but not before the Blair leadership had been exposed to more charges of "control freakery". Also ominous for the government was the deep unhappiness of the public sector unions with the proposed introduction of much more private-sector finance in the provision of public services.

The Labour Party is a founder member of the Socialist International. Its representatives in the European Parliament sit in the Party of European Socialists group.

Liberal Democrats

Address. 4 Cowley Street, London, SWIP 3NB
Telephone. (+44–20) 7222–7999
Fax. (+44–20) 7799–2170
Email. libdems@cix.co.uk
Website. www.libdems.org.uk
Leadership. Leadership. Charles Kennedy (leader); Alan Beith (deputy leader); Lord (Navnit) Dholakia (president); Baroness (Shirley) Williams (leader in Lords); Hugh Rickard (chief executive)

The Liberal Democrats are directly descended from the historic Liberal Party, by way of an alliance and then merger between the latter and the bulk of the new Social Democratic Party, initially under the title Social and Liberal Democrats, which was shortened in late 1989 to Liberal Democrats. The party's federal constitution states that the party "exists to build and defend a fair, free and more equal society, shaped by the values of liberty, justice and community, in which no-one shall be enslaved by poverty, ignorance or conformity". The party is committed to continued British membership of the European Union (EU) and of the North Atlantic Treaty Organization (NATO), while advocating the freezing of Britain's nuclear deterrent capacity at the existing level. It also advocates devolution of power to Scotland, Wales and the English regions, an elected second chamber at Westminster and the introduction of a form of proportional representation.

Of the two components of the Liberal Democrats, the Liberal Party traced its earliest origins to the 17th-century struggle by English Whigs in favour of freedom of conscience and civil rights, which led ultimately to parliament rather than the monarch being accepted as the country's supreme authority. (The Scottish term Whig was applied to those who opposed the succession of James II in 1685 on account of his Catholic sympathies.) The term Liberal Party was first formally used by Lord John Russell in 1839 in letters to Queen Victoria, Liberal governments holding office for over 50 of the 83 years up to 1914. The National Liberal Federation, set up in 1877, was the national political organization and Liberals were the first to produce party manifestos; they also introduced a national system of education, the secret ballot, the foundations of the welfare state and a reform of the House of Lords. During World War I, when the party led a coalition government under David Lloyd-George, it became divided and began to decline, a process accelerated by the rise of the →Labour Party on the strength of universal adult suffrage and its trade union base.

Liberals held office in the World War II coalition government, and Sir William Beveridge, a Liberal MP in 1944–45, was the architect of the post-war National Health Service and other welfare state structures created by the

Labour government. By now the Liberals' representation in the Commons was tiny, remaining at six seats in the three elections of the 1950s, rising to nine in 1964 and 12 in 1966, and then falling back to six in 1970. In this period the party was led by Clement Davies (1945–56), Jo Grimond (1956–67) and Jeremy Thorpe (1967–76). Under Thorpe's leadership the Liberals obtained over 6 million votes (19.3% of the total) and 14 seats in the February 1994 elections, when →Conservative Prime Minister Edward Heath, having narrowly lost his majority, tried and failed to entice them into a coalition. The result was a minority Labour government and further elections in October 1974, in which the Liberals fell back to 5.3 million votes (18.3%) and 13 seats.

Undone by scandal, Thorpe was succeeded in July 1976 by David Steel, who became the first Liberal leader to be elected directly by party members. Steel took the party into the 1977–78 "Lib-Lab pact", under which the Liberals supported the minority Labour government in its pursuit of economic recovery between March 1977 and July 1978. But his hope that the Liberals would thereby acquire a beneficial "governmental" aura was disappointed in the May 1979 elections, in which the party won only 11 seats on a 13.8% vote share.

With the Conservative Party now in power under the radical right-wing leadership of Margaret Thatcher and the Labour Party having moved sharply to the left following its election defeat, the Liberal Party's hopes of presenting a viable centrist alternative appeared to be strengthened in early 1981 when a right-wing Labour faction broke away to form the Social Democratic Party (SDP). In June 1981 the Alliance of the Liberals and the SDP was launched in a joint statement entitled *A Fresh Start for Britain*, in which the two parties agreed not to oppose each other in elections. After winning a number of Commons by-elections on the basis of this agreement, the Alliance contested the June 1983 general elections with an agreed distribution of candidates between the two parties. However, although it garnered 7.8 million votes (25.4% of the total), the yield in seats was only 23, of which the Liberals took 17.

The Alliance was nevertheless maintained and contested the June 1987 elections under the uneasy joint leadership of Steel and former Labour Foreign Secretary David Owen (who had become leader of the SDP immediately after the 1983 elections). However, a further decisive Conservative victory and a partial Labour recovery denied the Alliance its minimum target of securing the balance of power between the two major parties: its aggregate support fell to 22.6%, with the Liberals winning 4.2 million votes (12.8%) and 17 seats and the SDP 3.2 million (9.8%) and five seats.

Three days after the June 1987 elections Steel unexpectedly proposed a "democratic fusion" of the two Alliance parties, a proposal supported with some reservations within his own party but which divided the SDP into pro-merger and anti-merger factions, the latter including Owen and, at that stage, three of the other four SDP MPs. A subsequent ballot of the SDP membership showed a 57.4% majority in favour of merger negotiations, whereupon Owen resigned as SDP leader in August 1987 and launched an anti-merger Campaign for Social Democracy. His successor was Robert Maclennan, a former Labour MP who had joined the SDP on its formation, had initially opposed merger with the Liberals but was now prepared to negotiate in good faith. After both the SDP and Liberal 1987 annual conferences had given overwhelming approval to the concept of a merger, detailed negotiations on the constitution and platform of a unified party took place. After one false start, these resulted in a modified policy document (published in January 1988) and agreement that the new party should be called the Social and Liberal Democrats (and Democrats for short). Whereas a first policy document had pledged firm support for British acquisition of the Trident nuclear missile system (despite the Liberal Party's commitment to nuclear disarmament), the revised version called for the freezing of Britain's nuclear deterrent at a level no greater than the existing Polaris force.

Later in January 1988 special conferences of the two parties each voted heavily in favour of proceeding to a further ballot of their memberships to secure final approval of the merger plan. Both of these ballots showed large majorities in favour, enabling the new SLD to be formally launched in March 1988, under the joint interim leadership of Steel and Maclennan pending an election for a single leader. This resulted in July 1988 in the elections of Paddy Ashdown, who proceeded to rename the merged party the Liberal Democrats. On the declaration of the SDP's final ballot decision in favour of merger, Dr Owen announced the relaunching of the Social Democratic Party as an independent formation. It did not prosper and was dissolved in June 1990.

Ashdown led the Liberal Democrats to some improvement in the April 1992 general elections, when the party won 20 seats and almost 6 million votes (17.9% of those cast) on a platform which included a commitment to a general increase in the basic income tax. By June 1994 its Commons representation had risen to 23 seats on the strength of a series of stunning by-election victories in hitherto "safe" Conservative seats. In the same month the party at last achieved European Parliament representation, winning two of the 87 UK seats, although its share of the national vote fell back to 16.1%. Thereafter the Liberal Democrats were somewhat eclipsed by Tony Blair's "new" Labour Party, which gained ascendancy as the main opposition party, although the Liberal Democrats were boosted to 26 Commons seats by two Conservative defectors in 1995–96.

The response of the Liberal Democrat leadership to the resurgence of Labour was to make increasingly explicit offers of support for a future Labour government in the event that the Liberal Democrats held the balance of power. In the event, the Labour landslide meant that Liberal Democrats did not hold the balance of power after the May 1997 general elections, although thanks to anti-Conservative tactical voting their seat tally rose sharply to 46 (the highest since 1929) on the basis of a reduced vote share of 17.2%. Liberal Democrats thereafter accepted appointment to a special Cabinet committee of the new Labour government concerned with constitutional and electoral reform (later extended to cover other issues); but the party's influence was limited in the face of Labour's large majority and it made no progress on its aim of bringing in proportional representation for general elections.

A form of PR was introduced for elections to the new devolved legislatures of Scotland and Wales in May 1999, the Liberal Democrats winning 17 Scottish seats (and joining a formal coalition with Labour) and six Welsh seats. Regional PR also operated in the European elections in June 1999, when the Liberal Democrats lifted their seat tally to 10, though on a reduced vote share of 12.7%. Meanwhile, Ashdown had in January 1999 announced his imminent departure as Liberal Democrat leader after 11 years in the post. His successor, elected in August, was Scottish MP and former SDP member Charles Kennedy(39), whose nearest challenger was London MP Simon Hughes. Kennedy pledged that he would seek to build a "strong, independent, progressive" party, while backing the continuation of political co-operation with the Labour government.

In May 2000 the Liberal Democrats had a spectacular by-election success, capturing the "safe" Conservative seat of Romsey in Hampshire with assistance from tactical Labour voters. In simultaneous elections for the new mayor of London, Liberal Democrat candidate Susan Kramer came fourth with 11.9% of the vote, while the party won four of the 25 seats in the new Greater London Assembly and opted to join the mayoral administration of Ken Livingstone (independent). In October 2000 the Liberal Democrats in Wales joined a majority coalition with the dominant Labour Party.

In March 2001 Kennedy concluded an agreement with Prime Minister Tony Blair that the forthcoming Labour election manifesto would promise a review of UK electoral systems to establish whether a referendum should be held on the introduction of proportional representation for Westminster elections. The formula kept alive the Liberal Democrats' holy grail of national PR, although party leaders had no illusions about the lack of real Labour support for a change. The Labour pledge did not feature prominently in the Liberal Democrat campaign for the June 2001 general elections, in which the party consolidated its position by winning 52 seats (a net gain of six) and 18.8% of the vote (up 1.6%). In the Wyre Forest constituency in Worcestershire the Liberal Democrats opted to support the successful candidate of →Independent Kidderminster Hospital and Health Concern.

In September 2001 Kennedy withdrew his party from the Cabinet committee in which it had co-operated with Labour since 1997, thereby signalling his intention that the Liberal Democrats would become a genuine party of opposition. Speaking to the annual party conference in Bournemouth later in the month, Kennedy called upon moderate Conservatives and dissident Labour voters to join the Liberal Democrats.

With an official membership of 90,000, the Liberal Democrats are affiliated to the Liberal International. Their representatives in the European Parliament sit in the European Liberal, Democratic and Reformist group.

Plaid Cymru–The Party of Wales

Address. Ty Gwynfor, 18 Park Grove, Caerdydd/Cardiff, CF10 3BN, Wales
Telephone. (+44–29) 2064–6000
Fax. (+44–29) 2064–6001
Email. post@plaidcymru.org
Website. www.plaidcymru.org
Leadership. Ieuan Wyn Jones (president); Marc Phillips (chairman); Karl Davies (general secretary)

Founded in August 1925, *Plaid Cymru* seeks self-government for Wales based on socialist principles, Welsh membership of the European Union and restoration of the Welsh language and culture. It has contested all elections to the Westminster parliament since 1945 but remained unrepresented until July 1966, when its then president, Dafydd Elis Thomas, won a by-election at Carmarthen. Although the party lost that seat in 1970, it won two others in the February 1974 elections (Carnarvon and Merioneth) and added the Carmarthen seat in October of that year, for a tally of three. The party also built up significant representation in local government. In light of this performance, the then →Labour Party government tabled proposals for an elected Welsh Assembly, but the idea was rejected by Welsh voters in a referendum of March 1979.

In the May 1979 general elections *Plaid Cymru* held the Carnarvon and Merioneth seats but lost Carmarthen to Labour. It retained its two seats in the 1983 elections, winning a total of 125,309 votes. In the June 1987 elections the party again moved up to three Commons seats by winning Ynys Mon in North Wales, although its total vote slipped to 123,595 (7.3% of the Welsh total). The April 1992 general elections yielded the party's best result to date, four of the 32 seats contested being won, including Pembroke North, with an aggregate vote of 148,232 (about 8.5% of the Welsh total). In the June 1994 European Parliament elections, moreover, *Plaid Cymru* advanced to over 17% of the Welsh vote, although without winning any seats.

In the May 1997 general elections *Plaid Cymru* presented 40 candidates, winning four seats with an aggregate vote of 161,030 (9.9% in Wales). It thereafter backed the new Labour government's introduction of a devolved Assembly for Wales and sought to explain the very narrow referendum vote in favour in September 1997 (in a turnout of only 50%) by citing the legislature's lack of tax-raising powers. In the Welsh Assembly elections in May 1999 *Plaid Cymru* made inroads in Labour strongholds in south Wales, taking second place with 17 of the 60 seats on a vote share of 30.5%. In the

June 1999 European elections the *Plaid Cymru* share of the vote in Wales leapt forward to 29.6%, giving it representation (two seats) for the first time.

Plaid Cymru Assembly members contributed to the ousting of Labour first secretary Alun Michael in February 2000 and saw the formation of a Labour-Liberal coalition administration in October as confirming the party's status as the only genuine opposition in Wales. In the UK general elections of June 2001 *Plaid Cymru* again won four seats, but its increased popular vote (195,892) represented a significant advance to 14.3% in Wales.

In August 2001 Ieuan Wyn Jones, Westminster MP for Ynys Mon, was elected leader of *Plaid Cymru* in succession to Dafydd Wigley, who had announced his retirement after 10 years in the post. In September 2001 the party's annual conference in Cardiff formally dropped the goal of independence from the *Plaid Cymru* programme, instead setting full membership of a regionalized EU as the party's aim for Wales. The conference also urged that the Welsh Assembly should be given tax-raising powers.

Plaid Cymru is a member of the Democratic Party of the Peoples of Europe–European Free Alliance. Its representatives in the European Parliament sit in the Greens/European Free Alliance group.

Scottish National Party (SNP)

Address. 6 North Charlotte Street, Edinburgh, EH2 4JH, Scotland
Telephone. (+44–131) 226–3661
Fax. (+44–131) 226–9597
Email. snp.hq@snp.org.uk
Website. www.snp.org.uk
Leadership. John Swinney (leader/national convenor); Winifred Ewing (president); Stewart Hosie (national secretary)

The SNP's basic aim is Scottish independence within the European Union (EU) and the Commonwealth, while on economic and social questions it identifies itself as "moderate, left-of-centre". The party was founded in 1934 as a merger of the National Party of Scotland and the Scottish Party. It won a House of Commons by-election at Motherwell in April 1945 but lost this seat to the →Labour Party in the general elections three months later. Over the next three decades the SNP held only single seats in the House of Commons: Hamilton in 1967-70, Western Isles in 1970–74 and Govan in 1973–74. In the February 1974 elections, however, the party won seven seats with 21.9% of the vote in Scotland, boosted by the discovery of oil in the North Sea and the prospect that an independent Scotland would be financially viable on the basis of oil revenues.

In the October 1974 elections the SNP advanced further to 11 seats with 30.4% of the Scottish vote, whereupon the then Labour government tabled proposals for the creation of a devolved Scottish assembly. But the tide of pro-independence feeling had ebbed somewhat by the time of the March 1979 referendum on the plans, the outcome being that the 52% vote in favour represented only 32.8% of those entitled to vote (the turnout having been 63.7%). Basing itself on an earlier decision that a higher real vote in favour would be required, the UK parliament thereupon refused to set up the assembly. In the May 1979 general elections the SNP lost all but two of its seats, although it still polled 17.2% of the Scottish vote. Both of these seats were retained in the 1983 elections, but the SNP's share of the Scottish vote contracted to 11.8%. In the June 1987 elections the SNP polled 416,873 votes (14% of the Scottish total) and won three parliamentary seats. Immediately prior to the 1987 general elections, the SNP signed an agreement with →*Plaid Cymru* (Welsh Nationalists) pledging mutual support in parliament.

By-election successes increased the SNP's representation in the Commons to five seats in the course of the 1987–92 parliament, but the party fell back to three in the April 1992 general elections despite increasing its share of the Scottish vote to 21.5% (629,564 votes), just behind the

→Conservative Party. The SNP established itself as Scotland's second party (after Labour) in the June 1994 European Parliament elections, obtaining nearly a third of the Scottish vote and winning two Euro-seats (compared with one in 1979). In May 1995, moreover, the party increased its Commons representation to four seats as a result of a by-election victory over the Conservatives in which it took 40% of the vote.

In the May 1997 general elections the SNP increased its representation in the Commons to six seats and its share of the Scottish vote to 22.1%, although in a lower turnout its vote aggregate fell to 621,550. It thereafter opted to work with the incoming Labour government's devolution plan for Scotland, although it fell far short of core SNP aims, and helped to secure 74% approval for the proposals in a referendum in September 1997. In elections to the new Scottish Parliament in May 1999 the SNP came second behind Labour, winning 35 of the 129 seats with a 27.3% share of the list vote and becoming the principal opposition to a coalition of Labour and the →Liberal Democrats. In the June 1999 European elections the SNP again won two seats on a UK vote share of 2.7%.

In March 2000 the SNP published plans for a referendum on independence for Scotland if the party came to power in the 2003 Scottish elections. In July 2000 Alex Salmond unexpectedly announced his decision to vacate the SNP leadership after 10 years in the post. In a leadership ballot three months later John Swinney, who advocated a "gradualist" approach to the goal of independence, easily defeated Alex Neil, a "fundamentalist", by winning 67% of delegates' votes at the party's annual conference in Inverness. In a Commons by-election in December 2000, the SNP narrowly failed to capture the Falkirk West seat, although it achieved a 16% swing from Labour.

Its priority now being the Scottish Parliament, the SNP mounted a low-key campaign for the UK general elections in June 2001. It lost one of its six seats (to the Conservatives) and its share of the Scottish vote fell to 20.1% (464,305). At its annual conference in Dundee in September 2001, the SNP called for a comprehensive review of the "inefficient" UK tax system to make it simpler and more progressive in Scotland. The party also declared its opposition to any attempt by the Labour government in London to combine a cut in the number of Scottish seats in the Commons with a reduction in the size of the Scottish Parliament.

The SNP is a member of the Democratic Party of the Peoples of Europe–European Free Alliance. Its representatives in the European Parliament sit in the Greens/European Free Alliance group.

UK Independence Party (UKIP)

Address. Suite 407, Triumph House, 189 Regent Street, London, W1R 7WF
Telephone. (+44–20) 7434–4559
Fax. (+44–20) 7439–4659
Email. mail@independence.org.uk
Website. www.independence.org.uk
Leadership. Jeffrey Titford (leader); Michael Nattrass (chairman); Michael Harvey (secretary)

The UKIP was founded at the London School of Economics in 1993 by Alan Sked to oppose what it regards as the unacceptable surrender of British sovereignty to the European Union (EU). Having contested the 1992 general elections as the Anti-Federalist League (whose 16 candidates all lost their deposits), the UKIP fought most UK seats in the 1994 European Parliament elections, winning an overall vote share of 1%. In the May 1997 general elections 193 UKIP candidates took only 0.3% of the vote, all but one losing their deposits. However, the party broke through in the June 1999 European elections (held under a form of proportional representation), winning 7.0% of the national vote and returning three MEPs.

The UKIP split in April 2000 when the election of MEP Jeffrey Titford as leader (in succession to Michael Holmes) was seen by a minority faction as confirming the party's drift to the far right. The defectors established the →Reform 2000 Party but failed to attract much rank-and-file support. In the June 2001 general elections the UKIP fielded 428 candidates (all unsuccessful, although six saved their desposits), who obtained an aggregate of 390,576 votes, representing a 1.5% share.

The UKIP representatives in the European Parliament joined the Europe of Democracies and Diversities group.

Other Parties

In addition to the seven parties covered above, 151 other parties in Great Britain were registered with the Electoral Commission as at October 2001, of which 66 had contested the June 2001 general elections. The listing below focuses on those perceived to be more than purely local groupings.

British National Party (BNP), an extreme right-wing formation standing for "rights for whites", a cessation of non-white immigration, encouragement of the "repatriation" of non-whites and a halt to "multiculturalism" in the UK. The party was founded in 1960 as an alliance of the League of Empire Loyalists, the White Defence League and the National Labour Party. A split in the mid-1960s resulted in the formation of a paramilitary elite corps (named "Spearhead") under the leadership of Colin Jordan and John Tyndall, the rump BNP being one of the founder members of the →National Front in 1967. In 1982 the BNP re-emerged as an independent party under Tyndall's leadership, contesting 53 seats in the 1983 general elections (losing 53 deposits) and a smaller number in 1987 (with the same result). Although Tyndall had been sentenced to 12 months' in prison in 1986 for incitement to racial hatred, the party subsequently sought to give a "respectable" face to extreme right-wing politics and to develop contacts with like-minded movements in continental Europe. The 13 BNP candidates all lost their deposits in the 1992 general elections (achieving an aggregate vote of 7,005), but in September 1993 the party won its first local council seat in the east London borough of Tower Hamlets, an area of high Bangladeshi settlement. It lost the seat in the May 1994 local elections, although its overall vote in the borough increased. In the 1997 general elections 57 BNP candidates won 35,832 votes (0.1%), all but three losing their deposits. In June 2001 the BNP's 33 candidates won 47,129 votes (0.2%), five saving their deposits by benefiting from racial tension in northern English constituencies with high Asian populations, notably in Oldham, where BNP chairman Nick Griffin took 16.4%.
Address. PO Box 14, Welshpool, Powys, SY21 0WE
Telephone/Fax. (+44–374) 454–893
Email. letters@bnp.net
Website. www.bnp.net
Leadership. Nick Griffin (chairman); Scott McLean (deputy chairman)

Christian People's Alliance (CPA), founded in 1999 by Kenyan Asian businessman Ram Gidoomal as an attempt to create a continental-style Christian democratic party in Britain. In the May 2000 London elections Gidoomal won 2.5% in the mayoral race, ahead of the →Green Party and →UK Independence Party candidates, while the CPA list took 3.2%, without securing representation.
Address. PO Box 932, Sutton, Surrey, SM1 1HQ
Email. info@cpalliance.net
Website. www.cpalliance.net
Leadership. Ram Gidoomal (leader); David Campanale (president)

Communist Party of Britain (CPB), originally founded in 1920, the present party deriving from a 1988 breakaway by

a minority faction of the Communist Party of Great Britain (→Socialist Alliance) which opposed the CPGB's espousal of "Euro-communism" and later rejected any theoretical accommodation with the collapse of communism in Eastern Europe. The new CPB is closely aligned with the co-operative which has retained control of *The Morning Star* (once the official daily newspaper of the old CPGB). The party's six candidates in the 2001 elections all lost their deposits.
Address. Unit F11, Cape House, 787 Commercial Road, London, E14 7HG
Telephone. (+44–20) 7517–9722
Fax. (+44–20) 7517–9733
Email. cp-of-britain@mcr1.poptel.org.uk
Leadership. Robert Griffiths (general secretary); Anita Halpin (chairperson)

Co-operative Party, founded in 1917 by the British Co-operative Union (the central body representing British consumer and other co-operatives) in order to secure for the co-operative movement direct representation. The party has been represented in parliament ever since, in alliance with the →Labour Party whereby its representatives stand as "Labour and Co-op" candidates. There have been Co-operative members in all Labour governments since 1924.
Address. Victory House, 10–14 Leicester Square, London, WC2H 7QH
Telephone. (+44–20) 7439–0123
Fax. (+44–20) 7439–3434
Email. p.hunt@co-op-party.org.uk
Leadership. James Lee (chairman); Peter Hunt (secretary)

Countryside Party, founded in 2000 "out of a feeling that recognized political parties were at best neglecting or at worst ignoring the feelings of the countryside, and the people who work in the country, or enjoy country sports and the rural way of life". It contested one Scottish seat in June 2001, winning 265 votes.
Address. The Croft, Sunnyside, Culloden Moor, Inverness, IV2 5EE
Email. cparty@btinternet.com
Website. www.countrysideparty.org
Leadership. James Crawford (leader)

Fellowship Party (FP), founded in 1955 on a pacifist, social justice and environmentalist platform, claims to have been instrumental in the establishment of the Campaign for Nuclear Disarmament (CND). It has contested numerous elections without any real success.
Address. Woolacombe House, 141 Woolacombe Road, Blackheath, London, SE3 8QP
Leadership. Sidney Fagan (chairman)

Independent Kidderminster Hospital and Health Concern, created to campaign against the proposed downgrading of Kidderminster NHS hospital in Worcestershire. Its chairman contested the Wyre Forest constituency in June 2001, winning the seat from the →Labour Party with the support of the →Liberal Democrats.
Address. 13 Telford Drive, Bewdley, Worcestershire, DY12 2EP
Leadership. Dr Richard Taylor (chairman)

Islamic Party of Britain (IPB), founded in 1989 in part to campaign for the banning of Salman Rushdie's *Satanic Verses* but also for other religions to be brought under the protection of the blasphemy laws currently only giving (notional) protection to the established Protestant Christian faith. Advocating state funding for Muslim schools (achieved under the post-1997 Labour government), the IPB fielded four candidates in the 1992 elections, obtaining a total of 1,085 votes and losing all four deposits. It did not contest the 1997 and 2001 elections.
Address. PO Box 844, Oldbrook, Milton Keynes, MK6 2YT
Email. info@islamicparty.com

Website. www.islamicparty.com
Leadership. David Musa Pidcock (leader)

Legalize Cannabis Alliance (LCA), founded by convicted cannabis smuggler Howard Marks, presented its first parliamentary candidate in the Kensington and Chelsea by-election in November 1999. Its 13 candidates in the 2001 elections all lost their deposits in winning 8,677 votes in total.
Address. PO Box 198, Norwich, NR2 2DH
Telephone. (+44–1603) 442–215
Email. lca@-uk.org
Website. www.lca-uk.org
Leadership. Alun Buffry (co-ordinator)

Liberal Party (LP), founded by former Liberal MP Michael Meadowcroft as an attempt to keep the historic LP in existence following the formation in 1989 of what became the →Liberal Democrats. The LP obtained 64,744 votes in the 1992 general elections, although only one of its 73 candidate saved his/her deposit. In 1997 its 55 candidates obtained a total of 45,166 votes (0.1%), all but two losing their deposits. Less ambitiously, it contested nine seats in 2001, losing deposits in eight in winning 10,920 votes.
Address. PO Box 263, Southport, Lancashire, PR9 9AQ
Telephone/Fax. (+44–1704) 500–115
Email. libparty@libparty.demon.co.uk
Website. www.libparty.demon.co.uk
Leadership. Michael Meadowcroft (leader)

Mebyon Kernow (Party for Cornwall), founded in 1951 to campaign for the self-government of Cornwall. By 1960 it claimed to have the active support of three Cornish MPs of other parties, although such people became ineligible for membership following the movement's 1974 decision to contest parliamentary elections itself. It has gained representation in Cornish local government, often under the "independent" label, but has failed at national level, its three candidates in 2001 all losing their deposits in winning 3,199 votes.
Address. Lanhainsworth, Fraddon Hill, St Columb, Cornwall, TR9 6PQ
Email. dickcole@tinyworld.co.uk
Website. members.tripod.co.uk/trebell
Leadership. Dick Cole (leader); Colin Lawry (deputy leader)

Monster Raving Loony Party (MRLP), Britain's premier "alternative" party, founded in the early 1960s by David ("Screaming Lord") Sutch (a former rock musician). Sutch contested over 40 by-elections before he committed suicide in June 1999, never saving a deposit but sometimes registering a not insignificant vote, as when he obtained 4.8% in a 1994 contest, outpolling the candidate of the Social Democratic Party (→Liberal Democrats). Sutch was succeeded by publican Alan ("Howling Lord") Hope, who bestowed joint party leadership on his ginger tomcat Mandu. Known by many variants of its historic title and currently calling itself the "Official" MRLP, the party has some support in the West Country, Hope having been mayor of Ashburton when he became leader. It fielded 18 candidates in the 1997 general elections, all of whom lost their deposits. In 2001 its 15 candidates suffered the same fate in winning a total of 6,655 votes.
Address. The Dog and Partridge, 105 Reading Road, Yateley, Hampshire, GU46 7LR
Leadership. Alan Hope (leader)

Muslim Party, contending that the 2-million-strong UK Muslim community needs separate political representation; it ran four candidates in 2001 and won 1,003 votes in total.
Address. First Base, Calthorpe House, 30 Hagley Road, Birmingham, B16 8QY
Leadership. Abdul Aziz (leader)

National Democratic Resistance (NDR), far-right formation opposed to non-white immigration, also campaigning against abuse of the political asylum system, for more vigorous action against paedophiles and against membership of the European Union. The party presented 21 candidates in the 1997 general elections, all but one losing their deposits, winning an aggregate vote of 10,829. Under the chairmanship of Ian Anderson (a former leader of the →National Front), it did not present candidates in 2001, preferring to back other far-right parties.

Address. BCM Natdems, London, WC1N 3XX
Telephone. (+44–7071) 226–074
Email. natdems@swnd.freeserve.co.uk
Website. www.natdems.org.uk
Leadership. Ian Anderson (chairman)

National Front (NF), far-right formation founded in 1967, seeking the restoration of Britain as an ethnically homogeneous state by means of the "repatriation" of coloured immigrants and their descendants. It also seeks to liberate Britain from international ties such as the United Nations, NATO and the European Union, and opposes the international financial system and "big business capitalism", favouring instead small privately-owned enterprises and workers' co-operatives. The NF was founded as a merger of the →British National Party (BNP), the League of Empire Loyalists and the Racial Preservation Society. It has nominated candidates in all general elections since its formation, rising to 303 in 1979, but has received only negligible support, although a 1973 by-election in West Bromwich yielded 16% of the vote. In the 1970s NF meetings frequently led to violence, as opponents mounted counter-demonstrations. The right of NF candidates to hire halls for election meetings was upheld by the High Court in November 1982, but many NF marches have been banned under the Public Order Act since then, while some NF leaders have been convicted of "incitement to racial hatred" under the Race Relations Act. In 1984–85 the NF gained publicity when one of its activists, Patrick Harrington, registered at a North London college, provoking a long confrontation with anti-fascist students. The Front then sought to improve its image by electing a new generation of university-educated leaders who developed an intellectual basis for the movement (described as "new positivism") and publicly distanced themselves from the violent street activism previously associated with Martin Webster (the controversial NF organizer ousted from the party in 1983–84). Nevertheless, internal divisions continued, leading to a split between a "revolutionary nationalist" group and a "radical nationalist" group in 1986–87, by which time the NF had largely been eclipsed on the far right by the revived BNP. The NF's 14 candidates in the 1992 elections all lost their deposits, obtaining a total of 4,816 votes. In 1997 six NF candidates won 2,716 votes, all losing their deposits and in 2001 five NF candidates also failed, winning 2,484 votes in total.

Address. PO Box 5475, Hinckley, LE10 2WD
Telephone. (+44–7932) 509–805
Email. britishnationalfront@hotmail.com
Website. www.natfront.com
Leadership. Tom Holmes (chairman)

Pro-Life Alliance, anti-abortion movement which fielded 56 candidates in the May 1997 elections, all losing their deposits in winning an aggregate vote of 19,332 (0.1%). In 2001 37 Pro-Life candidates took only 9,453 votes and all lost their deposits.

Address. PO Box 13395, London, SW3 6XE
Telephone. (+44–20) 7351–9955
Fax. (+44–20) 7349–0450
Email. info@prolifealliance.org.uk
Website. www.prolifealliance.org.uk
Leadership. Bruno Quintavalle (chairman)

Reform 2000 Party, formed by a dissident anti-right faction of the →UK Independence Party. Its five candidates in 2001 all lost their deposits in winning 1,418 votes.

Address. PO Box 394, Waltham Cross, Hertfordshire, EN8 8DX
Leadership. Erol Basarik (leader)

Revolutionary Communist Party of Britain–Marxist-Leninist (RCPB–ML), leftist grouping founded in 1981. Its eight candidates all lost their deposits in the 1992 general elections, obtaining an aggregate vote of 745 electors. The party did not contest the 1997 and 2001 elections.

Address. 170 Wandsworth Road, London, SW8 2LA
Telephone. (+44–20) 7627–0599
Email. office@rcpbml.org.uk
Website. www.rcpbml.org.uk
Leadership. Chris Coleman (chairman)

Scottish Green Party, autonomous environmentalist party in Scotland linked fraternally with the →Green Party of England and Wales. Its one successful candidate for the new Scottish Parliament in May 1999 was the first for the Greens in a major UK election. In the 2001 general elections three of the party's four candidates lost their deposits, the aggregate party vote being 4,551.

Address. 14 Albany Street, Edinburgh, EH1 3QB
Telephone/Fax. (+44–131) 478–7896
Email. info@scottishgreens.org.uk
Website. www.scottishgreens.org.uk
Leadership. Mark Ballard (convenor); Robin Harper (principal spokesperson)

Scottish Socialist Party (SSP), left-wing formation in Scotland opposed to the "revisionism" of Blair's →Labour Party. It failed to make an impact in 1997 general elections, but was joined by Labour MP Dennis Canavan, who won a seat in the Scottish Parliament elections in May 1999 (and whose Westminster seat was regained by Labour in a December 2000 by-election following his expulsion from the party). In the 2001 general elections the 72 SSP candidates were all unsuccessful (62 losing their deposits), mustering an aggregate vote of 72,279 (3.1% in Scotland).

Address. 73 Robertson Street (2nd floor), Glasgow, G2 8QD
Leadership. Tommy Sheridan (leader)

Socialist Alliance, formed prior to the 2001 elections as a broad front of some 15 groupings to the left of the Labour Party, including (i) the **Communist Party of Great Britain (CPGB),** descended from the "moderate" majority wing of the historic Communist Party by way of the Democratic Left formation of the 1990s; the **Socialist Party (SP),** led by former Labour MP Dave Nellist; and the **Socialist Workers' Party (SWP),** founded in 1950 as the International Socialists and known under that name until 1977. The Alliance ran 98 candidates, who won a total of 60,496 votes (0.2%), with only three saving their deposits. In September 2001 the Alliance launched a campaign against the US–UK military action in Afghanistan.

Address. Wickham House, 10 Cleveland Way, London, E1 4TR
Telephone. (+44–20) 7791–3138
Email. office@socialistalliance.net
Website. www.socialistalliance.net
Leadership. Dave Nellist (chairman)

Socialist Equality Party (SEP), British section of the (Trotskyist) International Committee of the Fourth International, fighting against "the post-Soviet school of falsification which seeks to draw an equals sign between the bloody dictatorship of Stalin and genuine socialism". The SEP strongly opposes the US-UK military action in Afghanistan.

Address. PO Box 1306, Sheffield, S9 3UW
Telephone. (+44–114) 244–3545
Fax. (+44–114) 244–0224

Email. sep@socialequality.org.uk
Website. www.socialequality.org.uk

Socialist Labour Party (SLP), launched by Arthur Scargill in 1996 to provide a radical left-wing alternative to the "new" →Labour Party of Tony Blair. As president of the National Union of Mineworkers, Scargill had led abortive opposition to the policies of the Thatcher government in the 1980s, becoming disenchanted with the line of the Labour leadership. In the new party's first electoral contest, at the Hemsworth by-election in February 1996, the SLP candidate won 5.4% of the vote. In the 1997 general elections 61 of 64 SLP candidates lost their deposits, the party's aggregate vote being 52,109. In 2001 all but one of the 114 SLP candidates lost their deposits, their aggregate vote being 57,536 (0.2%).
Address. 9 Victoria Road, Barnsley, S. Yorks, S70 2BB
Telephone/Fax. (+44) 1226) 770–957
Leadership. Arthur Scargill (chairman)

Socialist Party of Great Britain (SPGB), a Marxist formation founded in 1904 in quest of "a world-wide community based on the common ownership and democratic control of the means of wealth distribution and production". In the course of its long history the SPGB opposed both world wars. Its parliamentary and local election forays have also met with regular lack of success. The SPGB has links with similarly named and orientated parties in a number of other developed countries, together constituting the World Socialist Movement.
Address. 52 Clapham High Street, London SW4 7UN
Telephone. (+44–20) 7622–3811
Fax. (+44–20) 7720–3665
Email. spgb@worldsocialism.org
Website. www.worldsocialism.org/spgb
Leadership. Julian Vein (chairman)

Workers' Revolutionary Party (WRP), far-left formation which rejects "the parliamentary road to socialism" but has contested recent general elections. Descended from the pre-war Militant Group, by way of the Workers' International League and the Revolutionary Communist Party (among other earlier formations), the WRP succeeded the Socialist Labour League (founded in 1959) and at first worked inside the Labour Party. The party ran six candidates in the 2001 elections, garnering a total of 607 votes.
Address. BCM Box 747, London, WC1N 3XX
Telephone. (+44–20) 7928–3218
Fax. (+44–20) 7620–1221
Email. info@wrp.org.uk
Website. www.wrp.org.uk
Leadership. Sheila Torrance (general secretary)

Northern Ireland

Capital: Belfast

Population: 1,665,000 (2000E)

Northern Ireland was created in 1921 as an autonomous component of the United Kingdom of Great Britain and Northern Ireland, its territory comprising six counties (four with a Protestant majority) of the historic nine-county Irish province of Ulster. Amid a descent into sectarian violence between Protestants and the Catholic minority and the launching by the Irish Republican Army (IRA) of an armed campaign against British rule, the Northern Ireland parliament was suspended in 1972. For the next 27 years (apart from a brief period in 1974) Northern Ireland was ruled directly from Westminster, the responsible member of the UK Cabinet being the Secretary of State for Northern Ireland. However, the multi-party Good Friday Agreement signed in Belfast on April 10, 1998, provided for the restoration of a Northern Ireland legislature and government (executive) with substantial economic and social powers, the executive to be constituted under power-sharing arrangements giving all major parties representation.

Elections to a new Northern Ireland Assembly were held on June 25, 1998, the 108 seats being filled by the single transferable vote method in 18 six-member constituencies, as follows: Ulster Unionist Party (UUP) 28 seats (with 21.3% of the vote), Social Democratic and Labour Party (SDLP) 24 (22.0%), Democratic Unionist Party (DUP) 20 (18.1%), *Sinn Féin* 18 (17.6%), Alliance Party of Northern Ireland 6 (6.5%), United Kingdom Unionist Party 5 (4.5%), Independent Unionists 3 (3.0%), Progressive Unionist Party 2 (2.5%), Northern Ireland Women's Coalition 2 (1.6%).

A year and a half later, on Dec. 2, 1999, the new power-sharing executive was formally established, whereupon the Irish government promulgated amendments to the Republic's 1937 constitution (approved by referendum on May 22, 1998) formally enshrining the principle of popular consent to any change in the status of the North (see introduction to Ireland chapter). Also inaugurated on Dec. 2, 1999, were a consultative North–South Ministerial Council, a re-launched UK-Irish Intergovernmental Council and a "Council of the Isles" (representing the parliaments of the UK, the Irish Republic, Northern Ireland, Scotland, Wales, the Channel Islands and the Isle of Man).

In the UK general elections of June 7, 2001, the 18 Northern Ireland seats (filled by simple majority in single-member constituencies) were distributed as follows: UUP 6 (with 26.8% of the Northern Ireland vote), DUP 5 (22.5%), *Sinn Féin* 4 (21.7%), SDLP 3 (21.0%).

Alliance Party of Northern Ireland (Alliance/APNI)
Address. 88 University Street, Belfast, BT7 1HE
Telephone. (+44–28) 9032–4274
Fax. (+44–28) 9033–3147
Email. alliance@allianceparty.org
Website. www.allianceparty.org
Leadership. (Sean) Neeson (leader); Seamus Close (deputy leader); Richard Good (general secretary)

Alliance, as the party is usually known, was founded in April 1970 as a centrist, non-sectarian unionist party, drawing support from the moribund Ulster Liberal Party and the moderate (Faulknerite) Unionist Party of Northern Ireland. It advocates the restoration of a devolved government with the sharing of power between the Catholic and Protestant sections of the community. The party, which has tended to have a mainly Protestant following but Catholic leaders, is generally regarded as a liberal middle-class formation, and is strongly opposed to political violence. It was the only unionist party to support the Anglo-Irish Agreement of November 1985.

Alliance first contested elections in 1973, winning 9.2% of the vote for the Northern Ireland Assembly. In January 1974 it joined a power-sharing executive (provincial government) with Brian Faulkner's faction of the →Ulster Unionist Party and with the →Social Democratic and Labour Party (SDLP). That executive collapsed in May 1974. In the May 1975 Constitutional Convention elections Alliance obtained 9.8% of the vote, and its support peaked in the 1977 local government elections, when it came third with 14.3%. In the Assembly elections of October 1982 it won 10 of the 78 seats, with 9.3%. In the June 1983 UK general elections Alliance polled 8% of the vote, and in those of June 1987 9.9%.

John Cushnahan, who had succeeded Oliver Napier as party leader in 1984, resigned in October 1987 and was succeeded by John T. Alderdice. In the 1989 local, 1992 general and 1993 local elections the party secured 6%, 8.7% and 7.7% of the vote respectively. It fell to 4.1% in the 1994 European polls but recovered to 6.5% in the 1996 Forum elections. Strongly supportive of the April 1998 Good Friday Agreement, the party again won 6.5% of the vote in the June 1998 Assembly elections, which gave it six seats, insufficient for representation on the new power-sharing executive. Sean Neeson was elected party leader in September 1998 after Lord Alderdice (as he now was) had resigned on his appointment as initial presiding officer (speaker) of the new Assembly. In the June 2001 UK general elections Alliance fielded 10 candidates, who took 3.6% of the Northern Ireland vote without winning a seat.

Alliance is a full member of the Liberal International, which it joined in 1991, and of the European Liberal Democratic and Reformist Party (ELDR). It has had close relations, but no organic link, with the Liberal Party in Great Britain, and subsequently with the →→Liberal Democrats.

Democratic Unionist Party (DUP)

Address. 91 Dundela Avenue, Belfast, BT4 3BU
Telephone. (+44–28) 9047–1155
Fax. (+44–28) 9047–1797
Email. info@dup.org.uk
Website. www.dup.org.uk
Leadership. Rev. Ian Richard Kyle Paisley (leader); Peter Robinson (deputy leader); Jim McClure (chairman); Nigel Dodds (secretary)

The DUP is a loyalist party closely identified with its leader's brand of fundamentalist Protestantism and drawing its main support from the urban working class and small farmers. The DUP is more populist than the →Ulster Unionist Party (UUP, formerly OUP). It is vehemently opposed to any involvement of the Dublin government, which it regards as alien and Catholic-controlled, in the administration of the North. It also opposes the European Union, which it has denounced as a Catholic conspiracy, although the party has accepted representation in the European Parliament.

The holder of an honorary doctorate from the Bob Jones University of South Carolina (USA), Paisley founded and leads the Free Presbyterian Church, a fiery sect which provides much of the DUP's support. He was also founder and leader of the DUP's predecessor, the Protestant Unionist Party (PUP), which was formed in 1969 (by the amalgamation of the Ulster Constitution Defence Committee with Ulster Protestant Action) and which in 1970 won two seats in the Northern Ireland parliament and one in the UK parliament. The DUP was founded in 1971 (formally known as the Ulster Democratic Unionist Party, UDUP) and won eight of the 78 seats in the Northern Ireland Assembly in 1973. Paisley was re-elected to the UK House of Commons in February and October 1974, when the DUP and other groups combined as the United Ulster Unionist Council (UUUC). He was re-elected in 1979, when the DUP gained

two other seats, and in the same year Paisley was elected to the European Parliament. In 1975–76 the party held 12 of the 46 UUUC seats in the inconclusive Northern Ireland Constitutional Convention.

In the October 1982 elections to a Northern Ireland Assembly the DUP secured 21 of the 78 seats (with 23% of the vote). The DUP's Westminster MPs, re-elected in 1983 (when the party secured 20% of the vote), resigned their seats along with their OUP colleagues in January 1986, forcing by-elections as a form of referendum on the 1985 Anglo-Irish Agreement: all three held their seats, as they did in the June 1987 UK general elections, when the DUP declined to 11.7% (having agreed not to contest any OUP-held seats). Peter Robinson, who had lost prestige in unionist circles by paying a fine imposed for participating in a riot in the Republic of Ireland, resigned after seven years as deputy leader in October 1987, but was re-appointed in early 1988.

In the 1992 UK general elections the DUP increased its vote to 13.1%, retaining its three MPs, and in 1993 it won 17.2% in local elections (down from 17.7% in 1989). After the IRA ceasefire first declared in 1994 and reinstated in 1996, the DUP resolutely opposed any negotiations by political parties or government representatives with →Sinn Féin. In the 1996 Forum elections it increased its vote to 18.8%, winning 24 of the 110 seats.

The DUP slipped to two seats and a 12.3% vote share in the UK general elections in May 1997. It refused to participate in the negotiations that produced the Good Friday Agreement of April 1998 and claimed that only a minority of Protestants had endorsed it in the referendum held in May 1998. In the June 1998 Assembly elections the DUP won 18.0% of the vote and 20 of the 108 seats, therefore becoming entitled to two posts in the new power-sharing executive. In the June 1999 European elections the DUP again won one seat (heading the Northern Ireland poll with 28.0% of the vote). Having called unsuccessfully for the expulsion of *Sinn Féin* from the peace process, the two DUP ministers (Peter Robinson and Nigel Dodds), took their seats when the executive was eventually inaugurated in December 1999, although they refused to sit in meetings with *Sinn Féin* representatives.

Maintaining its opposition to the power-sharing arrangements as they ran into serious difficulties in 2000, the DUP was rewarded in a September by-election for the Westminster seat of South Antrim, which it captured from the UUP by 822 votes. In the June 2001 UK general elections, moreover, the DUP advanced strongly to five Commons seats and 22.5% of the Northern Ireland vote, its gains being at the expense of the UUP. In October 2001 Paisley and other DUP leaders were entirely unconvinced by the long-delayed start of arms decommissioning by the IRA.

The DUP representative in the European Parliament is one of the non-attached members.

Northern Ireland Women's Coalition (NIWC)

Address. 50 University Street, Belfast, BT7 1HB
Telephone. (+44–28) 9068–1118
Fax. (+44–28) 9068–1118
Email. niwc@iol.ie
Leadership. Monica McWilliams, Pearl Sagar & Jane Morrice

The NIWC began as an ad hoc grouping formed to raise the profile of women's issues in the May 1996 Forum elections and the subsequent discussions. It obtained just over 1% of the vote and its regional-list nominees, Monica McWilliams and Pearl Sagar, were among only 14 women elected to the 110–seat body, in which they frequently protested that their interventions were not taken seriously. Strongly supportive of the April 1998 Good Friday Agreement, the NIWC won two seats and a 1.6% vote share in the June 1998 Assembly elections. In the June 2001 UK elections the NIWC fielded only one candidate, who obtained 2,968 votes.

Progressive Unionist Party (PUP)

Address. 182 Shankill Road, Belfast, BT13 2BL
Telephone. (+44–28) 9032–6233
Fax. (+44–28) 9024–9602
Website. www.pup.org
Leadership. Hugh Smyth (leader); David Ervine (spokesperson); Billy Hutchinson (press officer)

Formed in 1977 (succeeding the Volunteer Political Party, VPP), the PUP is the political wing of one of the two largest "loyalist" paramilitary groupings, namely the Ulster Volunteer Force (UVF), and also speaks for the Red Hand Commando (RHC). Although the UVF has been illegal almost since its formation, the existence of the PUP permitted the British government to engage openly in ministerial-level negotiations with it from late 1994, the declared aim of the government being to secure the disarmament of the loyalist groups. It was widely accepted that the electoral system for the 1996 Forum elections, in which the PUP secured 3.5% of the vote and two seats, was designed to ensure representation for the two parties euphemistically described as "close to the thinking of" the loyalist paramilitaries.

The PUP was strongly supportive of the peace process which resulted in the April 1998 Good Friday Agreement, being regarded as the most left-wing of the unionist parties. In the June 1998 elections to a new Northern Ireland Assembly it won two seats on a vote share of 2.5%. In the June 2001 UK elections its two candidates, both unsuccessful, won 0.6% of the Northern Ireland vote.

Sinn Féin (SF)

Address. 51–55 Falls Road, Belfast, BT12 4PD
Telephone. (+44–28) 9062–4421
Fax. (+44–28) 9062–2112
Email. sinnfein@iol.ie
Website. www.sinnfein.ie
Leadership. Gerry Adams (president); Martin McGuinness (vice-president); Mitchel McLaughlin (chairman)

Sinn Féin (meaning "ourselves" or "we alone" in Irish) is one of a small number of parties active in both jurisdictions on the island of Ireland (see also entry in Ireland chapter). The Northern membership, which forms a majority within the party, is formally integrated in the all-Ireland structure, although a Northern executive deals with matters specific to what the party calls "the occupied area" or "the six counties".

Founded in 1905 as a nationalist pressure group, *Sinn Féin* in 1918 won 73 of the 105 Irish seats in the UK House of Commons, refusing to take them and instead formed a Constituent Assembly for an independent state in Dublin. After the partition of Ireland in 1922 it was the political wing of the militant republican movement, supporting the periodic guerrilla campaigns of the Irish Republican Army (IRA) against British rule. The main party of the Catholic electorate in the North after 1922 was the Nationalist Party, as *Sinn Féin* candidates stood on a policy of refusing to recognize or participate in any of the three parliaments claiming jurisdiction on the island. In the 1955 Northern Ireland parliamentary elections, however, SF won 150,000 votes (some 56% of the Catholic total). The party was banned in Northern Ireland in 1956 (and remained so until 1973).

A period of left-wing activity from 1967 moved *Sinn Féin* to an overtly socialist position, but communal violence in 1969 led to a resurgence of the traditional nationalist tendency. A split in 1970 led to the creation of a "Provisional" Army Council, which rebuilt the IRA to pursue a military campaign against British rule; the political wing of this more militant faction became known as Provisional or (after its Dublin headquarters) Kevin Street *Sinn Féin*, to distinguish it from "Official" (Gardiner Place) *Sinn Féin*. The latter group evolved into the Workers' Party, leaving only one *Sinn Féin* and making redundant the Provisional prefix (which was never formally adopted but is still widely used in the abbreviated "Provos" form).

The Provisional tendency portrayed itself through the 1970s as a classic national liberation movement, adopting Marxist rhetoric for non-American audiences, but in fact having almost no party political activity because of its principle of abstention from the institutions of the "partitionist" states. In the early 1980s, however, the movement was transformed by the emotional reaction and mass demonstrations generated by the hunger strikes of IRA (and other) prisoners, and by the election of abstentionist republican (not, formally, *Sinn Féin*) candidates to the Westminster and Dublin parliaments. *Sinn Féin* capitalized on the hunger strike issue to involve a new generation in its political activities, which broadened to include participation in community issues and contesting local and parliamentary elections. It continued to demand British disengagement from the North and the negotiation of a new all-Ireland framework. In 1981 it won the UK Commons seat which had been held by an IRA volunteer, Bobby Sands, who had died on hunger strike.

In the 1982 elections to the Northern Ireland Assembly, SF candidates secured 10.1% of the vote. In the 1983 UK general elections SF won 13.1% in Northern Ireland (43% of the Catholic vote), with Gerry Adams (who had become national leader of SF in 1983) being the only SF candidate elected (and holding to the abstentionist policy). By late 1987 SF had some 60 seats on local councils in the North, having won its first in 1983. In the UK general elections of June 1987, SF received 11.2% of the vote, with Adams holding his seat in West Belfast. In the 1992 elections, however, he lost it to the →Social Democratic and Labour Party (SDLP) and the SF vote slipped to 10%.

From January 1988 *Sinn Féin* had a series of discreet meetings with the SDLP, much to the consternation of the unionist camp, which spoke of a "pan-nationalist pact". The contacts were instrumental in bringing about secret negotiations with the British government in 1991–93, and the announcement of an IRA ceasefire in August 1994. During the ceasefire the party sought to become involved in ministerial-level negotiations with Britain and in all-party talks on a new constitutional framework, but the British government and most unionist parties insisted that substantive talks had to be preceded by the partial or complete disarmament of the IRA. The IRA resumed its bombings in February 1996, following which *Sinn Féin* continued to press for unconditional inclusion in negotiations. It was bolstered by its increased share of the vote (15.5%) in the June 1996 elections to a consultative Northern Ireland Forum (the proceedings of which SF boycotted because of its continued exclusion from constitutional talks).

Sinn Féin scored a major success in the May 1997 UK elections, returning two candidates (Adams and deputy SF leader Martin McGuinness) and securing 16.1% of the vote. Both declined to swear the oath of allegiance and so were barred from taking up their seats (their attempt to obtain members' facilities at Westminster being rebuffed by Speaker Betty Boothroyd). The reinstatement of the IRA ceasefire in July 1997 and the referral of the arms decommissioning issue to an international commission facilitated the inclusion of *Sinn Féin* in peace talks which yielded the Good Friday Agreement of April 1998. In elections to a new Northern Ireland Assembly in June 1998, SF candidates took 17.6% of the vote, winning 18 of the 108 seats, which entitled the party to two seats on the new power-sharing executive. In the June 1999 European elections the SF vote held up at 17.1%, but the party did not gain representation.

On the eventual implementation of the April 1998 accord in December 1999, McGuinness and Bairbre de Brun became the two SF ministers in the new Northern Ireland executive, responsible respectively for education and health. *Sinn Féin* deplored the reimposition of direct rule in February 2000 and welcomed the restoration of the executive 108 days later. It thereafter accused the →Ulster Unionist Party (UUP) of seeking to sabotage the peace process by insisting on IRA arms decommissioning as a condition for its continued participation, arguing that general demilitarization was required, applying also to British forces. In April 2001 McGuinness for the first time acknowledged publicly that he had been an IRA commander in the 1960s. This did not harm *Sinn Féin* in the UK general elections in June, when the party outpolled the SDLP by winning 21.7% of the Northern Ireland vote and doubling its seat tally from two to four.

In October 2001 Adams announced that the *Sinn Féin* leadership had urged the IRA to begin arms decommissioning in the interests of saving the peace process. The confirmation within days that the IRA had responded positively was seen as an historic renunciation of armed struggle by the mainstrean republican movement. Most commentators related the decision to the Sept. 11 terrorist attacks on the USA and the resultant US denunication of all forms of terrorism.

Sinn Féin has no formal international affiliations, although it corresponds with many overseas socialist parties and nationalist movements. It has a particular affinity with the →→We Basques (*Eukal Herritarrok*) separatist party in Spain.

Social Democratic and Labour Party (SDLP)

Address. 121 Ormeau Road, Belfast, BT7 1SH
Telephone. (+44–28) 9024–7700
Fax. (+44–28) 9023–6699
Email. sdlp@indigo.ie
Website. www.sdlp.ie
Leadership. Mark Durkan (leader); Séamus Mallon (deputy leader); Jonathan Stephenson (chairman); Gerry Cosgrove (general secretary)

The nationalist, centre-left SDLP is the main party of the Catholic minority, and has as its long-term objective the reunification of Ireland by consent; it rejects political violence and seeks co-operation with the Protestant majority. It was for some years the only major party in Northern Ireland committed to the maintenance of the 1985 Anglo–Irish Agreement, and to the institutionalization of the Dublin government's advisory role in respect of Northern affairs; subsequently it became a driving-force in the peace process which led to the Good Friday Agreement of April 1998. There are within the SDLP various currents of opinion committed to greater or lesser degrees to traditional nationalism; the social democratic aspect of its ideology has tended to be understated.

The SDLP grew out of the civil rights agitation of the late 1960s; it was formed in August 1970 by members of the then Northern Ireland Parliament. Two of its founders sat for the Republican Labour Party (including Gerry Fitt, also a Westminster MP, who became leader), one for the Northern Ireland Labour Party, one for the Nationalist Party and three as independents. Having rapidly overtaken the Nationalist Party as the main party of the Catholic community, the SDLP participated with moderate unionist members of the Northern Ireland Assembly in the short-lived power-sharing executive formed in 1974. SDLP candidate John Hume was elected to the European Parliament in 1979, in which year he won the party leadership from Fitt (who left the party, lost his Westminster seat and was later appointed to the UK House of Lords). In the 1982 Assembly elections the SDLP won 14 seats, with 18.8% of the vote, but did not take them up because of the opposition of the unionist parties to power-sharing. Hume entered the UK House of Commons in the 1983 elections, when the SDLP's advantage over the radical republican →*Sinn Féin* (SF) fell to 4.5 percentage points (17.9% to 13.4%), although it recovered ground in the Catholic community thereafter.

The SDLP won an additional Westminster seat in the 15 by-elections held in Northern Ireland in early 1987, and a third seat in the 1987 UK general elections, with 21.6% of the vote. In the 1992 UK general elections the party took 23.5% of the Northern Ireland vote and captured a fourth seat, winning back West Belfast from *Sinn Féin*. However, Hume's central role in bringing about the IRA ceasefire of

1994–96 and its reinstatement in July 1997, and in persuading *Sinn Féin* to commit itself publicly to a negotiated settlement, proved of more electoral benefit to *Sinn Féin* than to the SDLP. In the 1996 Forum elections the decline in the SDLP vote (to 21.4%) contributed significantly to the dramatic increase in the *Sinn Féin* vote. In the May 1997 UK general elections the SDLP fell back to three seats, although its share of the Northern Ireland vote improved to 24.1%, eight points ahead of *Sinn Féin*.

Strongly supportive of the April 1998 Good Friday Agreement, the SDLP won 24 of the 108 seats in the new Northern Ireland Assembly elected in June 1998, taking a 22.0% vote share. Hume was the joint recipient, with →Ulster Unionist Party (UUP) leader David Trimble, of the 1998 Nobel Peace Prize. He was again elected to the European Parliament in June 1999, the SDLP winning 27.7% of the Northern Ireland vote, well ahead of the UUP. In the new power-sharing executive inaugurated in December 1999, Séamus Mallon became Deputy First Minister and three SDLP ministers were appointed, namely Mark Durkan (finance), Seán Farren (higher education and employment) and Brid Rodgers (agriculture).

Through the repeated crises in the peace process in 2000-01, the SDLP consistently called on the IRA to begin arms decommissioning in advance of the general demilitarization demanded by *Sinn Féin*. This brought in no reward in the June 2001 UK general elections, in which the SDLP retained three seats but fell back to 21% of the Northern Ireland and was overtaken by *Sinn Féin*. In September 2001 Hume announced his retirement as SDLP leader for health reasons (although not as a Westminster MP and MEP) and was succeeded in November by Durkan (41).

The SDLP is a full member of the Socialist International. Its representative in the European Parliament sits in the Party of European Socialists group.

Ulster Unionist Party (UUP)

Address. 3 Glengall Street, Belfast, BT12 5AE
Telephone. (+44–28) 9032–4601
Fax. (+44–28) 9024–6738
Email. uup@uup.org
Website. www.uup.org
Leadership. David Trimble (leader); John Taylor (deputy leader); Sir Josias Cunningham (president)

Dating from 1905, the UUP is the largest party of the (mainly Protestant) unionist majority in Northern Ireland and stands for the maintenance of the union with Great Britain, while also accepting in recent years the need for power-sharing with the Catholic minority and a consultative all-Ireland dimension in the governance of the province. Generally conservative on social and economic issues, the party was closely linked for most of its existence with the British →→Conservative Party, but those ties were considerably weakened during the early 1970s and were terminated as a result of the Conservative Party's commitment to the 1985 Anglo–Irish Agreement.

The original Unionist Party, which with the semi-secret Orange Order mobilized the Protestant majority in north-eastern Ireland in defence of the union with Britain, was founded in 1905. It was the monolithic ruling party from the creation of Northern Ireland in 1921 (by the partition treaty which gave the rest of the country autonomy within the British Empire) until the prorogation of the regional parliament and the introduction of direct rule from London in 1972. During this period of Protestant unionist hegemony, which was challenged from time to time by upsurges of republican violence, the region was ruled by a parliament and government based at Stormont, although it continued to be represented in the UK legislature at Westminster.

The party fragmented in 1970–73 under pressures arising from the agitation of the Catholic minority for civil rights. The faction informally known as the Official Unionist Party (OUP) was the largest and the most successful in claiming historical continuity with the old Unionist Party, whereas the →Democratic Unionist Party (DUP) was the only break-away party to achieve and retain a significant electoral following. James Molyneaux succeeded Harry West as OUP leader in 1974, and was himself succeeded in September 1995 by David Trimble.

During the 1980s the OUP gradually reasserted the original title of Ulster Unionist Party (although legally constituted as the Ulster Unionist Council, UUC) and consistently won a large proportion of parliamentary and local council seats, sometimes in coalition with other unionist parties. In 1982 it secured 26 of the 78 seats in the Northern Ireland Assembly, with 29.7% of the vote; in 1983 it won 34% and 11 of the 17 Northern Ireland seats in the UK House of Commons (losing one in a subsequent by-election). In June 1987 it won nine Westminster seats, with 37.7% of the vote, holding them in 1992 with a 34.5% vote share). In 1994 it held its European Parliament seat with 23.8% of first-preference votes. In the June 1996 Northern Ireland Forum elections it headed the list of successful parties, winning 30 of the 110 seats on a 24.7% vote share.

In the May 1997 UK general elections the UUP advanced to 10 out of 18 seats, although its share of the Northern Ireland vote slipped to 32.7%. The party was a leading participant in the subsequent multi-party peace negotiations which yielded the Good Friday Agreement of April 1998, although a substantial section of the party persistently opposed accommodation with the nationalist minority on the terms proposed and in particular any dealings with →Sinn Féin. In the June 1998 elections for a new Northern Ireland Assembly, the UUP headed the poll by winning 28 of the 108 seats, but its share of the vote fell to 21.3% because of defections by anti-agreement unionists. In the June 1999 European elections the UUP slipped further to 17.4% of the Northern Ireland vote, although it retained its single seat. Meanwhile, Trimble was the joint recipient, with →Social Democratic and Labour Party leader John Hume, of the 1998 Nobel Peace Prize in recognition of their role in the peace process.

Seeking to preserve unionist support for the April 1998 agreement, Trimble subsequently demanded that arms decommissioning by the IRA must precede the creation of a power-sharing executive containing *Sinn Féin* representatives. His eventual acceptance in November 1999 that decommissioning would follow the establishment of the executive was endorsed by the UUP party council, although with significant minority dissent. Trimble became First Minister of the new executive inaugurated in early December 1999, the other UUP ministers being Sir Reg Empey (enterprise and trade), Sam Foster (environment) and Michael McGimpsey (culture and leisure).

During the protracted crises in the power-sharing arrangements in 2000–01, Trimble was assailed both on the unionist side, for "appeasing" the republicans, and on the republican side, for endangering the peace process by insisting on IRA arms decommissioning. In March 2000 Trimble only narrowly survived a challenge to his UUP leadership by hardliner Martin Smyth, while the following month he attracted fierce unionist criticism for proposing that the UUP should end its institutional links with the Orange Order. In a by-election in September 2000 the OUP suffered the humiliating loss of its "safe" Westminster seat of South Antrim to the DUP.

A month before the UK general elections of June 2001 Trimble announced that he would resign as First Minister at the end of June if arms commissioning had not been delivered. His stance did the UUP little good at the polls, its representation slumping to six seats on a 26.8% share of the Northern Ireland vote, with most of its lost support going to the DUP. Trimble thereupon carried out his resignation threat, forcing the UK government to suspend the power-sharing arrangements. The resultant deadlock was broken in October 2001 by the *Sinn Féin*/IRA decision to begin arms commissioning, whereupon Trimble secured UUP approval for his return to the post of First Minister.

The UUP representative in the European Parliament is a member of the European People's Party–European Democrats group.

United Kingdom Unionist Party (UKUP)

Address. 10 Hamilton Road, Bangor, BT20 4LE
Telephone. (+44–28) 9147–9538
Fax. (+44–28) 9146–5037
Email. webmaster@ukup.org
Website. www.ukup.org
Leadership. Robert McCartney (leader); Anne Moore (secretary)

Not so much a party as the personal vehicle of McCartney, a leading barrister, the UKUP arose to support his successful bid to succeed the similarly independent-minded unionist Sir James Kilfedder as MP for the affluent constituency of North Down after the latter's death in 1995. McCartney, formerly a leading member of the Campaign for Equal Citizenship, fought the by-election in June 1995 as an independent "United Kingdom Unionist" candidate on a platform of resolute opposition to the involvement of the Republic in what he saw as the internal affairs of Northern Ireland. Thus he opposed the Anglo–Irish Agreement of 1985, the Downing Street Declaration issued by the UK and Irish governments in 1993 and the post-1997 peace process which yielded the April 1998 Good Friday Agreement. He is identified with hardline unionism and opposed to the line of the →Ulster Unionist Party (UUP), although vigorously rejecting the religious sectarianism associated with others of that tendency.

In the June 1996 Northern Ireland Forum elections, McCartney headed a list which became known as the UKUP, although it was not formally constituted as a party. McCartney was the only UKUP candidate elected to a constituency seat, but two regional-list seats went to the curious UKUP pairing of Conor Cruise O'Brien (a former Foreign Minister in the Dublin government representing the Irish →→Labour Party and latterly a journalist sympathetic to the Northern unionists) and Cedric Wilson (an inveterate protester against "Dublin interference", formerly a member of the →Democratic Unionist Party and subsequently founder of the →Northern Ireland Unionist Party). McCartney retained his Westminster seat in the May 1997 UK general elections.

Opposed to the Good Friday Agreement, the UKUP won five seats and 4.5% of the vote in the Northern Ireland Assembly elections in June 1998. In the UK general elections in June 2001 the UKUP narrowly lost the North Down seat to the UUP.

The UKUP describes itself as a sister party of the London-based anti-EU →→UK Independence Party.

Other Parties

Communist Party of Ireland (*Páirtí Cumannach na hÉireann, CPI*), based in Dublin (see Ireland section), but its Northern area, based in Belfast has a degree of autonomy. The CPI has contested many elections without success, most recently the 1996 Forum elections, in which it won 66 votes.
Address. PO Box 85, Belfast, BT1 1SR
Telephone/Fax. (+44–28) 9023–0669
Leadership. Margaret Bruton (regional secretary)

Conservative Party and Unionist Party, an attempt to extend the British →→Conservative and Unionist Party to Northern Ireland in the late 1980s, following the breakdown of the Conservatives' long relationship with the →Ulster Unionist Party. The party in Northern Ireland has failed to achieve a significant following in terms of membership or electoral support. It has constituency associations in several parts of the region, but has local council representation only in the commuter belt of North Down. Despite securing 5.7% in the 1992 general election, and several council seats in

1993, it won less than 0.5% in the 1996 Forum elections. In the 2001 UK elections its three candidates won 0.3% of the Northern Ireland vote and lost their deposits.

Address. 2 May Avenue, Bangor, Co. Down
Telephone. (+44–28) 9146–9210

Green Party, an ecologist group present in elections since 1981, receiving 0.5% of the vote in the 1996 Forum elections; has close links with other Green parties, especially in Britain and the Irish Republic.

Address. 537 Antrim Road, Belfast, BT7 1JR
Telephone. (+44–28) 9077–6731
Email. nigreens@belfast.co.uk
Website. www.belfast.co.uk/nigreens
Leadership. Peter Emerson

Irish Republican Socialist Party (IRSP), a small revolutionary formation founded in 1974 by dissident members of the "Official" republican movement (later the →Workers' Party). Damaged by allegations of gangsterism and drug dealing, and by frequent and bloody feuding among members of its armed wing (the Irish National Liberation Army, INLA) and between the INLA and other republican groups, the IRSP has never been numerically significant and by 1999 had only a few dozen active members in Northern Ireland (and others in the Republic, being established, like other republican organizations, on an all-Ireland basis). The IRSP currently calls for a broad front of republican and socialist groupings to oppose what it regards as the unduly moderate position of →Sinn Féin and to speak for "the subject people of the six counties and the oppressed working class of Ireland".

Address. 392 Falls Road, Belfast, BT12
Email. irsp-web@irsm.org
Website. www.irsm.org/irsp

Northern Ireland Labour, post-1999 attempt to create a socialist party across the sectarian divide. Although a single Labour Coalition list was put forward in the 1996 Forum elections, securing 0.8% of the vote and two regional-list seats, its subsequent internal wrangles illustrated the difficulties which have frustrated all efforts to organize an inclusive region-wide socialist party. The Labour Coalition brought together a wide range of formations, including (i) the semi-defunct Northern Ireland Labour Party (NILP), a former affiliate of the Socialist International which had had no significant electoral support since 1975; (ii) the Labour and Trade Union Groups (L&TU), a network of local democratic socialist formations which had contested elections in Belfast, Derry and other centres without success from 1975 onwards; (iii) the Newtownabbey Labour Party, which had won a single council seat in 1993 for Mark Langhammer (then the only public representative elected on any Labour ticket); (iv) the Labour Party '87, which had also contested the 1993 local elections; (v) the Labour Co-ordinating Committee, chaired by Langhammer, which joined and then broke away from the Coalition; (vi) the Labour Movement in Local Government, which had been formed by Paddy Devlin and Robert Clarke in May 1984 as an anti-sectarian socialist group; (vii) the Labour Representation Committee (LRC), which had been formed in 1984 to seek the extension of the British →Labour Party to Northern Ireland; and (viii) Militant Labour. Following the disintegration of the Labour Coalition, several activists established Labour Northern Ireland (LNI), which in 1998 entered into ultimately abortive discussions with other tendencies. The latest attempt to unite the various socialist groupings led to the launch of Northern Ireland Labour in May 1999, when a conference elected a steering group.

Address. 16 Garland Heights, Lurgan, BT66 6BZ
Telephone/Fax. (+44–28) 3832–4303
Email. secretary@labourni.org
Website. www.labourni.org
Leadership. Oliver Frawley (chairman); Alan Evans (secretary)

Northern Ireland Unionist Party (NIUP), small unionist formation opposed to the Good Friday Agreement; its two candidates won 1,794 votes (0.2%) in the 2001 UK elections, both losing their deposits.

Address. 38 Main Street, Ballyclare, Antrim, BT39 9AA
Leader. Cedric Wilson (leader)

Ulster Democratic Party (UDP), founded in the 1970s (as the Ulster Loyalist Democratic Party, ULDP, dropping the second word in 1992) as a political front for the Ulster Defence Association (UDA). The UDA, a loyalist paramilitary group responsible for many hundreds of murders, mainly of Catholic non-combatants, was eventually declared illegal in 1992; by that time the party had established some distance between itself and the parent organization, presenting itself as quite independent. The UDP has contested local government elections, securing a handful of council seats by election or defection, but its main role is as a channel of communication with the UDA and the Protestant underclass which supports it. In that capacity it participated in talks with the British government, some at ministerial level, following the loyalist ceasefire declared in October 1994, four months after that of the IRA. It secured only 2.2% of the poll in the 1996 Forum elections, winning no constituency seats, but was accorded two at-large seats under the formula designed to bring the UDP and its associated party, the PUP, into negotiations.

Address. 36 Castle Street, Lisburn, BT27 4XE
Telephone. (+44–28) 9266–7056
Fax. (+44–28) 9260–5159
Email. info@udp.org
Website. www.udp.org
Leadership. Gary McMichael (leader)

United Unionist Assembly Party (UUAP), launched in September 1998 by Denis Watson, who had been elected to the new Northern Ireland Assembly in June 1998 as an independent unionist candidate.

Address. Room 149, Parliament Buildings, Stormont, Belfast, BT4 3XX
Leadership. Denis Watson (leader)

The Workers' Party (WP), a semi-autonomous Northern section of the Dublin-based WP, a Marxist republican party which arose from the "Official" majority faction which remained loyal to the then leadership of →Sinn Féin in the 1969–70 split, at which time the Northern section of Sinn Féin operated under the name Republican Clubs. The associated armed faction known as the Official IRA wound down its activities during the 1970s and was said to have disbanded in the 1980s. The movement's attempts to develop radical anti-sectarian socialist politics in the North, reflected in its change of name to The Workers' Party–Republican Clubs and its subsequent abandonment of the suffix, were hampered not only by the climate of violence in the 1970s and 1980s but by allegations of gangsterism associated with the Official IRA and by factionalism within the political wing, leading to the breakaway of what became the →Democratic Left. The WP, which campaigns for peace, full employment and class politics, has been represented on local councils, with one remaining councillor in 1996, but has rarely secured more than 2% of the parliamentary poll, and only 0.6% in 1992; in the 1996 Forum elections its share fell to 0.5%. Having won 0.4% of the Northern Ireland vote in the 1997 UK elections, the WP ran six candidates in 2001, winning a total of 2,352 votes (0.3%).

Address. 6 Springfield Road, Belfast, BT12 7AG
Telephone. (+44–28) 9032–8663
Fax. (+44–28) 9033–3475
Email. info@workers-party.org
Website. www.workers-party.org
Leadership. John Lowry (regional secretary)

UK Crown Dependencies

The three crown fiefdoms of Jersey and Guernsey (the Channel Islands) and of the Isle of Man are historically distinct from the United Kingdom, although to all intents and purposes they are British territory and accepted as being such by the vast majority of their inhabitants and under international law. Legally, both entities are under the jurisdiction of the crown rather than the Westminster Parliament (in which they are not represented) and neither is part of the European Union *de jure*.

Channel Islands

Located in the English Channel off the French coast, the Channel Islands (capital: St Helier, Jersey; 2000E population: 150,000), consisting of Jersey and Guernsey with dependencies, have been attached to the crown of England since 1106. Each of the two islands has a Lieutenant-Governor representing the British monarch and a Bailiff (appointed by the crown) as president of each of the States (legislatures) and of the royal courts. Elections to the States are not held on British party political lines, although in Jersey some elected members have represented the Jersey Democratic Movement.

Isle of Man

Situated in the Irish Sea between Britain and Ireland, the Isle of Man (capital: Douglas; 2000E population: 70,000) has been a dependency of the crown for four centuries, but retaining its own laws administered by the Court of Tynwald, consisting of a Governor (appointed by the crown), an 11-member Legislative Council and the House of Keys, which is a 24-member representative assembly elected for a five-year term by adult suffrage and which elects eight of the Legislative Council members. In elections to the House of Keys in November 1996 all successful candidates stood without official party attribution, although five were identified with the Alliance for Progressive Government (APG) and two with the Manx Labour Party (MLP). Also in existence is the pro-independence *Mec Vannin* (Sons of Mann) movement.

UK Dependent Territories

At end-2001 the United Kingdom retained sovereignty over 13 overseas territories, of which three (British Antarctic Territory, British Indian Ocean Territory, and South Georgia and the South Sandwich Islands) have no settled population. The other 10, each of which is described in the following pages, all enjoy substantial autonomy in their internal affairs and several have a flourishing party system.

Anguilla

Capital: The Valley

Population: 10,000 (2000E)

The Caribbean island of Anguilla was a British colony from 1650 to 1967, when it became part of the new Associated State of St Christopher/St Kitts–Nevis–Anguilla. However, the Anguillans repudiated government from St Kitts, and in 1969 a British commissioner was installed following a landing by British security forces. In 1976 Anguilla was given a new status and separate constitution, formally becoming a UK dependent territory in 1980. Constitutional amendments introduced in 1982 (and in 1990) provide for a Governor (as the representative of the British sovereign) with wide-ranging powers, an Executive Council and a House of Assembly. The Executive Council consists of the Chief Minister and three other ministers (appointed by the Governor from among the elected members of the House of Assembly), together with the Deputy Governor and the Attorney-General as *ex-officio* members. The House of Assembly includes seven representatives elected by universal adult suffrage, two *ex-officio* members (the Deputy Governor and Attorney-General) and two nominated members.

In general elections on March 3, 2000, an alliance of the Anguilla National Alliance (ANA) and the Anguilla Democratic Party (ADP) came to power by winning, respectively, three seats (with 34.1% of the vote) and one seat (10.8%), while the Anguilla United Party (AUP) won two (12.1%) and an independent took the remaining seat.

Anguilla Democratic Party (ADP)

Address. c/o House of Assembly, The Valley
Leadership. Victor Banks (leader)

The conservative ADP was founded in 1981 (as the Anguilla People's Party) by then Chief Minister Ronald Webster on his expulsion from the then ruling →Anguilla United Party (AUP). The party won five seats in the House of Assembly in subsequent elections that year and Webster was reappointed Chief Minister. In the 1984 polls the party held only two seats, and Webster resigned as leader, to be replaced by Victor Banks. The ADP remained in opposition until the 1994 elections, winning two seats and forming a coalition government with the AUP.

The AUP–ADP coalition remained in power after the March 1999 elections, in which the ADP again won two seats. In June 1999, however, Banks resigned as Minister of Finance and took the ADP into opposition, provoking a constitutional crisis which led to early elections in March 2000. These resulted in the United Front of the ADP and the Anguilla National Alliance (ANA) winning a majority of four of the seven seats. Although the ADP itself slipped to a single seat, Banks regained the finance portfolio in a new government headed by the ANA.

Anguilla National Alliance (ANA)

Address. c/o House of Assembly, The Valley
Leadership. Osbourne Fleming (leader)

The conservative ANA was created in 1980 as the successor to the People's Progressive Party, whose leader Ronald Webster had headed Anguilla's government from the separation from St Kitts–Nevis in 1967 until 1977. Having lost power in the 1980 elections, the ANA again became the ruling party in 1984 under Sir Emile Gumbs, who remained Chief Minister until his retirement in February 1994. In the ensuing elections the ANA won two of the seven elective seats and went into opposition to a government headed by the →Anguilla United Party (AUP).

The ANA remained in opposition after the March 1999 elections, although its improved representation of three seats enabled it to block government business when the ruling coalition collapsed in June 1999. In early general elections in March 2000 the ANA again won three seats in alliance with the →Anguilla Democratic Party (ADP), which took one, so that party leader Osbourne Fleming was able to form a majority government.

The ANA is associated with the International Democrat Union through its membership of the Caribbean Democrat Union.

Anguilla United Party (AUP)

Address. c/o House of Assembly, The Valley
Leadership. Hubert Hughes (leader)

The conservative AUP was formed in 1977 by Ronald Webster after he had lost the leadership of the then ruling People's Progressive Party. The AUP won the elections in 1980 and Webster returned as Chief Minister, but after disagreements within the party he was expelled from the AUP in May 1981. In early elections the following month the AUP lost all its seats. Under the leadership of Hubert Hughes, the revived party won two seats in the March 1994 elections and formed a coalition administration with the →Anguilla Democratic Party (ADP), with the AUP leader as Chief Minister. This coalition continued after the March 1999 elections, in which the AUP again won two seats, but collapsed in June 1999. Hughes then tried to govern as a minority administration but was eventually forced to agree to new elections in March 2000. The AUP retained two seats but went into opposition to a new coalition headed by the →Anguilla National Alliance.

Other Parties

Anguilla Patriotic Movement (APM), won 3.9% of the vote and no seats in the March 2000 elections.
Leadership. Franklin Richardson & Quincy Gumbs

Movement For Grassroots Democracy (MFGD), won 3.6% of the vote and no seats in the March 2000 elections.
Leadership. John Benjamin & Joyce Kentish

Bermuda

Capital: Hamilton   **Population:** 62,000 (2000E)

First settled by the British in 1609 and located in the western Atlantic, the crown colony of Bermuda has enjoyed internal self-government since 1968. The Governor, representing the British sovereign, has responsibility for external affairs, defence, internal security and police. Internal executive authority in most matters is exercised by the Premier and the Cabinet, who are appointed by the Governor but are responsible to the 40-member House of Assembly, which is popularly elected for a five-year term. The Governor also appoints the 11-member Senate, including five on the recommendation of the Premier and three on the advice of the Leader of the Opposition.

In the most recent general elections to the House of Assembly on Nov. 9, 1998, the Progressive Labour Party came to power for the first time by winning 26 seats (and 54.2% of the vote), and 14 (44.1%) for the United Bermuda Party.

National Liberal Party (NLP)
Address. POB HM 1704, Hamilton HM HX
Telephone. (+1–441) 292–8587
Leadership. Gilbert Darrell (leader)
The centrist NLP was formed in 1985 by a breakaway group of →Progressive Labour Party members of the House of Assembly led by Gilbert Darrell. The party lost one of its two seats in the 1989 elections and failed to win any representation in 1993 and 1998, achieving only 0.8% of the vote in the latter contest.

Progressive Labour Party (PLP)
Address. PO Box HM 1367, Hamilton HMFX
Telephone. (+1–441) 292–2264
Fax. (+1–809) 295–7890
Email. plp@plp.bm
Website. www.plp.bm
Leadership. Jennifer Smith (leader); C. Eugene Cox (deputy leader); Neville Tyrell (chairman); Roderick Burchall (secretary-general)
Founded in 1963 (and therefore Bermuda's oldest party) and drawing most of its support from the black population, the left-leaning PLP was the runner-up to the →United Bermuda Party (UBP) in successive elections from 1968 to 1993, when it won 18 of the 40 seats in the House of Assembly. While favouring an end to British sovereignty, the party urged its supporters to abstain in the August 1995 referendum on the principle of independence, which was rejected by a 58.8% majority. Since then the PLP has regarded independence as a long-term goal rather than an immediate objective.

On the death of Frederick Wade in December 1996, he was succeeded as PLP leader by Jennifer Smith. Under her leadership the party achieved a decisive victory in parliamentary elections in November 1998, ousting the 30-year-old UBP government by winning 26 of the 40 seats. Smith accordingly formed a PLP government pledged to enhancing Bermuda's attractiveness to foreign companies and to maintaining its existing favourable tax regime.

United Bermuda Party (UBP)
Address. PO Box HM 715, Hamilton HMCX
Telephone. (+1–441) 295–0729
Fax. (+1–441) 292–7195
Email. info@ubp.bm
Website. www.ubp.bm
Leadership. Pamela Gordon (leader); Wayne Furbert (chairman); Gwyneth Rawlins (secretary)
The conservative and multi-racial UBP gained its eighth successive general election victory in October 1993 under the leadership of Sir John Swan (since 1982), although with a much reduced share of the vote which yielded 22 of the 40 seats. In the August 1995 referendum on the principle of independence, the UBP as a party remained neutral but Swan and some other UBP leaders advocated a "yes" vote, promising to resign in the event of a "no" verdict. He honoured his pledge and was succeeded as Premier and UBP leader by the Finance Minister, David Saul.

Saul sought to heal UBP divisions over the independence question; but these and other issues resulted in his downfall in March 1997 and the election of Pamela Gordon to replace him. She also failed to restore the party's popular standing. The UBP's dominance came to an end in the November 1998 elections, following which it went into opposition for the first time, to a government of the →Progressive Labour Party.

British Virgin Islands

Capital: Road Town, Tortola   **Population:** 18,500 (2000E)

Located in the Caribbean and under British rule since 1672, the 60 or so islands comprising the British Virgin Islands are a crown colony, with an appointed Governor representing the British sovereign. Under the present constitution, which took effect from 1977, the Governor is responsible for defence, internal security, external affairs and the civil service. The Legislative Council consists of a Speaker, chosen from outside the Council, one *ex-officio* member (the Attorney-General) and 13 directly elected members, representing nine constituency seats and four territory-wide ("at large") seats. The Executive Council, chaired by the Governor, has one *ex-officio* member (the Attorney-General) and four ministers (including a Chief Minister) drawn from the elected members of Legislative Council.

In Legislative Council elections on May 17, 1999, the Virgin Islands Party retained power, winning seven of the 13 elective seats (with 38.0% of the vote). The National Democratic Party took five (36.9%) and the Concerned Citizens' Movement one (4.0%).

National Democratic Party (NDP)

Address. c/o Legislative Council, Road Town, Tortola
Leadership. Orlando Smith (leader)

The NDP was founded in 1998 in a move to rally opposition to the ruling →Virgin Islands Party (VIP). It won a creditable five of the 13 elective seats in the May 1999 Council elections, thereby becoming the principal opposition to a further VIP government.

Virgin Islands Party (VIP)

Address. c/o Legislative Council, Road Town, Tortola
Leadership. Ralph O'Neal (leader)

Until his sudden death in May 1995, H. Lavity Stoutt had been the long-time leader of the VIP, serving as the islands' Chief Minister from 1967 to 1971, Deputy Chief Minister under an independent Chief Minister from 1975 to 1979, and Chief Minister again between 1979 and 1983 and from 1986 until 1995. Having been returned to power in 1986, the VIP increased its majority in the 1990 election, and then retained power with the support of an independent following the February 1995 poll. Stoutt was succeeded as Chief Minister by his deputy, Ralph O'Neal, and the government majority in the Legislative Council was maintained by the recruitment of another independent member. The May 1999 elections confirmed O'Neal and the VIP in power with a legislative majority of seven seats. In September 2000 O'Neal dismissed his deputy, Eileen Parsons, for allegedly conspiring with the opposition →National Democratic Party and appointed J. Alvin Christopher in her stead.

Other Parties

Concerned Citizens' Movement (CCM), formed in 1994 as successor to the Independent People's Movement, which had itself been formed by party leader Omar Hodge in 1989. In the 1995 general elections the CCM won two Legislative Council seats, but only one in 1998.
Leadership. Omar Hodge (leader)

United Party (UP), has fought successive general elections since the mid-1970s and was briefly in government from 1983 to 1986 in a coalition under the premiership of an independent. Having won two Legislative Council seats in 1995, the UP failed to retain representation in 1998.
Leadership. Conrad Maduro (leader)

Cayman Islands

Capital: George Town, Grand Cayman

Population: 28,000 (2000E)

Under British rule from 1670, the Caribbean Cayman Islands were governed from Jamaica until its independence in 1962, when the islands opted to remain under the British crown. The constitution, which was most recently revised in 1994, provides for a Governor, Executive Council and Legislative Assembly. The Governor represents the British sovereign and is responsible for external affairs, defence, internal security and the civil service. The Executive Council, chaired by the Governor, consists of three official members (Chief Secretary, Financial Secretary and Attorney-General) and five other members elected by the Legislative Assembly from their own number. The Assembly includes the three official members of the Executive Council and 15 directly elected members.

There are no formally constituted political parties in the Caymans. Elections to the Legislative Assembly have been contested by loose groupings or "teams" of candidates, as well as by independents, but all candidates have been committed to the economic development of the islands and the maintenance of colonial status. The most recent general elections were held on Nov. 8, 2000.

Falkland Islands

Capital: Stanley

Civilian population: 2,200 (2000E)

Situated in the South Atlantic, the Falklands Islands have been under continuous British rule since 1833, except for a brief period in 1982 when Argentina (which calls them Las Malvinas) asserted its claim to sovereignty by military occupation in early April but surrendered to British forces in June. Under the 1985 constitution, the Falkland Islands and their former dependencies (South Georgia and the South Sandwich Islands) are administered by a Governor representing the British monarch. The Governor presides over an Executive Council with two other (non-voting) ex officio members and three elected by and from the Legislative Council. The latter body has two (non-voting) ex officio members and eight elected by universal adult suffrage. Decisions of the Executive Council are subject to veto by the Governor and the British Foreign Secretary.

All candidates elected to the Legislative Council on Oct. 9, 1997, stood as independents favouring the maintenance of British status and avoidance of unnecessary contact with Argentina until the latter abandoned its claim to sovereignty.

Gibraltar

Capital: Gibraltar   **Population:** 34,000 (2000E)

Located on the southern tip of the Iberian Peninsula, Gibraltar became a British possession under the 1713 Treaty of Utrecht. Under its 1969 constitution, the dependency has a crown-appointed Governor exercising executive authority, a Gibraltar Council under a Chief Minister and a House of Assembly of two ex-officio and 15 elected members serving a four-year term. The franchise is held by British subjects and citizens of the Republic of Ireland resident in Gibraltar for at least six months prior to registration as voters. Each voter has the right to vote for up to eight candidates, which is the maximum number that any one party can present in Assembly elections.

In elections to the House of Assembly held on Feb. 10, 2000, the Gibraltar Social Democrats retained power by taking eight of the elective seats (with 58.3% of the popular vote), an alliance of the Gibraltar Socialist Labour Party and the Liberal Party being allocated the remaining seven (with 41.6%). A major issue in these and earlier elections was the Spanish claim to sovereignty over Gibraltar and the local response to ongoing UK–Spanish negotiations seeking to resolve the dispute.

Gibraltar Social Democrats (GSD)

Address. 3/5 Horse Barrack Court, Gibraltar
Telephone. (+350) 70786
Fax. (+350) 70786
Website. www.gibnynex.gi/home/gsd
Leadership. Peter Caruana (leader); Terry Cartwright (general secretary)

The GSD was launched in 1989 as a centre–right party advocating that the government should participate in the ongoing UK–Spanish negotiations on Gibraltar, thus differing sharply from the boycott policy of the then ruling →Gibraltar Socialist Labour Party (GSLP). Drawing support that had previously gone to the Gibraltar Labour Party–Association for the Advancement of Civil Rights (later disbanded), the new party won seven of the 15 elective seats in the January 1992 Assembly elections and became the opposition to a further GSLP government.

Assisted by economic problems and a deterioration in relations with Spain, the GSD won the May 1996 elections, taking the maximum possible eight seats with a vote share of 48% and forming a government headed by Peter Caruana. The new Chief Minister took a higher profile in ongoing UK–Spanish exchanges on the territorial issue, while remaining firmly opposed to any concessions to Spain's claim to sovereignty. In the February 2000 elections Caruana led the GSD to a second term, with an impressive 58.3% share of the popular vote.

Gibraltar Socialist Labour Party (GSLP)

Address. Line Wall Road, Gibraltar
Telephone. (+350) 42359
Leadership. Joe Bossano (leader)

The GSLP's constitution is modelled on that of the →→Labour Party of Britain, as it was when the GSLP was founded in 1976. The party's basic aim is "the creation of a socialist decolonized Gibraltar based on the application of self-determination", so that it vigorously opposes Spain's claim to Gibraltar as well as the 1984 UK–Spanish Brussels agreement providing for negotiations on the sovereignty issue. The party was formed as the Gibraltar Democratic Movement (GDM), which contested the 1976 elections with the statutory maximum of eight candidates, of whom four were elected on a platform of "working for the decolonization of the Rock [of Gibraltar] and the creation of a new constitutional arrangement which will guarantee the future of the territory and the people". In 1977 three of these GDM members crossed the floor, only one remaining when the GDM changed its name to GSLP.

The party contested the 1980 elections on a socialist programme, obtaining 20% of the vote and one of the 15 elec-

tive seats in the House of Assembly. In January 1984, however, when it fielded eight candidates, it gained all seven opposition seats in the House. The GSLP finally came to power in the March 1988 Assembly elections, when it won eight seats and approaching 60% of the popular vote. As Gibraltar's new Chief Minister, Joe Bossano reiterated his party's election pledge that a GSLP government would not participate in the negotiating process initiated under the 1984 Brussels agreement. The GSLP was confirmed in power in the January 1992 elections, retaining the maximum permissible eight seats but with a vote share of over 70%.

Economic and other difficulties during Bossano's second term, including lack of any progress on the GSLP's self-determination aim, resulted in a seepage of popular support, amidst worsening relations with London over the rise of drug-trafficking and money-laundering in Gibraltar. In the May 1996 elections the GSLP was soundly defeated by the →Gibraltar Social Democrats (GSD), winning seven of the 15 elective seats on a greatly reduced popular vote of 39%. The popularity of the GSD government impelled the GSLP to contest the February 2000 Assembly elections in alliance with the newly organized →Liberal Party, with only negligible results in terms of the popular. Of the seven seats allocated to the alliance, the GSLP took five.

Liberal Party

Address. 95 Irish Town, PO Box 225, Gibraltar
Telephone. (+350) 76959
Fax. (+350) 74664
Email. libparty@gibnet.gi
Website. www.gibraltar.gi/liberalparty
Leadership. Joseph García (leader); Steven Linares (secretary-general)

The Liberal Party was launched in 1998 as successor to the Gibraltar National Party (GNP), which had been founded in December 1991 to promote the idea of self-determination for Gibraltar from a centre–right perspective. Despite rising from 5% of the vote in 1992 to 13% in 1996, the GNP had remained without representation. For the February 2000 Assembly elections the new Liberal Party formed an alliance with the →Gibraltar Socialist Labour Party (GSLP), being allocated two of the seven seats won by the joint list and becoming part of the parliamentary opposition to the ruling →Gibraltar Social Democrats.

The Liberal Party is a member of the Liberal International and the European Liberals, Democrats and Reformists (ELDR).

Montserrat

Capital: Plymouth

Population: 5,000 (2000E)

The Caribbean island of Montserrat formed part of the British federal colony of the Leeward Islands from 1871 until 1956, when it became a separate dependent territory. Under the 1960 constitution as amended, Montserrat has a Governor who represents the British sovereign and is responsible for defence, internal security and external affairs (including, from 1989, regulation of the "offshore" financial sector in response to a banking scandal). The Legislative Council consists of the Speaker, nine elected representatives, two official members (the Attorney-General and Financial Secretary) and two nominated members. Executive authority in most internal matters is exercised by a seven-member Executive Council, presided over by the Governor and including the Attorney-General, Financial Secretary and four ministers (including the Chief Minister) drawn from the Legislative Council.

The massive eruption of the Soufrière Hills volcano in June 1997 severely disrupted economic and political life, leading directly to the resignation of the government in face of protest against its handling of the crisis. By the end of 1997 about three-quarters of the previous population of some 12,500 had fled from the island. Some returned as reconstruction was put in hand, but regular minor eruptions in subsequent years prevented a return to anything like normalcy.

In general elections on April 2, 2001, the New People's Liberation Movement won seven seats (against two for the National Progressive Party) and thus returned to power after a decade in opposition.

National Progressive Party (NPP)

Address. PO Box 280, Plymouth
Telephone. (+1–809) 491–2444
Leadership. Reuben T. Meade (leader)

The NPP was formed just prior to the general elections in October 1991, when it won a majority in the Legislative Council, securing four out of the seven seats. Party leader Meade became Chief Minister. In the November 1996 elections the party was reduced to one seat and went into opposition. It partially recovered to two seats in further elections in April 1999 but remained in opposition, this time to the →New People's Liberation Movement.

New People's Liberation Movement (NPLM)

Address. c/o Legislative Council, Plymouth
Leadership. John A. Osborne (leader)

The centre-right NPLM is descended from the PLM, which was the governing party from 1978 until 1991 under John A. Osborne, seeking to promote economic development of the island with a view to eventual independence. In the October 1991 elections, amidst allegations of mismanagement and corruption against Osborne's administration, the PLM retained only one Legislative Council seat and went into opposition to the →National Progressive Party (NPP). In February 1993 Osborne and Noel Tuitt, a former PLM minister, were cleared of corruption and conspiracy charges following a police investigation. Although an opposition member, Tuitt was appointed to the NPP administration in March 1994.

For the 1996 elections Osborne formed the People's Progressive Alliance (PPA), incorporating the PLM, winning two seats and joining a coalition with the Movement for National Reconstruction (MNR) led by Bertrand Osborne. The crisis arising from the Soufrière volcanic eruption in mid-1997 forced the resignation of the MNR–PPA government in August and the appointment of an independent Chief Minister. Osborne subsequently organized the NPLM as successor to the PPA and the MNR. The new formation swept to victory in the April 2001 elections with seven seats, so that Osborne again became Chief Minister.

The NPLM is associated with the International Democrat Union through its membership of the Caribbean Democrat Union.

Pitcairn Islands

Population: 50 (2000E)

Britain's only remaining Pacific dependency, Pitcairn Island was settled in 1790 by the mutineers of *The Bounty* and became an official British possession in 1887, together with three nearby uninhabited islands. Under the 1940 constitution, the Governor (since 1970 the UK High Commissioner in New Zealand) represents the British monarch. An Island Magistrate elected every three years presides over the Island Court and the Island Council of 10 members, five of whom are elected annually. There is no party activity among Pitcairn's small and dwindling population.

St Helena and Dependencies

Capital: Jamestown   **Population:** 6,500 (2000E)

Situated in the South Atlantic, St Helena was governed by the British East India Company from 1673 and brought under the control of the crown in 1834. The constitution in force since 1989, applying to St Helena and its dependencies of Ascension Island and the Tristan da Cunha island group, provides for a crown-appointed Governor and Commander-in-Chief, who presides over an Executive Council, which includes five members selected from among their number by a popularly-elected Legislative Council of 12 members. Elections to the latter in the 1970s and early 1980s were contested on a party basis reflecting differing views on the constitutional future of the islands. More recently, however, there has been no party activity, the most recent elections on July 9, 1997, being conducted on a non-partisan basis.

Turks and Caicos Islands

Capital: Cockburn Town, Grand Turk   **Population:** 14,500 (2000E)

A Jamaican dependency from 1873 until 1959, the Turks and Caicos Islands became a separate British colony in 1962, following Jamaican independence. From 1965 the islands were administratively associated with the Bahamas, until Bahamian independence in 1973. Under the 1976 constitution as amended, executive power is vested in the Governor, who represents the British sovereign and is responsible for external affairs, defence and internal security. The Governor presides over the Executive Council, which includes ministers appointed from among the elected members of the Legislative Council and also *ex-officio* members. The Legislative Council is made up of the Speaker, three nominated members, the *ex-officio* members of the Executive Council and 13 directly-elected representatives.

In general elections to the Legislative Council on March 4, 1999, the People's Democratic Movement retained power by winning nine seats (with 52.4% of the vote) against four for the Progressive National Party (40.3%).

People's Democratic Movement (PDM)
Address. PO Box 38, Grand Turk
Leadership. Derek Taylor (leader)
Founded in the mid-1970s, the centre-left PDM favours internal self-government and eventual independence for the islands. The party won the first elections held under the 1976 constitution, but then went into opposition following defeat in 1980 on an explicitly pro-independence manifesto. Having overwhelmingly won the 1988 elections, and then lost to the →Progressive National Party in 1991, the PDM returned to power in the January 1995 poll, in which it gained eight Legislative Council seats. It advanced to nine seats in March 1999 and thus remained in office with Derek Taylor as Chief Minister.

Progressive National Party (PNP)
Address. c/o Legislative Council, Grand Turk
Leadership. Washington Misick (leader)
The conservative PNP is committed to continued dependent status for the islands. It was the ruling party from 1980 until the suspension of ministerial government and its replacement by a nominated executive headed by the Governor in 1986. This followed a period of domestic political tension in the islands and investigations by a commission of inquiry into political and administrative malpractices. At the 1988 elections, preceding the islands' return to constitutional rule, the PNP suffered a heavy defeat by the →People's Democratic Movement. Having been returned to power in 1991, the party retained only four seats in the January 1995 elections and again went into opposition. It remained in opposition after again winning four seats in March 1999.

United States of America

Capital: Washington DC   **Population:** 280,000,000 (2000)

The United States of America has under the "separation of powers" laid down in its founding Constitution three branches of national government, the executive, the legislative and the judicial. The President is the head of the executive branch and is elected for a four-year term (for a maximum of two terms): the President nominates Cabinet officers, the heads of government agencies, and federal judges, subject to confirmation (not automatically or always accorded) by the Senate. The legislative branch is Congress, comprising the House of Representatives and the Senate, whose members are elected on a first past the post basis. The 435 members of the House are elected for two-year terms and represent districts of approximately equal population. The composition of the Senate reflects the federal character of the Union, with each of the 50 states having two Senators, elected for six-year terms (with one-third of the Senate standing for re-election every two years). This has the effect that rural states with small populations are comparatively over-represented in the Senate, an imbalance reflected in its somewhat more conservative composition. The judicial branch has at its apex the US Supreme Court. The nine Supreme Court justices are nominated by the President, and their appointments ratified by the Senate, but once appointed enjoy lifetime tenure with considerable powers to strike down and interpret legislation on the basis of a judicial reading of the Constitution. Parallel systems (with small variations) prevail in the 50 states of the Union, in which elected Governors head the executive branch: the degree of autonomy enjoyed by the individual states is constantly under debate, but in general has declined steadily over the past two centuries.

Under the separation of powers the President, although the nation's chief executive, does not necessarily command a majority in either House of Congress. A tradition of bi-partisan agreement underpins the effective functioning of government: when this breaks down over controversial issues and the President cannot win the support of Congress, deadlock may ensue. Equally, although the President does not control the initiation of legislation, he does have powers of veto to override the wishes of Congress. To a degree unaccustomed in many parliamentary systems, therefore, the enactment of legislation is often disrupted. The President may not in the event of an impasse dissolve Congress to call elections (legislators sitting for fixed terms), nor may the Congress vote out a President other than in the extreme circumstance of impeachment and conviction.

Two parties, the Democrats and the Republicans, have dominated the American political landscape (both nationally and at state level) since the middle of the nineteenth century. While numerous third-party challengers have appeared over the years none has come close to threatening the hegemony of the two main parties, which have also enjoyed overall a remarkable parity in terms of office-holding. The parity between the two parties in the popular vote has reached exceptional levels in recent years: in the last three elections to the House of Representatives (1996, 1998 and 2000) the rounded percentage share of the vote has been split 49:49, 48:49 and 49:49, while the 2000 presidential election was so close that its outcome remained in dispute for several weeks.

Neither of the main parties has an accepted single political leader. Presidential candidates are selected as the outcome of a vigorously contested process of primary elections, state by state, taking place over several months and culminating in a nominating convention, and the presidential nomination is sometimes won by an individual who emerges from comparative obscurity. Traditionally presidential aspirants have often built a successful run for their party's nomination from a base in state rather than national politics, with four of the last five Presidents having been former state Governors who had never sat in Congress. Similarly, Presidents select their Cabinet members from a disparate constituency (sometimes including individuals with a non-partisan background), rather than from among a coherent party leadership. It is in consequence difficult to ascribe a clear policy programme to the major US parties in the way that is possible in the majority of developed democratic countries that have straightforward leadership structures and national policy-making processes. At the same time party loyalties and machines tend to be notably strong and cases of politicians in the main parties switching allegiance are rare: only seven US Senators have switched parties since World War II. In addition, when a party holds the presidency, the President generally sets a course and defines the image for the party in the country as a whole regardless of the party's internal divisions; it is in the nominating process, and when a party does not hold the White House, that the lack of a single leader is most apparent.

Campaign finance has been a matter of controversy since the Watergate affair of 1972–74 included revelations of large-scale donations by wealthy individuals to the re-election campaign of President Richard M. Nixon. Following Nixon's resignation in August 1974, in the face of a threatened vote of impeachment, Congress enacted comprehensive legislation, aimed at increasing transparency in election financing by limiting both campaign contributions and expenditures. The legislation also provided for public financing of presidential campaigns and established an independent commission to administer the legislation. In 1976, however, citing the 1st Amendment to the Constitution, which guarantees freedom of expression and association, the Supreme Court threw out the imposition of spending limits in federal elections, other than in the case of presidential candidates who voluntarily accepted public funding. Other aspects of the 1974 legislation were upheld, however, leaving a situation where, in broad terms, campaign contributions were limited (and subject to disclosure) but spending was not. At federal level (elections for the presidency and Congress) the amount an individual may donate to a candidate during a campaign has been fixed at $1,000 since 1974. In addition an individual may contribute $5,000 per year to a political action committee and $20,000 per year to a political party.

The significance of the distinction between campaign contributions and expenditures was illustrated in 1992 when billionaire H. Ross Perot took 18.9% of the vote in the presidential election on the basis of a campaign funded mainly from his own personal fortune. In contrast other third-party initiatives have been severely hampered by the need, without strong grass-roots organization, to raise donations in relatively small amounts.

Campaign finance reform assumed renewed prominence in 2000 when it was put onto the agenda by Sen. John McCain (Arizona) in his (unsuccessful) campaign to win the Republican presidential nomination. Particular attention was focused on so-called "soft money", unregulated payments to parties, nominally for general promotional purposes rather than to support individual candidates, by corporations and individuals. An estimated $500 million in soft money was raised by the two major parties for the 2000 elections, split fairly evenly between the parties, compared with $477 million raised by the Republicans and $270 million raised by the Democrats in (regulated) "hard money". On Apr. 4, 2001, the Senate adopted legislation by 59 to 41 co-sponsored by McCain and Sen. Russ Feingold (D., Wisconsin) banning soft money contributions to national parties but raising ceilings on hard money contributions to candidates and parties. However, parallel legislation in the House subsequently stalled.

Parties that win more than 5% of the vote in federal elections are entitled to financial subsidies in the next election. In the 2000 election campaign George W. Bush (Republican) and Al Gore (Democrat) each received $67.6m. in federal funding. In the primaries Gore also received matching funding although Bush declined this in order not to face limits on his spending.

Following three terms of Republican Presidents (Ronald Reagan 1981-1989 and George Bush 1989-1993), Bill Clinton won two successive terms for the Democrats (1993–2001). The presidential election held on Nov. 7, 2000, resulted in extreme controversy arising from the closeness of the vote between the two main candidates. According to official results later compiled by the Federal Election Commission based on state reports, the total of votes won by the leading candidates were (in descending order): Al Gore (Democrat) 50,992,335 (48.38%); George W. Bush (Republican) 50,455,156 (47.87%); Ralph Nader (Green candidate) 2,882,897 (2.74%); Patrick J. Buchanan (Reform Party) 448,892 (0.42%); Harry Browne (Libertarian Party) 384,429 (0.36%). No other candidate gained more than 100,000 votes. Total turnout at 105,396,641 was only just over 51%, although this was more than two percentage points higher than in 1996. The number of votes given to the various third-party candidates in 2000 was widely seen as having been depressed by the much anticipated closeness of the vote between Bush and Gore. The 2000 election was the third in a row in which the victorious candidate had taken less than 50% of the popular vote.

It became clear in the immediate aftermath of voting that Gore would narrowly win the popular vote. However, the President is not elected directly but by an Electoral College to which each state sends delegates who by law or convention vote en bloc for the candidate who won the popular vote in their state. The number of Electoral College seats per state is determined on the basis of the combined representation of each state in the Senate and the House of Representatives which means (given that each state has two Senators) it has a small bias in favour of the less populated rural states, where Bush had run comparatively strongly. Attention quickly focused particularly on the exceptionally close race in Florida, which controlled a decisive number (25) of Electoral College votes, all of which would go to the candidate declared the victor in the state. The controversy was exacerbated by the fact that the state Governor, Jeb Bush, was the Republican candidate's brother. On Nov. 8, the Florida Division of Elections reported that Bush had beaten Gore by 2,909,135 votes to 2,907,351, and there then followed a period in which the Democratic campaign sought manual recounts in a series of counties where disputes existed over the reliability of the count, while the Republican campaign resisted such recounts. Over several weeks there was a series of court-ordered partial recounts against a background of suits and counter-suits in state and federal courts brought by the two main parties and others. The controversy was marked by conflicting judgements in both state and federal courts and focused in particular on the issue of whether voter intent could be determined in the case of ballots that had been imperfectly perforated by the voting machines, although broader issues of ballot access also surfaced. On Dec. 8 the Florida Supreme Court (with a Democratic-appointed majority) ordered a lower state court to hand count 9,000 disputed ballots in Miami-Dade County. On Dec. 12, however, the US Supreme Court, voted in effect to overrule the Florida Supreme Court, end the counting, and leave Florida's electoral votes with Bush. While the issues decided were nominally largely technical in character, relating to the feasibility of staging an accurate re-count with each ballot assessed equally, the split in the Court was unambiguously ideological, with the five most conservative judges (all Republican appointees) voting to block the recount process altogether, two centre-ground justices taking a middle position that there were serious problems with the recount process but that these potentially could be rectified if more time was allowed, and the two most liberal justices dissenting entirely. While Justice John Paul Stevens, for the liberal wing, declared that the decision would cost "the nation's confidence in the judge as an impartial guardian of the rule of law", the majority decision was immediately accepted by Gore as marking the end of the controversy. The Electoral College went on to award 271 college votes (from 30 states) to Bush while Gore took 266 (from 20 states and the District of Columbia).

The November 2000 congressional elections were also extremely close. In the elections to the House the two parties took an almost identical share of the vote but the Republicans retained a reduced majority, holding 221 seats to the Democrats' 212 (with two seats going to independents). The Senate races resulted in the Democrats and Republicans each holding 50 seats, but with the Republicans retaining effective control by virtue of the casting vote of the Vice-President. This was the first time since 1954 that the Republicans had simultaneously controlled the presidency and both Houses of Congress. In May 2001, however, the defection of a Republican senator to become an independent handed control of the Senate, and the key positions of chairs of its legislative committees, to the Democrats.

As of October 2001 the Republicans held 29 state governorships, the Democrats 19 and independents 2. The Democrats held the governorship of the most populous state, California, but most of the other major states (including New York, Texas, Illinois, Ohio, Pennsylvania, New Jersey, Michigan and Florida) had Republican governors.

Democratic Party

Address. Democratic National Committee, 430 South Capitol Street, SE, Washington, DC 20003
Telephone. (+1–202) 863–8000
Website. www.democrats.org
Leadership. Terry McAuliffe (national chair); Thomas A. Daschle (Senate majority leader); Richard Gephardt (House minority leader)

The Democratic Party may be broadly defined as occupying the centre–left of the US political spectrum. Supportive of a free-market economy, the party also places emphasis on equality of opportunity and civil, labour and minority rights. Like the Republicans, however, the Democrats are a broad coalition and the party embraces individuals who in Europe would affiliate to socialist and radical parties as well as those who are ideologically sympathetic to most Republican positions but have a traditional Democratic allegiance.

The Democratic Party traces its origins back to the late

18th century; it adopted the present name and set up the Democratic National Committee (DNC) in the 1840s, making it one of the longest established political parties in the world. However, much of its contemporary character took shape during the New Deal of the 1930s when, under President Franklin D. Roosevelt (1933–45), it initiated a wide range of spending and welfare programmes to help counter economic depression. Since then the Democrats have been identified as the more liberal of the two main parties, with a greater belief in the role of the federal government in combating poverty and discrimination.

In common with the Republicans, the Democrats do not have a single accepted "leader". When the party holds the presidency, the President is the leading individual voice, but the President does not automatically command the support of all or most of his party in Congress. Leading figures in the party tend to be long-standing members of Congress (especially if they chair key committees), and sometimes state Governors, but there is considerable fluidity without a well-defined leadership group. Holders of major Cabinet offices are not necessarily major figures within the party. Similarly none of the current members of the DNC are nationally first-rank political figures in their own right. It is arguable that no Democratic President since Roosevelt has been able to "lead" his party in the way that characterizes British Prime Ministers or German Chancellors.

Internal ideological conflicts within the party climaxed in the 1960s and early 1970s. Under Presidents John F. Kennedy (1961–63) and Lyndon B. Johnson (1963–69), the party addressed the long-ignored issue of Southern segregation and the denial of civil rights to blacks. Since the Civil War the Republicans, as the party of Lincoln, had been anathema to the (white) South: the region had become known as the "solid South" in its allegiance to the Democrats. However, the impact of Democratic sponsorship of civil rights legislation in Washington was to break up Democratic support in the South. At the same time the party was challenged from a "new left" bitterly opposed to Johnson's prosecution of the war in Vietnam and which found increasing numbers of allies on the liberal wing of the party. The 1968 Democratic convention in Chicago was marked by violent division in the conference hall and on the streets and the Republican candidate for the presidency, Richard M. Nixon, went on to secure election on a platform emphasizing his appeal to the non-radical "silent majority". In 1972 a chaotic Democratic convention nominated George McGovern, who stood far outside what had hitherto been the party mainstream and slumped to defeat by Nixon. In 1974 Nixon was forced to resign over the Watergate scandal (which originated in a 1972 break-in at the DNC offices by individuals linked to the White House). Watergate and the legislation it spawned (including sweeping restrictions on the powers of the President and the CIA) marked the high water mark of radicalism, however. The party's successful nomination of Jimmy Carter (President 1977–81) as its presidential candidate in 1976 marked a quest to recover the ideological centre ground and (as Carter, the Governor of Georgia and a peanut farmer, was very much an "outsider" from the Washington political establishment) to re-connect with the concerns of heartland America. From the end of the 1970s, however, the political agenda was set by the newly energized Republican right-wing and the Republicans went on to hold the presidency, under Ronald Reagan and George Bush, through three terms from 1981-93. The Democrats regained the presidency with the election of Bill Clinton in 1992, and in 1996 Clinton became the first Democratic President to be re-elected since Roosevelt.

The Clinton era confirmed a re-positioning of the party. While substantial parts of the liberal social agenda from the 1960s and 1970s have been absorbed by the mainstream Democratic Party (notably in areas such as the treatment of minorities and personal morality) much of the Republican agenda on issues such as taxation, balanced budgets, and freedom of enterprise has also been accepted. Indeed,

although Clinton inherited a \$290 billion budget deficit he was able, following several years of rapid growth, to leave office with a considerable budget surplus, something the Republicans had previously made a touchstone for political success but failed to achieve. George W. Bush's victory in the 2000 presidential election was notable in that it came against a background where the Democratic contender, Vice-President Al Gore, could point to a record of several years of sustained economic growth, record employment, low inflation and balanced budgets, positive elements lacking when the Republicans re-captured the presidency in 1980. Among the factors suggested as tipping an extremely close contest to the Republicans were distaste for the air of sleaze and scandal surrounding the second term of the Clinton presidency, Gore's lack of charisma, and his late-campaign rhetoric which seemed to be aimed more at traditional Democratic voters than the undecided.

The party's contemporary hard-core base of support lies particularly among minorities, in the inner cities, in older industrial regions, among organized labour and among public sector workers. Although the Democratic Party is not a socialist party its support base closely resembles that of democratic socialist parties in western Europe. The support of blacks (representing 12% of the population) for the party is overwhelmingly high. The party is also the preferred choice of most Hispanics (also about 12% of the population), with the notable exception of Cuban Americans. While the business community tends to be heavily Republican in sympathies, it is the custom for big corporations to fund both of the major parties. The AFL–CIO labour confederation is strongly supportive of the party and assists in organizing grass-roots campaigning: it, however, affiliates fewer than 10% of private sector workers and its main strength is in public services, to which the Democrats show much greater commitment than do the Republicans. A key consideration for the Democrats is ensuring that they attract support beyond their core constituencies by ensuring balanced tickets that reach out to all sections of the country. Although the Democrats have put up presidential candidates from various parts of the country since Kennedy, the only candidates to win have been from the South (Johnson, Texas, in 1964; Carter, Georgia, in 1976; Clinton, Arkansas, in 1992 and 1996). With the two main parties taking virtually identical shares of the popular vote in national elections since the mid-1990s, the Democrats (as the Republicans) regard it as essential to maximize their support in the centre ground while also ensuring that they mobilize their core constituency on polling day, objectives that can come into conflict as was witnessed during Al Gore's campaign in 2000.

With the election of Bill Clinton in 1992 the party gained simultaneous control of the presidency and both Houses of Congress for the first time since the 1970s. At the congressional mid-term elections of 1994, however, the Democrats suffered a major setback, losing control of the Senate and, more dramatically, losing their majority in the House of Representatives for the first time since 1954. The Republicans' control of Congress subsequently enabled them to frustrate unpalatable aspects of Clinton's legislative programme, even though he secured re-election in 1996, and during his second term Clinton was put on the defensive by the Monica Lewinsky affair. This climaxed in the vote of the (Republican-controlled) House in December 1998 to impeach him (requiring a trial before the Senate). However, despite widespread criticism of Clinton's moral conduct within his own party, the effort to remove him from office never (unlike in the Watergate affair) developed any bi-partisan character, without which (a Senate vote for conviction requiring a 2/3 majority) it was bound to fail, given that there were then 45 Democratic and 55 Republican Senators. When on Feb. 13, 1999, the Senate came to vote on the two articles of impeachment (Article 1, perjury before a grand jury; Article 2, obstruction of justice) all 45 Democrats voted for acquittal on both counts and they were even joined by 10 Republicans on Article 1 and five on Article 2. Despite the heated rhetoric surrounding the Lewinsky affair its lasting impact (in contrast to Watergate) was slight; it resulted in no landmark legislation, and it did not result in any major shift in voting patterns in the 2000 elections, where the parties remained very evenly balanced. In the November 2000 elections the Republicans retained control of the House but with a reduced majority; in the Senate the parties were left in a dead heat (50 seats each) but the Republicans retained control by virtue of the Vice-President's casting vote. However, in May 2001 the defection of a Republican senator (who became an independent) handed the Democrats control of the Senate and the key positions of the chairmanships of its committees.

The conflict surrounding the 2000 presidential election underscored the divergence of approach within the Democratic Party and its character as a coalition. To sections of organized labour, some representatives of minorities, and party liberals with a radical agenda, the effort to prevent a Bush victory had an intense urgency as he was seen as a mouthpiece for unrestrained right-wing politics and the big corporations. To these elements of the party Bush's election victory was irreversibly tainted by his second-place in the popular vote, electoral practices that worked against minorities, and perceived bias in the US Supreme Court decision (swung by a majority of Republican appointees) that had effectively handed him the contest. Centrist Democrats, in contrast, including most in Congress, were disinclined to continue the controversy beyond the Supreme Court decision, putting their emphasis on the need for national reconciliation.

Different currents within the party find a degree of formal organization. Most significant is the Democratic Leadership Council (DLC), spearheading the New Democrat Movement that seeks to transcend "stale left-right debate" and define a "Third Way" in politics. Past chairs of the DLC include former President Bill Clinton and current House minority leader Richard Gephardt. An offshoot of the New Democrat Movement is the New Democrat Coalition, which has 72 members in the House and 20 in the Senate. The left-wing of the party associates in the Congressional Progressive Caucus; its much smaller membership is based in the House of Representatives and includes Jesse Jackson Jr. The party's conservative wing in Congress includes adherents of the 32-member Blue Dog Coalition, so-named because their views had been "choked blue" in the party before 1994, and who particularly emphasize fiscal responsibility; it lacks major names, however.

The Democratic Party is an observer member of the Christian Democrat International and of the Liberal International.

Republican Party

Address. Republican National Committee, 310 First Street SE, Washington, DC 20003
Telephone. (+1–202) 863–5000
Fax. (+1–202) 863–8820
Email. info@rnc.org
Website. www.rnc.org
Leadership. Jim Gilmore, Ann L. Wagner (national co-chairmen); Trent Lott (Senate minority leader); Richard (Dick) K. Armey (House majority leader); George W. Bush (President of the United States)

The Republican Party represents the centre-right of the American political spectrum. Ideologically it favours small government and fiscal restraint (although in practice often acting as a party of "big government"), free enterprise and conservative social values. In foreign affairs it has traditionally been somewhat less interventionist than the Democratic Party although the isolationist wing of the party, a significant factor immediately after World War II, has been a marginal force in recent decades.

Informally known as the "Grand Old Party (GOP)", the Republican Party was founded in 1854 by opponents of

Southern slavery. In 1860 its candidate, Abraham Lincoln, was elected President with the votes of the northern states, with the subsequent civil war between North and South (1861-65) resulting in victory for the North. The Republicans then held the presidency for all but 16 years in the period through to the election of Democrat Franklin D. Roosevelt in 1932, since when the presidency has been fairly evenly shared between the two main parties. The 1930s New Deal also marked a watershed in that thenceforth the Republicans were far more clearly seen as standing to the right of the Democrats. The once prominent progressive wing of the party largely disintegrated or re-located to the Democrats in this period, although a small minority tradition of liberal Republicanism continued until the 1970s. In the 1960s the allegiance of much of the once solidly Democratic white vote in the South also shifted to the Republicans in protest at the civil rights legislation of the Kennedy and Johnson presidencies.

In 1968 and 1972 Richard M. Nixon was elected on platforms that promised to speak for the "silent majority" at a time of national strife over Vietnam and race, but he was forced to resign in August 1974 as a consequence of the Watergate scandal. His (unelected) successor, Gerald Ford, seen as representing traditional moderate establishment Republicanism, was defeated in the 1976 election by Jimmy Carter. By this time, however, a "new right", in some respects representing an ideological counter-point to the "new left" that had influenced the Democrats over the past decade, was an increasing force in the party. In 1980, former California Governor Ronald Reagan, with the backing of the new right, captured the party nomination and went on to win successive presidential terms (1981–89). "Reaganism", like Thatcherism in the United Kingdom, gave the nation's main conservative party an ideological dynamic that had been lacking for several decades during which the Democrats had set the agenda for change while the Republicans had fought a rearguard action in favour of the status quo. Reagan's successor (from 1989), George Bush (as Thatcher's successor from 1990, John Major), represented a dilution of the more radical and ideological aspects of Reaganism. In 1992 Bush was defeated for re-election by Bill Clinton, who went on to win a second term in 1996 when he defeated moderate Senator Bob Dole of Kansas. In 2000, however, George W. Bush, the Governor of Texas and son of the former President, recaptured the presidency for the Republicans (with Richard Cheney as his running mate for Vice-President) in an election in which he gained a majority in the Electoral College despite taking a smaller share of the popular vote than the Democratic candidate Al Gore.

In 1994, the Republicans won control of both Houses of Congress, substantially weakening the effectiveness of the Clinton presidency. Congressional powers of investigation were subsequently employed to undermine Clinton, culminating in his impeachment over the Monica Lewinsky affair. However, while the threat to drive Clinton from office was often compared with the process that led to the resignation of Nixon over Watergate, the national mood of contentment and prosperity could not be compared with the febrile and self-doubting atmosphere of the last days of the Vietnam War, when many members of Nixon's own party turned against him. When the Senate came to vote on Feb. 13, 1999, at the end of a trial on the two articles of impeachment (requiring a 2/3 majority for conviction) the 45 Democrats voted en bloc for acquittal on both counts, and they were joined by 10 Republicans on one count and five on the other. The fact that the Republicans voting for acquittal came from the moderate wing of the party, including figures such as Olympia Snowe of Maine and Arlen Specter of Pennsylvania, underscored that the Senate had split on grounds of ideological orientation rather than on the merits of the case. The Senate vote reflected the fact that in the country as a whole, the campaign to bring down Clinton had not built a constituency beyond the ranks of those who had previously been implacably hostile to him in any case.

In November 2000, with the election of George W. Bush as President, the Republicans briefly enjoyed simultaneous control of the presidency and both Houses of Congress for the first time since 1954. However, with the Senate tied 50:50, control in the Senate relied on the exercise of the casting vote of the Vice-President. In May 2001 a hitherto obscure liberal Republican Senator, James Jeffords (Vermont), quit the party, saying he would sit as an independent, and as a consequence the Democrats gained control of the chamber, creating potential difficulties for the Bush agenda on a wide range of issues, including appointments requiring Senate approval.

Since the election of Ronald Reagan in 1980 many of the major political issues have been resolved on terms favoured by the Republicans: balanced budgets have become an orthodoxy, as have tax cuts; commitment to a strong military and foreign policy has been renewed; and the worldwide challenge of communism has collapsed. The most potent issues on the political right now tend to be in the areas of domestic social concern and personal morality, such as opposition to abortion, stem cell research and gun controls, and with a dimension of (Christian) religious fundamentalism that sits uncomfortably with the values of suburban voters central to Republican electoral success. While the "Republican landslide" of 1994 was hailed by the right as representing a decisive victory, the realities of the virtual dead heat nationwide between the two parties in vote share over the following years have driven Republican campaign managers to attempt to win the centre ground while not driving right-wing radicals into third-party activity.

In common with the Democrats, the Republicans do not have a single accepted "leader"; individual members of Congress have considerable autonomous influence and principal Cabinet officers are not necessarily leading members of the party. Different streams within the party find representation within a range of pressure groups. The Republican Leadership Council is an independent group of centrist Republicans, established in 1997 to resist the pressure on the party from an "intolerant vocal minority" and seen as a mirror of the Democratic Leadership Council in its association with the party establishment. On the liberal wing the Republican Mainstream Committee seeks to expand the party's appeal to centrist, women, independent, young and minority voters. The Republican Main Street Partnership, founded in 1998, aims to give voice to the "principled but pragmatic centre" within the party: it emphasizes fiscal conservatism but moderation on social issues and has strong support from numerous leaders of major corporations. The Republican Liberty Caucus represents a libertarian, laissez-faire current. The National Federation of Republican Assemblies stands on the right and the agenda is also influenced from the right by non-partisan organizations such as the American Conservative Union and Pat Robertson's Christian Coalition, although the latter is a much diminished force. Leading figures often identified with the religious right include Attorney General John Ashcroft, former Senate foreign relations committee chairman Jesse Helms and Senate minority leader Trent Lott. Despite the continuing vigour of the religious right, however, the dominant stream of pro-big business, traditionalist conservatism has since the late 1980s found continuity in the successive presidencies of Bush father and son.

The Republican Party is a member of the International Democrat Union.

Other Parties

There are numerous US would-be third parties, particularly at the ideological poles. The most successful in recent years have been the Reform Party, the Libertarian Party and the green movement, now crystallized into the Green Party of the United States; each of these has had some influence on the national political agenda (although none has elected a candidate to Washington). The Democrats and Republicans are dominant throughout the country and there are no important regional parties. The listing below includes all the more significant minor parties with operations or influence beyond the single-state level; it does not include the various political-education lobbies that do not refer to themselves as political parties but endorse favoured candidates on a non-partisan basis.

American Heritage Party, founded in June 2000 on the basis of the breakaway Washington State section of the →Constitution Party and taking the Bible as its "political textbook".
Address. PO Box 241, Leavenworth, Washington 98826-0241
Telephone. (+1–509) 548–2319
Fax. (+1–509) 548–8709
Email. ahp@nwi.net
Website. www.americanheritageparty.org
Leadership. Daniel Eby (national chairman)

American Independent Party, originated in California in 1967 as a vehicle for the third-party presidential aspirations of anti-Washington segregationist Gov. George Wallace of Alabama (who won five Southern states in 1968); claiming to have some 300,000 registered members in California it last fielded a presidential candidate in 1980 and is now affiliated nationally to the right-wing →Constitution Party; favours small government, abolition of the Internal Revenue Service, disengagement from NAFTA and the WTO, an "America First" non-interventionist foreign policy and ending abortion rights.
Address. 1084 West Marshall Blvd, San Bernadino, California 92405
Website. www.aipca.org
Leadership. Nathan Johnson (chairman)

American Party, right-wing formation dating from 1972, advocating an isolationist foreign policy, restrictions on the federal government, and an end to gun controls; has declined since the 1970s and its 2000 presidential aspirant failed to get on the ballot in a single state.
Address. 47 East Kensington Avenue, Salt Lake City, Utah 84115
Email. liberty@theamericanparty.org
Website. www.theamericanparty.org
Leadership. Arly Pedersen (national chairman)

American Reform Party (ARP), formed in 1997 by a faction of the →Reform Party (RP) that had wanted to nominate former Colorado Governor Dick Lamm rather than Ross Perot for president in 1996; subsequently attracted supporters of Minnesota Governor Jesse Ventura and other RP defectors; adopted reformist, centrist programme calling for paying down the national debt, reduced immigration, and economic protectionism, but also advocating continued engagement in international affairs, payment of dues to the UN, universal health care, environmental protection and restoration of diplomatic relations with Cuba. In 2000 joined the loose coalition backing Ralph Nader's presidential bid.
Website. www.americanreform.org
Leadership. David Repko (chairman)

Communist Party–USA (CP–USA), founded in 1919 and historically aligned with the Soviet Union (which subsidized the party's operations); at its peak during the 1930s depression and World War II alliance between the USA and Soviet Union, but of negligible influence since then; retains Marxism-Leninism as its "guiding theory" and currently emphasizes efforts to build a united front of progressive forces against →Republican President Bush and the "ultra-right". Last put forward a presidential candidate (who took 36,000 votes) in 1984 and in 2000 elections called for a vote for →Democrat Al Gore to prevent the "greater evil" of Bush in the White House.

Address. 235 W. 23rd Street, New York, NY 10011
Telephone. (+1-212) 989-4994
Website. www.cpusa.org
Leadership. Sam Webb (national chair)

Conservative Party of New York State, founded in 1962 to oppose liberalism and collectivism and has had national influence on the American right; runs its own candidates but more commonly endorses favoured candidates from the major parties; claims 170,000 members.
Address. 486 78th Street, Brooklyn, NY 11209
Email. info@cpnys.org
Website. www.cpnys.org

Constitution Party, founded in 1992 as the US Taypayers' Party (calling for abolition of the US Internal Revenue Service) and adopted present name in 1999. This is a right-wing formation that wants to limit the federal government to activities specifically authorized by the Constitution and has a programme shaped by the concerns of the religious right. Howard Phillips, the party's three-time presidential candidate was a leading figure in the ideological "new right" that influenced the Reagan presidency; he took 98,020 votes (0.09% of the total) in the 2000 presidential election.
Address. 23 North Lime Street, Lancaster, Pennsylvania 17602
Telephone. (+1–717) 390–1993
Fax. (+1–717) 390–1996
Email. info@constitutionparty.com
Website. www.constitutionparty.com
Leadership. Jim Clymer(chairman); Howard Phillips (presidential candidate)

Democratic Socialists of America (DSA), established under its present name in 1983 as a coalition of old-style socialists, New Deal progressives and new left elements, including defectors from the old Socialist Party (which had in 1972 become →Social Democrats USA); the principal US affiliate of the Socialist International but an insignificant force in domestic politics; does not put forward its own candidates and generally works within the left-wing of the →Democratic Party.
Address. 180 Varick Street, New York, NY 10014
Telephone. (+1–212) 727–8610
Fax. (+1–212) 727–8616
Email. dsa@dsausa.org
Website. www.dsausa.org
Leadership. Horace Small (national director)

Green Party of the United States (GPUS), describing itself as a "confederation of state green parties", the GPUS was founded in July 2001 at a national conference of the Association of State Green Parties (ASGP). The ASGP had itself been created as a network of state green parties in November 1996 as a development from Ralph Nader's first presidential bid, when he took over 700,000 votes. Its membership overlapped with that of the →Greens/Green Party USA although ASGP was sometimes seen as the more moderate wing of the movement. In 2000 the ASGP again endorsed Nader as its presidential candidate (although Nader ran with a far wider constituency of support than just the Green movement, including some former supporters of the →Reform Party). Nader was on the ballot in 44 states and took 2,882,897 votes (2.74% of the total) on a platform that emphasized opposition to the "special interests", capitalist globalization and the power of big corporations: his success was widely blamed by Democrats as having brought about Bush's narrow victory. The high national profile the Nader campaign created encouraged the ASGP to launch the GPUS. The agenda defined by GPUS leaders included opposition to global corporate power and the IMF, World Bank and WTO; boycotting the major oil companies to force the Bush administration to re-join the Kyoto accord; demanding universal health care; ending the death penalty, and the

expansion of local democracy. The GPUS opposed the military campaign launched against Afghanistan in the wake of the Sept. 11, 2001, terrorist attacks in the USA, calling for "international co-operation" to bring the perpetrators of the Sept. 11 attacks before an international tribunal.

As of October 2001 91 Greens held elective office on city councils and other local bodies in 20 states but there were no members of state legislatures or Congress. Greens had had the most success in the states of California (34 current officials), Wisconsin (reflecting the progressive tradition in Madison) 16, and Oregon, 8.
Address. PO Box 18452, Washington DC 20036
Telephone. (+1–202) 232–0335
Email. capeconn@home.com
Website. www.gpus.org

The Greens/Green Party USA (G/GPUSA), locally based green groups, focusing on community and environmental issues and inspired by the German Greens, formed the Green Committees of Correspondence in 1984, held their first full delegated congress in 1989, and adopted the present name in 1991. The G/GPUSA, which calls itself an "anti-party party", and is more inclined to direct action than electoral politics, has a small membership base and has been seen as the left-wing of the Green movement in its strongly anti-capitalist orientation compared with the Association of State Green Parties, which in July 2001 founded the →Green Party of the United States (GPUS). The G/GPUSA backed Nader's 2000 presidential campaign although Nader did not accept its nomination. The 2001 G/GPUSA convention failed to produce the necessary 2/3 majority for merger into the new GPUS but a sizeable proportion of the membership reportedly joined the new party.
Address. PO Box 1406, Chicago, Illinois 60690
Telephone. (+1–866) 473–3672
Email. gpusa@greens.org
Website. www.greenparty.org

Independence Party, founded by Jesse Ventura after he left the →Reform Party (RP) in February 2000 (having been elected Governor of Minnesota as its candidate in 1998); more centrist than the RP rump; currently based almost entirely in Minnesota but organizing elsewhere and with national ambitions.
Address. 113 Monroe Avenue, North Mankato, Minnesota 56003
Telephone. (+1–507) 387–2657
Website. www.eindependence.org
Leadership. Jesse Ventura (leader)

Independent American Party, founded in 1998 on the basis of the Utah Independent American Party (the latter with origins in the American Independent Party of Utah set up to support George Wallace's presidential bid in 1968), emphasizing patriotism and conservative Christian values; in 2000 it endorsed the presidential candidacy of Howard Phillips of the →Constitution Party.
Address. 793 W. Green Oaks Drive, Murray, Utah 84123
Email. contact@usiap.org
Website. www.usiap.org
Leadership. Bruce Bangerter (chair)

Labor Party, held its first constitutional convention in November 1998 with backing from some labour unions; campaigning reflects union agenda on issues such as labour law and health care; neither ran nor endorsed a presidential candidate in 2000.
Address. PO Box 53177, Washington DC 20009
Telephone. (+1–202) 234–5190
Fax. (+1–202) 234–5266
Website. www.igc.org

Libertarian Party (LP), founded in 1971 in Colorado, organized in every state, and among the most significant of the various third parties over the last two decades. It represents a distinctive American ideological stream, rooted in traditions of individualism, hostility to big government, and isolationism in international affairs. The LP believes in shrinking the role of the government, including ending corporate and farm subsidies and the complete withdrawal of the federal government from areas such as health, education and welfare. It promises to reduce government spending to a level where income taxes are unnecessary. It is hostile to government interference in personal conduct, opposing gun control laws, compulsory wearing of seat belts, laws on under-age drinking and street security cameras. It opposes the government's war on drugs saying that this has undermined civil liberties. In foreign relations it advocates a foreign policy based on non-intervention, peace and free trade. It opposes foreign aid as creating welfare dependence in the recipient countries and US involvement in countries such as Iraq and former Yugoslavia, and believes defence spending should be confined to defending the USA. Following the Sept. 11, 2001, attacks on the USA it re-iterated its view that the underlying solution lay in US non-intervention internationally, arguing that Switzerland had never suffered a terrorist attack; a poll of LP members showed, however, that most also supported military action against Osama bin Laden on the ground that it was a response to a direct attack on the USA.

The LP has nearly 500 elected officials at local level but has never won an election for a seat in the US Congress (although its 1988 presidential candidate, Ron Paul, is now a Republican congressman). In the 2000 elections it put up candidates in 255 of the 435 House districts, winning an aggregate of 1.7 million votes. Its presidential candidates have had little impact. The most successful year was 1980 when Ed Clark won 921,199 votes. In 2000, Harry Browne won 384,429 votes (0.36% of votes cast), representing a decline from 1996 when he gained 485,798 votes.

Address. 2600 Virginia Avenue, NW, Suite 100, Washington DC 20037
Telephone. (+1–202) 333–0008
Fax. (+1–202) 333–0072
Email. hq@lp.org
Website. www.lp.org
Leadership. Harry Browne (presidential candidate); Steve Dasbach (national director); Ron Crickenberger (political director)

Natural Law Party (NLP), founded in 1992 by followers of the Maharishi Mahesh Yogi; sees social and economic problems as a resulting from violations of "natural law"; practical policy positions tend to be centrist or ambiguous with emphasis on achieving "harmony" with natural law as the solution. After the Sept. 11 terrorist attacks called on President Bush to train US troops in the "peace-promoting techniques of transcendental meditation". Unlike most Natural Law parties worldwide has some perceptible political identity: its leader and presidential candidate, physicist John Hagelin (described as "Minister of Science and Technology of the Global Country of World Peace"), won 110,000 votes in 1996; in 2000 he gained support from a disaffected section of the →Reform Party, but polled only 83,555 votes (0.08% of the total).

Address. PO Box 1900, Fairfield, Iowa 52556
Telephone. (+1–641) 472–2040
Fax. (+1–641) 472–2011
Email. info@natural-law.org
Website. www.natural-law.org
Leadership. John Hagelin (leader)

New Party, a progressive formation founded in 1992 and active particularly at municipal level in a number of states on issues such as affordable housing, tenants' rights, campaign finance and urban sprawl. In elections it has generally endorsed left–liberal →Democrats rather than run its own candidates.

Address. 88 Third Avenue, Suite 313, Brooklyn, NY 11217
Telephone. (+1–718) 246–3713
Fax. (+1–718) 246–3718
Email. Newparty@newparty.org
Website. www.newparty.org
Leadership. Jim Fleischmann (executive director)

Prohibition Party (PP), originating in 1869 it has since then run a presidential candidate in every election; in the late nineteenth and early twentieth century the party had great influence in many states; maintains its historic opposition to the commercial sale of alcohol and emphasizes a conservative moral and social agenda. Earl Dodge, its 2000 presidential candidate, appeared on the ballot only in Colorado, winning 208 votes.

Website. www.prohibition.org
Leadership. Earl Dodge (national chairman)

Reform Party (RPUSA), for a period in the 1990s the ideologically diffuse conservative–populist movement inspired by Texas billionaire H. Ross Perot constituted the most significant third-party challenge for decades. It called for paying down the national debt, balanced budgets, electoral and campaign reform, and opposed the North American Free Trade Agreement (NAFTA) as exporting American jobs.

Perot announced on a TV show in February 1992 that he would run as an independent in that year's presidential election if the citizens would put him on the ballot in all 50 states. An ad hoc grass-roots movement, which coalesced as "United We Stand America" (UWSA), aided by heavy spending on advertising by Perot, propelled him to 18.9% of the vote in the November 1992 election. Perot's expenditure from his personal fortune was estimated at \$60 million. Perot was thought to have taken votes disproportionately from the →Republican candidate, George Bush, thereby contributing to the victory of →Democrat Bill Clinton. Following the election, UWSA continued in existence as a "watchdog group" with chapters in every state. In the 1994 congressional elections, in which the Republicans took control of both Houses, Perot urged his supporters to vote for Republican candidates. In September 1995 Perot announced he would assist UWSA supporters to create a Reform Party to challenge the country's two-party structure. In the 1996 campaign, as Reform Party presidential candidate, Perot had the benefit of federal matching funds because of his success in taking above 5% of the national vote in 1992 but was excluded (unlike in 1992) from the live televised presidential debates; he took less than 9% of the vote.

In November 1998 former professional wrestler Jesse Ventura was elected as Governor of Minnesota on a Reform Party ticket, the first time since 1916 that a candidate from a nationally-organized third party had won a state governorship. In 1999-2000, however, with Perot now remaining aloof from its affairs, the party was split by a series of personality and ideological conflicts, with hostile factions claiming to represent the RP nationally. In February 2000 Ventura resigned from the party calling it "hopelessly dysfunctional" and warning that its likely presidential candidate, former conservative Republican commentator Patrick J. Buchanan, was "an anti-abortion extremist and unrealistic isolationist". The party nonetheless went on to nominate Buchanan at its convention in August 2000, although a minority faction held a rival convention which nominated John Hagelin, the leader of the →Natural Law Party, who claimed to be the heir to the Reform Party of Perot. Although the Federal Election Commission awarded Buchanan the \$12.6 million in matching federal funding to which the party was eligible based on its 1996 electoral performance, Hagelin's backers succeeded in keeping Buchanan off the ballot in some states. Other former RP supporters, in the →American Reform Party, backed Ralph Nader, the most left-wing of the main candidates, while Perot himself ultimately endorsed the Republican candidate,

George W. Bush. In the November 2000 presidential election Buchanan won only 0.42% of the vote. The result meant that the party would not attract matching federal campaign funds in the next presidential election.
Address. 3281 N. Meadow Mine Place, Tucson, AZ 85745
Website. www.reformparty.org
Leadership. Gerald Moan (national chair)

Social Democrats USA (SDUSA), claiming descent from the Socialist Party (SP) founded in 1901 that had some influence in the early decades of the 20th century when leader Eugene Debs won nearly one million votes running for President in 1912 and 1920; its 1932 presidential candidate, Norman Thomas, took 896,000 votes but thereafter much of its support moved to the New Deal →Democratic Party. In 1972 the party, which stood to the right of the contemporary new left movement, adopted its current name; leftists within the SP subsequently formed the →Socialist Party USA. The SDUSA is, with the →Democratic Socialists of America, one of the two US member parties of the Socialist International but a minor force in US politics; it is close to the liberal wing of the Democratic Party.
Address. 815 15th Street, NW, Suite 921, Washington DC 20005
Telephone. (+1-202) 638-1515
Fax. (+1-202) 347-2531
Email. info@socialdemocrats.org

Website. www.idsonline.com/sdusa
Leadership. David Jessup (president)

Socialist Party USA, small radical democratic socialist formation founded in 1973 by left-wingers opposed to the renaming of the original Socialist Party as →Social Democrats USA; focuses mainly on local and grass-roots activism but puts forward presidential candidates to raise awareness, its 2000 candidate, David McReynolds, winning 5,602 votes.
Address. 339 Lafayette Street, #303, New York, NY 10012
Telephone/Fax. (+1-212) 982-4586
Email. socialistparty@sp-usa.org
Website. sp-usa.org
Leadership. Greg Pason (national secretary)

The Southern Party, ultra-conservative formation founded in 1999 to demand the restoration of sovereignty for the Southern states lost with the defeat of the Confederacy in 1865; adopted Confederate flag as symbol and compares its position to that of the →→*Parti Québécois* in Canada and the →→Scottish National Party in the United Kingdom; a rare example of a regionalist party in the USA; says that it is open to all races, though the membership is reported as overwhelmingly white.
Website. www.southernparty.org
Leadership. Jerry Baxley (chairman)

US Dependencies

The achievement of independence by Palau in October 1994 effectively terminated the US government's administration of the United Nations Trust Territory of the Pacific Islands, the other components of which had either achieved full independence or, in the case of the Northern Marianas, opted for US Commonwealth status on the same basis as Puerto Rico. These two territories are covered below, together with the other US dependencies of significance in the Pacific and the Caribbean.

American Samoa

Capital: Pago Pago   **Population:** 67,000 (2001E)

The South Pacific islands known collectively as American Samoa form an unincorporated territory of the United States, administered since 1951 under the US Department of the Interior. Executive authority is vested in a Governor, who is popularly elected for a four-year term. The bicameral legislature (*Fono*) consists of a Senate, whose 18 members are chosen for four-year terms by traditional clan leaders, and a popularly elected 21-member House of Representatives. The territory sends one non-voting delegate to the US House of Representatives, with election to this position contested by the (US) Republican and Democratic parties, as well as by independents; the Democratic candidate was elected in November 2000.

In legislative elections held in November 1998 and November 2000 only non-partisans were elected. In the gubernatorial election held on Nov. 7, 2000, Tauese Sunia was re-elected, taking 6,110 votes, 341 more than the runner-up, Lealaifuaneva P. Reid. The result was subsequently upheld in the territory's High Court, dismissing a complaint by the runner-up that the management of the vote had been open to fraud.

Guam

Capital: Hagatna (Agana)   **Population:** 157,000 (2001E)

The Pacific island of Guam is an unincorporated territory of the United States and is administered under the US Department of the Interior. Executive power is exercised by a Governor popularly elected for a four-year term. The unicameral Guam Legislature has 15 members who are popularly elected for a two-year term. The territory elects one non-voting delegate to the US House of Representatives. Political activity mirrors that on the US mainland and is therefore dominated by the Democratic and Republican parties.

The gubernatorial election of November 1998 resulted in the re-election of Democratic incumbent, Carl Gutierrez, with a 53.2% share of the vote. In the November 2000 legislative elections, the Republican Party won 8 seats and the Democrats 7 in the Guam Legislature, while Robert A.Underwood (Democrat) was re-elected with 78% of the vote as the territory's delegate to the US House of Representatives.

Northern Mariana Islands

Capital: Sapian   **Population:** 75,000 (2001E)

Originally part of the UN Trust Territory of the Pacific administered by the United States, the Northern Mariana Islands voted to become a US Commonwealth Territory in 1975, following which a new constitution came into effect in 1978. One of two US Commonwealth Territories (the other being Puerto Rico), its inhabitants have US citizenship. The territory does not send a delegate to the US Congress but has a "resident representative" in Washington. Executive authority is held by the Governor, elected by universal adult suffrage for a four-year term. The bicameral legislature consists of a directly elected Senate, with nine members elected for four-year terms, and a House of Representatives, with 18 members elected for two-year terms.

The US Democratic and Republican parties have traditionally dominated political activity. Elections held on Nov. 3, 2001, resulted in victory for the Republicans, with their candidate Juan Nekai Babauta retaining the governorship for the party in a four-way race with 43% of the vote, while the Republicans also retained control of both Houses of the legislature.

Covenant Party, founded in 2001 to challenge the dominance of the US-based Democratic and Republican parties in the territory, its name referring to the 1975 Covenant under which the islands' constitutional status was established; in elections in November 2001 the party's candidate for Governor, former Republican House Speaker Benigno R. Fitial, came second with 24% of the vote, while the party also secured minority representation in both legislative Houses.

Leadership. Eloy Inos (chairman); Benigno R. Fitial (leader)

Puerto Rico

Capital: San Juan   **Population:** 3,937,000 (2001E)

The Caribbean island of Puerto Rico was ceded by Spain to the United States as a result of the Spanish–American War of 1898 and has had Commonwealth status since 1952. While this status has been often described as one of "free association" with the USA, the US House of Representatives in 1998 concluded that Puerto Rico was in effect an unincorporated territory that did not meet the US or international definition of free association. Although Puerto Ricans have been US citizens since 1917 they do not have a vote in US congressional or presidential elections and are instead represented in the US Congress by a Resident Commissioner, elected for a four-year term, who may vote on committees but not from the floor. The US President is head of state. The head of government is the Governor, who is elected for a four-year term and assisted by an appointed Cabinet. There is a bicameral Legislative Assembly comprising a Senate and a House of Representatives; both chambers are directly elected for a four-year term, with the majority of seats decided by direct election from single-seat districts.

Two parties, the Popular Democratic Party (PPD) and the New Progressive Party (PNP) have dominated Puerto Rican politics since the late 1960s, alternating in power. The principal political issue in Puerto Rico for several decades has been its constitutional status. The PPD favours continued Commonwealth status and the PNP seeks statehood within the USA. The only other party of any current significance is the Puerto Rican Independence Party (PIP), which favours full independence. In 1967, a plebiscite resulted in 60.4% supporting continued Commonwealth status, 39% statehood within the USA, and 0.6% independence. In November 1993, 48.6% of voters opted for continued Commonwealth status, 46.3% for statehood and 4.4% for independence. A further plebiscite was held on Dec. 13, 1998. However, while the PNP and PIP supported the statehood and independence options on the ballot, respectively, the PPD rejected the terminology for the continuation of Commonwealth status. The result was that votes were cast as follows for the main options: 787,900 (50.3%) for "none of the above" (i.e. the PPD's position); 728,157 (46.5%) for statehood; and 39,838 (2.5%) for independence. The 1998 plebiscite was locally organized and the US Congress while endorsing the principle of self-determination for Puerto Rico had not, however, defined what options it was in practice prepared to accept.

The most recent general election, held Nov. 7, 2000, resulted in a clean sweep of victories for the PPD, which won back control from the PNP. The results were as follows: House of Representatives, PPD 30, PNP 20, PIP 1; Senate, PPD 19, PNP 8, PIP 1. The PPD gubernatorial candidate, Sila María Calderón was likewise victorious (taking 48.6% of the vote, compared with the 45.7% taken by the PNP candidate and 5.2% by the PIP candidate) as was its candidate for Resident Commissioner, Aníbel Acevedo Vlá. Voter turnout, at close to 90%, was markedly higher than in the simultaneous national elections in the USA, where only 51% cast their vote in the presidential election.

New Progressive Party
Partido Nuevo Progresista (PNP)
Address. PO Box 1992, Fernández Juncos Station, San Juan, PR 00910–1992
Telephone. (+1–787) 289–2000
Website. www.pnp.org
Leadership. Pedro Rosselló (leader)
Formed in 1967 as a break-away away from the →Popular Democratic Party (PPD), since when it has rivalled the PPD as one of the two major parties. It has won the governorship for five four-year terms (in 1968, 1976, 1980, 1992 and 1996).

The PNP since its formation has advocated statehood for Puerto Rico within the USA. It maintains that Commonwealth status deprives Puerto Ricans of the full opportunities and obligations of their US citizenship. In a plebiscite on the issue held in 1967, 39.0% voted in favour of statehood. In a further plebiscite held in 1993 after the PNP returned to office in 1992 the gap narrowed, with 46.3% voting for statehood. However, a further plebiscite held in December 1998 following an intensive campaign by the PNP, showed that the PNP had been unable to capitalize on its then control of the legislature and governorship, the proportion of the electorate favouring statehood remaining virtually unchanged at 46.5%. The US Congress, while acknowledging the right of self-determination for Puerto Rico, has never indicated that it is prepared to accept Puerto Rico's admission as the 51st state and it is generally considered that there is no majority support for such an option in Congress.

The PNP held comfortable majorities in both House and Senate following the 1992 and 1996 elections, but lost control of both chambers to the PPD in November 2000. Pedro Rosselló won the gubernatorial elections of 1992 and 1996 for the PNP, but in 2000 the PNP candidate, Carlos I. Pesquera, lost to the PPD's Sila María Calderón, while the PNP's candidate for Resident Commissioner, Carlos Romero Barceló (a former Governor) was also defeated.

Popular Democratic Party
Partido Popular Democrático (PPD)
Address. 403 Ponce de León Ave, POB 5788, Puerta de Tierra, San Juan, PR 00906
Leadership. Sila María Calderón (Governor of Puerto Rico)
The PPD was founded in 1938 and was the dominant political formation from 1940 until a split in the party in 1968 resulted in the →New Progressive Party (PNP) gaining power, since when the PPD and PNP have alternated in office. The PPD won the first election for Governor in 1948 and then held the governorship until it was captured by the PNP in 1968. Since then the PPD has won the governorship for four four-year terms (in 1972, 1984, 1988 and 2000).

The PPD has traditionally embraced a wide range of views on social and economic issues, including strongly pro-business and pro-American conservatives and left-liberals who favour greater autonomy from the USA, although the majority tend to identify with the →→Democratic Party in the USA. In the early years the PPD, while emphasizing social and economic reform, favoured independence, but with the onset of the Cold War in the mid-1940s repudiated this position (with disaffected supporters then joining the →Puerto Rican Independence Party, PIP) and then became a framer and consistent defender of the Commonwealth status granted in 1952. Perceived benefits of Commonwealth status include automatic US citizenship, federal tax breaks for investors, welfare benefits paid for by the US taxpayer but exemption of Puerto Ricans from federal taxes, a common market with the USA, and US military defence, while also providing sufficient autonomy to enable Puerto Rico to retain its distinctive Hispanic culture and identity. In successive plebiscites (most recently in December 1998) the electorate has, though in 1993 and 1998 by narrow majorities, rejected the quest for statehood favoured by the PNP. In the 1998 plebiscite, the PPD rejected the terminology adopted, which it said was biased in favour of the statehood option, and backed a vote for "none of the above", which won 50.3% of the ballot.

In the 1992 elections the PPD lost control of both the House and Senate to the PNP and failed to recover any ground in 1996. In November 2000, however, the PPD recovered strongly, capturing both Houses and with its candidates being elected for the posts of Governor and Resident Commissioner. Sila María Calderón (the Mayor of San Juan) became the island's first woman Governor.

Puerto Rican Independence Party
Partido Independentista Puertorriqueño (PIP)
Address. 963 Ave. Roosevelt, San Juan, PR 00920-2901
Email. pipnacional@independencia.net
Website. www.independencia.net
Leadership. Rubén Berríos Martínez (president)
The democratic socialist PIP was formed in 1946 by defectors opposed to the movement of the ruling →Popular Democratic Party (PPD) away from advocacy of independence. The PIP regards the status of Puerto Rico as being that of a colony, and campaigns to achieve "national freedom". The independence issue was at its most potent in the late 1930s through to the early 1950s, with terrorist attacks in both Puerto Rico and the USA and widespread detentions in Puerto Rico, but independence is now favoured by only a small minority (being supported by only 2.5% in the most recent plebiscite, held in December 1998). In the 1992, 1996 and 2000 elections the PIP won one seat in both the House and Senate on each occasion, while its 2000 candidates for

Governor and Resident Commissioner took just over and just under 5% of the vote, respectively.

The PIP believes that Puerto Rico's status has fostered a culture of dependence on federal welfare payments and tax reliefs for US investors; it argues that statehood for Puerto Rico (as favoured by the PNP) would inevitably be on second-class basis as its per capita income is only one-third of the US average and it is overwhelmingly Hispanic, with only a minority adequately speaking English; likewise it regards the existing Commonwealth status, as supported by the PPD, as an "outmoded remnant of the Cold War" when the USA was concerned that it should ensure control. The party also rejects "free association" on the model of the Marshall Islands, Micronesia and Palau as a diluted form of independence.

The PIP opposes the "militarization" of Puerto Rico and has waged a campaign of non-violent resistance against the Navy's use of the island of Vieques as a bombing range. Following a mass trespass, party leader Rubén Berríos (a law professor) was tried in May 2001 and sentenced to four months' imprisonment; however, in June 2001, US President George W. Bush said the Navy would halt the bombing on Vieques in "a reasonable period of time", an announcement seen as a gesture to the Hispanic vote. In a referendum held on July 29, 2001, on Vieques nearly 70% voted in favour of the immediate and permanent cessation of Navy bombing.

The PIP is a member party of the Socialist International.

Other Organizations

PROELA, describing itself as a civic organization and recognized by the Election Commission in the December 1998 plebiscite as the advocate of free association (a formula employed in the case of the Pacific territories of Palau and Micronesia), which option received only 0.3% of votes cast. *Leadership.* Luis Vega-Ramos (president)

US Virgin Islands

Capital: Charlotte Amilie (St Thomas)

Population: 122,000 (2001E)

Located in the Caribbean east of Puerto Rico, the US Virgin Islands were purchased from Denmark and proclaimed US territory in 1917. The group is an unincorporated territory administered under the US Department of the Interior. Executive authority is vested in a Governor, directly elected for a four-year term, and legislative authority in a unicameral 15-member Senate, popularly elected every two years.

The main parties currently are the US Democratic Party and the local Independent Citizens' Movement (ICM); although the US Republican Party exists locally it has no representation in the legislature. The gubernatorial election of November 1998 was won by the Democratic candidate Charles W. Turnbull, who took 58.9% of the vote, with Roy Schneider of the ICM, the incumbent, taking 41.1%. Following the Senate elections of November 2000, the Democrats held six seats, the ICM two and independents seven. The islands also send one non-voting delegate (currently a Democrat) to the US House of Representatives.

Independent Citizens' Movement (ICM), formed by a breakaway from the Democratic Party, and has held the governorship for periods since 1974; in 1998, however, incumbent ICM Governor Roy Schneider was defeated by the Democratic Party candidate, while the party holds only two Senate seats following the November 2000 elections. *Address.* c/o Senate, Charlotte Amilie

Uruguay

Capital: Montevideo

Population: 3,337,000 (2000E)

The independence of the Republic of Uruguay was recognized in 1830 after a period in which its territory was the subject of a dispute between Argentina and Brazil. Internal politics were then dominated by the struggle between the liberal Colorado (red) (PC) and conservative Blanco (white) (or National, PN) parties, giving rise to civil wars throughout the 19th century. The Colorados held power continuously from 1865 to 1958 before giving way to the Blancos. The illusion that Uruguay was "the Switzerland of Latin America" was shattered when in 1971 laws curtailing civil liberties were introduced to give the army a free hand in fighting the *Tupamaro* guerrillas. Two years later in 1973 the armed forces took power, dissolving Congress and replacing it with an appointed Council of State. Although by 1976 the military promised a return to democracy, their regime of terror continued, with an estimated 6,000 political opponents imprisoned and subjected to torture.

With an eye on eventually transferring power to a civilian government, the military regime drafted a new constitution meant to assure the army's say in all national security matters. This was rejected by a plebiscite in November 1980. Amidst mass protests, demonstrations and strikes and an economic crisis, the military finally agreed to elections being held in November 1984, which were won by the Colorado candidate, Julio María Sanguinetti. His government was marked by a major controversy over whether an amnesty should be given to all military and police personnel accused of human rights infringements, which was finally approved in a referendum in April 1989. The first fully free elections since the coup were held in November 1989, from which the Blancos emerged as the winners, with their leader, Luis Alberto Lacalle, becoming President.

In November 1994 Sanguinetti was elected President for a second time, then presiding over a coalition government between the Colorados and the Blancos. In November 1999 Jorge Batlle of the Colorado Party was elected President in a run-off against the candidate of the Progressive Encounter–Broad Front (*Encuentro Progresista–Frente Amplio*) (EP–FA), Tabaré Vázquez. Batlle won the second round election with the support of the Blancos, taking 54.1% of the vote compared with the 45.9% vote for Vázquez. However, the EP–FA in the legislative elections held on Oct. 31, 1999, emerged as the largest party in Congress. The EP–FA won 12 seats in the Senate, against 10 for the Colorados, 7 for the Blancos and 1 for the New Space (*Nuevo Espacio*). In the Chamber of Deputies the EP–FA won 40 seats, the Colorados 33, the Blancos 22 and the New Space 4. President Batlle took office for a five-year term on March 1, 2000 leading a coalition government with the Blancos.

Under the 1966 constitution, the Republic has an executive President who is assisted by a Vice-President and an appointed Council of Ministers. Legislative power is vested in a National Congress consisting of a 99-member Chamber of Deputies and a 31-member Senate (30 senators plus the Vice-President, who presides over Senate business but is also permitted to vote). The President and Vice-President are elected for a five-year term by direct universal suffrage on a run-off system. The President cannot be re-elected. Under a constitutional reform passed in 1996, parties must choose their presidential candidates by open primary elections that take place simultaneously for all parties on the last Sunday of April of the year of the presidential election. Senators and deputies are elected by proportional representation for fixed five-year terms. Senators are elected from a national constituency and deputies from the 19 departmental (provincial) sub-divisions. Under Uruguayan electoral law, the electorate votes in parliamentary elections for factions within each party itself. Parties usually present a large number of lists of candidates for the two chambers of parliament and congressmen represent both their faction and their party. Parliamentary party discipline necessitates coordination between the party's factions. Provincial (departmental) elections take place in May of the year following the general election. Voting is compulsory for all citizens who are 18 or older.

Broad Front
Frente Amplio (FA)

Address. Colonia 1367, Montevideo
Email. info@epfaprensa.org
Website. www.epfaprensa.org
Leadership. Tabaré Vázquez (party president, presidential candidate 1994 and 1999); Jorge Brovetto (party vice-president)

The main constituent of the →Progressive Encounter alliance, the FA is a broad alliance of left and left-of-centre political forces. It is currently formed by 19 different political parties and movements although not all its constituent members have parliamentary representation. The Front has campaigned vigorously against the government's neo-liberal policies but has lately moderated its own political programme to attract centre ground voters.

Founded in 1971 the coalition originally consisted of 17 parties of such diverse allegiances as the →Christian Democratic Party (PDC), the →Uruguayan Socialist Party (PSU) and the →Communist Party of Uruguay (PCU) plus various dissident →Colorado and →National (Blanco) factions.

Internal divisions caused by political differences and over the nomination of a presidential candidate led to a serious split in March 1989 and the formation of the →New Space. The Front nevertheless scored considerable success in the November 1989 elections: Líber Seregni, its presidential candidate, came third with 21% of the vote. The Front also won the municipal (departmental) election in the capital Montevideo and came third in the congressional elections with 21 seats in the Chamber and seven seats in the Senate. The Front supported a broad campaign against the Blanco government's privatization programme and in Congress voted against proposed austerity measures.

By April 1992 the Socialists had displaced the Communists as the dominant grouping in the FA. In parallel, the influence of the popular mayor of Montevideo, the Socialist Tabaré Vázquez grew. In March 1994 he was declared the alliance's presidential candidate.

In 1994 the Front fought the election in alliance with a dissident Blanco leader, Rodolfo Nin Novoa, forming the Progressive Encounter-Broad Front alliance (EP–FA), a kind of front within a front. In an extremely closely fought contest the EP–FA came third in the presidential election,

with 30.6% of the votes, against 32.3% for the winning Colorados and 31.2% for the second-placed Blancos. The Front also comfortably retained the government of Montevideo and increased their parliamentary representation. In 1999 Vázquez lost the presidential contest against Jorge Batlle of the Colorados in a run-off but the EP–FA became Uruguay's largest formation in the legislature, taking 40 of the 99 Assembly seats, and 12 of the 31 Senate seats, on a 40.1% share of the vote.

Christian Democratic Party
Partido Demócrata Cristiano (PDC)

Address. Aquiles Lanza 1318bis Montevideo
Telephone. (+598–2) 9030704
Email. pdc@chasque.apc.org
Website. www.chasque.net/pdc
Leadership. Héctor Lescano (president); Francisco Ottonelli (secretary general)

A centre–left party within the →Progressive Encounter alliance (alongside the →Broad Front), the PDC was founded in 1962. The party was formed as a successor to the Civic Union of Uruguay, a Catholic party founded in 1872. The majority decision to join the Broad Front in 1971 caused a more conservative section to split away and re-form the →Civic Union (UC). Like all Broad Front parties, the PDC was banned after the coup in 1973 but was legalized again in July 1984.

In 1988 the Christian Democrats opposed the inclusion of the former *Tupamaros* guerrillas (by now called the →National Liberation Movement) in the Broad Front. Soon afterwards, the party had further disagreements with the more left-wing members of the Front when the candidacy of Hugo Batalla (leader of the Party for the Government of the People, PGP) was not approved for the 1989 presidential elections. The Christian Democrats, together with the PGP and the Civic Union, withdrew from the Broad Front in March 1989 and together formed the →New Space alliance, which came fourth in the November 1989 general election. The PDC left the New Space and joined the Progressive Encounter alliance in 1994. The PDC has one deputy in the 2000–2005 legislature.

The PDC is an affiliate of the Christian Democrat International.

Colorado Party
Partido Colorado (PC)
Address. Martinez Trueba 1271, Montevideo
Telephone. (+598–2) 4090180
Website. www.partido-colorado.org
Leadership. Julio María Sanguinetti *(Foro Batllista* faction, president 1985-90 and 1995-2000); Jorge Batlle Ibáñez *(1994 Battlismo Unido* faction, presidential candidate 1989, president 2000-2005)

The Colorado party has dominated Uruguayan politics throughout most of the country's history. One of Uruguay's two so-called traditional parties, it is a broad-based, catch-all, centrist political force. It is composed of different organized factions with their own leaders, which compete among themselves. The Colorados emerged from the 1836–48 civil war and were named after the red flag of one of the warring factions. The party first came to power in 1865 and governed Uruguay uninterruptedly for 93 years. In the early twentieth century its leader and two-term president José Batlle y Ordóñez (1903–07 and 1911–15), introduced a wide-ranging social welfare system. Since then *Batllismo,* as the party's dominant strand came to be known, became associated with welfarism and industrial development. Having lost a national election for the first time in the twentieth century in 1958, the Colorados regained power in the 1966 elections and won again in 1971. In 1973, however, the constitutional government was deposed by the military, which then ruled the country for over a decade.

The November 1984 election, which marked the end of military rule, was won by the Colorado party and the leader of its largest faction "Unity and Reform", Julio María Sanguinetti, became the country's President. Sanguinetti's most controversial policy was the *caducidad* ("no punishment") law, granting immunity from prosecution to military and police officers accused of gross human rights violations during the military rule of 1973–85. Although widely opposed, mollification of the military was uppermost in the government's mind and the amnesty law was passed by Congress in December 1986 with the assistance of the →National Party (Blancos).

The Colorados lost the November 1989 elections to the Blancos but won the subsequent 1994 (Sanguinetti) and 1999 (Jorge Batlle) presidential elections. However, the party failed to gain a parliamentary majority of its own in both elections, forcing it to forge a coalition with the Blancos. The party is divided between a neo-liberal faction headed by President Batlle and a social democratic one, led by former President Sanguinetti. The party has 10 senators (plus the Vice-President) and 33 deputies in the 2000–2005 legislature.

Communist Party of Uruguay
Partido Comunista del Uruguay (PCU)
Address. Rio Negro 1525, Montevideo
Telephone. (+598–2) 917171
Fax. (+598–2) 911050
Email. pcu@i.com.uy
Leadership. Marina Arismendi (secretary-general)

Founded in 1921, the PCU was once a major force in the →Broad Front but is now in decline. Unusually for a Latin American Communist party, the PCU remained legally recognized for 52 years and regularly had candidates elected to Congress. The party has also had a strong representation in the trade union movement throughout its history.

In 1971 the PCU set up the Broad Front (FA) in conjunction with 16 other left-wing and centre-left parties and groups, and in the general election of the same year the Communists won two of the 18 FA seats in the Chamber. As a result of the 1973 military coup, the PCU was banned and fiercely persecuted. The party's secretary-general, Rodney Arismendi, was permitted to go into exile in the Soviet Union in 1975 but many other members were subjected to torture in prison. The PCU continued to be the dominant left-wing force in the Broad Front after the restoration of

civilian government. It took a major part in the campaign for a referendum on the *punto final* amnesty law and contributed to the Front's success in the November 1989 general election, in which 21 Broad Front deputies and seven senators were elected. However the fall of the Berlin Wall and the dissolution of the Soviet Union caused divisions and splits within the party, which remained under the control its orthodox faction under the leadership of Arismendi's daughter, Marina. The party has since entered in a process of decline but remains a well organized and disciplined political force with influence in the trade union movement. It has one senator in the legislature elected in October 1999.

National Liberation Movement
Movimiento de Liberación Nacional (MLN)
Email. mln@chasque.apc.org
Leadership. José Mujica (secretary-general)

The left-wing MLN has its roots in the guerrilla movement of the 1960s and 1970s. Although it is now committed to democratic politics the movement has never renounced its past. It campaigns for radical economic reforms and represents the more left-wing faction within the →Broad Front as part of an alliance known as the Popular Participation Movement *(Movimiento de Participación Popular,* MPP).

The MLN was founded by Raúl Sendic Antonaccio as the political wing of the *Tupamaros* guerrilla group (named in honour of the 18th century Peruvian Indian leader Tupac Amaru). It was originally concentrated in rural areas, motivated by the plight of the sugar cane cutters (whom Sendic had helped to organize in strikes of 1961–62) and fought for agrarian reform and rural workers' rights. The group switched its attention to the cities in 1966 and became engaged in armed struggle. Between 1966 and 1972 the *Tupamaros* became one of Latin America's most successful urban guerrilla groups.

Following the army offensive launched against them in 1972, and the ensuing military dictatorship, the MLN was virtually annihilated. On the return to civilian rule, all guerrillas were released in an amnesty in 1985, Sendic announcing that the MLN would now be working within the democratic political system. While piloting MLN towards parliamentary involvement, Sendic founded a movement to promote rural reform but he died shortly afterwards. Although at first excluded from the Broad Front, the MLN was finally permitted to join in late 1988. In May 1989 it obtained legal recognition as a political party.

The MLN has become an influential although minority faction of the →Progressive Encounter-Broad Front alliance. As part of the umbrella Movement for Popular Participation *(Movimiento de Participación Popular,* MPP) the MLN has 2 senators and 5 deputies in the legislature elected in October 1999.

National Party
Partido Nacional (PN)–Blancos
Address. Juan Carlos Gómez 1380, Montevideo
Telephone. (+598–2) 916–3831
Email. partidonacional@partidonacional.com.uy
Website. www.partidonacional.com.uy
Leadership. Luis Alberto Lacalle Herrera *(Herrerista* faction; president of the party's directorate, president of the Republic 1990–95, presidential candidate 1999); Juan Andrés Ramirez (leader *Desafío Nacional* faction)

Like the other so-called traditional party, the →Colorados, the PN is a catch-all, centrist party composed of several organized factions. Deriving their name from the white flag of one of the factions in the 1836–48 civil war, the Blancos were founded by an alliance of rural chieftains *(caudillos)* and urban elites. With a mainly rural base of support, the National Party was for a long time the permanent opposition party to the ruling Colorados and only fully turned to parliamentary politics after an unsuccessful uprising in 1904. The PN did not win national power in the 20th century until 1958, when it obtained six of the nine seats on the then collective executive, the National Governing Council (CNG). The party retained a majority in this collective executive in the elections of 1962. However, in 1966, when the presidential system was reinstated, the PN lost the elections to the Colorados. In the 1970s the party began a process of renewal and adopted a left-of-centre programme that appealed to a more modern, urban constituency. The party leader, Wilson Ferreira Aldunate, won the most votes of any single candidate in the 1971 presidential elections, but lost the election under the aggregate party vote system. He was forced into exile after the 1973 military coup and was imprisoned for six months on his return in 1984. Other reformist PN members who had remained in the country suffered persecution and imprisonment. Ferreira Aldunate was not allowed by the military to run for president in the 1984 elections but nonetheless he acknowledged the legitimacy of the victory of the Colorado candidate, Julio María Sanguinetti, and gave parliamentary support to his administration. He seemed certain to be the party's 1989 presidential candidate but died of cancer before the election.

For the presidential elections of November 1989, the party selected Luis Alberto Lacalle Herrera, representing the neo-liberal right-wing, as its candidate, who won the election although with only 37% of the ballot. The Lacalle government's programme of economic liberalization and austerity measures met with sustained opposition not only from the Inter-Union Workers' Assembly–Workers' National Convention (PIT–CNT) labour confederation, which staged numerous general strikes between 1990 and 1992, but also from sections of the Colorado Party and even a faction of the Blancos.

In the 1994 elections the Blancos lost power to the Colorados. Lacalle was again the party's presidential candidate in 1999 but fared poorly, coming a distant third to the Broad Front and Colorado parties' candidates. He supported the Colorado Party candidate Jorge Batlle in the run-off presidential election. In 1999 the party had its worst-ever electoral result taking only 22% of the national vote, resulting in the party holding 22 seats in the Chamber and 7 in the Senate, behind the →Progressive Encounter-Broad Front alliance and the Colorados. Since 1995 the Blancos have served in governing coalitions with the ruling Colorados.

New Space
Nuevo Espacio (NE)
Address. Eduardo Acevedo 1615, Montevideo
Website. nuevoespacio.org.uy
Leadership. Rafael Michelini
This electoral alliance was originally formed by the →Christian Democratic Party (PDC), the Party for the Government of the People (PGP) and the →Civic Union (UC), after the PDC and PGP left the →Broad Front (FA) in March 1989 following disagreements over the presence in it of former *Tupamaros* guerrillas, its policies and the choice of presidential candidate for the forthcoming elections.

The New Space alliance backed the moderate campaign of Hugo Batalla, the leader of the PGP, who came fourth in the November 1989 elections with 8.5% of the national vote. The alliance together won nine seats in the Chamber and two seats in the Senate.

In the run-up to the 1994 elections, the PDC left the alliance to join the →Progressive Encounter alliance and the Civic Union withdrew to campaign separately. The PGP in turn split and Batalla left the NE to join the →Colorado Party as Sanguinetti's vice-presidential candidate. A faction led by congressman Rafael Michelini remained the backbone of the NE and came in fourth in the 1994 election. In 1999 Michelini again came fourth, with only 4.4% of the vote, in the first round of the presidential election while the party won one seat in the Senate and 4 in the Chamber.

The NE is a consultative member of the Socialist International.

Progressive Encounter
Encuentro Progresista (EP)
Website. www.epfaprensa.org
Leadership. Tabaré Vázquez (1994 and 1999 presidential candidate), Rodolfo Nin Noboa (1994 and 1999 vice-presidential candidate)
The EP was formed prior to the 1994 election. It is effectively an electoral appendix of the →Broad Front with no political influence of its own. The constituent parties in this left-of-centre alliance are the →Broad Front (FA), the →Christian Democratic Party (PDC), a dissident →National Party (Blanco) faction led by Rodolfo Nin Noboa (who was the EP's vice presidential candidate in 1994 and 1999) and several small groups with no electoral weight. In the 1999 elections the EP–FA broke the Blancos' and Colorados' historical domination of Uruguayan politics by effectively becoming Uruguay's leading political force after it gathered 40% of the vote in the first round presidential and congressional elections. However the EP's presidential candidate, Tabaré Vázquez, lost a run-off election against the Colorado Jorge Batlle. The EP–FA has 12 out of 30 seats in the Senate and 40 out of 99 seats in the Chamber of Deputies in the 2000–2005 legislature elected in October 1999.

Uruguayan Socialist Party
Partido Socialista del Uruguay (PSU)
Address. Casa del Pueblo Soriano, 1218 Montevideo
Telephone. (+598–2) 9013344
Fax. (+598–2) 9082548
Email. ps@chasque.apc.org
Website. chasque.apc.org/ps
Leadership. Manuel Laguarda (secretary general)
The PSU was founded in 1910 and reorganized after the majority split away to form the →Communist Party (PCU) in 1921. The PSU moved to the left in 1959 and became a founder member of the →Broad Front (FA) in 1971. Currently the party is divided between its more orthodox left-wing faction and the social-democrat modernizers. One of its leaders, Tabaré Vázquez, became the first left-wing mayor of Montevideo in the November 1989 elections. Subsequently Vázquez became the president of the →Progressive Encounter-Broad Front (EP–FA) and the Front's presidential candidate in the 1994 and 1999 elections. Benefiting from Vázquez's popularity and the decline of the Communists, the PSU has become the largest party within the EP–FA with 4 senators and 14 deputies in the legislature elected in 1999.

The PSU is a member party of the Socialist International.

Other Parties

Civic Union (*Unión Cívica*, UC), taking the name of a Catholic formation dating back to 1872, it originated as a centre-right faction of the →Christian Democratic Party (PDC) that broke away when the PDC joined the →Broad Front in 1971. In 1989 it joined the Christian Democrat-led →New Space alliance.
Address. Rio Branco 1486, Montevideo
Telephone. (+598–2) 905535
Email. info@unioncivica.com
Website. www.unioncivica.com

Party for the Victory of the Poor (*Partido por la Victoria del Pueblo, PVP*), participates in the →Broad Front.
Email. casi@adinet.com.uy
Leadership. Hugo Cores (president)

Uzbekistan

Capital: Tashkent

Population: 5,700,000 (2001E)

The Republic of Uzbekistan declared its independence from the Soviet Union at the end of August 1991 and became a member of the Commonwealth of Independent States (CIS) in December of that year. In direct presidential elections on Dec. 29, 1991, Islam Karimov (who had been elected to the newly established post of President by the then Supreme Soviet in March 1990) was confirmed in office, winning 86% of the vote. A new constitution, adopted in December 1992, provided for a smaller legislature, the 250-member Supreme Assembly (*Oly Majlis*), consisting of 83 directly elected members and 167 indirectly elected by local administrative bodies and various citizens' groups.

Elections to the Supreme Assembly were held for the first time in January 1994–January 1995 and were contested by only two parties, of which the ruling People's Democratic Party (PDP) won a large majority of directly and indirectly elected seats. Five registered parties took part in the next parliamentary elections on Dec. 5 and 19, 1999, and each gained representation. The PDP retained a substantial majority, the second-largest bloc being that of the Self-Sacrifice Party, followed by Progress of the Fatherland. However, since all five parties are supportive of government and presidential policies, there is no opposition as such.

Meanwhile, in a referendum held in March 1995, the electorate had almost unanimously approved an extension of President Karimov's term of office to the year 2000. In a presidential election held on Jan. 9, 2000, the incumbent was credited with receiving 91.9% of the vote against one other candidate, thus being returned to office for a further five-year term.

Justice–Social Democratic Party of Uzbekistan
Adolat

Address. c/o Oly Majlis, Tashkent
Leadership. Turgunpulat Daminov (first secretary)
Adolat was registered as a political party in February 1995, establishing a parliamentary faction claiming to have the support of nearly 50 deputies in the Supreme Assembly. The party advocates greater social justice and the consolidation of democratic reform. In the December 1999 elections it was credited with 11 seats in its own right, but as after the 1994 polling its faction attracted deputies elected without party affiliation.

National Revival Party
Milli Tiklanish

Address. c/o Oly Majlis, Tashkent
Leadership. Ibrahim Gafurov (chairman)
Including several prominent Uzbek intellectuals, *Milli Tiklanish* was formed in May 1995 (and registered the following month), favouring democracy and the establishment of a law-based state. It was credited with winning 10 seats in its own right in the December 1999 elections.

People's Democratic Party (PDP)
Khalk Demokratik Partijasi

Address. c/o Oly Majlis, Tashkent
Leadership. Abdulhafiz Jalalov (first secretary)
The PDP was formed under the leadership of President Karimov in November 1991, as effectively the successor to the Communist Party of Uzbekistan (of which Karimov had been the last Soviet-era first secretary). It has since remained the dominant political force, directly or indirectly. One of only two parties permitted to register for the legislative elections in December 1994 and January 1995, the PDP secured a large majority in the Supreme Assembly. Karimov resigned his position as party leader in June 1996, bowing to the view that it was incompatible with that of head of state.

The PDP was less dominant in the official results of the December 1999 legislative elections, returning 48 candidates under its own label, but was again assured of commanding a majority by virtue of support from other pro-government parties and deputies. To give a semblance of democratic competition to presidential elections in

January 2000, party leader Abdulhafiz Jalalov was the nominal PDP candidate against President Karimov. It was reported that Jalalov's only appearance was on election day, when he came out to vote for Karimov.

Progress of the Fatherland
Vatan Tarakkiyoti

Address. c/o Oly Majlis, Tashkent
Leadership. Anwar Yoldashev (chairman)
Progress of the Fatherland was formed in 1992 to advocate the development of a market economy and has been supportive of the dominant →People's Democratic Party (PDP). It was the only party, other than the PDP, permitted to contest the legislative elections in December 1994 and January 1995, gaining 14 seats in the Supreme Assembly. In the December 1999 elections it advanced to 20 seats.

Self-Sacrifice Party
Fidokorlor

Address. c/o Oly Majlis, Tashkent
Leadership. Erkin Norbotaev (general secretary)
Established in December 1998, *Fidokorlor* came second in the December 1999 legislative elections, returning 34 deputies under its party label. It subsequently formally nominated President Karimov as candidate in the presidential elections held in January 2000.

Other Parties

Freedom (*Erk*), opposition party established in 1990 as an offshoot of →Unity (*Birlik*). Its leader, Mohammad Salih, was President Karimov's only rival in the December 1991 presidential elections, winning 12% of the vote. After independence *Erk* had a brief period of co-operation with the government. However, relations soon soured and the party was banned in December 1992; many of its activists, including Salih, sought asylum abroad. Several members of *Erk* were allegedly implicated in an assassination attempt on President Karimov in February 1999, Salih being publicly named as one of the organizers; he was subsequently tried and sentenced for terrorism *in absentia*.
Leadership. Mohammad Salih (chairman)

Unity (*Birlik*), a nationalist and secular organization formed in the late 1980s as the first significant non-communist political grouping in Uzbekistan. After independence it was subjected to repressive measures by the Uzbek government and was finally banned in 1992. Several of members, including its leader, sought asylum abroad.

Website. www.birlik.net

Leadership. Abdurahim Pulatov (chairman)

Vanuatu

Capital: Port Vila   **Population:** 182,000 (2000E)

Vanuatu, the former Anglo-French condominium of the New Hebrides, became an independent republic in July 1980. Legislative authority is vested in a unicameral Parliament, the 52 members of which are elected for four years from 14 multi-member constituencies on the basis of universal adult suffrage. Executive power is exercised by the Prime Minister (who is elected by Parliament from among its members) and by the Council of Ministers, which consists of members of Parliament appointed by the Prime Minister. The President, the republic's head of state, is elected for five years by an electoral college composed of the Parliament and the presidents of the regional councils (local government bodies to which a considerable degree of power is constitutionally devolved).

In general elections held on March 6, 1998, the *Vanua'aku Pati* (VP) regained power by winning 18 seats (with 20.8% of the vote), while the Union of Moderate Parties won 12 (18.4%), the National United Party 11 (15.7%), the Melanesian Progressive Party 6 (10.8), John Frum Movement 2 (2.2%), the Vanuatu Republican Party 1 (6.7%) and independents 2.

Melanesian Progressive Party (MPP)
Address. c/o Parliament, Port Vila
Leadership. Barak Sope (chairman)
The anglophone MPP was formed in mid-1988 by an expelled faction of the →*Vanua'aku Pati* (VP) led by Barak Sope (previously VP secretary-general), who in April 1989 was released from prison when sedition convictions against him were overturned. In the November 1995 general elections the MPP was part of the opposition Unity Front (UF), also including the VP and the →Tan Union, which won 20 of the then 50 seats and went into opposition to a coalition of the →Union of Moderate Parties (UMP) and the →National United Party (NUP). In February 1996, however, the UF joined a faction of the divided UMP to oust the UMP-NUP government and form a new coalition administration, with Sope as Finance Minister.

Dismissed from the government in August 1996, Sope took the MMP out of the UF and the following month accepted appointment as Deputy Prime Minister in a new coalition headed by the other UMP faction. Sope was again dismissed in October 1996 after being involved in the temporary abduction of the President by unpaid security force members. He again returned to government in May 1997, in a coalition headed by a temporarily reunited UMP. But protracted political chicanery eventually resulted in new elections in March 1998, in which the MPP won only six seats and went into opposition to a coalition led by the VP.

On the collapse of the VP-led government in November 1999, Soke became Prime Minister in a new coalition of the MPP and the UMP. However, amidst increasingly murky corruption and other controversies, the withdrawal of the UMP resulted in Soke being defeated in a confidence vote in April 2001, whereupon the MPP reverted to opposition to a new government headed by the VP.

National United Party (NUP)
Address. c/o Parliament, Port Vila
Leadership. Willie Titongoa (chairman)
The centre-left NUP was launched in 1991 by former Prime Minister Fr. Walter Lini following his removal as leader of the then ruling →*Vanua'aku Pati* (VP). In the December 1991 general elections the NUP gained 10 parliamentary seats and joined a coalition supporting the premiership of Maxime Carlot Korman of the →Union of Moderate Parties (UMP). The UMP-NUP coalition was beset by internal problems during 1993 and in August a majority NUP faction led by Lini withdrew its support from Carlot Korman. Some NUP members defied instructions by continuing to support the government, and were expelled from the party in May 1994. In the November 1995 general elections the NUP won nine seats and, in December, joined a faction of the divided UMP in a new coalition government. This survived only until February 1996, but in October 1996 the NUP joined a new coalition headed by another faction of the UMP and continued in government when the UMP factions were temporarily reunited in May 1997.

In the March 1998 general elections the NUP advanced slightly to 11 seats, whereupon Lini overcame his differences with his former party and became Deputy Prime Minister in a new coalition headed by the VP. In October 1998, however, Lini and his party were ejected from the government because of collusion with the opposition. Lini died in February 1999 at the age of 56 and was succeeded as NUP leader by Willie Titongoa.

Union of Moderate Parties (UMP)
Union des Partis Modérés (UPM)
Address. PO Box 698, Port Vila
Leadership. Serge Vohor (chairman)
The conservative francophone UMP was formed in 1980 as a coalition of groups opposed to the →*Vanua'aku Pati* (VP) government. Under the leadership of Vincent Boulekone, it came second to the VP in both the 1983 and the 1987 elections. Boulekone was replaced as leader of the coalition by Maxime Carlot Korman after the 1987 polling and subsequently broke away from the UMP as leader of the →Tan Union. Following the UMP's success in the December 1991 election, in which it won 19 out of 46 seats, the party joined with the Fr. Walter Lini's →National United Party (NUP) to form a coalition under Carlot Korman's premiership. A majority NUP group under Lini went into opposition in August 1993, but a minority NUP faction remained in the coalition as the UMP's junior partner.

In the November 1995 general elections the UMP won 17 out of 50 seats, whereupon the UMP became seriously split between factions led respectively by Carlot Korman and by party chairman Serge Vohor. The party's executive council eventually opted for the NUP as a coalition partner and chose Vohor for the post of Prime Minister. In February 1996 Carlot Korman's supporters, together with the opposition Unity Front, succeeded in bringing down Vohor's administration and forming a new coalition under the premiership of Carlot Korman. However, amidst fierce party infighting, Carlot Korman lost a no-confidence vote in September 1996 and was replaced as Prime Minister by Vohor.

An apparent reconciliation between Vohor and Carlot Korman resulted in the formation in May 1997 of a coalition between both UMP factions, the NUP and the →Melanesian Progressive Party (MPP). Hostility between Vohor and Carlot Korman soon resurfaced, resulting in the collapse of the government in November 1997 and the formation of the breakaway →Vanuatu Republican Party by Carlot Korman. In early elections in March 1998 the UMP declined to 12 seats out of 52 and went into opposition to a coalition headed by the VP. In October 1998 a faction of the UMP led by Willie Jimmy joined a new VP-led coalition. But the main Vohor faction remained in opposition until November 1999, when it joined a new coalition under an MPP Prime Minister. In April 2001 the UMP was instrumental in bringing the government down, whereupon Vohor overcame his longstanding antipathy to the VP and became Deputy Prime Minister in a VP–UMP coalition.

Vanua'aku Pati (VP)

Address. c/o Parliament, Port Vila
Leadership. Edward Nipake Natapei (president)

The left-wing *Vanua'aku Pati* was established in the early 1970s as the New Hebrides National Party, adopting its present title (which means something like "Party of Our Land") in 1977. Under the leadership of Fr. Walter Lini, the party won a majority of seats in the Representative Assembly in November 1979, following which a VP government headed by Lini led the country to independence as Vanuatu the following year. Despite the emergence of internal dissent, the VP retained power in the 1983 and 1987 elections. In 1988 the former VP secretary-general, Barak Sope, and four colleagues resigned from the VP and announced the formation of a rival →Melanesian Progressive Party (MPP). By 1991 there was diminishing support for Lini's leadership and in the autumn of that year he was ousted and replaced as party leader and Prime Minister by Donald Kalpokas, whereupon Lini and his supporters formed the →National United Party (NUP). In the wake of the party split, the VP was defeated in the December 1991 general election.

The VP contested the November 1995 elections as a constituent of the opposition Unity Front (UF), including the MPP and the →Tan Union, which won 20 of the then 50 seats and went into opposition to a coalition of the →Union of Moderate Parties (UMP) and the NUP. In February 1996, however, the UF joined a faction of the divided UMP to oust

the UMP-NUP government and form a new coalition administration. The ejection of the MMP in August 1996 resulted in that party's withdrawal from the UF and the defeat of the government in September. The successor administration lasted less than a month and was replaced in October 1996 by a coalition headed by a faction of the UMP and including the VP and the NUP. In May 1997, however, Kalpokas took the VP into opposition to a new coalition of the UMP, the NUP and the MPP.

In early elections in March 1998 the VP became substantially the largest party by winning 18 of the 52 seats, so that Kalpokas became Prime Minister of a coalition between the VP and the NUP. In October 1998 Kalpokas ejected the NUP because of its collusion with the opposition, bringing a faction of the UMP and the tiny →John Frum Movement into a new coalition. In March 1999 a Kalpokas ally, Fr. John Bennett Bani (an Anglican minister), was elected President by the Parliament. However, defections and by-election defeats reduced the government to minority status, so that Kalpokas resigned in November 1999 and was replaced by an MPP Prime Minister in coalition with the main UMP.

The VP leadership passed to Edward Nipake Natapei, who eventually succeeded in detaching the UMP from the government, which fell in April 2001. Natapei then formed a VP-UMP majority coalition, whose members were at first locked out of Parliament by the Speaker on the grounds that Natapei's election as Prime Minister had been irregular. In May 2001, however, the new government gained access to the legislature after the Speaker and his two deputies had been charged with sedition.

Other Parties

John Frum Movement, based on the southern island of Tanna, won two seats in the March 1998 elections and was part of the 1998-99 government headed by the →*Vanua'aku Pati*.

Tan Union, broke away from the →Union of Moderate Parties after the 1987 elections; was part of the Unity Front headed by →*Vanua'aku Pati* in the 1995 elections, but has not been represented since the 1998 contest.
Leadership. Vincent Boulekone (chairman)

Vanuatu Republican Party, founded in January 1998 by former Prime Minister Maxime Carlot Korman following his break with the →Union of Moderate Parties. He was the new party's only successful candidate in the March 1998 elections.
Leadership. Maxime Carlot Korman (chairman)

Venezuela

Capital: Caracas

Population: 23,500,000 (2000E)

The Republic of Venezuela achieved full independence from Spain in 1830. It was mostly ruled by *caudillos* ("strong men") and the military until 1945, when Gen. Enisaías Medina Angarita was removed by a coup led by progressive young army officers and supported especially by an ambitious middle class. An interim revolutionary junta was established and a new constitution introduced which for the first time provided for the election of the President and Congress by universal suffrage. The first President elected under the new constitution, Rómulo Gallegos, was deposed by a military coup in 1948, however, and a period of military rule followed. Gen. Marcos Pérez Jiménez, who proclaimed himself President in 1952, alienated all sections of opinion by his corrupt and repressive rule, and was overthrown in 1958 by a popular uprising. The two strongest parties, Democratic Action (AD) and the Social Christian Party (COPEI), subsequently alternated in office until the rise to power of the radical populist Lt.-Col. Hugo Chávez Frías. Chávez, as leader of the Fifth Republic Movement (MVR), was elected as President in December 1998, defeating Henrique Salas Römer, an independent endorsed by the AD and COPEI.

A new constitution, drafted by a Constituent Assembly composed mainly of supporters of Chávez, was promulgated in December 1999. It permits the President to serve two consecutive six-year terms (the constitution previously mandating five-year terms and barring immediate re-election), and increased the executive branch's control over the legislature, the military and the central bank. The new constitution replaced Congress (the bicameral legislature) with a unicameral, 165-member National Assembly, thereby eliminating the Senate (the upper house) and with it the position of lifetime senator, a position traditionally granted to former heads of state.

Chávez was re-elected in July 2000 for a new six-year term, in a presidential election called under the terms of the new constitution. Elections were also held for the newly-created National Assembly. The MVR won the largest number of seats (76), but fell short of the absolute two-thirds majority Chávez required to effectively overrule any opposition. Contrary to some expectations the outcome did not spell the demise of the old parties, with the AD emerging as the second largest bloc in the legislature.

Democratic Action
Acción Democrática (AD)
Address. Calle los Cedros, Entre Avenida Los Jabillos y Samanes, La Florida, Caracas 1050
Telephone. (+58–2) 749855
Leadership. Henry Ramos Allup (president); Timoteo Zambrano (secretary-general)
Founded in 1936, the AD is nominally social democratic but has tended to adopt conservative policies when in office. The party was formed by Rómulo Betancourt under the name of the National Democratic Party *(Partido Democrático Nacional,* PDN) and was registered under its present name in 1941. Its grass-roots support came mainly from organized labour. The party's charismatic and populist leader Carlos Andrés Pérez served as President from 1973 to 1978 and again from 1988 to 1993. Alongside the →Social Christian Party (COPEI), the AD dominated Venezuelan politics for the four decades prior to the emergence of Lt.-Col. Hugo Chávez Frías as a political force.

In what was widely regarded as a major setback for the AD and the other much discredited traditional parties, a coalition headed by Chávez's →Movement for the Fifth Republic (MVR), virtually matched the performance of the AD in legislative elections held in November 1998. In presidential elections held a month later Chávez defeated Henrique Salas Römer, an independent endorsed by both the AD and COPEI. In the last days of the election campaign, the AD had withdrawn its support for its candidates in order to rally behind Salas. (The AD's candidate and secretary general, Luis Alfaro Ucero, refused to step down and was promptly expelled from the party.) Elections to a Constituent Assembly, charged with formulating a new constitution, were held in July 1999 and resulted in a crushing defeat for the AD, which failed to win a single seat in the Assembly. The entire leadership of the party, including president Carlos Canache Mata, resigned a month later in the aftermath of the party's devastating defeat in the elections. Canache was replaced by David Morales Bello, hitherto first vice-president of the party. However, Morales and the party's entire national executive committee resigned in January 2000. Henry Ramos Allup was appointed as the new party president in June, ahead of presidential and legislative elections in July. The party performed better than expected in the legislative elections, emerging as the second-largest party in the new National Assembly by taking 29 seats in its own right and four in alliance with COPEI. In-fighting within the party continued in the wake of the elections, however, with new secretary general Timoteo Zambrano challenging Allup's leadership.

The AD is a member party of the Socialist International.

Movement for the Fifth Republic
Movimiento V República (MVR)
Address. Calle Lima, cruce con Av. Libertador, Los Caobos, Caracas
Telephone. (+58-2) 7931521
Fax. (+58-2) 7829720
Leadership. Hugo Chávez Frías (leader)
The MVR was launched by Lt.-Col. (retd.) Hugo Chávez Frías in July 1997. Chávez, a former paratroop commander

who had tried to storm the presidential palace in a failed coup attempt in 1992, had spent two years in prison before being released in 1994 by President Rafael Caldera Rodríguez. Chávez was a populist figure who drew strong support amongst the poor and those disillusioned with traditional politics in Venezuela, which had been dominated for the previous four decades by the →Democratic Action (AD) party and the →Social Christian Party (COPEI).

At the launch of the MVR Chávez made the bold prediction that his new party would enable him to win the forthcoming presidential election, which he duly did with apparent ease. During the election campaign he frightened the business establishment with his pledges of radical economic and political change. His programme included the dissolution of the legislature, the suspension of foreign debt payments, and the revision of recent privatization contracts. After his election in December 1998, however, the stock market soared as he showed signs that he would abandon some of his radical leftist proposals, whilst pledging to tackle the country's growing fiscal deficit.

Chávez was re-elected in July 2000 for a new six-year term, polling close to 60% of the vote in the election called under a new constitution approved by referendum in late 1999. He easily defeated his main challenger and erstwhile comrade-in-arms Fransisco Arias Cárdenas, who had helped him carry out the failed 1992 coup. Following his victory, Chávez promised to launch an ambitious new economic policy aimed at pushing through a social revolution for the poor.

The July 2000 elections were also called to elect a new 165-member unicameral National Assembly. The MVR won 77 seats in the new Assembly, short of the absolute two-thirds majority required to effectively overrule any opposition. The party created a *Cambio* (Change) bloc in the Assembly that provided it with the support of 114 deputies. However, the MVR's main ally, the left-wing →Movement Towards Socialism (MAS), withdrew its support in May 2001 after accusing President Chávez of attempting to extend his powers.

Movement Towards Socialism
Movimiento al Socialismo (MAS)
Address. Urb. Las Palmas, Av. Valencia, Qta.Alemar, Caracas
Telephone. (+58–2) 782 7309
Fax. (+58–2) 782 9720
Leadership. Leopoldi Puchi (leader)
This democratic socialist party was founded in 1971. The MAS was formed by the bulk of the membership of the →Communist Party of Venezuela (PCV), a majority of Communist trade union leaders, and almost the entire PCV youth movement, following a split in 1970. The split had occurred after the expulsion of PCV leader and former guerrilla leader Teodoro Petkoff Maleo for his open condemnation of the 1968 Soviet invasion of Czechoslovakia and his rejection of both Soviet and Eurocommunist models for the development of Venezuelan socialism.

The party's growing success, however, was hampered in the run-up to the 1983 election when it split into supporters of Petkoff and those who, backing José Vicente Rangel as the representative of a broad left alliance, broke away from the party. Petkoff, with the support of the Movement of the Revolutionary Left (MIR), won 4.2% (as opposed to Rangel's 3.3%) but the MAS's representation in the Chamber of Deputies fell to 10 seats and to only two in the Senate.

The two parties formed an alliance in 1988 when Petkoff once more stood for the presidency in the December elections, although one sector of the party wanted to support the →Democratic Action (AD) candidate, Carlos Andrés Pérez, in order to concentrate the alliance's efforts on the congressional elections. Petkoff came third with less than 3% of the presidential vote, as did the MAS–MIR alliance, which obtained 18 seats in the Chamber and three in the Senate. Because the ruling AD failed to retain its congressional majority the MAS gained considerable influence as part of the congressional opposition block.

After Lt-Col Hugo Chávez Frías's attempted military coup in early February 1992, the MAS leadership was invited by President Pérez to take part in a "Cabinet of National Unity" but the MAS rejected the offer. MAS joined the →Social Christian Party (COPEI) in a 1992 coalition that won ten state governorships and supported the →National Convergence's campaign for Rafael Caldera Rodríguez in his successful 1993 presidential bid.

The presidential prospects of former coup leader Chávez were enhanced by his endorsement in June 1998 by MAS. The decision was passed at a MAS convention by 264 votes to 128, against the recommendations of three prominent MAS leaders who had served as members of Caldera's Cabinet, including Petkoff, who announced the following month that he was resigning his membership of the party that he had co-founded.

Immediately prior to the December 1998 presidential poll (won by Chávez) MAS fought elections to the National Congress (the old bicameral legislature) as part of the Patriotic Front coalition, a grouping of parties led by Chávez's →Movement for the Fifth Republic (MVR). The new coalition won the most votes, with MAS taking almost 9% of the vote and 17 seats in the Chamber of Deputies (the lower chamber). MAS continued to support Chávez in the July 2000 elections, winning 21 seats in the new legislature and thereafter helping to provide the President with the necessary votes to achieve a two-thirds majority in the National Assembly (the MVR having won only 77 out of the total 165 seats). However, in May 2001 the alliance between MAS and the MVA broke down, following an announcement by President Chávez that he was considering the declaration of a state of emergency and the assumption of emergency powers. Announcing the ending of the alliance, MAS leader Leopoldo Puchi challenged Chávez to hold a referendum on the issue of the granting of further emergency powers to the presidency.

Project Venezuela
Proyecto Venezuela (Proven)

Address. C/o Asamblea Nacional, El Silencio, Caracas 1010
Website. www.proyectovenezuela.org.ve
Leadership. Henrique Salas Römer (leader)
This new party was founded by Salas Römer, an independent candidate for the presidency in 1998 who won the backing of →Democratic Action and the →Social Christian Party but was defeated by Hugo Chávez. It won seven National Assembly seats in the July 2000 legislative election. It is a member of the *Cambio* (Change) bloc in the National Assembly, dominated by the ruling →Movement for the Fifth Republic (MVR).

Social Christian Party
Partido Social Cristiano (COPEI)

Address. Erb. El Bosque, Quinta Cuijito, detras Jefe de Camaras, Calle Gloria, Caracas
Telephone. (+58–2) 7313393
Fax. (+58–2) 7313990

Email. copei@infoline.wtfe.com
Website. www.copei.org
Leadership. Rosana Ordonez (president); Edgar Mora-Contreras (secretary-general)
Founded in 1946, COPEI is a centrist, Christian democratic party. The party was founded by Rafael Caldera as the Organizing Committee for Independent Electoral Policy (*Comité de Organización Politica Electoral Independiente),* whose acronym COPEI is still in use despite the party's change of name. Alongside the →Democratic Action (AD) party, COPEI dominated Venezuelan politics for the four decades prior to the rise of Lt.-Col. Hugo Chávez Frías in the late 1990s.

As one of the country's traditional parties, COPEI's influence was seriously undermined by Chávez and his →Movement for the Fifth Republic (MVR). In the November 1998 legislative elections the party came fourth with little over 10% of the vote and 27 seats in the lower house (down from almost 70 seats a decade earlier). In the last days of the campaign for the December 1998 presidential election, COPEI and the AD both withdrew their support for their candidates in order to rally behind the independent, Henrique Salas Römer. Despite such desperate measures, Chávez won the election. COPEI plunged into deep disarray. A faction led by Oswaldo Alvarez Paz broke away, proclaiming that the "death of the party should be definitive". In the July 2000 legislative election the party again performed poorly, winning only five seats in its own right and four in alliance with the AD. In the aftermath of the election the party formed a small and relatively insignificant social-Christian parliamentary bloc, alongside →National Convergence.

COPEI is a member party of the Christian Democrat International.

Other Parties

A New Time (*Un Nuevo Tiempo, UNT*)), won three National Assembly seats in the July 2000 legislative election and is a member of the *Cambio* (Change) bloc in the National Assembly dominated by the ruling →Movement for the Fifth Republic (MVR).

Alliance of Brave People (*Alianza Bravo Pueblo, ABP*)), won one National Assembly seat in the July 2000 legislative election; it is not a member of either the ruling or the main opposition blocs in the National Assembly.

Communist Party of Venezuela (*Partido Comunista de Venezuela, PCV*)), founded in 1931, now a negligible force and unrepresented in the legislature.

The Fatherland for Everybody (*Patria por Todos, PPT*), won one National Assembly seat in the July 2000 legislative election; it is not a member of either the ruling or the main opposition blocs in the National Assembly.
Website. www.patriaparatodos.org
Leadership. Pablo Medina (secretary-general)

First Justice (*Primero Justicia, PJ*), political reform party that won five National Assembly seats in the July 2000 legislative election; it is not a member of either the ruling or the main opposition blocs in the National Assembly.
Website. www.primerojusticia.net

Integration, Renewal, New Hope (*Integración y Renovación Nueva Esperanza, IRENE*), founded in 1995 to promote the presidential aspirations of former beauty queen Irene Saez, who took under 3% of the vote in the 1998 presidential election; in March 1999 she won the governorship of Nueva Esparta (Isla Margarita).

Lapy, a regional party that won three National Assembly seats in the July 2000 legislative election; it is not a member of either the ruling or the main opposition blocs in the National Assembly.

National Council of Venezuelan Indians (*Consejo Nacional Indio de Venezuela, CONIVE*), won three National Assembly seats in the July 2000 legislative election; a member of the *Cambio* (Change) bloc in the National Assembly dominated by the ruling →Movement for the Fifth Republic (MVR).

National Convergence (*Convergencia Nacional, CN*), launched in 1993 as a (successful) presidential campaign vehicle for Rafael Caldera Rodríguez; won one National Assembly seat in the July 2000 legislative election (for its leader, Juan José Caldera); it is a member of the opposition social-Christian bloc in the National Assembly, alongside the →Social Christian Party (COPEI).

Organization of Forces in Movement (*Organisation Fuerza en Movimiento, OFM*)), won one National Assembly seat in the July 2000 legislative election; a member of the *Cambio* (Change) bloc in the National Assembly dominated by the ruling →Movement for the Fifth Republic (MVR).

The Radical Cause (*La Causa Radical, LCR*), has its main support base in the Guayana industrial region and won three National Assembly seats in the July 2000 legislative election; it is not a member of either the ruling or the main opposition blocs in the National Assembly.
Leadership. Lucas Matheus (secretary-general)

Union Party, formed in May 2001 by Francisco Arias Cárdenas, a former governor of Zulia state and a one-time comrade-in-arms of President Chávez, who had finished second to him in the July 2000 presidential election.

United Multiethnic People of the Amazon (*Pueblos Unidos Multietnicos de Amazonas, PUAMA*), won one National Assembly seat in the July 2000 legislative election and is a member of the *Cambio* (Change) bloc dominated by the ruling →Movement for the Fifth Republic (MVR).

We All Gain All Independent Movement (*Movimiento Independiente Ganamos Todos, MIGATO*), won one National Assembly seat in the July 2000 legislative election; a member of the *Cambio* (Change) bloc dominated by the ruling →Movement for the Fifth Republic (MVR).

Vietnam

Capital: Hanoi

Population: 78,770,000 (2000E)

The Socialist Republic of Vietnam was proclaimed in July 1976, following the reunification of Vietnam after two decades of warfare between North and South Vietnam. In 1954 Vietnam had been partitioned following protracted Communist-led resistance to French colonial authority. Effective political power has since been exercised by the Communist Party of Vietnam (CPV), the sole legal political party.

In 1992 a new constitution entered into force, which enshrined the market-oriented economic reforms undertaken since the mid-1980s, while ensuring that the CPV maintained its position as "a leading force of the state and society". Under the constitution the National Assembly (*Quoc Hoi*), the highest organ of state power, elects the President (from among its own deputies for a five-year term), the Vice-President and the Prime Minister, and ratifies the Prime Minister's proposals for appointing members of the government.

Elections to the 395-member National Assembly were last held in July 1997. Candidates were nominated by a variety of organizations and approved by the Vietnam Fatherland Front, the CPV-controlled body embracing the country's various mass organizations. In September 1997 the National Assembly elected Gen. Tran Duc Luong as President and Phan Van Khai as Prime Minister.

Communist Party of Vietnam (CPV)
Dang Cong San Viet Nam
Address. 1C Hoang Van Thu Street, Hanoi
Telephone. (+84–4) 431472
Email. cpv@hn.vnn.vn
Website. www.cpv.org.vn
Leadership. Nong Duc Manh (secretary-general)
The CPV is descended from the Communist Party of Indo-China (CPIC), founded in 1930 by Ho Chi Minh and other Communists, which in April 1931 was recognized as an autonomous section of the Third (Communist) International (or Comintern). Born in 1890 as Nguyen Tat Thanh in Nghe Tinh province in the central region of what was then French Indo-China, Ho Chi Minh (literally "Ho the seeker of enlightenment") had been a founder member of the →→French Communist Party in 1920 and had subsequently worked as an agent of the Comintern in Asia. Simultaneously with the formation of the CPIC, a peasant rebellion broke out in Indo-China which then received Communist backing. It was suppressed and Ho was sentenced to death *in absentia* by the French authorities. After the failure of a further Communist-led uprising in 1940, Ho joined Vietnamese exiles on the Chinese border and in 1941 formed the Communist-dominated Viet Minh guerrilla

organization, which harried the Japanese during World War II.

Immediately after the Japanese surrender in August 1945, the Viet Minh set up a provisional government in coalition with other nationalist groups and on Sept. 2, 1945, the Democratic Republic of Vietnam was proclaimed in Hanoi with Ho as its President as well as Prime Minister and Foreign Minister. Various attempts to reach a compromise settlement with the re-established French authorities broke down and from late 1946 Ho's Viet Minh guerrillas engaged in bitter hostilities with the French forces which culminated in the decisive defeat of the latter at Dien Bien Phu in May 1954. Meanwhile, at its second congress in February 1951, the CPIC was dissolved; its Vietnamese members joined the Vietnam Workers' Party (VWP). Separate communist parties later emerged in Laos and Cambodia. Under the 1954 Geneva agreements Vietnam was temporarily divided at the 17th parallel and Ho Chi Minh became both President and Prime Minister of North Vietnam, relinquishing the premiership in 1955 but retaining the presidency and party chairmanship until his death in September 1969.

At its third congress in 1960 the party decided "to promote the national people's democratic revolution in South Vietnam" and "to unify the country on the basis of independence and democracy". The ensuing war against the then government of the Republic of Vietnam, which was supported by the United States, ended in the conquest of South Vietnam in April 1975 followed by the reunification of the country as the Socialist Republic of Vietnam. At the fourth party congress held in December 1976, the party's name was changed to the Communist Party of Vietnam. In 1977 other mass organizations led by the party were merged with the Vietnam Fatherland Front. At the fifth party congress, held in Hanoi in March 1982, Le Duan, then CPV general secretary, declared that the party had established "the dictatorship of the proletariat in the whole country" and had fought two wars—"against the expansionism and hegemonism of the Chinese reactionary leadership" (in 1979) and against aggression in the South by the Cambodian "Pol Pot clique"—and that "a militant alliance between Cambodia, Laos and Vietnam" had also strengthened "militant solidarity with the Soviet Union". He described the task of the party during the 1980s as being to guide the people and the army "to build socialism successfully and to defend the socialist Vietnamese fatherland". His report also emphasized the need of consolidating party unity, and he criticized members who had "damaged the prestige of the party", warning that they would be expelled.

In the political report presented to the sixth CPV congress in December 1986 by Truong Chinh (general secretary in succession to Le Duan, who had died in July 1986), it was admitted that existing serious shortcomings in the country's economy and social life had "lessened the confidence of the masses in the party leadership and the functioning of state organs". It was expressly acknowledged that the central committee, the political bureau, the secretariat and the Council of Ministers were "primarily responsible for the above-mentioned errors and shortcomings". The report addressed a number of these errors, in particular in economic planning for investment allocation and capital construction in 1976–80, acknowledging that the targets set by the fifth party congress had not been met. Truong Chinh retired as general secretary during the sixth congress, and

Nguyen Van Linh (real name Nguyen Van Cuc) was elected as his successor. The sixth congress adopted a major reform program known as *doi moi*, or renovation. Vietnam abandoned Soviet-style central planning and moved towards creating a market economy under state direction. Vietnam's reform efforts slowed in the late 1980s particularly after the collapse of socialism in Eastern Europe and as the Soviet Union began to disintegrate. Do Muoi replaced reformist Nguyen Van Linh as party secretary general at the seventh national congress in June 1991. This congress set as its main objective "to emerge from crisis, [and to] stabilize the socioeconomic situation." This objective was accomplished and at the party's first mid-term conference in January 1994 priority was now given to the goal of industrialization and modernization. The eighth congress in June 1996 endorsed the objective of "accelerating industrialization and modernization" by the year 2020.

Internal party factionalism resulted in a delay in replacing the party's top leaders until December 1997. At that time Le Kha Phieu, a former army political commissar, became secretary general. Phieu provided lackluster leadership at a time when Vietnam was experiencing the effects of the Asian financial crisis and a series of internal disturbances. In preparation for the ninth party congress, in May 1999 Phieu initiated a two-year campaign of "criticism and self-criticism" in order to strengthen the party.

On the eve of the ninth party congress (held in April 2001) it was revealed that 69,000 party members, out of a total membership of 2.4 million, had been found guilty of corruption since the last congress. Phieu told the congress that public anger over corruption and decadence had become a "major danger" to the regime.

At the ninth congress the septuagenarian Phieu was replaced as secretary general by Nong Duc Manh, 61, a member of the Tay ethnic minority with long service in Vietnam legislature, where he served as chairman of the National Assembly's Standing Committee. The ninth congress vowed to continue pursuing the objective of industrialization and with the goal of doubling GDP by 2010.

Western Sahara

Capital: El Aaiún

Population: 245,000 (2000E)

The former Spanish Western Sahara (consisting of Saguia el Hamra and Rio de Oro) was partitioned between Morocco and Mauritania under a 1975 treaty following Spain's decision to withdraw from a region which it had controlled since the 19th century. However, this decision was not accepted by the territory's principal national liberation movement, the Popular Front for the Liberation of Saguia el Hamra and Rio de Oro (Polisario Front), which proclaimed the Sahrawi Arab Democratic Republic (SADR) in 1976. The SADR has since been recognized by more than 75 countries (and was admitted to the Organization of African Unity in 1982), despite Morocco's extension of sovereignty over the whole territory when Mauritania officially renounced all claims in 1979.

The protracted and militarily inconclusive conflict between Morocco and the Polisario Front has been the subject of United Nations mediation efforts, envisaging the holding of a UN-sponsored referendum to determine the future status of the territory. However, preparations for such a referendum have repeatedly stalled over the issue of voter eligibility, with each side accusing the other of falsifying voter registration lists. After the renewal in April 2001 of the mandate of the UN Mission for the Referendum in Western Sahara (MINURSO, which had been set up in 1991 to help facilitate a settlement), the UN Secretary-General warned the parties to negotiate or risk an end to UN involvement.

Popular Front for the Liberation of Saguia el Hamra and Rio de Oro (Polisario Front)
Frente Popular para la Liberación de Saguia el Hamra y Rio de Oro (Frente Polisario)
Address. BP 10, El-Mouradia, Algiers
Leadership. Mohammed Abdelazziz (secretary-general)
Formed in 1973 to pursue independence for Spanish Sahara,

the socialist Polisario Front was initially based in Mauritania, but its political leadership has operated since the mid-1970s from Algeria, although with diminishing backing from the government of that country. A congress in 1982 elected the Front's secretary-general, Mohammed Abdelazziz, as President of the SADR. The National Secretariat elects the secretary-general for a three-year mandate and the deputies of a 101-member National Assembly. Executive power is vested in the secretary-general and a 13-member government.

In a post-Cold War climate much less friendly to liberation movements, the military stalemate and reduced financial and material support from Algeria and Libya caused serious problems for Polisario, which suffered from a stream of defections to Morocco, including the SADR

foreign minister, Brahim Hakim in August 1992. Fears of a resumption of hostilities remain, although many observers believe that Polisario does not have sufficient military and manpower resources to mount a major campaign. However, the organization continues to maintain that the conflict cannot be resolved without the right of the Sahrawi people to self-determination.

Yemen

Capital: Sana'a

Population: 17,249,000 (2000E)

The Republic of Yemen was established in May 1990 through the unification of the Yemen Arab Republic (North Yemen) and the People's Democratic Republic of Yemen (South Yemen). A referendum held in May 1991 approved the country's new constitution. There had previously been no political parties in North Yemen, while South Yemen had been a one-party state. Unification and political liberalization led to the creation of large number of political groups.

Executive power is held by the President, who is directly elected every seven years and who appoints the Prime Minister and Council of Ministers. Legislative power is vested in a bicameral parliament consisting of the 301-member House of Representatives (*Majlis al-Nuwab*), which is elected for a six-year term, and a second chamber, the 111-member *Shura* Council, appointed by the President.

At elections to the House of Representatives held on April 17, 1993, 80% of the seats were won by the three major parties—the General People's Congress (GPC), the Yemeni *Islah* Party (YIP) and the Yemen Socialist Party (YSP)—which subsequently signed an agreement providing for the creation of a coalition government. Smaller parties won 12 seats, independent candidates 47 and one seat was undeclared. In October 1993 the House elected a five-member Presidential Council, which in turn elected the GPC's leader, Lt.-Gen. Ali Abdullah Salih, as the country's President.

Mounting tensions between the YSP, with its power base in former South Yemen, and the GPC from the North erupted into full-scale civil war between forces from the two former territories in May 1994. The southern leader and former Vice-President of unified Yemen, Ali Salim al-Bid, proclaimed the formation of the independent Democratic Republic of Yemen (DRY) in the South. In the North, which continued to designate itself the Republic of Yemen, YSP members were dismissed from political office and the armed forces. The DRY forces were defeated by the North in early July 1994 and its leadership fled abroad. In October 1994 the Presidential Council was abolished, President Salih was confirmed in office and a new GPC/YIP coalition, excluding the YSP, was formed.

Twelve parties contested the parliamentary elections held on April 27, 1997, which returned the GPC with the majority (187) of seats. The YIP took 54 seats and independent candidates 55. The YSP boycotted the elections. Salih was re-elected on Sept. 23, 1999, in the country's first direct presidential election. He claimed 96.3% of the vote, although overall turnout was about 66% (and was believed to be less than 10% in the south).

Seven months before the next parliamentary elections were scheduled to be held, parliament voted for a series of significant constitutional amendments, which were put to a referendum on Feb. 20, 2001. About 77% of the electorate voted for the changes which extended the presidential term from five to seven years and the parliamentary mandate from four to six years (rescheduling the next election from 2001 to 2003). The establishment of the *Shura* Council was also approved (this body being appointed in May 2001).

Baath Arab Socialist Rebirth Party
Address. c/o House of Representatives, Sana'a
Leadership. Dr. Qassim Salaam (leader)
This Yemeni version of the historic pan-Arab *Baath* returned seven successful candidates in the 1993 elections to the House of Representatives. In early 1995 the party was reportedly a constituent of a Democratic Coalition of Opposition. It retained only two seats in the 1997 elections. Although Dr. Salaam was appointed to the new *Shura* Council in 2001, his party joined the →Co-ordination Council of Opposition Parties (CCOP).

General People's Congress (GPC)
Mutamar al-Shabi al-Am
Address. c/o House of Representatives, Sana'a
Leadership. Lt.-Gen. Ali Abdullah Salih (leader); Sultan Al-Barakani (chairman of the parliamentary party)
Website. www.gpc.org.ye
The GPC was formed in 1982 in what was then North

Yemen (the Yemen Arab Republic) as a 1,000-member consultative body rather than a political party. Lt.-Gen. Salih, the long-time President of the Yemen Arab Republic, relinquished his position as secretary-general of the GPC upon assuming the presidency of the unified Republic of Yemen in May 1990. With the →Yemen Socialist Party (YSP, based in the former South Yemen) the GPC was responsible for guiding the new republic through a transitional period culminating in the 1993 legislative elections. In the elections the GPC was the most successful party, taking 123 seats. It subsequently formed a coalition government with the YSP and the →Yemeni *Islah* Party (YIP), and took two seats on the Presidential Council. However, the GPC and the YSP became increasingly estranged, leading to the 1994 civil war. In October 1994, with the southern rebellion quashed, the GPC formed a new coalition government with the YIP, further strengthening its position as the dominant partner in a ministerial reshuffle in June 1995.

The GPC was returned as the dominant party with a substantial majority, taking 187 seats in the 1997 parliamentary elections. In 1999 President Salih opened up the presidency to directly contested elections, although his only opponent, Najeeb Qahtan Al-Sha'abi, who gained less than 4% of the poll, was a relatively unknown parliamentarian from his own party. In an attempt to appease opposition parties following the result of the referendum in February 2001 extending the presidential and legislative terms, President Salih proposed further amendments to make elections to the presidency more competitive, including reducing the percentage of parliamentary support required for nominations from 10% to 5%.

Nasserite Unionist People's Organization (NUPP)
Address. c/o House of Representatives, Sana'a
Recognized as a legal party in 1989, the extreme left NUPP won three seats in the 1997 parliamentary elections.

Yemen Socialist Party (YSP)
Hizb al-Ishtirakiya al-Yamaniya
Leadership. Ali Salih Myqbil (leader); Ali Saleh Obad (secretary-general)
The YSP was formed in 1978 as a Marxist-Leninist "vanguard" party for the People's Democratic Republic of Yemen (South Yemen), and maintained one-party control despite several leadership conflicts until unification with the North in 1990. Upon unification the then YSP secretary-general, Ali Salim al-Bid, was named Vice-President of the new republic, in which the YSP, together with the →General People's Congress (GPC) from the North, was charged with the management of the transitional period prior to elections.

Having won 56 seats in the 1993 legislative elections, the YSP was allocated nine cabinet posts in the subsequent coalition government and took two seats on the Presidential Council. However, increasing political tensions between the YSP and the GPC led to the outbreak of civil war in mid-1994 and the short-lived secession of the Democratic Republic of Yemen. Despite the election of a new party leadership after the civil war, the YSP was excluded from the new coalition government which was formed in October 1994.

The YSP boycotted the 1997 elections, alleging unfairness, and therefore had no parliamentary support to nominate a candidate for the presidential election in 1999. The party opposed the referendum in February 2001, particularly criticizing those amendments giving the president power to dissolve the parliament and to appoint the members of the new *Shura* Council.

The YSP's fourth general conference, held in 2000 without government restriction, voted to elect former members, exiled since 1994, to its central committee. This included individuals sentenced to death or imprisonment for their role in the 1994 civil war. The party joined the →Co-ordination Council of Opposition Parties (CCOP) in 2001.

Yemeni Islah Party (YIP)
Islah
Address. POB 23090, Sana'a
Leadership. Sheikh Abdullah bin Hussein al-Ahmar (leader)
The YIP, also known as the Yemeni Alliance for Reform, was established in September 1990, attracting support from the conservative pro-Saudi population in northern tribal areas. The party campaigned against the new constitution adopted in May 1991 in alliance with several other groups advocating strict adherence to Islamic law. In the 1993 legislative elections the YIP emerged with 62 seats, subsequently assuming six cabinet posts in the coalition government and taking one seat on the Presidential Council. The party leader was also elected speaker of the House of Representatives.

In the 1994 civil war the YIP strongly supported President Salih and the northern forces. It formed a new coalition with the dominant →General People's Congress in the government announced in October 1994, although it lost ground in a ministerial reshuffle in June 1995.

The YIP reportedly formed a co-operation agreement with the ruling GPC, winning 54 seats in the 1997 elections and supporting President Saleh's nomination for the presidential election in 1999. However, it joined the →Co-ordination Council of Opposition Parties (CCOP) in 2001.

Other Parties

Co-ordination Council of Opposition Parties (CCOP), established in 2001, its members seeking full participation in the political process and opposing the constitutional amendments proposed in the February 2001 referendum.

Truth Party (*Al-Haq*), established by Islamic religious scholars in 1991. It secured two seats in the House of Representatives in the 1993 elections which were lost in the 1997 polling.
Leadership. Sheikh Ahmad ash-Shami (secretary-general)

Yugoslavia

Capital: Belgrade

Population: 10,700,000 (2000E)

The one-party regime of the former League of Communists of Yugoslavia (LCY) collapsed in 1989–90, heralding the break-up of the Yugoslav federation established in 1945. Four of the former constituent republics (Slovenia, Croatia, Bosnia and Hercegovina, and Macedonia) seceded during 1991–92. The remaining two republics of Serbia and Montenegro declared themselves the Federal Republic of Yugoslavia (FRY) in April 1992. Within the Serbian Republic, meanwhile, the overwhelmingly ethnic Albanian province of Kosovo and the Hungarian-populated province of Vojvodina had lost the autonomous status that they had enjoyed under LCY rule.

Under the 1992 constitution as amended in 2000, executive authority at federal level is vested in the federal President, who is directly elected for a four-term renewable once, and in the federal government headed by a Prime Minister appointed by the President subject to parliamentary endorsement. Legislative authority is vested in the bicameral Federal Assembly (*Savezna Skupština*), consisting of the (i) the Chamber of Citizens (*Veće Gradjana*), whose 138 members (108 from Serbia and 30 from Montenegro) are directly elected for a four-year term, 78 by proportional representation in 36 multi-member constituencies and 60 from single-member constituencies; and (ii) the Chamber of Republics (*Veće Republika*), whose 40 members (20 from Serbia and 20 from

Montenegro) are indirectly elected for a four-year term by the republican Assemblies of Serbia and Montenegro. Within the federal structure substantial powers reside in the two constituent republics, with the much larger Serbian Republic dominating. The unicameral Serbian and Montenegrin National Assemblies (of 250 and 77 members respectively) are themselves directly elected for four-year terms and each republic has its own directly-elected President, who appoints the republican Prime Minister subject to Assembly approval.

The FRY was dominated from its creation by the Socialist Party of Serbia (SPS), successor to the Serbian branch of the LCY and led by Slobodan Milošević, who was President of Serbia in 1989–97 and President of the FRY from July 1997. The SPS and its allies remained dominant in legislative elections in November 1996, but from early 1998 the Milošević regime faced insurrection by separatists in Kosovo and mounting international concern over escalating violence between ethnic Albanians and Serbian security forces. In March 1999 forces under the command of the North Atlantic Treaty Organization (NATO) launched a bombing campaign against Serbian government targets, forcing the withdrawal of Serbian forces from Kosovo, which was placed under interim UN administration. Although most Serbs had backed his resistance to NATO's demands, Milošević in 2000 came under intense opposition pressure for new elections, which were called after the enactment in July 2000 of federal constitutional amendments providing for direct presidential elections and thus enabling Milošević (who had been elected by the Federal Assembly in 1997) to seek re-election.

Despite widespread intimidation and ballot-rigging by Milošević's supporters, federal presidential elections on Sept. 24, 2000, were generally believed to have produced an outright first-round victory for the candidate of the multi-party Democratic Opposition of Serbia (DOS), Vojislav Koštunica. Prevarication by the government, which at first insisted that a second round of voting was needed and then sought to annul the elections, provoked massive popular protest, which in early October forced Milošević to vacate the presidency in favour of Koštunica. Equally flawed elections to the federal Chamber of Citizens also held on Sept. 24, 2000, resulted in the DOS alliance being credited with 58 seats, an alliance of the SPS and the Yugoslav United Left 44, the Socialist People's Party of Montenegro (SNPCG) 28, the Serbian Radical Party (SRS) 5, the Serbian People's Party of Montenegro 2 and the Union of Vojvodina's Hungarians 1. The Democratic Party of Socialists of Montenegro (DPSCG), the republic's main ruling party, boycotted both federal elections.

Freer and fairer elections to the Serbian Assembly on Dec. 23, 2000, resulted in the DOS alliance winning 176 seats, the SPS 37, the SRS 23 and the Serbian Unity Party 14. Elections to the Montenegrin Assembly on April 22, 2001, resulted in a pro-independence alliance headed by the DPSCG winning 36 seats, an anti-independence alliance headed by the SNPCG 33, the Liberal Alliance of Montenegro 6 and others 2.

Christian Democratic Party of Serbia
Demohrišćanska Stranka Srbije (DhSS)
Address. Zmaja od Noćaja br. 7, 11000 Belgrade
Telephone. (+381–11) 184–568
Fax. (+381–11) 184–568
Email. dhss@net.yu
Website. www.dhss.org.yu
Leadership. Vladan Batić (chairman)
The DhSS was part of the victorious →Democratic Opposition of Serbia (DOS) alliance in the late 2000 federal and Serbian elections, party leader Vladan Batić being appointed Justice Minister in the new Serbian republican government.

In October 2000 the DhSS was admitted as an observer member of the Christian Democrat International.

Civic Alliance of Serbia
Gradjanski Savez Srbije (GSS)
Address. Terazije 3, 11000 Belgrade
Telephone. (+381–11) 334–1696
Fax. (+381–11) 334–1478
Email. gss@gradjanskisavez.org.yu
Website. www.gradjanskisavez.org.yu
Leadership. Goran Svilanović (chairman)
The radical liberal GSS was founded in 1992 by peace campaigner Vesna Pešić, who was elected to the Serbian Assembly in 1993 within the DEPOS opposition coalition. It subsequently joined the *Zajedno* ("Together") alliance with the →Democratic Party (DS), the →Democratic Party of Serbia (DSS) and the →Serbian Renewal Movement (SPO), which won 22 lower house seats in the November 1996 federal elections, but boycotted the Serbian Assembly elections in September 1997 in protest against media manipulation by the Milošević regime. In late 1998 the GSS joined a new opposition grouping called the Alliance for Change, which formed the core of the anti-Milošević→Democratic Opposition of Serbia (DOS) alliance launched in January 2000, by which time Pešić had left the country and been succeeded as GSS leader by Goran

Svilanović. When the DOS alliance came to power in October 2000, Svilanović was appointed Foreign Minister in the federal government.

Democratic Alternative
Demokratska Alternativa (DA)
Address. Makedonska 5, 11000 Belgrade
Telephone. (+381–11) 334–3471
Fax. (+381–11) 334–3192
Email. da@da.org.yu
Website. www.da.org.yu
Leadership. Nebojsa Čović (chairman)
The DA formed part of the victorious →Democratic Opposition of Serbia (DOS) alliance in the late 2000 federal and Serbian elections, party leader Nebojsa Čović being appointed a Deputy Prime Minister in the new Serbian republican government.

Democratic Centre
Demokratski Centar (DC)
Address. Terazije 3/II, 11000 Belgrade
Telephone. (+381–11) 322–9925
Fax. (+381–11) 322–3321
Email. dcentar@infosky.net
Website. www.dc.org.yu
Leadership. Dragoljub Mićunović (chairman)
The DC was formed in 1996 by a moderate splinter group of the →Democratic Party (DS) aspiring to "maintain the original spirit" of the DS. It formed part of the victorious →Democratic Opposition of Serbia (DOS) alliance in the late 2000 federal and Serbian elections.

Democratic Opposition of Serbia
Demokratska Opozicija Srbije (DOS)
Address. Simina 41, 11000 Belgrade
Telephone. (+381–11) 334–0620
Fax. (+381–11) 334–1924
Email. info@dos.org.yu
Website. www.dos.org.yu

Leadership. Vojislav Koštunica (chairman)

The DOS was launched in early 2000 in the wake of the 1999 Kosovo crisis as a broad-based alliance of parties and groups seeking the removal of Slobodan Milošević from power and an end to the dominance of his →Socialist Party of Serbia (SPS). The alliance eventually embraced 19 parties and organizations, including the nationalist →Democratic Party (DS) and →Democratic Party of Serbia (DSS); the radical liberal →Civic Alliance of Serbia (GSS); the pro-business →New Democracy (ND); the centrist →Christian Democratic Party of Serbia, →Democratic Centre and →Movement for a Democratic Serbia; the centre-left →Social Democratic Union and →Social Democracy; the regional →League for Sumadia–Sumadia Coalition; the →Union of Vojvodina's Hungarians and three other parties representing ethnic Hungarians; the ethnic Albanian →Party of Democratic Action (PDA); the Serb Resistance Movement–Democratic Movement (of Serbs in Kosovo); and the Association of Free and Independent Trade Unions (ASNS).

The DOS candidate for the September 2000 federal presidential elections was Vojislav Koštunica of the DSS, regarded as the most right-wing of the alliance components. Despite widespread intimidation and vote-rigging, Koštunica was widely believed to have obtained an outright first-round victory over Milošević. Attempts by the regime to resist the democratic verdict prompted a DOS-orchestrated national uprising, which forced Milošević to hand over power in early October. Concurrent (and equally flawed) federal parliamentary elections resulted officially in the DOS alliance winning 58 of the 138 lower house seats.

Inaugurated as federal President, Koštunica appointed Zoran Žižić of the →Socialist People's Party of Montenegro (SNPCG) as federal Prime Minister, heading a transitional government which consisted mainly of DOS ministers. In elections to the Serbian Assembly in December 2000, the DOS alliance displayed its real popular strength by winning 176 of the 250 seats with 65.8% of the valid vote. A new Serbian government appointed in January 2001 was headed by DS leader Zoran Djindjić and included representatives of all of the main DOS components. Despite being in government, the alliance continued to use the DOS appellation pending a possible decision to adopt a more appropriate title and/or to create a unitary movement from the component formations, which in the meantime all maintained their individual identities. Analysts subsequently predicted that Koštunica's DSS would become the core of a new centre-right party of Christian democratic orientation and Djindjić's DS the mainspring of a new centre-left party of social democratic orientation.

The coming to power of the DOS and Koštunica was welcomed by the international community, although the new President declared that his administration would be nationalist in orientation, notably in that it would resist any move to detach Kosovo from Serbia and would not co-operate with the international war crimes tribunal at The Hague in its pursuit of Yugoslavs indicted for alleged crimes, including Milošević. He also came out strongly in favour of maintenance of Serbia's federation with Montenegro and against the latter's moves towards independence.

Western pressure and the threat to withhold economic aid quickly persuaded Djindjić's Serbian government not only to arrest Milošević but also to hand him over to the tribunal at The Hague in late June. This action, on which Koštunica complained that he had not been consulted, provoked serious strains in the DOS alliance, with the DSS and two other right-wing components taking their parliamentary deputies out of the DOS caucus in late July, thereby reducing it to minority status. The following month, however, the divisions were patched up sufficiently for the three dissident groupings to return to the DOS fold.

Democratic Party
Demokratska Stranka (DS)

Address. Kruška 69, 11000 Belgrade
Telephone. (+381–11) 344–3003
Fax. (+381–11) 344–2946
Email. info@ds.org.yu
Website. www.ds.org.yu
Leadership. Zoran Djindjić (chairman)

The right-wing DS was founded in 1990 as Serbia's first opposition party under the leadership of prominent academic Dragoljub Mićunović, adopting a nationalistic programme and advocating Serbian intervention in support of Serb separatists in Bosnia and Hercegovina. Weakened by the defection of its nationalist wing to form the →Democratic Party of Serbia (DSS), the DS won five lower house seats in the December 1992 federal elections. It advanced to 29 seats in the Serbian Assembly elections in December 1993 and subsequently joined a coalition government headed by Slobodan Milošević's →Socialist Party of Serbia (SPS), hoping to reform the system from within. In January 1994 Mićunović was succeeded as DS chairman by Zoran Djindjić, then mayor of Belgrade.

The DS reverted to opposition in 1996, joining the *Zajedno* ("Together") alliance with the DSS, the →Serbian Renewal Movement (SPO) and the →Civic Alliance of Serbia, which won only 22 lower house seats in the November 1996 federal elections. The alliance collapsed in mid-1997 when Djindjić refused to back the SPO leader as opposition candidate for the Serbian presidency, whereupon the SPO retaliated by helping to eject the DS leader from the Belgrade mayorship. The DS then boycotted the Serbian Assembly elections in September 1997 in protest against media manipulation by the Milošević regime.

In late 1998 the DS joined a new opposition grouping called the Alliance for Change, which formed the core of the anti-Milošević →Democratic Opposition of Serbia (DOS) alliance launched in January 2000. The eventual victory of the DOS candidate in the September 2000 federal presidential elections resulted in DS representatives joining the federal government. Moreover, following a landslide DOS victory in Serbian Assembly elections in December 2000, Djindjić was appointed Prime Minister of the Serbian government in January 2001.

Whereas the DOS election platform had ruled out handing over indicted Yugoslav war criminals such as Milošević to the international tribunal at The Hague, Djindjić quickly pushed through a Serbian government decree authorizing co-operation with the tribunal, thereby attracting criticism from the more nationalist DOS components that he was bowing to Western economic blackmail.

Democratic Party of Serbia
Demokratska Stranka Srbije (DSS)

Address. Braće Jugovića 2a/I, 11000 Belgrade
Telephone. (+381–11) 328–2886
Fax. (+381–11) 182–535
Email. info@dss.org.yu
Website. www.dss.org.yu
Leadership. Vojislav Koštunica (chairman)

The DSS was founded in 1992 by a right-wing faction of the nationalist →Democratic Party (DS) and contested the December 1992 federal elections as part of the DEPOS opposition alliance, which won 20 lower house seats. In the December 1993 Serbian Assembly elections, the DSS won seven seats in its own right, remaining in opposition. It subsequently joined the *Zajedno* ("Together") alliance with the DS, the →Serbian Renewal Movement (SPO) and the →Civic Alliance of Serbia, which won 22 lower house seats in the November 1996 federal elections. The party joined the DS in boycotting the Serbian Assembly elections in September 1997 in protest against media manipulation by the Milošević regime.

In late 1998 the DSS joined a new opposition grouping called the Alliance for Change, which formed the core of the anti-Milošević →Democratic Opposition of Serbia (DOS) alliance launched in January 2000. DSS leader Vojislav Koštunica became the DOS candidate in the September 2000 federal presidential elections, winning an outright majority in the first round according to independent estimates and eventually being installed as President in early October. Following a landslide DOS victory in Serbian Assembly elections in December 2000, the DSS was represented by two ministers in the resultant Serbian government headed by the DS leader.

The Serbian government's decision in June 2001 to extradite Milošević to the war crimes tribunal at The Hague provoked serious strains between the DSS and the DS. Although the DOS alliance survived, Koštunica took the DSS out of the Serbian government in August 2001, claiming that it was already compromised by corruption.

League for Sumadia–Sumadia Coalition
Liga za Šumadiju–Koalicija Šumadija

Address. Branka Radićevića 18/2, 34000 Kragujevac
Telephone. (+381–34) 367–973
Fax. (+381–34) 367–973
Email. sumadija@infoky.net
Website. www.sumadija.org.yu
Leadership. Branislav Kovačević (chairman); Snežana Zekavica (secretary-general)
This regional Serb party formed part of the victorious →Democratic Opposition of Serbia (DOS) alliance in the late 2000 federal and Serbian elections, following which party leader Branislav Kovačević was elected chairman of the DOS group in the new Serbian National Assembly.

Movement for a Democratic Serbia
Pokret za Demokratsku Srbiju (PDS)

Address. Božidara Adžije 21, 11000 Belgrade
Telephone. (+381–11) 444–6248
Fax. (+381–11) 436–857
Email. info@pokret.org.yu
Website. www.pokret.org.yu
Leadership. Momčilo Perišić (chairman)
The PDS was launched in August 1998 by Momcilo Perišić following his dismissal as Chief of Staff of the Yugoslav army because he had questioned the policy of the Milošević regime in Kosovo. The party formed part of the victorious →Democratic Opposition of Serbia (DOS) alliance in the late 2000 federal and Serbian elections, following which Perišić was appointed a Deputy Prime Minister in the new Serbian republican government. The Serbian government's decision in June 2001 to extradite Slobodan Milošević to the war crimes tribunal at The Hague was opposed by the PDS, which joined with the →Democratic Party of Serbia and the →New Serbia in temporarily withdrawing from the DOS parliamentary caucus. However, the DOS alliance survived and the NS did not join the DSS in withdrawing from the Serbian government.

New Democracy
Nova Demokratija (ND)

Address. Proleterskih brigada 76, 11000 Belgrade
Telephone. (+381–11) 444–0677
Fax. (+381–11) 444–9778
Email. izv.odbor@novademokratija.org.yu
Website. www.novademokratija.org.yu
Leadership. Dušan Mihajlović (chairman)
The ND was established in 1990 as the successor to the official youth organization of the communist-era, subsequently attracting support in the business community. Claiming to be both social democratic and liberal, the party contested the 1992 federal and 1993 Serbian Assembly elections as part of the DEPOS opposition alliance, but in February 1994 deserted DEPOS to join the Serbian government led by the →Socialist Party of Serbia

(SPS) of Slobodan Milošević. It remained allied with the SPS in the 1996 federal and 1997 Serbian elections (winning five seats in the latter contest), but later joined what became the anti-Milošević →Democratic Opposition of Serbia (DOS) alliance. It therefore participated in the DOS victories in the elections of late 2000, with ND leader Dušan Mihailović becoming a Deputy Prime Minister in the new Serbian government appointed in January 2001.

New Serbia
Nova Srbija (NS)

Address. Dragoslava Jovanovića 7, 11000 Belgrade
Telephone. (+381–11) 323–8225
Fax. (+381–11) 334–3914
Email. info@nova-srbija.org.yu
Website. www.nova-srbija.org.yu
Leadership. Velimir Ilić & Mihajlo Marković (co-chairmen)
The NS formed part of the victorious →Democratic Opposition of Serbia (DOS) alliance in the late 2000 federal and Serbian elections, party co-chairman Velimir Ilić being appointed a Deputy Prime Minister in the new Serbian republican government. The Serbian government's decision in June 2001 to extradite Slobodan Milošević to the war crimes tribunal at The Hague was opposed by the NS, which joined with the →Democratic Party of Serbia and the →Movement for a Democratic Serbia in temporarily withdrawing from the DOS parliamentary caucus. However, the DOS alliance survived and the NS did not join the DSS in withdrawing from the Serbian government.

Party of Democratic Action
Partija Demokratske Akcije (PDA)

Address. Poštanski fah 101, 36300 Novi Pazar
Telephone. (+381–20) 311–454
Leadership. Rasim Ljajić (chairman)
The moderate ethnic Muslim PDA in Yugoslavia is linked to the (formerly ruling) party of the same name in Bosnia and Hercegovina. Distinct PDA factions have operated in Kosovo, Montenegro and other Yugoslav regions with significant ethnic Albanian/Muslim populations, winning three seats in the Montenegrin Assembly and one federal lower house seat in 1996 and three seats in the Serbian Assembly in 1997.

Under the new leadership of Rasim Ljajić, the DPA joined the anti-Milošević →Democratic Opposition of Serbia (DOS) alliance and therefore participated in the DOS victories in the elections of late 2000, Ljajić becoming Minister of National and Ethnic Communities in the new federal government.

Serbian Radical Party
Srpska Radikalna Stranka (SRS)

Address. Ohridska 1, 11000 Belgrade
Telephone. (+381–11) 457–745
Leadership. Vojislav Šešelj (president)
Founded in 1991, the ultra-nationalist SRS advocates the creation of a Greater Serbia stretching from the Adriatic to the Aegean. The party won 34 federal lower house seats in December 1992 and subsequently co-operated with the dominant →Socialist Party of Serbia (SPS) until September 1993. Its representation in the Serbian Assembly was almost halved to 39 seats in December 1993, following which the party disbanded its paramilitary wing (named after the Chetniks of the World War II resistance), which had been accused of atrocities in Serb separatist campaigns elsewhere in former Yugoslavia. In the November 1996 federal elections SRS lower house representation fell to 16 seats on a 17.9% vote share. In the September 1997 Serbian Assembly elections, however, the SRS advanced strongly to 82 seats and 29.3% of the vote and in March 1998 was included in a Serbian coalition government headed by the SPS.

Meanwhile, SRS leader Vojislav Šešelj had stood in the protracted Serbian presidential elections in late 1997, his victory in the first contest being annulled because of a low turnout, following which his losing vote share against the SPS candidate in the second was 40%.

The SRS strongly backed President Milošević's intransigence in the 1998-99 Kosovo crisis, and therefore opposed the withdrawal of Serbian forces in June 1999. The party remained part of the ruling coalition and in June 2000 forced the withdrawal of a controversial new "anti-terrorism" bill seen as intended to curb any opposition to the Milošević regime. The party opted to run Tomislav Nikolić in the September 2000 federal presidential elections, but he was believed to have obtained only 6% of the first-round vote.

In the post-election crisis surrounding Milošević's initial reluctance to accept his defeat by Vojislav Koštunica of the →Democratic Opposition of Serbia (DOS), a crucial factor was Šešelj's endorsement Koštunica's claim of victory. Having won only five lower house seats in the simultaneous federal parliamentary elections, the SRS slumped to 23 seats (and 8.5% of the vote) in Serbian Assembly elections in December 2000. Having been indicted by the international war crimes tribunal for alleged participation in ethnic cleansing in Croatia in 1991-92, Šešelj in October 2001 declared his readiness to go to The Hague to explain why he was proud of what he and "thousands of Serbian Radical Party volunteers" had done to defend "Serbdom".

Serbian Renewal Movement
Srpski Pokret Obnove (SPO)

Address. Nušićeva 8/III, 11000 Belgrade
Leadership. Vuk Drašković (chairman)

The relatively moderate Serb nationalist SPO was formed in 1990 as a merger of four previous groups. The party became the lynchpin of the DEPOS opposition alliance in the 1992 and 1993 elections, in which the DEPOS parties won 20 federal lower house seats and 45 seats in the Serbian Assembly. The SPO subsequently joined the *Zajedno* ("Together") alliance with the →Democratic Party (DS), the →Democratic Party of Serbia (DSS) and the →Civic Alliance of Serbia (GSS), which won 22 lower house seats in the November 1996 federal elections. In late 1997 the SPO was the only moderate opposition party to contest the Serbian presidential and parliamentary elections, Drašković coming third in the former contest with 15.4% of the first-round vote and the party winning 45 seats and 20% of the vote in the latter.

In January 1999 Drašković took the SPO into the federal government headed by the →Socialist Party of Serbia (SPS), becoming a Deputy Prime Minister. Three months later the party withdrew in opposition to President Milošević's hardline policy on →Kosovo. In the September 2000 federal presidential elections which ousted Milošević from power, SPO candidate Vojislav Mihajlović obtained only about 3% of the vote, while the party failed to obtain representation in either the federal lower house or the Serbian Assembly, winning 4% of the vote in the latter elections.

Serbian Unity Party
Partija Srpskog Ujedinjenja (PSU)

Address. c/o Skupština Srbije, 11000 Belgrade
Leadership. Borisav Pelević (chairman)

The PSU was founded in 1992 with support from the then ruling →Socialist Party of Serbia (SPS) led by Sloboban Milošević, who reportedly saw the party's paramilitary provenance as a counterweight to the →Serbian Radical Party (SRS) and its paramilitary wing. The PSU's founder, Željko Ražnjatović (known universally by his *nom de guerre* Arkan), had previously created the Tigers paramilitary group, which had been linked with many of the worst atrocities and ethnic cleansing in the regional conflicts then raging. Arkan also gained the reputation of being the "boss of bosses" of the organized criminal gangs which came to dominate Yugoslav economic life in the late 1990s.

The PSU won five seats in the December 1992 elections for the Serbian Assembly, receiving strong support from ethnic Serbs in Kosovo. It failed to obtain representation in the December 1993 Serbian elections and made little impact in subsequent contests in the 1990s, as relations between Arkan and the ruling elite cooled. In March 1999 the international war crimes tribunal at The Hague disclosed that it had indicted Arkan and sent a warrant for his arrest to the Belgrade government (which took no action). The gunning-down of Arkan and two associates in a Belgrade hotel in January 2000 provoked a torrent of speculation about responsibility for the murders, much of it centring on Arkan's reported readiness to give evidence against Milošević to the war crimes tribunal.

Under the new leadership of Borisav Pelević, the PSU unexpectedly made a political comeback in the post-Milošević Serbian Assembly elections in December 2000, winning 14 seats (and 5.3% of the vote) and becoming part of the parliamentary opposition to the new government of the →Democratic Opposition of Serbia. In October 2001 a Belgrade court convicted three men of Arkan's murder, although the judge noted that they had been paid hitmen and that it remained unclear who had ordered the assassination.

Social Democracy
Socijaldemokratija (Sd)

Address. Terazije 3/I, 11000 Belgrade
Telephone. (+381–11) 334–2753
Fax. (+381–11) 334–2289
Email. info@socijaldemokratija.org.yu
Website. www.socijaldemokratija.org.yu
Leadership. Vuk Obradović (chairman)

Founded in 1997 by Gen. (retd) Vuk Obradović, the Sd combines a social democratic orientation with a tinge of nationalism. It was part of the victorious →Democratic Opposition of Serbia (DOS) alliance in the late 2000 federal and Serbian elections.

Social Democratic Union
Socijaldemokratska Unija (SdU)

Address. Beogradska 8/II, 11000 Belgrade
Telephone. (+381–11) 434–107
Fax. (+381–11) 434–107
Email. info@sdu.org.yu
Website. www.sdu.org.yu
Leadership. Žarko Korać (chairman); Vlatko Sekulović (chairman of executive)

Founded in May 1996 by a social democratic splinter group of the →Civic Alliance of Serbia, the SdU opposed the policies of the Milošević regime in Kosovo in 1998-99 and called for full Yugoslav co-operation with the war crimes tribunal at The Hague. It formed part of the victorious →Democratic Opposition of Serbia (DOS) alliance in the late 2000 federal and Serbian elections, following which party leader Žarko Korać was appointed a Deputy Prime Minister in the new Serbian republican government.

Socialist Party of Serbia
Socijalistička Partija Srbije (SPS)

Address. Studentski trg 15, 11000 Belgrade
Telephone. (+381–11) 328–2575
Fax. (+381–11) 328–2491
Email. info@sps.org.yu
Website. www.sps.org.yu
Leadership. Slobodan Milošević (chairman); Živadin Jovanović (deputy chairman); Oskar Kovač (parliamentary leader); Zoran Andjelković (secretary-general)

The SPS was created in July 1990 by the merging of the Serbian wings of the former ruling League of Communists of Yugoslavia (LCY) and the associated Socialist Alliance of the Working People, with Milošević (who had become leader of the Serbian LCY in 1986 and Serbian President in 1989) as its chairman. While acknowledging its origins in the communist-era ruling structure, the SPS officially subscribed to democratic socialism, favouring a continuing state economic role and preservation of the social security system. In reality, the SPS became the political vehicle for the hardline Serbian nationalist policies of Milošević in the regional conflicts of the 1990s and for an increasingly repressive response to domestic opposition.

Having won an overwhelming majority in the Serbian Assembly in December 1990 (when Milošević was re-elected Serbian President with 65% of the vote), the SPS obtained a narrow lower house majority in the May 1992 federal elections. The imposition of UN sanctions from mid-1992 resulted in reduced popular support for the SPS, which lost its overall majorities in the federal lower house and the Serbian Assembly in December 1992, although it remained the largest single party in both and Milošević was re-elected President of Serbia with 56% of the vote. In further Serbian elections in December 1993, the SPS increased its lower house representation from 101 to 123 seats out of 250, subsequently forming a government with the →New Democracy (ND) party.

Milošević's reluctant acceptance of the November 1995 Dayton peace agreement for Bosnia and Hercegovina brought him into conflict with ultra-hardliners within the SPS, several of whom defected or were expelled. In federal elections in November 1996 a Joint List alliance of the SPS, the →Yugoslav United Left (JUL) led by Milošević's wife and the ND won 64 of the 138 lower house seats, so that the SPS continued to dominate the federal government. In simultaneous local elections, however, opposition parties captured Belgrade and most other Serbian cities – results which the government-controlled courts tried to annul but which Milošević eventually accepted in the face of mass popular protests and strikes.

Being constitutionally barred from a third term as Serbian President, Milošević was in July 1997 elected as federal President by the Federal Assembly, under the then prevailing system of indirect election. Serbian Assembly elections in September 1997 resulted in the SPS/JUL/NS alliance winning 110 seats, the outcome being a coalition government of the SPS, the JUL and the ultra-nationalist →Serbian Radical Party (SRS) under the continued premiership of Mirko Marjanović. In protracted Serbian presidential elections in late 1997, SPS candidate Milan Milutinović was eventually returned with 59% of the vote, in balloting regarded as deeply flawed by international observers.

The Kosovo crisis of 1998–99 and the eventual bombardment of Serbia by NATO initially appeared to strengthen Milošević and the SPS politically. However, following the withdrawal of Serbian forces from Kosovo in June 1999 and the indictment of Milošević for alleged war crimes, growing popular pressure for a change of government was orchestrated by what became the →Democratic Opposition of Serbia (DOS). Milošević and his coterie resisted the pressure, the President being re-elected to the SPS chairmanship unopposed in February 2000 and telling a party congress that the Kosovo conflict had been "a struggle for freedom and independence". In July 2000, moreover, Milošević secured the enactment of constitutional amendments providing for the direct election of the federal President, which meant that the ban on a second federal presidential term no longer applied.

However, in balloting in September 2000 intimidation and vote-rigging by Milošević supporters failed to prevent what observers regarded as an outright victory for the DOS candidate in the first round, with Milošević's vote being estimated at little more than 37%. After last-ditch attempts by the regime to resist the verdict had provoked a massive popular uprising, Milošević eventually surrendered the federal presidency in early October. In simultaneous federal parliamentary elections, themselves marred by irregularities, the SPS/JUL alliance declined to 44 lower house seats out of 138. Three months later Serbian Assembly elections in December revealed the true state of opinion by reducing the SPS/JUL to only 37 of the 250 seats and 14% of the vote.

Milošević remained defiant after losing power, asserting that he would lead a revitalized SPS back to government in the near future. At the beginning of April, however, he was arrested at his Belgrade home and charged with misappropriation of funds and other abuses as President. The following month Serbian President Milutinović, whose signature was one of those on the arrest warrant for Milošević, resigned from his SPS leadership posts. Worse was to follow for Milošević, because the new Serbian government headed by Zoran Djindjić of the →Democratic Party, contrary to the DOS election pledge that those charged with war crimes should be tried in Yugoslavia, in late June 2001 unexpectedly handed Milošević over to the international war crimes tribunal at The Hague. There the former President refused to accept the tribunal's right to try him, claiming that he had always acted in accordance with his constitutional duty to defend the interests of the Serbian people and the Serbian/Yugoslav state.

Incarcerated in the Netherlands pending the start of his trial, Milošević sought to direct the SPS by telephone. In August 2001, however, the SPS executive in Belgrade voted to disregard his instruction that the SPS should not co-operate with the UN-sponsored interim administration in Kosovo.

Union of Vojvodina's Hungarians
Savez Vojvodjanskih Madjara (SVM)
Vajdasági Magyar Szövetsége (VMSz)

Address. Age Mamuzica 13/II, 24000 Subotica
Telephone. (+381–24) 553–801
Email. office@vmsz.org.yu
Website. www.vmsz.org.yu
Leadership. Jozef Kasza (chairman)

The SVM/VMSz was launched in mid-1994, effectively succeeding the Democratic Community of Vojvodina Hungarians (DZVM). Campaigning for the restoration of autonomy to Vojvodina (which had been abolished by the Milošević regime), the formation won three federal parliamentary seats in 1996 and four in the Serbian Assembly in 1997. In early 2000 the SVM/VMSz joined the multi-party →Democratic Opposition of Serbia (DOS), in which three ethnic Hungarian formations had separate membership status, namely the Reform Democratic Party of Vojvodina (*Reformska Demokratska Stranka Vojvodine*, RDSV) led by Miodrag Isakov, the League of Social Democrats of Vojvodina (*Liga Socijaldemokrata Vojvodine*, LSdV) led by Nenad Čanak and the Vojvodina Coalition (*Koalicija Vojvodina*, KV) led by Dragan Veselinov.

As well as participating in the victory of the DOS alliance in the late 2000 federal and Serbian elections, the SVM/VMSz also won one federal lower house in its own right. SVM/VMSz leader Jozef Kasza was appointed a Deputy Prime Minister in the new DOS government of Serbia, while Veselinov became Minister of Agriculture. Kasza subsequently expressed confidence that agreement would be reached on the restoration of autonomy to Vojvodina, while threatening to "internationalize" the issue if the government dragged its feet.

Yugoslav United Left
Jugoslovenska Ujedinjena Levica (JUL)

Address. c/o Savezna Skupština, Nikole Pašića 13, 11000 Belgrade
Email. info@jul.org.yu
Website. www.jul.org.yu
Leadership. Mira Marković (executive chairperson); Ljubisa Ristić (president)

The JUL was launched in July 1995 under the leadership of Mira Marković, the wife of then Serbian President Slobodan Milošević, as a Marxist-oriented alliance of over 20 groups mostly derived from the former ruling League of Communists of Yugoslavia. The formation's political role was to rally unreconstructed communists to the cause of the dominant →Socialist Party of Serbia (SPS). It later came to be accused of being the party of war profiteers and those corruptly benefiting from the disposal of state assets. In federal elections in November 1996 a Joint List alliance of the JUL, the SPS and →New Democracy (ND) won 64 of the 138 lower house seats. Serbian Assembly elections in September 1997 resulted in the SPS/JUL/NS alliance winning 110 of the 250 seats, the outcome being a coalition government of the SPS, the JUL and the ultra-nationalist →Serbian Radical Party (SRS). A month after the elections JUL secretary-general Zoran Todorović (who was also manager of Yugoslavia's second-largest petrol company) was shot dead in Belgrade.

In the controversial September 2000 elections which resulted in the downfall of Milošević, the JUL was allied only with the SPS in the balloting for federal parliamentary seats, their joint list returning 44 members to the lower house. Serbian Assembly elections in December 2000 reduced the SPS/JUL to only 37 seats and 14% of the vote. The extradition of Milošević in June 2001 to stand trial before the war crimes tribunal at The Hague raised a question-mark over the continued existence of the JUL. According to SPS officials in Belgrade in August, Milošević was seeking from his cell in the Netherlands to install his wife as SPS leader in his absence.

Parties in Kosovo

The 1998–99 Kosovo crisis and the aftermath of UN administration stimulated even greater proliferation of already numerous political parties in the province, particularly those based in the majority ethnic Albanian population. A total of 26 lists (several being alliances of individual parties) were registered for elections to a new 120-member Kosovo Assembly in November 2001. The four groupings covered below (three ethnic Albanian and one Serb) emerged as the leading formations in their respective communities.

Alliance for the Future of Kosovo
Aleanca për Ardhmërinë e Kosovës (AAK)
Leadership. Ramush Haradinaj (chairman)
One of the three main ethnic Albanian formations in Kosovo, the AAK was created in the aftermath of the 1998-99 crisis as an alliance of various pro-independence groupings, taking a line somewhere between those of the "moderate" →Democratic League of Kosovo (LDK) and the militant →Democratic Party of Kosovo (PDK). In launching the formation's campaign for the November 2001 Kosovo elections, Ramush Haradinaj told voters that by supporting the AAK "you will make your dream of freedom, dignity and economic well-being . . . come true".

Democratic League of Kosovo
Lidhja Demokratike e Kosovës (LDK)
Address. Beogradi PN, 8000 Pristina
Telephone. (+381–38) 32992
Fax. (+381–38) 27660
Leadership. Ibrahim Rugova (chairman)
Advocating independence for Kosovo, the LDK was launched in 1990 when the Belgrade government ended the province's autonomous status, thus provoking widespread ethnic Albanian protest against Serb rule. Calling for a negotiated settlement and officially opposing armed struggle, the LDK won a majority of seats in provincial assembly elections organized by Albanians in May 1992, following which Rugova was declared "President of Kosovo". However, the elections were declared illegal by the Serbian and federal authorities and the assembly was prevented from holding its inaugural session. Subsequent Serbian and federal elections were boycotted by the LDK.

Although Rugova and the LDK won large majorities in further presidential and assembly elections organized illegally in Kosovo in March 1998, he and his party appeared to

be marginalized as conflict in the province intensified and the Kosovo Liberation Army (UCK) emerged as the fighting arm of Albanian separatism. Rugova continued to support a negotiated settlement, attracting criticism from ethnic Albanians when he appeared on television with President Slobodan Milošević in April 1999 (possibly under duress), soon after the start of the NATO bombardment of Serbia. He was also criticized for spending the rest of the conflict in Italy.

Following the withdrawal of Serb forces from Kosovo in June 1999 and Rugova's return a month later, the LDK recovered its status as the principal political representative of Kosovar Albanians. In August 1999 it joined the Kosovo Transitional Council set up by the new UN administration, thereafter working with the UN to promote inter-ethnic peace and reconciliation. In municipal elections in Kosovo in October 2000, the LDK obtained 58% of the vote and won control of 21 of the 30 municipalities at issue. In the same month the LDK welcomed the ousting of the Milošević regime in Belgrade, although the successor government of the →Democratic Opposition of Serbia (DOS) was also resolutely opposed to independence for Kosovo.

Facing strong competition from militant pro-independence parties in elections to a new Kosovo Assembly in November 2001, Rugova sought to match their rhetoric. Launching the LDK's campaign, he said that the elections would "show that it is about time that the independence of Kosovo was recognized and that its people are capable of building a democratic society and state".

The LDK is a member of the Christian Democrat International.

Democratic Party of Kosovo
Partija Demokratike e Kosovës (PDK)
Leadership. Hashim Thaci (chairman)
The PDK was founded in the wake of the 1998-99 Kosovo crisis as the party political manifestation of the militant separatist Kosovo Liberation Army (UCK), in which Hashim Thaci had been "head of the political directorate". Standing for immediate independence for Kosovo, the PDK was heavily outpolled in municipal elections in October 2000 by the more moderate (but also pro-independence) →Democratic League of Kosovo (LDK), winning 27% of the vote and taking control in six of the 30 municipalities at issue.

In the run-up to the UN-sponsored elections to a new Kosovo Assembly in November 2001, the PDK in June 2001 joined with the LDK and the →Alliance for the Future of Kosovo (AAK) in rejecting a proposal by President Putin of Russia for a Balkan conference to affirm the inviolability of existing national borders. In launching the PDK's election campaign, Thaci said that the party was "ready to govern with all those . . . who are sincerely committed to Kosovo's independence".

Return Coalition
Koalicija "Povratak" (KP)
Leadership. Sima Garikalović (chairman)
The KP was created by some 20 ethnic Serb parties demanding that Serbs who had fled or been forcibly expelled from Kosovo during the 1998-99 hostilities should be guaranteed safe return to their homes and that Kosovo should remain under Serbian/Yugoslav sovereignty. The alliance received the backing of the ruling →Democratic Opposition of Serbia (DOS) in Belgrade, which urged Kosovo Serbs to overcome their reluctance to vote in the elections for a new Kosovo Assembly in November 2001.

Other formations which presented over 50 candidates in the November 2001 elections were the **Kosovo Centre Liberal Party** (*Partia Qendra Liberale e Kosovës*, PQLK) led by Ibrahim Shala; the **Kosovo Christian Democratic Party** (*Partia Shqiptare Demokristiane e Kosovës*, PSHDK) led by Mark Krasniqi (a member of the Christian Democrat International); the **Kosovo Green Party** (*Partia e të*

Gjelbërve e Kosovës, PGjK) led by Daut Maloku; the **Kosovo Liberal Party** (*Partia Liberale e Kosovës*, PLK) led by Gjergj Dedaj (an observer member of the Liberal International); the **Kosovo National Liberation Movement** (*Lëvizja Kombëtare për Çlirimin e Kosovës*, LKÇK) led by Fatmir Humolli; the **Kosovo People's Movement** (*Lëvizja Popullore e Kosovës*, LPK) led by Bedrush Çollaku and the **National Front** (*Balli Kombëtar*, BK) led by Kajtaz Fazlia.

Parties in Montenegro

Democratic Alliance of Montenegro
Demokratska Savez Crne Gore (DSCG)
Address. c/o Skupština Crne Core, Podgorica
Leadership. Mehmet Bardahi (chairman)
One of several parties representing the 6% ethnic Albanian component of Montenegro's population, the DSCG obtained one of the five Assembly seats reserved for ethnic minorities in both the May 1998 and the April 2001 Montenegrin elections.

Democratic Party of Socialists of Montenegro
Demokratska Partija Socijalista Crne Gore (DPSCG)
Address. Jovana Tomaševića 66, 81000 Podgorica
Telephone. (+381–81) 243–952
Fax. (+381–81) 243–347
Email. webmaster@dps.cg.yu
Website. www.dps.cg.yu
Leadership. Milo Djukanović (chairman)
The DPSCG is the successor to the League of Communists of Montenegro, which changed its name in 1991, and was in favour of the federation with Serbia until the late 1990s, thereafter moving to a pro-independence stance. The party obtained an overall majority in the Montenegrin Assembly in December 1992, also winning 17 lower house seats in simultaneous federal elections and joining a coalition government led by the →Socialist Party of Serbia (SPS) of Slobodan Milošević. The following month the then DPSCG leader, Momir Bulatović, was elected President of Montenegro. The DPSCG retained its Montenegrin Assembly majority in November 1996, when it also advanced to 20 federal lower house seats.

Increasing internal opposition to Bulatović for his pro-federation stance culminated in October 1997 in his narrow defeat by Prime Minister Milo Djukanović in Montenegrin presidential elections in which both stood as DPSCG candidates. Djukanović also became undisputed DPSCG chairman, while Bulatović launched the breakaway →Socialist People's Party of Montenegro (SNPCG). Advocating greater independence for Montenegro, the DPSCG contested the May 1998 Montenegrin Assembly elections as leader of the "For a Better Life" alliance, which included the →People's Party of Montenegro (NSCG) and the →Social Democratic Party of Montenegro (SdPCG) and which won 42 out of 78 seats and therefore formed a new government with Filip Vujanović as Prime Minister.

Relations between the DPSCG and the Milošević regime deteriorated during the 1998–99 Kosovo crisis, when the Montenegrin government received strong Western backing for a proposed loose "association" with Serbia. When Milošević enacted constitutional amendments in July 2000 which were seen as reducing Montenegrin powers in the federation, the DPSCG came out in favour of full separation and boycotted the September 2000 federal elections, in which Milošević and the SPS were defeated by the →Democratic Opposition of Serbia (DOS). In Montenegro the consequence was that the NSCG withdrew from the ruling coalition, leaving the DPSCG and the SdPCG without a majority.

In early Montenegrin Assembly elections in April 2001 the DPSCG headed an alliance of pro-independence parties called "Victory for Montenegro", including the SdPCG and indirectly the →Democratic Union of Albanians. The alliance emerged as the largest bloc with 36 of the 77 seats

(and 42% of the vote) in a close result in which the overall pro-separation vote was only 5,000 higher than that against. Lacking an overall majority and failing to reach a coalition agreement with the pro-independence →Liberal Alliance of Montenegro (LSCG), the DPSCG-led bloc opted to form a minority government (with LSCG external support) and to announce that a referendum on independence would be held in March 2002. However, the new DOS government in Belgrade, broadly enjoying Western support, was as opposed to the break-up of the federation as its predecessor and argued that there were historic, economic and security reasons for maintaining a single state.

Democratic Union of Albanians (DUA)
Address. c/o Skupština Crne Core, Podgorica
Leadership. Gezim Hajdinaga
Based in Montenegro's ethnic Albanian population (about 6% of the total), the DUA obtained representation in the 1996 and 1998 republican Assembly elections. In the April 2001 contest it obtained one of the five seats reserved for ethnic minorities and became part of the subsequent minority government headed by the →Democratic Party of Socialists of Montenegro, in which Gezim Hajdinaga was appointed Minister for the Protection of National and Ethnic Minorities.

Liberal Alliance of Montenegro
Liberalni Savez Crne Gore (LSCG)
Address. Milacica 101, 81000 Podgorica
Telephone. (+381–81) 624–213
Fax. (+381–81) 623–509
Email. lscginfo@crnagora.com
Website. www.lscg.crnagora.com
Leadership. Slavko Perović (leader); Miodrag Živković (deputy leader); Miroslav Vicković (spokesman); Vesna Perović (chairperson)
Strongly in favour of the withdrawal of Montenegro from the Yugoslav federation, the LSCG was founded in 1990 and gained third place in the December 1992 Montenegrin Assembly elections by winning 13 seats. The party contested the November 1996 elections within the People's Unity alliance with the →People's Party of Montenegro, which won 19 Montenegrin seats and eight in the federal lower house. Reverting to independent status for the next Montenegrin elections in May 1998, it won five seats on a platform of secession from the Yugoslav federation.

Following the defeat of the Milošević regime in Belgrade in late 2000, the LSCG contested the April 2001 Montenegrin Assembly elections outside the pro-independence alliance led by the →Democratic Party of Socialists of Montenegro (DPSCG), because it doubted that the DPSCG was deeply committed to separation. The narrowness of the result between the pro-independence and pro-federation sides left the LSCG, which won six seats from 7.9% of the vote, able to give the DPSCG-led bloc an overall majority. However, coalition talks foundered on the LSCG's demand for additional seats in the Assembly, whereupon the party pledged external support to a DPSCG-led minority government which promised to hold an independence referendum in March 2002. Under the agreement, Vesna Perović of the LSCG was elected Speaker of the new Assembly. By September 2001, however, the LSCG was in deep dispute with the government on the wording of the referendum question.

The LSCG is a member party of the Liberal International.

People's Party of Montenegro
Narodna Stranka Crne Gore (NSCG)
Address. c/o Skupština Crne Gore, Podgorica
Leadership. Novak Kilibarda (chairman)
Advocating the maintenance of federal ties with Serbia, the NSCG won 14 seats in the Montenegrin assembly elections and four seats in the federal Chamber of Citizens in 1992. In the 1996 elections an unlikely alliance between the NSCG and the pro-separation →Liberal Alliance of Montenegro

won 19 Montenegrin seats and eight in the federal lower house. For the May 1998 Montenegrin elections the NSCG was part of the victorious "For a Better Life" alliance headed by the →Democratic Party of Socialists of Montenegro (DPSCG) and including the →Social Democratic Party of Montenegro (SdPCG), winning seven seats itself and joining a three-party coalition government.

The NSCG withdrew from the Montenegrin government in late 2000 when its two coalition partners adopted a platform calling for Montenegro's relationship with Serbia to be redefined as a union of two independent states which should each receive international recognition. In early Montenegrin elections in April 2001 the NSCG was a component of the anti-separation bloc headed by the →Socialist People's Party of Montenegro (SNPCG), which was narrowly defeated by the pro-independence bloc led by the DPSCG.

Serbian People's Party of Montenegro
Srpska Narodna Partija Crne Gore (SNPCG)
Address. c/o Skupština Crne Gore, Podgorica
Leadership. Božidar Bojović (chairman)
The pan-Serbian SNPCG won two federal lower house seats in the disputed September 2000 elections, on a platform of opposition to the separation of Montenegro and Serbia. In the April 2001 Montenegrin Assembly elections it was part of the narrowly defeated anti-independence alliance headed by the →Socialist People's Party of Montenegro.

Social Democratic Party of Montenegro
Socijaldemokratska Partija Crne Gore (SdPCG)
Address. c/o Skupština Crne Gore, Podgorica
Leadership. Ranko Krivokapić (chairman)
The SdPCG was created in June 1993 from a merger of the Social Democratic Reform Party and the Socialist Party of Montenegro. Having won one federal lower house seat in 1996, the SdPCG contested the May 1998 Montenegrin Assembly elections in alliance principally with the →Democratic Party of Socialists of Montenegro (DPSCG), winning five seats and becoming a member of the subsequent republican government. In the April 2001 Montenegrin elections the party was part of the pro-independence "Victory for Montenegro" alliance headed by the DPSCG, whose narrow plurality resulted in the formation of a minority government in which then SdPCG chairman Žarko Rakočević became a Deputy Prime Minister and one other SdPCG minister was appointed. In view of his government participation, Rakočević was succeeded as party chairman by Ranko Krivokapić in October 2001.

The SdPCG is a consultative member of the Socialist International.

Socialist People's Party of Montenegro
Socijalistička Narodna Partija Crne Gore (SNPCG)
Address. c/o Skupština Crne Gore, Podgorica
Leadership. Predrag Bulatović (chairman)
The pro-federation SNPCG was launched in early 1998 by a breakaway faction of the →Democratic Party of Socialists of Montenegro (DPSCG) led by Momir Bulatović, following his narrow defeat by an anti-federation DPSCG candidate in Montenegrin presidential elections of October 1997. The SNPCG drew on substantial pro-federation opinion to take second place in the May 1998 Montenegrin Assembly elections, winning 29 of the 78 seats with 36% of the vote. Shortly before the elections, Momir Bulatović had been appointed federal Prime Minister by President Slobodan Milošević of the →Socialist Party of Serbia (SPS), charged with maintaining the federation at a time of national crisis over the status of Kosovo.

The SNPCG maintained its pro-federation stance in the September 2000 federal elections, in which Milošević and the SPS were defeated by the →Democratic Opposition of Serbia (DOS). The dubious official results of a contest boycotted by the DPSCG gave the SNPCG 28 of the 138 lower house seats, following which the new federal President, Vojislav Koštunica, appointed Zoran Žižić of the SNPCG as federal Prime Minister (in accordance with the rule that if the President was from Serbia the Prime Minister must be from Montenegro). The luckless Momir Bulatović was then ousted from the chairmanship of his new party, being succeeded in February 2001 by Predrag Bulatović (no relation), who was more aligned with the new government in Belgrade.

In early elections to the Montenegrin Assembly in April 2001 the SNPCG headed the "Together for Yugoslavia" pro-federation alliance (including the →People's Party of Montenegro and the →Serbian People's Party of Montenegro). The alliance lost very narrowly, winning 33 of the 77 seats with 40.6% of the vote, and therefore contended that the resultant minority DPSCG-led government had no mandate for independence. The results showed that the ousted Momir Bulatović had gained some revenge, in that his independent SNPCG list had taken 2.9% of the vote, thus depriving the official SNPCG-led alliance of a plurality.

Žižić resigned from the federal premiership in late June 2001 in protest against the Serbian government's decision to hand Milošević over to the war crimes tribunal at The Hague. He was succeeded in July by Dragiša Pešić, also of the SNPCG.

Zambia

Capital: Lusaka

Population: 9,580,000 (2000E)

After Zambia gained independence from the United Kingdom in 1964, the next 27 years of its political life were dominated by the republic's first President, Kenneth Kaunda, and the United National Independence Party (UNIP), which was declared the sole legal political organization in 1972. However, in September 1990, in line with developments in much of Africa at that time, the party agreed to the termination of its monopoly on power and to contest elections on a multi-party basis. Accordingly, a new democratic constitution was approved in August 1991, under which executive authority is vested in the President, who is elected by universal adult suffrage for a five-year term (once renewable) at the same time as elections to the 150-member National Assembly. The President appoints a Vice-President and a Cabinet from members of the National Assembly. The constitution also provides for a 27-member consultative House of Chiefs.

Multi-party presidential and legislative elections on Oct. 31, 1991, resulted in a clear victory for Frederick Chiluba and the Movement for Multi-Party Democracy (MMD) over Kaunda and the UNIP. In May 1996 the National Assembly approved a constitutional amendment requiring presidential candidates to be Zambian nationals of Zambian parentage. In protest at this amendment (which effectively prevented Kenneth Kaunda from standing as a candidate) and other electoral issues, the UNIP boycotted Zambia's 1996 elections, as did a number of other opposition parties. The presidential election of Nov. 18, 1996, was won by Chiluba with 72.5% of the vote in a five-way contest. Simultaneous National Assembly elections gave the MMD 131 seats; of the remaining seats, ten were won by independents and nine by candidates of small opposition parties (National Party 5, Agenda for Zambia 2, Zambia Democratic Congress 2). The Zambia Democratic Congress subsequently merged into the Zambia Alliance for Progress.

Agenda for Zambia (AZ)

Address. PO Box 50303, Lusaka
Leadership. Akashambatwa Lewanika (president)
The AZ was founded in 1996 by former members of the →National Party. In the November 1996 elections its candidate for the presidency won 4.6% of the vote; two AZ members were elected to the National Assembly. In 1999 the AZ agreed to join the →Zambia Alliance for Progress but reversed this decision when it became clear that such a move would necessitate the disbanding of the AZ as a separate party.

Movement for Multi-Party Democracy (MMD)

Address. Private Bag E365, Lusaka
Leadership. Frederick Chiluba (president); Michael Sata (secretary)
The MMD was formed in July 1990 as an informal alliance of groups opposed to the then ruling →United National Independence Party, and was granted legal recognition the following December. In February 1991 Frederick Chiluba, the head of the Zambian Congress of Trade Unions, was elected party president. In the elections held in October 1991 the MMD, having focused its campaign on UNIP's poor record of economic management, secured 125 seats in the National Assembly, an overwhelming majority. In the presidential poll Chiluba dislodged Kenneth Kaunda, winning just over 75% of the votes cast.

The MMD government's rigorous IMF-directed economic policies proved unpopular and caused increasing discord within the MMD, as evidenced by the emergence during 1992–93 of new opposition groups, including the →National Party (NP), following splits in the ruling party. Further tensions within the MMD led in July 1995 to the expulsion of the party treasurer (who announced the formation of the Zambia Democratic Congress and stood as that party's candidate in the 1996 presidential election, winning 12.5% of the vote compared with 72.5% for Chiluba). In the November 1996 Assembly elections (which were boycotted by UNIP and some of the other opposition parties) the MMD increased its representation to 131 seats. Criticism of Chiluba's record in office intensified during his second presidential term, which included major confrontations with public sector trade unions and widespread arrests of suspects during a five-month state of emergency following an abortive coup attempt in October 1997.

The internal politics of the MMD remained volatile amid much speculation that Chiluba would seek to amend the constitution in 2001 to allow him to stand for a third presidential term. In early May 2001, following a change in MMD party rules to permit the re-adoption of Chiluba as a presidential candidate, 22 prominent opponents of this move (including the Vice-President and eight other Cabinet ministers) were expelled from the MMD. This provoked major protests in the Assembly (where some MMD members called for the impeachment of Chiluba), street demonstrations by students and condemnation from influential churchmen and lawyers. Chiluba then stated that he would not seek a third term as President of Zambia, although he did wish to stay on as MMD party president after 2001.

The MMD is a member of the Democrat Union of Africa, a regional organization of the International Democrat Union.

National Party (NP)

Address. PO Box 32599, Lusaka

Leadership. Samuel Nyangu Chipungu
The National Party was founded in 1993 by dissident members of the ruling →Movement for Multi-Party Democracy (MMD). It won five seats in the November 1996 National Assembly elections. Its candidate came third, with 7% of the vote, in the 1996 presidential election.

United National Independence Party (UNIP)

Address. PO Box 30302, Lusaka
Telephone. (+260–1) 221197
Fax. (+260–1) 221327
Leadership. Tilyenji Kaunda (president); Mulondwe Muzungu (acting secretary-general)
Dating from 1958, the UNIP under Kenneth Kaunda ruled Zambia from independence in 1964 until 1991, for most of that period as the country's sole legal political organization. In the multi-party elections held in October 1991, Kaunda suffered a resounding defeat, taking only about 25% of the presidential vote, while UNIP candidates secured only 25 of the 150 National Assembly seats in the legislative elections. Kaunda resigned as party leader in January 1992, although he continued to take an active interest in political developments. In March 1993 the →Movement for Multi-Party Democracy government accused radical elements within UNIP of plotting a coup with foreign backing.

In June 1994 the UNIP joined six other parties in launching a Zambia Opposition Front. Also in mid-1994, Kaunda announced his intention to return to active politics, being elected UNIP president in June the following year. In October 1995 the government raised questions about Kaunda's nationality, since he had failed to register as a Zambian citizen at independence in 1964 and had retained citizenship of Malawi (his birthplace) until 1970. In May 1996 the constitution was amended to impose a citizenship qualification which effectively prevented Kaunda from standing again as a presidential candidate. UNIP boycotted Zambia's November 1996 presidential and legislative elections and did not resume electoral participation until 1998, when it won 15% of the seats in municipal elections. Kenneth Kaunda resigned as UNIP president in March 2000. His son, Tilyenji Kaunda (appointed secretary-general of the party in May 2000) became president of UNIP in April 2001.

United Party for National Development (UPND)

Address. PO Box 33199, Lusaka
Leadership. Anderson Mazoka
Formed in 1998 by a former senior business executive, the UPND enjoyed some success in municipal elections held at the end of that year. It subsequently fielded candidates at parliamentary by-elections, and had five seats in the National Assembly by September 2000.

Other Parties

Republican Party, launched in August 2000 by dissident members of the ruling →Movement for Multi-Party Democracy (MMD) following the expulsion from the MMD of Benjamin Mwila, a former minister who had publicly expressed an ambition to seek the MMD nomination for the presidency in 2001. In February 2001 the Republican Party announced its intention to merge with the →Zambia Alliance for Progress (ZAP), under the name Zambia Republican Party, before the 2001 elections.
Leadership. Benjamin Mwila

Social Democratic Party (SDP), launched in August 2000 by a former Zambian ambassador to Germany.
Leadership. Gwendoline Konie

Zambia Alliance for Progress (ZAP), founded in 1999 through the merger of several opposition parties, among which the Zambia Democratic Congress had won two seats

in the 1996 legislative elections and had fielded the runner-up in the 1996 presidential election (namely Dean Mung'omba, who received 12.5% of the vote). In February 2001 the ZAP announced its intention to merge with the →Republican Party, under the name Zambia Republican Party, before the 2001 elections in Zambia.
Leadership. Dean Mung'omba

Zimbabwe

Capital: Harare

Population: 11,342,500 (2000E)

The white minority regime in Rhodesia, which had declared unilateral independence from the United Kingdom in 1965, ended in 1979 with the adoption of the Lancaster House Agreement. The following year the country gained full independence as the Republic of Zimbabwe. It has since been ruled by the Zimbabwe African National Union-Patriotic Front (ZANU–PF).

An amendment in 1987 to the 1980 pre-independence constitution vested executive power in the President, who is both head of state and head of government, with a six-year mandate. Previously executive authority had been held by the Prime Minister. When the Lancaster House Agreement on the constitution expired in April 1990, the former bicameral legislature set up at independence was replaced by a single-chamber House of Assembly with a six-year term of office and 150 members (120 elective, 10 traditional chiefs, eight provincial governors appointed by the President and 12 other presidential appointees).

Robert Mugabe (ZANU–PF), who had been Prime Minister since independence, was elected President by the House of Assembly in December 1987. In March 1990 he was directly elected to the presidency for the first time, being re-elected for a second six-year term in March 1996 as the sole candidate. In legislative elections in April 1995 ZANU–PF won an overwhelming victory, taking all but two of the 120 elective seats. A proposed new constitution for Zimbabwe (the final drafting of which was overseen by ZANU–PF) was rejected in a national referendum held on Feb. 12-13, 2000. In legislative elections held on June 24–25, 2000, ZANU–PF won 62 of the elective seats with 48.6% of the vote, while the Movement for Democratic Change (MDC) won 57 seats with 47% of the vote. The remaining elective seat was won by the ZANU–*Ndonga* party. The June 2000 election results in 38 constituencies were challenged by the MDC, whose constitutional right to mount such a challenge was upheld by the Supreme Court in January 2001.

Movement for Democratic Change (MDC)
Address. 6th Floor, Robinson House, Angwa Street/Union Ave., Harare
Telephone. (+263–4) 781138
Email. support@mdc.co.zw
Website. www.mdczimbabwe.com
Leadership. Morgan Tsvangirai (president); Welshman Ncube (secretary-general)
The MDC was founded in September 1999 to offer a broad-based alternative to the →ZANU–PF party of President Mugabe, which the MDC accused of ruling in an increasingly oppressive manner since its overwhelming victory in the 1995 National Assembly elections. The MDC president, Morgan Tsvangirai (then secretary-general of the Zimbabwe Congress of Trade Unions) was part of a multi-ethnic leadership made up of academics, trade unionists, businessmen, churchmen and human rights activists. Politically centrist, the MDC favoured industrialization, privatization, dialogue with international agencies on Zimbabwe's economic situation, and strict adherence to the rule of law in the land redistribution process in Zimbabwe. The MDC contested all 120 elective seats in the June 2000 National Assembly elections and won 57 of them, receiving 47% of the recorded vote in what international observers agreed were far from satisfactory polling conditions. A total of 32 MDC supporters were killed during the election campaign, and Tsvangirai himself failed to be elected. The results in 38 constituencies were challenged by the MDC. By early June 2001 three results (including that in the constituency contested by Tsvangirai) had been annulled, while a further three seats had become vacant through deaths of sitting members. In early May 2001 Tsvangirai, facing prosecution for treason as a result of an anti-Mugabe speech at a political rally in

September 2000, mounted a legal challenge to the constitutionality of the pre-independence law under which he had been charged. He described the action against him as "politically motivated", with the aim of preventing him from standing as a candidate in the 2002 presidential election (which he would be barred from contesting if he received a sentence of more than six months' imprisonment).

Zimbabwe African National Union–Ndonga (ZANU-Ndonga)
Address. PO Box UA525, Union Avenue, Harare
Rev. Ndabaningi Sithole, the founding president of the Zimbabwe African National Union, broke away from that party in 1977 to form ZANU-*Ndonga*, which he led until his death in 2000. Right-wing in outlook and hostile to the ruling ZANU–PF party, ZANU-*Ndonga* was the only opposition party to gain parliamentary representation in the April 1995 elections, winning two House of Assembly seats with 6.5% of the vote. In October 1995 Sithole was arrested and charged with conspiracy to assassinate President Mugabe and overthrow the government. His conviction (handed down in 1997) was quashed on appeal. In December 1995 a Sithole lieutenant, Simon Mhlanga, was found guilty of undergoing illegal guerrilla training in Mozambique, the court finding that he was leader of the *Chimwenje* armed dissident movement. In January 1996 the Mozambique government ordered the expulsion of all *Chimwenje* members from its territory. ZANU-*Ndonga* won one seat in the June 2000 elections.

Zimbabwe African National Union-Patriotic Front (ZANU–PF)
Address. PO Box 4530, Harare

Telephone. (+263–4) 750516
Fax. (+263–4) 752389
Email. info@zanupf.net
Website. www.zanupf.net

Leadership. Robert Mugabe (president); Simon Muzenda (vice-president); Joseph Msika (vice-president)

Originally a black nationalist liberation movement, the party was founded in 1963 as the Zimbabwe African National Union (ZANU), a breakaway group from Joshua Nkomo's Zimbabwe African People's Union (ZAPU), which had itself been formed in 1961. In the mid-1970s ZAPU and ZANU organized military wings to conduct guerrilla operations against the white minority regime. In 1976 Mugabe and Nkomo agreed to set up the Patriotic Front alliance with the objective of achieving genuine black majority rule, although in practice ZANU and ZAPU remained separate organizations. The following year Rev. Ndabaningi Sithole broke away from the Mugabe faction of ZANU to form the →Zimbabwe African National Union–*Ndonga*.

In the pre-independence elections in 1980 (consequent upon the Lancaster House settlement) and in several subsequent elections, Mugabe's ZANU–PF won substantial parliamentary majorities, culminating in its securing 118 of the 120 elective House of Assembly seats in April 1995. In the first direct presidential election in 1990, Mugabe retained office with 78% of the votes cast. Nkomo's PF–ZAPU was formally incorporated into ZANU–PF in 1989. In 1991 Mugabe announced that he had abandoned plans to introduce a one-party state structure, and the party agreed to delete references to Marxism, Leninism and scientific socialism from its constitution.

Having been nominated as ZANU–PF's candidate in December 1995, Mugabe registered a somewhat hollow triumph in the presidential election of March 1996, the withdrawal of other candidates leaving him effectively unopposed. In a 32% turnout, he was credited with receiving 93% of the votes cast, the residue going to two names that had remained on ballot papers. In February 2000 the electorate rejected (on a 54.6% "no" vote) a proposed new constitution that would have increased the power of the President, weakened civil liberties and redistributed white-owned land. The government nevertheless introduced legislation (passed in April 2000) to amend the existing constitutional provisions on land ownership. Having legalized the compulsory transfer of white-owned land to landless blacks, the authorities made little effort to prevent or punish acts of violence and intimidation by pro-government "war veterans" who carried out forcible seizures of land. Known supporters of the recently formed →Movement för Democratic Change (MDC) were among the white farmers attacked (and in some cases killed) by war veterans and suspected ZANU–PF activists in the weeks preceding the June 2000 legislative elections, which also brought an upturn in attacks on black MDC organizers and supporters. Despite the physical danger facing campaigners in some parts of Zimbabwe, the MDC (with 47% of the vote and 57 seats) drastically reduced the ZANU–PF majority (to 48.6% of the vote and 62 seats) in an election that seemed to represent a significant turning point in Zimbabwe's post-independence politics.

Other Parties

Conservative Alliance of Zimbabwe (CAZ), the name adopted in 1984 by a party founded in 1962 as the Rhodesian Front (a coalition of right-wing white parties) and known from 1981 as the Republican Front. As the Rhodesian Front, it was the party responsible for the 1965 unilateral declaration of independence and the subsequent period of white minority rule. As the CAZ, it ended its whites-only membership policy. With the abolition of reserved white seats in 1987 the CAZ ceased to be represented in the legislature.

United Parties (UP), established in 1994 by Bishop Abel Muzorewa, who had briefly been Prime Minister prior to independence. Having boycotted the April 1995 House of Assembly elections, Muzorewa announced his withdrawal from the 1996 presidential election on the grounds that the contest was unfairly weighted in favour of the ruling →Zimbabwe African National Union–Patriotic Front. The UP is unrepresented in the legislature elected in 2000.

APPENDIX A: INTERNATIONAL PARTY ORGANIZATIONS

Christian Democrat International

The Christian Democrat International (CDI) was established at a conference in Quito (Ecuador) in November 1982, as successor to the Christian Democratic World Union founded in 1961, with the aim of expanding international co-operation between Christian democratic parties and promoting the formation of new parties. CDI affiliates in European Union and EU candidate countries are members or associate members of the European People's Party (EPP), which provides the first part of the name of the European Parliament group in which MEPs from these parties and some others sit (see Appendix B). Latin American and Caribbean member parties are grouped in the regional Christian Democratic Organization of America (ODCA), which dates from 1949.

Address. 67 rue d'Arlon, 1047 Brussels, Belgium
Telephone. (+32–2) 285–4145
Fax. (+32–2) 285–4166
Email. idc@idc–cdi.org
Website. www.idc–cdi.org
Leadership. Wilfried Martens (president); Alejandro Agag Longo (executive secretary)

Affiliated Parties

Albania	Christian Democratic Party of Albania
Argentina	Christian Democratic Party of Argentina
Argentina	Justicialist Party
Austria	Austrian People's Party
Belarus	Belarusan Popular Front–Renaissance
Belarus	Christian Democratic Party of Belarus*
Belgium	Christian People's Party
Belgium	Christian Social Party
Bolivia	Christian Democratic Party
Bosnia & Hercegovina	New Croatian Initiative
Brazil	Brazilian Social Democratic Party†
Brazil	Liberal Front Party
Brazil	National Solidarity Party of Brazil†
Bulgaria	Bulgarian Agrarian People's Union*
Bulgaria	Democratic Party*
Bulgaria	Union of Democratic Forces
Cameroon	Democratic Progressive Party of Cameroon*
Chile	Christian Democratic Party
Colombia	Conservative Party of Colombia
Congo	Movement for Democracy and Solidarity
Congo, Dem. Rep. of	Democratic and Social Christian Party
Costa Rica	Social Christian Unity Party
Cuba	Christian Democratic Party
Cyprus	Democratic Rally
Czech Republic	Christian Democratic Union–Czechoslovak People's Party
Denmark	Christian People's Party
Dominican Republic	Social Christian Reformist Party
Ecuador	Popular Democracy–Christian Democratic Union
El Salvador	Christian Democratic Party
El Salvador	Social Christian Union
Equatorial Guinea	Popular Union*
Equatorial Guinea	Progress Party of Equatorial Guinea
Estonia	Fatherland Union
France	New Union for French Democracy
Georgia	Christian Democratic Union of Georgia
Georgia	National Democratic Alliance
Georgia	People's Party
Greece	New Democracy
Guatemala	Guatemalan Christian Democratic Party

Haiti	Progressive Democratic and National Rally
Honduras	Christian Democratic Party of Honduras
Honduras	National Party of Honduras
Hungary	Hungarian Democratic Forum
Indonesia	Christian Catholic Indonesia
Ireland	*Fine Gael*
Italy	Christian Democratic Centre
Italy	Italian Popular Party
Italy	United Christian Democrats
Lebanon	Lebanese Christian Democratic Union
Lithuania	Lithuanian Christian Democrats
Luxembourg	Christian Social People's Party
Malta	Nationalist Party
Mauritius	Democratic Union of Mauritius
Mexico	National Action Party
Moldova	Christian Democratic People's Party
Mozambique	Mozambique National Resistance (RENAMO)
Netherlands	Christian Democratic Appeal
Netherlands: Aruba	Aruban People's Party
Netherlands Antilles	Bonaire Patriotic Union
Netherlands Antilles	National People's Party
Netherlands Antilles	Windward Islands People's Movement
Nicaragua	Christian Social Union Party
Norway	Christian People's Party
Panama	Christian Democratic Party
Paraguay	Christian Democratic Party
Peru	Christian Democratic Union
Philippines	People's Struggle (*Lakas*)
Portugal	Social Democratic Party
Romania	Christian Democratic National Peasants' Party
Romania	Hungarian Democratic Union of Romania*
Russia	Christian Democratic Union–Christians of Russia
San Marino	Christian Democratic Party of San Marino
Slovakia	Christian Democratic Movement*
Slovakia	Hungarian Coalition Party*
Slovenia	New Slovenia–Christian People's Party
Spain	Democratic Union of Catalonia
Spain	Popular Party
Suriname	Progressive People's Party of Suriname
Sweden	Christian Democratic Community Party
Switzerland	Christian People's Party of Switzerland
Switzerland	Evangelical People's Party
Trinidad & Tobago	United National Congress
Uganda	Democratic Party
Ukraine	Christian Popular Union Party*
Uruguay	Christian Democratic Party
Venezuela	Christian Social Party
Yugoslavia	Christian Democratic Party of Serbia*
Yugoslavia	Democratic League of Kosovo
Yugoslavia	Kosovo Christian Democratic Party

*Observer member of CDI
†Observer member of ODCA

European Federation of Green Parties

A European Greens organization was first established in January 1984, on the basis of earlier policy co-ordination between such parties. As membership and Green electoral strength grew in the late 1980s and early 1990s, the challenges of European Union integration and the collapse of communism in Eastern Europe stimulated demands for a more sophisticated European-wide Green structure. The outcome was the foundation of the European Federation of Green Parties (EFGP) at a conference in Helsinki in June 1993.
Address. EP–PHS 2C85, Rue Wiertz, 1047 Brussels, Belgium
Telephone. (+32–2) 284–5135

Fax. (+32–2) 284–9135
Email. efgp@europarl.eu.int
Website. www.europeangreens.org
Leadership. Marian Coyne & Pekka Haavisto (spokespersons); Arnold Cassola (secretary-general)

Member Parties

Austria	The Greens–Green Alternative
Belgium	Ecologist Party
Belgium	Live Differently
Bulgaria	Green Party
Czech Republic	Green Party
Cyprus	Cyprus Green Party
Denmark	Green Party
Estonia	Estonian Greens
Finland	Green Union
France	The Greens
Georgia	Georgia Greens
Germany	Alliance 90/The Greens
Greece	Green Party
Hungary	Green Alternative
Ireland	Green Party
Italy	Green Federation
Latvia	Latvian Green Party
Luxembourg	The Greens
Malta	Democratic Alternative
Netherlands	Green Left
Netherlands	The Greens
Norway	Green Party of Norway
Portugal	Ecologist Party The Greens
Romania	Ecologist Federation of Romania
Russia	Inter-regional Green Party
Slovakia	Green Party in Slovakia
Spain	The Greens
Switzerland	Green Party–Greens
Ukraine	Green Party of Ukraine
United Kingdom	Green Party of England and Wales
United Kingdom	Scottish Green Party

International Democrat Union

The *International Democrat Union (IDU)* was established in London in June 1983 with the aim of promoting co-operation between conservative and centre-right parties. The IDU currently embraces five regional unions, namely the Americas Democrat Union (ADU), the Asia-Pacific Democrat Union (APDU), the Caribbean Democrat Union (CDU), the Democrat Union of Africa/African Dialogue Group (DUA/ADG) and the European Democrat Union (EDU). Parties can be members of regional unions without being members of the IDU itself. For ease of reference, IDU members and regional union members are all listed below by alphabetical order of country, those with regional union membership only being identified by the appropriate abbreviation in parentheses.

Address. 32 Smith Square, London, SW1P 3HH, UK
Telephone. (+44–20) 7984–8052
Fax. (+44–20) 7976–0486
Email. rnormington@idu.org
Website. www.idu.org
Leadership. William Hague (chairman); Richard Normington (executive secretary)

Affiliated and Associated Parties

Albania	Democratic Party of Albania (EDU)
Angola	National Democratic Union of Angola (DUA/ADG)
Argentina	Justicialist Party
Australia	Liberal Party of Australia

Austria	Austrian People's Party
Azerbaijan	Azerbaijan National Independence Party
Belarus	United Civic Party of Belarus (EDU)
Belize	United Democratic Party (CDU)
Bolivia	Nationalist Democratic Action*
Botswana	Botswana Democratic Party (DUA/ADG)
Bulgaria	Democratic Party (EDU)
Bulgaria	Union of Democratic Forces
Bulgaria	United Christian Democratic Centre (EDU)
Canada	Progressive Conservative Party
Chile	National Renewal (ADU)
Chile	New Democratic Force (ADU)
Colombia	Conservative Party of Colombia
Congo, Dem. Rep. of	Union for Democracy and Social Progress (DUA/ADG)
Côte d'Ivoire	Democratic Party of Côte d'Ivoire (DUA/ADG)
Cyprus	Democratic Rally
Czech Republic	Civic Democratic Alliance (EDU)
Czech Republic	Civic Democratic Party
Denmark	Conservative People's Party
Denmark: Faroe Islands	People's Party (EDU)
Dominica	Dominica Freedom Party (CDU)
Dominican Republic	Social Christian Reformist Party
El Salvador	Nationalist Republican Alliance
Estonia	Fatherland Union
Finland	National Coalition
France	Rally for the Republic
Gabon	Rally of Woodcutters (DUA/ADG)
Gambia	United Democratic Party (DUA/ADG)
Germany	Christian Democratic Union
Germany	Christian Social Union
Ghana	New Patriotic Party (DUA/ADG)
Greece	New Democracy
Grenada	New National Party*
Guatemala	National Advancement Party
Honduras	National Party of Honduras
Hungary	Federation of Young Democrats–Hungarian Civic Party (EDU)
Hungary	Hungarian Democratic Forum (EDU)
Hungary	Independent Party of Smallholders, Agrarian Workers and Citizens (EDU)
Iceland	Independence Party (EDU)
Italy	*Forza Italia* (EDU)
Italy	South Tyrol People's Party (EDU)
Italy	United Christian Democrats (EDU)
Jamaica	Jamaica Labour Party (CDU)
Kenya	Democratic Party (DUA/ADG)
Korea, South	Grand National Party
Lesotho	Basotho National Party (DUA/ADG)
Liechtenstein	Fatherland Union (EDU)
Liechtenstein	Progressive Citizens' Party in Liechtenstein (EDU)
Lithuania	Homeland Union–Lithuanian Conservatives (EDU)
Luxembourg	Christian Social People's Party (EDU)
Macedonia	Democratic Party of Albanians (EDU)
Macedonia	Internal Macedonian Revolutionary Organization–Democratic Party for Macedonian National Unity (EDU)
Malawi	Malawi Congress Party (DUA/ADG)
Malta	Nationalist Party*
Mongolia	Democratic Party*
Mozambique	Mozambique National Resistance (DUA/ADG)
Namibia	Democratic Turnhalle Alliance of Namibia*
New Zealand	New Zealand National Party
Nicaragua	National Conservative Party (ADU)
Norway	Conservative Party
Poland	Freedom Union (EDU)
Portugal	Social Democratic Party
Romania	Christian Democratic National Peasants' Party (EDU)
Romania	Hungarian Democratic Union of Romania (EDU)
Russia	Union of Rightist Forces
St Christopher & Nevis	Nevis Reformation Party (CDU)

St Christopher & Nevis	People's Action Movement*
St Lucia	United Workers' Party (CDU)
St Vincent & Grenadines	New Democratic Party*
Seychelles	Democratic Party (DUA/ADG)
Slovakia	Christian Democratic Movement (EDU)
Slovakia	Hungarian Coalition Party (EDU)
Slovenia	Slovenian People's Party (EDU)
South Africa	New National Party*
Spain	Popular Party
Sri Lanka	United National Party
Sweden	Moderate Party
Switzerland	Christian Democratic People's Party of Switzerland (EDU)
Taiwan	Nationalist Party (*Kuomintang*)
Tanzania	Party for Democracy and Development (DUA/ADG)
Turkey	Motherland Party (EDU)
Turkey	True Path Party (EDU)
Uganda	Democratic Party (DUA/ADG)
United Kingdom	Conservative and Unionist Party
UK: Anguilla	Anguilla National Alliance (CDU)
UK: Montserrat	People's Liberation Movement (CDU)
United States	Republican Party
Zambia	Movement for Multi-Party Democracy (DUA/ADG)

*Associate member of IDU

Liberal International

The Liberal International (LI) was established in its present form at a conference held in Oxford (England) in April 1947 but traces its origins back to pre-war international co-operation between Liberal parties. LI membership increased only slowly for four decades, but accelerated sharply following the end of communist rule in Eastern Europe and the formation or re-emergence of many liberal parties. LI affiliates in Europe are members of the European Liberals, Reformists and Democrats (ELDR) organization, which gives its name to the European Parliament group in which MEPs from these parties and some others sit (see Appendix B).

Address. 1 Whitehall Place, London, SW1A 2HD, UK
Telephone. (+44–20) 7839–5905
Fax. (+44–20) 7925–2685
Email. all@liberal–international.org
Website. www.liberal–international.org
Leadership. Annemie Neyts-Uyttebroeck (president); Jan Weijers (secretary-general)

Affiliated Parties

Andorra	Liberal Party of Andorra
Angola	Liberal Democratic Party
Austria	Liberal Forum
Belgium	Flemish Liberals and Democrats–Citizens' Party
Belgium	Liberal Reformist Party
Bosnia & Hercegovina	Liberal Democratic Party*
Bulgaria	Radical Democratic Party*
Canada	Liberal Party of Canada
Croatia	Croatian Social Liberal Party
Croatia	Liberal Party
Cuba	Cuban Liberal Union
Cuba	Democratic Solidarity Party*
Cuba	Liberal Democratic Party*
Denmark	Liberal Party
Denmark	Radical Liberal Party
Dominican Republic	Liberal Party for Restructuring
Ecuador	Movement of Ecuadorian Forces*
Equatorial Guinea	Democratic National Union
Estonia	Estonian Coalition Party
Estonia	Estonian Reform Party

Finland	Centre Party of Finland
Finland	Liberal People's Party
Finland	Swedish People's Party
Germany	Free Democratic Party–The Liberals
Honduras	Liberal Party of Honduras
Hungary	Alliance of Free Democrats
Iceland	Progressive Party
Israel	*Shinui*
Italy	Federation of Liberals/Liberal Party*
Japan	Liberal Party*
Latvia	Latvia's Way
Lithuania	Lithuanian Centre Union*
Lithuania	Lithuanian Liberal Union
Luxembourg	Democratic Party
Macedonia	Liberal Democratic Party
Malawi	United Democratic Front
Netherlands	Democrats 66
Netherlands	People's Party for Freedom and Democracy
Nicaragua	Constitutional Liberal Party
Norway	Liberal Party (*Venstre*)
Panama	National Liberal Party*
Paraguay	Authentic Radical Liberal Party
Philippines	Liberal Party
Romania	National Liberal Party
Russia	*Yabloko**
Senegal	Senegalese Democratic Party
Seychelles	Seychelles National Party*
Slovakia	Democratic Union of Slovakia
Slovakia	Coexistence (Hungarian Coalition Party)
Slovenia	Liberal Democracy of Slovenia
South Africa	Democratic Party
Spain	Democratic and Social Centre
Spain	Liberty and Democracy
Spain	Majorca Union*
Sri Lanka	Liberal Party
Sweden	Liberal People's Party
Switzerland	Radical Democratic Party of Switzerland
Switzerland	Liberal Party of Switzerland
Taiwan	Democratic Progress Party*
Tanzania	Civic United Front*
Tanzania	United Democratic Party*
Tunisia	Liberal Social Party*
Turkey	Liberal Democratic Party*
Ukraine	Liberal Party of Ukraine*
United Kingdom	Liberal Democrats
UK: N. Ireland	Alliance Party
UK: Gibraltar	Liberal Party
Yugoslavia	Liberal Alliance of Montenegro
Yugoslavia	Liberal Party of Kosovo*

*Observer member

Socialist International

The present-day Socialist International (SI) dates from 1951 but traces its origins back to the First International (1864–76) and more particularly to the Second International founded in Paris in 1889. Seriously weakened by the outbreak of World War I in 1914, the Second International was irrevocably split by the formation of the Third (Communist) International, or Comintern, in 1919. Four years later, in 1923, the socialist parties which rejected the Soviet revolutionary model established the Labour and Socialist International (LSI), which itself finally collapsed in 1940 when German forces occupied Brussels, where its secretariat was located.

After World War II efforts spearheaded by the British Labour Party to revive a democratic socialist world organization culminated in the foundation of the Socialist International (SI) at a congress held in Frankfurt

(Germany) in mid-1951. Originally consisting mainly of European parties, the SI steadily expanded its membership in the Third World, notably after the relaunching of the organization in 1976 under the presidency of Willy Brandt (Social Democratic Party of Germany). A further influx of new members followed the collapse of communism in Europe in 1989–91, many of the new entrants being democratic socialist successors to the former ruling communist parties. In 1992 Brandt was succeeded as SI president by Pierre Mauroy (Socialist Party of France), who was in turn succeeded by António Gutteres (Socialist Party of Portugal) at the SI's 21st congress held in Paris in November 1999. SI affiliates in Europe are members of the Party of European Socialists (PES), which gives its name to the European Parliament group in which MEPs from these parties and some others sit (see Appendix B).

Address. Maritime House, Old Town, London SW4 OJW, UK

Telephone. (+44–20) 7627–4449

Fax. (+44–20) 7720–4448

Email. secretariat@socialistinternational.org

Website. www.socialistinternational.org

Leadership. António Gutteres (president); Luis Ayala (secretary-general)

Affiliated Parties

Albania	Social Democratic Party
Albania	Socialist Party of Albania*
Algeria	Socialist Forces Front
Andorra	Social Democratic Party*
Angola	Popular Movement for the Liberation of Angola†
Argentina	Popular Socialist Party
Argentina	Radical Civic Union
Armenia	Armenian Revolutionary Federation (*Dashnak*)*
Australia	Australian Labor Party
Austria	Social Democratic Party of Austria
Azerbaijan	Social Democratic Party†
Barbados	Barbados Labour Party
Belarus	Belarusan Social Democratic Party†
Belgium	Socialist Party (PS)
Belgium	Socialist Party (SP)
Benin	Social Democratic Party*
Bolivia	Movement of the Revolutionary Left
Bosnia & Hercegovina	Social Democratic Party of Bosnia & Hercegovina
Botswana	Botswana National Front†
Brazil	Democratic Labour Party
Bulgaria	Bulgarian Social Democratic Party
Bulgaria	Euro-Left Coalition†
Burkina Faso	Party for Democracy and Progress
Cameroon	Social Democratic Front
Canada	New Democratic Party
Cape Verde	African Party for the Independence of Cape Verde
Central African Rep.	Patriotic Front for Progress
Chile	Party for Democracy
Chile	Radical Social Democratic Party
Chile	Socialist Party of Chile
Colombia	Democratic Alliance–April 19 Movement*
Colombia	Liberal Party of Colombia
Costa Rica	National Liberation Party
Côte d'Ivoire	Ivorian Popular Front
Croatia	Social Democratic Party of Croatia
Cyprus	Movement of Social Democrats
Czech Republic	Czech Social Democratic Party
Denmark	Social Democratic Party
Denmark: Greenland	Forward (*Siumut*)*
Dominica	Dominica Labour Party*
Dominican Republic	Dominican Revolutionary Party
Ecuador	Democratic Left
Egypt	National Democratic Party
El Salvador	Democratic Party†
Equatorial Guinea	Social Democratic Convergence
Estonia	Moderates
Fiji	Fiji Labour Party*
Finland	Finnish Social Democratic Party

France	Socialist Party
Gabon	Gabonese Progress Party*
Georgia	Citizens' Union of Georgia‡
Germany	Social Democratic Party of Germany
Greece	Pan-Hellenic Socialist Movement
Guinea	Rally of the Guinean People*
Guyana	Working People's Alliance*
Haiti	Organization of Struggling People†
Haiti	Party of the National Congress of Democratic Movements
Haiti	Revolutionary Progressive Nationalist Party
Hungary	Hungarian Social Democratic Party
Hungary	Hungarian Socialist Party
Iceland	Social Democratic Alliance
India	Janata Dal‡
Iran	Democratic Party of Iranian Kurdistan‡
Ireland	Labour Party
Israel	Israel Labour Party
Israel	Meretz
Italy	Democrats of the Left
Italy	Italian Democratic Socialists
Jamaica	People's National Party
Japan	Social Democratic Party of Japan
Latvia	Latvian Social Democratic Workers' Party
Lebanon	Progressive Socialist Party
Lithuania	Lithuanian Social Democratic Party
Luxembourg	Luxembourg Socialist Workers' Party
Macedonia	Social Democratic Union of Macedonia‡
Malaysia	Democratic Action Party
Mali	Alliance for Democracy in Mali
Malta	Malta Labour Party
Mauritius	Labour Party
Mauritius	Mauritian Militant Movement†
Mexico	Institutional Revolutionary Party†
Mexico	Party of the Democratic Revolution
Moldova	Social Democratic Party of Moldova‡
Mongolia	Mongolian People's Revolutionary Party‡
Morocco	Socialist Union of Popular Forces
Mozambique	Front for the Liberation of Mozambique
Nepal	Nepali Congress Party
Netherlands	Labour Party
Netherlands: Aruba	People's Electoral Movement
Netherlands Antilles	New Antilles Movement
New Zealand	New Zealand Labour Party
Nicaragua	Sandinista National Liberation Front
Niger	Niger Party for Democracy and Socialism†
Norway	Norwegian Labour Party
Pakistan	Pakistan People's Party†
Palestinian Entity	Al-Fatah*
Panama	Democratic Revolutionary Party*
Paraguay	Febrerista Revolutionary Party
Peru	Peruvian Aprista Party
Philippines	Philippines Democratic Socialist Party
Poland	Democratic Left Alliance
Portugal	Socialist Party
Romania	Democratic Party
Romania	Social Democratic Party‡
St Christopher & Nevis	St Kitts–Nevis Labour Party*
St Lucia	St Lucia Labour Party*
St Vincent & Grenadines	Unity Labour Party*
San Marino	Socialist Party of San Marino
Senegal	Senegal Socialist Party
Slovakia	Party of the Democratic Left
Slovakia	Social Democratic Party of Slovakia
Slovenia	United List of Social Democrats
South Africa	African National Congress
Spain	Spanish Socialist Workers' Party
Sweden	Swedish Social Democratic Labour Party

Switzerland	Social Democratic Party of Switzerland	
Togo	Democratic Convention of African Peoples*	
Tunisia	Democratic Constitutional Rally	
Tunisia	Popular Unity Movement*	
Turkey	Republican People's Party	
United Kingdom	Labour Party	
UK: Northern Ireland	Social Democratic and Labour Party	
United States	Democratic Socialists of America	
United States	Social Democrats USA	
USA: Puerto Rico	Puerto Rican Independence Party	
Uruguay	New Space*	
Uruguay	Uruguayan Socialist Party	
Venezuela	Democratic Action	
Yugoslavia	Social Democratic Party of Montenegro*	

*Consultative member
†Observer member
‡Permanent guest

APPENDIX B: EUROPEAN PARLIAMENT PARTY GROUPS

Covered below are the party groups established in the 625-member European Parliament as a result of the direct elections held in the 15 European Union (EU) member states in June 1999, showing the composition of the groups as at early November 2001. For ease of cross-reference, the party names shown in the tables correspond to the English versions used in the country sections of the present volume. It should be noted that in some cases the party name changed after the June 1999 European elections, while in others the list title used in the elections was not the same as the official party name.

European People's Party–European Democrats (EPP/ED)

The EPP/ED group dates from June 1953 and was called the Christian Democratic Group until 1979. The original Christian democratic core has been diluted in recent years by the sometimes controversial adhesion of other centre-right parties, notably the British and Scandinavian Conservatives and *Forza Italia*. The group has provided over half of the presidents of the Parliament, including the two most recent, José Maria Gil-Robles of Spain (1994–99) and the present incumbent, Nicole Fontaine of France. The 1999 elections resulted in the EPP/ED group becoming substantially the largest in the European Parliament (for the first time since 1975), with members from every EU country, representing a total of 33 political parties and movements.
Address. European Parliament, Rue Wiertz, B-1047 Brussels, Belgium
Telephone. (+32–2) 284–2111
Fax. (+32–2) 230–9793
Email. epp-ed@europarl.eu.int
Website. www.europarl.eu.int/ppe
Leadership. Hans-Gert Pöttering (chairman); Klaus Welle (secretary-general)

Austria	Austrian People's Party	7
Belgium	Christian People's Party	3
Belgium	Christian Social Party	1
Belgium	Citizens' Movement for Change	1
Belgium	Christian Social Party	1
Denmark	Conservative People's Party	1
Finland	National Coalition	4
Finland	Swedish People's Party	1
France	New Union for French Democracy	9
France	Rally for the Republic	6
France	Liberal Democracy	4
France	Civil Society	1
France	Ecology Generation	1
Germany	Christian Democratic Union	43
Germany	Christian Social Union	10
Greece	New Democracy	9
Ireland	*Fine Gael*	4
Ireland	Rosemary Scallon (Dana) (ind.)	1

Italy	*Forza Italia*	22
Italy	Italian Popular Party	4
Italy	Christian Democratic Centre	2
Italy	United Christian Democrats	2
Italy	Democratic Union for the Republic	1
Italy	Italian Renewal	1
Italy	Pensioners' Party	1
Italy	South Tyrol People's Party	1
Luxembourg	Christian Social People's Party	2
Netherlands	Christian Democratic Appeal	9
Portugal	Social Democratic Party	9
Spain	Popular Party	27
Spain	Democratic Union of Catalonia	1
Sweden	Moderate Party	5
Sweden	Christian Democratic Community Party	2
United Kingdom	Conservative and Unionist Party	35
UK: Northern Ireland	Ulster Unionist Party (UUP)	1

Total 232

Party of European Socialists (PES)

The PES group dates from June 1953 and was known as the Socialist Group until the formation of the PES in 1993 as a supranational grouping of the European member parties of the Socialist International. The Socialists were the largest group in the European Parliament from the first direct elections in 1979 until 1999, when the collapse of the representation of the British Labour Party (from 62 to 29 members) was the main reason for its relegation to the status of second largest group.

Address. European Parliament, Rue Wiertz, B-1047 Brussels, Belgium
Telephone. (+32–2) 284–2111
Fax. (+32–2) 230–6664
Email. pesnet@europarl.eu.int
Website. www.europarl.eu.int/pes
Leadership. Enrique Baron Crespo (chairman); Christine Verger (secretary-general)

Austria	Social Democratic Party of Austria	7
Belgium	Socialist Party (PS)	3
Belgium	Socialist Party (SP)	2
Denmark	Social Democratic Party	3
Finland	Finnish Social Democratic Party	3
France	Socialist Party	18
France	Left Radical Party	2
France	Citizens' Movement	2
Germany	Social Democratic Party of German	33
Germany	Alliance 90–The Greens	2
Greece	Pan-Hellenic Socialist Movement	9
Ireland	Labour Party	1
Italy	Democrats of the Left	14
Italy	Italian Democratic Socialists	2
Luxembourg	Luxembourg Socialist Workers' Part	2
Netherlands	Labour Party	6
Portugal	Socialist Party	12
Spain	Spanish Socialist Workers' Party	22
Spain	Democratic Party of the New Left	2
Sweden	Social Democratic Labour Party	6
United Kingdom	Labour Party	29
UK: Northern Ireland	Social Democratic and Labour Party	1

Total 181

European Liberal, Democratic and Reformist Group (ELDR)

The ELDR group dates from the foundation in 1953 of the Liberal Group, which became the Liberal and Democratic Group in 1976 and the ELDR group in 1986. Its size as the third largest European Parliament group has remained relatively stable in recent years, although in the 1999 elections the number of EU countries represented in it fell from 13 to 10.

Address. European Parliament, Rue Wiertz, B-1047 Brussels, Belgium
Telephone. (+32–2) 284–3169
Fax. (+32–2) 231–1907

Email. eldrparty@europarl.eu.int
Website. www.eurolib.org/eldrparty
Leadership. Pat Cox (chairman); Bo Manderup Jensen (secretary-general)

Belgium	Flemish Liberals and Democrats	3
Belgium	Liberal Reformist Party/Democratic Front of French-Speakers	2
Denmark	Liberal Party	5
Denmark	Radical Liberal Party	1
Finland	Centre Party of Finland	4
Finland	Swedish People's Party	1
Ireland	Pat Cox (ind.)	1
Italy	Democrats for the New Olive Tree	6
Italy	Italian Republican Party	1
Italy	Marco Formentini (ind.)	1
Luxembourg	Democratic Party	1
Netherlands	People's Party for Freedom and Democracy	6
Netherlands	Democrats 66	2
Spain	Democratic Convergence of Catalonia	2
Spain	Canarian Coalition	1
Sweden	Centre Party	1
Sweden	Liberal People's Party	3
United Kingdom	Liberal Democrats	10

Total 51

Greens/European Free Alliance (G/EFA)

The Greens first founded a European Parliament group after the 1989 elections but remained relatively small until more than doubling its size in the 1999 elections, thanks in part to the adhesion of regionalist parties of the European Free Alliance (EFA). The combined Greens/EFA group includes representatives from 12 of the 15 EU countries.
Address. European Parliament, LEO 2C, Rue Wiertz, B-1047 Brussels, Belgium
Telephone. (+32–2) 284–3045
Fax. (+32–2) 230–7837
Email. jkutten@europarl.eu.int
Website. www.europarl.eu.int/greens
Leadership. Heidi Hautala & Paul Lannoye (co-chairpersons); Juan Behrend & Vula Tsetsi (co-secretaries-general)

Austria	The Greens	2
Belgium	Ecologist Party (ECOLO)	3
Belgium	Live Differently (AGALEV)	2
Belgium	People's Union/Complete Democracy for the 21st Century	2
Finland	Green Union	2
France	The Greens	9
Germany	Alliance 90–The Greens	4
Ireland	Green Party	2
Italy	Green Federation	2
Luxembourg	The Green Alternative	1
Netherlands	Green Left	4
Spain	Andalusian Party	1
Spain	Basque Solidarity	1
Spain	Basque Nationalist Party	1
Spain	Galician Nationalist Bloc	1
Sweden	Green Ecology Party	2
United Kingdom	Green Party	2
UK: Scotland	Scottish National Party (SNP)	2
UK: Wales	*Plaid Cymru*–The Party of Wales	2

Total 45

European United Left/Nordic Green Left (GUE/NGL)

The GUE/NGL group dates from the formation of the Communist and Allies Group in October 1973 and has gone through many complex changes, as ex-Communist parties embraced democratic socialism and in some cases joined the Party of European Socialists. The GUE title was adopted after the 1994 European elections, the suffix "Nordic Green Left" being added on the accession of leftist parties from Finland and Sweden following EU enlargement in 1995. The 1999 elections produced an overall advance for the group, which now has member parties from 10 EU countries.

Address. European Parliament, Rue Wiertz 45, B-1047 Brussels, Belgium
Telephone. (+32–2) 284–2683
Fax. (+32–2) 230–5582
Email. guewebmaster@europarl.eu.int
Website. www.europarl.eu.int/grue
Leadership. Francis Wurtz (chairman); Maria d'Alimonte (secretary-general)

Denmark	Socialist People's Party	1
Finland	Left Alliance	1
France	French Communist Party	6
France	Workers' Struggle/Revolutionary Communist League	5
Germany	Party of Democratic Socialism	6
Germany	Alliance 90–The Greens	1
Greece	Communist Party of Greece	3
Greece	Coalition of the Left and Progress	2
Greece	Democratic Social Movement	2
Italy	Communist Refoundation Party	4
Italy	Party of Italian Communists	2
Netherlands	Socialist Party	1
Portugal	Portuguese Communist Party	2
Spain	United Left	4
Sweden	Left Party	3
	Total	43

Union for a Europe of Nations (UEN)

The UEN group was formed after the June 1999 European elections as an expansion of earlier groupings with reservations about further European integration, although the French Gaullist Rally for the Republic switched to the European People's Party/European Democrats and was replaced by the more electorally successful and Eurosceptic Rally for France and the Independence of Europe (RPF–IE), whose leader, Charles Pasqua, became chairman of the group. Divisions within the RPF–IE subsequently resulted in nine of its 12 MEPs defecting from the UEN group, three joining the Europe of Democracies and Diversities (EDD) group and six opting to sit as Non-Attached Members. A split in the UK Independence Party in April 2000 resulted in one of its three MEPs leaving the UEN to become non-attached.
Address. European Parliament, Rue Wiertz, B-1047 Brussels, Belgium
Telephone. (+32–2) 284–2111
Fax. (+32–2) 230–9793
Email. fwurtz@europarl.eu.int
Website. www.europarl.eu.int/groups
Leadership. Charles Pasqua (chairman); Frank Barrett (secretary-general)

Denmark	Danish People's Party	1
France	Rally for France and the Independence of Europe	3
Ireland	*Fianna Fáil*	6
Italy	National Alliance/Segni Pact	10
Portugal	Popular Party	2
	Total	22

Europe of Democracies and Diversities (EDD)

The EDD is a new group consisting of parties from four EU countries that are highly critical of the EU and further European integration. The 1999 European elections yielded notable gains for such parties in France and the UK.
Address. European Parliament, Rue Wiertz, B-1047 Brussels, Belgium
Telephone. (+32–2) 284–2111
Fax. (+32–2) 230–9793
Email. jpbonde@europarl.eu.int
Website. http://www.europarl.eu.int/groups
Leadership. Jens-Peter Bonde (acting chairman); Claudine Vangrunderbeeck (secretary-general)

Denmark	June Movement	3
Denmark	People's Movement against the European Union	1
France	Hunting, Fishing, Nature, Traditions	6
France	Rally for France and the Independence of Europe	3
Netherlands	Reformational Political Federation/Reformed Political Association/Reformed Political Party	3
United Kingdom	UK Independence Party	2
	Total	18

Non-Attached Members

Listed below are the parties represented in the 1999–2004 European Parliament which are not members of any of the above groups, largely because they are regarded as being too extreme to qualify for such membership.

Austria	Freedom Movement	5
Belgium	Flemish Bloc	2
France	Rally for France and the Independence of Europe	6
France	National Front	5
France	Marie-France Garaud (ind.)	1
Italy	Radical Party (Bonino List)	7
Italy	Northern League	3
Italy	Tricolour Flame Social Movement	1
Spain	We Basques	1
United Kingdom	UK Independence Party	1
UK: Northern Ireland	Democratic Unionist Party (DUP)	1
		Total 33

INDEX OF PERSONAL NAMES

INDEX OF PARTY NAMES

This index provides a page reference to the main entry for each party. Where there are parties of the same name in different countries the country name is given.

575

592